Greenland
Godthab
Iceland
Reykjavik
Quebec
St. John's
Ottawa
Montreal
Halifax
Toronto
Cleveland
New York
Philadelphia
Washington
Charlotte
Jacksonville
Miami
Bahamas
Dom. Rep.
Haiti
Caracas
Trinidad & Tobago
Guyana
Paramaribo
French Guiana
Suriname
Venezuela
Georgetown
Bogota
Colombia
Belem
Peru
Brazil
Recife
Lima
La Paz
Brasilia
Salvador
Bolivia
Belo Horizonte
Rio De Janeiro
Sao Paulo
Chile
Paraguay
Asuncion
Cordoba
Porto Alegre
Santiago
Argentina
Uruguay
Buenos Aires
Montevideo
Trondheim
Norway
Sweden
Finland
Bergen
Oslo
Tampere
Helsinki
St. Petersburg
Stockholm
Estonia
Aberdeen
United Kingdom
Copenhagen
Denmark
Latvia
Lithuania
Dublin
Manchester
Ireland
Neth.
Berlin
Germany
Poland
London
Bel.
Lux.
Czech Rep.
Slovakia
Paris
Austria
Hungary
Switz.
Ukraine
Moldova
Romania
France
Italy
Croatia
Bos. & Herz.
Serb.
Bulgaria
Bucharest
Odesa
Kiev
Warsaw
Belarus
Minsk
Moscow
Ryazan'
Kostroma
Voronezh
Russia
Perm'
Yekaterinburg
Omsk
Novosibirsk
Oufa
Chelyabinsk
Astana
Kazakhstan
Bishkek
Kyrgyzstan
Tashkent
Uzbekistan
Tajikistan
Turkmenistan
Ashgabat
China
Spain
Portugal
Madrid
Lisbon
Rome
Albania
Mace.
Naples
Greece
Istanbul
Ankara
Turkey
Georgia
Armenia
Azerb.
Tunis
Athens
Algiers
Malta
Tripoli
Tunisia
Rabat
Morocco
Algeria
Libya
Cyprus
Lebanon
Israel
Syria
Tehran
Iran
Baghdad
Iraq
Jordan
Kuwait
Shiraz
Kabul
Afghanistan
Islamabad
Ludhiana
Lahore
New Delhi
Nepal
Kathmandu
Pakistan
Karachi
Ahmadabad
Bhopal
Calcutta
India
Bombay
Hyderabad
Bangalore
Chennai
Madurai
Colombo
Sri Lanka
Cairo
Egypt
Riyadh
Qatar
U.A.E.
Saudi Arabia
Muscat
Jeddah
Oman
Yemen
San'a
Western Sahara
(Occupied by Morocco)
Mauritania
Mali
Nouakchott
Niger
Chad
Khartoum
Eritrea
Cape Verde
Senegal
Gambia
Guinea-Bissau
Guinea
Sierra Leone
Liberia
Bamako
Niamey
Burkina Faso
Benin
Nigeria
Abuja
N'Djamena
Sudan
Djibouti
Addis Ababa
Ethiopia
Somalia
Cote d'Ivoire
Ghana
Togo
Cameroon
Central African Republic
Bangui
Equatorial Guinea
Sao Tome & Principe
Yaounde
Libreville
Gabon
Congo
Brazzaville
Dem. Rep. of Congo
Kinshasa
Uganda
Kampala
Rwanda
Kenya
Mogadishu
Nairobi
Burundi
Dodoma
Dar es Salaam
Tanzania
Luanda
Angola
Zambia
Malawi
Lusaka
Harare
Zimbabwe
Mozambique
Antananarivo
Mauritius
Madagascar
Namibia
Windhoek
Botswana
Gaborone
Pretoria
Johannesburg
Swaziland
Lesotho
South Africa
Cape Town
Port Elizabeth

peng

global business

peng

global business

Mike W. Peng

Provost's Distinguished Professor of Global Business Strategy

University of Texas at Dallas

SOUTH-WESTERN
CENGAGE Learning™

Australia • Brazil • Japan • Korea • Mexico • Singapore • Spain • United Kingdom • United States

Global Business
Dr. Mike W. Peng

VP/Editorial Director: Jack W. Calhoun

Editor-in-Chief: Melissa Acuña

Senior Acquisitions Editor: Michele Rhoades

Developmental Editor: Jennifer King

Marketing Manager: Clint Kernen

Content Project Manager: Heather Mann

Manager, Editorial Media: John Barans

Technology Project Editor: Rob Ellington

Senior Marketing Communications Manager: Jim Overly

Senior Buyer – Manufacturing: Doug Wilke

Production Service: Lachina Publishing Services

Compositor: Lachina Publishing Services

Senior Art Director: Tippy McIntosh

Cover Design: Tippy McIntosh

Internal and Logo Design: Mike Stratton, Stratton Design

Cover Image: Fry Design Ltd/Getty Images

Senior Permissions Rights Acquisitions Account Manager – Images: Deanna Ettinger

Photo Researcher: Terri Miller

Library of Congress Control Number: 2008920890

Student Edition ISBN-13: 978-0-324-36073-8

Student Edition ISBN-10: 0-324-36073-8

Instructor's Edition ISBN 13: 978-0-324-58509-4

Instructor's Edition ISBN 10: 0-324-58509-8

South-Western Cengage Learning
5191 Natorp Boulevard
Mason, OH 45040
USA

Cengage Learning products are represented in Canada by Nelson Education, Ltd.

For your course and learning solutions, visit **academic.cengage.com**

Purchase any of our products at your local college store or at our preferred online store **www.ichapters.com**

Printed in Canada
1 2 3 4 5 6 7 12 11 10 09 08

Credits appear on page 577, which constitutes a continuation of the copyright page.

To Agnes, Grace, and James

BRIEF CONTENTS

Part 1 Laying Foundations 1

1 Globalizing Business 2
2 Understanding Formal Institutions: Politics, Laws, and Economics 28
3 Emphasizing Informal Institutions: Cultures, Ethics, and Norms 54
4 Leveraging Resources and Capabilities 86
Integrative Cases 110

Part 2 Acquiring Tools 121

5 Trading Internationally 122
6 Investing Abroad Directly 152
7 Dealing with Foreign Exchange 180
8 Capitalizing on Global and Regional Integration 206
Integrative Cases 236

Part 3 Strategizing around the Globe 251

9 Growing and Internationalizing the Entrepreneurial Firm 252
10 Entering Foreign Markets 276
11 Managing Global Competitive Dynamics 302
12 Making Alliances and Acquisitions Work 328
13 Strategizing, Structuring, and Learning around the World 358
Integrative Cases 386

Part 4 Building Functional Excellence 409

14 Competing on Marketing and Supply Chain Management 410
15 Managing Human Resources Globally 436
16 Governing the Corporation around the World 462
17 Managing Corporate Social Responsibility Globally 488
Integrative Cases 512

CONTENTS

Part 1 Laying Foundations 1

Chapter 1
Globalizing Business 2

International Business and Global Business 4

Why Study Global Business? 7

A Unified Framework 8

One Fundamental Question 9 / First Core Perspective: An Institution-Based View 10 / Second Core Perspective: A Resource-Based View 10 / A Consistent Theme 11

What Is Globalization? 11

Three Views of Globalization 12 / The Pendulum View of Globalization 12 / Semiglobalization 13

Global Business and Globalization at a Crossroads 14

A Glance of the World Economy 14 / The Globalization Debate and You 16

Organization of the Book 21

Chapter 2
Understanding Formal Institutions: Politics, Laws, and Economics 28

Formal and Informal Institutions 31

What Do Institutions Do? 32

An Institution-based View of Global Business 33

Two Political Systems 34

Democracy 34 / Totalitarianism 34 / Political Risk 35

Three Legal Systems 36

Civil Law, Common Law, and Theocratic Law 36 / Property Rights 37 / Intellectual Property Rights 38

Three Economic Systems 39

Debates and Extensions 41

Drivers of Economic Development: Culture, Geography, or Institutions? 41 / Speed and Effectiveness of Institutional Transitions: China versus Russia 43 / Measures of Political Risk: Perception versus Objective Measures 44

Management Savvy 46

Chapter 3
Emphasizing Informal Institutions: Cultures, Ethics, and Norms 54

Where Do Informal Institutions Come From? 56

Culture 57

Definition of Culture 57 / Language 58 / Religion 59

Classifying Cultural Differences 61

The Context Approach 61 / The Cluster Approach 62 / The Dimension Approach 64 / Culture and Global Business 66

Ethics 68

Definition and Impact of Ethics 68 / Managing Ethics Overseas 69 / Ethics and Corruption 70

Norms and Ethical Challenges 72

Debates and Extensions 73

Economic Development: Western Values versus Eastern Values 73 / Cultural Change: Convergence versus Divergence 74 / Opportunism versus Individualism/Collectivism 75

Management Savvy 77

Chapter 4
Leveraging Resources and Capabilities 86

Understanding Resources and Capabilities 89

Analyzing the Value Chain: In-house versus Outsource 91

Analyzing Resources and Capabilities with a VRIO Framework 95

The Question of Value 95 / The Question of Rarity 96 / The Question of Imitability 97 / The Question of Organization 98

Debates and Extensions 99

Domestic Resources versus International (Cross-Border) Capabilities 99 / Offshoring versus Not Offshoring 100

Management Savvy 102

Integrative Cases 110

1.1 The Chinese Menu (For Development) 110 / 1.2 DP World 111 / 1.3 Tips about Corruption around the Pacific 116 / 1.4 Private Military Companies: Dogs of War or Pussycats of Peace? 118

Part 2 Acquiring Tools 121

Chapter 5
Trading Internationally 122

Why Do Nations Trade? 124

Theories of International Trade 127

Mercantilism 127 / Absolute Advantage 127 Comparative Advantage 129 / Product Life Cycle 132 / Strategic Trade 132 / National Competitive Advantage of Industries 135 / Evaluating Theories of International Trade 136

Realities of International Trade 138

Tariff Barriers 138 / Nontariff Barriers (NTBs) 139 / Economic Arguments against Free Trade 140 / Political Arguments against Free Trade 142

Debates and Extensions 142

Trade Deficit versus Trade Surplus 142 / Classical Theories versus New Realities 143

Management Savvy 146

Chapter 6
Investing Abroad Directly 152

Understanding the FDI Vocabulary 154

The Key Word Is D 155 / Horizontal and Vertical FDI 155 / FDI Flow and Stock 156 / MNE versus non-MNE 156

Why Do Firms Become MNEs By Engaging in FDI? 158

Ownership Advantages 159

The Benefits of Direct Ownership 159 / FDI versus Licensing 159

Location Advantages 161

Location, Location, Location 161 / Acquiring and Neutralizing Location Advantages 162

Internalization Advantages 163

Market Failure 163 / Overcoming Market Failure through FDI 163

Realities of FDI 165

Political Views on FDI 165 / Benefits and Costs of FDI to Host Countries 166 / Benefits and Costs of FDI to Home Countries 168

How MNEs and Host Governments Bargain 168

Debates and Extensions 170

FDI versus Outsourcing 170 / Facilitating versus Confronting Inbound FDI 171

Management Savvy 172

Chapter 7
Dealing with Foreign Exchange 180

Factors Behind Foreign Exchange Rates 183

Basic Supply and Demand 183 / Relative Price Differences and Purchasing Power Parity 184 / Interest Rates and Money Supply 186 / Productivity and Balance of Payments 186 / Exchange Rate Policies 188 / Investor Psychology 189

Evolution of the International Monetary System 190

The Gold Standard (1870–1914) 190 / The Bretton Woods System (1944–1973) 190 / The Post–Bretton Woods System (1973–present) 190 / The International Monetary Fund (IMF) 191

Strategic Responses to Foreign Exchange Movements 192

Strategies for Financial Companies 193 / Strategies for Nonfinancial Companies 195

Debates and Extensions 196

Fixed versus Floating Exchange Rates 196 / A Strong Dollar versus a Weak Dollar 197 / Currency Hedging versus Not Hedging 198

Management Savvy 200

Chapter 8
Capitalizing on Global and Regional Integration 206

Global Economic Integration 209

Political Benefits for Global Economic Integration 209 / Economic Benefits for Global Economic Integration 210

General Agreement on Tariffs and Trade: 1948–1994 211

World Trade Organization: 1995–present 211

Trade Dispute Settlement 212 / The Doha Round: The "Doha Development Agenda" 213

Five Types of Regional Economic Integration 215

The Pros and Cons for Regional Economic Integration 215 / Types of Regional Economic Integration 217

Regional Economic Integration in Europe 218

Origin and Evolution 218 / The EU Today 218 / The EU's Challenges 222

Regional Economic Integration in the Americas 223

North America: North American Free Trade Agreement (NAFTA) 223 / South America: Andean Community, Mercosur, FTAA, and CAFTA 224

Regional Economic Integration in Asia Pacific 226

Australia-New Zealand Closer Economic Relations Trade Agreement (ANZCERTA or CER) 226 / Association of Southeast Asian Nations (ASEAN) 226 / Asia-Pacific Economic Cooperation (APEC) 227

Regional Economic Integration in Africa 228

Debates and Extensions 228

Building Blocks versus Stumbling Blocks 228 / Does the WTO Really Matter? 230

Management Savvy 230

Integrative Cases 236

2.1 Which Is More American? 236 / 2.2 Soybeans in China 238 / 2.3 AGRANA: From a Local Supplier to a Global Player 241 / 2.4 Competing in the Chinese Automobile Industry 245

Part 3 Strategizing around the Globe 251

Chapter 9
Growing and Internationalizing the Entrepreneurial Firm 252

Entrepreneurship and Entrepreneurial Firms 254

How Institutions and Resources Affect Entrepreneurship 255

Institutions and Entrepreneurship 255 / Resources and Entrepreneurship 256

Growing the Entrepreneurial Firm 258

Growth 258 / Innovation 258 / Financing 259

Internationalizing the Entrepreneurial Firm 261

Transaction Costs and Entrepreneurial Opportunities 261 / International Strategies for Entering Foreign Markets 262 / International Strategies for Staying in Domestic Markets 265

Debates and Extensions 266

Traits versus Institutions 266 / Slow Internationalizers versus Born Global Start-Ups 267 / Antifailure Bias versus Entrepreneur-Friendly Bankruptcy Laws 268

Management Savvy 269

Chapter 10
Entering Foreign Markets 276

Overcoming Liability of Foreignness 278

Where to Enter? 279

Location-Specific Advantages and Strategic Goals 279 / Cultural/Institutional Distances and Foreign Entry Locations 283

When to Enter? 284

How to Enter? 285

Scale of Entry: Commitment and Experience 286 / Modes of Entry: The First Step on Equity versus Nonequity Modes 286 / Modes of Entry: The Second Step on Making Actual Selections 286

Debates and Extensions 291

Liability versus Asset of Foreignness 291 / Global versus Regional Geographic Diversification 291 / Cyberspace versus Conventional Entries 293

Management Savvy 293

Chapter 11
Managing Global Competitive Dynamics 302

Competition, Cooperation, and Collusion 305

War and Peace 305 / Cooperation and Collusion 305

Institutions Governing Domestic and International Competition 309

Formal Institutions Governing Domestic Competition: A Focus on Antitrust 309 / Formal Institutions Governing International Competition: A Focus on Antidumping 310

Resources Influencing Competitive Dynamics 311

Value 311 / Rarity 312 / Imitability 312 / Organization 312 / Resource Similarity 313

Attack, Counterattack, and Signaling 314

Three Main Types of Attack 314 / Attack and Counterattack 315 / Cooperation and Signaling 316

Local Firms versus Multinational Enterprises 317

Debates and Extensions 319

Competition versus Antidumping 319 / Managers versus Antitrust Policymakers 319

Management Savvy 320

Chapter 12
Making Alliances and Acquisitions Work 328

Defining Alliances and Acquisitions 330

How Institutions and Resources Affect Alliances and Acquisitions 332

Institutions, Alliances, and Acquisitions 332 / Resources and Alliances 333 / Resources and Acquisitions 335

Alliances and Acquisitions 337

Formation of Alliances 338

Stage One: To Cooperate or Not to Cooperate? 338 / Stage Two: Contract or Equity? 339 / Stage Three: Specifying the Relationship 340

Evolution of Alliances 341

Combating Opportunism 341 / From Corporate Marriage to Divorce 341

Performance of Alliances 343

Motives for Acquisitions 344

Performance of Acquisitions 345

Debates and Extensions 347

M&As + Alliances 347 / Majority JVs as Control Mechanisms versus Minority JVs as Real Options 347

Management Savvy 349

Chapter 13
Strategizing, Structuring, and Learning around the World 358

Multinational Strategies and Structures 360

Pressures for Cost Reductions and Local Responsiveness 360 / Four Strategic Choices 361 / Four Organizational Structures 363 / The Reciprocal Relationship between Multinational Strategy and Structure 366

How Institutions and Resources Affect Multinational Strategy, Structure, and Learning 367

Institution-Based Considerations 367 / Resource-Based Considerations 370

The Challenge of Managing Learning, Innovation, and Knowledgement Worldwide 370

Knowledge Management 370 / Knowledge Management in Four Types of MNEs 371 / Globalizing Research and Development 372 / Problems and Solutions in Knowledge Management 374

Debates and Extensions 375

Corporate Controls versus Subsidiary Initiatives 375 / Customer-Focused Dimensions versus Integration, Responsiveness, and Learning 376

Management Savvy 377

Integrative Cases 386

3.1 Dentek's UK Decision 386 / 3.2 The LG-Nortel Joint Venture 390 / 3.3 Ocean Park Confronts Hong Kong Disneyland 393 / 3.4 Global Knowledge Management at Accenture 400 / 3.5 DHL Bangladesh 403

Part 4 Building Functional Excellence 409

Chapter 14
Competing on Marketing and Supply Chain Management 410

Three of the Four Ps in Marketing 412

Product 413 / Price 415 / Promotion 416

From Distribution Channel to Supply Chain Management 418

The Triple As in Supply Chain Management 419

Agility 419 / Adaptability 419 / Alignment 420

How Insititutions and Resources Affect Marketing and Supply Chain Management 423

Institutions, Marketing, and Supply Chain Management 423 / Resources, Marketing, and Supply Chain Management 425

Debates and Extensions 426

Manufacturing versus Services 426 / Market Orientation versus Relationship Orientation 427

Management Savvy 428

Chapter 15
Managing Human Resources Globally 436

Staffing 438

Ethnocentric, Polycentric, and Geocentric Approaches to Staffing 439 / The Role of Expatriates 440 / Expatriate Failure and Selection 441

Training and Development Needs 442

Training for Expatriates 442 / Development for Returning Expatriates (Repatriates) 443 / Training and Development for Host Country Nationals 444

Compensation and Performance Appraisal 444

Compensation for Expatriates 445 / Compensation for Host Country Nationals 446 / Performance Appraisal 448

Labor Relations 448

Managing Labor Relations at Home 448 / Managing Labor Relations Abroad 449

How Institutions and Resources Affect Human Resource Management 450

Institutions and Human Resource Management 450 / Resources and Human Resource Management 453

Debates and Extensions 453

Best Fit versus Best Practice 453 / Expatriation versus Inpatriation 454 / Across-the-Board Pay Cut versus Reduction in Force 454

Management Savvy 455

Chapter 16
Governing the Corporation around the World 462

Owners 465

Concentrated versus Diffused Ownership 465 / Family Ownership 465 / State Ownership 466

Managers 466

Principal-Agent Conflicts 466 / Principal-Principal Conflicts 467

The Board of Directors 469

Key Features of the Board 469 / The Role of Boards of Directors 470

Governance Mechanisms as a Package 471

Internal (Voice-Based) Governance Mechanisms 471 / External (Exit-Based) Governance Mechanisms 472 / Internal Mechanisms + External Mechanisms = Governance Package 473

A Global Perspective on Governance Mechanisms 473

How Institutions and Resources Affect Corporate Governance 475

Institutions and Corporate Governance 475 / Resources and Corporate Governance 477

Debates and Extensions 478

Opportunistic Agents versus Managerial Stewards 478 / Global Convergence versus Divergence 478

Management Savvy 480

Chapter 17
Managing Corporate Social Responsibility Globally 488

A Stakeholder View of the Firm 491

A Big Picture Perspective 491 / Primary and Secondary Stakeholder Groups 494 / A Fundamental Debate 494

Institutions and Corporate Social Responsibility 496

Reactive Strategy 497 / Defensive Strategy 498 / Accommodative Strategy 498 / Proactive Strategy 499

Resources and Corporate Social Responsibility 500

Value 500 / Rarity 501 / Imitability 501 / Organization 501 / The CSR-Economic Performance Puzzle 502

Debates and Extensions 502

Domestic versus Overseas Social Responsibility 502 / Race to the Bottom ("Pollution Haven") versus Race to the Top 503 / Active versus Inactive CSR Engagement Overseas 504

Management Savvy 505

Integrative Cases 512

4.1 Shakira: The Dilemma of Going Global 512 / 4.2 Kalashnikov: Swords into Vodka 514 / 4.3 Computime 515 / 4.4 Shakti: Unilever Collaborates with Women Entrepreneurs in Rural India 524

Glossary 530

Name Index 543

Organization Index 555

Subject Index 561

Credits 577

PREFACE

Global Business intends to set a new standard for international business (IB) textbooks. Written for undergraduate and MBA students around the world, this book will make IB teaching and learning (1) more engaging, (2) more comprehensive, (3) more fun, and (4) more relevant.

More Engaging

For the first time in the history of IB textbooks, a unified framework integrates all chapters. Given the wide range of topics in IB, most textbooks present the discipline in a fashion that "Today is Tuesday, it must be Luxembourg." Very rarely do authors address: "*Why* Luxembourg today?" More important, what is it that we do in IB? What is the big question that the field is trying to address? Our unified framework suggests that the discipline can be united by one big question and two core perspectives. The big question is: What determines the success and failure of firms around the globe? This focus on firm performance around the globe defines our field. To address this question, we introduce two core perspectives: (1) an institution-based view and (2) a resource-based view, in *all* chapters. It is this relentless focus on our big question and core perspectives that enables this book to engage a variety of IB topics in an integrated fashion. This provides great continuity in the learning process.

Global Business further engages readers through an *evidence-based* approach. I have endeavored to draw on the latest research, as opposed to the latest fads. As an active researcher myself, I have developed the unified framework not because it just popped up in my head when I wrote the book. Rather, this is an extension of my own research that consistently takes on the big question and leverages the two core perspectives. This work has been published in the *Journal of International Business Studies* and other leading academic journals.[1]

Another vehicle used to engage students is debates. Virtually all textbooks uncritically present knowledge "as is" and ignore debates. However, it is debates that drive the field of practice and research forward. Obviously, our field has no shortage of debates, ranging from outsourcing to social responsibility. It is the responsibility of textbook authors to engage students by introducing cutting-edge debates. Thus, I have written a beefy "Debates and Extensions" section for *every* chapter (except Chapter 1, which is a big debate in itself).

Finally, this book engages students by packing rigor with accessibility. There is no "dumbing down." No other competing IB textbook exposes students to an article authored by a Nobel laureate (Douglass North—Integrative Case 1.1), commentary pieces by Jack Welch (former GE chairman—In Focus 15.2) and Laura Tyson (former economic advisor to President Clinton—In Focus 5.3), and a *Harvard Business Review* article (authored by me—In Focus 12.2). These are not excerpts but full-blown, original articles—the first in an IB (and in fact in any management) textbook. These highly readable short pieces directly give students a flavor of the original insights. In general, the material is presented in an accessible manner to facilitate learning.

---

[1] M. W. Peng, 2004, Identifying the big question in international business research, *Journal of International Business Studies*, 35: 99-108; M. W. Peng, D. Wang, & Y. Jiang, 2008, An institution-based view of international business strategy: A focus on emerging economies, *Journal of International Business Studies* (in press); M. W. Peng, 2001, The resource-based view and international business, *Journal of Management*, 27: 803-829.

More Comprehensive

Global Business offers the most comprehensive and innovative coverage of IB topics available on the market. Unique chapters not found elsewhere are:

- Chapter 9 on entrepreneurship and small firms' internationalization
- Chapter 11 on competitive dynamics
- Chapter 16 on corporate governance
- Chapter 17 on corporate social responsibility (in addition to one full-blown chapter on ethics, cultures, and norms, Chapter 3)
- Half of Chapter 12 (alliances and acquisitions) deals with the under-covered topic of acquisitions. Approximately 70% of market entries based on foreign direct investment (FDI) around the world use acquisitions. Yet, no other IB textbook has a chapter on acquisitions—a missing gap that Chapter 12 fills.

The most comprehensive topical coverage is made possible by drawing on the most comprehensive range of the literature. Specifically, every article in each issue in the past ten years in the *Journal of International Business Studies* and other leading IB journals has been read and coded. In addition, I have endeavored to consult numerous specialty journals. For example:

- The trade and finance chapters (Chapters 5–7) draw on the *American Economic Review* and *Quarterly Journal of Economics*
- The entrepreneurship chapter (Chapter 9) consults with the *Journal of Business Venturing* and *Entrepreneurship Theory and Practice*
- The marketing and supply chain chapter (Chapter 14) draws heavily from the *Journal of Marketing*, *Journal of International Marketing*, and *Journal of Operations Management*
- The human resource chapter (Chapter 15) heavily cites from *Human Resource Management*, *International Journal of Human Resource Management*, *Journal of Applied Psychology*, and *Personnel Psychology*
- The corporate governance chapter (Chapter 16) is visibly guided by research published in the *Journal of Finance* and *Journal of Financial Economics*
- The corporate social responsibility chapter (Chapter 17) borrows from work that appeared in the *Journal of Business Ethics* and *Business Ethics Quarterly*

As research for the book progressed, my respect and admiration for the diversity of insights of our field grew tremendously. The end result is the unparalleled, most comprehensive set of evidence-based insights on the IB market. While citing every article is not possible, I am confident that I have left no major streams of research untouched. Feel free to check the authors found in the Name Index to verify this claim.

Finally, *Global Business* also has the most comprehensive set of cases contributed by scholars from around the world—an innovation on the IB market. Virtually all other IB textbooks have cases written by book authors. In comparison, this book has been blessed by a global community of case contributors who are based in Canada, China, Hong Kong, Singapore, and the United States. Many of them are experts who are located in or are from the countries in which the cases take place—for example, among all IB textbooks, *Global Business* has the very first China case written by China-based case authors (see Integrative Case 2.2, Soybeans in China). Additionally, the Video Cases bring you the insights and expertise of noted business leaders from England, Scotland, India, France, and the United States.

More Fun

In case you think that this book must be very boring because it draws so heavily on current research, you are wrong. I have used a clear, engaging, conversational style to tell the "story." Relative to rival books, my chapters are generally more lively and shorter. For example, most books use two chapters to go over topics such as trade, FDI, and foreign exchange. I cut out a lot of "fat" and use one chapter to cover each of these topics, thus enhancing the "weight-to-contribution" ratio. Some reviewers (other professors) commented that reading my chapters is like reading a good magazine. Just check out any chapter to see for yourself.

Throughout the text, I have woven a large number of interesting, non-traditional anecdotes, ranging from ancient Chinese military writings (Sun Tzu) to the Roman Empire's import quotas, and from quotes in *Anna Karenina* to mutually assured destruction (MAD) strategy in the Cold War. Popular movies, such as *High School Musical, Lord of the Rings, The Full Monty*, and *The Hunt for Red October* are also discussed.

In addition, numerous Opening Cases, Closing Cases, and In Focus boxes spice up the book. Check out the following fun-filled features:

- The Dell theory of world peace (Chapter 2, In Focus 2.1)
- Comparative advantage and *you* (Chapter 5, In Focus 5.1)
- Who wants to be a trillionaire? (Chapter 7, In Focus 7.3)
- Sew What? (Chapter 9, Opening Case)
- A fox in the hen house (Chapter 11, In Focus 11.2)
- Blunders in international marketing (Chapter 14, Table 14.2) and in international HRM (Chapter 15, Table 15.6)
- List in New York? No, thanks! (Chapter 16, Opening Case)
- Have you offset your carbon emission? (Chapter 17, Closing Case)

Finally, there is one video case to support every chapter. While virtually all competing books have some videos, none has a video package that is so integrated with the learning objectives of *every* chapter.

More Relevant

So what? Chapters in most textbooks leave students (and professors) to figure out the crucial "so what?" question for themselves. In contrast, I conclude every chapter with an action-packed section titled Management Savvy. Each section has at least one table (sometimes two or three tables) that clearly summarizes the key learning points from a *practical* standpoint. No other competing IB book is so savvy and so relevant.

Further, ethics is a theme that cuts through the book, with each chapter having at least one Ethical Dilemma feature and a series of Critical Discussion Questions on ethics to engage students.

Finally, many chapters offer *career* advice for students. For example:

- Chapter 4 develops a resource-based view of the individual—that is, about you, the student. The upshot? You want to make yourself into an "untouchable," who adds valuable, rare, and hard-to-imitate capabilities indispensable to an organization. In other words, you want to make sure your job cannot be outsourced.
- Chapter 15 offers tips on how to strategically and proactively invest in your career now—as a student—for future international career opportunities.

Support Materials

A full set of supplements is available for students and adopting instructors, all designed to facilitate ease of learning, teaching, and testing.

Instructor's Resource DVD-ROM. Instructors will find all of the teaching resources they need to plan, teach, grade, and assess student understanding and progress at their fingertips with this all-in-one resource for *Global Business*. The IR-DVD-ROM contains:

- Instructor's Manual—Written by John Bowen (Ohio State University, Newark and Columbus State Community College), this valuable, time-saving Instructor's Manual includes comprehensive resources to streamline course preparation, including teaching suggestions, lecture notes, and answers to all chapter questions. Also included are discussion guidelines and answers for the Integrative Cases found at the end of each part.
- Testbank—Prepared by Ann Langlois (Palm Beach Atlantic University), the *Global Business* Testbank in ExamView® software allows instructors to create customized texts by choosing from 25 True/False, 25 Multiple Choice, and at least 5 short answer/essay questions for each of the 17 chapters. Ranging in difficulty, all questions have been tagged to the text's Learning Objectives and AASCB standards to ensure students are meeting the course criteria.
- PowerPoint® Slides—Mike Giambattista (University of Washington) has created a comprehensive set of more than 250 PowerPoint® slides that will assist instructors in the presentation of the chapter material, enabling students to synthesize key global concepts.
- Video Cases—Perhaps one of the most exciting and compelling bonus features of this program, these 17 short and powerful video clips, produced by 50 Lessons, provide additional guidance on international business strategies. The video clips offer real-world business acumen and valuable learning experiences from an array of internationally known business leaders.

Product Support Website. We offer a *Global Business* product support website at academic.cengage.com/peng, where instructors can download files for the Instructor's Manual, Testbank, ExamView® software, and PowerPoint® slides. Also through this website, students will have access to their own set of PowerPoint® slides, as well as the Glossary. Found only on the Product Support Website, a set of auto-gradable, interactive quizzes—written by Yi Jiang (California State University, East Bay)—will allow students to instantly gauge their comprehension of the material. The quizzes are all tagged to the book's Learning Objectives and AACSB standards.

WebTutor on BlackBoard® and WebTutor on WebCT™. Available on two different platforms, *Global Business* WebTutor enhances students' understanding of the material by featuring the Opening Cases and Video Cases, as well as e-lectures, the Glossary, study flashcards, and a set of four engaging, interactive maps that delve more deeply into key concepts presented in the book.

CengageNOW™ Course Management System. Designed by instructors for instructors, CengageNOW™ mirrors the natural teaching workflow with an easy-to-use online suite of services and resources, all in one program. With this system, instructors can easily plan their courses, manage student assignments, automatically grade, teach with dynamic technology, and assess student progress with pre- and post-tests tagged to AACSB standards. For students, study tools including e-lectures, flashcards, PowerPoint® slides, and a set of four interactive maps enhance comprehension of the material, while diagnostic tools create a personalized study plan for each student that focuses their study efforts. CengageNOW™ operates seamlessly with WebCT™, Blackboard®, and other course management tools.

Acknowledgments

Undertaking a project of this magnitude makes me owe a great deal of debt—intellectual, professional, and personal—to many people, whose contributions I would like to acknowledge. Intellectually, I am grateful to Charles Hill (University of Washington), my former PhD advisor, who inspired my interest in global business. At UT Dallas, I thank my colleagues George Barnes, Tev Dalgic, Dave Deeds, Anne Ferrante, Dave Ford, John Fowler, Richard Harrison, Jonathan Hochberg, Marilyn Kaplan, Seung-Hyun Lee, John Lin, Livia Markoczy, Kumar Nair, Joe Picken, Orlando Richard, Jane Salk, Eric Tsang, Davina Vora, Habte Woldu, Laurie Ziegler, and the leadership team—Hasan Pirkul (dean), Varghese Jacobs (senior associate dean), and Greg Dess (area coordinator)—for creating and nurturing a supportive intellectual environment. In addition, this research has been supported by a National Science Foundation Faculty Career Grant (SES 0552089) and a Provost's Distinguished Research Professorship, for which I am grateful.

At South-Western Cengage Learning (formerly South-Western Thomson), I thank the dedicated team that turned this book from vision to reality: Melissa Acuna, Editor-in-Chief; Michele Rhoades, Senior Acquisitions Editor; Joe Sabatino, Senior Acquisitions Editor; John Abner, Managing Developmental Editor; Jennifer King, Developmental Editor; Kimberly Kanakes, Executive Marketing Manager; Clinton Kernen, Marketing Manager; Sara Rose, Marketing Coordinator; Tippy McIntosh, Senior Art Director; and Terri Coats, Executive Director, International.

In the academic community, I thank Ben Kedia (University of Memphis) for inviting me to conduct faculty training workshops in Memphis *every* year since 1999 on how to most effectively teach IB and Michael Pustay (Texas A&M University) for co-teaching the workshops with me—known as the "M&M Show" in the field. Interactions and discussions (and debates) with more than 120 colleagues who have come to these faculty workshops over the last eight years have helped shape this book into a better product.

I would also like to thank the text reviewers, who provided excellent and timely feedback:

Richard Ajayi (University of Central Florida, Orlando)
Lawrence A. Beer (Arizona State University)
Tefvik Dalgic (University of Texas at Dallas)
Tim R. Davis (Cleveland State University)
Ann L. Langlois (Palm Beach Atlantic University)
Ted London (University of Michigan)
Martin Meznar (Arizona State University, West)
Dilip Mirchandani (Rowan University)
William Piper (Alcorn State University)
Tom Roehl (Western Washington University)
Bala Subramanian (Morgan State University)
Susan Trussler (University of Scranton)

In addition, I thank a number of friends and colleagues, who informally commented on and critiqued certain chapters:

Irem Demirkan (Northeastern University)
Greg Dess (University of Texas at Dallas)
Dharma deSilva (Wichita State University)
Kiran Ismail (St. Johns University)
Yung Hua (University of Texas at Dallas)
Seung-Hyun Lee (University of Texas at Dallas)
Klaus Meyer (University of Bath)
Bill Newburry (Florida International University)
Mine Ozer (SUNY Oneonta)
Barbara Parker (Seattle University)
Jane Salk (University of Texas at Dallas)
Muthu Subbiah (University of Texas at Dallas)
Sunny Li Sun (University of Texas at Dallas)
Paul Vaaler (University of Illinois at Urbana-Champaign)
Davina Vora (SUNY New Paltz)
Habte Woldu (University of Texas at Dallas)
Fang Wu (University of Texas at Dallas)
Yasu Yamakawa (University of Texas at Dallas)
Toru Yoshikawa (McMaster University)
Kevin Zheng Zhou (University of Hong Kong)
Jessie Qi Zhou (Southern Methodist University)

My students' contributions have been invaluable to me. Most of my ideas in this book have been classroom tested in Beijing, Columbus, Dallas, Hanoi, Hong Kong, Honolulu, Memphis, Seattle, and Xian. A number of PhD students have worked on this book as my assistants and made the book significantly better. They are Ted Khoury, Kenny Oh, Erin Pleggenkuhle-Miles, and Sunny Li Sun. In addition, the following PhD students volunteered to help me proofread: Ramya Aroul, Hao Chen, Martina Quan, Yasu Yamakawa, and David Weng.

A total of 33 colleagues have contributed cases that have significantly enhanced this book. They are:

Bill Bentz (University of Texas at Dallas)
Steve Caudill (University of Texas at Dallas)
Masud Chand (Simon Fraser University)
David Choi (Loyola Marymount University)
Bee-Leng Chua (Hawaii Pacific University)
Andrew Delios (National University of Singapore)
C. Gopinath (Suffolk University)
Yi Jiang (California State University, East Bay)
Ted Khoury (University of Texas at Dallas)
Donald Liu (University of Washington)
Yi Liu (Xi'an Jiaotong University, China)
Ted London (University of Michigan)
Hemant Merchant (Florida Atlantic University)
John Ness (*Newsweek*)
Douglass North (Washington University)—Nobel laureate
Kenny K. Oh (University of Texas at Dallas)
Yongsun Paik (Loyola Marymount University)
Christine Pepermintwalla (University of Texas at Dallas)
Erin Pleggenkuhle-Miles (University of Texas at Dallas)
Amber Galbraith Quinn (University of Tennessee)
Anne Smith (University of Tennessee)
Charles Stevens (Ohio State University)
Sunny Li Sun (University of Texas at Dallas)
Tom Tao (Lehigh University)
Bill Turner (University of Texas at Dallas)
Maulin Vakil (University of North Carolina at Chapel Hill)
Ken Williamson (University of Texas at Dallas)
Chris Woodyard (*USA TODAY*)
Wei Yang (Xi'an Jiaotong University, China)
Arthur Yeung (University of Michigan/China Europe International Business School)
Michael Young (Hong Kong Baptist University)—2 cases
Xi Zou (Columbia University)

I would also like to thank the following academicians, who provided input and guidance on the presentation of the material:

Basil Al-Hashimi (Mesa Community College)
John Anderson (Christopher Newport University)
Brian Bartel (Mid-State Technical College, Steven's Point)
Tim Bryan (University of West Florida)
Martin Carrigan (University of Findlay)
Ping Deng (Maryville University)

Zahi Haddad (Georgetown College)
Pol Herrmann (Iowa State University)
Joe Horton (University of Central Arkansas)
H. Rika Houston (California State University, Los Angeles)
Samira Hussein (Johnson County Community College)
Ralph Jagodka (Mount San Antonio College)
Larry Maes (Davenport University, Warren)
Bill Motz (Lansing Community College)
Lilach Nachum (Baruch College, CUNY)
Braimoh Oseghale (Fairleigh Dickinson University, Teaneck)
Daria Panina (Texas A&M University)
Diane Scott (Wichita State University)
Amit Sen (Xavier University)
Gladys Torres-Baumgarten (Kean University)

Last, but by no means least, I thank my wife Agnes, my daughter Grace, and my son James—to whom this book is dedicated. Grace was three and James was one when the book was conceived. Grace is now a five-year-old. She calls this book "Daddy's storybook," and she has told me that she wants to become a writer when she grows up (so that she doesn't have to go to sleep at night!). My three-year-old James has now developed a strong body of knowledge in fish and all kinds of sea creatures. As a third-generation professor in my family, I can't help but wonder whether one (or both) of them will become a fourth-generation professor. A great deal of thanks also go to my two in-laws, who came to help. Without such instrumental help, the writing of this book would have been significantly delayed. To all of you, my thanks and my love.

MWP
November 5, 2007

AUTHOR

Mike W. Peng is the Provost's Distinguished Professor of Global Business Strategy at the University of Texas at Dallas. At UT Dallas, he founded the Center for Global Business, where he serves as the Executive Director. He holds a bachelor's degree from Winona State University, Minnesota and a PhD degree from the University of Washington, Seattle, where he was advised by Professor Charles Hill. Prior to joining UTD, Professor Peng had been on the faculty at the Ohio State University, Chinese University of Hong Kong, and University of Hawaii. In addition, he has held visiting or courtesy appointments in Australia (University of Sydney and Queensland University of Technology), Britain (University of Nottingham), China (Xi'an Jiaotong University, Sun Yat-sen University, and Cheung Kong Graduate School of Business), Denmark (Copenhagen Business School), Hong Kong (Chinese University of Hong Kong and Hong Kong Polytechnic University), Vietnam (Foreign Trade University), and the United States (University of Memphis, University of Michigan, and Seattle Pacific University).

Professor Peng is widely regarded as one of the most prolific and most influential scholars in global business—both the United Nations and the World Bank have cited his work in major publications. Truly global in scope, his research focuses on firm strategies in regions such as Asia, Central and Eastern Europe, and North America, covering countries such as China, Hong Kong, Japan, Russia, South Korea, Thailand, and the United States. He has published approximately 50 articles in leading academic journals and previously authored three books. The first two are *Behind the Success and Failure of US Export Intermediaries* (Quorum, 1998) and *Business Strategies in Transition Economies* (Sage, 2000). His third book is *Global Strategy* (Thomson South-Western, 2006), which has become the world's best-selling global strategy book and has been translated into Chinese (Posts and Telecom Press, 2007). *Global Business* builds on and leverages the success of *Global Strategy*.

Professor Peng is active in leadership positions in his field. At the Academy of International Business, he was a Co-Program Chair for the Research Frontiers Conference in San Diego (2006) and is currently guest editing a *Journal of International Business Studies* special issue on "Asia and global business." At the Strategic Management Society, he was the first elected Program Chair of the Global Strategy Interest Group (2005-07). At the Academy of Management, he was in charge of the Junior Faculty Consortium for the International Management Division at the Atlanta meetings (2006). Professor Peng has served on the editorial boards of the *Academy of Management Journal, Academy of Management Review, Journal of International Business Studies, Journal of World Business*, and *Strategic Management Journal*. He has also guest edited the *Journal of Management Studies*. At present, he is Editor-in-Chief of the *Asia Pacific Journal of Management*.

On a worldwide basis, Professor Peng has taught students at all levels—undergraduate, MBA, PhD, EMBA, executive, and faculty training programs. Some of his former PhD students are now professors at California State University, Chinese University of Hong Kong, Georgia State University, Hong Kong University of Science and Technology, Lehigh University, Northeastern University, Southern

Methodist University, St. John's University, University of Colorado at Boulder, and University of Texas at Dallas.

Professor Peng is also an active faculty trainer and consultant. He has provided on-the-job training to over 200 professors around the world. Every year since 1999, he has conducted faculty training workshops on how to teach international business at the University of Memphis with faculty participants from around the country. He has consulted for organizations such as BankOne, Berlitz International, Chinese Chamber of Commerce, Greater Dallas Asian American Chamber of Commerce, Hong Kong Research Grants Council, Manufacturers Alliance/MAPI, National Science Foundation, Nationwide Insurance, Ohio Polymer Association, SAFRAN, US-China Business Council, and The World Bank. His practitioner oriented research has been published in the *Harvard Business Review, Academy of Management Executive*, and *China Business Review*.

Professor Peng has received numerous awards and recognitions. He has been recognized as a Foreign Expert by the Chinese government. One of his *Academy of Management Review* papers has been found to be a "new hot paper" (based on citations) representing the entire field of Economics and Business by the Institute for Scientific Information (ISI), which publishes the Social Sciences Citation Index (SSCI). One of his Babson conference papers won a Small Business Administration (SBA) Award for the best paper exploring the importance of small businesses to the US economy. Professor Peng is a recipient of the Scholarly Contribution Award from the International Association for Chinese Management Research (IACMR). He has also been quoted in *Newsweek, The Exporter Magazine, Business Times* (Singapore), and Voice of America.

In addition, Professor Peng's high-impact, high-visibility research has also attracted significant external funding, totaling more than half a million dollars from sources such as the (US) National Science Foundation, Hong Kong Research Grants Council, and Chinese National Natural Science Foundation. At present, his research is funded by a five-year, prestigious National Science Foundation CAREER Grant. At $423,000, this is reportedly the largest grant the NSF has awarded to a business school faculty member.

PART 1

Laying Foundations

CHAPTERS

1 Globalizing Business
2 Understanding Formal Institutions: Politics, Laws, and Economics
3 Emphasizing Informal Institutions: Cultures, Ethics, and Norms
4 Leveraging Resources and Capabilities

Globalizing Business

OPENING CASE

Which Country Made This Book?

Let us start with a quiz: Which country made your book—yes, the very copy you are reading now? If you answer, "Of course, the United States!," I would respond, "Not so fast." Some of you will look at the copyright page (the page after the title page) and point out the publisher, South-Western, and its address in Mason, Ohio (just outside Cincinnati), as evidence that this book is a US product. But how do you know for sure?

Not only is the nationality of our publisher difficult to track down, but it has also been *changing*. Founded in 1902, South-Western had been an independent US publisher until it was acquired in 1986 by the Thomson Corporation, an $8 billion Canadian firm whose shares are listed in Toronto (TSX: TOC) and New York (NYSE: TOC). South-Western thus became a wholly owned subsidiary of Thomson. The book contract that I signed in 2005 was with Thomson (or specifically with Thomson Learning South-Western, a unit of Thomson Learning, which had been one of the four major divisions within Thomson with approximately $2.47 billion in sales in 2006). So technically, the book would have been Canadian—at least when it was conceived.

However, the winds of global change extensively discussed in this book have also directly impacted this book. In 2007 (before the book was finished), the Thomson Corporation sold its Thomson Learning division for $7.75 billion to two private equity groups: the London-based Apax Partners and Toronto-based OMERS Partners.* Apax Partners is one of the oldest and largest private equity firms in the world with more than $30 billion under its management. OMERS is one of the largest and most sophisticated asset management entities in Canada with over $45 billion in assets. (Chapters 12 and 16 present more details on acquisitions and private equity.)

In July 2007, Thomson Learning, now under joint British and Canadian ownership, changed its name to Cengage Learning. The new name was based on being at the "center of engagement" for its customers worldwide. Cengage Learning is a multinational publisher with operations in 39 countries. In the academic marketplace, it serves elementary, secondary, and postsecondary students, teachers, professors, and learning institutions. Cengage Learning will continue to emphasize its brands, including Heinle, Gale, Wadsworth, Delmar Learning, and our very own South-Western. In our own segment for business and economics college textbooks with the South-Western brand, Cengage Learning is number one in the world in terms of market share, followed by McGraw-Hill (with the Irwin brand) and Pearson (with the Prentice Hall brand). While Cengage Learning is now UK and Canadian owned, Pearson is also UK owned and McGraw-Hill is US owned. However, because Cengage Learning's corporate headquarters is in Stamford, Connecticut, it can also be labeled a US-based publisher.

So, given the global nature of your publisher, Cengage Learning, "Which country made this book?" becomes a very tricky question to answer definitively. Now, let us try a more straightforward one: Which country *produced* this book? In the jargon of publishing, "production" means the transformation of a manuscript into printable plates by a production house, which is neither a publisher nor a printer. The actual printing and binding of books is called "manufacturing." Although the majority of the production and manufacturing of this book was indeed done in the United States, the

* The Thomson Corporation used the proceeds of the sale of Thomson Learning as a part of its $17 billion funds to acquire Reuters, a UK-based financial data and news service provider. The combined entity later became Thomson-Reuters.

LEARNING OBJECTIVES

After studying this chapter, you should be able to

1. explain the concepts of international business and global business
2. articulate what you hope to learn by reading this book and taking this course
3. identify one most fundamental question and two core perspectives that provide a framework for studying this field
4. participate in the debate on globalization with a reasonably balanced and realistic view and a keen awareness of your likely bias in favor of globalization
5. have a basic understanding of the future of the global economy and its broad trends

publisher accepted bids on the project from production houses in India and printers in China. Does it surprise you that a US-based publisher would ask a production house in India to produce its books? Or that it would negotiate with a Chinese printing company to print a book in English? What would prompt a US-based publisher to turn to service companies abroad? It is because these firms can offer benefits to their customers such as cost and quality.

A few years ago, a majority of the Thomson textbooks were handled by US production houses. Since 2000, offshore outsourcing of support and services, primarily to Indian production houses, has been growing at 8% a year at Thomson (now Cengage Learning). In response, US production houses fight back by becoming "Indian"—through subsidiary operations in India. In this very global business, Indian production houses not only need to fend for themselves against US rivals but also need to watch out for rivals from other emerging economies. For now, non-English-speaking competitors from Brazil, China, and Poland have a hard time winning contracts from Cengage Learning. In the short run, the Philippines, with its large supply of low-cost, English-speaking professionals, seems determined to eat some of India's lunch. In the long run, Bulgaria, China, and Pakistan may emerge as global contenders. For managers at current and would-be competitors in these companies, there is no doubt that how to take advantage of the globalization of their business is their job number one.

Sources: Based on (1) author's interviews with Cengage (formerly Thomson) executives, 2005, 2006, and 2007; (2) Cengage Learning, http://en.wikipedia.org (accessed August 16, 2007); (3) M. W. Peng, 2006, Competing in and out of India, *Global Strategy* (pp. 3–4), Cincinnati, OH: Thomson South-Western; (4) Thomson Investor Day presentations, October 6, 2005, and October 6, 2006; (5) http://www.thomson.com.

How do firms compete around the globe? For British, Canadian, Indian, and US firms involved in the production of your textbook, how do they strengthen their competitive advantage? For Brazilian, Bulgarian, Chinese, Pakistani, Philippine, and Polish firms that want to have a piece of the action, how can they overcome their disadvantage? What determines the success and failure of these firms around the world? This book will address these and other important questions on global business.

LEARNING OBJECTIVE 1

explain the concepts of international business and global business

INTERNATIONAL BUSINESS AND GLOBAL BUSINESS

Traditionally, **international business (IB)** is defined as (1) a business (firm) that engages in international (cross-border) economic activities and/or (2) the action of doing business abroad. Consequently, a previous generation of IB textbooks almost always takes the foreign entrant's perspective, often dealing with issues such as how to enter foreign markets and how to select alliance partners. The most frequently discussed foreign entrant is the **multinational enterprise (MNE)**, defined as a firm that engages in **foreign direct investment (FDI)** by directly investing in, controlling, and managing value-added activities in other countries.[1] As important as MNEs and their cross-border activities are, they only cover one side of IB—namely, the foreign side. Students educated by these books often come away with the impression that the other side of IB does not exist. Of course, the other side, consisting of domestic firms, does exist. Facing foreign entrants such as MNEs, domestic firms do not just sit around. They actively compete and/or collaborate with foreign entrants. In other words, focusing on the foreign entrant side captures, at best, only one side of the coin.[2]

international business (IB)
(1) A business (firm) that engages in international (cross-border) economic activities and/or (2) the action of doing business abroad.

multinational enterprise (MNE)
A firm that engages in foreign direct investments and operates in multiple countries.

foreign direct investment (FDI)
Investments in, controlling, and managing value-added activities in other countries.

It seems uncontroversial to suggest that there are two key words in IB: *international* (I) and *business* (B). However, previous textbooks all focus on "international" (the foreign entrant) to the extent that the "business" part (that also includes domestic business) almost disappears. This is unfortunate because IB is most fundamentally about B before I. To put it differently, in the undergraduate and MBA curriculum at numerous business schools, the IB course is probably the *only* course with the word *business* in its title. All other courses are labeled as management, marketing, finance, and so on, representing one function but not the overall picture of business. Does it matter? Of course! It means that your IB course is an *integrative* course that has the potential to provide you with an overall business perspective (as opposed to a functional view) grounded in a global environment. Consequently, it makes sense that your textbook should give you both the I and B parts—instead of just the I part.

This is exactly why this book, which covers both I and B parts, is titled *Global Business*—not merely "international" business. **Global business**, consequently, is defined in this book as business around the globe. The activities include both (1) international (cross-border) activities covered by traditional IB books and (2) domestic business activities.

global business
Business around the globe.

Such deliberate blurring of the traditional boundaries separating international and domestic business is increasingly important today because many previously national (domestic) markets are now globalized. In college textbook publishing, not long ago, competition was primarily on a nation-by-nation basis. South-Western (before its acquisition by Canada's Thomson and more recently by Britain's Apax Partners and Canada's OMERS Partners), Prentice Hall (before its acquisition by Britain's Pearson), and McGraw-Hill fought each other largely in the United States. A different set of publishers competed in other countries. Now, thanks to rising demand for high-quality business textbooks in English, Cengage (formerly Thomson), Pearson, and McGraw-Hill have significantly globalized their competition. It becomes difficult to tell in this competition what is international and what is domestic. *Global* does seem to be a better word to capture the essence of this competition.

Moreover, this book has gone substantially beyond competition in developed economies by devoting extensive space to competitive battles waged throughout **emerging economies**, a term that has gradually replaced the term *developing countries* since the 1990s.[3] Another often used term is **emerging markets** (see Closing Case). How important are emerging economies? Shown in Figure 1.1, collectively, they now contribute approximately 50% of the global **gross domestic product (GDP)**.[4] Note that this percentage is adjusted for **purchasing power parity (PPP)**, which is an adjustment to reflect the differences in cost of living (see In Focus 1.1). Using official (nominal) exchange rates without adjusting for PPP, emerging economies contribute about 26% of the global GDP. Why is there such a huge difference between the two measures? This is because cost of living in emerging economies, such as housing and haircuts, tends to be lower than

emerging economies
A term that has gradually replaced the term *developing countries* since the 1990s. Another often used term is **emerging markets**.

gross domestic product (GDP)
The sum of value added by resident firms, households, and governments operating in an economy.

purchasing power parity (PPP)
A conversion that determines the equivalent amount of goods and services different currencies can purchase. This conversion is usually used to capture the differences in cost of living in different countries.

FIGURE 1.1 THE CONTRIBUTIONS OF EMERGING ECONOMIES

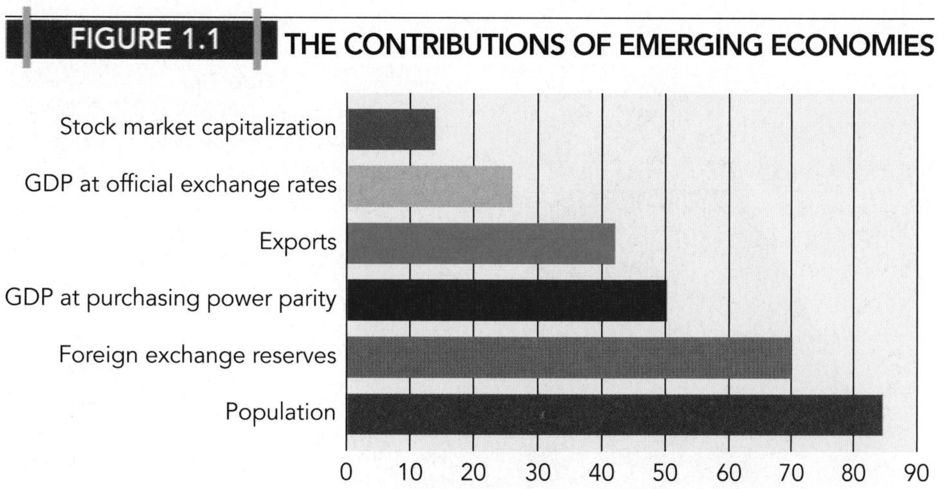

Source: Adapted from *Economist*, 2006, Climbing back (p. 69), January 21: 69-70. Original data are from the International Monetary Fund's World Economic Outlook database.

IN FOCUS 1.1 Setting the Terms Straight

GDP, GNP, GNI, PPP—there is a bewildering variety of acronyms that are used to measure economic development. It is useful to set these terms straight before proceeding. Gross domestic product (GDP) is measured as the sum of value added by *resident* firms, households, and government operating in an economy. For example, the value added by foreign-owned firms operating in Mexico would be counted as part of Mexico's GDP. However, the earnings of *nonresident* sources that are sent back to Mexico (such as earnings of Mexicans who do not live and work in Mexico and dividends received by Mexicans who own non-Mexican stocks) are not included in Mexico's GDP. One measure that captures this is **gross national product (GNP)**. More recently, the World Bank and other international organizations have used a new term, **gross national income (GNI)**, to supersede GNP. Conceptually, there is no difference between GNI and GNP. What exactly is GNI/GNP? It comprises GDP plus income from nonresident sources abroad.

Although GDP, GNP, and now GNI are often used as yardsticks of economic development, differences in cost of living make such a direct comparison less meaningful. A dollar of spending in, say, Thailand can buy a lot more than in Japan. Therefore, conversion based on purchasing power parity (PPP) is often necessary (Chapter 7 has more details). The Swiss per capita GNI is $54,930 based on official (nominal) exchange rates—*higher* than the US per capita GNI of $43,740. However, everything is more expensive in Switzerland. A Big Mac costs $5.20 in Switzerland versus $3.41 in the United States. Thus, Switzerland's per capita GNI based on PPP becomes $37,080—*lower* than the US per capita GNI based on PPP, $41,950. On a worldwide basis, measured at official exchange rates, emerging economies' share of global GDP is approximately 26%. However, measured at PPP, it had doubled by 2005 to about *half* of the global GDP. Overall, when we read statistics about GDP, GNP, and GNI, always pay attention to whether these numbers are based on official exchange rates or PPP, which can make a huge difference.

Sources: Based on (1) *Economist*, 2007, The Big Mac index: Sizzling, July 7: 74; (2) *Economist*, 2006, Climbing back, January 21: 69; (3) *Economist*, 2006, Grossly distorted picture, February 11: 72; (4) World Bank, 2007, *World Development Report* 2007, Washington, DC: World Bank.

gross national product (GNP)
Gross domestic product plus income from nonresident sources abroad.

gross national income (GNI)
GDP plus income from nonresident sources abroad. GNI is the term used by the World Bank and other international organizations to supersede the term GNP.

Triad
Three regions of developed economies (North America, Western Europe, and Japan).

that in developed economies. For example, $1 spent in Mexico can buy a lot more than that in $1 spent in the United States. The rapid growth of some emerging economies is evident.[5] A recent *Economist* survey of 555 executives from 68 countries reports that emerging economies command their utmost attention.[6]

The global economy can be viewed as a pyramid (Figure 1.2). The top consists of about one billion people with per capita annual income of $20,000 or higher. They are mostly in developed economies in the **Triad**, three regions that consist of North America, Western Europe, and Japan. The second tier consists of another billion people making $2,000 to $20,000 a year. The vast majority of humanity, about four billion people, live at the base of this pyramid making less than $2,000 a year. Most

FIGURE 1.2 THE GLOBAL ECONOMIC PYRAMID

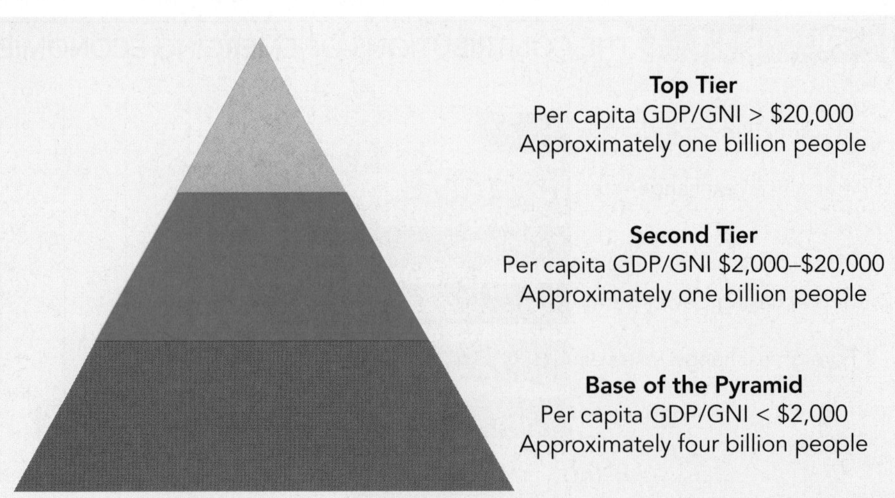

Sources: Adapted from (1) C. K. Prahalad & S. Hart, 2002, The fortune at the bottom of the pyramid, *Strategy + Business*, 26: 54–67, and (2) S. Hart, 2005, *Capitalism at the Crossroads* (p. 111), Philadelphia: Wharton School Publishing.

MNEs (and most traditional IB books) focus on the top and second tiers. They end up ignoring the **base of the pyramid**.[7] An increasing number of such low-income countries have shown a great deal of economic opportunities with rising income levels (In Focus 1.2). Today's students—and tomorrow's business leaders—will ignore these opportunities at the base of the pyramid at their own peril. This book will help ensure that you will not ignore these opportunities (see Closing Case).

base of the pyramid
The vast majority of humanity, about four billion people, who make less than $2,000 a year.

WHY STUDY GLOBAL BUSINESS?

LEARNING OBJECTIVE 2
articulate what you hope to learn by reading this book and taking this course

Global business (or IB) is one of the most exciting, challenging, and relevant subjects offered by business schools. In addition to the requirements at your business school that usually classify this course as a required (compulsory) or recommended course, there are at least two compelling reasons you should study it.

First, because many ambitious students aspire to join the top ranks of large firms, expertise in global business is often a prerequisite. Today, it is increasingly difficult, if not impossible, to find top managers at large firms without significant global competence. Of course, eventually, hands-on global experience, not merely knowledge acquired from this course, will be required.[8] However, mastery of the knowledge of, and demonstration of interest in, global business during your education will set you apart as a more ideal candidate to be selected as an **expatriate manager**—a manager who works abroad, or "**expat**" in short—to gain such experience (see Chapter 15 for details).

expatriate manager (expat)
A manager who works abroad.

Thanks to globalization, low-level jobs not only command lower salaries but are also more vulnerable. However, top-level jobs, especially those held by expats, are both financially rewarding and relatively secure. Expats often command a

IN FOCUS 1.2 It's the Base of the Pyramid Calling

What magical device can boost entrepreneurship, provide an alternative to bad roads, widen farmers' and fishermen's access to markets, and allow swift and safe transfers of money? It is . . . a mobile (cell) phone! At the base of the global economic pyramid, where fixed-line phones are rare or nonexistent, mobile phones are often the very first telephone networks widely deployed. In a typical country at the base of the pyramid, an increase of ten mobile phones per 100 people reportedly boosts GDP growth by 0.6%. Not surprisingly, the most explosive growth is found in the poorest region of the world: sub-Saharan Africa. In 2006, subscriber growth rates in Chad, Liberia, and Zambia were 292%, 172%, and 138%, respectively. Of course, such growth was based on a very low penetration level: In sub-Saharan Africa, there were three mobile phones per 100 people in 2001. Now there are eight mobile phones per 100. In comparison, the ratio is above 50 mobile phones per 100 people in developed economies.

As the demand takes off at the base of the pyramid, mobile phone makers and service providers cannot be happier. The reason is simple: At the top of the pyramid, market penetration is reaching saturation. The "race to the bottom" is challenging because customers demand rock-bottom prices of $50 or less per handset. For now, the only serious contenders for this segment, which is predicted to grow 100% annually for the next five years, are Nokia and Motorola, the world's number one and number two makers, respectively. Their tremendous volume gives them hard-to-beat economies of scale. Samsung, LG, and Sony Ericsson have not yet announced plans to sell less-than-$50 handsets, preferring to rake in profits at the high end. Chinese makers such as Bird and TCL find that their volume is not high enough to match the efficiencies enjoyed by Nokia and Motorola, so they lose money on low-end phones. Many customers at the base may be illiterate, but they are brand conscious. At the same price, they prefer Nokia and Motorola over unknown brands. Already, both Nokia and Motorola are further consolidating their position by making models for as little as $25, while still maintaining margins at approximately 30%, which is comparable to their margin around the world. Overall, this is a win-win solution for numerous emerging economies eager to develop and for the few farsighted and capable mobile phone makers to do what C. K. Prahalad, a guru on the base of the pyramid, preaches: serving the world's poor, *profitably*.

Sources: Based on (1) *Business Week*, 2005, Cell phones for the people, November 14: 65; (2) *Economist*, 2005, Calling across the divide, March 12: 74; (3) *Economist*, 2006, Mobile phones in Africa, February 4: 94; (4) C. K. Prahalad & A. Hammond, 2002, Serving the world's poor, profitably, *Harvard Business Review*, September: 48–57; (5) C. K. Prahalad & S. Hart, 2002, The fortune at the bottom of the pyramid, *Strategy + Business*, 26 (1): 2–14.

What are some of the benefits you might enjoy as an expatriate manager?

significant **international premium** in compensation—a significant pay raise when working overseas. In US firms, their total compensation package is approximately $250,000 to $300,000 (including benefits; not all is take-home pay). To put it bluntly, if a 2,000-employee ball-bearing factory in Lima, Ohio is shut down and the MNE sets up a similar factory in Lima, Peru, only about ten to twenty jobs would be saved. Yes, you guessed it: These jobs are a few top-level positions such as the CEO, CFO, CIO, factory director, and chief engineer. These managers will be sent by the MNE as expats to Peru to start up operations there. Because it is regarded as a "hardship" assignment, the MNE has to give them many more perks in Peru than in Ohio. How about company-subsidized luxury housing plus maid services, free tuition for children in American or international schools in Peru, and all-expenses paid vacation for the whole family to see their loved ones in Ohio? Moreover, these expats do not live in Peru forever. When they return to the United States after a tour of duty (usually two or three years), if their current employer does not provide attractive career opportunities, they are often hired by competing firms. This is because competing firms are also interested in globalizing their business by tapping into the expertise and experience of these former expats. And yes, to hire away these internationally experienced managers, competing firms will have to pay them an even larger premium. This indeed is a virtuous cycle.

international premium
A significant pay raise commanded by expats when working overseas.

This hypothetical example serves two purposes in motivating you: (1) Study hard, and someday you can become one of these sought-after, globetrotting managers. (2) If you do not care about being expats, do you really want to join the ranks of the unemployed due to such layoffs? If this scenario is too hypothetical, check out the 1998 movie *The Full Monty*. It portrays how laid-off steelworkers, to make a living, pick up an "alternative" line of work that my editors do not allow me to mention here—psst . . . it's male strip dancing.

Second, even for graduates at large companies with no aspiration to compete for the top job and for individuals who work at small firms or are self-employed, you may find yourself dealing with foreign-owned suppliers and buyers, competing with foreign-invested firms in your home market, and perhaps even selling and investing overseas. Alternatively, you may find yourself working for a foreign-owned firm, your domestic employer acquired by a foreign player, or your unit ordered to shut down for global consolidation. This is a very likely scenario because approximately 80 million people worldwide, including 18 million Chinese, six million Americans, and one million British, are employed by foreign-owned firms. Understanding how global business decisions are made may facilitate your own career in such firms.[9] If there is a strategic rationale to downsize your unit, you would want to be able to figure this out and be the first one to post your résumé on Monster.com. In other words, it is your career that is at stake. Don't be the last in the know!

In short, in this age of global competition, "how do you keep from being Bangalored? Or Shanghaied?"[10] (That is, have your job outsourced to India or China.) A good place to start is to study hard and do well in your IB course.

LEARNING OBJECTIVE **3**

identify one most fundamental question and two core perspectives that provide a framework for studying this field

A UNIFIED FRAMEWORK

Global business is a vast subject area. It is one of the few courses that will make you appreciate why your university requires you to take a number of (seemingly unrelated) courses in general education. Here, we draw on major social sciences that you have probably studied in general education, such as economics, geography, history, psychology, political science, and sociology, as well as a number of business disciplines such as finance and marketing. It is very easy to lose sight of the "forest" while scrutinizing various "trees" or even "branches." The subject is not difficult, and most students find it to be fun. The number one student complaint (based on previous student feedback) is an overwhelming amount of information, which is also my number one complaint as your author.

To proactively address your possible complaint and make your learning more manageable (and ideally, more fun), we will develop a unified framework as a consistent theme to cover *all* chapters (Figure 1.3). This will provide great continuity to facilitate your learning. Specifically, we will discipline ourselves by focusing on only one most fundamental question. A fundamental question acts to define a field and to orient the attention of students, practitioners, and scholars in a certain direction. Our "big question" is: *What determines the success and failure of firms around the globe?*[11] To answer this question, we will introduce only two core perspectives throughout this book: (1) an institution-based view and (2) a resource-based view. The remainder of this section outlines why this is the case.

One Fundamental Question

What is it that we do in global business? Why is it so important that practically every student in a business school around the world is either required or recommended to take this course? Although there are certainly a lot of questions to raise, a relentless interest in "what determines the success and failure of firms around the globe?" serves to unify the energy of our field. Global business, fundamentally, is about not limiting yourself to your home country and about treating the entire global economy as your potential playground (or battlefield). Some firms may be successful domestically. However, when they venture abroad, they fail miserably. Other firms successfully translate their strengths from their home market to other countries. If you were to lead your firm's efforts to enter a particular foreign market, wouldn't you want to find out what is behind the success and failure of other firms in that market?

Overall, the focus on firm performance around the globe, more than anything else, defines the field of global business. Numerous other questions all relate in one way or another to this most fundamental question. Therefore, the primary focus of this book is to answer this question: What determines the success and failure of firms around the globe?

FIGURE 1.3 A UNIFIED FRAMEWORK FOR GLOBAL BUSINESS

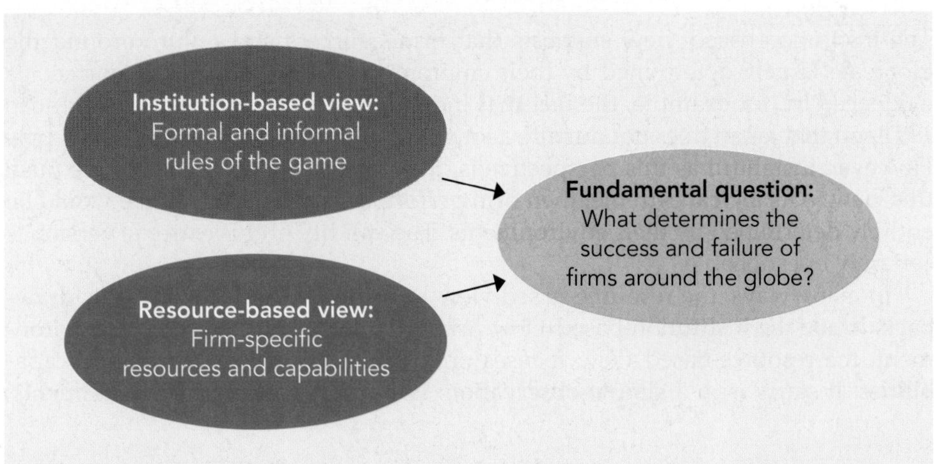

First Core Perspective: An Institution-Based View[12]

In layperson's terms, institutions are the "rules of the game." Doing business around the globe requires intimate knowledge about the formal and informal rules governing competition in various countries. It is difficult to imagine that ignorant firms not doing their "homework" to know the rules of the game in a certain country will emerge as winners. In a nutshell, an institution-based view suggests that success and failure of firms are enabled and constrained by the different rules of the game.

Some *formal* rules of the game, such as the requirements to treat domestic and foreign firms as equals, would enhance the potential odds for foreign firms' success. Hong Kong is well known to treat all comers, ranging from neighboring mainland China (whose firms are still technically regarded as "nondomestic") to far-away Chile, the same as it treats indigenous Hong Kong firms. It is thus not surprising that Hong Kong attracts a lot of outside firms. Other rules of the game, which may discriminate against foreign firms, would undermine the chances for foreign entrants. India's recent attraction as a site for foreign investment in IT/BPO (see Opening Case) was only possible after it changed its FDI regulations from confrontational to accommodating. Prior to 1991, India's rules severely discriminated against foreign firms. As a result, few foreign firms bothered to show up there, and the few that did had a hard time. For example, in the 1970s, Coca-Cola was confronted by the Indian government to either get out of India or hand over the recipe for its secret syrup, which it did not (and still does not) share even with the US government. Painfully, Coca-Cola chose to leave India. Its return to India since the 1990s speaks volumes about the changing rules of the game in India.

In addition to formal rules, *informal* rules such as cultures, ethics, and norms play an important part in shaping the success and failure of firms around the globe. For example, because founding new firms tends to deviate from the social norm of working for other bosses, individualistic societies, led by the English-speaking countries such as Australia, Britain, and the United States, tend to have a relatively higher level of entrepreneurship as reflected in the number of business start-ups. Conversely, collectivistic societies such as Japan often have a hard time fostering entrepreneurship; most people there refuse to stick their neck out to found new businesses, which is against the norm.[13]

Overall, an institution-based view suggests that the formal and informal rules of the game, known as institutions, shed a great deal of light on what is behind firm performance around the globe.[14]

Second Core Perspective: A Resource-Based View[15]

The institution-based view suggests that firms' success and failure around the globe are largely determined by their environments. This is certainly correct, as evidenced by, for example, the fact that India failed to attract much FDI prior to 1991 and that Japan does not nurture a lot of internationally competitive start-ups. However, insightful as this perspective is, there is a major drawback. If we push this view to its logical extreme, then firm performance around the globe would be entirely determined by their environments. The validity of this extreme version is certainly questionable.

In many ways, the resource-based view has emerged to overcome this drawback. While the institution-based view primarily deals with the *external* environment, the resource-based view focuses on a firm's *internal* resources and capabilities. It starts with a simple observation: In harsh, unattractive environments, most firms either suffer or exit. However, against all odds, a few superstars thrive in these environments. For instance, despite the former Soviet Union's declared hostility toward the United States during the Cold War, PepsiCo had been successfully operating in the former Soviet Union starting in the 1970s (!). In the global airline industry, where most of the major airlines around the world have been losing money since September 11, 2001, a small number of players, such as Southwest in the United States and Ryanair in Ireland, have been raking in profits year after year. How can these firms succeed in highly unattractive and often hostile environments? A short answer is that PepsiCo, Southwest, and Ryanair must have certain valuable and unique *firm-specific* resources and capabilities that are not shared by competitors in the same environments.

Doing business outside one's home country is challenging. Foreign firms have to overcome a **liability of foreignness**, which is the *inherent* disadvantage that foreign firms experience in host countries because of their nonnative status.[16] Just think about all the differences in regulations, languages, cultures, and norms. Against such significant odds, the primary weapon foreign firms employ is overwhelming resources and capabilities that after offsetting the liability of foreignness, still result in some significant competitive advantage. Today, many of us take it for granted that year in and year out, Toyota Camry is the best-selling car in the United States, Coca-Cola is the best-selling soft drink in Mexico, and Microsoft Word is the market-leading word processing software around the world. We really shouldn't take it for granted because it is *not* natural for these foreign firms to dominate nonnative markets. Behind such remarkable success stories, these firms must possess some very rare and powerful firm-specific resources and capabilities that are the envy of their rivals around the globe.

liability of foreignness
The inherent disadvantage that foreign firms experience in host countries because of their non-native status.

What are some factors that have contributed to JetBlue's success, despite a challenging business environment?

A Consistent Theme

Given our focus on the fundamental question of what determines the success and failure of firms around the globe, we will develop a unified framework by organizing the materials in *every* chapter according to the two core perspectives—namely, institution- and resource-based views. This is the *first* time a global business (or IB) textbook has developed such a consistent theme across all its chapters. Insightful as some of the previous books are, they probably collect too many "trees" or "branches" without assembling a coherent "forest." Our unified framework—an innovation in IB books—guides our exploration of the global business "forest."

WHAT IS GLOBALIZATION?

LEARNING OBJECTIVE 4
participate in the debate on globalization with a reasonably balanced and realistic view and a keen awareness of your likely bias in favor of globalization

The rather abstract five-syllable word **globalization** is now frequently heard and debated.[17] Those who approve of globalization count its contributions to include higher economic growth and standards of living, increased sharing of technologies, and more extensive cultural integration. Critics argue that globalization undermines wages in rich countries, exploits workers in poor countries, and gives MNEs too much power. So, what exactly is globalization? This section (1) outlines three views of globalization, (2) recommends the "pendulum" view, and (3) introduces the idea of "semiglobalization."

globalization
The close integration of countries and peoples of the world.

Three Views of Globalization

Depending on what sources you read, globalization could be

- A new force sweeping through the world in recent times
- A long-run historical evolution since the dawn of human history
- A pendulum that swings from one extreme to another from time to time

An understanding of these views helps put things in perspective. First, opponents of globalization suggest that it is a new phenomenon since the late 20th century, driven by both the recent technological innovations and Western hypocrisy designed for MNEs to exploit and dominate the world. While presenting few clearly worked-out alternatives to the present economic order, other than an ideal world free of environmental stress, social injustice, and branded sportswear (allegedly made in "sweatshops"), pundits of this view nevertheless often argue that globalization needs to be slowed down if not stopped.[18] Most antiglobalization protesters seem to share this view.

A second view contends that globalization has always been part and parcel of human history.[19] Some historians are debating whether globalization started 2,000 or 8,000 years ago. MNEs existed for more than two millennia, with their earliest traces discovered in Assyrian, Phoenician, and Roman Empires.[20] International competition from low-cost countries is nothing new. In the first century A.D., so concerned was the Roman Emperor Tiberius about the massive quantity of low-cost Chinese silk imports that he imposed the world's first known import quota of textiles.[21] Today's most successful MNEs do not come close to wielding the historical clout of some MNEs such as Britain's East India Company during colonial times. In a nutshell, globalization is nothing new and will always march on.

A third view suggests that globalization is the "closer integration of the countries and peoples of the world which has been brought about by the enormous reduction of the costs of transportation and communication, and the breaking down of artificial barriers to the flows of goods, services, capital, knowledge, and (to a lesser extent) people across borders."[22] Globalization is neither recent nor one directional. It is, more accurately, a process similar to the swing of a pendulum.

The Pendulum View of Globalization

The third, pendulum view probably makes the most sense because it can help us understand the ups and downs of globalization. The current era of globalization originated in the aftermath of World War II, when major Western nations committed to global trade and investment. However, between the 1950s and 1970s, this view was not widely shared. Communist countries, such as China and the (former) Soviet Union, sought to develop self-sufficiency. Many noncommunist developing countries, such as Argentina, Brazil, India, and Mexico, focused on fostering and protecting domestic industries. However, refusing to participate in global trade and investment ended up breeding uncompetitive industries. In contrast, four developing economies in Asia—namely, Hong Kong, Singapore, South Korea, and Taiwan—earned their stripes as the "Four Tigers" by participating in the global economy. They become the *only* economies once recognized as less developed (low-income) by the World Bank to have subsequently achieved developed (high-income) status.

Inspired by the Four Tigers, more and more countries, such as China in the late 1970s, Latin America in the mid-1980s, Central and Eastern Europe in the late 1980s, and India in the 1990s, realized that joining the world economy was a must. As these countries started to emerge as new players in the world economy, they become collectively known as "emerging economies" (as discussed earlier).[23] As a result, globalization rapidly accelerated. For example, between 1990 and 2000, while world output grew by 23%, global trade expanded by 80% and the total flow of FDI increased fivefold.[24]

However, as a pendulum, globalization is unable to keep going in one direction. The 1990s, a period of very rapid globalization, saw some significant backlash against it. First, the rapid growth of globalization led to the historically inaccurate view that globalization is new. Second, it created fear among many people in developed economies because emerging economies not only seem to compete away many low-end manufacturing jobs but also increasingly appear to threaten some high-end jobs. Finally, some factions in emerging economies complained against the onslaught of MNEs, which allegedly not only destroy local companies but also local cultures and values as well as the environment. Many people in Indonesia, South Korea, and Thailand devastated by the 1997 Asian economic crisis bitterly resented the pre-1997 policies of rapid capital market liberalization, which made these countries subject to both the irrational exuberance and pessimism of the global investment community. They further resented the "rescue" policies of the International Monetary Fund (IMF) that might have exacerbated the downturns[25] (see Chapter 7).

Although small-scale acts of vandalizing McDonald's restaurants are reported in a variety of countries, the December 1999 antiglobalization protests in Seattle and the September 2001 terrorist attacks in New York and Washington are undoubtedly the most visible and most extreme acts of antiglobalization forces at work. As a result, international travel was curtailed, and global trade and investment flows slowed in the early 2000s.[26]

More recently, worldwide economic growth has again been humming on all cylinders. World GDP, cross-border trade, and per capita GDP have all soared to historically high levels. More than half of the world GDP growth now comes from emerging economies, whose per capita GDP grew 4.6% annually in the decade ending 2007. **BRIC** (a newly coined acronym for Brazil, Russia, India, and China) has become a new buzzword. Developed economies are also doing well, averaging 2% per capita GDP growth during the same period. *Fortune* in 2007 declared that "for your average globetrotting *Fortune* 500 CEO, right now is about as good as it gets."[27] Yet, the same article cautioned, "Assuming history at some point proves yet again unkind . . . it pays to be vigilant."

BRIC
A newly coined acronym for the emerging economies of Brazil, Russia, India, and China.

Overall, like the proverbial elephant, globalization is seen by everyone and rarely comprehended. All of us felt sorry when we read the story of a bunch of blindmen trying to figure out the shape and form of an elephant. Although we are not blind, our task is more challenging than the blindmen who study a standing animal. This is because we (1) try to live with, (2) avoid being crushed by, and (3) even attempt to profit from a rapidly moving (back and forth!) beast called globalization. We believe that the view of globalization as a pendulum is a more balanced and realistic perspective. Like the two-faced Janus (a Roman god), globalization has both rosy and dark sides.[28]

Semiglobalization

Most measures of market integration (such as trade and FDI) have recently scaled new heights but still fall far short of complete globalization. In other words, what we have may be labeled **semiglobalization**, which is more complex than extremes of total isolation and total globalization. Semiglobalization suggests that barriers to market integration at borders are high but not high enough to completely insulate countries from each other.[29] Semiglobalization calls for more than one way for doing business around the globe. Total isolation on a nation-state basis would suggest localization (treating each country as a unique market) and total globalization would lead to standardization (treating the entire world as one market), but there is no single correct strategy in the world of semiglobalization, which results in a wide variety of experimentations.[30] Overall, (semi)globalization is neither to be opposed as a menace nor to be celebrated as a panacea; it is to be *engaged*.[31]

semiglobalization
A perspective that suggests that barriers to market integration at borders are high but not high enough to completely insulate countries from each other.

LEARNING OBJECTIVE 5

have a basic understanding of the future of the global economy and its broad trends

GLOBAL BUSINESS AND GLOBALIZATION AT A CROSSROADS

The challenge confronting a new generation of business leaders in the 21st century is enormous. This book will provide you with a road map. As a backdrop for the remainder of this book, this section makes two points. First, a basic understanding of the world economy is necessary. Second, it is important to critically examine your own personal views and biases on globalization.

A Glance of the World Economy

The world economy at the beginning of the 21st century is an approximately $48 trillion economy (total global GDP calculated at official, nominal exchange rates). Although there is no need to memorize a lot of statistics, it is useful to remember this $48 trillion figure to put things in perspective.

A frequent observation in the globalization debate is the enormous size of MNEs. Table 1.1 ranks sales of the world's largest MNEs alongside the GDP of the world's largest countries. The size of these leading MNEs is indeed striking: 47 of the world's top 100 economic entities are companies. If the two largest MNEs, US-based Wal-Mart and Exxon Mobil, were independent countries, they would be the 22nd and 23rd largest economies, respectively (their sales are smaller than

TABLE 1.1 TOP 100 ECONOMIES (GDP) AND COMPANIES (SALES)

Rank	Company	Country	US $ Millions	Rank	Company	Country	US $ Millions
1		United States	13,201,819	21		Indonesia	364,459
2		Japan	4,340,133	22	Wal-Mart Stores	(US)	351,139
3		Germany	2,906,681	23	ExxonMobil	(US)	347,254
4		China	2,668,071	24		Poland	338,733
5		United Kingdom	2,345,015	25		Austria	322,444
6		France	2,230,721	26	Royal Dutch Shell	(UK/ Netherlands)	318,845
7		Italy	1,844,749	27		Norway	310,960
8		Canada	1,251,463	28		Saudi Arabia	309,778
9		Spain	1,223,988	29		Denmark	275,237
10		Brazil	1,067,962	30	BP	(UK)	274,316
11		Russian Federation	986,940	31		South Africa	254,992
12		India	906,268	32		Greece	244,951
13		South Korea	888,024	33		Iran	222,889
14		Mexico	839,182	34		Ireland	222,650
15		Australia	768,178	35		Argentina	214,058
16		Netherlands	657,590	36		Finland	209,445
17		Turkey	402,710	37	General Motors	(US)	207,349
18		Belgium	392,001	38		Thailand	206,247
19		Sweden	384,927	39	Toyota Motor	(Japan)	204,746
20		Switzerland	379,758	40	Chevron	(US)	200,567

Table 1.1, *continued*

Rank	Company	Country	US $ Millions	Rank	Company	Country	US $ Millions
41		Portugal	192,572	71	AIG	(US)	113,194
42	Daimler Chrysler	(Germany)	190,191	72		Hungary	112,899
43		Hong Kong, China	189,798	73	China National Petroleum	(China)	110,520
44		Venezuela	181,862	74	BNP Paribas	(France)	109,214
45	Conoco-Phillips	(US)	172,451	75	ENI	(Italy)	109,014
46	Total	(France)	168,351	76	UBS	(Switzerland)	107,835
47	General Electric	(U.S)	168,307	77		Egypt	107,484
48	Ford Motor	(US)	160,126	78	Siemens	(Germany)	107,342
49	ING Group	(Netherlands)	158,274	79	State Grid	(China)	107,182
50		Malaysia	148,940	80		Ukraine	106,111
51	Citigroup	(US)	146,777	81		New Zealand	103,873
52		Chile	145,841	82	Assicurazioni Generali	(Italy)	101,811
53		Czech Republic	141,801	83	J. P. Morgan Chase	(US)	99,973
54	AXA	(France)	139,738	84	Carrefour	(France)	99,015
55		Colombia	135,836	85	Berkshire Hathaway	(US)	98,539
56	Volkswagen	(Germany)	132,323	86	Pemex	(Mexico)	97,469
57		Singapore	132,158	87	Deutsche Bank	(Germany)	96,152
58	Sinopec	(China)	131,636	88	Dexia Group	(Belgium)	95,847
59		United Arab Emirates	129,702	89	Honda Motor	(Japan)	94,790
60		Pakistan	128,830	90	McKesson	(US)	93,574
61	Crédit Agricole	(France)	128,481	91		Peru	93,269
62	Allianz	(Germany)	125,346	92	Verizon	(US)	93,221
63		Israel	123,434	93	NTT	(Japan)	91,998
64		Romania	121,609	94	Hewlett-Packard	(US)	91,658
65	Fortis	(Belgium/ Netherlands)	121,202	95	IBM	(US)	91,424
66	Bank of America	(US)	117,017	96	Valero Energy	(US)	91,051
67		Philippines	116,931	97	Home Depot	(US)	90,837
68	HSBC Holdings	(Britain)	115,361	98	Nissan Motor	(Japan)	89,502
69		Algeria	114,727	99	Samsung Electronics	(South Korea)	89,476
70		Nigeria	114,686	100	Credit Suisse	(Switzerland)	89,354

Sources: Adapted from (1) World Development Indicators database, World Bank, http://www.worldbank.org (accessed July 12, 2007) and (2) *Fortune*, 2007, The *Fortune* Global 500, http://www.fortune.com (accessed July 12, 2007). Numbers are rounded by the author. All numbers refer to 2006 data.

Indonesia's GDP but larger than Poland's). The sales of the largest EU-based MNE, Royal Dutch Shell, were larger than the GDP of Norway, Denmark, Greece, and Ireland—all EU members. The sales of the largest Asia-Pacific-based MNE, Toyota, were greater than the GDP of Malaysia, Singapore, and New Zealand.

In 2006, over 77,000 MNEs controlled at least 770,000 subsidiaries overseas.[32] Total annual sales of the largest 500 MNEs exceed $20 trillion (about 40% of global output). Table 1.2 documents the change in the makeup of the 500 largest MNEs. Figure 1.4 tracks the changes between 1996 and 2006, during which revenues nearly doubled. In general, over 80% of the 500 largest MNEs come from the Triad. Since 1990, the United States has contributed about one-third of these firms, the European Union has maintained a reasonably steady increase, and Japan has experienced the most dramatic variation (roughly corresponding to its economic boom and bust with several years of delay).

Among MNEs from emerging economies, those from South Korea and Brazil have largely maintained their presence in the *Fortune* Global 500. MNEs from China have come on strong—Beijing is now headquarters of 18 *Fortune* Global 500 firms, four fewer than New York City. Table 1.3 shows that in select industries, these MNEs, often regarded as "Third World multinationals" or "dragon multinationals," have joined the top ranks.[33] Clearly, Western rivals cannot afford to ignore them, and students reading this book need to pay attention to these emerging multinationals.

The Globalization Debate and You

At the dawn of the 21st century, the seemingly one-directional march of globalization started to show its color as a pendulum, which has direct ramifications for you as a future business leader, a consumer, and a citizen. At least two sets of sudden, high-profile events have occurred that have significant ramifications for business around the world: (1) antiglobalization protests and (2) terrorist attacks. First,

TABLE 1.2 CHANGES IN THE *FORTUNE* GLOBAL 500, 1990–2006

Country/bloc	1990	1991	1992	1993	1994	1995	1996	1997
United States	164	157	161	159	151	153	162	175
European Union	129	134	126	126	149	148	155	155
Japan	111	119	128	135	149	141	126	112
Canada	12	9	8	7	5	6	6	8
South Korea	11	13	12	12	8	12	13	12
Switzerland	11	10	9	9	14	16	14	12
China	0	0	0	0	3	2	3	4
Australia	9	9	9	10	3	4	5	7
Brazil	3	1	1	1	2	4	5	5
Others	50	48	46	41	16	14	11	10
Total	**500**	**500**	**500**	**500**	**500**	**500**	**500**	**500**

large-scale antiglobalization protests began in December 1999, when more than 50,000 protesters blocked downtown Seattle in an attempt to derail a ministerial meeting of the World Trade Organization (WTO). The demonstrators were protesting against a wide range of issues, including job losses resulting from foreign competition, downward pressure on unskilled wages, and environmental destruction. Since Seattle, antiglobalization protestors have turned up at just about every major globalization meeting, and some protests have become violent. It is obvious that numerous individuals in many countries believe that globalization has detrimental effects on living standards and the environment. As shown throughout this book, the debate on globalization has numerous dimensions, and neither the proglobalization forces nor the antiglobalization forces have won the debate.[34]

A second set of events center on terrorist attacks in New York and Washington on September 11, 2001, and the resultant war on terror in Afghanistan, Iraq, and elsewhere. Since then, terrorists struck Indonesia, Spain, and Britain. Terrorism, which used to be "a random political risk of relatively insignificant proportions,"[35] is now a leading concern for business leaders around the globe.[36] Heightened risk of terrorism has (1) reduced freedom of international movement as various countries curtail visas and immigration, (2) enhanced security checks at airports, seaports, and land border crossing points (see In Focus 1.3), and (3) canceled or scaled down trade and FDI deals, especially in high-risk regions such as the Middle East.

As a future business leader, you are not reading this book as a disinterested reader—as you would when reading a history book. The globalization debate directly affects *your* future.[37] Therefore, it is imperative that you participate in the globalization debate, instead of letting other people make decisions on globalization that will significantly affect your career, your consumption, and your country. Although this book does not advocate any particular view for your participation in the debate, it is important to know your own biases when joining the debate. By your very act of now taking an IB course and reading this book, you probably already have some proglobalization biases relative to nonbusiness majors elsewhere on campus and the general public in your country.

Table 1.2, *continued*

Country/bloc	1998	1999	2000	2001	2002	2003	2004	2005	2006
United States	185	179	185	178	192	189	176	170	162
European Union	156	148	136	139	150	147	161	165	165
Japan	100	107	95	88	88	100	81	70	67
Canada	12	12	13	5	14	12	13	14	16
South Korea	9	12	8	12	13	9	11	12	14
Switzerland	11	11	10	9	11	12	11	12	13
China	6	10	10	10	11	14	16	20	24
Australia	7	7	7	6	6	7	9	8	8
Brazil	4	3	3	4	4	3	3	4	5
Others	10	11	33	49	11	7	19	25	26
Total	**500**	**500**	**500**	**500**	**500**	**500**	**500**	**500**	**500**

Sources: Based on data from various issues of *Fortune Global 500*. Finland and Sweden are included as "others" prior to 1996 and as European Union after 1996.

FIGURE 1.4 THE *FORTUNE* GLOBAL 500

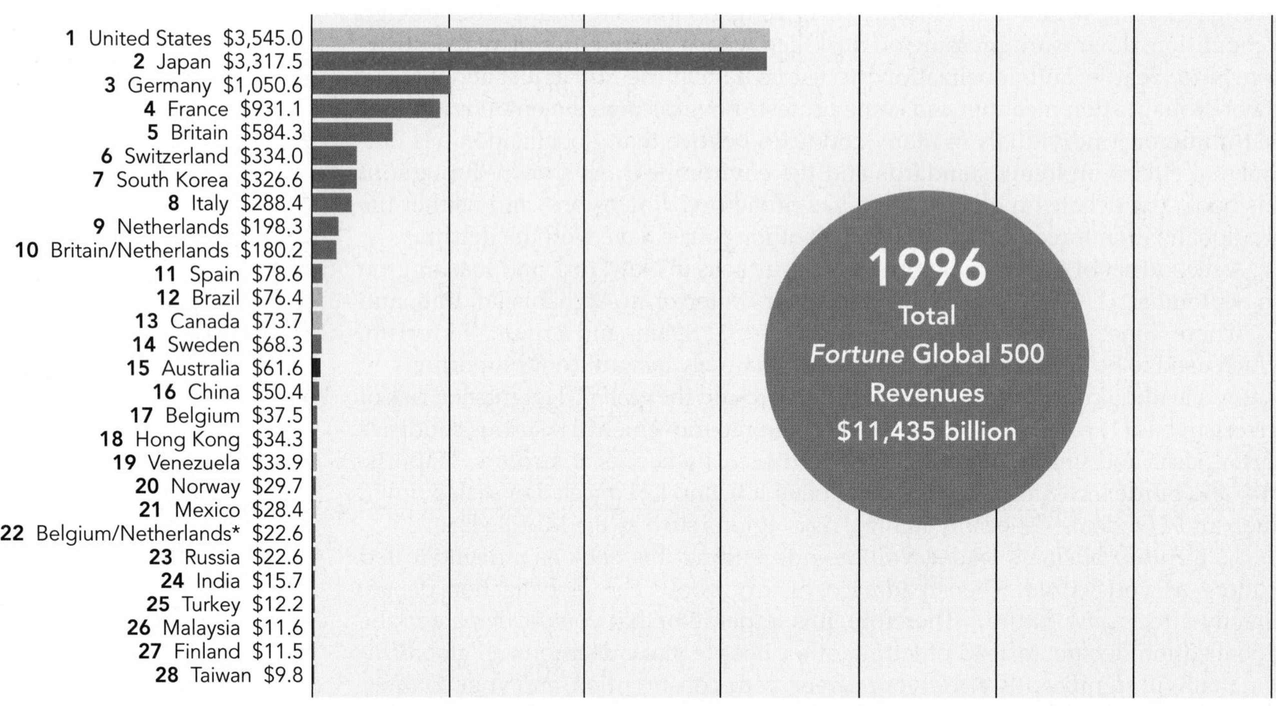

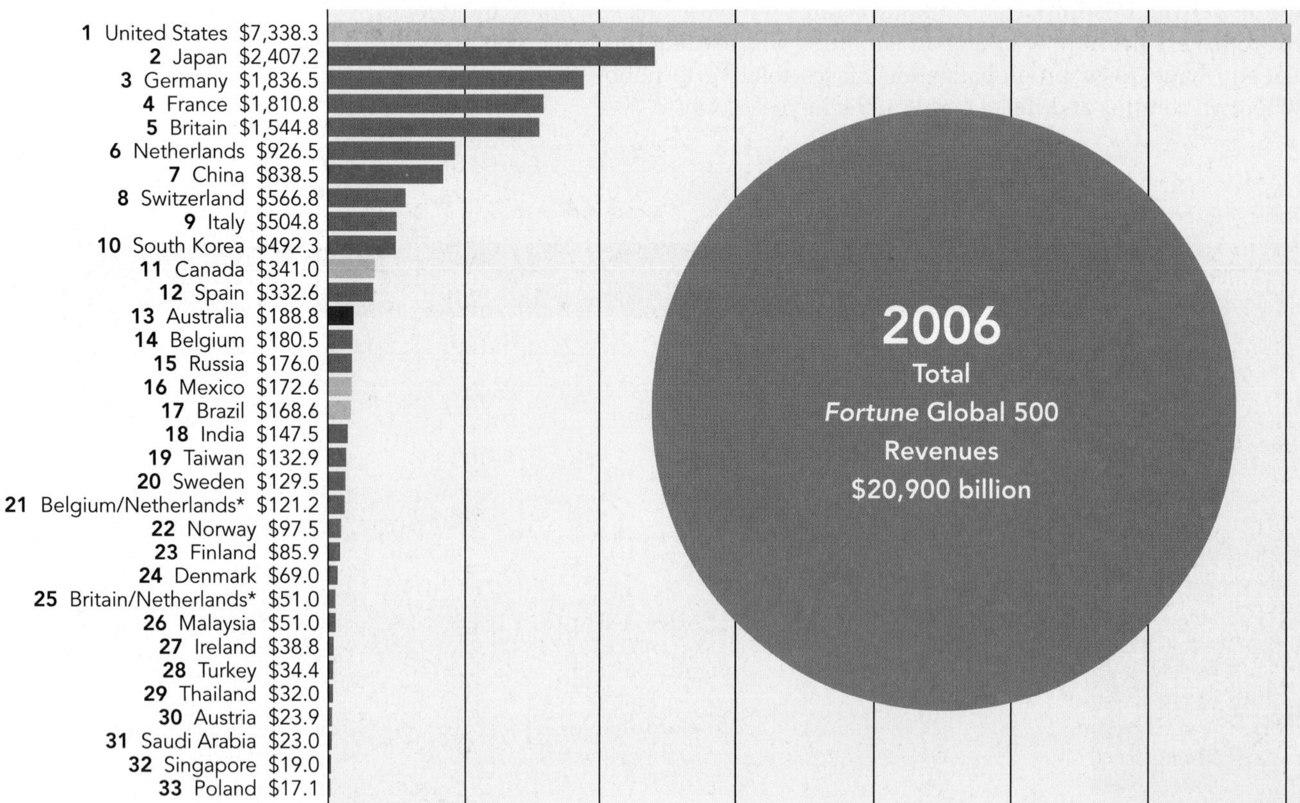

* Dual listings indicate companies headquartered in two countries.

Source: *Fortune*, 2007, The world's largest corporations (p. 101), July 23: 100–103. Revenues of firms headquartered in one country are consolidated into one circle for 1996 and another one for 2006.

TABLE 1.3 TOP TEN MNEs (BASED ON REVENUES) IN SELECT INDUSTRIES

(Companies in **bold** typeface are based in emerging economies)

	Container shipping	Electronics	Mining	Petroleum refining	Steel
1	A.P. Moller-Maersk	Siemens	BHP Billiton	ExxonMobil	Arcelor Mittal
2	Mediterranean	Hitachi	Alcoa	BP	Nippon Steel
3	CMA CGM	Matsushita	Alcan	Shell	JFE Steel
4	**Evergreen**	**Samsung Electronics**	Rio Tinto	Total	**POSCO**
5	Hapag-Lloyd	Sony	**Vale do Rio Doce**	Chevron	**Baosteel**
6	**China Shipping**	Toshiba	Phelps Dodge	Conoco-Philips	US Steel
7	**APL**	Tyco	Commercial Metals	**Sinopec**	Corus
8	**Hanjin**	**LG Electronics**	Furukawa	ENI	Nucor
9	**COSCO**	Royal Philips	Inco	**CNPC**	ThyssenKrupp
10	NYK	Mitsubishi Electric	**Aluminum Corp. of China**	Valero	Riva

Source: Adapted from United Nations, 2006, *World Investment Report 2006* (p. 123), New York and Geneva: United Nations.

You are not alone. In the last several decades, most elites in both developed and emerging economies—executives, policymakers, and scholars—are biased toward acknowledging the benefits of globalization.[38] Although it has long been known that globalization carries both benefits and costs, many elites have failed to take into sufficient account the social, political, and environmental costs associated with globalization. However, that these elites share certain perspectives on globalization does *not* mean that most other members of the society share the same views. Unfortunately, many elites fail to understand the limits of their beliefs and mistakenly

IN FOCUS 1.3 ETHICAL DILEMMA: Terrorism, Protectionism, and Homeland Security

In 2004, in response to terrorist attacks, the US Department of Homeland Security awarded a major contract to Accenture LLP to design and implement the US Visitor and Immigrant Status Indicator Technology (US-VISIT) program, which would be deployed at the nation's more than 400 ports of entry. However, several members of Congress noted that Accenture LLP is *not* a US firm and argued that the contract should have been awarded to bona fide US firms—in other words, better homeland security protection calls for protectionism. Accenture LLP is the US-based subsidiary of Accenture Ltd., which is a global technology consulting firm with $15 billion revenues in 2005. Accenture Ltd. has 123,000 employees in 48 countries, and 25,000 of them are in the United States. Despite Accenture Ltd.'s strong US roots (as part of the now-defunct Arthur Andersen until 1989) and its US stock listing (NYSE: ACN), it is incorporated in Bermuda, and its SEC filings disclose it as a "Bermuda holding company." The dilemma thus boils down to whether outsourcing US-VISIT to the US subsidiary of a Bermuda firm, as opposed to a "pure" US firm, compromises the effectiveness of the program.

© Tim Brakemeier/dpa /Landov

Sources: Based on (1) J. Carafano, 2005, Global terrorism and the global economy, in *2005 Index of Economic Freedom*, Washington, DC: Heritage Foundation, http://www.heritage.org; (2) SEC filings by Accenture Ltd., 2005; (3) http://www.accenture.com.

nongovernment organizations (NGO)
Organizations, such as environmentalists, human rights activists, and consumer groups that are not affiliated with governments.

assume that the rest of the world is like "us." To the extent that powerful economic and political institutions are largely controlled by these elites in almost every country, it is not surprising that some powerless antiglobalization groups end up resorting to unconventional tactics (such as mass protests) to make their point.

A lot of opponents of globalization are **nongovernment organizations (NGOs)**, such as environmentalists, human rights activists, and consumer groups. Ignoring them will be a grave failure in due diligence when doing business around the globe.[39] Instead of viewing NGOs as opponents, many firms view them as partners.[40] NGOs do raise a valid point on the necessity of firms, especially MNEs, to have a broader concern for various stakeholders affected by their actions around the world.[41] At present, this view is increasingly moving from the periphery to the mainstream (see Chapter 17).

It is certainly interesting and perhaps alarming to note that as would-be business leaders who will shape the global economy in the future, current business school students already exhibit values and beliefs in favor of globalization similar to those held by executives, policymakers, and scholars and different from those held by the general public. Shown in Table 1.4, relative to the general public, US business students have significantly more positive (almost one-sided) views toward globalization. While these data are based on US business students, my teaching and lectures around the world suggest that most business students worldwide—regardless of their nationality—seem to share such positive views on globalization. This is not surprising. Both self-selection to study business and socialization within the curriculum, in which free trade is widely regarded as positive, may lead to certain attitudes in favor of globalization. Consequently, business students may focus more on the economic gains of globalization and be less concerned with its darker sides.

Current and would-be business leaders need to be aware of their own biases embodied in such one-sided views of globalization. Since business schools aspire to train future business leaders by indoctrinating students with the dominant values managers hold, these results suggest that business schools may have largely succeeded in this mission. However, to the extent that there are strategic blind spots in the views of the current managers (and professors), these findings are potentially alarming. They reveal that business students already share these blind spots. Despite possible self-selection in choosing to major in business, there is no denying that student values are shaped, at least in part, by the educational experience business schools provide. Knowing such limitations, business school professors and students need to work especially hard to break out of this straightjacket.[42]

TABLE 1.4 VIEWS OF GLOBALIZATION: AMERICAN GENERAL PUBLIC VS. BUSINESS STUDENTS

Percentage answering "good" for the question: Overall, do you think globalization is *good* or *bad* for	General public[1] (*N* = 1,024)	Business students[2] (*N* = 494)
• US consumers like you	68%	96%
• US companies	63%	77%
• The US economy	64%	88%
• Strengthening poor countries' economies	75%	82%

Sources: Based on (1) A. Bernstein, 2000, Backlash against globalization, *Business Week*, April 24: 43; (2) M. W. Peng & H. Shin, 2008, How do future business leaders view globalization? *Thunderbird International Business Review* (in press). All differences are statistically significant.

To combat the widespread tendency to have one-sided, rosy views of globalization, a significant portion of this book is devoted to numerous debates. Beyond this chapter (which illustrates a big debate in itself), debates are systematically introduced in *every* chapter to provoke more critical thinking and discussion. Virtually all textbooks uncritically present knowledge "as is" and ignore the fact that the field is alive with numerous debates. No doubt, it is debates that drive practice and research forward. Therefore, it is imperative that you be exposed to cutting-edge debates and encouraged to form your own views when engaging in these debates.[43] In addition, ethics is emphasized throughout the book. A featured Ethical Dilemma and a series of Critical Discussion Questions on ethics can be found in every chapter. In addition, two full-blown chapters are devoted to ethics, norms, and cultures (Chapter 3) and corporate social responsibility (Chapter 17).

ORGANIZATION OF THE BOOK

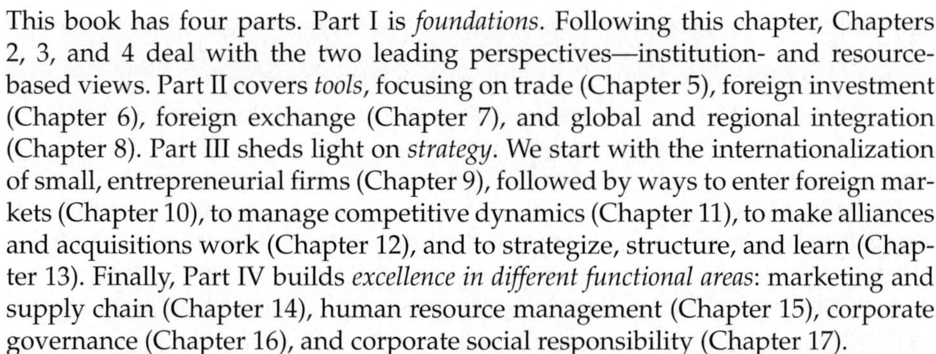

This book has four parts. Part I is *foundations*. Following this chapter, Chapters 2, 3, and 4 deal with the two leading perspectives—institution- and resource-based views. Part II covers *tools*, focusing on trade (Chapter 5), foreign investment (Chapter 6), foreign exchange (Chapter 7), and global and regional integration (Chapter 8). Part III sheds light on *strategy*. We start with the internationalization of small, entrepreneurial firms (Chapter 9), followed by ways to enter foreign markets (Chapter 10), to manage competitive dynamics (Chapter 11), to make alliances and acquisitions work (Chapter 12), and to strategize, structure, and learn (Chapter 13). Finally, Part IV builds *excellence in different functional areas*: marketing and supply chain (Chapter 14), human resource management (Chapter 15), corporate governance (Chapter 16), and corporate social responsibility (Chapter 17).

In closing, most of you were probably surprised by the Opening Case on the global nature of your textbook. Globalization is fascinating, isn't it? This book will reduce the element of surprise by providing a road map as you embark on this journey. Welcome aboard!

CHAPTER SUMMARY

1. Explain the concepts of international business (IB) and global business
   - IB is typically defined as (1) a business (firm) that engages in international (cross-border) economic activities and (2) the action of doing business abroad.
   - Global business is defined in this book as business around the globe.
   - This book goes beyond competition in developed economies by devoting extensive space to competitive battles waged in emerging economies and the base of the global economic pyramid.
2. Articulate what you hope to learn by reading this book and taking this course
   - To better compete in the corporate world that will require global expertise.
   - To enhance your understanding of what is going on in the global economy.
3. Identify one most fundamental question and two core perspectives that provide a framework for studying this field
   - Our most fundamental question is: What determines the success and failure of firms around the globe?
   - The two core perspectives are (1) the institution-based view and (2) the resource-based view.

- We develop a unified framework by organizing materials in *every* chapter according to the two perspectives guided by the fundamental question.

4. Participate in the debate on globalization with a reasonably balanced and realistic view and a keen awareness of your own likely bias in favor of globalization
   - Some view globalization as a recent phenomenon, and others believe that it is a one-directional evolution since the dawn of human history.
   - We suggest that globalization is best viewed as a process similar to the swing of a pendulum.

5. Have a basic understanding of the future of the global economy and its broad trends
   - MNEs, especially large ones from developed economies, are sizable economic entities.
   - Current and would-be business leaders need to be aware of their own hidden proglobalization biases.

KEY TERMS

Base of the pyramid 7
BRIC 13
Emerging economies (emerging markets) 5
Expatriate manager (expat) 7
Foreign direct investment (FDI) 4
Global business 5
Globalization 11
Gross domestic product (GDP) 5
Gross national income (GNI) 6
Gross national product (GNP) 6
International business (IB) 4
International premium 8
Liability of foreignness 11
Multinational enterprise (MNE) 4
Nongovernment organization (NGO) 20
Purchasing power parity (PPP) 5
Semiglobalization 13
Triad 6

REVIEW QUESTIONS

1. What is the difference between international business and global business, as defined in this book?
2. Referring to Figure 1.1, how important are emerging economies in the overall global economy?
3. Referring to Figure 1.2, what observations can you make about the three tiers of people in the global economic pyramid?
4. What is your interest in studying global business? How do you think it might apply to your future?
5. If you were to work as an expatriate manager, where would you like to go and what would you like to do?
6. What is the fundamental question driving your study of global business, and why is it important?
7. How would you describe an institution-based view of global business?
8. How would you describe a resource-based view of global business?
9. After comparing the three views of globalization described in this book, which seems the most logical or sensible to you and why?

10. What is semiglobalization, and what factors contribute to it?
11. What do Table 1.2 and Figure 1.4 tell you about changes in the global economy over the last ten to fifteen years?
12. Why do some people protest against globalization? What point do they make that all people, whether for or against globalization, should consider?
13. What can people who are in favor of global business learn from NGOs such as environmentalists, human rights activists, and consumer groups?

CRITICAL DISCUSSION QUESTIONS

1. A classmate says: "Global business is relevant for top executives such as CEOs in large companies. I am just a lowly student who will struggle to gain an entry-level job, probably in a small domestic company. Why should I care about it?" How do you convince her that she should care about it?
2. In his book *The World Is Flat* (2005), Thomas Friedman suggests that the world is flattening—meaning it is increasingly interconnected by new technology such as the Internet. This can raise the poor from poverty, nurture a worldwide middle class, and even spread democracy. On the other hand, this presents significant challenges for developed economies, whose employees may feel threatened by competition from low-cost countries. How does this flattening world affect you?
3. ON ETHICS: What are some of the darker sides (in other words, costs) associated with globalization? How can business leaders make sure that the benefits of their various actions (such as outsourcing discussed in Opening Case) outweigh their drawbacks (such as job losses in developed economies)?
4. ON ETHICS: Some argue that aggressively investing in emerging economies is not only economically beneficial but also highly ethical because it may potentially lift many people out of poverty (see Closing Case). However, others caution that in the absence of reasonable hopes of decent profits, rushing to emerging economies is reckless. How would you participate in this debate?

VIDEO CASE

Watch "International Business" by Sir Bob Reid of Halifax Bank of Scotland.

1. How does the experience of the Nigerians in Japan illustrate what has been covered in this chapter regarding the "informal rules of the game?"
2. What did Sir Reid say that would suggest that "foreignness" is less an issue in West Africa than adaptability?
3. This chapter covered a range of economically developed nations but Sir Reid focused on West Africa—to what extent do his ideas apply to doing business in developed economies?
4. Why did Sir Reid mention the importance of listening?
5. If your school has students from other countries, how does this video help improve the effectiveness of the interaction among them?

CLOSING CASE

Global Business and Emerging Economies

The bulk of international business takes place among developed economies—also described as high-income countries, Western (plus Japanese) economies, and the First World—which contribute approximately 74% of the global GDP by official (nominal) exchange rates. The UN defines these 44 countries as having per capita incomes in excess of $9,000. Is it appropriate to continue to focus on them in the 21st century?

Referred to as developing economies, less developed countries, low-income nations, and the Third World, the term *emerging economies* has caught on since the 1990s. One side of the debate argues that emerging economies are the markets of tomorrow, and they are also frequently labeled "emerging markets." This argument is certainly both true *and* false. Emerging economies consist of 156 countries in various stages of development, accounting for 84% of the world's population but only approximately 26% of its GDP by official exchange rates. Some of them grow rapidly, whereas many others will be submerging in the years to come. In short, much of the base of the global economic pyramid will remain the base. Advocates for emerging economies concede that the relative economic firepower of even some of the largest emerging economies is limited. For example, Russia's GDP is smaller than Italy's and Mexico's GDP is smaller than Texas's.

© RAUL VASQUEZ/Bloomberg News/Landov

However, what is exciting seems to be the growth potential of some (although not all) emerging economies, especially Brazil, Russia, India, and China—known as BRIC. During the Industrial Revolution, it took America and Britain 50 years to double their GDP. Today, China is achieving that in a single decade. Therefore, if Western firms want to grow, they will have to participate in such growth. For instance, demand for durables such as washers, dryers, and cars is primarily based on replacement needs in the West, whereas in many emerging economies, rising income levels afford numerous first-time purchases of these big-ticket items.

At present, FDI inflows to emerging economies command about one-third of global FDI inflows, $334 billion of the global total of $916 billion in 2006. Since FDI inflows to emerging economies trail those to developed economies, the argument goes, Western firms need to *disproportionately* invest in emerging economies. To support this argument, experts note that measured at purchasing power parity (PPP), emerging economies already command 50% of global GDP (see Figure 1.1). More than half of the world GDP *growth* now comes from emerging economies, whose per capita GDP grew 4.6% annually in the decade ending 2007 (developed economies averaged 2% per capita annual GDP growth during the same period). As a result, more and more job descriptions for CEOs in Western MNEs call for explicit business experience on the ground in emerging economies. Boards increasingly are looking for CEOs with passports showing frequent visits to BRIC.

On the other hand, strong arguments have been made against aggressively moving into emerging economies, given their uncertainties. Emerging economies often experience tremendous booms and busts. The Asian "miracle" was suddenly replaced by a major crisis in 1997. Central and Eastern Europe experienced the euphoria of the removal of communism in 1989, which was quickly replaced by a deep recession worsened by the Russian default in 1998. Since 1995, every major Latin America economy was hit by a significant crisis: Mexico (1995), Brazil (1998), Argentina (2002), and Venezuela (2006). China has been periodically hit by crises, ranging from SARS (2003) to the product safety mess (2007).

Overall, emerging economies represent the classic combination of high risk and high (potential) return. A sensible strategy for Western MNEs is to strike a balance between developed and emerging economies. Strong performance in emerging economies may significantly contribute to the worldwide corporate bottom line. Volkswagen, for instance, derives approximately one-third of its *worldwide* profits from China alone.

For another example, consider water. General Electric (GE) is working on water-desalination systems in the Middle East at $0.001 per millimeter, which, according to GE's CEO Jeff Immelt, is "off-the-charts low cost." "We will never hit that in the US." Immelt continued, "But we'll hit it someplace outside. And the second we do, a huge market is going to open up inside as well." Likewise, GE is working in China on a magnetic resonance imaging (MRI) scanner that could cut price in half. "At the right cost point, you not only sell it in China," Immelt commented, "you open up a market among the 35% of US hospitals that today cannot afford to have an MRI scanner."

However, the expertise of Western MNEs, profiting from high-income customers at the top of the global pyramid, requires significant adaptation. For instance, bragging about shampoo-and-conditioner-in-one (otherwise known as 2-in-1) is of little relevance to customers who have never used shampoo or conditioner. Entering emerging economies with a warehouse-style retail format suitable for markets with a high level of car ownership (such as Costco and Sam's Club) is unlikely to reach the masses, who usually do not have cars.

Despite significant differences, emerging economies have enough common underlying logic to justify developing an alternative business model based on price/value trade-offs different from those in developed economies. General Motors and Honda are racing to develop $5,000 entry-level cars for China. Given these MNEs' inability to profitably produce such models in the United States and Japan, imagine the profit potential these models developed in China may have back home where entry-level cars now sell for $10,000.

To the extent Western MNEs often find it tough going in these unfamiliar territories, it is not surprising that some new MNEs from emerging economies—called Third World multinationals or "dragon multinationals"—well versed in such an alternative business model are capturing the hearts, minds, and wallets of customers in emerging economies. In India, Tata Motors is striving to unleash a "one lakh" car (one lakh equals 100,000 rupees, roughly $2,500). In the Philippines, Jollibee beats the mighty McDonald's and is now venturing out to Southeast Asia and the Middle East. In Africa, Asia, and Central America, South African Breweries (now SABMiller) runs neck and neck with Anheuser-Busch, Carlsberg, and Heineken. Out of China, Lenovo aspires to become "king of the hill" in the PC battle. In a nutshell, there is money to be made in and out of emerging economies. The million (or billion) dollar challenge for global business in the 21st century is: How to make such money?

Case Discussion Questions

1. From an institution-based view, what determines firm performance in emerging economies?
2. From a resource-based view, what determines firm performance in emerging economies?
3. What are the main concerns that prevent Western MNEs from aggressively investing in emerging economies? What are the costs if they choose not to focus on emerging economies?

Sources: Based on (1) P. Aulakh, 2007, Emerging multinationals from developing economies, *Journal of International Management*, 13: 235–240; (2) L. Brouthers, E. O'Donnell, & J. Hadjimarcou, 2005, Generic product strategies for emerging market exports into Triad nation markets, *Journal of Management Studies*, 42: 225–245; (3) N. Dawar & A. Chattopadhyay, 2002, Rethinking marketing programs for emerging markets, *Long Range Planning*, 35: 457–474; (4) Economist Intelligence Unit, 2006, *Corporate Priorities for 2006 and Beyond*, London: *The Economist*; (5) *Fortune*, 2007, The greatest economic boom ever, July 23: 75–80; (6) S. Hart & T. London, 2005, Developing native capability, *Stanford Social Innovation Review*, summer: 28–33; (7) J. Mathews, 2006, Dragon multinationals as new features of globalization in the 21st century, *Asia Pacific Journal of Management*, 23: 5–27; (8) R. Wooster, 2006, U.S. companies in transition economies, *Journal of International Business Studies*, 37: 179–195; (9) M. Wright, I. Filatotchev, R. Hoskisson, & M. W. Peng, 2005, Strategy research in emerging economies, *Journal of Management Studies*, 42: 1–33.

NOTES

Journal acronyms: AME – *Academy of Management Executive;* **AMJ** – *Academy of Management Journal;* **AMR** – *Academy of Management Review;* **APJM** – *Asia Pacific Journal of Management;* **BW** – *Business Week;* **CMR** – *California Management Review;* **HBR** – *Harvard Business Review;* **JIBS** – *Journal of International Business Studies;* **JIM** – *Journal of International Management;* **JM** – *Journal of Management;* **JMS** – *Journal of Management Studies;* **JWB** – *Journal of World Business;* **LRP** – *Long Range Planning;* **MIR** – *Management International Review;* **SMJ** – *Strategic Management Journal;* **TIBR** – *Thunderbird International Business Review*

[1] This definition of the MNE can be found in R. Caves, 1996, *Multinational Enterprise and Economic Analysis*, 2nd ed. (p. 1), New York: Cambridge University Press; J. Dunning, 1993, *Multinational Enterprises and the Global Economy* (p. 30), Reading, MA: Addison-Wesley. Other terms are multinational corporation (MNC) and transnational corporation (TNC), which are often used interchangeably with MNE. To avoid confusion, in this book, we use MNE.

[2] O. Shenkar, 2004, One more time: International business in a global economy (p. 165), *JIBS*, 35: 161–171. See also J. Boddewyn,

B. Toyne, & Z. Martinez, 2004, The meanings of "international management," *MIR*, 44: 195–215.

[3] M. W. Peng, 2005, From China strategy to global strategy, *APJM*, 22: 123–141; M. W. Peng, 2003, Institutional transitions and strategic choices, *AMR*, 28: 275–296.

[4] *Economist*, 2006, Climbing back, January 21: 69–70.

[5] T. Hasfi & M. Farashahi, 2005, Applicability of management theories to developing countries, *MIR*, 45: 483–513; R. Hoskisson, L. Eden, C. Lau, & M. Wright, 2000, Strategy in emerging economies, *AMJ*, 43: 249–267; K. Meyer, 2004, Perspectives on multinational enterprises in emerging economies, *JIBS*, 35: 259–276; K. Meyer & M. W. Peng, 2005, Probing theoretically into Central and Eastern Europe, *JIBS*, 36: 600–621; R. Ramamurti, 2004, Developing countries and MNEs, *JIBS*, 35: 277–283; M. Wright, I. Filatotchev, R. Hoskisson, & M. W. Peng, 2005, Strategy research in emerging economies, *JMS*, 42: 1–33.

[6] Economist Intelligence Unit, 2006, *CEO Briefing: Corporate Priorities for 2006 and Beyond*, London: The Economist.

[7] S. Hart, 2005, *Capitalism at the Crossroads*, Philadelphia: Wharton School Publishing; T. London & S. Hart, 2004, Reinventing strategies for emerging markets, *JIBS*, 35: 350–370; C. K. Prahalad, 2005, *The Fortune at the Bottom of the Pyramid*, Philadelphia: Wharton School Publishing.

[8] A. Yan, G. Zhu, & D. Hall, 2002, International assignments for career building, *AMR*, 27: 373–391.

[9] W. Newburry, 2001, MNC interdependence and local embeddedness influences on perceptions of career benefits from global integration, *JIBS*, 32: 497–508.

[10] *BW*, 2007, The changing talent game (p. 68), August 20: 68–71.

[11] M. W. Peng, 2004, Identifying the big question in international business research, *JIBS*, 35: 99–108.

[12] M. W. Peng, D. Wang, & Y. Jiang, 2008, An institution-based view of international business strategy: A focus on emerging economies, *JIBS* (forthcoming).

[13] S. Lee, M. W. Peng, & J. Barney, 2007, Bankruptcy laws and entrepreneurship development, *AMR*, 32: 257–272.

[14] W. Henisz & B. Zelner, 2005, Legitimacy, interest group pressures, and change in emergent institutions, *AMR*, 30: 361–382; B. Kim & J. Prescott, 2005, Deregulatory forms, variations in the speed of governance adaptation, and firm performance, *AMR*, 30: 414–425; I. Mahmood & C. Rufin, 2005, Government's dilemma, *AMR*, 30: 338–360; P. Ring, G. Bigley, T. D'Aunno, & T. Khanna, 2005, Perspectives on how governments matter, *AMR*, 30: 308–320; P. Rodriguez, K. Uhlenbruck, & L. Eden, 2005, Government corruption and the entry strategies of multinationals, *AMR*, 30: 383–396.

[15] M. W. Peng, 2001, The resource-based view and international business, *JM*, 27: 803–829.

[16] J. Mezias, 2002, Identifying liabilities of foreignness and strategies to minimize their effects, *SMJ*, 23: 229–244; S. Miller & A. Parkhe, 2002, Is there a liability of foreignness in global banking? *SMJ*, 23: 55–75; S. Zaheer, 1995, Overcoming the liability of foreignness, *AMJ*, 38: 341–363.

[17] T. Clark & L. Knowles, 2003, Global myopia, *JIM*, 9: 361–372.

[18] A. Giddens, 1999, *Runaway World*, London: Profile; S. Strange, 1996, *The Retreat of the State*, Cambridge: Cambridge University Press.

[19] B. Husted, 2003, Globalization and cultural change in international business research, *JIM*, 9: 427–433.

[20] K. Moore & D. Lewis, 1999, *Birth of the Multinational*, Copenhagen: Copenhagen Business School Press.

[21] D. Yergin & J. Stanislaw, 2002, *The Commanding Heights* (p. 385), New York: Simon & Schuster.

[22] J. Stiglitz, 2002, *Globalization and Its Discontents* (p. 9), New York: Norton.

[23] The term *emerging economies* was probably coined in the 1980s by Antonie van Agtmael, a Dutch officer at the World Bank's International Finance Corporation (IFC). See Yergin & Stanislaw, 2002, *The Commanding Heights* (p. 134).

[24] United Nations, 2000, *World Investment Report 2000*, New York and Geneva: United Nations.

[25] This view is not only shared by ordinary critics of globalization but also by Joseph Stiglitz, former chair of the Presidential Council of Economic Advisers, former senior vice president and chief economist of the World Bank, and 2001 winner of the Nobel prize in economics. See Stiglitz, 2002, *Globalization and Its Discontents* (esp. chap. 4).

[26] J. Oxley & K. Schnietz, 2001, Globalization derailed? *JIBS*, 32: 479–496.

[27] All information and quotes in this paragraph are from *Fortune*, 2007, The greatest economic boom ever, July 23: 75–80.

[28] L. Eden & S. Lenway, 2001, Multinationals: The Janus face of globalization, *JIBS*, 32: 383–400.

[29] P. Ghemawat, 2003, Semiglobalization and international business strategy, *JIBS*, 34: 138–152.

[30] J. Ricart, M. Enright, P. Ghemawat, & S. Hart, 2004, New frontiers in international strategy, *JIBS*, 35: 175–200; A. Rugman & A. Verbeke, 2004, A perspective on regional and global strategies of multinational enterprises, *JIBS*, 35: 3–18.

[31] M. Guillen, 2001, *The Limits of Convergence* (p. 232), Princeton, NJ: Princeton University Press; W. Stanbury & I. Vertinsky, 2004, Economics, demography and cultural implications of globalization, *MIR*, 44: 131–151.

[32] United Nations, 2006, *World Investment Report 2006* (p. 10), New York and Geneva: United Nations.

[33] P. Aulakh, 2007, Emerging multinationals from developing economies, *JIM*, 13: 235–240; A. Cuervo-Cazurra, 2007, Sequence of value-added activities in the multinationalization of developing country firms, *JIM*, 13: 258–277; B. Elango & C. Pattnaik, 2007, Building capabilities for international operations through networks, *JIBS*, 38: 541–555; I. Filatotchev, R. Strange, J. Piesse, & Y. Lien, 2007, FDI by firms from newly industrialized economies in emerging markets, *JIBS*, 38: 556–572; M. Garg & A. Delios, 2007, Survival of the foreign subsidiaries of TMNCs, *JIM*, 13: 278–295; S. Klein & A. Worcke, 2007, Emerging global contenders, *JIM*, 13: 319–337; J. Lee & J. Slater, 2007, Dynamic capabilities, entrepreneurial rent-seeking, and the investment development path, *JIM*, 13: 241–257; P. Li, 2007, Toward an integrated theory of multinational evolution, *JIM*, 13: 296–318; Y. Luo & R. Tung, 2007, International expansion of emerging market enterprises, *JIBS*, 38: 481–498; J. Mathews, 2006, Dragon multinationals as new features of globalization in the 21st century, *APJM*, 23: 5–27; D. Yiu, C. Lau, & G. Bruton, 2007, International venturing by emerging economy firms, *JIBS*, 38: 519–540.

[34] J. Bhagwati, 2004, *In Defense of Globalization*, New York: Oxford University Press; R. Rajan & L. Zingales, 2003, *Saving Capitalism from the Capitalists*, New York: Crown.

[35] M. Kotabe, 2005, Global security risks and international competitiveness (p. 453), *JIM*, 11: 453–455.

[36] P. Barnes & R. Oloruntoba, 2005, Assurance of security in maritime supply chains, *JIM*, 11: 519–540; M. Czinkota, G. Knight, P. Liesch, & J. Steen, 2005, Positioning terrorism in management and marketing, *JIM*, 11: 581–604; N. Kshetri, 2005, Pattern of global cyber war and crime, *JIM*, 11: 541–562; S. Li, S. Tallman, & M. Ferreira, 2005, Developing the eclectic paradigm as a model of global strategy, *JIM*, 11: 479–496; R. Spich & R. Grosse, 2005, How does homeland security affect U.S. firms' international competitiveness? *JIM*, 11: 457–478.

[37] T. Friedman, 2005, *The World Is Flat*, New York: Farrar, Straus & Giroux.

[38] A. Bird & M. Stevens, 2003, Toward an emergent global culture and the effects of globalization on obsolescing national cultures, *JIM*, 9: 395–407.

[39] H. Teegen, J. Doh, & S. Vachani, 2004, The importance of nongovernmental organizations (NGOs) in global governance and value creation, *JIBS*, 35: 463–483.

[40] D. Rondinelli & T. London, 2003, How corporations and environmental groups cooperate, *AME*, 17 (1): 61–76; S. Hart & M. Milstein, 2003, Creating sustainable value, *AME*, 17 (2): 56–67.

[41] A. Peredo & J. Chrisman, 2006, Toward a theory of community-based enterprise, *AMR*, 31: 309–328; C. Robertson & W. Crittenden, 2003, Mapping moral philosophies, *SMJ*, 24: 385–392.

[42] J. Pfeffer & C. Fong, 2004, The business school "business," *JMS*, 41: 1501–1520; K. Starkey, A. Hatchuel, & S. Tempest, 2004, Rethinking the business school, *JMS*, 41: 1521–1531.

[43] B. Kedia & A. Mukherji, 1999, Global managers, *JWB*, 34: 230–251; D. Ricks, 2003, Globalization and the role of the global corporation, *JIM*, 9: 355–359.

CHAPTER 2

Understanding Formal Institutions: Politics, Laws, and Economics

O P E N I N G   C A S E

Managing Risks in the New South Africa

With a population of 46 million, South Africa represents 10% of Africa's population and 45% of the continent's gross domestic product (GDP). Its GDP is almost as big as the rest of sub-Saharan Africa's 47 countries *combined*. As the engine of growth for Africa, South Africa recently has been growing at 5% annually. Its GDP ranks 20th in the world and is among the top-ten emerging economies.

Before 1994, South Africa had been ruled by a white minority government that earned notoriety for its apartheid (racial segregation) policy. In 1986, the US imposition of sanctions led many American multinationals such as AIG and IBM to divest their South African operations. In 1994, South Africa accomplished a peaceful transition of power, with the black majority party, African National Congress (ANC), taking over power. ANC's leader, Nelson Mandela, a Nobel peace prize laureate, served as its first post-apartheid president. Since then, South Africa has embarked on a new journey toward political reconciliation and economic liberalization.

Yet, doing business in South Africa has always been risky. Although the risks associated with apartheid are well known, managing risks in the post-apartheid era is no less challenging. Since 1994, South Africa has introduced fundamental and comprehensive changes to its "rules of the game," unleashing both uncertainties and opportunities. The new democratically elected ANC government has adopted a Black Economic Empowerment (BEE) policy aiming to increase blacks' share in the economy. Although neighboring Zimbabwe has violently expropriated land from white farmers and redistributed it to blacks, the South African government is committed to protecting property rights. BEE aims to accomplish its goals through peaceful means.

In principle, few South Africans disagree with BEE. Yet, there has been much grumbling over the way BEE has been implemented. This is because BEE is clearly intrusive, setting quotas and timetables in terms of black ownership, executive position, employment, and affirmative action procurement. South African firms, which are predominantly owned and managed by whites, are compelled to sell a substantial percentage (25% to 50%) of their equity to black-owned businesses and investors often at discounted prices. A number of leading South African firms listed on the New York Stock Exchange, such as AngloGold, SAPPI, Sasol, and Telkom, have disclosed BEE as a risk to shareholders because these firms cannot guarantee that BEE transactions would take place at fair market price. BEE also affects foreign firms. Foreign firms interested in securing government contracts in excess of $10 million are required to invest at least 30% of the sales in local black-owned firms. In the case of defense contracts, the percentage increases to 50%. Firms such as Sasol complain that in a country whose official unemployment rate is stubbornly high at 25% (which may really be as high as 40%), BEE scares away investment and deters foreign firms. Further, although BEE has rapidly created a new black business elite, it has not created jobs for the millions of poor and unemployed blacks. In other words, BEE has sliced up the economic cake differently but has done little to expand it. President Thabo Mbeki labeled firms such as SASOL "bigoted" and accused them of bad-mouthing South Africa's attempt to address the legacy of racism.

In addition to BEE, heavy-handed labor regulations are another area attracting business complaints. Unions are given broad power to block layoffs and limit the outsourcing of contracts, making a lot of firms reluctant to hire in the first place. The HIV/AIDS epidemic has reached epic proportions, affecting 5.5 million individuals, one-ninth of the population. Since laid-off

LEARNING OBJECTIVES

After studying this chapter, you should be able to

1. explain the concept of institutions and their key role in reducing uncertainty
2. articulate the two core propositions underpinning an institution-based view of global business
3. identify the basic differences between democracy and totalitarianism
4. outline the differences among civil law, common law, and theocratic law
5. understand the importance of property rights and intellectual property rights
6. appreciate the differences among market economy, command economy, and mixed economy
7. participate in three leading debates on politics, laws, and economics
8. draw implications for action

HIV-positive employees will be on government support, the government has more incentive to make it harder to fire employees. The upshot? Skyrocketing absenteeism and healthcare costs. Crime is another problem. Security expenditures and crime-related losses cost South African firms approximately 1% of sales, higher than in Russia or Brazil.

Despite the risks, many firms—both domestic and foreign—are charging ahead. For large domestic firms, noncompliance with BEE may not be an option in the long run. Thus, they adopt two strategies. The first is "fronting": relying on businesses controlled by blacks to acquire procurement contracts. Second, lobbying to renegotiate the BEE terms becomes a frequent coping strategy. The Chamber of Mines, an industry association for the important mining sector, successfully reduced the targeted ten-year equity quota for black ownership from 51% to 26%. Many foreign firms find it attractive to form joint ventures (JVs) or merge with black-owned firms. For instance, Tsavliris Salvage Group of Greece formed a JV with Cape Diving & Salvage of South Africa that has a 66% black equity stake. This JV thus is well positioned to go after government contracts in the offshore oil industry. PricewaterhouseCoopers's South African subsidiary merged with MSGM Masuku Jeena, the largest black-owned accounting firm in the country. The merger opened doors for more lucrative contracts.

Sources: I thank Professor Steve Burgess (University of Cape Town) for his insights and assistance on this case. This case is based on (1) S. Burgess, 2003, Within-country diversity: Is it key to South Africa's prosperity in a changing world? *International Journal of Advertising*, 22: 157–182; (2) *Economist*, 2006, Chasing the rainbow, April 8: 1–12; (3) Economist, 2006, South Africa, January 14: 51; (4) *Economist*, 2006, The way to BEE, December 23: 99; (5) *Economist*, 2007, The long journey of a young democracy, March 3: 32–34; (6) J. van Wyk, W. Dahmer, & M. Custy, 2004, Risk management and the business environment in South Africa, *Long Range Planning*, 37: 259–276.

Although South Africa is clearly the country to be in if one wants to do business with Africa, the country's post-apartheid transitions present numerous uncertainties. For domestic and foreign firms, pressing questions include: How do they play the game when the rules of the game are uncertain and keep changing? While there is a proposition that democracy usually goes hand in hand with a functioning market economy, does the government's insistence on BEE, often involving nonmarket-based quotas and below-market prices for equity sales to black firms and investors, support or refute this proposition? Should foreign firms be or not be interested in entering South Africa?

Fundamentally, doing business around the globe boils down to "location, location, location." As the Opening Case illustrates, different locations have different **institutions**, popularly known as "the rules of the game." Overall, the success and failure of firms around the globe are to a large extent determined by firms' ability to understand and take advantage of the different rules of the game. In other words, how firms play the game and win (or lose), at least in part, depends on how the rules are made and enforced. This calls for firms to constantly monitor, decode, and adapt to the changing rules of the game to survive and prosper. As a result, such an **institution-based view** has emerged as a leading perspective on global business.[1] This chapter first introduces the institution-based view. Then, we focus on *formal* institutions (such as political systems, legal systems, and economic systems). *Informal* institutions (such as cultures, ethics, and norms) will be discussed in Chapter 3.

institutions
Formal and informal rules of the game.

institution-based view
A leading perspective in global business that suggests that firm performance is, at least in part, determined by the institutional frameworks governing firm behavior around the world.

FORMAL AND INFORMAL INSTITUTIONS

LEARNING OBJECTIVE 1

explain the concept of institutions and their key role in reducing uncertainty

Building on the rules of the game metaphor, Douglass North, a Nobel laureate in economics, more formally defines institutions as "the humanly devised constraints that structure human interaction."[2] An **institutional framework** is made up of formal and informal institutions governing individual and firm behavior. These institutions are supported by three "pillars" identified by Richard Scott, a leading sociologist. They are (1) regulatory, (2) normative, and (3) cognitive pillars.[3]

Shown in Table 2.1, **formal institutions** include laws, regulations, and rules. In global business, such formal institutions may be imposed by home countries and host countries. Their primary supportive pillar, **regulatory pillar**, is the coercive power of governments. For example, the South African government has explicitly set targeted quotas and timetables in terms of black ownership, executive position, and employment ratio. Domestic and foreign firms failing to meet BEE targets have to pay fines and are disqualified from government contracts (see Opening Case).

On the other hand, **informal institutions** include norms, cultures, and ethics. There are two main supportive pillars: normative and cognitive. **Normative pillar** refers to how the values, beliefs, and actions of other relevant players—collectively known as norms—influence the behavior of focal individuals and firms. For instance, the recent norms centered on rushing to invest in China and India prompt many Western firms to imitate each other without a clear understanding of how to make such moves.[4] Cautious managers resisting such "herding" are often confronted by board members, investors, and reporters: "Why don't you invest in China and India?"

Also supporting informal institutions, **cognitive pillar** refers to the internalized, taken-for-granted values and beliefs that guide individual and firm behavior. For example, what triggered whistle-blowers to report Enron's wrongdoing is their beliefs in what is right and wrong. Although most employees may not feel comfortable with organizational wrongdoing, the norms are not to "rock the boat." Essentially, whistle-blowers choose to follow their internalized personal beliefs on what is right by overcoming the norms that encourage silence.

For firms doing business abroad, formal and informal institutional forces primarily stem from home countries and host countries, but international and regional organizations—such as the World Trade Organization (WTO), the International Monetary Fund (IMF), and the European Union (EU)—may also influence firm conduct in terms of do's and don'ts (see Chapters 7 and 8 for more details).

institutional framework
Formal and informal institutions governing individual and firm behavior.

formal institutions
Institutions represented by laws, regulations, and rules.

regulatory pillar
The coercive power of governments.

informal institutions
Institutions represented by norms, cultures, and ethics.

normative pillar
The mechanism through which norms influence individual and firm behavior.

cognitive pillar
The internalized, taken-for-granted values and beliefs that guide individual and firm behavior.

TABLE 2.1 DIMENSIONS OF INSTITUTIONS

Degree of formality	Examples	Supportive pillars
Formal institutions	• Laws • Regulations • Rules	• Regulatory (coercive)
Informal institutions	• Norms • Cultures • Ethics	• Normative • Cognitive

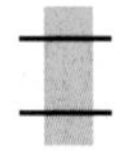

WHAT DO INSTITUTIONS DO?

Although institutions do many things, their key role, in two words, is to *reduce uncertainty*.[5] Specifically, institutions influence individuals' and firms' decision making by signaling which conduct is legitimate and acceptable and which is not. Basically, institutions constrain the range of acceptable actions. Why is it so important to reduce uncertainty? Because uncertainty can be potentially devastating.[6] Political uncertainty such as a coup may render long-range planning obsolete. Economic uncertainty such as failure to carry out transactions as spelled out in contracts may result in economic losses. An extreme case of political and economic uncertainty can be seen in Argentina in 2002, when the government defaulted on its $155 billion public debt, a world record. Desperate to maximize revenue, the government clumsily changed the rules of the economy. All dollar-denominated assets, despite previous legal assurances, were simply turned into pesos by a new government decree against the wishes of the asset holders. This caused the peso to slip fourfold against the dollar within a few months. During 2002, Argentina's GDP shrank 15%, unemployment rose to 23%, and riots broke out.

transaction costs
The costs associated with economic transactions—or more broadly, costs of doing business.

Uncertainty surrounding economic transactions can lead to **transaction costs**, which are defined as costs associated with economic transactions—or more broadly, costs of doing business. A leading theorist, Oliver Williamson, refers to frictions in mechanical systems: "Do the gears mesh, are the parts lubricated, is there needless slippage or other loss of energy?" He goes on to suggest that transaction costs can be regarded as "the economic counterpart of frictions: Do the parties to exchange operate harmoniously, or are there frequent misunderstandings and conflicts?"[7]

opportunism
Self-interest seeking with guile.

An important source of transaction costs is **opportunism**, defined as self-interest seeking with guile. Examples include misleading, cheating, and confusing other parties in transactions that will increase transaction costs. Attempting to reduce such transaction costs, institutional frameworks increase certainty by spelling out the rules of the game so that violations (such as failure to fulfill a contract) can be mitigated with relative ease (such as through formal arbitration and courts).

Without stable institutional frameworks, transaction costs may become prohibitively high, to the extent that certain transactions simply would not take place. For example, in the absence of credible institutional frameworks that protect investors, domestic investors may choose to put their money abroad. Rich Russians often choose to purchase a soccer club in London or a seaside villa in Cyprus instead of investing in Russia. In the aftermath of the 2002 crisis in Argentina, many foreign investors left and went to "greener pastures" elsewhere.

institutional transitions
Fundamental and comprehensive changes introduced to the formal and informal rules of the game that affect organizations as players.

Institutions are not static. **Institutional transitions**, defined as "fundamental and comprehensive changes introduced to the formal and informal rules of the game that affect organizations as players,"[8] are widespread in the world, especially in emerging economies (see Chapter 1 Closing Case). Institutional transitions in some emerging economies, particularly those moving from central planning to market competition (such as China, Poland, Russia, and Vietnam), are so pervasive that these countries are simply called "transition economies" (a *subset* of "emerging economies"). Institutional transitions in countries such as China, India, Russia (see Closing Case), and South Africa (see Opening Case) create both huge challenges and tremendous opportunities for domestic and international firms. For example, a Swedish manager working for IKEA in Russia complained that "Russia is a bit of a rollercoaster, you don't know exactly what will happen tomorrow."[9] But such unpredictability did not deter IKEA from investing $2.4 billion to operate eight megastores in Russia.

Having outlined the definitions of various institutions and their supportive pillars as well as their key role in uncertainty reduction, next we will introduce the first core perspective on global business: an institution-based view.

AN INSTITUTION-BASED VIEW OF GLOBAL BUSINESS

LEARNING OBJECTIVE 2

articulate the two core propositions underpinning an institution-based view of global business

Shown in Figure 2.1, an institution-based view of global business focuses on the dynamic interaction between institutions and firms and considers firm behaviors the outcome of such an interaction.[10] Specifically, firm behaviors are often a reflection of the formal and informal constraints of a particular institutional framework.[11] In short, institutions matter.

How do institutions matter? The institution-based view suggests two core propositions (Table 2.2). First, managers and firms *rationally* pursue their interests and make choices within institutional constraints. In the railway industry in China and India that is not affected by international competition, managers at the state-owned railways are eager to ask for help from the government and reluctant to improve service. In contrast, in the IT industry in China and India, managers have to excel in the game of market responsiveness and innovation because the rules of the game are defined by the global heavyweights. Both strategies are perfectly rational.

The second proposition is that formal and informal institutions combine to govern firm behavior, but in situations where formal constraints are unclear or fail, informal constraints play a *larger* role in reducing uncertainty and providing constancy to

FIGURE 2.1 INSTITUTIONS, FIRMS, AND FIRM BEHAVIORS

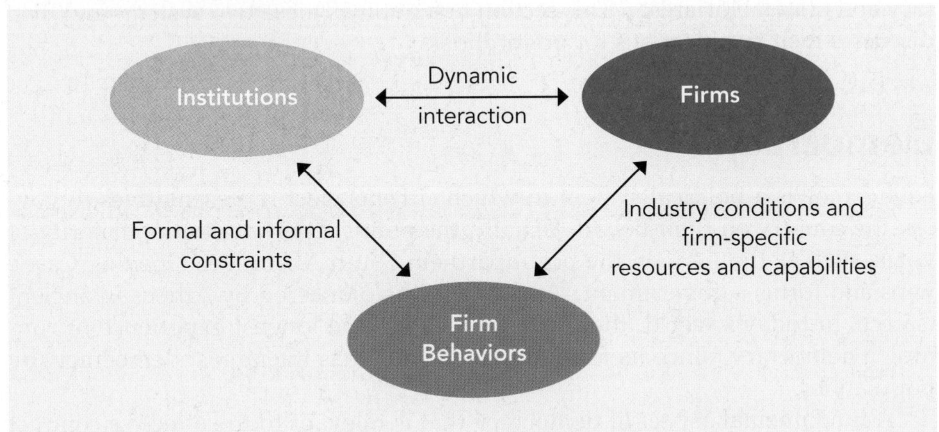

TABLE 2.2 TWO CORE PROPOSITIONS OF THE INSTITUTION-BASED VIEW

Proposition 1	Managers and firms *rationally* pursue their interests and make choices within the formal and informal constraints in a given institutional framework.
Proposition 2	Although formal and informal institutions combine to govern firm behavior, in situations where formal constraints are unclear or fail, informal constraints will play a *larger* role in reducing uncertainty and providing constancy to managers and firms.

managers and firms. For example, when the formal regime collapsed with the disappearance of the former Soviet Union, it is largely the informal constraints, based on personal relationships and connections (called *blat* in Russian) among managers and officials, that have facilitated the growth of many entrepreneurial firms.[12]

Many observers have the impression that relying on informal connections is only relevant to firms in emerging economies and that firms in developed economies only pursue "market-based" strategies. This is far from the truth. Even in developed economies, formal rules only make up a small (although important) part of institutional constraints, and informal constraints are pervasive. Just as firms compete in product markets, they also fiercely compete in the political marketplace characterized by informal relationships.[13] Basically, if a firm cannot be a market leader, it may still beat the competition on another ground—namely, the nonmarket, political environment.[14] The skillful use of a country's institutional frameworks to acquire advantage is at the heart of the institution-based view.

Although there are numerous formal and informal institutions, in this chapter we focus on *formal* institutions (informal institutions will be covered in Chapter 3). Chief among formal institutions are (1) political systems, (2) legal systems, and (3) economic systems. Each is briefly described next.

LEARNING OBJECTIVE 3

identify the basic differences between democracy and totalitarianism

TWO POLITICAL SYSTEMS

political system

A system of the rules of the game on how a country is governed politically.

A **political system** refers to the rules of the game on how a country is governed politically. At the broadest level, there are two primary political systems: (1) democracy and (2) totalitarianism. This section first outlines these two systems and then discusses their ramifications for political risk.

Democracy

democracy

A political system in which citizens elect representatives to govern the country on their behalf.

Democracy is a political system in which citizens elect representatives to govern the country on their behalf. Usually, the political party with the majority of votes, such as the ANC in the post-apartheid South Africa (see Opening Case), wins and forms a government. Democracy was pioneered by Athens in ancient Greece. In today's world, the United States has the longest experience of running a democracy (since its founding), and India has the largest democracy (by population).

A fundamental aspect of democracy that is relevant to the effective conduct of global business is an individual's right to freedom of expression and organization. For example, starting up a firm is an act of economic expression, essentially telling the rest of the world: "I want to be my own boss! And I want to make some money!" In most modern democracies, this right to organize economically has not only been extended to domestic individuals and firms but also to *foreign* individuals and firms that come to do business. Those of us fortunate enough to be brought up in a democracy take the right to found a firm for granted, but we should remember that this may not necessarily be the case under other political systems. Before the 1980s, if someone dared to formally found a firm in the former Soviet Union, he or she would have been arrested and *shot* by the authorities.

Totalitarianism

totalitarianism (or **dictatorship**)

A political system in which one person or party exercises absolute political control over the population.

At the opposite end of democracy is **totalitarianism** (also known as **dictatorship**), which is defined as a political system in which one person or party exercises absolute political control over the population. This section outlines four major types of totalitarianism.

- **Communist totalitarianism** centers on a communist party. This system had been embraced throughout Central and Eastern Europe and the former Soviet Union until the late 1980s. It is still practiced in China, Cuba, Laos, North Korea, and Vietnam.
- **Right-wing totalitarianism** is characterized by its intense hatred of communism. One party, typically backed by the military, restricts political freedom, arguing that such freedom would lead to communism. In the postwar decades, the Philippines, South Africa (see Opening Case), South Korea, Taiwan, and most Latin American countries practiced right-wing totalitarianism. Most of these countries have recently become democracies.
- **Theocratic totalitarianism** refers to the monopolization of political power in the hands of one religious party or group. Iran and Saudi Arabia are leading examples. Taliban-ruled Afghanistan, until 2001 when US forces removed the Taliban, is another example.
- **Tribal totalitarianism** refers to one tribe or ethnic group (which may or may not be the majority of the population) monopolizing political power and oppressing other tribes or ethnic groups. Rwanda's bloodbath in the 1990s was due to some of the most brutal practices of tribal totalitarianism.

Political Risk

Although the degree of hostility toward business varies among different types of totalitarianism (some can be more probusiness than others), totalitarianism in general is not as good as democracy for business. Totalitarian countries often experience wars, riots, protests, chaos, and breakdowns, which result in higher **political risk**—risk associated with political changes that may negatively impact domestic and foreign firms.[15] The most extreme political risk may lead to nationalization (expropriation) of foreign assets.[16] This happened in many totalitarian countries during the 1950s–1970s. Consider the oil industry in Argentina. The government in 1955 canceled international contracts signed by a previous president, Peron, in 1952. The next president signed new contracts in 1958, which were nullified in 1963 by a different president. Foreign oil companies were invited to return in 1966, expelled in 1973, and again encouraged to enter after 1976.[17] It is hardly surprising that foreign oil companies are sick and tired and would rather go to "greener pastures" elsewhere.

political risk
Risk associated with political changes that may negatively impact domestic and foreign firms.

Firms operating in democracies also confront political risk. However, such risk is qualitatively lower than that in totalitarian states. For example, Quebec's possible independence from the rest of Canada creates some political risk. Although firms highly exposed to Quebec may experience some drop in their stock price, there is no general collapse of stock prices in Canada or flight of capital out of Canada.[18] Investors are confident that should Quebec become independent, the Canadian democracy is mature enough to manage the breakup process in a relatively nondisruptive way.

No two democracies have reportedly gone to war with each other (see In Focus 2.1 for an interesting extension). Obviously, when two countries are at each other's throat, we can forget about doing business between them (perhaps other than smuggling). In this regard, the recent advance of democracy and retreat of totalitarianism are highly beneficial for global business. It is not a coincidence that globalization took off in the 1990s, a period when both communist and right-wing totalitarianism significantly lost their power and democracy expanded around the world (see Chapter 1).

IN FOCUS 2.1 McDonald's, Dell, and World Peace

Thomas Friedman, a *New York Times* columnist and author of the 1999 book *The Lexus and the Olive Tree*, reported that no two countries that both had McDonald's had ever fought a war against each other since they got their McDonald's. He theorized that the country does not necessarily have to operate a democracy, but if its political system can foster a middle class whose population is large enough to support a chain of McDonald's, people don't like to fight wars anymore. They prefer to wait in line for burgers. While this "theory" was offered slightly tongue in cheek, Friedman wrote that the serious point was that as countries are woven into the fabric of global trade and rising standards of living, which are symbolized by McDonald's, the cost of war becomes too prohibitive.

More recently, in a 2005 bestseller, *The World Is Flat*, Friedman upgraded his McDonald's theory and suggested a new Dell theory: No two countries that are both part of a major global supply chain, like Dell's, will ever fight a war against each other as long as they are both part of the same global supply chain. Countries involved in major global supply chains focus on just-in-time deliveries of goods and services, which raise standards of living. In the case of Dell (which, incidentally, is the computer your author is using when writing this textbook), the following countries are involved: China, Costa Rica, Germany, Israel, Malaysia, Philippines, South Korea, Taiwan, Thailand, and the United States. The biggest test of this theory is whether China will go to war with Taiwan, which is regarded as a renegade province by Beijing.

Sources: Based on (1) T. Friedman, 1999, *The Lexus and the Olive Tree*, New York: Farrar, Straus and Giroux; (2) T. Friedman, 2005, *The World Is Flat*, New York: Farrar, Straus and Giroux.

LEARNING OBJECTIVE  4

outline the differences among civil law, common law, and theocratic law

THREE LEGAL SYSTEMS

A **legal system** refers to the rules of the game on how a country's laws are enacted and enforced. By specifying the do's and don'ts, a legal system reduces transaction costs by minimizing uncertainty and combating opportunism. This section first introduces the three legal traditions and then discusses crucial issues associated with property rights and intellectual property.

legal system
The rules of the game on how a country's laws are enacted and enforced.

Civil Law, Common Law, and Theocratic Law

Laws in different countries typically are not enacted from scratch but are often transplanted—voluntarily or otherwise—from three legal traditions (or legal families): (1) civil law, (2) common law, and (3) theocratic law (Table 2.3). Each is briefly described here.

Civil law was derived from Roman law and strengthened by Napoleon's France. It is "the oldest, the most influential, and the most widely distributed around the world."[19] It uses comprehensive statutes and codes as a primary means to form legal judgments. More than 80 countries practice civil law. **Common law**, which is English in origin, is shaped by precedents and traditions from previous judicial decisions. Common law has spread to all English-speaking countries and their (former) colonies.

civil law
A legal tradition that uses comprehensive statutes and codes as a primary means to form legal judgments.

common law
A legal tradition that is shaped by precedents and traditions from previous judicial decisions.

Relative to civil law, common law has more flexibility because judges have to resolve specific disputes based on their *interpretation* of the law, and such interpretation may give new meaning to the law, which will shape future cases. Civil law has less flexibility because judges only have the power to *apply* the law. On the other hand, civil law is less confrontational because comprehensive statutes and codes serve to guide judges. Common law is more confrontational because plaintiffs and defendants, through their lawyers, must argue and help judges to favorably interpret the law largely based on precedents. In addition, contracts in common law countries tend to be long and detailed to cover all possible contingencies because common law tends to be relatively underdefined. In contrast, contracts in civil law countries are usually shorter and less specific because many issues typically articulated in common law contracts are already covered in comprehensive civil law codes.

TABLE 2.3 THREE LEGAL TRADITIONS[1]

Civil law countries	Common law countries	Theocratic law countries
Argentina, Austria, Belgium, Brazil, Chile, China, Egypt, France, Germany, Greece, Indonesia, Italy, Japan, Mexico, Netherlands, Russia, South Korea, Sweden, Switzerland, Taiwan	Australia, Canada, Hong Kong, India, Ireland, Israel, Kenya, Malaysia, New Zealand, Nigeria, Singapore, South Africa, Sri Lanka, United Kingdom, United States, Zimbabwe	Iran, Saudi Arabia

1. The countries are examples and do not exhaustively represent all countries practicing a particular legal system.

The third legal family is **theocratic law**, a legal system based on religious teachings. Examples include Jewish and Islamic laws. Although Jewish law is followed by some elements of the Israeli population, it is *not* formally embraced by the Israeli government. Only Islamic law is the surviving example of a theocratic legal system that is formally practiced by some governments, such as those of Iran and Saudi Arabia. Despite popular characterization that Islam is antibusiness, it is important to note that Muhammad was a merchant trader, and the tenets of Islam are probusiness in general. However, the holy book of Islam, the Koran, advises against *certain* business practices. In Saudi Arabia, McDonald's operates "ladies only" fast-food restaurants to be in compliance with the Koran's ban on direct, face-to-face contact between women (who often wear a veil) and men in public. Also in Saudi Arabia, banks have to maintain two retail branches: one for male customers staffed by men and another for female customers staffed by women. This requirement obviously increases the property, overhead, and personnel costs. To reduce costs, some foreign banks, such as HSBC, staff their back office operations with both male and female employees who work side by side.[20]

theocratic law
A legal system based on religious teachings.

Overall, as an important component of the first, regulatory pillar, legal systems are a crucial component of the institutional framework. They directly impose do's and don'ts on businesses around the globe. Under the broad scope of a legal system, there are numerous components. Two of these, property rights and intellectual property, are discussed next.

Property Rights

LEARNING OBJECTIVE 5
understand the importance of property rights and intellectual property rights

Regardless of which legal family a country's legal system belongs to, a most fundamental economic function that a legal system serves is to protect **property rights**—the legal rights to use an economic property (resource) and to derive income and benefits from it. Examples of property include homes, offices, and factories (intellectual property will be discussed in the next section).

property rights
The legal rights to use an economic property (resource) and to derive income and benefits from it.

What difference do property rights supported by a functioning legal system make? A lot. Why did developed economies become developed (remember, for example, the United States was a "developing" or "emerging" economy 100 years ago)? There are many answers, but a leading answer, which is most forcefully put forward by Hernando de Soto, a Peruvian economist, focuses on the role played by formal institutions, in particular, the protection of property rights afforded by a functioning legal system.[21] In developed economies, every parcel of land, every

intellectual property
Intangible property that results from intellectual activity (such as books, videos, and websites).

intellectual property rights
Rights associated with the ownership of intellectual property.

patents
Legal rights awarded by government authorities to inventors of new products or processes, who are given exclusive (monopoly) rights to derive income from such inventions through activities such as manufacturing, licensing, or selling.

copyrights
Exclusive legal rights of authors and publishers to publish and disseminate their work.

building, and every trademark are represented in a property document that entitles the owner to derive income and benefits from it and prosecutes violators through legal means. Because of the stability and predictability of such a legal system, tangible property can lead an invisible, parallel life alongside its material existence. It can be used as collateral for credit. For example, the single most important source of funds for new start-ups in the United States is the mortgage of entrepreneurs' houses.

However, if you live in a house but cannot produce a title document specifying that you are the legal owner (which is a very common situation throughout the developing world, especially in "shantytowns"), no bank in the world will allow you to use your house as collateral for credit. To start up a new firm, you end up having to borrow funds from family members, friends, and other acquaintances through *informal* means. But funds through informal means are almost certainly more limited than funds that could have been provided formally by banks. As a result, in the aggregate, because of such underfunding, the average firm size in the developing world is smaller than that in the developed world. Such insecure property rights also result in using technologies that employ little fixed capital and do not entail long-term investment (such as R&D). These characteristics do not bode well in global competition where leading firms reap benefits from economies of scale, capital-intensive technologies, and sustained investment in R&D. What the developing world lacks and desperately needs is formal protection of property rights to facilitate economic growth.

© BABU/Reuters /Landov

Why do officials in India use this bulldozer to crush thousands of illegal CDs? Do you think it is acceptable to make an unauthorized copy of copyrighted material, such as a movie, music, or software program?

Intellectual Property Rights

Although the term *property* traditionally refers to *tangible* pieces of property (such as land), **intellectual property** specifically refers to *intangible* property that results from intellectual activity (such as books, videos, and websites). **Intellectual property rights** (IPRs) are rights associated with the ownership of intellectual property. IPRs primarily include rights associated with (1) patents, (2) copyrights, and (3) trademarks. **Patents** are legal rights awarded by government authorities to inventors of new products or processes, who are given exclusive (monopoly) rights to derive income from such inventions through activities such as manufacturing, licensing, or selling. **Copyrights** are the exclusive legal rights of authors and publishers to publish and disseminate their work (such as this book). **Trademarks** are the exclusive legal rights of firms to use specific names, brands, and designs to differentiate their products from others.

Because IPRs are usually asserted and protected on a country-by-country basis, a pressing issue arises internationally: How are IPRs protected when countries have uneven levels of, and willingness associated with, IPR enforcement? The Paris Convention for the Protection of Industrial Property is the "gold standard" for a higher level of IPR protection. Adopting the Paris Convention is required to become a signatory country to the WTO's Agreement on Trade-Related Aspects of Intellectual Property Rights (TRIPS). Given the global differences in the formal rules, much stricter IPR protection is provided by TRIPS. Once countries join TRIPS, firms are often forced to pay more attention to innovation (see In Focus 2.2).

IPRs need to be asserted and enforced through a *formal* system, which is designed to provide an incentive for people and firms to innovate and to punish violators. However, the intangible nature of IPRs makes their protection difficult.[22]

IN FOCUS 2.2 The Paris Convention in Latin America

Does better protection of intellectual property rights (IPRs) lead to more foreign direct investment (FDI) inflows? During the 1990s, 15 Latin American countries adopted the Paris Convention for the Protection of Industrial Property in order to join the WTO TRIPS agreement. There is no evidence of immediate increase in FDI after adoption of the Paris Convention. However, over time, FDI gradually increased. This means that the earlier the countries adopted the Paris Convention, the more FDI they were able to attract later.

The primary mandate of the Paris Convention is to foster more innovation through better IPR protection. In addition to FDI, one crucial measure is the rate of domestic innovation, often captured by the number of patents that are filed by resident individuals and firms. In Latin America, there is a positive correlation between the number of patents filed in a given country and the amount of FDI it attracts. This suggests that some multinationals may be seeking innovations that take place in Latin American countries via FDI. As a result, a high level of IPR protection afforded by the Paris Convention and TRIPS would seem beneficial.

Sources: This case was written by **Theodore A. Khoury** (University of Texas at Dallas), under the supervision of Professor Mike W. Peng. It is based on (1) T. A. Khoury & M. W. Peng, 2006, Institutional change and strategic response: Exploring intellectual property reform in Latin America, Working paper, University of Texas at Dallas; (2) M. W. Peng & D. Wang, 2000, Innovation capability and foreign direct investment, *Management International Review*, 40 (1): 79–93.

Around the world, **piracy**—the unauthorized use of IPRs—is widespread, ranging from unauthorized sharing of music files to deliberate counterfeiting of branded products (see In Focus 2.3). Different countries have developed "distinctive competencies." For example, Russia is emerging as a powerhouse for counterfeit software. Ukraine is famous for bootlegged optical discs. Paraguay is well known for imitation cigarettes. Italy is a leading producer of counterfeit luxury goods. Florida has developed a strong reputation for fake aircraft parts.[23]

Overall, an institution-based view suggests that the key to understanding IPR violation is realizing that IPR violators are not amoral monsters but ordinary people and firms. Given an institutional environment of weak IPR protection, IPR violators have made a rational decision by investing their skills and knowledge in this business (see In Focus 2.3). When filling out a survey on "What is your dream career?" no high school graduate will answer, "My dream career is counterfeiting." Nevertheless, thousands of individuals and firms *voluntarily* choose to be involved in this business worldwide. Stronger IPR protection may reduce their incentive to do so. For example, counterfeiters in China will be criminally prosecuted only if their profits exceed approximately $10,000. However, IPR reforms to criminalize *all* counterfeiting activities regardless of the amount of profits, currently being discussed in China, may significantly reduce counterfeiters' incentive.[24]

trademarks
Exclusive legal rights of firms to use specific names, brands, and designs to differentiate their products from others.

piracy
The unauthorized use of intellectual property rights.

THREE ECONOMIC SYSTEMS

LEARNING OBJECTIVE 6
appreciate the differences among market economy, command economy, and mixed economy

An **economic system** refers to the rules of the game on how a country is governed economically. At the two ends of a spectrum, we can find (1) a market economy and (2) a command economy. In between, there is a mixed economy.

A pure **market economy** is characterized by the "invisible hand" of market forces first noted by Adam Smith in *The Wealth of Nations* in 1776. The government takes a hands-off approach known as *laissez faire*. Specifically, all factors of production should be privately owned. The government only performs functions the private sector cannot perform (such as providing roads and defense).

A pure **command economy** is defined by a government taking, in the words of Lenin, the "commanding height" in the economy. All factors of production should be government- or state-owned and controlled, and all supply, demand,

economic system
Rules of the game on how a country is governed economically.

market economy
An economy that is characterized by the "invisible hand" of market forces.

IN FOCUS 2.3 ETHICAL DILEMMA: Dealing with Counterfeiting

Counterfeiting is a thriving global business. Close to 10% of *all* world trade is reportedly in counterfeits. Counterfeiting is generally regarded as a byproduct of an entrepreneurial boom, such as the boom unfolding in China. A fundamental issue is while most entrepreneurs pursue legitimate business, why do many individuals and firms choose a counterfeiting strategy? Experts generally agree that the single largest determinant lies in institutional frameworks. A lack of effective formal IPR protection seems to be a prerequisite of counterfeiting. As a WTO member since 2001, China has significantly strengthened its IPR laws in line with the WTO TRIPS Agreement. However, what is lacking is enforcement. In America, convicted counterfeiters face fines of up to $2 million and ten years in prison for a *first* offense. In China, counterfeiters will not be criminally prosecuted if their profits do not exceed approximately $10,000; few counterfeiters are dumb enough to keep records showing that they make that much money. If they are caught and are found to make less than $10,000, they can usually get away with a $1,000 fine, which is widely regarded as a (small) cost of doing business. In many cases, local governments and police have little incentive to enforce IPR laws, in fear of losing tax revenues and increasing unemployment. China is not alone in this regard. For example, in Thailand, a 2000 raid to shut down counterfeiters was blocked by 1,000 angry people organized by local officials.

To stem the tide of counterfeits, four "Es" are necessary. The first E, enforcement, even if successful, is likely to be short-lived as long as demand remains high. The other three Es (education, external pressures, and economic growth) require much more patient work. Education not only refers to educating IPR law enforcement officials but also the general public about the perils of counterfeits (fake drugs can kill and so can fake auto parts). Educational efforts ideally will foster new norms among a new generation of entrepreneurs who will have internalized the values in favor of more ethical and legitimate businesses.

External pressures have to be applied skillfully. Confronting host governments is not likely to be effective. For example, Microsoft, when encountering extensive software piracy in China, chose to collaborate with the Ministry of Electronics to develop new software instead of challenging it head on. Microsoft figured that once the government has a stake in the sales of legitimate Microsoft products, it may have a stronger interest in cracking down on pirated software.

Finally, economic growth and homegrown brands are the most effective remedies in the long run. In the 1500s, the Netherlands (an *emerging* economy at that time) was busy making counterfeit Chinese porcelain. In the 1960s, Japan was the global leader in counterfeits. In the 1970s, Hong Kong grabbed this dubious distinction. In the 1980s, South Korea and Taiwan led the world. Now it is China's turn. As these countries developed their own industries, they also strengthened IPR laws. If past experience around the world is any guide, then there is hope that someday China and other leading counterfeiting nations will follow the same path.

Sources: Based on (1) *Business Week*, 2005, Fakes! February 7: 54–64; (2) D. Clark, 2006, Counterfeiting in China, *China Business Review*, January–February: 14–15; (3) *Economist*, 2003, Imitating property is theft, May 17: 52–54; (4) C. Hill, 2007, Digital piracy: Causes, consequences, and strategic responses, *Asia Pacific Journal of Management*, 24: 9–24; (5) M. W. Peng, 2001, How entrepreneurs create wealth in transition economies, *Academy of Management Executive*, 15: 95–108; (6) T. Trainer, 2002, The fight against trademark counterfeiting, *China Business Review*, November–December: 20–24.

command economy
An economy in which all factors of production are government- or state-owned and controlled, and all supply, demand, and pricing are planned by the government.

mixed economy
An economy that has elements of both a market economy and a command economy.

and pricing are planned by the government. During the heydays of communism, the former Soviet Union and China approached such an ideal.

A **mixed economy**, by definition, has elements of both a market economy and a command economy. It boils down to the relative distribution of market forces versus command forces. In practice, no country has ever completely embraced Adam Smith's ideal *laissez faire*. Here is a quiz: Which economy has the highest degree of economic freedom (the lowest degree of government intervention in the economy)? Hint: It is not the United States. A series of surveys report that it is Hong Kong (the post-1997 handover to Chinese sovereignty does not make a difference).[25] The crucial point here is that even in Hong Kong, there is still some noticeable government intervention in the economy. During the aftermath of the 1997 economic crisis when the share price of all Hong Kong–listed firms took a nosedive, the Hong Kong government took a highly controversial action. It used government funds to purchase 10% of the shares of all the "blue-chip" firms listed under the Hang Seng index. This action did slow down the sliding of share prices and stabilized the economy, but it turned all the blue-chip firms into state-owned enterprises (SOEs)—at least 10% owned by the state.

Likewise, no country has ever practiced a complete command economy despite the efforts of communist zealots throughout the Eastern bloc during the Cold War. Poland never nationalized its agriculture. Hungarians were known to have second (and private!) jobs while all of them theoretically worked only for the state. Black markets hawking agricultural produce and small merchandise existed in practically all (former) communist countries. While the former Soviet Union and Central and Eastern European countries have recently thrown away communism, even ongoing practitioners of communism, such as China and Vietnam, have embraced market reforms. Cuba has a lot of foreign-invested hotels. Even North Korea is now interested in attracting foreign investment.

Overall, the economic system of most countries is a mixed economy. In practice, when we say a country has a market economy, it is really a shorthand version for a country that organizes its economy *mostly* (but not completely) by market forces and that still has certain elements of a command economy. China, Russia, Sweden, and the United States all claim to have a market economy now, but the meaning is different in each country. In short, free markets are not totally free. It boils down to a matter of degree.

DEBATES AND EXTENSIONS

LEARNING OBJECTIVE 7

participate in three leading debates on politics, laws, and economics

Formal institutions such as political, legal, and economic systems represent some of the broadest and most comprehensive forces affecting global business. They provoke some significant debates. In this section, we focus on three major debates: (1) drivers of economic development, (2) speed and effectiveness of institutional transitions, and (3) measures of political risk.

Drivers of Economic Development: Culture, Geography, or Institutions?

The differences in economic development around the globe are striking. Based on gross national income (GNI) using official exchange rates, Table 2.4 shows the highest and lowest per capita income countries to be Norway ($59,590) and Burundi ($100), respectively. Based on purchasing power parity (PPP—see In Focus 1.1 for definition), the richest and poorest countries are the United States ($41,950) and Burundi ($640), respectively. Why are countries such as Norway and the United States so developed (rich) and some African countries such as Burundi so underdeveloped (poor)? More generally, what drives economic development in different countries?

Scholars and policymakers have debated this very important question since Adam Smith. One side argues that rich countries tend to have smarter and harder working populations driven by a stronger motivation for economic success (such as the Protestant work ethic identified by Max Weber—see Chapter 3). However, it is difficult to imagine that on average, Norwegians are nearly *600 times* smarter and harder at work than Burundians. This line of thinking, bordering on racism, is no longer acceptable in the 21st century. Another voice in this debate suggests that rich countries (such as the United States) tend to be well endowed with natural resources. However, one can easily point out that some poor countries (such as the Democratic Republic of Congo [Zaire]) also possess rich natural resources and that some rich countries (such as Denmark and Japan) are very poor in natural resources. In addition, some countries are believed to be cursed by their poor geographic location, which may be landlocked (such as Malawi) and/or located near the hot equator zone infested with tropical diseases (such as Burundi). This argument is not convincing either because some landlocked countries are

TABLE 2.4 RICHEST AND POOREST COUNTRIES BY PER CAPITA GROSS NATIONAL INCOME (GNI)

Per capita GNI based on official exchange rates	US $	Per capita GNI based on purchasing power parity (PPP)	US $
Richest Five		**Richest Five**	
Norway	$59,590	United States	$41,950
Switzerland	$54,930	Norway	$40,420
Denmark	$47,390	Switzerland	$37,080
United States	$43,740	Ireland	$34,720
Sweden	$41,060	Hong Kong, China	$34,670
Poorest Five		**Poorest Five**	
Sierra Leone	$220	Republic of Congo	$810
Malawi	$160	Tanzania	$730
Ethiopia	$160	Democratic Republic of Congo (Zaire)	$720
Democratic Republic of Congo (Zaire)	$120	Malawi	$650
Burundi	$100	Burundi	$640

Source: Adapted from The World Bank, 2006, *World Development Report 2007: Development and the Next Generation*, Washington, DC: The World Bank. GNI is gross domestic product (GDP) plus net receipts of primary income (compensation of employees and property income) from nonresident sources.

phenomenally well developed (such as Switzerland), and some countries near the equator have accomplished enviable growth (such as Singapore). Geography is important but not destiny.

The other side of the debate argues that institutions are "the basic determinants of the performance of an economy."[26] Because institutions provide the incentive structure of a society, formal political, legal, and economic systems have a significant impact on economic development by affecting the costs of doing business. In short, rich countries are rich because they have developed better market-supporting institutional frameworks. Specifically, several points can be made:

- It is economically advantageous for individuals and firms to grow and specialize to capture the gains from trade. This is the "division of labor" thesis first advanced by Adam Smith (see Chapter 5).
- A lack of strong, formal, market-supporting institutions forces individuals to trade on an informal basis with a small neighboring group and forces firms to remain small, thus foregoing the gains from a sharper division of labor by trading on a large scale with distant partners. For example, most of the transactions in Africa are local in nature, and most firms are small. More than 40% of Africa's economy is reportedly informal, the highest proportion in the world.[27]
- Emergence of formal, market-supporting institutions encourages individuals to specialize and firms to grow in size to capture the gains from complicated long-distance trade (such as transactions with distant, foreign countries). For example, as China's market institutions progress, many Chinese firms have grown substantially.

- When formal, market-supporting institutions protect property rights, they will fuel more innovation, entrepreneurship, and thus economic growth. Spontaneous innovation has existed throughout history, but why has its pace accelerated significantly since the Industrial Revolution starting in the 1700s? In no small measure, this was because of the Statute of Monopolies enacted in Great Britain in 1624, which was the world's first patent law to formally protect the IPRs of inventors and make innovation financially lucrative.[28] This law has been imitated around the world. Its impact is still felt today, as we now expect continuous innovation to be the norm. This would not have happened had there not been a system of IPR protection.

These arguments, of course, are the backbone of the institution-based view of global business. Championed by Douglass North, the Nobel laureate quoted earlier, this side has clearly won the debate on the drivers of economic development.[29] However, the debate does not end because it is still unclear *exactly* what kind of political system facilitates economic development.

Is a democracy conducive for economic growth? While champions of democracy shout yes, the fastest growing economy in the last three decades, China, remains totalitarian. The growth rate of India, the world's largest democracy, in the same period is only about half of China's. On the other hand, no one in his or her right mind can seriously argue a case for totalitarianism to facilitate economic development. The few examples of "benign" totalitarian regimes that protected property rights and delivered strong growth, such as South Korea and Taiwan, have become democracies in the last two decades. Overall, there is no doubt that democracy has spread around the world (from 69 countries in the 1980s to 117 in the 2000s). However, whether democracy necessarily leads to strong economic development is still subject to debate (see Closing Case and Integrative Case 1.1).

Speed and Effectiveness of Institutional Transitions: China versus Russia

market transition debate
The debate about how to make the transition to a market economy work in most effective and least disruptive way.

Although countries make different political choices (ranging from China's insistence on communism to Russia's determination to abandon communism), their economic policies have been remarkably similar: They are all interested in stimulating market development and economic growth. In many emerging economies, it was not long ago that competition was all but absent. Markets were closed, industries protected, and strategizing not necessary. Now, the only constant seems to be change—formally known as institutional transitions (as discussed earlier in this chapter).

Practically, however, how to make the transitions work in a most effective and least disruptive way has led to a fierce debate, known as the **market transition debate**. China and Russia are usually cited as two examples of contrasting approaches. The Chinese transitions are known for their slow, incremental, "gradualist" approach, whereas the Russian transitions are noted for their fast, radical, and "big bang" characteristic. Related to our first debate on the merits of democracy (see previous section), one side of the current debate, such as advocates of radical reforms in Russia in the 1990s, argues that a country needs to rapidly democratize in order to have any hope for having a true market economy. Another side, impressed by China's economic accomplishments, points out that a country can build a market-friendly economy without necessarily becoming a democracy.

Are the income and jobs of these automobile workers in China affected by the transitions toward a market economy in that country?

path dependency
The present choices of countries, firms, and individuals are constrained by the choices made previously.

Because of the choices made earlier, countries undergoing institutional transitions do not have the full range of choices. This is known as **path dependency**; namely, the present choices of countries (as well as firms and individuals) are constrained by the choices made previously. Given the different path dependencies, it seems difficult to argue whether China or Russia has chosen a better approach. Let us look at some simple measures of economic performance. China's total GNI is approximately $1.7 trillion (sixth largest in the world), and Russia's is $487 billion (sixteenth largest). China thus outperforms Russia by a 4:1 ratio. However, because of population difference (China's 1.3 billion versus Russia's 140 million), China's per capita GNI, $1,290 (134th in the world), trails Russia's, $3,410 (97th in the world), by about two-thirds. Using PPP-adjusted per capita GNI does not change the picture: Russia's is $9,620 (82nd in the world), whereas China's is only half that level, $5,530 (119th).[30] Of course, there is a lot more complexity beyond such simple measures—see both the Closing Case (on Russia) and Integrative Case 1.1 (on China) to engage this debate more.

Measures of Political Risk: Perception versus Objective Measures

Although there is hardly any controversy on the importance of monitoring political risk, how to actually measure political risk has led to a significant debate.[31] One side of the debate suggests that political risk is all based on perception and that the best measures can be found through surveys of international executives on their perceptions. A number of rating agencies, such as the Economist Intelligence Unit, *Euromoney*, and World Bank, produce rankings of political risk. For example, they generally show that China has a moderate and declining level of political risk (Table 2.5).

However, critics argue that perception can be deceiving and misleading. They point out that perception-based rankings in the 1990s failed to provide warning of sudden political changes in Indonesia, Malaysia, South Korea, and Thailand triggered by the 1997 East Asian financial crisis. In fact, these had often been rated as the *least* risky countries. This was hardly surprising as prior to the 1997 crisis, East Asia had been widely regarded as a "miracle" region, and foreign investors had flocked in. The velocity of the 1997 crisis shocked the vast majority of investors and politicians in these countries as well as international executives and political risk experts. Malaysia, for example, suspended the tradability of its currency and jailed its vice prime minister, forcing a dramatic change in the perception of its political risk. The underlying political risk in these countries was eventually picked up by the perception-based rankings, but it was too late to help prevent losses. Critics of the perception-based measures thus ask: If more FDI flocks into a country because more investors believe that the political risk is low (which will be captured by the perception-based rankings), has the true level of political risk actually decreased? Their answer, of course, is no![32]

In response, critics have advocated objective measures of political risk that takes into account a country's underlying political and regulatory structures.[33] A leading objective measure of political risk is the political constraint index (POLCON).[34] It focuses on the identifiable and measurable number of veto points in a political system, such as multiple branches of the government and judicial independence (see Table 2.5). The assumption is that a political system with no checks and balances would have no constraints on the leading politicians because nobody possesses the power to veto key decisions. This is the essence of totalitarianism. In such a system, political change may become highly unpredictable, thus presenting a lot of risk.

For example, China's POLCON measure has remained at 0, the worst possible score (the maximum being 1). In other words, the rising level of FDI flocking to

TABLE 2.5 MEASURES OF POLITICAL RISK: PERCEPTION VERSUS OBJECTIVITY

	Perception measure: *Euromoney*[1] (1994)	Perception measure: *Euromoney* (2004)	Objective measure: POLCON[2] (1994)	Objective measure: POLCON (2004)
Argentina	10.56	4.88	0.76	0.51
Canada	23.91	24.56	0.86	0.86
China	17	18.01	0	0
India	14.68	15.23	0.76	0.74
Indonesia	16.34	10.67	0	0.52
Japan	23.14	23.62	0.77	0.76
Malaysia	21.15	18.69	0.77	0.77
Mexico	14.85	16.99	0.28	0.39
Pakistan	11.05	8.60	0.54	0
Poland	11.47	17.47	0.70	0.74
Russia	7.29	13.53	0.10	0.19
Singapore	22.26	24.25	0.68	0.67
South Africa	15.28	15.29	0.84	0.74
South Korea	21.74	19.99	0.75	0.74
Taiwan	22.83	21.34	0.74	0.76
Thailand	19.19	17.32	0.78	0.45
United Kingdom	21.56	24.52	0.74	0.74
United States	21.74	24.12	0.74	0.76
Vietnam	11.67	12.61	0	0.13

1. The *Euromoney* measure is between 0 and 25—the lower the number, the higher the risk.
2. The political constraints (POLCON) measure is between 0 and 1—the lower the number, the higher the risk (0 means no constraints on political actors, and 1 means maximum constraints on political actors).

Sources: Adapted from (1) *Euromoney*, March 2005 and (2) POLCON V database—the latter used by permission by Witold Henisz. See http://www-management.wharton.upenn.edu/henisz. For more details, see W. Henisz, 2000, The institutional environment for economic growth, *Economics and Politics*, 12: 1–31; W. Henisz, 2002, The institutional environment for infrastructure investment, *Industrial and Corporate Change*, 11: 355–389.

China does not necessarily reduce its political risk. For example, in 1998, without any consultation or warning, the Chinese government suddenly imposed a nationwide ban on direct marketing, giving American cosmetics firms such as Avon and Mary Kay more than a huge headache. On a larger scale, although we all hope the following will not be the case, the Chinese leadership, in the words of Douglass North, "could perceive the evolving open society as a threat to the existing vested interests, and halt the course of the past decades."[35] In another example, South Africa's POLCON measures improved from 0.33 in 1993 (not shown in Table 2.5) to 0.84 in 1994 (shown in Table 2.5), indicating that the democratization of the country during that time introduced more political constraints on the new politicians and that the country's political risk was reduced (see Opening Case). Finally, Indonesia is generally perceived to have a higher political risk in the aftermath of the 1997–1998 financial and political crisis (according to *Euromoney*, from 16.34 in 1994 to 10.67 in 2004—see Table 2.5). However, using the POLCON measure, one can argue that Indonesia's political risk is *lower* now (from 0 in 1994 to 0.52 in 2004) because Indonesia recently installed a democracy that has added layers of political constraints.

Overall, perceptual measures will always lag political changes because such changes must be experienced by survey respondents who will then change their perception. In comparison, an objective measure based on systematic differences in political systems may provide a more objective estimate of the likelihood of the direction of future political changes.[36] Of course, both measures overlap and support each other in many cases. Therefore, a combination of both may yield better insights.

LEARNING OBJECTIVE 8

draw implications for action

MANAGEMENT SAVVY

Focusing on *formal* institutions, this chapter has sketched the contours of an institution-based view of global business, which is one of the two core perspectives we present throughout this book (Chapter 3 will reinforce this view with a focus on *informal* institutions). How does the institution-based view help us answer the fundamental question that is of utmost managerial concern worldwide: What determines the success and failure of firms around the globe? In a nutshell, this chapter suggests that firm performance is, at least in part, determined by the institutional frameworks governing firm behavior. It is the growth of the firm that, in the aggregate, leads to the growth of the economy. Not surprisingly, most developed economies are supported by strong, effective, and market-supporting formal institutions, and most underdeveloped economies are pulled back by weak, ineffective, and market-depressing formal institutions. In other words, when markets work smoothly in developed economies, formal market-supporting institutions are almost invisible and taken for granted. However, when markets work poorly, the absence of strong formal institutions may be conspicuous.

For managers doing business around the globe, this chapter suggests two broad implications for action (Table 2.6). First, managerial choices are made rationally within the constraints of a given institutional framework. Therefore, when entering a new country, managers need to do their homework by having a thorough understanding of the formal institutions affecting their business. The rules for doing business in a democratic market economy are certainly different from the rules in a totalitarian command economy. In short, "when in Rome, do as the Romans do." Although this is a good start, managers also need to understand *why* Romans do things in a certain way by studying the formal institutions governing Roman behavior. A superficial understanding may not get you very far and may even be misleading or dangerous. Managers should especially guard against the **herd mentality**—a behavior influenced by the movement of the crowd (or the herd) with little independent judgment. As the debate on the measures of political

herd mentality
A behavior influenced by the movement of the crowd (or the herd) with little independent judgment.

TABLE 2.6 IMPLICATIONS FOR ACTION

- When entering a new country, do your homework by having a thorough understanding of the formal institutions governing firm behavior
- When doing business in countries with a strong propensity for informal relational exchanges, insisting on formalizing the contract right away may backfire

risk indicates, the fact that a large number of firms are rushing to do business in a certain country does not necessarily mean that its political risk is lower.

Second, although this chapter has focused on the role of formal institutions, managers should follow the advice of the second proposition of the institution-based view: In situations where formal constraints are unclear or fail, informal constraints (such as relationship norms) will play a *larger* role in reducing uncertainty. This means that when doing business in countries with a strong propensity for informal, relational exchanges, insisting on formalizing the contract right away may backfire. Because these countries often have relatively weak legal systems, personal relationship building is often a substitute for the lack of strong legal protection. Attitudes such as "business first, relationship afterward" (have a drink after the negotiation) may clash with a norm of "relationship first, business afterward" (lavish entertainment first, talk about business later). For example, we often hear that because of their culture, the Chinese prefer to cultivate personal relationships (*guanxi*) first. This is *not* entirely true because in the absence of a strong and credible legal and regulatory regime in China, investing in personal relationships up front may simply be the initial cost one has to pay if interested in eventually doing business together. Such investment in personal relationships is a must in countries ranging from Argentina to Zimbabwe. The broad range of these countries with different cultural traditions suggests that the interest in cultivating what the Chinese call *guanxi*, which is a word found in almost every culture (such as *blat* in Russia and *guan he* in Vietnam), is not likely to be driven by culture alone but, more significantly, by common institutional characteristics—in particular, the lack of formal market-supporting institutions.

CHAPTER SUMMARY

1. Explain the concept of institutions and their key role in reducing uncertainty
   - Institutions are commonly defined as "the rules of the game."
   - Institutions have formal and informal components, each with different supportive pillars.
   - Their key functions are to reduce uncertainty, curtail transaction costs, and combat opportunism.
2. Articulate the two core propositions underpinning an institution-based view of global business
   - Proposition 1: Managers and firms *rationally* pursue their interests and make choices within formal and informal institutional constraints in a given institutional framework.
   - Proposition 2: When formal constraints are unclear or fail, informal constraints will play a *larger* role.
3. Identify the basic differences between democracy and totalitarianism
   - Democracy is a political system in which citizens elect representatives to govern the country.
   - Totalitarianism is a political system in which one person or party exercises absolute political control.

4. Outline the differences among civil law, common law, and theocratic law
   - Civil law uses comprehensive statutes and codes as a primary means to form legal judgments.
   - Common law is shaped by precedents and traditions from previous judicial decisions.
   - Theocratic law is a legal system based on religious teachings.
5. Understand the importance of property rights and intellectual property rights
   - Property rights are legal rights to use an economic resource and to derive income and benefits from it.
   - Intellectual property refers to intangible property that results from intellectual activity.
6. Appreciate the differences among market economy, command economy, and mixed economy
   - A pure market economy is characterized by *laissez faire* and total control by market forces.
   - A pure command economy is defined by government ownership and control of all means of production.
   - Most countries operate mixed economies, with a different emphasis on market versus command forces.
7. Participate in three leading debates
   - These are (1) What drives economic development? (2) What are the most effective and least disruptive institutional transitions toward more market competition? (3) How to best measure political risk?
8. Draw implications for action
   - Managers considering working abroad should have a thorough understanding of the formal institutions before entering a country.
   - In situations where formal constraints are unclear, managers can reduce uncertainty by relying on informal constraints, such as relationship norms.

KEY TERMS

Civil law 36
Cognitive pillar 31
Command economy 39
Common law 36
Copyrights 38
Democracy 34
Economic system 39
Formal institutions 31
Herd mentality 46
Informal institutions 31
Institutional framework 31
Institutional transitions 32
Institution-based view 30
Institutions 30
Intellectual property 38
Intellectual property rights 38
Legal system 36
Market economy 39
Market transition debate 43
Mixed economy 40
Normative pillar 31
Opportunism 32
Patents 38
Path dependency 44
Piracy 39
Political risk 35
Political system 34
Property rights 37
Regulatory pillar 31
Theocratic law 37
Totalitarianism (dictatorship) 34
Trademarks 38
Transaction costs 32

REVIEW QUESTIONS

1. Name and describe the one pillar that supports formal institutions and the two additional pillars that support informal institutions.

2. In what ways do institutions influence individuals' and firms' behaviors? Explain your answer.
3. Define institutional transitions, and give three examples of where they can be found.
4. Explain the two core propositions behind the institution-based view of global business.
5. Which are generally more significant: formal or informal constraints? Explain your answer.
6. What fundamental aspect of democracy is relevant to the effective conduct of global business?
7. Name and describe the four types of totalitarianism.
8. How does political risk affect global business?
9. Describe the differences among the three types of legal systems.
10. Give an example of how theocratic law affects daily business operations.
11. Name three types of economic property, and explain how they could be used in business.
12. Name three types of intellectual property, and explain how they could be used in business.
13. What is TRIPS?
14. Name and describe the three economic systems.
15. Which economic system is the most common and why?
16. Our current system of intellectual property protection stems from what early patent law?
17. Describe two contrasting examples of market transitions.
18. Explain path dependency, how a country's present choices are often constrained by earlier choices.
19. Which do you think offers a more accurate measure of political risk: one based on perception or one based on political and regulatory structures? Explain your answer.
20. Generally speaking, what is the result of strong, effective, market-supporting formal institutions?
21. Why should managers guard against a herd mentality?
22. If formal constraints are unclear or ineffective, what else can managers use to reduce uncertainty?

CRITICAL DISCUSSION QUESTIONS

1. Without looking at any references, please identify the top-three countries with the most significant change in political risk in the last five years. Then consult references based on both perception and objective measures. How do your own intuition and the two kinds of measures differ?

2. ON ETHICS: As manager, you discover that your firm's products are counterfeited by small family firms that employ child labor in rural Bangladesh. You are aware of the corporate plan to phase out these products soon. You also realize that once you report to the authorities, these firms will be shut down, employees will be out of work, and families and children will be starving. How would you proceed?
3. ON ETHICS: Your multinational is the largest foreign investor and enjoys good profits in (1) Sudan, where government forces are reportedly cracking down on rebels and killing civilians, and (2) Vietnam, where religious leaders are reportedly being prosecuted. As country manager, you understand that your firm is pressured by activists to exit these countries. The alleged government actions, which you personally find distasteful, are not directly related to your operations. How would you proceed?

VIDEO CASE

Watch "Monitor Your Business Environment and Anticipate Change" by Paul Skinner of Rio Tinto.

1. How did formal institutions impact Mr. Skinner's organization?
2. How did his contingency planning give him an advantage over those with a herd mentality and enable his firm to profit from the change in formal institutions?
3. Based on Mr. Skinner's experience, how do the economic system and the regulatory pillar interact in affecting the organization?
4. According to this chapter, "managers and firms rationally pursue their interests and make choices within institutional constraints." Based on that, how might firms in Mr. Skinner's industry maximize their position before and after deregulation?
5. What is the main message of this video, and how might it relate to experiences you could have in the future?

CLOSING CASE

The Russia Puzzle

Since the collapse of the former Soviet Union in 1991, Russia has undergone a series of extraordinary institutional transitions. Led by two presidents, Boris Yeltsin (1991–2000) and Vladimir Putin (2000–2008), Russia changed from a communist totalitarian state into a democracy with regular elections. Its centrally planned economy was transformed into a capitalist economy of mostly private firms. Yet, Russia has remained a huge puzzle to policymakers, scholars, and business practitioners both in Russia and abroad, thus provoking a constant debate.

The debate centers on political, economic, and legal dimensions. Politically, does Russia really have a democracy? Even before Putin's recent consolidation of power, some critics labeled Russia's democracy "phony." In 2004, Russia was *downgraded* from "Partly Free" to "Not Free"—on a

1 to 3 scale of "Free," "Partly Free," and "Not Free"—by Freedom House, a leading nongovernment organization (NGO) promoting political freedom. This was driven by Russia's recent steady drift toward more authoritarian rule under Putin. Yet, Russia under Putin since 2000 grew 7% annually, whereas Russia under Yeltsin during the 1990s, when it was "Partly Free," experienced a catastrophic economic decline. Most Russians, who were economically better off in the 2000s, do not seem to mind living in a "less democratic" country (relative to what Russia was in the 1990s).

Economically, just how bad was the decline? Official statistics indicated that GDP fell approximately 40% in the 1990s. One side of the debate argues that the actual decline might have been far worse. However, the other side suggests that Russia's economic performance was actually far better because some decline in output, by reducing military goods and shoddy consumer products for which there was no demand, was good for the economy. For example, there was no reason that the former Soviet Union should produce 80% more steel than the United States. Also, the level of output at the outset of reforms was exaggerated because the central planning system rewarded managers who *overreported* their output. However, managers now *underreport* output to reduce their tax bill. Thus, the real decline was probably smaller than officially reported. In addition, Russia's unofficial economy blossomed since the early 1990s, significantly compensating for the decline of the official sector. Hence, Russia's decline might not have been as bad as commonly thought. Today's Russian economy, fueled by the rising price of oil, is much stronger, growing at 7% annually.

Legally, establishing the rule of law that respects private property is one of the main goals of Russia's institutional transitions. However, in a society where nobody had any significant private property, how a small number of individuals become super rich oligarchs (tycoons) almost overnight is intriguing. By 2003, the top-ten families or groups owned 60% of Russia's total market capitalization. Should the government protect private property if it is acquired through illegitimate or "gray" means? Most oligarchs obtained their wealth during the chaotic 1990s. Once these oligarchs have acquired assets, they demand that the government respect and protect their assets. The government thus faces a dilemma: Redistributing wealth by confiscating assets from the oligarchs creates more uncertainty, whereas respecting and protecting the property rights of the oligarchs result in more resentment among the population. Thus far, except when a few oligarchs, notably Mikhail Khodorkovsky, threatened to politically challenge the government, the Putin administration sided with the oligarchs. Not surprisingly, oligarchs have emerged as a strong force in favor of property rights protection. In Russia, oligarchs run their firms more efficiently than other types of business owners (except foreign owners). Although the emergence of oligarchs no doubt has increased income inequality and caused mass resentment, on balance, oligarchs are often argued to have contributed to Russia's more recent boom.

Where exactly is Russia heading? Key to solving this puzzle is to understand the government of Putin and his successor. Some even suggest that there are two Putins: the autocrat and the reformer. If the reformer gained the upper hand, a stronger, more democratic Russia might emerge. However, it seems that Putin the autocrat clearly won the battle. While Russia becomes economically richer and stronger (thanks to high oil prices), the government is bolder and more assertive in foreign affairs and willing to challenge the United States. At home, the government is also sliding back to more authoritarian ways. But one argument goes, if the government delivers economic growth, so what?

Finally, another group of writers point out that despite its former superpower status, Russia has become a "normal" middle-income country. With GDP per capita around $8,000, Russia in 2007 is at a level similar to that of Argentina in 1991 and Mexico in 1999. Democracies in this income range are rough around the edges. They tend to have corrupt governments, high income inequality, concentrated corporate ownership, and turbulent economic performance. In all these aspects, Russia may be quite "normal." However, these flaws are not necessarily incompatible with further political, economic, and legal progress down the road. For example, consumers in normal, middle-income countries naturally demand bank loans, credit cards, and mortgages, which have only appeared in Russia for the first time and created lucrative opportunities for Russian and foreign firms. Despite some political fluctuation, overall, big political risks, which might deter foreign investors, seem reasonably remote. More and more foreign firms are now rushing into Russia, which is the R in BRIC—a group of attractive major emerging economies consisting of Brazil, Russia, India, and China.

Case Discussion Questions

1. Does the Russian experience support or refute the claim that democracy is conducive to economic growth?
2. Although a stable legal framework that protects property rights reportedly can remove uncertainty and thus facilitate economic growth, the government's protection of oligarchs is not without controversies. If you were to advise the Russian government on property rights reforms, what would be your advice?
3. If you were a board member at one of the major Western multinational retailers (such as Carrefour, IKEA, Metro, or Wal-Mart), would you vote yes or no for a new project to set up your firm's first major store in Russia?

Sources: I thank Professors Sheila Puffer and Dan McCarthy (both at Northeastern University) for sharing their work on Russia with me. Based on (1) *Economist*, 2006, Richer, bolder—and sliding back, July 15: 23–25; (2) *Economist*, 2007, Dancing with the bear, February 3: 63–64; (3) *Economist*, 2007, Russia and America, February 17: 60–61; (4) S. Guriev & A. Rachinsky, 2005, The role of oligarchs in Russian capitalism, *Journal of Economic Perspectives*, 19: 131–150; (5) D. McCarthy & S. Puffer, 2006, Ilim Pulp: Corporate governance battles in Russia, in M. W. Peng (ed.), *Global Strategy* (pp. 540–546), Cincinnati, OH: Thomson South-Western; (6) S. Puffer & D. McCarthy, 2007, Can Russia's state-managed, network capitalism be competitive? *Journal of World Business*, 42: 1–13; (7) A. Shleifer & D. Treisman, 2005, A normal country: Russia after communism, *Journal of Economic Perspectives*, 19: 151–174; (8) http://www.freedomhouse.org.

NOTES

Journal acronyms: **AMR** – *American Economic Review;* **AME** – *Academy of Management Executive;* **AMJ** – *Academy of Management Journal;* **AMR** – *Academy of Management Review;* **APJM** – *Asia Pacific Journal of Management;* **ASQ** – *Administrative Science Quarterly;* **BW** – *Business Week;* **CBR** – *China Business Review;* **JIBS** – *Journal of International Business Studies;* **JIM** – *Journal of International Management;* **JM** – *Journal of Management;* **JMS** – *Journal of Management Studies;* **JPE** – *Journal of Political Economy;* **JWB** – *Journal of World Business;* **LRP** – *Long Range Planning;* **OSc** – *Organization Science;* **SMJ** – *Strategic Management Journal;* **WSJ** – *Wall Street Journal*

[1] M. W. Peng, D. Wang, & Y. Jiang, 2008, An institution-based view of international business strategy, *JIBS* (in press).

[2] D. North, 1990, *Institutions, Institutional Change, and Economic Performance* (p. 3), New York: Norton.

[3] W. R. Scott, 1995, *Institutions and Organizations*, Thousand Oaks, CA: Sage.

[4] M. Guillen, 2003, Experience, imitation, and the sequence of foreign entry, *JIBS*, 34: 185–198; J. Lu, 2002, Intra- and inter-organizational imitative behavior, *JIBS*, 33: 19–37.

[5] M. W. Peng, 2000, *Business Strategies in Transition Economies* (pp. 42–44), Thousand Oaks, CA: Sage.

[6] S. Elbanna & J. Child, 2007, Influences on strategic decision making, *SMJ*, 28: 431–453; D. Elenkov, 1997, Strategic uncertainty and environmental scanning, *SMJ*, 18: 287–302; T. Murtha & S. Lenway, 1994, Country capabilities and the strategic state, *SMJ*, 15: 113–129; R. Ramamurti, 2003, Can governments make credible promises? *JIM*, 9: 253–269; O. Sawyerr, 1993, Environmental uncertainty and environmental scanning activities of Nigerian manufacturing executives, *SMJ*, 14: 287–299.

[7] O. Williamson, 1985, *The Economic Institutions of Capitalism* (pp. 1–2), New York: Free Press.

[8] M. W. Peng, 2003, Institutional transitions and strategic choices (p. 275), *AMR*, 28: 275–296. See also E. George, P. Chattopadhyay, S. Sitkin, & J. Barden, 2006, Cognitive underpinning of institutional persistence and change, *AMR*, 31: 347–365.

[9] *Economist*, 2007, Dancing with the bear (p. 63), February 3: 63–64.

[10] M. W. Peng, 2002, Towards an institution-based view of business strategy, *APJM*, 19: 251–267.

[11] N. Biggart & R. Delbridge, 2004, Systems of exchange, *AMR*, 29: 28–49; R. Greenwood & R. Suddaby, 2006, Institutional entrepreneurship in mature fields, *AMR*, 49: 27–46; U. Haley, 2003, Assessing and controlling business risks in China, *JIM*, 9: 237–253; M. Kotabe & R. Mudambi, 2003, Institutions and international business, *JIM*, 9: 215–217; P. Moran & S. Ghoshal, 1999, Markets, firms, and the process of economic development, *AMR*, 24: 390–412; R. Mudambi & C. Paul, 2003, Domestic drug prohibition as a source of foreign institutional instability, *JIM*, 9: 335–349; T. Ozawa, 2003, Japan in an institutional quagmire, *JIM*, 9: 219–235; A. Parkhe, 2003, Institutional environments, institutional change, and international alliances, *JIM*, 9: 305–316.

[12] M. W. Peng, 2001, How entrepreneurs create wealth in transition economies, *AME*, 15: 95–108; S. Puffer & D. McCarthy, 2007, Can Russia's state-managed, network capitalism be competitive? *JWB*, 42: 1–13.

[13] A. Hillman & W. Wan, 2005, The determinants of MNE subsidiaries' political strategies, *JIBS*, 36: 322–340; M. Lord, 2003, Constituency building as the foundation for corporate political strategy, *AME*, 17: 112–124; A. McWilliams, D. van Fleet, & K. Cory, 2002, Raising rivals' costs through political strategy, *JMS*, 39: 707–723; D. Schuler, K. Rehbein, & R. Cramer, 2002, Pursuing strategic advantage through political means, *AMJ*, 45: 659–672.

[14] J. Bonardi, G. Holburn, & R. Bergh, 2006, Nonmarket strategy performance, *AMJ*, 49: 1209–1228; J. Boddewyn & T. Brewer, 1994, International-business political behavior, *AMR*, 19: 119–143.

[15] K. Butler & D. Joaquin, 1998, A note on political risk and the required return on foreign direct investment, *JIBS*, 29: 599–608; T. Brewer, 1993, Government policies, market imperfections, and foreign direct investment, *JIBS*, 24: 101–120.

[16] R. Click, 2005, Financial and political risks in US direct foreign investment, *JIBS*, 36: 559–575.

[17] M. Guillen, 2001, *The Limits of Convergence* (p. 135), Princeton, NJ: Princeton University Press.

[18] M. Beaulieu, J. Cosset, & N. Essaddam, 2005, The impact of political risk on the volatility of stock returns, *JIBS*, 36: 701–718.

[19] R. La Porta, F. Lopez-de-Silanes, A. Shleifer, & R. Vishny, 1998, Law and finance (p. 1118), *JPE*, 106: 1113–1155.

[20] The author's interview, Middle East Women's Delegation visiting the University of Texas at Dallas, January 23, 2006.

[21] H. de Soto, 2000, *The Mystery of Capital*, New York: Basic Books.

[22] C. W. L. Hill, 2007, Digital piracy, *APJM*, 24: 9–25.

[23] M. W. Peng, 2006, Dealing with counterfeiting, in M. W. Peng (ed.), *Global Strategy* (pp. 137–138), Cincinnati, OH: Thomson.

[24] J. Simone, 2006, Silk market fakes, *CBR*, January–February: 16–17.

[25] Heritage Foundation, http://www.heritage.org.

[26] D. North, 2005, *Understanding the Process of Economic Change* (p. 48), Princeton, NJ: Princeton University Press.

[27] *Economist*, 2005, Doing business in Africa, July 2: 61.

[28] D. North, 1981, *Structure and Change in Economic History* (p. 164), New York: Norton.

[29] D. Acemoglu, S. Johnson, & J. Robinson, 2001, The colonial origins of comparative development, *AER*, 91: 1369–1401; R. Barro & X. Sala-i-Martin, 2003, *Economic Growth*, Cambridge, MA: MIT Press; D. North, 1994, Economic performance through time, *AER*, 84: 359–368; G. Roland, 2000, *Transition and Economics*, Cambridge, MA: MIT Press.

[30] World Bank, 2006, *World Development Report 2006* (p. 292), Washington, DC: World Bank.

[31] M. Calhoun, 2006, Exposing illusions and questioning controls, Working paper, Ohio State University.

[32] W. Henisz & B. Zelner, 2005, Measures of political risk, Working paper, Wharton School.

[33] P. Vaaler, B. Schrage, & S. Block, 2005, Counting the investor vote, *JIBS*, 36: 62–88.

[34] W. Henisz & A. Delios, 2001, Uncertainty, imitation, and plant location, *ASQ*, 46: 443–475; W. Henisz & J. Macher, 2004, Firm and country-level tradeoffs and contingencies in the evaluation of foreign investment, *OSc*, 15: 537–554.

[35] D. North, 2005, The Chinese menu (for development), *WSJ*, April 7: A14.

[36] A. Delios & P. Beamish, 2004, *International Business: An Asia Pacific Perspective*, Singapore: Pearson.

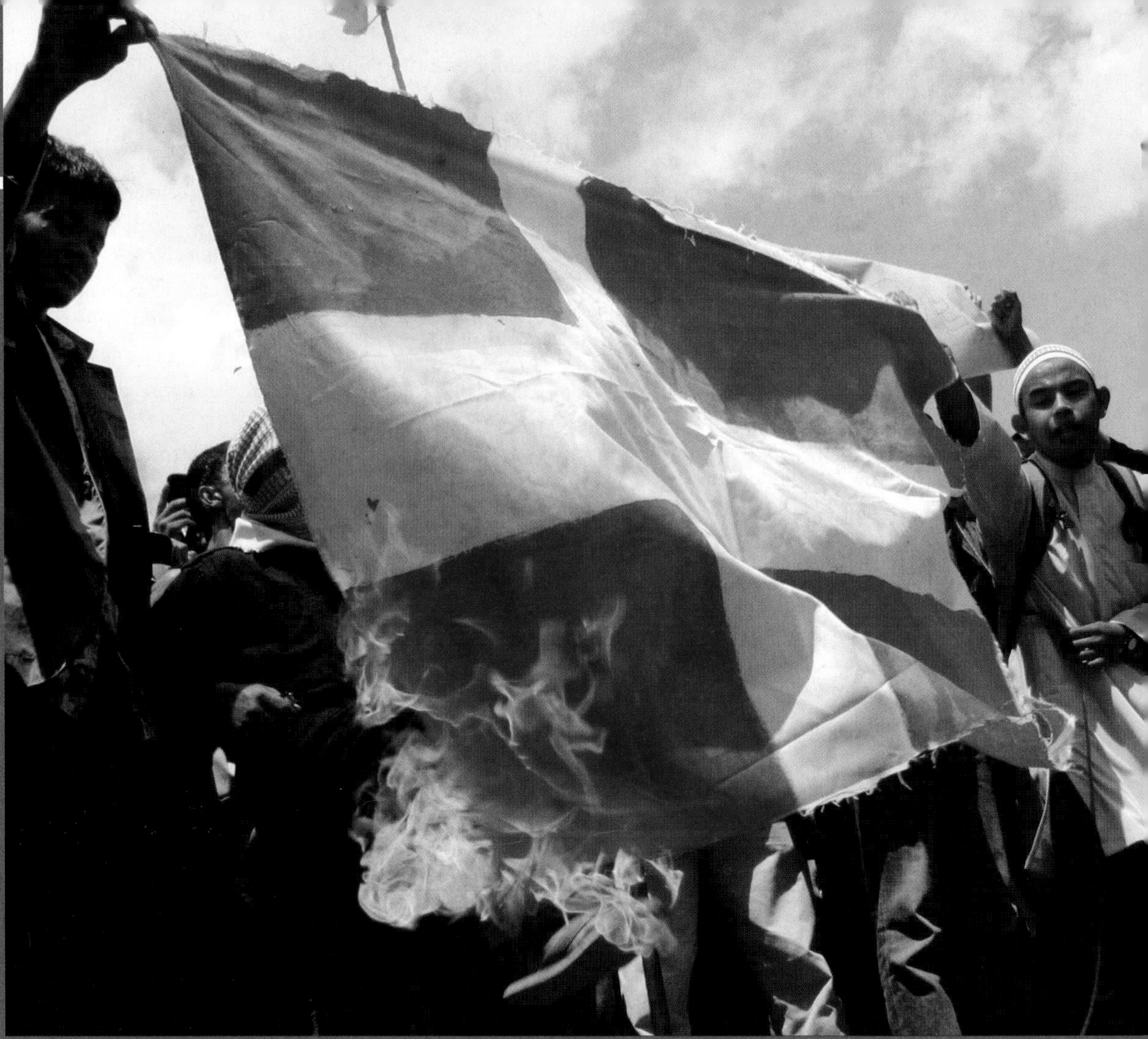

Emphasizing Informal Institutions: Cultures, Ethics, and Norms

OPENING CASE

Cartoons That Exploded

In September 2005, Danish newspaper *Jyllands-Posten* (*The Jutland Post*) published a dozen cartoons of the Muslim prophet Muhammad. These cartoons not only violated the Muslim norm against picturing prophets, but also portrayed Muhammad in a highly negative, insulting light, especially those that pictured him as a terrorist. *Jyllands-Posten* knew that it was testing the limits of free speech and good taste. But it had no idea about the ferociousness of the explosion its cartoons would ignite. For Denmark itself, this incident became the biggest crisis since the Nazi occupation during World War II. Beyond Denmark, publishers in a total of 22 countries, such as Belgium, France, Germany, the Netherlands, and Norway, reprinted these cartoons to make a point about their right to do so in the name of freedom of expression. Muslims around the world were outraged, protests were organized, Danish flags were burned, and Western embassies in Indonesia, Iran, Lebanon, and Syria were attacked. In Khartoum, Sudan, a crowd of 50,000 chanted "Strike, strike, bin Laden!" At least ten people were killed in protests against the cartoons, as police in Afghanistan shot into crowds besieging Western installations.

In addition to mob reactions in the street, Muslim governments took action. In protest against the cartoons, Iran, Libya, Saudi Arabia, and Syria withdrew their ambassadors from Denmark. The justice minister of the United Arab Emirates argued: "This is cultural terrorism, not freedom of expression." However, Anders Rasmussen, the Danish Prime Minister, when meeting ambassadors from ten Muslim countries, indicated that however distasteful the cartoons were, the government could not apologize on behalf of the newspaper. This was because, in principle, freedom of speech was enshrined in Denmark (and the West), and in practice, even if the Danish government preferred to take action against the newspaper, there were no laws empowering it to do so.

While acknowledging the importance of freedom of speech, Western governments expressed sympathy to Muslims. French President Jacques Chirac issued a plea for "respect and moderation" in exercising freedom of expression. British Foreign Minister Jack Straw called the cartoons "insensitive." US President George W. Bush called on world governments to stop the violence and be "respectful." Carsten Juste, editor of *Jyllands-Posten*, who received death threats, said that the drawings "were not in violation of Danish law but offended many Muslims, for which we would like to apologize."

While Muslim feelings were hurt, Danish firms active in Muslim countries were devastated. Arla Foods, one of Denmark's (and Europe's) largest dairy firms, had been selling to the Middle East for 40 years, had had production in Saudi Arabia for 20 years, and normally had sold approximately $465 million a year to the region, including the best-selling butter in the Middle East. Arla's sales to the region plummeted to zero in a matter of days after the protests began. Arla lost $1.8 million every *day* and was forced to send home 170 employees. Other affected firms included Carlsberg (a brewer), Lego (a toy maker), and Novo Nordisk (an insulin maker). In addition, Carrefour, a French supermarket chain active in the region, voluntarily pulled Danish products from shelves in its Middle East stores and boasted about it to customers.

In response, Arla took out full-page advertisements in Saudi newspapers, reprinting the news release from the Danish Embassy in Riyadh saying that Denmark respected all religions. That failed to stop the boycott. Other Danish firms kept a low profile. Some switched "Made in Denmark" labels to "Made in European Union." Others used foreign subsidiaries to camouflage

LEARNING OBJECTIVES

After studying this chapter, you should be able to

1. define what culture is and articulate its two main manifestations: language and religion
2. discuss how cultures systematically differ from each other
3. understand the importance of ethics and ways to combat corruption
4. identify norms associated with strategic responses when firms deal with ethical challenges
5. participate in three leading debates on cultures, ethics, and norms
6. draw implications for action

their origin. Danish shipping companies, such as Maersk, took down the Danish flag when docking in ports in Muslim countries. Overall, although Muslim countries represented only approximately 3% of all Danish exports, a worst-case scenario would lead to 10,000 job losses, which would be a significant blow to a small country with a population of only 5.4 million.

Sources: I thank Professor Klaus Meyer (formerly at Copenhagen Business School, now at the University of Bath) for his assistance. Based on (1) A. Browne, 2006, Denmark faces international boycott over Muslim cartoons, *Times Online*, January 31, http://www.timesonline.co.uk; (2) *Economist*, 2006, Mutual incomprehension, mutual outrage, February 11: 29–31; (3) *Economist*, 2006, When markets melted away, February 11: 56; (4) E. Pfanner, 2006, Danish companies endure snub by Muslim consumers, *New York Times*, February 27: 2; (5) P. Reynolds, 2006, A clash of rights and responsibilities, *BBC News Website*, February 6, http://news.bbc.co.uk.

Publishing the offending cartoons is legal in Denmark, but is it ethical? Should the editor of *Jyllands-Posten*, the Danish prime minister, and managers at Arla have reacted differently? Why should many Danish firms, which had nothing to do with the cartoons, suffer major economic losses in Muslim countries? Why did non-Danish and non-Muslim firms, such as Carrefour, withdraw Danish products from their shelves in the Middle East? More fundamentally, what informal institutions govern individual and firm behavior in different countries?

informal institutions
Institutions represented by cultures, ethics, and norms.

Following Chapter 2, this chapter continues our coverage on the institution-based view with a focus on **informal institutions** represented by cultures, ethics, and norms. Of the two propositions in the institution-based view, the first proposition—managers and firms rationally pursue their interests within a given institutional framework—deals with both formal and informal institutions. The second proposition—in situations where formal institutions are unclear or fail, informal institutions play a larger role in reducing uncertainty—is more important and relevant in this chapter. Shown in the Opening Case, this chapter is more than about how to present business cards correctly and wine and dine differently (as portrayed by chapters on "cultural differences" in other textbooks). Informal institutions can make or break firms, thus necessitating a great deal of our attention.[1]

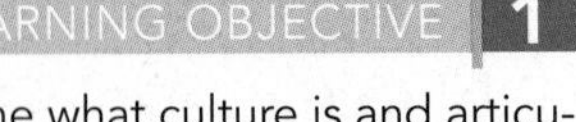
LEARNING OBJECTIVE 1

define what culture is and articulate its two main manifestations: language and religion

WHERE DO INFORMAL INSTITUTIONS COME FROM?

Recall that any institutional framework consists of formal and informal institutions. Although formal institutions such as politics, laws, and economics (see Chapter 2) are important, they make up a small (although important) part of "the rules of the game" that govern individual and firm behavior. As pervasive features of every economy, informal institutions can be found almost everywhere.

ethnocentrism
A self-centered mentality by a group of people who perceive their own culture, ethics, and norms as natural, rational, and morally right.

Where do informal institutions come from? They come from socially transmitted information and are part of the heritage that we call culture, ethics, and norms. Those within a society tend to perceive their own culture, ethics, and norms as "natural, rational, and morally right."[2] This self-centered mentality is known as **ethnocentrism**. For example, many Americans believe in "American exceptionalism"—that is, the United States is exceptionally well endowed to lead the world. The Chinese call China *zhong guo*, which literally means "the country in the middle" or "middle kingdom." Ancient Scandinavians called their country by a similar name (*midgaard*). Some modern Scandinavians, such as some Danes, believe in their freedom to publish whatever they please. Unfortunately, as shown in the Opening Case, those from other societies may feel differently. In other words, common sense in one society may become uncommon elsewhere.[3]

Recall from Chapter 2 that informal institutions are underpinned by the two normative and cognitive pillars, whereas formal institutions are supported by the regulatory pillar. While the regulatory pillar clearly specifies the do's and don'ts, informal institutions, by definition, are more elusive. Yet, they are no less important.[4] Thus, it is imperative that we pay attention to informal institutions. Here, we are going to discuss three aspects of informal institutions: culture, ethics, and norms.

CULTURE

Of many informal institutions, culture probably is most frequently discussed. This section first defines culture and then highlights two major components: language and religion.

Definition of Culture

Although hundreds of definitions of culture have appeared, we will use the definition proposed by the world's foremost cross-cultural expert, Geert Hofstede, a Dutch professor. He defines **culture** as "the collective programming of the mind which distinguishes the members of one group or category of people from another."[5] Before proceeding, it is important to make two points to minimize confusion. First, although it is customary to talk about American culture or Brazilian culture, there is no strict one-to-one correspondence between cultures and nation-states. Within many multiethnic countries such as Belgium, China, India, Indonesia, Russia, South Africa, Switzerland, and the United States, many subcultures exist.[6] In Focus 3.1 shows that North Vietnam and South Vietnam, 30 years after unification, continue to be different. Second, there are many layers of culture, such as regional, ethnic, and

culture
The collective programming of the mind that distinguishes the members of one group or category of people from another.

IN FOCUS 3.1 North Vietnam versus South Vietnam: After Thirty Years

In 2005, Vietnam celebrated 30 years of unification. In 1975, North Vietnam "liberated" South Vietnam and renamed Saigon, capital city of the South, Ho Chi Minh City. With different dialects, food, and weather, the two regions have always been very different. Northerners are considered serious and bookish, whereas Southerners tend to be flexible and flamboyant—similar to the stereotypes of Scandinavians and Mediterraneans in Europe. The Vietnam War (which the Vietnamese call the "American War") exacerbated these differences. North Vietnam has been under communist rule since 1954. South Vietnam had much more recent experience with capitalism. The diaspora of Southerners, who fled from the northern communists in the 1970s, has become the *Viet Kieu* (overseas Vietnamese). *Viet Kieu* have flocked to the South since the beginning of the *Doi Moi* (market liberalization) policy in 1986. Despite the harsh communist reeducation programs to cleanse the Southerners of capitalist values, the economic center of gravity remains in the South. In 2005, Ho Chi Minh City, with 9% of the nation's population, contributed 17% of national output, 30% of foreign investment, and 40% of exports. Its per capita income was four times the national average.

Three decades after the war, Ho Chi Minh City's skyline is again emblazoned with American brands such as Citigroup and Sheraton. In 2004, when United Airlines resumed flights to Ho Chi Minh City, it was pleasantly surprised to find out that the city's code name was still SGN. When I taught in the country's first Executive MBA (EMBA) program (consisting of both Northerners and Southerners) in Hanoi in 1997, my South Vietnamese EMBA students advised me: "No need to call that city Ho Chi Minh City. It has too many words. Everybody just calls it Saigon in the South." It seems that in Vietnam—war or peace—old habits die hard.

Sources: I thank Yung Hua (University of Texas at Dallas) for her assistance. Based on (1) Author's interviews of the country's first class of EMBA students, Foreign Trade University, Hanoi, Vietnam, November 1997; (2) *Economist*, 2005, America lost, capitalism won, April 30: 37–38; (3) K. Meyer & H. Nguyen, 2005, Foreign investment strategies and sub-national institutions in emerging markets: Evidence from Vietnam, *Journal of Management Studies*, 42: 63–93; (4) D. Ralston, V. T. Nguyen, & N. Napier, 1999, A comparative study of the work values of North and South Vietnamese managers, *Journal of International Business Studies*, 30: 655–672.

religious cultures. Within a firm, one may find a specific organizational culture (such as the IKEA culture). Having acknowledged the validity of these two points, we will follow Hofstede by using the term *culture* when discussing *national culture*—unless otherwise noted. This is a matter of expediency, and it is also a reflection of the institutional realities of the world with about 200 nation-states.

Each one of us is a walking encyclopedia of our own culture. Due to space constraints, we will highlight only two major components of culture: language and religion.

Language

lingua franca
The dominance of one language as a global business language.

Among approximately 6,000 languages in the world, Chinese is the world's largest in terms of the number of native speakers.[7] English is a distant second, followed closely by Hindi and Spanish (Figure 3.1). Yet, the dominance of English as a global business language, known as the **lingua franca** in the jargon, is unmistakable. This is driven by two factors. First, English-speaking countries contribute the largest share of global output (Figure 3.2). Such economic dominance not only drives trade and investment ties between English-speaking countries and the rest of the world, but also generates a constant stream of products and services marketed in English. Think about the ubiquitous Hollywood movies, *Economist* magazines, and Google search engines.

Second, recent globalization has called for the use of one common language. For firms headquartered in English-speaking countries as well as Scandinavia and the Netherlands, using English to manage operations around the globe poses little difficulty. However, settling on a global language for the entire firm is problematic for firms headquartered in Latin Europe countries (such as France) or Asian countries (such as Japan). Yet, even in these firms, insisting on a language other than English as the global corporate lingua franca is still hard.[8] Around the world, nonnative speakers of English who can master English, such as the Taiwanese-born Hollywood director Ang Lee, Icelandic-born singer Björk, and Colombian-born pop star Shakira, increasingly command a premium in jobs and compensation. This fuels the rising interest in English. The European Union (EU) insists that documents in

FIGURE 3.1 WORLD POPULATION BY LANGUAGE

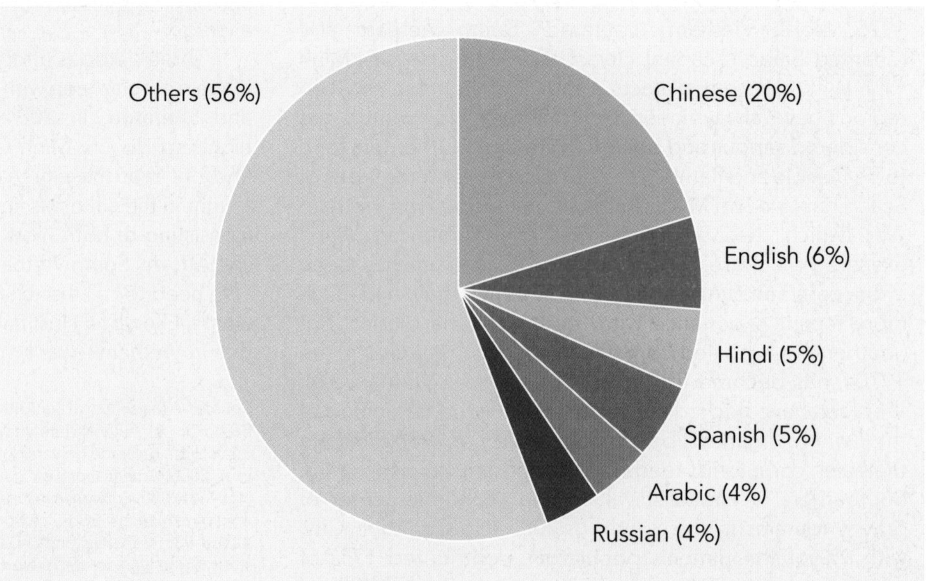

Sources: Author's estimates based on data in (1) *The Economist Atlas*, 2005, London: The Economist Books; (2) D. Graddol, 2004, The future of language, *Science*, 303: 1329–1331; (3) S. Huntington, 1996, *The Clash of Civilizations and the Remaking of World Order*, New York: Simon & Schuster.

FIGURE 3.2 WORLD OUTPUT BY LANGUAGE

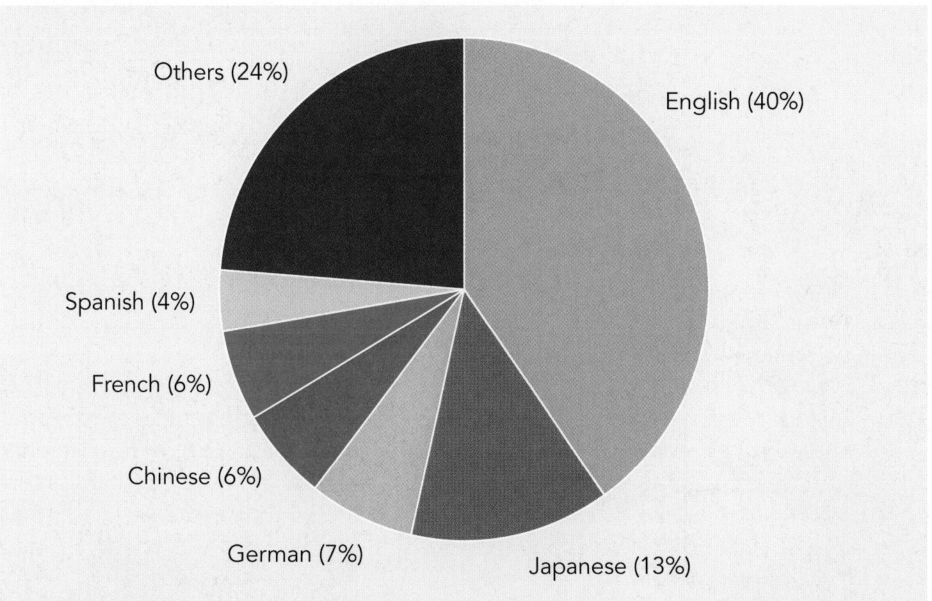

Sources: Author's estimates based on data in World Bank, 2005, World Development Indicators database, http://www.worldbank.org (accessed January 30, 2007).

every member country's official language be translated into all other official languages. The expanded set of 23 official languages for 27 member countries (since 2007) makes this requirement almost impossible to satisfy. For example, nobody can fluently translate Estonian into Portuguese. An Estonian document needs to be translated into English, which then can be translated into Portuguese. Thus, translators well versed in English are in great demand.

On the other hand, the dominance of English, which does give native speakers of English a large advantage in global business, may also lead to a disadvantage. An expatriate manager not knowing the local language misses a lot of cultural subtleties and can only interact with locals fluent in English. Weak (or no) ability in foreign languages makes it difficult (or impossible) to detect translation errors, which may result in embarrassments. For example, Rolls-Royce's Silver Mist was translated into German as "Silver Excrement." Coors Beer translated its slogan "Turn it loose!" into Spanish as "Drink Coors and get diarrhea!" Ford marketed its Nova car in Latin America with disastrous results: *No va* means "no go" in Spanish.[9] To avoid such embarrassments, you will be better off if you can pick up at least one foreign language during your university studies.

Religion

Religion is another major manifestation of culture. Approximately 85% of the world's population reportedly have some religious belief. Figure 3.3 shows the geographic distribution of different religious heritages. The four leading religions are (1) Christianity (approximately 1.7 billion adherents), (2) Islam (1 billion), (3) Hinduism (750 million), and (4) Buddhism (350 million). Of course, not everybody claiming to be an adherent actively practices a religion. For instance, some Christians may go to church only once every year—on Christmas.

Because religious differences have led to numerous challenges, knowledge about religions is crucial even for nonreligious managers. For example, in Christian countries, the Christmas season represents the peak in shopping and consumption. In the United States, half of the toys are sold in one month before Christmas. Since (spoiled) kids in America consume half of the world's toys and virtually all toys

FIGURE 3.3 RELIGIOUS HERITAGES OF THE WORLD

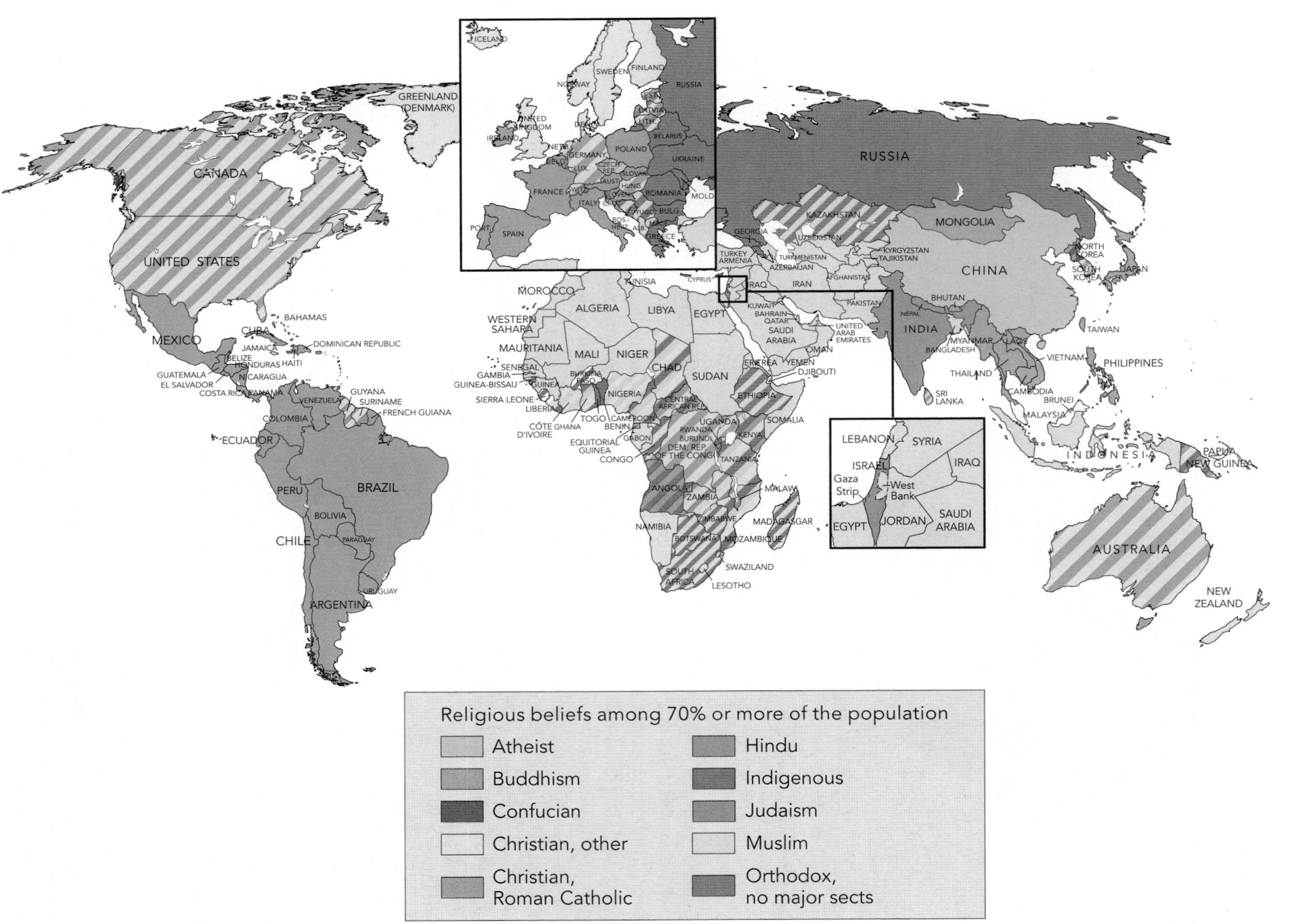

Source: CIA—*The World Factbook 2000.* Note that Confucianism, strictly speaking, is not a religion but a set of moral codes guiding interpersonal relationships.

are made outside the United States (mostly in Asia), this means 25% of the world toy output is sold in one country in one month, thus creating severe production, distribution, and coordination challenges. For toy makers and stores, "missing the boat" from Asia, whose transit time is at least two weeks, can literally devastate an entire season (and probably the entire year).

Managers and firms ignorant of religious traditions and differences may end up with embarrassments and, worse, disasters. A US firm blundered in Saudi Arabia by sending a meticulously prepared proposal bound with an expensive pigskin leather cover hoping to impress the clients. The proposal, an excellent one, was never read and soon rejected because Muslims avoid pig products.[10] While this is a relatively minor embarrassment, a similar incident with much graver consequences took place in India in 1857. In those days, bullets were encased in pig wax, and the tops had to be bitten off before firing the bullets. When Muslim soldiers discovered the stuff they bit off was pig wax, they revolted against British officers. Eventually, British insensitivity to religious traditions in India led to hundreds of casualties on both sides.[11] Fast forward through 150 years, Danish insensitivity to Muslim traditions sparked riots in many Muslim countries (see Opening Case). Ideally, historically and religiously sensitive managers and firms will avoid such blunders in the future.

In addition to language and religion, numerous other informal aspects, such as social structure, communication, and education, are also manifestations of culture. However, if we keep going with these differences, this chapter—in fact, this book—may never end, given the tremendous differences around the world. As a reader, it must be frustrating to feel that you are being bombarded with a seemingly random collection of the numerous informal "rules of the game": Do this in Muslim countries, don't do that in Catholic countries, and so on. These are all interesting "trees," but let us not forget that we are more interested in the "forest." The point about seeing the "forest" is to understand how cultures are *systematically* different. This is done next.

CLASSIFYING CULTURAL DIFFERENCES

LEARNING OBJECTIVE 2

discuss how cultures systematically differ from each other

This section outlines three ways to systematically understand cultural differences: (1) context, (2) cluster, and (3) dimension approaches. Then, culture is linked with different firm behavior.

context

The underlying background upon which interaction takes place.

low-context culture

A culture in which communication is usually taken at face value without much reliance on unspoken context.

The Context Approach

Of the three main approaches probing into cultural differences, the context approach is the most straightforward because it relies on a single dimension: context.[12] **Context** is the underlying background upon which interaction takes place. Figure 3.4 outlines the spectrum of countries along the dimension of low- versus high-context. In **low-context cultures** (such as North American and Western

FIGURE 3.4 HIGH-CONTEXT VERSUS LOW-CONTEXT CULTURES

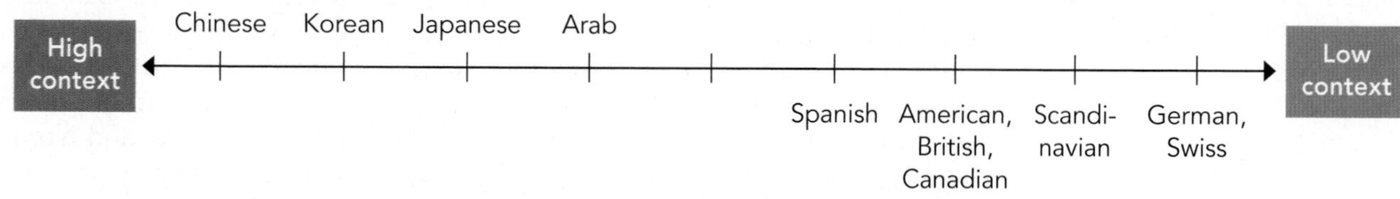

European countries), communication is usually taken at face value without much reliance on unspoken context. In other words, no means no. In contrast, in **high-context cultures** (such as Arab and Asian countries), communication relies a lot on the underlying unspoken context, which is as important as the words used. For example, no does not necessarily mean no.

high-context culture
A culture in which communication relies a lot on the underlying unspoken context, which is as important as the words used.

Why is context important? This is because failure to understand the differences in interaction styles may lead to misunderstandings. For instance, in Japan, a high-context culture, negotiators prefer not to flatly say "no" to a business request. They will say something like "We will study it" and "We will get back to you later." Their negotiation partners are supposed to understand the context of these responses that lack enthusiasm and figure out that these responses essentially mean no (although the word "no" is never mentioned). In another example, in the United States, a low-context culture, lawyers often participate in negotiations by essentially attempting to remove the "context." A contract should be as straightforward as possible, and parties are not supposed to "read between the lines." For this reason, negotiators from high-context countries (such as China) often prefer *not* to involve lawyers until the very last phase of contract drafting. In high-context countries, initial rounds of negotiations are supposed to create the "context" for mutual trust and friendship. For individuals brought up in high-context cultures, decoding the context and acting accordingly are their second nature. Straightforward communication and confrontation, typical in low-context cultures, often baffle them.

Why is it important to understand the context of business communications?

The Cluster Approach

The cluster approach groups countries that share similar cultures together as one **cluster**. There are three influential sets of clusters (Table 3.1). The first is the Ronen and Shenkar clusters, proposed by management professors Simcha Ronen and Oded Shenkar.[13] In alphabetical order, these clusters are (1) Anglo, (2) Arabic, (3) Far East, (4) Germanic, (5) Latin America, (6) Latin Europe, (7) Near Eastern, and (8) Nordic.

cluster
Countries that share similar cultures together.

The second set of clusters is called the GLOBE clusters, named after the Global Leadership and Organizational Behavior Effectiveness project led by management professor Robert House.[14] The GLOBE project identifies ten clusters, five of which use identical labels as the Ronen and Shenkar clusters: (1) Anglo, (2) Germanic Europe, (3) Latin America, (4) Latin Europe, and (5) Nordic Europe. In addition, GLOBE has (6) Confucian Asia, (7) Eastern Europe, (8) Middle East, (9) Southern Asia, and (10) Sub-Sahara Africa, which roughly (but not completely) correspond with the respective Ronen and Shenkar clusters.

The third set of clusters is the Huntington civilizations, popularized by political scientist Samuel Huntington. A **civilization** is "the highest cultural grouping of people and the broadest level of cultural identity people have."[15] Shown in Table 3.1, Huntington divides the world into eight civilizations: (1) African, (2) Confucian (Sinic), (3) Hindu, (4) Islamic, (5) Japanese, (6) Latin American, (7) Slavic-Orthodox, and (8) Western. Although this classification shares a number of similarities with the Ronen and Shenkar and GLOBE clusters, Huntington's Western civilization is a very broad cluster that is subdivided into Anglo, Germanic, Latin Europe, and Nordic clusters by Ronen and Shenkar and GLOBE. In addition to such an uncontroversial

civilization
The highest cultural grouping of people and the broadest level of cultural identity people have.

classification scheme, Huntington has advanced a highly controversial idea that the Western civilization will clash with the Islamic and Confucian civilizations in the years to come. Incidents such as 9/11, Iraq, and more recently the Danish cartoons (see Opening Case) have often been cited as evidence of such a clash.

For our purposes, we do not need to debate the validity of Huntington's provocative thesis of the "clash of civilizations." We will leave your political science or international relations classes to debate that. However, we do need to appreciate the underlying idea that people and firms are more comfortable doing business with other countries within the same cluster/civilization. This is because common language, history, religion, and customs within the same cluster/civilization reduce the liability of foreignness when operating abroad (see Chapter 1). For example, Hollywood movies are more likely to succeed in English-speaking countries. Most foreign investors in China are from Hong Kong and Taiwan—that is, they are not very "foreign." Conversely, Danish firms suffered in Muslim countries in the aftermath of the cartoon incident because of their high level of liability of foreignness in a culturally distant cluster (see Opening Case).

TABLE 3.1 CULTURAL CLUSTERS[1]

Ronen and Shenkar Clusters[2]	GLOBE Clusters[3]	Huntington Civilizations
Anglo	Anglo	Western (1)[4]
Arabic	Middle East	Islamic
Far East	Confucian Asia	Confucian (Sinic)
Germanic	Germanic Europe	Western (2)
Latin America	Latin America	Latin American
Latin Europe	Latin Europe	Western (3)
Near Eastern	Southern Asia	Hindu
Nordic	Nordic Europe	Western (4)
Central and Eastern Europe	Eastern Europe	Slavic-Orthodox
Sub-Sahara Africa	Sub-Sahara Africa	African
Independents: Brazil, India, Israel, Japan		Japanese

1. This table is the *first* time these three major systems of cultural clusters are compiled side by side. Viewing them together can allow us to see their similarities. However, there are also differences. Across the three systems (columns), even though some clusters share the same labels, there are still differences. For example, Ronen and Shenkar's Latin America cluster does not include Brazil (which is regarded as an "independent"), whereas GLOBE and Huntington's Latin America includes Brazil.
2. Ronen and Shenkar originally classified eight clusters (in alphabetical order, from Anglo to Nordic), covering 44 countries. They placed Brazil, India, Israel, and Japan as "independents." Upon consultation with Oded Shenkar, my colleagues and I more recently added Central and Eastern Europe and Sub-Sahara Africa as two new clusters—see Peng, Hill, and Wang, 2000, cited as (3) in the Sources.
3. GLOBE includes ten clusters, covering 62 countries.
4. Huntington includes eight civilizations, in theory covering *every* country. For the Western civilization, he does not use such labels as Western 1, 2, 3, and 4 as in the table. The present author added them to establish some rough correspondence with the respective Ronen and Shenkar and GLOBE clusters.

Sources: Based on (1) R. House, P. Hanges, M. Javidan, P. Dorfman, & V. Gupta (eds.), 2004, *Culture, Leadership, and Organizations: The GLOBE Study of 62 Societies*, Thousand Oaks, CA: Sage; (2) S. Huntington, 1996, *The Clash of Civilizations and the Remaking of World Order*, New York: Simon & Schuster; (3) M. W. Peng, C. Hill, & D. Wang, 2000, Schumpeterian dynamics versus Williamsonian considerations, *Journal of Management Studies*, 37: 167–184; (4) S. Ronen & O. Shenkar, 1985, Clustering countries on attitudinal dimension, *Academy of Management Review*, 10: 435–454.

The Dimension Approach

Although both the context and cluster approaches are interesting, the dimension approach is more influential. The reasons for such influence are probably twofold. First, insightful as the context approach is, context only represents one dimension. What about other dimensions? Second, the cluster approach has relatively little to offer regarding differences among countries *within* one cluster. For example, what are the differences between Italy and Spain, both of which belong to the same Latin Europe cluster according to Ronen and Shenkar and GLOBE? By focusing on multiple dimensions of cultural differences both within and across clusters, the

TABLE 3.2 HOFSTEDE'S DIMENSIONS OF CULTURE[1]

	1. Power distance	2. Individualism	3. Masculinity	4. Uncertainty avoidance	5. Long-term orientation
1	Malaysia (104)[2]	USA (91)	Japan (95)	Greece (112)	China (118)
2	Guatemala (95)	Australia (90)	Austria (79)	Portugal (104)	Hong Kong (96)
3	Panama (95)	UK (89)	Venezuela (73)	Guatemala (101)	Taiwan (87)
4	Philippines (94)	Canada (80)	Italy (70)	Uruguay (100)	Japan (80)
5	Mexico (81)	Netherlands (80)	Switzerland (70)	Belgium (94)	South Korea (75)
6	Venezuela (81)	New Zealand (79)	Mexico (69)	El Salvador (94)	Brazil (65)
7	Arab countries (80)	Italy (76)	Ireland (68)	Japan (92)	India (61)
8	Ecuador (78)	Belgium (75)	Jamaica (68)	Yugoslavia (88)	Thailand (56)
9	Indonesia (78)	Denmark (74)	UK (66)	Peru (87)	Singapore (48)
10	India (77)	Sweden (71)	Germany (66)	France (86)	Netherlands (44)
11	West Africa (77)	France (71)	Philippines (64)	Chile (86)	Bangladesh (40)
12	Yugoslavia (76)	Ireland (70)	Colombia (64)	Spain (86)	Sweden (33)
13	Singapore (74)	Norway (69)	South Africa (63)	Costa Rica (86)	Poland (32)
14	Brazil (69)	Switzerland (68)	Ecuador (63)	Panama (86)	Germany (31)
15	France (68)	Germany (67)	USA (62)	Argentina (86)	Australia (31)
16	Hong Kong (68)	South Africa (65)	Australia (61)	Turkey (85)	New Zealand (30)
17	Colombia (67)	Finland (63)	New Zealand (58)	South Korea (85)	USA (29)
18	El Salvador (66)	Austria (55)	Greece (57)	Mexico (82)	UK (25)
19	Turkey (66)	Israel (54)	Hong Kong (57)	Israel (81)	Zimbabwe (25)
20	Belgium (65)	Spain (51)	Argentina (56)	Colombia (80)	Canada (23)
21	East Africa (64)	India (48)	India (56)	Venezuela (76)	Philippines (19)
22	Peru (64)	Japan (46)	Belgium (54)	Brazil (76)	Nigeria (16)
23	Thailand (64)	Argentina (46)	Arab countries (53)	Italy (75)	Pakistan (0)
24	Chile (63)	Iran (41)	Canada (52)	Pakistan (70)	
25	Portugal (63)	Jamaica (39)	Malaysia (50)	Austria (70)	
26	Uruguay (61)	Brazil (38)	Pakistan (50)	Taiwan (69)	
27	Greece (60)	Arab countries (38)	Brazil (49)	Arab countries (68)	
28	South Korea (60)	Turkey (37)	Singapore (48)	Ecuador (67)	

dimension approach has endeavored to overcome these limitations. While there are several competing frameworks,[16] the work of Hofstede and his colleagues is by far the most influential[17] and thus is our focus here.

Hofstede and his colleagues have proposed five dimensions (Table 3.2). First, **power distance** is the extent to which less powerful members within a country expect and accept that power is distributed unequally. For example, in high power distance Brazil, the richest 10% of the population receives approximately 50% of the national income, and everybody accepts this as "the way it is." In low power distance Sweden, the richest 10% only gets 22% of the national income.[18] Even within the same cluster, there are major differences. For instance, in the United

power distance
The extent to which less powerful members within a country expect and accept that power is distributed unequally.

Table 3.2, *continued*

	1. Power distance	2. Individualism	3. Masculinity	4. Uncertainty avoidance	5. Long-term orientation
29	Iran (58)	Uruguay (36)	Israel (47)	Germany (65)	
30	Taiwan (58)	Greece (35)	Indonesia (46)	Thailand (64)	
31	Spain (57)	Philippines (32)	West Africa (46)	Iran (59)	
32	Pakistan (55)	Mexico (30)	Turkey (45)	Finland (59)	
33	Japan (54)	East Africa (27)	Taiwan (45)	Switzerland (58)	
34	Italy (50)	Yugoslavia (27)	Panama (44)	West Africa (54)	
35	Argentina (49)	Puerto Rico (27)	Iran (43)	Netherlands (53)	
36	South Africa (49)	Malaysia (26)	France (43)	East Africa (52)	
37	Jamaica (45)	Hong Kong (25)	Spain (42)	Australia (51)	
38	USA (40)	Chile (23)	Peru (42)	Norway (50)	
39	Canada (39)	West Africa (20)	East Africa (41)	South Africa (49)	
40	Netherlands (38)	Singapore (20)	El Salvador (40)	New Zealand (49)	
41	Australia (36)	Thailand (20)	South Korea (39)	Indonesia (48)	
42	Cost Rica (35)	El Salvador (19)	Uruguay (38)	Canada (48)	
43	Germany (35)	South Korea (18)	Guatemala (37)	USA (46)	
44	UK (35)	Taiwan (17)	Thailand (34)	Philippines (44)	
45	Switzerland (34)	Peru (16)	Portugal (31)	India (40)	
46	Finland (33)	Costa Rica (15)	Chile (28)	Malaysia (36)	
47	Norway (31)	Pakistan (14)	Finland (26)	UK (35)	
48	Sweden (31)	Indonesia (14)	Yugoslavia (21)	Ireland (35)	
49	Ireland (28)	Colombia (13)	Costa Rica (21)	Hong Kong (29)	
50	New Zealand (22)	Venezuela (12)	Denmark (16)	Sweden (29)	
51	Denmark (18)	Panama (11)	Netherlands (14)	Denmark (23)	
52	Israel (13)	Ecuador (8)	Norway (8)	Jamaica (13)	
53	Austria (11)	Guatemala (6)	Sweden (8)	Singapore (8)	

1. When scores are the same, countries are tied according to their alphabetical order. Arab, East Africa, and West Africa are clusters of multiple countries. Germany and Yugoslavia refer to the former West Germany and the former Yugoslavia, respectively.
2. Scores reflect relative standing among countries, not absolute positions. They are measures of differences only.

Sources: Adapted from G. Hofstede, 1997, *Cultures and Organizations: Software of the Mind* (pp. 25, 26, 53, 84, 113, 166), New York: McGraw-Hill.

States, subordinates often address their bosses on a first-name basis, which reflects a relatively low power distance. While this boss, Mary or Joe, still has the power to fire you, the distance appears to be shorter than if you have to address this person as Mrs. Y or Dr. Z. In low power distance American universities, all faculty members, including the lowest ranked assistant professors, are commonly addressed as "Professor A." In high power distance British universities, only full professors are allowed to be called "Professor B" (everybody else is called "Dr. C" or "Ms. D" if D does not have a PhD). German universities are perhaps most extreme: Full professors with PhDs need to be honored as "Prof. Dr. X"; your author would be "Prof. Dr. Peng" if I worked at a German university.

individualism
The perspective that the identity of an individual is fundamentally his or her own.

collectivism
The idea that the identity of an individual is primarily based on the identity of his or her collective group.

masculinity
A relatively strong form of societal-level sex-role differentiation whereby men tend to have occupations that reward assertiveness and women tend to work in caring professions.

femininity
A relatively weak form of societal-level sex-role differentiation whereby more women occupy positions that reward assertiveness and more men work in caring professions.

uncertainty avoidance
The extent to which members in different cultures accept ambiguous situations and tolerate uncertainty.

long-term orientation
A perspective that emphasizes perseverance and savings for future betterment.

Second, **individualism** refers to the perspective that the identity of an individual is fundamentally his or her own, whereas **collectivism** refers to the idea that the identity of an individual is primarily based on the identity of his or her collective group (such as family, village, or company). In individualist societies (led by the United States), ties between individuals are relatively loose, and individual achievement and freedom are highly valued. In contrast, in collectivist societies (such as many countries in Africa, Asia, and Latin America), ties between individuals are relatively close, and collective accomplishments are often sought after.

Third, the **masculinity** versus **femininity** dimension refers to sex-role *differentiation*. In every traditional society, men tend to have occupations that reward assertiveness, such as politicians, soldiers, and executives. Women, on the other hand, usually work in caring professions, such as teachers and nurses, in addition to being homemakers. High masculinity societies (led by Japan) continue to maintain such a sharp role differentiation along gender lines. In low masculinity societies (led by Sweden), women increasingly become politicians, scientists, and soldiers (think about the movie *GI Jane*), and men frequently assume the role of nurses, teachers, and *househusbands*.

Fourth, **uncertainty avoidance** refers to the extent to which members in different cultures accept ambiguous situations and tolerate uncertainty. Members of high uncertainty avoidance cultures (led by Greece) place a premium on job security and retirement benefits. They also tend to resist change, which, by definition, is uncertain. Low uncertainty avoidance cultures (led by Singapore) are characterized by a greater willingness to take risks and less resistance to change.

Finally, **long-term orientation** emphasizes perseverance and savings for future betterment. China, which has the world's longest continuous written history of approximately 4,000 years and the highest contemporary savings rate, leads the pack. On the other hand, members of short-term orientation societies (led by Pakistan) prefer quick results and instant gratification.

Overall, Hofstede's dimensions are interesting and informative. They are also largely supported by subsequent work.[19] It is important to note that Hofstede's dimensions are not perfect and have attracted some criticisms (see In Focus 3.2).[20] However, it is fair to suggest that these dimensions represent a *starting point* for trying to figure out the role of culture in global business.

Culture and Global Business

A great deal of global business activities is consistent with the context, cluster, and dimension approaches to cultural differences.[21] For instance, the average length of contracts is longer in low-context countries (such as Germany) than in high-context countries (such as Vietnam). This is because in high-context countries a lot of agreements are unspoken and not necessarily put in a legal contract.

Also, as pointed out by the cluster approach, firms are a lot more serious in preparation when doing business with countries in other clusters, compared with how they deal with countries within the same cluster. Recently, countless new books have been published on how to do business in China. Two decades ago,

IN FOCUS 3.2 Criticizing Hofstede's Framework

Despite the influence of Hofstede's framework, it has attracted a number of criticisms.

- Cultural boundaries are not the same as national boundaries.
- Although Hofstede was careful to remove some of his own cultural biases, "the Dutch software" of his mind, as he acknowledged, "will remain evident to the careful reader." Being more familiar with Western cultures, Hofstede might inevitably be more familiar with dimensions relevant to Westerners. Thus, crucial dimensions relevant to Easterners could be missed.
- Hofstede's research was based on surveys of more than 116,000 IBM employees working at 72 national subsidiaries during 1967–1973. This had both pros and cons. On the positive side, it not only took place in the same industry but also in the same company. Otherwise, it would have been difficult to attribute whether findings were due to differences in national cultures or industrial/organizational cultures. However, because of such a single firm/single industry design, it was possible that Hofstede's findings captured what was unique to that industry or to IBM. Given anti-American sentiments in some countries, some individuals might refuse to work for an American employer. Thus, it was difficult to ascertain whether employees working for IBM were true representatives of their respective national cultures.
- Because the original data are now 40 years old, critics contend that Hofstede's framework would simply fail to capture aspects of cultural change.

Hofstede responded to all four criticisms. First, he acknowledged that his focus on national culture was a matter of expediency with all its trappings. Second, since the 1980s, Hofstede and colleagues relied on a questionnaire derived from cultural dimensions most relevant to the Chinese and then translated it from Chinese to multiple languages. That was how he uncovered the fifth dimension, long-term orientation (originally labeled "Confucian dynamism"). In response to the third and fourth criticisms, Hofstede pointed out a large number of studies conducted by other scholars using a variety of countries, industries, and firms. Most results were supportive of his original findings. Overall, Hofstede's work is not the Holy Bible and is imperfect, but on balance, its values seem to outweigh its drawbacks.

Sources: I thank Professor Geert Hofstede for working with me on an article for the *Asia Pacific Journal of Management*, where I serve as Editor-in-Chief—see (4) cited below—and Professor Tony Fang (Stockholm University) for his assistance. Based on (1) T. Fang, 2003, A critique of Hofstede's fifth national culture dimension, *International Journal of Cross-Cultural Management*, 3: 347–368; (2) G. Hofstede, 1997, *Cultures and Organizations*, New York: McGraw-Hill; (3) G. Hofstede, 2006, What did GLOBE really measure? *Journal of International Business Studies*, 37: 882–896; (4) G. Hofstede, 2007, Asian management in the 21st century, *Asia Pacific Journal of Management*, 24: 411–420; (5) M. Javidan, R. House, P. Dorfman, P. Hanges, & M. Luque, 2006, Conceptualizing and measuring cultures and their consequences, *Journal of International Business Studies*, 37: 897–914; (6) B. McSweeney, 2002, Hofstede's model of national cultural differences and their consequences, *Human Relations*, 55: 89–118; (7) B. Kirkman, K. Lowe, & C. Gibson, 2006, A quarter century of *Culture's Consequences*, *Journal of International Business Studies*, 37: 285–320; (8) K. Leung, R. Bhagat, N. Buchan, M. Erez, & C. Gibson, 2005, Culture and international business, *Journal of International Business Studies*, 36: 357–378; (9) P. Smith, 2006, When elephants fight, the grass gets trampled, *Journal of International Business Studies*, 37: 915–921.

gurus wrote about how to do business in Japan. Evidently, there is a huge demand for English-speaking business people to read such books before heading to China and Japan. But has anyone ever seen a book on how to do business in Canada in English?

Hofstede's dimension approach is also often supported in the real world. For instance, managers in high power distance countries such as France and Italy have a greater penchant for centralized authority.[22] Solicitation of subordinate feedback and participation, widely practiced in low power distance Western countries (known as empowerment), is often regarded as a sign of weak leadership and low integrity in high power distance countries such as Egypt, Russia, and Turkey.[23]

Individualism and collectivism also affect business activities. Individualist US firms may often try to differentiate themselves, whereas collectivist Japanese firms tend to follow each other.[24] Because entrepreneurs "stick their neck out" by founding new firms, individualist societies tend to foster a relatively higher level of entrepreneurship.[25]

Likewise, masculinity and femininity affect managerial behavior. The stereotypical manager in high masculinity societies is "assertive, decisive, and 'aggressive' (only in masculine societies does this word carry a positive connotation)," whereas the stylized manager in high femininity societies is "less visible, intuitive rather than decisive, and accustomed to seeking consensus."[26]

Managers in low uncertainty avoidance countries (such as Britain) rely more on experience and training, whereas managers in high uncertainty avoidance countries (such as China) rely more on rules.[27] For example, the 1998 crash of a Swissair flight is indicative of high uncertainty avoidance. The Swissair pilots took their smoke-filled aircraft to the sea to dump fuel before attempting an emergency landing. Unfortunately, the aircraft crashed in the sea and everyone on board was killed. A controversy thus broke out as to whether the pilots should have first attempted to land with more fuel (which could explode during landing). With 20/20 hindsight, some US pilots commented that Swissair pilots should have landed the plane as soon as smoke was detected. Swissair officials argued that their pilots did exactly what was required by the written rules. US commentators suggested that pilots should have exercised independent judgment regardless of the rules; in other words, "rules are there to be broken during an emergency like this," an attitude typical of Americans' uncertainty-accepting norms. Swissair officials, on the other hand, argued that "rules exist exactly for such emergencies."[28]

In addition, cultures with a long-term orientation are likely to nurture firms with long horizons. For instance, Japan's Matsushita has a 250-year plan, which was put together in the 1930s.[29] While this is certainly an extreme case, Japanese and Korean firms tend to focus more on the long term.[30] In comparison, Western firms often focus on relatively short-term profits (often on a *quarterly* basis).[31]

Overall, there is strong evidence pointing out the importance of culture.[32] Sensitivity to cultural differences does not guarantee success, but it can at least avoid blunders. For instance, a Chinese manufacturer exported to the West a premium brand of battery called White Elephant, while not knowing the meaning of this term. In another example, when a French manager was transferred to a US subsidiary and met his American secretary (a woman) the first time, he greeted her with an effusive kiss on the cheek—a "hello" that would be harmless in France. However, the secretary later filed a complaint for sexual harassment.[33] More seriously, Mitsubishi Motors, coming from Japan that leads the world in masculinity, encountered major problems when operating in the United States, where there is more female participation in the labor force (indicative of a relatively higher level of femininity). In 1998, its North American division paid $34 million to settle sexual harassment charges.

Although "what is different" cross-culturally can be interesting, it can also be unethical—all depending on the institutional frameworks in which firms are embedded. This is dealt with next.

LEARNING OBJECTIVE **3**

understand the importance of ethics and ways to combat corruption

ETHICS

Definition and Impact of Ethics

ethics
The principles, standards, and norms of conduct governing individual and firm behavior.

Ethics refers to the principles, standards, and norms of conduct governing individual and firm behavior.[34] Ethics is not only an important part of informal institutions but is also deeply reflected in formal laws and regulations. To the extent that laws reflect a society's minimum standards of conduct, there is a substantial overlap between what is ethical and legal and between what is unethical and illegal. However, there is a gray area because what is legal may be unethical (see Opening Case).

Recent scandals (such as those at Citigroup discussed in Closing Case) have pushed ethics to the forefront of global business discussions. Numerous firms have introduced a **code of conduct**—a set of guidelines for making ethical decisions.[35] There is a debate on firms' ethical motivations. A negative view suggests that firms may simply jump onto the ethics "bandwagon" under social pressures to appear

code of conduct
A set of guidelines for making ethical decisions.

more legitimate without necessarily becoming better. A positive view maintains that some (although not all) firms may be self-motivated to "do it right" regardless of pressures. An instrumental view believes that good ethics may simply be a useful instrument to help make money.[36]

Perhaps the best way to appreciate the value of ethics is to examine what happens after some crisis. As a "reservoir of goodwill," the value of an ethical reputation is *magnified* during a time of crisis. One study finds that all US firms engulfed in crises (such as the *Exxon Valdez* oil spill) took an average hit of 8% of their market value in the first week. However, after ten weeks, stock of firms with ethical reputations actually *rose* 5%, whereas those without such reputations dropped 15%.[37] Paradoxically, catastrophes may allow more ethical firms to shine. The upshot seems to be that ethics pays.

What do you think a company's code of conduct should say about respect for people's religious beliefs and practices?

Managing Ethics Overseas

Managing ethics overseas is challenging because what is ethical in one country may be unethical elsewhere.[38] There are two schools of thought.[39] First, **ethical relativism** follows the cliché, "When in Rome, do as the Romans do." If women in Muslim countries are discriminated against, so what? Likewise, if industry rivals in China can fix prices, who cares? Isn't that what the "Romans" do in "Rome"? Second, **ethical imperialism** refers to the absolute belief that "There is only one set of Ethics (with the capital E), and we have it." Americans are especially renowned for believing that their ethical values should be applied universally.[40] For example, since sexual discrimination and price fixing are wrong in the United States, they must be wrong everywhere else. In practice, however, neither of these schools of thought is realistic. At the extreme, ethical relativism would have to accept any local practice, whereas ethical imperialism may cause resentment and backlash among locals.

ethical relativism
A perspective that suggests that all ethical standards are relative.

ethical imperialism
The absolute belief that "there is only one set of Ethics (with the capital E), and we have it."

Three "middle-of-the-road" guiding principles have been proposed by Thomas Donaldson, a business ethicist (Table 3.3). First, respect for human dignity and basic rights (such as those concerning health, safety, and the need for education instead of working at a young age) should determine the absolute minimal ethical thresholds for *all* operations around the world.

Second, respect for local traditions suggests cultural sensitivity. If gifts are banned, foreign firms can forget about doing business in China and Japan, where gift giving is part of the business norm. Although hiring employees' children

TABLE 3.3 MANAGING ETHICS OVERSEAS: THREE "MIDDLE-OF-THE-ROAD" APPROACHES

- Respect for human dignity and basic rights
- Respect for local traditions
- Respect for institutional context

Sources: Based on text in (1) T. Donaldson, 1996, Values in tension: Ethics away from home, *Harvard Business Review*, September–October: 4–11; (2) J. Weiss, 2006, *Business Ethics*, 4th ed., Cincinnati, OH: Thomson South-Western.

and relatives instead of more qualified applicants is illegal according to US equal opportunity laws, Indian companies routinely practice such nepotism, which would strengthen employee loyalty. What should US companies setting up subsidiaries in India do? Donaldson advises that such nepotism is not necessarily wrong, at least in India.

Finally, respect for institutional context calls for a careful understanding of local institutions. Codes of conduct banning bribery are not very useful unless accompanied by guidelines for the scale and scope of appropriate gift giving and receiving. Citigroup allows employees to accept noncash gifts valued at less than $100. The *Economist* allows its journalists to accept any gift that can be consumed in a single day—a bottle of wine is acceptable, but a case of wine is not.[41] Rhone-Poulenc Rorer, a French pharmaceutical firm, has invited foreign subsidiaries to add locally appropriate supplements to its corporate-wide code of conduct. Overall, these three principles, although far from perfect, can help managers make decisions about which they may feel relatively comfortable.

Ethics and Corruption

corruption
The abuse of public power for private benefits, usually in the form of bribery.

Ethics helps combat **corruption**, often defined as the abuse of public power for private benefits, usually in the form of bribery (in cash or in kind).[42] Corruption distorts the basis for competition that should be based on products and services, thus causing misallocation of resources and slowing economic development.[43] According to Transparency International, which is headquartered in Berlin, Germany, and is probably the most influential anticorruption nongovernment organization (NGO), the correlation between a high level of corruption and a low level of economic development is strong (Table 3.4). In other words, corruption and poverty go together. There is some evidence that corruption discourages foreign direct investment (FDI).[44] If the level of corruption in Singapore (very low) hypothetically increases to the level in Mexico (in the middle range), it reportedly would have the same negative effect on FDI inflows as raising the tax rate by 50%.[45]

However, there are exceptions. China is an obvious case, where corruption is often reported. Another exception seems to be Indonesia, whose former President Suharto was known as "Mr. Ten Percent," which refers to the well-known (and transparent!) amount of bribes foreign firms were expected to pay him or members of his family. Why are these two countries popular FDI destinations? There are two explanations. First, the vast potential of these two economies may outweigh the drawbacks of corruption. Second, overseas Chinese (mainly from Hong Kong and Taiwan) and Japanese firms are leading investors in mainland China and Indonesia, respectively. Hong Kong, Taiwan, and Japan may be relatively "cleaner," but they are not among the "cleanest" countries (Table 3.4). It is possible that "acquiring skills in managing corruption [at home] helps develop a certain competitive advantage [in managing corruption overseas]."[46]

Foreign Corrupt Practices Act (FCPA)
A US law enacted in 1977 that bans bribery to foreign officials.

If that is indeed the case, it is not surprising that many US firms complained that they were unfairly restricted by the **Foreign Corrupt Practices Act (FCPA)**, a law enacted in 1977 that bans bribery to foreign officials. They also pointed out that overseas bribery expenses had often been tax deductible (!) in many EU countries such as Austria, France, and Germany—at least until the late 1990s. However, even with the FCPA, there is no evidence that US firms are inherently more ethical than others. The FCPA itself was triggered by investigations in the 1970s of many corrupt US firms. Even the FCPA makes exceptions for small "grease" payments to go through customs abroad. Most alarmingly, the World Bank recently reports that despite over two decades of FCPA enforcement, US firms "exhibit systematically *higher* levels of corruption" than other OECD firms (original italics).[47]

TABLE 3.4 TRANSPARENCY INTERNATIONAL RANKINGS OF CORRUPTION PERCEPTIONS

Rank	Least corrupt countries of 163	Index: 10 (highly clean) – 0 (highly corrupt)	Rank	Most corrupt countries of 163	Index: 10 (highly clean) – 0 (highly corrupt)
1	Finland	9.6	163	Haiti	1.8
	Iceland	9.6	160	Guinea	1.9
	New Zealand	9.6		Iraq	1.9
4	Denmark	9.5		Myanmar	1.9
5	Singapore	9.4	156	Bangladesh	2
6	Sweden	9.2		Chad	2
7	Switzerland	9.1		Democratic Republic of Congo	2
8	Norway	8.8		Sudan	2
9	Australia	8.7	151	Belarus	2.1
	Netherlands	8.7		Cambodia	2.1
11	Austria	8.6		Côte d'Ivoire	2.1
	Luxembourg	8.6		Equatorial Guinea	2.1
	United Kingdom	8.6		Uzbekistan	2.1
14	Canada	8.5	142	Angola	2.2
15	Hong Kong	8.3		Republic of Congo	2.2
16	Germany	8		Kenya	2.2
17	Japan	7.6		Kyrgyzstan	2.2
18	France	7.4		Nigeria	2.2
	Ireland	7.4		Pakistan	2.2
20	Belgium	7.3		Sierra Leone	2.2
	Chile	7.3		Tajikistan	2.2
	USA	7.3		Turkmenistan	2.2

Source: Adapted from Transparency International *Corruption Perceptions Index 2006*, http://www.transparency.org (accessed June 16, 2007).

Overall, the FCPA can be regarded as an institutional weapon in the global fight against corruption. Despite the FCPA's formal *regulatory* "teeth," for a long time, there was neither a *normative* pillar nor a *cognitive* pillar. Until recently, the norms among other OECD firms had seemed to be to pay bribes first and get tax deductions later—a clear sign of ethical relativism. Only in 1997 did the OECD Convention on Combating Bribery of Foreign Public Officials commit all 30 member countries (essentially all developed economies) to criminalize bribery. It went into force in 1999. A more ambitious campaign is the UN Convention against Corruption, signed by 106 countries in 2003 and activated in 2005. If every country criminalizes bribery and every investor resists corruption, their combined power will eradicate it.[48] However, this will not happen unless FCPA-type legislation is institutionalized *and* enforced in every country.

LEARNING OBJECTIVE 4

identify norms associated with strategic responses when firms deal with ethical challenges

norms

The prevailing practices of relevant players that affect the focal individuals and firms.

NORMS AND ETHICAL CHALLENGES

As an important informal institution, **norms** are the prevailing practices of relevant players—the proverbial "everybody else"—that affect the focal individuals and firms. How firms strategically respond to ethical challenges is often driven, at least in part, by norms. Four broad strategic responses are (1) reactive, (2) defensive, (3) accommodative, and (4) proactive strategies (see Table 3.5).

A reactive strategy is passive. Even when problems arise, firms do not feel compelled to act, and denial is usually the first line of defense. In the absence of formal regulation, the need to take necessary action is neither internalized through cognitive beliefs, nor does it become any norm in practice. For example, Ford marketed the Pinto car in the early 1970s knowing that its gas tank had a fatal design flaw that could make the car susceptible to exploding in rear-end collisions. Citing high costs, Ford decided not to add an $11 per car improvement. Sure enough, accidents happened and people were killed and burned in Pintos. Still, for several years, Ford refused to recall the Pinto, and more lives were lost. Only in 1978, under intense formal pressures from the government and informal pressures from the media and consumer groups, did Ford belatedly recall all 1.5 million Pintos.[49]

A defensive strategy focuses on regulatory compliance. In the absence of regulatory pressures, firms often fight informal pressures coming from the media and activists. In the early 1990s, Nike was charged for running "sweatshops," although these incidents took place in its contractors' factories in Indonesia and Vietnam. Although Nike did not own or manage these factories, its initial statement, "We don't make shoes," failed to convey any ethical responsibility. Only when several senators began to suggest legislative solutions did Nike become more serious.

An accommodative strategy features emerging organizational norms to accept responsibility and a set of increasingly internalized cognitive beliefs and values toward making certain changes (see Closing Case). These normative and cognitive values may be shared by a number of firms, thus leading to new industry norms. In other words, it becomes legitimate to accept a higher level of ethical and moral responsibility beyond what is minimally required legally. In this fashion, Nike and the entire sportswear industry became more accommodative toward the late 1990s.

In another example, in 2000, when Ford Explorer vehicles equipped with Firestone tires had a large number of fatal rollover accidents, Ford evidently took the painful lesson from its Pinto fire fiasco in the 1970s. It aggressively initiated a speedy recall, launched a media campaign featuring its CEO, and discontinued its 100-year relationship with Firestone. While critics argue that Ford's accommodative strategy was to place blame squarely on Firestone, the institution-based view

TABLE 3.5 STRATEGIC RESPONSES TO ETHICAL CHALLENGES

Strategic responses	Strategic behaviors	Examples in the text
Reactive	Deny responsibility; do less than required	Ford Pinto fire (the 1970s)
Defensive	Admit responsibility but fight it; do the least that is required	Nike (the early 1990s)
Accommodative	Accept responsibility; do all that is required	Ford Explorer rollovers (the 2000s)
Proactive	Anticipate responsibility; do more than is required	BMW (the 1990s)

(especially Proposition 1 in Chapter 2) suggests that such highly rational actions are to be expected. Even if Ford's public relations campaign was only "window dressing," publicizing a set of ethical criteria against which it can be judged opens doors for more scrutiny by concerned stakeholders. It probably is fair to say that Ford became a better corporate citizen in 2000 than what it was in 1975.

Finally, proactive firms anticipate institutional changes and do more than is required. In 1990, BMW anticipated its emerging responsibility associated with the German government's proposed "take-back" policy, requiring automakers to design cars whose components can be taken back by the same manufacturers for recycling. BMW not only designed easier-to-disassemble cars but also signed up the few high-quality dismantler firms as part of an exclusive recycling infrastructure. Further, BMW actively participated in public discussions and succeeded in establishing its approach as the German national standard for automobile disassembly. Other automakers were thus required to follow BMW's lead. However, they had to fight over smaller, lower quality dismantlers or develop in-house dismantling infrastructure from scratch.[50] Through such a proactive strategy, BMW has set a new industry standard, facilitating the emergence of new environmentally friendly norms in both car design and recycling. Overall, while there is probably a certain element of "window dressing," the fact that proactive firms are going beyond the current regulatory requirements is indicative of the normative and cognitive beliefs held by many managers at these firms on the importance of doing the "right thing."[51]

DEBATES AND EXTENSIONS

LEARNING OBJECTIVE 5

participate in three leading debates on cultures, ethics, and norms

Informal institutions such as cultures, ethics, and norms provoke a series of significant debates. In this section, we focus on three: (1) Western values versus Eastern values, (2) cultural convergence versus divergence, and (3) opportunism versus individualism/collectivism.

Economic Development: Western Values versus Eastern Values

This is another component of the debate on the drivers of economic development first discussed in Chapter 2. Here, our focus is on the role of informal cultural values. About 100 years ago, at the apex of Western power (which ruled the majority of Africans and Asians in colonies), German sociologist Max Weber argued that it was the Protestant work ethic that led to the "spirit of capitalism" and strong economic development. As a branch of Christianity (the other two branches are Catholic and Orthodox), Protestantism is widely practiced in English-speaking countries, Germany, the Netherlands, and Scandinavia. This is where the Industrial Revolution (and modern capitalism) took off. Weber suggested that the Protestant emphasis on hard work and frugality is necessary for capital accumulation—hence the term *capitalism*. Adherents of other religious beliefs, including Catholicism, are believed to lack such traits. At that time, Weber's view was widely accepted.

Such belief in the superiority of Western values has recently been challenged by two sets of Eastern values: (1) Islam and (2) Asian (Confucian). The first is the challenge from Islamic fundamentalism, which, rightly or wrongly, argues that Western dominance *causes* the lackluster economic performance of Muslim countries. Aggressive marketing of Western products in these countries is seen as a cultural invasion. Islamic fundamentalists prefer to go "back to the roots" by moving away from Western influence. Although the majority of Islamic fundamentalists are peaceful, a small number of radical fundamentalists have become terrorists (such as those involved in 9/11).

A second challenge comes from East Asia, whose values center on Confucianism, based on the teachings of Kong Fu Zi (Confucius is the Anglicized spelling of his name), an ancient Chinese scholar who lived more than 2,000 years ago. Confucianism is not a religion but a set of moral codes guiding interpersonal relationships, which emphasize respect, loyalty, and reciprocity. A hundred years ago, Confucianism was criticized by Weber as a leading cause of Asian backwardness. However, winds change. In postwar decades, while Western economic growth has been relatively stagnant, it is Confucian Asia—first led by Japan in the 1960s, then the Four Tigers in the 1970s, and China since the 1980s—that generated the fastest economic growth in the world and for the longest time. Interestingly, the same Confucianism, trashed by Weber, has been widely viewed as the engine behind such an "Asian economic miracle." Not only do Asians proudly proclaim the validity of such "Asian values," but leading Western scholars also increasingly endorse such a view. For example, Hofstede's fifth dimension, long-term orientation, was originally labeled simply as "Confucian dynamism."[52] In 1993, the World Bank published a major study, entitled *The East Asian Miracle*, with one underlying theme: Confucianism.[53]

While Islamic fundamentalists prefer to drop out of the game of economic development, Asian value proponents claim to have beaten the West in its own game. However, any declaration of winning the game needs to be viewed with caution. By 1997, much of Asia was suddenly engulfed in a financial crisis. Then—guess what—Confucianism has been blamed, by both Asians and non-Asians, for having *caused* such hardship (!). Respect, loyalty, and reciprocity become inertia, nepotism, and cronyism.[54] Ten years after the crisis, now with much recovery throughout Asia and with the emergence of both China and India (although India has very little Confucian influence), the Asian value gurus again are practicing their craft—although with a softer voice this time.

As we can see from this wide-ranging debate, our understanding of the connection between cultural values and economic development is very superficial. To advocate certain cultural values as key to economic development may not be justified. A new generation of students and managers needs to be more sophisticated and guard against such ethnocentric thinking. One speculation is that if there ever will be an African economic takeoff, there will be no shortage of gurus pontificating on how the African cultural values provide such a booster behind Africa's yet-to-happen economic takeoff.

Cultural Change: Convergence versus Divergence

Every culture evolves and changes. A great debate thus erupts on the *direction* of cultural change. In this age of globalization, one side of the debate argues that there is a great deal of convergence, especially toward more "modern" Western values such as individualism and consumerism.[55] As evidence, convergence gurus point out the worldwide interest in Western products such as Levi jeans, iPods, and MTV, especially among the youth.[56]

However, another side suggests that Westernization in consumption does not necessarily mean Westernization in values. In a most extreme example, on the night of September 10, 2001, terrorists enjoyed some American soft drinks, pizzas, and movies and then went on to kill thousands of Americans the next day.[57] More broadly, the popularity of Western brands in the Middle East does not change Muslim values (see Opening Case). In another example, the increasing popularity of Asian foods and games in the West does not necessarily mean that Westerners are converging toward "Asian values" (see In Focus 3.3). In short, cultural divergence may continue to characterize the world.

A middle-of-the-road group makes two points. First, the end of the Cold War, the rise of the Internet, and the ascendance of English all offer evidence of some cultural convergence—at least on the surface and among the youth. For example, relative to the average citizens, younger Chinese, Georgian, Japanese, and Russian managers are becoming more individualist and less collectivist.[58] Second, deep down, cultural divergence may continue to be the norm. Therefore, perhaps a better term is *cross-vergence,* which acknowledges the validity of both sides of the debate.[59] This idea suggests that when marketing products and services to younger customers around the world, a more "global" approach (featuring uniform content and image) may work, whereas when dealing with older, more tradition-bound consumers, local adaptation may be a must (see Chapter 14).

Opportunism versus Individualism/Collectivism[60]

As noted in Chapter 2, opportunism is a major source of uncertainty that adds to transaction costs, and institutions emerge to combat opportunism.[61] However, critics argue that emphasizing opportunism as "human nature" may backfire in practice.[62] This is because if a firm assumes that employees will steal and places surveillance cameras everywhere, then employees who otherwise would not steal may become alienated and decide to do exactly that. For another example, if firm A insists on specifying minute details in an alliance contract to prevent firm B from behaving opportunistically *in the future,* B is likely to regard A as being untrustworthy and

IN FOCUS 3.3 Are We All "Asians" Now?

Around the world, there is now a rising popularity of Asian foods (such as tofu and sushi), martial arts (such as kung fu, tae kwon do, and judo), toys (such as Pokemon), cartoons (such as *Astro Boy*), and belief systems (such as feng shui). Asian business words, such as *guanxi, keiretsu,* and *chaebol,* now routinely appear in English publications without any definition provided in brackets. In the main pedestrian shopping street in Copenhagen, Denmark, there are two competing Chinese restaurants: one called Beijing and another called Shanghai. When watching a sport as quintessentially American as baseball, you can buy a box of sushi to wash down with your beer at the ballpark. School kids in the West can't get enough of toys, cartoons, comics, and video games originating from Japan—ranging from Hello Kitty for girls and Godzilla for boys. To combat declining reader interest in newspapers, especially among young readers, a number of US newspapers, including the *Los Angeles Times,* have introduced *manga*-style comics (Japanese comics with wide-eyed characters) to their Sunday funny pages. The lead theme is *Peach Fuzz,* a playful chronicle of a nine-year-old girl and her pet ferret. The sight of a ferret where Snoopy once reigned may lead some old-timers to exclaim: "Good grief!"

Until recently, the United States had been the only place that had muscle to generate significant "cultural exports," such as movies, music, and food. But winds are changing. Japan now sells approximately $15 billion cultural exports, three times the value of its exports of TV sets. Publishers, toy makers, and game developers increasingly look East to spot new trends. Hasbro, a leading US toymaker, teamed with Shogakukan, a major *manga* publisher, to create *Duel Masters,* a new TV show and trading card game. Sony synched *Astro Boy* characters' lips with both Japanese and English to maximize their appeal.

Some have long argued that consumption of Western products, ranging from Coca-Cola to credit cards, would "Westernize" the world. Obviously, not everyone agrees. Now, if you are not an Asian, ask yourself: If you carried a Samsung mobile (cell) phone, had fried rice and egg rolls for lunch, enjoyed *Peach Fuzz* comics, and practiced tae kwon do for your exercise, are you really becoming more "Asian" in values and outlook?

Sources: Based on (1) T. Bestor, 2000, How sushi went global, *Foreign Policy,* December: 54–63; (2) *Business Week,* 2005, Can *manga* ferret out young readers? November 28: 16; (3) *Business Week,* 2004, Is Japanese style taking over the world? July 26: 56–58; (4) C. Robertson, 2000, The global dispersion of Chinese values, *Management International Review,* 40: 253–268; (5) E. Tsang, 2004, Superstition and decision-making, *Academy of Management Executive,* 18 (4): 92–104.

© SCOTT OLSON/ Stringer/ AFP/ Getty Image

What are the advantages and disadvantages of airport security checkpoints?

opportunistic *now*. This is especially the case if B is from a high-context (or collectivist) society.[63] Thus, attempts to combat opportunism may beget opportunism.

Transaction cost theorists acknowledge that opportunists are a minority in any population. However, theorists contend that because of the difficulty in identifying such a minority of opportunists *before* they cause any damage, it is imperative to place safeguards that, unfortunately, treat everybody as a potential opportunist. For example, thanks to the work of only 19 terrorists, millions of air travelers around the world since September 11, 2001, now have to go through heightened security. Everybody hates it, but nobody argues that it is unnecessary. This debate, therefore, seems deadlocked.

in-group
Individuals and firms regarded as part of "us."

out-group
Individuals and firms not regarded as part of "us."

One cultural dimension, individualism/collectivism, may hold the key to an improved understanding of opportunism. A common stereotype is that players from collectivist societies (such as China) are more collaborative and trustworthy, and those from individualist societies (such as America) are more competitive and opportunistic.[64] However, this is not necessarily the case. Collectivists are more collaborative *only* when dealing with **in-group** members—individuals and firms regarded as part of their own collective. The flip side is that collectivists discriminate more harshly against **out-group** members—individuals and firms not regarded as part of "us." On the other hand, individualists, who believe that every person (firm) is on his or her (its) own, make less distinction between in-group and out-group. Therefore, while individualists may indeed be more opportunistic than collectivists when dealing with in-group members (this fits the stereotype), collectivists may be *more* opportunistic when dealing with out-group members. Thus, on balance, the average Chinese is not inherently more trustworthy than the average American. The Chinese motto regarding out-group members is: "Watch out for strangers. They will screw you!"

This helps explain why the United States, the leading individualist country, is among societies with a higher level of spontaneous trust, whereas there is greater interpersonal and interfirm *distrust* in the large society in China.[65] This also explains why it is so important to establish *guanxi* (relationship) for individuals and firms in China; otherwise, life can be very challenging in a sea of strangers. In another example, one study published in 2004 reported that although Britain and Hong Kong have comparable levels of per capita income, 24% of the Internet users shopped online in Britain, whereas only 7% did so in Hong Kong.[66] Of course, numerous factors may be at play (such as the availability of broadband), but one crucial point is that shopping online means having some trust in the out-group—the anonymous "system" that processes payment. Not surprisingly, collectivists in Hong Kong (most are ethnic Chinese) are reluctant to do so.

This insight is not likely to help improve airport security screening, but it can help managers and firms better deal with one another. Only through repeated social interactions can collectivists assess whether to accept newcomers as in-group members.[67] If foreigners who, by definition, are from an out-group refuse to show any interest in joining the in-group, then it is fair to take advantage of them. For example, don't ever refuse a friendly cup of coffee from a Saudi businessman, which is considered an affront. Most of us do not realize that "Feel free to say no when offered food or drink" reflects the cultural underpinning of individualism, and folks in collectivist societies do not view this as an option (unless one wants to offend the host). This misunderstanding, in part, explains why many cross-culturally naive Western managers and firms often cry out loud for being taken advantage of in collectivist societies. In reality, they are simply being treated as "deserving" out-group members.

MANAGEMENT SAVVY

LEARNING OBJECTIVE 6

draw implications for action

A contribution of the institution-based view is to emphasize the importance of informal institutions—cultures, ethics, and norms—as the bedrock propelling or constraining business around the world. How does this perspective answer our fundamental question: What determines the success and failure of firms around the globe? The institution-based view argues that firm performance is, at least in part, determined by the informal cultures, ethics, and norms governing firm behavior.

For managers around the globe, this emphasis on informal institutions suggests two broad implications. First, enhancing **cultural intelligence**, defined as an individual's ability to understand and adjust to new cultures, is necessary.[68] Nobody can become an expert, the chameleon in Table 3.6, in all cultures. However, a genuine interest in foreign cultures will open your eyes. Acquisition of cultural intelligence passes through three phases: (1) awareness, (2) knowledge, and (3) skills.[69] *Awareness* refers to the recognition of both the pros and cons of your "mental software" and the appreciation of people from other cultures. *Knowledge* refers to ability to identify the symbols, rituals, and taboos in other cultures—also known as cross-cultural literacy. Although you may not share (or may disagree) with their values, you will at least obtain a road map of the informal institutions governing their behavior. Finally, *skills* are based on awareness and knowledge, plus good practice (Table 3.7). Of course, culture is not everything. It is advisable not to read too much into culture, which is one of many variables affecting global business.[70] However, it is imprudent to ignore culture.

cultural intelligence
An individual's ability to understand and adjust to new cultures.

TABLE 3.6 FIVE PROFILES OF CULTURAL INTELLIGENCE

Profiles	Characteristics
The Local	A person who works well with people from similar backgrounds but does not work effectively with people from different cultural backgrounds.
The Analyst	A person who observes and learns from others and plans a strategy for interacting with people from different cultural backgrounds.
The Natural	A person who relies on intuition rather than on a systematic learning style when interacting with people from different cultural backgrounds.
The Mimic	A person who creates a comfort zone for people from different cultural backgrounds by adopting their general posture and communication style. This is not pure imitation, which may be regarded as mocking.
The Chameleon	A person who may be mistaken for a native of the foreign country. He/she may achieve results that natives cannot, due to his/her insider's skills and outsider's perspective. This is very rare.

Sources: Based on (1) P. C. Earley & S. Ang, 2003, *Cultural Intelligence: Individual Interactions across Cultures*, Palo Alto, CA: Stanford University Press; (2) P. C. Earley & E. Mosakowski, 2004, Cultural intelligence, *Harvard Business Review*, October: 139–146; (3) P. C. Earley & E. Mosakowski, 2004, Toward culture intelligence: Turning cultural differences into a workplace advantage, *Academy of Management Executive*, 18 (3): 151–157.

TABLE 3.7 IMPLICATIONS FOR ACTION: SIX RULES OF THUMB WHEN VENTURING OVERSEAS

- Be prepared
- Slow down
- Establish trust
- Understand the importance of language
- Respect cultural differences
- Understand that no culture is inherently superior in all aspects

While skills can be taught, the most effective way is total immersion within a foreign culture. Even for gifted individuals, learning a new language and culture to function well at a managerial level will take at least several months of full-time studies. Most employers do not give their managers that much time to learn before sending them abroad. Thus, most expat managers are inadequately prepared, and the costs for firms, individuals, and families are tremendous (see Chapter 15). This means that you, a student studying this book, are advised to invest in your own career by picking up at least one foreign language, spending one semester (or year) abroad, and reaching out to make some international friends who are taking classes with you (and perhaps sitting next to you). Such an investment during university studies will make you stand out among the crowd and propel your future career to new heights.

Second, managers need to be aware of the prevailing norms and their transitions globally. The norms around the globe in the 2000s are more culturally sensitive and ethically demanding than, say, in the 1970s. This is not to suggest that every local norm needs to be followed. However, failing to understand and adapt to the changing norms by "sticking one's neck out" in an insensitive and unethical way may lead to unsatisfactory or disastrous results (see Opening and Closing Cases). The best managers expect norms to shift over time by constantly deciphering the changes in the informal rules of the game and by taking advantage of new opportunities. How BMW managers proactively shaped the automobile recycling norms serves as a case in point. Firms that fail to realize the passing of old norms and fail to adapt accordingly are likely to fall behind or even go out of business.

CHAPTER SUMMARY

1. Define what culture is and articulate its two main manifestations: language and religion
   - Culture is the collective programming of the mind that distinguishes one group from another.
   - Managers and firms ignorant of foreign languages and religious traditions may end up with embarrassments and, worse, disasters when doing business around the globe.

2. Discuss how cultures systematically differ from each other
   - The context approach differentiates cultures based on the high- versus low-context dimension.
   - The cluster approach groups similar cultures together as clusters and civilizations.

- Hofstede and colleagues have identified five cultural dimensions: (1) power distance, (2) individualism/ collectivism, (3) masculinity/femininity, (4) uncertainty avoidance, and (5) long-term orientation.

3. Understand the importance of ethics and ways to combat corruption
   - When managing ethics overseas, two schools of thought are ethical relativism and ethical imperialism.
   - Three "middle-of-the-road" principles help guide managers to make ethical decisions.
   - The fight against corruption around the world is a long-term, global battle.
4. Identify norms associated with strategic responses when firms deal with ethical challenges
   - When confronting ethical challenges, individual firms have four strategic choices: (1) reactive, (2) defensive, (3) accommodative, and (4) proactive strategies.
5. Participate in three leading debates on cultures, ethics, and norms
   - These are (1) Western values versus Eastern values, (2) cultural convergence versus divergence, and (3) opportunism versus individualism/collectivism.
6. Draw implications for action
   - It is important to enhance cultural intelligence, leading to cross-cultural literacy.
   - It is crucial to understand and adapt to changing norms globally.

KEY TERMS

Civilization 62
Cluster 62
Code of conduct 68
Collectivism 66
Context 61
Corruption 70
Cultural intelligence 77
Culture 57
Ethical imperialism 69
Ethical relativism 69
Ethics 68
Ethnocentrism 56
Femininity 66
Foreign Corrupt Practices Act (FCPA) 70
High-context culture 62
Individualism 66
Informal institutions 56
In-group 76
Lingua franca 58
Long-term orientation 66
Low-context culture 61
Masculinity 66
Norms 72
Out-group 76
Power distance 65
Uncertainty avoidance 66

REVIEW QUESTIONS

1. Where do informal institutions come from, and how do they lead to ethnocentrism?
2. What language is considered the lingua franca of the modern business world? Why?
3. Using Figure 3.3, identify the four major religions in the world and where they are distributed geographically.
4. Name two major components and three minor components of a country's culture.
5. What is the difference between a low-context culture and a high-context culture? How would you classify your home country's culture?
6. Name and describe the three systems for classifying cultures by clusters.

7. Describe the differences among the five dimensions of Hofstede's framework for classifying cultures.
8. Give three examples of how your own personal ethics might be reflected in a firm's code of conduct.
9. What is the difference between ethical relativism and ethical imperialism?
10. Name and describe Thomas Donaldson's three guiding ethical principles.
11. How would you define corruption in a business setting?
12. Explain the difference between a reactive strategy and a defensive strategy when dealing with an ethical challenge.
13. What might be the outcome if several firms within an industry decide to adopt the same accommodative strategy to a shared ethical challenge?
14. Give an example of a proactive strategy to an ethical challenge that demonstrates your understanding of the concept.
15. What was Max Weber's view of the connection between Protestantism and capitalism?
16. How is Western capitalism viewed by two major sets of Eastern values, Islam and Confucianism?
17. Explain the concept of cross-vergence.
18. In general, how do collectivists typically behave toward in-group members and out-group members?
19. Explain the concept of cultural intelligence using at least two examples from Table 3.6.
20. Describe the three phases that lead to cultural intelligence.

CRITICAL DISCUSSION QUESTIONS

1. When you take an airline flight, the passenger sitting next to you tries to strike up a conversation. He or she asks: "What do you do?" You would like to be nice but don't want to disclose too much information about yourself (such as your name). How would you answer this question?
2. Based on Table 3.6, which best describes your cultural intelligence profile: a Local, Analyst, Natural, Mimic, or Chameleon? Why?
3. ON ETHICS: Assume you work for a New Zealand company exporting a container of kiwis to Azerbaijan or Haiti. The customs official informs you that there is a delay in clearing your container through customs, and it may last a month. However, if you are willing to pay an "expediting fee" of US$200, he will try to make it happen in one day. What are you going to do?
4. ON ETHICS: Most developed economies have some illegal immigrants. The United States has the largest number: approximately 10 to 11 million. Without legal US identification (ID) documents, they cannot open bank accounts or buy houses. Many US firms have targeted this population, accepting the ID issued by their native countries and selling them products and services. Some Americans are furious with these business practices. Other Americans suggest that illegal immigrants represent a growth engine in an economy with relatively little growth elsewhere. How would you participate in this debate?

VIDEO CASE

Watch "The Six Components of Ethical Decision Making" by John Abele of Boston Scientific.

1. Mr. Abele stated that the Golden Rule might be one guideline for ethical decision-making. What difficulty might be encountered if its application is tailored to the unique aspects of each culture?
2. Mr. Abele indicated that transparency and public disclosure could be used as a guide to ethical decisions. What did he mean by that and how could its application be affected by the diversity of cultures?
3. Mr. Abele suggested that you consider what a person you trust would do in making an ethical decision. What aspects of culture could impact the application of that guideline?
4. What is the Categorical Imperative and how does the existence of various cultures and norms affect its application?
5. Suppose you were the CEO of a global corporation operating in a variety of countries and cultures. Suppose also that you wished to use Mr. Abele's Six Components of Ethical Decision Making as your guide. How would you make that application? Would it involve only one or certain components or all components and would the applications be affected (or sometimes be changed) due to time and place?

CLOSING CASE

ETHICAL DILEMMA: Citigroup Needs to Clean Up around the Globe

Citigroup is the world's largest financial services company. Its history dates back to 1812. Now, it does business in more than 100 countries. In many countries, Citigroup has been active for more than 100 years. Citigroup's 2005 annual report proudly claimed that it had "the best international footprint of any US financial services company and the best US presence of any international financial services company." Yet, recently, Citigroup found itself engulfed in a number of ethical crises around the globe. Most alarmingly, these new crises erupted *after* it was criticized for its failure to have a "firewall" separating analysts and investment bankers and for its involvement in the Enron bankruptcy in the United States in the early 2000s.

© KIM KYUNG-HOON/Reuters /Landov

In London, on the morning of August 2, 2004, Citigroup's bond trading unit dumped $13.3 billion worth of European government bonds onto the market. Such a huge volume caused immediate chaos in the market and resulted in lower prices. Then, within about a half hour, Citigroup's bond traders bought back a third of the bonds they just sold, raking in a $24 million profit. The traders were jubilant. Their actions were legal, but they broke an unwritten norm of the industry not to stimulate major turbulence of the thin summer trading. When a puzzled rival trader called to ask what was up, the Citigroup crew laughed and hung up. Nobody was laughing now. The profits were not worth the damage to its reputation. Citigroup angered governments in countries such as Belgium and Italy that relied on the international bond markets and offered Citigroup lucrative contracts to handle their deals. Overall, European regulators would no longer tolerate such behavior.

In Japan, a worse disaster struck. In September 2004, regulators ordered Citigroup to shut down its private bank in Japan because of a series of abuses in selling securities at "unfair" prices to clients. Citigroup sales force pushed sales to many Japanese clients without explaining the underlying risk. Regulators charged the bank with fostering "a management environment in which profits are given undue importance by the bank headquarters." This drastic action followed repeated warnings in previous years. While Citigroup was still allowed to run a retail bank and a corporate bank in Japan, the damage to its reputation was significant.

The ramifications were profound. On the first page of the 2004 annual report, Chuck Prince, Citigroup's CEO, apologized to shareholders. Around the world, Prince met with employees and stressed the importance of ethical integrity. Prince, a lawyer by training, had assumed his position to deal with the legal and ethical turbulence in the United States. Now, he had his hands full around the world. In response to the European and Japanese scandals, a new code of conduct was implemented and a Global Compliance unit was established. Every employee would receive ethics training, and a toll-free ethics hotline was aggressively marketed to employees. Prince wrote in his letter to shareholders in the 2004 annual report:

> These failures [in Europe and Japan] do not reflect the kind of company we are or want to be . . . We are already the most profitable and the largest financial institution in the world. We believe that when we add "most respected" to that résumé, there is no limit to what we will accomplish.

Talk is cheap, according to critics. Many critics are suspicious of whether the transformation pushed by Prince will be successful. It is not an accident that Citigroup has become a global industry leader in sales and profits. The competitive instinct permeates the corporate DNA. Job number one for Prince—and indeed for the entire organization—is how to become a more ethical firm without losing its competitive edge. [POSTSCRIPT: Before this book went to press, in November 2007, Prince resigned.]

Case Discussion Questions

1. What are the costs and benefits of breaking industry norms around the world?
2. What strategic response does Citigroup's top management undertake? Is it adequate?
3. Are some of Citigroup's employees "bad apples" or is Citigroup a "bad barrel"?

Sources: I thank Yasuhiro Yamakawa (University of Texas at Dallas) for his assistance. Based on (1) *Business Week*, 2004, Can Chuck Prince clean up Citi? October 4: 32–35; (2) *Business Week*, 2006, For Citi, "no more excuses," April 3: 134; (3) *Citigroup 2004 Annual Report*, (4) *Economist*, 2004, Sayonara, September 25: 88; (5) *Economist*, 2006, A mixed week, April 8: 73; (6) Financial Services Agency, 2004, Administrative actions on Citibank NA Japan branch, http://www.fsa.go.jp.

NOTES

Journal acronyms: **AME** – *Academy of Management Executive;* **AMJ** – *Academy of Management Journal;* **AMR** – *Academy of Management Review;* **APJM** – *Asia Pacific Journal of Management;* **CMR** – *California Management Review;* **HBR** – *Harvard Business Review;* **IJHRM** – *International Journal of Human Resource Management;* **JIBS** – *Journal of International Business Studies;* **JIM** – *Journal of International Management;* **JM** – *Journal of Management;* **JMS** – *Journal of Management Studies;* **JWB** – *Journal of World Business;* **MIR** – *Management International Review;* **OD** – *Organizational Dynamics;* **OSt** – *Organization Studies;* **PB** – *Psychological Bulletin;* **RES** – *Review of Economics and Statistics;* **SMJ** – *Strategic Management Journal.*

[1] J. Salk & M. Brannen, 2000, National culture, networks, and individual influence in a multinational management team, *AMJ*, 43: 191–202; H. Woldu, P. Budhwar, & C. Parkes, 2006, A cross-national comparison of cultural value orientations of Indian, Polish, Russian, and American employees, *IJHRM*, 17: 1076–1094.

[2] G. Hofstede, 1997, *Cultures and Organizations* (p. xii), New York: McGraw-Hill.

[3] S. Michailova, 2002, When common sense becomes uncommon, *JWB*, 37: 180–187.

[4] L. Busenitz, C. Gomez, & J. Spencer, 2000, Country institutional profiles, *AMJ*, 43: 994–1003; M. Hitt, V. Franklin, & H. Zhu, 2006,

Culture, institutions, and international strategy, *JIM*, 12: 222–234; T. Kostova & S. Zaheer, 1999, Organizational legitimacy under conditions of complexity, *AMR*, 24: 64–81; M. Lounsbury, 2007, A tale of two cities, *AMJ*, 50: 289–307; S. Rangan & A. Drummond, 2002, Explaining outcomes in competition among foreign multinationals in a focal host market, *SMJ*, 25: 285–293; D. Xu, Y. Pan, & P. Beamish, 2004, The effect of regulative and normative distances on MNE ownership and expatriate strategies, *MIR*, 44: 285–307; D. Xu & O. Shenkar, 2002, Institutional distance and the multinational enterprise, *AMR*, 27: 608–618.

[5] Hofstede, 1997, *Cultures and Organizations* (p. 5).

[6] K. Au, 1999, Intra-cultural variation, *JIBS*, 30: 799–813; G. Cheung & I. Chow, 1999, Subcultures in Greater China, *APJM*, 16: 369–387.

[7] D. Graddol, 2004, The future of language, *Science*, 303: 1329–1331.

[8] P. Rosenzweig, 2004, Tomorrow's global workforce, in S. Chowdhury (ed.), *Next Generation Business Handbook* (pp. 1007–1027), New York: Wiley.

[9] D. Ricks, 1999, *Blunders in International Business*, 3rd ed., Oxford, U.K.: Blackwell.

[10] Ricks, 1999, *Blunders* (p. 31).

[11] L. James, 1994, *The Rise and Fall of the British Empire*, London: Abacus.

[12] E. Hall & M. Hall, 1987, *Hidden Differences*, Garden City, NY: Doubleday.

[13] S. Ronen & O. Shenkar, 1985, Clustering countries on attitudinal dimension, *AMR*, 10: 435–454.

[14] R. House, P. Hanges, M. Javidan, P. Dorfman, & V. Gupta (eds.), 2004, *Culture, Leadership, and Organizations: The GLOBE Study of 62 Societies*, Thousand Oaks, CA: Sage.

[15] S. Huntington, 1996, *The Clash of Civilizations and the Remaking of World Order* (p. 43), New York: Simon & Schuster.

[16] S. Schwartz, 1994, Cultural dimensions of values, in U. Kim et al. (eds.), *Individualism and Collectivism* (pp. 85–119), Thousand Oaks, CA: Sage; F. Trompenaars, 1993, *Riding the Waves of Culture*, Chicago: Irwin.

[17] K. Sivakumar & C. Nakata, 2001, The stampede toward Hofstede's framework, *JIBS*, 32: 555–574.

[18] World Bank, 2004, *World Development Indicators*, http://www.worldbank.org.

[19] House et al., 2004, *Culture, Leadership, and Organizations*; B. Kirkman, K. Lowe, & C. Gibson, 2006, A quarter century of *Culture's Consequences*, *JIBS*, 37: 285–320; K. Leung, R. Bhagat, N. Buchan, M. Erez, & C. Gibson, 2005, Culture and international business, *JIBS*, 36: 357–378.

[20] D. Dow & A. Karunaratna, 2006, Developing a multidimensional instrument to measure psychic distance stimuli, *JIBS*, 37: 578–602; D. Oyserman, H. Coon, & M. Kemmelmeier, 2002, Rethinking individualism and collectivism, *PB*, 128: 3–72; R. Yeh & J. Lawrence, 1995, Individualism and Confucian dynamism, *JIBS*, 26: 655–669.

[21] K. Brouthers & L. Brouthers, 2001, Explaining the national cultural distance paradox, *JIBS*, 32: 177–189; J. Evans & F. Mavondo, 2002, Psychic distance and organizational performance, *JIBS*, 33: 515–532; J. Hennart & J. Larimo, 1998, The impact of culture on the strategy of MNEs, *JIBS*, 29: 515–538; B. Kogut & H. Singh, 1988, The effect of national culture on the choice of entry mode, *JIBS*, 19: 411–432; J. Lee, T. Roehl, & S. Choe, 2000, What makes management style similar or distinct across borders? *JIBS*, 31: 631–652; J. Li, K. Lam, & G. Qian, 2001, Does culture affect behavior and performance of firms? *JIBS*, 32: 115–131; R. S. Marshall & D. Boush, 2001, Dynamic decision-making, *JIBS*, 32: 873–893; P. Morosini, S. Shane, & H. Singh, 1998, National cultural distance and cross-border acquisition performance, *JIBS*, 29: 137–158; S. O'Grady & H. Lane, 1996, The psychic distance paradox, *JIBS*, 27: 309–333; V. Pothukuchi, F. Damanpour, J. Choi, C. Chen, & S. Park, 2002, National and organizational culture differences and international joint venture performance, *JIBS*, 33: 243–265; J. West & J. Graham, 2004, A linguistic-based measure of cultural distance and its relationship to managerial values, *MIR*, 44: 239–260.

[22] M. K. Erramilli, 1996, Nationality and subsidiary ownership patterns in multinational corporations, *JIBS*, 27: 225–248.

[23] C. Fey & I. Bjorkman, 2001, The effect of HRM practices on MNC subsidiary performance in Russia, *JIBS*, 32: 59–75; J. Parnell & T. Hatem, 1999, Behavioral differences between American and Egyptian managers, *JMS*, 36: 399–418; E. Pellegrini & T. Scandura, 2006, Leader-member exchange (LMX), paternalism, and delegation in the Turkish business context, *JIBS*, 37: 264–279.

[24] S. Kotha, R. Dunbar, & A. Bird, 1995, Strategic action generation, *SMJ*, 16: 195–220.

[25] T. Begley & W. Tian, 2001, The socio-cultural environment for entrepreneurship, *JIBS*, 32: 537–553; A. Thomas & S. Mueller, 2000, A case for comparative entrepreneurship, *JIBS*, 31: 287–301.

[26] Hofstede, 1997, *Cultures and Organizations* (p. 94).

[27] P. Smith, M. Peterson, & Z. Wang, 1996, The manager as mediator of alternative meanings, *JIBS*, 27: 115–137.

[28] R. Griffin & M. Pustay, 2003, *International Business*, 3rd ed. (p. 109), Upper Saddle River, NJ: Prentice Hall.

[29] C. Bartlett & S. Ghoshal, 1989, *Managing across Borders* (p. 41), Boston: Harvard Business School Press.

[30] R. Peterson, C. Dibrell, & T. Pett, 2002, Long- vs. short-term performance perspectives of Western European, Japanese, and U.S. companies, *JWB*, 37: 245–255; L. Thomas & G. Waring, 1999, Competing capitalism, *SMJ*, 20: 729–748.

[31] J. Child, D. Faulkner, & R. Pitkethly, 2000, Foreign direct investment in the U.K., *JMS*, 37: 141–166; K. Laverty, 1996, Economic "short-termism," *AMR*, 21: 825–860.

[32] X. Chen & S. Li, 2005, Cross-national differences in cooperative decision-making in mixed-motive business contexts, *JIBS*, 36: 622–636; R. Friedman, S. Chi, & L. Liu, 2006, An expectancy model of Chinese-American differences in conflict-avoiding, *JIBS*, 37: 76–91; D. Griffith, M. Hu, & J. Ryans, 2000, Process standardization across intra- and inter-cultural relationships, *JIBS*, 31: 303–324; K. Lee, G. Yang, & J. Graham, 2006, Tension and trust in international business negotiations, *JIBS*, 37: 623–641; S. Makino & K. Neupert, 2000, National culture, transaction costs, and the choice between joint venture and wholly owned subsidiary, *JIBS*, 31: 705–713; L. Metcalf, A. Bird, M. Shankarmahesh, Z. Aycan, J. Larimo, & D. Valdelamar, 2006, Cultural tendencies in negotiation, *JWB*, 41: 382–394; W. Newburry & N. Yakova, 2006, Standardization preferences, *JIBS*, 37: 44–60; G. Van der

Vegt, E. Van de Vliert, & X. Huang, 2005, Location-level links between diversity and innovative climate depend on national power distance, *AMJ*, 48: 1171–1182.

[33] P. C. Earley & E. Mosakowski, 2004, Toward culture intelligence (p. 155), *AME*, 18 (3): 151–157.

[34] L. Trevino & K. Nelson, 2004, *Managing Business Ethics*, 3rd ed. (p. 13), New York: Wiley; L. Trevino, G. Weaver, & S. Reynolds, 2006, Behavioral ethics in organizations, *JM*, 32: 951–990.

[35] R. Durand, H. Rao, & P. Monin, 2007, Code of conduct in French cuisine, *SMJ*, 28: 455–472; A. Kolk & R. Tulder, 2004, Ethics in international business, *JWB*, 39: 49–60; I. Maignan & D. Ralston, 2002, Corporate social responsibility in Europe and the US, *JIBS*, 33: 497–514; J. Stevens, H. K. Steensma, D. Harrison, & P. Cochran, 2005, Symbolic or substantive document? *SMJ*, 26: 181–195.

[36] T. Jones, 1995, Instrumental stakeholder theory, *AMR*, 20: 404–437.

[37] C. Fombrun, 2001, Corporate reputations as economic assets, in M. Hitt, R. E. Freeman, & J. Harrison (eds.), *The Blackwell Handbook of Strategic Management* (pp. 289–312), Cambridge, U.K.: Blackwell.

[38] K. Lee, G. Qian, J. Yu, & Y. Ho, 2005, Trading favors for marketing advantage, *JIM*, 13: 1–35; S. Puffer & D. McCarthy, 1995, Finding common ground in Russian and American business ethics, *CMR*, 37: 29–46; K. Parboteeah, J. Cullen, B. Victor, & T. Sakano, 2005, National culture and ethical climates, *MIR*, 45: 459–519; A. Spicer, T. Dunfee, & W. Bailey, 2004, Does national context matter in ethical decision making? *AMJ*, 47: 610–620.

[39] This section draws heavily from T. Donaldson, 1996, Values in tension, *HBR*, September–October: 4–11.

[40] D. Vogel, 1992, The globalization of business ethics, *CMR*, Fall: 30–49.

[41] *Economist*, 2006, How to grease a palm (p. 116), December 23: 115–116.

[42] A. Cuervo-Cazurra, 2006, Who cares about corruption? *JIBS*, 37: 807–822; N. Khatri, E. Tsang, & T. Begley, 2006, Cronyism, *JIBS*, 37: 61–75; S. Lee & K. Oh, 2007, Corruption in Asia, *APJM*, 24: 97–114; P. Rodriguez, K. Uhlenbruck, & L. Eden, 2004, Government corruption and the entry strategies of multinationals, *AMR*, 30: 383–396.

[43] C. Dirienzo, J. Das, K. Cort, & J. Burbridge, 2006, Corruption and the role of information, *JIBS*, 38: 320–332; J. Doh, P. Rodriguez, K. Uhlenbruck, J. Collins, & L. Eden, 2003, Coping with corruption in foreign markets, *AME*, 17: 114–127; C. Robertson & A. Watson, 2004, Corruption and change, *SMJ*, 25: 385–396; P. Rodriguez, D. Siegel, A. Hillman, & L. Eden, 2006, Three lenses on the multinational enterprise, *JIBS*, 37: 733–746; U. Weitzel & S. Berns, 2006, Cross-border takeovers, corruption, and related aspects of governance, *JIBS*, 37: 786–806; J. H. Zhao, S. Kim, & J. Du, 2003, The impact of corruption and transparency on foreign direct investment, *MIR*, 43: 41–62.

[44] S. Globerman & D. Shapiro, 2003, Governance infrastructure and U.S. foreign direct investment, *JIBS*, 34: 19–39; D. Loree & S. Guisinger, 1995, Policy and non-policy determinants of U.S. equity foreign direct investment, *JIBS*, 26: 281–299.

[45] S. Wei, 2000, How taxing is corruption on international investors? *RES*, 82: 1–11.

[46] M. Habib & L. Zurawicki, 2002, Corruption and foreign direct investment (p. 295), *JIBS*, 33: 291–307.

[47] J. Hellman, G. Jones, & D. Kaufmann, 2002, Far from home: Do foreign investors import higher standards of governance in transition economies? (p. 20), Working paper, Washington, DC: World Bank, http://www.worldbank.org.

[48] C. Kwok & S. Tadesse, 2006, The MNC as an agent of change for host-country institutions, *JIBS*, 37: 767–785.

[49] D. Gioia, 2004, Pinto fires, in Trevino & Nelson (eds.), *Managing Business Ethics* (pp. 105–108).

[50] S. Hart, 2005, *Capitalism at the Crossroads*, Philadelphia: Wharton School Publishing.

[51] A. King, M. Lenox, & A. Terlaak, 2005, The strategic use of decentralized institutions, *AMJ*, 48: 1091–1106.

[52] R. Franke, G. Hofstede, & M. Bond, 1991, Cultural roots of economic performance, *SMJ*, 12: 165–173; G. Hofstede & M. Bond, 1988, The Confucian connection, *OD*, 16 (4): 4–21.

[53] World Bank, 1993, *The East Asian Miracle*, Washington, DC: World Bank.

[54] M. W. Peng, 2007, Celebrating 25 years of Asia Pacific management research, *APJM*, 24: 385–394.

[55] M. Heuer, J. Cummings, & W. Hutabarat, 1999, Cultural change among managers in Indonesia? *JIBS*, 30: 599–610.

[56] T. Levitt, 1983, The globalization of markets, *HBR*, May–June: 92–102.

[57] National Commission on Terrorist Attacks on the United States, 2004, *The 9/11 Report* (p. 364), New York: St Martin's.

[58] A. Ardichvili & A. Gasparishvili, 2003, Russian and Georgian entrepreneurs and non-entrepreneurs, *OSt*, 24: 29–46; C. Chen, 1995, New trends in allocation preferences, *AMJ*, 38: 408–428; D. Ralston, C. Egri, S. Stewart, R. Terpstra, & K. Yu, 1999, Doing business in the 21st century with the new generation of Chinese managers, *JIBS*, 30: 415–428.

[59] C. Carr, 2005, Are German, Japanese, and Anglo-Saxon strategic decision styles still divergent in the context of globalization? *JMS*, 42: 1155–1188; D. Ralston, D. Holt, R. Terpstra, & K. Yu, 1997, The impact of national culture and economic ideology on managerial work values, *JIBS*, 28: 177–207.

[60] This section draws heavily on C. Chen, M. W. Peng, & P. Saparito, 2002, Individualism, collectivism, and opportunism: A cultural perspective on transaction cost economics, *JM*, 28: 567–583.

[61] O. Williamson, 1985, *The Economic Institutions of Capitalism*, New York: Free Press.

[62] S. Ghoshal & P. Moran, 1996, Bad for practice, *AMR*, 21: 13–47.

[63] P. Doney, J. Cannon, & M. Mullen, 1998, Understanding the influence of national culture on the development of trust, *AMR*, 23: 601–620.

[64] J. Cullen, K. P. Parboteeah, & M. Hoegl, 2004, Cross-national differences in managers' willingness to justify ethically suspect behaviors, *AMJ*, 47: 411–421.

[65] F. Fukuyama, 1995, *Trust*, New York: Free Press; G. Redding, 1993, *The Spirit of Chinese Capitalism*, New York: Gruyter.

[66] K. Lim, K. Leung, C. Sia, & M. Lee, 2004, Is e-commerce boundaryless? (p. 546), *JIBS*, 35: 545–559.

[67] J. Graham & N. Lam, 2003, The Chinese negotiation, *HBR*, 81 (10): 82–91.

[68] P. C. Earley & E. Mosakowski, 2004, Cultural intelligence, *HBR*, October: 139–146; J. Johnson, T. Lenartowicz, & S. Apud, 2006, Cross-cultural competence in international business, *JIBS*, 37: 525–543.

[69] Hofstede, 1997, *Cultures and Organizations* (p. 230).

[70] O. Shenkar, 2001, Cultural distance revisited, *JIBS*, 32: 519–535; K. Singh, 2007, The limited relevance of culture to strategy, *APJM*, 24: 421–428; L. Tihanyi, D. Griffith, & C. Russell, 2005, The effect of cultural distance on entry mode choice, international diversification, and MNE performance, *JIBS*, 36: 270–283.

CHAPTER 4

Leveraging Resources and Capabilities

OPENING CASE

The Rise of Hainan Airlines

Because of external shocks such as 9/11, SARS, and the rising price of oil, airlines around the world have had a hard time, and an increasing number of them, such as Delta, Swissair, and United, have flown into bankruptcy. In China, rapid growth has made the country the second largest aviation market behind the United States. Disappointingly, the growth has largely been profitless, and collectively, the Chinese airline industry barely breaks even. Yet, the young Hainan Airlines, which started in 1993, has defied gravity. From obscure roots, Hainan has not only risen to become the fourth largest airline in China but also the most profitable one.

In China, until the mid 1980s, there had been only one service provider for the entire country, Civil Aviation Administration of China (CAAC). As a state-owned monopoly, CAAC was known for its arrogance, high price, sloppy service, and frequent cancellations, earning its nickname as "Chinese Airlines Always Cancels." In the 1980s, CAAC reformed itself to become a regulator. As a result, CAAC formed three large airlines known as the Big Three: Air China headquartered in Beijing, China Eastern based in Shanghai, and China Southern centered on Guangzhou. Through deregulation, CAAC also allowed for the entry of approximately two dozen new airlines, including Hainan.

In the crowd of new entrants and the Big Three (still owned and controlled by CAAC), 15 years ago few people would have predicted that Hainan, headquartered in Hainan island, the remote, southernmost part of China, would emerge as a winner in this increasingly competitive industry. Hainan's accomplishments are impressive: Every year since 2000, it not only has the best profitability and best on-time departure record in the industry but also wins the coveted Best Airline Award voted by passengers every year.

What are Hainan Airlines' secrets? Plenty. First, keeping costs to a bare minimum is its hallmark. Like its role model, Southwest Airlines in the United States, Hainan specializes in point-to-point flights primarily using a single type of aircraft, Boeing 737. Flying point-to-point allows Hainan to turn around flights much faster than hub-and-spoke operators such as the Big Three. The worldwide average ratio of employees per aircraft is about 170:1. The ratio for China's Big Three is 280:1. In contrast, Hainan's ratio is only 80:1.

Second, as an independent airline, Hainan is able to build a uniform fleet by focusing on the Boeing 737 (for larger markets) and the Dornier 328 regional jet (for smaller markets), thus enjoying great economies of scale. In contrast, the Big Three have to accept aircraft centrally purchased by CAAC often on political grounds. When China and the United States have some diplomatic arguments, CAAC often buys jets from Airbus, which the Big Three are then forced to absorb. Historically strong with Boeing jets, the Big Three thus have a mixture of Boeing and Airbus, significantly jacking up maintenance, components, and training costs.

Third, headquartered in a remote region, Hainan had not been on the radar screen of the Big Three until recently. Hainan deliberately avoids head-on competition. Instead of flying into the Shanghai Hongqiao airport (a popular domestic hub only 30 minutes away from city center), Hainan flies into the newer, less popular Shanghai Pudong airport (mostly for international flights, 90 minutes away from city center). Hainan has also gone international by identifying unfilled gaps instead of going after popular but crowded markets (such as the US-China routes). In Asia, it flies to Bangkok, Kuala Lumpur, Osaka, Seoul, and Singapore. It also flies to Budapest, becoming the first Chinese airline to offer nonstop service to Central Europe.

LEARNING OBJECTIVES

After studying this chapter, you should be able to

1. explain what firm resources and capabilities are
2. undertake a basic SWOT analysis of the value chain to decide whether to keep an activity in-house or outsource it
3. analyze the value, rarity, imitability, and organizational aspects of resources and capabilities
4. participate in two leading debates on cross-border capabilities and offshoring
5. draw implications for action

Fourth, not having any historical baggage associated with CAAC, Hainan from the beginning has emphasized service quality. Passengers can participate in a fun-filled auction for a return ticket, with a flight attendant serving as the auctioneer-cum-game-show-host. Since the auction starts at a tantalizingly low price of 10 yuan ($1.25), even the winning bid, which is announced with much fanfare on board, is similar to winning a lottery. For many passengers, a flight on Hainan becomes a chance to relax, unwind, and perhaps win a cheap ticket. In addition, there are 25 full-time quality inspectors, who do nothing other than appear as regular passengers to fly around and "crack the whip." Every year, crews rated at the bottom 10% of their peers are automatically fired, quite a (ruthless) change for this industry renowned for its "iron rice bowls" (job security). Since 1999, Hainan has become the first Chinese airline to be ISO 9000 certified for excellent service quality.

Last but not least, Hainan has attracted a strategic investor—George Soros, a renowned global financier. In 1995, Soros, through American Aviation, which is a subsidiary of his Quantum Fund (a leading hedge fund), invested $25 million in Hainan's shares (15% equity) and became its largest shareholder. Instead of quickly selling for profits, Soros kept his Hainan shares for ten years, with enviable returns worth $60 million by 2005. Of thousands of firms in China, Hainan is the only lucky one to have been picked by Soros. In October 2005, Soros visited Hainan for the first time, bringing with him another $25 million investment. On the day of his arrival, Hainan's shares jumped 9% on the Shanghai Stock Exchange. Although Soros sent two representatives to sit on Hainan's board, he has essentially left the management alone. Emboldened by Soros's vote of confidence, Hainan executives have announced that their goal is to build a world-class airline by blending Chinese culture and Western management.

Sources: I thank Sunny Li Sun (University of Texas at Dallas) for his assistance. Based on (1) *Economist*, 2006, On a wing and a prayer, February 25: 66–67; (2) *Expression* (Hainan in-flight magazine), 2005, Soros raises stake in Hainan Airlines, December: 35–42; (3) D. Li, J. Leong, & M.-J. Chen, 2003, Hainan Airlines: En route to direct competition, Case study, University of Virginia; (4) S. L. Sun & S. R. Cao, 2005, *Zhang Da de Xie Zi [Shoes That Fit]*, Beijing: Chinese Social Sciences Press; (5) http://www.hnair.com.

Why are Hainan Airlines and its role model, Southwest Airlines, able to outcompete rivals in a difficult industry? Because airline service is hard to differentiate, price competition is the norm, thus devastating profits for the entire industry. Then, how can a few high flyers soar in such an unattractive industry? The answer is that there must be certain resources and capabilities specific to firms such as Hainan Airlines that are not shared by competitors. This insight has been developed into a **resource-based view**, which has emerged as one of the two core perspectives on global business.[1]

resource-based view
A leading perspective in global business that posits that firm performance is fundamentally driven by differences in firm-specific resources and capabilities.

One leading tool in global business is **SWOT analysis**, delineating one firm's strengths (S), weaknesses (W), opportunities (O), and threats (T). In global business, the institution-based view deals with the *external* O and T, enabled and constrained by formal and informal rules of the game (see Chapters 2 and 3). The resource-based view builds on the SWOT analysis[2] and concentrates on the *internal* S and W to identify and leverage sustainable competitive advantage.[3] In this chapter, we first define resources and capabilities and then discuss the value chain analysis, concentrating on the decision to keep an activity in-house or outsource it. We then focus on value (V), rarity (R), imitability (I), and organization (O) through a VRIO framework. Debates and extensions follow.

SWOT analysis
An analytical tool for delineating one firm's strengths (S), weaknesses (W), opportunities (O), and threats (T).

UNDERSTANDING RESOURCES AND CAPABILITIES

LEARNING OBJECTIVE 1

explain what firm resources and capabilities are

A basic proposition of the resource-based view is that a firm consists of a bundle of productive resources and capabilities.[4] **Resources** are defined as "the tangible and intangible assets a firm uses to choose and implement its strategies."[5] There is some debate regarding the definition of capabilities. Some argue that capabilities are a firm's capacity to dynamically deploy resources. They suggest a crucial distinction between resources and capabilities and advocate a "dynamic capabilities" view.[6]

resources
The tangible and intangible assets a firm uses to choose and implement its strategies.

Scholars may debate the fine distinctions between resources and capabilities, but these distinctions are likely to "become badly blurred" in practice.[7] For example, is Hainan Airlines' low cost structure a resource or capability? How about its ability to quickly turn around aircraft? Its ability to attract George Soros as a strategic investor? For current and would-be managers, the key is to understand how these attributes help improve firm performance, as opposed to figuring out whether they should be defined as resources or capabilities. Therefore, in this book, we will use the terms "resources" and "capabilities" *interchangeably* and often in *parallel*. In other words, **capabilities** are defined here the same way as resources.

capability
The tangible and intangible assets a firm uses to choose and implement its strategies.

All firms, including the smallest ones, possess a variety of resources and capabilities. How do we meaningfully classify such diversity? A useful way is to separate them into two categories: tangible and intangible ones (Table 4.1). **Tangible resources and capabilities** are assets that are observable and more easily quantified. They can be broadly organized in four categories:

tangible resources and capabilities
Assets that are observable and easily quantified.

- **Financial resources and capabilities:** the depth of a firm's financial pockets. Examples include abilities to generate internal funds and raise external capital, such as Hainan's ability to tap into Soros's pool of funds. Thus far, no other Chinese airline has been able to do that.
- **Physical resources and capabilities:** plants, offices, and equipment, their geographic locations, and access to raw materials and distribution channels. For example, although many people attribute the success of Amazon to its online savvy (which makes sense), a crucial reason Amazon has emerged as the largest bookseller is because it has built some of the largest physical, *brick-and-mortar* book warehouses in key locations throughout the United States.
- **Technological resources and capabilities:** skills and assets that generate leading-edge products and services supported by patents, trademarks, copyrights, and trade secrets.[8] For instance, over 60% of Canon's products on the market today, including popular digital cameras and digital copiers, have been introduced since 2005.
- **Organizational resources and capabilities:** a firm's planning, command, and control systems and structures. In general, younger firms tend to rely more on the visions of managers (often founders), whereas more established firms usually have more formalized systems and structures. In the early days of Hainan Airlines (founded in 1993), executives often followed hunches with new initiatives unsubstantiated by formal analysis. However, those days are long gone. A more elaborate set of formal evaluation criteria have now been developed.

Intangible resources and capabilities, by definition, are harder to observe and more difficult (or sometimes impossible) to quantify (see Table 4.1). Yet, it is widely acknowledged that they must be "there" because no firm is likely to generate competitive advantage by relying on tangible resources and capabilities alone.[9] Examples of intangible assets include:

intangible resources and capabilities
Assets that are hard to observe and difficult (or sometimes impossible) to quantify.

- **Human resources and capabilities:** the knowledge, trust, and talents embedded within a firm that are not captured by its formal, tangible systems and structures.[10] For instance, Hainan Airlines' top management is well known for

TABLE 4.1 EXAMPLES OF RESOURCES AND CAPABILITIES

Tangible resources and capabilities	Examples
Financial	• Ability to generate internal funds • Ability to raise external capital
Physical	• Location of plants, offices, and equipment • Access to raw materials and distribution channels
Technological	• Possession of patents, trademarks, copyrights, and trade secrets
Organizational	• Formal planning, command, and control systems • Integrated management information systems
Intangible resources and capabilities	**Examples**
Human	• Managerial talents • Organizational culture
Innovation	• Research and development capabilities • Capacities for organizational innovation and change
Reputational	• Perceptions of product quality, durability, and reliability among customers • Reputation as a good employer • Reputation as a socially responsible corporate citizen

Sources: Adapted from (1) J. Barney, 1991, Firm resources and sustained competitive advantage, *Journal of Management*, 17: 101; (2) R. Hall, 1992, The strategic analysis of intangible resources, *Strategic Management Journal*, 13: 135–144.

their (relative) youth, competitive orientation, and Western training, which are head and shoulders above that at competing Chinese airlines.

- **Innovation resources and capabilities:** a firm's assets and skills to (1) research and develop new products and services and (2) innovate and change ways of organizing.[11] Some firms are renowned for innovations. For instance, Sony often pioneers new *classes* of products, such as the Walkman, the Discman, and the Aibo (e-pet). Sony's archrival, Samsung Electronics, has recently emerged as a new powerhouse for cool designs and great gadgets.
- **Reputational resources and capabilities:** a firm's abilities to develop and leverage its reputation as a solid provider of goods/services, an attractive employer, and/or a socially responsible corporate citizen. Reputation can be regarded as an outcome of a competitive process in which firms signal their attributes to constituents.[12] For example, L'Oreal's acquisition of The Body Shop was driven in part by an attempt to acquire some reputational resources (In Focus 4.1). While firms do not become reputable overnight, it makes sense to leverage reputation after acquiring it.[13] That is why Toyota, Honda, and Nissan launched three luxury brands—Lexus, Acura, and Infiniti, respectively. Conversely, ambitious Chinese firms such as Haier and TCL are handicapped by their lack of reputation outside China.

It is important to note that all resources and capabilities discussed here are merely examples and that they do not represent an exhaustive list. As firms forge ahead, discovery and leveraging of new resources and capabilities are likely.

IN FOCUS 4.1 ETHICAL DILEMMA: L'Oreal Acquires The Body Shop

L'Oreal of Paris is the global leader in cosmetics, with strong capabilities in virtually all areas of this industry, except ethics. Among social activists, L'Oreal is often labeled the "evil empire," insisting on animal testing and other "unethical" practices. On the other hand, UK-based The Body Shop had been the poster child for corporate social responsibility toward the environment, human rights, and fair trade. It built its reputation selling eco-friendly products made of natural ingredients and standing against animal testing. In fact, The Body Shop founder Anita Roddick had harshly criticized L'Oreal's unethical practices before the acquisition. Therefore, many people were surprised when in 2006, L'Oreal announced that it would acquire The Body Shop for $1.15 billion, representing a 34% premium. Roddick personally pocketed approximately $210 million. Shaken to the core were some ideologues, who believed that The Body Shop, a $732 million, publicly traded corporation, existed primarily to validate their anticorporate beliefs. They consequently labeled The Body Shop and Roddick "unethical." In defense, Roddick argued, "I have done what any founder ought to do. I have done all I can to protect the future of thousands of employees and community trade suppliers . . . I do not believe that L'Oreal will compromise the ethics of The Body Shop. That is after all what they are paying for and they are too intelligent to mess with our DNA." The business world largely applauded this deal. L'Oreal was in desperate need of diversification, and acquiring some reputational resources from The Body Shop as an ethical and socially responsible corporate citizen could prove to be the right move. (More recently, before the book went to press, Roddick passed away in 2007.)

Sources: Based on (1) *Brand Week*, 2006, L'Oreal goes green with Body Shop acquisition, http://www.brandweek.com; (2) *Economist*, 2006, The body beautiful, March 25: 68; (3) S. Pitman, 2006, L'Oreal Body Shop acquisition meets with mixed reaction, http://www.cosmeticsdesign.com; (4) S. Silvers, 2006, Body Shop acquisition polarizes corporate reformists, http://www.stevensilvers.com.

ANALYZING THE VALUE CHAIN: IN-HOUSE VERSUS OUTSOURCE

LEARNING OBJECTIVE 2

undertake a basic SWOT analysis of the value chain to decide whether to keep an activity in-house or outsource it

If a firm is a bundle of resources and capabilities, how do they come together to add value? A value chain analysis allows us to answer this question. Shown in Figure 4.1 panel A, most goods and services are produced through a chain of vertical activities (from upstream to downstream) that add value—in short, a **value chain**. The value chain typically consists of two areas: primary activities and support activities.[14]

value chain
A chain of vertical activities used in the production of goods and services that add value.

Each activity requires a number of resources and capabilities. Value chain analysis forces managers to think about firm resources and capabilities at a very micro, activity-based level.[15] Given that no firm is likely to have enough resources and capabilities to be good at all primary and support activities, the key is to examine whether the firm has resources and capabilities to perform a *particular* activity in a manner superior to competitors—a process known as **benchmarking** in SWOT analysis.

benchmarking
An examination as to whether a firm has resources and capabilities to perform a particular activity in a manner superior to competitors.

If managers find that their firm's particular activity is unsatisfactory, a two-stage decision model shown in Figure 4.2 can remedy the situation. In the first stage, managers ask: "Do we really need to perform this activity in-house?" Figure 4.3 introduces a framework to take a hard look at this question, whose answer boils down to (1) whether an activity is industry-specific or common across industries and (2) whether this activity is proprietary (firm-specific) or not. The answer is no when the activity is found in cell 2 of Figure 4.3 with a great deal of commonality across industries and little need for keeping it proprietary—known in the recent jargon as a high degree of **commoditization**. The answer may also be no if the activity is in cell 1 of Figure 4.3, which is industry-specific but also with a high level of commoditization. Then the firm may want to outsource this activity, sell the unit involved, or lease the unit's services to other firms (see Figure 4.2). This is because operating multiple stages of activities in the value chain may be cumbersome.

commoditization
A process of market competition through which unique products that command high prices and high margins gradually lose their ability to do—these products thus become "commodities."

Think about steel, definitely a crucial component for automobiles. But the question for automakers is: Do we need to make the steel ourselves? The requirements for steel are common across end-user industries; that is, the steel for automakers is essentially the same for construction, defense, and other steel-consuming end users (ignoring minor technical differences for the sake of our discussion). For automakers, while it

FIGURE 4.1 THE VALUE CHAIN

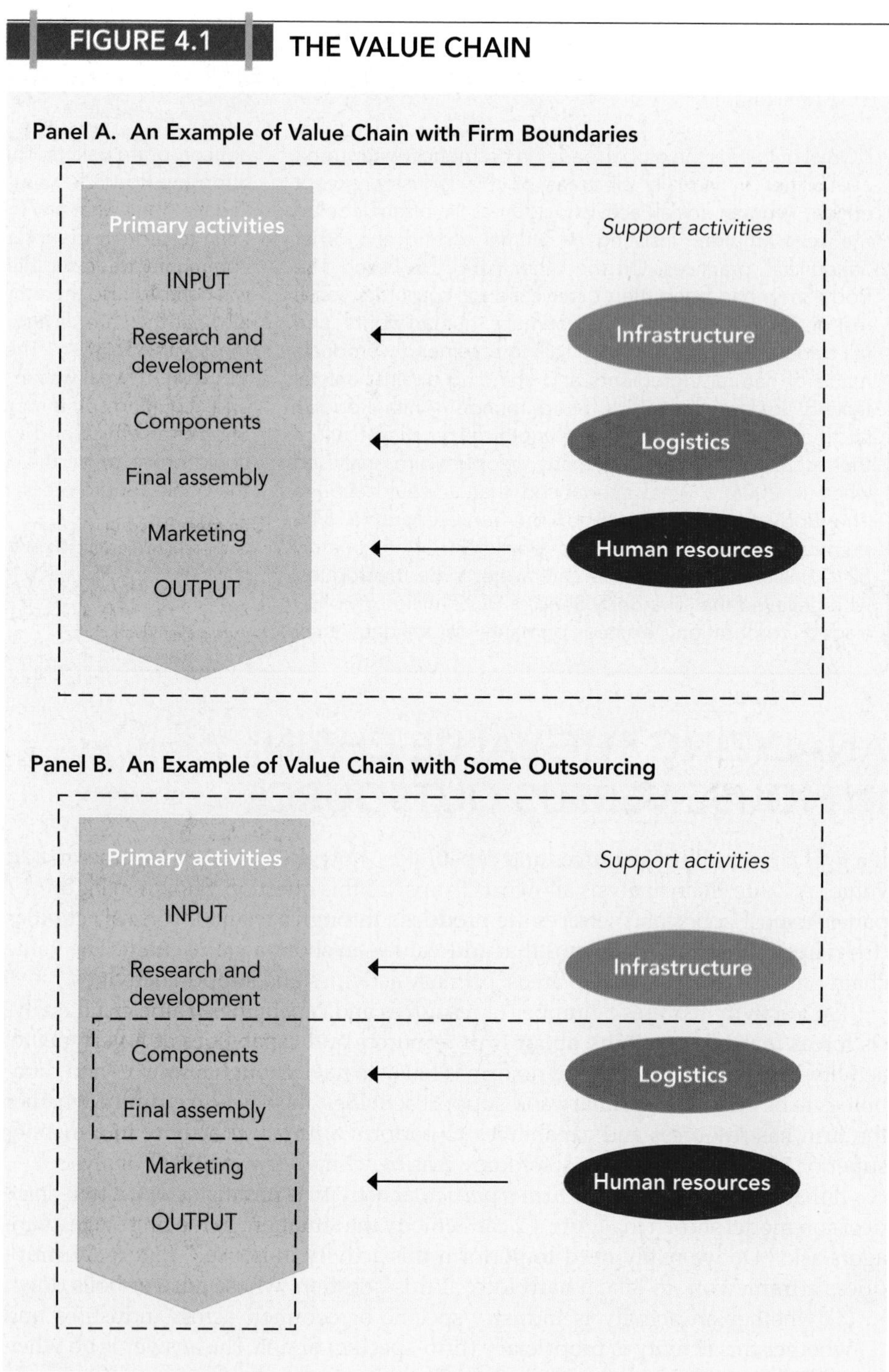

Note: Dashed lines represent firm boundaries.

is imperative to keep the automaking activity (especially engine and final assembly) proprietary (cell 3 of Figure 4.3), there is no need to keep steelmaking in-house. Therefore, although many automakers such as Ford and GM historically were involved in steelmaking, none of them does it now. In other words, steelmaking is outsourced and steel commoditized.

outsourcing
Turning over an organizational activity to an outside supplier that will perform it on behalf of the focal firm.

Outsourcing is defined as turning over an organizational activity to an outside supplier that will perform it on behalf of the focal firm.[16] For example, many consumer products companies (such as Nike), which possess strong capabilities in upstream activities (such as design) and downstream activities (such as marketing),

FIGURE 4.2 A TWO-STAGE DECISION MODEL IN VALUE CHAIN ANALYSIS

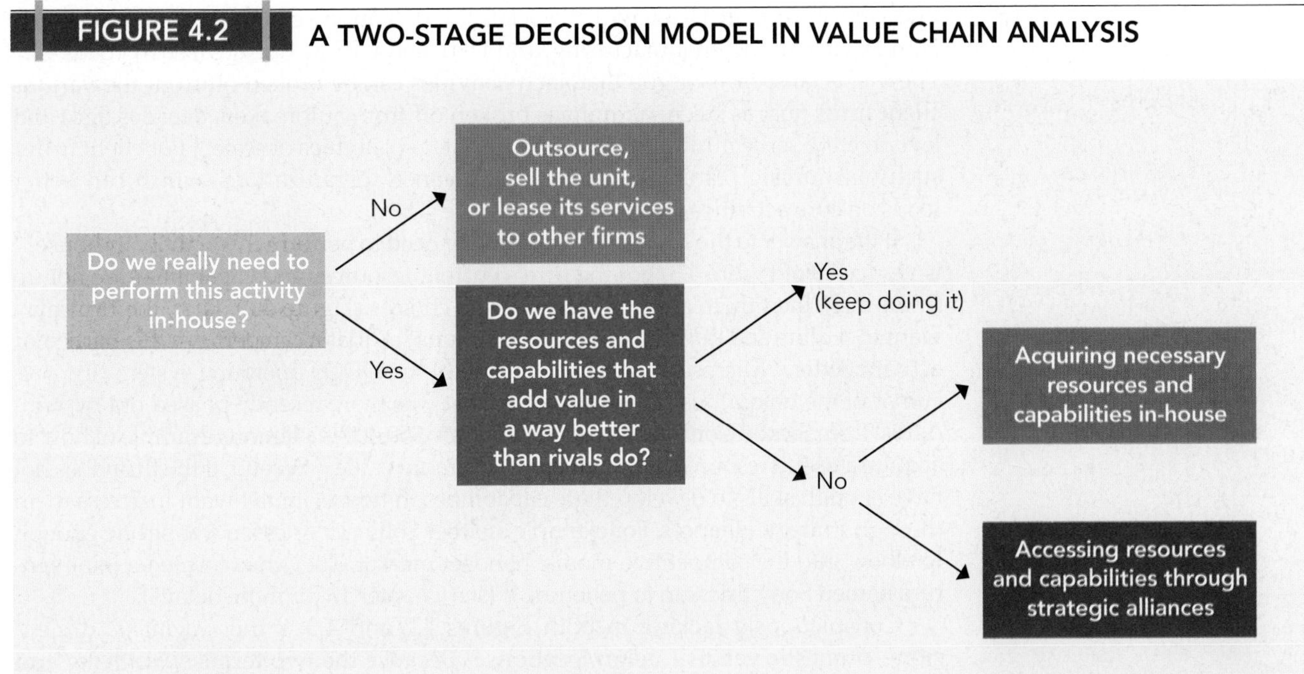

FIGURE 4.3 IN-HOUSE VERSUS OUTSOURCE

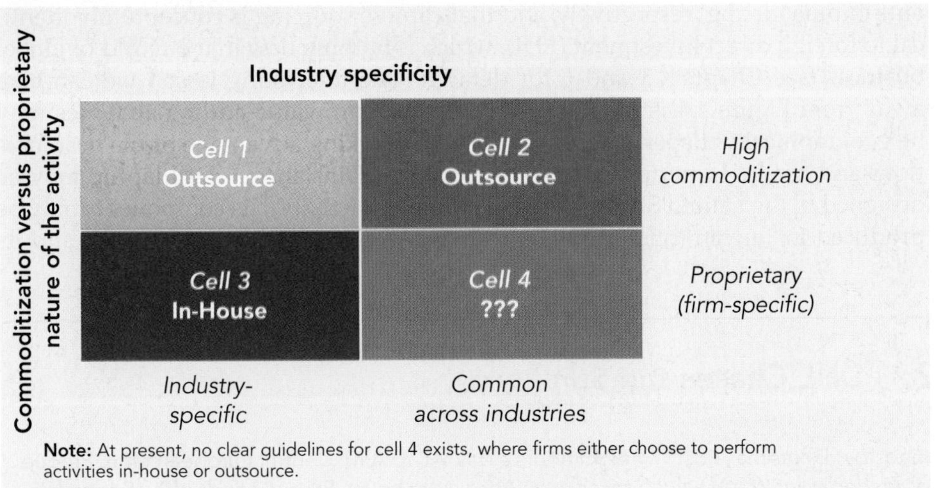

Note: At present, no clear guidelines for cell 4 exists, where firms either choose to perform activities in-house or outsource.

have outsourced manufacturing to suppliers in low-cost countries. A total of 80% of the value of Boeing's new 787 Dreamliner is provided by outside suppliers. This compares with 51% for existing Boeing aircraft.[17] Recently, not only is manufacturing often outsourced, a number of service activities, such as information technology (IT), human resources (HR), and logistics, are also outsourced. The driving force is that many firms, which used to view certain activities as a very special part of their industries (such as airline reservations and bank call centers), now believe that these activities have relatively generic attributes that can be shared across industries. Of course, this changing mentality is fueled by the rise of service providers, such as

EDS and Infosys in IT, Hewitt Associates and Manpower in HR, Flextronics and Hon Hai in contract manufacturing, and DHL and UPS in logistics (see In Focus 4.2). These specialist firms argue that such activities can be broken off from the various client firms (just as steelmaking was broken off from automakers decades ago) and leveraged to serve multiple clients with greater economies of scale.[18] For client firms, such outsourcing results in "leaner and meaner" organizations, which can better focus on core activities (see panel B of Figure 4.1).

If the answer to the question "Do we really need to perform this activity in-house?" is yes (cell 3 of Figure 4.3) but the firm's current resources and capabilities are not up to the task, then there are two second-stage choices (Figure 4.2). First, the firm may want to acquire and develop capabilities in-house so that it can perform this particular activity better.[19] Microsoft's 1980 acquisition of the QDOS operating system (the precursor of the ubiquitous MS-DOS system that was more recently phased out by Windows) from Seattle Computer Products for only $50,000 is a famous example of how to acquire a useful resource upon which to add more value.[20] Second, if the firm does not have enough skills to develop these capabilities in-house, it may want to access them through strategic alliances. For example, neither Sony nor Ericsson was strong enough to elbow into the competitive mobile handset market. They thus formed a joint venture named Sony Ericsson to penetrate it (see Chapter 12 for more details).

Conspicuously lacking in both Figures 4.2 and 4.3 is the *geographic* dimension—domestic versus foreign locations.[21] Because the two terms *outsourcing* and *offshoring* have emerged rather recently, there is a great deal of confusion, especially among some journalists, who often casually equate them. So to minimize confusion, we go from two terms to four in Figure 4.4 based on locations and modes (in-house versus outsource): (1) **offshoring** (international/foreign outsourcing), (2) **inshoring** (domestic outsourcing), (3) **captive sourcing** (setting up subsidiaries abroad—the work done is in-house but the location is foreign), and (4) domestic in-house activity. Despite this set of new labels, we need to clearly be aware that offshoring and inshoring are simply international and domestic variants of outsourcing, respectively, and that captive sourcing is conceptually identical to foreign direct investment (FDI), which is nothing new in the world of global business (see Chapters 1 and 6 for details). One interesting lesson we can take away from Figure 4.4 is that even for a single firm, value-adding activities may be geographically dispersed around the world, taking advantage of the best locations and modes to perform certain activities. For instance, a Dell laptop may be designed in the United States (domestic in-house activity), its components may be produced in Taiwan (offshoring) as well as the United States (inshoring), and its

offshoring
Outsourcing to an international or foreign firm.

inshoring
Outsourcing to a domestic firm.

captive sourcing
Setting up subsidiaries abroad—the work done is in-house but the location is foreign. Conceptually, this is also known as foreign direct investment (FDI).

IN FOCUS 4.2 DHL Chases the Sun

DHL, which has been 100% owned by Deutsche Post World Net since 2002, is the global leader in international express and contract logistics. Its network links more than 220 countries and territories, with approximately 285,000 employees delivering to 120,000 destinations every day. How many packages does it deliver a year? An astounding one *billion*. Key to managing this widest possible scope of global coverage is DHL's capability to track shipments at all times in all locations during transit. DHL has built three centers that house such capabilities in strategic locations: Scottsdale, Arizona; Cyberjaya, Malaysia; and most recently, Prague, the Czech Republic. "Chasing the sun," Cyberjaya manages the network for eight hours a day. At 10 A.M. Central European time, Prague takes over. After eight hours, Prague hands off to Scottsdale. "This is not a call center," proclaimed Prague's managing director. "What we do is high-end IT." Prague's combination of affordability (average IT engineers earn $23,000) and quality of its highly skilled IT workers convinced DHL in 2003 to set up the third crucial leg of its global "tripod" in Prague. In this business where reliability is key, DHL no doubt believes that Prague is one of the most optimal locations on earth to chase the sun.

© UWE GERIG/dpa /Landov

Sources: Based on (1) *Business Week*, 2005, Sitting pretty in Prague: DHL's tech triumph, December 12: 56; (2) http://www.dhl.com; (3) http://www.dpwn.com.

FIGURE 4.4 LOCATION, LOCATION, LOCATION

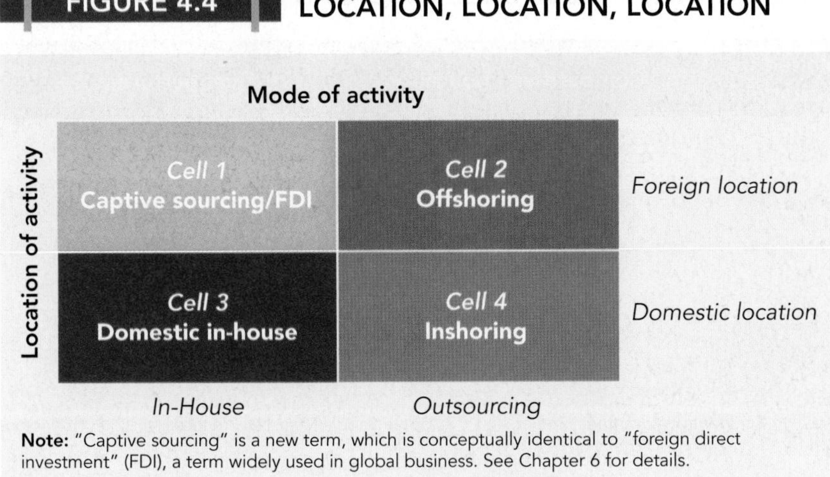

Note: "Captive sourcing" is a new term, which is conceptually identical to "foreign direct investment" (FDI), a term widely used in global business. See Chapter 6 for details.

final assembly may be in China (captive sourcing/FDI). When customers call for help, the call center may be in India, Ireland, Jamaica, or the Philippines staffed by an outside service provider—Dell may have outsourced the service activities through offshoring.

Overall, a value chain analysis engages managers to ascertain a firm's strengths and weaknesses on an activity-by-activity basis, *relative to rivals*, in a SWOT analysis. The recent proliferation of new labels is intimidating, causing some gurus to claim that "twenty-first century offshoring really is different."[22] In reality, under the skin of the new vocabulary, we still see the time-honored SWOT analysis at work. The next section introduces a framework on how to do this.

ANALYZING RESOURCES AND CAPABILITIES WITH A VRIO FRAMEWORK[23]

LEARNING OBJECTIVE 3

analyze the value, rarity, imitability, and organizational aspects of resources and capabilities

The resource-based view focuses on the value (V), rarity (R), imitability (I), and organizational (O) aspects of resources and capabilities, leading to a **VRIO framework**. Summarized in Table 4.2, addressing these four important questions has a number of ramifications for competitive advantage.

VRIO framework

The resource-based framework that focuses on the value (V), rarity (R), imitability (I), and organizational (O) aspects of resources and capabilities.

The Question of Value

Do firm resources and capabilities add value? The value chain analysis suggests that this is the most fundamental question.[24] Only value-adding resources can possibly lead to competitive advantage, whereas nonvalue-adding capabilities may lead to competitive *disadvantage*. With changes in the competitive landscape, previously value-adding resources and capabilities may become obsolete. The evolution of IBM is a case in point. IBM historically excelled in making hardware, including tabulating machines in the 1930s, mainframes in the 1960s, and personal computers (PCs) in the 1980s. However, as competition for hardware heats up, IBM's core capabilities in hardware not only add little value but also increasingly become core rigidities that stand in the way of the firm to move into new areas.[25] Since the 1990s, under two new CEOs, IBM has been transformed to focus on more lucrative software and services, where it has developed new value-adding capabilities, aiming to become an on-demand computing *service* provider for corporations. As part of this new strategy, IBM sold its PC division to China's Lenovo in 2004.

TABLE 4.2 THE VRIO FRAMEWORK: IS A RESOURCE OR CAPABILITY . . .

Valuable?	Rare?	Costly to imitate?	Exploited by organization?	Competitive implications	Firm performance
No	—	—	No	Competitive disadvantage	Below average
Yes	No	—	Yes	Competitive parity	Average
Yes	Yes	No	Yes	Temporary competitive advantage	Above average
Yes	Yes	Yes	Yes	Sustained competitive advantage	Persistently above average

Sources: Adapted from (1) J. Barney, 2002, *Gaining and Sustaining Competitive Advantage*, 2nd ed. (p. 173), Upper Saddle River, NJ: Prentice Hall; (2) R. Hoskisson, M. Hitt, & R. D. Ireland, 2004, *Competing for Advantage* (p. 118), Cincinnati, OH: Thomson South-Western

The relationship between valuable resources and capabilities and firm performance is straightforward. Instead of becoming strengths, nonvalue-adding resources and capabilities, such as IBM's historical expertise in hardware, may become weaknesses. If firms are unable to get rid of nonvalue-adding resources and capabilities, they are likely to suffer below-average performance.[26] In the worst case, they may become extinct, a fate IBM narrowly skirted during the early 1990s. Similarly, Nintendo exited its earlier lines of business (toys and playing cards) and developed new value-adding capabilities first in arcade games and more recently in video games. "Continuous strategic renewal," in the words of Gary Hamel, a strategy guru, "is the only insurance against irrelevance."[27]

The Question of Rarity

Simply possessing valuable resources and capabilities may not be enough. The next question asks: How rare are valuable resources and capabilities? At best, valuable but common resources and capabilities will lead to competitive parity but not to an advantage. Consider the identical aircraft made by Boeing and Airbus used by Southwest, Ryanair, Hainan, and most other airlines. They are certainly valuable; yet, it is difficult to derive competitive advantage from these aircraft alone. Airlines have to compete on how to use these same aircraft differently. The same is true for bar codes, enterprise resource planning (ERP) software, and radio frequency identification (RFID) tags. Their developers are too willing to sell them everywhere, thus undermining their novelty (rarity) value.

Only valuable and rare resources and capabilities have the potential to provide some temporary competitive advantage.[28] Western IT firms increasingly rely on intellectual property (IP) to provide streams of revenue by licensing their patents to others. For instance, IBM now earns $1 billion a year from its IP portfolio, and Microsoft files approximately 3,000 patents a year—up from a mere five patents in 1990.[29] However, there is always a danger that their licensees (or their licensees' employees) may use the technology for purposes other than those originally intended. Although blatant patent infringement is illegal, smart reverse engineering, by inventing "around" a given patent, is legal. In contrast, Indian IT companies prefer to hold on to their innovations rather than patenting and licensing them. For example, Wipro calls these inventions "IP blocks," which are bits of software or processes taken from work for one client that it can draw on to serve multiple clients better. A total of around 10,000 Wipro engineers are involved with such high-end design and development work for numerous clients, but Wipro only has fewer than 10 patents.[30] By developing and keeping the technology (mostly) in-house, Wipro can use such expertise for many contracts, lowering the cost for everyone while not worrying (too much) about its leakage.

Overall, the question of rarity is a reminder of the cliché: If everyone has it, you can't make money from it. For example, the quality of the American Big Three automakers is now comparable with the best Asian and European rivals. However, even in their home country, Big Three's quality improvements have not translated into stronger sales. Instead, their US market share has declined from 80% in 1975 to barely above 50% recently. The point is simple: Flawless high quality is now expected among car buyers, is no longer rare, and thus provides no advantage. In Focus 4.3 reports a similar story about Hyundai's uphill battle.

The Question of Imitability

Valuable and rare resources and capabilities can be a source of competitive advantage only if competitors have a difficult time imitating them. It is relatively easy to imitate a firm's *tangible* resources (such as plants), but it is a lot more challenging and often impossible to imitate *intangible* capabilities (such as tacit knowledge, superior motivation, and managerial talents).[31] In an effort to maintain a high-quality manufacturing edge, many Japanese firms intentionally employ "supertechnicians" (or *supaa ginosha*)—an honor designated by the Japanese government—to handle mission-critical work, such as mounting tiny chips onto circuit boards for laptops at Sharp, whose quality is better than robots.[32] Although robots can be purchased by rivals, no robots, and few humans elsewhere, can imitate the skills and dedication of the supertechnicians in Japan.

Imitation is difficult. Why? In two words: **causal ambiguity**, which refers to the difficulty of identifying the causal determinants of successful firm performance.[33] For three decades, Toyota has been meticulously studied by all automakers and numerous nonautomakers around the world. Yet, none has figured out what exactly leads to its prominence, and thus, none has been able to challenge it. If anything, Toyota has *widened* the performance gap between itself and the rest

causal ambiguity
The difficulty of identifying the causal determinants of successful firm performance.

IN FOCUS 4.3 Hyundai's Uphill Battle

Would you believe that South Korea's Hyundai has better quality than Toyota and Honda? The automobile industry's authoritative J. D. Power survey in 2006 found that Hyundai indeed had the third highest quality in the industry (behind only Lexus and Porsche). Trouble is, just like you, most American car buyers don't buy it. Only 23% of all new-car buyers in the United States bother to consider buying a Hyundai. This compares with 65% and 50% for Toyota and Honda, respectively.

Make no mistake: Hyundai is very capable. It was the fastest growing automaker in the US market from 2000 to 2005. Elbowing its way into the entry-level market, Hyundai captured many value conscious buyers, who appreciated the more *tangible* equipment and performance at lower prices (6% to 10% lower than those of rivals). However, with the won appreciating 25% against the dollar over the past three years, the price gap was narrowing between imports of entry-level Hyundai cars from South Korea and more highly regarded brands. Hyundai thus was forced to go after the higher margin, high-end market. To offset the won appreciation, Hyundai's two-year-old, $1 billion plant in Montgomery, Alabama, beefed up production. Yet, it turned out cars twice as fast as dealers ordered them. The problem? "When we don't have a price story," said David Zuchowski, Hyundai's vice president for sales, "we have no story." For high-end buyers, it is the *intangible* reputation and mystique that count. In 2007, Hyundai launched its upscale Genesis sedan (in the $30,000 to $35,000 price range) and audaciously compared it with both the BMW 5 series and the Lexus ES350. Does Hyundai have what it takes to win the hearts, minds, and wallets of high-end car buyers?

Sources: Based on (1) *Business Week*, 2007, Hyundai still gets no respect, May 21: 68–70; (2) http://www.jdpower.com.

of the pack, rising to (almost) become the number-one automaker by volume in the world. Market capitalization says it all: Toyota is now worth more than the American Big Three combined, and more than Honda and Nissan put together. Its net profits are far bigger than the combined total of the American Big Three. In the past 25 years during which every firm is allegedly "learning from Toyota," Toyota's productivity has grown sevenfold, twice as much as Detroit's finest despite their serious efforts to keep up.[34]

A natural question is: How can Toyota do it? Usually, a number of resources and capabilities will be nominated, including its legendary Toyota production system, its aggressive ambition, and its mystical organizational culture. While all of these resources and capabilities are plausible, what *exactly* is it? Knowing the answer to this question is not only intriguing to scholars and students, but it can also be hugely profitable for Toyota's rivals. Unfortunately, outsiders usually have a hard time understanding what a firm does inside its boundaries. We can try, as many rivals have, to identify Toyota's recipe for success by drawing up a long list of possible reasons labeled as "resources and capabilities" in our classroom discussion. But in the final analysis, as outsiders, we are not sure.[35]

What is even more fascinating for scholars and students and more frustrating for rivals is that often managers of a focal firm such as Toyota do not know exactly what contributes to their success. When interviewed, they can usually generate a long list of what they do well, such as a strong organizational culture, a relentless drive, and many other attributes. But to make matters worse, different managers of the same firm may have different lists. When probed as to which resource or capability is "it," they usually suggest that it is all of the above in *combination*. This is probably one of the most interesting and paradoxical aspects of the resource-based view: If insiders have a hard time figuring out what unambiguously contributes to their firm's performance, it is not surprising that outsiders' efforts in understanding and imitating these capabilities are usually flawed and often fail.[36]

Overall, valuable, rare, but imitable resources and capabilities may give firms some temporary competitive advantage, leading to above-average performance during some time. However, such advantage is not likely to be sustainable. Shown by the Toyota example, only valuable, rare, and *hard-to-imitate* resources and capabilities may potentially lead to sustained competitive advantage.

The Question of Organization

Even valuable, rare, and hard-to-imitate resources and capabilities may not give a firm sustained competitive advantage if the firm is not properly organized. Although movie stars represent some of the most valuable, rare, and hard-to-imitate as well as highest paid resources, *most* movies flop. More generally, the question of organization asks: How can a firm (such as a movie studio) be organized to develop and leverage the full potential of its resources and capabilities?

Numerous components within a firm are relevant to the question of organization.[37] In a movie studio, these components include talents in "smelling" good ideas, photography crews, musicians, singers, makeup specialists, animation artists, and managers on the business side who deal with sponsors, distributors, and local sites. These components are often called **complementary assets**[38] because, considered by themselves, they cannot generate box office hits. For the favorite movie you saw most recently, do you still remember the names of makeup artists? Of course, not—you probably only remember the stars. However, stars alone cannot generate hit movies either. It is the *combination* of star resources and complementary assets that create hit movies.[39] "It may be that not just a few resources and capabilities enable a firm to gain a competitive advantage but that literally thousands of these organizational attributes, bundled together, generate such advantage."[40]

complementary assets
The combination of numerous resources and assets that enable a firm to gain a competitive advantage.

Another idea is **social complexity**, which refers to the socially complex ways of organizing typical of many firms. Many multinationals consist of thousands of people scattered in many different countries. How they overcome cultural differ-

social complexity
Refers to the socially complex ways of organizing typical of many firms.

ences and are organized as one corporate entity and achieve organizational goals is profoundly complex (see In Focus 4.2 and Closing Case).[41] Often, it is their invisible relationships that add value.[42] Such organizationally embedded capabilities are thus very difficult for rivals to imitate. This emphasis on social complexity refutes what is half-jokingly called the "Lego" view of the firm, in which a firm can be assembled (and disassembled) from modules of technology and people (à la Lego toy blocks). By treating employees as identical and replaceable blocks, the Lego view fails to realize that the social capital associated with complex relationships and knowledge permeating many firms can be a source of competitive advantage.

Overall, only valuable, rare, and hard-to-imitate resources and capabilities that are organizationally embedded and exploited can possibly lead to sustained competitive advantage and persistently above-average performance.[43] Because resources and capabilities cannot be evaluated in isolation, the VRIO framework presents four interconnected and increasingly difficult hurdles for them to become a source of sustainable competitive advantage (Table 4.2). In other words, these four aspects come together as one "package."

DEBATES AND EXTENSIONS

LEARNING OBJECTIVE 4

participate in two leading debates on cross-border capabilities and offshoring

Like the institution-based view outlined in Chapters 2 and 3, the resource-based view has its fair share of controversies and debates. Here, we introduce two leading debates: (1) domestic resources versus international (cross-border) capabilities and (2) offshoring versus not offshoring.

Domestic Resources versus International (Cross-Border) Capabilities

Do firms that are successful domestically have what it takes to win internationally? If you ask managers at The Limited Brands, their answer would be no. The Limited Brands is the number-one US fashion retailer, which has a successful retail empire of 4,000 stores throughout the country with brands such as The Limited, Victoria's Secret, and Bath & Body Works. Yet, it has refused to go abroad—not even to Canada. On the other hand, the ubiquitous retail outlets of LVMH, Gucci, and United Colors of Benetton in major cities around the world suggest that their answer would be yes!

Some domestically successful firms continue to succeed overseas. For example, Swedish furniture retailer IKEA has found that its Scandinavian style of furniture combined with do-it-yourself flat packaging is very popular around the globe. IKEA thus has become a global cult brand. However, many other domestically formidable firms are burned badly overseas. Wal-Mart withdrew from Germany and South Korea recently. Similarly, Wal-Mart's leading global rival, France's Carrefour, had to exit the Czech Republic, Japan, Mexico, South Korea, and Slovakia recently. Starbucks' bitter brew has failed to turn into sweet profits overseas. In media, four US giants—Disney, Time Warner, Viacom, and News Corporation (which hailed from Australia)—believe that they need to be global in reach. Following this path, one French company, Vivendi Universal, aggressively entered the United States and imploded spectacularly. Likewise, Germany's Bertelsmann was forced to pull back from America. But the US media giants have hardly done any better. Thanks to their "go global" strategy, their average shareholder returns during 1991–2004 were merely 6%, barely half of the S&P 500 average of 11%. In sharp contrast, old-fashioned, locally based newspaper companies in the United States, which had no international capabilities to speak of, delivered far superior shareholder returns, averaging 13% during 1991–2004.[44]

In recent years, some firms have offshored their customer service operations. What are the advantages and disadvantages of this practice?

Are domestic resources and cross-border capabilities essentially the same? The answer can be either yes or no.[45] This debate is an extension of the larger debate on whether international business (IB) is different from domestic business. On the yes side, this is precisely the argument for having stand-alone IB courses in business schools. On the no side, it is possible to argue that IB fundamentally is about "business," which is well covered by strategy, finance, and other courses (most textbooks in these areas have at least one chapter on "international topics"). This question is obviously very important for companies and business schools. However, there is no right or wrong answer. It is important to emphasize the advice *think global, act local*. In practice, this means that despite grand global strategic designs, companies have to concretely win one local market (country) after another.

Offshoring versus Not Offshoring

As noted earlier, offshoring—or more specifically, international (offshore) outsourcing—has emerged as a leading corporate movement in the 21st century. While outsourcing manufacturing to countries such as China and Mexico is now largely accepted, what has become very controversial recently is the outsourcing of increasingly high-end services, starting with IT and now encompassing all sorts of "business process outsourcing" (BPO) to countries led by India (see Chapter 1 Opening Case). Because digitization and commoditization of service work is only enabled by the very recent rise of the Internet and the reduction of international communication costs, whether such offshoring proves to be a long-term benefit or hindrance to Western firms and economies is debatable.[46]

Proponents argue that offshoring creates enormous value for firms and economies. Western firms are able to tap into low-cost and high-quality labor, translating into significant cost savings. They can also focus on their core capabilities, which may add more value than dealing with noncore (and often uncompetitive) activities. In turn, offshoring service providers, such as Infosys and Wipro, develop *their* core competencies in IT/BPO. Focusing on offshoring between the United States and India, a McKinsey study reports that for every $1 of spending by US firms on India, US firms save 58 cents (see Table 4.3). Overall, $1.46 in new wealth is cre-

TABLE 4.3 BENEFIT OF $1 US SPENDING ON OFFSHORING TO INDIA

Benefit to the United States	$	Benefit to India	$
Savings accruing to US investors/customers	0.58	Labor	0.10
Exports of US goods/services to providers in India	0.05	Profits retained in India	0.10
Profit transfer by US-owned operations in India back to the US	0.04	Suppliers	0.09
Net direct benefit retained in the United States	0.67	Central government taxes	0.03
Value from US labor reemployed	0.46	State government taxes	0.01
Net benefit to the United States	1.13	**Net benefit to India**	0.33

Source: Based on text in D. Farrell, 2005, Offshoring: Value creation through economic change, *Journal of Management Studies*, 42: 675–683. Farrell is director of the McKinsey Global Institute, and she refers to a McKinsey study.

ated, of which the US economy captures $1.13 through cost savings and increased exports to India (which buys made-in-USA equipment, software, and services). India captures the other 33 cents through profits, wages, and additional taxes.[47] While acknowledging that some US employees may lose their jobs, offshoring proponents suggest that on balance, offshoring is a win-win solution for both US and Indian firms and economies. In other words, offshoring can be conceptualized as the latest incarnation of international trade (in tradable services), which theoretically will bring mutual gains to all countries involved (see Chapter 5).

Critics of offshoring make three points on strategic, economic, and political grounds. Strategically, if, according to some outsourcing gurus, "even core functions like engineering, R&D, manufacturing, and marketing can—and often should—be moved outside,"[48] what is left of the firm? In manufacturing, US firms have gone down this path before with disastrous results. For example, Radio Corporation of America (RCA), having invented the color TV, outsourced its production to Japan in the 1960s, a *low*-cost country at that time. Fast forward to the 2000s: the United States no longer has any US-owned color TV producer left. The nationality of RCA itself, after being bought and sold several times, is now *Chinese* (France's Thomson sold RCA to China's TCL in 2003). More recently, Eastman Kodak outsourced the manufacturing of its cameras to Singapore's Flextronics. Critics argue such offshoring nurtures rivals.[49] Why, after 2000, are Indian IT/BPO firms emerging as strong rivals challenging EDS and IBM? It is in part because these Indian firms built up their capabilities doing work for EDS and IBM in the 1990s—remember Y2K (the IT industry's race before the year 2000 to fix the "millennium bug" problem)?

In manufacturing, many Asian firms, which used to be **original equipment manufacturers (OEMs)** executing design blueprints provided by Western firms, now want to have a piece of the action in design by becoming **original design manufacturers (ODMs)** (see Figure 4.5). Having mastered low-cost and high-quality manufacturing, Asian firms such as BenQ, Compal, Flextronics, Hon Hai, HTC, and Huawei are indeed capable of capturing some design function from

original equipment manufacturer (OEM)
A firm that executes the design blueprints provided by other firms and manufactures such products.

original design manufacturer (ODM)
A firm that both designs and manufactures products.

FIGURE 4.5 FROM ORIGINAL EQUIPMENT MANUFACTURER TO ORIGINAL DESIGN MANUFACTURER

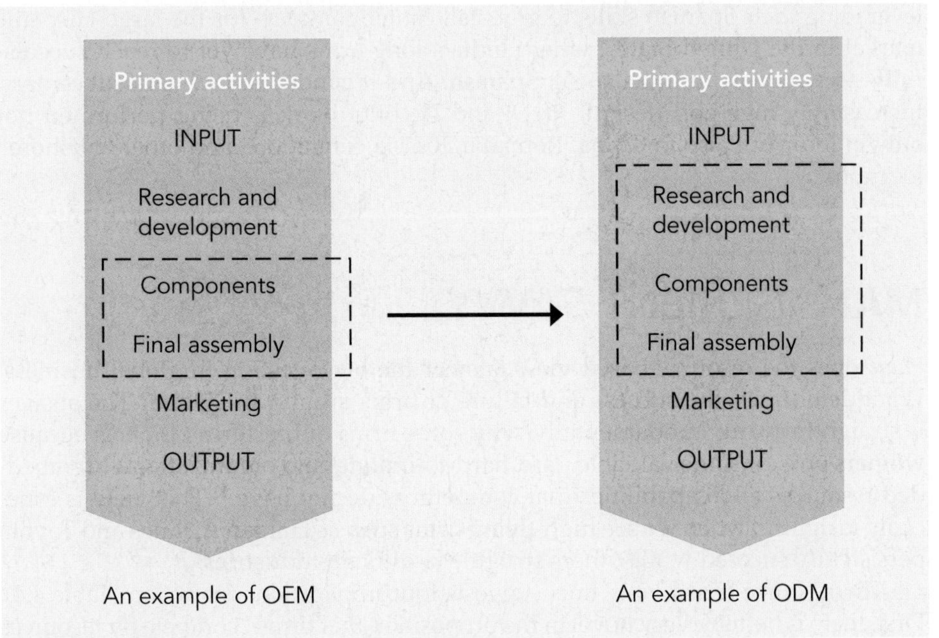

Note: Dashed lines represent organizational boundaries. A further extension is to become an original *brand* manufacturer (OBM), which would incorporate brand ownership and management in the marketing area. For graphic simplicity, it is not shown here.

Western firms such as Dell, HP, Kodak, Nokia, Nortel, and PalmOne. Therefore, increasing outsourcing of design work by Western firms may accelerate their own long-run demise. A number of Asian OEMs, now quickly becoming ODMs, have openly announced that their real ambition is to become **original brand manufacturers (OBMs)**. Thus, according to critics of offshoring, isn't enough writing on the wall?

original brand manufacturer (OBM)
A firm that designs, manufactures, and markets branded products

Economically, critics contend that in addition to Western firms reducing their firm-level capabilities and competitiveness, critics are not sure whether developed economies, as a whole, actually gain more. Although shareholders and corporate high flyers embrace offshoring (see Chapter 1), offshoring increasingly results in job losses in high-end areas such as design, R&D, and IT/BPO. While white-collar individuals who lose jobs will naturally hate it, the net impact (consolidating all economic gains and losses, including job losses) on developed economies may still be negative.

Finally, critics argue politically that many large US firms claim that they are "global companies" and that they do not represent or are not bound by American values any more. All these firms are interested in is the "cheapest and most exploitable" labor. Not only is work commoditized, but people (such as IT programmers) are degraded as "tradable commodities" that can be jettisoned. As a result, large firms that outsource work to emerging economies are often accused of being unethical, destroying jobs at home, ignoring corporate social responsibility, violating customer privacy (for example, by sending tax returns and credit card numbers to be processed overseas), and in some cases, undermining national security. Not surprisingly, the debate often becomes political, emotional, and explosive when such accusations are made.

For firms in developed economies, the choice is not really offshoring versus not offshoring but *where* to draw the line on offshoring. It is important to note that this debate primarily takes place in developed economies. There is relatively little debate in emerging economies because they clearly stand to gain from such offshoring to them. Taking a page from the Indian playbook, the Philippines, with its large army of English-speaking professionals, is trying to eat some of India's lunch. Northeast China, where Japanese is widely taught, is positioning itself as an ideal location for call centers for Japan. Central and Eastern Europe naturally gravitate toward serving Western Europe. South Africa is also entering the game, playing up its English and Dutch skills. Central and South American countries are leveraging their Spanish skills to grab call center contracts for the large Hispanic market in the United States, where India's long arms have yet to reach successfully—few people in India speak Spanish. And it is not just low-end call centers. Increasingly high-end design, R&D, and IT/BPO work is being performed not only in India but also in China, Romania, Russia, Singapore, and other "offshore" locations.

LEARNING OBJECTIVE **5**
draw implications for action

MANAGEMENT SAVVY

How does the resource-based view answer the big question in global business: What determines the success and failure of firms around the globe? The answer is straightforward: Fundamentally, why some firms outperform others is because winners possess some valuable, rare, hard-to-imitate, and organizationally embedded resources and capabilities that competitors do not have.[50] This view is especially insightful when we see high-flying firms such as Hainan Airlines and Toyota persistently succeed while others struggle in difficult industries.

The resource-based view thus suggests four implications for action (Table 4.4). First, there is nothing very novel in the proposition that firms "compete on resources and capabilities." The subtlety comes when managers attempt, via the VRIO frame-

TABLE 4.4 IMPLICATIONS FOR ACTION

- Managers need to build firm strengths based on the VRIO framework
- Relentless imitation or benchmarking, while important, is not likely to be a successful strategy
- Managers need to develop strategic foresight for future competition
- Students need to make themselves "untouchables" whose jobs cannot be easily outsourced

work, to distinguish resources and capabilities that are valuable, rare, hard to imitate, and organizationally embedded from those that do not share these attributes. In other words, the VRIO framework can greatly aid the time-honored SWOT analysis, especially the S (strengths) and W (weaknesses) part. Managers, who cannot pay attention to every resource and capability, must have some sense of what really matters. A common mistake that managers often make when evaluating their firms' capabilities is failing to assess them relative to rivals', thus resulting in a mixed bag of both good and mediocre capabilities. Using the VRIO framework, a value chain analysis helps managers make decisions on what capabilities to focus on in-house and what to outsource. Increasingly, what really matters is not tangible resources that are relatively easy to imitate but intangible capabilities that are harder for rivals to lay their arms around. At present, as much as 75% of the value of publicly traded corporations in the United States comes from intangible, knowledge-based assets, up from approximately 40% in the early 1980s.[51] Firms in other parts of the world have experienced similar growth in intangible assets. This is a crucial reason that we increasingly label the new global economy as a "knowledge-based economy." Therefore, managers need to focus on the identification, development, and leveraging of valuable, rare, hard-to-imitate, and organizationally embedded resources and capabilities, which are often intangible. It is thus not surprising that capabilities not meeting these criteria are increasingly outsourced.

Second, relentless imitation or benchmarking, while important, is not likely to be a successful strategy. Follower firms have a tendency to mimic the most visible, the most obvious, and consequently, the *least* important practices of winning firms. At best, follower firms that meticulously replicate every resource possessed by winning firms can hope to attain competitive parity. Firms so well endowed with resources to imitate others may be better off by developing their own unique capabilities. The best performing firms often create new ways of adding value.

Third, a competitive advantage that is sustained does not imply that it will last forever, which is not realistic in today's global competition. All a firm can hope for is a competitive advantage that can be sustained for as long as possible. However, over time, all advantages may erode. As noted earlier, each of IBM's product-related advantages associated with tabulating machines, mainframes, and PCs was sustained for a period of time. But eventually, these advantages disappeared. Therefore, the lesson for all firms, including current market leaders, is to develop strategic *foresight*—"over-the-horizon radar" is a good metaphor—that enables them to anticipate future needs and move early to identify, develop, and leverage resources and capabilities for future competition.[52]

Finally, here is a very personal and relevant implication for action. As a student who is probably studying this book in a developed (read: high-wage and thus high-cost!) country such as the United States, you may be wondering: What do I get out of this? How do I cope with the frightening future of global competition? There are two lessons you can learn. First, the whole debate on offshoring, a part of the larger debate on globalization, is very relevant and directly affects your future as a manager, a consumer, and a citizen (see Chapter 1). So don't be a couch potato. Be active, get involved, and be prepared because it is not only *their* debate; it is *yours* as well. Second, be very serious about the VRIO advice of the resource-based view. Although this view has been developed to advise firms, there is no reason you cannot develop that into a resource-based view of the *individual*. That is, you want to make yourself an "untouchable," who is defined by Thomas Friedman in *The World Is Flat* (2005) as an individual whose job cannot be outsourced. This is because an untouchable individual possesses valuable, rare, and hard-to-imitate capabilities indispensable to an organization. This won't be easy. But you really don't want to be mediocre. A generation ago, parents told their kids: "Eat your food—kids in China and India are starving." Now, Friedman would advise you (and I fully agree): "Study this book and leverage your education—students in China and India are starving for your job."[53]

CHAPTER SUMMARY

1. Explain what firm resources and capabilities are
   - Resources and capabilities are tangible and intangible assets a firm uses to choose and implement its strategies.
2. Undertake a basic SWOT analysis of the value chain to decide whether to keep an activity in-house or outsource it
   - A value chain consists of a stream of activities from upstream to downstream that add value.
   - A SWOT analysis engages managers to ascertain a firm's strengths and weaknesses on an activity-by-activity basis relative to rivals.
   - Outsourcing is defined as turning over all or part of an organizational activity to an outside supplier.
   - An activity with a high degree of industry commonality and a high degree of commoditization can be outsourced, and an industry-specific and firm-specific (proprietary) activity is better performed in-house.
   - On any given activity, the four choices for managers in terms of modes and locations are (1) offshoring, (2) inshoring, (3) captive sourcing/FDI, and (4) domestic in-house activity.
3. Analyze the value, rarity, imitability, and organizational aspects of resources and capabilities
   - A VRIO framework suggests that only resources and capabilities that are valuable, rare, inimitable, and organizationally embedded will generate sustainable competitive advantage.
4. Participate in two leading debates on cross-border capabilities and offshoring
   - Are domestic capabilities the same as international (cross-border) capabilities?
   - For Western firms and economies, is offshoring beneficial or detrimental in the long run?
5. Draw implications for action
   - Managers need to build firm strengths based on the VRIO framework.
   - Relentless imitation or benchmarking, while important, is not likely to be a successful strategy.
   - Managers need to develop strategic foresight for future competition.
   - Students are advised to make themselves "untouchables" whose jobs cannot be outsourced.

KEY TERMS

Benchmarking 91
Capability 89
Captive sourcing 94
Causal ambiguity 97
Commoditization 91
Complementary assets 98
Inshoring 94
Intangible resources and capabilities 89
Offshoring 94
Original brand manufacturer (OBM) 102
Original design manufacturer (ODM) 101
Original equipment manufacturer (OEM) 101
Outsourcing 92
Resources 89
Resource-based view 88
Social complexity 98
SWOT analysis 88
Tangible resources and capabilities 89
Value chain 91
VRIO framework 95

REVIEW QUESTIONS

1. Describe the four types of tangible resources and capabilities.
2. Describe the three types of intangible resources and capabilities.
3. Explain the difference between primary activities and support activities in a value chain.
4. Using Figure 4.3, explain the meaning of commoditization.
5. Redraw Figure 4.4, add definitions to each of the four terms.
6. When analyzing a value chain with a VRIO framework, what is the most important question to begin with and why?
7. How does the rarity of a firm's resources and capabilities affect its competitive advantage?
8. Which is more difficult: imitating a firm's tangible resources or its intangible resources?
9. Why is imitation difficult?
10. How do complementary assets and social complexity influence a firm's organization?
11. If a firm is successful domestically, is it likely to be successful internationally? Why or why not?
12. After reviewing the arguments for and against offshoring, state your opinion on this issue.
13. What is one common mistake that managers often make when evaluating their firm's capabilities?
14. What is the likely result of relentless imitation or benchmarking?
15. How would you characterize strategic foresight?

CRITICAL DISCUSSION QUESTIONS

1. Pick any pair of rivals (such as Samsung/Sony, Nokia/Motorola, and Boeing/Airbus) and explain why one outperforms another. Apply both a SWOT analysis and a VRIO framework to the chosen pair.

2. Conduct a VRIO analysis of your business school in terms of (1) perceived reputation (such as rankings), (2) faculty strength, (3) student quality, (4) administrative efficiency, (5) IT, and (6) building maintenance relative to the top-three rival schools. If you were the dean with a limited budget, where would you invest precious financial resources to make your school number one among rivals. Why?
3. ON ETHICS: Ethical dilemmas associated with offshoring are numerous. Pick one of these dilemmas and make a case either to defend your firm's offshoring activities or to argue against such activities (assuming you are employed at a firm headquartered in a developed economy).
4. ON ETHICS: Since firms read information posted on competitors' websites, is it ethical to provide false information on resources and capabilities on corporate websites? Do the benefits outweigh the costs?

VIDEO CASE

Watch "Bright Ideas" by Perween Warsi of S&A Foods.

1. Explain the firm's resources and capabilities as covered in the video. What is the relative importance of managerial and worker resources as discussed by Ms. Warsi?
2. According to this chapter, "managers need to build firm strengths based on the VRIO framework." What technique does Ms. Warsi use to enhance the V (value) of her human resources? Do you think that approach would work with equal effectiveness around the world?
3. How could Ms. Warsi's recommendations be affected by a firm's policy regarding outsourcing?
4. How might a firm that uses Ms. Warsi's approach develop and enable employees to make even more innovative suggestions? Apply your answer to a global work force.
5. How might you take the approach used by Ms. Warsi to improve your leadership in some student group or other nonprofit organization?

CLOSING CASE

PolyGram/Universal Music Group's Star Search

Universal Music Group (UMG), formerly PolyGram, is the world's largest music company with a 26% global market share. In North America, its lineup includes Bon Jovi, Mariah Carey, Shania Twain, and Sting. In Europe, stars include Snow Patrol and U2. In Asia, stars such as Jacky Cheung and Alan Tam are enlisted.

How did PolyGram (now UMG) outperform previously better known and historically larger rivals such as EMI and Sony Music to attain global leadership? There are many intriguing answers, but one key distinction seems to be PolyGram's unique structure that allowed it to turn selected local artists into international stars. Originally with a decentralized, country-based structure, PolyGram tried to be a leading player in each country in which it competed. Its talent spotters made nightly forays to local bars, clubs, and concert halls, searching for raw material with star potential. If its talent spotters found a promising young artist in Hong Kong, for example, the Hong Kong subsidiary would produce a record for the local market.

While successful, this country-based structure missed out on the profit potential to make national stars into regional or even global stars. Some (although not all) star performers in Hong Kong, for example, might also succeed in China, Taiwan, Southeast Asia, and perhaps elsewhere. If the company could identify and leverage these talents with international potential, it could earn very attractive returns. This was because most competitors such as EMI and Sony sourced the majority of their talents from just two "mainstream" countries: Great Britain and the United States. Intense competition for talent inflated the cost of signing new artists in these two countries. Consequently, it would be much more profitable to unlock the international potential of an artist or group popular in a nonmainstream market—for example, Björk from Iceland, who sang at the opening ceremony of the 2004 Athens Olympics. As a result, a record company can sign artists who are local stars in Iceland, Hong Kong, or Venezuela at a fraction of the cost for a similar star in Great Britain or the United States.

© MONTY BRINTON/CBS /Landov

The challenge, of course, lies in how to identify such local talent with international potential. Searching for a new star, even locally, is always like looking for the proverbial needle in a haystack. Each new song is an inherently risky innovation, and very few local artists would have international appeal. PolyGram thus confronted the challenge of how to combine some very complex, tacit, and hard-to-describe knowledge—namely, linking its understanding of what made an artist successful locally with its knowledge of whether this distinctiveness would sell records in other countries. Although such knowledge has no written rules, it is not entirely based on "gut feelings" or "hunches" either. PolyGram would have to call on the combined knowledge of talent spotters, producers, and promotional specialists dispersed in far-flung places around the globe.

Having decided to embark on this more international strategy, PolyGram has formed a new structure, featuring a network of International Repertoire Centers (IRCs). This network consists of 75 professionals located in 21 sourcing centers—seven centers in Great Britain, five in the United States, and one each in Australia, Canada, France, Germany, Hong Kong, Italy, Japan, the Netherlands, and Switzerland. IRC professionals have a single mandate: to analyze repertoire sourced by their local colleagues and then identify and exploit those with international potential. They were evaluated and rewarded on the basis of their success in generating international sales from local acts. Experts suggest that what has propelled PolyGram (now UMG) to the top of the global music industry is such deeply embedded, knowledge-based capabilities in identifying, sourcing, and leveraging local repertoire internationally through its network of IRCs.

Case Discussion Questions

1. What is the main source of PolyGram/UMG's competitive advantage? Is it tangible or intangible?
2. Why do rivals find it very difficult to imitate PolyGram/UMG's capabilities?
3. Are PolyGram/UMG's domestic resources and international (cross-border) capabilities the same?
4. In this case, why is the question of organization in the VRIO framework so important?

Sources: Based on (1) Y. Doz, J. Santos, & P. Williamson, 2001, *From Global to Metanational* (pp. 17–18), Boston: Harvard Business School Press; (2) http://new.umusic.com; (3) M. W. Peng, 2006, PolyGram/Universal Music Group makes local stars shine globally, in M. W. Peng, *Global Strategy* (pp. 403–404), Cincinnati, OH: Thomson South-Western.

NOTES

Journal acronyms: **AME** – *Academy of Management Executive;* **AMJ** – *Academy of Management Journal;* **AMR** – *Academy of Management Review;* **BW** – *Business Week;* **HBR** – *Harvard Business Review;* **JIBS** – *Journal of International Business Studies;* **JM** – *Journal of Management;* **JMS** – *Journal of Management Studies;* **MIR** – *Management International Review;* **OSc** – *Organization Science;* **SMJ** – *Strategic Management Journal*

[1] M. W. Peng, 2001, The resource-based view and international business, *JM*, 27: 803–829. For historical development of this view, see J. Barney, 1991, Firm resources and sustained competitive advantage, *JM*, 17: 99–120; B. Wernerfelt, 1984, A resource-based view of the firm, *SMJ*, 5: 171–180.

[2] G. Dess, T. Lumpkin, & M. Eisner, 2007, *Strategic Management*, 3rd ed. (p. 78), Chicago: McGraw-Hill.

[3] F. Acedo, C. Barroso, & J. Galan, 2006, The resource-based theory, *SMJ*, 27: 621–636; S. Newbert, 2007, Empirical research on the resource-based view of the firm, *SMJ*, 28: 121–146; D. Sirmon, M. Hitt, & R. D. Ireland, 2007, Managing firm resources in dynamic environments to create value, *AMR*, 32: 273–292.

[4] M. W. Peng & P. Heath, 1996, The growth of the firm in planned economies in transition, *AMR*, 21: 492–528; E. Penrose, 1959, *The Theory of the Growth of the Firm*, London: Blackwell. See also A. Goerzen & P. Beamish, 2007, The Penrose effect, *MIR*, 47: 221–239; P. Buckley & M. Casson, 2007, Edith Penrose's theory of the growth of the firm and the strategic management of multinational enterprises, *MIR*, 47: 151–173; M. Pettus, 2001, The resource-based view as a developmental growth process, *AMJ*, 44: 878–896; C. Pitellis & A. Verbeke, 2007, Edith Penrose and the future of the multinational enterprise, *MIR*, 47: 139–149; J. Steen & P. Liesch, 2007, A note on Penrosian growth, resource bundles, and the Uppsala model of internationalization, *MIR*, 47: 193–206; D. Tan & J. Mahoney, 2007, The dynamics of Japanese firm growth in US industries, *MIR*, 47: 259–279; A. Verbeke & W. Yuan, 2007, Entrepreneurship in multinational enterprises, *MIR*, 47: 241–258.

[5] J. Barney, 2001, Is the resource-based view a useful perspective for strategic management research? (p. 54), *AMR* 26: 41–56.

[6] C. Helfat & M. Peteraf, 2003, The dynamic resource-based view, *SMJ*, 24: 997–1010; D. Teece, G. Pisano, & A. Shuen, 1997, Dynamic capabilities and strategic management, *SMJ*, 18: 509–533.

[7] J. Barney, 2002, *Gaining and Sustaining Competitive Advantage*, 2nd ed. (p. 157), Upper Saddle River, NJ: Prentice Hall.

[8] E. Danneels, 2007, The process of technological competence leveraging, *SMJ*, 28: 511–533; A. Phene, K. Fladmoe-Lindquist, & L. Marsh, 2006, Breakthrough innovations in the US biotechnology industry, *SMJ*, 27: 369–388.

[9] A. Carmeli & A. Tishler, 2004, The relationships between intangible organizational elements and organizational performance, *SMJ*, 25: 1257–1278; S. Dutta, O. Narasimhan, & S. Rajiv, 2005, Conceptualizing and measuring capabilities, *SMJ*, 26: 277–285; H. Itami & T. Roehl, 1987, *Mobilizing Invisible Assets*, Cambridge, MA: Harvard University Press.

[10] N. Hatch & J. Dyer, 2004, Human capital and learning as a source of competitive advantage, *SMJ*, 25: 1155–1178.

[11] B. Allred & H. K. Steensma, 2005, The influence of industry and home country characteristics on firms' pursuit of innovation, *MIR*, 45: 383–412; J. Birkinshaw, R. Nobel, & J. Ridderstrale, 2002, Knowledge as a contingency variable, *OSc*, 13: 274–289; H. Cho & V. Pucik, 2005, Relationship among innovativeness, quality, growth, profitability, and market value, *SMJ*, 26: 555–575; S. McEvily, K. Eisenhardt, & J. Prescott, 2004, The global acquisition, leverage, and protection of technologies competencies, *SMJ*, 25: 713–722; K. Smith, C. Collins, & K. Clark, 2005, Existing knowledge, knowledge creation capability, and the rate of new product introduction in high-technology firms, *AMJ*, 48: 346–357; M. Subramaniam & M. Youndt, 2005, The influence of intellectual capital on the types of innovative capabilities, *AMJ*, 48: 450–463.

[12] N. Gardberg & C. Fombrun, 2006, Corporate citizenship, *AMR*, 31: 329–346; K. Mayer, 2006, Spillovers and governance, *AMJ*, 49: 69–84; V. Rindova, T. Pollock, & M. Hayward, 2006, Celebrity firms, *AMR*, 31: 50–71.

[13] P. Lee, 2001, What's in a name.com? *SMJ*, 22: 793–804; P. Roberts & G. Dowling, 2002, Corporate reputation and sustained superior financial performance, *SMJ*, 23: 1077–1093.

[14] M. Porter, 1985, *Competitive Advantage*, New York: Free Press; C. Stabell & O. Fjeldstad, 1998, Configuring value for competitive advantage, *SMJ*, 19: 413–437.

[15] G. Johnson, L. Melin, & R. Whittington, 2003, Micro strategy and strategizing, *JMS*, 40: 3–22; A. Parmigiani, 2007, Why do firms both make and buy? *SMJ*, 28: 285–311.

[16] J. Barthelemy, 2003, The seven deadly sins of outsourcing, *AME*, 17 (2): 87–98; F. Rothaermel, M. Hitt, & L. Jobe, 2006, Balancing vertical integration and strategic outsourcing, *SMJ*, 27: 1033–1056.

[17] *BW*, 2006, The 787 encounters turbulence, June 19: 38–40.

[18] M. Jacobides & S. Winter, 2005, The co-evolution of capabilities and transaction costs (p. 404), *SMJ*, 26: 395–413.

[19] A. Ranft & M. Lord, 2002, Acquiring new technologies and capabilities, *OSc*, 13: 420–441.

[20] R. Makadok, 2001, Toward a synthesis of the resource-based and dynamic capability views of rent creation (p. 388), *SMJ*, 22: 387–401.

[21] J. Anand & A. Delios, 2002, Absolute and relative resources as determinants of international acquisitions, *SMJ*, 23: 119–134; M. K. Erramilli, S. Agarwal, & S. Kim, 1997, Are firm-specific advantages location-specific too? *JIBS*, 28: 735–757; A. Madhok & T. Osegowitsch, 2000, The international biotechnology industry, *JIBS*, 31: 325–335.

[22] D. Levy, 2005, Offshoring in the new global political economy (p. 687), *JMS*, 42: 685–693.

[23] This section draws heavily on Barney, 2002, *Gaining and Sustaining* (pp. 159–174).

[24] R. Adner & P. Zemsky, 2006, A demand-based perspective on sustainable competitive advantage, *SMJ*, 27: 215–239; J. Anderson, J. Narus, & W. Van Rossum, 2006, Customer value propositions in business markets, *HBR*, March: 91–99; S. Lippman & R. Rumelt, 2003, A bargaining perspective on resource advantage, *SMJ*, 24: 1069–1086; J. Morrow, D. Sirmon, M. Hitt, & T. Holcomb, 2007, Creating value in the face of declining performance, *SMJ*, 28: 271–283.

[25] D. Leonard-Barton, 1992, Core capabilities and core rigidities, *SMJ*, 13: 111–125.

[26] D. Lavie, 2006, Capability reconfiguration, *AMR*, 31: 153–174; N. Siggelkow, 2001, Change in the presence of fit, *AMJ*, 44: 838–857; G. P. West & J. DeCastro, 2001, The Achilles heel of firm strategy, *JMS*, 38: 417–442.

[27] G. Hamel, 2006, Management innovation (p. 78), *HBR*, February: 72–84.

[28] N. Carr, 2003, *Does IT Matter?* Boston: Harvard Business School Press.

[29] *Economist*, 2005, A market for ideas (p. 4), October 22: 3–6.

[30] *Economist*, 2005, Thinking for themselves (p. 16), October 22: 14–17; S. Ethiraj, P. Kale, M. Krishnana, & J. Singh, 2005, Where do capabilities come from and how do they matter? *SMJ*, 26: 25–45.

[31] A. Knott, D. Bryce, & H. Posen, 2003, On the strategic accumulation of intangible assets, *OSc*, 14: 192–208; D. Miller, 2003, An asymmetry-based view of advantage, *SMJ*, 24: 961–976; G. Ray, J. Barney, & W. Muhanna, 2004, Capabilities, business processes, and competitive advantage, *SMJ*, 25: 23–37; R. Schroeder, K. Bates, & M. Junttila, 2002, A resource-based view of manufacturing strategy, *SMJ*, 23: 105–118; B. Skaggs & M. Youndt, 2004, Strategic positioning, human capital, and performance in service organizations, *SMJ*, 25: 85–99.

[32] *BW*, 2005, Better than robots, December 26: 46–47.

[33] A. King, 2007, Disentangling interfirm and intrafirm causal ambiguity, *AMR*, 32: 156–178; T. Powell, D. Lovallo, & C. Caringal, 2006, Causal ambiguity, management perception, and firm performance, *AMR*, 31: 175–196.

[34] *Economist*, 2005, The quick and the dead, January 29: 10–11.

[35] M. Lieberman & S. Asaba, 2006, Why do firms imitate each other? *AMR*, 31: 366–385.

[36] A. Lado, N. Boyd, P. Wright, & M Kroll, 2006, Paradox and theorizing within the resource-based view, *AMR*, 31: 115–131.

[37] G. Hoetker, 2006, Do modular products lead to modular organizations? *SMJ*, 27: 501–518; M. Kotabe, R. Parente, & J. Murray, 2007, Antecedents and outcomes of modular production in the Brazilian automobile industry, *JIBS*, 38: 84–106.

[38] N. Stieglitz & K. Heine, 2007, Innovations and the role of complementarities in a strategic theory of the firm, *SMJ*, 28: 1–15.

[39] D. Miller & J. Shamsie, 1996, The resource-based view of the firm in two environments, *AMJ*, 39: 519–543.

[40] J. Barney, 1997, *Gaining and Sustaining Competitive Advantage* (p. 155), Reading, MA: Addison-Wesley. See also J. Jansen, F. Van den Bosch, & H. Volberda, 2005, Managerial potential and related absorptive capacity, *AMJ*, 48: 999–1015; Y. Kor & J. Mahoney, 2005, How dynamics, management, and governance of resource deployments influence firm-level performance, *SMJ*, 26: 489–496; Y. Mishina, T. Pollock, & J. Porac, 2004, Are more resources always better for growth? *SMJ*, 25: 1179–1197; S. Thomke & W. Kuemmerle, 2002, Asset accumulation, interdependence, and technological change, *SMJ*, 23: 619–635; P. Yeoh & K. Roth, 1999, An empirical analysis of sustained advantage, *SMJ*, 20: 637–653.

[41] J. Birkinshaw & N. Hood, 1998, Multinational subsidiary evolution, *AMR*, 23: 773–795; A. Delios & P. Beamish, 2001, Survival and profitability, *AMJ*, 44: 1028–1038; A. Rugman & A. Verbeke, 2001, Subsidiary-specific advantages in multinational enterprises, *SMJ*, 22: 237–250; S. Tallman, 1991, Strategic management models and resource-based strategies among MNEs in a host market, *SMJ*, 12: 69–82.

[42] T. Kostova & K. Roth, 2003, Social capital in multinational corporations and a micro-macro model of its formation, *AMR*, 28: 297–317; P. Moran, 2005, Structural vs. relational embeddedness, *SMJ*, 26: 1129–1151.

[43] J. Fahy, G. Hooley, J. Beracs, K. Fonfara, & V. Gabrijan, 2003, Privatization and sustainable advantage in the emerging economies of Central Europe, *MIR*, 43: 407–428; S. McEvily & B. Chakravarthy, 2002, The persistence of knowledge-based advantage, *SMJ*, 23: 285–305; S. Zahra & A. Nielsen, 2002, Sources of capabilities, integration, and technology commercialization, *SMJ*, 23: 377–398.

[44] B. Greenwald & J. Kahn, 2005, All strategy is local, *HBR*, September: 95–103.

[45] J. Boddewyn, B. Toyne, & Z. Martinez, 2004, The meanings of "international management," *MIR*, 44: 195–212; L. Nachum, 2003, International business in a world of increasing returns, *MIR*, 43: 219–245; M. W. Peng, 2004, Identifying the big question in international business research, *JIBS*, 35: 99–108.

[46] J. Doh, 2005, Offshore outsourcing, *JMS*, 42: 695–704.

[47] D. Farrell, 2005, Offshoring: Value creation through economic change, *JMS*, 42: 675–683.

[48] M. Gottfredson, R. Puryear, & S. Phillips, 2005, Strategic sourcing (p. 132), *HBR*, February: 132–139.

[49] C. Rossetti & T. Choi, 2005, On the dark side of strategic sourcing, *AME*, 19 (1): 46–60.

[50] W. DeSarbo, C. Nenedetto, M. Song, & I. Sinha, 2005, Revisiting the Miles and Snow strategic framework, *SMJ*, 26; 47–74; G. T. Hult, D. Ketchen, & S. Slater, 2005, Market orientation and performance, *SMJ*, 26: 1173–1181.

[51] *Economist*, 2005, A market for ideas, October 22: 3.

[52] G. Hamel & C. K. Prahalad, 1994, *Competing for the Future*, Boston: Harvard Business School Press.

[53] The author's paraphrase based on T. Friedman, 2005, *The World Is Flat* (p. 237), New York: Farrar, Straus & Giroux.

INTEGRATIVE CASE 1.1

THE CHINESE MENU (FOR DEVELOPMENT)

Douglass C. North
Washington University

In the years since the end of World War II, we, and other developed nations, have devoted immense amounts of resources to the development of poor countries. The result has not been a success story. This is puzzling, since during that time we have learned a great deal about the process of economic and political change: not only the underlying source of economic growth—productivity increase—but also the factors that make for such increase. And in the past several decades, as economists have become aware of the role of institutions in providing the correct incentives for economic growth, we have incorporated an understanding of the significance of well-specified and -enforced property rights as key structural requirements in that process.

Despite our increased understanding, the record at promoting development is not impressive, largely because we fail to see the importance of open-access political systems as well as open-access competitive markets. Yes, the world has gotten richer, the percentage of the world's population subsisting on less than a dollar a day has fallen, and there have been a few spectacular success stories, most particularly China. But sub-Saharan Africa remains a part of the world where per capita income has absolutely fallen, Latin America continues to have stop-and-go development, and the efforts at promoting development by the World Bank have been, to put it politely, nothing to brag about.

Yet, none of the standard models of economic and political theory can explain China. After a disastrous era of promoting collective organization, in which approximately 30 million people died of starvation, China gradually fumbled its way out of the economic disaster it had created by instituting the Household Responsibility System which provided peasants with incentives to produce more. This system in turn led to the town-village enterprises (TVEs) and sequential development built on their cultural background. But China still does not have well-specified property rights, TVEs hardly resembled the standard firm of economics, and it remains to this day a communist dictatorship.

What kind of a model is that for the developing world? It is not a good model and it is still not clear what the outcome will be, but the Chinese experience should force economists to rethink some of the fundamental tenets of economics as they apply to development. Two features stand out: (1) While the institutions China employed are different from developed nations, the incentive implications were similar; and (2) China has been confronting new problems and pragmatically attempting new solutions.

Two implications are clear. First, there are many paths to development. The key is creating an institutional structure derived from your particular cultural institutions that provide the proper incentives—not slavishly imitating Western institutions. Second, the world is constantly changing in fundamental ways. The basics of economic theory are essential elements of every economy, but the problems countries face today are set in new and novel frameworks of beliefs, institutions, technologies, and radically lower information costs than ever before. The secret of success is the creation of adaptively efficient institutions—institutions that readily adapt to changing circumstances. Just how do we create such an institutional framework?

Institutions are the way we structure human interaction—political, social, and economic—and are the incentive framework of a society. They are made up of formal rules (constitutions, laws, and rules), informal constraints (norms, conventions, and codes of conduct), and their enforcement characteristics. Together they define the way the game is played, whether as a society or an athletic game. Let me illustrate from professional football. There are formal rules defining the way the game is supposed to be played; informal norms—such as not deliberately injuring the quarterback of the opposing team; and enforcement characteristics—umpires, referees—designed to see that the game is played according to the intentions underlying the rules. But enforcement is always imperfect and it frequently pays for a team to violate rules. Therefore, the way a game is actually played is a function of the underlying intentions embodied in the rules, the strength of informal codes of conduct, the perception of the umpires, and the severity of punishment for violating rules.

It is the same way with societies. Poorly performing societies have rules that do not provide the proper incentives, lack effective informal norms that would

This case was written by Douglass C. North (Washington University, St. Louis, MO) and first published as "The Chinese Menu (for Development)" in *The Wall Street Journal*, April 7, 2005, A14. North received the Nobel prize in economics in 1993. Case discussion questions were added by Mike Peng.

encourage productivity, and/or have poor enforcement. Underlying institutions are belief systems that provide our understanding of the world around us and, therefore, the incentives that we face. Creating institutions that will perform effectively is, thus, a difficult task. Effective performance entails the creation of open-access societies—the essential requirement for the dynamic market that Adam Smith envisioned. Let me illustrate from the contrasting histories of North and South America.

North America was settled by British colonists bringing with them the property-rights structure that had evolved by that time in the home country. Because the British did not regard the colonies as critical to their own development, they were allowed a large measure of self-government. In the context of relative political and economic freedom with a setting of endless resource opportunities, the result was the gradual evolution of an open-access society in the decades following independence.

Latin America, in contrast, was settled by the Spanish (and Portuguese) to exploit the discovery and extraction of treasure. The resultant institutional structure was one of monopoly and political control from Madrid and Lisbon. Independence in the 19th century led to efforts to follow the lead of the United States and constitutions were written with that objective. The results, however, were radically different. With no heritage of self-government (political and economic), the result was a half-century of civil wars to attempt to fill the vacuum left by Iberian rule. It also was the creation of political and economic institutions dominated by personal exchange that led to political instability and economic monopolies that persist in much of that continent to this day, with adverse consequences for dynamic economic growth.

The perpetuation of open-access societies like the United States in a world of continuous novel change raises a fundamental institutional dilemma at the heart of the issue of economic development and of successful dynamic change. By uncertainty, we mean that we do not know what is going to happen in the future, and that condition characterizes the world we have been creating. How can our minds make sense of new and novel conditions that are continually occurring? The answer that in fact has proven successful in the case of the United States and other open-access societies is the creation of an institutional structure that maximizes trials and eliminates errors and, therefore, maximizes the potential for achieving a successful outcome—a condition first prescribed by Friedrich Hayek many years ago and still the prescription for an adaptively efficient society. Such an institutional structure is derived from an underlying belief system that recognizes the tentative nature of our understanding of the world around us.

What about China? China partially opened competitive access to its economic markets. But China is barely halfway there. The society is still dominated by a political dictatorship and, as a result, personal exchange rather than impersonal rules dominate the economy. How will China evolve? It could continue to evolve open-access economic markets built on impersonal rules and gradually dissolve the barriers to open political markets. . . . Or the political dictatorship could perceive the evolving open-access society as a threat to the existing vested interests, and halt the course of the past decades.

Case Discussion Questions

1. What role do institutions play in economic development?
2. What is behind the differences in economic development between North and South America?
3. Some argue that a democratic political system is conducive to economic growth. How does the experience of recent Chinese economic development support or refute this statement?
4. If you were a policymaker in a poor country or a World Bank official, what would be your advice, based on North's article and China's experience, for the most effective economic development?

INTEGRATIVE CASE 1.2

DP WORLD

C. Gopinath
Suffolk University

On February 13, 2006, the shareholders of Peninsular & Oriental Steam Navigation Co. of London (P&O) confirmed sale of their company to Dubai Ports World (DP World). Through this act, the management of port operations in five US ports also came under DP World's purview. On March 9, DP World announced that it would divest the US port operations.

The intervening 25 days saw a flurry of activity in the United States with politicians of all shades of opinion, news programs, administration officials, and assorted experts debating the pros and cons of the deal. The outcome of the deal was seen to have much larger implications than mere port management. It raised issues of national security, the investments of petrodollars around the world, US policy toward foreign investment, political risk, and the attitudes of Americans toward the Arabs.

A Dubai Company

Since 1999, DP World, a Dubai government-owned company, had begun a strategy of aggressive growth. With the acquisition of P&O, it became the world's third largest port operator, with operations in 13 countries, including China, India, Germany, Australia, the United Kingdom, and the Dominican Republic. The acquisition of P&O was the successful outcome of a bidding war against Singapore's Temasek Holdings for $6.8 billion. (Being privately owned, DP World's revenues and profit figures are not publicly accessible.)

Dubai is the second largest of a federation of seven semiautonomous city-states, which became the United Arab Emirates (UAE) in 1971. It has a population of about four million, of whom only about 20% are citizens. Like most of the other countries in the region, Dubai depends on a large number of expatriate workers from South Asia (India, Pakistan, and Bangladesh) to run the country. Its has also attracted a number of British, Australian, and Americans who have come to work or retire.

Dubai attempts to balance the demands on its being a Middle Eastern state with its desire to play a larger role in the world. The UAE is a part of the boycott of Israel called by the Arab League since the early 1990s, although it ignores this in practice. It also does not recognize US sanctions against Iran. As the UAE does not have any direct links with Israel, products are not shipped directly from Israel but are allowed to enter from third countries.

Unlike some of its neighboring states, Dubai gets only a small share of its income from oil and has worked hard over the years to build the country as a business hub and tourism destination. It does not have income taxes. Dubai is a popular shopping center in the region with glitzy malls, extravagant hotels, and amusement parks. All major luxury brands of the world have outlets there. Apart from tourism, it is also the regional headquarters of many of the world's large financial institutions. Dubai built its port to world-class levels, and it also operates the biggest airline of the area, Emirates Air. More than 500 US companies operate in the UAE.

The Dubai government has been using its oil revenues to make major investments around the world. It has purchased hotels and property in the US and UK. It recently purchased a $1 billion stake in DaimlerChrysler AG and became the third largest shareholder.[1]

Given its strategic geographic location and small size, the country has tried to maintain good relations with countries in the region and outside. It stayed neutral during the Iran-Iraq war in the 1980s. The UAE is considered a key ally by the US administration. It cooperates militarily and hosts US naval vessels since its ports are capable of receiving large aircraft carriers and nuclear submarines. It also has an airbase for refueling US military planes.

On the other hand, two of the hijackers who participated in the September 11, 2001, terrorist attacks in the United States were from the UAE. Even before that, it was one of three countries (apart from Pakistan and Saudi Arabia) that officially recognized the Taliban regime in Afghanistan. The UAE was also seen as a transit point for Iran and Pakistan to move contraband nuclear materials, and its banking facilities are believed to be used by terrorist groups. After the terrorist attacks, the country had worked hard to strengthen controls on its financial system.

Investment in US Ports

Through this purchase, the operations by P&O in five ports in the US passed on to DP World's hands. These included New York/New Jersey, Philadelphia, Baltimore, Miami, and New Orleans. Of these, the New York/New Jersey and Miami terminals are considered the more attractive ones, and in these two, P&O shared ownership with other operators. Apart from the five marine terminal operations, P&O's operations included cargo handling and cruise ship services in 22 ports in the United States.[2]

The management of the five ports was not the first venture of DP World in the US. In a previous deal, DP World had purchased the international terminal business of CSX Corp. of Jacksonville, Florida, for $1.15 billion in December 2004.

All foreign investment in the United States needs to be approved by the US Committee on Foreign Investment (CFIUS). The late 1980s saw a lot of debate in the US about increasing Japanese investments. In response, US Congress passed the Omnibus Trade and Competitiveness Act of 1988 (Exon-Florio Amendment) to the Defense Production Act of 1950, which empowered the president to block foreign acquisition proposals on grounds of national security. This role was assigned to CFIUS.

CFIUS comes under the Department of Treasury and is an interagency committee chaired by the department's Secretary. There are 12 members including the Secretaries of State, Defense, Commerce, and Homeland Security, Attorney General, Director of the Office of Management and Budget, US Trade Representative, Chairman of the Council of Economic Advisers, Assis-

---

This case was written by C. Gopinath (Suffolk University, Boston, MA).

tant to the President for Economic Policy, Assistant to the President for National Security, and Director of the Office of Science and Technology. On receipt of notification, it undertakes a 30-day review, and in some cases, an additional 45-day period for investigation is allowed, after which it makes a recommendation to the president. The committee since 1988 had reviewed about 1,600 transactions. Of these, only about 25 were investigated further.

In mid-October 2005, even before formally approaching P&O about the acquisition, DP World retained the services of two lawyers in Washington, DC, to informally negotiate with CFIUS and seek its approval. This is normal practice, and often a lot of the work involved in such reviews is undertaken even before a formal application. After completing the deal with P&O and formally announcing the deal, DP World, in mid-November 2005, made its formal application to CFIUS, which was approved on January 16, 2006. At that time, the company also put forward a package of commitments on security, such as allowing US officials to examine company records and check the background of its employees and to separate the port terminal operations from the rest of the country.

When information about the deal appeared in the press, Eller & Co., a stevedoring company in Miami that had a joint venture with P&O, decided it did not want to be an "involuntary partner" of DP World[3] pursuant to the acquisition. Therefore, Eller retained the services of a lobbyist in Washington, Mr. Joe Muldoon, who began researching the issues involved in the P&O acquisition and contacted several legislators in February, when they returned from their January recess. One of those senators was Mr. Charles Schumer, Democrat from New York (where one of the ports is situated), who was also on the Banking Committee in the Senate. Meanwhile, the Associated Press also contacted Mr. Schumer and issued a report making a connection between the acquisition, the country of Dubai, terrorists, and the vulnerability of the ports to terrorism.[4]

Politicians of different hues were quick to react to the deal. Mr. Schumer addressed a press conference along with the families of those who suffered from the terrorist attacks on September 11, 2001, calling the president to step in and prevent the deal. On February 17, Senator Hillary Clinton, the other senator from New York and also a Democrat, said, "Our port security is too important to place in the hands of foreign governments." Even Republicans (the same party as the president) were opposed to the deal, saying, "Dubai can't be trusted with our critical infrastructure." Another said, "It is my intention to lay the foundation to block the deal."[5] Senator Lindsey Graham (Republican) said, "It's unbelievably tone-deaf politically . . . four years after 9/11, to entertain the idea of turning port security over to a company based in the UAE, [a country that] vows to destroy Israel."[6]

Some political observers felt that the president's low standing in public opinion polls due to dissatisfaction on the progress in the war in Iraq was making some Republican lawmakers challenge and distance themselves from him in preparation for their own reelection battles in November 2006.

News commentators began to raise alarms about the deal. On the same day that P&O announced its purchase, Lou Dobbs, a business anchor on the CNN News channel said, "a country with ties to the Sept. 11 terrorists could soon be running significant operations at some of our most important and largest seaports with full blessing of the Bush White House."[7] Mr. Dobbs was known for taking a nationalist position on issues like immigration and outsourcing and the effects on jobs in the United States. Several radio talk shows picked up the story and filled the airwaves with different interpretations. Moreover, many public and security professionals who had been concerned that the government had not been doing enough for port safety and scanning of containers found the ports takeover as another example of a government that was slackening on security.

In an effort to manage the debate around the deal, the administration clarified that it had asked and received additional security commitments from DP World before giving its clearance. An Israeli shipping company, ZIM Integrated Shipping Services Ltd., even sent a letter to US senators stating that they have used the services of DP World at Dubai and have had no concern about their level of security.[8]

Officials also clarified that security screening was not the responsibility of the commercial port operators but that of US law enforcement agents. However, the misperception that the Middle East company would be responsible for port security persisted in the public impression and was repeated on talk shows.

Ports and Container Operations

Container shipping was pioneered by a US company, Sea Land, in the 1950s. However, during the 1980s, US companies found it difficult to face the competition from companies that were operating under flags of convenience, were thus subject to less stringent tax and regulatory policies, and also used less expensive labor. The shipping industry has been globalized for some time now. None of the major global container shipping companies is US owned. Shipping companies often have subsidiaries to manage terminals to facilitate the cargo they carry.

Most ports are owned by port authorities that are set up by local governments. The authorities lease a terminal to an individual company, which is responsible for port management and operations such as moving the containers from the ships to the warehouses.

Large ports have multiple terminals, and these are operated by different companies. US companies have exited from this business over time because it requires heavy investment, and returns are seen only over the long term. At the Los Angeles port, the terminals are managed by companies from China, Denmark, Japan, Singapore, and Taiwan. The big ports of the United States—namely, Los Angeles, Long Beach, and Oakland in California and New York/New Jersey—handle about half of all containers that pass through the US. At these ports, about 80% of the container terminals are handled by foreign companies, and some are owned by foreign governments.

Companies that manage terminals were often subsidiaries of shipping companies. About 80% of global cargo was handled by five companies around the world, headquartered in Hong Kong (Hutchison Whampoa), Singapore (PSA), Dubai (DP World), Denmark (A.P. Moller-Maersk Terminals), and Germany (Eurogate).

Security[9]

Regardless of whether a US or a foreign company operates the terminal, security at the ports, including inspection of containers, is the responsibility of federal agencies such as the US Coast Guard and the US Customs and Border Protection. The Coast Guard is also authorized to inspect a vessel at sea or at the harbor entrance. About 26,000 containers arrive at US ports every day, and customs agents inspect about 5% of them. About 37% of containers that leave the ports for the highways are screened. Security in the area surrounding the ports is part of the responsibility of the local police.

There are several areas that can do with strengthening to improve security, and they have very little to do with who manages port operations. There is a voluntary program operated by the US government to protect incoming shipments. Many companies have signed up for this, under which the companies develop voluntary security procedures to protect the shipment from the factory to the port. In return, their cargo is processed at a faster pace at the port. Shipments from companies that don't take part in the program may not always be inspected. Even for those who do participate, security is not perfect because the cargo may be open to tampering in transit.

About 40 ports around the world ship approximately 80% of the cargo entering the United States. At the port of shipment, the carrier is required to electronically provide the manifest (list of items being shipped) at least 24 hours before loading. This list is analyzed in a screening center in the US, and customs agents who identify any suspicious items can ask their counterparts at the port of dispatch to screen the containers. However, the US Government Accountability Office reports that as of 2005 about one-third of the containers were not being analyzed, and about one-fourth of those identified as high-risk were not being inspected. Scanners and radiation detectors to screen every single container are available, and their use was estimated to add about $20 to the container.

Opposition Gathers Momentum

Faced with rising criticism, DP World also had a crew of lobbyists and attorneys working on its behalf in Washington. Officials of the UAE embassy were also working closely with people like Senator John Warner (Republican) who was in favor of the deal. Legislation was also being planned to permit the deal subject to conditions such as the terminals being operated by US citizens.

When some members of Congress threatened to pass legislation blocking the sale, President George W. Bush responded on February 21 by saying that he would veto it. He also said that he learned about the deal only after it was approved by his administration. Expressing concern about the implications of the deal, he was quoted as saying, "I want those who are questioning to step up and explain why all of a sudden a Middle Eastern company is held to a different standard than a British company. I am trying to say to the people of the world, 'We'll treat you fairly.'"[10]

By the end of February, a CBS News poll revealed that 70% of participants said that a UAE company should not be permitted to operate US shipping ports. With political objections mounting, DP World on February 26 requested a fresh 45-day review of the deal and offered to hold the American operations separate until the review was completed. The administration agreed to undertake the review.

Although the administration had taken a hard stand initially in supporting the deal, the opposition from within the president's party was strong. Both the leader of the party in the Senate and the speaker in the House of Representatives were opposed to the president on the issue.

Although the US operations only accounted for about 10% of P&O's profits, DP World was keen on making the deal work. The US operations of the company were the destination of cargo from its more significant holdings in Asia, and the company wanted this as a foothold to expand its US operations in the future. Its CEO, Mr. Ted Bilkey, told a US news channel, "We'll do anything possible to make sure this deal goes through."[11]

In keeping with this, the company, on March 7, offered three Republican senators a package of security measures[12] titled "Proposed Solution to the DP World Issue." These proposals, which were in addition to the commitments the company made earlier in January, included:

- Paying for screening devices at all current and future ports the company operates around the world.

- Giving the Department of Homeland Security the right to disapprove the choice of chief executive, board members, security officials, and all senior officers.
- A "supermajority" of the board would be US citizens.
- All records pertaining to its security operations would be maintained on US soil, and these records would be turned over at the request of the US government.
- Its US subsidiary, now managed by a British citizen, would in the future also be headed only by a US or British citizen.
- A Security and Financial Oversight Board would be established, headed by a prominent American who would report annually to the Department of Homeland Security.

Some observers felt that this was truly extraordinary for a foreign company to offer. Although such an offer, if made earlier, may have swayed the debate, by the time it came, positions had already hardened. On March 8, the House Appropriations Committee voted 62 to 2 to block the DP World deal. To make the president's threat of a veto more difficult, the committee attached this as an amendment to a spending bill for the wars in Iraq and Afghanistan. The next day, the Republican congressional leaders conveyed to the president that Congress would kill the deal.

The Bush administration then conveyed a request to Dubai's ruler to sever the US operations to allay fears in the US about security. Officials in the UAE saw this as a situation where President Bush was incurring a loss of face in his dealings with Congress. Consequently, DP World on March 9, 2006, offered to divest the US port operations.

Case Discussion Questions

1. From a resource-based view, why was DP World interested in acquiring US ports? What advantages did it have or was interested in acquiring?
2. From an institution-based view, did this acquisition violate any *formal* laws, rules, and regulations?
3. Also from an institution-based view, what *informal* rules and norms did this acquisition "violate" that triggered such a strong negative reaction in the United States?
4. Did DP World and its American lawyers and other advisors do enough homework?
5. Combining the institution- and resource-based views, what advantages did Eller have that DP World did not have? Did Eller's political strategy make sense?
6. If you were CEO of Hong Kong's Hutchison Whampoa, Singapore's PSA, Denmark's Maersk, or Germany's Eurogate, what lessons would you draw from this case when entertaining the idea of acquiring US port operations?

Notes

[1] Dubai: Business partner of terrorist hotbed, *Wall Street Journal*, February 25–26, 2006, p. A9.

[2] D. Machalaba, DP World's ports sale may not pinch, *Wall Street Journal*, March 11–12, 2006, p. A6.

[3] P. Overby, Lobbyist's last-minute bid set off ports controversy, All Things Considered, National Public Radio (NPR), March 8, 2006, http://www.npr.org/templates/story/story.php?storyId=5252263.

[4] T. Bridis, Associated Press, United Arab Emirates firm may oversee 6 US ports, *Washington Post*, February 12, 2006, p. A17.

[5] D. E. Sanger, Under pressure, Dubai company drops port deal, *New York Times*, March 10, 2006, p. 1

[6] Dubai: Business partner of terrorist hotbed.

[7] G. Hitt & S. Ellison, Dubai firm bows to public outcry, *Wall Street Journal*, March 26, 2006, p. A1.

[8] T. Al-Issawi, Port company ignores boycott, *Boston Globe*, March 3, 2006.

[9] Much of the data in this section is from Our porous port protections, *New York Times*, March 10, 2006, p. A18.

[10] Dubai: Business partner of terrorist hotbed.

[11] In ports furor, a clash over Dubai, *Wall Street Journal*, February 23, 2006, p. A1.

[12] N. King Jr., DP World tried to soothe US waters, *Wall Street Journal*, March 14, 2006, p. A4.

INTEGRATIVE CASE 1.3

TIPS ABOUT CORRUPTION AROUND THE PACIFIC

Andrew Delios
National University of Singapore

"Hey! Wait! Wait! Wait a minute, will you? You forgot something," the stylishly clad waiter yelled at Mr. Biswas, Mr. Lee, and Mr. Lai as they exited the wharf-side restaurant in Monterey, California, in early September 2006.

"Thanks, what'd we forget?" inquired Mr. Biswas of the waiter.

"You left some junk on the table," replied the waiter as he tossed their $1.50 tip at the trio. "Next time leave nothing, or leave a real tip. Don't insult me by leaving a few quarters. Why don't you learn the local customs before you come here again!"

Mr. Lee turned to Mr. Biswas and asked, "What was that all about? I thought we were quite generous to the waiter. What we left could pay for a decent meal in any of our home countries."

"Apparently, we were not," piped in the pragmatic Mr. Lai. "He's obviously angry with our tip. I never know how much to tip. I like the situation in China much better. We never have to tip, and never have to worry about the service. None of this silly calculation of some odd percentage and not knowing who to tip and when."

"It's the same for me in India," said Mr. Biswas. "I go to a restaurant and I don't have to worry about some extra charge to the base price. The waiters just do their jobs, the taxi drivers do their jobs, the bellboy does his job, and I don't have to pay them some bribe to have them do their job. In the US, I don't even know who I am supposed to tip: the waiter, the bellboy, the taxi driver, the hair stylist, the maid, the concierge; and the list just goes on and on."

"Tipping is a crazy custom," Mr. Lee reinforced. "The proprietors should just pay them for the work they do, and they should just do their work without trying to draw extra money from us. Instead, this doesn't happen and I always end up paying too little or too much and I don't even know if it improves the service at all."

"The US is an odd country," continued Mr. Biswas. "It harps on us about corrupt practices in our parts of the world, yet it continues to not only allow, but support, this private sector corruption. Tipping, forget it. It's unnecessary and it's an archaic custom. The Americans should follow our lead and legislate it out of existence."

Mr. Biswas

Mr. Biswas was a 55-year-old home construction contractor from the large city of Mumbai, located on the central west coast of India. He had worked in the housing industry from a young age, driven by a desire to build his own home. Mr. Biswas had experienced several eras in the industry, most recently the opening up of the construction industry following liberalization and other free market reforms in India.

Although the market was opening up in India, Mr. Biswas still felt there was a high degree of bureaucracy in the market. State-level and local municipal officials wielded considerable power when it came to the sale of land necessary for Mr. Biswas's increasingly large developments.

Mr. Biswas did not let this feature of the business environment deter him. He was familiar with the procedures necessary to secure the cooperation of local officials in his land purchases. He understood the expectations of the local officials:

India is large country with a strong bureaucracy. From the days of the British Raj, through independence, to the days of liberalization, there has always been a great deal of power concentred in the civil service and government officials. Even today, with the national government pushing for reforms and liberalization, there is still resistance at the state and local levels to the reforms. The local bureaucrats have entrenched power. They have a long legacy of power, and they aren't afraid to use their power to say yes, to say no, or to say nothing at all. The latter is the worst, when you put in an application or a form or a filing to do business in a particular area, and they just sit on the application.

As they say, sometimes you need to put grease in the wheels. Putting in the grease does not make the wheels turn in ways they are not supposed to turn; it just makes

This case was written by Andrew Delios (National University of Singapore) to provide material for class discussion. It was first published by Ivey Publishing at the University of Western Ontario as "A Few Tips about Corruption in the US" as Case 9B06M089. The author does not intend to illustrate either effective or ineffective handling of a managerial situation. The author may have disguised certain names and other identifying information to protect confidentiality.

the wheels turn better. I don't want the bureaucrats to do something they are not supposed to do, like rig a contract or a bid for my company. I just want them to do what they are supposed to do and to do it fast.

I know what they would like, and I trust that what I give to them will help move the business process forward. Look, in the market today, you can't afford to sit and wait and let your competitors leapfrog you. If that requires me to secure the cooperation of bureaucrats to do the job they are supposed to do, then so be it. In any case, all these problems are caused by the politicians, who refuse to provide enough resources to upgrade the civil service and its staff. I should not have to pay the price for their incompetence, but a bit of money from me will help these poorly paid civil servants lead a better life.

Mr. Lee

Mr. S. M. Lee was a fifth-generation Malaysian with distant Hokkien roots in China, who had founded and operated a large textile business. Although he originally began his business in the island-state of Penang in the 1970s, the commercial growth of this island through the 1980s soon made manufacturing in his local textile plants prohibitively costly.

Mr. Lee's response to the increasingly high-cost environment in Malaysia was rather dramatic. Recognizing the trend toward the development of electronic and high-technology industries in Malaysia, Mr. Lee made the decision to relocate his textile factory to Surabaya in Indonesia.

Mr. Lee relocated this plant in the mid-1980s. He subsequently expanded this plant in the early 1990s, as growth in Asia spurred growth in textile demand. As with many businesses in Asia, Mr. Lee's grew rapidly through the mid-1990s, only to face a severe downturn following the Asian Economic Crisis in the late 1990s. With the return to growth in Asia in the early 2000s, Mr. Lee wanted to set up a new facility to replace his already aged textile factory.

Mr. Lee commented on the process of trying to establish another foreign-owned plant in Indonesia:

When I set up my first plant in Indonesia in 1986, it was quite a challenge. Foreign direct investment (FDI) from Malaysia to Indonesia was not that common. There was a lot I had to learn about operating in Indonesia. I had to find local managers; I had to learn how to pay, train, and motivate the textile workers. Should I use a piece-rate system or should I pay them a flat rate? Operational questions such as these arose nearly every day. I made my share of mistakes, but fortunately, through hard work and some luck, I was able to succeed. Being able to understand Bahasa Indonesia, because I speak Malay, certainly helped.

If I can speak frankly, part of the reason I was able to succeed is that I knew who to partner with. Setting up a plant in Indonesia at that time could not be done as a wholly owned subsidiary; I had to use a joint venture. I also had to obtain the agreement of the government for the plant. At that time, it was not a secret about what one had to do when establishing a foreign business in Indonesia. You had to go to Suharto and his family and somehow get them involved in the business. Either they were involved as a joint venture partner, most often in a silent role, or you involved them at the start-up stage, and after that, they left you alone.

The good thing is that with the Suharto family's involvement, I knew which government official I had to work with, and I knew what the outcome would be. Remember the saying at that time: All would be good if you covered the standard 10% requested by Suharto's wife, Madam Tien, or as she came to be known, Madam Ten.

When making this payment, I had very little worry that I would be cheated or the official would not do what he said he would do. I could run the textile operation with my eyes closed. My friends questioned whether it was right for me to do this with the Suharto family, but I think they did much for Indonesia's development and helped reduce poverty greatly. So I was actually helping the country through my investments.

These days, the situation is quite difficult. Now I know all the operational details. But the big problem for me is securing official approvals for the land and construction of the new plant. I don't know what my tax rates will be, and I don't know who to contact in the government to help me with this. Also, previous Indonesian President Megawati Soekarnoputri began the crackdown on corruption, collusion, and nepotism that were prevalent during the Suharto regime. That said, corruption is still practiced collectively by those sitting in provincial legislative bodies, but now it is riskier to work with local government officials, and there is no guarantee that they will do what you have arranged with them to do. There was none of this uncertainty in the time of Suharto.

Mr. Lai

Mr. X. C. Lai's family has a long and colorful history, as do many families in a country with as long a history as China. Originally from the inland province of Sichuan, Mr. Lai's family moved to the coastal city of Shanghai in the late 19th century. After three generations in Shanghai, in the late 1940s, the generation of Mr. Lai's grandparents went on a diaspora, with one brother moving to Hong Kong, another to Taiwan, and a third to the United States. Mr. Lai's grandfather remained in Shanghai, where Mr. Lai was raised.

Mr. X. C. Lai was raised in a tumultuous period in China's history. With the many changes that took place in China since the communists achieved power in the late-1940s, the country that Mr. Lai grew up in was quite different from present-day China, as echoed in Mr. Lai's comments:

When the open-door policies began to gain traction in the late 1970s, I became acutely aware of the possibilities that existed should these reforms hold. I heard from my extended family in Hong Kong, Taiwan, and the United States of the kinds of opportunities that could arise, and I wanted to be in a position to capitalize on these.

With a bit of effort in the early 1980s, I was able to travel to Shenzhen, and I saw the opportunity for developing manufacturing operations. My cousin in Hong Kong ran a series of small manufacturing operations that produced toys for major companies in the US. My cousin saw that the rising wage costs in Hong Kong were at risk of pricing him out of his contracts.

My cousin and I agreed that the proximity of Shenzhen to Hong Kong, coupled with the plentiful supply of low-cost labor in Shenzhen, as coupled with its status as a Special Economic Zone, could make for a very competitive manufacturing operation. My cousin had the contacts with the Western companies, and he had the knowledge of how to develop the manufacturing plant. It was my task to secure the resources to actually build and operate the plant.

At this time in China's open-door era, there was no real market for me to gather everything I needed to run even a small, labor-intensive manufacturing plant. Many resource decisions such as the supply of electricity, the supply of building materials to build the facility, and even the supply of the plastics and other raw materials to make the toys were still centrally allocated.

Fortunately, I was not the only one who had wanted to develop manufacturing operations in Shenzhen. Through my associates from Shanghai, I was introduced to various officials in Shenzhen. Over time, I began to know these officials. Whenever I visited their offices, I was sure to bring along a gift, such as foreign wine or cigarettes or other items, often secured for me by my cousin in Hong Kong. This practice of gift-giving was nothing out of the ordinary in China at this time. Instead, it would be more unusual if I hadn't brought gifts. I also hosted these officials to dinners and festive occasions. It was a nice way of thanking the officials for their service to the country, since they were paid so poorly by the government.

Occasionally, there was pressure on me to deliver a bit more, especially once our operations started and we were known as being modestly successful, but I resisted this. I wanted to do what was necessary to maintain a good relationship and to be fair and operate by normal practices, but I didn't want to engage in any overtly unusual practices.

Back to the United States

Mr. Biswas, Mr. Lee, and Mr. Lai all agreed that what they were doing was not really different from tipping in the United States. They merely paid a small proportion of their full costs to ensure faster and better assistance from service staff in the government. Surely, this could not be wrong.

Case Discussion Questions

1. What is the definition of corruption? Is tipping in the private sector corruption? Why or why not?
2. Why do Mr. Lee, Mr. Biswas, and Mr. Lai have such difficulty understanding the practice of tipping? Should it not be second nature to know how to tip?
3. Is what Mr. Biswas does in India corruption? Why or why not?
4. Is what Mr. Lee does in Indonesia corruption? Why or why not?
5. Is what Mr. Lai does in China corruption? Why or why not?
6. Is corruption good or bad? Can it be both? Be prepared to defend your answer. Can this answer be used to develop a company policy for guiding its employees in their business decisions when operating domestically or abroad?

INTEGRATIVE CASE 1.4

PRIVATE MILITARY COMPANIES: DOGS OF WAR OR PUSSYCATS OF PEACE?

Mike W. Peng
University of Texas at Dallas

This industry dates back to thousands of years ago, is visible in TV news almost every day (at least since September 11, 2001), is global in nature, and has annual sales of $100 billion. Yet, participants do not even agree on how to label it, and most outsiders are clueless about its entrepreneurial nature and ethical dilemma. So, what industry is this? Many journalists and scholars call it the "private military industry." Others label it the "private security industry"—a leading British industry association, formed in 2006, calls itself the British Association of Private Security Companies (BAPSC). A leading American industry association, founded in 2001, names itself the International Peace Operations Association (IPOA) and has coined post-modern labels the "peace and stability industry" and the "peace operations industry." For compositional simplicity, in this case, we call this industry "private military industry" to emphasize its twin nature of private and military. Companies in this industry are thus called "private military companies" (PMCs).

From Rome to Iraq

The roots of this industry can be found in mercenaries. In fact, the very word "soldier" derives from *solidus*, the Roman gold coin. In other words, a soldier, by classical definition, is one who fought for money. During the American Revolution, mercenaries from Germany fought on the British side. The stereotype of mercenaries is the "dogs of war" who help win civil wars and topple governments (usually in resource-rich African countries).

However, modern PMCs hate to be associated with mercenaries. Today's PMCs are proud of their professionalism and value added. Led by entrepreneurs who are often retired military officers, PMCs compete globally. There are three main types. First, closest to the battlefield are "military provider firms" that supply hired guns (often known as "private contractors") who serve alongside national military forces. Blackwater (see Postscript) is perhaps the best-known military provider firm. Second, "military consulting firms" offer assistance but do not engage in the battlefield. One example is Military Professional Resources, Inc. Third, "military support firms," such as Halliburton, provide non-lethal support, such as intelligence, logistics, technical support, and transportation. One of the rare publicly listed PMCs is DynCorp that went public in May 2006 (NYSE: DCP). It has more than 14,400 employees and generates about $2 billion revenue around the world.

A DynCorp employee guards an Afghan official.

Entrepreneurs thrive on chaos. To PMCs, the war in Iraq has been a pot of gold. While US allies have been withdrawing their forces, PMCs rush in. They have grown into the second *largest* military contingent in Iraq (about 20,000 to 30,000 personnel), after the US (national) forces. Private soldiers drive convoy trucks, build camps, guard dignitaries, and gather intelligence. The most lucrative job is not "guns on trucks" but the less glamorous but more steady work such as logistics. Well-muscled men with wraparound sunglasses may steal headlines (especially after they allegedly shoot Iraqi civilians), but the real money is in other lines of work.

Long before Iraq, the use of PMCs alongside US troops had become an indispensable component of America's "total force." In an age of outsourcing, the Pentagon has followed suit, contracting dozens of PMCs to carry out essential military work that was once exclusively performed by uniformed soldiers. Not surprisingly, the driver behind such outsourcing is cost—both political and financial. Dead private soldiers mean fewer dead uniformed soldiers. Military casualties in Iraq are carefully recorded and provoke fierce antiwar protests. Neither the media nor the public seem to care about PMC casualties, although about 700 have died in Iraq.

Global Competition and Challenges

While well-connected American PMCs often win big contracts handed out by the US government, the competition is global. British PMCs, whose services represent Britain's biggest export to Iraq, grab more work from the private sector. Why are the British so competitive in this line of work? Three reasons. First, many British PMCs are first movers, tracing their roots to the days when they were real mercenaries active in Africa when the British Empire collapsed in the 1950s and 1960s. Second, British PMCs benefit from the clustering of many energy and mining companies in London, whose dangerous work often demands more security services. Third, British PMCs recruit from the British army, whose soldiers patrolled the mean streets of Northern Ireland without killing too many civilians. Such portable skills are highly sought after in Iraq now.

There are two ethical challenges associated with PMCs. The first is the morality issue associated with their deployment. For regular soldiers, aid workers, and government officials, an instinctive reaction is: Why should we respect these people who fight for money? Nevertheless, privatization of government services is a global trend in general. In the military arena, the cost effectiveness of PMCs is compelling. Some argue that the UN Security Council should have contracted PMC services to limit the Rwanda genocide in the 1990s, as it was contemplating at the time but failed to do so. The new genocide in Sudan's Darfur region and UN member countries' hesitation to commit national troops as

---

This case was written by Mike W. Peng (University of Texas at Dallas) for educational purposes. Its preparation was supported in part by a National Science Foundation CAREER grant (SES 0552089). This case is based entirely on published sources. The views expressed are those of the author and not those of the NSF.

Blue Helmets have again led to calls for PMCs, which, in theory, can be deployed more rapidly and at a lower cost than Blue Helmets.

The second and probably larger challenge confronting PMCs is accountability—or the apparent lack of it. For example, private contractors were involved in the torture scandal at the Abu Ghraib prison in Baghdad, but only military personnel were court-martialed while private contractors were outside the scope of court-martial jurisdiction. Further, contracts are often impossible to monitor, particularly when private soldiers are deployed in dangerous situations. Where there is no accountability, "rogue" firms and individuals may enter, severely undermining the industry's reputation.

The presence of PMCs in conflict and post-conflict environments creates a significant institutional challenge as to what and whose rules of the game should govern PMCs. During a traditional war, national militaries are governed by the law of war—or more specifically the law of armed conflicts—whose most famous institution is the Geneva Convention. At all other times, the law of peace prevails and civilian casualties are not acceptable. However, the distinction between "war" and "peace" has broken down. Technically, US Congress has never issued a declaration of war against Iraq, but nobody can argue there is "peace" in Iraq since 2003. Given such ambiguity of "neither war nor peace," PMCs are essentially unregulated.

However, as the industry aspires to become a "mature" one by diversifying into post-conflict reconstruction and risk management (after all, there are only so many shooting wars to fight), its current unregulated nature is not sustainable. In the absence of regulation, PMCs' seemingly secretive nature prevents them from being recognized as legitimate players. In response, the PMC community has recently set up the IPOA and BAPSC in order to advocate self-regulation. A very unmercenary Code of Conduct governing all IPOA members went into effect in 2001. Its 11th revision, publicized in 2006, promised that member PMCs only work for legitimate governments and organizations and that all rules of engagement must "emphasize appropriate restraint and caution to minimize casualties and damage." In the long run, PMCs adhering to "aggressive self-regulation" hope to be perceived as reliable, professional, and high-quality service providers. Far from being the dogs of war, declared BAPSC's director-general, "we are actually the pussycats of peace." This thought-provoking statement is indicative of the ethical dilemma of PMCs: while they prefer to dispel any mercenary notion that they are dogs of war, they also thrive on the mean-and-tough warrior mystique. After all, wrote the *Economist*, "who would use a pussycat as a guard-dog?"

Postscript

Before this book went to press in October 2007, Blackwater, a leading PMC, found itself in hot water. The Iraqi government alleged that on September 16, 2007, Blackwater personnel opened fire indiscriminately at a Baghdad crossroads and killed 17 innocent civilians. Blackwater maintained that its men were under fire. Because Blackwater (and other PMCs) were formally immune from Iraqi law, the best that the Iraqi government could do was to demand that Blackwater leave the country. US Congress was in an uproar concerning such an embarrassing incident, and in October 2007 held a hearing on Blackwater—and in fact on the entire private military industry. Naturally, Blackwater's staunchest defenders tended to be the US officials protected by its private soldiers. US officials preferred Blackwater and other PMCs because PMC personnel were regarded as more highly trained than (national) military guards. Blackwater's founder, Erik Prince, told the Congressional committee that "no individual protected by Blackwater has ever been killed or seriously injured," while 30 of its staff died while on the job. While measures for increased legal and regulatory oversight were called for by the highest levels of the US government, whether these measures would be implemented on the messy and dangerous ground in Iraq (and elsewhere) remains to be seen.

Case Discussion Questions:

1. From an institution-based view, explain what is behind the rise of this industry.
2. From a resource-based standpoint, explain why certain PMCs outperform others.
3. Why are industry associations such as the IPOA and BAPSC so interested in self-regulation?
4. As an investor, would you consider buying stock in a PMC such as DynCorp? Why or why not? Do you have any ethical reservations?
5. As an oil company executive setting up operations in a politically unstable and dangerous country, would you consider hiring security personnel from Blackwater?

Sources: Based on (1) A. Bearpark & S. Schulz, 2006, The regulation of the private security industry and the future of the market, http://bapsc.org.uk (accessed January 8, 2007); (2) *Business Week*, 2006, Tainted past? No problem, July 17: 71–72; (3) *Economist*, 2006, Blood and treasure, November 4: 70; (4) *Economist*, 2006, Who dares profits? May 20: 60; (5) *Economist*, 2007, Blackwater in hot water, October 13: 51; (6) International Peace Operations Association, 2006, Code of conduct, http://ipoaonline.org (accessed January 8, 2007); (7) *Newsweek*, 2007, Blackwater is soaked, October 15: 30; (7) C. Ortiz, 2007, Assessing the accountability of private security provision, *Journal of International Peace Operations*, January: 9; (8) P. Singer, 2003, *Corporate Warriors*, Ithaca, NY: Cornell University Press.

PART 2

Acquiring Tools

CHAPTERS

5 Trading Internationally

6 Investing Abroad Directly

7 Dealing with Foreign Exchange

8 Capitalizing on Global and Regional Integration

North Korea

South Korea

Satellite image of North Korea, South Korea, and neighboring countries at night.

Trading Internationally

OPENING CASE

North Korea versus South Korea

How much difference does international trade make? A lot. The comparison between North Korea and South Korea provides an interesting clue. In 1945, at the time of Korea's liberation from Japanese colonial occupation, the North was slightly more advantageous economically because the North had more industry, whereas the South had only agriculture. However, this mattered very little because the Korean War (1950–1953) devastated the economic fundamentals of both. After the war, both countries essentially started from scratch and were roughly equal in terms of backwardness. Fast forward to 2006 and the differences were striking. North Korea's per capita GDP in 2006 was $1,800 (based on purchasing power parity, PPP), 187th in the world. In contrast, South Korea had a per capita GDP of $22,045 (based on PPP), 16th in the world. So what happened to these two equally devastated countries populated by the same people sharing the same cultural heritage?

After the Korean War, North Korea adopted an isolationist policy of self-sufficiency. Although North Korea received aid from the Soviet Union and China, it refused to join the communist "common market"—the Council for Mutual Economic Assistance (CMEA), which was hardly a practitioner of free trade. The collapse of the Soviet Union has exacerbated North Korea's economy, which has suffered from chronic food shortages. At present, North Korea's only reliable exports are illegal drugs, weapons, and counterfeits. North Korea's nuclear weapons are viewed by experts as an *economic*, not a military, weapon. This is because, sadly, with nothing else to trade with the rest of the world, North Korea's only bargaining chip to extract more donations of rice, oil, and technology from its reluctant donor countries (led by the United States) is to wave its nukes.

In contrast, South Korea undertook a strong export strategy. Since the early 1960s, the government provided extensive export subsidies, adopted policies to encourage inflows of foreign capital, and reduced import barriers. As a result, South Korea became one of the Four Tigers in East Asia, known for its economic prowess (the other three were Hong Kong, Singapore, and Taiwan). This is not to say that the South Korean economy is perfect. It is not, as illustrated by the devastation of the 1997–1998 financial crisis that showed its structural problems. Nevertheless, economically, a weakened South Korea is still much stronger than North Korea. In the last decade, South Korea has bounced back from the crisis and embraced the Internet era. Since 1996, South Korea has been a proud member of the Organization for Economic Cooperation and Development (OECD)—known as "the rich (developed) countries' club," whose only other Asian members are Japan and Singapore. At present, South Korea is the world leader in per capita broadband usage.

Overall, between 1965 and 2004, the average annual GDP growth rate in South Korea was approximately 8%, whereas North Korea trailed increasingly behind, averaging about 3%. Although there are many reasons for the radically different economic performance of the two Koreas, international trade is a crucial component of any answer offered. In 1965, North Korea's international trade volume was about two-thirds of South Korea's. By 2005, South Korea's trade volume beat North Korea's by 170 times.

Sources: This case was prepared by **Kenny K. Oh** (University of Texas at Dallas) under the supervision of Professor Mike W. Peng. It was based on (1) *Business Week*, 2003, The other Korean crisis, January 20: 44–52; (2) *CIA— World Factbook*, http://www.cia.gov; (3) S. Kim, B. Kim, & K. Lee, 2006, Assessing the economic performance of North Korea, 1954–1989, *Proceedings of Annual Meetings of Allied Social Sciences Association.*

LEARNING OBJECTIVES

After studying this chapter, you should be able to

1. use the resource- and institution-based views to explain why nations trade
2. understand classical and modern theories of international trade
3. realize the importance of political and economic realities governing international trade
4. participate in two leading debates on international trade
5. draw implications for action

Why does North Korea choose to isolate itself economically? Why does South Korea embrace international trade? Why has North Korea remained very poor, whereas South Korea has become a developed economy? International trade is the oldest and still the most important building block of international business. It has never failed to generate debates. Debates on international trade tend to be very ferocious because, as powerfully illustrated by our Opening Case, so much is at stake.

We begin by addressing the crucial issue of why nations trade. Then we outline how the two core perspectives introduced in earlier chapters—namely, resource- and institution-based views—can help us understand this issue. The remainder of the chapter deals with (1) theories and (2) realities of international trade. As before, debates and implications for action follow.

LEARNING OBJECTIVE 1

use the resource- and institution-based views to explain why nations trade

WHY DO NATIONS TRADE?

Other than a few extreme cases such as North Korea, most nations are like South Korea: They actively participate in international trade—consisting of **exporting** (selling abroad) and **importing** (buying from abroad). Table 5.1 provides a snapshot of the top-ten exporting and importing nations in the two main sectors: **merchandise** and **services**. In merchandise trade, China exhibited the strongest growth in 2006, with 27% and 20% annual growth in its exports and imports, respectively. In service trade (whose volume is about one-fourth of merchandise trade) in 2006, India had the strongest export growth (34%) and Spain had the strongest import growth (18%).

exporting
Selling abroad.

importing
Buying from abroad.

merchandise
Tangible products being traded.

services
Intangible services being traded.

Relative to domestic trade, international trade entails much greater complexities. So why do nations go through these troubles to trade internationally? Without getting into details, we can safely say that there must be economic gains from trade. More important, such gains must be shared by *both* sides; otherwise, there will be no willing exporters and importers. In other words, international trade is a *win-win* deal. Figure 5.1 shows that world trade growth (averaging about 6% during 1996–2006) routinely outpaces GDP growth (averaging 3% during 1996–2006), suggesting that the gains from trade must be increasing. Otherwise, international trade would not have grown.

Why are there gains from trade? How do nations benefit from such gains? The remainder of the chapter will answer these questions. Before proceeding, it is important to clarify that "nations trade" is a misleading statement. A more accurate expression would be: "Firms from different nations trade."[1] Unless different governments directly buy and sell from each other (such as arms sales), the majority of trade is conducted by firms, which pay little attention to country-level ramifications. For example, Wal-Mart imports a lot into the United States and does not export much. Wal-Mart thus directly contributes to the US **trade deficit** (a nation imports more than it exports), which is something the US government does not like. However, in most countries, governments cannot tell firms, such as Wal-Mart, what to do (and not to do) unless firms engage in illegal activities. Therefore, we need to be aware that when we ask "Why do nations trade?" we are really asking "Why do firms from different nations trade?" When discussing the US-China trade whereby China runs a **trade surplus** (a nation exports more than it imports), we are really referring to thousands of US firms buying from and selling to China, which also has thousands of firms buying from and selling to the United

trade deficit
An economic condition in which a nation imports more than it exports.

trade surplus
An economic condition in which a nation exports more than it imports.

TABLE 5.1 LEADING TRADING NATIONS

	Top-10 merchandise exporters	Value ($ billion)	World share	Annual change		Top-10 merchandise importers	Value ($ billion)	World share	Annual change
1	Germany	1,112	9.2%	15%	1	United States	1,920	15.5%	11%
2	United States	1,037	8.6%	14%	2	Germany	910	7.4%	17%
3	China	969	8.0%	27%	3	China	792	6.4%	20%
4	Japan	647	5.4%	9%	4	United Kingdom	601	4.9%	17%
5	France	490	4.1%	6%	5	Japan	577	4.7%	12%
6	Netherlands	462	3.8%	14%	6	France	533	4.3%	6%
7	United Kingdom	443	3.7%	15%	7	Italy	436	3.5%	13%
8	Italy	410	3.4%	10%	8	Netherlands	416	3.4%	14%
9	Canada	388	3.2%	8%	9	Canada	357	2.9%	11%
10	Belgium	372	3.1%	11%	10	Belgium	356	2.9%	12%
	World total	**12,062**	**100%**	**15%**		**World total**	**12,380**	**100%**	**14%**

	Top-10 service exporters	Value ($ billion)	World share	Annual change		Top-10 service importers	Value ($ billion)	World share	Annual change
1	United States	387	14.3%	9%	1	United States	307	11.7%	9%
2	United Kingdom	223	8.2%	9%	2	Germany	215	8.2%	7%
3	Germany	164	6.1%	11%	3	United Kingdom	169	6.5%	6%
4	Japan	121	4.5%	12%	4	Japan	143	5.5%	8%
5	France	112	4.1%	-2%	5	France	108	4.1%	3%
6	Italy	101	3.7%	13%	6	Italy	101	3.9%	14%
7	Spain	100	3.7%	8%	7	China	100	3.8%	15%
8	China	87	3.2%	7%	8	Netherlands	78	3.0%	7%
9	Netherlands	82	3.0%	4%	9	Ireland	77	3.0%	11%
10	India	73	2.7%	34%	10	Spain	77	2.9%	18%
	World total	**2,710**	**100%**	**11%**		**World total**	**2,620**	**100%**	**10%**

Source: World Trade Organization, 2007, *World trade 2006*, Press release, April 12, http://www.wto.org. All data are for 2006.

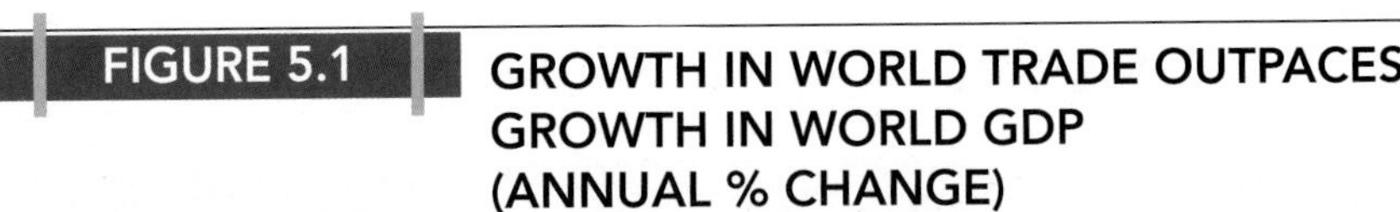

FIGURE 5.1 GROWTH IN WORLD TRADE OUTPACES GROWTH IN WORLD GDP (ANNUAL % CHANGE)

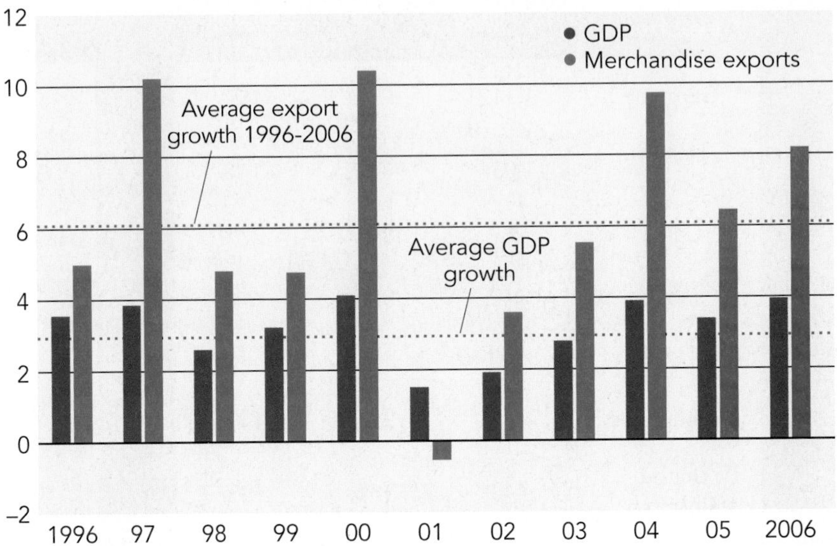

Source: World Trade Organization, 2007, *World trade 2006, prospects for 2007*, press release, April 12, http://www.wto.org.

balance of trade
The aggregation of importing and exporting that leads to the country-level trade surplus or deficit.

States. The aggregation of such buying (importing) and selling (exporting) by both sides leads to the country-level **balance of trade**—namely, whether a country has a trade surplus or deficit.

Having acknowledged the limitations of statements such as "nations trade," we will still use them. This is not only because these expressions have been commonly used but also because they serve as a shorthand version of the more accurate but more cumbersome ones such as "firms from different nations trade." This clarification does enable us to use the two *firm-level* perspectives introduced earlier—namely, the resource- and institution-based views—to shed light on why nations trade.

Recall from Chapter 4 that it is valuable, rare, inimitable, and organizationally derived (VRIO) products that determine the competitive advantage of a firm. Applying this insight, we can suggest that valuable, rare, and inimitable products generated by organizationally strong firms in one nation can lead to the competitive advantage of a nation's exports.[2] Further, recall from Chapters 2 and 3 that numerous politically and culturally derived rules of the game, known as institutions, constrain individual and firm behavior. For example, although American movies are the best in the world, Canada, France, and South Korea limit the market share of American movies to protect their domestic movies. Likewise, although oil from Saudi Arabia may be of the highest quality, most oil-importing nations cry out loud in fear of "dangerous" foreign oil dependence. Thus, various regulations create trade barriers around the world. On the other hand, we also see the rise of rules that facilitate trade, such as those promoted by the World Trade Organization (WTO—see Chapter 8).

Overall, why are there economic gains from international trade? According to the resource-based view, this is because some firms in one nation generate exports that are valuable, unique, and hard to imitate that firms from other nations find it beneficial to import. How do firms and nations benefit from such gains? According to the institution-based view, different rules governing trade are designed to share such gains. The remainder of this chapter expands on these two perspectives.

THEORIES OF INTERNATIONAL TRADE

LEARNING OBJECTIVE 2

understand classical and modern theories of international trade

Theories of international trade provide one of the oldest, richest, and most influential bodies of economics, whose founding is usually associated with the publication of Adam Smith's *The Wealth of Nations* in 1776. Theories of international trade predate Adam Smith; in fact, Adam Smith wrote *The Wealth of Nations* to challenge an earlier theory: mercantilism. In this section, we briefly review major theories of international trade: (1) mercantilism, (2) absolute advantage, (3) comparative advantage, (4) product life cycle, (5) strategic trade, and (6) national competitive advantage. The first three are often regarded as **classical trade theories**, and the last three are viewed as **modern trade theories**.

classical trade theories
The major theories of international trade that were advanced before the 20th century, which consist of mercantilism, absolute advantage, and comparative advantage.

modern trade theories
The major theories of international trade that were advanced in the 20th century, which consist of product life cycle, strategic trade, and national competitive advantage.

Mercantilism

Widely practiced during the 1600s and 1700s, the **theory of mercantilism** viewed international trade as a zero-sum game. Its theorists, led by French statesman Jean-Baptiste Colbert, believed that the wealth of the world (measured in gold and silver at that time) was fixed and that a nation that exported more and imported less would enjoy the net inflows of gold and silver and thus become richer. On the other hand, a nation experiencing a trade deficit would see its gold and silver flowing out and, consequently, would become poorer. The upshot? Self-sufficiency would be best.

Although mercantilism is the oldest theory in international trade, it is not an extinct dinosaur. Very much alive, mercantilism is the direct intellectual ancestor of modern-day **protectionism**, which is the idea that governments should actively protect domestic industries from imports and vigorously promote exports. Even today, many modern governments may still be mercantilist at heart.

theory of mercantilism
A theory that holds the wealth of the world (measured in gold and silver) is fixed and that a nation that exports more and imports less would enjoy the net inflows of gold and silver and thus become richer.

protectionism
The idea that governments should actively protect domestic industries from imports and vigorously promote exports.

Absolute Advantage

The theory of absolute advantage, advocated by Adam Smith in 1776, opened the floodgates of the free trade movement that is still going on today. Smith argued that in the aggregate, it is the "invisible hand" of markets, rather than governments, that should determine the scale and scope of economic activities. This is known as *laissez faire* (see Chapter 2). By trying to be self-sufficient and to (inefficiently) produce a wide range of goods, mercantilist policies *reduce* the wealth of a nation in the long run. Smith thus argued for **free trade**, which is the idea that free market forces should determine how much to trade with little (or no) government intervention.

Specifically, Smith proposed a **theory of absolute advantage**: Under free trade, each nation gains by specializing in economic activities in which a nation has absolute advantage. What is **absolute advantage**? It is the economic advantage one nation enjoys that is absolutely superior to other nations. For example, Smith argued that because of better soil, water, and weather, Portugal enjoyed an absolute advantage over England in the production of grapes and wines. Likewise, England had an absolute advantage over Portugal in the production of sheep and wool. England could grow grapes at a greater cost and with much lower quality—has anyone heard of any world famous English wines? Smith suggested that England should specialize in sheep and wool, Portugal should

free trade
A theory that suggests that under free trade, each nation gains by specializing in economic activities in which it has absolute advantage.

theory of absolute advantage
A thoery that suggests that under free trade, each nation gains by specializing in economic activities in which it has absolute advantage.

absolute advantage
The economic advantage one nation enjoys that is absolutely superior to other nations.

specialize in grapes and wines, and they should trade with each other. Smith's greatest insights were in the argument (1) that by specializing in the production of goods for which each has an absolute advantage, both can produce more, and (2) that by trading, both can benefit more. In other words, international trade is not a zero-sum game as suggested by mercantilism. It is a *win-win* game.

How can this be? Let us use an example with hypothetical numbers (Figure 5.2 and Table 5.2). For the sake of simplicity, assume there are only two nations in the world: China and the United States. They perform only two economic activities: grow wheat and make aircraft. Production of wheat or aircraft, naturally, requires resources such as labor, land, and technology. Assume that both are equally endowed with 800 units of resources. Between the two activities, the United States has an absolute advantage in the production of aircraft—it takes 20 resources to produce an aircraft (for which China needs 40 resources) and the total US capacity is 40 aircraft if it does not produce wheat (point D in Figure 5.2). China has an absolute advantage in the production of wheat—it takes 20 resources to produce 1,000 tons of wheat (for which the United States needs 80 resources) and the total Chinese capacity is 40,000 tons of wheat if it does not make aircraft (point A). It is important to note that the United States can grow wheat and China can make aircraft, albeit inefficiently. But because both nations need wheat and aircraft, without trade, they pro-

FIGURE 5.2 ABSOLUTE ADVANTAGE

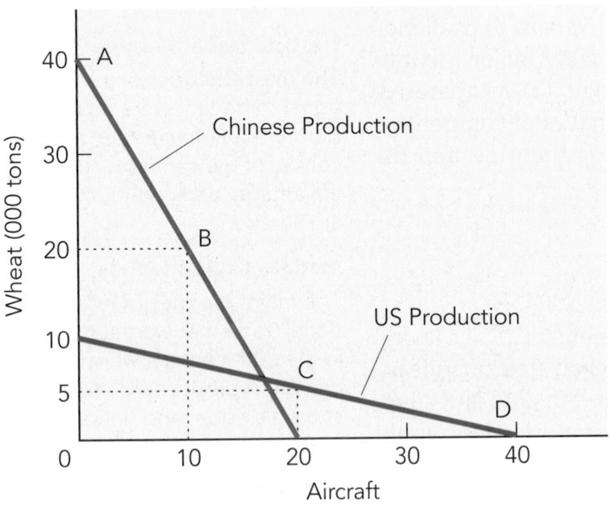

TABLE 5.2 ABSOLUTE ADVANTAGE

Total units of resources = 800 for each country		Wheat	Aircraft
1. Resources required to produce 1,000 tons of wheat and 1 aircraft	China	20 resources	40 resources
	US	80 resources	20 resources
2. Production and consumption with no specialization and without trade (each country devotes *half* of its resources to each activity)	China (point B)	20,000 tons	10 aircraft
	US (point C)	5,000 tons	20 aircraft
	Total production	**25,000 tons**	**30 aircraft**
3. Production with specialization (China specializes in wheat and produces no aircraft, and the United States specializes in aircraft and produces no wheat)	China (point A)	40,000 tons	0
	US (point D)	0	40 aircraft
	Total production	**40,000 tons**	**40 aircraft**
4. Consumption after each country trades one-fourth of its output while producing at points A and D, respectively (Scenario 3)	China	30,000 tons	10 aircraft
	US	10,000 tons	30 aircraft
	Total consumption	**40,000 tons**	**40 aircraft**
5. *Gains* from trade: Increase in consumption as a result of specialization and trade (Scenario 4 versus 2)	China	+10,000 tons	0
	US	+5,000 tons	+10 aircraft

Is it necessary for a country to have an absolute advantage in some activity, such as the production of a particular crop, in order to participate in international trade?

duce both by spending half of their resources on each—China at point B (20,000 tons of wheat and 10 aircraft) and the United States at point C (5,000 tons of wheat and 20 aircraft). Interestingly, if they stay at points A and D, respectively, and trade one-quarter of their output with each other (that is, 10,000 tons of Chinese wheat with 10 American aircraft), these two countries, and by implication the global economy, both produce more and consume more (Table 5.2). In other words, there are *net* gains from trade based on absolute advantage.

Comparative Advantage

According to Adam Smith, each nation should look for absolute advantage. However, what can nations do when they do *not* possess absolute advantage? Continuing our two-country example of China and the United States, what if China is absolutely inferior to the United States in the production of both wheat and aircraft (which is the real case today)? What should China do? What should the United States do? Obviously, the theory of absolute advantage runs into a dead end.

In response, British economist David Ricardo developed a **theory of comparative advantage** in 1817. This theory suggests that even though the United States has an absolute advantage over China in both wheat and aircraft, as long as China is not equally less efficient in the production of both goods, China can still choose to specialize in the production of one good (such as wheat) in which it has **comparative advantage**—defined as the relative (not absolute) advantage in one economic activity that one nation enjoys in comparison with other nations. Figure 5.3 and Table 5.3 show that China's comparative advantage lies in its *relatively less inefficient* production of wheat: If China devotes all resources to wheat, it can produce 10,000 tons, which is four-fifths of the 12,500 tons the United States can produce. However, at a maximum, China can produce only 20 aircraft, which is merely one-half of the 40 aircraft the United States can make. By letting China specialize in the production of wheat and importing some wheat from China, the United States is able to leverage its strengths by devoting its resources to aircraft. For example, if (1) the United States devotes four-fifths of its resources to aircraft and one-fifth to wheat (point C of Figure 5.3), (2) China concentrates 100% of its

theory of comparative advantage
A theory that focuses on the relative (not absolute) advantage in one economic activity that one nation enjoys in comparison with other nations.

comparative advantage
Relative (not absolute) advantage in one economic activity that one nation enjoys in comparison with other nations.

opportunity cost
Given the alternatives (opportunities), the cost of pursuing one activity at the expense of another activity.

resources on wheat (point E), and (3) trading with each other, both countries produce and consume more than what they would produce and consume if they inefficiently devote half of their resources to each activity (see Table 5.3).

Again, there are net gains from trade, this time from comparative advantage. One crucial concept here is **opportunity cost**—given the alternatives (opportunities), the cost of pursuing one activity at the expense of another activity. For the United States, the opportunity cost of concentrating on wheat at point A in Figure 5.3 is tremendous relative to producing aircraft at point D, because it is only 25% more productive in wheat than China but is 100% more productive in aircraft.

Relative to absolute advantage, the theory of comparative advantage seems counterintuitive. However, this theory is far more realistic and useful in the real world. This is because it is easy to identify an absolute advantage in a highly simplified, two-country world, as in Figure 5.2, but how can each nation decide what to specialize in when there are more than 200 nations in the world? It is simply too challenging to ascertain that one nation is absolutely better than all others in one activity. Is the United States *absolutely* better than not only China but also all other 200 nations in aircraft production? European nations that produce Airbus obviously beg to differ. The theory of comparative advantage suggests that even without an absolute advantage, the United States can still profitably specialize in aircraft as long as it is relatively more efficient than others. This insight has greatly

FIGURE 5.3 COMPARATIVE ADVANTAGE

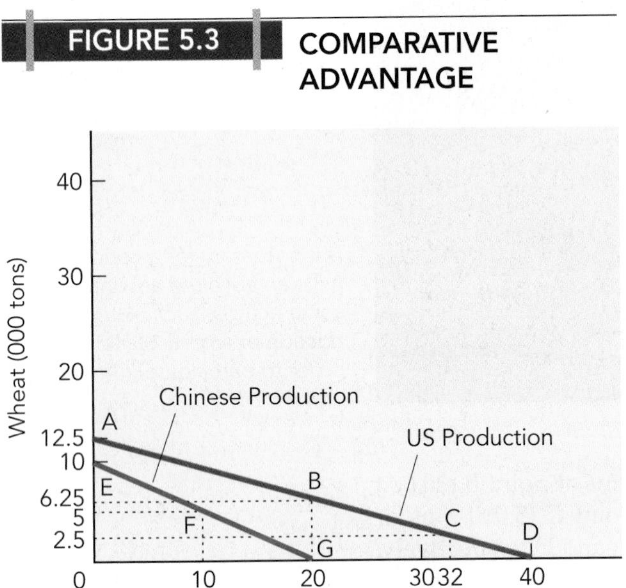

TABLE 5.3 COMPARATIVE ADVANTAGE

Total units of resources = 800 for each country		Wheat	Aircraft
1. Resources required to produce 1,000 tons of wheat and 1 aircraft	China	80 resources	40 resources
	US	64 resources	20 resources
2. Production and consumption with no specialization and without trade (each country devotes *half* of its resources to each activity)	China (point F)	5,000 tons	10 aircraft
	US (point B)	6,250 tons	20 aircraft
	Total production	**11,250 tons**	**30 aircraft**
3. Production with specialization (China devotes all resources to wheat, and the United States devotes one-fifth of its resources to wheat and four-fifths of its resources to aircraft)	China (point E)	10,000 tons	0
	US (point C)	2,500 tons	32 aircraft
	Total production	**12,500 tons**	**32 aircraft**
4. Consumption after China trades 4,000 tons of wheat for 11 US aircraft while producing at points E and C, respectively (Scenario 3)	China	6,000 tons	11 aircraft
	US	6,500 tons	21 aircraft
	Total consumption	**12,500 tons**	**32 aircraft**
5. *Gains* from trade: Increase in consumption as a result of specialization and trade (Scenario 4 versus 2)	China	+1,000 tons	+1 aircraft
	US	+250 tons	+1 aircraft

lowered the threshold for specialization because absolute advantage is no longer required (see In Focus 5.1).

Where do absolute and comparative advantages come from? In one word, productivity. Smith looked at *absolute* productivity differences, and Ricardo emphasized *relative* productivity differences. In this sense, absolute advantage is really a special case of comparative advantage. But what leads to such productivity differences? In the early 20th century, Swedish economists Eli Heckscher and Bertil Ohlin argued that absolute and comparative advantages stem from different **factor endowments**—namely, the extent to which different countries possess various factors, such as labor, land, and technology. This **factor endowment theory** (or **Heckscher-Ohlin theory**) proposed that nations will develop comparative advantage based on their *locally abundant* factors.[3] Numerous examples support the theories of comparative advantage and factor endowments. For instance, Brazil is blessed by its abundant factors of land, water, and weather that enable it to become an agricultural powerhouse. For another example, when Indian firms set up call centers to service Western clients, they use human labor, a factor that is very abundant in India, to replace some automation functions when answering the phone. But in the West, telephone automation technology has been developed because of a labor shortage. Western clients are happier talking with a live person instead of talking to or pressing buttons on a machine (press 1 for this, press 2 for that).

factor endowments
The extent to which different countries possess various factors, such as labor, land, and technology.

factor endowment theory (or **Heckscher-Ohlin theory**)
A theory that suggests that nations will develop comparative advantage based on their locally abundant factors.

In summary, *classical* theories, (1) mercantilism, (2) absolute advantage, and (3) comparative advantage (which includes factor endowments), had evolved from approximately 300 to 400 years ago to the beginning of the 20th century. More recently, three *modern* theories, outlined next, emerged.

IN FOCUS 5.1 Comparative Advantage and You

Despite the seemingly abstract reasoning, the theory of comparative advantage is very practical. Although you may not be aware of it, you have been a practitioner of this theory almost *every day*. How many of you grow your own food, knit your own sweaters, and write your own software? Hardly any! You probably buy everything you consume. By doing this, you are actually practicing this theory. This is because buying your food, sweaters, and software from producers frees up the time it would have taken you to grow your own food, knit sweaters, and write software—even assuming you are multitalented and capable of doing all of the above. As students, you are probably using this time wisely to pursue a major (ranging from accounting to zoology) in which you may have some comparative advantage. After graduation, you will trade your skills (via your employer) with others who need these skills from you. By specializing and trading, rather than producing everything yourself, you help channel the production of food, sweaters, and software to more efficient producers. Some of them may be foreign firms. You and these producers mutually benefit because they can produce more for everyone to consume, and you can concentrate on your studies and build your tradable skills.

Let's assume that at your school, you are the best student receiving all As. At the same time, you also drive a cab at night to earn enough money to put you through school. In fact, you become the best cab driver in town, knowing all the side streets, never getting lost, and making more money than other cab drivers. Needless to say, by studying during the day and driving a cab at night, you don't have a life. However, your efforts are handsomely rewarded when the best company in town hires you after graduation, and very soon, as a fast tracker, you become the best manager in town. Of course, you quit driving a cab after joining the firm. The best cab driver (who doesn't sleep) can earn about $50,000 a year, whereas the best manager (who does sleep) can make $500,000, so your choice would be obvious. One day, you leave your office and jump into a cab to rush to the airport. The cab driver doesn't speak English, misunderstands your instruction, gets lost, and is unnecessarily stuck in a bad traffic jam. As soon as you become irritated because you may miss your flight, you start to smile because you remember today's lecture. "Yes, I have an absolute advantage both in driving a cab and being a good manager compared with this poor cab driver. But by focusing on my comparative advantage in being a good manager," you remember what your professor said, "this cab driver, whose abilities are nowhere near my cab driving skills, can tap into his comparative advantage (funny, he has one!), trade his skills with me, and can still support his family." With this pleasant thought, you end up giving the driver a big tip when arriving at the airport.

Product Life Cycle

Up to this point, classical theories all paint a *static* picture: If England has an absolute or comparative advantage in textiles (mostly because of its factor endowments such as favorable weather and soil), it should keep producing them. However, this assumption of no change in factor endowments and trade patterns does not always hold in the real world. While Adam Smith's England, over 200 years ago, was a major exporter of textiles, today England's textile industry is very insignificant. So what happened? One may argue that in England, weather has changed and soil has become less fertile, but it is difficult to believe that weather and soil have changed so much in 200 years, which is a relatively short period for long-run climatic changes. For another example, since the 1980s, the United States turned from a net exporter to a net importer of personal computers (PCs), while Malaysia transformed itself from a net importer to a net exporter—and this example has nothing to do with weather or soil change. Why do patterns of trade in PCs change over time? Classic theories would have a hard time answering this intriguing question.

product life cycle theory
A theory that accounts for changes in the patterns of trade over time by focusing on product life cycles.

In 1966, American economist Raymond Vernon developed the **product life cycle theory**, which is the first *dynamic* theory to account for changes in the patterns of trade over time.[4] Vernon divided the world into three categories: (1) lead innovation nation (which, according to him, is typically the United States), (2) other developed nations, and (3) developing nations. Further, every product has three life cycle stages: new, maturing, and standardized. Shown in Figure 5.4, in the first stage, production of a new product (such as a VCR) that commands a price premium will concentrate in the United States, which exports to other developed nations. In the second, maturing stage, demand and ability to produce grow in other developed nations (such as Australia and Italy) so it is now worthwhile to produce there. In the third stage, the previously new product is standardized (or commoditized). Therefore, much production will now move to low-cost developing nations, which export to developed nations. In other words, comparative advantage may change over time.

While this theory was first proposed in the 1960s, some later events (such as the migration of PC production) have supported its prediction. However, this theory has been criticized on two accounts. First, it assumes that the United States will always be the lead innovation nation for new products. This may be increasingly invalid. For example, the fanciest cell phones are now routinely pioneered in Asia and Europe. Second, this theory assumes a stage-by-stage migration of production that takes at least several years (if not decades). In reality, however, an increasing number of firms now *simultaneously* launch new products (such as iPods) around the globe.

Strategic Trade

Except for mercantilism, all the theories that have been discussed have nothing to say about the role of governments. Since the days of Adam Smith, government intervention is usually regarded by economists as destroying value because it allegedly distorts free trade. However, government intervention is extensive and is not going away. Can government intervention actually add value? Since the 1970s, a new theory, **strategic trade theory**, has been developed to address this question.[5]

strategic trade theory
A theory that suggests that strategic intervention by governments in certain industries can enhance their odds for international success.

first-mover advantage
Advantage that first entrants enjoy and do not share with late entrants.

Strategic trade theory suggests that strategic intervention by governments in certain industries can enhance their odds for international success. What are these industries? They tend to be highly capital-intensive, high entry-barrier industries that domestic firms may have little chance without government assistance. These industries also feature substantial **first-mover advantages**—namely, advantages that first entrants enjoy and do not share with late entrants. A leading example is the commercial aircraft industry. Founded in 1915 and strengthened

FIGURE 5.4 THEORY OF PRODUCT LIFE CYCLES

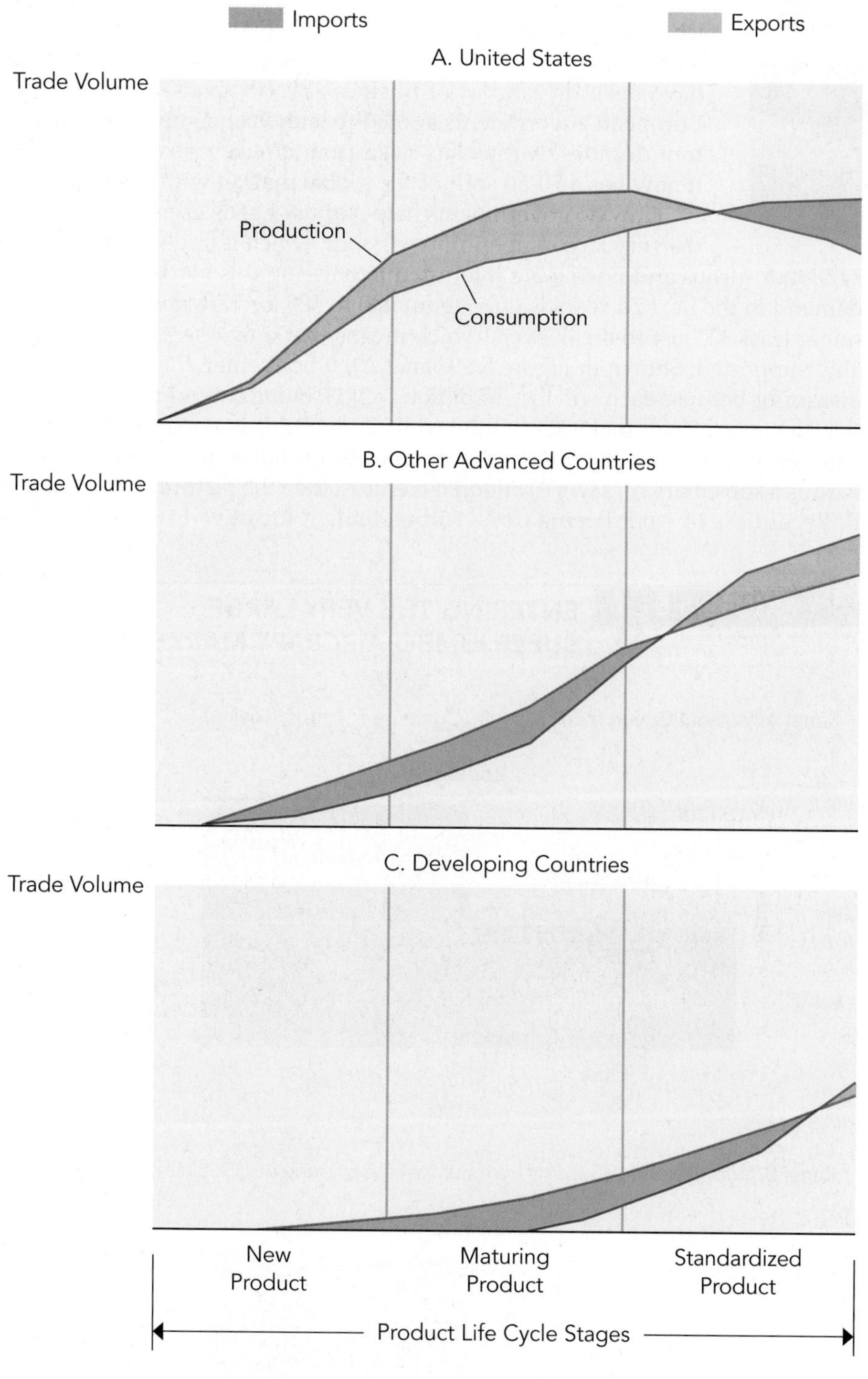

© PASCAL ROSSIGNOL/Reuters /Landov

How did strategic trade policy contribute to the creation of the Airbus A380?

by large military orders during World War II, Boeing has long dominated this industry. In the jumbo jet segment, Boeing's first-mover advantages associated with its 400-seat 747, first launched in the late 1960s, are still significant today. Alarmed by such US dominance, in the late 1960s, British, French, German, and Spanish governments realized that if they had not intervened in this industry, individual European aerospace firms on their own might have been driven out of business by US rivals. Therefore, these European governments agreed to launch and subsidize Airbus. In four decades, Airbus has risen from nowhere to a position where it now has a 50-50 split of the global market with Boeing.

How do governments help Airbus? Let us use a recent example: the very large, superjumbo aircraft, which is larger than the Boeing 747. Both Airbus and Boeing are interested in entering this market. However, the demand in the next 20 years is only about 400 to 500 aircraft, and a firm needs to sell at least 300 just to break even, which means that only one firm can be profitably supported. Shown in Figure 5.5 (panel A), if both enter, the outcome will be disastrous because each will lose $5 billion (cell 1). If one enters and the other does not, the entrant will make $20 billion (cells 2 and 3). It is possible that both will enter and clash (see Chapter 11). If a number of European governments promise Airbus a subsidiary of, say, $10 billion if it enters, then the picture changes to panel B. Regardless of what Boeing does, Airbus finds it lucrative to enter. In cell 1, if

FIGURE 5.5 ENTERING THE VERY LARGE, SUPERJUMBO AIRCRAFT MARKET?

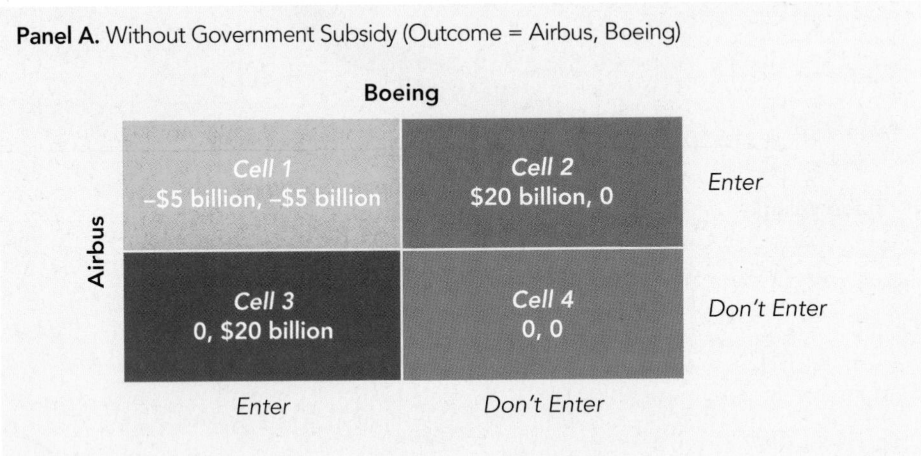

Panel B. With $10 Billion Subsidy from European Governments (Outcome = Airbus, Boeing)

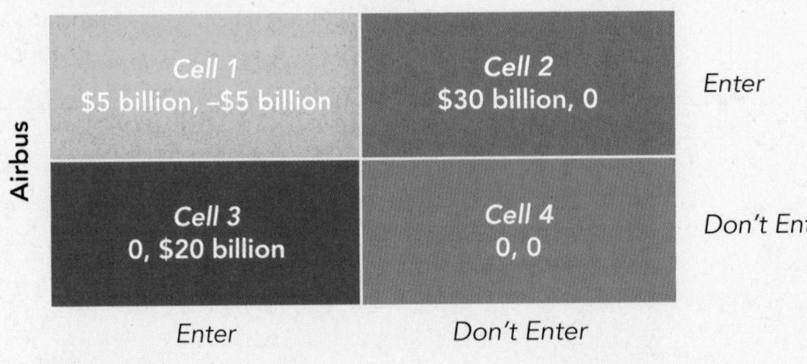

Boeing enters, it will lose $5 billion as before, whereas Airbus will make $5 billion ($10 billion subsidy minus $5 billion loss). So Boeing has no incentive to enter. Therefore, the more likely outcome is cell 2, where Airbus enters and enjoys a profit of $30 billion. Thus, the subsidy has given Airbus a *strategic* advantage, and the policy to assist Airbus is known as a **strategic trade policy**.[6] This has indeed been the case, as the 550-seat A380 will enter service when this book is published.

strategic trade policy
A theory that advocates economic policies to provide companies a strategic advantage through government subsidies.

Strategic trade theorists do not advocate a mercantilist policy to promote all industries. They only propose to help a few strategically important industries. However, this theory has been criticized on two accounts. Ideologically, many scholars and policymakers are uncomfortable. What if governments are not sophisticated and objective enough to do this job? Practically, a lot of industries claim that they are strategically important. For instance, after 9/11, American farmers successfully argued that agriculture is a strategic industry (guarding food supply against terrorists) and extracted more subsidies. Overall, where to draw the line between strategic and nonstrategic industries is tricky.

National Competitive Advantage of Industries

The most recent theory is known as the **theory of national competitive advantage of industries**. This is popularly known as the **"diamond" theory** because its principal architect, Harvard strategy professor Michael Porter, presents it in a diamond-shaped diagram[7] (Figure 5.6). This theory focuses on why certain *industries* (but not others) within a nation are competitive internationally. For example, although Japanese electronics and automobile industries are global winners, Japanese service industries are notoriously inefficient. Porter is interested in finding out why.

theory of national competitive advantage of industries (or "diamond" theory)
A theory that suggests that the competitive advantage of certain industries in different nations depends on four aspects that form a "diamond."

Porter argues that the competitive advantage of certain industries in different nations depends on four aspects that form a "diamond." First, he starts with factor endowments, which refer to the natural and human resource repertoires noted by the Heckscher-Ohlin theory. Some countries (such as Saudi Arabia) are rich in natural resources but short on population, and others (such as Singapore) have a well-educated population but few natural resources. Not surprisingly, Saudi

FIGURE 5.6 NATIONAL COMPETITIVE ADVANTAGE OF INDUSTRIES: THE PORTER DIAMOND

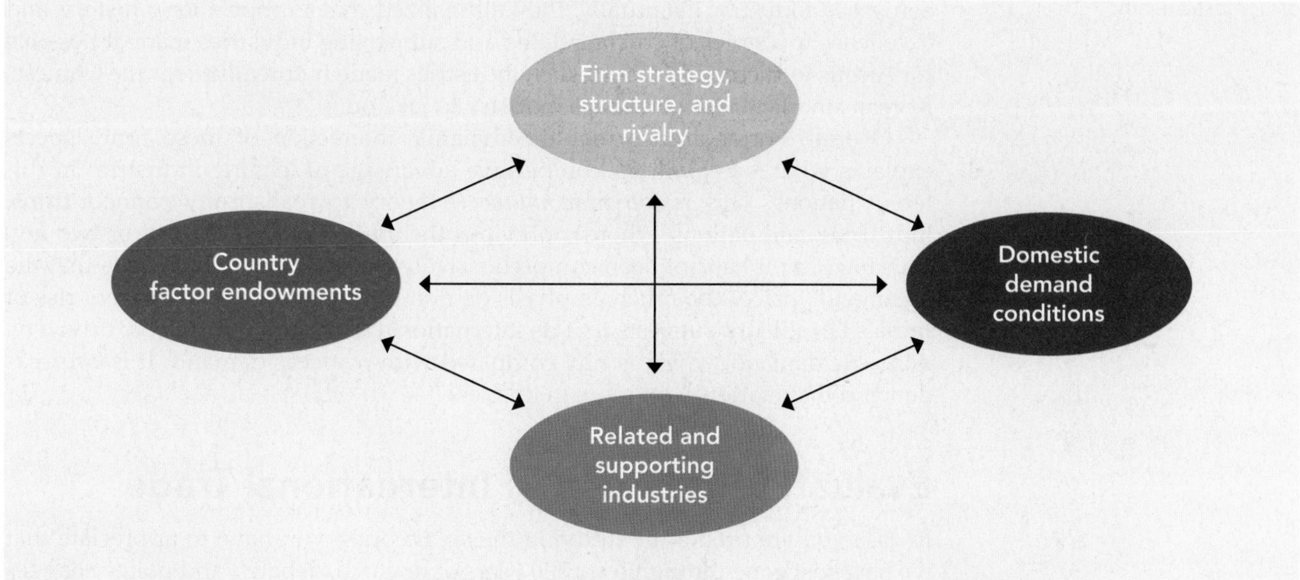

Source: M. Porter, 1990, The competitive advantage of nations (p. 77), *Harvard Business Review*, March–April: 73–93. Reprinted with permission.

Arabia exports oil, and Singapore exports semiconductors (which need abundant skilled labor). While building on these insights from previous theories, Porter argues that factor endowments are not enough.

Second, tough domestic demand propels firms to scale new heights. Why are American movies so competitive worldwide? One reason is that American moviegoers demand the very best "sex and violence" (two themes that sell universally if artfully packaged). Endeavoring to satisfy such domestic demand, movie studios unleash *High School Musical 2* after *High School Musical* and *Spiderman 3* after *Spiderman 1* and *Spiderman 2*—each time packing more excitement. Most movies, in fact, most products, are created to satisfy domestic demand first. Thus, abilities to satisfy a tough domestic crowd may make it possible to successfully deal with less demanding overseas customers.

Third, domestic firm strategy, structure, and rivalry in one industry play a huge role in its international success or failure. One reason the Japanese electronics industry is so competitive globally is because its *domestic* rivalry is probably the most intense in the world. When shopping for digital cameras or camcorders, if you are tired with some 20 models in an average American electronics store, you will be more exhausted when shopping in Japan: The average store there carries about 200 models (!). Most firms producing such a bewildering range of models do not make money. However, the few top firms (such as Canon) that win the tough competition domestically may have a relatively easier time when venturing abroad because overseas competition is less demanding.

© TOMOHIRO OHSUMI/Bloomberg News/Landov

What are some of the outcomes of domestic rivalry?

Finally, related and supporting industries provide the foundation upon which key industries can excel. In the absence of strong related and supporting industries such as engines, avionics, and materials, a key industry such as aerospace cannot become globally competitive. Each of these related and supporting industries requires years (and often decades) of hard work. For instance, emboldened by the Airbus experience, Chinese, Korean, and Japanese governments poured money into their own aerospace industry. Eventually, they all realized that Europe's long history and excellence in a series of crucial related and supporting industries made it possible for Airbus to succeed. A lack of such industries made it unrealistic for the Chinese, Korean, and Japanese aerospace industry to take off.

Overall, Porter argues that the dynamic interaction of these four aspects explains what is behind the competitive advantage of leading industries in different nations. This is the first *multilevel* theory to realistically connect firms, industries, and nations, whereas previous theories only work on one or two levels. However, it has not been comprehensively tested. Some critics argue that the "diamond" places too much emphasis on domestic conditions.[8] The recent rise of India's IT industry suggests that its international success is not entirely driven by domestic demand, which is tiny compared with overseas demand. It is overseas demand that matters a lot more in this case.[9]

Evaluating Theories of International Trade

In case you are tired after studying the six theories, you have to appreciate that we have just gone through over 300 years of research, debates, and policy changes around the world in about ten pages (!). As a student, that is not a small accomplishment. Table 5.4 enables you to see the "forest."

TABLE 5.4 THEORIES OF INTERNATIONAL TRADE: A SUMMARY

	Main points	Strengths and influences	Weaknesses and debates
Classical theories			
Mercantilism (Colbert, 1600s–1700s)	• International trade is a zero-sum game—trade deficit is dangerous • Governments should protect domestic industries and promote exports	• Forerunner of modern-day protectionism	• Inefficient allocation of resources • Reduces the wealth of the nation in the long run
Absolute advantage (Smith, 1776)	• Nations should specialize in economic activities in which they have an absolute advantage and trade with others • By specializing and trading, each nation produces more and consumes more • The wealth of all trading nations, and the world, increases	• Birth of modern economics • Forerunner of the free trade movement • Defeats mercantilism, at least intellectually	• When one nation is absolutely inferior to another, the theory is unable to provide any advice • When there are many nations, it may be difficult to find an absolute advantage
Comparative advantage (Ricardo, 1817; Heckscher, 1919; Ohlin, 1933)	• Nations should specialize in economic activities in which they have a comparative advantage and trade with others • Even if one nation is absolutely inferior to another, the two nations can still gainfully trade • Factor endowments underpin comparative advantage	• More realistic guidance to nations (and their firms) interested in trade but having no absolute advantage • Explains patterns of trade based on factor endowments	• Relatively static, assuming that comparative advantage and factor endowments do not change over time
Modern theories			
Product life cycle (Vernon, 1966)	• Comparative advantage first resides in the lead innovation nation, which exports to other nations • Production migrates to other advanced nations and then developing nations in different product life cycle stages	• First theory to incorporate dynamic changes in patterns of trade • More realistic with trade in industrial products in the 20th century	• The United States may not always be the lead innovation nation • Many new products are now launched simultaneously around the world
Strategic trade[1] (Brander, Spencer, Krugman, 1980s)	• Strategic intervention by governments may help domestic firms reap first-mover advantages in certain industries • First-mover firms, aided by governments, may have better odds at winning internationally	• More realistic and positively incorporates the role of governments in trade • Provides direct policy advice	• Ideological resistance from many "free trade" scholars and policymakers • Invites all kinds of industries to claim they are strategic
National competitive advantage of industries (Porter, 1990)	• Competitive advantage of different industries in different nations depends on the four interacting aspects of a "diamond" • The four aspects are (1) factor endowments, (2) domestic demand, (3) firm strategy, structure, and rivalry, and (4) related and supporting industries	• Most recent, most complex, and most realistic among various theories • As a multilevel theory, it directly connects research on firms, industries, and nations	• Has not been comprehensively tested • Overseas (not only domestic) demand may stimulate the competitiveness of certain industries

1. This theory is sometimes referred to as "new trade theory." However, it is now more than 25 years old and no longer that new. In some ways, all the modern trade theories can be regarded as "new" trade theories relative to classical theories. Therefore, to avoid confusion, we label this "strategic trade theory."

Today, the classical pro-free trade theories seem like common sense. However, we need to appreciate that they were *revolutionary* in the late 1700s and early 1800s in a world of mercantilism. These theories attracted numerous attacks. But eventually, they defeated mercantilism, at least intellectually. Influenced by these classic theories, England in the 1830s dismantled its protectionist Corn Laws, which triggered the global movement for free trade that is still going on today.

resource mobility
The assumption that a resource removed from one industry can be moved to another.

All theories simplify to make their point. Classical theories rely on highly simplistic assumptions of a model consisting of only two nations and two goods. They also assume perfect **resource mobility**—that is, one resource removed from wheat production can be moved to make aircraft. In reality, farmhands probably will have a hard time assembling modern aircraft. Further, classical theories assume no foreign exchange complications and zero transportation costs. So, in the real world of many countries, numerous goods, imperfect resource mobility, fluctuating exchange rates, high transportation costs, and product life cycle changes, is free trade still beneficial as Smith and Ricardo suggested? The answer is still yes, as worldwide data support the *basic* arguments of free traders such as Smith and Ricardo.[10] (See the section on Debates and Extensions for disagreements.)

Instead of relying on simple factor analysis, modern theories rely on more realistic product life cycles, first-mover advantages, and the "diamond" to explain and predict patterns of trade. Overall, classical and modern theories have significantly contributed to today's ever deepening trade links. Yet, the victory of classic and modern pro-free trade theories is not complete. The political realities governing international trade, outlined next, indicate that mercantilism is alive and well.

LEARNING OBJECTIVE 
realize the importance of political and economic realities governing international trade

REALITIES OF INTERNATIONAL TRADE

The political realities of the world suggest that as "rules of the game," plenty of trade barriers exist. Although some are being dismantled, many will remain. Let us examine why this is the case.

Tariff Barriers

tariff barrier
Trade barriers that rely on tariffs to discourage imports.

nontariff barrier (NTB)
Trade barriers that rely on nontariff means to discourage imports.

import tariff
A tax imposed on imports.

deadweight costs
Net losses that occur in an economy as the result of tariffs.

There are two broad types of trade barriers: (1) **tariff barriers** and (2) **nontariff barriers (NTBs)**. As a major tariff barrier, an **import tariff** is a tax imposed on imports. Figure 5.7 uses rice tariffs in Japan to show that there are *unambiguously* net losses—known as **deadweight costs.**

- Panel A: In the absence of international trade, the domestic price is P_1 and domestic rice farmers produce Q_1, determined by the intersection of domestic supply and demand curves.
- Panel B: Because Japanese rice price P_1 is higher than world price P_2, foreign farmers export to Japan. In the absence of tariffs, Japanese farmers reduce output to Q_2. Japanese consumers enjoy more rice at Q_3 at a much lower price P_2.
- Panel C: The government imposes an import tariff, effectively raising price from P_2 to P_3. Japanese farmers increase production from Q_2 to Q_4, and consumers pay more at P_3 and consume less by reducing consumption from Q_3 to Q_5. Imports fall from Q_2Q_3 in panel B to Q_4Q_5 in panel C.

Classical theorists such as Smith and Ricardo would have advised Japan to enjoy the gains from trade in panel B. But political realities land Japan in panel C, which, by limiting trade, introduces total inefficiency represented by the area consisting of A, B, C, and D. However, Japanese rice farmers gain the area of A, and the government pockets tariff revenues in the area of C. Therefore:

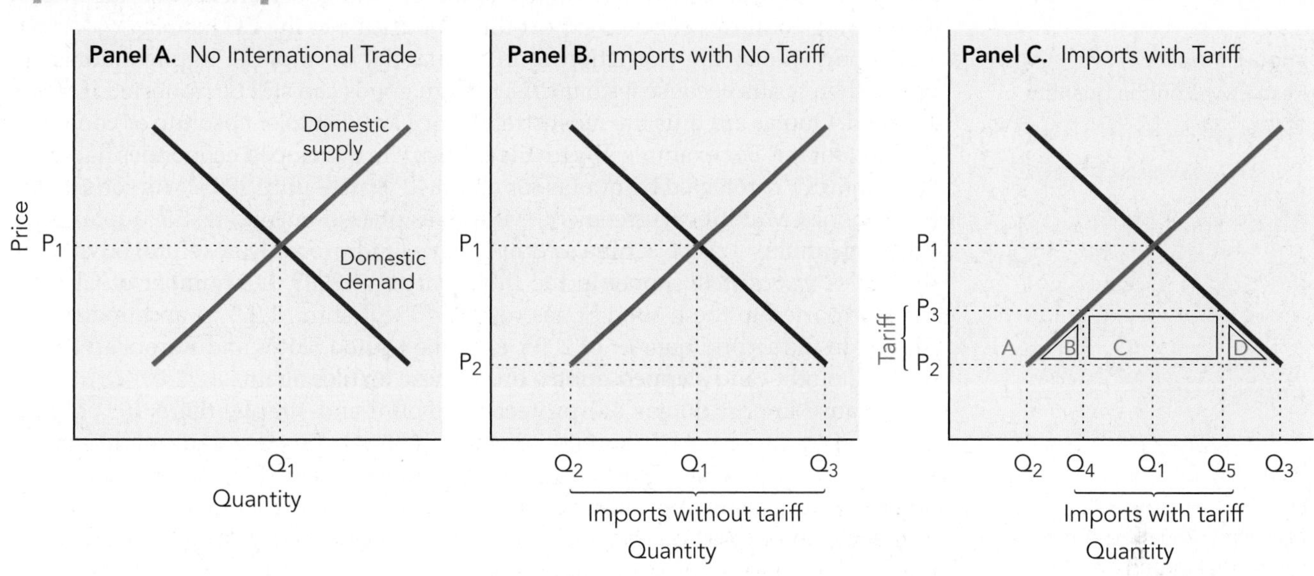

Net losses (deadweight) = Total inefficiency – net gain

= Area (A + B + C + D) – Area (A + C)

= Area (B + D)

The net losses (areas B and D) represent unambiguous economic inefficiency to the nation as a whole. Japan is not alone in this regard. During 2002–2004, the US government levied tariffs on steel. US steelmakers gained $240 million and saved 5,000 jobs. But steel consumers lost $600 million and 26,000 jobs.[11] This helped push auto components maker Delphi into bankruptcy and General Motors almost into bankruptcy. Consumers who bought cars, appliances, and houses paid more as well.

Given the well-known net losses, why are tariffs imposed? The answer boils down to the political realities. Although almost everybody in a country is hurt because of higher rice and steel prices, it is extraordinarily costly, if not impossible, to politically organize geographically scattered individuals and firms to advance the case for free trade.[12] On the other hand, certain special interest groups tend to be geographically concentrated and skillfully organized to advance their interest. In Japan, although farmers represent less than 5% of the population, they represent disproportionate votes in the Diet (Japanese congress). Why? Diet districts were drawn up in the aftermath of World War II, when most Japanese lived in rural areas. Such districts were never rezoned, although the majority of the population now lives in urban areas. Thus, when the powerful farm lobby speaks, the Japanese government listens. Likewise, in the United States, Big Steel controlled votes in key states, and President George W. Bush was eager to get reelected in 2004. Does that make sense?

Nontariff Barriers (NTBs)

Today, tariff barriers are often criticized around the world. NTBs are now increasingly the weapon of choice in trade wars. NTBs include (1) subsidies, (2) import quotas, (3) export restraints, (4) local content requirements, (5) administrative policies, and (6) antidumping duties.

Subsidies, as noted earlier, are government payments to domestic firms. Similar to their colleagues in Japan, European farmers, who represent 2% of the EU population, are masters of extracting subsidies. The EU's Common Agricultural

subsidy
Government payments to domestic firms.

Policy (CAP) costs European taxpayers $47 billion a year, eating up 40% of the EU budget.[13] European consumers do not like CAP, and governments and farmers in developing countries eager to export their foodstuffs to the EU hate it.

import quota
Restrictions on the quantity of imports.

Import quotas are restrictions on the quantity of imports. Import quotas are worse than tariffs because with tariffs, foreign goods can still be imported if tariffs are paid. Quotas are thus the most straightforward denial of absolute or comparative advantage. For example, the textile industry in developed economies had been "temporarily" protected by quotas for about 40 years—until 2005.[14] As soon as the protectionist Multifiber Agreement (MFA) was phased out and textile quotas were lifted on January 1, 2005, China's comparative (and probably absolute) advantage in textiles *immediately* shone. In the first quarter of 2005, the number of Chinese pants exported to the United States rose 1,573%, T-shirts 1,277%, and underwear 318%.[15] In the second quarter of 2005, both the United States and European Union said "Enough!" and slapped quotas on Chinese textiles again.

voluntary export restraint (VER)
An international agreement that shows that exporting countries voluntarily agree to restrict their exports.

Because import quotas are protectionist pure and simple, there are political costs that countries have to shoulder in today's largely pro-free trade environment. In response, **voluntary export restraints (VERs)** have been developed to show that on the surface, exporting countries *voluntarily* agree to restrict their exports. VERs in essence are export quotas. One of the most (in)famous examples is the VERs that the Japanese government agreed upon in the early 1980s to restrict US-bound automobile exports. This, of course, was a euphemism because the Japanese did not volunteer to restrict their exports. Only when faced with concrete threats did the Japanese reluctantly agree.

local content requirement
A requirement that a certain proportion of the value of the goods made in one country originate from that country.

Another NTB is **local content requirements**, which require a certain proportion of the value of the goods made in one country to originate from that country. The Japanese automobile VERs are again a case in point here. Starting in the mid-1980s, because of VERs, Japanese automakers switched to producing cars in the United States through foreign direct investment (FDI—see Chapter 6). However, initially, such factories were "screwdriver plants" because a majority of components were imported from Japan and only the proverbial screwdrivers were needed to tighten the bolts. To deal with this issue, many countries impose local content requirements, mandating that a "domestically produced" product will still be treated as an "import" subject to tariffs and NTBs unless a certain fraction of its value (such as 51% specified by the Buy America Act) is produced locally.

administrative policy
Bureaucratic rules that make it harder to import foreign goods.

Administrative policies refer to bureaucratic rules that make it harder to import foreign goods. For example, regular chewing gum imports are banned in Singapore, whose government is concerned about the mess created by improperly disposed used gum. Only gums with documented health benefits can be sold. Further, customers will have to give their names to the seller so that the authorities, if necessary, may be able to hold someone accountable in case of a chewing gum mess (In Focus 5.2).

antidumping duty
Costs levied on imports that have been "dumped" (selling below costs to "unfairly" drive domestic firms out of business).

Finally, the arsenal of trade warriors also includes **antidumping duties** levied on imports that have been "dumped" (selling below costs to "unfairly" drive domestic firms out of business). Chapter 11 will expand the discussion on antidumping in much greater detail.

Taken together, trade barriers reduce or eliminate international trade. Although certain domestic industries and firms benefit, the entire country—or at least a majority of its consumers—tends to suffer. Given these well-known negative aspects, why do people make arguments against free trade? The next two sections outline economic and political arguments against free trade.

Economic Arguments against Free Trade

Prominent among economic arguments against free trade include (1) the need to protect domestic industries and (2) the necessity to shield infant industries. The oldest and most frequently used economic argument against free trade is the urge

IN FOCUS 5.2 Sticky Business in Singapore

Singapore is famous for its high standards of tidiness and for the stringent policies that support public cleanliness. Beginning in 1992, policymakers, anxious to avoid the messy and unsightly problem of improperly disposed used chewing gum, banned the sale of gum. US gum manufacturers missed the opportunity to sell their products to four million Singaporeans. Wrigley, maker of several leading chewing-gum brands, pressured US legislators and trade representatives to do something. The ban didn't discriminate against foreign gum because no producer existed in Singapore, nor did it violate any of Singapore's other WTO responsibilities. So the only way for the United States to get Singapore to remove or loosen the antigum policy was to negotiate. In 2001, the two countries began talks to reach a broad US-Singapore Free Trade Agreement. Wrigley made sure that the agenda included an unlikely item that turned out to be quite sticky: the chewing-gum ban.

© Tim Boyle/ Staff/ Getty Images

At first, Singapore agreed to allow only medicinal-purpose gums prescribed by a doctor (for example, products to help stop smoking or to treat chronic dry mouth). Wrigley and its supporters were not satisfied. More negotiations followed. Finally, Singapore agreed to permit sales but only of gums with proven health benefits, only by licensed dentists or pharmacists, and only if the customer gave his or her name to the seller. This sufficed to gain entry for Wrigley's sugar-free Orbit brand of gum, which claims to strengthen tooth enamel. Singapore's stiff penalties for gum-related littering remain. Fines of more than US$200 plus a trip to court are common. Some pharmacists seem a bit puzzled. After all, they sell more serious drugs with fewer restrictions.

Source: Adapted from B. V. Yarbrough & R. M. Yarbrough, 2006, Sticky business in Singapore, in *The World Economy,* 7th ed. (p. 237), Cincinnati, OH: Thomson South-Western. Reprinted with permission.

to protect domestic industries, firms, and jobs from "unfair" foreign competition—in short, protectionism. The following excerpt is from an 1845 petition of the French candle makers to the French government:

> We are subject to the intolerable competition of a foreign rival, who enjoys such superior capabilities for the production of light, that he is flooding the domestic market at an incredibly low price. From the moment he appears, our sales cease, all consumers turn to him, and a branch of French industry whose ramifications are innumerable is at once reduced to complete stagnation. This rival is nothing other than the sun. We ask you to be so kind as to pass a law requiring the closing of all windows, skylights, shutters, curtains, and blinds—in short, all openings, holes, chinks, and fissures through which sunlight penetrates . . .[16]

Although this was a hypothetical satire written by a French free trade advocate Fredric Bastiat 160 years ago, similar points are often heard today. Such calls for protection are not limited to commodity producers like candle makers. Highly talented individuals, such as American mathematicians and Japanese sumo wrestlers, have also called for protection. Foreign math PhDs grab 40% of US math jobs, and recent US math PhDs face a jobless rate of 11%. Thus, many American math PhDs have called for protection of their jobs. Similarly, Japanese sumo wrestlers insist that foreign sumo wrestlers should not be allowed to throw their weight in Japan.[17]

Another argument is the **infant industry argument**. If domestic firms are as young as "infants," in the absence of government intervention, they stand no chance of surviving and will be crushed by mature foreign rivals. Thus, it is imperative that governments level the playing field by assisting infant industries. This argument is legitimate sometimes, but governments and firms have a tendency to abuse it. Some protected infant industries may never grow up—why bother?[18] When Airbus was a true infant in the 1960s, it no doubt deserved some subsidies. However, by the 2000s, Airbus has become a giant that can take on Boeing (in some years, Airbus *outsells* Boeing). Nevertheless, Airbus continues to ask for subsidies, which European governments continue to provide.

infant industry argument
The argument that if domestic firms are as young as "infants," in the absence of government intervention, they stand no chance of surviving and will be crushed by mature foreign rivals.

Political Arguments against Free Trade

Political arguments against free trade advance a nation's political, social, and environmental agenda regardless of possible economic gains from trade. These arguments include (1) national security, (2) consumer protection, (3) foreign policy, and (4) environmental and social responsibility.

First, national security concerns are often invoked to protect defense-related industries. Many nations fear that if they rely on arms imports, their national security may be compromised if there are political or diplomatic disagreements between them and the arms-producing nation. France has always insisted on maintaining an independent defense industry to produce nuclear weapons, aircraft carriers, and combat jets. Although the French can often purchase such weapons at lower costs from the United States, which is eager to sell them, the French answer has usually been: "No, thanks!"

Second, consumer protection has frequently been used as an argument for nations to erect trade barriers. In the early 2000s, a single case of mad cow disease in Canada led the United States to completely ban beef imports from Canada. For another example, American hormone-treated beef was banned by the European Union (EU) between 1989 and 1995 because of the alleged health risks. Even though the United States won a WTO battle on this, the EU still has refused to remove the ban.

trade embargo
Politically motivated trade sanctions against foreign countries to signal displeasure.

Third, foreign policy objectives are often sought through trade intervention. **Trade embargoes** are politically motivated trade sanctions against foreign countries to signal displeasure. The United States had enforced its embargoes against Cuba and North Korea (although exceptions are sometimes made). Many Arab countries maintain embargoes against Israel. During the cartoon incident in 2005–2006, a number of Muslim countries initiated embargoes against Denmark (see Chapter 3 Opening Case).

Finally, environmental and social responsibility can be used as political arguments to initiate trade intervention against certain countries. In a "shrimp-turtle" case, the United States banned shrimp imports from India, Malaysia, Pakistan, and Thailand because shrimp were caught in their waters using a technique that also accidentally trapped sea turtles, an endangered species protected by the United States. These nations were upset and brought the case to the WTO, alleging that the United States invoked an environmental law as a trade barrier. The WTO sided with these nations and demanded that the US ban be lifted, with which the United States later complied (see In Focus 8.2).

LEARNING OBJECTIVE 4
participate in two leading debates on international trade

DEBATES AND EXTENSIONS

As has been shown, international trade has a substantial mismatch between theories and realities, resulting in numerous debates. This section highlights two leading debates: (1) trade deficit versus surplus and (2) classic theories versus new realities.

Trade Deficit versus Trade Surplus

Smith and Ricardo would probably turn in their graves if they heard that one of today's hottest trade debates still echoes the old debate between mercantilists and free traders 200 years ago. Nowhere is the debate more ferocious than in the United States, which runs the world's largest trade deficit (combining the US deficit in merchandise trade with its surplus in service trade). In 2006, it reached a record-breaking \$760 billion (6% of GDP) and is likely to deteriorate further. Should this increasing trade deficit be of concern? Free traders argue that this is not a grave concern. They suggest that the United States and its trading partners mutually benefit by developing a deeper division of labor based on comparative advantage. Former Treasury Secretary Paul O'Neill went so far as to say that trade deficit was "an antiquated theoretical construct."[19] Economist Paul Krugman argued:

> International trade is not about competition, it is about mutually beneficial exchange . . . Imports, not exports, are the purpose of trade. That is, what a country gains from trade is the ability to import things it wants. Exports are not an objective in and of themselves: the need to export is a burden that a country must bear because its import suppliers are crass enough to demand payment.[20]

Critics strongly disagree. They argue that international trade *is* about competition—about markets, jobs, and incomes. Trade deficit has always been blamed on a particular country with which the United States runs the largest deficit: Japan in the 1980s and 1990s and China in the 2000s. Therefore, the recent trade deficit debate is otherwise known as the China trade debate. Unlike Japan, which is a democratic, military ally of the United States, China's status as the last surviving communist power makes matters a lot worse when the US trade deficit with it reached $233 billion in 2006. "China bashing" thus is in vogue among some US politicians, journalists, and executives. The United States runs trade deficits with all of its major trading partners—Canada, the EU, Japan, and Mexico—and is in trade disputes with them most of the time (see Closing Case). Nevertheless, the China trade debate is by far the most emotionally charged and politically explosive (see In Focus 5.3).

Major arguments and counterarguments in the debate are in Table 5.5. It is obvious that in this seemingly intractable debate, emotions are high, and cool heads and convincing answers are few.[21] Two things are certain: (1) Given Americans' seemingly endless appetite for imports, the US trade deficit is difficult to eliminate. (2) Drastic measures proposed by some protectionist members of US Congress (such as slapping all Chinese imports with 20% to 30% tariffs if the yuan does not appreciate "satisfactorily") are unrealistic and would violate US commitments to the WTO. As China's export drive continues, according to the *Economist*, China will be the "scapegoat of choice" for America's economic problems for a long time.[22] (We will discuss the currency issue in Chapter 7.)

Classical Theories versus New Realities

While the first debate (mostly on China) is primarily about *merchandise* trade and unskilled manufacturing jobs that classical theories talk about, the second debate (mostly on India) is about *service* trade and high-skill jobs in high technology such as IT. Typically dealing with wheat from Australia to Britain on a slow boat, classical theorists certainly could not have dreamed about using the Internet to send *this* manuscript to India to be typeset and counted as India's service exports.

We already discussed a part of this debate in Chapter 4 when focusing on outsourcing. That debate deals with *firm*-level capabilities; here, let us examine *nation*- and *individual*-level ramifications. Classical theorists and their modern-day disciples argue that the United States and India trade by tapping into each other's comparative advantage. India leverages its abundant, high-skill, and low-wage labor. Americans will channel their energy and resources to higher skill, higher paying jobs. Regrettably, certain Americans will lose jobs, but the nation as a whole benefits, so the theory goes.[23]

But not so fast, argued retired MIT economics professor Paul Samuelson. In an influential 2004 paper, Samuelson suggested that in a more realistic world, India can innovate in the area that the United States traditionally enjoys comparative

IN FOCUS  5.3

ETHICAL DILEMMA: The Folly of Slapping Quotas on China—Laura D'Andrea Tyson

America's trade deficit with China is emerging as an issue in the presidential campaign [*of 2004—editor*]. The Bush administration has slapped unilateral quotas on imports of Chinese textile products, with the threat of more to come in other sectors. Congress is buzzing with lobbying efforts and legislative initiatives to address the specters of unfair trading practices and currency manipulation attributed to China. And China has become the target for half of all of the antidumping cases brought by US companies. Protectionist sentiment is not surprising in an election year featuring a jobless economic recovery and close votes in swing states with large labor constituencies. But there is no economic justification for protectionism. Even protectionist rhetoric risks destabilizing the global capital flows on which the US expansion depends. China does indeed have a huge and ballooning trade surplus with the United States, but it runs sizable deficits with other countries, and its overall trade surplus is small and shrinking. More important, China has flung open its doors to foreign direct investment. Last year [*2002—editor*] it was the second largest target for such flows. And the International Monetary Fund (IMF) recently said there is no evidence that the Chinese currency is substantially undervalued. Indeed, if the currency were floated, it might well decline as Chinese convert their domestic currency holdings into dollars.

China is a daunting export machine. Its exports grew eightfold between 1990 and 2003. It is a source of both labor-intensive traditional products like textiles, toys, and shoes and an exporter of technology-intensive products as well. While American textile workers may be getting hit, China's export surge overall is not displacing American workers but alternative suppliers around the world. Because labor is four times more expensive in Mexico than in China, China has overtaken Mexico as America's second largest trading partner. China's exports in the electronics industry have driven out similar exports from competing higher cost Asian economies. The real victims of China's formidable production cost advantages are its emerging-market competitors. And American consumers have been the beneficiaries. Since 1997, US consumers have saved about $100 billion a year in import bills as lower priced goods, primarily from China, have supplanted goods from other regions.

US businesses have been a force behind China's export performance. Foreign-owned companies and joint ventures between Chinese and foreign investors, many of them American, produced much of China's exports over the last decade. Foreign companies currently account for about 50% of China's exports and about 60% of its imports.

China's large trade surplus with the United States, heading toward $130 billion this year [*2003; it reached $233 billion in 2006—editor*], obscures the fact that China is also a voracious importer. Since 1995, China's imports have grown twice as fast as US imports. This year, sales to China will account for nearly three-quarters of the increase in Japan's exports, 40% of the rise in Korea's exports, 99% of the boost in Taiwan's exports, and about a quarter of the increase in US exports. China is America's fastest growing export market, expanding at an annual rate of about 20%. American companies sell $20 billion worth of goods to China.

Finally, China is nurturing America's economic expansion by helping to keep US interest rates low through substantial purchases of government debt. During the past year and a half [*2002–2003—editor*], China bought more than $100 billion in US government securities. China is a primary source of funding for the US fiscal and current-account deficits.

The US current-account deficit [*$760 billion in 2006—editor*] is large and rising. It is financed by the Chinese, Japanese, and other central banks of Asia that are channeling the substantial domestic savings of their populations into funding the spendthrift, debt-ridden ways of Washington. The growth of the world economy today depends on a simple logic: The United States spends, and Asia lends. Protectionism threatens to upset this logic, as the recent sell-off in dollar assets following the unilateral imposition of quotas on Chinese textiles by the Bush administration indicates. Alan Greenspan [*chairman of the US Federal Reserve Bank at that time—editor*] recently warned that new protectionist initiatives in the context of wide current-account imbalances could erode the flexibility of the global economy. Such initiatives could roil currency markets, undermine capital flows, and strangle the nascent global expansion. Are a few votes in a few swing states really worth the risk?

Source: L. D. Tyson, 2003, The folly of slapping quotas on China, *Business Week*, December 8: 30. © 2003 The McGraw-Hill Companies, reprinted with permission. Tyson chaired President Clinton's Council of Economic Advisors. At the time of this writing, she was dean of London Business School in Britain.

advantage, such as IT.[24] Indian innovation can reduce the price of US software exports and curtail the wage of US IT workers. Despite the availability of cheaper goods (which is a plus), the net effect may be that the United States is *worse* off as a whole. Samuelson is not an antiglobalization ideologue. Rather, he won a Nobel prize for his penetrating research on the gains from international trade,[25] and his mainstream economics textbook has trained generations of students (including this author). Now, even Samuelson is not so sure about one of the founding pillars of modern economics, comparative advantage.

TABLE 5.5 DEBATE ON THE US TRADE DEFICIT WITH CHINA[1]

US trade deficit with China is a huge problem	US trade deficit with China is not a huge problem
Naive trader versus unfair protectionist • The United States is a "naive" trader with open markets. China has "unfairly" protected its markets	*Market reformer versus unfair protectionist* • China's markets are already unusually open. Its trade volume (merchandise and services) is 75% of GDP, whereas the US volume is only 25%—so is Japan's
Greedy exporters • Unscrupulous Chinese exporters are eager to gut US manufacturing jobs and drive US rivals out of business	*Eager foreign investors* • Two-thirds of Chinese exports are generated by foreign-invested firms in China, and numerous US firms have invested in and benefited from such operations in China
The demon who has caused deflation • Cheap imports sold at "the China price" push down prices and cause deflation	*Thank China (and Wal-Mart) for low prices* • Every consumer benefits from cheap prices brought from China by US firms such as Wal-Mart
Intellectual property (IP) violator • China is a blatant violator of IP rights, and US firms lose $2 billion a year	*Inevitable step in development* • True, but (1) the US did that in the 19th century (to the British), and (2) IP protection will improve in China
Currency manipulator[2] • The yuan is severely undervalued (maybe up to 40%), giving Chinese exports an "unfair" advantage in being priced at an artificially low level	*Currency issue is not relevant* • The yuan is somewhat undervalued, but (1) US and other foreign firms producing in China benefit, and (2) yuan appreciation will not eradicate US trade deficit
Trade deficit will make the United States poorer • Since imports have to be paid, the United States borrows against its future with disastrous outcomes	*Trade deficit does not cause a fall in the US standard of living* • As long as the Chinese are willing to invest in the US economy (such as Treasury bills), what's the worry?
Something has to be done • If the Chinese don't do it "our way," the United States should introduce drastic measures (such as slapping 20% to 30% tariffs on all Chinese imports)	*Remember the gains from trade argued by classical theories?* • Tariffs will not bring back US jobs, which will simply go to Mexico or Malaysia, and will lead to retaliation from China, a major *importer* of US goods and services

1. This table is a representative sample—but not an exhaustive list—of major arguments and counterarguments in this debate. Other issues include (1) statistical reporting differences, (2) environmental damage, (3) human rights, and (4) national security, which are not discussed to make this table manageable.
2. The currency issue will be discussed at length in Chapter 7 (see especially Opening Case and In Focus 7.3).

Sources: Based on (1) *Business Week*, 2004, The China price, December 6: 102–112; (2) *Business Week*, 2006, The runaway trade giant, April 24: 30–33; (3) *Economist*, 2003, Tilting at dragons, October 25: 65–66; (4) *Economist*, 2005, From T-shirts to T-bonds, July 30: 61–63; (5) *Economist*, 2005, The dragon comes calling, September 3: 24–25; (6) O. Shenkar, 2005, *The Chinese Century*, Philadelphia: Wharton School Publishing; (7) *South China Morning Post*, 2007, US visit aims for progress on yuan, July 30; (8) L. Tyson, 2003, The folly of slapping quotas on China, *Business Week*, December 8: 30.

The reaction has been swift. Within the same year (2004), Jagdish Bhagwati, an Indian-born, Columbia University trade expert, and his colleagues countered Samuelson by arguing that classical pro-free trade theories still hold.[26] Bhagwati and colleagues wrote:

> Imagine that you are exporting aircraft, and new producers of aircraft emerge abroad. That will lower the price of your aircraft, and your gains from trade will diminish. You have to be naïve to believe that this can never happen. But

> you have to be even more naïve to think that the policy response to the reduced gains from trade is to give up the remaining gains as well. The critical policy question we must address is: When external developments, such as the growth of skills in China and India, for instance, do diminish the gains from trade to the US, is the harm to the US going to be reduced or increased if the US turns into Fortress America? The answer is: The US will only increase its anguish if it closes its markets.[27]

In any case, according to Bhagwati and colleagues, the "threat" posed by Indian innovation is vastly exaggerated, and offshoring is too small to matter much. Although approximately 3.4 million US jobs may be outsourced by 2015 (see Chapter 4), we have to realize that in any given year, the US economy destroys 30 million jobs and creates slightly more, thus dwarfing the effect of offshoring. Further, Bhagwati argues that higher level jobs will replace those lost to offshoring.

However, here is a huge problem: Where are such higher level jobs? Will there be enough of these jobs so that the United States will not suffer from a huge burden of unemployment among its highly educated? Bhagwati has no concrete answer. For example, in an industry where the United States is the undisputed "king of the hill," movies, the single greatest project in recent history, the *Lord of the Rings* trilogy, was crafted in New Zealand—not in Hollywood.[28] In Auckland, New Zealand, Academy Award-winning director Peter Jackson built a film complex and attracted hundreds of the best cinematographers, costume designers, computer-graphic artists, editors, and animators, who more recently produced the remake of *King Kong*. In case you think this is a trivial, "nonstrategic" industry that would not matter much, remember "Show Biz is big business." George Lucas's *Star Wars* movies almost single-handedly sparked a series of jobs from video games to product tie-ins in marketing. Because *Star Wars* movies were produced in the United States, a majority of such related and supporting jobs were held by Americans. While the competition for top-level film jobs is highly visible, numerous other industries are also competing. In the United States, not only do the nation's 15 million factory hands in manufacturing jobs face rivals elsewhere, 57 million white-collar workers in service jobs may also feel threatened—combined, that is more than half of the US work force of 130 million.[29] What does the future hold?

LEARNING OBJECTIVE **5**

draw implications for action

MANAGEMENT SAVVY

How does this chapter answer the big question in global business adapted for the context of international trade: What determines the success and failure of firms' exports around the globe? The two core perspectives lead to two answers. Fundamentally, the various economic theories underpin the resource-based view, suggesting that successful exports are valuable, unique, and hard-to-imitate products generated by certain firms from a nation. However, the political realities stress the explanatory and predictive power of the institution-based view: As rules of the game, institutions such as laws and regulations promoted by various special interest groups can protect certain domestic industries, firms, and individuals, erect trade barriers, and make the nation as a whole worse off.

As a result, three implications for action emerge (Table 5.6). First, location, location, location! In international trade, savvy managers' job number one is to leverage comparative advantage of world-class locations. For instance, as managers aggressively tapped into Argentina's comparative advantage in wine production, its wine exports grew from $6 million in 1987 to $170 million in 2003.[30]

Second, comparative advantage is not fixed. Managers need to constantly monitor and nurture the current comparative advantage of a location and take advantage of new promising locations. Managers who fail to realize the departure of comparative advantage from certain locations are likely to fall behind. For

TABLE 5.6 IMPLICATIONS FOR ACTION

- Discover and leverage comparative advantage of world-class locations
- Monitor and nurture the current comparative advantage of certain locations and take advantage of new locations
- Be politically active to demonstrate, safeguard, and advance the gains from international trade

instance, numerous German managers have moved production elsewhere, citing Germany's reduced comparative advantage in basic manufacturing. However, they still concentrate top-notch, high-end manufacturing in Germany, leveraging its excellence in engineering.

Third, managers need to be politically active if they are to gain from trade. Although managers at many uncompetitive firms have long mastered the game of twisting politicians' arms for more protection, managers at competitive firms, who tend to be pro-free trade, have a tendency to shy away from "politics." They often fail to realize that free trade is *not* free—it requires constant efforts and sacrifices to demonstrate, safeguard, and advance the gains from such trade. For example, the US-China Business Council, a pro-free trade (in particular, pro-China trade) group consisting of 250 large US corporations, has stood up and spoken out against various China bashers.

CHAPTER SUMMARY

1. Use the resource- and institution-based views to explain why nations trade
   - The resource-based view suggests that nations trade because some firms in one nation generate valuable, unique, and hard-to-imitate exports that firms in other nations find it beneficial to import.
   - The institution-based view argues that as "rules of the game," different laws and regulations governing international trade aim to share gains from trade.
2. Understand classical and modern theories of international trade
   - Classical theories include (1) mercantilism, (2) absolute advantage, and (3) comparative advantage.
   - Modern theories include (1) product life cycles, (2) strategic trade, and (3) "diamond."
3. Realize the importance of political and economic realities governing international trade
   - The net impact of various tariffs and NTBs is that the whole nation is worse off while certain special interest groups (such as certain industries, firms, and regions) benefit.
   - Economic arguments against free trade center on (1) protectionism and (2) infant industries.
   - Political arguments against free trade focus on (1) national security, (2) consumer protection, (3) foreign policy, and (4) environmental and social responsibility.
4. Participate in two leading debates on international trade
   - The first debate deals with whether persistent trade deficit is of grave concern or not.
   - The second deals with whether service trade will benefit or hurt rich countries.

5. Draw implications for action
   - Discover and leverage comparative advantage of world-class locations.
   - Monitor and nurture current comparative advantage of certain locations and take advantage of new locations.
   - Be politically active to demonstrate, safeguard, and advance the gains from international trade.

KEY TERMS

Absolute advantage 127
Administrative policy 140
Antidumping duty 140
Balance of trade 126
Classical trade theories 127
Comparative advantage 129
Deadweight costs 138
Exporting 124
Factor endowments 131
Factor endowment theory (Heckscher-Ohlin theory) 131
First-mover advantage 132
Free trade 127
Import quota 140
Import tariff 138
Importing 124
Infant industry argument 141
Local content requirement 140
Merchandise 124
Modern trade theories 127
Nontariff barrier (NTB) 138
Opportunity cost 130
Product life cycle theory 132
Protectionism 127
Resource mobility 138
Services 124
Strategic trade policy 135
Strategic trade theory 132
Subsidy 139
Tariff barrier 138
Theory of absolute advantage 127
Theory of comparative advantage 129
Theory of mercantilism 127
Theory of national competitive advantage of industries ("diamond" theory) 135
Trade deficit 124
Trade embargo 142
Trade surplus 124
Voluntary export restraint (VER) 140

REVIEW QUESTIONS

1. International trading is quite complex, so why do nations routinely engage in this activity?
2. Name and describe the two key components of a balance of trade.
3. Briefly summarize the three classical theories of international trade.
4. Compare and contrast the three modern theories of international trade.
5. How is the concept of opportunity cost related to the theories of absolute advantage and comparative advantage?
6. Is it possible for all of a country's resources to be completely mobile? Why or why not?
7. Devise your own examples that demonstrate your understanding of tariff and nontariff barriers.
8. What are the two primary economic arguments that critics use against free trade?
9. Summarize the four political arguments against free trade.
10. Do you agree with economist Paul Krugman that international trade is not about competition? Explain your answer.
11. What are some of the contemporary debates that affect international trade theories and policies?

12. What are some of the factors managers might need to consider when assessing the comparative advantage of various locations around the world?
13. Why is it necessary for business people to monitor and participate in political activity concerning international trade?

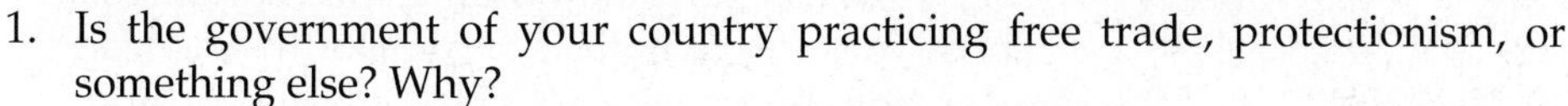

CRITICAL DISCUSSION QUESTIONS

1. Is the government of your country practicing free trade, protectionism, or something else? Why?
2. What is the ratio of total volume of international trade (exports + imports) to GDP in your country? How about the ratio for the following: the United States, the European Union, Japan, Russia, China, and Singapore? Do these ratios help you answer question 1?
3. ON ETHICS: As a foreign policy tool, trade embargoes, such as US embargoes against Cuba, Iraq (until 2003), and North Korea, are meant to discourage foreign governments. But they also cause a great deal of misery among the population (such as shortage of medicine and food). Are embargoes ethical?
4. ON ETHICS: Although the nation as a whole may gain from free trade, there is no doubt that certain regions, industries, firms, and individuals may lose their jobs and livelihood due to foreign competition. How can the rest of the nation help the unfortunate ones cope with the impact of international trade?

VIDEO CASE

Watch "Local Versus Global" by Maurice Levy of Publicis Groupe.

1. What does Maurice Levy mean when he says that one cannot have only a global view?
2. Mr. Levy said that sometimes one may have a branding strategy that will work with several countries and that at other times the strategy must be local. Does that support or contradict the theories of Smith and Ricardo or modern theories such as the resource-based view?
3. How does his illustration of taking a client to dinner and the comments during the resulting conversation illustrate the benefits of trade?
4. Although Mr. Levy was very supportive of trade, he said it does have dangers. Have you or anyone you know experienced the problems he mentioned?
5. He mentioned the impact of different cultures and values in international trade. Do you think such differences will increase or decrease in the years to come?

C L O S I N G C A S E

Canada and the United States: Fighting over Salmon and Softwood

Sharing the world's longest undefended border, Canada and the United States are the best of friends. Their bilateral trading relationship is the world's largest, with $700 billion in volume. About 80% of Canada's exports (approximately one-third of its GDP) go to its southern neighbor, making it the largest exporter to the United States. Canadian products command approximately 20% of the US import market share. In comparison, China, the second largest exporter to the United States, only commands less than 10%. Canada is also the largest import market of US products, absorbing about one-fourth of US exports. The United States runs a sizable trade deficit with Canada, at approximately $82 billion in 2006. Despite such a close trade relationship, they fight like "cats and dogs" in trade disputes. Salmon and softwood serve as two cases in point.

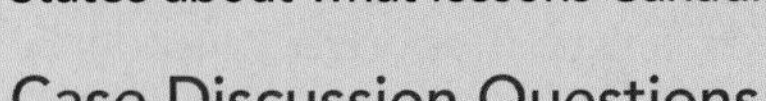
© National Geographic/Getty Images

Salmon migrate for thousands of miles, from Canadian and US rivers to the Pacific Ocean and then back to their original river to spawn. Because salmon swimming in the ocean do not sport a national color, Canadian fishing boats would inevitably catch some "US fish," and American boats likewise would innocently net some "Canadian fish." In 1985, both countries signed a treaty. Both agreed that US interceptions of Canadian fish and Canadian interceptions of US fish should be balanced. However, measurement was a huge issue. Canada alleged that US boats were catching more Canadian salmon. The Canadian government seized several US boats and British Columbia fishing boats temporarily blockaded an Alaska-bound US ferry. Finally, in 1999, both countries signed another treaty, based on abundance-based management with flexible catch limits based on a species' abundance or scarcity in a given year. Since then, clash at sea has not been reported very frequently.

Lately, Canada's number-one hot button is the softwood dispute. American timber firms argued that Canadian rivals, which cut trees mostly from publicly owned Crown lands, paid artificially low cutting fees that essentially were an unfair subsidy. In 2002, the United States, for the fourth time since 1982, imposed hefty tariffs on Canadian lumber. Canada formally complained to a North American Free Trade Agreement (NAFTA) panel. In 2004, a NAFTA panel issued a "final" decision, finding (1) that Canadian firms had not injured US rivals and (2) that approximately $4 billion in US tariffs collected needed to be refunded.

However, the United States ignored the "final" ruling and launched a postfinal decision "extraordinary challenge" (allowed by the NAFTA rules), alleging that the first panel was unfair. In 2005, NAFTA's extraordinary challenge committee upheld the original panel's verdict. However, the United States ignored even that ruling. Although most Americans hardly noticed this, most Canadians were upset. "Unacceptable," thundered (then) Prime Minister Paul Martin. Because a major selling point of NAFTA to Canadians was that it would set up an institutional framework to adjudicate trade disputes like this, Canadian newspapers questioned whether America's signature meant anything at all. Although US Secretary of State Condoleezza Rice insisted that America's record on honoring treaties was "as good as gold," Canadian radicals called for cutting off oil and gas exports in retaliation. The Canadian government, not so radical, launched an information campaign to inform other countries seeking trade treaties with the United States about what lessons Canadians learned.

Case Discussion Questions

1. Why do Canada and the United States have the largest bilateral trading relationship in the world?
2. Based on resource- and institution-based views, explain why Canadian products have such a large market share in the United States.
3. Some argue that the Canadians have overreacted. Even with controversial US tariffs, Canadian lumber still has 34% of the US market and lumber represents only 3% of Canada's exports. What do you think?

Sources: Based on (1) J. Baggs & J. Brander, 2006, Trade liberalization, profitability, and financial leverage, *Journal of International Business Studies*, 37: 196–211; (2) *Economist*, 2005, Hard talk on softwood, September 10: 38; (3) *Economist*, 2005, Living with number one, December 3: 10–12; (4) World Trade Organization, 2005, Merchandise trade of the United States by region and economy, 2004, http://www.wto.org; (5) B. V. Yarbrough & R. M. Yarbrough, 2006, *The World Economy*, 7th ed. (p. 238), Cincinnati, OH: Thomson South-Western.

NOTES

Journal acronyms: **AER** – *American Economic Review;* **AME** – *Academy of Management Executive;* **BW** – *Business Week;* **EJ** – *Economic Journal;* **IBR** – *International Business Review;* **JEP** – *Journal of Economic Perspectives;* **JIBS** – *Journal of International Business Studies;* **JIE** – *Journal of International Economics;* **JM** – *Journal of Management;* **JMS** – *Journal of Management Studies;* **QJE** – *Quarterly Journal of Economics*

[1] J. Baggs & J. Brander, 2006, Trade liberalization, profitability, and financial leverage, *JIBS*, 37: 196–211.

[2] M. W. Peng, 2001, The resource-based view and international business, *JM*, 27: 803–829.

[3] B. Ohlin, 1933, *Interregional and International Trade*, Cambridge, MA: Harvard University Press. In this work, Ohlin summarized and extended E. Heckscher's research first published in 1919.

[4] R. Vernon, 1966, International investments and international trade in product life cycle, *QJE*, May: 190–207.

[5] J. Brander & B. Spencer, 1985, Export subsidies and international market share rivalry, *JIE*, 18: 83–100; P. Krugman (ed.), 1986, *Strategic Trade Policy and the New International Economics*, Cambridge, MA: MIT Press.

[6] P. Krugman, 1994, *Peddling Prosperity* (p. 238), New York: Norton.

[7] M. Porter, 1990, *Competitive Advantage of Nations*, New York: Free Press.

[8] H. Davies & P. Ellis, 2001, Porter's *Competitive Advantage of Nations*: Time for the final judgment? *JMS*, 37: 1189–1215; J. Dunning, 1993, *The Globalization of Business*, London: Routledge; H. Moon, A. Rugman, & A. Verbeke, 1998, A generalized double diamond approach to the global competitiveness of Korea and Singapore, *IBR*, 7: 135–151.

[9] D. Kapur & R. Ramamurti, 2001, India's emerging competitive advantage in services, *AME*, 15 (2): 20–32.

[10] D. Bernhofen & J. Brown, 2005, An empirical assessment of the comparative advantage gains from trade, *AER*, 95: 208–225.

[11] *Economist*, 2003, Sparks fly over steel, November 15: 67–68.

[12] J. Bhagwati, 2004, *In Defense of Globalization*, New York: Oxford University Press.

[13] *Economist*, 2005, Europe's farm follies, December 10: 25; *Economist*, 2005, The farmers' friend, November 5: 58.

[14] H. Nordas, 2004, The global textile and clothing industry beyond the Agreement on Textiles and Clothing (p. 34), Discussion paper no. 5, Geneva: WTO Secretariat.

[15] *Economist*, 2005, The great stitch-up, May 28: 61–62.

[16] F. Bastiat, 1964, *Economic Sophisms*, A. Goddard (ed. and trans.), New York: Van Nostrand.

[17] M. Kreinin, 2006, *International Economics*, 10th ed. (p. 82), Cincinnati, OH: Thomson South-Western.

[18] S. Lenway, R. Morck, & B. Yeung, 1996, Rent seeking, protectionism, and innovation in the American steel industry, *EJ*, 106: 410–421.

[19] Quoted in *BW*, 2005, America's trade deficit: Expect some storm damage, October 3: 31.

[20] P. Krugman, 1993, What do undergrads need to know about trade? (p. 24), *AER*, 83: 23–26.

[21] L. Dobbs, 2004, *Exporting America: Why Corporate Greed Is Shipping American Jobs Overseas*, New York: Warner; O. Shenkar, 2005, *The Chinese Century*, Philadelphia: Wharton School Publishing.

[22] *Economist*, 2003, Tilting at dragons (p. 65), October 25: 65–66.

[23] C. Mann, 2003, *Globalization of IT Services and White Collar Jobs*, Washington, DC: Institute for International Economics.

[24] P. Samuelson, 2004, Where Ricardo and Mill rebut and confirm arguments of mainstream economists supporting globalization, *JEP*, 18 (3): 135–146.

[25] P. Samuelson, 1962, The gains from international trade once again, *EJ*, 72: 820–829.

[26] J. Bhagwati, A. Panagariya, & T. Sribivasan, 2004, The muddles over outsourcing, *JEP*, 18 (4): 93–114.

[27] J. Bhagwati & A. Panagariya, 2004, Trading opinions about free trade (p. 20), *BW*, December 27: 20.

[28] R. Florida, 2005, *The Flight of the Creative Class*, New York: Harper.

[29] *BW*, 2004, Shaking up trade theory (p. 120), December 6: 116–120.

[30] *Economist*, 2004, Use your brains, June 5: 10–11.

CHAPTER 6

Investing Abroad Directly

OPENING CASE

German Firms Invest Abroad Directly

Germany is the world's export champion, whose export volume (approximately $1 trillion a year) routinely outperforms other powerhouses such as the United States, China, and Japan. Yet, German firms increasingly find it necessary to reduce production at home and to invest abroad. The reason? The "Made in Germany" label has become both a blessing and a curse. As a blessing, German engineering, craftsmanship, and emphasis on reliability and durability have won customers all over the world. As a curse, such a quest for perfection, obsession with details, and (over)engineering come at a price that Germany may not be able to afford. Expensive products built to last do not bring much repeat business. While BMW and Mercedes cars set global standards, Germany has a lot of less visible but equally successful champion products in their respective domains. For example, Neumann microphones, which have captured songs from singers ranging from Elvis Presley to Céline Dion, will last 22 years before they need repair. But they don't come cheap: A single top-of-the-line, made-in-Germany Neumann microphone costs $6,450.

The little Neumann microphone is a good reflection of many German firms' dilemma. Shown in Table 6.1, it is often too expensive to produce in Germany, especially for labor-intensive products and processes, which cost close to $20 an hour (Table 6.1). The labor market is also inflexible, often guarded by prolabor government regulations and unions. In response, German firms have undertaken two coping strategies. First, many German firms, via foreign direct investment (FDI), perform much of the labor-intensive manufacturing abroad and then bring components home to add a magical German finishing touch, which adds value. As a result, the share of imported inputs to German exports increased from 30% to 40% between 1995 and 2005.

A second strategy, also via FDI, is to simply produce the whole thing abroad. Even when servicing the domestic German market, firms find that China can be ideal to handle time-insensitive goods. For time-sensitive goods, FDI in Central European countries such as Bulgaria, Hungary, and Poland can largely get the job done. When servicing overseas customers, producing in locations closer to them, especially for bulky products such as automobiles, can not only save labor costs but also hefty transportation and insurance bills. In 1990, BMW was synonymous with "Made in Germany." In 2006, in addition to Germany, BMW made cars in Austria, Brazil, Britain, China, Egypt, Indonesia, Malaysia, Philippines, Russia, South Africa, Thailand, United States, and Vietnam. While labor costs go down, does quality suffer? A little, but not much. For example, Continental, a tire maker, makes tire sensors in both China and Germany. The only difference is a slightly higher failure rate of two parts per million in China, compared with 0.8 parts per million in Germany.

FDI recipient economies are naturally happy. Central Europe, in particular, has recently accomplished strong growth thanks to German (and other EU) firms' "nearshoring." Yet, Germany has been suffering from chronically high and rising unemployment rates above 10%. More than 50% of the German job seekers have been looking for more than one year, but few of them are interested in migrating to Poland or Bulgaria (let alone India, South Africa, or China) to accept lower wages. Because of the welfare needs to support the army of unemployed, the tax burdens for firms and employees who have jobs end up becoming more crushing. Because of this vicious circle, out of necessity, many German firms have to shut down factories and move abroad. Recently, Continental closed a plant near Hanover, losing 320 jobs and

LEARNING OBJECTIVES

After studying this chapter, you should be able to

1. understand the vocabulary associated with foreign direct investment (FDI)
2. use the resource- and institution-based views to explain why FDI takes place
3. understand how FDI results in ownership, location, and internalization (OLI) advantages
4. identify different political views on FDI based on an understanding of FDI's benefits and costs to host and home countries
5. participate in two leading debates on FDI
6. draw implications for action

attracting political criticisms. In response, its CEO argued, "My duty is to my 80,000 workers worldwide." He further commented that if wages were set by the market (as opposed to being jacked up by inflexible rules), more German jobs would be saved.

TABLE 6.1 ESTIMATED AVERAGE HOURLY WAGE (US$)

	Factory worker	Engineer	Middle manager
Germany	19.80	38.90	40.40
Poland	3.07	4.32	6.69
Czech Republic	2.81	5.38	4.10
Hungary	1.96	5.09	7.44
Slovakia	2.21	4.15	5.48
Bulgaria	0.73	1.43	0.83
China	0.80	3.50	4.24
India	0.43	2.40	3.13
United States	13.50	35.00	45.00

Sources: Based on (1) http://www.bmwgroup.com; (2) *Business Week*, 2005, The rise of Central Europe, December 12: 50–54; (3) *Economist*, 2006, The problem with solid engineering, May 20: 71–73; (4) *Economist*, 2005, The rise of nearshoring, December 3: 65–67; (5) *Economist*, 2006, Waiting for a wunder, February 11: 1–16.

foreign direct investment (FDI) Investment in, controlling, and managing value-added activities in other countries.

multinational enterprise (MNE) A firm that engages in foreign direct investment and operates in multiple countries.

Why are German firms increasingly interested in outbound FDI? Is it because of the push of high labor costs at home? The pull of low labor costs and lucrative markets abroad? Or both? Recall from Chapter 1 that **foreign direct investment (FDI)** is defined as directly investing in activities that control and manage value creation in other countries.[1] Also recall from Chapter 1 that firms that engage in FDI are known as **multinational enterprises (MNEs)**. This chapter continues our coverage of international trade in Chapter 5. International trade and FDI are closely related. About 40% of US merchandise trade is between (1) overseas subsidiaries of US MNEs and US-based units and (2) US subsidiaries of non-US MNEs and their non-US-based units.[2] Approximately 60% of Chinese exports are generated by MNE affiliates producing in that country.

This chapter starts by clarifying the terms. Then we address a crucial question: Why do firms engage in FDI? We outline how the core perspectives introduced earlier—namely, resource- and institution-based views—can help answer this question. Debates and implications for action follow.

LEARNING OBJECTIVE 1

understand the vocabulary associated with foreign direct investment (FDI)

UNDERSTANDING THE FDI VOCABULARY

Part of FDI's complexity is associated with the vocabulary. We will try to reduce this complexity by setting the terms straight. Specifically, we will discuss (1) the key word in FDI, (2) horizontal versus vertical FDI, (3) FDI flow and stock, and (4) MNE versus non-MNE.

The Key Word Is D

There are two primary kinds of international investment: FDI and **foreign portfolio investment (FPI)**. FPI refers to investment in a portfolio of foreign securities such as stocks and bonds that do not entail the active management of foreign assets. Essentially, FPI is "foreign *indirect* investment." In contrast, the key word in FDI is D (direct)—namely, the direct hands-on management of foreign assets. While reading this book, some of you may have some FPI at the same time; as long as you own some foreign stocks and bonds, you don't need to do anything else. However, when reading this book, it is by definition impossible that you are also engaging in FDI at the same time, which requires that you as a manager get your feet "wet" by actively managing foreign operations.

foreign portfolio investment (FPI)
Investment in a portfolio of foreign securities such as stocks and bonds.

For statistical purposes, FDI is defined by the United Nations as involving an equity stake of 10% or more in a foreign-based enterprise.[3] Without a sufficiently large equity, it is difficult to exercise **management control rights**—namely, the rights to appoint key managers and establish control mechanisms. Many firms invest abroad for the explicit purpose of managing foreign operations, and they need a large equity, sometimes up to 100%, to be able to do that.

management control rights
The rights to appoint key managers and establish control mechanisms.

Horizontal and Vertical FDI

There are two main types of FDI: horizontal and vertical. Recall the value chain introduced in Chapter 4, through which firms perform value-adding activities stage by stage in a vertical fashion (from upstream to downstream). When a firm *duplicates* its home country-based activities at the same value chain stage in a host country through FDI, we call this **horizontal FDI** (see Figure 6.1). For example, BMW assembles cars in Germany. Through horizontal FDI, it does the same thing in host countries such as Russia, Thailand, and the United States. Overall, horizontal FDI refers to producing the same products or offering the same services in a host country as firms do at home.

horizontal FDI
A type of FDI in which a firm duplicates its home country-based activities at the same value chain stage in a host country.

If a firm through FDI moves upstream or downstream in different value chain stages in a host country, we label this **vertical FDI** (Figure 6.2). For instance, if BMW (hypothetically) only assembles cars and does not manufacture components

vertical FDI
A type of FDI in which a firm moves upstream or downstream in different value chain stages in a host country.

FIGURE 6.1 HORIZONTAL FDI

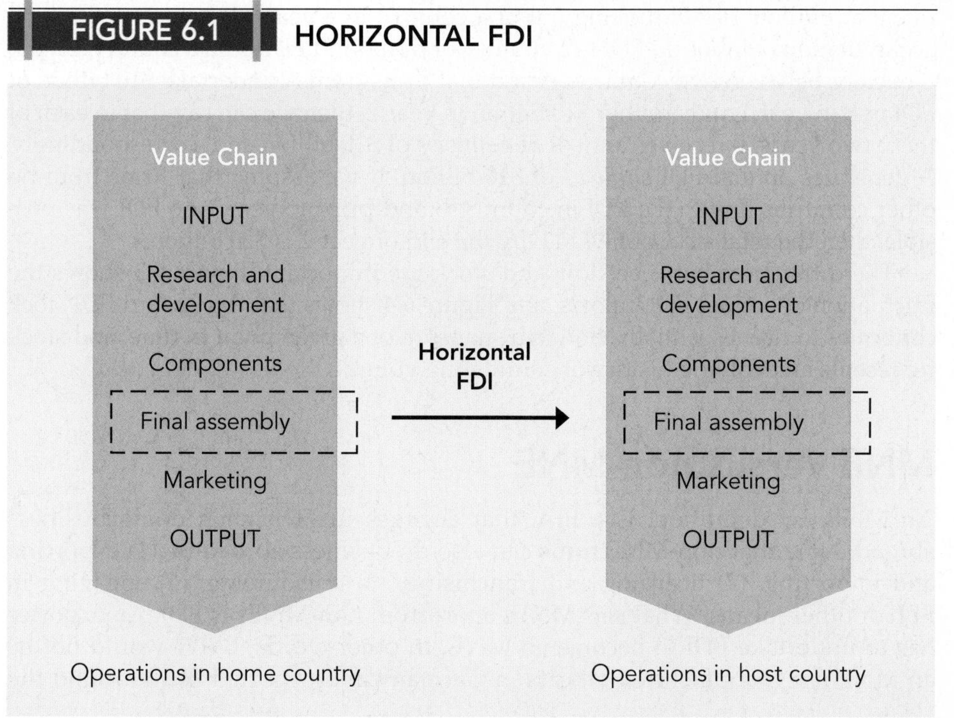

FIGURE 6.2 VERTICAL FDI

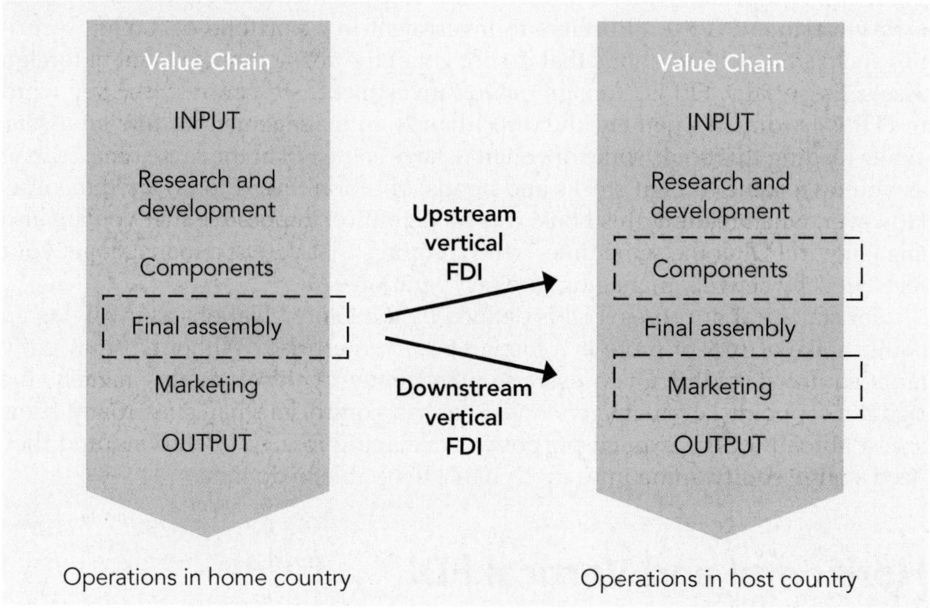

in Germany, but in the United States, it enters into components manufacturing through FDI (an upstream activity), this would be **upstream vertical FDI.** Likewise, if BMW does not engage in car distribution in Germany but invests in car dealerships in Egypt (a downstream activity), it would be **downstream vertical FDI.**

upstream vertical FDI
A type of vertical FDI in which a firm engages in an upstream stage of the value.

downstream vertical FDI
A type of vertical FDI in which a firm engages in a downstream stage of the value chain in two different countries.

FDI Flow and Stock

Another pair of words often used is flow and stock. **FDI flow** is the amount of FDI moving in a given period (usually a year) in a certain direction. **FDI inflow** usually refers to inbound FDI moving into a country in a year, and **FDI outflow** typically refers to outbound FDI moving out of a country in a year. **FDI stock** is the total accumulation of inbound FDI in a country or outbound FDI from a country. Hypothetically, between two countries A and B, if firms from A undertake $10 billion of FDI in B in year 1 and another $10 billion in year 2, then we can say that in each of these two years, B receives annual FDI *inflows* of $10 billion and, correspondingly, A generates annual FDI *outflows* of $10 billion. If we assume that firms from no other countries undertake FDI in country B and prior to year 1 no FDI was possible, then the total *stock* of FDI in B by the end of year 2 is $20 billion.

The differences between flow and stock are important. Figure 6.3 shows the fluctuation of annual FDI inflows, and Figure 6.4 shows that the inward FDI stock continues to rise. Essentially, flow is a snapshot of a given point in time, and stock represents an evolving history of cumulating volume.

FDI flow
The amount of FDI moving in a given period (usually a year) in a certain direction.

FDI inflow
Inbound FDI moving into a country in a year.

FDI outflow
Outbound FDI moving out of a country in a year.

FDI stock
The total accumulation of inbound FDI in a country or outbound FDI from a country across a given period of time (usually several years).

MNE versus non-MNE

An MNE, by definition, is a firm that engages in FDI when doing business abroad. Note that non-MNE firms can also do business abroad by (1) exporting and importing, (2) licensing and franchising, (3) outsourcing, (4) engaging in FPI, or other means. What sets MNEs apart from non-MNEs is FDI. An exporter has to undertake FDI to become an MNE. In other words, BMW would not be an MNE if it manufactured all cars in Germany and exported them around the

FIGURE 6.3 ANNUAL FDI INFLOWS

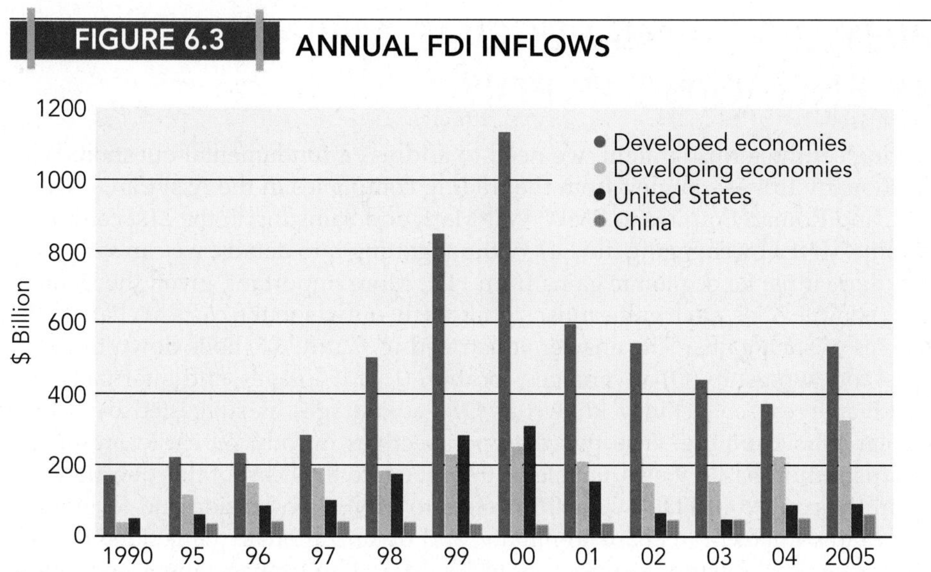

Source: Based on data from United Nations Conference on Trade and Development, 2006, *World Investment Report 2006*, New York and Geneva: UNCTAD, with additional data from http://stats.unctad.org. China refers to mainland China (the People's Republic of China) only and does not include Hong Kong, China and Macao, China.

FIGURE 6.4 INWARD FDI STOCK

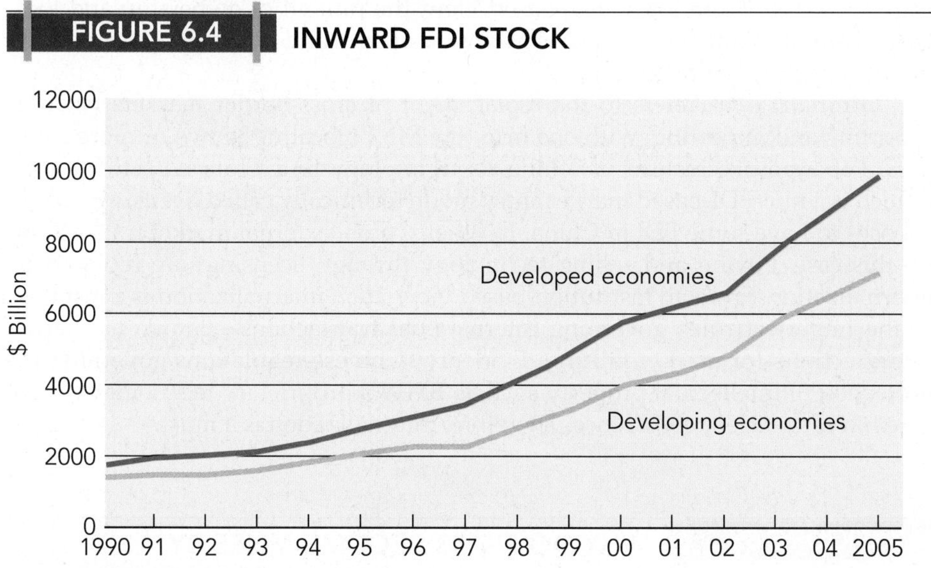

Source: Based on data from United Nations Conference on Trade and Development, 2006, *World Investment Report 2006*, New York and Geneva: UNCTAD, with additional data from http://stats.unctad.org.

world. BMW became an MNE only when it started to directly invest abroad (see Opening Case).

Although a lot of people believe that MNEs are a new organizational form that emerged after World War II, that is not true. MNEs existed for at least 2,000 years, with their earliest traces discovered in the foreign trading posts of the Assyrian, Phoenician, and Roman Empires.[4] In 1903 when Ford Motor Company was founded, it exported its sixth car. Ford almost immediately engaged in FDI by having a factory in Canada that produced its first car in 1904.[5] In postwar decades, MNEs have experienced significant growth. In 1970, there were approximately 7,000 MNEs worldwide.[6] In 1990, there were 37,000 MNEs, with 170,000 foreign affiliates. By 2006, more than 77,000 MNEs (*two times* the 1990 number) controlled 690,000 foreign affiliates (*four times* the 1990 number). The share of FDI-based value-added of foreign affiliates of MNEs in world GDP rose from 7% in 1990 to 10% in 2006.[7] Clearly, there is a proliferation of MNEs lately.

LEARNING OBJECTIVE 2

use the resource- and institution-based views to explain why FDI takes place

WHY DO FIRMS BECOME MNEs BY ENGAGING IN FDI?

Having set the terms straight, we need to address a fundamental question: Why do so many firms—ranging from the trading companies in the Assyrian, Phoenician, and Roman Empires to BMW, Wal-Mart, and Samsung in the 21st century—become MNEs by engaging in FDI? Without getting into details, we can safely say that there must be economic gains from FDI. More important, given the tremendous complexities, such gains must significantly outweigh the costs.[8] What are the sources of such gains? The answer, illustrated in Figure 6.5, boils down to firms' quest for ownership (O) advantages, location (L) advantages, and internalization (I) advantages—collectively known as **OLI advantages** as suggested by British scholar John Dunning.[9] The two core perspectives introduced earlier, resource- and institution-based views, enable us to probe into the heart of this question.

OLI advantages
A firm's quest for ownership (O) advantages, location (L) advantages, and internalization (I) advantages via FDI.

In the context of FDI, **ownership** refers to MNEs' possession and leveraging of certain valuable, rare, hard-to-imitate, and organizationally embedded (VRIO) assets overseas. Owning proprietary technological and management know-how that makes a BMW helps ensure that the MNE can beat rivals abroad. **Location** refers to advantages enjoyed by firms operating in certain areas. For instance, BMW's operations in South Africa provide a convenient platform to cover sub-Saharan Africa. From a resource-based view, the pursuit of ownership and location advantages can be regarded as MNEs' resources and capabilities flexing their muscles in global competition.

ownership
The MNEs' possession and leveraging of certain valuable, rare, hard-to-imitate, and organizationally embedded (VRIO) assets overseas in the context of FDI.

location
Advantages enjoyed by firms operating in certain locations.

Internalization refers to the replacement of cross-border markets (such as exporting and importing) with one firm (the MNE) locating in two or more countries. For example, instead of selling its technology to a Chinese firm for a fee (which is a non-FDI-based market entry mode technically called **licensing**), BMW chooses to have some FDI in China. In other words, external market transactions (in this case, buying and selling technology through licensing) are replaced by internalization. From an institution-based view, such internalization is a response to the imperfect rules governing international transactions—known as **market imperfections** (or **market failure**). Evidently, Chinese regulations governing the protection of intellectual property such as BMW's proprietary technology do not give BMW sufficient confidence. Therefore, internalization is a must.

internalization
The replacement of cross-border markets (such as exporting and importing) with one firm (the MNE) locating in two or more countries—essentially internalizing the external market transaction and turning it in-house.

licensing
An external market transaction in which firms buy and sell technology and intellectual property rights.

market imperfections (or **market failure**)
The imperfect rules governing international transactions.

FIGURE 6.5 WHY DO FIRMS BECOME MNES BY ENGAGING IN FDI? AN OLI FRAMEWORK

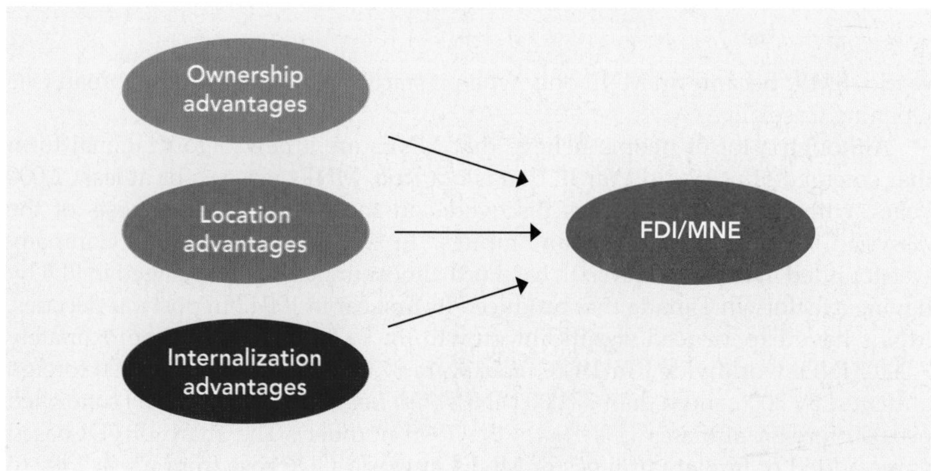

Overall, firms become MNEs because FDI provides ownership, location, and internalization advantages that they otherwise would not obtain. The next three sections outline why this is the case.

OWNERSHIP ADVANTAGES

LEARNING OBJECTIVE 3

understand how FDI results in ownership, location, and internalization (OLI) advantages

All investments, including both FDI and FPI, entail ownership of assets. So, what is unique about FDI? This section (1) highlights the benefits of direct ownership and (2) compares and contrasts FDI with licensing when entertaining market entries abroad.

The Benefits of Direct Ownership

Remember the key word in FDI is *direct*, and it requires a significant equity ownership position. The benefits of ownership lie in the *combination* of equity ownership rights and management control rights. Specifically, it is significant ownership rights that provide much needed management control rights.[10] In contrast, FPI represents essentially insignificant ownership rights and no management control rights. To compete successfully, firms need to deploy overwhelming resources and capabilities to overcome their liabilities of foreignness (see Chapters 1 and 4). FDI provides one of the best ways to facilitate such extension of firm-specific resources and capabilities abroad.

FDI versus Licensing

When entering foreign markets, basic entry choices include (1) exporting, (2) licensing, or (3) FDI. Successful exporting may provoke protectionist responses from host countries, thus forcing firms to choose between licensing and FDI. Between licensing and FDI, which is better? Three reasons may compel firms to prefer FDI to licensing (Table 6.2).

First, FDI affords a high degree of direct management control that reduces the risk of firm-specific resources and capabilities being opportunistically taken advantage of. One of the leading risks abroad is **dissemination risks**, defined as the risks associated with unauthorized diffusion of firm-specific know-how. If a foreign company grants a license to a local firm to manufacture or market a product, "it runs the risk of the licensee, or an employee of the licensee, disseminating the know-how or using it for purposes other than those originally intended."[11] For instance, Pizza Hut found out that its long-time licensee in Thailand disseminated its know-how and established a direct competitor, called The Pizza Company, that recently controlled 70% of the market in Thailand.[12] Owning and managing proprietary assets through FDI do not completely shield firms from dissemination risks (after all, their employees can quit and join competitors), but FDI is better

dissemination risks
The risks associated with unauthorized diffusion of firm-specific know-how.

TABLE 6.2 WHY FIRMS PREFER FDI TO LICENSING

- FDI reduces dissemination risks
- FDI provides tight control over foreign operations
- FDI facilitates the transfer of tacit knowledge through "learning by doing"

Does Wal-Mart's competitive advantage in this store in China come from its tacit knowledge?

than licensing that provides no such management control. Understandably, FDI is extensively used in knowledge-intensive, high-tech industries, such as automobiles, electronics, chemicals, and IT.[13]

Second, FDI provides more direct and tighter control over foreign operations. Even when licensees (and their employees) harbor no opportunistic intention to take away "secrets," they may not follow the wishes of the foreign firm that provides the know-how. Without FDI, the foreign firm cannot order or control its licensee to move ahead. For example, Starbucks entered South Korea by licensing its format to ESCO. Although ESCO soon opened ten stores, Starbucks felt that ESCO was not aggressive enough in growing the chain. But there was very little Starbucks could do. Eventually, Starbucks switched from licensing to FDI, which allowed Starbucks to directly call "the shots" and promote the aggressive growth of the chain in South Korea.

Finally, certain knowledge (or know-how) calls for FDI as opposed to licensing. Even if there is no opportunism on the part of licensees and if they are willing to follow the wishes of the foreign firm, certain know-how may be too difficult to transfer to licensees without FDI. Knowledge has two basic categories: (1) explicit and (2) tacit (implicit). Explicit knowledge is codifiable (that is, it can be written down and transferred without losing much of its richness). Tacit (implicit) knowledge, on the other hand, is noncodifiable, and its acquisition and transfer require hands-on practice. For instance, a driving manual represents a body of explicit knowledge. However, mastering this manual without any road practice does not make you a good driver. Tacit knowledge is evidently more important and harder to transfer and learn; it can only be acquired through learning by doing (in this case, driving practice supervised by an experienced driver). Likewise, operating a Wal-Mart store entails a great deal of knowledge, some explicit (often captured in an operational manual) and some tacit. However, simply giving foreign licensees a copy of the Wal-Mart operational manual will not be enough. Foreign employees will need to learn from Wal-Mart personnel side by side (learning by doing).

From a resource-based standpoint, it is Wal-Mart's tacit knowledge that gives it competitive advantage (see Chapter 4). Wal-Mart owns such crucial tacit knowledge, and it has no incentive to give it away to licensees without having some management control over how such tacit knowledge is used. Therefore, properly transferring and controlling tacit knowledge calls for FDI.[14] Overall, ownership advantages enable the firm, now becoming an MNE, to more effectively extend, transfer, and leverage firm-specific capabilities abroad.[15] Next, we discuss location advantages.

LOCATION ADVANTAGES

The second key word in FDI is F and refers to a foreign location. Given the well-known liability of foreignness, foreign locations must offer compelling advantages.[16] This section (1) highlights the sources of location advantages and (2) outlines ways to acquire and neutralize location advantages.

Location, Location, Location

Certain locations possess geographic features that are difficult for others to match. We may regard the continuous expansion of international business, such as FDI, as an unending saga in search of location-specific advantages. For example, Vienna is an attractive site as MNE regional headquarters for Central and Eastern Europe. Miami advertises itself as the Gateway of the Americas. These locations, naturally, attract a lot of FDI.

Beyond natural geographic advantages, location advantages also arise from the clustering of economic activities in certain locations—referred to as **agglomeration**.[17] For instance, the Netherlands grows and exports two-thirds of the worldwide exports of cut flowers. Slovakia produces more cars per capita than any other country in the world, thanks to the quest for agglomeration benefits by global automakers. In Focus 6.1 highlights how agglomeration has made Wichita, Kansas, the Air Capital of the World. Overall, agglomeration advantages stem from:

agglomeration
The location advantages that arise from the clustering of economic activities in certain locations.

IN FOCUS 6.1 Air Capital of the World: Wichita, Kansas

Although Wichita, Kansas only has a population of approximately 400,000 people, the *entire* population of major aerospace companies in the Western world is represented here: Airbus (North American Wing Design), Boeing (Integrated Defense Systems), Bombardier Aerospace/Learjet, Cessna Aircraft, Raytheon/Beech Aircraft, and Spirit AeroSystems. While Boeing, Cessna, and Raytheon are US owned, Airbus, Bombardier, and Spirit have come to Wichita via FDI—the latter two companies are Canadian owned. The city proudly claims itself to be the Air Capital of the World. Why is Wichita so attractive? In one word, agglomeration (clustering of economic activities). In Wichita, the aerospace industry employs 35,000 workers and makes up 60% of manufacturing earnings. In Kansas, $22 of every $100 in earnings comes from this industry.

Wichita's aerospace industry started in the 1920s. Flat land, good winds, and excellent year-round flying weather were initially important. In 1929, Boeing came by acquiring a local start-up. During World War II, Boeing produced numerous military aircraft, including the famous B-29 bomber, in Wichita. In postwar decades, Wichita has become one of Boeing's prime engineering, fabrication, assembly, and modification centers. The two US presidential Boeing 747s, known as Air Force One when the president is on board, were made in Everett, Washington, but modified, equipped, and serviced in Wichita. In addition to large aircraft made by Boeing, Wichita is also the undisputed leader in small aircraft for general aviation (often known as business jets). All the top-three players, Learjet, Cessna, and Beech, are here. Cessna and Beech were acquired by US-owned Textron and Raytheon, respectively, and Learjet was bought by Canada's Bombardier. Airbus does not manufacture in Wichita. Instead, it set up an R&D center that employs 200 engineers. In 2005, Boeing spun off its commercial aircraft division in Wichita and sold it, for $1.5 billion, to a Canadian company that nobody had heard of in the aerospace industry, Onex Corporation. Although Onex (TSX: OCX) is one of Canada's largest diversified companies with $16 billion annual sales, it had never operated in the aerospace industry before. Onex named its new Wichita-based subsidiary Spirit AeroSpace. Spirit has continued to be a major supplier to Boeing. In addition, exercising the spirit of an independent company, Spirit has also secured new contracts to supply Airbus in Europe. Since then, Boeing's work in Wichita has been entirely focusing on the military side.

Sources: I thank Professor Dharma DeSilva (Wichita State University) for his assistance on this case. Based on (1) R. Whyte, 2006, Competitiveness in the global aircraft industry, Presentation at Wichita State University, May 20; (2) http://www.boeing.com; (3) http://www.learjet.com; (4) http://www.cessna.com; (5) http://www.onex.com; (6) http://www.raytheon.com; (7) http://www.wingsoverkansas.com.

knowledge spillover
Knowledge diffused from one firm to others among closely located firms.

- **Knowledge spillovers** (knowledge diffused from one firm to others) among closely located firms that attempt to hire individuals from competitors
- Industry demand that creates a skilled labor force whose members may work for different firms without having to move out of the region
- Industry demand that facilitates a pool of specialized suppliers and buyers also located in the region[18]

Beyond the quest for geographic and agglomeration advantages, some firms undertake FDI in search of markets. Airbus is building an assembly plant in China not because it is cheap to make planes in China. The country's inefficiencies in advanced aerospace manufacturing and in related and supporting industries more than offset the savings brought by cheap labor (see Chapter 5). Airbus has one clear goal: seeking greater access to the Chinese aviation market.[19] Although some products can be made in the home country and exported to host countries, firms have to consider transportation costs, which can be very high for bulky products such as automobiles and appliances. Thus, high transportation costs often justify FDI, as illustrated by China's Haier in In Focus 6.2.

Acquiring and Neutralizing Location Advantages

Note that from a resource-based view, location advantages do not entirely overlap with country-level advantages such as factor endowments discussed in Chapter 5. Location advantages refer to the advantages one firm obtains when operating in one location due to its *firm-specific* capabilities. In 1982, General Motors (GM) ran its Fremont, California, plant to the ground and had to close it. Reopening the same plant, Toyota in 1984 initiated its first FDI project in the United States (in a joint venture [JV] with GM). Since then, Toyota (together with GM) has leveraged this plant's location advantages by producing award-winning cars that American customers particularly like, the Toyota Corolla and Tacoma. The point here is that it is Toyota's unique capabilities, applied to the California location, that literally saved this plant from its demise. The California location in itself does not provide location advantages per se, as shown by GM's inability to make it work prior to 1982.

Firms do not operate in a vacuum. When one firm enters a foreign country through FDI, its rivals are likely to follow by undertaking additional FDI in a host

IN FOCUS  6.2 Haier Invests in America

Haier is China's largest and the world's fifth largest appliance maker. Since the early 1990s, Haier has launched an export push. Although Haier manufactures 250 product lines at home, its US entry, starting in 1994, sidestepped market leaders such as GE and Whirlpool by focusing on a very narrow segment—small (sub-180 liter) refrigerators that serve hotel rooms and dorms. Incumbents had dismissed this segment as peripheral and low margin. Since then, the Haier brand has successfully penetrated nine of the ten largest US retail chains, including Wal-Mart and Target.

Haier has also become a foreign direct investor by setting up factories in India, Indonesia, and Iran. Since 2000, it has invested more than $30 million to build a factory in Camden, South Carolina. One wonders why a Chinese multinational, blessed with a low-wage work force at home, would want to open a plant in high-wage America. Haier officials suggest that shipping refrigerators across the Pacific is costly and can take 40 days, thus offsetting China's wage advantage. Better to build close to the customer and place the "Made-in-USA" tag on the product, which is a tiebreaker among American consumers. The factory brings other less tangible benefits as well. It shows a commitment to the US market, which increases retailers' confidence in carrying the brand. Also, it is "politically correct" when Chinese exports are being criticized for taking away American jobs.

Sources: Based on (1) R. Crawford & L. Paine, 1998, The Haier Group (A), Harvard Business School case 9-398-101; (2) B. Wysocki, 2002, Chinese firms aim for global market, *Asian Wall Street Journal*, January 29: 1; (3) M. Zeng & P. Williamson, 2003, The hidden dragons, *Harvard Business Review*, 81 (10): 92–104.

country to (1) acquire location advantages themselves or (2) at least neutralize the first mover's location advantages. These actions to imitate and follow competitors are especially likely in industries characterized by **oligopoly**—industries populated by a small number of players (such as aerospace and semiconductors).[20] The automobile industry is a typical oligopolistic industry. In China, Volkswagen was the first foreign entrant, starting production in 1985 and enjoying a market share of 60% in the 1990s. Now, every self-respecting global automaker has entered China trying to eat some of Volkswagen's "lunch" (see Integrative Case 2.4). Overall, competitive rivalry and imitation, especially in oligopolistic industries, underscore the importance of acquiring and neutralizing location advantages around the world.

oligopoly
Industries populated by a small number of players.

INTERNALIZATION ADVANTAGES

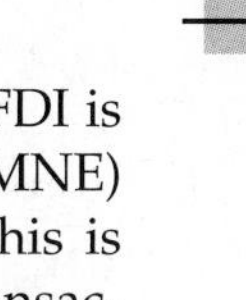

Known as internalization, another set of great advantages associated with FDI is the ability to replace the external market relationship with one firm (the MNE) owning, controlling, and managing activities in two or more countries. This is important because of significant imperfections in international market transactions. The institution-based view suggests that markets are governed by rules, regulations, and norms that are designed to reduce uncertainties. Uncertainties introduce transaction costs—costs associated with doing business (see Chapter 2). This section (1) outlines the necessity to combat market failure and (2) describes the benefits brought by internalization.

Market Failure

Compared with domestic transaction costs, international transaction costs tend to be higher. Because laws and regulations are typically enforced on a nation-state basis, if one party from country A behaves opportunistically, the other party from country B will have a hard time enforcing the contract. Suing the other party in a foreign country is not only costly but also uncertain. In the worst case, such imperfections are so grave that markets fail to function, and many firms choose not to do business abroad to avoid being "burned." Thus, high transaction costs can result in market failure—the imperfections of the market mechanisms that make transactions prohibitively costly and sometimes prevent transactions from taking place. However, recall from Chapter 5 that there are gains from trade. In response, MNEs emerge to overcome and combat such market failure through FDI.

Overcoming Market Failure through FDI

How do MNEs combat market failure through internalization? Let us use a simple example: an oil importer, BP in Britain, and an oil exporter, Nigerian National Petroleum Corporation (NNPC) in Nigeria. For the sake of our discussion, assume that BP does all its business in Britain and NNPC does all its business in Nigeria; in other words, neither is an MNE. BP and NNPC negotiate a contract which specifies that NNPC will export from Nigeria a certain amount of crude oil to BP's oil refinery facilities in Britain for a certain amount of money. Shown in Figure 6.6, this is both an export contract (from NNPC's perspective) and an import contract (from BP's standpoint) between two firms.

However, this market transaction between an importer and an exporter may suffer from high transaction costs. What is especially costly is the potential opportunism on both sides. For example, *after* the deal is signed, NNPC may demand higher than agreed-upon prices, citing a variety of reasons such as inflation, natural disasters, or simply rising oil prices. BP thus has to either (1) pay more than the agreed-upon price or (2) refuse to pay and suffer from the huge costs of keeping

FIGURE 6.6 **AN INTERNATIONAL MARKET TRANSACTION BETWEEN TWO COMPANIES IN TWO COUNTRIES**

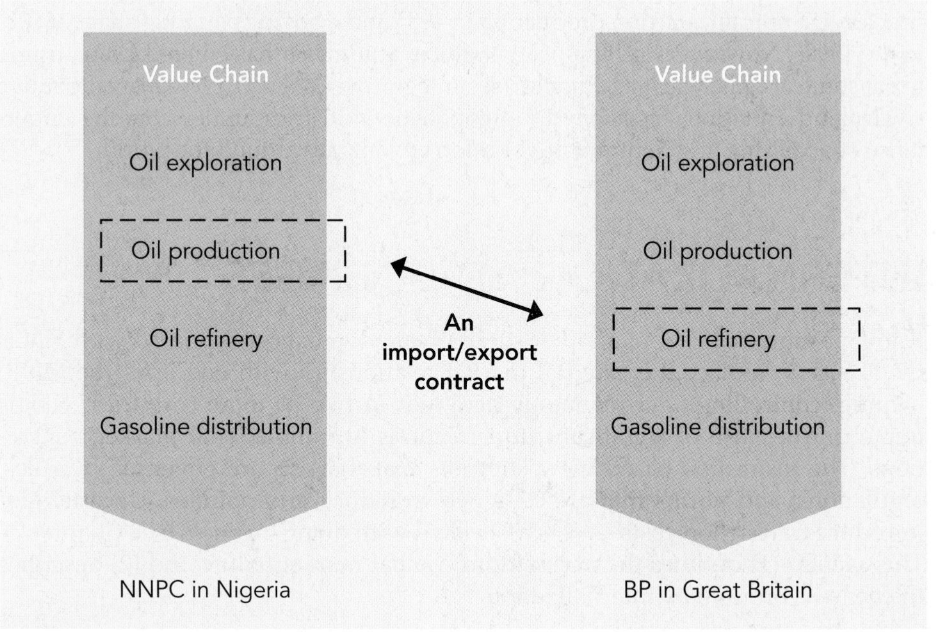

expensive refinery facilities idle. In other words, NNPC's opportunistic behavior can cause a lot of BP's losses.

However, the point here is not to suggest that Nigerians are always opportunistic (this is only an example). The British can also behave opportunistically. For instance, BP may refuse to accept a shipment after its arrival from Nigeria citing unsatisfactory quality, but the real reason could be BP's inability to sell refined oil downstream because gasoline demand is going down (perhaps people are driving less). NNPC is thus forced to find a new buyer for a huge tanker load of crude oil on a last-minute, "fire sale" basis with a deep discount, losing a lot of money.

Overall, in a market (export/import) transaction, once one side behaves opportunistically, the other side will not be happy and will threaten or initiate lawsuits. Because the legal and regulatory frameworks governing such international transactions are generally not as effective as those governing domestic transactions, the injured party will usually be frustrated while the opportunistic party often gets away with it. All these are examples of transaction costs that increase international market inefficiencies and imperfections, ultimately resulting in market failure.

While the default is not undertaking such hazardous international trade and giving up potential gains from trade, FDI combats such market failure through internalization. By replacing an external market relationship with a single organization spanning both countries (a process called internalization, transforming the external market with in-house links), the MNE thus reduces cross-border transaction costs and increases efficiencies.[21] In theory, there can be two possibilities: (1) BP undertakes upstream vertical FDI by owning oil production assets in Nigeria, or (2) NNPC undertakes downstream vertical FDI by owning oil refinery assets in Great Britain

What advantages does LukOil of Russia obtain by engaging in FDI in the US?

FIGURE 6.7 **COMBATING MARKET FAILURE THROUGH FDI: ONE COMPANY (MNE) IN TWO COUNTRIES***

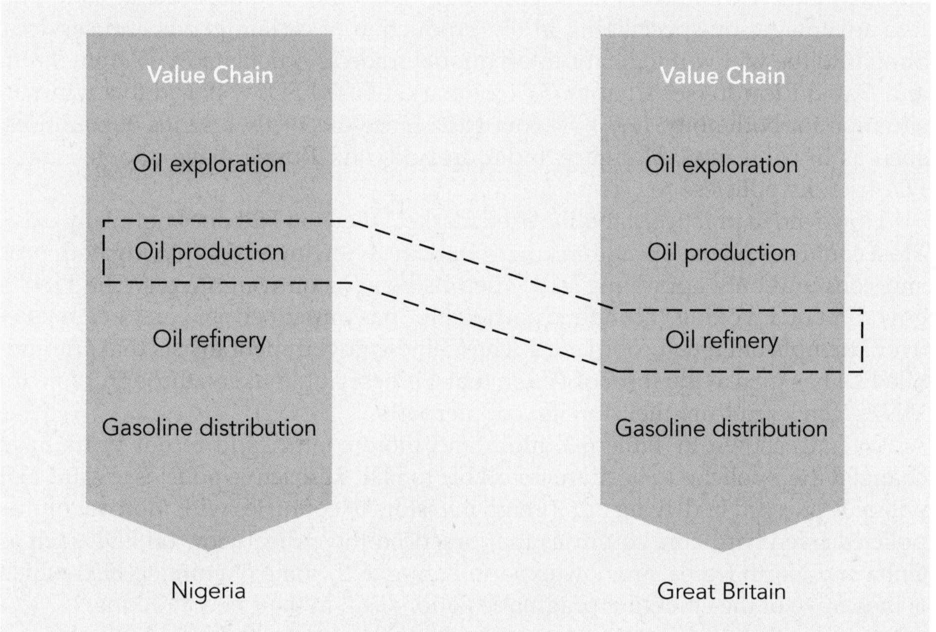

* In theory, there can be two possibilities: (1) BP undertakes *upstream* vertical FDI by owning oil production assets in Nigeria, or (2) NNPC undertakes *downstream* vertical FDI by owning oil refinery assets in Great Britain. In reality, the first scenario is more likely.

(Figure 6.7). As a real-life example, the photo on page 164 shows Russian firm LukOil's FDI in US gas stations. FDI essentially transforms the international trade between two independent firms in two countries to **intrafirm trade** between two subsidiaries in two countries controlled by the same MNE.[22] The MNE is thus able to coordinate cross-border activities better. Such advantage is called internalization advantage.

intrafirm trade
International trade between two subsidiaries in two countries controlled by the same MNE.

Overall, motivations for FDI are complex. The quest for OLI advantages, while analytically distinct as discussed, may overlap in practice.[23] Based on resource- and institution-based views, we can view FDI as a reflection of (1) firms' motivation to extend firm-specific capabilities abroad and (2) their responses to overcome market imperfections and failures.

REALITIES OF FDI

LEARNING OBJECTIVE 4
identify different political views on FDI based on an understanding of FDI's benefits and costs to host and home countries

The realities of FDI are intertwined with politics. This section starts with three political views on FDI, followed by a discussion of the pros and cons of FDI for home and host countries.

Political Views on FDI

There are three primary political views. First, the **radical view** is hostile to FDI. Tracing its roots to Marxism, the radical view treats FDI as an instrument of imperialism and as a vehicle for exploitation of domestic resources, industries, and people by foreign capitalists and firms. Governments embracing the radical view often nationalize MNE assets or simply ban (or discourage) inbound MNEs. Between the 1950s and the early 1980s, the radical view was influential throughout Africa, Asia, Eastern Europe, and Latin America.[24] However, the popularity of this view is in decline worldwide because (1) economic development in these countries

radical view on FDI
A political view that is hostile to FDI.

free market view on FDI
A political view that suggests that FDI, unrestricted by government intervention, will enable countries to tap into their absolute or comparative advantages by specializing in the production of certain goods and services.

pragmatic nationalism
A political view that approves FDI only when its benefits outweigh its costs.

was poor in the absence of FDI, and (2) the few developing countries (such as Singapore) that embraced FDI attained enviable growth.

On the other hand, the **free market view** suggests that FDI, unrestricted by government intervention, will enable countries to tap into their absolute or comparative advantages by specializing in the production of certain goods and services. Similar to the win-win logic for international trade as articulated by Adam Smith and David Ricardo (see Chapter 5), free market-based FDI will lead to a win-win situation for both home and host countries. Since the 1980s, a series of countries, such as Brazil, China, Hungary, India, Ireland, and Russia, have adopted more FDI-friendly policies.

However, in practice, a totally "free market" view on FDI does not really exist. Most countries practice **pragmatic nationalism**—viewing FDI as having both pros and cons and only approving FDI when its benefits outweigh costs. The French government, invoking "economic patriotism," has torpedoed several foreign takeover attempts of French companies. The Chinese government insists that automobile FDI has to take the form of JVs so that Chinese automakers, through JVs with MNEs, can learn from their foreign counterparts.

Overall, shown in Table 6.3, more and more countries in recent years have changed their policies to be more favorable to FDI. Restrictive policies toward FDI will only succeed in driving out foreign investors to countries with more favorable policies. Even hard-core countries that practiced the radical view on FDI, such as Cuba and North Korea, are now experimenting with some opening to FDI, which is indicative of the emerging pragmatic nationalism in their new thinking.

Benefits and Costs of FDI to Host Countries

Underpinning pragmatic nationalism is the need to assess the various benefits and costs of FDI to host (recipient) countries and home (source) countries. In a nutshell, Figure 6.8 outlines these considerations. This section focuses on host countries, and the next section deals with home countries.

Cell 1 in Figure 6.8 shows four primary benefits to host countries:

- Capital inflow can help improve a host country's balance of payments. The balance of payments records a country's payments to and receipts from other countries. Japanese firms undertake FDI by acquiring US-based assets. By bringing more capital into the United States, such FDI helps improve the US balance of payments.[25] (See Chapter 7 for more coverage on balance of payments.)

TABLE 6.3 CHANGES IN NATIONAL REGULATIONS OF FOREIGN DIRECT INVESTMENT (FDI)

	1991	1995	2000	2001	2002	2003	2004	2005
Number of countries	35	64	69	71	70	82	102	93
Number of changes	82	112	150	208	248	244	271	205
More favorable to FDI	80	106	147	194	236	220	235	164
Less favorable to FDI	2	6	3	14	12	24	36	41

Source: Adapted from United Nations Conference on Trade and Development, *World Investment Report 2005* (p. 26) and *World Investment Report 2006* (p. 24), New York and Geneva: UNCTAD.

FIGURE 6.8 EFFECTS OF FDI ON HOME AND HOST COUNTRIES

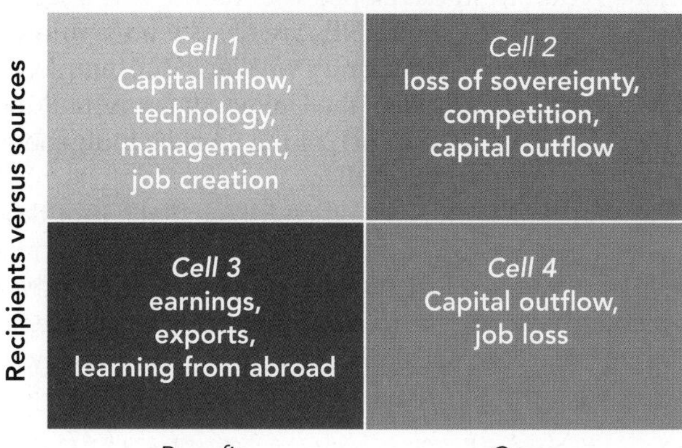

- Technology, especially more advanced technology from abroad, can create **technology spillovers** (foreign technology diffused domestically) that benefit domestic firms and industries.[26] Local rivals, after observing such technology, may recognize its feasibility and strive to imitate it. This is known as the **demonstration effect**—sometimes also called the **contagion** (or **imitation**) **effect**.[27] It underscores the important role that MNEs play in stimulating competition in host countries.[28]
- Advanced management know-how may be highly valued. It is often difficult for indigenous development of management know-how to reach a world-class level in the absence of FDI.[29]
- Finally, FDI creates jobs both directly and indirectly.[30] Direct benefits arise when MNEs employ individuals locally. For example, more than 50% of the Irish manufacturing employees work for MNEs.[31] Indirect benefits include jobs created when local suppliers increase hiring and when MNE employees spend money locally resulting in more jobs. For instance, in 2006, Toyota directly employed 32,000 employees in the United States. Indirectly, it created 386,000 jobs.

technology spillover
Foreign technology diffused domestically that benefits domestic firms and industries.

demonstration effect (contagion or imitation effect)
The reaction of local firms to rise to the challenge demonstrated by MNEs through learning and imitation.

Cell 2 in Figure 6.8 outlines three primary costs of FDI to host countries: (1) loss of sovereignty, (2) adverse effects on competition, and (3) capital outflow. The first concern is the loss of some (but not all) economic sovereignty associated with FDI. Because of FDI, foreigners are making decisions to invest, produce, and market products and services in a host country, or if locals serve as heads of MNE subsidiaries, they represent the interest of foreign firms. Will foreigners and foreign firms make decisions in the best interest of host countries? This is truly a "billion-dollar" question. According to the radical view, the answer is no because foreigners and foreign firms are likely to maximize their own profits by exploiting people and resources in host countries. Such deep suspicion of MNEs leads to policies that discourage or even ban FDI. On the other hand, countries embracing free market and pragmatic nationalism views agree that despite some acknowledged differences between foreign and host country interests, there is a sufficient overlap of interests between MNEs and host countries. Thus, host countries are willing to live with some loss of sovereignty.

How does this high-performance Nokia mobile device affect the motivation and capabilities of indigenous mobile phone makers in emerging economies?

A second concern is associated with the negative effects on local competition. We have just discussed MNEs' positive effects on local competition, but it is possible that MNEs may drive some domestic firms out of business. Having driven domestic firms out of business, MNEs, in theory, may be able to monopolize local markets. Although this is a relatively minor concern in developed economies, it is a legitimate concern for less developed economies, where MNEs are of such a magnitude in size and strength and local firms tend to be significantly weaker. For example, as Coca-Cola and PepsiCo extend their "cola wars" from the United States around the world, they have almost "accidentally" wiped out much of the world's indigenous beverages companies, which are—or were—much smaller.

A third concern is associated with capital outflow. When MNEs make profits in host countries and repatriate (send back) such earnings to headquarters in home countries, host countries experience a net outflow in the capital account in their balance of payments. As a result, some countries have restricted MNEs' ability to repatriate funds. Another issue arises when MNE subsidiaries spend a lot of money to import components and services abroad, which also results in capital outflow.

Benefits and Costs of FDI to Home Countries

As exporters of capital, technology, management, and (in some cases) jobs, home (source) countries often reap benefits and endure costs associated with FDI that are *opposite* those experienced by host countries. In cell 3 of Figure 6.8, three benefits to home countries are:

- Repatriated earnings from profits from FDI
- Increased exports of components and services to host countries
- Learning via FDI from operations abroad

Shown in cell 4 of Figure 6.8, costs of FDI to home countries primarily center on (1) capital loss and (2) job loss. First, since host countries enjoy capital inflow because of FDI, home countries naturally suffer from some capital outflow. Less confident home country governments often impose capital controls to prevent or reduce FDI from flowing abroad. For example, in the 1960s, the US government imposed "voluntary capital restraints" on US MNEs' outbound FDI.[32] But this concern is now less significant, as many governments realize the benefits eventually brought by FDI outflows.[33]

The second concern is now more prominent: job loss. Many MNEs simultaneously invest abroad by adding employment overseas and curtail domestic production by laying off employees. Delphi, through its bankruptcy filing, planned to drastically reduce its US employment from 32,000 to 7,000, leaving the bulk of its production abroad (see Closing Case). It is not surprising that restrictions on FDI outflows have been increasingly vocal, called for by politicians, union members, journalists, and social activists in developed economies such as the United States and Germany.

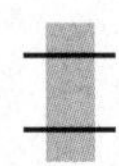

HOW MNEs AND HOST GOVERNMENTS BARGAIN

bargaining power
The ability to extract a favorable outcome from negotiations due to one party's strengths.

MNEs react to various policies by bargaining with host governments. The outcome of the MNE-host government relationship, namely, the scale and scope of FDI in a host country, is a function of the relative **bargaining power** of both sides—the ability to extract a favorable outcome from negotiations due to one party's strengths.[34] MNEs typically prefer to minimize the intervention from host governments and maximize the incentives provided by host governments. Host governments usually want to ensure a certain degree of control and minimize the incentives provided to MNEs. Sometimes, host governments "must coerce or cajole the multinationals into undertaking roles that they would otherwise abdicate,"[35] such as investing in advanced manufacturing and R&D in high-risk areas. However, host governments have to "induce, rather than command," because MNEs have options elsewhere.[36] Different countries, in effect, are competing with each other for precious FDI dollars.[37]

Shown in In Focus 6.3 (Intel Bargains with Israel), FDI is not a zero-sum game.[38] The negotiations are characterized by the "three Cs": common interests, conflicting interests, and compromises[39] (Figure 6.9). The upshot is that despite a variety of conflicts, there are conditions within which the interests of both sides may converge on an outcome that makes each side better off.[40]

Moreover, such bargaining is not one round only. After the initial FDI entry, both sides may continue to exercise bargaining power. A well-known phenomenon is the **obsolescing bargain**, referring to the deal struck by MNEs and host

obsolescing bargain
Refers to the deal struck by MNEs and host governments, which change their requirements after the initial FDI entry.

IN FOCUS 6.3 Intel Bargains with Israel

Intel began operating in Israel in 1974 with five employees. By 2000, Intel had a major facility in Kiryat Gat in southern Israel. Intel had invested $1.5 billion in this facility and had benefited from a previous law supportive of FDI by receiving a grant worth 32% of the investment. The law subsequently was changed, and the maximum level of a grant was reduced to 20% of the investment for new FDI projects. In 2000, Intel decided to invest in three new production facilities: one in the United States, one outside the United States, and the third one to be either inside or outside the United States. Intel approached the Israeli government, suggesting that it would be ready to build a new facility in Israel, provided that it would receive a *reasonable* amount of support.

Because of the security conflicts, Israel is usually regarded as a high-risk country for FDI. However, the security issue has two sides. In addition to the risk side, a positive side is the large and continuous investment in security by the Israeli government, which has generated a high-quality work force capable of performing cutting-edge, high-tech work, which is desirable for Intel. Israel, on the other hand, was interested in securing Intel's further investment to attract other MNEs. Therefore, both sides shared some common interests.

However, the negotiations quickly revealed the conflicting interests. Intel, fully aware of the new law, asked the Israeli government to specify the level and nature of support. The government refused prior to receiving a request from Intel on what Intel deemed the minimum level of support. In other words, both sides refused to be precise. Intel wanted to maximize the support, which the government preferred to minimize.

The Israeli government knew that Intel was interested but was also considering other sites, such as Ireland. The government's main problem was the limited budget to support FDI and the opportunity cost of not being able to support other projects should Intel be supported. The government team came back offering to replace the grant by a tax relief with the same present value. Intel rejected this offer, arguing that switching from a grant to a tax relief would have a negative effect on the operational profit, which was the main performance measure. The Israeli team responded by offering a grant to be paid against tax payments over time. This would allow Intel to reduce the capital investment by the present value and the depreciation. This would have a positive impact on operational profit. Intel eventually accepted the new offer and invested $2 billion on a new facility next to the existing one in Kiryat Gat and another $1 billion to upgrade the existing facility.

These negotiations were successful because both sides reached a number of compromises. Intel not only accepted a substantially lower level of support (from 32% to 20% of the investment) but also agreed not to bargain for a cash grant up front. Israel agreed to maximize the level of support per the new law and also shifted the cost for supporting this much needed, high-profile project from a high opportunity cost area (a direct cash grant for large-scale support) to a lower opportunity cost area (lower tax receipts in the future). Today, the new Kiryat Gat manufactures Pentium® 4 processors, which are exported around the world. Intel is Israel's largest private employer with 6,600 employees in production and R&D facilities in Kiryat Gat and five other locations.

Sources: Based on (1) T. Agmon, 2003, Who gets what: The MNE, the nation state, and the distributional effects of globalization, *Journal of International Business Studies*, 34: 416–427; (2) http://www.intel.com.

FIGURE 6.9 HOW MNEs NEGOTIATE WITH HOST GOVERNMENTS: THE THREE Cs

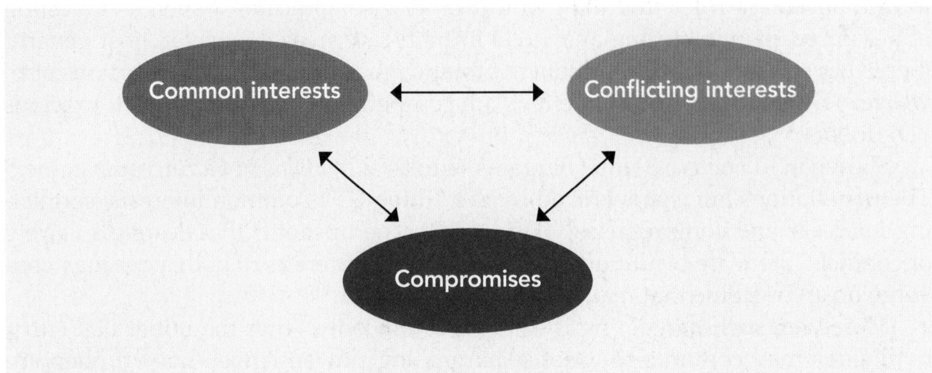

governments, which change their requirements *after* the initial FDI entry.[41] It typically unfolds in three rounds:

- In round one, the MNE and the government negotiate a deal. The MNE usually is not willing to enter in the absence of some government assurance of property rights and incentives (such as tax holidays).
- In round two, the MNE enters and, if all goes well, earns profits that may become visible.
- In round three, the government, often pressured by domestic political groups, may demand renegotiations of the deal that seems to yield "excessive" profits to the foreign firm (which, of course, regards these as "fair" and "normal" profits). The previous deal, therefore, becomes obsolete. The government's tactics include removing incentives, demanding a higher share of profits and taxes, and even confiscating foreign assets—in other words, **expropriation**.
- At this time, the MNE has already invested substantial sums of resources (called **sunk costs**) and often has to accommodate some new demands. Otherwise, it may face expropriation or exit at a huge loss. Not surprisingly, MNEs do not appreciate the risk associated with such obsolescing bargains.[42] Unfortunately, recent actions in Venezuela, Bolivia, and Ecuador suggest that obsolescing bargains are not necessarily becoming obsolete (see the next section for details).

expropriation
Government's confiscation of foreign assets.

sunk cost
Cost that a firm has to endure even when its investment turns out to be unsatisfactory.

LEARNING OBJECTIVE **5**
participate in two leading debates on FDI

DEBATES AND EXTENSIONS

MNEs, defined by FDI, are widely regarded as the embodiment of globalization (see Chapter 1). Not surprisingly, FDI has stimulated a lot of debates. This section highlights two: (1) FDI versus outsourcing and (2) facilitating versus confronting inbound FDI.

FDI versus Outsourcing

Although this chapter has focused on FDI, we need to be aware that FDI is *not* the only mode of foreign market entry. Especially when undertaking a value chain analysis regarding specific activities (see Chapter 4), a decision to undertake FDI will have to be assessed relative to the benefits and costs of outsourcing. Recall from Chapter 4 that in a foreign location, overseas outsourcing becomes "offshoring," whereas FDI—that is, performing an activity in-house at an overseas location—has been recently labeled "captive sourcing" by some authors (see Figure 4.4). A strategic debate is whether FDI (captive sourcing) or outsourcing will serve firms' purposes better.

The answer boils down to (1) how critical the activity being considered to perform abroad is to the core mission of the firm, (2) how common the activity is being undertaken by multiple end-user industries, and (3) how readily available the overseas talents to perform this activity are. If the activity is marginal to the firm's source of competitive advantage, is common (or similar) across multiple end-user industries (such as certain functions of IT), and is able to be provided by proven talents overseas, then outsourcing is called for. Otherwise, FDI is often necessary. The litmus test is whether FDI will provide ownership, location, and internalization advantages. For instance, when Travelocity outsourced its call center operations to India, its rival Sabre carefully considered its options. It eventually decided to avoid outsourcing and to initiate FDI in a new location—Uruguay (see In Focus 6.4). While this is but one example, it is important to understand that similar debates unfold at numerous firms.

Facilitating versus Confronting Inbound FDI

Despite the general trend toward friendlier policies to facilitate inbound FDI around the world (see Table 6.3), debates continue to rage among various host countries. Recent debates in the 21st century echo debates in the 20th century. At the heart of these debates is the age-old question discussed earlier: Can we trust foreigners and foreign firms in making decisions important to our economy?

In developed economies, backlash against inbound FDI from certain countries is not unusual. In the 1960s, Europeans were concerned about the massive US FDI in Europe. In the 1980s, Americans were alarmed by the significant Japanese FDI inroads into the United States. Over time, such concerns subsided. More recently, in 2006, a controversy erupted when DP World, which stands for Dubai Ports World, a Dubai government-owned company, purchased US ports from another *foreign* firm, Britain's P&O. This entry gave DP World control over terminal operations at the ports of New York/New Jersey, Philadelphia, Baltimore, Miami, and New Orleans. Although Dubai has been a US ally for three decades, Senator

IN FOCUS 6.4 Sabre Travel Network: FDI versus Outsourcing

Sabre Travel Network, headquartered in Southlake, Texas (near Dallas), is the world's largest marketer and distributor of travel-related products and services. More than 53,000 travel agencies subscribe to Sabre's services, which provide access to more than 400 airlines, 72,000 hotels, 32 car rental companies, 11 cruise lines, 35 railroads, and 220 tour operators worldwide. With one of every two travelers with trips originating in the United States using Sabre in some fashion, Sabre's 2006 revenues were $1.6 billion.

Because 9/11 attacks devastated the travel industry, Sabre was forced to have its first layoffs and pay careful attention to its cost structure. In 2003, Travelocity, a leading rival, outsourced its call center operations to India, forcing Sabre to weigh its options between outsourcing and FDI. Sabre viewed its proprietary systems and its relationships with travel agencies to be its key assets. Therefore, it ruled out outsourcing and focused on FDI. Then it searched Canada, India, and Poland and eventually decided to move its customer service center and software and hardware help desks to Uruguay. Unlike its bigger neighbor Argentina, Uruguay is politically stable. It offered significant incentives. Uruguay's well-educated labor force, thanks to universal free college tuition, is 40% cheaper than the United States. Better yet, the country is in the same time zone with most of the United States.

Sources: Based on (1) *Economist*, 2006, Uruguay: Paper dreams, October 8: 47; (2) M. Tapp, 2006, Sabre Travel Network, MBA case study, University of Texas at Dallas; (3) http://www.sabretravelnetwork.com.

Bolivian president Evo Morales denounces MNEs that allegedly "plunder" Bolivian oil and gas assets. Can you name other examples of tension over foreign ownership?

Hillary Clinton from New York argued, "Our port security is too important to place in the hands of foreign governments." She was not alone; many politicians, journalists, and activists opposed such FDI. In this "largest political storm over US ports since the Boston Tea Party,"[43] DP World eventually withdrew (see Integrative Case 1.2 for details). Cases such as these make many wonder whether a wave of protectionism is emerging in developed economies.

In some parts of the developing world, tension over foreign ownership can heat up. There were numerous incidents of nationalization and expropriation against MNE assets throughout the developing world between the 1950s and 1970s. Given the recent worldwide trend toward more FDI-friendly policies (see Table 6.3), many people thought that such actions were a thing of the past. During 2006, individuals holding such a view had a rude awakening. In March 2006, Venezuelan President Hugo Chavez ordered Chevron, Royal Dutch, Total, ENI, and other oil and gas MNEs to convert their operations in the country into forced JVs with state-owned Venezuelan firm PDVSA with PDVSA holding at least 60% of the equity. When France's Total and Italy's ENI rejected such terms, their fields were promptly seized by the government.[44] On May 1 (May Day in the socialist world), 2006, the Bolivian military stormed MNEs' oil fields and proclaimed control, and President Evo Morales declared, "The plunder [by MNEs] has ended."[45] Soon after, in late May 2006, Ecuador expropriated the oil fields run by America's Occidental Petroleum.

Although the rapidity of the anti-MNE events in Latin America was surprising, it is important to note that these actions were not sudden impulsive policy changes. The politicians leading these actions were all democratically elected. These actions were the result of lengthy political debates concerning FDI in the region, and such takeovers were mostly popular among the public. Bolivian President Morales's action in fact fulfilled his campaign promise. Until the 1970s, Latin American governments had often harshly confronted and dealt with MNEs. Only in the 1990s, when these countries became democratic, did they open their oil industry to inbound FDI. Therefore, the 180 degree policy reversal is both surprising (considering how recently these governments welcomed MNEs' arrival) and not surprising (considering the history of how MNEs were dealt with in the region). Some argue that the recent actions were driven by industry-specific dynamics (oil prices skyrocketed so that governments could not resist the urge of their "grabbing hands"), but others suggest that these actions represent the swing of a "pendulum," whose movement, after a period of pro-FDI policies, will inevitably move toward more confrontation (for the "pendulum" on globalization, see Chapter 1).

Given the general tendency for host country governments to facilitate more inbound FDI, the incidents just discussed—in both developed and developing economies—are relatively rare. Debates continue as to whether these incidents represent mere aberrations or routine occurrences in the future.

LEARNING OBJECTIVE **6**

draw implications for action

MANAGEMENT SAVVY

The big question in global business, adapted to the context of FDI, is: What determines the success and failure of FDI around the globe? The answer boils down to two components. First, from a resource-based view, some firms are very good at FDI because they leverage ownership, location, and internalization advantages in a way that is valuable, unique, and hard to imitate by rival firms. Second, from an institution-based view, the political realities either enable or constrain FDI from reaching its full economic potential. Therefore, the success and failure of FDI also significantly depend on institutions governing FDI as "rules of the game."

As a result, three implications for action emerge (Table 6.4). First, carefully assess whether FDI is justified in light of other possibilities such as outsourcing and licensing. This exercise needs to be conducted on an activity-by-activity basis as part of the value chain analysis (see Chapter 4). If ownership and internalization advantages are deemed not crucial, then FDI is not recommended.

Second, once a decision to undertake FDI is made, pay attention to the old adage: "Location, location, location!" The quest for location advantages has to create a fit with the firm's strategic goals. For example, if a firm is searching for the best "hot spots" for innovations, certain low-cost locations that do not generate sufficient innovations will not become very attractive (see Chapters 10 and 13).

Finally, given the political realities around the world, be aware of the institutional constraints. Recent events suggest that savvy MNE managers should not take FDI-friendly policies for granted. Setbacks are likely. In the long run, MNEs' interests in host countries can be best safeguarded if they accommodate rather than neglect or dominate host countries' interests. In practical terms, contributions to local employment, job training, education, pollution control, and financial support for local infrastructure, schools, research, and sports will demonstrate MNEs' commitment to host countries.[46] These actions will reduce liabilities of foreignness and enhance MNEs' legitimacy in the eyes of host country governments and the public.

TABLE 6.4 IMPLICATIONS FOR ACTION

- Carefully assess whether FDI is justified in light of other foreign entry modes such as outsourcing and licensing
- Pay careful attention to the location advantages in combination with the firm's strategic goals
- Be aware of the institutional constraints and enablers governing FDI and enhance legitimacy in host countries

CHAPTER SUMMARY

1. Understand the vocabulary associated with FDI
   - FDI refers to directly investing in activities that control and manage value creation in other countries.
   - MNEs are firms that engage in FDI.
   - FDI can be classified as horizontal FDI and vertical FDI.
   - Flow is the amount of FDI moving in a given period in a certain direction (inflow or outflow).
   - Stock is the total accumulation of inbound FDI in a country or outbound FDI from a country
2. Use the resource- and institution-based views to explain why FDI takes place
   - The resource-based view suggests that the key word of FDI is D (direct), which reflects firms' interest in directly managing, developing, and leveraging their firm-specific resources and capabilities abroad.
   - The institution-based view argues that recent expansion of FDI is indicative of generally friendlier policies, norms, and values associated with FDI (despite some setbacks).
3. Understand how FDI results in ownership, location, and internalization (OLI) advantages
   - Ownership refers to MNEs' possession and leveraging of certain valuable, rare, hard-to-imitate, and organizationally embedded (VRIO) assets overseas.

- Location refers to certain locations' advantages that can help MNEs attain strategic goals.
- Internalization refers to the replacement of cross-border market relationship with one firm (the MNE) locating in two or more countries. Internalization helps combat market imperfections and failures.

4. Identify different political views on FDI based on an understanding of FDI's benefits and costs to host and home countries
   - The radical view is hostile to FDI, and the free market view calls for minimum intervention in FDI.
   - Most countries practice pragmatic nationalism, weighing the benefits and costs of FDI.
   - FDI brings a different (and often opposing) set of benefits and costs to host and home countries.
5. Participate in two leading debates on FDI
   - The first debate deals with whether FDI should be undertaken as opposed to outsourcing.
   - The second debate focuses on whether recent anti-FDI incidents represent mere aberrations in the larger environment of having FDI friendlier policies or represent some routine occurrences in the future.
6. Draw implications for action
   - Carefully assess whether FDI is justified, in light of other options such as outsourcing and licensing.
   - Pay careful attention to the location advantages in combination with the firm's strategic goals.
   - Be aware of the institutional constraints governing FDI and enhance legitimacy in host countries.

KEY TERMS

Agglomeration 161
Bargaining power 168
Contagion (imitation) effect 167
Demonstration effect 167
Dissemination risks 159
Downstream vertical FDI 156
Expropriation 170
FDI flow 156
FDI inflow 156
FDI outflow 156
FDI stock 156
Foreign direct investment (FDI) 154
Foreign portfolio investment (FPI) 155
Free market view on FDI 166
Horizontal FDI 155
Knowledge spillover 162
Internalization 158
Intrafirm trade 165
Licensing 158
Location 158
Management control rights 155
Market imperfections (market failure) 158
Multinational enterprise (MNE) 154
Obsolescing bargain 169
OLI advantages 158
Oligopoly 163
Ownership 158
Pragmatic nationalism 166
Radical view on FDI 165
Sunk cost 170
Technology spillover 167
Upstream vertical FDI 156
Vertical FDI 155

REVIEW QUESTIONS

1. What is the primary difference between FDI and FPI?
2. How does horizontal FDI compare to vertical FDI?

3. Devise an example that demonstrates your understanding of upstream and downstream vertical FDI.
4. What distinguishes an MNE from a non-MNE?
5. Briefly summarize each of the three OLI advantages.
6. Why do market imperfections (or market failure) exist? What are some examples?
7. What is the primary benefit of ownership?
8. Describe at least two of the three reasons firms may choose FDI over licensing.
9. Devise your own example of agglomeration that demonstrates your understanding of the concept.
10. In oligopolistic industries, what two advantages often prompt rivals to imitate a leading firm that has entered a foreign country through FDI?
11. Briefly explain how FDI can be used to overcome high transaction costs and prevent market failure.
12. Compare and contrast the three political views of FDI.
13. Describe two benefits and two costs of FDI on a host country.
14. Of the two primary costs of FDI on a home country, which is the more prominent?
15. Briefly summarize how the "three Cs" influence negotiations between MNEs and host countries.
16. Given that outsourcing is a viable alternative to FDI, what issues should be considered before a firm decides between the two?
17. Why do some countries object to inbound FDI?
18. What process could a manager use to evaluate the merits of FDI for any given situation? How would that work?
19. What qualities should a savvy manager consider when evaluating a particular location for FDI?

CRITICAL DISCUSSION QUESTIONS

1. Identify the top-five (or -ten) *source* countries of FDI into your country. Then identify the top-ten (or -20) foreign MNEs that have undertaken inbound FDI in your country. Why do these countries and companies provide the bulk of FDI into your country?
2. Identify the top-five (or -ten) *recipient* countries of FDI from your country. Then identify the top-ten (or -20) MNEs headquartered in your country that have made outbound FDI elsewhere. Why do these countries attract FDI from the top MNEs in your country?
3. Worldwide, which countries were the largest recipient and source countries of FDI *last year*? Why? Will this situation change in five years? Ten years? How about 20 years down the road? Why?

4. ON ETHICS: Undertaking FDI, by definition, means not investing in the MNE's home country (see Closing Case). What are the ethical dilemmas here? What are your recommendations, as (1) MNE executives, (2) labor union leaders of your domestic (home country) labor forces, (3) host country officials, and (4) home country officials?

VIDEO CASE

Watch "Work on What You Can Control" by Sir Nick Scheele of Ford Motor Co. of Mexico.

1. How did the institution-based view affect Sir Nick Scheele when he took charge at Ford Motor of Mexico?
2. In what way did Sir Nick Scheele focus on the resource-based view?
3. In what way did he stress the V and R in VRIO?
4. In what ways did Sir Nick Scheele manage FDI so as to make use of the O in OLI?
5. What guideline did he provide for making use of FDI under changing environmental conditions?

CLOSING CASE

ETHICAL DILEMMA
Delphi: Go Bankrupt, Then Go Overseas

Delphi Corporation's battle with the United Auto Workers (UAW) has all the earmarks of a conventional labor showdown. CEO Robert S. "Steve" Miller Jr. has demanded up to 40% pay cuts, which he says are necessary to lift the world's largest auto parts maker out of bankruptcy and make it globally competitive. The UAW has agreed in principle but is adamantly resisting the scope of changes Miller wants.

© Adam Bird/Bloomberg News /Landov

But what's different in this battle is that Miller wants to use the bankruptcy courts to drastically slash Delphi's US presence, thus freeing it up to focus on its already vast overseas production. Miller filed for Chapter 11 (bankruptcy) protection only for his US operations, which employ 32,000 UAW and other union workers. He was careful to exclude Delphi's 115,000-worker foreign factories, many of which operate in low-wage countries such as Mexico and China. If Miller gets his way, court filings show, Delphi will end up with a US work force of perhaps 7,000, leaving the bulk of its production abroad.

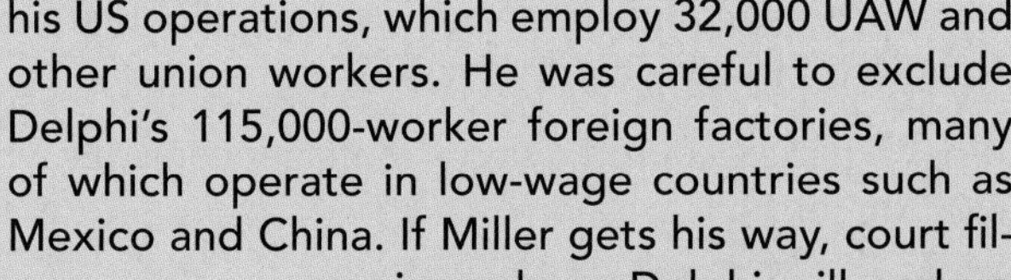

Miller's is an unorthodox approach that paves a new road for US employers striving to compete in a globalizing economy. After all, US bankruptcy laws were written before globalization and intended to give companies a chance to reorganize and start over—not flee overseas, says Sean McAlinden, chief economist with the Center for Automotive Research. He says other auto parts companies, a handful of which already are in bankruptcy, are likely to follow suit if Miller's strategy succeeds. That means the $170 billion annual auto parts business could shift overseas even faster, jeopardizing more of the industry's 695,000 jobs.

Critics are trying to throw up all the roadblocks they can. On April 6, 2006, two UAW allies, Senator Evan Bayh (a Democrat from Indiana) and Representative John Conyers Jr. (a Democrat from Michigan), introduced legislation in Congress to tighten up the bankruptcy laws in response to Delphi's moves. The bills would require the courts to factor in a bankrupt company's overseas operations when determining whether it can abrogate union contracts and retiree healthcare plans in the United States. "Some international corporations that are struggling domestically use their losses at home to justify breaking contracts with American workers while their overall company is still thriving," the two lawmakers proclaimed in their joint announcement of the legislation.

Miller doesn't talk much publicly about his goals for fear of further inflaming an already outraged UAW, but the gist of Delphi's plan is apparent in its bankruptcy filings. Right now, the company produces about two-thirds of its $28 billion in annual revenue in the United States. This includes everything from high-tech engine controls and satellite radios to low-tech commodities such as air filters and brake parts. Its reorganization plan would ditch everything in the United States except safety technology, radios, information and entertainment systems, electronics, wiring, and engine controls. That would leave Delphi with US revenues as low as $5 billion.

To pull off a downsizing of that scale, Delphi would close or sell 21 of 29 plants it has identified as noncore businesses, according to the filings. An additional 12 plants are not named in the reorganization plan, but a company spokesman says some of those will go, too. It's not just $27-an-hour union wage scales at issue. Even if the UAW agrees to slash pay to $22 per hour this year and to $16.50 per hour next year, as Miller has demanded, many of Delphi's plants are inefficient and would take huge investments to bring up to world-class standards. Bottom line: Delphi's plan would slice away 27,000 US union jobs by 2010.

For Miller, the preferred outcome is clear: exit high-cost US operations in which Delphi is not competitive. McAlinden figures other suppliers—even healthy ones—will take similar steps.

Case Discussion Questions

1. From a resource-based view, explain why Delphi is not competitive.
2. From an institution-based view, is Miller's unorthodox approach ethical?
3. What would you do if you were the governor of Indiana or Michigan?
4. If you were CEO of a struggling US manufacturing firm, would you follow Delphi's example?

Source: D. Welch, 2006, Go bankrupt, then go overseas, *Business Week*, April 24: 52–53.

NOTES

Journal acronyms: **AER** – *American Economic Review;* **AMR** – *Academy of Management Review;* **BW** – *Business Week;* **EJ** – *Economic Journal;* **FEER** – *Far Eastern Economic Review;* **HBR** – *Harvard Business Review;* **IBR** – *International Business Review;* **JB** – *Journal of Business;* **JIBS** – *Journal of International Business Studies;* **JWB** – *Journal of World Business;* **LRP** – *Long Range Planning;* **MIR** – *Management International Review;* **MS** – *Management Science;* **NI** – *National Interest;* **OSc** – *Organization Science;* **SMJ** – *Strategic Management Journal*

[1] R. Caves, 1996, *Multinational Enterprise and Economic Analysis*, 2nd ed. (p. 1), New York: Cambridge University Press.

[2] US Census Bureau, 2006, *US goods trade: Imports and exports by related parties, 2005*, News release, May 12.

[3] United Nations, 2005, *World Investment Report 2005* (p. 4), New York and Geneva: United Nations.

[4] K. Moore & D. Lewis, 1999, *Birth of the Multinational*, Copenhagen: Copenhagen Business School Press.

[5] M. Wilkins, 2001, The history of multinational enterprise (p. 13), in A. Rugman & T. Brewer (eds.), *The Oxford Handbook of International Business*, 3–35, New York: Oxford University Press.

[6] P. Drucker, 2005, Trading places (p. 104), *NI*, Spring: 101–107.

[7] United Nations, 2006, *World Investment Report 2006* (p. 10), New York and Geneva: United Nations.

[8] A. Madhok, 1997, Cost, value, and foreign market entry mode, *SMJ*, 18: 39–61.

[9] J. Dunning, 1993, *Multinational Enterprises and the Global Economy*, Reading, MA: Addison-Wesley.

[10] Y. Pak & Y. Park, 2004, Global ownership strategy of Japanese multinational enterprises, *MIR*, 44: 3–17.

[11] C. Hill, P. Hwang, & C. Kim, 1990, An eclectic theory of the choice of international entry mode (p. 124), *SMJ* 11: 117–128.

[12] R. Tasker, 2002, Pepperoni power, *FEER*, November 14: 59–60.

[13] M. Cannice, R. Chen, & J. Daniels, 2004, Managing international technology transfer risk, *MIR*, 44: 129–139; J. Denekamp, 1995, Intangible assets, internalization, and foreign direct investment in manufacturing, *JIBS*, 26: 493–504.

[14] X. Martin & R. Salomon, 2003, Tacitness, learning, and international expansion, *OSc*, 14: 297–311.

[15] B. Kogut & U. Zander, 1993, Knowledge of the firm and the evolutionary theory of the multinational corporation, *JIBS*, 24: 625–646. See also B. Elango & C. Pattnaik, 2007, Building capabilities for international operations through networks, *JIBS*, 38: 541–555; D. Yiu, C. M. Lau, & G. Bruton, 2007, International venturing by emerging economy firms, *JIBS*, 38: 519–540.

[16] P. Buckley & N. Hashai, 2004, A global system view of firm boundaries, *JIBS*, 35: 33–45; J. Dunning, 1998, Location and the multinational enterprise, *JIBS*, 29: 45–66; R. Grosse & L. Trevino, 2005, New institutional economics and FDI location in Central and Eastern Europe, *MIR*, 45: 123–135.

[17] W. Chung & A. Kalnins, 2001, Agglomeration effects and performance, *SMJ*, 22: 969–988; E. Maitland, S. Nicholas, W. Purcell, & T. Smith, 2004, Regional learning networks, *MIR*, 44: 87–100; J. M. Shaver & F. Flyer, 2000, Agglomeration economies, firm heterogeneity, and foreign direct investment in the United States, *SMJ*, 21: 1175–1193.

[18] A. Kalnins & W. Chung, 2004, Resource-seeking agglomeration, *SMJ*, 25: 689–699; L. Nachum, 2000, Economic geography and the location of TNCs, *JIBS*, 31: 367–385; M. Porter, 1998, *On Competition*, Boston: Harvard Business School Press; R. Pouder & C. St. John, 1996, Hot spots and blind spots, *AMR*, 21: 1192–1225; S. Tallman, M. Jenkins, N. Henry, & S. Pinch, 2004, Knowledge, clusters, and competitive advantage, *AMR*, 29: 258–271.

[19] *BW*, 2006. Airbus may hit an air pocket over China, April 24: 44.

[20] F. Knickerbocker, 1973, *Oligopolistic Reaction and Multinational Enterprise*, Boston: Harvard Business School Press; J. Yu & K. Ito, 1988, Oligopolistic reaction and foreign direct investment, *JIBS*, 18: 449–460.

[21] P. Buckley & M. Casson, 1976, *The Future of the Multinational Enterprise*, London: Macmillan; J. Campa & M. Guillen, 1999, The internalization of exports, *MS*, 45: 1463–1478.

[22] L. Eden, L. Juarez, & D. Li, 2005, Talk softly but carry a big stick, *JIBS*, 36: 398–414; L. Eden & P. Rodriguez, 2004, How weak are the signals? *JIBS*, 35: 61–74; I. Filatotchev, R. Strange, J. Piesse, & Y. Lien, 2007, FDI by firms from new industrialized economies in emerging markets, *JIBS*, 38: 556–572.

[23] J. Galan & J. Gonzalez-Benito, 2006, Distinctive determinant factors of Spanish foreign direct investment in Latin America, *JWB*, 41: 171–189.

[24] T. Poynter, 1982, Government intervention in less developed countries, *JIBS*, 13: 9–25; R. Vernon, 1977, *Storm over the Multinationals*, Cambridge, MA: Harvard University Press.

[25] L. Brouthers, S. Werner, & T. Wilkinson, 1996, The aggregate impact of firms' FDI strategies on the trade balances of host countries, *JIBS*, 27: 359–373.

[26] S. Feinberg & S. Majumdar, 2001, Technology spillovers from foreign direct investment in the Indian pharmaceutical industry, *JIBS*, 32: 421–437; H. Gorg & E. Strobl, 2001, Multinational companies and productivity spillovers, *EJ*, 111: 723–739; X. Liu, P. Siler, C. Wang, & Y. Wei, 2000, Productivity spillovers from foreign direct investment, *JIBS*, 31: 407–425; Y. Wei & X. Liu, 2006, Productivity spillovers from R&D, exports, and FDI in China's manufacturing sector, *JIBS*, 37: 544–557.

[27] B. Aitken & A. Harrison, 1999, Do domestic firms benefit from direct foreign investment? *AER*, 89: 605–618; R. Banga, 2006, The export-diversifying impact of Japanese and US foreign direct investments in the Indian manufacturing sector, *JIBS*, 37: 558–568; P. Buckley, J. Clegg, & C. Wang, 2002, The impact of inward FDI on the performance of Chinese manufacturing firms, *JIBS*, 33: 637–655; B. Javorcik, 2004, Does foreign direct investment increase the productivity of domestic firms? *AER*, 94: 605–627.

[28] M. Hanafi & S. Rhee, 2004, The wealth effect of foreign investor presence, *MIR*, 44: 157–167; K. Meyer, 2004, Perspectives on multinational enterprises in emerging economies, *JIBS*, 35: 259–276.

[29] N. Camiah & G. Hollinshead, 2003, Assessing the potential for effective cross-cultural working between "new" Russian managers and Western expatriates, *JWB*, 38: 245–261; W. Danis, 2003, Differences in values, practices, and systems among Hungarian managers and Western expatriates, *JWB*, 38: 224–244; J. Engelhard & J. Nagele, 2003, Organizational learning in subsidiaries of multinational companies in Russia, *JWB*, 38: 262–277; S. Michailova, 2003, Constructing management in Eastern Europe, *JWB*, 38: 165–167.

[30] T. Wilkinson & L. Brouthers, 2000, Trade shows, trade missions, and state governments, *JIBS*, 31: 725–734.

[31] F. Barry & C. Kearney, 2006, Multinational enterprises and industrial structure in host countries, *JIBS*, 37: 392–406.

[32] J. Behrman, 2006, A career in the early limbo of international business, *JIBS*, 37: 432–444.

[33] P. Braunerhjelm, L. Oxelheim, & P. Thulin, 2005, The relationship between domestic and outward foreign direct investment, *IBR*, 14: 677–694; W. Hejazi & P. Pauly, 2003, Motivations for FDI and domestic capital formation, *JIBS*, 34: 282–289.

[34] D. Lecraw, 1984, Bargaining power, ownership, and profitability of transnational corporations in developing countries, *JIBS*, 15: 27–43; T. Murtha & S. Lenway, 1994, Country capabilities and the strategic state, *SMJ*, 15: 113–129.

[35] P. Evans, 1979, *Dependent Development* (p. 44), Princeton, NJ: Princeton University Press.

[36] C. Lindblom, 1977, *Politics and Markets* (p. 173), New York: Basic Books.

[37] A. Bevan, S. Estrin, & K. Meyer, 2004, Foreign investment location and institutional development in transition economies, *IBR*, 13: 43–64.

[38] J. Boddewyn & T. Brewer, 1994, International business political behavior, *AMR*, 19: 119–143.

[39] T. Agmon, 2003, Who gets what, *JIBS*, 34: 416–427; H. Aswicahyono & H. Hill, 1995, Determinants of foreign ownership in LDC manufacturing, *JIBS*, 26: 139–158.

[40] M. W. Peng, 2000, Controlling the foreign agent, *MIR*, 40: 141–165.

[41] T. Brewer, 1992, An issue-area approach to the analysis of MNE-government relations, *JIBS*, 23: 295–309.

[42] J. Doh & R. Ramamurti, 2003, Reassessing risk in developing country infrastructure, *LRP*, 36: 337–353.

[43] *Economist*, 2006, Trouble on the waterfront, February 25: 33–34.

[44] *BW*, 2006, Venezuela: You are working for Chavez now, May 15: 76–78.

[45] *Economist*, 2006, Bolivia: Now it's the people's gas, May 6: 37–38.

[46] E. Iankova & J. Katz, 2003, Strategies for political risk mediation by international firms in transition economies, *JWB*, 38: 182–203.

CHAPTER 7

Dealing with Foreign Exchange

OPENING CASE

The Yuan and Wal-Mart

Before picking up this book, most of you probably knew that the value of the Chinese yuan has caused a great deal of controversy. According to US critics (including plenty of politicians in the US Congress), the Chinese government has "artificially" kept the yuan at a lower value (maybe up to 40%), making China's exports cheaper and thus representing an "unfair" advantage. Therefore, the yuan needs to appreciate, and the dollar will consequently depreciate. As a result, Americans will benefit because, with a cheap dollar, US exports will be more price competitive when sold in China and elsewhere. This "us versus them" story seems straightforward, and US firms, according to this story, should applaud the efforts to push China to raise the value of its yuan. Well, not so fast! Plenty of US firms may not like this idea. Wal-Mart is one US company standing in the middle of the debate. Wal-Mart is not an average American company. It is the largest company in America and in the world (by sales).

Estimating the impact of Wal-Mart on the US and global economy has become a cottage industry in itself. Wal-Mart is unrivaled; it is as big as Costco, Home Depot, Kmart, Kroger, Sears, and Target *combined*. In 2007, it operates 3,900 stores in the United States and 2,700 stores in 14 other countries. Beyond sales, Wal-Mart is the nation's and the world's largest private employer. It employs an army of 1.8 million employees worldwide, including 1.3 million in the United States. It is now the largest corporate employer in both Mexico and Canada and the second largest grocer in Britain. Worldwide, more than 176 million people, including 127 million Americans, shop at Wal-Mart every week. Why is Wal-Mart so attractive? Its tag line says it all: "Always low prices. *Always*." The second *always* is italicized and underlined in case there is any confusion. Wal-Mart claims that it saves the average American household more than $2,300 every year.

How can Wal-Mart deliver consistently attractive and low prices? In one word, *China*. Suppliers and competitors of Wal-Mart widely acknowledge that there exist a wholesale price, a retail price, and a Wal-Mart price, but what they really mean is an unbeatable *China price*. Although Wal-Mart sources from suppliers in more than 70 countries, China is no doubt at the center of Wal-Mart's supplier base. Of Wal-Mart's 6,000 suppliers, at least 80% produce in China, often at Wal-Mart's urging in an effort to cut costs. China is the largest exporter to the US economy in consumer goods, and Wal-Mart is the leading retailer in consumer goods. Therefore, China and Wal-Mart, according to an influential PBS documentary, are a "joint venture made in heaven." It is not a coincidence that the rise of Wal-Mart and the rise of China have taken place during roughly the same period.

At present, the United States runs the largest trade deficit with China, totaling $233 billion in 2006 (about one-third of the record high $760 billion US trade deficit). A China trade debate is thus in rage in the United States on how to deal with the deficit (see Chapter 5, especially Table 5.5). However, the debate is complicated because it is much more than just "us versus them." It is "us versus them + our Wal-Mart + Wal-Mart's suppliers producing in China" (!). Over 60% of "Chinese exports" are not produced by Chinese-owned companies but by foreign-invested enterprises producing in China. If Wal-Mart were an independent country, it would rank as China's eighth largest trading partner, ahead of Russia, Australia, and Canada. Regardless of whether the yuan is "unfairly" low or not, all foreign-invested enterprises in China, including about 5,000 of Wal-Mart's

LEARNING OBJECTIVES

After studying this chapter, you should be able to

1. understand the determinants of foreign exchange rates
2. track the evolution of the international monetary system
3. identify firms' strategic responses to deal with foreign exchange movements
4. participate in three leading debates on foreign exchange movements
5. draw implications for action

non-Chinese-owned suppliers producing in China, benefit from the yuan's low valuation. Standing in the middle, Wal-Mart has made this "us versus them" debate more complicated.

In July 2005, China abandoned the yuan's peg to the dollar at 8.3 yuan per dollar. Since then, the pace of yuan appreciation has gathered steam, reaching 7.6 yuan per dollar in July 2007, an 8.6% increase in two years. However, if the yuan appreciates sharply, Wal-Mart's entire business model may be in jeopardy. Because approximately 70% of the Wal-Mart products are made in China, if the yuan (hypothetically) appreciates by 30%, it means that 70% of its products may experience a 30% price *jump* (holding everything else constant). A strong yuan can potentially wipe out Wal-Mart's entire profit margin almost overnight. The leading practitioner of "always low prices" will naturally do everything possible to prevent this from happening. Although Wal-Mart strongly guards its corporate plans, it makes sense to imagine that Wal-Mart may have a two-pronged strategy. First, Wal-Mart will work with its suppliers to lobby extensively against efforts to push the yuan to appreciate sharply. Second, some appreciation of the yuan seems inevitable, as acknowledged by the Chinese government itself, which denies the influence of US political pressure but cites the reasons for China's own good (such as cooling off the overheated economy—see In Focus 7.3). As a result, Wal-Mart may seek to minimize the damage caused by a stronger yuan by currency hedging and strategic hedging (diversifying its supplier base).

Sources: Based on (1) *Business Week*, 2004, The China price, December 6: 102–112; (2) C. Fishman, 2006, *The Wal-Mart Effect*, New York: Penguin; (3) R. E. Freeman, 2006, The Wal-Mart effect and business, ethics, and society, *Academy of Management Perspectives*, 20: 38–40; (4) PBS/Frontline, 2004, Is Wal-Mart good for America? http://www.pbs.org; (5) *South China Morning Post*, 2007, Yuan soars to highest level since 2005, July 20: 1; (6) http://www.wakeupwalmart.com (an unofficial "Wal-Mart watcher" website); (7) http://www.walmartfacts.com (an official Wal-Mart website).

Why is the value of the yuan so important? Why are some US politicians so interested in depreciating the dollar (which will happen if the yuan appreciates)? What determines foreign exchange rates? How do foreign exchange rates affect trade and investment? What is the role of global institutions such as the **International Monetary Fund (IMF)**? Finally, how do firms strategically respond? Continuing from our two previous chapters on trade (Chapter 5) and foreign direct investment (FDI) (Chapter 6), this chapter addresses these crucial questions. At the heart of our discussion are the two core perspectives introduced earlier: the institution- and resource-based views. Essentially, the institution-based view suggests that as the "rules of the game," domestic and international institutions (such as the IMF) influence foreign exchange rates and affect capital movements. In turn, the resource-based view sheds light on how firms, such as Wal-Mart and its suppliers, can profit from favorable foreign exchange movements by developing their own firm-specific resources and capabilities.

International Monetary Fund (IMF)
An international organization that was established to promote international monetary cooperation, exchange stability, and orderly exchange arrangements.

We start with a basic question: What determines foreign exchange rates? Then, we track the evolution of the international monetary system culminating in the IMF. How firms strategically respond is outlined next. We conclude with some discussion on debates and extensions.

FACTORS BEHIND FOREIGN EXCHANGE RATES

LEARNING OBJECTIVE 1

understand the determinants of foreign exchange rates

A **foreign exchange rate** is the price of one currency, such as the dollar ($), in terms of another, such as the euro (€). Table 7.1 provides some examples. This section addresses a key question: What determines foreign exchange rates?

foreign exchange rate
The price of one currency in terms of another.

Basic Supply and Demand

The concept of an exchange rate as the price of a commodity—one country's currency—helps us understand its determinants. Basic economic theory suggests that the price of a commodity is most fundamentally determined by its supply and demand. Strong demand will lead to price hikes, and oversupply will result in price drops. Of course, we are dealing with a most unusual commodity here, money, but the basic underlying principles still apply. When the United States sells products to China, US exporters often demand that they be paid in US dollars because the Chinese yuan is useless (technically, nonconvertible) in the United States. Chinese importers of US products will somehow have to generate US dollars to pay for US imports. The easiest way to generate US dollars is to *export* to the United States, whose buyers will pay in US dollars. In this example, the dollar is the common transaction currency involving both US imports and US exports. As a result, the demand for dollars is much stronger than the demand for yuan (while holding the supply constant). Worldwide, a wide variety of users, such as Chinese exporters, Russian mafia members, and Swiss bankers, prefer to hold and transact in US dollars, thus fueling the demand for dollars. Such a strong demand explains why the US dollar is the most sought after currency in postwar decades (see Table 7.2). At present, approximately 65% of the world's foreign exchange holdings are in US dollars, followed by 25% in euros, 4% in yen, and 3% in pounds.[1]

TABLE 7.1 EXAMPLES OF KEY CURRENCY EXCHANGE RATES

	US Dollar (US$)	Euro (€)	UK Pound (£)	Swiss Franc (SFr)	Mexican Peso	Japanese Yen (¥)	Canadian Dollar (C$)
Canadian Dollar (C$)	1.0574	1.4444	2.1369	0.88315	0.09591	0.00897	—
Japanese Yen (¥)	117.86	161.00	238.18	98.438	10.691	—	111.46
Mexican Peso	11.024	15.059	22.279	9.2078	—	0.09354	10.426
Swiss Franc (SFr)	1.1973	1.6355	2.4196	—	0.10860	0.01016	1.1323
UK Pound (£)	0.49483	0.67594	—	0.41329	0.04488	0.00420	0.46797
Euro (€)	0.73206	—	1.4794	0.61143	0.06640	0.00621	0.69232
US Dollar (US$)	—	1.3660	2.0209	0.83521	0.09071	0.00848	0.94572

Source: These examples are from August 9, 2007. The rates may change. Adapted from *Wall Street Journal*, 2007, Key currency cross rates, August 9, http://www.wsj.com. Reading *vertically*, the first column means US$1 = C$1.06 = ¥118 = Mexican Peso 11.02 = SFr 1.20 = £0.49 = €0.73. Reading *horizontally*, the last row means €1 = US$1.37; £1 = US$2.02; SFr 1 = US$0.84; Mexican Peso 1 = US$0.09; ¥1 = US$0.008; C$1 = US$0.95.

TABLE 7.2 THE ROLE OF THE US DOLLAR OUTSIDE THE UNITED STATES

Common reference	Most international statistics (such as exports, imports, and GDP) reported by national governments and international organizations (such as the UN and WTO) are expressed in US dollars.
Intervention currency	Most central banks buy and sell US dollars in their respective foreign exchange markets to influence their exchange rates. Many countries peg their currencies to the dollar.
Reserve currency	Most central banks hold US dollars as official reserves to intervene in their respective markets. (The US Federal Reserve System maintains its foreign currency reserves in euros and yen.)
Vehicle currency	Transaction between two less commonly used ("exotic") currencies, such as the Brazilian real and the Czech koruna, is often through dollars. There is always an active market for dollars in every country.

Because foreign exchange is such a unique commodity, its markets are influenced not only by economic factors but also by a lot of political and psychological factors. The next question is: What determines the supply and demand of foreign exchange? Figure 7.1 sketches the five underlying building blocks: (1) relative price differences, (2) interest rates and monetary supply, (3) productivity and balance of payments, (4) exchange rate policies, and (5) investor psychology.

Relative Price Differences and Purchasing Power Parity

purchasing power parity (PPP) A conversion that determines the equivalent amount of goods and services different currencies can purchase. This conversion is usually used to capture the differences in cost of living in different countries.

Some countries (such as Switzerland) are famously expensive, and others (such as the Philippines) are known to have cheap prices. How do these price differences affect exchange rate? An answer is provided by the theory of **purchasing power parity (PPP)**, which is essentially the "law of one price." The theory suggests that in the absence of trade barriers (such as tariffs), the price for identical products sold in different countries must be the same. Otherwise, arbitragers may "buy low" and "sell high," eventually driving different prices for identical products

FIGURE 7.1 WHAT DETERMINES FOREIGN EXCHANGE RATES?

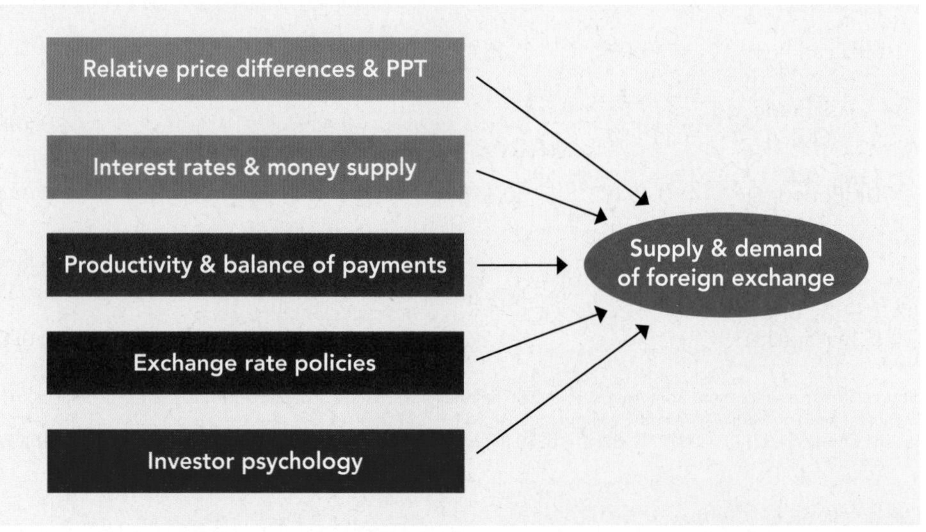

to the same level around the world. The PPP theory argues that in the long run, exchange rates should move toward levels that would equalize the prices of an identical basket of goods in any two countries.[2]

One of the most influential and most fun-filled applications of the PPP theory is the Big Mac index, popularized by the *Economist* magazine. The *Economist*'s "basket" is McDonald's Big Mac hamburger produced in about 120 countries. According to the PPP theory, a Big Mac should cost the same everywhere around the world. In reality, it does not. In July 2007, a Big Mac cost $3.41 in the United States and 11 yuan in China. If the Big Mac indeed cost the same, the de facto exchange rate based on the Big Mac became 3.23 yuan to the dollar (that is, 11 yuan/$3.41), whereas the nominal (official) rate at that time was 7.6 yuan to the dollar. According to this calculation, the yuan was 58% "undervalued" against the dollar—the most extreme in the Big Mac universe (Table 7.3). In other words, the Big Mac sold in China has the best "value" in the world, costing only $1.45 (!) based on the official exchange rate.

Although the Big Mac index is never a serious exercise, it has been cited by some US politicians as "evidence" that the yuan is artificially undervalued. This claim has been disavowed by the *Economist* itself. More seriously, we can make four observations:

- The Big Mac index confirms that prices in some European countries are very expensive. A Big Mac in Switzerland and Denmark was the most expensive in the world, costing $5.20 and $5.08, respectively.

TABLE 7.3 THE BIG MAC INDEX

	Big Mac price in local currency	Big Mac price in US dollars	Implied PPP of the US dollar[1]	Official exchange rate of the US dollar (July 2, 2007)	Under (–) / over (+) valuation of the US dollar
United States	$3.41	$3.41	—	—	—
Brazil	Real 6.90	$3.61	2.02	1.91	+6%
Britain	£1.99	$4.01	1.71	2.01	+18%
Canada	C$3.88	$3.68	1.14	1.05	+8%
China	Yuan 11.0	$1.45	3.23	7.60	–58%
Denmark	DKr 27.75	$5.08	8.14	5.46	+49%
Egypt	Pound 9.54	$1.68	2.80	5.69	–51%
Euro area	€3.06	$4.17	1.12	1.36	+22%
Hong Kong	HK$12	$1.54	3.52	7.82	–55%
Japan	¥280	$2.29	82.1	122	–33%
Mexico	Peso 29.00	$2.69	8.50	10.8	–21%
Philippines	Peso 85.00	$1.85	24.9	45.9	–46%
Russia	Ruble 52.00	$2.03	15.2	25.6	–41%
Singapore	S$3.95	$2.50	1.16	1.52	–24%
Sweden	SKr 33.00	$4.86	9.68	6.79	+42%
Switzerland	SFr 6.30	$5.20	1.85	1.21	+53%

1. PPP = Price in local currency divided by price in the United States ($3.41).

Source: Adapted from *Economist*, 2007, The Big Mac index: Sizzling, July 5, http://www.economist.com.

- Prices in developing countries are cheaper. A Big Mac in Egypt and the Philippines cost only $1.68 and $1.85, respectively. This makes sense because a Big Mac is a product with both traded and nontraded inputs. To simplify our discussion, let us assume that the costs for traded inputs (such as flour for the bun) are the same; it is obvious that nontraded inputs (such as labor and real estate) are cheaper in developing countries.
- The Big Mac is not a traded product. No large number of American hamburger lovers would travel to China simply to get the best deal on the Big Mac and then somehow take with them large quantities of the made-in-China Big Mac (perhaps in portable freezers). If they did that, the Big Mac price in China would be driven up, and the price in the United States would be pushed down—remember supply and demand?
- After having a laugh, we shouldn't read too much into this index. PPP signals where exchange rates may move in the *long run*. But it does not suggest that the yuan should appreciate by 58% or the Swiss franc should depreciate by 53% next year. According to the *Economist*, anyone interested in the PPP theory "would be unwise to exclude the Big Mac from their diet, but Super Size servings would equally be a mistake."[3]

Interest Rates and Money Supply

The PPP theory suggests the long-run direction of exchange rate movement, but what about the short run? In the short run, variations in interest rates have a powerful effect. If one country's interest rate is high relative to other countries, the country will attract foreign funds. Because inflows of foreign funds usually need to be converted to the home currency, a high interest rate will increase the demand for the home currency, thus enhancing its exchange value.

In addition, a country's rate of inflation, relative to that prevailing abroad, affects its ability to attract foreign funds and hence its exchange rate. A high level of inflation is essentially too much money chasing too few goods in an economy—technically, an expansion of a country's money supply. A government, when facing budgetary shortfalls, may choose to print more currency, which tends to stimulate inflation. In turn, this would cause its currency to depreciate. This makes sense because as the supply of a given currency (such as the Mexican peso) increases while the demand stays the same, the per unit value of that currency (such as one peso) goes down. Therefore, the exchange rate is very sensitive to changes in monetary policy. It responds swiftly to changes in money supply. To avoid losses from holding assets in a depreciated currency, investors sell them for assets denominated in other currencies. Such massive sell-offs may worsen the depreciation. This happened in Argentina during 2001–2002, when numerous investors sold off assets held in the Argentinian peso and forced it to hit from parity to a low of 3.5 to the dollar.

Productivity and Balance of Payments

In international trade, the rise of a country's productivity, relative to other countries, will improve its competitive position—this is a basic proposition of the theories of absolute and comparative advantage discussed in Chapter 5. More FDI will be attracted to the country, fueling demand for its home currency. One recent example is China. All the China-bound FDI inflows in dollars, euros, and pounds have to be converted to local currency, boosting the demand for the yuan and hence its value. Other examples are not hard to find. The rise in relative Japanese productivity over the past three decades led to a long-run appreciation of the yen, which rose from about ¥310 = $1 in 1975 to ¥118 = $1 in 2007.

Recall from Chapter 5 that changes in productivity will change a country's balance of trade. A country highly productive in manufacturing may generate a merchandise trade surplus, whereas a country less productive in manufacturing may end up with a merchandise trade deficit. These have ramifications for the **balance of payments**—officially known as a country's international transaction statement, including merchandise trade, service trade, and capital movement. Table 7.4 shows that in 2006, the United States had a merchandise trade deficit

balance of payments
A country's international transaction statement, including merchandise trade, service trade, and capital movement.

TABLE 7.4 THE US BALANCE OF PAYMENTS, 2006 (BILLION DOLLARS)

I. Current Account		
1. Exports of goods (merchandise)	1,023	
2. Imports of goods (merchandise)	–1,861	
3. Balance on goods (merchandise trade—lines 1 + 2)		**–838**
4. Exports of services	422	
5. Imports of services	–343	
6. Balance on services (service trade—lines 4 + 5)		**79**
7. Balance on goods and services (trade deficit/surplus—lines 3 + 6)		**–759**
8. Income receipts on US-owned assets abroad	650	
9. Income payments on foreign-owned assets in the US	–613	
10. Government grants and private remittances	–90	
11. Balance on current account (current account deficit/surplus—lines 7 + 8 + 9 + 10)		**–811**
II. Financial Account		
12. US-owned private assets abroad (increase/financial outflow = – [negative sign])	–1,063	
13. Foreign-owned private assets in the US	1,419	
14. Financial derivatives[1]	29	
15. Statistical discrepancy	–18	
16. Balance on financial account (lines 12 + 13 + 14 + 15)		**367**
17. Overall balance of payments[2] (Official reserve transactions balance—lines 11 + 16)		**–444**
18. Increase in US official reserves (increase = – [negative sign]/decrease = + [positive sign])	3	
19. Increase in foreign official reserves in the US (increase = + [positive sign])	441	

1. As a new item, financial derivatives were added for the first time in 2006. The number was based on a new methodology for estimating interest received and paid on bonds.
2. Overall balance of payments (line 17) must be settled—via instruments such as gold, official debt, and official foreign currency reserves. Technically, lines 18 and 19 must equal the imbalance shown in line 17 but bear the opposite sign, resulting in a zero ("balance") for the entire statement. In reality, the overall deficit of $444 billion was financed by (1) a small $3 billion decrease in US official reserves (line 18—note: a positive sign means a *decrease*) and (2) a massive $441 billion increase in foreign official reserves in the US (line 19—note: a positive sign means an *increase*). The latter was primarily due to foreign central banks' purchase of US government securities (such as Treasury bills).

Source: Adapted from US Department of Commerce, Bureau of Economic Analysis, 2007, *US International Transactions*, Table 1, June 15, Washington, DC: BEA, http://www.bea.gov. Numbers may not add due to rounding.

of $838 billion and a service trade surplus of $79 billion. In addition to merchandise and service trade, we add receipts on US assets abroad (such as repatriated earnings from US multinational enterprises [MNEs] in China and dividends paid by Japanese firms to American shareholders), subtract payments on US-based foreign assets (such as repatriated earnings from Canadian MNEs in the United States to Canada and dividends paid by US firms to Dutch shareholders), and government grants and private remittances (such as US foreign aid thrown at Iraq and the money that Mexican farmhands in America send home). After doing all the math, we can see that the United States ran an $811 billion current account deficit. Technically, the current account balance consists of exports minus imports of merchandise and services, plus income on US assets abroad minus payments on foreign assets in the United States, plus unilateral government transfers and private remittances.

A current account deficit has to be financed by a financial account—consisting of purchases and sales of assets. This is because a country needs to balance its accounts in much the same way as a family deals with its finances. Any deficit in a family budget has to be financed by spending from savings or by borrowing.[4] In a similar fashion, the overall US deficit of $444 billion in 2006 (combining the $811 billion current account deficit and the $367 billion financial account surplus) was financed by (1) spending from savings (a small $3 billion decrease in official reserves) and (2) borrowing (selling $441 billion US government securities to foreign central banks).

To make a long story short, a country experiencing a current account surplus will see its currency appreciate; conversely, a country experiencing a current account deficit will see its currency depreciate. This may not happen overnight, but it will happen in a span of years and decades. The current movement between the yuan (appreciating) and the dollar (depreciating) is but one example (see Opening Case). Going back to the 1950s and 1960s, the rise of the dollar was accompanied by a sizable US surplus on merchandise trade. By the 1970s and 1980s, the surplus gradually turned into a deficit. By the 1990s and 2000s, the US current account deficit became ever increasing, forcing the dollar to depreciate relative to other currencies, such as the yuan, the euro, and the Canadian dollar. Broadly speaking, the value of a country's currency is an embodiment of its economic strengths, as reflected in its productivity and balance of payments positions. Overall, the recent pressure for the US dollar to depreciate is indicative of the relative (not absolute) decline of US economic strengths compared with its major trading partners.

floating (or **flexible**) **exchange rate policy**
The willingness of a government to let the demand and supply conditions determine exchange rates.

clean (or **free**) **float**
A pure market solution to determine exchange rates.

dirty (or **managed**) **float**
The common practice of determining exchange rates through selective government intervention.

target exchange rates (or **crawling bands**)
A limited policy of intervention, occurring only when the exchange rate moves out of the specified upper or lower bounds.

Exchange Rate Policies

There are two major exchange rate policies: (1) floating rate and (2) fixed rate. Governments adopting the **floating** (or **flexible**) **exchange rate policy** tend to be free market believers, willing to let the demand and supply conditions determine exchange rates—usually on a daily basis via the foreign exchange market. However, few countries adopt a **clean** (or **free**) **float**, which would be a pure market solution. Most countries practice a **dirty** (or **managed**) **float**, with selective government interventions. Of the major currencies, the US, Canadian, and Australian dollars, the yen, and the pound have been under managed float since the 1970s (after the collapse of the Bretton Woods system; see next section). Since the late 1990s, several developing countries, such as Brazil, Mexico, and South Korea, have also joined the managed float regime.

The severity of intervention is a matter of degree. Heavier intervention moves the country closer to a fixed exchange rate policy, and less intervention enables a country to approach the free float ideal. A main objective of intervention is to prevent the emergence of erratic fluctuations that may trigger macroeconomic turbulence. Some countries do not adhere to any particular rates. Others choose **target exchange rates**—known as **crawling bands** or more vividly "snake in a tube" (intervention will only occur when the snake crawls out of a tube's upper or lower bounds).

Another major exchange rate policy is the **fixed exchange rate policy**—countries fix the exchange rate of their currencies relative to other currencies. Both political and economic rationales may be at play. During the German reunification in 1990, the West German government, for political considerations, fixed the exchange rate between the West and East German mark as 1:1. In economic terms, the East German mark was not worth that much. Politically, this exchange rate reduced the feeling of alienation and resentment among East Germans, thus facilitating a smoother unification process. Of course, West Germans ended up paying more for the costs of unification.

During reunification with East Germany, what were some of the economic consequences of West Germany's decision to fix the exchange rate between the West and East German marks at parity (a 1:1 rate)?

Economically, many developing countries **peg** their currencies to a key currency (often the US dollar). There are two benefits for a peg policy. First, a peg stabilizes the import and export prices for developing countries. Second, many countries with high inflation have pegged their currencies to the dollar (the United States has relatively low inflation) to restrain domestic inflation. (See Debates and Extensions for more discussion.)

Investor Psychology

Although theories on price differences (PPP), interest rates and money supply, balance of payments, and exchange rate policies predict long-run movements of exchange rates, they often fall short of predicting short-run movements. It is investor psychology, some of which is fickle and thus very hard to predict, that largely determines short-run movements. Professor Richard Lyons at the University of California, Berkeley, is an expert on exchange rate theories. However, he was baffled when he was invited by a friend to observe currency trading firsthand:

> As I sat there, my friend traded furiously all day long, racking up over $1 billion in trades each day. This was a world where the standard trade was $10 million, and a $1 million trade was a "skinny one." Despite my belief that exchange rates depend on macroeconomics, only rarely was news of this type his primary concern. Most of the time he was reading tea leaves that were, at least to me, not so clear . . . It was clear my understanding was incomplete when he looked over, in the midst of his fury, and asked me: "What should I do?" I laughed. Nervously.[5]

Investors—currency traders (such as the one Lyons observed), foreign portfolio investors, and average citizens—may move as a "herd" at the same time in the same direction, resulting in a **bandwagon effect**. The bandwagon effect seemed to be at play in the second half of 1997, when the Thai baht, Malaysian ringgit, Indonesian rupiah, and South Korean won lost approximately 50% to 70% of their value against the US dollar. Essentially, a large number of individuals and companies exchanged domestic currencies for US dollars to exit these countries—a phenomenon known as **capital flight**. This would push down the demand for, and thus the value of, domestic currencies. Then, more individuals and companies joined the herd, further depressing the exchange rate and setting off a major economic crisis.

Overall, economics, politics, and psychology are all involved. The stakes are high, yet consensus is rare regarding the determinants of foreign exchange rates. As a result, predicting the direction of currency movements remains an art or at best a highly imprecise science.

fixed exchange rate policy
Fixing the exchange rate of a currency relative to other currencies.

peg
A stabilizing policy of linking a developing country's currency to a key currency.

bandwagon effect
The result of investors moving as a herd in the same direction at the same time.

capital flight
A phenomenon in which a large number of individuals and companies exchange domestic currencies for a foreign currency.

LEARNING OBJECTIVE 2

track the evolution of the international monetary system

EVOLUTION OF THE INTERNATIONAL MONETARY SYSTEM

Having outlined the basic determinants of exchange rates, let us undertake a historical excursion to trace the three eras in the evolution of the international monetary system: (1) the gold standard, (2) the Bretton Woods system, and (3) the post–Bretton Woods system.

The Gold Standard (1870–1914)

gold standard
A system in which the value of most major currencies was maintained by fixing their prices in terms of gold, which served as the common denominator.

The **gold standard** was a system in place between 1870 and 1914, when the value of most major currencies was maintained by fixing their prices in terms of gold. Gold was used as the common denominator for all currencies. This was essentially a global peg system, with little volatility and every bit of predictability and stability. To be able to redeem its currency in gold at a fixed price, every central bank needed to maintain gold reserves. The system provided powerful incentives for countries to run current account surpluses, resulting in net inflows of gold.

The Bretton Woods System (1944–1973)

The gold standard was severely undermined in 1914 when World War I broke out and several combatant countries printed excessive amounts of currency to finance their war efforts. After World War I, especially during the Great Depression (1929–1933), countries engaged in competitive devaluations in an effort to boost exports at the expense of trading partners. But no country could win such a "race to the bottom," and the gold standard eventually had to be jettisoned.

Bretton Woods system
A system in which all currencies were pegged at a fixed rate to the US dollar.

Toward the end of World War II, at an allied conference in Bretton Woods, New Hampshire, a new system—known as the **Bretton Woods system**—was agreed upon by 44 countries. The Bretton Woods system was centered on the US dollar as the new common denominator. All currencies were pegged at a fixed rate to the dollar. Only the dollar was convertible into gold at $35 per ounce. Other currencies were not required to be gold convertible.

It was the Bretton Woods system that propelled the dollar to the commanding heights of the global economy (see Table 7.2). This was also a reflection of the higher US productivity level and the large US trade surplus with the rest of the world in the first two postwar decades. This was not surprising because the US economy contributed approximately 70% of the global GDP at the end of World War II and was the export engine of the world at that time.

The Post–Bretton Woods System (1973–present)

By the late 1960s and early 1970s, a combination of rising productivity elsewhere and US inflationary policies led to the demise of Bretton Woods. First, West Germany and other countries got caught up in productivity and exported more, and the United States ran its first post-1945 trade deficit in 1971. This pushed the West German mark to appreciate and the dollar to depreciate—a situation very similar to the yen-dollar relationship in the 1980s and the yuan-dollar relationship in the 2000s. Second, in the 1960s, to finance both the Vietnam War and Great Society welfare programs, President Lyndon Johnson increased government spending not by additional taxation but by increasing the money supply. These actions led to rising inflation levels and strong pressures for the dollar to depreciate.

As currency traders bought more German marks, Germany's central bank, the Bundesbank, had to buy billions of dollars to maintain the dollar/mark exchange rate fixed by Bretton Woods. Being stuck with massive amounts of the dollar that was worth less now, Germany unilaterally allowed its currency to float in May 1971.

Likewise, the Bretton Woods system became a pain in the neck for the United States because it was not allowed to unilaterally change the exchange rate of the dollar. Per Bretton Woods agreements, the US Treasury was obligated to dispense one ounce of gold for every $35 brought by a foreign central bank such as the Bundesbank. Consequently, there was a hemorrhage of US gold flowing into the coffers of foreign central banks. In August 1971, to stop such hemorrhaging, President Richard Nixon unilaterally announced that the dollar was no longer convertible into gold. After tense negotiations, major countries collectively agreed to hammer the coffin nails of the Bretton Woods system by allowing their currencies to float in 1973. In retrospect, the Bretton Woods system had been built on two conditions: (1) the US inflation rate had to be low and (2) the US could not run a trade deficit. When both these conditions were violated, the demise of the system was inevitable.

As a result, today we live in the **post–Bretton Woods system**. The strengths lie in its flexibility and diversity of exchange rate regimes described earlier (ranging from various floating systems to various fixed rates). Its drawback is turbulence and uncertainty. Since the early 1970s, the US dollar is no longer the official common denominator. However, it has retained a significant amount of "soft power" as a key currency (see Table 7.2).

post–Bretton Woods system
A system of flexible exchange rate regimes with no official common denominator.

The International Monetary Fund (IMF)

Although the Bretton Woods system is no longer with us, one of its most enduring legacies is the IMF, founded in 1944 as a "Bretton Woods institution."[6] With 184 member countries now, the IMF is very much alive today (Figure 7.2). Its mandate is to promote international monetary cooperation and provide temporary financial assistance to member countries to help overcome balance of payments problems. The IMF performs three primary activities: (1) monitoring the global economy, (2) providing technical assistance to developing countries, and (3) lending.

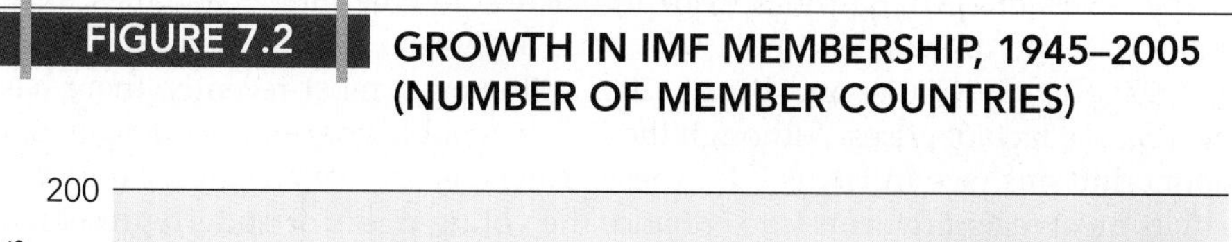

GROWTH IN IMF MEMBERSHIP, 1945–2005 (NUMBER OF MEMBER COUNTRIES)

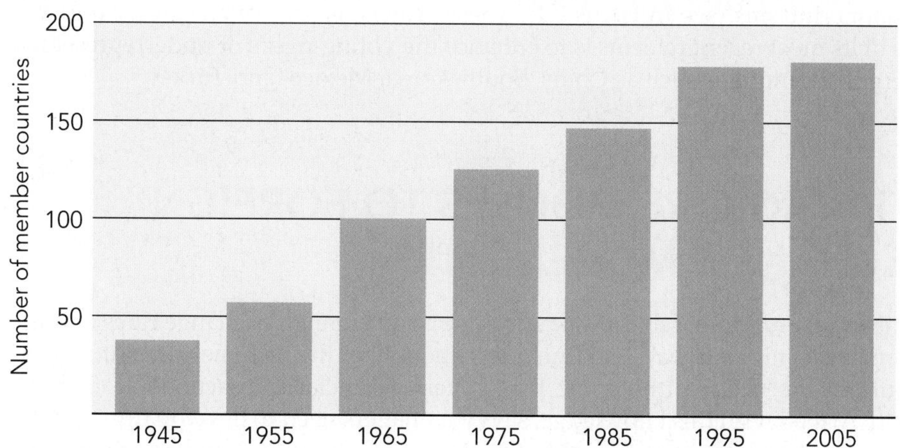

Source: International Monetary Fund, 2006, *About the IMF* (p. 1), Washington, DC: IMF, http://www.imf.org. The IMF had 44 member countries in 1945 and 186 member countries in 2006.

TABLE 7.5 TYPICAL IMF CONDITIONS ON LOAN RECIPIENT COUNTRIES

- Balance budget by slashing government spending (often entails cutting social welfare programs)
- Enhance tax revenues
- Raise interests to slow monetary growth and inflation

Lending is a core responsibility of the IMF. It provides loans to countries experiencing balance of payments problems. The IMF can be viewed as a lender of last resort to assist member countries should they get into financial difficulty. Where does the IMF get its funds? The answer boils down to the same principle of where insurance companies get their funds to pay for insurance coverage. For the same reason that insurance companies obtain their funds from insurance subscribers who pay a premium, the IMF collects funds from member countries. Each member country is assigned a quota, based broadly on its relative size in the global economy, that determines its financial contribution to the IMF, its capacity to borrow, and its voting power.

By definition, the IMF's lending refers to loans, not free grants. IMF loans usually have to be repaid in one to five years. Although there are some extensions for payments, no member country has defaulted. The ideal scenario for the IMF to make a difference is that when a country suffers from a balance of payments crisis (for example, importing more than it exports) that may trigger a financial crisis, the IMF can step in and inject funds in the short term.

While an IMF loan provides short-term financial resources, it also comes with strings attached—long-term policy reforms that recipient countries must undertake as conditions of receiving the loan. These conditions usually entail belt-tightening by pushing governments to embark on reforms that they otherwise probably would not have undertaken (Table 7.5). For instance, when the IMF provided a $30 billion loan to Brazil in 2002, the Brazilian government agreed to maintain a budget surplus of 3.75% of GDP or higher to pay for government debt. Since the 1990s, the IMF has often gone into action in emerging economies, such as Mexico (1994), Russia (1996 and 1998), Asia (Indonesia, South Korea, and Thailand, 1997), Turkey (2001), and Brazil (2002). However, most recently, there has been a relative lack of crises. Although the IMF has noble goals, its actions are not without criticisms (see In Focus 7.1). These criticisms thus often call for reforms. One of its most recent reforms is to enhance the voting rights of underrepresented emerging economies such as China, South Korea, Mexico, and Turkey.[7]

LEARNING OBJECTIVE 3

identify firms' strategic responses to deal with foreign exchange movements

STRATEGIC RESPONSES TO FOREIGN EXCHANGE MOVEMENTS

From an institution-based view, knowledge about foreign exchange rates and the international monetary system (including the role of the IMF) helps paint a broad picture of the rules of the game that govern financial transactions around the world. Armed with this knowledge, savvy managers need to develop firm-specific resources and capabilities to rise to the challenge—or at least to keep their firms from being crushed by unfavorable currency movements. This section outlines the strategic responses of two types of firms: financial and nonfinancial companies.

IN FOCUS 7.1 ETHICAL DILEMMA: The IMF's Actions and Criticisms

The complexity of the IMF's actions means that it cannot please everyone. First, critics argue that the IMF's lending may *facilitate* more problems because of moral hazard. **Moral hazard** refers to recklessness when people and organizations (including governments) do not have to face the full consequences of their actions. Moral hazard is inherent in all insurance arrangements, including the IMF. Basically, knowing that the IMF would come to the rescue, certain governments may behave more recklessly. For example, between 1958 and 2001, Turkey was rescued by 18 IMF loans.

A second criticism centers on the IMF's lack of accountability. By 2002, the IMF managed loans in 88 developing countries with a total population of 1.4 billion people. On average, there are only about 11 officials to deal with crucial economic decisions in each country, and the IMF has a staff of fewer than 1,000. None of these officials is democratically elected, and most of them do not have any deep knowledge of the host country. Consequently, they sometimes make disastrous decisions. For example, in 1997–1998, the IMF forced the Indonesian government to drastically cut back on food subsidies for the poor. Riots exploded the next day. Hundreds of people were killed, and property was damaged. Then, the IMF reversed its position by restoring food subsidies. However, in some quarters, the bitterness was all the greater. Many protesters argued: If food subsidies could have been continued, why were they taken away in the first place?

A third and perhaps most challenging criticism is that the IMF's "one-size-fits-all" strategy may be inappropriate. Since the 1930s, to maintain more employment, most Western governments have abandoned the idea of balancing the budget. Deficit spending has been used as a major policy weapon to pull a country out of an economic crisis. Yet, the IMF often demands governments in more vulnerable developing countries, in the midst of a major economic crisis, to balance their budgets by slashing spending (such as cutting food subsidies). These actions often make the crisis far worse than it needs to be. After the IMF came to "rescue" countries affected by the 1997 Asian financial crisis, the unemployment rate was up threefold in Thailand, fourfold in South Korea, and tenfold in Indonesia. Many scholars are surprised that the IMF would pursue its agenda in the absence of conclusive research and with the knowledge of repeated failures. Since then, the IMF has admitted some mistakes. Since no two countries—or two crises—are identical, the IMF constantly faces a dilemma when going into action: Should it apply its rigid "formula" or modify it?

Sources: Based on (1) J. Sachs, 1997, Power unto itself, *Financial Times*, December 11: 11; (2) J. Stiglitz, 2002, *Globalization and Its Discontents*, New York: Norton.

Strategies for Financial Companies

One of the leading strategic goals for financial companies is to profit from the foreign exchange market. The **foreign exchange market** is a market where individuals, firms, governments, and banks buy and sell foreign currencies. Unlike a stock exchange, the foreign exchange market has no central physical location. This market is truly global and transparent. Buyers and sellers are geographically dispersed but constantly linked (quoted prices change as often as 20 times a minute).[8] The market opens on Monday morning first in Tokyo and then Hong Kong and Singapore, when it is still Sunday evening in New York. Gradually, Frankfurt, Zurich, Paris, London, New York, Chicago, and San Francisco "wake up" and come online.

Operating on a 24/7 basis, the foreign exchange market is the largest and most active market in the world. On average, the worldwide volume exceeds $2 trillion a *day*. To put this mind-boggling number in perspective, the amount of one single *day* of foreign exchange transactions roughly doubles the amount of entire worldwide FDI outflows in one *year* ($916 billion in 2005) and roughly equals close to one-quarter of worldwide merchandise exports in one *year* (over $9 trillion in 2005). Of course, trade and FDI are directly related to foreign exchange transactions because traders and investors need to convert currencies. However, the strikingly large scale of the foreign exchange market, relative to the more "modest" levels of trade and FDI, suggests that something else must be going on beyond the needs to service trade and FDI. Specifically, there are two functions of the foreign exchange market: (1) to service the needs of trade and FDI and (2) to trade in its own commodity, namely, foreign exchange.

moral hazard
Recklessness when people and organizations (including governments) do not have to face the full consequences of their actions.

foreign exchange market
A market where individuals, firms, governments, and banks buy and sell foreign currencies.

spot transaction
The classic single-shot exchange of one currency for another.

forward transaction
A foreign exchange transaction in which participants buy and sell currencies now for future delivery, typically in 30, 90, or 180 days, after the date of the transaction.

currency hedging
A transaction that protects traders and investors from exposure to the fluctuations of the spot rate.

forward discount
A condition under which the forward rate of one currency relative to another currency is higher than the spot rate.

forward premium
A condition under which the forward rate of one currency relative to another currency is lower than the spot rate.

currency swap
A foreign exchange transaction between two firms in which one currency is converted into another in Time 1, with an agreement to revert it back to the original currency at a specific Time 2 in the future.

offer rate
The price offered to sell a currency.

bid rate
The price offered to buy a currency.

spread
The difference between the offered price and the bid price.

There are three primary types of foreign exchange transactions: (1) spot transactions, (2) forward transactions, and (3) swaps. **Spot transactions** are the classic single-shot exchange of one currency for another. For example, through spot transactions, Australian tourists buying several thousand euros in Italy with Australian dollars will get their euros from a bank right away.

Forward transactions allow participants to buy and sell currencies now for future delivery, typically in 30, 90, or 180 days, after the date of the transaction. The primary benefit of forward transactions is to protect traders and investors from exposure to the fluctuations of the spot rate, an act known as **currency hedging**. Currency hedging is essentially a way to minimize the foreign exchange risk inherent in all nonspot transactions, which characterize most trade and FDI deals. Traders and investors expecting to make or receive payments in a foreign currency in the future are concerned whether they will have to make a greater payment or receive less in terms of the domestic currency should the spot rate change. For example, if the forward rate of the euro (€/US$) is exactly the same as the spot rate, the euro is "flat." If the forward rate of the euro per dollar is *higher* than the spot rate, the euro has a **forward discount**. If the forward rate of the euro per dollar is *lower* than the spot rate, the euro then has a **forward premium**.

Hypothetically, assume that (1) today's exchange rate of €/US$ is 1, (2) a US firm expects to be paid €1 million six months later, and (3) the euro is at a 180-day forward discount of 1.1. The US firm may take out a forward contract now and convert euro earnings into a dollar revenue of $909,091 (€1 million/1.1) after six months. Does such a move make sense? There can be two answers. Yes, if the firm knew in advance that the future spot rate would be 1.25. With the forward contract, the US firm would make $909,091 instead of $800,000 (€1 million/1.25)—the difference is $109,091 (14% of $800,000). However, the answer would be no if the spot rate after six months was below 1.1. If the spot rate remained at 1, the firm could have earned $1 million, *without* the forward contract, instead of only $909,091. This simple example suggests a powerful observation: Currency hedging *requires* firms to have expectations or forecasts of future spot rates relative to forward rates (see Closing Case).

A third major type of foreign exchange transaction is a swap. A **currency swap** is the conversion of one currency into another in Time 1, with an agreement to revert it back to the original currency at a specific Time 2 in the future. Deutsche Bank may have an excess balance of pounds but needs dollars. At the same time, Union Bank of Switzerland (UBS) may have more dollars than it needs at the moment but is looking for more pounds. They can negotiate a swap agreement in which Deutsche Bank agrees to exchange with UBS pounds for dollars today and dollars for pounds at a specific point in the future.

The primary participants of the foreign exchange market are large international banks that trade among themselves (led by Deutsche Bank, UBS, and Citigroup—in descending order of volume in 2006). How do these banks make money by trading money? They make money by capturing the difference between their **offer rate** (the price to sell) and **bid rate** (the price to buy)—the bid rate is *always* lower than the offer rate. The difference of this "buy low, sell high" strategy is technically called the **spread**. For example, Citigroup may quote offer and bid rates for the Swiss franc at $0.5854 and $0.5851, respectively, and the spread is $0.0003. That is, Citigroup is willing to sell 1 million francs for $585,400 and buy 1 million francs for $585,100. If Citigroup can simultaneously buy and sell 1 million francs, it can make $300 (the spread of $0.0003 × 1 million francs). Given the instantaneous and transparent nature of the electronically linked foreign exchange market around the globe (one new quote in London can reach New York before you finish reading this sentence), the opportunities for trading, or arbitrage, can come and go very quickly. The globally integrated nature of this market leads to three outcomes:

- Razor-thin spread
- Quick (often literally split-second) decisions on buying and selling (remember Professor Lyons's observation earlier)
- Ever increasing volume to make more profits (recall the daily volume of $2 trillion). In the earlier example, $300 is obviously just a few "peanuts" for Citigroup. Do a little math: How much trading in Swiss francs does Citigroup have to do to make $1 million in profits for itself?

Strategies for Nonfinancial Companies

How do nonfinancial companies cope with the fluctuations of the foreign exchange market—broadly known as **currency risks**? There are two primary strategies: (1) currency hedging (as discussed earlier) and (2) strategic hedging.[9] Currency hedging is risky if there are wrong bets of currency movements. For example, Japan Airlines (JAL) needed US dollars to purchase Boeing aircraft, but its revenues were mostly in yen. In 1985, it entered a ten-year contract with foreign exchange traders at a rate of $1 to 185 yen. This looked like a great deal given the 1985 exchange rate of $1 to 240 yen. However, by 1994, the yen had surged against the dollar to $1 to 99 yen. Because JAL was bound by the contract to purchase dollars at the rate of $1 to 185 yen, it was paying 86% (!) more than it needed to for every Boeing aircraft it bought.[10]

currency risk
The fluctuations of the foreign exchange market.

Strategic hedging means spreading out activities in a number of countries in different currency zones to offset the currency losses in certain regions through gains in other regions.[11] Therefore, strategic hedging can be considered currency diversification. It reduces exposure to unfavorable foreign exchange movements. Strategic hedging is conceptually different from currency hedging. Currency hedging focuses on using forward contracts and swaps to contain currency risks, a financial management activity that can be performed by in-house financial specialists or outside experts (such as currency traders). Strategic hedging refers to geographically dispersing operations—through sourcing or FDI—in multiple currency zones. By definition, this is more strategic, involving managers from many functional areas (such as production, marketing, and sourcing) in addition to those from finance. Strategic hedging was one of the key motivations behind Toyota's 1998 decision to set up a new factory in France instead of expanding its existing British operations (which would cost less in the short run). France is in the euro zone that the British refused to join.

strategic hedging
Spreading out activities in a number of countries in different currency zones to offset the currency losses in certain regions through gains in other regions.

Overall, the importance of foreign exchange management cannot be overstressed for firms of all stripes interested in doing business abroad. Firms whose performance is otherwise stellar can be devastated by unfavorable currency movements. For instance, Nestlé's sales volume in Brazil grew by 10% during 1998–2002. But because of currency deterioration, its Brazil revenues in Swiss francs actually went *down* by 30% during the same period.[12] Honda is similarly hurt by the strong yen, which appreciated against the dollar since 2000. Since Honda made 80%

© LUCAS SCHIFRES/BLOOMBERG NEWS /Landov

What foreign exchange considerations prompted Toyota to locate a new factory in France instead of Great Britain?

of its profits in the United States, their value, when translated into the Japanese yen, became much lower.[13]

From a resource-based view, it seems imperative that firms develop resources and capabilities that can combat currency risks in addition to striving for excellence in, for example, operations and marketing.[14] MNE subsidiary managers in certain countries may believe that there are lucrative opportunities to expand production. However, if these countries suffer from high currency risks, it may be better—for the multinational as a whole—to curtail such expansion and channel resources to other countries whose currency risks are more manageable. Developing such expertise is no small accomplishment because, as noted earlier, prediction of currency movements remains an art or a highly imprecise science. Because of such challenges, firms able to profit from (or at least avoid being crushed by) unfavorable currency movements will possess some valuable, rare, and hard-to-imitate capabilities that are the envy of rivals.

LEARNING OBJECTIVE 4

participate in three leading debates on foreign exchange movements

DEBATES AND EXTENSIONS

In the highly uncertain world of foreign exchange movements, stakes are high, yet consensus is rare and debates are numerous. We review three major debates here: (1) fixed versus floating exchange rates, (2) a strong versus a weak dollar, and (3) hedging versus not hedging.

Fixed versus Floating Exchange Rates[15]

Since the collapse of the Bretton Woods system in the early 1970s, debate has never ended on whether fixed or floating exchange rates are better. Proponents of fixed exchange rates argue that these rates impose monetary discipline by preventing governments from engaging in inflationary monetary policies (essentially, printing more money). Proponents also suggest that fixed exchange rates reduce uncertainty and thus encourage trade and FDI, not only benefiting the particular economy but also helping the global economy.

Proponents of floating exchange rates believe that market forces should take care of supply, demand, and thus the price of any currency. Floating exchange rates may avoid large balance of payment deficits, surprises, and even crises. In other words, flexible exchange rates may help avoid the crises that occur under fixed exchange rates when expectations of an impending devaluation arise. For example, Thailand probably would not have been devastated so suddenly in July 1997 (generally regarded as the triggering event for the 1997 Asian financial crisis) had it operated a floating exchange rate system. In addition, floating exchange rates allow each country to make its own monetary policy. A major problem associated with the Bretton Woods system was that other countries were not happy about fixing their currencies to the currency of a country with inflationary monetary policies, as practiced by the United States in the late 1960s.

There is no doubt that floating exchange rates are more volatile than fixed rates. Many countries have no stomach for such volatility. The most extreme fixed rate policy is through a **currency board**, which is a monetary authority that issues notes and coins convertible into a key foreign currency at a *fixed* exchange rate. Usually, the fixed exchange rate is set by law, making changes to the exchange rate politically very costly for governments. To honor its commitment, a currency board must back the domestic currency with 100% of equivalent foreign exchange. In the case of Hong Kong's currency board, every HK$7.8 in circulation is backed by US$1. By design, a currency board is passive. When more US dollars flow in, the board issues more Hong Kong dollars and interest rates fall. When more US

currency board
A monetary authority that issues notes and coins convertible into a key foreign currency at a fixed exchange rate.

dollars flow out, the board reduces money supply and interest rates rise. The Hong Kong currency board has been jokingly described as an Asian outpost of the US Federal Reserve. This is technically accurate because interest rates in Hong Kong are essentially determined by the US Federal Reserve. While the Hong Kong currency board was a successful bulwark against speculative attacks on the Hong Kong dollar in 1997 and 1998, a currency board is not necessarily a panacea, as evidenced by Argentina's experience (In Focus 7.2).

A Strong Dollar versus a Weak Dollar

The debate on the Chinese yuan discussed in the Opening Case is part of a larger debate on the value of the US dollar. Under the Bretton Woods system (1944–1973), the US dollar was the only common denominator. Since the demise of Bretton Woods in 1973, the importance of the US dollar has been in gradual decline. This does not mean that the US dollar is no longer important; it still is (see Table 7.2). It is the dollar's relative importance—in particular, its value—that is at the heart of this debate. Table 7.6 outlines the pros and cons of a strong dollar versus a weak dollar.

As noted earlier in the section on the determinants of foreign exchange rates, the value of a currency is a broad reflection of a country's economic strengths. In December 2006, the value of the dollar sharply dropped against the euro, the pound, the yen, and the yuan—falling to a 20-month low of $1.32 per euro. The *Economist* remarked that "the only real surprise was that the dollar had not slipped sooner."[16] What are the implications of a weak dollar for the rest of the world? Although a weak dollar hurts exporters in Asia and Europe, it helps remedy the US balance of payments and results in more global balancing. As the US economy slows down and thus is unable to absorb more imports (the United States already

IN FOCUS 7.2 Hong Kong and Argentina: A Tale of Two Currency Boards

Hong Kong is usually cited as an example that has benefited from a currency board. In the early 1980s, Hong Kong had a floating exchange rate. As Britain and China intensified their negotiations over the colony's future, the fear that the "Hong Kong way of life" might be abandoned after 1997 shook business confidence, pushed down real estate values, and caused panic buying of vegetable oil and rice. The result was 16% depreciation in the Hong Kong dollar against the US dollar. In 1983, the Hong Kong government ended the crisis by adopting a currency board that pegged the exchange rate at HK$7.8 = US$1. The currency board almost immediately restored confidence. The second major test of the currency board came in 1997, in the first autumn after Hong Kong was returned to Chinese sovereignty. During the Asian financial crisis of 1997–1998, Hong Kong's currency board stood like a rock, successfully repelled speculative attacks, and maintained its peg to the US dollar.

In Argentina, hyperinflation was rampant in the 1980s. Prices increased by more than 1,000% (!) in both 1989 and 1990. In 1991, to tame its tendency to finance public spending by printing pesos, Argentina adopted a currency board and pegged the peso at parity to the US dollar (1 peso = US$1). At first, the system worked, as inflation was brought down to 2% by 1995. However, by the late 1990s, Argentina was hit by multiple problems. First, appreciation of the dollar made its exports less competitive. Second, rising US interest rates spilled over to Argentina. Third, depreciation of Brazil's real resulted in more imports from Brazil and fewer exports from Argentina to Brazil. To finance budget deficits, Argentina borrowed dollars on the international market, as printing more pesos was not possible under the currency board. When further borrowing became impossible in 2001, the government defaulted on its $155 billion public debt (a world record), ended the peso's convertibility, and froze most dollar-denominated deposits in banks. In 2002, Argentina was forced to give up its currency board. After the delink, the peso plunged, hitting a low of 3.5 to the dollar. Riots broke out as people voiced their displeasure with politicians.

Sources: Based on (1) R. Carbaugh, 2007, *International Economics*, 11th ed. (pp. 492–495), Cincinnati, OH: Thomson South-Western; (2) F. Gunter, 2004, Why did Argentina's currency board collapse? *The World Economy*, May: 697–704; (3) M. W. Peng, 2006, Coping with institutional uncertainty in Argentina, in M. W. Peng, *Global Strategy* (p. 111), Cincinnati, OH: Thomson South-Western.

TABLE 7.6 A STRONG DOLLAR VERSUS A WEAK DOLLAR

PANEL A. A STRONG (APPRECIATING) DOLLAR

Advantages	Disadvantages
• US consumers benefit from low prices on imports • Lower prices on foreign goods help keep US price level and inflation level low • US tourists benefit from lower prices when traveling abroad	• US exporters have a hard time competing on price competitiveness abroad • US firms in import-competing industries have a hard time competing with low-cost imports • Foreign tourists find it more expensive when visiting the United States

PANEL B. A WEAK (DEPRECIATING) DOLLAR

Advantages	Disadvantages
• US exporters find it easier to compete on price competitiveness abroad • US firms face less competitive pressure to keep prices low • Foreign tourists benefit from lower prices when visiting the United States	• US consumers face higher prices on imports • Higher prices on imports contribute to higher price level and inflation level in the United States • US tourists find it more expensive when traveling abroad

Source: Adapted from R. Carbaugh, 2007, *International Economics*, 11th ed. (p. 373), Cincinnati, OH: Thomson South-Western.

has the world's largest import bill and largest current account deficit), a weak dollar forces Asian and European economies to boost their domestic demand. Thus, the world economy may benefit from a gradual slide of the dollar.

However, the rest of the world has two reasons to support a strong dollar. First, the rest of the world holds so many greenbacks that most countries fear the capital loss they would suffer if the dollar falls too deep. China leads the world by holding $1 trillion foreign reserve, most of which is in dollars (In Focus 7.3). Second, many countries prefer to keep the value of their currencies down to promote exports. Unfortunately, the more and the longer they pile up dollars, the bigger the eventual losses in the event of a dollar depreciation. Around the world, how to manage the dollar's slide without causing too much pain remains a "trillion-dollar" question.

Currency Hedging versus Not Hedging

Given the unpredictable nature of foreign exchange rates (at least in the short run), it seems natural that firms that deal with foreign transactions—both financial and nonfinancial types, both large and small firms—would engage in currency hedging (see Closing Case). Firms that fail to hedge are at the mercy of the spot market. In 1997, Siam Cement, a major chemicals firm in Thailand, had $4.2 billion debt denominated in foreign currencies and hedged none of it. When the Thai baht sharply depreciated against the US dollar in July 1997, Siam Cement had to absorb a $517 million loss, which wiped out all the profits it made during 1994–1996.[17]

Yet, surprisingly, many firms do not bother to engage in currency hedging. Among America's largest firms, only approximately one-third hedge. The standard argument for currency hedging is increased stability of cash flows and earn-

IN FOCUS 7.3 Who Wants to Be a Trillionaire? Not China's Central Bank

By the end of October 2006, China's foreign-exchange reserves are likely to top $1 trillion, twice their level two years ago and more than one-fifth of global reserves. This handsome sum would be enough to buy all the gold sitting in central banks' vaults (indeed, twice over) or almost all of London's residential property. China's massive hoard is the result of its large current account surplus, significant inward FDI, and big inflows of speculative capital over the past couple of years. In theory, flows of foreign money into China should push up the yuan, but China has resisted this, forcing the central bank—the People's Bank of China—to buy up the surplus foreign currency. The growth in reserves has slowed in recent months, but it is still averaging a hefty $16 billion a month.

China's official reserves already far exceeded what is required to ensure financial stability. As a rule of thumb, a country needs enough foreign exchange to cover three months' imports or settle its short-term foreign debt. China's reserves are equivalent to 15 months of imports and are six times bigger than its short-term debt. The explosion of reserves is also a headache for the central bank. It creates excess liquidity, which risks fueling higher inflation, asset-price bubbles, and imprudent bank lending.

There are two simple ways to stop reserve rising. China could set free its exchange rate, or it could relax restrictions on capital outflows and allow private citizens to hold foreign assets. Significant moves of either kind seem unlikely in the near future. As long as China runs a large external surplus (the natural result of its high savings rate) and refuses to set its currency free, its stash of foreign currency will probably continue to mount.

How that money is invested has big implications for the world economy, not just for China. About 70% of it is invested in dollars, mainly Treasury securities. This has popped up the dollar and reduced American bond yields by up to 1.5% according to some estimates. A big shift out of dollars could therefore push up bond yields and hence mortgage rates, damaging America's already crumbling housing market. China's central bank is thought to be switching from Treasury bonds to American mortgage-backed securities and corporate bonds in an attempt to earn higher yields. Chinese officials have also discussed in private the need to diversify reserves out of dollars to reduce exposure to a big drop in the greenback. The bank may be putting a bigger slice of any increase in reserves into euros and emerging Asian currencies, but so far, there is little sign of a shift out of its existing stock of dollars. One problem is that China's investments are so big that they move markets. Shifting money into euros would push down the dollar. China would then not only suffer a capital loss on its remaining dollar reserves, but it could also be forced to buy yet more reserves to hold its currency down against a weak dollar.

Fear of a capital loss and dissatisfaction with unrewarding yields have triggered a flurry of ideas on how to put the money to better use. One popular idea is to use some of China's reserves to buy oil and other commodities. The snag is that stockpiling oil would push up prices, yet absorb only a tiny portion of the sums at China's disposal. Buying the equivalent of six-months' oil consumption would take only 8% of total reserves at current prices, but the extra oil bought would amount to three times the growth in global oil demand this year. Buying gold would have similar results: If China invested just 5% of its reserves in gold, it could buy the world's entire annual gold mine production.

Another proposal is to spend more money on infrastructure investment, which would yield a much higher return than American bonds. However, since China's investment already accounts for 40% of GDP, it is not clear that China needs more. Writing off banks' nonperforming loans might seem more sensible. In 2004 and 2005, the People's Bank of China did indeed shift $60 billion to state banks. The remaining stock of bad loans is now around $250 billion, according to UBS.

By buying American bonds, China is subsidizing rich American consumers while China's healthcare, education, and social safety net are starved for funds. So why not use reserves to relieve rural poverty, improve healthcare, or inject money into the underfunded pension system? Unfortunately, all of these proposals to spend money at home misunderstand the nature of foreign reserves. The problem is that conversion of the foreign currency into yuan would put upward pressure on the yuan and so force the central bank to buy yet more foreign currency to hold it down. Reserves would return to their original level.

The only real solution to the poor return on China's reserves is to stop accumulating them. That requires policy reforms to reduce China's massive savings, which drives its current account surplus, and a more flexible exchange rate system. But before that happens, China's reserves could well hit $2 trillion.

Source: *Economist*, 2006, Who wants to be a trillionaire? Not China's central bank, October 28: 85.

ings. In essence, currency hedging may be regarded as a form of insurance, whose cost may be outweighed by the protection it provides. However, many large firms, such as 3M, Deere, Eastman Kodak, ExxonMobil, and IBM, do not care about such insurance. Managers argue that currency hedging eats into profits. A simple forward contract may cost up to half a percentage point per year of the revenue being hedged. More complicated transactions may cost more. As a result, many firms believe that the ups and downs of various currencies balance out in the long run. Some, such as IBM, focus on strategic hedging (geographically dispersing activities) but refrain from currency hedging. Whether such a "no currency hedging" strategy outperforms a currency hedging strategy remains to be seen.

LEARNING OBJECTIVE 5

draw implications for action

MANAGEMENT SAVVY

The big question in global business, adapted to the context of foreign exchange movements, is: What determines the success and failure of currency management around the globe? The answer boils down to two components. First, from an institution-based standpoint, the changing rules of the game—economic, political, and psychological—enable or constrain firms. Shown in the Opening Case, Wal-Mart's low-cost advantage from made-in-China products stems at least in part from the Chinese government's policy to peg its yuan at a favorable level against the dollar. Consequently, Wal-Mart's low-cost advantage may be eroded as the yuan appreciates. Second, from a resource-based perspective, how firms develop valuable, unique, and hard-to-imitate capabilities in currency management may make or break them. As illustrated in the Closing Case, Markel's wrong bets on the currency movements resulted in painful pay cuts for its employees.

As a result, three implications for action emerge (Table 7.7). First, foreign exchange literacy must be fostered. Savvy managers need not only pay attention to the broad long-run movements informed by PPP, productivity changes, and balance of payments, but also to the fickle short-run fluctuations triggered by interest rate changes and investor mood swings.

Second, risk analysis of any country must include its currency risks. Previous chapters have advised managers to pay attention to the political, regulatory, and cultural risks of various countries. Here, a crucial currency risk dimension is added. An otherwise attractive country may suffer from high inflation, resulting in devaluation of its currency on the horizon. Countries in Southeast Asia prior to 1997 represented such a scenario. Numerous firms ignoring such a currency risk dimension were burned badly in the Asian financial crisis of 1997–1998.

Finally, a country's high currency risks do not necessarily suggest that this country needs to be totally avoided. Instead, it calls for a prudent currency risk management strategy via currency hedging, strategic hedging, or both. Not every firm has the stomach or capabilities to do both. Smaller, internationally inexperienced firms (such as Markel) may outsource currency hedging to specialists such as currency traders. Strategic hedging may be unrealistic for such smaller, inexperienced firms. On the other hand, many larger, internationally experienced firms (such as 3M) choose not to touch currency hedging, citing its unpredictability. Instead, they focus on strategic hedging. Although there is no fixed formula, firms not having a well-thought-out currency management strategy will be caught off guard when currency movements take a wrong turn.

TABLE 7.7 IMPLICATIONS FOR ACTION

- Fostering foreign exchange literacy is a must
- Risk analysis of any country must include an analysis of its currency risks
- A currency risk management strategy is necessary via currency hedging, strategic hedging, or both

CHAPTER SUMMARY

1. Understand the determinants of foreign exchange rates
   - A foreign exchange rate is the price of one currency expressed in another.
   - Basic determinants of foreign exchange rates include (1) relative price differences and PPP, (2) interest rates, (3) productivity and balance of payments, (4) exchange rate policies, and (5) investor psychology.
2. Track the evolution of the international monetary system
   - The international monetary system evolved from the gold standard (1870–1914), to the Bretton Woods system (1944–1973), and eventually to the current post-Bretton Woods system (1973–present).
   - The IMF serves as a lender of last resort to help member countries fight balance of payments problems.
3. Identify firms' strategic responses to deal with foreign exchange movements
   - Three foreign exchange transactions are: (1) spot transactions, (2) forward transactions, and (3) swaps.
   - Firms' strategic responses include (1) currency hedging, (2) strategic hedging, or (3) both.
4. Participate in three leading debates on foreign exchange movements
   - These are: (1) fixed versus floating exchange rates, (2) a strong versus a weak dollar, and (3) currency hedging versus not hedging.
5. Draw implications for action
   - Fostering foreign exchange literacy is a must.
   - Risk analysis of any country must include an analysis of its currency risks.
   - A currency risk management strategy is necessary via currency hedging, strategic hedging, or both.

KEY TERMS

Balance of payments 187
Bandwagon effect 189
Bid rate 194
Bretton Woods system 190
Capital flight 189
Clean (free) float 188
Currency board 196
Currency hedging 194
Currency risk 195
Currency swap 194
Dirty (managed) float 188
Fixed exchange rate policy 189
Floating (flexible) exchange rate policy 188
Foreign exchange market 193
Foreign exchange rate 183
Forward discount 194
Forward premium 194
Forward transaction 194
Gold standard 190
International Monetary Fund (IMF) 182
Moral hazard 193
Offer rate 194
Peg 189
Post–Bretton Woods system 191
Purchasing power parity (PPP) 184
Spot transaction 194
Spread 194
Strategic hedging 195
Target exchange rates (crawling bands) 188

REVIEW QUESTIONS

1. Briefly summarize the six major factors that influence foreign exchange rates.
2. How would you describe the theory of purchasing power parity (PPP)?
3. What is the relationship between a country's current account balance and its currency?

4. What is the difference between a floating exchange rate policy and a fixed exchange rate policy?
5. How is the phenomenon of capital flight an example of the bandwagon effect or herd mentality?
6. Why did the gold standard evolve to the Bretton Woods system? Then why did the Bretton Woods system evolve to the present post-Bretton Woods system?
7. Describe the IMF's roles and responsibilities.
8. Name and describe the three primary types of foreign exchange transactions made by financial companies.
9. Name and describe two ways nonfinancial companies can cope with currency risks.
10. Which do you think is a better policy to adopt: a floating exchange rate or a fixed rate?
11. Why is the strength of the American dollar important to the rest of the world?
12. Devise your own example of a way a firm might engage in currency hedging.
13. What concepts must a savvy manager understand to be considered literate about foreign exchange?
14. What skills might a manager need to develop to devise strategies for managing currency risk?

CRITICAL DISCUSSION QUESTIONS

1. If US$1 = €0.73 in New York and US$1 = €0.75 in Paris, how can foreign exchange traders profit from these exchange rates? Which of their actions may result in the same dollar/euro exchange rate in New York and Paris?
2. Identify the currencies of the top-three trading partners of your country in the last ten years. Find the exchange rates of these currencies, relative to your country's currency, ten years ago and now. Explain the changes. Then predict the movement of these exchange rates ten years from now.
3. As a manager, you are choosing to do business in two countries: One has a fixed exchange rate, and the other has a floating rate. Which country would you prefer? Why?
4. Should China revalue the yuan against the dollar? If so, what impact may this have on (1) US balance of payments, (2) Chinese balance of payments, (3) relative competitiveness of Mexico and Thailand, (4) firms such as Wal-Mart, and (5) US and Chinese retail consumers?
5. ON ETHICS: You are an IMF official going to a country whose export earnings are not able to pay for imports. The government has requested a loan from the IMF. Which areas would you recommend the government to cut: (1) education, (2) salaries for officials, (3) food subsidies, and/or (4) tax rebates for exporters?

VIDEO CASE

Watch "Creating Financial Acumen within Your Company" by Blythe McGarvie of Leadership International Finance.

1. Blythe McGarvie stressed that all employees are affected by finance and can affect finance. As a result, she felt that there is a need for all to understand some-

thing about finance so that everyone can have a "common language" on financial issues. One aspect of finance is the topic for this chapter on dealing with foreign exchange. Do her comments apply to understanding the currency market?

2. How can employee understanding of the currency aspect of finance contribute to corporate strategy and strategic response?
3. Ms. McGarvie pointed out that the amount of financial acumen could affect decision-making assumptions. What acumen involving the currency aspect of finance could affect such assumptions?
4. Ms. McGarvie indicated that results are key in evaluating financial decisions but that it might take years before the results can be adequately measured. Based on what you have learned in this chapter, do you think decisions in the currency market take that long to evaluate?
5. Ms. McGarvie gave an example in which one person was given responsibility for both financial decisions and monitoring the decisions. What would be the danger of allowing one expert to make all the decisions concerning foreign exchange?

CLOSING CASE

Markel Corporation Fights Currency Fluctuations

Markel Corporation is a family-owned tubing maker based in Plymouth Meeting, Pennsylvania. Its tubing and insulated lead wire are used in appliances, automobiles, and water purifiers. Approximately 40% of its $30 million sales are exported, mainly to Europe. To protect itself from currency fluctuations, Markel has two strategies: (1) charge customers stable prices in their own currencies and (2) use forward contracts.

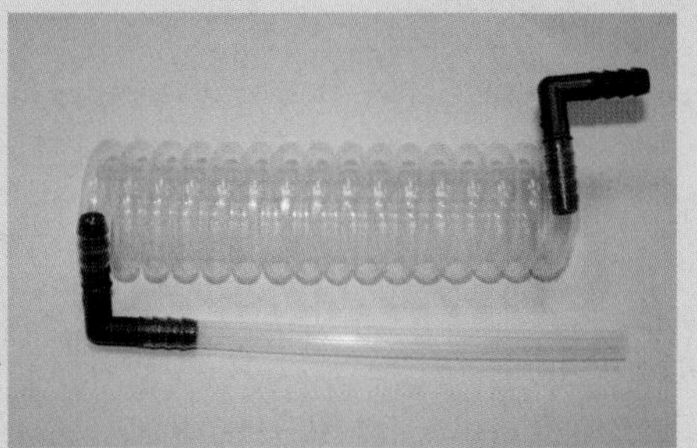
© Courtesy of Markel Corporation

Markel executives believe that their strategy of setting prices in foreign currencies, mainly the euro, has helped it attain 70% of the world market share in its specialty market. But this also means that Markel signs contracts that will be paid in a lot of euros months or even years down the road. There is always the danger that the value of these euros in dollars may be much less than what it is when contracts are signed.

To combat the uncertainty associated with exchange rates, Markel purchases forward contracts from PNC Financial Services Group in Pittsburgh. Markel agrees to pay PNC, for example, one million euros in 30 (or 90 or 180) days, and PNC guarantees a certain amount of dollars regardless of what happens to the exchange rate. When Markel's chief financial officer (CFO) believes that the dollar would appreciate against the euro, he may hedge his entire expected euro earnings with a forward contract. If he feels that the dollar would depreciate, he may hedge, for example, half of the euro earnings and take a chance that Markel will make more dollars by doing nothing with the other half of the euro earnings. Unfortunately, the CFO does not always make the right bet. In April 2003, for instance, Markel had to pay PNC 50,000 euros from a contract that Markel purchased three months earlier. PNC paid $1.05 per euro or $52,500. If Markel had waited, it could have made an additional $1,500 by selling at the going rate, $1.08.

How an export-intensive firm such as Markel deals with exchange rates can directly make or break its bottom line. In 1998, Markel signed a five-year export deal with a German firm and set the sales price assuming the euro would be $1.18

by 2003, about the same level as the euro was traded when introduced officially in 1999. But the euro declined sharply, hitting a low of 82 cents in 2000. Thus, each euro Markel received was worth far less in dollars than anticipated. During 2000–2002, Markel had to swallow more than $650,000 in currency losses, which contributed to its overall losses. Consequently, Markel employees had to endure pay cuts, and the firm had to redouble its efforts to boost efficiency and cut costs.

By 2003, Markel signed most of its currency deals assuming that the euro would be valued between 90 and 95 cents. When the euro soared to $1.08, helped by the war in Iraq and nervousness about the US trade deficit, Markel began to reap windfalls. Executives estimated that if the euro remained between $1.05 and $1.07, the company would profit from $400,000 to $500,000 in currency gains in 2003, significantly recovering from the losses in 2000–2002.

Case Discussion Questions

1. Some argue that given the complexity and unpredictability, currency hedging is not worth it. Is currency hedging worth it for Markel?
2. Can Markel improve the performance of its currency hedging?
3. Other than currency hedging, what other currency management strategies can Markel choose?

Sources: Based on (1) R. Carbaugh, 2007, *International Economics*, 11th ed. (pp. 381–382), Cincinnati, OH: Thomson South-Western; (2) http://www.markelcorporation.com.

NOTES

Journal acronyms: **AMLE** – *Academy of Management Learning & Education;* **BW** – *Business Week;* **JEP** – *Journal of Economic Perspectives;* **JIBS** – *Journal of International Business Studies;* **MS** – *Management Science*

[1] International Monetary Fund (IMF), 2005, *IMF Annual Report* (p. 109), Washington, DC: IMF.

[2] A. Taylor & M. Taylor, 2004, The purchasing power parity debate, *JEP*, 18: 135–158.

[3] *Economist*, 2006, McCurrencies, May 27: 74.

[4] M. Kreinin, 2006, *International Economics* (p. 183), Cincinnati, OH: Thomson South-Western.

[5] R. Lyons, 2001, *The Microstructure Approach to Exchange Rates* (p. 1), Cambridge, MA: MIT Press.

[6] The other Bretton Woods institution is the World Bank.

[7] *Economist*, 2006, Monetary misquotations, August 26: 56–57; *Economist*, 2006, Reshaping the IMF, April 22: 69–70.

[8] R. Carbaugh, 2007, *International Economics*, 11th ed. (p. 360), Cincinnati, OH: Thomson South-Western.

[9] F. Carrieri & B. Majerbi, 2006, The pricing of exchange risk in emerging stock markets, *JIBS*, 37: 372–391; L. Jacque & P. Vaaler, 2001, The international control conundrum with exchange risk, *JIBS*, 32: 813–832; D. Miller & J. Reuer, 1998, Firm strategy and economic exposure to foreign exchange rate movements, *JIBS*, 29: 493–514.

[10] C. Hill, 2003, *International Business*, 4th ed. (p. 307), Chicago: Irwin McGraw-Hill.

[11] B. Kogut & N. Kulatilaka, 1994, Operating flexibility, global manufacturing, and the option value of a multinational network, *MS*, 40: 123–139; C. Pantzalis, B. Simkins, & P. Laux, 2001, Operational hedges and the foreign exchange exposure of US multinational corporations, *JIBS*, 32: 793–812.

[12] *Economist*, 2003, Selling to the developing world, December 13: 8.

[13] *BW*, 2004, How Honda is stalling in the US, *BW*, May 24: 62–63.

[14] R. Faff & A. Marshall, 2005, International evidence on the determinants of foreign exchange rate exposure of multinational corporations, *JIBS*, 36: 539–558; R. Weiner, 2005, Speculation in international crises, *JIBS*, 36: 576–587.

[15] This section draws heavily on B. Yarbrough & R. Yarbrough, 2006, *The World Economy*, 7th ed. (p. 683), Cincinnati, OH: Thomson South-Western.

[16] *Economist*, 2006, The falling dollar (p. 13), December 2: 13.

[17] Carbaugh, 2007, *International Economics* (p. 380).

Capitalizing on Global and Regional Integration

OPENING CASE

A Closer Continent

When Kurt Wilson's pals told him they were throwing him a bachelor party in Vilnius, Lithuania, back in 2002, the British entrepreneur was less than thrilled. Aside from cheap beer, what could this grim former Soviet bloc city offer? Plenty, as it turned out. Wilson, now 32, fell so in love with Vilnius, with its friendly people and beautiful medieval old town, that he has since made it his second home.

A Brit commuting to Lithuania? A few years ago, such an idea would have been unthinkable. Now, thanks to airfare as low as $100 round-trip on Ryanair or its local competitor, Air Baltic, Wilson and his wife travel between London and Vilnius at least once a month. The couple owns two apartments in Vilnius. And Wilson, impressed with the skilled and inexpensive local workforce, opened a local office of Advansys, his Reading-based software development company. "When I first came here, my friends thought I was mad," he says. "Low-cost airlines are opening up places that used to be beyond most people's comfort zones."

Ryanair, easyJet, and nearly 40 other low-cost airlines across Europe are accomplishing what the politicians in the expanding European Union couldn't. Not until the discount airlines came on strong did millions of Europeans start to cross borders en masse for business and pleasure. Airlines last year [*2005—editor*] logged more than 420 million passengers on intra-European flights, an increase of some 40% from five years ago. In the process, they've played a major role in breaking down cultural barriers, revitalizing local economies, and opening up new business opportunities. "Bureaucrats in Brussels have been blathering on about European unity for ages," says Michael O'Leary, CEO of Dublin-based Ryanair. "But low-cost airlines are at the forefront of delivering it."

Jetting around Europe used to be a luxury. Now it's possible to criss-cross the region for as little as $30 round-trip—less than the fare on a taxi ride to the local airport. The British pop over to Budapest for budget root canals and cut-price nip-and-tucks. Irish property speculators fly to Estonia to bag a bargain. Latvian construction workers head to Dublin to cash in on that city's construction boom, while Polish doctors and nurses jet over to Britain to fill hospital shortages. "I've been to places I've never even heard of just because it's so cheap," says Dave Marsden, a 38-year-old dispatch manager at a Manchester printing company who recently spent a weekend in Santiago de Compostela in Spain.

The explosion in low-cost flights has given rise to a new group of Euro-commuters. For six years, Herman Bynke, a 34-year-old Swede who runs London-based Hela Ltd., a maker of ergonomic computer accessories, endured the stress and high cost of living in London. But when Ryanair began offering direct flights from London to Gothenburg, Bynke decided it was time to move back home. Now for $85 or less round-trip, he makes the three-hour door-to-door trip from his home in Sweden to his office in London biweekly. "I can spend more time with my family, save more money, and have a better quality of life," he says.

The trend originated in 1997 when Brussels deregulated the aviation industry, enabling discounters to get airborne. Ryanair was one of the first. The Irish carrier launched service from Britain to the Continent in 1997, keeping fares low by flying to smaller, out-of-the-way airports, a model pioneered by Southwest Airlines in the United States. Today, Ryanair is Europe's leading discounter, flying 334 routes to 23 countries. The company is on course to log a 6% increase in pretax profit in 2006, to $409 million, on revenues of $2.1 billion. O'Leary's fleet of 105 Boeing 737s will ferry some 42 million passengers

LEARNING OBJECTIVES

After studying this chapter, you should be able to

1. make the case for global economic integration
2. understand the evolution of the GATT and the WTO, including current challenges
3. describe the advantages and disadvantages of regional economic integration
4. understand regional economic integration efforts in Europe, the Americas, Asia Pacific, and Africa
5. participate in two debates on global and regional economic integration
6. draw implications for action

this year, more than British Airways (BA). To fight back, BA, Air France, Lufthansa, and the other flag carriers have been slashing their own fares. The fare wars could set the stage for an industrywide European shakeout, but for now consumers are the big winners. In Sweden, for instance, the average international airfare fell from $160 in 2001 to $110 last year.

The resulting surge in European travel is turning once-sleepy backwaters into boomtowns. Bratislava's airport used to be a grim, deserted place. But that was before Slovakian upstart SkyEurope turned it into its hub four years ago. Traffic has more than quadrupled since 2002, from 300,000 passengers a year to more than 1.3 million, as easyJet and Ryanair have followed SkyEurope's lead and added Bratislava to their routes.

To cater to Europe's new commuters, savvy entrepreneurs are setting up businesses that offer every service imaginable. Frances Sargent, a 56-year-old Briton, discovered Slovenia after vacationing there a decade ago. Now she and her family spend weekends at their second home, in the Julian Alps, and she runs Slovenian Properties, a company that helps Slovenian real estate agents market their properties to English-speaking buyers. Since low-cost flights to Slovenia started two years ago, values in areas such as the tiny lakeside town of Bled have risen 30%. Sargent's own property has doubled in value since she bought it 18 months ago. "I realized that Slovenes hadn't anticipated the interest from British buyers," she says.

Thanks to low fares, Britons are even flocking to dentists in Budapest. Hungarian Dental Travel Ltd., a one-year-old London-based outfit, has built a brisk business referring travelers to English-speaking dentists in Hungary. "In Britain the average cost of an implant is $3,500, but in Hungary you can get it done for $1,000," says Managing Director Christopher Hall. British consumers aren't just stopping in Hungary for their teeth—they're also headed to the Czech Republic for the rest of their bodies. Tamara Zdinakova, 28, runs Beauty in Prague, a Web site that refers English-speaking patients to plastic surgeons in the Czech Republic, where prices are a fraction of those in the West. British builder Tony Barham and his wife, Maureen, both 55, flew easyJet to Prague for a 17-day holiday—and Maureen's face-lift. "It should be called Plastic Surgery Airline," Tony says. At $3,700, they'll pay one-quarter what they would for the same procedure back in Britain. Zdinakova says the business wouldn't exist without discount airlines. "It just wipes out the barriers," she says of the cheap airlines. "Prague has not been this close ever before."

By all accounts, low-cost carriers will only keep shrinking Europe. Cheap air travel has "changed my life for the better," says Peter Allegretti, a 44-year-old Italian hypnotherapist who regularly commutes from his home in Barcelona to work in London. "National boundaries are disappearing." Now, that sounds like a true European Union.

Source: K. Capell. 2006. A closer continent. *Business Week*, May 8: 44–45. © 2006 McGraw-Hills. Reprinted with permission.

regional economic integration
Efforts to reduce trade and investment barriers within one region.

European Union (EU)
The official title of European economic integration since 1993.

global economic integration
Efforts to reduce trade and investment barriers around the globe.

Why are Ryanair, easyJet, Air Baltic, SkyEurope, and 40 other low-cost airlines able to bring Europe "closer"? Why are firms such as Advansys, Beauty in Prague, Hungarian Dental Travel, and Slovenian Properties thriving? In two words: economic integration—both regionally and globally. **Regional economic integration** refers to efforts to reduce trade and investment barriers within one region, such as the **European Union (EU)**. **Global economic integration**, in turn, refers to efforts to reduce trade and investment barriers around the globe.

Most fundamentally, this chapter is about how the two core perspectives in global business interact. Specifically, how do changes in the rules of the game via global and regional economic integration, as emphasized by the institution-based view, lead firms to better develop and leverage their capabilities, as highlighted by the resource-based view? In other words, how do firms around the world capitalize on global and regional economic integration? We start with a description of global economic integration. Next we introduce regional economic integration. Debates and extensions follow.

GLOBAL ECONOMIC INTEGRATION

LEARNING OBJECTIVE 1
make the case for global economic integration

Current frameworks of regional and global economic integration date back to the end of World War II. The world community, mindful of the mercantilist trade wars during the 1930s, which worsened the Great Depression and eventually led to World War II, initiated two developments. Globally, the **General Agreement on Tariffs and Trade (GATT)** was created in 1948. In Europe, regional integration started in 1951. Both developments proved so successful that they have now expanded considerably: One became the **World Trade Organization (WTO)**, and the other is the European Union.

General Agreement on Tariffs and Trade (GATT)
A multilateral agreement governing the international trade of goods (merchandise).

World Trade Organization (WTO)
The official title of the multilateral trading system and the organization underpinning this system since 2005.

Political Benefits for Global Economic Integration[1]

Recall from Chapters 5 and 6 that, theoretically, there are economic gains when firms from different countries can freely trade and engage in foreign direct investment (FDI). However, until the end of World War II, these insights had not been accepted by most governments. In the late 1920s and early 1930s, virtually all governments imposed protectionist policies through tariffs and quotas trying to protect domestic industries. Collectively, these beggar-thy-neighbor policies triggered retaliation that further restricted trade (Figure 8.1). Eventually, trade wars turned into World War II.

FIGURE 8.1 DOWN THE TUBE: CONTRACTION OF WORLD TRADE DURING THE GREAT DEPRESSION (1929–1933, MILLIONS $)

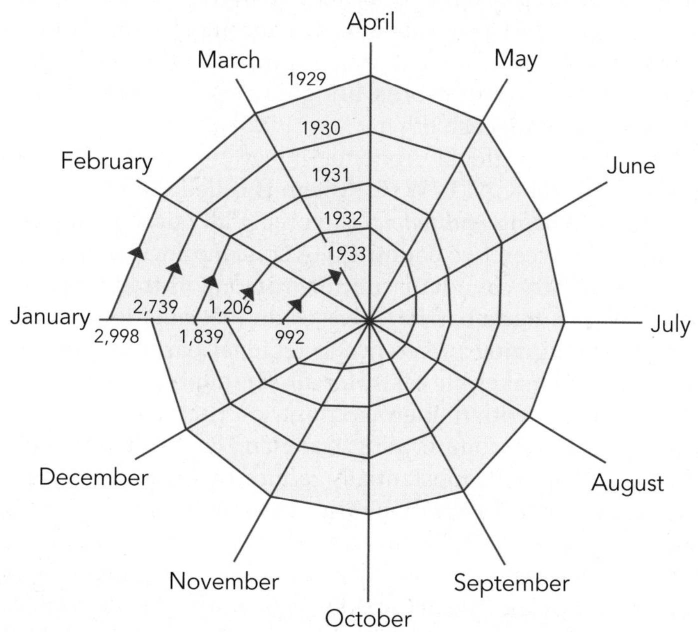

Source: C. Kindleberger, 1973, *The World in Depression* (p. 170), Berkeley: University of California Press.

TABLE 8.1 BENEFITS OF GLOBAL ECONOMIC INTEGRATION

Political benefits
• Promote peace by promoting trade and investment
• Build confidence in a multilateral trading system
Economic benefits
• Disputes are handled constructively
• Rules make life easier and discrimination impossible for all participating countries
• Free trade and investment raise incomes and stimulate economic growth

The postwar urge for global economic integration grew out of the painful lessons of the 1920s and 1930s. While emphasizing economic benefits, global economic integration is *political* in nature. Its most fundamental goal is to promote peace (Table 8.1). Simply put, buyers and sellers are usually reluctant to fight or kill each other. On the other hand, in 1941, when the United States cut off oil sales to Japan (in protest of its aggression in China), Japan attacked Pearl Harbor. Global economic integration seeks to build confidence. The trade wars in the 1930s were triggered by a lack of confidence. Building confidence is key to avoiding the tragedies of the 1930s. Governments, if they are confident that other countries will not raise trade barriers, will not be tempted to do the same.

Economic Benefits for Global Economic Integration

There are at least three other compelling economic reasons for global economic integration. One is to handle disputes constructively. This is especially evident in the WTO's dispute resolution mechanisms (discussed later in this chapter). Although there is an escalation in the number of disputes brought to the WTO, such an increase, according to the WTO, "does not reflect increasing tension in the world. Rather, it reflects the closer economic ties throughout the world, the WTO's expanding membership, and the fact that countries have faith in the system to solve their differences."[2] In other words, bringing disputes to the WTO is so much better than declaring war on each other.

multilateral trading system
The global system that governs international trade among countries—otherwise known as the GATT/WTO system.

nondiscrimination
A principle that a country cannot discriminate among its trading partners (a concession given to one country needs to be made available to all other GATT/WTO members).

Another benefit is that global economic integration makes life easier for all participants. Officially, the GATT/WTO system is called the **multilateral trading system**—the key word being *multilateral* (involving all participating countries) as opposed to *bilateral* (between two countries). A crucial principle is **nondiscrimination**. Specifically, a country cannot discriminate among its trading partners. Every time a country lowers a trade barrier, it has to do the same for *all* WTO member countries (except when giving preference to regional partners—discussed later). Such nondiscrimination makes life easier for all. The alternative would be continuous bilateral negotiations with numerous countries. Each pair may end up with a different deal, significantly complicating trade and investment. Small countries may individually end up with substantially reduced bargaining power.

Finally, global economic integration raises incomes, generates jobs, and stimulates economic growth. The WTO estimates that cutting global trade barriers by a third may raise worldwide income by approximately $600 billion—equivalent to contributing an economy the size of Canada to the world.[3] While countries benefit, individuals also benefit because more and better jobs are created. In the United

States, 12 million people owe their jobs to exports.[4] In China, 18 million people work for foreign-invested firms, which have the highest level of profits and pay among all China-based firms.[5]

Of course, global economic integration has its share of problems. Critics may not be happy with the environmental impact and distribution of the fruits from more trade and investment among the haves and have-nots in the world. However, when weighing all the pros and cons, most governments and people agree that global economic integration generates enormous benefits, ranging from preserving peace to generating jobs. Next, let us examine its two principal mechanisms: the GATT and WTO.

GENERAL AGREEMENT ON TARIFFS AND TRADE: 1948–1994

LEARNING OBJECTIVE 2

understand the evolution of the GATT and the WTO, including current challenges

The GATT was created in 1948. Unlike the WTO, the GATT was technically an agreement but *not* an organization. Its major contribution was to reduce the level of tariffs by sponsoring "rounds" of multilateral negotiations. As a result, the average tariff in developed economies dropped from 40% in 1948 to 3% in 2005. In other words, the GATT facilitated some of the highest growth rates in international trade recorded in history. Between 1950 and 1995 (when the GATT was phased out to become the WTO), world GDP grew about fivefold, but world merchandise exports grew about 100 times (!). During the GATT era, trade growth consistently outpaced GDP growth.

Despite the GATT's phenomenal success in bringing down tariff barriers, by the mid-1980s when the Uruguay Round was launched, it was clear that reforms would be necessary. Such reforms were triggered by three concerns. First, because of the GATT's declared focus on merchandise trade, neither trade in services nor intellectual property protection was covered. Both of these areas were becoming increasingly important. Second, in merchandise trade, there were a lot of loopholes that called for reforms. The most (in)famous loophole was the Multifibre Arrangement (MFA) designed to *limit* free trade in textiles, which was a direct violation of the letter and spirit of the GATT. Finally, the GATT's success in reducing tariffs, combined with the global recessions in the 1970s and 1980s, led many governments to invoke nontariff barriers (NTBs), such as subsidies and local content requirements (see Chapter 5). Unlike tariff barriers that were relatively easy to verify and challenge, NTBs were subtler but pervasive, thus triggering a growing number of trade disputes. The GATT, however, lacked effective dispute resolution mechanisms. Thus, at the end of the Uruguay Round, participating countries agreed in 1994 to upgrade the GATT and to launch the WTO.

WORLD TRADE ORGANIZATION: 1995–PRESENT

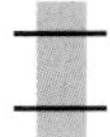

Established on January 1, 1995, the WTO has become the GATT's successor. This transformation turned the GATT from a provisional treaty serviced by an ad hoc secretariat to a full-fledged international organization, headquartered in Geneva, Switzerland. Although the WTO is technically one of the youngest major international organizations, it is not so young considering its history since 1948 as the GATT. One interesting question is: What happened to the GATT? Did it "die"? Not really, because the GATT is still in existence as part of the WTO. But this is confusing. A straightforward way to distinguish the new GATT (as part of the WTO) from the original GATT is to identify the new one as "GATT 1994" and the old one as "GATT 1947."

FIGURE 8.2 **SIX MAIN AREAS OF THE WTO**

Umbrella	Agreement Establishing the WTO		
Three main areas	Goods (GATT)	Services (GATS)	Intellectual Property (TRIPS)
Dispute settlement	Dispute Settlement Mechanisms		
Transparency	Trade Policy Reviews		

Source: Adapted from World Trade Organization, 2003, *Understanding the WTO* (p. 22), Geneva: WTO.

Significantly broader than the GATT, the WTO has six main areas (Figure 8.2):

- An umbrella agreement, simply called the Agreement Establishing the WTO.
- An agreement governing the international trade of goods, still using the old title as the General Agreement on Tariffs and Trade (GATT)—technically, as noted, it is GATT 1994.
- An agreement governing the international trade of services, the **General Agreement on Trade in Services (GATS)**.
- An agreement governing intellectual property rights, the **Trade-Related Aspects of Intellectual Property Rights (TRIPS)**—see Chapter 2.
- Trade dispute settlement mechanisms, which allow for the WTO to adjudicate trade disputes among countries in a more effective and less time-consuming way (discussed next).
- Trade policy reviews, which enable the WTO and other member countries to "peer review" a country's trade policy (see In Focus 8.1).

General Agreement on Trade in Services (GATS)
A WTO agreement governing the international trade of services.

Trade-Related Aspects of Intellectual Property Rights (TRIPS)
A WTO agreement governing intellectual property rights.

Overall, the WTO has a far wider scope, bringing into the multilateral trading system—for the first time—trade in services, intellectual property, dispute settlement, and peer review of policy.[6] The next two sections outline two of its major initiatives: dispute settlement and the Doha Round.

Trade Dispute Settlement

One of the main objectives for establishing the WTO was to strengthen the trade dispute settlement mechanisms. The old GATT mechanisms experienced (1) long delays, (2) blocking by accused countries, and (3) inadequate enforcement. The WTO addresses all three problems. First, it sets time limits for a panel, consisting of three neutral countries, to reach a judgment. Second, it removes the power of the accused countries to block any unfavorable decision. WTO decisions will be final. Third, in terms of enforcement, although the WTO has earned the nickname of "the world's supreme court in trade," it does *not* have real enforcement capability. The WTO simply recommends that the losing countries change their laws or practices and authorizes the winning countries to use tariff retaliation to compel the offending countries' compliance with the WTO rulings.

Understandably, it is the WTO's enforcement area that has attracted significant controversies because the losing countries experience some loss of sovereignty. As shown in the "shrimp-turtle" case (In Focus 8.2), even some of the most powerful countries, such as the United States, have lost cases and have painfully adjusted their own laws and practices to be in compliance with the WTO rulings.

IN FOCUS 8.1 China's First Five Years in the WTO

China became a new member of the WTO in 2001 and went through its first trade policy review in 2006. The review focused on three areas: trade, services, and intellectual property rights (IPRs). In terms of trade (GATT 1994), fellow members commended China's efforts to revise over 2,000 laws and regulations to comply with its WTO commitments. The average tariff was reduced from 16% in 2001 to 10% in 2005. Import quotas were virtually eliminated. In terms of services (GATS), members acknowledged that commitments undertaken by China were more extensive than those of other developing countries. However, liberalization of key service sectors, such as banking and insurance, was slower than other sectors. In terms of IPRs (TRIPS), many members expressed concern that, despite China's efforts, enforcement remained problematic. Overall, China's record of WTO implementation was generally considered good, despite some room for improvement.

By most statistical measures, China's first five years in the WTO were very successful. China's GDP growth averaged 9%. It became the world's third largest trading nation (after the United States and Germany) and one of the largest recipients of FDI (averaging $55 billion annually). US exports to China more than doubled. China is now the second largest exporter to the United States (behind Canada) and the fourth largest market for US exports—third largest, when combined with Hong Kong, trailing only Canada and Mexico.

Overall, several experts noted that China on the whole met the letter, if not the full spirit, of its WTO commitments. In particular, commitments that were easy to implement, such as tariff reductions, were largely met. In more difficult areas such as IPRs, implementation fell short. In a critical published statement, US Trade Representative Susan Schwab wrote: "it is apparent that China has not yet fully embraced the key WTO principles of nondiscrimination and national treatment." In theory, foreign banks could open branches in most parts of the country as of 2006. But here is a catch: They could open only one branch a year, and each branch must have operating capital of $50 million, a burden that local banks do not have to shoulder.

After five years, internal Chinese debates center on two issues. First, is China now too dependent on trade, especially exports? Strong export growth often leads to foreign resentment and antidumping actions. During the WTO's first decade (1995–2005), Chinese exporters were the most frequent targets for antidumping actions worldwide, commanding approximately 15% of all such cases. China complained to the WTO, in its official report as part of the trade policy review, that "discriminatory measures against a particular member is contrary to the spirit of free trade and the principle of non-discrimination enshrined in the multilateral trading system." Second, do foreign-invested enterprises (FIEs) benefit too much? In 2005, FIEs accounted for more than 60% of Chinese exports. FIEs enjoy lower tax rates than domestic firms. Taxpayers in a developing country such as China are effectively subsidizing FIEs, many of which come from developed countries. To many Chinese, this does not seem fair and calls for equalization in taxation between FIEs and domestic firms.

Sources: Based on (1) *Business Week*, 2006, How Beijing is keeping banks at bay, October 2: 42; (2) K. Lieberthal, 2006, Completing WTO reforms, *China Business Review*, September: 52–58; (3) S. Schwab, 2006, A message from the US Trade Representative, *China Business Review*, September: 30; (4) Y. Wang, 2006, China in the WTO, *China Business Review*, September: 42–48; (5) WTO, 2006, *Trade Policy Review Report by the People's Republic of China*, Geneva: WTO; (6) WTO, 2006, *Trade Policy Review Report by the Secretariat: People's Republic of China*, Geneva: WTO.

In the absence of real enforcement "teeth" of the WTO, a country, which has lost a dispute case, chooses its own options: (1) change its laws or practices to be in compliance or (2) defy the ruling by doing nothing and be willing to suffer trade retaliation by winning countries known as "punitive duties." Fundamentally, the WTO ruling is a *recommendation* but not an order; no higher level entity can order a sovereign government to do something against its wishes. In other words, the offending countries retain full sovereignty in their decision on whether or not to implement a panel recommendation. Most of the WTO's trade dispute rulings indeed are resolved without resorting to trade retaliation. This supports the first proposition in the institution-based view (see Chapter 2): Most offending countries have made a *rational* decision to respect the rules of the game, believing that the benefits of being in compliance with the rulings unfavorable to them outweigh the costs.

The Doha Round
A round of WTO negotiations to reduce agricultural subsidies, slash tariffs, and strengthen intellectual property protection that started in Doha, Qatar, in 2001—officially known as the "Doha Development Agenda." It was suspended in 2006 due to disagreements.

The Doha Round: The "Doha Development Agenda"

The Doha Round (2001–2006) was the only round of trade negotiations sponsored by the WTO. In 1999, a WTO meeting in Seattle intended to start a new round of trade talks was not only devastated by the appearance of 30,000 protesters, but

IN FOCUS 8.2 The WTO's "Shrimp-Turtle" Case

In 1997, India, Malaysia, Pakistan, and Thailand brought a joint complaint to the WTO against a US ban on shrimp imports from these countries. The protection of sea turtles was at the heart of the ban. Shrimp trawlers from these countries often caught shrimp with nets that trapped and killed an estimated 150,000 sea turtles each year. The US Endangered Species Act, enacted in 1989, listed as endangered or threatened five species of sea turtles and required US shrimp trawlers to use turtle excluder devices (TEDs) in their nets when fishing in areas where sea turtles may be found. It also placed embargoes on shrimp imports from countries that do not protect sea turtles from deadly entrapment in nets. The complaining countries, unwilling to equip their fleets with TEDs, argued that the US Endangered Species Act was an illegal trade barrier. The WTO panel ruled in favor of the four Asian countries and provoked a firestorm of criticisms from environmentalists, culminating in some violence in the Seattle protests against the WTO in 1999. The United States appealed but lost again. In its final ruling, the WTO Appellate Body argued that the United States lost the case *not* because it sought to protect the environment but because it violated the principle of nondiscrimination. It provided countries in the Western Hemisphere, mainly in the Caribbean, technical and financial assistance to equip their fishermen with TEDs. However, it did not give the same assistance to the four complaining countries. The WTO opined:

> We have not decided that the protection and preservation of the environment is of no significance to members of the WTO. Clearly, it is. We have not decided that the sovereign nations that are members of the WTO cannot adopt effective measures to protect endangered species, such as sea turtles. Clearly, they can and should . . . What we decided in this appeal is simply this: although the measure of the United States in dispute in this appeal serves an environmental objective that is recognized as legitimate . . . this measure has been applied by the United States in a manner which constitutes arbitrary and unjustifiable discrimination between members of the WTO . . . WTO members are free to adopt their own policies aimed at protecting the environment as long as, in so doing, they fulfill their obligations and respect the rights of other members under the WTO Agreement.

After its appeal failed, the United States reached agreements with the four complaining countries to provide technical and financial assistance on TEDs to be implemented on their shrimp boats.

Sources: Based on (1) R. Carbaugh, 2005, *International Economics*, 10th ed. (pp. 186–187), Cincinnati, OH: Cengage South-Western; (2) WTO, 2003, *Understanding the WTO* (pp. 68–69), Geneva: WTO.

also derailed by significant differences between developed and developing countries. The meeting, thus, became known as the "Battle of Seattle" (see Chapter 1).

Undeterred by the backlash, WTO member countries went ahead to launch a new round of negotiations in Doha, Qatar, in November 2001. The Doha Round was significant for two reasons. First, it was launched in the aftermath of the 9/11 attacks. There was a strong resolve to make free trade work around the globe to defeat the terrorist agenda to divide and terrorize the world. Second, this was the first round in the history of GATT/WTO to specifically aim at promoting economic development in developing countries. This would make globalization more inclusive and help the world's poor. Consequently, the official title of the Doha Round was the "Doha Development Agenda." The agenda was ambitious: Doha would (1) reduce agricultural subsidies in developed countries to facilitate exports from developing countries, (2) slash tariffs, especially in industries that developing countries might benefit (such as textiles), (3) free up trade in services, and (4) strengthen intellectual property protection. Note that in the Doha Round, *not* all meetings were held in Doha. Subsequent meetings took place in Cancún, Mexico (2003), Hong Kong (2005), and Geneva (2006).

Unfortunately, in the Cancún meeting in September 2003, numerous countries failed to deliver what they had signed up for two years before in Doha. The "hot potato" turned out to be agriculture (see Closing Case). Australia, Argentina, and most developing countries demanded that Japan, the EU, and the US reduce farm subsidies. Japan rejected any proposal to cut rice tariffs. The EU refused to significantly reduce farm subsidies, which consumed 40% of its budget. The US actually *increased* farm subsidies. On the other hand, many developing countries, led by India, refused to tighten protection for intellectual property, citing their needs for cheap generic drugs to combat diseases such as HIV/AIDS. Overall, developing

What were some factors that led to the collapse of the Doha Round?

countries refused to offer concessions in intellectual property and service trade in part because of the failure of Japan, the EU, and the US to reduce farm subsidies.

After the failed Cancún meeting, member countries tried again in Hong Kong in December 2005. Their only agreement was to keep talking. Finally, in Geneva in July 2006, it was evident that they could not talk any more because they were still miles apart. The Doha Round was thus officially suspended, and hopes of lifting millions out of poverty through free trade derailed. Labeled "the biggest threat to the postwar [multilateral] trading system" by the *Economist*,[7] the Geneva fiasco of the Doha Round disappointed almost every country involved.[8] Finger pointing naturally started immediately. To be fair, no country was totally responsible for the collapse of the Doha Round, and all members collectively were culpable. The sheer complexity of reaching an agreement on "everything" among 149 member countries (as of 2006) in the Doha Round was indeed mind boggling.

What happens next? Officially, Doha was "suspended" but not "terminated" or "dead." Multilateral trade negotiations are notoriously challenging. In 1990, the Uruguay Round was similarly suspended, only to rise again in 1994 with a far-reaching agreement that launched the WTO. Whether history will repeat itself remains to be seen. On the other hand, although a global deal might be lost, regional deals are moving "at twice the speed and with half the fuss."[9] The upshot of Doha's failure is stagnation of multilateralism and acceleration of regionalism—a topic we turn to next.

FIVE TYPES OF REGIONAL ECONOMIC INTEGRATION

LEARNING OBJECTIVE 3

describe the advantages and disadvantages of regional economic integration

There is now a proliferation of regional trade deals. Except for Mongolia, all WTO members are now involved in some regional trade arrangement. This section introduces the benefits for regional economic integration and discusses its major types.

The Pros and Cons for Regional Economic Integration

Similar to global economic integration, the benefits for regional economic integration center on both political and economic dimensions (see Table 8.1). Politically, regional economic integration promotes peace by fostering closer economic ties and building confidence. Only in the last six decades did Europeans break away from their deadly habit of war and violence against one another dating back hundreds of years. A leading cause of this dramatic behavioral change is economic integration. In addition, regional integration enhances the collective political weight of a region. Postwar European integration has been fueled by such a desire when dealing with superpowers such as the United States.

Economically, the three benefits associated with regional economic integration are similar to those associated with global economic integration. (1) Disputes are handled constructively. (2) Consistent rules make life easier and discrimination impossible for participating countries within one region. (3) Free trade and investment raise incomes and stimulate economic growth (see Table 8.1). In addition, regional economic integration may bring additional benefits, such as a larger market, simpler standards, reduced distribution costs, and economies of scales for firms based in that region.

However, not everything is rosy in regional integration. A case can be made *against* it. Politically, regional integration, centered on preferential treatments for firms within a region, discriminates against firms outside a region, thus undermining global integration (In Focus 8.3). Of course, in practice, global deals (such as the Doha Round) are very challenging to accomplish, and regional deals emerge

IN FOCUS 8.3 Is Japan Being Left Out?

As of 2002, Japan was one of the only four WTO members not a party to any preferential regional trade agreement. Since then, Japan has concluded agreements with Singapore and Mexico, and negotiations are currently underway with ASEAN and South Korea. Japan's sudden interest in preferential regional trade agreements, after two decades of shunning the growing trend, suggests that the country might be worried about being left out. This raises an important question: How have the major preferential trade agreements of which Japan is not a member affected Japan's trade? The map presents some estimates of six major trade groups' effects on Japan's trade. For each group, the figure indicates two percentage changes: the change in Japan's exports to a trade group's members calculated as a percentage of Japan's trade with that group and Japan's imports from group member countries also calculated as a percentage of Japan's trade with that group. Most of the numbers are negative, indicating that trade groups tended to *reduce* members' imports from and exports to Japan. The major exception is the large increase in Japanese imports from the EU. So far, the Asian economic integration group, AFTA, has had the smallest effect on Japanese trade.

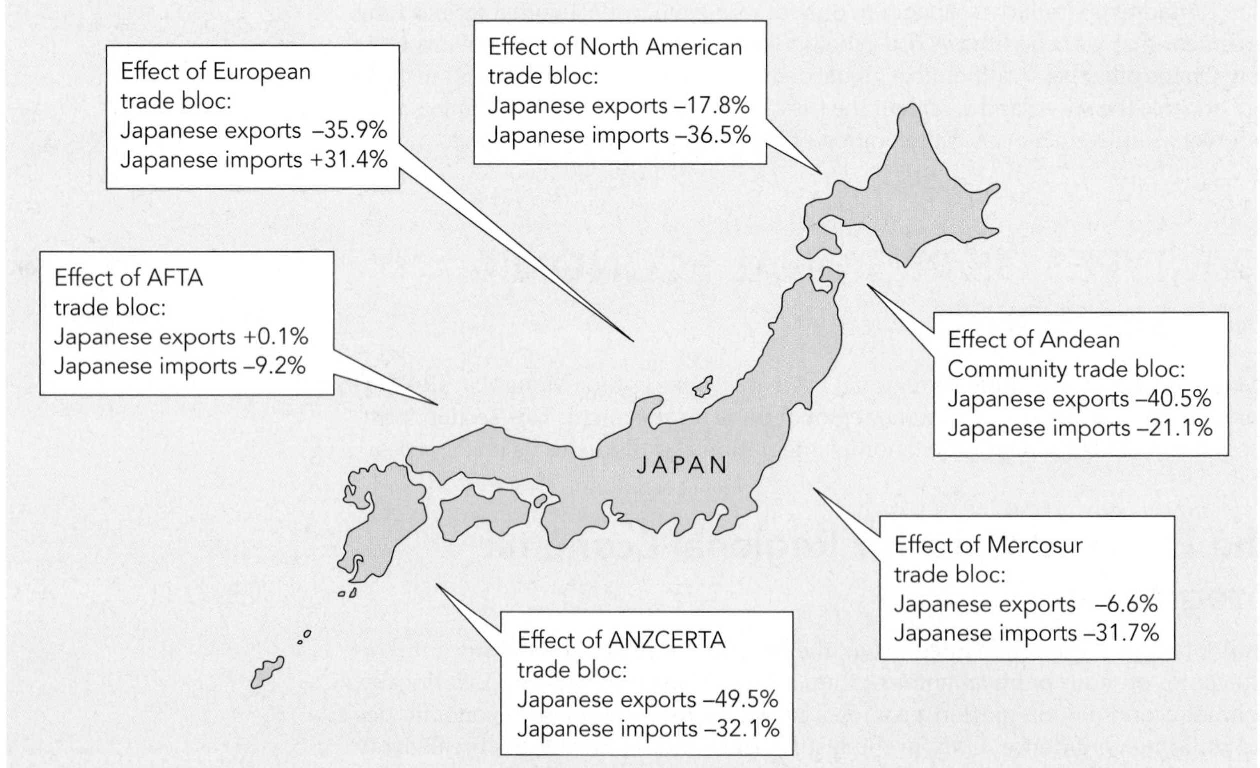

Sources: Adapted from B. Yabrough & R. Yabrough, 2006, *The World Economy* (pp. 275–276), Cincinnati, OH: Cengage South-Western. Reprinted with permission. Data are from H. Wall, 2003, NAFTA and the geography of North American trade, *Federal Reserve Bank of St. Louis Review*, 85 (March–April): 13–26. AFTA—ASEAN Free Trade Area; ANZCERTA—Australia and New Zealand Closer Economic Relations Trade Agreement.

as realistic alternatives. Economically, regional integration may result in some loss of sovereignty. For example, the 12 EU members adopting the euro can no longer implement independent monetary policies.

Because of the simultaneous existence of pros and cons, countries are often cautious of joining regional economic integration. Norway and Switzerland chose not to join the EU. Even when countries are part of a regional deal, they sometimes choose to stay out of certain areas. For example, three EU members, Britain, Denmark, and Sweden, refused to adopt the euro. Overall, different levels of enthusiasm call for different types of regional economic integration, which are outlined next.

Types of Regional Economic Integration

Figure 8.3 shows five main types of regional economic integration.

- A **free trade area (FTA)** is a group of countries that remove trade barriers among themselves. Each still maintains different external policies regarding nonmembers. An example is NAFTA.
- A **customs union** is one step beyond an FTA. In addition to all the arrangements of an FTA, a customs union imposes common external policies on nonparticipants to combat trade diversion. One example is Benelux—consisting of Belgium, the Netherlands, and Luxembourg.
- A **common market** combines everything a customs union has. In addition, a common market permits the free movement of goods and people. Today's EU used to be a common market.
- An **economic union** has all the features of a common market. Members also coordinate and harmonize economic policies (in areas such as monetary, fiscal, and taxation) to blend their economies into a single economic entity. Today's EU is an economic union. One possible dimension of an economic union is to establish a **monetary union**, which has been accomplished by 12 EU members through the adoption of the euro (see next section).
- A **political union** is the integration of political and economic affairs of a region. The United States and the former Soviet Union are two examples. Whether the EU will eventually turn into a political union is subject to debate. At present, the EU is not a political union.

free trade area (FTA)
A group of countries that remove trade barriers among themselves.

customs union
One step beyond a free trade area (FTA), a customs union imposes common external policies on nonparticipating countries.

common market
Combining everything a customs union has, a common market, in addition, permits the free movement of goods and people.

economic union
Has all the features of a common market. Members also coordinate and harmonize economic policies (in areas such as monetary, fiscal, and taxation) to blend their economies into a single economic entity.

monetary union
A group of countries that use a common currency.

political union
The integration of political and economic affairs of a region.

FIGURE 8.3 TYPES OF REGIONAL ECONOMIC INTEGRATION

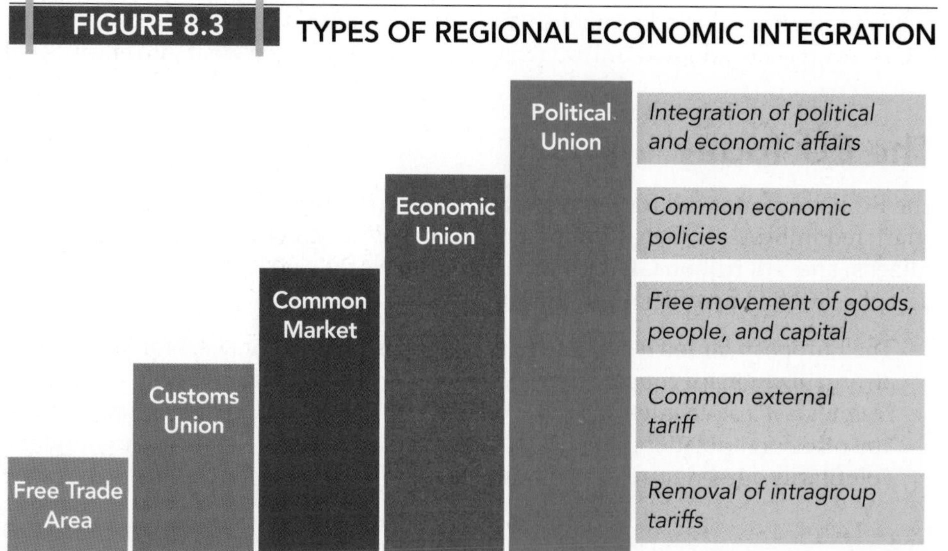

Overall, these five major types feature an intensification of the level of regional economic integration. Next, we take a tour around the world to visit concrete examples of these arrangements.

LEARNING OBJECTIVE 4

understand regional economic integration efforts in Europe, the Americas, Asia Pacific, and Africa

REGIONAL ECONOMIC INTEGRATION IN EUROPE

At present, the most ambitious economic integration takes place in Europe. This section (1) outlines its origin and evolution, (2) introduces its current structure, and (3) discusses its challenges.

Origin and Evolution

Although European economic integration is now often noted for its economic benefits, its origin was political in nature. More specifically, it was an effort by European politicians to stop the vicious cycle of hatred and violence. In 1951, Belgium, France, Germany (then known as West Germany), Italy, Luxembourg, and the Netherlands signed the European Coal and Steel Community (ECSC) Treaty, which was the first step toward what is now the European Union. There was a good reason for the six founding members and the two industries to be involved. France and Germany were the main combatants in World Wars I and II (and major previous European wars), each having lost millions of soldiers and civilians. Reflecting the public mood, politicians in both countries realized that such killing needed to stop. Italy had the misfortune of being dragged along and devastated whenever France and Germany went to war. The three small countries known as Benelux had the unfortunate geographic location of being sandwiched between France and Germany and were usually wiped out when France and Germany fought. For Italy and Benelux, they would naturally be happy to do anything to stop France and Germany from firing their guns again. In addition, the specific industry focus on coal and steel was no accident: These two industries would supply the raw materials for war. Integrating them among six members might help prevent future hostilities from breaking out.

In 1957, six member countries of ECSC signed the Treaty of Rome, which launched the European Economic Community (EEC), later known as the European Community (EC). Starting as an FTA, the EEC/EC progressed to become a customs union and eventually a common market. In 1991, 12 member countries signed the Treaty on European Union in Maastricht, Netherlands (in short, the Maastricht treaty) to complete the single market and establish an economic union. The title European Union (EU) was officially adopted in 1993 when the Maastricht treaty went into effect.

The EU Today

The EU has experienced four waves of expansion (Figure 8.4 and Table 8.2). Headquartered in Brussels, Belgium, today's EU has 27 member countries, 480 million citizens, and $13 trillion GDP—a quarter of the world's GDP. Here is how the EU describes itself in an official publication:

> The European Union is not a federation like the United States. Nor is it simply an organization for cooperation between governments, like the United Nations. Neither is it a state intended to replace existing states, but it is much more than any other organization. The EU is, in fact, unique. Never before have countries voluntarily agreed to set up common institutions to which they delegate some

FIGURE 8.4 THE EUROPEAN UNION

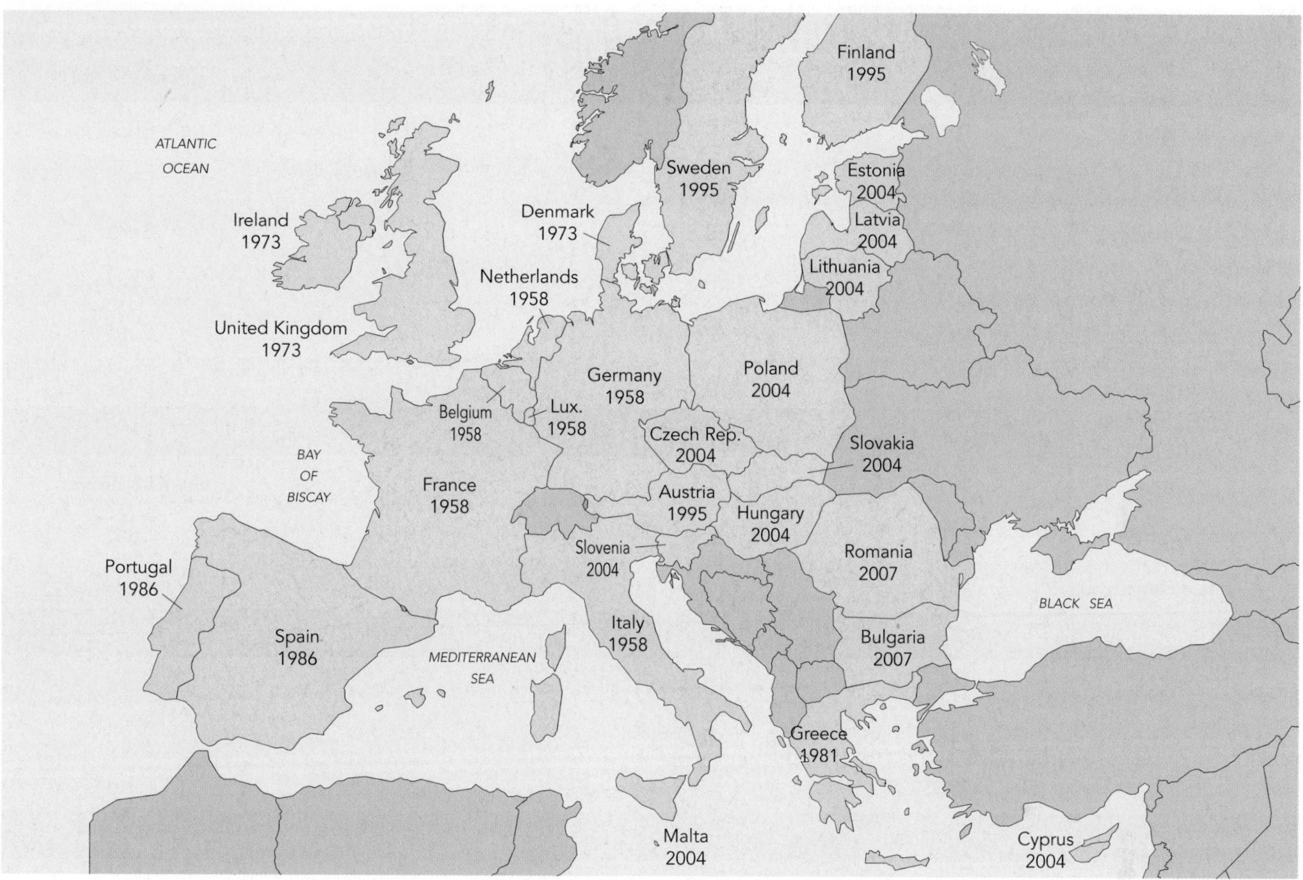

of their sovereignty so that decisions on specific matters of joint interest can be made democratically at a higher, in this case European, level. This pooling of sovereignty is called "European integration."[10]

The EU today is an economic union. Most internal trade barriers have been removed. In aviation, the EU now has a single market, which means all European carriers compete on equal terms across the EU (including domestic routes in a foreign country). US airlines are not allowed to fly between pairs of cities within Germany. However, non-German EU airlines can fly between any pair of cities within Germany. Such deregulation has allowed discount airlines such as Ryanair and easyJet to thrive (see Opening Case). On the ground, it used to take French truck drivers 24 hours to cross the border to enter Spain due to numerous paperwork requirements and checks. Since 1992, passport and customs control within 12 member countries of the EU has been disbanded, and checkpoints at border crossings are no longer manned—the area became known as the **Schengen** passport-free travel zone. Now French trucks can move from France to Spain nonstop, similar to how American trucks go from Texas to Oklahoma. Citizens of the EU 15 (the 15 "core" countries that joined between 1957 and 1995), but not those of the newer members, are free to live and work throughout the EU. Thus, when Germany did not generate enough jobs, a lot of Germans went to Ireland to seek employment.

As an economic union, the EU's proudest accomplishment is the introduction of a common currency, the **euro**, in 12 of the EU 15 countries—known as the **euro zone**. The euro zone accounts for approximately 21% of world GDP (relative to

Schengen
A passport-free travel zone within the EU.

euro
The currency currently used in 12 EU countries.

euro zone
The 12 EU countries that currently use the euro as the official currency.

TABLE 8.2 THE EUROPEAN UNION: WAVES OF EXPANSION

Member countries	Year of entry	Population (millions) 2005	GDP (billion US$) 2006	Current currency
Six founding members				
Belgium	1957	10.4	353.3	Euro
France	1957	60.6	1998.2	Euro
Germany	1957	82.5	2698.7	Euro
Italy	1957	58.5	1791.0	Euro
Luxembourg	1957	0.5	35.2	Euro
Netherlands	1957	16.3	549.7	Euro
Expansion in the 1970s				
Denmark	1973	5.4	203.5	Danish crown
Ireland	1973	4.1	191.7	Euro
United Kingdom	1973	60.0	2004.4	Pound sterling
Expansion in the 1980s				
Greece	1981	10.7	274.5	Euro
Portugal	1986	10.5	217.9	Euro
Spain	1986	43	1203.4	Euro
Expansion in the 1990s				
Austria	1995	8.2	298.7	Euro
Finland	1995	5.2	179.1	Euro
Sweden	1995	9.0	296.7	Swedish crown
Expansion in the 2000s				
Cyprus	2004	0.7	19.7	Cyprus pound
Czech Republic	2004	0.7	210.4	Czech koruna
Estonia	2004	1.3	25.8	Estonian kroon
Hungary	2004	10.1	190.3	Forint
Latvia	2004	2.3	34.4	Lats
Lithuania	2004	3.4	57.0	Litas
Malta	2004	0.4	8.5	Maltese lira
Poland	2004	38.2	556.9	Zloty
Slovakia	2004	5.4	101.2	Slovak koruna
Slovenia	2004	2.0	49.1	Tolar
Bulgaria	2007	7.3	28.1	Lev
Romania	2007	22.3	80.1	Leu

Sources: Based on (1) Key facts and figures about Europe and the Europeans 2006, http://europa.eu (accessed June 15, 2007) and (2) for Bulgaria and Romania data, *CIA—The World Factbook.*

30% for the United States). The euro was introduced in two phases. First, it became available in 1999 as "virtual money" only used for financial transactions but not in circulation. Exchange rates with various national currencies were also fixed at that point. Second, in 2002, the euro was introduced as banknotes and coins. To meet the cash needs of over 300 million people, the EU printed 14.25 billion banknotes and minted 56 billion coins—with a total value of 660 billion euros ($558 billion). The new banknotes would cover the distance between the earth and the moon *five* times (!).[11] Overall, the introduction of the euro was a great success.[12]

Adopting the euro has three great benefits (Table 8.3). First, it reduces currency conversion costs. Travelers and businesses no longer need to pay processing fees to convert currencies for tourist activities or hedging purposes (see Chapter 7). Second, direct and transparent price comparison is now possible, thus channeling more resources toward more competitive firms. Third, adopting the euro imposes strong macroeconomic discipline on participating governments. Prior to adopting the euro, different governments independently determined exchange rates. Italy, for example, sharply devalued its lira in 1992 and 1995. Although Italian exports became cheaper and more competitive overseas, other EU members, especially France, were furious.[13] Also, when confronting recessions, governments often printed more currency and increased government spending. Such actions cause inflation, which may spill over to neighboring countries. By adopting the euro, euro zone countries agreed to abolish monetary policy (such as manipulating exchange rates and printing more currency) as a tool to solve macroeconomic problems. These efforts provide much needed macroeconomic stability. Overall, the euro has boosted intra-EU trade by approximately 10%. Commanding 25% of global foreign currency reserves, the euro has quickly established itself as the only plausible rival to the dollar.[14]

© Sean Gallup/ Stringer/ Getty Images

What are some advantages to the adoption of the euro as the EU's common currency?

However, there are also significant costs involved. The first, noted earlier, is the loss of ability to implement independent monetary policy. The second cost is the lack of flexibility in implementing fiscal policy in areas such as deficit spending. When a country runs into fiscal difficulties, it may be faced with inflation, high interest rates, and a run on its currency. When a number of countries share a common currency, the risks are spread. But some countries can become "free riders" because they may not need to fix their own fiscal problems; other more responsible members will shoulder the burden. To prevent such free riding, euro zone governments signed the Stability and Growth Pact (SGP) in 1997, which committed them to bringing their budget deficit to be no more than 3% of GDP. Otherwise, countries could be fined. Essentially, the tools of fighting a recession, namely, tax

TABLE 8.3 BENEFITS AND COSTS OF ADOPTING THE EURO

Benefits	Costs
• Reduce currency conversion costs • Facilitate direct price comparison • Impose monetary discipline on governments	• Unable to implement independent monetary policy • Limit the flexibility in fiscal policy (in areas such as deficit spending)

reductions and deficit spending, are severely constrained by the SGP. The SGP thus forced Portugal, the first country to exceed the 3% deficit, to dutifully and painfully slash public spending, thus making its own recession and unemployment worse. However, the SGP failed to prevent free riding. When France and Germany failed to curtail their deficit to be less than 3%, they were in open defiance of the SGP, essentially free riding. In 2004, the case went to the highest court in the EU, the European Court of Justice, which opined that France and Germany indeed violated the SGP but recommended no corrective action. Since the EU's two founding members broke the rules and got away with it, the SGP, which offers too little fiscal flexibility, has been seriously undermined.

The EU's Challenges

In 2007, the EU celebrated its 50th anniversary since the signing of the Treaty of Rome in 1957. Politically, the EU has delivered more than half a century of peace and prosperity and turned some opponents in the Cold War into members. Anyone complaining about the huge expenses and bureaucratic meetings of the EU needs to be reminded that one day spent on such meetings is one day member countries are not shooting at one another—a more prohibitively costly outcome. Economically, the EU has launched a single currency and built a single market in which people, goods, services, and capital can move freely—known as the "four freedoms of movement"—within the core Schengen area (not completely within the EU though). The accomplishments are enviable in the eyes of other regional organizations, but the EU seems to be engulfed in a midlife crisis.[15] Significant challenges lie ahead, especially in terms of (1) internal divisions and (2) enlargement concerns.

Internally, there is a significant debate on whether the EU should be an economic and political union or just an economic union. One school of thought, led by France, argues that an economic union should inevitably evolve toward a political union, through which Europe speaks as "one voice." Proponents of this view frequently invoke the famous term enshrined in the 1957 Treaty of Rome, "ever closer union." In this spirit, a Constitution for Europe was drafted in 2004, urging more centralization of power at the EU level. Another school of thought, led by Britain, views the EU as primarily an economic union, which should focus on free trade, pure and simple. Nowhere was such an internal division more visible than the debate on Iraq in 2003. France and Germany were adamantly against the US-led invasion of Iraq, whereas Britain, Denmark, Italy, Poland, and Spain sent forces to Iraq to support the US military. Evidently, the EU had more than one voice. For the Constitution to enter into force, it would have to be ratified by every member country. In 2005, "no" votes in popular referendum prevailed by wide margins in two of the founding members of the EU, France and the Netherlands, thus torpedoing further progress to move toward a political union.[16]

There are also significant concerns associated with enlargement. The EU's largest expansion took place in 2004, with 10 new members, eight of which were former eastern bloc Central and Eastern Europe (CEE) countries, including three Baltic states that were part of the former Soviet Union (Table 8.2). Although taking on 10 new members was a political triumph, it was an economic burden. The 10 new members added 20% to the population but only 9% to the GDP, with 46% of the average GDP per capita relative to EU 15.[17] While CEE displayed the strongest economic growth rates within the EU and provided low-cost production sites for EU 15 firms,[18] the rich EU 15 countries had to provide billions of euros in aid to bring CEE up to speed. For average voters in France and the Netherlands, who experienced low economic growth and high unemployment, their "no" votes on the Constitution were indicative of them being sick and tired of taking on an additional burden to absorb new members. Many citizens in other EU 15 countries felt the same way.

In the same spirit, of the EU 15 countries, only Britain, Ireland, and Sweden opened their labor markets to citizens from the 10 new member countries. The rest of the EU 15, where unemployment stood at 9%, were fearful of an onslaught of job seekers from CEE taking away scarce jobs.[19] There are good reasons to fear. In two years (2004–2006), approximately 200,000 CEE job seekers came to Ireland and about 600,000 (including half a million Poles) showed up in Britain—the *biggest* single wave of migration in British history.[20] Despite the relatively vibrant growth of the British and Irish economies, there is a limit to the absorptive capacity of their labor markets, resulting in second thoughts on the wisdom of such an open-door policy.[21] When Bulgaria and Romania joined the EU in 2007, they brought down the EU average further and would likely send another wave of job seekers, if they were allowed to come. Even Britain now restricted immigration from Bulgaria and Romania.

Another major debate regarding enlargement is Turkey, whose average income is even lower. In addition, its large Muslim population is a concern for a predominantly Christian EU. If Turkey were to join, its population of 73 million would make it the second most populous EU country behind only Germany, whose population is 83 million now. Given the current demographic trends (high birthrates in Turkey and low birthrates in Germany and other EU 15 countries), by 2020, Turkey, if it were to join the EU, would become the most populous and thus the most powerful member, by commanding the most significant voting power. It is not surprising that existing members of the club are concerned.

Overall, we can view the EU enlargement as a miniature version of globalization and the "enlargement fatigue" as part of the recent backlash against globalization.[22] Given the accomplishments and challenges, what does the future of the EU hold? One possible scenario is that there will be an "EU à la carte": Different members pick and choose certain mechanisms to join and opt out of other mechanisms.[23] Practically, seeking consensus among 27 members during negotiations may be impractical. If every country's representative spends 10 minutes on opening remarks, 4.5 *hours* will have passed before discussions even begin. The translation and interpretation among the 23 official languages as of 2007 cost the EU €1.1 billion ($1.4 billion) a year.[24] Since not every country needs to take part in everything, ad hoc grouping of member countries, due to similar interests, are increasingly common and discussions are more efficient. To some extent, EU à la carte has already taken place, as evidenced by the three countries that refused to adopt the euro and 12 countries that blocked job seekers from CEE. Although EU à la carte is at odds with the ideal of an "ever closer union," it seems a more realistic outcome given the recent backlash.

REGIONAL ECONOMIC INTEGRATION IN THE AMERICAS

Two sets of regional economic integration efforts in the Americas have taken place along geographic lines, one in North America and the other in South America.

North America: North American Free Trade Agreement (NAFTA)

North American Free Trade Agreement (NAFTA)
A free trade agreement among Canada, Mexico, and the United States.

Because of the very different levels of economic development, NAFTA, consisting of Canada, Mexico, and the United States, was labeled "one of the most radical free trade experiments in history."[25] Politically, the Mexican government was interested in cementing market liberalization reforms by demonstrating its commitment to free trade. Economically, Mexico was interested in securing preferential treatment for 80% of its exports. Consequently, by the stroke of a pen, Mexico declared itself a *North* American country. In the United States, when unemployment was 7% in the early 1990s, many Americans thought it did not seem to be the best time to open up borders. H. Ross Perot, a presidential candidate in 1992, coined the term "giant sucking sound" to refer to NAFTA's potential destruction of thousands of US jobs.

As NAFTA went into effect in 1994, tariffs on half of the exports and imports among members were removed immediately. Remaining tariffs would be phased out by 2010. These changes in the rules of the game significantly shaped the strategies of NAFTA and non-NAFTA firms.[26]

NAFTA celebrated its 10th anniversary in 2004. By most statistical measures, it was a great success. In its first decade, trade between Canada and the United States grew twice as fast as it did before NAFTA. Expanding even faster, US exports to Mexico grew threefold, from $52 billion to $161 billion. US FDI in Mexico averaged $12 billion a year, three times what India took in. Mexico's US-bound exports grew threefold, and its GDP rose to become the ninth in the world, up from 15th in 1992. Mexico's GDP per capita rose 24% during 1993–2003 to over $4,000, several times China's.[27]

What about jobs? *Maquiladora* (export assembly) factories blossomed under NAFTA, with jobs peaking at 1.3 million in 2000. Beyond *maquiladoras*, the export boom NAFTA caused reportedly accounted for more than half of the 3.5 million jobs created in Mexico since 1994. However, there has been no sign of a "giant sucking sound." Approximately 300,000 US jobs were lost due to NAFTA, which, on the other hand, added about 100,000 jobs. The net loss was small since the US economy generated 20 million new jobs during the first decade of NAFTA. NAFTA's impact on job destruction versus creation in the United States was essentially a "wash."[28] However, a hard count on jobs misses a pervasive but subtle benefit. NAFTA has allowed US firms to *preserve* more US jobs because 82% of the components used in Mexican assembly plants are US-made, whereas factories in Asia use far fewer US parts. Without NAFTA, entire industries might be lost rather than just the labor-intensive portions.[29]

Although economic theory suggests that trade benefits all partners (see Chapter 5), the impact of trade is different among members. More than 85% of Canadian and Mexican exports go to the United States, but only 40% of US exports go to NAFTA partners (about 22% to Canada and 18% to Mexico). Despite the explosion in trade, US imports from Mexico amounted to less than 1.5% of US GDP, and consequently, their impact was relatively small. Low-priced Mexican imports helped hold down inflation but only modestly, shaving about 0.1% off the annual inflation rate in the United States.[30]

As NAFTA approaches its 15th anniversary in 2009, not all is rosy. Opponents of globalization in both Canada and the United States no longer focus on the negative impact of competition from Mexico but rather on China and India. Despite the impressive gains, many Mexicans feel betrayed by NAFTA. Because of Chinese competition, Mexican real wages in manufacturing have stagnated. Many US, Canadian, European, and Japanese multinationals are shifting some of their factory work to China, which has now replaced Mexico as the second largest exporter to the United States (after Canada).[31] About 1,000 *maquiladora* factories have closed down since 2000. One reason many Mexicans are disappointed is that the deal might have been oversold by its sponsors as a cure-all for Mexico to become the next South Korea. If NAFTA has disappointed, it may be in part because the Mexican government has not capitalized on the tremendous opportunities NAFTA has offered. There is only so much free trade can do; other reforms in infrastructure and education need to keep up.[32]

South America: Andean Community, Mercosur, FTAA, and CAFTA

Andean Community
A customs union in South America that was launched in 1969.

Mercosur
A customs union in South America that was launched in 1991.

However imperfect NAFTA is, it is much more effective than the two customs unions in South America: **Andean Community** and **Mercosur**. Members of the Andean Community (launched in 1969) and Mercosur (launched in 1991) are mostly countries on the *western* and *eastern* sides of the Andean mountains, respectively (Figure 8.5). There is much mutual suspicion and rivalry between both orga-

FIGURE 8.5 **REGIONAL ECONOMIC INTEGRATION IN SOUTH AMERICA**

nizations as well as within each of them. Mercosur is relatively more protectionist and suspicious of the United States, whereas the Andean Community is more pro-free trade.[33] When Colombia and Peru, both Andean Community members, signed trade deals with the United States, Venezuela, led by its anti-American President Hugo Chavez, pulled out of the Andean Community in protest and joined Mercosur in 2006. At the same time, Uruguay, a Mercosur member, demanded permission from the group to sign a separate trade deal with the United States; otherwise, it threatened to quit Mercosur.[34]

Both regional initiatives have not been effective, in part because only about 5% and 20% of members' trade is within the Andean Community and Mercosur, respectively. Their largest trading partner, the United States, lies outside the region. It is a free trade deal with the United States, not among themselves, that would generate the most significant benefits. Emboldened by NAFTA, in 1998, all Latin American countries (except Cuba) launched negotiations with Canada and the United States for a possible **Free Trade Area of the Americas (FTAA)**. However, by November 2005, Argentina, Brazil, Paraguay, Uruguay, and Venezuela changed their mind and announced that they opposed FTAA, thus undermining the chances that FTAA would ever be set up.[35]

Free Trade Area of the Americas (FTAA)
A proposed free trade area for the entire Western Hemisphere.

In the absence of the FTAA, one recent accomplishment is the **United States-Dominican Republic-Central America Free Trade Agreement (CAFTA)**, which took effect in 2005. Modeled after NAFTA, CAFTA is "between a whale and six minnows" (five Central American countries—Guatemala, Honduras, El Salvador, Nicaragua, and Costa Rica—plus the Dominican Republic).[36] Although small, the six CAFTA countries collectively represent the second largest US export market in Latin America (behind only Mexico). Globally, CAFTA is the 10th largest US export market, importing more than Russia, India, and Indonesia *combined*.[37]

United States-Dominican Republic-Central America Free Trade Agreement (CAFTA)
A free trade agreement between the United States and five Central American countries and Dominican Republic.

How do certain industries in the six smaller CAFTA members benefit from their trade agreement with the United States?

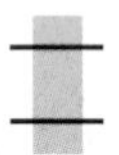

REGIONAL ECONOMIC INTEGRATION IN ASIA PACIFIC

This section introduces regional integration efforts (1) between Australia and New Zealand, (2) in Southeast Asia, and (3) throughout Asia Pacific. Their scale and scope differ.

Australia-New Zealand Closer Economic Relations Trade Agreement (ANZCERTA or CER)

The CER, launched in 1983, turned the historical rivalry between Australia and New Zealand into a partnership. As an FTA, the CER over time removed tariffs and NTBs. For example, both countries agreed not to charge exporters from another country for "dumping." Citizens from both countries can also freely work and reside in the other country. Mostly due to the relatively high level of geographic proximity and cultural homogeneity, CER has been regarded as a very successful FTA.

Association of Southeast Asian Nations (ASEAN)
The organization underpinning regional economic integration in Southeast Asia.

Association of Southeast Asian Nations (ASEAN)

Founded in 1967, ASEAN (Figure 8.6) had not been economically active until 1992. Encouraged by the EU, ASEAN in 1992 set up the ASEAN Free Trade Area (AFTA). Despite the setback of the 1997 Asian economic crisis, intra-ASEAN trade has grown by 12% annually since 1992.[38]

Although the gains are impressive, ASEAN suffers from a similar problem that Latin American countries face: ASEAN's main trading partners, the United States, the European Union, Japan, and China, are outside the region. Intra-ASEAN trade usually accounts for less than a quarter of total trade. The benefits of AFTA, thus, may be limited. In response, ASEAN in 2001 launched a more ambitious agenda: ASEAN + 3 (China, Japan, and South Korea). In 2002, ASEAN and China signed an ASEAN-China Free Trade Agreement (ACFTA) to be launched by the early 2010s. Given the

FIGURE 8.6 REGIONAL ECONOMIC INTEGRATION IN ASIA PACIFIC

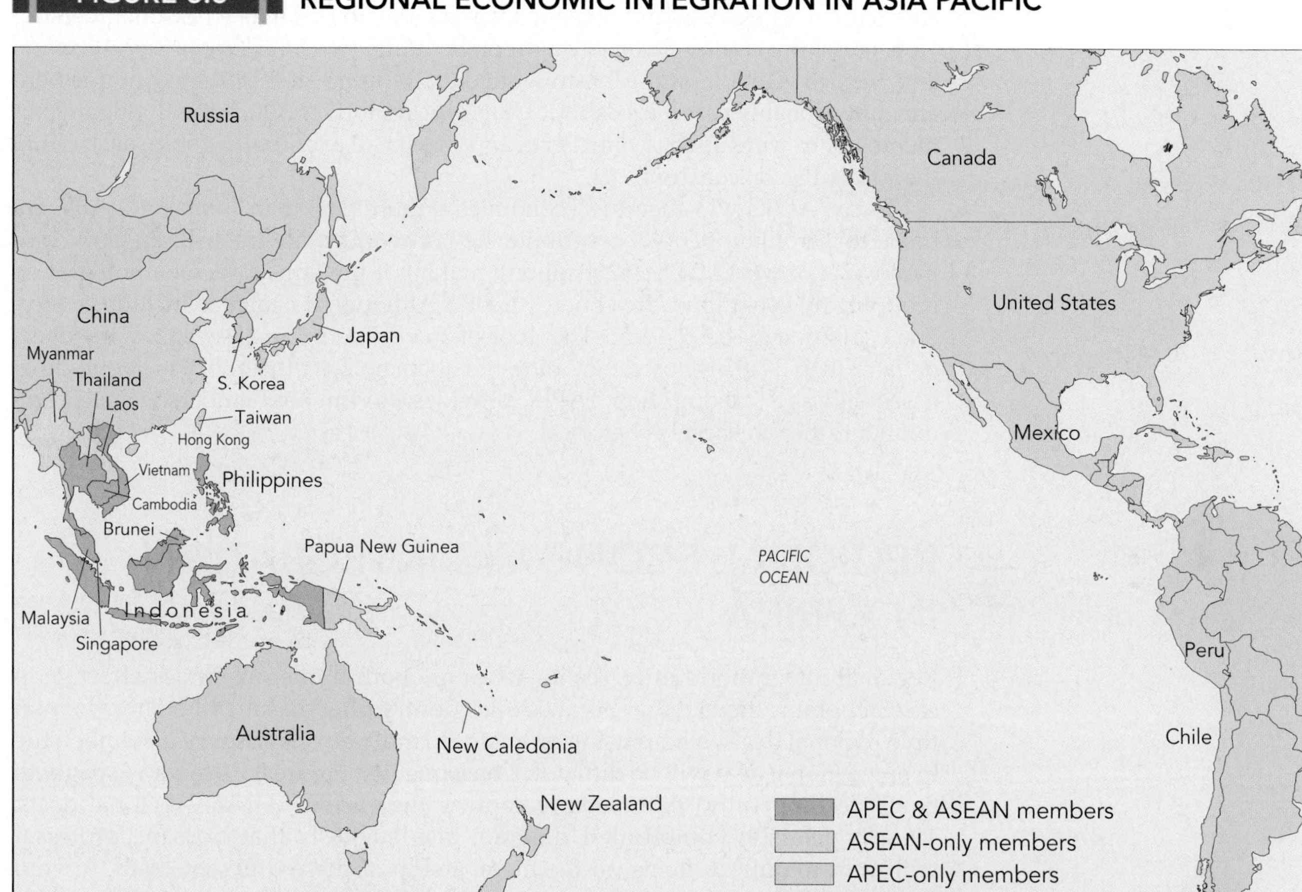

increasingly strong competition in terms of Chinese exports and China-bound FDI that could have come to ASEAN, ACFTA may potentially turn such rivalry into a partnership. ACFTA is estimated to boost ASEAN's exports to China by 48% and China's exports to ASEAN by 55%, thus raising ASEAN's GDP by 0.9% and China's by 0.3%.[39] Similar FTAs are being negotiated with Japan and South Korea.

Asia-Pacific Economic Cooperation (APEC)

Asia-Pacific Economic Cooperation (APEC)
The official title for regional economic integration involving 21 member economies around the Pacific.

While ASEAN was deepening its integration, in 1989, Australia was afraid that it might be left out and suggested that ASEAN and CER countries form APEC. Given the lack of a global heavyweight in both ASEAN and CER, Japan was invited. The Japanese happily agreed to join, but ASEAN and CER countries feared that Japan might dominate the group and create a de facto "yen bloc." Japan invaded most countries in the region during World War II to exercise such leadership, and bitter memories of Japanese wartime atrocities seemed to die hard. China in 1990 was economically far less significant than it is now and thus could hardly counterbalance Japan. The United States requested to join APEC, citing its long West Coast that would qualify it as a Pacific country. Economically, the United States did not want to be left out of the most dynamically growing region in the world. Politically, the United States was interested in containing Japanese influence in any Asian regional deals. Although the United States could certainly serve as a counterweight for Japan, US membership would change the character of APEC centered on ASEAN and CER. To make its APEC membership "less odd," the United States brought on board its two NAFTA partners, Canada and Mexico. Canada and Mexico were equally interested in the economic benefits but probably cared less about US political motives. Once the floodgates for membership were open, Chile, Peru, and Russia all eventually got in, each citing their long Pacific coastlines (!).

Today, APEC's 21 member economies (Figure 8.6) span four continents, are home to 2.6 billion people, contribute 46% of world trade ($7 trillion), and command 57% of world GDP ($21 trillion), making it the largest regional integration grouping by geographic area and by GDP.[40] Although it is nice to include "everyone," APEC may be too big. The goal of free trade by industrialized members no later than 2010 and by developing members no later than 2020 is *not* binding. Essentially as a "talking shop," APEC provides a forum for members to make commitments that are largely rhetorical.

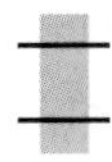

REGIONAL ECONOMIC INTEGRATION IN AFRICA

Regional integration initiatives in Africa are both numerous and ineffective. A case in point is the fact that because one country often has memberships in multiple regional deals, a map using one color to indicate one country's membership in one regional deal will be difficult. Consequently, Figure 8.7 draws a "spaghetti bowl" to (hopefully) more clearly capture the various African regional deals. This (hopelessly) complicated diagram also suggests that no sane professor will want to quiz students on the membership of these different deals on your exam (!). While various African countries are interested in reaping the benefits from regional economic integration, there is relatively little trade within Africa (amounting to less than 10% of the continent's total trade), where protectionism often prevails. Frustration with a current regional deal often leads to a new deal, usually with a different set of countries, eventually leading to the messy "spaghetti bowl" in Figure 8.7.

LEARNING OBJECTIVE 

participate in two debates on global and regional economic integration

DEBATES AND EXTENSIONS

As discussed earlier, global and regional economic integration is characterized by numerous debates (What caused Doha to collapse? How to enlarge the EU?). This section outlines two additional major debates: (1) building blocks versus stumbling blocks and (2) impact of the WTO.

Building Blocks versus Stumbling Blocks

In the absence of global economic integration, regional economic integration is often regarded as the next best thing to facilitate free trade—at least within a region. Some may even argue that regional integration represents building blocks for eventual global integration. For example, the EU now participates in WTO negotiations as one entity, which seems like a building block for global integration. Individual EU member countries no longer enter such talks.

However, another school of thought argues that regional integration has become stumbling blocks for global integration. By design, regional integration

FIGURE 8.7 **REGIONAL ECONOMIC INTEGRATION IN AFRICA**

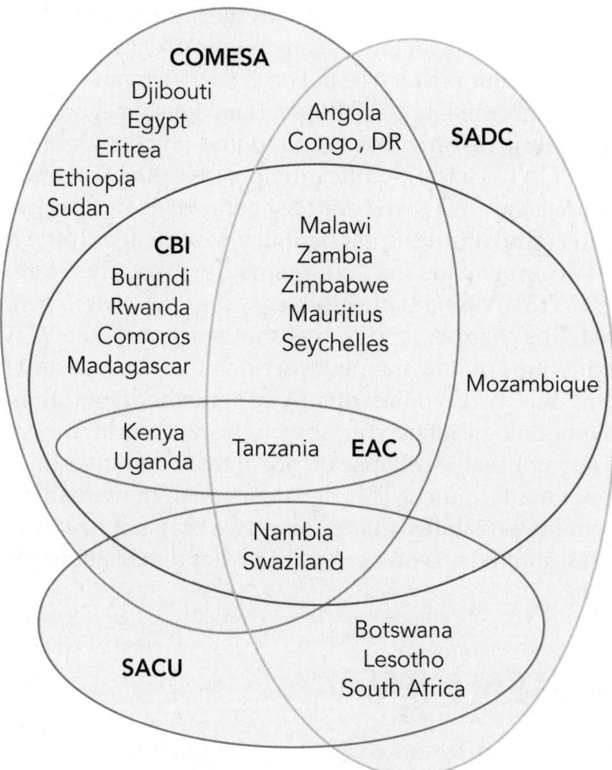

Source: J. Bhagwati, 2002, *Free Trade Today* (p. 115), Princeton, NJ: Princeton University Press. CBI—Cross Border Initiative; COMESA—Common Market for Eastern and Southern Africa; EAC—Commission for East Africa Co-operation; SADC—Southern African Development Community; SACU—Southern African Customs Union.

provides preferential treatments to members and, at the same time, *discriminates* against nonmembers (which is allowed by WTO rules). It is still a form of protectionism centered on "us versus them," except "us" is now an expanded group of countries. The proliferation of regional trade deals thus may be alarming. In the first few decades after World War II, the United States avoided regional deals. In part alarmed by the EU, the United States, with Canada and Mexico, launched NAFTA. NAFTA was more recently extended to CAFTA and may eventually lead to FTAA. Likewise, Japan, alarmed by the rising protectionist sentiments with the EU and NAFTA, abandoned its long-standing policy of avoiding regional deals (see In Focus 8.3). Similarly, China signed its first FTA agreement (ACFTA) in 2002 with ASEAN. Further, in 2004, China signed Closer Economic Partnership Agreements (CEPA) with Hong Kong and Macao, and in 2005, it signed FTA deals with Chile and Pakistan.[41] Clearly, the trend is accelerating.

Of course, all countries party to some regional deals participate in WTO talks, arguing that they are walking on two legs (regional and global). Yet, "instead of walking on two legs," critics such as Columbia professor Jagdish Bhagwati argued, "we have wound up on all fours"—crawling with slow progress.[42] This sorry state is triggered by the pursuit of countries' individual interest in a globally uncoordinated fashion. As regional deals proliferate, nonmembers feel that they are squeezed out and begin plotting their own regional deals. Very soon, the world ends up having a global "spaghetti bowl."

Does the WTO Really Matter?

Frustration associated with the collapse of the Doha Round and other WTO initiatives hinges on a crucial assumption that the WTO actually matters. However, this assumption itself is now subject to debate. On the surface, the impact of the WTO seems unambiguous. China's first five years in the WTO (2001–2006) coincide with its rise as a global economic power (see In Focus 8.1). Vietnam was happy to become the WTO's 150th member in late 2006. Russia is anxiously negotiating to get in.

However, academic research has failed to find any compelling evidence that the WTO (and the GATT) has a significantly positive effect on trade.[43] True, trade has blossomed since the GATT was established in 1948. But Andrew Rose, a professor at the University of California, Berkeley, reports that trade has blossomed for the GATT/WTO members and nonmembers alike. Therefore, it is difficult to find that the GATT/WTO membership *caused* more trade. The *Economist* thus commented that "the 'hoopla' and 'hype' that surrounds the WTO's successes, failure, and admissions of new members are just that: hoopla and hype."[44]

Defenders of the WTO point out Rose's methodological imperfections.[45] Beyond such methodological hair splitting, in the real world, the collapse of Doha has not caused any noticeable collapse of global trade and investment. So, perhaps the WTO does not matter much. This debate is much more than just academic. It directly speaks to the possibility that perhaps we may not need to place so much hope on the WTO, and there is no need to be so depressed about Doha's collapse.

LEARNING OBJECTIVE 6

draw implications for action

MANAGEMENT SAVVY

Of the two major perspectives on global business (institution- and resource-based views), this chapter has focused on the institution-based view. To address the question, "What determines the success and failure of firms around the globe?" the entire chapter has been devoted to an introduction of the rules of the game as institutions governing global and regional economic integration. How does this knowledge help managers? Managers need to combine the insights from the institution-based view with those from the resource-based view to come up with strategies and solutions on how their firms can capitalize on opportunities presented by global and regional economic integration. Two broad implications for action emerge (Table 8.4).

First, given the slowdown of multilateralism and the acceleration of regionalism, managers are advised to focus their attention more at regional than global levels.[46] To a large extent, they are already doing that. The majority of the multinational enterprises (MNEs) generate most of their revenues in their home region (such as within the EU or NAFTA).[47] The largest MNEs may have a presence all over the world, but their center of gravity (measured by revenues) is often still their home region. Thus, they are not really very global. Regional strategies make sense because most countries within a region share some cultural, economic, and

TABLE 8.4 IMPLICATIONS FOR ACTION

- Think regional, downplay global
- Understand the rules of the game and their transitions at both global and regional levels

geographic similarities, which can lower the liability of foreignness when moving within one region—as opposed to moving from one region to another. From a resource-based standpoint, most firms are better prepared to compete on regional as opposed to global levels. Despite the hoopla associated with "global strategies," managers, in short, need to think local and downplay global (while not necessarily abandoning global).

Second, managers also need to understand the rules of the game and their transitions at both global and regional levels. Although trade negotiations involve a lot of politics that many managers think they can hardly care less about, managers ignore these rules and their transitions at their own peril. When the MFA was phased out in 2005, numerous managers at textile firms who had become comfortable under the MFA's protection complained about their lack of preparation. In fact, they had 30 years to prepare for such an eventuality. When the MFA was signed in 1974, it was agreed that it would be phased out by 2005. The typical attitude that "we don't care about (trade) politics" can lead to a failure in due diligence. The best managers expect their firm strategies to shift over time by constantly deciphering the changes in the "big picture" and being willing to take advantage of new opportunities brought by global and regional trade deals.[48] Ryanair and Hungarian Dental Travel (see Opening Case) represent some interesting examples of such firms.

CHAPTER SUMMARY

1. Make the case for global economic integration
   - There are both political and economic benefits for global economic integration.
2. Understand the evolution of the GATT and the WTO, including current challenges
   - The GATT (1948–1994) significantly reduced tariff rates on merchandise trade.
   - The WTO (1995–present) was set up not only to incorporate the GATT but also to cover trade in services, intellectual property, trade dispute settlement, and peer review of trade policy.
   - The Doha Round to promote more trade and development thus far failed to accomplish its goals.
3. Describe the advantages and disadvantages of regional economic integration
   - Political and economic benefits for regional integration are similar to those for global integration.
   - Regional integration may undermine global integration and lead to some loss of countries' sovereignty.
4. Understand regional economic integration efforts in Europe, the Americas, Asia Pacific, and Africa
   - The EU has delivered more than half a century of peace and prosperity, launched a single currency, and constructed a single market. Its challenges include internal divisions and enlargement concerns.
   - Despite problems, NAFTA has significantly boosted trade and investment among members.
   - In South America, the prominent regional deals are Andean Community, Mercosur, and CAFTA.
   - Regional integration in Asia Pacific centers on CER, ASEAN, and APEC.
   - Regional integration deals in Africa are both numerous and ineffective.

5. Participate in two debates on global and regional economic integration
   - Is regional integration building blocks or stumbling blocks for global integration?
   - Does the WTO really matter?
6. Draw implications for action
   - Given the acceleration of regionalism, managers are advised to focus more at regional than global levels.
   - Managers also need to understand the rules of the game and their transitions at both global and regional levels.

KEY TERMS

Andean Community 224
Asia-Pacific Economic Cooperation (APEC) 227
Association of Southeast Asian Nations (ASEAN) 226
Common market 217
Customs union 217
The Doha Round 213
Economic union 217
Euro 219
Euro zone 219
European Union (EU) 208
Free trade area (FTA) 217
Free Trade Area of the Americas (FTAA) 225
General Agreement on Tariffs and Trade (GATT) 209
General Agreement on Trade in Services (GATS) 212
Global economic integration 208
Mercosur 224
Monetary union 217
Multilateral trading system 210
Nondiscrimination 210
North American Free Trade Agreement (NAFTA) 223
Political union 217
Regional economic integration 208
Schengen 219
Trade-Related Aspects of Intellectual Property Rights (TRIPS) 212
United States-Dominican Republic-Central America Free Trade Agreement (CAFTA) 225
World Trade Organization (WTO) 209

REVIEW QUESTIONS

1. Name and describe three compelling economic benefits of global economic integration.
2. List two disadvantages of global economic integration.
3. Briefly summarize the history of the WTO.
4. What are the six main areas of concern for the WTO?
5. Describe two outcomes of the failure of the Doha Development Agenda.
6. In what ways are the benefits of regional economic integration similar to global economic integration?
7. What is one possible negative outcome of regional integration?
8. Referring to Figure 8.3 as needed, name and describe the five main types of regional economic integration.
9. What are the advantages and disadvantages of the EU's adoption of the euro?
10. After reviewing the two sides of the debate over whether the EU should be just an economic union or also a political union, state your opinion on the issue and explain your reasons.

11. What achievements do NAFTA supporters point to as evidence of NAFTA's success?
12. What achievements do CAFTA supporters point to as evidence of its success?
13. Why is the FTAA largely considered a failure?
14. Name and describe three examples of regional integration in Asia and the Pacific.
15. Some countries involved in regional deals say they are "walking on two legs" with both the WTO and regional economic integration, and others say they have "wound up on all fours." Why?
16. What evidence suggests that the WTO may not be as significant as its supporters claim it is?
17. What two trends indicate that managers should focus more on regional as opposed to global issues?
18. How important is it for a manager to understand the political ramifications of global and regional trade negotiations?

CRITICAL DISCUSSION QUESTIONS

1. The Doha Round collapsed because many countries believed that no deal was better than a bad deal. Do you agree or disagree with this approach? Why?
2. Will Turkey become a full-fledged member of the EU? Why or why not?
3. ON ETHICS: Critics argue that the WTO single-mindedly promotes trade at the expense of the environment (see In Focus 8.2). Therefore, trade, or more broadly, globalization, needs to slow down. What is your view on the relationship between trade and the environment?
4. ON ETHICS: Critics argue that because of NAFTA, a flood of subsidized US food imports wiped out Mexico's small farmers. Some 1.3 million farm jobs disappeared. Consequently, the number of illegal immigrants in the United States skyrocketed. What is your view on NAFTA, CAFTA, and FTAA?

VIDEO CASE

Watch "Messiness" by Sir Martin Sorrell of WPP.

1. This chapter deals with global and regional integration. To what extent did Sir Martin Sorrell indicate political limits on such integration?
2. In view of efforts to achieve economic integration among countries, does Sir Sorrell support or oppose global integration?
3. What did he mean by the pendulum swinging too far? How does that affect the future of global and regional integration?
4. Sir Martin Sorrell seems to feel that the impact of the United States internationally may have peaked. If that is true, how might it affect global and regional integration?
5. The title of the video is "Messiness." What is messy and what does Sir Sorrell suggest as the solution?

CLOSING CASE

ETHICAL DILEMMA: Cotton Farmers in West Africa and Mississippi

During 2004–2006, the United States was the world's largest exporter of cotton, and West Africa—consisting of 10 sub-Saharan countries, Benin, Burkina Faso, Cameroon, Central African Republic, Chad, Côte d'Ivoire, Mali, Niger, Senegal, and Togo—was the second largest. Both export regions were subject to market forces that slashed prices by 66% from 1995 to 2002. In 2002, the price being offered to West Africa's cotton farmers was 10% lower than the previous year's—a meager amount, given that world cotton prices had declined to the most unprofitable level in 30 years. After the harvest, once the costs were paid, the typical West African farmer was left with less than $2,000 for the year to support two dozen family members and relatives.

© MARKOS DOLOPIKOS / Alamy

At the same time, cotton seedlings in the United States pushed up through thick black soil of Perthshire Farms, a 10,000-acre cotton plantation on the Mississippi Delta. Farmers climbed into the air-conditioned cabs of their $130,000 Caterpillar tractors and prepared to apply fertilizer to the seedlings. There were no obvious indications in Mississippi that world cotton prices were depressed. Why? Because US farmers receive government subsidies in abundance, whereas West African growers don't.

Armed with almost $3.5 billion in subsidy checks, which constituted about half of their income, US cotton farmers in 2002 harvested a record crop of about 10 billion pounds of cotton, aggravating a US surplus and pushing prices below the breakeven price of most farmers around the world. However, West Africa's governments, hard-pressed to provide even the most basic education and healthcare to their people, can't keep up with subsidies of their own.

The reason Mississippi's farmers are so dependent on subsidies is that they are among the highest cost cotton producers in the world. They could grow corn, soybeans, and wheat much more cheaply, but switching would render much of their investment worthless. For example, a cotton-picking machine costs about $300,000 and is useless for other crops. Analysts estimate that if the US subsidies were removed, the world price of cotton would rise, and revenue to West African countries would increase by about $250 million. But in Mississippi, there is little sympathy for the removal of subsidies. Cotton is king in Mississippi, and its growers don't want competition from West Africa's farmers. Simply put, American cotton farmers maintain that they cannot survive without subsidies. In 2004, the WTO issued an interim ruling that declared America's subsidies to its cotton farmers illegal. In 2007, the WTO upheld the earlier decision. It remains to be seen whether these rulings result in a dismantling of America's agricultural subsidies as well as the subsidies of other nations.

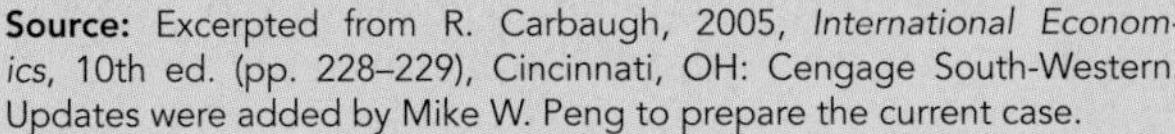

Source: Excerpted from R. Carbaugh, 2005, *International Economics*, 10th ed. (pp. 228–229), Cincinnati, OH: Cengage South-Western. Updates were added by Mike W. Peng to prepare the current case.

Case Discussion Questions

1. Subsidies stimulate higher US production, which depresses global prices. If subsidies were removed, cotton prices would go up, and textile products would be more expensive. As both a US taxpayer and a textile consumer, do you recommend that subsidies (1) be increased, (2) be maintained at current levels, or (3) be eliminated?
2. Agricultural subsidies have been blamed for having caused the collapse of the Doha Round of the WTO. If you were (1) a US cotton farmer or (2) West African cotton farmer, do you think this criticism is fair?
3. As governor of Mississippi or CEO of Perthshire Farms, how would you prepare for a possible subsidy-free future?

NOTES

Journal acronyms: **AER** – *American Economic Review;* **AMR** – *Academy of Management Review;* **BW** – *Business Week;* **JIBS** – *Journal of International Business Studies;* **JWB** – *Journal of World Business*

[1] This section draws heavily on World Trade Organization, 2005, *10 Benefits of the WTO Trading System*, Geneva: WTO.

[2] *10 Benefits of the WTO Trading System* (p. 3).

[3] *10 Benefits of the WTO Trading System* (p. 8). However, some argue that these estimates may be too optimistic. See J. Stiglitz & A. Charlton, 2005, *Fair Trade for All* (p. 46), New York: Oxford University Press.

[4] *10 Benefits of the WTO Trading System* (p. 10).

[5] D. Xu, Y. Pan, C. Wu, & B. Yim, 2006, Performance of domestic and foreign-invested enterprises in China (p. 268), *JWB*, 41: 261–274.

[6] R. Carbaugh, 2005, *International Economics*, 10th ed. (p. 181), Cincinnati, OH: Cengage South-Western.

[7] *Economist*, 2006, The future of globalization (p. 11), July 29: 11.

[8] World Trade Organization, 2006, Talks suspended, news release, July 24, http://www.wto.org (accessed July 24, 2006).

[9] *Economist*, 2006, In the twilight of Doha (p. 63), July 29: 63–64.

[10] Delegation of the European Commission to the USA, 2005, *The European Union: A Guide for Americans* (p. 2), Washington, DC: Delegation of the European Commission to the USA.

[11] G. Zestos, 2006, *European Monetary Integration: The Euro* (p. 64), Cincinnati, OH: Cengage South-Western.

[12] P. Whyman, 2002, Living with the euro, *JWB*, 37: 208–215.

[13] *Economist*, 2005, A survey of Italy (p. 6), November 25: 1–16.

[14] *Economist*, 2007, The quest for prosperity, March 17: 6–9.

[15] *Economist*, 2007, Europe's mid-life crisis, March 17: 13.

[16] *Economist*, 2005, The Europe that died, June 4: 13–14.

[17] *Economist*, 2004, A club in need of a new vision (p. 26), May 1: 25–27.

[18] K. Meyer & M. W. Peng, 2005, Probing theoretically in Central and Eastern Europe, *JIBS*, 36: 600–621.

[19] *Economist*, 2006, When East meets West, February 11: 47–48.

[20] *Economist*, 2006, A survey of Poland (p. 3), May 13: 3–12.

[21] *Economist*, 2006, Second thoughts, August 26: 45–46.

[22] *Economist*, 2006, A case of enlargement fatigue, May 13: 64; L. Tyson, 2005, Behind the EU backlash, *BW*, July 11: 94.

[23] *Economist*, 2004, Europe à la carte, September 25: 14–16.

[24] *Economist*, 2006, Babelling on, December 16: 50.

[25] *BW*, 2003, Mexico: Was NAFTA worth it? December 22, http://www.businessweek.com (accessed September 30, 2006).

[26] A. Rugman & J. Kirton, 1998, Multinational enterprise strategy and the NAFTA trade and environment regime, *JWB*, 33: 438–454.

[27] *BW*, 2003, Happy birthday, NAFTA, December 22; *BW*, 2003, Mexico: Was NAFTA worth it?

[28] J. Garten, 2003, At 10, NAFTA is ready for an overhaul, *BW*, December 22, http://www.businessweek.com (accessed September 30, 2006).

[29] *BW*, 2001, NAFTA's scorecard: So far, so good, July 9, http://www.businessweek.com (accessed September 30, 2006).

[30] *BW*, 2001, NAFTA's scorecard.

[31] J. Sargent & L. Matthews, 2006, The drivers of evolution/upgrading in Mexico's maquiladoras, *JWB*, 41: 233–246.

[32] Stiglitz & Charlton, 2005, *Free Trade for All* (p. 23).

[33] *Economist*, 2006, Trade in South America, August 26: 30.

[34] *Economist*, 2006, Mercosur's summit: Downhill from here, July 29: 36.

[35] United Nations, 2006, *World Investment Report 2006* (p. 75), New York and Geneva: United Nations/UNCTAD.

[36] *Economist*, 2005, Another such victory, July 30: 66.

[37] US Trade Representative, 2005, *The Case for CAFTA*, February, http://www.ustr.gov (accessed October 1, 2006).

[38] ASEAN Secretariat, 2002, *Southeast Asia: A Free Trade Area*, Jakarta: ASEAN Secretariat, http://www.aseansec.org (accessed October 1, 2006).

[39] ASEAN Secretariat, 2002, *Southeast Asia: A Free Trade Area.*

[40] APEC Secretariat, 2005, *APEC at a Glance*, Singapore: APEC Secretariat, www.apec.org (accessed October 20, 2007)

[41] World Trade Organization, 2006, *Trade Policy Review Report by the People's Republic of China*, Geneva: WTO.

[42] J. Bhagwati, 2002, *Free Trade Today* (p. 119), Princeton, NJ: Princeton University Press.

[43] A. Rose, 2004, Do we really know that the WTO increases trade? *AER*, 94: 98–114.

[44] *Economist*, 2005, Is there any point to the WTO? August 6: 62.

[45] M. Tomz, J. Goldstein, & D. Rivers, 2005, Membership has its privileges, Working paper, Stanford University; A. Subramanian & S. Wei, 2005, The WTO promotes trade strongly but unevenly, Working paper, IMF.

[46] A. Rugman, 2005, *The Regional Multinationals* (p. 215), Cambridge, UK: Cambridge University Press.

[47] A. Rugman & A. Verbeke, 2004, A perspective on regional and global strategies of multinational enterprises, *JIBS*, 35: 3–18.

[48] M. W. Peng, 2003, Institutional transitions and strategic choices (p. 292), *AMR*, 28: 275–296.

INTEGRATIVE CASE 2.1

WHICH IS MORE AMERICAN?

Chris Woodyard
USA TODAY

Joe Luehrmann likes American cars, has owned a string of them, and is considering buying another. But he faces a problem in trying to figure out what's American anymore. His brother just bought a Chevy Equinox, but some of its parts are from China. And he knows all about the Kentucky-built Camry, but buying a Toyota ships the profit to Japan. Toyota brags in ads about its growing list of US plants, yet it imported 37% more cars from Japan last year [*2006—editor*] to meet increased demand. General Motors promotes its trucks in TV commercials to strains of "This Is Our Country" but makes some of its best-known SUVs in Mexico.

"What's American vs. what's foreign? I can't really say," says the frustrated Luehrmann, a Chicago accountant. "It's not that easy. It's very shades of gray." The ambiguity creates a quandary for the many who consider "Made in the USA" a badge of honor. To them, the label means putting fellow countrymen to work at decent wages and supporting the US economy in wartime. Some domestic-brand dealers use patriotic appeals to try to rev up the Buy American spirit. But many consumers are increasingly confused. The world is no longer as simple as us vs. them, Detroit against the Asians and Europeans. It's a global industry now, in which all manufacturers are touching their automaking toes on the shores of just about every industrialized nation. Even GM, long the icon of American industry, hedges its bets. "We're very proud for the economic role we play in this country," says GM spokesman Greg Martin. "However, we're a global car company that happens to be based in the United States."

The contradictions of a borderless automotive economy are borne out by government figures that track where vehicles are made and their domestic parts content. The search for the American car leads to:

- **Foreign cars made in the USA.** Honda's Ohio-built Accord is 70% domestic parts. Toyota's Corolla is made in a California plant alongside General Motors models.
- **American cars made abroad.** Ford's hit Fusion sedan is made in Mexico; only half its parts are from the USA or Canada. GM pitches its small HHR sport utility and giant Suburban straight at the American market, but they, too, are built in Mexico. HHR has only 41% American and Canadian parts.
- **Famous American names and foreign owners.** More than three-quarters of the parts in Dodge's new Nitro SUV, which is assembled in Toledo, Ohio, are American or Canadian. But the profits go to Germany because Dodge is part of DaimlerChrysler. Chrysler Group, meanwhile, just became the first major automaker to announce it's going to make small cars for the US market in China.

Despite the confusion, about half of Americans surveyed say they still try to buy products made in the USA, says Britt Beemer of America's Research Group. The government makes it easy for buyers wandering sales lots to figure out which vehicles are most American. The location of the plant where a vehicle was assembled and its amount of US or Canadian parts—they aren't separated out—are pasted on the window sticker (Table 1).

Arguably, the most American of all vehicles right now is Ford's hulking 2007 Ford Expedition, a *USA TODAY* check of government listings, manufacturers, and dealer sales lots reveals. The SUV is composed of 95% US or Canadian parts, and it was made in Michi-

TABLE 1 HOW AMERICAN ARE THESE CARS?

Car Manufacturer and Model	Percentage of Content Made in US or Canada	Assembly Location
Chevy HHR	41%	Mexico
Toyota Sienna	85%	Indiana, USA
Ford Expedition	95%	Michigan, USA

This case was written by Chris Woodyard and first published as "Which Is More American?" in *USA TODAY*, March 22, 2007, Money Section B1 and B2.

gan. Ford's new Edge crossover and the Crown Victoria sedan also have 95% components, but both they and their corporate cousins are assembled in Canada. Even though individual models vary widely, Detroit automakers overall still had more domestic parts in their vehicles when weighted according to sales, says an analysis from a pro-Detroit trade group (Table 2).

Detroit's Big Three derived about 77% of their parts from US and Canadian factories from domestic sources. That compares with slightly less than half for Japanese brands overall, according to the Automotive Trade Policy Council, which represents the domestic manufacturers in trade issues. Among Japanese brands, Honda had the most domestic content at 59%. "The data is clear: Domestic auto plants create more jobs in this country than overseas producers who locate here," says United Auto Workers President Ron Gettelfinger in a statement to *USA TODAY*. But he was quick to note that foreign automakers have created more jobs in the USA by opening plants here, and he respects their workers.

Many auto dealers selling domestic brands are playing to the patriotism theme. In Tampa, Florida, Bill Currie Ford credits pro-USA ad themes for contributing to fast growth. A billboard posted along Interstate 275 shows an American flag and outlines of Japan and South Korea. The message: "Whose country are you supporting?" "We've had some compliments," says Currie's community relations director, Danny Lewis. And, he adds, "very little criticism." In Roseville, Minnesota, Cadillac dealer Wally McCarthy runs radio ads on WCCO-AM in Minneapolis that say, "Buying a vehicle from GM, quite simply, helps support Americans."

Manufacturers—and not just those in Detroit—have picked up on the patriotism theme lately, especially when it comes to pickups. To crack the full-size pickup market with its new Tundra, Toyota doesn't hold back in promoting how American it has become. The new Texas truck plant where the Tundra is built "is just one more example of our commitment to America," Toyota touts in colorful newspaper ads that mention lots of new jobs and a $15 billion US investment. GM counters with its Our Country campaign, filled with images of vintage Americana, for its Chevy Silverado pickups.

Consumers who care the most about patriotism when it comes to purchases are usually working-class white men—thus the emphasis on the pickup market, says Dana Frank, a history professor at the University of California, Santa Cruz, and author of *Buy American: The Untold Story of Economic Nationalism*. Pickup buyers also are notoriously loyal, another reason the campaigns are targeting them. They'll wear a Chevy belt buckle with pride, notes Honda Senior Vice President John Mendel, adding, "Not a lot of Lexus owners have an 'L' tattooed on their arm." Half the domestic pickup buyers surveyed by J. D. Power and Associates cited not wanting to own a foreign-made truck as the chief reason for their purchase decision, even more than the one out of three who said they didn't like foreign-truck styling.

TABLE 2 WHICH AUTOMAKERS USE THE MOST AMERICAN AND CANADIAN PARTS?

US	Japanese	European
Chrysler Group 77.7%	Honda/Acura 59.1%	BMW 9.7%
Ford 78.0%	Nissan/Infiniti 45.5%	Porsche 1.9%
General Motors 77.7%	Toyota/Lexus 47.1%	Volkswagen/ Audi 4.4%

Pickup buyers "tend to be flag wavers, and they aren't convinced that Toyota is an American company," says Art Spinella of CNW Marketing Research. Consumers may be a little predisposed against Toyota, with 61% of those participating in CNW focus group panels in five cities saying they don't consider Toyota to be a US company despite efforts to tint its image more red, white, and blue. "It does bother me that they have a series of ads showing they are part of the heartland of America, yet their imports increased," says building contractor Jim Urbano, 53, of Woodbridge, Connecticut, who also researches car-buying options on Edmunds.com. He says he prefers American-made vehicles, because, "It troubled me to see so many US autoworkers being laid off."

Besides its flag-waving Tundra ads, Toyota has been running a public relations campaign in greater Washington, DC, to cultivate an apple pie, not sushi, image among policymakers. It helps that Toyota announced that a new assembly plant will be built in Tupelo, Mississippi, its fifth in the USA, with a goal of increasing production by 600,000 vehicles by 2010. Honda is also building a new assembly plant in Indiana. "We are committed to building where we sell," says Toyota spokeswoman Martha Voss. "No one is adding more capacity than we are." Voss cites demand for small cars last year as the reason Toyota's Japanese imports rose by so much. Altogether, Toyota imported close to half of all the vehicles it sold in the USA last year from Japan, including all of its gas-electric hybrids and most of its luxury Lexus division vehicles.

Honda's imports soared 30% last year, Mazda's rose 19%, and Suzuki's were up 23%, the Congressional Research Service finds in a new report. It says Japanese makers are simply trying to meet customer demand while running their US plants at full tilt. Japanese automakers encountered "capacity restraints in their existing US plants as a sharp increase in the price of gasoline sparked greater consumer demand for fuel-efficient, environmentally friendly vehicles," says William Duncan, general director of the Japan Automobile Manufacturers Association's office in Washington, DC.

All told, each of the Detroit automakers supports $2\frac{1}{2}$ times more US jobs than Toyota, says Jim Doyle, president of the Level Field Institute, a Washington research group. He acknowledges, however, that "people are trying to define what an American car is, and they are having a tough time."

The confusion pains Luehrmann, 48. Hoping to reach a decision soon about his next car, he's looking at everything. He's a believer in American cars, but, says with a tinge of regret, "I don't feel any great loyalty anymore."

Case Discussion Questions

1. What are the pros and cons of inbound foreign direct investment (FDI) in the US automobile industry? Discuss this question from the perspective of (1) the US economy, (2) US car consumers, and (3) US car companies.
2. Toyota tries very hard to advertise itself as an "American" company. Recently, it has been adding more production capacity than any automaker in the United States. Yet, it still confronts significant liability of foreignness. If you were (1) a Toyota spokesperson, (2) a GM spokesperson, (3) the governor of California, Kentucky, Mississippi, or Texas (where Toyota makes cars), or (4) a US car buyer who drives a Toyota or Lexus, do you think it is fair to label Toyota a "non-American" company?
3. A number of Japanese companies have increased US-bound FDI and exports (or imports from the US perspective) at the same time. What does that tell us in terms of the relationship between FDI and trade?
4. In this age of globalization, is it still relevant to identify an "American" car? Should patriotic American consumers continue to look for "American" cars?

INTEGRATIVE CASE 2.2

SOYBEANS IN CHINA

Liu Yi and Yang Wei
Xi'an Jiaotong University, China

Soybeans were first grown in China over 5,000 years ago, and today, China is the world's largest producer of non-genetically modified (non-GM) soybeans. China's northeast region (Manchuria), the Inner Mongolian Autonomous Region, and the Yellow River and Huaihai River valleys are some of the best locations in the world to grow soybeans.

In 1938, the soybean growing area in China reached 9.07 million hectares and the total output was 12.1 million tons, accounting for 93% of world output. Since then, other countries have caught up, with the United States, Brazil, and Argentina all progressing greatly. Soybean production is concentrated in Asia and the Americas, accounting for 96% of total area and 90% of total output. At present, the United States, Brazil, China, and Argentina are the world's top-four soybean producing countries (in that order), with North America accounting for 45% total area and 49% output, followed by Latin America and then Asia.

Soybeans in China: From Exporter to Importer

As economic growth increases, so does the demand of soybean production. Before 1995, China was a net exporting country of soybeans. However, since 1996, it has become a net importing country. From 2003 to 2005, the annual import amount was more than 20 million tons. In 2005, China produced 17.8 million tons, and it imported 26.6 million tons, which accounted for one-third of global trade. China thus became the largest soybean importing country. Experts estimate that by 2020, China will need to import 36 million tons of soybeans—in other words, about 80% of China's soybeans will be imported.

Unfortunately, this strong increase in demand brings no benefits to the soybean farmers in China. In

This case was written by Professor Liu Yi and Yang Wei (both at Xi'an Jiaotong University, Xi'an, China) for teaching purposes. The authors thank Professor Mike W. Peng and Erin Pleggenkuhle-Miles for editorial assistance on the English version. A Chinese version is available upon request from the authors. Please e-mail Professor Liu Yi at liuyi@mail.xjtu.edu.cn.

2005, the acreage of soybean planting in Heilongjiang Province (China's northernmost province located in the Northeast [Manchuria]) decreased from 108 million mu[1] to 82 million mu, a 24% decrease from the previous year. During the same period, the soybean acreage in the Inner Mongolian Autonomous Region also decreased by 17%, from 28 million mu in 2004 to 23 million mu in 2005. At the same time, soybean supplies stockpiled due to low prices. Many farmers who had planted and harvested soybeans with the expectation of increased income lost profits instead. For example, in Heilongjiang, which had the largest acreage and highest output of soybeans, the average sales price was only $0.271 per kilogram, which was lower than the farmers' cost. Consequently, farmers in Heilongjiang collectively lost $419.26 million, had incentive to reduce output, and the number of unemployed soybean farmers soared to approximately 1.2 million.

Subsidies and Imports

Soybean farmers suffer, but farmers who grow wheat and corn are "lucky." To encourage farmers' enthusiasm toward wheat and corn, the government offers subsidies every year. For example, in 2005, the Henan provincial government gave $1.23 for every mu of wheat grown, resulting in $3.627 million of total subsidies to wheat farmers in the province. In 2006, the Beijing municipality government adjusted its subsidies for corn growers upward to $1.88 per mu. One county in the Chongqing municipality announced that it would subsidize $0.64 per mu to wheat growers in 2007. At the national level, the central government uses strategic storage of wheat and corn to ensure that the sales prices farmers command are not lower than minimum prices. In contrast, subsidies for soybeans are negligible.

Falling soybean prices and the rise of imports also affect downstream soybean oil processing firms. No. 93 Seed-Oil Corporation was set up by one of the state-owned farms in Heilongjiang in China's Northeast (Manchuria) with the specific purpose of absorbing and processing soybeans produced by farms in the province. The annual soybean output of Heilongjiang Province is about six million tons, and the company purchases two million tons (one-third of the total output from that province). Yet, even such a firm crucial to soybean production and processing in the Northeast had to yield to the pressures from the rise of imports. In 2004, five of its soybean oil processing subsidiaries in the Northeast went bankrupt. As a result, two new subsidiaries were built in 2005: one in Tianjin and another in Dalian. However, both these new soybean oil processing subsidiaries exclusively used *imported* soybeans, which commanded more than half of all the soybeans processed by No. 93 Seed-Oil Corporation.

Aside from the lack of subsidies, one crucial reason that domestic soybeans are not as competitive as imports is because soybeans are primarily grown in China's Northeast, whereas soybean oil processing companies concentrate along the coast. If No. 93 Seed-Oil Corporation used locally grown soybeans, taking into account transportation, storage, and capital requirements, the cost of domestic soybeans is $20.54 more than imported soybeans per ton. Because of economies of scale, industrialized production, foreign government subsidies, and topographical and climatic conditions, the cost of imported soybeans is far lower than that of domestic soybeans. In 2003, the production cost of soybeans per ton in the United States was $168, in Brazil $119, and in China $192. Table 1 has a more detailed comparison of prices between domestic and imported soybeans in recent years.

More than half this huge difference in price can be attributed to agriculture subsidies. Among the 30 OECD members, the ratio of agriculture subsidies

TABLE 1 SOYBEAN PRODUCTION, CONSUMPTION, AND IMPORTS IN CHINA

Year	Planting area (million hectare)	Output (million tons)	Consumption (million tons)	Import (million tons)	Domestic Purchase Price ($/kg)	Import Price ($/kg)
1998	8.500	15.152	22.020	3.196	0.273	0.181
1999	7.962	14.245	26.290	4.317	0.297	0.183
2000	9.299	15.300	31.810	10.420	0.261	0.193
2001	8.700	15.000	30.700	13.940	0.266	0.242
2002	8.720	16.507	32.690	11.320	0.267	0.220
2003	9.133	16.400	37.900	20.740	0.346	0.312
2004	9.600	18.000	38.150	20.229	0.326	0.338
2005	9.103	17.800	40.000	26.590	0.331	0.278

Source: http://www.93.com.cn

(percentage of subsidies over total agricultural income) varies tremendously (see Table 2). In many competing countries, agricultural subsidy ratios are over 20%, but in China, the overall agricultural subsidy ratio is only 8.5%, as pledged by the government's commitment to the WTO in 2001.

The quality of soybeans depends on the quantity of oil that can be extracted from the bean. A 1% variance can lead to a profit difference of $1.9 million for every 100,000 tons of soybeans produced. At present, the ratio of oil extraction from domestic soybeans is only 16%–17%, which is 2%–3% lower than imported soybeans. Not surprisingly, when confronting higher prices and lower quality domestic soybeans, oil processing firms in China, such as No. 93 Seed-Oil Corporation, choose to import soybeans.

TABLE 2 SUBSIDY RATIO VARIANCES

Country	Subsidy Ratio[a]
Switzerland	71%
Iceland	69%
Norway	68%
South Korea	63%
Japan	56%
EU	33%
Canada	21%
United States	18%
China	8.5%

[a] Subsidy ratio = percentage of subsidies over total agricultural income.

International Competition

In the international agricultural market for basic foodstuffs such as soybeans, about 80% of the market share is dominated by four *Fortune* Global 500 companies: Archer Daniels Midland (ADM), Bunge, and Cargill of the United States and Louis Dreyfus of France—collectively known as "ABCD." Since 2005, these multinational firms have intensified their acquisitions in the Chinese soybean oil processing industry. In 2000, the number of Chinese soybean oil processing firms exceeded 1,000. In 2006, there were only 90, and 64 of them were wholly or partially controlled by foreign investors. These 64 foreign-invested firms command 85% of the production capability.

In 2005, Baogang Seed-Oil Corporation, once a leading seed oil manufacturing company in Jiangsu Province, declared bankruptcy as a result of capital shortage. The company could not pay its debt, so the Nantong municipality government authorized it to be leased by Cargill. However, employees clearly knew that the "lease" was just a transition form and that the company's eventual fate would be an acquisition by Cargill. In addition to acquisitions, foreign firms are shifting some attention to soybean research. For example, Kwok Brothers Corporation of Singapore held talks with the Academy of Agricultural Sciences in Heilongjiang Province, hoping that the academy would license the output of its research to the Singapore company. By popularizing the new breed of soybeans pioneered by the academy, the Singapore company hoped to purchase such soybeans directly from farmers when harvested and then to gradually monopolize the soybean industry of Heilongjiang Province (and perhaps even the whole country).

The Soybean Value Chain

An extensive industry value chain can be derived from soybeans. First, soybeans can be made into a variety of food products, including tofu and other bean curd-based products, soy milk, and soy-protein drinks. Second, oil can be pressed from soybeans. Finally, the soybean oil extraction process generates a byproduct, soybean residue, which contains abundant proteins. Soybean residue is a main ingredient in feed for livestock and poultry. Animal feed, in turn, connects soybeans with livestock and poultry production, another crucial component of the agricultural industry.

Nowadays, foreign direct investment (FDI) has mainly penetrated the soybean oil production process (other than some attempts to be involved in upstream production as noted earlier). What is the attitude of other players in the soybean value chain toward FDI? Consider Qinghe Technology, Ltd., a large animal-feed producer. Because soybean residue represents 60% of the raw materials used in production, the market price of soybeans directly affects the company's production cost. Obviously, the low price of imported soybeans makes Qinghe happy. Therefore, managers in the animal-feed industry are interested in more imported soybeans.

The Future of Soybeans in China

As the country that proudly pioneered soybean production, China has been producing non-GM soybeans for more than 5,000 years. Except for Qinghai Province, soybeans are grown everywhere in China, and the variety of soybean categories in China is the most complete in the world. We can say, without exaggeration, that China cultivates soybeans, and in turn, soybeans nurture our country. At present, soybeans are at a crucial historical crossroads between progress and decline. Fortunately, on October 1, 2006, the central government passed new regulations on the labeling standards of edible oil, requiring that "GM-based" or "non-GM-based" soybeans be clearly labeled for consumers. Can this "institutional change" in the rules of the game governing soybean oil labeling and consumption bring new hope to domestic soybeans?

Case Discussion Questions

1. Does China have an absolute or comparative advantage in soybean production?
2. In China, what is the current crisis of the soybean industry? Do you think the government should or should not intervene? If intervention is called for, what measures should be taken?
3. What difficulties do Chinese soybean farmers face? How can they compete with international producers?
4. Will the new labeling standards for non-GM-based soybeans used for edible oil production have any impact on domestic soybeans?
5. Facing the imminent wave of consolidations fueled by FDI, what can the soybean oil processing companies do to promote locally grown soybeans? Is this their responsibility?

[1] Mu is the standard Chinese unit for acreage. The conversion is: 1 mu = $^1/_{15}$ hectare = $^1/_6$ acre.

INTEGRATIVE CASE 2.3

AGRANA: FROM A LOCAL SUPPLIER TO A GLOBAL PLAYER

Erin Pleggenkuhle-Miles
University of Texas at Dallas

Although most readers of this book probably have never heard of AGRANA, virtually everybody has heard of Nestlé, Coca-Cola, Danone, PepsiCo, Archer Daniels Midland (ADM), Tyson Foods, and Hershey Foods. Headquartered and listed in Vienna, Austria, AGRANA is one of the leading suppliers to these multinational brands around the world. With revenues of US$2.6 billion and capitalization of $1.4 billion, AGRANA is the world's leader in fruit preparations and one of Central Europe's leading sugar and starch companies.

AGRANA was formed in 1988 as a holding company for three sugar factories and two starch factories in Austria. In the last two decades, it has become a global player with 52 production plants in 26 countries with three strategic pillars: sugar, starch, and fruit. AGRANA supplies most of its fruit preparations and fruit juice concentrates to the dairy, baked products, ice-cream, and soft-drink industries. In other words, you may not know AGRANA, but you have probably enjoyed many AGRANA products. How did AGRANA grow from a local supplier serving primarily the small Austrian market to a global player?

From Central and Eastern Europe to the World

In many ways, the growth of AGRANA mirrors the challenges associated with regional integration in Europe and then with global integration of multinational production in the last two decades. There are two components of European integration. First, EU integration accelerated throughout Western Europe in the 1990s. This means that firms such as AGRANA, based in a relatively smaller country, Austria (with a population of 8.2 million), needed to grow its economies of scale to fend off the larger rivals from other European countries blessed with larger home country markets and hence larger scale economies. Second, since 1989, Central and Eastern European (CEE)[1] countries, formerly off limits to Western European firms, have opened their markets. For Austrian firms such as AGRANA, the timing of CEE's arrival as potential investment sites was fortunate. Facing powerful rivals from larger Western European countries but being constrained by its smaller home market, AGRANA has aggressively expanded its foreign direct investment (FDI) throughout CEE. Most CEE countries have become EU members since then. As a result, CEE provides a much larger playground for AGRANA, allowing it to enhance its scale, scope, and thus competitiveness.

At the same time, multinational production by global giants such as Nestlé, ConAgra, Coca-Cola, PepsiCo, and Danone has been growing by leaps and bounds, thus reaching more parts of the world. Emerging as a strong player not only in Austria and CEE but also in the EU, AGRANA has further "chased" its corporate buyers by investing in and locating supplier operations around the world. This strategy has allowed AGRANA to better cater to the expanding needs of its corporate buyers.

This case was written by Erin Pleggenkuhle-Miles (University of Texas at Dallas) under the supervision of Professor Mike Peng.

Until 1918, Vienna had been capital of the Austro-Hungarian Empire, whose territory not only included today's Austria and Hungary but also numerous CEE regions. Although formal ties were lost (and in fact cut during the Cold War), informal ties through cultural, linguistic, and historical links had never disappeared. These ties have been reactivated since the end of the Cold War, thus fueling a rising interest among Austrian firms to enter CEE.

Overall, from an institution-based view, it seems natural that Austrian firms would be pushed by pressures arising from the EU integration and pulled by the attractiveness of CEE. However, among hundreds of Austrian firms that have invested in CEE, not all are successful and some have failed miserably. Then, how can AGRANA emerge as a winner from its forays into CEE? The answer boils down to AGRANA's firm-specific resources and capabilities, a topic that we turn to next.

Product-Related Diversification

AGRANA has long been associated with sugar and starch production in CEE. Until 2003, AGRANA's focus on the sugar and starch industries worked well. However, the reorganization of the European sugar market by the European Union (EU) Commission in recent years motivated AGRANA to look in new directions for future growth opportunities.[2] This new direction—fruit—has since become the third and largest division at AGRANA (see Table 1).

How to diversify? As a well-known processor in the sugar and starch industries, AGRANA wanted to capitalize on its core competence—the refining and processing of agricultural raw materials (sugar beets, cereals, and potatoes). To capitalize on its accumulated knowledge of the refinement process, AGRANA decided to diversify into the fruit-processing sector (Table 2 gives a brief description of each of the three current divisions). First, entry into the fruit sector ensured additional growth and complemented AGRANA's position in the starch sector. Since the Starch Division was already a supplier to the food and beverage industry, this allowed AGRANA to benefit from those relationships previously developed when it entered the fruit sector. Second, because the fruit sector is closely related to AGRANA's existing core sugar and starch businesses, AGRANA could employ the expertise and market knowledge it has accumulated over time, thus benefiting its new Fruit Division. AGRANA's core competence of the refinement process allowed it to diversify into this new segment smoothly.

AGRANA's CEO, Johann Marihart, believes that growth is an essential requirement for the manufacturing of high-grade products at competitive prices. Econo-

TABLE 1 AGRANA PLANT LOCATIONS

Segment	1988–1989	2002–2003	2006–2007
Sugar	4	15	10
Starch	2	5	4
Fruit	0	0	39
Total	**6**	**20**	**53**

Source: AGRANA company presentation, June 2007, http://www.agrana.com.

TABLE 2 AGRANA DIVISIONS

Sugar: AGRANA Sugar maintains nine sugar factories in five EU countries (Austria, Czech Republic, Slovakia, Hungary, and Romania) and is one of the leading sugar companies in Central Europe. The sugar AGRANA processes is sold to both consumers (via the food trade) and manufacturers in the food and beverage industries. Within this sector, AGRANA maintains customer loyalty by playing off its competitive strengths, which include high product quality, matching product to customer needs, customer service, and just-in-time logistics.

Starch: AGRANA operates four starch factories in three countries (Austria, Hungary, and Romania). The products are sold to the food and beverage, paper, textile, construction chemicals, pharmaceutical, and cosmetic industries. To maintain long-term client relationships, AGRANA works in close collaboration with its customers and develops "made-to-measure solutions" for its products. As a certified manufacturer of organic products, AGRANA is Europe's leading supplier of organic starch.

Fruit: This third segment was added to the core sugar and starch segments to ensure continued growth during a time when AGRANA reached the limits allowed by competition law in the sugar segment. The Fruit Division operates 39 production plants across every continent. Like the Starch Division, the Fruit Division does not make any consumer products, limiting itself to supplying manufacturers of brand-name food products. Its principal focus is on fruit preparations and the manufacturing of fruit juice concentrates. Fruit preparations are special customized products made from a combination of high-grade fruits and sold in liquid or lump form. Manufacturing is done in the immediate vicinity of AGRANA customers to ensure a fresh product. Fruit juice concentrates are used as the basis for fruit juice drinks and are supplied globally to fruit juice and beverage bottlers and fillers.

Source: AGRANA International website, http://www.agrana.com.

mies of scale have become a decisive factor for manufacturers in an increasingly competitive environment. In both the sugar and starch segments, AGRANA developed from a locally active company to one of Central Europe's major manufacturers in a very short timespan. Extensive restructuring in the Sugar and Starch divisions has allowed AGRANA to continue to operate efficiently and competitively in the European marketplace. Since its decision to diversify into the fruit-processing industry in 2003, Marihart has pursued a consistent acquisitions policy to exploit strategic opportunities in the fruit preparations and fruit juice concentrates sectors.

Acquisitions

How does AGRANA implement its expansion strategy? In one word, acquisitions. Between 1990 and 2001, AGRANA focused on dynamic expansion into CEE sugar and starch markets by expanding from five plants to 13 and almost tripling its capacity. As the Sugar Division reached a ceiling to its growth potential due to EU sugar reforms, AGRANA began searching for a new opportunity for growth. Diversifying into the fruit industry aligned with AGRANA's goal to be a leader in the industrial refinement of agricultural raw materials. AGRANA began its diversification into the fruit segment in 2003 with the acquisitions of Denmark's Vallø Saft and Austria's Steirerobst. By July 2006, AGRANA's Fruit Division had acquired three additional holding firms and was reorganized so all subsidiaries were operating under the AGRANA brand.

AGRANA diversified into the fruit segment in 2003 through the acquisition of five firms. With the acquisition of Denmark's Vallø Saft Group (fruit juice concentrates) in April 2003, AGRANA gained a presence in Denmark and Poland. The acquisition of an interest (33%) in Austria's Steirerobst (fruit preparations and fruit juice concentrates) in June 2003 gave AGRANA an increased presence in Austria, Hungary, and Poland, while also establishing a presence in Romania, Ukraine, and Russia. AGRANA fully acquired Steirerobst in February 2006. AGRANA first began acquiring France's Atys Group (fruit preparations) in July 2004 (25%). The acquisition of Atys Group was complete in December 2005 (100%) and was AGRANA's largest acquisition as Atys had 20 plants across every continent. In November 2004, AGRANA acquired Belgium's Dirafrost (fruit preparations) under the Atys Group and two months later (January 2005) acquired Germany's Wink Group (fruit juice concentrates) under the Vallø Saft Group. AGRANA's most recent expansion was a 50-50 joint venture under the Vallø Saft Group with Xianyang Andre Juice Co. Ltd. (fruit juice concentrates) in China. These acquisitions allowed AGRANA to quickly (within two years!) become a global player in the fruit segment. Table 3 provides an overview of AGRANA's present locations around the globe.

TABLE 3 AGRANA PLANT LOCATIONS AS OF 2007

	Sugar	Starch	Fruit	Ethanol
Argentina			1	
Australia			1	
Austria	2	2	3	1
Belgium			1	
Bosnia Herzegovina	1 (50%)*			
Brazil			1	
Bulgaria			1 (50%)	
China			2	
Czech Republic	2		1	
Denmark			1	
Fiji			1	
France			2	
Germany			1	
Hungary	2	1 (50%)	3	X**
Mexico			1	
Morocco			1	
Poland			5	
Romania	2	1	2	
Russia			1	
Serbia			1	
Slovakia	1			
South Africa			1	
South Korea			1	
Turkey			1	
Ukraine			2	
USA			4	
Total Plants	**10**	**4**	**39**	**1**

* AGRANA's holding is given in parentheses when not 100%.

** Hungrana, Hungary, plant also produces some ethanol.

Source: AGRANA 2006–2007 Annual Report.

The strategy of AGRANA is clearly laid out in its 2006–2007 annual report: "AGRANA intends to continue to strengthen its market position and profitability in its core business segments . . . and to achieve a sustainable increase in enterprise value. This will be done by concentrating on growth and efficiency, by means of investments and acquisitions that add value, with the help of systematic cost control and through sustainable enterprise management." AGRANA's growth strategy, consistent improvement in productivity, and value added approach have enabled it to provide continual increases in its enterprise value and dividend distributions to shareholders. The key to AGRANA's global presence in the fruit segment is not only its many acquisitions but its ability to quickly integrate those acquired into the group to realize synergistic effects.

In Table 4, the annual revenue is given for each sector. Although the Sugar Division was the leader in 2005–2006 (contributing 50% of the revenue), AGRANA's 2006–2007 annual report announced the Fruit Division as the new revenue leader (48%), surpassing the projected expectations. AGRANA attributes its growth in the fruit sector to increases in dietary awareness and per capita income, two trends that are assumed to continue to rise in the future.

Diversifying into Biofuel

In light of further EU sugar reforms, AGRANA has continually looked for new growth opportunities. On May 12, 2005, the supervisory board of AGRANA gave the go-ahead for the construction of an ethanol facility in Pichelsdorf, Austria. Construction is estimated to be completed in October 2007. AGRANA first began making alcohol in 2005 in addition to starch and isoglucose at its Hungrana, Hungary, plant in a preemptive move to accommodate forthcoming EU biofuel guidelines. This move into ethanol was seen as a logical step by CEO Marihart. Similar to its move into the fruit sector, the production of ethanol allows AGRANA to combine its extensive know-how of processing agricultural raw materials with its technological expertise and opens the door for further growth.

Case Discussion Questions

1. From an institution-based view, what opportunities and challenges have been brought by the integration of EU markets in both Western Europe and CEE?
2. From a resource-based view, what is behind AGRANA's impressive growth?
3. From an international perspective, what challenges do you foresee AGRANA facing as it continues its expansion into other regions such as East Asia?

Sources: Based on media publications and company documents. The following sources were particularly helpful: (1) AGRANA investor information provided by managing director, Christian Medved, to Professor Mike Peng at the Strategic Management Society Conference, Vienna, October 2006; (2) AGRANA Company Profile 2007; (3) AGRANA Annual Report 2005–2006 and 2006–2007, http://www.agrana.com (accessed August 1, 2007); (4) Sugar Traders Association, http://www.sugartraders.co.uk/ (accessed May 4, 2007); (5) N. Merret, 2007, Fruit segment drives Agrana growth, Food Navigator.com Europe, January 12; (6) N. Merret, 2006, Agrana looks east for competitive EU sugar markets, Confectionery News.com, November 29; (7) AGRANA Preliminary Results for Financial Year 2006–2007, press release, May 7, 2007; (8) C. Blume, N. Strang, & E. Farnstrand, *Sweet Fifteen: The Competition on the EU Sugar Markets*, Swedish Competition Authority Report, December 2002.

[1] Central and Eastern Europe (CEE) typically refers to (1) Central Europe (former Soviet bloc countries such as the Czech Republic, Hungary, Poland, and Romania and three Baltic states of the former Soviet Union) and (2) Eastern Europe (the European portion of the 12 post-Soviet republics such as Belarus, Russia, and Ukraine).

[2] One component of the Common Agricultural Policy (CAP) of the EU is the common organization of the markets in the sugar sector (CMO Sugar). CMO Sugar regulates both the total EU quantity of sugar production and the quantity of sugar production in each sugar-producing country. It also controls the range of sugar prices, essentially limiting competition by assigning quotas to incumbent firms, such as AGRANA. In 2006, the EU passed sugar reforms reducing subsidies and price regulation, influencing the competition in the marketplace. These reforms included a reduction of sugar production by six million tons over a four-year transition period. Sugar reforms such as these have forced some of AGRANA's competitors to close a number of sugar facilities. However, AGRANA's executives are optimistic about AGRANA's future due to its investments in the fruit and starch markets.

TABLE 4 AGRANA BY DIVISION

	Sugar	Starch	Fruit	Total
Staff	2723	776	4724	8223
2005–2006 Revenue*	1040.04** (50%)	314.01 (15%)	730.62 (35%)	2084.67
2006–2007 Revenue	1059.34 (41%)	292.27 (11%)	1234.71 (48%)	2586.33

* Reported in USD, May 17, 2007, exchange rate used in calculation (US $1 = €0.74).

** Figures are reported in millions.

Source: AGRANA 2006–2007 Annual Report.

INTEGRATIVE CASE 2.4

COMPETING IN THE CHINESE AUTOMOBILE INDUSTRY

Qingjiu (Tom) Tao
Lehigh University

The Red-hot Market

For automakers seeking relief from a global price war caused by overcapacity and recession, China is the only game in town. With just ten vehicles per 1,000 residents in China as of 2006 (as opposed to 940 in the United States and 584 in Western Europe), there seem to be plenty of growth opportunities. Not surprisingly, nearly every major auto company has jumped into China, quickly turning the country into a new battleground for dominance in this global industry. In addition, China has become a major auto parts supplier. Of the world's top-100 auto parts suppliers, 70% have a presence in China.

China vaulted past Japan in 2006 to become the world's number-two vehicle market (behind the United States). In 2006, car sales in China were up 37%, and sales of all vehicles including trucks and buses (7.2 million in total) were up 25%. Reports of record sales, new production, and new venture formations were numerous. After China's accession to the World Trade Organization (WTO) in 2001, the industry has been advancing by leaps and bounds. At the global level, China has moved to the third position in production behind the United States and Japan and is slated to produce 8.5 to 9 million vehicles in 2007 (see Table 1). Around 50% of the world's activity in terms of capacity expansion is seen in China.

Because the Chinese government does not approve wholly owned subsidiaries for foreign carmakers (even after the WTO accession), foreign firms interested in final-assembly operations have to set up joint ventures (JVs) or licensing deals with domestic players. By the mid-1990s, most major global auto firms had managed to enter the country through these means (Table 2). Among the European companies, Volkswagen (VW), one of the first entrants (discussed later), has dominated the passenger car market. In addition, Fiat-Iveco and Citroën are expanding.

Japanese and Korean automakers are relatively late entrants. In 2003, Toyota finally committed $1.3 billion to a 50/50 JV. Guangzhou Honda, Honda's JV, quadrupled its capacity by 2004. Formed in 2003, Nissan's new JV with Dongfeng, which is the same partner for the Citroën JV, is positioned to allow Nissan to make a full-fledged entry. Meanwhile, Korean auto players are also keen to participate in the China race, with Hyundai and Kia having commenced JV production recently.

American auto companies have also made significant inroads into China. General Motors (GM) has an important JV in Shanghai, whose cumulative investment by 2006 would be $5 billion. Although Ford does not have a high-profile JV as does GM, it nevertheless established crucial strategic linkages with several of China's second-tier automakers. DaimlerChrysler's Beijing Jeep venture, established since the early 1980s, has continued to maintain its presence.

The Evolution of Foreign Direct Investment (FDI) in the Automobile Industry

In the late 1970s, when Chinese leaders started to transform the planned economy to a market economy, they realized that China's roads were largely populated by inefficient, unattractive, and often

TABLE 1 AUTOMOBILE PRODUCTION VOLUME AND GROWTH RATE IN CHINA (1996–2006)

Year	1996	1997	1998	1999	2000	2001	2002	2003	2004	2005	2006
Volume (Million)	1.475	1.585	1.629	1.832	2.068	2.347	3.251	4.443	5.070	5.718	7.280
Growth rate	1.5%	7.5%	2.8%	12.5%	12.9%	13.2%	38.5%	37.7%	14.1%	12.8%	27.3%

Source: *Yearbook of China's Automobile Industry (1996–2006).*

TABLE 2 TIMING AND INITIAL INVESTMENT OF MAJOR CAR PRODUCERS

	Formation	Initial Investment ($ Million)	Foreign Equity	Chinese Partner	Foreign Partner
Beijing Jeep	1983	223.93	42.4%	Beijing Auto Works	Chrysler
Shanghai Volkswagen	1985	263.41	50%	SAIC	Volkswagen
Guangzhou Peugeot	1985	131.4	22%	Guangzhou Auto Group	Peugeot
FAW VW	1990	901.84	40%	First Auto Works	Volkswagen
Wuhan Shenlong Citroën	1992	505.22	30%	Second Auto Works	Citroën
Shanghai GM	1997	604.94	50%	SAIC	GM
Guangzhou Honda	1998	887.22	50%	Guangzhou Auto Group	Honda
Changan Ford	2001	100.00	50%	Changan Auto Motors	Ford
Beijing Hyundai	2002	338.55	50%	Beijing Auto Group	Hyundai
Tianjin Toyota	2003	1300.00	50%	First Auto Works	Toyota

unreliable vehicles that needed to be replaced. However, importing large quantities of vehicles would be a major drain on the limited hard currency reserves. China thus saw the need to modernize its automobile industry. Attracting FDI through JVs with foreign companies seemed ideal. However, unlike the new China at the dawn of the 21st century, which attracted automakers of every stripe, China in the late 1970s and early 1980s was not regarded as attractive by many global automakers. In the early 1980s, Toyota, for example, refused to establish JVs with Chinese firms even when invited by the Chinese authorities (Toyota chose to invest in a more promising market, the United States, in the 1980s). In the first wave, three JVs were established during 1983–1984 by VW, American Motors,[1] and Peugeot, in Shanghai, Beijing, and Guangzhou, respectively. These three JVs thus started the two decades of FDI in China's automobile industry.

There are two distinct phases of FDI activities in China's automobile industry. The first phase is from the early 1980s to the early 1990s, as exemplified by the three early JVs just mentioned. The second phase is from the mid-1990s to the present. Because of the reluctance of foreign car companies, only approximately 20 JVs were established by the end of 1989. FDI flows into this industry started to accelerate sharply from 1992. The accumulated number of foreign invested enterprises was 120 in 1993 and skyrocketed to 604 in 1998 with the cumulated investment reaching $20.9 billion.

The boom of the auto market, especially during the early 1990s, brought significant profits to early entrants such as Shanghai VW and Beijing Jeep. The bright prospect attracted more multinationals to invest. This new wave of investment had resulted in an overcapacity. Combined with the changing customer base from primarily selling to fleets (government agencies, state-owned enterprises, and taxi companies) to private buyers, the auto market has turned into a truly competitive arena. The WTO entry in 2001 has further intensified the competition as government regulations weaken. Given the government mandate for JV entries and the limited number of worthy local firms as partners, multinationals have to fight their way in to secure the last few available local partners. By the end of 2002, almost all major Chinese motor vehicle assemblers set up JVs with foreign firms. For numerous foreign automakers that entered China, the road to the Great Wall has been a bumpy and crowded one. Some firms lead, others struggle, and some had to drop out. The leading players are profiled next (see Figure 1).

Volkswagen

After long and difficult negotiations that began in 1978, VW in 1984 entered a 50/50 JV with the Shanghai Automotive Industrial Corporation (SAIC) to produce the Santana model using completely knocked down (CKD) kits. The Santana went on to distinguish itself as China's first mass-produced modern passenger car. As a result, VW managed to establish a solid market position. Four years later, VW built on its first-mover advantage and secured a second opening in the China market when the central authorities decided to establish two additional passenger car JVs. After competing successfully against GM, Ford, Nissan, Renault, Peugeot, and Citroën, VW was selected to set up a second JV with the First Auto Works (FAW) in Changchun in northeast China in 1988 for CKD assembly of the Audi 100 and the construction of a state-of-the-art auto plant to produce the VW Jetta in 1990.

Entering the China market in the early 1980s, VW took a proactive approach in spite of great potential risks. The German multinational not only committed enormous financial resources but also practiced a rather bold approach in its dealings in China. This involved a great deal of high-level political interaction with China's central and local government authorities for which the German government frequently lent its official support. Moreover, VW was willing to avail the Chinese partners a broad array of technical and financial resources from its worldwide operations. For example, in 1990, VW allowed FAW a 60% ownership stake in its JV while furnishing most of the manufacturing technology and equipment for its new FAW Volkswagen Jetta plant in Changchun. Moreover, VW has endeavored to raise the quality of locally produced components and parts. Undoubtedly, for the remainder of the 1980s and most of the 1990s, VW enjoyed significant first-mover advantages. With a market share (Shanghai VW and FAW VW combined) of more than 70% for passenger cars over a decade, VW, together with its Chinese partners, benefited considerably from the scarcity of high-quality passenger cars and the persistence of a sellers' market.

However, by the late 1990s, the market became a more competitive buyers' market. As the leading incumbent, VW has been facing vigorous challenges brought by its global rivals, which by the late 1990s made serious commitments to compete in China. Consequently, VW's passenger car market share in China dropped from over 70% in 1999 to 39% in 2004. In 2005, GM took the number-one position in China from VW. For VW, how to defend VW's market position thus is of paramount importance.

FIGURE 1 EVOLUTION OF RELATIVE MARKET SHARE AMONG MAJOR AUTO MANUFACTURERS IN CHINA

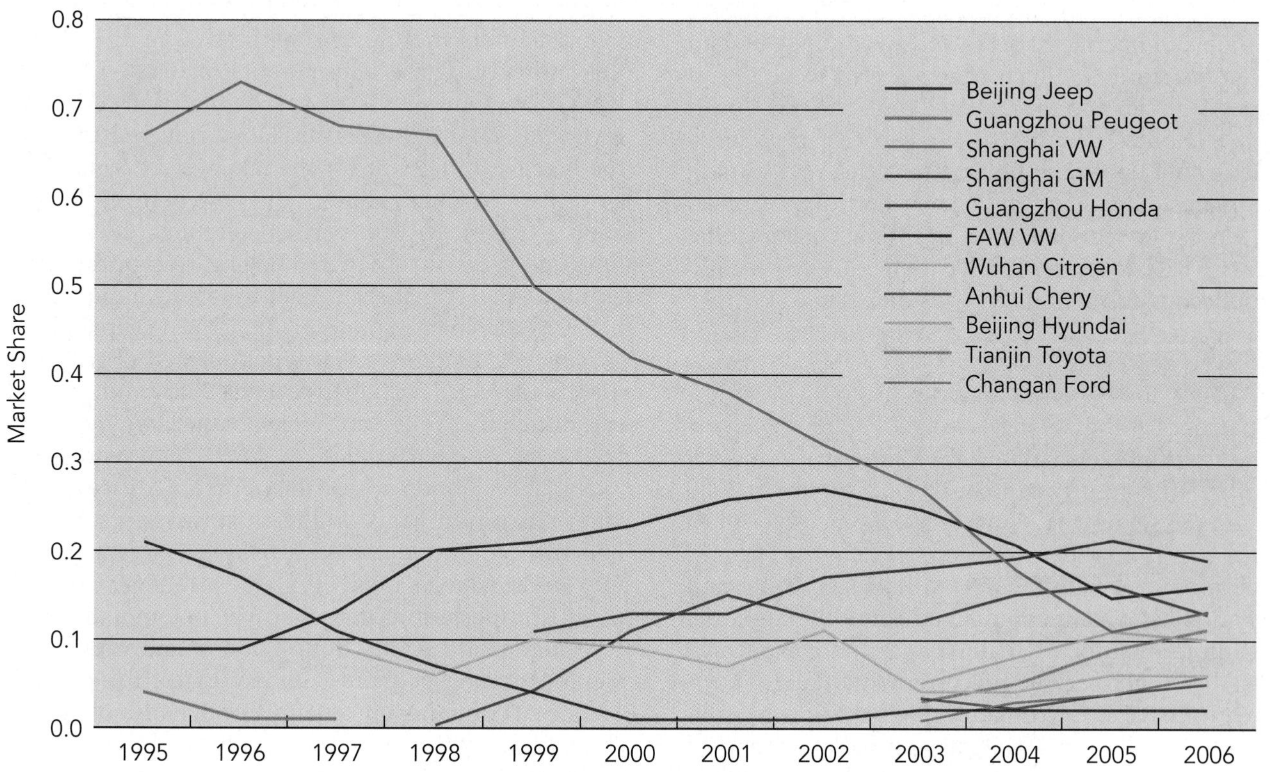

General Motors

In 1995, GM and SAIC, which was also VW's partner, signed a 50/50, $1.57 billion JV agreement—GM's first JV in China—to construct a green-field plant in Shanghai. The new plant was designed to produce 100,000 sedans per year, and it was decided to produce two Buick models modified for China. The plant was equipped with the latest automotive machinery and robotics and was furnished with process technology transferred from GM's worldwide operations. Initially, GM Shanghai attracted a barrage of criticisms about the huge size of its investment and the significant commitments to transfer technology and design capabilities to China. These criticisms notwithstanding, GM management reiterated on numerous occasions that China was expected to become the biggest automotive market in the world within two decades and that China represented the single most important emerging market for GM.

Since launching Buick in China in 1998, GM literally started from scratch. Unlike its burdens at home, GM is not saddled with billions in pensions and healthcare costs. Its costs are competitive with rivals, its reputation does not suffer, and it does not need to shell out $4,000 per vehicle in incentives to lure new buyers. Even moribund brands such as Buick are held in high esteem in China. Consequently, profits are attractive: The $437 million profits GM made in 2003 in China, selling just 386,000 cars, compares favorably with $811 million profits it made in North America on sales of 5.6 million autos. In 2004, GM had about 10,000 employees in China and operated six JVs and two wholly owned foreign enterprises (which were allowed to be set up more recently in nonfinal assembly operations). Boasting a combined manufacturing capacity of 530,000 vehicles sold under the Buick, Chevrolet, and Wuling nameplates, GM offers the widest portfolio of products among JV manufacturers in China. Seeing China sales rise 32% to nearly 880,000 vehicles, GM recently announced plans to build hybrids in China.

Peugeot

Together with VW and American Motors (the original partner for the Beijing Jeep JV), Peugeot was one of the first three entrants in the Chinese automobile industry. It started to search for JV partners in 1980 and in 1985 set up a JV, Guangzhou Peugeot, in south China. The JV mainly produced the Peugeot 504 and 505, both out-of-date models of the 1970s. Although many domestic users complained about the high fuel consumption, difficult maintenance, and expensive parts, the French car manufacturer netted huge short-term profits of approximately $480 million by selling a large amount of CKD kits and parts. Among its numerous problems, the JV also reportedly repatriated most of its profits and made relatively few changes to its 1970s era products, whereas VW in Shanghai reinvested profits and refined its production, introducing a new Santana 2000 model in the mid-1990s. Around 1991, Guangzhou Peugeot accounted for nearly a 16% share of the domestic passenger car market. But it began to go into the red in 1994 with its losses amounting to $349 million by 1997, forcing Peugeot to retreat from China. It sold its interest in the JV to Honda in 1998 (discussed later).

Although the sour memories of the disappointing performance of its previous JV were still there, Peugeot (now part of PSA Peugeot Citroën) decided to return to the battlefield in 2003. This time, the Paris-based carmaker seemed loaded with ambitious expectations to grab a slice of the country's increasingly appealing auto market sparked by the post-WTO boom. One of its latest moves is an agreement in 2003 under which PSA Peugeot Citroën would further its partnership with Hubei-based Dongfeng Motor, one of China's top-three automakers that originally signed up as a JV partner with Citroën to produce Peugeot vehicles in China. According to the new deal, a Peugeot production platform will be installed at the Wuhan plant of the JV, Dongfeng Citroën. Starting from 2004, the new facility has turned out car models tailored for domestic consumers, including the Peugeot 307, one of the most popular models in Europe since 2003.

Honda

Peugeot's 1998 pullout created a vacuum for foreign manufacturers that missed the first wave of FDI into this industry. These late entrants included Daimler-Benz, GM, Opel (a German subsidiary of GM), and Hyundai. Against these rivals, Honda entered and won the fierce bidding war for the takeover of an existing auto plant in Guangzhou of the now defunct Guangzhou Peugeot JV. The partner-selection process had followed a familiar pattern: Beijing was pitting several bidders against each other to extract a maximum of capital, technology, and manufacturing capabilities, as well as the motor vehicle types deemed appropriate for China. Honda pledged to invest $887 million and committed the American version of the Honda Accord, whose production started in 1999. Two years later, Guangzhou Honda added the popular Odyssey minivan to its product mix. In less than two years, Honda had turned around the loss-making Peugeot facility into one of China's most profitable passenger car JVs.

It is important to note that well before its JV with the Guangzhou Auto Group, Honda had captured a significant market share with exports of the popular Honda Accord and a most effective network of dealerships and service-and-repair facilities all over China. These measures helped Honda not only attain an excellent reputation and brand recognition but also strengthened Honda's bargaining power with the Chinese negotiators.

Emerging Domestic Players

The original thinking behind the open-door policy in China's auto market by forming JVs with multinationals was to access capital and technology and to develop Chinese domestic partners into self-sustaining independent players. However, this market-for-technology strategy failed to achieve its original goal. Cooperation with foreign car companies did bring in capital and technology but also led to overdependence on foreign technology and inadequate capacity (or even incentive) for independent innovations. By forming JVs with all the major domestic manufacturers and controlling brands, designs, and key technologies, multinational companies effectively eliminated the domestic competition for the most part of the last two decades. Only in the last few years did Chinese manufacturers start to design, produce, and market independent brands. In 2006, domestic companies controlled some 27% of the domestic market (mostly in entry- to midlevel segments). They have become masters at controlling costs and holding prices down, with a typical Chinese autoworker earning $1.95 an hour against a German counterpart making $49.50 an hour.

Ironically, the breakthrough came from newly established manufacturers without foreign partners. Government-owned Chery (Qirui) automobile, which started with $25 million using secondhand Ford production equipment, produced only 2,000 vehicles six years ago.[2] In 2006, it sold 305,236 cars, a surge of 118% over 2005, with plans to double that again by 2008. Privately owned Geely Group obtained its license in 2001 and began with crudely built copycat hatchbacks powered by Toyota-designed engines. With an initial output of 5,000 cars in 2001, Geely today produces 180,000 a year, with various models of sedans and sports cars, including those equipped with self-engineered six-cylinder engines.

Beyond the domestic market, Chery now exports cars to 29 countries. In 2006, the company produced 305,000 cars and exported 50,000. Chery cars are expected to hit the European market later in 2007. It signed a deal with DaimlerChrysler to produce Dodge brand vehicles for the US and Western Europe markets in the near future. Geely Group plans to buy a stake in the UK taxi maker Manganese Bronze Holdings and start producing London's black taxis in Shanghai. It also aims to sell its affordable small vehicles in the United States within several years.

In an effort to get closer to overseas markets, the Chinese players are starting to open overseas factories, too. Chery has assembly operations in Russia, Indonesia, Iran, and Egypt. The company now is planning to extend its reach in South America by opening an assembly plant to produce its Tigo brand sport utility vehicle in Uruguay. Brilliance produces vehicles in three overseas factories in North Korea, Egypt, and Vietnam, and Geely has a factory in Russia.

The Road Ahead

Looking ahead, the tariff and nontariff barriers will gradually be removed in post-WTO China. Increasing vehicle imports after trade liberalization will put pressure on the existing JVs that assemble cars in China and will force them to improve their global competitiveness. Otherwise, locally produced vehicles, even by JVs with multinational automakers, with little advantage with regard to models, prices, sales networks, components supply, and client services, will have a hard time surviving.

Despite China's low per capita income overall, there is a large, wealthy entrepreneurial class with significant purchasing power thanks to two decades of economic development. The average price of passenger cars sold in China in 2004 is about $20,000, whereas the average car price in countries such as Brazil, India, and Indonesia is $6,000 to $8,000. China, for example, is BMW's biggest market for the most expensive, imported 7-Series sedan, outstripping even the United States—even though Chinese buyers pay double what Americans pay and often in cash.

However, vehicle imports will not exceed 8% of the market in the foreseeable future. China's automobile industry, which has almost exclusively focused on the domestic market, still has much room for future development and will maintain an annual growth rate of 20% for the next few years. In the long run, as domestic growth inevitably slows down, there will be fiercer market competition and industry consolidation. The entry barrier will be higher and resource development will be more crucial to the sustainability of competitive advantage. To survive and maintain healthy and stable growth, China's JV and indigenous automobile companies, having established a solid presence domestically, must offer their own products that are competitive in the global market.

No doubt, the road to success in China's automobile industry is fraught with plenty of potholes. As latecomers, Hyundai, Toyota, Honda, and Nissan had fewer options in the hunt for appropriate JV partners and market positioning than did first-mover VW during the 1980s. All the way through the early 1990s, foreign auto companies were solicited to enter China and encountered very little domestic competition or challenge. This situation has changed significantly. Today, the industry is crowded with the world's top players vying for a share of this dynamic market.

Success in China may also significantly help contribute to the corporate bottom line for multinationals that often struggle elsewhere. For example, China, having surpassed the United States, is now Volkswagen's largest market outside Germany. One-quarter of Volkswagen's corporate-wide profits now come from China.

There are two competing scenarios confronting executives contemplating a move into China or expansion in China: (1) At the current rate of rapid foreign and domestic investment, the Chinese industry will rapidly develop overcapacity. Given the inevitable cooling down in the overall growth of the economy, a bloodbath propelled by self-inflicted wounds such as massive incentives looms large on the horizon. (2) Given the low penetration of cars among the vast Chinese population whose income is steadily on the rise, such a rising tide will be able to list all boats—or wheels—for a long while at least.

Case Discussion Questions

1. Why do all multinational automakers choose to use FDI to enter this industry? What are the drawbacks of using other entry modes such as exporting and licensing?
2. Some early entrants (such as Volkswagen) succeeded, but other early entrants (such as Peugeot) failed. Similarly, some late entrants (such as Honda) did well, but other late entrants (such as Ford) are struggling. From a resource-based standpoint, what role does entry timing play in determining performance?
3. From an institution-based view, explain the initial reluctance of most multinational automakers to enter China in the 1980s. Why happened that made them to change their mind more recently?
4. If you were a board member at one of the major multinational companies, you have just heard two presentations at a board meeting outlining the two contrasting scenarios for the outlook of the Chinese automobile industry in the last paragraph of the case. Would you vote yes or no for a $2 billion proposal to fund a major FDI project in China?

Sources: Based on (1) W. Arnold, 2003, The Japanese automobile industry in China, JPRI working paper no. 95; (2) *Economist*, 2003, Cars in China: The great leap forward, February 1: 53–54; (3) G. Edmondson, 2004, Volkswagen slips into reverse, *Business Week*, August 9: 40; (4) H. Huang, 1999, Policy reforms and foreign direct investment: The case of the Chinese automotive industry, *Fourin*, 9 (1): 3–66; (5) M. W. Peng, 2000, Controlling the foreign agent: How governments deal with multinationals in a transition economy, *Management International Review*, 40 (2): 141–166; (6) Q. Tao, 2004, The road to success: A resource-base view of joint venture evolution in China's auto industry, PhD dissertation, University of Pittsburgh; (7) D. Welch, 2004: GM: Gunning it in China, *Business Week*, June 21: 112–115; (8) G. Zeng & W. Peng, 2003, China's automobile industry boom, *Business Briefing: Global Automobile Manufacturing & Technology*, 20–22; (9) E. Thun, 2006. Changing lanes in China, *China Business Review* (online); (10) D. Roberts, 2007, China's auto industry takes on the world, *Business Week*, March 28 (online).

[1] American Motors was later acquired by Chrysler, which in turn was acquired by Daimler to form DaimlerChrysler. In 2007, DaimlerChrysler divested the Chrysler part. Between 1983 and 2005, the JV in China maintained its name as Beijing Jeep Corporation while experiencing ownership changes. In 2005, its name was changed to Beijing Benz-DaimlerChrysler Automotive Co., Ltd. At the time of this writing (late 2007), it is not clear how the JV's name may change further to reflect the divestiture of Chrysler.

[2] In May 2005, GM sued Chery in a Chinese court for counterfeiting the design of a vehicle developed by GM's South Korean subsidiary Daewoo. While this case created some media sensation, in November 2005, the parties, encouraged by the Chinese government, reached "an undisclosed settlement." The settlement terms were not revealed. It was not known whether Chery had to pay for its alleged infringement or whether it was barred from using the purportedly infringing design (http://iplaw.blogs.com/content/2005/11/gm_piracy_case_.html).

PART 3

Strategizing around the Globe

CHAPTERS

9 Growing and Internationalizing the Entrepreneurial Firm

10 Entering Foreign Markets

11 Managing Global Competitive Dynamics

12 Making Alliances and Acquisitions Work

13 Strategizing, Structuring, and Learning around the World

CHAPTER 9

Growing and Internationalizing the Entrepreneurial Firm

OPENING CASE

Sew What? A Global Brand

In 2002, frustrated after losing a major out-of-state contract for a car show, Megan Duckett wanted to expand her drapery business to clients outside California. She managed to transform her part-time business into an international operation.

Once the province of companies with extensive legal and sales departments, exporting is now growing among smaller companies. The costs of doing business abroad have fallen dramatically, making it feasible for even homegrown businesses to set up shops abroad. Twenty years ago, about 65,000 American companies with fewer than 500 employees exported, but in 2006, that number hit 226,000, according to the Small Business Exporters Association. Recent trade deals and dropping technology prices have made it easier for companies to export.

International trade wasn't on the horizon when Duckett got her start in 1991. She was sewing stage props at night while working at a concert production company by day. Her first job was sewing new linings into used coffins for a haunted-house set. "They want me to sew what?" Duckett recalls saying. And that gave birth to the name of her company, Sew What? Inc.

By 1997, she had moved out of her garage, and sales hit $25,000. The company grew quickly with jobs from musicians and clubs in southern California. But when she tried to win customers outside the area, most balked at working with such a small operation. The seamstress fashioned a crude website in 2002 and started studying web design. She hired someone for $1,500 to help the Sew What? site pop up in search engine results. Those moves helped push her sales past $1.27 million in 2003 from $895,000 in 2002.

At the same time, after visits to her native Australia, Duckett saw an opening for her business to sell US fabric down under. As a dual US and Australian citizen, she registered a parallel textile business, which she runs from California through another website. Boosted by that success, Duckett set up a Spanish-language section of her main website this year [*2006—editor*] after an employee from Mexico suggested it.

A personal connection abroad is the most common way business owners decide to move into international trade, says James Morrison, president of the Exporters Association. Immigrant entrepreneurs "feel like they can sell to other countries," he says. US free trade agreements and the growth of online storefronts have made it easier for small-business owners to become exporters.

Many small-business owners, like Duckett, can now install needed software on their own and at low cost. In 2005, she overhauled the Sew What? brand, sprucing up the website and logos to emphasize the company's music clients, such as Madonna and Sting.

Sew What? sales hit $2.4 million in 2005, and Duckett expects them to grow 65% in 2006 after the rebranding. Sharp-looking brochures and packaging are a key for US companies selling to other countries, which associate American goods with better quality.

With only 6% of her revenue from abroad, Duckett thinks that figure will climb. Just 18 months ago [*in early 2005—editor*], about 80% of her sales were in California. Since then, she has made 55 international transactions, and 66% of her clients are now from outside the state. Last year, she even got a call from Greek club owner Peter Young, who asked her to sew stage drapery for his all-night venue in Athens. She completed the whole deal without ever setting foot in Europe, finally sending a salesperson over to see the work in person and put in a bid for Young's next project.

Source: Adapted from R. Rayasam, 2006, Hemmed in no longer, this firm sews up a global brand, *US News & World Report*, July 31.

LEARNING OBJECTIVES

After studying this chapter, you should be able to

1. define entrepreneurship, entrepreneurs, and entrepreneurial firms
2. understand how institutions and resources affect entrepreneurship
3. identify the three characteristics of a growing entrepreneurial firm
4. differentiate international strategies that enter foreign markets and that stay in domestic markets
5. participate in three leading debates on growing and internationalizing the entrepreneurial firm
6. draw implications for action

small and medium-sized enterprises (SMEs)
Firms with fewer than 500 employees.

How do **small and medium-sized enterprises (SMEs)** such as Sew What? grow? SMEs are defined by the Organization for Economic Cooperation and Development (OECD), of which all developed economies such as the United States are members, as firms with fewer than 500 employees. How do they enter international markets? What are the challenges and constraints they face? This chapter deals with these important questions. This is different from many international business (IB) textbooks that typically focus on large firms. To the extent that *every* large firm today started small and that some (although not all) of today's SMEs may become tomorrow's multinational enterprises (MNEs), current and would-be managers will not gain a complete picture of the global business landscape if they focus only on large firms. In addition, since SMEs (in contrast to most large firms, which often have to downsize) generate most jobs now, most students will join SMEs. Some readers of this book will also start up SMEs, thus further necessitating our attention on these numerous "Davids" instead of on the smaller number of "Goliaths."

First, this chapter defines entrepreneurship. Next, we outline how our two leading perspectives, institution- and resource-based views, shed light on entrepreneurship. Then, we introduce characteristics of a growing entrepreneurial firm and multiple ways to internationalize. As before, debates and extensions follow.

LEARNING OBJECTIVE 1

define entrepreneurship, entrepreneurs, and entrepreneurial firms

ENTREPRENEURSHIP AND ENTREPRENEURIAL FIRMS

Although entrepreneurship is often associated with smaller and younger firms, there is no rule banning larger and older firms from being entrepreneurial. In fact, many large firms, which tend to be more established and bureaucratic, are often urged to become more entrepreneurial. Therefore, what exactly is entrepreneurship? Recent research suggests that firm size and age are *not* defining characteristics of entrepreneurship. Instead, **entrepreneurship** is defined as "the identification and exploitation of previously unexplored opportunities."[1] Specifically, it is concerned with "the sources of opportunities; the processes of discovery, evaluation, and exploitation of opportunities; and the set of individuals who discover, evaluate, and exploit them."[2] These individuals, thus, are **entrepreneurs**, who may be founders and owners of new businesses or managers of existing firms. Consequently, **international entrepreneurship** is defined as "a combination of innovative, proactive, and risk-seeking behavior that crosses national borders and is intended to create wealth in organizations."[3]

entrepreneurship
The identification and exploitation of previously unexplored opportunities.

entrepreneurs
Those who may be founders and owners of new businesses or managers of existing firms.

international entrepreneurship
A combination of innovative, proactive, and risk-seeking behavior that crosses national borders and is intended to create wealth in organizations.

Although our definitions suggest that SMEs are not the exclusive domain of entrepreneurship, the convention that many people often use is to associate entrepreneurship with SMEs, which, on average, may indeed be more entrepreneurial than large firms. To minimize confusion, in the remainder of this chapter, we follow such a convention, although it is not totally accurate. That is, while we acknowledge that some managers at large firms can be very entrepreneurial, we limit the use of the term *entrepreneurs* to owners, founders, and managers of SMEs. Further, we use the term *entrepreneurial firms* when referring to SMEs (fewer than 500 employees). We refer to firms with more than 500 employees as *large firms*.

SMEs are important. Worldwide, they account for over 95% of the number of firms, create approximately 50% of total value added, and generate 60% to 90%

of employment (depending on the country).[4] Obviously, there are both rewarding and punishing aspects of entrepreneurship.[5] Many entrepreneurs will try, and many SMEs will fail (for instance, approximately 60% of start-ups in the United States fail within six years).[6] Only a small number of entrepreneurs and SMEs will succeed.

HOW INSTITUTIONS AND RESOURCES AFFECT ENTREPRENEURSHIP

LEARNING OBJECTIVE 2

understand how institutions and resources affect entrepreneurship

Figure 9.1 shows that the institution- and resource-based views combine to shed interesting light on the entrepreneurship phenomenon.

Institutions and Entrepreneurship

First introduced in Chapters 2 and 3, both formal and informal institutional constraints, as rules of the game, affect entrepreneurship (see Figure 9.1). Although entrepreneurship is thriving around the globe in general, its development is unequal. Whether entrepreneurship is facilitated or retarded significantly depends on formal institutions governing how entrepreneurs start up new firms.[7] A recent World Bank study reports some striking differences in government regulations concerning start-ups such as registration, licensing, incorporation, taxation, and inspection (Table 9.1).[8] In general, governments in developed economies impose fewer procedures (as low as two procedures and two days in Canada and Australia) and a lower total cost (less than 2% of per capita GDP in New Zealand, Denmark, Ireland, and the United States). On the other hand, entrepreneurs confront harsher regulatory burdens in poor countries. As a class of its own, the Dominican Republic requires 21 procedures and a total cost of 4.63 times of per capita GDP. Other countries requiring a total cost more than their per capita GDP are Hungary, Nigeria, Egypt, Indonesia, Vietnam, and Bolivia. Madagascar leads the world in requiring entrepreneurs to spend 152 days to obtain legal clearance to start a new firm. Overall, it is not surprising that the more entrepreneur friendly these formal institutional requirements are, the more flourishing entrepreneurship is, and the more developed the economies will become—and vice versa.

FIGURE 9.1 INSTITUTIONS, RESOURCES, AND ENTREPRENEURSHIP

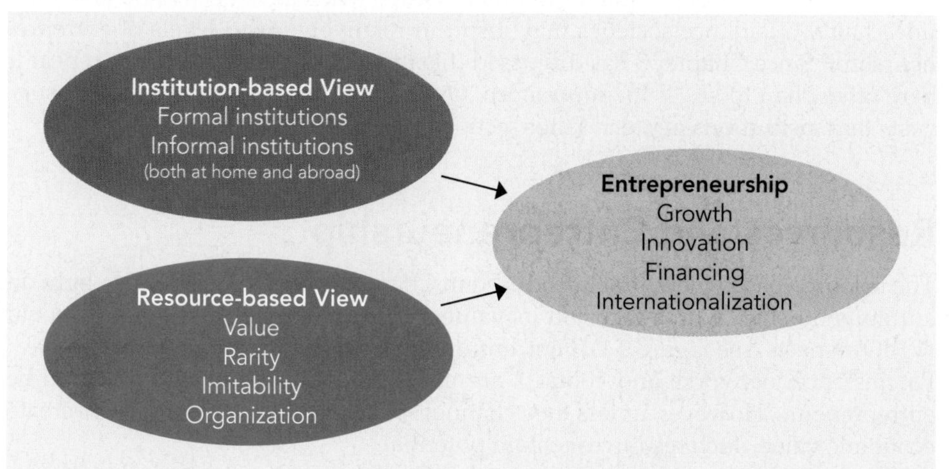

TABLE 9.1 THE COSTS OF STARTING UP A NEW FIRM IN 42 COUNTRIES

Country	Number of procedures	Time (days)	Direct costs (% of per capita GDP)	Time + direct costs (% of per capita GDP)
Canada	2	2	1.45	2.25
Australia	2	2	2.25	3.05
New Zealand	3	3	0.53	1.73
Denmark	3	3	1.00	1.12
Ireland	3	16	1.16	1.80
United States	4	4	0.50	1.69
Norway	4	18	4.72	11.92
United Kingdom	5	4	1.43	3.03
Hong Kong	5	15	3.33	9.33
Mongolia	5	22	3.31	12.11
Finland	5	24	1.16	10.76
Israel	5	32	21.32	34.12
Sweden	6	13	2.56	7.76
Zambia	6	29	60.49	72.09
Switzerland	7	16	17.24	23.64
Singapore	7	22	11.91	20.71
Latvia	7	23	42.34	51.54
Netherlands	8	31	18.41	30.81
Taiwan	8	37	6.60	21.40
Hungary	8	39	85.87	101.47
South Africa	9	26	8.44	18.84
Thailand	9	35	6.39	20.39
Nigeria	9	36	257.00	271.40

In addition to formal institutions, informal institutions such as cultural values and norms also affect entrepreneurship. For example, because entrepreneurs necessarily take more risks, individualistic and low uncertainty-avoidance societies tend to foster relatively more entrepreneurship, whereas collectivistic and high uncertainty-avoidance societies may result in relatively lower levels of entrepreneurship.[9] Since Chapter 3 has discussed this issue at length, we will not repeat it here other than to stress its importance. Overall, the institution-based view suggests that institutions matter.[10] Later sections will discuss how they matter.

Resources and Entrepreneurship

The resource-based view, first introduced in Chapter 4, sheds considerable light on entrepreneurship, with a focus on its value, rarity, imitability, and organizational (VRIO) aspects (see Figure 9.1). First, entrepreneurial resources must create *value*.[11] For instance, networks and contacts are great potential resources for would-be entrepreneurs. However, unless they channel such networks and contacts to create economic value, such resources remain potential.

Second, resources must be *rare*. As the cliché goes, "If everybody has it, you can't make money from it." The best-performing entrepreneurs tend to have the

Table 9.1, *continued*

Country	Number of procedures	Time (days)	Direct costs (% of per capita GDP)	Time + direct costs (% of per capita GDP)
Chile	10	28	13.08	24.28
Germany	10	42	15.69	32.49
Czech Republic	10	65	8.22	34.22
India	10	77	57.76	88.56
Japan	11	26	11.61	22.01
Egypt	11	51	96.59	116.99
Poland	11	58	25.46	48.66
Spain	11	82	17.30	50.10
Indonesia	11	128	53.79	104.99
China	12	92	14.17	50.97
South Korea	13	27	16.27	27.07
Brazil	15	63	20.14	45.34
Mexico	15	67	56.64	83.44
Italy	16	62	20.02	44.82
Vietnam	16	112	133.77	178.57
Madagascar	17	152	42.63	103.43
Russia	20	57	19.79	42.59
Bolivia	20	88	265.58	300.78
Dominican Republic	21	80	463.09	495.09
Global average	10.48	47.49	47.08	65.98

Source: Adapted from S. Djankov, R. La Porta, F. Lopez-de-Silanes, & A. Shleifer, 2002, The regulation of entry (pp. 18–20), *Quarterly Journal of Economics*, 67: 1–37. Drawing on a major World Bank study, the table is based on the ascending order of (1) the total number of procedures domestic entrepreneurs must fulfill, (2) the number of days to obtain legal status to start up a firm, and (3) the direct costs, as a percentage of per capita GDP, to do so. The measure of time + direct costs captures the monetized value of entrepreneurs' time in addition to direct costs. Global average is based on the full sample of 85 countries, and this table reports on 42 of them. Additional and updated data can be found at the World Bank's Doing Business website, http://www.doingbusiness.org.

rarest knowledge and deepest insights about business opportunities.[12] While there are numerous math geniuses out there, the ability to turn a passion for math into profit is rare. Google's two founders are such rare geniuses.

Third, resources must be *inimitable*. For instance, Amazon's success has prompted a number of online bookstores to directly imitate it. Amazon rapidly built the world's largest book warehouses, which ironically are bricks and mortar. It is Amazon's "best-in-the-breed" physical inventories—not its online presence—that are more challenging to imitate.

Fourth, entrepreneurial resources must be *organizationally* embedded. For example, individual mercenaries have always existed since the dawn of warfare, but only in modern times have private military companies (PMCs) become a global industry (see Integrative Case 1.4). Entrepreneurial PMCs thrive on their organizational capabilities to provide military and security services in dangerous conflict and postconflict environments, whereas individuals would shy away and, in some cases (as in Iraq), even national militaries would withdraw.

In sum, the resource-based view suggests that firm-specific (and in many cases entrepreneur-specific) resources and capabilities largely determine entrepreneurial success and failure (see In Focus 9.1 for an example in Africa). Overall, institution- and resource-based views combine to shed light on entrepreneurial strategies (see Figure 9.1).

IN FOCUS 9.1 Beefing Up Management Capabilities in Africa

According to the World Bank, over 40% of Africa's economy is informal—the highest proportion in the world. There are very few small and medium-sized enterprises (SMEs) to bridge the enormous gap between informal traders and large companies. A leading cause for such a gap is the lack of management capabilities that prevents entrepreneurs in Africa from growing their businesses into viable SMEs. Fortunately, help is on its way. The International Finance Corporation (the World Bank's private-sector arm), the UN Development Program, and the African Development Bank have jointly sponsored the founding of the nonprofit African Management Services Company (AMSCO), based in Johannesburg, South Africa. Its mission is to help African SMEs become competitive.

AMSCO selects struggling firms that have strong potential, where experienced managers can make a difference. Approximately 225 managers from all over the world, hired by AMSCO, are now working in 120 client firms in 21 countries. It is not easy work. At the Hotel Nord Sud in Mali, the first manager gave up after a few months. However, the second turned it around. Global Forest Products, a South African company, was losing money when it approached AMSCO. Outside experts introduced modern techniques and developed new products. Today, it is profitable. More important, long after the departure of AMSCO's management experts, their skills stay.

Sources: Based on (1) *Economist*, 2005, Different skills required, July 2: 61; (2) *Economist*, 2006, From online to helpline, August 5: 58.

LEARNING OBJECTIVE 3

identify the three characteristics of a growing entrepreneurial firm

GROWING THE ENTREPRENEURIAL FIRM

This section discusses three major characteristics associated with a growing entrepreneurial firm: (1) growth, (2) innovation, and (3) financing. A fourth characteristic, internationalization, will be highlighted in the next section. Before proceeding, it is important to note that these strategies are not mutually exclusive and that they are often pursued in combination by entrepreneurial firms.[13]

Growth

To many individuals, it is the excitement associated with a growing firm that has attracted them to become entrepreneurs.[14] Recall from the resource-based view that a firm can be conceptualized as consisting of a bundle of resources and capabilities. The growth of an entrepreneurial firm can thus be viewed as an attempt to more fully utilize currently underutilized resources and capabilities.[15] What are these resources and capabilities? For start-ups, they are primarily entrepreneurial vision, drive, and leadership, which compensate for these firms' shortage of tangible resources (such as financial capital and formal organizational structure).[16]

A hallmark of entrepreneurial growth is a dynamic, flexible, guerrilla strategy. As underdogs, entrepreneurial SMEs cannot compete against their larger and more established rivals head on. "Going for the crumbs" (at least initially), smaller firms often engage in indirect and subtle attacks that large rivals may not immediately recognize as competitive challenges.[17] In the lucrative market of US defense contracts, large firms such as Boeing and Raytheon like "doing the impossible," but a smaller firm, Alliant Techsystems (known for its stock symbol ATK), focuses on the possible and the cheap—upgrading missiles and making mortar munitions more accurate based on proven, off-the-shelf solutions. As a result, ATK is able to consistently beat a number of top guns to supply the US military, which has become increasingly concerned about cost overruns.[18]

Innovation

Innovation is at the heart of entrepreneurship.[19] There is evidence showing a positive relationship between a high degree of innovation and superior profitability.[20] Innovation allows for a more sustainable basis for competitive advantage. For example, Illycaffé is reportedly responsible for three of the seven major innovations in coffee making in the past century (see In Focus 9.2). Entrepreneurial firms that come up with "disruptive technologies" may define the rules of competition.[21] Google serves as a recent case in point.

Entrepreneurial firms are uniquely ready for innovation. Owners, managers, and employees at entrepreneurial firms tend to be more innovative and take more risks than those at large firms.[22] In fact, a key reason many SMEs are founded is because former employees of large firms are frustrated by their inability to translate innovative ideas into realities at large firms.[23] Intel, for instance, was founded by three former employees—one of them was Andy Grove—who quit Fairchild Semiconductor in 1968. Innovators at large firms also have limited ability to personally profit from innovations, whose property rights usually belong to the corporation. In contrast, innovators at entrepreneurial firms are better able to reap the financial gains associated with innovations, thus fueling their motivation to charge ahead.

Financing

All start-ups need to raise capital. Where are the sources? Here is a quiz (also a joke): Of the "4F" sources of entrepreneurial financing, the first three Fs are founders, family, and friends, but what is the other F source? The answer is . . . *fools* (!). While this is a joke, it strikes a chord in the entrepreneurial world: Given the well-known failure risks of start-ups (a *majority* of them will fail), why would anybody other than a fool be willing to invest in start-ups? In reality, most outside strategic investors, who can be angels (wealthy individual investors), venture capitalists, banks, foreign entrants, and government agencies, are not fools. They often demand some assurance (such as collateral), examine business plans, and require a strong management team.[24]

Around the world, the extent to which entrepreneurs draw on resources from outside investors (such as venture capitalists) vis-à-vis family and friends is different. Figure 9.2 shows that Sweden, South Africa, Belgium, and the United States lead the world in venture capital (VC) investment as a percentage of GDP. In contrast, Greece and China have the lowest level of VC investment. Figure 9.3 illustrates a different picture: informal investment (mostly by family and friends) as a percentage of GDP. In this case, China leads the world with the highest level of informal investment as a percentage of GDP. In comparison, Brazil and Hungary have the lowest level of informal investment. Although there is a lot of "noise"

IN FOCUS 9.2 Illycaffé: Perfection from Bean to Cup

"Starbucks has done an excellent job of raising consumer interest in coffee, especially in premium coffees," said 42-year-old Andrea Illy, owner of Illycaffé, headquartered in Trieste, Italy. Illycaffé's revenues of €227 million ($282 million) in 2005 are dwarfed by Starbucks' $7.8 billion. Illycaffé has opened Espressamente Illy cafés in over 120 cities in 18 countries, from New York to Palermo. However, these primarily serve as advertisements for the brand. Illycaffé's main business is coffee roasting and distribution to individuals and caterers through upscale retailers.

Unapologetically, Illy argues that his coffee represents the authentic flavor of Italian coffee. Founded by Andrea's grandfather, Illycaffé dates back to 1933, whereas Starbucks is just a recent imitator. Illy is obsessed with technical innovations. Illycaffé claims to be responsible for three of the seven main innovations in modern coffee-making, as a traditional Italian craft has become an industrial one. The first two are the standardization of espresso-making and development of the paper rod for espresso machines. Illycaffé is now implementing its third major innovation: a two-stage espresso-making process involving "hyper-fusion" (intensifying the drink's aroma) and "emulsification" (making it smoother). What is Illy's goal? Perfection from bean to cup.

© Kevin Clifford Photography / Alamy

Sources: Based on (1) *Economist*, 2006, Head barista, September 30: 76; (2) http://www.illy.com.

FIGURE 9.2 VENTURE CAPITAL INVESTMENT AS A PERCENTAGE OF GDP

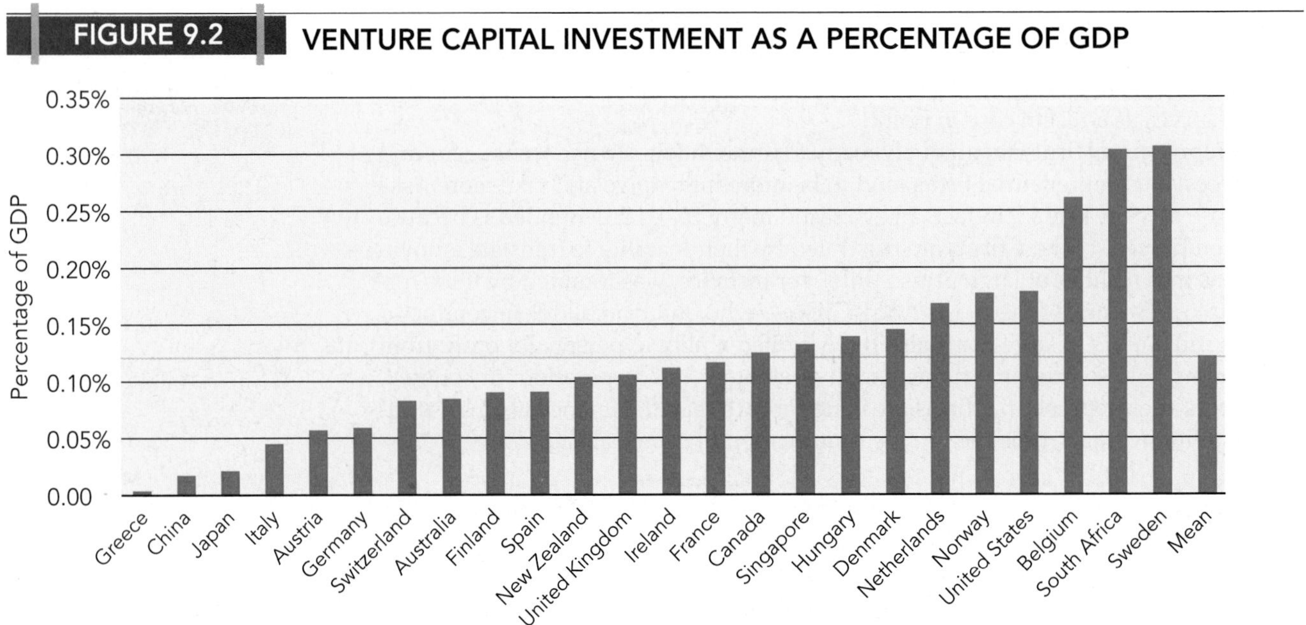

Source: Adapted from M. Minniti, W. Bygrave, & E. Autio, 2006, *Global Entrepreneurship Monitor 2006 Executive Report* (p. 49), Wellesley, MA: Babson College/GEM.

FIGURE 9.3 INFORMAL INVESTMENT AS A PERCENTAGE OF GDP

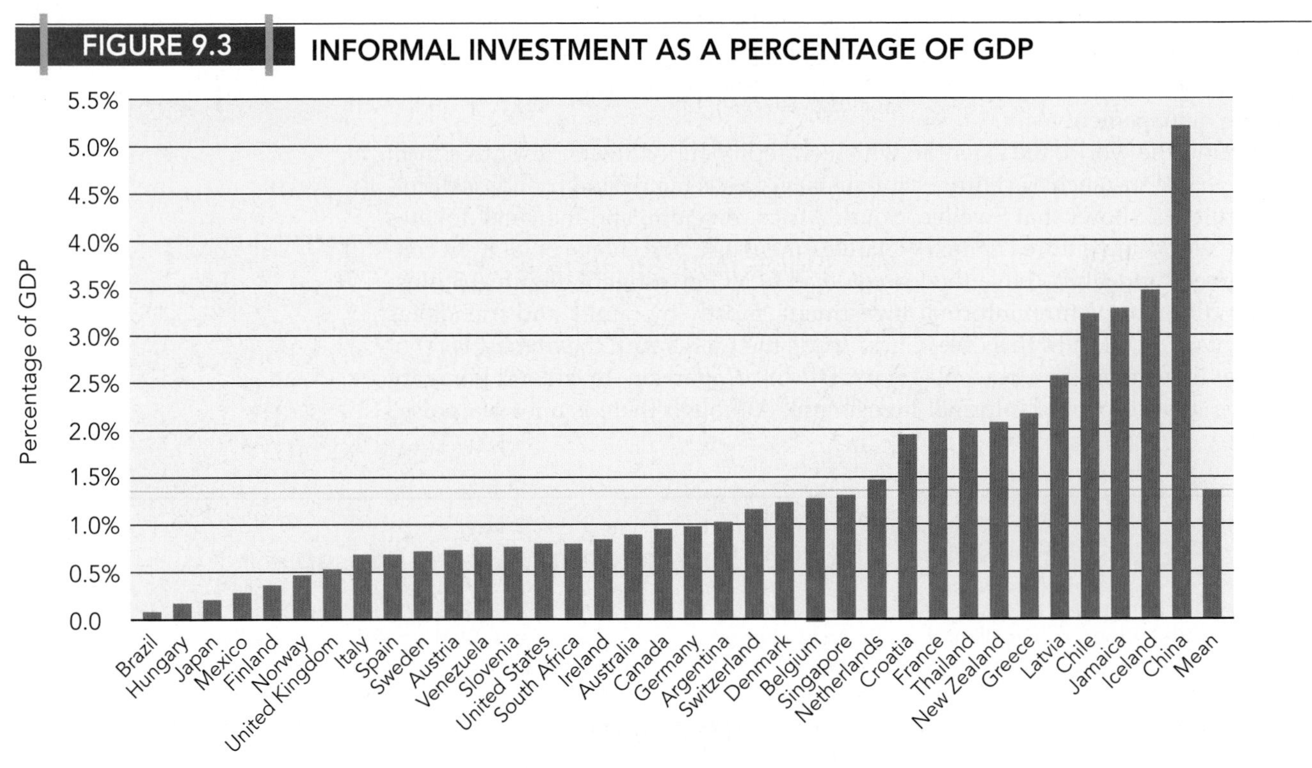

Source: Adapted from M. Minniti, W. Bygrave, & E. Autio, 2006, *Global Entrepreneurship Monitor 2006 Executive Report* (p. 53), Wellesley, MA: Babson College/GEM.

in such worldwide data, the case of China (second lowest in VC investment and highest in informal investment) is easy to explain: China's lack of formal market-supporting institutions such as venture capitalists and credit-reporting agencies, during a time of entrepreneurial boom in the country, necessitates a high level of informal investment for Chinese entrepreneurs and new ventures.[25]

In response to the lack of financing for entrepreneurial opportunities in many developing countries, a highly innovative solution—namely, **microfinance**—has emerged since the 1970s. Lending institutions in microfinance started by providing tiny loans ($50–$300) to entrepreneurs in countries such as Bangladesh and India that would lift them out of poverty. Shown in In Focus 9.3 and the Closing Case, microfinance has now become a global movement.

microfinance
Lending institutions provide tiny loans ($50–$300) to entrepreneurs in developing countries that would lift them out of poverty.

INTERNATIONALIZING THE ENTREPRENEURIAL FIRM

LEARNING OBJECTIVE 4

differentiate international strategies that enter foreign markets and that stay in domestic markets

There is a myth that only large MNEs do business abroad and that SMEs mostly operate domestically. This myth, based on historical stereotypes, is being increasingly challenged, as more and more SMEs, such as Sew What? (Opening Case), become internationalized. Further, some start-ups attempt to do business abroad from inception. These are often called **born global** firms (or international new ventures).[26] This section examines how entrepreneurial firms internationalize.

born global
Start-up companies that attempt to do business abroad from inception.

Transaction Costs and Entrepreneurial Opportunities

Compared with domestic transaction costs (the costs of doing business), international transaction costs are qualitatively higher.[27] On the one hand, there are numerous innocent differences in formal institutions and informal norms (see Chapters 2 and 3). On the other hand, there may be a high level of deliberate opportunism, which is hard to detect and remedy. For example, when an unknown Greek importer places an order with a US exporter, the US exporter may not be able to

IN FOCUS 9.3 ETHICAL DILEMMA: Microfinance, Macro Success

Teach a man to fish, and he'll eat for a lifetime. However, here is a catch: He has to afford a fishing rod. Sadly, in many poor developing countries, numerous eager "fishermen"—also known as entrepreneurs—cannot even afford a fishing rod. In 1976, Muhammad Yunus, a young economics professor in Bangladesh, loaned $27 out of his own pocket to a group of poor craftsmen and helped found a village-based enterprise called the Grameen Project. It never occurred to Yunus that he would inspire a global movement for entrepreneurial financing and would receive the Nobel peace prize 30 years later—in 2006, together with the Grameen Bank that he founded.

Microfinance is also known as "microloans," featuring a tiny sum of $50 to $300. In Bangladesh, where 2004 per capita GDP was $440, such loans are not small. Used to buy everything ranging from milk cows to mobile phones (to be used as pay phones by the entire village), these loans can make a huge difference. A powerful innovation is to overcome the obstacles of lending to the poor, who tend to have neither assets (necessary for collateral) nor credit history. A simple solution is to lend to women because women, on average, are more likely to use their earnings to support family needs than men, who may be more likely to indulge in drinking, gambling, or drugs. A more sophisticated solution is to organize the women in a village into a collective and lend money to the collective but not to individuals. Overall, 84% of microloan recipients are women and repayment rates are 95% to 98%. While interest rates average a hefty 35%, they are far below rates charged by local loan sharks. By 2006, there were 7,000 microfinance institutions, serving 113 million borrowers around the world.

However, the future of microfinance, as it grows from periphery to mainstream, is not all rosy. From an ethical standpoint, it is questionable whether clearly discriminatory lending practices against men can be sustained in the long run. In this age of gender equality, aspiring male entrepreneurs in the developing world probably do not appreciate being automatically discriminated against.

Source: Based on (1) *Business Week*, 2005, Microcredit missionary, December 26: 20; (2) *Business Week*, 2006, Taking tiny loans to the next level, November 27: 76–80.

ascertain that the Greek side will deliver payment upon receiving the goods. In comparison, most US firms are comfortable allowing domestic customers to pay within 30 or 60 days after receiving the goods. However, if foreign payment does not arrive on time (after 30, 60, or even more days), it is difficult to assess whether firms in Greece simply do not have the norm of punctual payment or if that particular importer is being deliberately opportunistic. If the latter is indeed the case, suing the Greek importer in a Greek court where Greek is the official language may be so costly that it is not an option for small US exporters.

As a result, many small firms (such as Sew What?) may simply say "Forget it!" when receiving an unsolicited order from abroad (such as the order from Greece). Conceptually, this is an example of transaction costs being so high that many firms may choose not to pursue international opportunities. Therefore, there are always entrepreneurial opportunities that can innovatively lower some of these transaction costs by bringing distant groups of people, firms, and countries together. Shown in Table 9.2, while entrepreneurial firms can internationalize by entering foreign markets, they can also add an international dimension without having to go abroad. Next, we discuss how they undertake some of these strategies.

International Strategies for Entering Foreign Markets

direct exports
The sale of products made by firms in their home country to customers in other countries.

sporadic (or passive) exporting
The sale of products prompted by unsolicited inquiries from abroad.

For SMEs, there are three broad modes for entering foreign markets: (1) direct exports, (2) licensing/franchising, and (3) foreign direct investment (FDI) (see Chapter 10 for more details). First, **direct exports** entail the sale of products made by entrepreneurial firms (such as Sew What? in Opening Case) in their home country to customers in other countries. This strategy is attractive because entrepreneurial firms are able to reach foreign customers directly. When domestic markets experience some downturns, sales abroad may compensate for such drops.[28] However, a major drawback is that SMEs may not have enough resources to turn overseas opportunities into profits. The way Sew What? reaches foreign customers is called **sporadic** (or **passive**) **exporting**, prompted by unsolicited inquiries, such as the order from Greece. To actively and systematically pursue export customers would be a different ball game.

Export transactions are complicated. A particular concern is how to overcome the lack of trust between exporters and importers when receiving an export order from unknown importers abroad. For example, in Figure 9.4, the US exporter does

TABLE 9.2 INTERNATIONALIZATION STRATEGIES FOR ENTREPRENEURIAL FIRMS

Entering foreign markets	Staying in domestic markets
• Direct exports • Franchising/licensing • Foreign direct investment (through strategic alliances, green-field wholly owned subsidiaries, and/or foreign acquisitions)	• Indirect exports (through export intermediaries) • Supplier of foreign firms • Franchisee/licensee of foreign brands • Alliance partner of foreign direct investors • Harvest and exit (through sell-off to and acquisition by foreign entrants)

FIGURE 9.4 AN EXPORT/IMPORT TRANSACTION

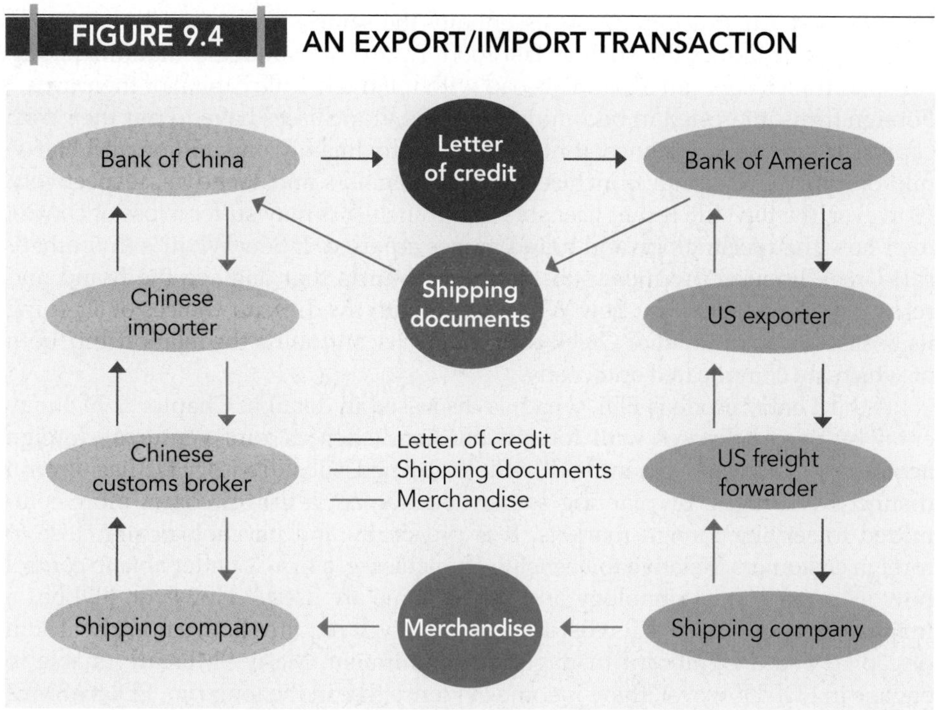

not trust the Chinese importer, but banks on both sides can facilitate this transaction by a **letter of credit (L/C)**, which is a financial contract that states that the importer's bank (Bank of China in this case) will pay a specific sum of money to the exporter upon delivery of the merchandise. It has several steps:

letter of credit (L/C)
A financial contract that states that the importer's bank will pay a specific sum of money to the exporter upon delivery of the merchandise.

- While the unknown Chinese importer's assurance that it will promptly pay for the merchandise may be questioned by the US exporter, a letter of credit from the highly reputable Bank of China will assure the US exporter that the importer has good creditworthiness and has sufficient funds for this transaction. If the US exporter is not sure about whether Bank of China is a credible bank, it can consult its own bank, Bank of America, which will confirm that a letter of credit from Bank of China is "as good as gold."
- With this assurance through the letter of credit, the US exporter can release the merchandise, which goes through a US freight forwarder, then a shipping company, and then a Chinese customs broker. Finally, the goods will reach the Chinese importer.
- Once the US exporter has shipped the goods, it will present to Bank of America the letter of credit from Bank of China and shipping documents. On behalf of the US exporter, Bank of America will then collect payment from Bank of China, which, in turn, will collect payment from the Chinese importer.

Overall, instead of having unknown exporters and importers deal with each other, transactions are facilitated by banks on both sides that have known each other quite well because of numerous such dealings. In other words, the letter of credit reduces transaction costs.

A second way to enter international markets is licensing/franchising. Usually used in *manufacturing* industries, **licensing** refers to Firm A's agreement to give Firm B the rights to use A's proprietary technology (such as a patent) or trademark (such as a corporate logo) for a royalty fee paid to A by B. Assuming (hypothetically) that Sew What? cannot keep up with demand in Greece, it may consider granting a Greek firm the license to use Sew What?'s technology and trademark

licensing
Firm A's agreement to give Firm B the rights to use A's proprietary technology (such as a patent) or trademark (such as a corporate logo) for a royalty fee paid to A by B. This is typically done in manufacturing industries.

franchising
Firm A's agreement to give Firm B the rights to use A's proprietary assets for a royalty fee paid to A by B. This is typically done in service industries.

for a fee. **Franchising** represents essentially the same idea, except it is typically used in *service* industries, such as fast food. A great advantage is that SME licensors and franchisors can expand abroad with relatively little capital of their own.[29] Foreign firms interested in becoming licensees/franchisees have to put their own capital up front. For instance, it now costs approximately one million and half-a-million dollars to earn a franchise from McDonald's and Wendy's, respectively. However, the flip side is that licensors and franchisors may suffer a loss of control over how their technology and brand names are used. If Sew What?'s (hypothetical) Greek licensee produces substandard products that damage the brand and refuses to improve quality, Sew What? is left with the difficult choices of (1) suing its licensee in an unfamiliar Greek court or (2) discontinuing the relationship, both of which are complicated and costly.

A third entry mode is FDI, which is discussed in detail in Chapter 6. FDI may entail strategic alliances with foreign partners (such as joint ventures), foreign acquisitions, and/or "green-field" wholly owned subsidiaries. FDI has several distinct advantages. By planting some roots abroad, a firm becomes more committed to serving foreign markets. It is physically and psychologically close to foreign customers. Relative to licensing/franchising, a firm is better able to control how its proprietary technology and brand name are used.[30] However, FDI has a major drawback, which is its cost and complexity. It requires both a nontrivial sum of capital and a significant managerial commitment. Many SMEs are unable to engage in FDI. However, there is some evidence that in the long run, FDI by SMEs may lead to higher performance and that some entrepreneurial SMEs can come up with sufficient resources to engage in FDI.[31]

stage models
Models of internationalization that portray the slow step-by-step (stage-by stage) process an SME must go through to internationalize its business.

In general, the level of complexity and required resources increases from direct exports, to licensing/franchising, and finally to FDI. Traditionally, it is thought that most firms will have to go through these different "stages" and that SMEs (perhaps with few exceptions) are unable to take on FDI. These ideas—collectively known as **stage models**—posit that even for some SMEs that eventually internationalize, it entails a very slow, stage-by-stage process.[32] A case in point: It took 15 years for Sew What?'s overseas sales to reach 6% of total sales (see Opening Case).

However, enough counterexamples of *rapidly* internationalizing entrepreneurial firms, known as the born globals, challenge stage models. Consider Logitech, now a global leader in computer peripherals.[33] It was established by entrepreneurs from Switzerland and the United States, where the firm set up dual headquarters. R&D and manufacturing were initially split between these two countries and then quickly spread to Ireland and Taiwan through FDI. Its first commercial contract was with a Japanese company. Another interesting example is a medical equipment venture, Technomed, which was set up in France. From its inception, the founder did not see it as a French company; instead, it was viewed as a global company with English as its official language, very uncharacteristic of French firms. Only nine months after its founding, Technomed established a subsidiary through FDI in a key market, the United States. Given the information technology advancements within the past decade, most Internet firms, because of their instant worldwide reach, have rapidly internationalized (see Closing Case).[34]

Given that most SMEs still fit the stereotype of slow (or no) internationalization and that some very entrepreneurial SMEs seem to be born global, a key question is: What leads to rapid internationalization? The key differentiator between rapidly and slowly (or no) internationalizing SMEs seems to be the international experience of entrepreneurs.[35] If entrepreneurs, such as Sew What?'s Megan Duckett, have solid previous experience abroad (such as working and studying overseas and/or immigrating from certain countries), then doing business internationally is not so intimidating. Otherwise, the "fear and loathing" factor associated with the unfamiliar foreign business world may take over, and entrepreneurs will simply want to avoid troubles overseas.

Although many entrepreneurial firms have aggressively gone abroad, it is probably true that a majority of SMEs will be unable to do so; struggling domestically is already giving them enough headache. However, as discussed next, some SMEs can still internationalize by staying at home.

International Strategies for Staying in Domestic Markets

Shown in Table 9.2, there are at least five strategies for entrepreneurial SMEs to internationalize without leaving their home country: (1) export indirectly, (2) become suppliers of foreign firms, (3) become licensees/franchisees of foreign brands, (4) become alliance partners of foreign direct investors, and (5) harvest and exit through sell-offs. First, whereas direct exports may be lucrative, many SMEs do not have the resources to handle such work. However, they still can reach overseas customers through **indirect exports**—exporting through domestic-based export intermediaries. **Export intermediaries** perform an important "middleman" function by linking sellers and buyers overseas that otherwise would not have been connected.[36] Being entrepreneurs themselves, export intermediaries facilitate the internationalization of many SMEs (In Focus 9.4). Intermediaries, such as trading companies and export management companies, handle about 50% of total exports in Japan and South Korea, 38% in Thailand, and 5% to 10% in the United States.[37]

indirect exports
A way for SMEs to reach overseas customers by exporting through domestic-based export intermediaries.

export intermediary
A firm that performs an important "middleman" function by linking sellers and buyers overseas that otherwise would not have been connected.

A second strategy is to become suppliers of foreign firms that come to do business in one's home country. To save costs, most foreign firms are interested in looking for local suppliers. For example, one Northern Irish bakery for chilled part-bake bread secured supply contracts with an American firm, Subway, that entered Ireland in the mid-1990s. So successful was this relationship that the firm now supplies Subway franchisees throughout Europe.[38] SME suppliers thus may be able to internationalize by "piggybacking" on the larger foreign entrants.

Third, entrepreneurial firms may consider becoming licensees or franchisees of foreign brands. Foreign licensors and franchisors will provide training and technology transfer—for a fee, of course. SMEs consequently can learn a great deal

IN FOCUS 9.4 Asia Trade Exports to the Russian Far East

Asia Trade is a small, Seattle-based export trading company founded by a recent Russian immigrant and his American wife in 1992. The collapse of the Soviet Union created chaos as well as opportunities. The breakdown hit the distant Russian Far East especially hard. Asia Trade took advantage of the general food shortage there by exporting canned foods, beverages, and flour, mostly sourced from the Pacific Northwest. As a virgin market, the Russian Far East had all the attractions for first movers. Yet, it also possessed all the dangers that would scare away the less determined. Locals would not do business with strangers unless they had become friends. Decades of communist rule resulted in deep suspicion of foreigners in a region guarded as a military reserve. Asia Trade had an advantage because one of the cofounders was born and raised there and had seven years of trading experience. Knowing whom to talk to, combined with the ability to reliably source products in America, enabled Asia Trade to thrive. Two years after its founding, its per capita export sales were more than double the average among the population of small US export intermediaries.

Source: Based on author's interviews, adapted from M. W. Peng, 1998, *Behind the Success and Failure of US Export Intermediaries: Transactions, Agents, and Resources* (pp. 86–87), Westport, CT: Quorum.

about how to operate at world-class standards. Further, licensees and franchisees do not have to be permanently under the control of licensors and franchisors. If enough learning has been accomplished and enough capital has been accumulated, it is possible to discontinue the relationship and to reap greater entrepreneurial profits. For example, in Thailand, Minor Group, which had held the Pizza Hut franchise for 20 years, broke away from the relationship. Its new venture, The Pizza Company, is now the market leader in Thailand.[39]

A fourth strategy is to become alliance partners of foreign direct investors. Facing an onslaught of aggressive MNEs, many entrepreneurial firms may stand little chance of successfully defending their market positions. Then it makes great sense to follow the old adage, "If you can't beat them, join them!" Although "dancing with the giants" is tricky, it seems to be a much better outcome than being crushed by the giants.

Finally, as a harvest and exit strategy, entrepreneurs may sell an equity stake or the entire firm to foreign entrants. An American couple, originally from Seattle, built a Starbucks-like coffee chain called Seattle Coffee with 60 stores in Britain. When Starbucks entered Britain, the couple sold the chain to Starbucks for a hefty $84 million. In light of the high failure rates of start-ups, being acquired by foreign entrants may help preserve the business in the long run.

LEARNING OBJECTIVE 5

participate in three leading debates on growing and internationalizing the entrepreneurial firm

DEBATES AND EXTENSIONS

Entrepreneurship throughout the world has attracted significant controversies and debates (see Closing Case). We discuss three leading debates: (1) traits versus institutions, (2) slow versus rapid internationalization, and (3) antifailure biases versus entrepreneur-friendly bankruptcy laws.

Traits versus Institutions

This is probably the oldest debate on entrepreneurship. It focuses on the question: What motivates entrepreneurs to establish new firms, while most others are simply content to work for bosses? The "traits" school of thought argues that it is personal traits that matter. Compared with nonentrepreneurs, entrepreneurs seem more likely to possess a stronger desire for achievement and are more willing to take risks and tolerate ambiguities. Overall, entrepreneurship inevitably deviates from the norm to work for others, and this deviation may be in the "blood" of entrepreneurs.[40]

Critics, however, argue that some of these traits, such as a strong achievement orientation, are not necessarily limited to entrepreneurs, but instead are characteristic of many successful individuals. Moreover, the diversity among entrepreneurs makes any attempt to develop a standard psychological or personality profile futile. Critics suggest it is institutions—namely, the environments that set formal and informal rules of the game—that matter.[41] For example, consider the ethnic Chinese, who have exhibited a high degree of entrepreneurship throughout Southeast Asia, where as a minority group (usually less than 10% of the population in countries such as Indonesia and Thailand), they control 70% to 80% of the wealth. Yet, in mainland China, for three decades (the 1950s through the 1970s), there had been virtually no entrepreneurship because of harsh communist policies. In the last two decades, as government policies have become relatively more entrepreneur friendly, the institutional transitions have opened the floodgates of entrepreneurship in China.

A high-profile recent case documents how institutions constrain or enable entrepreneurship. In 2005, Baidu, a Chinese Internet start-up, had its initial public offering (IPO) on NASDAQ, and its shares surged 354% on the same day (from $27 to $154), scoring the biggest one-day stock increase in US capital markets since 2000. Although there might have been some "irrational exuberance" among US investors chasing "China's Google," it is evident that they did not discriminate against Baidu. The sad reality for Baidu is that at home, it was blatantly discriminated against by the Chinese securities authorities. As a private start-up, it was not allowed to list its stock on China's stock exchanges—only state-owned firms need apply. Essentially, Baidu was pushed out of China to list in the United States, whose entrepreneur-friendly institutional frameworks, such as NASDAQ regulations, facilitate more entrepreneurial success.[42] In a nutshell, it is not what is in people's "blood" that makes or breaks entrepreneurship; it is institutions that encourage or constrain entrepreneurship.

Beyond the macro societal-level institutions, more micro institutions also matter. Family background and educational attainment have been found to correlate with entrepreneurship. Children of wealthy parents, especially parents who own businesses, are more likely to start their own firms. So are people who are better educated. Taken together, informal norms governing one's socioeconomic group, in terms of whether starting a new firm is legitimate or not, assert some powerful impact on the propensity to create new ventures.

Overall, this debate is an extension of the broader debate on "nature versus nurture." Most scholars now agree that entrepreneurship is the result of both nature *and* nurture.

Slow Internationalizers versus Born Global Start-Ups

There are two components here: (1) *Can* SMEs internationalize faster than what has been suggested by traditional stage models? (2) *Should* they rapidly internationalize? The dust has largely settled on the first component: It is possible for some (but not all) SMEs to make very rapid progress in internationalization. What is currently being debated is the second component.[43]

On the one hand, there are advocates who argue that every industry has become global and that entrepreneurial firms need to rapidly go after these opportunities.[44] On the other hand, stage models suggest that firms need to enter culturally and institutionally close markets first, spend enough time there to accumulate overseas experience, and then gradually move from more primitive modes such as exports to more sophisticated strategies such as FDI in distant markets. Consistent with stage models, Sweden's IKEA, for example, waited 20 years (1943–1963) before entering a neighboring country, Norway. Only more recently has it accelerated its internationalization.[45] Stage models caution that inexperienced swimmers may drown in unfamiliar foreign waters.

© LIU JIN/ Stringer/ AFP/ Getty Images

Although Sweden's IKEA is now active in distant markets such as China, it waited 20 years (1943–1963) before first entering a neighboring country, Norway. Did IKEA's slow, cautious approach in initial internationalization—suggested by stage models—make sense?

A key issue, therefore, is whether it is better for entrepreneurs to start the internationalization process soon after founding (as born global firms do) or to postpone until the firm has accumulated significant resources (as IKEA did). One study in Finland supports rapid internationalization.[46] Specifically, firms following the prescription of stage models, when eventually internationalizing, must overcome substantial inertia because of their domestic orientation. In contrast, firms that internationalize earlier need to overcome fewer of these barriers. Therefore, SMEs without an established domestic orientation (such as Logitech and Technomed discussed earlier) may outperform their rivals that wait longer to internationalize.[47] In other words, contrary to the inherent disadvantages in internationalization associated with SMEs as suggested by stage models, there may be inherent advantages of being small while venturing abroad.[48]

On the other hand, one study in the United States finds no performance difference between aggressive and passive internationalizers.[49] One study in Hungary reports that foreign sales during the first few years of the new venture may *reduce* its chances for survival.[50] Consequently, indiscriminate advice for new ventures to go global may not be warranted. Some scholars argue that "the born-global view, although appealing, is a dangerous half-truth." They maintain, "You must first be successful at home, then move outward in a manner that anticipates and genuinely accommodates local differences."[51] In other words, the teachings of stage models are still relevant.

Given the continuation of split findings, there are no hard-and-fast rules on whether entrepreneurial firms should rapidly internationalize or not. While the entrepreneurial urge to be bold should be encouraged, they also need to be reminded of the virtues of not being too bold.

Antifailure Bias versus Entrepreneur-Friendly Bankruptcy Laws[52]

Although a majority of entrepreneurial firms fail, entrepreneurs, scholars, journalists, and government officials all share an "antifailure" bias.[53] Everyone is interested in entrepreneurial success, and the attention to entrepreneurial failure is scant.

One of the leading debates is how to treat failed entrepreneurs who file for bankruptcy. Although we are confident that many start-ups will end up in bankruptcy, at present it is impossible to predict which ones will go under. Therefore, from an institutional standpoint, if entrepreneurship is to be encouraged, there is a need to ease the pain associated with bankruptcy by means such as allowing entrepreneurs to walk away from debt, a legal right that bankrupt American entrepreneurs appreciate. In contrast, bankrupt German entrepreneurs may remain liable for unpaid debt for up to 30 years. Further, German and Japanese managers of bankrupt firms can also be liable for criminal penalties, and some bankrupt Japanese entrepreneurs have committed suicide. Not surprisingly, many failed entrepreneurs in Germany and Japan try to avoid business exit despite escalating losses, while societal and individual resources cannot be channeled to more productive uses. Therefore, as rules of the "end game," harsh bankruptcy laws become grave *exit* barriers. They can also create significant *entry* barriers, as fewer would-be entrepreneurs may decide to launch their ventures.

At a societal level, if many would-be entrepreneurs, in fear of failure, abandon their ideas, there will not be a thriving entrepreneurial sector. Given the risks and uncertainties, it is not surprising that many entrepreneurs do not make it the first time. However, if they are given second, third, or more chances, some will succeed. For example, approximately 50% of American entrepreneurs who filed bankruptcy would resume a new venture in four years, in part due to the relatively more entrepreneur-friendly bankruptcy laws. On the other hand, a society that severely punishes failed entrepreneurs through harsh bankruptcy laws is not likely to foster widespread entrepreneurship. Failed entrepreneurs have nevertheless accumulated a great deal of experience and lessons on how to avoid their mistakes. If they drop out of the entrepreneurial game (or in the worst case, kill themselves), their wisdom will be permanently lost.[54]

Institutionally, there is an urgent need to remove some of our antifailure biases and design and implement entrepreneur-friendly bankruptcy policies so that failed entrepreneurs are given more chances. At a societal level, entrepreneurial failures may be beneficial because it is through a large number of entrepreneurial experiments—although many will fail—that winning solutions will emerge, that entrepreneurship will flourish, and that economies will develop.[55]

MANAGEMENT SAVVY

LEARNING OBJECTIVE 6

draw implications for action

Entrepreneurs and their firms are quintessential engines of the "creative destruction" process underpinning global capitalism first described by Joseph Schumpeter. What determines the success and failure of entrepreneurial firms around the globe? The answers boil down to two components. First, the institution-based view argues that the larger institutional frameworks explain a great deal about what is behind the differences in entrepreneurial and economic development around the world. Second, the resource-based view posits that it is largely intangible resources such as vision, drive, and willingness to take risks that fuel entrepreneurship around the globe. Overall, the performance of entrepreneurial firms depends on how they take advantage of formal and informal institutional resources and leverage their capabilities—at home, abroad, or both.

Two clear implications for action emerge (Table 9.3). First, institutions that facilitate entrepreneurship development—both formal and informal—are important. As a result, savvy entrepreneurs have a vested interest in pushing for more entrepreneur-friendly formal institutions in various countries, such as rules governing how to set up new firms (see Table 9.1). Entrepreneurs also need to cultivate strong informal norms granting legitimacy to entrepreneurs. Talking to high school and college students, taking on internships, and providing seed money as angels for new ventures are some of the actions that entrepreneurs can undertake.

Second, when internationalizing, entrepreneurs are advised to "be bold" to get their feet "wet" abroad. Thanks to globalization, the costs of doing business abroad have fallen recently. However, being bold does not mean being reckless. One specific managerial insight from this chapter is that it is possible to internationalize without venturing abroad. There are a variety of international strategies that enable entrepreneurial firms to stay in domestic markets. When the entrepreneurial firm is not ready to take on higher risk abroad, this more limited involvement may be appropriate. In other words, be bold but not too bold.[56]

TABLE 9.3 IMPLICATIONS FOR ACTION

- Push for institutions that facilitate entrepreneurship development—both formal and informal
- When internationalizing, be bold but not too bold

CHAPTER SUMMARY

1. Define entrepreneurship, entrepreneurs, and entrepreneurial firms
   - Entrepreneurship is the identification and exploration of previously unexplored opportunities.
   - Entrepreneurs may be founders and owners of new businesses or managers of existing firms.
   - Entrepreneurial firms in this chapter are defined as SMEs that employ fewer than 500 people.
2. Understand how institutions and resources affect entrepreneurship
   - Institutions—both formal and informal—enable and constrain entrepreneurship around the world.
   - Resources and capabilities largely determine entrepreneurial success and failure.
3. Identify the three characteristics of a growing entrepreneurial firm
   - These are (1) growth, (2) innovation, and (3) financing.
4. Differentiate international strategies that enter foreign markets and that stay in domestic markets
   - Entrepreneurial firms can internationalize by entering foreign markets through entry modes such as (1) direct exports, (2) licensing/franchising, and (3) foreign direct investment.
   - Entrepreneurial firms can also internationalize without venturing abroad by (1) exporting indirectly, (2) supplying foreign firms, (3) becoming licensees/franchisees of foreign firms, (4) joining foreign entrants as alliance partners, and (5) harvesting and exiting through sell-offs to foreign entrants.
5. Participate in three leading debates on growing and internationalizing the entrepreneurial firm
   - These are (1) traits versus institutions, (2) slow versus rapid internationalization, and (3) antifailure biases versus entrepreneur-friendly bankruptcy law.
6. Draw implications for action
   - Institutions that facilitate entrepreneurship development—both formal and informal—are important, so entrepreneurs need to proactively support them.
   - When internationalizing, the savvy entrepreneur should be bold but not too bold.

KEY TERMS

Born global 261
Direct exports 262
Entrepreneurs 254
Entrepreneurship 254
Export intermediary 265
Franchising 264
Indirect exports 265
International entrepreneurship 254
Letter of credit (L/C) 263
Licensing 263
Microfinance 261
Small and medium-sized enterprises (SMEs) 254
Sporadic (passive) exporting 262
Stage models 264

REVIEW QUESTIONS

1. How do you define entrepreneurship?
2. How prevalent and important are small entrepreneurial firms in economies around the globe? Use statistics to support your answer.

3. Referring to Table 9.1, to what extent do government regulations affect the start up of new firms in developed countries as opposed to developing countries?
4. Which societal norms tend to encourage entrepreneurship and which discourage it?
5. How important are an entrepreneur's resources and capabilities in determining his or her success?
6. Name and describe three major characteristics associated with an entrepreneurial firm's growth.
7. What qualities typically compensate for an entrepreneurial firm's lack of tangible resources?
8. What motivates strategic investors of all kinds to invest in start-ups when they are statistically quite risky?
9. Explain the genesis and role of microfinance.
10. Briefly summarize three modes an SME can use to enter foreign markets.
11. Name and describe at least three of the five ways entrepreneurial SMEs can internationalize without leaving their home countries.
12. In the entrepreneurial nature versus nurture debate, which do you think carries more power: traits (nature) or institutions (nurture)?
13. We know that it's possible for an SME to be born global by skipping immediately to the highest stage model, FDI, but do you think it's wise?
14. If an entrepreneur's start-up fails, should the entrepreneur be held accountable for all residual debts? Explain your answer.
15. Describe two or three examples of institutions that could be made friendlier and more supportive of entrepreneurs.
16. Devise your own example of an entrepreneurial action that demonstrates your understanding of the difference between being bold and being reckless.

CRITICAL DISCUSSION QUESTIONS

1. Given that most entrepreneurial start-ups fail, why do entrepreneurs found so many new firms? Why are (most) governments interested in promoting more start-ups?
2. Some suggest that foreign markets are graveyards for entrepreneurial firms to overextend themselves. Others argue that foreign markets represent the future for SMEs. If you were the owner of a small, reasonably profitable domestic firm, would you consider expanding overseas? Why?
3. ON ETHICS: Your former high school buddy invites you to join an entrepreneurial start-up that specializes in cracking the codes of protection software, which protect CDs and DVDs from being copied. He has developed the pioneering technology and lined up financing. The worldwide demand for this technology appears enormous. He offers you the job of CEO and 10% of the equity of the firm. How would you respond to his proposition?

VIDEO CASE

Watch "The DNA of an Entrepreneur" by Dame Anita Roddick of The Body Shop International.

1. Dame Anita Roddick pointed out that there are different skills needed when starting the business than later as the business grows. What did she mean by that? What was covered in the chapter as a solution for those entrepreneurs who wish to expand globally?
2. Would a passive or slow approach to internationalization be likely to work for the type of entrepreneur that she described?
3. Ms. Roddick recommended that the entrepreneur keep the organization private, but what challenges might make it difficult for an SME expanding globally to totally avoid going public?
4. Suppose you wished to help finance SME start-ups around the world and you wished to identify those people who would likely be the most successful entrepreneurs. Do you think that you could use Ms. Roddick's "The DNA of an Entrepreneur" as a means of identifying people from around the world who would likely be most successful?
5. Suppose you do not have the DNA suggested by Ms. Roddick. Nevertheless, was there anything that she said or anything in this chapter that might give you hope for success in a start-up SME focused on global expansion?

CLOSING CASE

Kiva Revolutionizes Microfinance

Yawa Aziaka, a hardworking but uneducated entrepreneur in Togo (Africa), needs a loan to buy chickens and feed to expand her poultry business. She will repay the loan in 15 months. If you could change her life with a $25 loan, would you? Well, now you can. Kiva, a San Francisco-based start-up, is using technology to connect small-stakes lenders around the world with impoverished entrepreneurs in developing countries—a feat that's helping to change the nature of microfinance. Kiva's approach is straightforward. Entrepreneurs working with established local microfinance institutions (MFIs) put their business plans, financing needs, and photos on Kiva's website. Investors from affluent countries visit Kiva.org, choose which entrepreneurs to back, and then finance the loans. The organization, which incorporated as a nonprofit in November 2005, has already raised more than $2 million in loans from 26,000 lenders. The idea is simple, yet Kiva insiders acknowledge that it's only feasible with today's technology.

The idea for Kiva, which means "agreement" in Swahili, dates back to early 2004, when cofounder Jessica Flannery worked in East Africa through the Village Enterprise Fund, a San Carlos, California-based nonprofit that provides business training, seed capital, and mentoring to people in that region. Inspired by her experience, Jessica and her husband, Matt Flannery, CEO and cofounder, tried to invest in microfinance ventures only to learn that they were priced out of the market. (The minimum investments for MFI funds are generally $50,000 or $100,000.) "We had seven businesspeople in Uganda we wanted to invest in, and we didn't find any organization that could help us do that," Matt Flannery says. So the Flannerys helped themselves. In March 2005, Matt created a website that featured the Ugandans' photos and stories. The couple then used the Internet to solicit "shares" in those businesses from family and friends. The shares sold in one weekend. Kiva was born, but it was just a side project at first. Matt kept his regular job as a computer programmer until December 2005. Meanwhile, Jessica spent a year raising money and researching legal issues related to their venture.

Around the same time, Jeremy Frazao, a software architect, and his wife, Fiona Ramsey, an executive assistant at a real estate company, were spending a year traveling. They arrived in Thailand just months after the catastrophic tsunami of December 2004. The couple sent e-mails to family and friends, asking for contributions for local entrepreneurs in need. In two days, they raised more than $3,000 via their PayPal account, some of which came from strangers to whom their original message had been forwarded. "That's what made my mind start spinning about the ability to raise money over the Internet," says Frazao. They returned to the United States in August 2005. Two months later, Frazao read about the nascent Kiva on a blog. "It just became clear to me that this is going to change everything," he says. Frazao started helping Matt Flannery write code. Weeks turned into months until Frazao finally became an official paid employee in August 2006. Ramsey became Kiva's community and operations manager.

Left to right: Olana Khan, chief operating officer; Jeremy Frazao, director of technology; Jessica Flannery, cofounder; Matt Flannery, CEO and cofounder; Fiona Ramsey, community and operations manager

Now Kiva's mission is to draw others into microfinance. Visitors to Kiva's site see that Juliet Igunbor in Nigeria needs $500 to expand her beauty salon. Francois Segbessi Akpatou in Togo is asking for $1,200 to grow his auto repair business. The entrepreneurs also say when they'll pay back the loans. Website visitors who decide to invest in a venture contribute online, going through a checkout process much like they would at a retail site. So far, there has been a 100% payback rate, but most lenders reinvest their money.

Kiva uses PayPal, a part of eBay Inc., to collect money from individual investors. PayPal reimburses Kiva for the transaction fees, essentially donating the service, which otherwise "far and away would be Kiva's greatest expense," Frazao says. Then Kiva wires the money overseas using San Francisco-based Wells Fargo & Co. PayPal is not available in many developing countries, making wire transfers the most efficient way of getting money there, according to Ramsey. One of the biggest challenges is slow Internet access in the developing world, Frazao says. "The infrastructure in places like Uganda is so bad that it makes things almost impossible."

Back in the United States, Kiva staffers face additional challenges. Among the biggest has been scaling the technology fast enough to meet the site's exploding popularity. A spike in interest after PBS ran a story highlighting Kiva in October 2006 caused the organization's servers to crash. "The organic growth works for a while, but there's a huge difference between organic, grass-roots architecture and a business-ready architecture," Matt Flannery says. In July 2006, Kiva finally acquired office space two doors down from a laundromat in San Francisco's Mission District. Its budget is increasing from just over $125,000 in 2006 to $500,000 for 2007, according to Chief Operating Officer Olana Khan. Loftier goals include expanding the marketplace and bringing more lenders and borrowers together, observes Matt Flannery. There's also a plan to pay investors back with interest. "We're just seeing the beginning," Frazao says. "Kiva is about to get really big."

Case Discussion Questions

1. From an institution-based view, explain what barriers Kiva is overcoming.
2. From a resource-based standpoint, explain why Kiva has rapidly emerged as a highly successful MFI among thousands of them.
3. Would you like to work for or invest in Kiva? Why? What might Kiva become in ten years?

Source: Adapted from M. Pratt, 2007, Kiva harnesses IT to revolutionize microfinance, *Computer World*, January 29: 31–32.

NOTES

Journal acronyms: **AME** – *Academy of Management Executive;* **AMJ** – *Academy of Management Journal;* **AMLE** – *Academy of Management Learning and Education;* **AMR** – *Academy of Management Review;* **APJM** – *Asia Pacific Journal of Management;* **ETP** – *Entrepreneurship Theory and Practice;* **FEER** – *Far Eastern Economic Review;* **HBR** – *Harvard Business Review;* **JBV** – *Journal of Business Venturing;* **JIBS** – *Journal of International Business Studies;* **JIE** – *Journal of International Entrepreneurship;* **JIM** – *Journal of International Management;* **JM** – *Journal of Management;* **JMS** – *Journal of Management Studies;* **JWB** – *Journal of World Business;* **MIR** – *Management International Review;* **MS** – *Management Science;* **OSc** – *Organization Science;* **QJE** – *Quarterly Journal of Economics;* **SMJ** – *Strategic Management Journal;* **SMR** – *MIT Sloan Management Review*

[1] M. Hitt, R. D. Ireland, S. M. Camp, & D. Sexton, 2001, Strategic entrepreneurship (p. 480), *SMJ*, 22: 479–491; J. McMullen & D. Shepherd, 2006, Entrepreneurial action and the role of uncertainty in the theory of the entrepreneur, *AMR*, 31: 132–152.

[2] S. Shane & S. Venkataraman, 2000, The promise of entrepreneurship as a field of research (p. 218) *AMR*, 25: 217–226.

[3] P. McDougall & B. Oviatt, 2000, International entrepreneurship (p. 903), *AMJ*, 43: 902–906; S. Young, P. Dimitratos, & L. Dana, 2003, International entrepreneurship research, *JIE*, 1: 31–42.

[4] Z. Acs & C. Armington, 2006, *Entrepreneurship, Geography, and American Economic Growth*, New York: Cambridge University Press; G. Knight, 2001, Entrepreneurship and strategy in the international SME, *JIM*, 7: 155–171; R. Wright & H. Etemad, 2001, SMEs and the global economy, *JIM*, 7: 151–154.

[5] V. Lau, M. Shaffer, & K. Au, 2007, Entrepreneurial career success from a Chinese perspective, *JIBS*, 38: 126–146; M. Hayward, D. Shepherd, & D. Griffin, 2006, A hubris theory of entrepreneurship, *MS*, 52: 160–172; R. Lowe & A. Ziedonis, 2006, Overoptimism and the performance of entrepreneurial firms, *MS*, 52: 173–186.

[6] J. Timmons, 1999, *New Venture Creation* (pp. 32–34), Boston: Irwin McGraw-Hill. See also R. Mudambi & S. Zahra, 2007, The survival of international new ventures, *JIBS*, 38: 333–352.

[7] A. Fadahunsi & P. Rosa, 2002, Entrepreneurship and illegality, *JBV*, 17: 397–429; F. Luthans & E. Ibrayeva, 2006, Entrepreneurial self-efficacy in Central Asian transition economies, *JIBS*, 37: 92–110.

[8] S. Djankov, R. La Porta, F. Lopez-de-Silanes, & A. Shleifer, 2002, The regulation of entry, *QJE*, 67: 1–37.

[9] W. Baumol, 2004, Entrepreneurial cultures and countercultures, *AMLE*, 3: 316–326; T. Begley & W. Tan, 2001, The socio-cultural environment for entrepreneurship, *JIBS*, 32: 537–553; L. Busenitz & C. Lau, 1996, A cross-cultural cognitive model of new venture creation, *ETP*, Summer: 25–39.

[10] A. Thomas & S. Mueller, 2000, A case for comparative entrepreneurship, *JIBS*, 31: 287–301.

[11] R. Doern & C. Fey, 2006, E-commerce developments and strategies for value-creation, *JWB*, 41: 315–327; D. Lepak, K. Smith, & M. S. Taylor, 2007, Value creation and value capture, *AMR*, 32: 180–194; E. Mosakowski, 1998, Entrepreneurial resources, organizational choices, and competitive outcomes, *OSc*, 9: 625–643.

[12] L. Busenitz & J. Barney, 1997, Differences between entrepreneurs and managers in large organizations, *JBV*, 12: 9–30.

[13] J. Baum, E. Locke, & K. Smith, 2001, A multidimensional model of venture growth, *AMJ*, 44: 292–303; B. Gilbert, P. McDougall, & D. Audretsch, 2006, New venture growth, *JM*, 32: 926–950.

[14] T. Nelson, 2003, The persistence of founder influence, *SMJ*, 24: 707–724; S. Park & Z. Bae, 2004, New venture strategies in a developing country, *JBV*, 19: 81–105.

[15] G. Bruton & Y. Rubanik, 2002, Resources of the firm, Russian high-technology start-ups, and firm growth, *JBV*, 17: 553–576.

[16] C. Nicholls-Nixon, 2005, Rapid growth and high performance, *AME*, 19: 77–88; G. Rowe, 2001, Creating wealth in organizations, *AME*, 15: 81–94; W. Sine, H. Mitsuhashi, & D. Kirsch, 2006, Revisiting Burns and Stalker, *AMJ*, 49: 121–132.

[17] M. Chen & D. Hambrick, 1995, Speed, stealth, and selective attack, *AMJ*, 38: 453–482; J. Ebben & A. Johnson, 2005, Efficiency, flexibility, or both? *SMJ*, 26: 1249–1259; G. George, 2005, Slack resources and the performance of privately held firms, *AMJ*, 48: 661–676.

[18] *Business Week*, 2005, The little contractor that could, July 4: 78–79.

[19] R. Katila & S. Shane, 2005, When does lack of resources make new firms innovative? *AMJ*, 48: 814–829; G. Lumpkin & G. Dess, 1996, Clarifying the entrepreneurial orientation construct and linking it to performance, *AMR*, 21: 135–172; R. McGrath & I. MacMillan, 2005, Market-busting strategies for exceptional business growth, *HBR*, March: 81–89.

[20] H. Lee, K. Smith, C. Grimm, & A. Schomburg, 2000, Timing, order, and durability of new product advantages with imitation, *SMJ*, 21: 23–30; T. Man, T. Lau, & K. Chan, 2002, The competitiveness of small and medium enterprises, *JBV*, 17: 123–142; A. Phene, K. Fladmoe-Lindquist, & L. Marsh, 2006, Breakthrough innovations in the US biotechnology industry, *SMJ*, 27: 369–388; P. Roberts, 1999, Product innovation, product-market competition, and persistent profitability, *SMJ*, 20: 655–670; N. Stieglitz & K. Heine, 2007, Innovations and the role of complementarities in a strategic theory of the firm, *SMJ*, 28: 1–15.

[21] C. Christensen, 1997, *The Innovator's Dilemma*, Boston: Harvard Business School Press.

[22] Z. Acs & D. Audretsch, 1990, *Innovation and Small Firms*, Cambridge, MA: MIT Press; G. Qian & L. Li, 2003, Profitability of small and medium-sized enterprises in high-technology industries, *SMJ*, 24: 881–887.

[23] S. Dobrev & W. Barnett, 2005, Organizational roles and transition to entrepreneurship, *AMJ*, 48: 433–449.

[24] A. Zacharakis & G. D. Meyer, 1998, A lack of insight, *JBV*, 13: 57–76.

[25] D. Ahlstrom, G. Bruton, & K. Yeh, 2007, Venture capital in China: Past, present, future, *APJM*, 24: 247–268; M. Wright, 2007, Venture capital in China: A view from Europe, *APJM*, 24: 269–282.

[26] G. Knight & S. T. Cavusgil, 2004, Innovation, organizational capabilities, and the born-global firm, *JIBS*, 35: 124–141; B. Oviatt & P. McDougall, 1994, Toward a theory of international new ventures, *JIBS*, 25: 45–64.

[27] A. Zacharakis, 1998, Entrepreneurial entry into foreign markets, *ETP*, Spring: 23–39.

[28] R. Chen & M. Martin, 2001, Foreign expansion of small firms, *JBV*, 16: 557–574.

[29] J. Combs & D. Ketcheb, 1999, Can capital scarcity help agency theory explain franchising? *AMJ*, 42: 196–207; A. Fosfuri, 2006, The licensing dilemma, *SMJ*, 27: 1141–1158; S. Michaels, 2000, Investments to create bargaining power, *SMJ*, 21: 497–515; O. Sorenson & J. Sorensen, 2001, Finding the right mix, *SMJ*, 22: 713–724.

[30] H. Boter & C. Holmquist, 1996, Industry characteristics and internationalization processes in small firms, *JBV*, 11: 471–487; S. Preece, G. Miles, & M. Baetz, 1998, Explaining the international intensity and global diversity of early-state technology-based firms, *JBV*, 14: 259–281.

[31] M. Jones, 2001, First steps in internationalization, *JIM*, 7: 191–210; J. Lu & P. Beamish, 2001, The internationalization and performance of SMEs, *SMJ*, 22: 565–586; S. Zahra, R. D. Ireland, & M. Hitt, 2000, International expansion by new venture firms, *AMJ*, 43: 925–950.

[32] J. Johanson & J. Vahlne, 1977, The internationalization process of the firm, *JIBS*, 4: 20–29; L. Li, D. Li, & T. Dalgic, 2004, Internationalization process of small and medium-sized enterprises, *MIR*, 44: 93–116.

[33] P. McDougall, S. Shane, & B. Oviatt, 1994, Explaining the formation of international new ventures, *JBV*, 9: 469–487.

[34] S. Kotha, V. Rindova, & F. Rothaermel, 2001, Assets and actions, *JIBS*, 32: 769–791; J. Tiessen, R. Wright, & I. Turner, 2001, A model of e-commerce use by internationalizing SMEs, *JIM*, 7: 211–233.

[35] S. Chetty, K. Eriksson, & J. Lindbergh, 2006, The effect of specificity of experience on a firm's perceived importance of institutional knowledge in an ongoing business, *JIBS*, 37: 699–712; N. Coviello, 2006, The network dynamics of international new ventures, *JIBS*, 37: 713–731; Z. Fernandez & M. Nieto, 2006, Impact of ownership on the international involvement of SMEs, *JIBS*, 37: 340–351; A. B. Reuber & E. Fischer, 1997, The influence of the management team's international experience on the internationalization behaviors of SMEs, *JIBS*, 28: 807–825; P. Westhead, M. Wright, & D. Ucbasaran, 2001, The internationalization of new and small firms, *JBV*, 16: 333–358.

[36] M. W. Peng & A. Y. Ilinitch, 1998, Export intermediary firms, *JIBS*, 29: 609–620; H. Trabold, 2002, Export intermediation: An empirical test of Peng and Ilinitch, *JIBS*, 33: 327–344.

[37] M. W. Peng & A. York, 2001, Behind intermediary performance in export trade, *JIBS*, 32: 327–346; M. W. Peng, Y. Zhou, & A. York, 2006, Behind make or buy decisions in export strategy, *JWB*, 41: 289–300.

[38] J. Bell, R. McNaughton, & S. Young, 2001, "Born-again global" firms (p. 184), *JIM*, 7: 173–189.

[39] R. Tesker, 2002, Pepperoni power, *FEER*, November 14: 59–60.

[40] B. Barringer, F. Jones, & D. Neubaum, 2005, A quantitative content analysis of the characteristics of rapid-growth firms and their founders, *JBV*, 20: 663–687.

[41] L. Busenitz, C. Gomez, & J. Spencer, 2000, Country institutional profiles, *AMJ*, 43: 994–1003; R. Mitchell, B. Smith, K. Seawright, & E. Morse, 2000, Cross-cultural cognitions and the venture creation decision, *AMJ*, 43: 974–993; J. Oxley & B. Yeung, 2001, E-commerce readiness, *JIBS*, 32: 705–724; H. K. Steensma, L. Marino, M. Weaver, & P. Hickson, 2000, The influence of national culture on the formation of technology alliances by entrepreneurial firms, *AMJ*, 43: 951–973; H. Yeung, 2002, Entrepreneurship in international business, *APJM*, 19: 29–61.

[42] Y. Yamakawa, M. W. Peng, & D. Deeds, 2008, What drives new ventures to internationalize from emerging to developed economies? *ETP* (in press).

[43] H. Sapienza, E. Autio, G. George, & S. Zahra, 2006, A capabilities perspective on the effects of early internationalization on firm survival and growth, *AMR*, 31: 914–933.

[44] V. Govindarajan & A. Gupta, 2001, *The Quest for Global Dominance*, San Francisco: Jossey-Bass.

[45] K. Kling & I. Goteman, 2003, IKEA CEO Anders Dahlvig on international growth, *AME*, 17: 31–45.

[46] E. Autio, H. Sapienza, & J. Almeida, 2000, Effects of age at entry, knowledge intensity, and imitability in international growth, *AMJ*, 43: 909–924.

[47] J. Mathews & I. Zander, 2007, The international entrepreneurial dynamics of accelerated internationalization, *JIBS*, 38: 387–403; S. Nadkarni & P. Perez, 2007, Prior conditions and early international commitment, *JIBS*, 38: 160–176.

[48] P. Liesch & G. Knight, 1999, Information internationalization and hurdle rates in small and medium enterprise internationalization, *JIBS*, 30: 383–394.

[49] P. McDougall & B. Oviatt, 1996, New venture internationalization, strategic change, and performance, *JBV*, 11: 23–40.

[50] M. Lyles, T. Saxton, & K. Watson, 2004, Venture survival in a transition economy, *JM*, 30: 351–373.

[51] S. Rangan & R. Adner, 2001, Profits and the Internet (pp. 49–50), *SMR*, Summer: 44–53.

[52] This section draws heavily on S. Lee, M. W. Peng, & J. Barney, 2007, Bankruptcy law and entrepreneurship development, *AMR*, 32: 257–272.

[53] R. McGrath, 1999, Falling forward: Real options reasoning and entrepreneurial failure, *AMR*, 24: 13–30.

[54] D. Shepherd, 2003, Learning from business failure, *AMR*, 28: 318–328.

[55] A. Knott & H. Posen, 2005, Is failure good? *SMJ*, 26: 617–641; S. Lee, Y. Yamakawa, & M. W. Peng, 2007, How does bankruptcy law affect entrepreneurship development? Working paper, University of Texas at Dallas.

[56] M. W. Peng, C. Hill, & D. Wang, 2000, Schumpeterian dynamics versus Williamsonian considerations, *JMS*, 37: 167–184.

CHAPTER 10

Entering Foreign Markets

OPENING CASE

A Warship Named Joint Venture

With a military budget larger than that of the next five powers combined, the United States is the world's largest defense market. For non-US firms, however, this is also the toughest nut to crack because the US military is famously protective of US firms. It is, therefore, remarkable that one Australian shipbuilder, Incat, has whetted the appetite of *all* branches of the US military except the Air Force.

Incat's secret? A world-leading technology in high-speed wave-piercing catamarans that allows it to have approximately 50% global market share of high-speed commercial ferries. Known as a "water jet," Incat's technology excels at high speeds in excess of 40 knots (40 sea miles per hour—one sea mile equals 1.852 kilometers), whereas traditional propeller technology can seldom perform at speeds higher than 30 knots. With relatively slight modifications, this technology can be adapted for military sealift and amphibious operations. A winning technology alone, however, is not enough. To enter the US defense market, in 2000 Incat set up a joint venture (JV) with Bollinger Shipyards, a Lockport, Louisiana-based builder of high-speed patrol boats. This JV was named Bollinger/Incat USA. In 2001, the US Navy, Army, Marines, and Coast Guard combined their resources to lease from the Bollinger/Incat USA JV a 96-meter (313-foot) high-speed craft, appropriately named the *Joint Venture* (HSV-X1), which was built by Incat in Tasmania, Australia.

In 2003, as part of Operation Iraqi Freedom, the *Joint Venture* successfully acted as a command, control, and staging platform for the special operations forces that assaulted and took the Iraqi port of Umm Qasr. Its sister ship built by Incat, the *Spearhead* (TSV-1X), also excelled in Iraq in 2003. Operating in shallow waters within sight of hostile shores, the *Joint Venture* and the *Spearhead* enabled special operations forces to independently operate a significant complement of troops and equipment for seven days unsupplied by the large Navy ships, which had to remain in safer, deep-water areas. These two ships thus significantly improved the efficiency, effectiveness, and safety of the forces deployed.

Action speaks louder than words. In 2003, overwhelming interests from US forces led Incat to build a third ship for the US military, the *Swift* (HSV-2), by incorporating the lessons learned from the *Joint Venture* and the *Spearhead*. In 2005, as part of the Hurricane Katrina relief force, the *Swift* served as a fast shuttle ship for other Navy ships in the Gulf of Mexico. Its higher payload required fewer trips than a smaller craft, and its shallow draft enabled it to enter ports that were inaccessible to deep-draft ships—a valuable and rare capability at a time when many port facilities were damaged by the hurricane.

Particularly useful in the war on terrorism and humanitarian missions, these leased ships led the US Navy to formally establish a Joint High Speed Vessel (JHSV) program. A contract for eight ships, at $200 million each, is scheduled to be awarded in 2008. Although the Navy will administer an open competition, guess which JV has the best odds for winning this contract to build the next generation *Joint Venture*?

Sources: Based on (1) http://www.bollinger-incatusa.com; (2) http://www.incat.com.au.

LEARNING OBJECTIVES

After studying this chapter, you should be able to

1. understand how institutions and resources affect liability of foreignness
2. match the quest for location-specific advantages with strategic goals (*where* to enter)
3. compare and contrast first- and late-mover advantages (*when* to enter)
4. follow the comprehensive model of foreign market entries (*how* to enter)
5. participate in three leading debates on foreign market entries
6. draw implications for action

How do numerous companies such as Incat enter foreign markets? Why do they enter certain countries but not others? Why did Incat establish a JV with a host-country firm (Bollinger) instead of setting up a wholly owned subsidiary? These are some of the key questions in this chapter. Entering foreign markets is one of the most important topics in international business. This chapter first draws on the institution- and resource-based view to discuss ways to overcome liability of foreignness. Then we focus on three crucial dimensions: where, when, and how—known as the 2W1H dimensions. Our discussion culminates in a comprehensive model, followed by debates and extensions.

LEARNING OBJECTIVE 1

understand how institutions and resources affect liability of foreignness

OVERCOMING LIABILITY OF FOREIGNNESS

It is not easy to succeed in an unfamiliar environment. Recall from Chapter 1 that foreign firms have to overcome liability of foreignness, which is the *inherent* disadvantage foreign firms experience in host countries because of their nonnative status.[1] Such a liability is manifested in at least two dimensions. First, there are numerous differences in formal and informal institutions governing the rules of the game in different countries. Local firms are already well versed in these rules, but foreign firms have to learn the rules quickly. For instance, EADS, Airbus's parent company, hired a number of retired US military officers to better compete for US defense contracts. Many governments ban foreigners from owning assets in certain strategic sectors. Media mogul Rupert Murdoch (owner of News Corporation) had to become a US citizen in order to acquire US broadcast properties. Emilio Azcárraga (owner of Grupo Televista, Mexico's leading broadcaster) is reportedly considering doing the same—becoming a US citizen—to better push across the US border.[2]

Second, although customers in this age of globalization *supposedly* no longer discriminate against foreign firms, the reality is that foreign firms are often still discriminated against, sometimes formally and other times informally. In government procurement, "buy national" (such as "buy American") is often required. In consumer products, the discrimination against foreign firms is less frequent but is still far from disappearing. For years, American rice and beef, suspected (although never proven) to contain long-term health hazards because of genetic modification, are informally resisted by individual consumers in Japan and Europe, *after* formal discriminatory policies imposed by their governments were removed. In India, activists singled out both Coca-Cola and Pepsi products as containing pesticides higher than permitted levels. However, they chose not to test any Indian soft drinks that might contain even higher pesticide levels in a country where pesticide residues are present in virtually all groundwater. Although both Coca-Cola and Pepsi denied these charges, their sales suffered.

Against such significant odds, how do foreign firms crack new markets? The answer boils down to our two core perspectives introduced earlier (see Figure 10.1). The institution-based view suggests that firms need to undertake actions deemed legitimate and appropriate by the various formal and informal institutions governing market entries. Differences in formal institutions may lead to regulatory risks due to differences in political, economic, and legal systems (see Chapter 2). There may be numerous trade and investment barriers on a national or regional basis (see Chapters 5, 6, and 8). In addition, we may view the existence of multiple currencies—and currency risks as a result—as another formal barrier (see Chapter 7). The experience of the euro shows how much more trade and investment can take place when multiple countries remove such a barrier by adopting the same currency (see Chapter 8). Informally, numerous differences in cultures, norms, and values create another major source of liability of foreignness (see Chapter 3). In addition, there are norms within one industry and among firms from the same

FIGURE 10.1 **INSTITUTIONS, RESOURCES, AND FOREIGN MARKET ENTRIES**

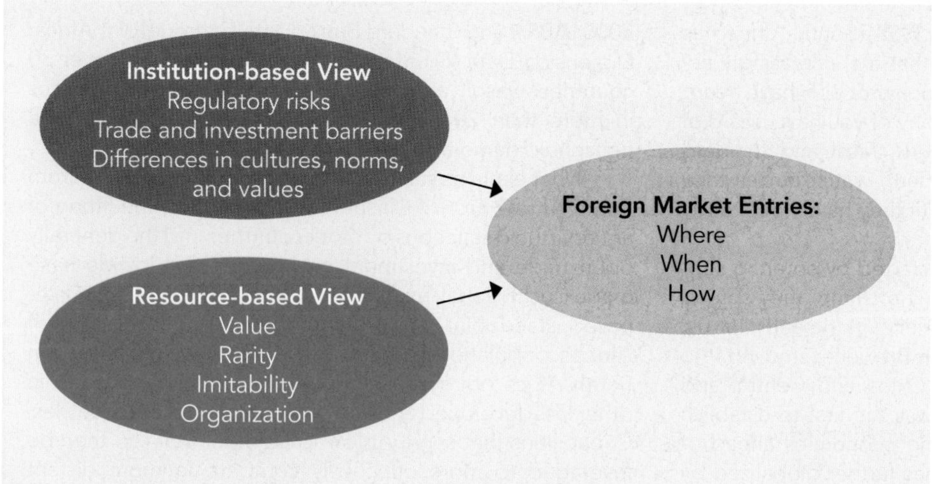

home country that may drive foreign market entries. For instance, the seven Baby Bells, offspring of the 1984 breakup of AT&T, intensely benchmarked against each other in their expansion into Latin America.[3]

The resource-based view argues that foreign firms need to deploy *overwhelming* resources and capabilities so that, after offsetting the liability of foreignness, there is still some competitive advantage.[4] Using the VRIO framework introduced in Chapter 4, we can suggest that Incat's technology is overwhelmingly valuable and rare. Its warships were first deployed by the Royal Australian Navy and caught the eyes of the US military in joint operations. Yet, no US rivals are able to imitate Incat's technology. Finally, Incat's strong organizational capability in not only designing and manufacturing but also servicing these high-tech warships around the world has proven to be a tremendous asset.

Overall, our two core perspectives shed a lot of light on firms' internationalization.[5] For example, In Focus 10.1 illustrates why there is a recent surge of multinational enterprises (MNEs) from South Africa. Next, we investigate the 2W1H dimensions associated with foreign market entries.

WHERE TO ENTER?

LEARNING OBJECTIVE 2

match the quest for location-specific advantages with strategic goals (*where* to enter)

Like real estate, the motto for international business is "Location, location, location." In fact, such a *spatial* perspective (that is, doing business outside one's home country) is a defining feature of international business.[6] Two sets of considerations drive the location of foreign entries: (1) strategic goals and (2) cultural and institutional distances. Each is discussed next.

Location-Specific Advantages and Strategic Goals

Favorable locations in certain countries may give firms operating there what are called **location-specific advantages**. We may regard the continuous expansion of international business as an unending saga in search of location-specific advantages. Certain locations possess geographic features that are difficult for others to match. Singapore, for instance, is an ideal stopping point for sea and air traffic connecting Europe and the Middle East on the one hand and East Asia and Australia

location-specific advantages Favorable locations in certain countries may give firms operating there an advantage.

IN FOCUS 10.1 South African Firms Spread Their Wings Abroad

Since apartheid was removed in 1994, South Africa has brewed a series of multinationals that are increasingly active abroad. Most readers of this book probably have heard of De Beers diamonds, but how many of you have heard of ABSA, Didata, MTN, Old Mutual, SAB, Sasol, and Standard Bank? If you have not heard of them, watch out as they soon may come to a city near you (if they have not already arrived).

Naturally, South African firms started by entering sub-Saharan African countries. After a short time, they spread their wings beyond the shores of Africa. In the early 1990s, SAB, the acronym for South African Breweries, moved into five African countries as well as China and Central and Eastern Europe. This meant SAB was the first to establish strong positions in major emerging economies ahead of other big brewers. Since then, it has further globalized by acquiring Miller, an American firm, in 2002. More recently, SABMiller—as the company is now known—has become the second largest brewer in South America when it bought Bavaria based in Colombia. Although SABMiller is a global leader in its industry, it is not alone among firms based in South Africa. Old Mutual, South Africa's biggest financial services firm, bought Sweden's oldest insurance firm in 2005. ABSA and Standard Bank operate throughout Africa. Dimension Data (Didata), an IT firm, competes in over 30 countries. Sasol, a chemicals and energy firm, operates in more than 20 countries. MTN, a telecom giant, is a household name throughout Africa.

What explains such a surge of internationalization from South Africa? From an institution-based view, the lifting of antiapartheid sanctions by other countries and the generally open trade and investment environment worldwide have made such global expansion possible. From a resource-based standpoint, since South Africa represents 5% of Africa's population but 45% of its GDP, winning firms in South Africa not surprisingly have a competitive edge in other less developed and less competitive African countries. Capabilities that serve African customers well can then be leveraged to more effectively compete in more distant emerging economies such as China, Central and Eastern Europe, and South America.

Sources: Based on (1) S. Burgess, 2003, Within-country diversity: Is it key to South Africa's prosperity in a changing world? *International Journal of Advertising*, 22: 157–182; (2) *Economist*, 2006, Chasing the rainbow: A survey of South Africa, April 8: 1–12; (3) *Economist*, 2006, Going global, July 15: 59–60.

on the other hand. Vienna is an attractive site as MNE regional headquarters for Central and Eastern Europe. Miami, which advertises itself as the Gateway of the Americas, is an ideal location both for North American firms looking south and Latin American companies coming north.

Beyond geographic advantages, location-specific advantages also arise from the clustering of economic activities in certain locations, usually referred to as **agglomeration**. The basic idea dates back at least to Alfred Marshall, a British economist who first published it in 1890. Essentially, location-specific advantages stem from (1) knowledge spillovers among closely located firms that attempt to hire individuals from competitors, (2) industry demand that creates a skilled labor force whose members may work for different firms without having to move out of the region, and (3) industry demand that facilitates a pool of specialized suppliers and buyers to also locate in the region.[7] Agglomeration explains why certain cities and regions, in the absence of obvious geographic advantages, can attract businesses. For example, due to agglomeration, financial services firms flock to Ireland (see Figure 10.2), and Slovakia produces more cars per capita than any other country in the world (see In Focus 10.2).

agglomeration
Beyond geographic advantages, location-specific advantages also arise from the clustering of economic activities in certain locations.

Given that different locations offer different benefits, it is imperative that strategic goals be matched with locations (Table 10.1).

natural resource seeking
Firms' quest to pursue natural resources in certain locations.

market seeking
Firms' quest to go after countries that offer strong demand for their products and services.

- Firms interested in **natural resource seeking** have to go after certain resources that are tied to particular foreign locations, such as oil in the Middle East, Russia, and Venezuela. Although the Venezuelan government is more hostile now, Western oil firms have to put up with it.
- **Market seeking** firms go after countries that offer strong demand for their products and services. For example, the Japanese appetite and willingness to pay for seafood have motivated seafood exporters around the world—ranging from

FIGURE 10.2 AGGLOMERATION OF FINANCIAL SERVICES FIRMS IN IRELAND

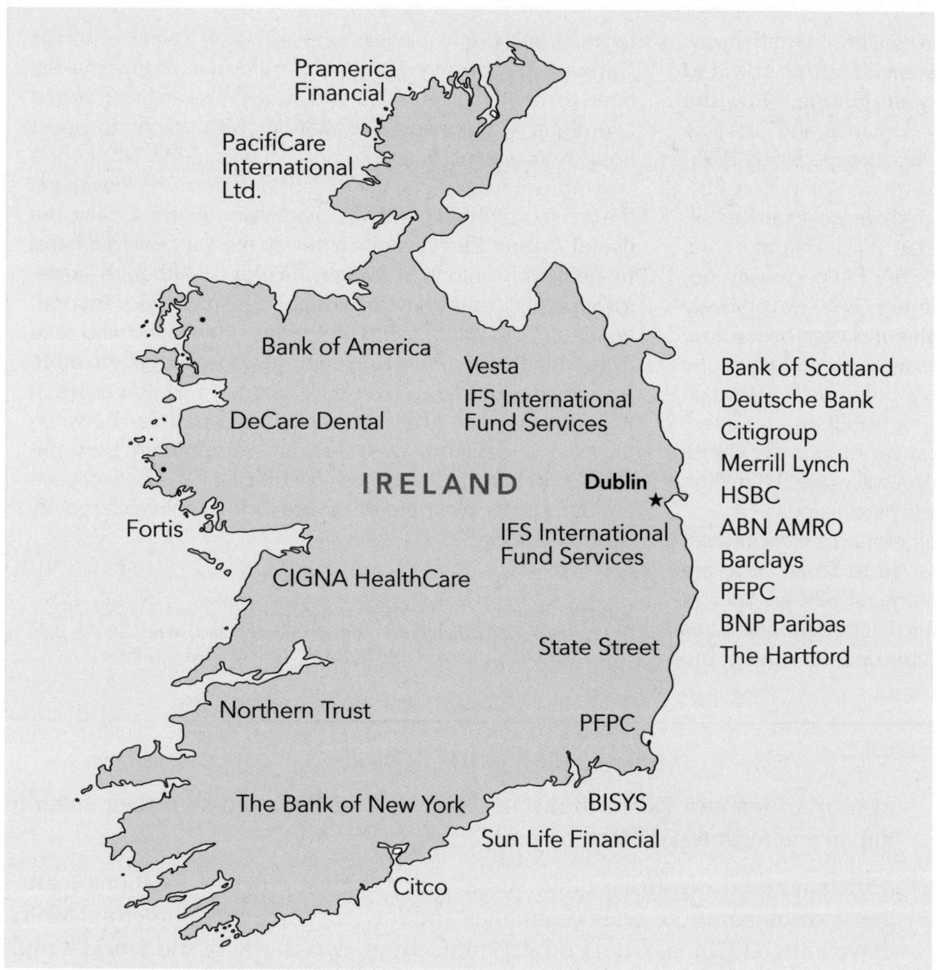

Source: IDA Ireland—Irish government's inward investment agency.

TABLE 10.1 MATCHING STRATEGIC GOALS WITH LOCATIONS

Strategic goals	Location-specific advantages	Illustrative locations mentioned in the text
Natural resource seeking	Possession of natural resources and related transport and communication infrastructure	Oil in the Middle East, Russia, and Venezuela
Market seeking	Abundance of strong market demand and customers willing to pay	Seafood in Japan
Efficiency seeking	Economies of scale and abundance of low-cost factors	Manufacturing in China
Innovation seeking	Abundance of innovative individuals, firms, and universities	IT in Silicon Valley and Bangalore; financial services in New York and London; aerospace in Russia

IN FOCUS 10.2 Making Cars in Central Europe

Central Europe is a centuries-old geopolitical term that was seldom used during the Cold War, when Europe was divided between Western Europe and Eastern Europe. Now, the Czech Republic, Hungary, Poland, Romania, and Slovakia are collectively labeled Central Europe again. Since 1995, automakers have pumped in more than $24 billion FDI, transforming the region into the world's newest car capital, nicknamed "Detroit East." Audi, Fiat, Ford, Hyundai, Kia, Opel (GM's German subsidiary), PSA Peugeot Citroën, Renault, Suzuki, Toyota, Volkswagen (VW)—everybody who wants to be somebody in this industry has come. The hub of this corridor from Warsaw to Budapest is tiny Slovakia, whose population is only 5.4 million. Slovakia produces close to one million cars, or about one for every six residents. It thus has the *highest* car output per capita in the world. By 2010, Central Europe will make 3.8 million cars, about 20% of Western Europe's production.

The advantages for such agglomeration are enormous. First, labor costs in Central Europe, $3 to $6 an hour, are significantly cheaper than the average of $29 an hour in Western Europe. Second, work ethic is stronger and rules more flexible in the east. At VW's plants on both sides of the former Iron Curtain, Slovaks work 40 hours a week, whereas Germans put in only 28 hours. In Slovakia, if automakers need to meet a surge in demand, new shifts can be arranged overnight. In Germany, negotiations with unions to boost hours may take up to six *months*. Thanks to low labor costs and motivated workers, VW's Bratislava factory in Slovakia is the most profitable of 42 VW plants worldwide. Finally, the rise of Detroit East has given automakers a powerful hand to deal with unions in Western Europe. Although large-scale plant closures have not happened in Western Europe, no union boss will demand pay raises when faced with such a credible threat. Moreover, competition will become more ferocious as the first China-built cars from Honda arrive in Western Europe. "This isn't about competition between Slovakia and Germany. It's about competition between China and Europe," said one VW official. "The only chance for Europe to compete is to use advantages offered by Central Europe."

Sources: Based on (1) *Business Week*, 2005, Detroit East, July 25: 48–51; (2) *Economist*, 2004, European carmaking: Going east, March 26: 60; (3) L. Johnson, 1996, *Central Europe*, New York: Oxford University Press.

nearby China and Korea to distant Norway and Peru—to ship their catch to Japan and fetch top dollars (or yen).

efficiency seeking
Firms' quest to single out the most efficient locations featuring a combination of scale economies and low-cost factors.

- **Efficiency seeking** firms often single out the most efficient locations featuring a combination of scale economies and low-cost factors.[8] Numerous MNEs have entered China. China now manufactures two-thirds of the world's photocopiers, shoes, toys, and microwave ovens; half of its DVD players, digital cameras, and textiles; one-third of its desktop computers; and a quarter of its mobile phones, TV sets, and steel.[9] Shanghai alone reportedly has a cluster of over 300 of the *Fortune* Global 500 firms there. It is important to note that China does not present the absolutely lowest labor costs in the world, and Shanghai is the *highest* cost city in China. However, its attractiveness lies in its ability to enhance foreign entrants' efficiency by lowering *total* costs. Since the key efficiency concern is lowest total costs, it is also not surprising that some nominally "high-cost" countries (such as the United States) continue to attract significant FDI. For instance, Grupo Mexico, the world's third largest copper producer, has moved some of its energy-thirsty refining operations from "high-cost" Mexico to "low-cost" Texas, where electricity costs 4 cents per kilowatt hour as opposed to 8.5 cents in Mexico.[10]

© Iain Masterton / Alamy

What makes China so attractive to MNEs as a manufacturing location?

- **Innovation seeking** firms target countries and regions renowned for generating world-class innovations, such as Silicon Valley and Bangalore (IT), New York and London (financial services), and Russia (aerospace). Such entries can be viewed as "an option to maintain access to innovations resident in the host country, thus generating information spillovers that may lead to opportunities for future organizational learning and growth"[11] (see Chapter 13 for details).

innovation seeking
Firms target countries and regions renowned for generating world-class innovations.

It is important to note that these four strategic goals, while analytically distinct, are not mutually exclusive. Also, location-specific advantages may grow, evolve, and/or decline. If policymakers fail to maintain the institutional attractiveness (for example, by raising taxes) and if companies overcrowd and bid up factor costs such as land and talents, some firms may move out of certain locations previously considered advantageous.[12] For instance, Mercedes and BMW had proudly projected a 100% "Made-in-Germany" image until the early 1990s. Both are now replacing it with "Made-by-Mercedes" and "Made-by-BMW" products manufactured in a series of countries such as Brazil, China, Mexico, South Africa, United States, and Vietnam. Such an emphasis on firm-specific (as opposed to location-specific) advantages illustrates both the relative decline of Germany's location-specific advantages and the rise of other countries' advantages (see Chapter 6 Opening Case).

Cultural/Institutional Distances and Foreign Entry Locations

In addition to strategic goals, another set of considerations centers on cultural/institutional distances (see also Chapters 2 and 3). **Cultural distance** is the difference between two cultures along some identifiable dimensions (such as individualism).[13] Considering culture as an informal part of institutional frameworks governing a particular country, **institutional distance** is "the extent of similarity or dissimilarity between the regulatory, normative, and cognitive institutions of two countries."[14] Many Western consumer products firms have shied away from Saudi Arabia, citing its stricter rules of personal behavior—in essence, cultural and institutional distance is too large.

cultural distance
The difference between two cultures along some identifiable dimensions (such as individualism).

institutional distance
The extent of similarity or dissimilarity between the regulatory, normative, and cognitive institutions of two countries.

Two schools of thought have emerged. The first is associated with stage models, arguing that firms will enter culturally similar countries during their first stage of internationalization and that they may gain more confidence to enter culturally distant countries in later stages.[15] This idea is intuitively appealing: It makes sense for Belgian and Russian firms to first enter, respectively, France and Ukraine, taking advantage of common cultural and linguistic traditions. Business between countries that share a language on average is three times greater than between countries without a common language. Firms from common-law countries (English-speaking countries and Britain's former colonies) are more likely to be interested in other common-law countries. Colony-colonizer links (such as Britain's ties with the Commonwealth, France's with the franc zone of West Africa, and Spain's with Latin America) boost trade significantly. In general, MNEs from emerging economies perform better in other developing countries, presumably because of their closer institutional distance and similar stages of economic development.[16] There is some evidence documenting certain performance benefits of competing in culturally and institutionally adjacent countries.[17]

Citing numerous counterexamples, a second school of thought argues that considerations of strategic goals such as market and efficiency are more important than cultural/institutional considerations.[18] For instance, natural resource seeking firms have some compelling reasons to enter culturally and institutionally distant countries (such as Papua New Guinea for bauxite, Zambia for copper, and Nigeria for oil). On Sakhalin Island, a very remote part of the Russian Far East rich with energy reserves, Western oil majors have to live with Russia's unfriendly, strong-arm tactics to grab more shares and profits that are recently described as "thuggish ways" by the *Economist*.[19] Because Western oil majors have few alternatives elsewhere, cultural, institutional, and geographic distance in this case does not seem relevant; these firms simply have to be there and let the Russians dictate the terms. Further, there is some counterintuitive (although inconclusive) evidence that in a particular host country, firms from distant countries do not necessarily underperform those from neighboring countries.[20] Overall, in the complex calculus underpinning entry decisions, locations represent but one of several important sets of considerations. As shown next, entry timing and modes are also crucial.

LEARNING OBJECTIVE 3

compare and contrast first- and late-mover advantages (*when* to enter)

first-mover advantages
Advantages that first movers obtain and that later movers do not enjoy.

late-mover advantages
Advantages that late movers obtain and that first movers do not enjoy.

WHEN TO ENTER?

Unless a firm is approached by unsolicited foreign customers that may lead to "passive" entries, conscientious entry timing considerations center on whether there are compelling reasons to be early or late entrants in certain countries.[21] There is often a quest for **first-mover advantages**, defined as the advantages that first movers obtain and that later movers do not enjoy.[22] However, first movers may also encounter significant disadvantages, which in turn become **late-mover advantages**. Table 10.2 shows a number of first-mover advantages.

- First movers may gain advantage through proprietary technology. They also ride down the learning curve in pursuit of scale and scope economies in new countries, as evidenced by Incat in wave-piercing technology (Opening Case).
- First movers may make preemptive investments. A number of Japanese MNEs have "cherry picked" leading local suppliers and distributors as new members of the expanded *keiretsu* networks in Southeast Asia and blocked access to them by late entrants from the West.[23]
- First movers may erect significant entry barriers for late entrants, such as customer switching costs. Parents, having bought one brand of disposable diapers (such as Huggies or Pampers) for their first child, often stick with this brand for their other children. Buyers of expensive equipment are likely to stick with the same producers for components, training, and other services for a long time. That is why American, British, French, German, and Russian aerospace firms competed intensely for Poland's first post–Cold War order of fighters. America's F-16 eventually won.

TABLE 10.2 FIRST-MOVER ADVANTAGES AND LATE-MOVER ADVANTAGES

First-mover advantages	Late-mover advantages (or first-mover disadvantages)
• Proprietary, technological leadership • Preemption of scarce resources • Establishment of entry barriers for late entrants • Avoidance of clash with dominant firms at home • Relationships and connections with key stakeholders such as customers and governments	• Opportunity to free ride on first-mover investments • Resolution of technological and market uncertainty • First mover's difficulty to adapt to market changes

- Intense domestic competition may drive some nondominant firms to seek fortunes abroad to avoid clashing with dominant firms head on in their home market. Among Japanese MNEs active in the United States, Sony, Honda, and Epson all entered ahead of their domestic industry leaders, Matsushita, Toyota, and NEC, respectively.
- First movers may build precious relationships with key stakeholders such as customers and governments. Motorola, for example, entered China in the early 1980s and benefited from its long-time presence in the country. Later, China adopted Motorola's technology as its national paging standard, locking out other rivals (at least for the initial period).

On the other hand, the potential advantages of first movers may be counterbalanced by various disadvantages (see Table 10.2). There are numerous examples of first-mover firms that have lost, such as EMI in CT scanner, de Haviland in jet airliner, and Netscape in Internet browser. It is such late-mover firms as GE, Boeing, and Microsoft (Explorer), respectively, that won. Specifically, late-mover advantages are manifested in three ways.

- Late movers may be able to free ride on first movers' huge pioneering investments. For example, a first mover in 3G telecommunications technology, such as Hong Kong's Hutchison Whampoa that is trying to introduce 3G in nine countries simultaneously, needs to incur huge advertising expenses to educate customers on *both* what 3G technology is and why its offering is the best. A late mover can free ride on such customer education by only focusing on why its particular product is the best.
- First movers face greater technological and market uncertainties. After some of these uncertainties are removed, late movers may join the game with massive firepower. Some MNEs such as IBM and Matsushita are known to have such a tendency.
- As incumbents, first movers may be locked into a given set of fixed assets or reluctant to cannibalize existing product lines in favor of new ones. Late movers may be able to take advantage of first movers' inflexibility by leapfrogging first movers.

Overall, there is some evidence pointing out first-mover advantages,[24] but there is also evidence supporting a late-mover strategy.[25] Unfortunately, a mountain of research is still unable to conclusively recommend a particular entry timing strategy. Although first movers may have an *opportunity* to win, their pioneering status is not a birthright for success.[26] For example, among all three first movers that entered the Chinese automobile industry in the early 1980s, Volkswagen captured significant advantages, Chrysler had very moderate success, and Peugeot failed and had to exit. Among late movers that entered in the late 1990s, while many are struggling, GM, Honda, and Hyundai have gained significant market shares. It is obvious that entry timing cannot be viewed in isolation, and entry timing per se is not the sole determinant of success and failure of foreign entries. It is through *interaction* with other strategic variables that entry timing has an impact on performance.[27]

HOW TO ENTER?

LEARNING OBJECTIVE 4

follow the comprehensive model of foreign market entries (*how* to enter)

This section first focuses on the large- versus small-scale entry. Then it introduces a comprehensive model. The first step is to determine whether to pursue equity or nonequity modes of entry. This crucial decision differentiates MNEs (involving equity modes) from non-MNEs (relying on nonequity modes). Finally, we outline the pros and cons of various equity and nonequity modes.

Scale of Entry: Commitment and Experience

scale of entry
The amount of resources committed to foreign market entry.

One key dimension in foreign entry decisions is the **scale of entry**. A number of European financial services firms, such as ABN Amro, HSBC, and ING Group, have recently spent several billion dollars to enter the United States by making a series of acquisitions. The benefits of these large-scale entries demonstrate strategic commitment to certain markets. This both helps assure local customers and suppliers ("We are here for the long haul!") and deters potential entrants. The drawbacks of such hard-to-reverse strategic commitment are (1) limited strategic flexibility elsewhere and (2) huge losses if these large-scale "bets" turn out wrong.

Small-scale entries are less costly. They focus on organizational learning by getting firms' feet "wet"—learning by doing—while limiting the downside risk.[28] For example, to enter the market of Islamic finance in which no interest can be charged (per teaching of the Koran), Citibank set up a subsidiary Citibank Islamic Bank, HSBC established Amanah, and UBS launched Noriba. They were all designed to experiment with different interpretations of the Koran on how to make money while not committing religious sins. It is simply not possible to acquire such ability outside the Islamic world. Overall, there is evidence that the longer foreign firms stay in host countries, the less liability of foreignness they experience.[29] The drawbacks of small-scale entries are a lack of strong commitment, which may lead to difficulties in building market share and capturing first-mover advantages.

Modes of Entry: The First Step on Equity versus Nonequity Modes

modes of entry
The format of foreign market entry.

Modes of entry are the format of foreign market entries. Among numerous modes of entry, managers are unlikely to consider all of them at the same time. Given the complexity of entry decisions, it is imperative that managers *prioritize* by considering only a few manageable, key variables first and then considering other variables later. Therefore, a comprehensive model shown in Figure 10.3 and explained in Table 10.3 is helpful.[30]

nonequity mode
A mode of entry (exports and contractual agreements) that tends to reflect relatively smaller commitments to overseas markets.

equity mode
A mode of entry (JVs and wholly owned subsidiaries) that is indicative of relatively larger, harder to reverse commitments.

In the first step, considerations for small- versus large-scale entries usually boil down to the equity (ownership) issue. **Nonequity modes** (exports and contractual agreements) tend to reflect relatively smaller commitments to overseas markets, whereas **equity modes** (JVs and wholly owned subsidiaries) are indicative of relatively larger, harder to reverse commitments. Equity modes call for the establishment of independent organizations overseas (partially or wholly controlled). Nonequity modes do not require such independent establishments. Overall, these modes differ significantly in terms of cost, commitment, risk, return, and control (see numerous examples in the next section).

The distinction between equity and nonequity modes is not trivial. In fact, it is what defines an MNE: An MNE enters foreign markets via equity modes through foreign direct investment (FDI). A firm that merely exports/imports with no FDI is usually not regarded as an MNE. As discussed at length in Chapter 6, an MNE, relative to a non-MNE, enjoys the three-pronged advantages along ownership, location, and internalization dimensions—collectively known as the OLI advantages.[31] Overall, the first step in entry mode considerations is crucial. A strategic decision has to be made in terms of whether or not to undertake FDI and to become an MNE by selecting equity modes.

Modes of Entry: The Second Step on Making Actual Selections

During the second step, managers consider variables within *each* group of nonequity and equity modes.[32] If the decision is to export, then next on the agenda would be direct exports or indirect exports (also discussed in Chapter 9). Direct exports

TABLE 10.3 MODES OF ENTRY: ADVANTAGES AND DISADVANTAGES

Entry modes	Advantages	Disadvantages
1. Nonequity modes: Exports		
Direct exports	• Economies of scale in production concentrated in home country • Better control over distribution	• High transportation costs for bulky products • Marketing distance from customers • Trade barriers and protectionism
Indirect exports	• Concentration of resources on production • No need to directly handle export processes	• Less control over distribution (relative to direct exports) • Inability to learn how to operate overseas
2. Nonequity modes: Contractual agreements		
Licensing/ Franchising	• Low development costs • Low risk in overseas expansion	• Little control over technology and marketing • May create competitors • Inability to engage in global coordination
Turnkey projects	• Ability to earn returns from process technology in countries where FDI is restricted	• May create efficient competitors • Lack of long-term presence
R&D contracts	• Ability to tap into the best locations for certain innovations at low costs	• Difficult to negotiate and enforce contracts • May nurture innovative competitors • May lose core innovation capabilities
Co-marketing	• Ability to reach more customers	• Limited coordination
3. Equity modes: Partially owned subsidiaries		
Joint ventures	• Sharing costs, risks, and profits • Access to partners' knowledge and assets • Politically acceptable	• Divergent goals and interests of partners • Limited equity and operational control • Difficult to coordinate globally
4. Equity modes: Wholly owned subsidiaries		
Green-field operations	• Complete equity and operational control • Protection of know-how • Ability to coordinate globally	• Potential political problems and risks • High development costs • Add new capacity to industry • Slow entry speed (relative to acquisitions)
Acquisitions	• Same as green-field • Do not add new capacity • Fast entry speed	• Same as green-field, except adding new capacity and slow speed • Postacquisition integration problems

FIGURE 10.3 THE CHOICE OF ENTRY MODES: A COMPREHENSIVE MODEL

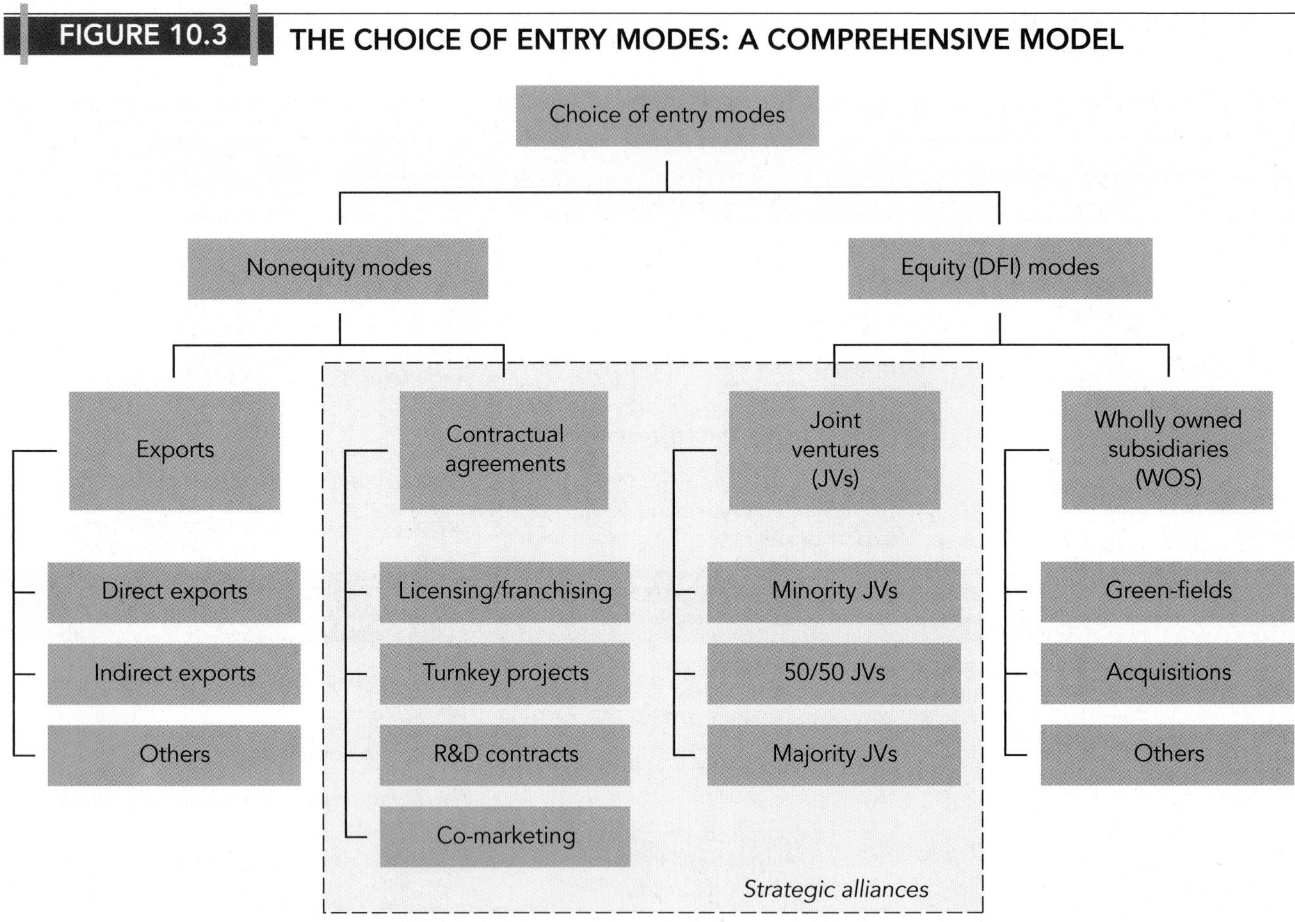

Source: Adapted from Y. Pan & D. Tse, 2000, The hierarchical model of market entry modes (p. 538), *Journal of International Business Studies*, 31: 535–554. The dotted area labeled "strategic alliances," including both nonequity modes (contractual agreements) and equity modes (JVs), is added by the present author.

represent the most basic mode, capitalizing on economies of scale in production concentrated in the home country and affording better control over distribution.[33] This strategy essentially treats foreign demand as an extension of domestic demand, and the firm is geared toward designing and producing for the domestic market first and foremost. Although direct exports may work if the export volume is small, it is not optimal when the firm has a large number of foreign buyers. "Marketing 101" suggests that the firm needs to be closer, both physically and psychologically, to its customers, prompting the firm to consider more intimate overseas involvement such as FDI. In addition, direct exports may provoke protectionism. In 1981, the success of direct automobile exports from Japan led the US government to impose a voluntary export restraint (VER) agreement on Japanese exports; never mind that in the absence of protectionist threats, the Japanese would not have voluntarily agreed to do so (see Chapter 5).

Another export strategy is indirect exports—namely, exporting through domestically based export intermediaries.[34] This strategy not only enjoys the economies of scale in domestic production (similar to direct exports), but it is also relatively worry-free. A significant amount of export trade in commodities (such as textiles, woods, and meats), which compete primarily on price, is indirect through intermediaries.[35] Indirect exports have some drawbacks because of the introduction of third parties such as export trading companies with their own agendas and objectives that are not necessarily the same as the exporter's.[36] The primary reason the exporter chooses intermediaries is because of information asymmetries concerning risks and uncertainties associated with foreign markets. Intermediaries with international contacts and knowledge essentially make a living by taking advantage of such information asymmetries. They may have a vested interest in making sure that such asymmetries are not reduced. Intermediaries, for example, may repackage the products under their own brand and insist on monopolizing the communication with overseas customers. If the exporter is interested in learning more about how its products perform overseas, indirect exports would not provide great opportunities for such learning.[37]

The next group of nonequity entry modes is contractual agreements consisting of (1) licensing/franchising, (2) turnkey projects, (3) R&D contracts, and (4) comarketing. First, as discussed in Chapter 9, in **licensing/franchising** agreements, the licensor/franchisor sells the rights to intellectual property such as patents and know-how to the licensee/franchisee for a royalty fee. Thus, the licensor/franchisor does not have to bear the full costs and risks associated with foreign expansion. On the other hand, the licensor/franchisor does not have tight control over production and marketing.[38] Its worst fear is to have nurtured a competitor, as Pizza Hut found out in Thailand. Its long-term licensee in Thailand, having learned the "tricks," terminated the licensing agreement and set up its own pizza restaurant chain that tried to eat Pizza Hut's lunch.

licensing/franchising
An agreement in which the licensor/franchisor sells the rights to intellectual property such as patents and know-how to the licensee/franchisee for a royalty fee.

Turnkey projects refer to projects in which clients pay contractors to design and construct new facilities and train personnel. At project completion, contractors will hand clients the proverbial "key" to facilities ready for operations—hence the term *turnkey*. The advantages entail the ability to earn returns from process technology in countries where FDI is restricted (such as power generation). The drawbacks are twofold. First, if foreign clients are competitors, selling them state-of-the-art technology through turnkey projects may boost their competitiveness. Second, turnkey projects do not allow for a long-term presence after the key is handed to clients. To obtain a longer term presence, **build-operate-transfer (BOT) agreements** are now often used instead of the traditional "build-transfer" type of turnkey projects. For instance, a consortium of German, Italian, and Iranian firms obtained a large-scale BOT power-generation project in Iran. After completion of the construction, the consortium will operate the project for 20 years before transferring it to the Iranian government.

turnkey project
A project in which clients pay contractors to design and construct new facilities and train personnel.

build-operate-transfer (BOT) agreement
A nonequity mode of entry used to build a longer term presence.

R&D contracts refer to outsourcing agreements in R&D between firms (that is, firm A agrees to perform certain R&D work for firm B). They allow firms to tap into the best locations for certain innovations at relatively low costs, such as IT work in India and aerospace research in Russia. However, three drawbacks may emerge. First, given the uncertain and multidimensional nature of R&D, these contracts are often difficult to negotiate and enforce. Although delivery time and costs are relatively easy to negotiate, quality is often difficult to assess. Second, such contracts may nurture competitors. A number of Indian IT firms, nurtured by such work, are now on a global offensive to take on their Western rivals (see Chapter 1 Opening Case). Finally, firms that rely on outsiders to perform a lot of R&D may in the long run lose some of their core R&D capabilities.

R&D contract
Outsourcing agreements in R&D between firms.

Co-marketing refers to efforts among a number of firms to jointly market their products and services. Fast-food chains such as McDonald's often launch co-marketing campaigns with movie studios and toy makers to hawk toys based on certain movie characters. Through code sharing, airline alliances such as One World and Star Alliance extensively engage in co-marketing. The advantages are the ability to reach more customers. The drawbacks center on limited control and coordination.

co-marketing
Efforts among a number of firms to jointly market their products and services.

The next group is equity modes, all of which entail some FDI, transforming the firm to become an MNE.[39] A **joint venture (JV)** is a "corporate child" that is a new entity given birth and jointly owned by two or more parent companies. It has three principal forms: minority JV (the focal firm holds less than 50% equity), 50/50 JV,

joint venture (JV)
A new corporate entity given birth and jointly owned by two or more parent companies.

and majority JV (more than 50% equity). JVs, such as Bollinger/Incat USA (see Opening Case), have three advantages. First, an MNE shares costs, risks, and profits with a local partner, possessing a certain degree of control while limiting risk exposure. Second, the MNE gains access to knowledge about the host country, and the local firm, in turn, benefits from the MNE's technology, capital, and management. Third, JVs may be politically more acceptable.

In terms of disadvantages, first, JVs often involve partners from different backgrounds and goals; conflicts are natural. Second, effective equity and operational control may be difficult to achieve because everything has to be negotiated (and in some cases, fought over). Finally, the nature of the JV does not give an MNE the tight control over a foreign subsidiary that it may need for global coordination (such as simultaneously launching new products around the world). Overall, all sorts of nonequity-based contractual agreements and equity-based JVs can be broadly considered as strategic alliances (within the *dotted area* in Figure 10.3). Chapter 12 will discuss them in detail.

wholly owned subsidiaries (WOS)
A subsidiary located in a foreign country that is entirely owned by the parent multinational.

green-field operation
Building factories and offices from scratch (on a proverbial piece of "green field" formerly used for agricultural purposes).

The last group of entry modes refers to **wholly owned subsidiaries (WOS)**. There are two primary means to set up a WOS.[40] The first is to establish **green-field operations**, building new factories and offices from scratch (on a proverbial piece of "green field" formerly used for agricultural purposes). There are three advantages. First, a green-field WOS gives an MNE complete equity and management control, thus eliminating the headaches associated with JVs. Second, this undivided control leads to better protection of proprietary technology. Third, a WOS allows for centrally coordinated global actions. Sometimes, a subsidiary will be ordered to launch actions that by design will *lose* money. For instance, Texas Instruments (TI) faced the low-price Japanese challenge in many countries, whereas rivals such as NEC and Toshiba were able to charge high prices in Japan and use domestic profits to cross-subsidize overseas expansion. By entering Japan and slashing prices there, TI retaliated by incurring a loss. However, this forced the Japanese firms to defend their profit sanctuary at home, where they had more to lose. Local licensees/franchisees or JV partners are unlikely to accept such a subservient role—being ordered to lose money (!). In terms of drawbacks, a green-field WOS tends to be expensive and risky not only financially but also politically. The conspicuous foreignness embodied in such a WOS may become a target for nationalistic sentiments. Another drawback is that green-field operations add new capacity to an industry, which will make a competitive industry more crowded—think of all the Japanese automobile transplants built in the United States. Finally, green-field operations, relative to acquisitions, suffer from a slow entry speed of at least one to two years.

The second way to establish a WOS is through an acquisition. Although this is the last mode we discuss here, it is probably the most important mode in terms of the amount of capital involved (representing approximately 70% of worldwide FDI). In addition to sharing all the benefits of green-field WOS, acquisitions enjoy two other advantages, namely, (1) adding no new capacity and (2) faster entry speed. For example, in less than a decade (the 1990s), two leading banks in Spain with little prior international experience, Santander and Bilbao Vizcaya, became the largest foreign banks in Latin America through some 20 acquisitions. In terms of drawbacks, acquisitions share all the disadvantages of green-field WOS, except adding new capacity and slow entry speed. In addition, acquisitions have to confront a unique and potentially devastating disadvantage—postacquisition integration problems (see Chapter 12).

Overall, while we have focused on one entry mode at a time, firms in practice are not limited by any single entry choice. For example, IKEA stores in China are JVs, and its stores in Hong Kong and Taiwan are separate franchises. In addition, entry modes may change over time.[41] Starbucks, for instance, first used franchising. It then switched to JVs and, more recently, to acquisitions.

DEBATES AND EXTENSIONS

LEARNING OBJECTIVE 5

participate in three leading debates on foreign market entries

This chapter has already covered some crucial debates, such as first- versus late-mover advantages. Here we discuss three heated *recent* debates: (1) liability versus asset of foreignness, (2) global versus regional geographic diversification, and (3) cyberspace versus conventional entries.

Liability versus Asset of Foreignness

While we do not need to spill more ink on the term "liability of foreignness," one contrasting view argues that under certain circumstances, being foreign can be an *asset* (that is, a competitive advantage). Japanese and German cars are viewed as of higher quality in the United States. Many American movies rake in more money overseas than at home. American cigarettes are "cool" among smokers in Central and Eastern Europe. Anything Korean—ranging from handsets and TV shows to *kimchi* (pickled cabbage) flavored instant noodles—is considered hip in Southeast Asia. Conceptually, this is known as the country-of-origin effect, which refers to the positive or negative perception of firms and products from a certain country.[42] However, whether foreignness is indeed an asset or a liability remains tricky. Disneyland Tokyo became wildly popular in Japan because it played up its American image. But Disneyland Paris received relentless negative press coverage in France because it insisted on its "wholesome American look."

Over time, the country-of-origin effect may shift. A number of UK firms used to proudly sport names such as British Telecom and British Petroleum. Recently, they have shied away from being "British" and rebranded themselves simply as BT and BP. In Britain, these changes are collectively known as the "B phenomenon." These costly rebranding campaigns are not casual changes. They reflect less confidence in the positive country-of-origin effect. Recently, BAE Systems, formerly British Aerospace, complained that its British origin is pulling its legs in its largest market, the US defense market. Only US citizens are allowed to know the details of its most sensitive US contracts, and even its British CEO cannot know such details. This is untenable now that two-fifths of its sales are in the United States. Thus, BAE Systems is giving serious consideration to becoming American. However, in an interesting twist, an Americanized BAE Systems may encounter liability of foreignness in Britain.[43] Not surprisingly, the B phenomenon is controversial in Britain. One lesson we can learn is that foreignness can either be a liability or an asset and that changes are possible.[44]

In Hong Kong Disneyland, is foreignness an asset or a liability?

Global versus Regional Geographic Diversification

In this age of globalization, there is a debate on the optimal geographic scope for MNEs. Despite the widely held belief (and frequently voiced criticism from anti-globalization activists) that MNEs are expanding "globally," Alan Rugman and Alain Verbeke report that, surprisingly, even among the largest *Fortune* Global 500 MNEs, few are truly "global."[45] Using some reasonable criteria (at least 20% of sales in *each* of the three regions of the Triad consisting of Asia, Europe, and North America but less than 50% in any one region), they find a total of only *nine* global MNEs (Column 1 of Table 10.4). Next to global MNEs, 25 firms are "biregional" MNEs that have at least 20% of sales in each of the two regions of the Triad but less

TABLE 10.4 GEOGRAPHIC DIVERSIFICATION OF THE LARGEST MULTINATIONAL ENTERPRISES (MNEs) BY SALES

	"Global" MNEs[1]		"Biregional" MNEs[2]		"Host-region-based" MNEs[3]
1	IBM	1	BP Amoco	1	DaimlerChrysler
2	Sony	2	Toyota	2	ING Group
3	Philips	3	Nissan	3	Royal Ahold
4	Nokia	4	Unilever	4	Honda
5	Intel	5	Motorola	5	Santander
6	Canon	6	GlaxoSmithKline	6	Delhaize "Le Lion"
7	Coca-Cola	7	EADS	7	AstraZeneca
8	Flextronics	8	Bayer	8	News Corporation
9	LVMH	9	Ericsson	9	Sodexho Alliance
		10	Alstom	10	Manpower
		11	Aventis	11	Wolseley
		12	Diageo		
		13	Sun Microsystems		
		14	Bridgestone		
		15	Roche		
		16	3M		
		17	Skanska		
		18	McDonald's		
		19	Michelin		
		20	Kodak		
		21	Electrolux		
		22	BAE		
		23	Alcan		
		24	L'Oreal		
		25	Lafarge		

1. Global MNEs have at least 20% of sales in each of the three regions of the Triad (Asia, Europe, and North America) but less than 50% in any one region.
2. Biregional MNEs have at least 20% of sales in each of the two regions of the Triad but less than 50% in any one region.
3. Host-region-based MNEs have more than 50% of sales in one of the Triad regions other than their home region.

Sources: Adapted from A. Rugman & A. Verbeke, 2004, A perspective on regional and global strategies of multinational enterprises (pp. 8–10), *Journal of International Business Studies*, 35: 3–18.

than 50% in any one. Interestingly, 11 MNEs are "host-region-based," with at least 50% of sales in one of the Triad regions other than their home region. The majority of the remaining *Fortune* Global 500 (over 450) are "home-region-oriented" MNEs; in other words, they may be labeled regional, but *not* global, firms.

Should most MNEs further globalize? There are two answers. First, most MNEs know what they are doing, and their current geographic scope is the maximum they can manage. Some of them may have already overdiversified and will need to downscope. Second, these data only capture a snapshot (the early 2000s), and some MNEs may become more globalized over time. While the debate goes on, it has at least taught us one important reason: Be careful when using the word "global."[46] The *majority* of the largest MNEs are not necessarily very global in their geographic scope.

Cyberspace versus Conventional Entries

From an institution-based view, the arrival of the Internet has sparked a new debate: Whose rules of the game should e-commerce follow? Although pundits argue that globalization is undermining the power of national governments, there is little evidence that the modern nation-state system, in existence since the 1648 Treaty of Westphalia, is retreating. Legally, one can argue that a *multinational* enterprise is a total fiction that does not exist. Since incorporation is only possible under national law, every MNE is essentially a bunch of *national* companies (subsidiaries) registered in various countries.

Although some suggest that geographic jurisdiction may be meaningless in cyberspace, others argue that the Internet is "no more a borderless medium than the telephone, the telegraph, postal service, facsimile, or smoke signal [of the ancient times]."[47] As the Yahoo! in France case (In Focus 10.3) illustrates, when the *formal* institutional constraints governing e-commerce clash, *informal* institutional constraints will rise, as predicted by the second proposition of the institution-based view (see Chapter 2). In the absence of harmonization among formal national regulations concerning cyberspace, such informal constraints will become more important in governing cross-border cyberspace activities.

MANAGEMENT SAVVY

LEARNING OBJECTIVE 6

draw implications for action

Foreign market entries represent a *foundation* for overseas actions. Without these crucial first steps, firms will remain domestic players. The challenges associated with internationalization are daunting, the complexities enormous, and the stakes high. Returning to our fundamental question, we ask: What determines the success and failure in foreign market entries? The answers boil down to the two core perspectives: institution- and resource-based views. Consequently, three implications for action emerge (Table 10.5). First, from an institution-based view, managers need to understand the rules of the game, both formal and informal, governing competition in foreign markets. Failure to understand these rules can be costly. Managers at Yahoo! initially ignored the rules of the game in France, ending up with a ton of bad press as the "defender of Nazi violence" that it could ill afford.

IN FOCUS 10.3 ETHICAL DILEMMA: Did Yahoo! Really Enter France?

In the late 1990s, Yahoo!, an American Internet portal, hosted third-party auctions, some of which sold Nazi memorabilia. Although perfectly legal, indeed protected under the First Amendment of the US Constitution, sales of Nazi items are illegal in France. Yahoo! was thus challenged in a French court. During the process, Yahoo! removed Nazi materials from its French language portal to comply with the French law. However, in November 2000, the French court ruled that Yahoo! must prevent French computer users from accessing any Yahoo! site—*in any language*—on which such items were sold or face a fine of 100,000 French francs (US$17,877) per day. Yahoo! first asked a US court to declare that this decision could not be enforced in the United States because it violated the First Amendment and that American firms were not obliged to follow French rules outside France. A US court supported this argument. However, by early 2001, Yahoo! changed its mind and decided to self-censor, removing all items that "promote or glorify violence or hatred" from its site.

© Richard Levine / Alamy

At the heart of this case is the controversy over whether France has the legal or ethical right to assert its law to order Yahoo!, which apparently had only a virtual presence in France, to change behavior that was in full compliance with US law. The fundamental question is whether national territorial jurisdiction applies to cyberspace. Some analysts saw the French decision as a dangerous one because taken to the extreme, it would imply that every jurisdiction on the planet regulates everything on the Internet. Others contend that cyberspace entries into foreign markets, just like bricks-and-mortar entries, have to follow local rules.

Sources: Based on (1) S. Kobrin, 2001, Territoriality and the governance of cyberspace, *Journal of International Business Studies*, 32: 687–704; (2) P. Lasserre, 2003, *Global Strategic Management* (p. 390), London: Palgrave.

TABLE 10.5 IMPLICATIONS FOR ACTION

- Understand the rules of game—both formal and informal—governing competition in foreign markets
- Develop overwhelming resources and capabilities to offset the liability of foreignness
- Match efforts in market entry and geographic diversification with strategic goals

Second, from a resource-based view, managers need to develop overwhelming capabilities to offset the liability of foreignness. In key emerging economies such as China, India, and Russia, which car company has the highest growth since 2005? Surprise—it is Hyundai! In both China and Russia, Hyundai is now the top-selling foreign brand car, and in India, it is a strong second. Hyundai's secret? The combination of its relatively advanced features (such as airbags and antilock brakes) that local rivals fall short and its more reasonable price tag ($15,000 for a Hyundai Elantra in Russia), which is cheaper than Japanese models. Such an unbeatable combination may eventually enable Hyundai to muscle its way to attain its stated goal—join the top five of global automakers.[48]

Finally, managers need to match entries with strategic goals. If the goal is to deter rivals in their home markets by slashing prices there (as TI did when entering Japan), then be prepared to fight a nasty price war and lose money. If the goal is to generate decent returns, then withdrawing from some tough nuts to crack may be necessary (as Wal-Mart withdrew from Germany and South Korea).

Overall, appropriate foreign market entries, while important, are only a beginning. To succeed overseas, postentry strategies are equally or more important. These would entail managing competitive dynamics (Chapter 11), making alliances and acquisitions work (Chapter 12), and creating dynamic and flexible structures (Chapter 13), all of which will be covered in later chapters.

CHAPTER SUMMARY

1. Understand how institutions and resources affect liability of foreignness
   - When entering foreign markets, firms confront liability of foreignness.
   - Both institution- and resource-based views advise managers on how to overcome such liability.
2. Match the quest for location-specific advantages with strategic goals (*where* to enter)
   - Where to enter depends on certain foreign countries' location-specific advantages and firms' strategic goals, such as seeking (1) natural resources, (2) market, (3) efficiency, and (4) innovation.
3. Compare and contrast first- and late-mover advantages (*when* to enter)
   - Each has pros and cons, and there is no conclusive evidence pointing in one direction.
4. Follow the comprehensive model of foreign market entries (*how* to enter)
   - How to enter depends on the scale of entry: large-scale versus small-scale entries.

- A comprehensive model of foreign market entries first focuses on the equity (ownership) issue.
- The second step focuses on making the actual selection, such as exports, contractual agreements, JVs, or wholly owned subsidiaries.

5. Participate in three leading debates on foreign market entries
   - The three leading debates are (1) liability versus asset of foreignness, (2) global versus regional geographic diversification, and (3) cyberspace versus conventional entries.
6. Draw implications for action
   - From an institution-based view, managers need to understand the rules of the game, both formal and informal, governing competition in foreign markets.
   - From a resource-based view, managers need to develop overwhelming capabilities to offset the liability of foreignness.
   - Managers must learn to match pre- and postentry efforts with the firm's strategic goals.

KEY TERMS

Agglomeration 280
Build-operate-transfer (BOT) agreement 289
Co-marketing 289
Cultural distance 283
Efficiency seeking 282
Equity mode 286
First-mover advantage 284
Green-field operation 290
Innovation seeking 282
Institutional distance 283
Joint venture (JV) 289
Late-mover advantage 284
Licensing/franchising 289
Location-specific advantage 279
Market seeking 280
Modes of entry 286
Natural resource seeking 280
Nonequity modes 286
R&D contract 289
Scale of entry 286
Turnkey project 289
Wholly owned subsidiary (WOS) 290

REVIEW QUESTIONS

1. Describe two ways in which foreign firms suffer from liability of foreignness.
2. What does the institution-based view indicate about how a firm should deal with the liability of foreignness? What does the resource-based view suggest?
3. What are some of the location-specific advantages found in agglomeration, the clustering of economic activities in a concentrated area?
4. Describe four attributes that can be found in foreign locations and how these might relate to a firm's strategic goals.
5. What is the difference between cultural distance and institutional distance?
6. Why might a firm choose to expand into a culturally similar country? Why might it choose to expand into a foreign country with very different qualities from its home location?
7. Summarize the five advantages of being a first mover.
8. What are three benefits of being a late mover?

9. How does a large-scale entry differ from a small-scale entry?
10. Name the two types of entry modes associated with exports, and explain how they differ.
11. Summarize four types of nonequity contractual agreements.
12. What are some of the hallmarks of each of the three types of equity modes?
13. How might the country-of-origin effect change for a firm over time?
14. Alan Rugman and Alain Verbeke assert that there are very few truly global firms. Why?
15. What type of institutional constraints is most important in governing business conducted in cyberspace?
16. Devise your own example of how a firm might use its capabilities to overwhelmingly offset the liability of foreignness as it moves into a new foreign market.
17. If you were a manager charged with choosing a new location for your firm's business, how would you go about matching the location options with your firm's strategic goals?

CRITICAL DISCUSSION QUESTIONS

1. During the 1990s, many North American, European, and Asian MNEs set up operations in Mexico, tapping into its location-specific advantages such as (1) proximity to the world's largest economy (the United States), (2) market-opening policies associated with NAFTA membership, and (3) abundant, low-cost, and high-quality labor. None of these has changed much. Yet, by the 15th anniversary of NAFTA (2009), there is a significant movement for MNEs to curtail operations in Mexico and move to China (see Chapter 8). Use institution- and resource-based views to explain why this is the case.
2. From institution- and resource-based views, identify the obstacles confronting MNEs from emerging economies interested in expanding overseas. How can such firms overcome them?
3. ON ETHICS: Entering foreign markets, by definition, means not investing in a firm's home country. For example, since 2000, GN Netcom shut down some operations in its home country, Denmark, while adding headcounts in China. Nissan closed factories in Japan and added a new factory in the United States. What are the ethical dilemmas here? What are your recommendations?

VIDEO CASE

Watch "Timing Your Entry into New Markets" by Lord Paul of The Caparo Group.

1. This chapter has three learning objectives pertaining to market entry that were covered in the video. They involved _______ to enter, _______ to enter, and _______ to enter. Which do you think is the most important?
2. Which of the three leaning objectives did Lord Paul indicate is most important? Why?
3. In making the "where" decision, Lord Paul chose India. What considerations were involved in that decision?

4. In covering how to enter, did Lord Paul seem to advocate large-scale or small-scale entry?
5. In answering the "where, when, and how" of market entry, what did Lord Paul say about making mistakes?

CLOSING CASE

Amazon in Japan

On November 11, 2000, American online bookstore Amazon opened its Japanese subsidiary, throwing wide "virtual doors" to a Japanese bookselling market that at $8 billion was larger than the $7 billion American market. Considering that the population of Japan is less than half of the American population, such a world-leading market size indicates that the Japanese are truly voracious readers.

By 2000, Amazon had already established itself as one of the three main booksellers in its domestic market, along with the much older Barnes & Noble and Borders. Amazon's success in the United States was based on its price advantage and wide selection, as it was able to offer a greater variety of books at a lower price than its bricks-and-mortar rivals. The Japanese retail bookselling industry was much less concentrated than the American market; the largest Japanese bookseller, Maruzen, was only one-fifth the size of Amazon's largest American rival, Barnes & Noble. By opening its new subsidiary, Amazon appeared to be in a position to feast on a Japanese bookselling industry characterized by a large market but small competitors. However, optimism soured quickly when Amazon Japan's 2001 sales only reached a disappointing $150 million—a drop in the bucket compared to Amazon's worldwide sales of $4 billion. Amazon's struggles were puzzling given its great success in the United States. Why was it unable to replicate its success in Japan, at least initially?

© Richard Levine / Alamy

The primary source of Amazon's troubles stems from the unique institutional landscape of the Japanese bookselling industry. Laws have allowed publishers to fix the price of new books and newspapers since 1980. In other words, publishers alone, not retailers like Amazon, have discretionary power over pricing. This price-fixing system is known as the *Saihanbai Kakaku-iji Seido* ("Resale Price Maintenance System"—commonly known as the Saihan system), and it virtually outlaws price competition between bookstores. For Amazon, whose primary competitive advantage rested on its ability to offer the lowest prices, the *Saihan* system was a critical roadblock. Although this could have spelled doom for Amazon, by the end of 2005 Amazon stood on top of its Japanese competitors, passing Maruzen and raking in approximately $1 billion in sales (a 560% increase from 2001). In 2001, Amazon's sales in Japan made up only 4% of its total sales, yet by 2005, Amazon's Japan operations accounted for over 10%. How did Amazon do this?

First, even though Amazon was not the first online bookseller in Japan, it was the first to sell a wide variety of products besides books. Seven months after opening its Japanese entry, Amazon added music, DVDs, games, videos, and software to its selection of books. By 2005, the software and gaming division was Amazon's second largest source of sales after books. Games were not regulated by the *Saihan* system, which allowed Amazon to give its customary 20% to 30% discounts for these products. Between 2001 and 2006, many more products were added, including electronics, kitchen appliances, toys, sporting goods, and health and beauty products. By 2005, book sales made up less than half of Amazon Japan's total sales. By this time, Amazon's online sales presence was nearly as large as that of Yahoo!'s Japanese site and Rakuten, the Japanese equivalent of eBay. Unlike books, many of these products were not under *Saihan* regulations, allowing Amazon to offer a large variety of products at discount prices. Even though Amazon was unable to sell books at discount prices, it was able to differentiate itself by offering a larger selection of products than its competitors.

Second, Amazon made adjustments to the unique environment of Japan. For example, a fear of fraud has made the Japanese comparatively more hesitant to make Internet credit card purchases. In response, starting in April 2006, Amazon allowed its customers to make payments at any of more than 70,000 convenience stores and ATMs throughout the country, enabling customers to avoid the risk of online fraud (as of 2007, Amazon Japan is the *only* Amazon subsidiary to offer this service). Also in Japan, there is a long tradition of *tachiyomi* (standing and reading), where readers pick up a book or magazine and stand to read it for as long as an hour or two. Following its US online store, in November 2005, Amazon Japan began to offer the "look inside" option for many of its books, allowing customers to read excerpts and passages from books before they purchase them.

Finally, Amazon used three clever methods to indirectly bypass the *Saihan* system. (1) Amazon offered free shipping on purchases over 5,000 yen (approximately $45). Later, the minimum amount was lowered to 1,500 yen (about $13)—lower than even the $25 minimum offered by its US online store (as of 2007). Free shipping put Amazon on par with its bricks-and-mortar rivals but gave it an advantage over other online stores that did not (or could not) offer this service. (2) Late in 2003, Amazon Japan opened a Japanese version of its highly successful "Amazon Marketplace," where third-party users sell both new and used products to each other. This allowed Amazon to indirectly sell books and music at prices below *Saihan*-mandated prices as third-party users, not Amazon, made the transaction. Of course, Amazon profited by charging a commission on the sale. (3) Finally, Amazon used a system that allowed customers to accumulate points based on the price of items purchased that could be redeemed for a gift certificate—essentially offering a discount in disguise.

Despite a slow start, once Amazon adjusted its strategy to the unique institutional environment of Japan, its sales took off and allowed the company to enjoy the same success it had enjoyed in its home market. Should the *Saihan* system be repealed, Amazon is in a prime strategic position to capture any potential windfalls.

Case Discussion Questions

1. What are Amazon's firm-specific resources and capabilities in the United States and Japan?
2. What institutional barriers prevent Amazon from flexing its muscle in Japan?
3. How does Amazon leverage its capabilities to overcome institutional barriers in Japan?

Sources: This case was written by **Charles E. Stevens** (Ohio State University). It is based on (1) http://www.amazon.co.jp; (2) C. Stevens, 2006, Bookoff, Amazon Japan, and the Japanese retail bookselling industry, in M. W. Peng, *Global Strategy* (pp. 158–164), Cincinnati, OH: Cengage South-Western; (3) http://japan.cnet.com; (4) http://www.yomiuri.co.jp.

NOTES

Journal acronyms: **AME** – *Academy of Management Executive;* **AMJ** – *Academy of Management Journal;* **AMR** – *Academy of Management Review;* **APJM** – *Asia Pacific Journal of Management;* **BW** – *Business Week;* **HBR** – *Harvard Business Review;* **JIBS** – *Journal of International Business Studies;* **JIM** – *Journal of International Management;* **JM** – *Journal of Management;* **JMS** – *Journal of Management Studies;* **JWB** – *Journal of World Business;* **LRP** – *Long Range Planning;* **MIR** – *Management International Review;* **SMJ** – *Strategic Management Journal;* **TIBR** – *Thunderbird International Business Review*

[1] S. Hymer, 1976, *The International Operations of National Firms*, Cambridge, MA: MIT Press; A. Madhok, 1997, Cost, value, and foreign market entry, *SMJ*, 18: 39–61; J. Mezias, 2002, Identifying liabilities of foreignness and strategies to minimize their effects, *SMJ*, 23: 229–244; S. Miller & A. Parkhe, 2002, Is there a liability of foreignness in global banking, *SMJ*, 23: 55–75; S. Zaheer, 1995, Overcoming the liability of foreignness, *AMJ*, 38: 341–363.

[2] *BW*, 2004, Can Televisa conquer the US? October 4: 70–71.

[3] J. Gimeno, R. Hoskisson, B. Beal, & W. Wan, 2005, Explaining the clustering of international expansion modes, *AMJ*, 48: 297–319. See also C. Chan, S. Makino, & T. Isobe, 2006, Interdependent behavior in foreign direct investment, *JIBS*, 37: 642–665.

[4] M. W. Peng, 2001, The resource-based view and international business, *JM*, 27: 803–829. See also M. Augier & D. Teece, 2007, Dynamic capabilities and multinational enterprises, *MIR*, 47: 175–192; D. Brock, T. Yaffe, & M. Dembovsky, 2006, International diversification and performance, *JIM*, 12: 473–489; S. Chang & P. Rosenzweig, 2001, The choice of entry mode in sequential foreign direct investment, *SMJ*, 22: 747–776; M. Chari, S. Devaraj, & P. David, 2007, International diversification and firm performance, *JWB*, 42: 184–197; M. Hitt, L. Tihanyi, T. Miller, & B. Connelly, 2006, International diversification, *JM*, 32: 831–867; S. Miller &

M. Richards, 2002, Liability of foreignness and membership in a regional economic group, *JIM*, 8: 323–337; L. Nachum, 2003, Liability of foreignness in global competition? *SMJ*, 24: 1187–1208; B. Petersen & T. Pedersen, 2002, Coping with liability of foreignness, *JIM*, 8: 339–350.

[5] H. Berry, 2006, Shareholder valuation of foreign investment expansion, *SMJ*, 27: 1123–1140; D. Tan & J. Mahoney, 2007, The dynamics of Japanese firm growth in US industries, *MIR*, 47: 259–279; A. Verbeke & W. Yuan, 2007, Entrepreneurship in multinational enterprises, *MIR*, 47: 241–258.

[6] R. Belderbos & L. Sleuwaegen, 2005, Competitive drivers and international plant configuration strategies, *SMJ*, 26: 577–593; J. Dunning, 1998, Location and the multinational enterprise, *JIBS*, 29: 45–66.

[7] L. Canina, C. Enz, & J. Harrison, 2005, Agglomeration effects and strategic orientations, *AMJ*, 48: 565–581; E. Maitland, E. Rose, & S. Nicholas, 2005, How firms grow, *JIBS*, 36: 435–451; L. Nachum & C. Wymbs, 2005, Product differentiation, external economies, and MNE location choices, *JIBS*, 36: 415–434; S. Tallman, M. Jenkins, N. Henry, & S. Pinch, 2004, Knowledge, clusters, and competitive advantage, *AMR*, 29: 258–271.

[8] D. Sethi, S. Guisinger, S. Phelan, & D. Berg, 2003, Trends in FDI flows, *JIBS*, 34: 315–326.

[9] Economist Intelligence Unit, 2006, *CEO Briefing* (p. 9), London: EIU.

[10] G. Smith, 2003, Mexico: Was NAFTA worth it? (p. 72), *BW*, December 22: 66–72.

[11] M. W. Peng & D. Wang, 2000, Innovation capability and foreign direct investment (p. 80), *MIR*, 40: 79–93.

[12] N. Driffield & M. Munday, 2000, Industrial performance, agglomeration, and foreign manufacturing investment in the UK, *JIBS*, 31: 21–37; A. Kalnins & W. Chung, 2004, Resource-seeking agglomeration, *SMJ*, 25: 689–699; J. M. Shaver & F. Flyer, 2000, Agglomeration economies, firm heterogeneity, and foreign direct investment in the United States, *SMJ*, 21: 1175–1193.

[13] B. Kogut & H. Singh, 1988, The effect of national culture on the choice of entry mode, *JIBS*, 19: 411–432.

[14] D. Xu & O. Shenkar, 2002, Institutional distance and the multinational enterprise (p. 608), *AMR*, 27: 608–618.

[15] K. Gillespie, L. Riddle, E. Sayre, & D. Sturges, 1999, Diaspora interest in homeland investment, *JIBS*, 30: 623–634; J. Johansson & J. Vahlne, 1977, The internationalization process of the firm, *JIBS*, 8: 23–32; K. Meyer & M. Gelbuda, 2006, Process perspectives in international business research in CEE, *MIR*, 46: 143–164.

[16] E. Tsang & P. Yip, 2007, Economic distance and survival of foreign direct investments, *AMJ*, 50: 1156–1168.

[17] H. Barkema, J. Bell, & J. Pennings, 1996, Foreign entry, cultural barriers, and learning, *SMJ*, 17: 151–166; M. Myers, C. Droge, & M. Cheung, 2007, The fit of home to foreign market environment, *JWB*, 42: 170–183.

[18] J. Johanson & J. Vahlne, 2006, Commitment and opportunity development in the internationalization process, *MIR*, 46: 165–178; Meyer & Gelbuda, 2006, Process perspectives in international business research in CEE; J. Steen & P. Liesch, 2007, A note on Penrosian growth, resource bundles, and the Uppsala model of internationalization, *MIR*, 47: 193–206.

[19] *Economist*, 2006, Don't mess with Russia, December 16: 11.

[20] J. Evans & F. Mavondo, 2002, Psychic distance and organizational performance, *JIBS*, 33: 515–532; P. Morosini, S. Shane, & H. Singh, 1998, National cultural distance and cross-border acquisition performance, *JIBS*, 29: 137–158; S. O'Grady & H. Lane, 1996, The psychic distance paradox, *JIBS*, 27: 309–333.

[21] Y. Luo & M. W. Peng, 1998, First mover advantages in investing in transition economies, *TIBR*, 40: 141–163.

[22] G. Dowell & A. Swaminathan, 2006, Entry timing, exploration, and firm survival, *SMJ*, 27: 1159–1182; J. G. Frynas, K. Mellahi, & G. Pigman, 2006, First mover advantages in international business and firm-specific political resources, *SMJ*, 27: 321–345; M. Lieberman & D. Montgomery, 1988, First-mover advantages, *SMJ*, 9: 41–58.

[23] M. W. Peng, S. Lee, & J. Tan, 2001, The *keiretsu* in Asia, *JIM*, 7: 253–276.

[24] T. Isobe, S. Makino, & D. Montgomery, 2000, Resource commitment, entry timing, and market performance of foreign direct investments in emerging economies, *AMJ*, 43: 468–484; B. Tan & I. Vertinsky, 1996, Foreign direct investment by Japanese electronics firms in the United States and Canada, *JIBS*, 27: 655–681.

[25] L. Fuentelsaz, J. Gomez, & Y. Polo, 2002, Followers' entry timing, *SMJ*, 23: 245–264; J. Shamsie, C. Phelps, & J. Kuperman, 2004, Being late than never, *SMJ*, 25: 69–84.

[26] V. Gaba, Y. Pan, & G. Ungson, 2002, Timing of entry in international market, *JIBS*, 33: 39–55.

[27] M. W. Peng, 2000, Controlling the foreign agent: How governments deal with multinationals in a transition economy, *MIR*, 40: 141–165; F. Suarez & G. Lanzolla, 2007, The role of environmental dynamics in building a first mover advantage theory, *AMR*, 32: 377–392; T. Tao, 2006, Race to the Great Wall, in M. W. Peng, *Global Strategy*, Cincinnati, OH: Cengage.

[28] Y. Luo & M. W. Peng, 1999, Learning to compete in a transition economy, *JIBS*, 30: 269–296. See also M. Lord & A. Ranft, 2000, Organizational learning about new international markets, *JIBS*, 31: 573–589.

[29] A. Delios & W. Henisz, 2003, Political hazards, experience, and sequential entry strategies, *SMJ*, 24: 1153–1164; P. Padmansbhan & K. Cho, 1999, Decision specific experience in foreign ownership and establishment strategies, *JIBS*, 30: 25–44.

[30] Y. Pan & D. Tse, 2000, The hierarchical model of market entry modes, *JIBS*, 31: 535–554. See also C. Hill, P. Hwang, & W. C. Kim, 1990, An eclectic theory of the choice of international entry mode, *SMJ*, 11: 117–128.

[31] S. Chen, 2005, Extending internalization theory, *JIBS*, 36: 231–245; J. Galan & J. Gonzalez-Benito, 2006, Distinctive determinant factors of Spanish foreign direct investment in Latin America, *JWB*, 41: 171–189.

[32] K. Brouthers, L. Brouthers, and S. Werner, 2003, Transaction cost-enhanced entry mode choices and firm performance, *SMJ*, 24: 1239–1248; J. Doh, P. Rodriguez, K. Uhlenbruck, J. Collins, & L. Eden, 2003, Coping with corruption in foreign markets, *AME*, 17: 114–127; D. Dow, 2006, Adaptation and performance in foreign markets, *JIBS*, 37: 212–226; K. Meyer & S. Estrin, 2001, Brownfield entry in emerging markets, *JIBS*, 32: 575–584; H. Zhao, Y. Luo, & T. Suh, 2004, Transaction cost determinants and ownership-based entry mode choice, *JIBS*, 35: 524–544.

[33] L. Leonidou & C. Katsikeas, 1996, The export development process, *JIBS*, 27: 517–551; R. Salomon & J. M. Shaver, 2005, Export and domestic sales, *SMJ*, 26: 855–871.

[34] G. Balabanis, 2000, Factors affecting export intermediaries' service offerings, *JIBS*, 31: 83–99.

[35] M. W. Peng, Y. Zhou, & A. York, 2006, Behind make or buy decisions in export strategy, *JWB*, 41: 289–300; H. Trabold, 2002, Export intermediation: An empirical test of Peng and Ilinitch, *JIBS*, 33: 327–344.

[36] H. Lau, 2008, Export channel structure in a newly industrialized economy, *APJM*, 25 (in press); L. Li, 2003, Determinants of export channel intensity in emerging markets, *APJM*, 20: 501–516; D. Skarmeas, C. Katsikeas, & B. Schlegelmilch, 2002, Drivers of commitment and its impact on performance in cross-cultural buyer-seller relationships, *JIBS*, 33: 757–783; C. Zhang, S. T. Cavusgil, & A. Roath, 2003, Manufacturer governance of foreign distributor relationships, *JIBS*, 34: 550–566.

[37] F. Wu, R. Sinkovics, S. T. Cavusgil, & A. Roath, 2007, Overcoming export manufacturers' dilemma in international expansion, *JIBS*, 38: 283–302.

[38] A. Arora & A. Fosfuri, 2000, Wholly owned subsidiary versus technology licensing in the worldwide chemical industry, *JIBS*, 31: 555–572; P. Aulakh, S. T. Cavusgil, & M. Sarkar, 1998, Compensation in international licensing agreements, *JIBS*, 29: 409–420.

[39] S. Chen & J. Hennart, 2002, Japanese investors' choice of joint ventures versus wholly-owned subsidiaries in the US, *JIBS*, 33: 1–18; J. Hennart & Reddy, 1997, The choice between mergers/acquisitions and joint ventures, *SMJ*, 18: 1–12.

[40] H. Barkema & F. Vermeulen, 1998, International expansion through start-up or acquisition, *AMJ*, 41: 7–26; A. Harzing, 2002, Acquisitions versus greenfield investments, *SMJ*, 23: 211–227.

[41] J. Hagedoorn & B. Sadowski, 1999, The transition from strategic technology alliances to mergers and acquisitions, *JMS*, 36: 87–107; B. Peterson, D. Welch, & L. Welch, 2000, Creating meaningful switching options, *LRP*, 33: 688–705.

[42] L. Brouthers, E. O'Connell, & J. Hadjimarcou, 2005, Generic product strategies for emerging market exports into Triad nation markets, *JMS*, 42: 225–245; J. Knight, D. Holdsworth, & D. Mather, 2007, Country-of-origin and choice of food imports, *JIBS*, 38: 107–125; S. Samiee, T. Shimps, & S. Sharma, 2005, Brand origin recognition accuracy, *JIBS*, 36: 379–397; P. Verlegh, 2007, Home country bias in product evaluation, *JIBS*, 38: 361–373.

[43] *Economist*, 2006, BAE Systems: Changing places, October 28: 66–67.

[44] J. Birkinshaw, P. Braunerhjelm, U. Holm, & S. Terjesen, 2006, Why do some multinational corporations relocate their headquarters overseas? *SMJ*, 27: 681–700.

[45] A. Rugman, 2005, *The Regional Multinationals*, Cambridge, UK: Cambridge University Press; A. Rugman & A. Verbeke, 2004, A perspective on regional and global strategies of multinational enterprises, *JIBS*, 35: 3–18.

[46] R. Grosse, 2005, Are the largest financial institutions really "global"? *MIR*, 45: 129–144; L. Li, 2005, Is regional strategy more effective than global strategy in the US service industries? *MIR*, 45: 37–57; C. Miller, C. Choi, & S. Chen, 2005, Globalization rediscovered, *MIR*, 45: 121–128; E. Yin & C. Choi, 2005, The globalization myth, *MIR*, 45: 103–120.

[47] P. Lasserre, 2003, *Global Strategic Management* (p. 390), New York: Palgrave.

[48] *BW*, 2005, Hyundai: Crowding into the fast lane, June 20: 54.

CHAPTER 11

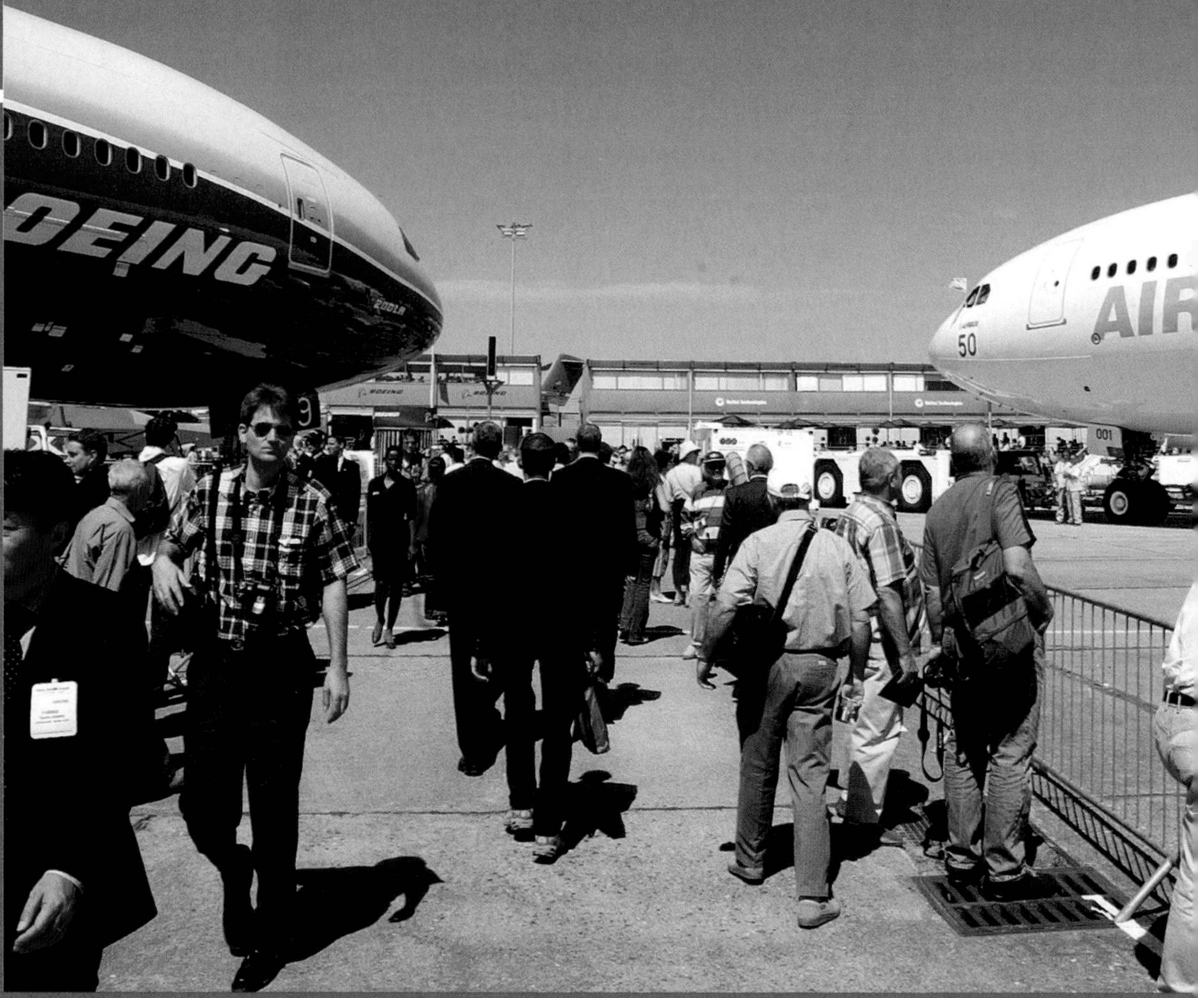

Managing Global Competitive Dynamics

Head to Head: Boeing versus Airbus

In October 2004, when a major trade dispute erupted between the United States and the European Union, on behalf of Boeing and Airbus, respectively, each of these two aerospace firms had 50% of the large civil aircraft market of the world. On May 31, 2005, the dispute escalated to the highest level, when both the US and EU sued each other on the *same* day (!) for unlawful subsidies at the World Trade Organization (WTO).

The Boeing-Airbus rivalry is legendary, and the latest exchange of blows is unlikely to be its last chapter. During the long rivalry, they have competed on (1) size, (2) technology, (3) marketing, and (4) political muscle. First, size matters. This industry is highly capital intensive, with astronomical R&D costs. Airbus's new A380 double-decker burned $12 billion before its maiden flight in 2005. Boeing's new 787 Dreamliner, scheduled to fly in 2007–2008, will cost $10 billion to develop. As a result, a firm needs to sell 500 to 600 aircraft in about 10 years before earning a profit. All other players whose pockets were not deep enough either dropped out or dropped dead. Founded in 1915, Boeing became "king of the hill" (by revenue) when it acquired its last US rival, McDonnell Douglas, in 1996. In comparison, Airbus is young. It was established in 1970 as a French-German consortium later joined by Spanish and UK firms. In 2000, in response to the new, bigger Boeing, Airbus became bigger as well. Three Airbus partners—Aerospatiale Matra of France, DaimlerChrysler Aerospace of Germany, and Construcciones Aerospatiale of Spain—merged to form a single integrated firm, European Aeronautic Defense and Space Company (EADS), that competes with the new Boeing. Airbus formally became a division owned by EADS (80% equity) and Britain's BAE Systems (20%), the remaining Airbus partner. (BAE Systems more recently sold its shares in 2006.)

Second, each firm is forced to charge ahead with risky technology. Throughout the 1990s, Airbus relentlessly pursued Boeing, moving from 20% of the market to snatching the lead in aircraft orders from Boeing in 2001. Having taken the initiative, Airbus in 2001 started to develop the 555-seat A380 to assault Boeing's last stronghold, the very large aircraft segment monopolized by the 415-seat 747 since the late 1960s. In response, Boeing made a series of technological errors. Its efforts to upgrade the 35-year-old 747 to fight the all-new A380 flopped. Its scheme to develop a supersonic (but fuel-thirsty) aircraft went nowhere. However, winds change. Through one gutsy, bet-the-company move, Boeing developed a game-changing technology—lightweight plastic composites. The airframe of its new midsize long-haul 787 is completely made of plastics. Most other planes are made of heavier aluminum. In the post-9/11 era when airlines suffer but oil prices skyrocket, airlines love the Dreamliner because they get tremendous bang for the buck—20% better fuel efficiency and 30% reduction in maintenance costs. In the four years (2004–2007) before the 787 took to the air, it became the fastest selling airliner in history, winning 700 orders. In a remarkable reversal of fortune, after five years on the top, Airbus's world in 2006 started falling apart. Its A380 was running late, upsetting angry customers that switched to buying Boeing. Its new A350 had a hard time finalizing its design.

Third, both firms approach essentially the same market differently. The A380 is based on the assumption that space at major hub airports will not increase; thus, packing more passengers into a four-engine superjumbo is the way to go. Boeing begs to differ. In the present hub-and-spoke system, the more people fly, the more likely that some of them will be stuck at hubs. Boeing believes that carriers prefer to fly relatively smaller, two-engine planes

LEARNING OBJECTIVES

After studying this chapter, you should be able to

1. understand the industry conditions conducive to cooperation and collusion
2. outline how antitrust and antidumping laws affect domestic and international competition
3. articulate how resources and capabilities influence competitive dynamics
4. identify the drivers for attacks, counterattacks, and signaling
5. discuss how local firms fight multinational enterprises (MNEs)
6. participate in two leading debates concerning competitive dynamics
7. draw implications for action

(such as the 787) nonstop between far-flung destinations, instead of having hundreds of passengers disembark from a huge plane and then change to smaller planes destined for various spokes.

Last but certainly not least, both firms compete on political muscle that they can mobilize. Airbus's early years were funded by the generous subsidies provided by French, German, Spanish, and UK governments. The "infant industry" argument posits that Airbus deserves such support in a high-risk industry. In fact, Airbus is the poster child for European governments' "strategic trade policy" (see Chapter 5). However, Boeing and the US government argue that there is no justification to *continue* to subsidize Airbus when it is no longer an "infant." Airbus and the EU point out that Boeing's lucrative defense contracts are subsidies as well. In 1992, the US and the EU signed an agreement, limiting the EU's launch aid to 33% of the development cost of new Airbus models and limiting US defense contracts to 4% of Boeing's civil aircraft turnover. Launch aid is no- or low-interest financing from EU governments that Airbus only needs to repay if the model is successful; otherwise, launch aid is forgiven. Not surprisingly, Boeing and the US government argue that such launch aid is "unfair" because it shifts commercial risk from Airbus to European taxpayers. The 1992 agreement referred to the aim of "reducing" launch aid. The Americans regarded it as a start toward eventual elimination, but the Europeans viewed the deal as validating launch aid within limits. By 2004 (before the launch of the 787), Boeing complained that launch aid enabled Airbus to unleash five new planes in ten years, while Boeing could only afford one (the 777 in the 1990s). After Airbus threatened Boeing with its A380 (funded in part by $3.7 billion launch aid), Boeing responded with its 787 in 2004. However, Airbus immediately launched the A350 to challenge the 787 and applied for $1.7 billion launch aid. Attributing Airbus's instant ability to challenge the 787 to generous launch aid, the US government unilaterally terminated the 1992 agreement with the EU in 2004.

The US and EU negotiations broke down in late 2004, and both went to court at the WTO in 2005 because, according to the EU, the US only wanted to talk about the immediate ending of launch aid and never wanted to "engage in a serious, even-handed discussion of the much larger subsidy program for Boeing." The EU calculated that since 1992, Boeing benefited from defense grants worth over $20 billion and from "unprecedented gifts" from Washington State worth $7 billion. The US pointed out that EADS and BAE Systems are the top defense contractors in Europe and the UK, respectively. Thus, any allegation that Boeing "illegally" benefits from defense work is irrelevant. As of this writing (October 2007), the WTO has not figured out how to solve this intractable case—or technically, two cases whose plaintiffs and defendants switch.

Sources: Based on (1) *Business Week*, 2005, A plastic dream machine, June 20: 32–35; (2) *Economist*, 2005, Air war, June 25: 12; (3) *Economist*, 2005, Nose to nose, June 25: 67–69; (4) European Commission, 2005, EU resumes WTO case against Boeing, May 31, Brussels: EU; (5) Office of the US Trade Representative, 2005, Airbus WTO litigation, May 30, Washington: USTR; (6) World Trade Organization, 2007, Dispute DS316 and Dispute DS317, Geneva: WTO.

---

competitive dynamics
The actions and responses undertaken by competing firms.

competitor analysis
The process of anticipating a rivals' actions in order to both revise a firm's plan and prepare to deal with rivals' responses.

In the long rivalry between Boeing and Airbus, why did they take certain actions but not others? Once one side initiates an action, how does the other respond? These are some of the key questions in this chapter, which focuses on such **competitive dynamics**—actions and responses undertaken by competing firms.[1] Since one firm's actions are rarely unnoticed by rivals, the initiating firm would naturally like to predict rivals' responses *before* making its own move. Anticipating rivals' actions, the initiating firm may want to both revise its plan and prepare to deal with rivals' responses in the next round. This process is called **competitor**

analysis, advocated a long time ago by the ancient Chinese strategist Sun Tzu's teaching to not only know "yourself" but also "your opponents."

As military officers have long known, a good plan never lasts longer than the first contact with the enemy because the enemy does not act according to our plan (!). The key word is *interaction*—how firms interact with rivals. This chapter first deals with competition, cooperation, and collusion. Then, we draw on institution- and resource-based views to shed light on competitive dynamics. Attack, counterattack, and signaling are then outlined, with one interesting extension on how local firms fight multinational enterprises (MNEs) in emerging economies. Debates and extensions follow.

COMPETITION, COOPERATION, AND COLLUSION

LEARNING OBJECTIVE 1

understand the industry conditions conducive to cooperation and collusion

War and Peace

While militaries fight over territories, waters, and airspaces, firms compete in markets. Note the military tone of terms such as *attacks* and *price wars*.[2] On the one hand, it often seems that "business is war." On the other hand, it is obvious that military principles cannot be completely applied in business because the marketplace, after all, is not a battlefield whose motto is "Kill or be killed." If fighting to the death destroys the "pie," there will be nothing left. In business, it is possible to compete and win without having to kill the opposition. In a nutshell, business is simultaneously war and peace.[3]

Alternatively, most competitive dynamics terms and concepts can also be explained in terms of sports analogies. Terms such as *offense* and *defense* should be very familiar to sports enthusiasts.

Cooperation and Collusion

"People of the same trade seldom meet together, even for merriment and diversion," wrote Adam Smith in *The Wealth of Nations* (1776), "but their conversation often ends in a conspiracy against the public." In modern jargon, this means that competing firms in an industry may have an incentive to engage in **collusion**, defined as collective attempts to reduce competition.

Collusion can be tacit or explicit. Firms engage in **tacit collusion** when they *indirectly* coordinate actions by signaling their intention to reduce output and maintain pricing above competitive levels. **Explicit collusion** exists when firms *directly* negotiate output and pricing and divide markets. Explicit collusion leads to a **cartel**—an output- and price-fixing entity involving multiple competitors. A cartel is also known as a trust, whose members have to trust each other for honoring agreements. Since the Sherman Act of 1890, cartels have often been labeled "anticompetitive" and outlawed by **antitrust laws** in many countries (see In Focus 11.1). Recent globalization, by fostering competition in many formerly protected markets, may have *increased* some firms' incentive to collude.[4]

In addition to antitrust laws, collusion is often crushed by the weight of its own incentive problems. The average duration of the cartels prosecuted in the 1990s is only six years. Chief among these problems is the **prisoners' dilemma**, which underpins **game theory**. The term "prisoners' dilemma" derives from a simple game in which two prisoners are suspected of a major joint crime (such

collusion
Collective attempts between competing firms to reduce competition.

tacit collusion
Firms indirectly coordinate actions by signaling their intention to reduce output and maintain pricing above competitive levels.

explicit collusion
Firms directly negotiate output, fix pricing, and divide markets.

cartel
An entity that engages in output- and price-fixing, involving multiple competitors.

antitrust laws
Laws that attempt to curtail anticompetitive business practices.

prisoners' dilemma
In game theory, a type of game in which the outcome depends on two parties deciding whether to cooperate or to defect.

game theory
A theory that studies the interactions between two parties that compete and/or cooperate with each other.

IN FOCUS 11.1 ETHICAL DILEMMA: The Global Vitamin Cartel

The largest and most wide-reaching cartel ever convicted is the global vitamin cartel in operation during 1990–1999. It mainly involved four firms that controlled more than 75% of worldwide production: (1) Hoffman-La Roche of Switzerland, (2) BASF of Germany, (3) Rhône-Poulenc of France (Now Aventis), and (4) Eisai of Japan. Four other Dutch, German, and Japanese firms were also involved. The ringleader was the industry leader, Hoffman-La Roche. This cartel was truly extraordinary: By 1999, prices were meticulously set in at least *nine* currencies. Its discovery led to numerous convictions and fines during 1999–2001 by US, EU, Canadian, Australian, and South Korean antitrust authorities. According to the US assistant attorney general:

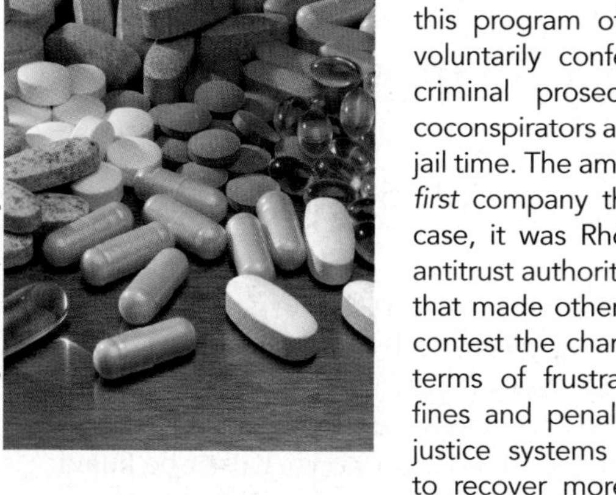
© Joe Pellegrini/ FoodPix/ Jupiterimages

> The criminal conduct of these companies hurt the pocketbook of virtually every American consumer—anyone who took a vitamin, drank a glass of milk, or had a bowl of cereal . . . These companies fixed the price; they allocated sales volumes; they allocated consumers; and in the United States they even rigged bids to make absolutely sure that their cartel would work. The conspirators actually held "annual meetings" to fix prices and to carve up world markets, as well as frequent follow-up meetings to ensure compliance with their illegal scheme.

While this statement only referred to the damage to the US economy, it is plausible to argue that *every* vitamin consumer in the world was ripped off. Average buyers paid 30% to 40% more. The total illegal profits—known as "global injuries"—were estimated to be $9 to $12 billion, of which 15% accrued in the United States and 26% in the European Union. Firms and managers in this conspiracy paid a heavy price: Worldwide, firms paid record fines of about $5 billion, including $500 million for Hoffman-La Roche and $225 million for BASF in the United States alone. In addition, for the first time in US antitrust history, Swiss and German executives working for Hoffman-La Roche and BASF served prison terms of three to four months and paid personal fines of $75,000 to $350,000.

This case has both triumphs and frustrations. A leading triumph stems from the US Corporate Leniency Program. Tapping into the powerful incentive to defect in this *real* prisoners' dilemma, this program offers the first company to voluntarily confess blanket amnesty from criminal prosecution while its fingered coconspirators are hit with criminal fines and jail time. The amnesty prize goes only to the *first* company that comes forward. In this case, it was Rhône-Poulenc that provided antitrust authorities overwhelming evidence that made other defendants decide not to contest the charges and to plead guilty. In terms of frustrations, despite the record fines and penalties, the criminal and civil justice systems of the world have failed to recover more than half of the cartel's illegal profits. In other words, given the low probability of detection, as experts noted, it may still be "utterly rational for would-be cartelists to form or join an international price-fixing conspiracy." Overall, the deterrence, as powerful as this case indicates, may still not be enough.

Sources: Based on (1) D. Bush et al., 2004, *How to Block Cartel Formation and Price-Fixing*, Washington, DC: AEI-Brookings Joint Center for Regulatory Studies; (2) *Guardian*, 2001, Vitamin cartel fined for price fixing, November 21; (3) C. Hobbs, 2004, The confession game, *Harvard Business Review*, September: 20–21; (4) US Department of Justice, 2000, Four foreign executives agree to plead guilty to participating in international vitamin cartel, April 6, Washington, DC: DOJ.

as burglary), but the police do not have strong evidence. The two prisoners are separately interrogated and told that if either one confesses, the confessor will get a one-year sentence while the other will go to jail for ten years. If neither confesses, both will be convicted of a lesser charge (such as trespassing) and go to jail for two years. If both confess, both will go to jail for ten years. At first glance, the solution seems clear enough. The maximum *joint* payoff would be for neither of them to confess. However, both prisoners have tremendous incentives to confess—otherwise known as defect.

Translated to an airline setting, Figure 11.1 illustrates the payoff structure for both airlines A and B in a given market, let's say, between Hong Kong and Singapore. Assuming a total of 200 passengers, cell 1 represents the ideal outcome for both airlines to maintain the price at $500, and each gets 100 passengers and makes $50,000; the "industry" revenue reaches $100,000. However, in cell 2, if B maintains its price at $500 while A drops it to $300, B is likely to lose all customers. Assuming perfectly transparent pricing information on the Internet, who would want to pay $500 when they can get a ticket for $300? Thus, A may make $60,000 on 200 passengers and B gets nothing. In cell 3, the situation is reversed. In both cells 2

FIGURE 11.1 A PRISONERS' DILEMMA FOR AIRLINES (ASSUMING A TOTAL OF 200 PASSENGERS)

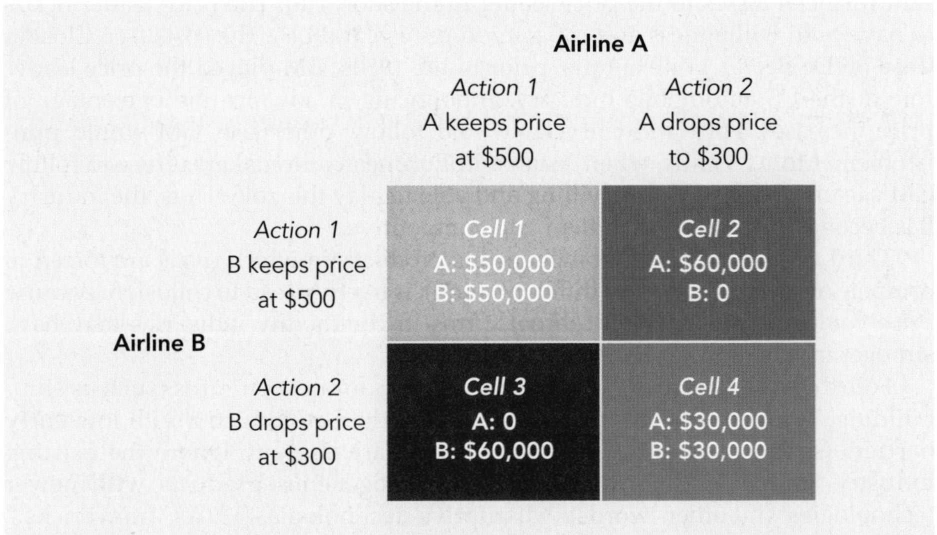

and 3, although the industry *decreases* revenue by 40%, the price dropper *increases* its revenue by 20%. Thus, both A and B have strong incentives to reduce price and hope the other side to become a "sucker." However, neither likes to be a sucker. Thus, both A and B may want to chop prices, as in cell 4, whereby each still gets 100 passengers. But both firms as well as the industry end up with a 40% reduction of revenue. A key insight of game theory is that even if A and B have a prior agreement to fix the price at $500, both still have strong incentives to cheat, thus pulling the industry to cell 4 where both are clearly worse off.

Given the benefits of collusion and incentives to cheat, which industries are conducive to collusion? Five factors emerge (Table 11.1). The first is the number of firms or, more technically, **concentration ratio**, the percentage of total industry sales accounted for by the top-four, eight, or twenty firms. In general, the higher the concentration, the easier it is to organize collusion. In the vitamin cartel, the top-four firms control 75% of global supply of bulk vitamins (In Focus 11.1).

Second, the existence of a **price leader**—defined as a firm that has a dominant market share and sets "acceptable" prices and margins in the industry—helps tacit collusion. The price leader needs to possess the **capacity to punish**, defined

concentration ratio
The percentage of total industry sales accounted for by the top four, eight, or twenty firms.

price leader
A firm that has a dominant market share and sets "acceptable" prices and margins in the industry.

capacity to punish
Sufficient resources possessed by a price leader to deter and combat defection.

TABLE 11.1 INDUSTRY CHARACTERISTICS AND POSSIBILITY OF COLLUSION VIS-À-VIS COMPETITION

Collusion possible	Collusion difficult (competition likely)
• Few firms (high concentration)	• Many firms (low concentration)
• Existence of an industry price leader	• No industry price leader
• Homogeneous products	• Heterogeneous products
• High entry barriers	• Low entry barriers
• High market commonality (mutual forbearance)	• Lack of market commonality (no mutual forbearance)

as sufficient resources to deter and combat defection. The most frequently used punishment entails undercutting the defector by flooding the market, thus making the defection fruitless. Such punishment is costly because it brings significant financial losses to the price leader in the short run. The price leader needs to have both willingness and capacity to punish and bear the costs (see Closing Case on De Beers). For example, prior to the 1980s, GM played the price leader role in the US automobile industry, announcing in advance the percentage of price increases. Ford and Chrysler would follow; otherwise, GM would punish them. More recently, when Asian and European automakers refuse to follow GM's lead, GM is no longer willing and able to play this role. Thus, the industry has become much more turbulent and competitive.

Third, an industry with homogeneous products, in which rivals are forced to compete on price (rather than differentiation), is likely to lead to collusion. Because price competition is often cut-throat, firms in commodity industries may have stronger incentives to collude (see In Focus 11.1).

Fourth, an industry with high entry barriers for new entrants (such as shipbuilding) is more likely to facilitate collusion than an industry with low entry barriers (such as restaurants).[5] New entrants are likely to ignore the existing industry "order" and to introduce less homogeneous products with newer technologies (in other words, "disruptive technologies").[6] As "mavericks," new entrants "can be thought of as loose cannons in otherwise placid and calm industries."[7]

market commonality
The overlap between two rivals' markets.

multimarket competition
Firms engage the same rivals in multiple markets.

mutual forbearance
Multimarket firms respect their rivals' spheres of influence in certain markets, and their rivals reciprocate, leading to tacit collusion.

cross-market retaliation
The ability of a firm to expand in a competitor's market if the competitor attacks in its original market.

Finally, **market commonality**, defined as the degree of overlap between two rivals' markets, also has a significant bearing on the intensity of rivalry.[8] A high degree of market commonality may restrain firms from aggressively going after each other. **Multimarket competition** occurs when firms engage the same rivals in multiple markets. Multimarket firms may respect their rivals' spheres of influence in certain markets, and their rivals may reciprocate, leading to tacit collusion—an outcome known as **mutual forbearance**.[9] Such mutual forbearance primarily stems from deterrence. A high degree of market commonality suggests that if a firm attacks in one market, its rivals have the ability to engage in **cross-market retaliation**, leading to a costly all-out war that nobody can afford.

Overall, the effectiveness of firm actions significantly depends on the domestic and international institutions governing competitive dynamics as well as firm-specific resources and capabilities. The next two sections expand on these points, which are summarized in Figure 11.2.

FIGURE 11.2 INSTITUTIONS, RESOURCES, AND COMPETITIVE DYNAMICS

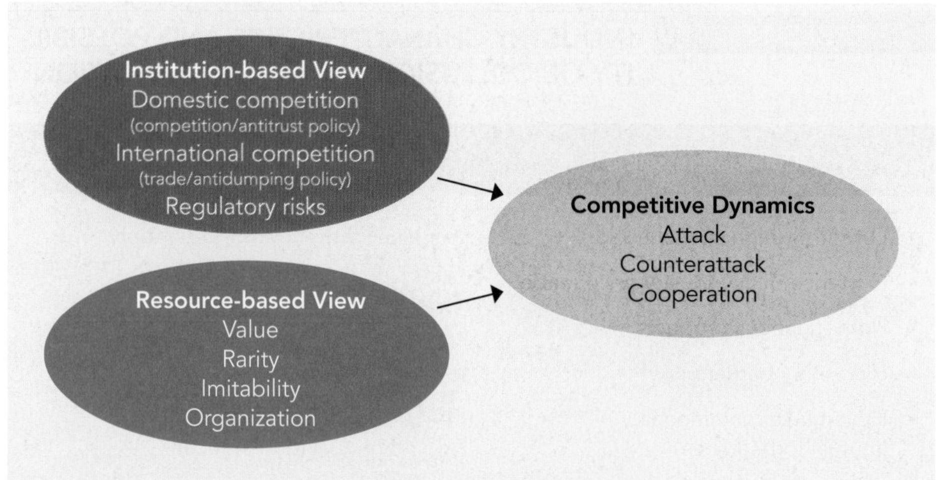

INSTITUTIONS GOVERNING DOMESTIC AND INTERNATIONAL COMPETITION

LEARNING OBJECTIVE 2

outline how antitrust and antidumping laws affect domestic and international competition

In a nutshell, the institution-based view advises managers to be well versed in the rules of the game governing domestic and international competition. A lack of understanding of these institutions may land otherwise successful firms (such as Microsoft) in deep trouble.

Formal Institutions Governing Domestic Competition: A Focus on Antitrust

competition policy
Policy governing the rules of the game in competition in a country.

antitrust policy
Laws designed to combat monopolies and cartels.

Formal institutions governing domestic competition are broadly guided by **competition policy**, which "determines the institutional mix of competition and cooperation that gives rise to the market system."[10] Of particular relevance to us is one branch called **antitrust policy** designed to combat monopolies and cartels.[11] Competition/antitrust policy seeks to balance efficiency and fairness. Although efficiency is relatively easy to understand, it is often hard to agree on what constitutes fairness. In the United States, fairness means equal opportunities for incumbents and new entrants. It is "unfair" for incumbents to raise entry barriers to shut out new entrants. However, in Japan, fairness means the *opposite*; that is, incumbents that have invested in and nurtured an industry for a long time deserve protection from the intrusion brought by new entrants. What Americans approvingly describe as "market dynamism" is negatively labeled by Japanese as "market turbulence"; the Japanese ideal is "orderly competition" (a euphemism for incumbent dominance—see Chapter 10 Closing Case).

Overall, the American antitrust policy is *procompetition* and *proconsumer*, whereas the Japanese approach is *proincumbent* and *proproducer*. It is difficult to argue about who is right or wrong here, but we need to be aware of such crucial differences. Overall, because of stronger, proconsumer antitrust laws, competitive forces have been stronger in the United States than in most other developed economies. As a result, on average, American consumers enjoy the lowest prices (except for drugs). Conversely, Japanese consumers endure the highest prices (except for cars) (see Table 11.2).

TABLE 11.2 INTERNATIONAL PRICE COMPARISONS (RATIO OF DOMESTIC RETAIL PRICES TO WORLD PRICES)

	Australia	Canada	Germany	Japan	Netherlands	UK	US
Agriculture and fisheries	**1.067**	1.112	1.529	1.584	1.080	1.648	1.158
Processed food	**1.086**	1.192	1.447	2.099	1.299	1.202	1.090
Textiles	1.111	1.163	1.101	1.478	1.140	1.237	**1.051**
Printing and publishing	1.120	1.205	1.024	1.186	1.342	1.029	**1.005**
Drugs and medicines	**1.001**	2.680	2.643	1.217	3.349	1.845	3.105
Petroleum and coal	2.127	1.320	2.847	3.359	4.335	4.067	**1.007**
Motor vehicles	1.224	1.197	1.315	**1.000**	1.648	1.680	1.106
Professional goods	1.125	1.082	1.379	1.077	1.369	1.586	**1.074**
Weighted means	1.266	1.270	1.539	1.567	1.541	1.48	**1.118**

Source: Adapted from OECD, 2004, Product market competition and economic performance in the United States (p. 14), Economics Department working paper no. 398, Paris: OECD. **Bold** typeface indicates the lowest price in this category.

collusive price setting
Price setting by monopolists or collusion parties at a higher than competitive level.

predatory pricing
An attempt to monopolize a market by setting prices below cost and intending to raise prices to cover losses in the long run after eliminating rivals.

Competition/antitrust policy focuses on (1) collusive price setting and (2) predatory pricing. **Collusive price setting** refers to price setting by monopolists or collusion parties at a higher than competitive level. The largest case prosecuted on collusive pricing is the global vitamin cartel of the 1990s, artificially jacking up prices by 30% to 40% (see In Focus 11.1).

Another area of concern is **predatory pricing**, defined as (1) setting prices below cost *and* (2) intending to raise prices to cover losses in the long run after eliminating rivals ("an attempt to monopolize"). This is an area of significant contention. First, it is not clear what exactly is "cost." Second, even when firms are found to be selling below costs, US courts have ruled that if rivals are too numerous to eliminate, one firm cannot recoup its losses due to low prices by jacking up prices. Then its pricing cannot be labeled "predatory." This seems to be the case in most industries. Thus, the two legal tests have made it extremely difficult to win a predation case in the United States.

Formal Institutions Governing International Competition: A Focus on Antidumping

dumping
An exporter selling below cost abroad and planning to raise prices after eliminating local rivals.

This section primarily deals with antidumping. In the same spirit of predatory pricing, **dumping** is defined as (1) an exporter selling below cost abroad and (2) planning to raise prices after eliminating local rivals. Although domestic predation is usually labeled "anticompetitive," cross-border dumping is often emotionally accused of being "unfair" (see Chapter 5).

Consider the following two scenarios. First, a steel producer in *Indiana* enters a new market, Texas. In Texas, it offers prices lower than those in Indiana, resulting in a 10% market share in Texas. Texas firms have two choices. The first is to initiate a lawsuit against the Indiana firm for predatory pricing. However, it is difficult to prove (1) that the Indiana firm is selling below cost *and* (2) that its pricing is an attempt to monopolize. Under US antitrust laws, a predation case like this will have no chance of succeeding. In other words, domestic competition/antitrust laws offer no hope for protection. Thus, Texas firms are most likely to opt for their second option—to retaliate in kind by offering lower prices to customers in Indiana, leading to lower prices in both Texas and Indiana.

Now in the second scenario, the "invading" firm is not from Indiana but *India*. Holding everything else constant, Texas steel firms can argue that the Indian firm is dumping. Under US antidumping laws, Texas steel producers "would almost certainly obtain legal relief on the very same facts that would not support an antitrust *claim*, let alone antitrust relief."[12] Note that imposing antidumping duties on Indian steel imports reduces the incentive for Texas firms to counterattack by entering India, resulting in *higher* prices in both Texas and India, where consumers are hurt. These two scenarios are not merely hypothetical; they are highly realistic. An OECD study in Australia, Canada, the EU, and the US reports that 90% of the practices found to be unfairly dumping in these countries would never have been questioned under their own antitrust laws if used by a domestic firm in making a domestic sale.[13] In a nutshell, foreign firms are discriminated against by the formal rules of the game.

Discrimination is also evident in the actual investigation of antidumping. A case is usually filed by a domestic firm with the relevant government authorities. In the United States, they are the International Trade Administration (a unit of the Department of Commerce) and International Trade Commission (an independent government agency). Then these government agencies send lengthy questionnaires to accused foreign firms, requesting comprehensive, proprietary data on their cost and pricing, in English, using US generally accepted accounting principles (GAAP), within 45 days. Many foreign defendants fail to provide such data on time because they are not familiar with US GAAP. The investigation can have the four following outcomes.

- If no data are forthcoming from abroad, the data provided by the accusing firm become the evidence, and the accusing firm can easily win.
- If foreign firms do provide data, the accusing firm can still argue that these "unfair" foreigners have lied—"There is no way their costs can be so low!" In the case of Louisiana versus Chinese crawfish growers, the authenticity of the $9 per *week* salary made by Chinese workers was a major point of contention.
- Even if the low-cost data are verified, US (and EU) antidumping laws allow the complainant to argue that these data are not "fair." In the case of China, the argument goes, its cost data reflect huge distortions due to government intervention because China is still a "nonmarket" economy; the wage may be low, but workers may be provided with low-cost housing and benefits subsidized by the government. The crawfish case thus boiled down to how much it would cost to raise hypothetical crawfish in a market economy (in this particular case, Spain was mysteriously chosen). Because Spanish costs were about the same as Louisiana costs, the Chinese, despite their vehement objections, were found guilty of dumping in America by selling below *Spanish* costs. Thus, 110% to 123% import duties were levied on Chinese crawfish.
- The fourth possible outcome is that the defendant wins the case. But this happens to only 5% of the antidumping cases in the United States.[14]

Simply filing an antidumping petition (regardless of the outcome), one study finds, may result in a 1% increase of the stock price for US listed firms (an average of $46 million increase in market value).[15] Evidently, Wall Street knows that Uncle Sam is "on your side." It is thus not surprising that antidumping cases have now proliferated throughout the world. Although the EU and the US have initiated the largest number of cases, on per dollar of imports, Argentina and South Africa have 20 times more cases than the US, India has seven times, and Brazil has five times.[16]

Overall, institutional conditions such as the availability of antidumping protection are not just the "background." They directly determine what weapons a firm has in its arsenal to wage competitive battles. In addition to formal institutions, informal norms and beliefs also play a significant role. Since many previous chapters have already dealt with these issues, we will not expand on this point here.

RESOURCES INFLUENCING COMPETITIVE DYNAMICS

LEARNING OBJECTIVE 3

articulate how resources and capabilities influence competitive dynamics

A number of resource-based imperatives, informed by the VRIO framework first outlined in Chapter 4, drive decisions and actions associated with competitive dynamics (see Figure 11.2).

Value

Firm resources must create value when engaging rivals. For example, the ability to attack in multiple markets—of the sort that enabled Gillette to launch its Sensor razors in 23 countries *simultaneously*—throws rivals off balance, thus adding value. Likewise, the ability to rapidly respond to challenges also adds value.[17] Another example is a dominant position in key markets (such as flights in and out of Dallas/Fort Worth by American Airlines). Such a strong sphere of influence poses credible threats to rivals, which understand that the firm will defend its core markets vigorously.

One way to add value is patenting. Patents are obviously valuable, and firms are expanding their scale and scope of patenting, resulting in a "patent race."[18] Microsoft now files approximately 3,000 patents a year, up from a mere five in 1990. Intel sits on 10,000 patents. Only about 5% of patents end up having any economic value. So why do firms spend so much money on the patent race (on average, half a million dollars in R&D for one patent)? The answer is purely defensive and competitive. The proliferation of patents makes it very easy for one firm to unwittingly infringe on rivals' patents. When being challenged, a firm without a defensive portfolio of patents is at a severe disadvantage: It has to pay its rivals for using their patents. On the other hand, a firm with strong patents can challenge rivals for their infringements, thus making it easier to reach some understanding—or mutual forbearance. Patents thus become a valuable weapon in fighting off rivals. For this reason, China's Huawei now files about 2,500 patents a year (Closing Case).

Rarity

Either by nature or nurture (or both), certain assets are very rare, thus generating significant advantage. Saudi Arabia's vast oil reserves enable it to become the enforcer (price leader) of OPEC cartel agreements. Singapore Airlines, in addition to claiming one of the best locations connecting Europe and Asia Pacific as its home base, has often been rated as the world's best airline. This combination of both geographic advantage and reputational advantage is rare, thus allowing Singapore Airlines to always charge higher prices and equip itself with newer and better equipment. It is the first airline in the world to fly the all new A380.

Imitability

Most rivals watch each other and probably have a fairly comprehensive (although not necessarily accurate) picture of how their rivals compete. However, the next hurdle lies in how to imitate successful rivals. It is well known that fast-moving rivals tend to perform better.[19] Even when armed with this knowledge, competitively passive and slow-moving firms will find it difficult to imitate rivals' actions. Many major airlines have sought to imitate successful discount carriers such as Southwest, Ryanair, and Hainan (see Chapter 4 Opening Case) but failed repeatedly.

Organization

Some firms are better organized for competitive actions, such as stealth attacks and willingness to answer challenges "tit-for-tat."[20] The intense "warrior-like" culture not only requires top management commitment but also employee involvement down to the "soldiers in the trenches." It is such a self-styled "wolf" culture that has propelled Huawei to become Cisco's leading challenger (Closing Case). It is difficult for slow-moving firms to suddenly wake up and become more aggressive.[21]

On the other hand, more centrally coordinated firms may be better mutual forbearers than firms whose units are loosely controlled. For an MNE competing with rivals across many countries, a mutual forbearance strategy requires some units, out of respect for rivals' sphere of influence, to sacrifice their maximum market gains by withholding some efforts. Of course, such coordination helps other units with dominant market positions to maximize performance, thus helping the MNE as a whole. Successfully carrying out such mutual forbearance calls for organizational reward systems and structures (such as those concerning bonuses and promotions) that encourage cooperation between units (see Chapter 13). Conversely, if a firm has competitive reward systems and structures (for example, bonuses linked to unit performance), unit managers may be unwilling to give up market gains for the greater benefits of other units and the whole firm, thus undermining mutual forbearance.[22]

Resource Similarity

As a concept extended from the resource-based view, **resource similarity** is defined as "the extent to which a given competitor possesses strategic endowments comparable, in terms of both type and amount, to those of the focal firm."[23] Firms with a high degree of resource similarity are likely to have similar competitive actions. American Airlines and Japan Airlines may have a higher degree of resource similarity than the degree of resource similarity between American Airlines and Travelocity.

resource similarity The extent to which a given competitor possesses strategic endowments comparable, in terms of both type and amount, to those of the focal firm.

If we put together resource similarity and market commonality (discussed earlier), we can yield a framework of competitor analysis for any pair of rivals (Figure 11.3). In cell 4, because two firms have a high degree of resource similarity but a low degree of market commonality (little mutual forbearance), the intensity of rivalry is likely to be the highest. Conversely, in cell 1, because both firms have little resource similarity but a high degree of market commonality, the intensity of their rivalry may be the lowest. Cells 2 and 3 present an intermediate level of competition. Such conscientious mapping can help managers sharpen their analytical focus and allocate resources in proportion to the degree of threat each rival presents.

To illustrate, In Focus 11.2 describes why Fox's entry has intensified the rivalry in the US TV broadcasting industry. One lesson is that the Big Three TV networks should have gone abroad earlier to establish mutual forbearance with News Corporation in other countries. In other words, as in military and sports, the motto is: "The best defense is offense." The next section discusses how to launch an offensive attack.

FIGURE 11.3 A FRAMEWORK FOR COMPETITOR ANALYSIS BETWEEN A PAIR OF RIVALS

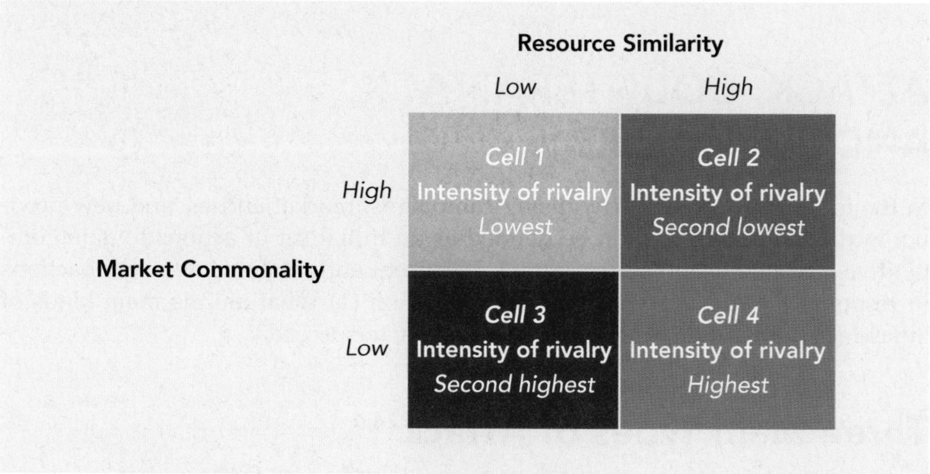

Market Commonality	Resource Similarity: Low	Resource Similarity: High
High	*Cell 1* Intensity of rivalry *Lowest*	*Cell 2* Intensity of rivalry *Second lowest*
Low	*Cell 3* Intensity of rivalry *Second highest*	*Cell 4* Intensity of rivalry *Highest*

Sources: Adapted from (1) M. Chen, 1996, Competitor analysis and interfirm rivalry: Toward a theoretical integration (p. 108), *Academy of Management Review*, 21: 100–134; (2) J. Gimeno & C. Y. Woo, 1996, Hypercompetition in a multimarket environment: The role of strategic similarity and multimarket contact in competitive de-escalation (p. 338), *Organization Science*, 7: 322–341.

IN FOCUS 11.2 A Fox in the Henhouse

Prior to 1996, the US TV broadcasting industry could be viewed as a relatively tranquil "henhouse." The Big Three networks (ABC, NBC, and CBS) dominated mainstream programming, and CNN ran its 24-hour news show. Like hens sharing a house, there was some rivalry. But there were well-understood rules of engagement, such as not raiding each other's affiliate stations. Overall, competition was gentlemanly.

However, the 1996 arrival of Fox News Channel, a subsidiary of Rupert Murdoch's News Corporation, has transformed the industry. First, violating industry norms, Fox raided Big Three affiliate stations by convincing some to switch and sign up with Fox. In some markets, Fox thus gained overnight at the expense of one of the Big Three whose affiliate station defected to join Fox. Second, Fox paid up to $11 per subscriber. This violated another norm of cable operators only paying stations carriage fees for programming. Third, having outfoxed the Big Three, Fox turned its guns on CNN. When Time Warner bought Ted Turner's CNN, it was required by an antitrust consent to carry a second news channel in addition to CNN. Time Warner chose MSNBC but not Fox, and Fox sued Time Warner. This media war became nasty, with Turner publicly comparing Murdoch to Adolf Hitler and Murdoch's *New York Post* questioning Turner's sanity. Perhaps controversy was exactly what Fox wanted. It had been repeatedly accused by critics of promoting a conservative (allegedly Republican) point of view. Viewers did not care. By 2006, Fox was the most watched news channel in the United States, reaching 96% of US households.

Using Figure 11.3, we can suggest that the pre-1996 industry was in cell 2. The intensity of rivalry was the second *lowest* because the Big Three and CNN had high market commonality (all focusing on the US) and high resource similarity (TV programming). However, Fox's entry has transformed the game. News Corporation is a global player that was historically headquartered in Australia but is now headquartered and listed in New York. In addition to its Australian roots, News Corporation has major presence in Asia, Canada, and Europe. Its first US acquisition took place in 1973, and Murdoch became an American citizen in 1985 to satisfy a requirement that only US citizens could own American TV stations. In other words, while Fox shares high resource similarity with the Big Three and CNN, it has low market similarity with the Big Three, which have very little non-US presence. The upshot? The industry is now in cell 4 with the *highest* intensity of rivalry. That is why Fox can beat up the Big Three, with little fear of its non-US markets being retaliated against. The Big Three thus pay a heavy price for their US-centric mentality. Being more international, CNN is in a better position to fight Fox. In 1997, Turner and Murdoch settled, with Time Warner agreeing to carry Fox and News Corporation, giving Time Warner access to News Corporation's satellites in Asia and Europe. In other words, they have established some mutual forbearance.

Sources: Based on (1) *Business Week*, 2006, Rupert Murdoch, August 21–28: 82; (2) Wikipedia, 2007, Fox News Channel, http://en.wikipedia.org.

LEARNING OBJECTIVE 

identify the drivers for attacks, counterattacks, and signaling

ATTACK, COUNTERATTACK, AND SIGNALING

In the form of price cuts, advertising campaigns, market entries, and new product introductions, **attack** can be defined as an initial set of actions to gain competitive advantage, and **counterattack** is consequently defined as a set of actions in response to an attack. This section focuses on (1) What are the main kinds of attack? (2) What kinds of attack are more likely to succeed?

attack
An initial set of actions to gain competitive advantage.

counterattack
A set of actions in response to an attack.

Three Main Types of Attack[24]

There are three main types of attack: (1) thrust, (2) feint, and (3) gambit. **Thrust** is the classic frontal attack with brute force.[25] A case in point is the browser war. In 1996, Netscape had 90% of the browser market, whereas Microsoft (Explorer) had less than 5%. Once Microsoft mobilized its formidable resources to launch a frontal attack, Netscape's market share fell to 14%, whereas Microsoft's rose to 86% in 1998.[26]

thrust
The classic frontal attack with brute force.

Feint, in basketball, is one player's effort to fool a defender by pretending he or she will go one way but actually charges ahead in another direction. In competitive dynamics, a feint is a firm's attack on a focal arena important to a competitor but not the attacker's true target area.[27] The feint is followed by the attacker's commitment of resources to its actual target area. Consider the Marlboro war between Philip Morris and R. J. Reynolds (RJR). In the early 1990s, both firms' traditional focal market, the United States, experienced a 15% decline over the previous decade. Both were interested in Central and Eastern Europe (CEE), which grew rapidly. Philip Morris executed a feint in the United States by dropping 20% off the price of its flagship brand, Marlboro, on one *day* (April 2, 1993, which became known as the Marlboro Friday). Confronting this ferocious and sudden move, RJR diverted substantial resources earmarked for CEE to defend its US market. Philip Morris was thus able to rapidly establish its dominant sphere of influence in CEE.[28]

feint
A firm's attack on a focal arena important to a competitor but not the attacker's true target area.

Gambit, in chess, is a move that sacrifices a low-value piece to capture a high-value piece. The competitive equivalent is to withdraw from a low-value market to attract rivals to divert resources into it and then to capture a high-value market. As a daring strategic move, gambit is not for the faint of heart. How Gillette battled Bic is indicative of a gambit. Both competed in razors and lighters. Gillette was stronger in razors and Bic was stronger in lighters. Gillette in 1984 withdrew *entirely* from lighters and devoted its attention to razors. Bic accepted the gambit and diverted razor resources to lighters. The gambit, in essence, can be regarded as an exchange of the spheres of influence between Gillette and Bic, each with a stronger position in one market.

gambit
To withdraw from a low-value market to attract rivals to divert resources into it and then to capture a high-value market.

Attack and Counterattack

Obviously, unopposed attacks are more likely to succeed. Thus, attackers need to be aware of the three drivers for counterattacks: (1) awareness, (2) motivation, and (3) capabilities.

- *Awareness* is a prerequisite for any counterattack. If an attack is so subtle that rivals are not aware of it, then the attacker's objectives are likely to be attained. One interesting idea is the "blue ocean strategy" that avoids attacking core markets defended by rivals.[29] A thrust on rivals' core markets is very likely to result in a bloody price war—in other words, a "red ocean." In the 1990s, Netscape drew tremendous publicity by labeling Microsoft the *Death Star* (of *Star Wars* movie fame) and predicting that the Internet would make Windows obsolete. Such a challenge helped make Netscape Microsoft's enemy number one, leading to the demise of Netscape (or its drowning in the red ocean).[30]
- *Motivation* is also crucial. If the attacked market is of marginal value, managers may decide not to counterattack. Consider Haier's entry into the US white goods market. Although Haier dominates in its home country, China, with a broad range of products, it chose to enter the US market in a most nonthreatening segment: compact refrigerators for hotels and dorms. Does anyone remember the brand of the compact refrigerator in the last hotel room you stayed in? Evidently, not only you failed to pay attention to that brand, but incumbents such as GE and Whirlpool also dismissed this segment as peripheral and low margin. In other words, they were not motivated to counterattack. Thanks in part to incumbents' lack of motivation to counterattack, Haier now commands a 50% US market share in compact refrigerators and has built a factory in South Carolina to go after more lucrative product lines (see In Focus 6.2).

© Kevin Casey/ Stringer/ Getty Images

How would you characterize the type of competitive move executed by the product manufacturer shown here?

- Finally, even if an attack is identified and a firm is motivated to respond, it requires strong *capabilities* to carry out counterattacks—as discussed in our earlier section on resources.

Overall, minimizing the awareness, motivation, and capabilities of the opponents is more likely to result in successful attacks. Carrying out frontal, infrequent, simple, and predictable attacks will find rivals to be prepared. Winning firms excel at making subtle, frequent, complex, but unpredictable moves. In Focus 11.3 illustrates how Lev Leviev maneuvers to challenge the mighty De Beers.

Cooperation and Signaling

Some firms choose to compete and attack, and others choose to cooperate. How can a firm signal its intention to cooperate to *reduce* competitive intensity? Short of illegally talking directly to rivals, firms have to resort to signaling; that is, "while you can't talk to your competitors on pricing, you can always *blink* at them." We outline five means of such blinking:

- A nonaggression strategy refers to active investment in nonthreatening ways so as not to provoke attacks on a firm's core markets. For example, IKEA actively invests in the wooden, self-assembly segment of the furniture market. At the

IN FOCUS 11.3 Lev Leviev Fights De Beers

In the diamond industry, De Beers of South Africa has been the undisputed "king of the hill" for more than 100 years. It has skillfully organized a cartel known as the Diamond Syndicate whose purposes were to keep supply low and price high. Historically dominating the global diamond production (mostly in South Africa), De Beers sold rough diamonds only to a select group of merchants (called "sightholders") from the world at take-it-or-leave-it prices. For independent producers, De Beers often urges them to sell rough diamonds only to De Beers. De Beers would purchase all of the output at prices it sets. In exchange, the producers reap the benefits of a cartel: stable prices, guaranteed purchases, and little competition. At present, De Beers still controls approximately 60% of the worldwide rough diamond sales.

As in all cartels, the incentives to cheat are tremendous. De Beers's reactions are typically swift. In 1981, Zaire broke away from De Beers to directly market its diamonds. De Beers drew on its stockpiles to flood the market, forcing the Zairians to change their mind. In 1978, some Israeli sightholders began hoarding rough diamonds. De Beers ruthlessly purged one-third of sightholders, forcing many Israeli buyers out of business.

It is against such formidable forces that the Lev Leviev Group of Israel has risen. Lev Leviev is a Russian-speaking, Uzbeki-born, Israeli citizen. As one of Israel's largest diamond polishers, Leviev was invited to become a sightholder by De Beers in 1985. However, Leviev has proven to be De Beers's worst enemy. His actions are characterized by their subtlety, complexity, and unpredictability. Leviev has subtly cultivated political connections in key countries. Dating back to the Soviet days, Russia had always sold its rough diamonds to De Beers. Leviev befriended Presidents Yeltsin and Putin and convinced the state-owned Russian producer, now called Alrosa, to set up a joint venture with him to cut $140 million worth of diamonds a year.

Leviev has cultivated a complex web of businesses scattered in numerous industries and countries. The Russian venture is only the tip of an iceberg of his deals in the former Soviet Union. In Angola, De Beers was engulfed in a public relations disaster associated with "conflict diamonds." In 1996, Leviev took advantage of the De Beers fiasco by putting together an Angola Selling Corporation, in which he gave the government a 51% share in exchange for exclusive rights to purchase Angolan rough diamonds. In Namibia where locals also preferred to process their own diamonds instead of selling them to De Beers, Leviev first set up a joint diamond polishing factory with local players and then bought out their shares.

Finally, Leviev's actions are often unpredictable in the tradition-bound diamond business largely dictated by De Beers. Leviev has become the first diamond dealer with his finger on every facet of the value chain, from mining and cutting to polishing and retailing. Leviev is innovatively branding his best stones dubbed the Vivid Collection. Outraged, De Beers kicked Leviev out as a sightholder in 1995. De Beers has also set up a diamond polishing factory in Namibia and sought to launch its own brand. Today, as the world's largest cutter and polisher and a primary source of rough diamonds, Leviev has become De Beers's enemy number one.

Sources: Based on (1) P. Berman & L. Goldman, 2003, The billionaire who cracked De Beers, *Forbes*, September 15: 108–115; (2) M. W. Peng, 2006, Lev Leviev, in *Global Strategy* (pp. 327–328), Cincinnati, OH: Cengage.

same time, it has announced that it has no intention to enter the traditional, factory-assembled furniture segment, thus discouraging traditional furniture firms from entering IKEA's core market.

- Although a nonaggression strategy reduces competition by *not* entering new markets, a second strategy, market entry, may have the same effect. Firms may enter new markets not really to challenge incumbents but to seek mutual forbearance by establishing multimarket contact. Thus, MNEs often chase each other, entering one country after another.[31] Airlines that meet on many routes are often less aggressive than airlines that meet on one or a few routes.[32]
- Firms can send an open signal for a truce. As GM faced grave financial difficulties in 2005, Toyota's chairman told the media *twice* that Toyota would "help GM" by raising Toyota prices in the United States. As far as signaling goes, Toyota's signal could not have been more unambiguous, short of talking directly to GM, which would be illegal. Toyota, of course, was self-interested. Should GM indeed declare bankruptcy, Toyota would attract all the "machine-gun fire" from protectionist backlash. Nevertheless, US antitrust authorities reportedly took note of Toyota's remarks—essentially an open message to GM for price fixing.[33]
- Sometimes, firms can send a signal to rivals by enlisting the help of governments. Because direct negotiations with rivals on what consists of "fair" pricing are often illegal, holding such discussions is legal under the auspices of government investigations. Thus, filing an antidumping petition or suing a rival does not necessarily indicate a totally hostile intent. Sometimes, it signals to the other side: "We don't like what you are doing; it's time to talk." Cisco, for instance, dropped its case against Huawei after both firms negotiated a solution, mediated by both Chinese and American governments (see Closing Case).
- Finally, firms can organize strategic alliances with rivals for cost reduction. Although price fixing is illegal, reducing cost by 10% through an alliance, which is legal, has the same impact on the financial bottom line as collusively raising price by 10%. See Chapter 12 for details.

LOCAL FIRMS VERSUS MULTINATIONAL ENTERPRISES

LEARNING OBJECTIVE 5

discuss how local firms fight multinational enterprises (MNEs)

While managers, students, and journalists are often fascinated by MNE rivals such as Coke/Pepsi, Intel/AMD, and Sony/Samsung, much less is known about how local firms cope when confronting the MNE onslaught. Given the broad choices of competing and/or cooperating, local firms can adopt four strategic postures depending on (1) the industry conditions and (2) the nature of competitive assets. Shown in Figure 11.4, these factors suggest four strategic actions.[34]

In cell 3, in some industries, the pressures to globalize are relatively low, and local firms' strengths lie in a deep understanding of local markets. Therefore, a **defender strategy**, by leveraging local assets in areas in which MNEs are weak, is often called for. For example, in Israel, facing an onslaught from MNE cosmetics firms, a number of local firms turned to focus on products suited to the Middle Eastern climate and managed to defend their turf. Ahava has been particularly successful, in part because of its unique components extracted from the Dead Sea that MNEs cannot find elsewhere.[35] In essence, we can view such a defender strategy as a *gambit*, through which local firms cede some markets (such as mainstream cosmetics) to MNEs while building strongholds in other markets.

defender strategy
This strategy centers on leveraging local assets in areas in which MNEs are weak.

In cell 4, in some industries where pressures for globalization are relatively low, local firms may possess some skills and assets that are transferable overseas, thus leading to an **extender strategy**. This strategy centers on leveraging homegrown

extender strategy
This strategy centers on leveraging homegrown competencies abroad.

FIGURE 11.4 **HOW LOCAL FIRMS IN EMERGING ECONOMIES RESPOND TO MNE ACTIONS**

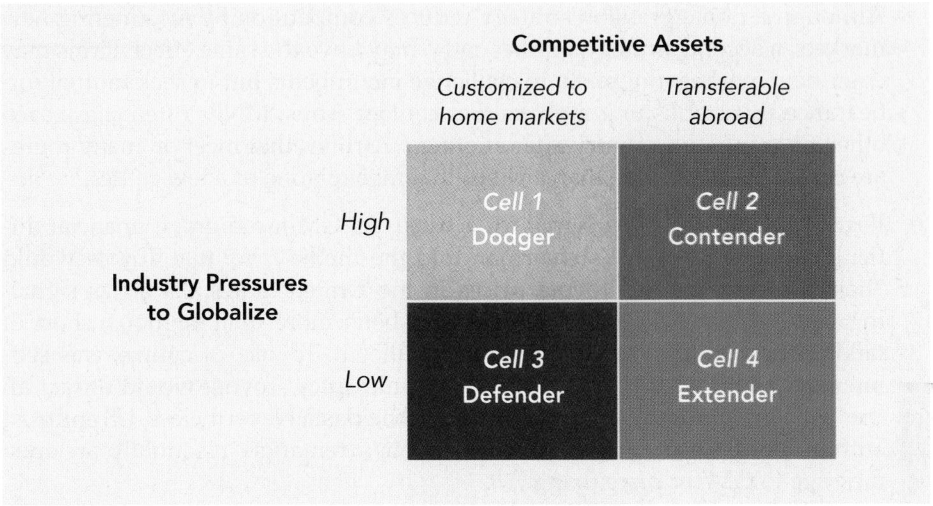

Source: Adapted from N. Dawar & T. Frost, 1999, Competing with giants: Survival strategies for local companies in emerging markets (p. 122), *Harvard Business Review*, March–April: 119–129.

competencies abroad. For instance, Asian Paints controls 40% of the house paint market in India. Asian Paints developed strong capabilities tailored to the unique environment in India, characterized by thousands of small retailers serving numerous dirt-poor consumers who only want small quantities of paint that can be diluted to save money. Such capabilities are not only a winning formula in India but also in much of the developing world. In contrast, MNEs, whose business model typically centers on affluent customers in developed economies, have had a hard time coming up with profitable low-end products (see Chapter 1 Closing Case). Overall, Asian Paints' strategy can be viewed as a *thrust* charging into new markets.

dodger strategy
This strategy centers on cooperating through joint ventures (JVs) with MNEs and sell-offs to MNEs.

Cell 1 depicts a most difficult situation for local firms that compete in industries with high pressures for globalization. Thus, a **dodger strategy** is necessary. This is largely centered on cooperating through joint ventures (JVs) with MNEs and sell-offs to MNEs. In the Chinese automobile industry, *all* major local automakers have entered JVs with MNEs. In the Czech Republic, Skoda was sold by the government to Volkswagen. The essence of this strategy is that to the extent that local firms are unable to successfully compete head on against MNEs, cooperation becomes necessary. In other words, if you can't beat them, join them!

contender strategy
This strategy centers on a firm engaging in rapid learning and then expanding overseas.

Finally, in cell 2, some local firms, through a **contender strategy**, engage in rapid learning and then expand overseas. A number of Chinese mobile phone makers such as TCL and Bird have rapidly caught up with global heavyweights such as Motorola and Nokia. By 2003, local firms, from a 5% market share five years earlier, commanded more than 50% market share in China. Engaging in a "learning race," TCL and Bird have now embarked on an overseas *thrust*.

Overall, how local firms respond is crucial for managers throughout emerging economies. In China, after the initial dominance, MNEs are not always "kings of the hill." In numerous industries (such as sportswear, cellular phone, personal computer, and home appliance), many MNEs have been "dethroned." Although weak local players are washed out, some of the leading local players (such as Huawei in Closing Case), having won the game in the highly competitive domestic environment, now challenge MNEs overseas. In the process, they become a new breed of MNEs themselves.[36] As a group, foreign MNEs in China are not as profitable as local firms (except state-owned ones).[37] The upshot is that when facing the onslaught of MNEs, local firms are not necessarily "sitting ducks."

DEBATES AND EXTENSIONS

LEARNING OBJECTIVE 6

participate in two leading debates concerning competitive dynamics

There are numerous debates in this sensitive area. We outline two of the most significant ones: (1) competition versus antidumping and (2) managers versus antitrust policymakers.

Competition versus Antidumping

There are two arguments against the practice of imposing antidumping restrictions on foreign firms. First, because dumping centers on selling below cost, it is often difficult (if not impossible) to prove the case, given the ambiguity concerning cost. The second argument is that if foreign firms are indeed selling below cost, so what? This is simply a commonly used competitive action. When entering a new market, virtually all firms lose money on Day 1 (and often Year 1). Until some point when the firm breaks even, it will lose money because it sells below cost. Domestically, there are numerous cases of such dumping, which are perfectly legal. For example, we all receive numerous coupons in the mail offering free or cheap goods. Coupon items are frequently sold (or given away) below cost. Do consumers complain about such good deals? Probably not. "If the foreigners are kind enough (or dumb enough) to sell their goods to our country below cost, why should we complain?"[38]

A classic response is: What if, through "unfair" dumping, foreign rivals drive out local firms and then jack up prices? Given the competitive nature of most industries, it is often difficult (if not impossible) to eliminate all rivals and then recoup losses by charging higher monopoly prices. The fear of foreign monopoly is often exaggerated by special interest groups who benefit at the expense of consumers in the entire country (see Chapter 5). Joseph Stiglitz, a Nobel laureate in economics and then chief economist of the World Bank, wrote that antidumping duties "are simply naked protectionism" and one country's "fair trade laws" are often known elsewhere as "unfair trade laws."[39]

One solution is to phase out antidumping laws and use the same standards against domestic predatory pricing. Such a waiver of antidumping charges has been in place between Australia and New Zealand, between Canada and the United States, and within the European Union. Thus, a Canadian firm, essentially treated as a US firm, can be accused of predatory pricing but cannot be accused of dumping in the United States. Since antidumping is about "us versus them," such harmonization represents essentially an expanded notion of "us." However, domestically, as noted earlier, a predation case is very difficult to make. In such a way, competition can be fostered, aggressiveness rewarded, and "dumping" legalized.

Managers versus Antitrust Policymakers

This debate is between managers and antitrust policymakers. Unfortunately, *none* of the other international business (IB) textbooks covers such a crucial debate. As a result, most business school students do not know antitrust policy, and when they graduate to become managers, they do not care either. Antitrust officials tend to be trained in economics and law but not in business. However, a background in these fields does not give antitrust officials an intimate sense of how firm-level competition and/or cooperation unfolds, which is something that a business school education provides. As a result, individuals trained in economics and law who have relatively little sense of how real companies make decisions end up making and enforcing the rules governing competition. Such a disconnect naturally breeds mutual suspicion and frustration from both sides. Business school students and managers will be better off if they know what the antitrust side talks about.

Because the United States has the world's oldest antitrust frameworks (dating back to the 1890 Sherman Act), the US debate is the most watched in the world and thus is the focus here. This does not mean that we are adopting a US-centric approach, which is a tendency this book endeavors to combat. We treat the US debate as a *case study* that may have global ramifications elsewhere.

On behalf of managers, concerned management scholars have made four arguments.[40] First, antitrust laws were often created in response to the old realities of mostly domestic competition—the year 1890 for the Sherman Act is *not* a typo for 1990 (!). However, the largely global competition today indicates that a large dominant firm in one country (think of Boeing) does not automatically translate into a dangerous monopoly. The existence of foreign rivals (such as Airbus) forces the large domestic incumbent to be more competitive (see Opening Case).

Second, the very actions accused to be "anticompetitive" may actually be highly "competitive" or "hypercompetitive." In the 1990s, the hypercompetitive Microsoft was charged for its "anticompetitive" behavior. Its alleged crime? *Not* voluntarily helping its competitors (!).

Third, US antitrust laws create strategic confusion. Because intent to destroy rivals is a smoking gun of antitrust cases, managers are forced to use milder language. Don't say or write a memo that "We want to beat competitors!" Otherwise, managers end up in court. In contrast, foreign firms often use warlike language: Komatsu is famous for "Encircling Caterpillar!" and Honda for "Annihilate, crush, and destroy Yamaha!" The inability to talk straight creates confusion among lower level managers and employees in US firms. A confused firm is not likely to be aggressive.

Finally, US antitrust laws may be unfair because these laws discriminate *against* US firms. If GM and Ford were to propose to jointly manufacture cars, antitrust officials would have turned them down, citing an (obvious!) intent to collude. Ironically, GM was allowed to make cars with Toyota starting in 1983. Now, after 25 years, Ford is no longer the second largest automaker in America. You guessed it, Toyota is now the second largest automaker in America. The upshot? American antitrust laws have helped Toyota but hurt Ford. This does not seem very fair, to say the least.

Given the importance of such a debate, it is unfortunate that *none* of the other IB textbooks discusses it. They may be doing the field a disservice by not confronting this debate head on. The outcome of this debate may to a large degree shape future competition in the world.

LEARNING OBJECTIVE 7
draw implications for action

MANAGEMENT SAVVY

Let us revisit our fundamental question: What determines the success and failure in managing competitive dynamics around the world? Drawing on the two core perspectives (institution- and resource-based views), we suggest that to successfully manage competitive dynamics, managers not only need to become masters of maneuvers (both confrontation and cooperation) but also experts in government regulations if they aspire to successfully navigate the global landscape.

Consequently, three clear implications for action emerge for savvy managers (Table 11.3). First, managers need to understand the rules of the game governing competition around the world. Domestically, aggressive language such as "Let's beat competitors" may not be allowed in countries such as the United States. However, carefully crafted ambitions such as Wal-Mart's "We want to be number one in grocery business" are legal because such wording (at least on paper) shows no illegal intention to destroy rivals. It's too bad that 31 US supermarket chains declared bankruptcy since Wal-Mart charged into groceries in the 1990s—just a tragic coincidence (!). Antitrust authorities cannot charge Wal-Mart's "every day low prices" as predatory pricing because after rivals drop out (or drop dead), Wal-Mart does *not* raise prices.[41]

The necessity of understanding the rules of the game is crucial when venturing abroad. What is legal domestically may be illegal elsewhere. Imagine the shock

TABLE 11.3 IMPLICATIONS FOR ACTION

- Understand the rules of the game governing domestic and international competition around the world
- Strengthen resources and capabilities that more effectively compete and/or cooperate
- Develop skills in competitor analysis that guide decision making on attacks, counterattacks, and cooperation

that Chinese managers may generate when they venture abroad and approach rivals in the United States to discuss pricing—legal in China. They would be prosecuted in the United States and may go to jail. Several German and Swiss managers involved in the vitamin cartel have served jail time in America (In Focus 11.1). Another crucial area is antidumping. Many Chinese managers are surprised that their low-cost strategy is labeled "illegal" dumping in the very countries that often brag about "free market" competition. In reality, free markets are not free. However, managers well versed in the rules of the game may launch subtle attacks without incurring the wrath of antidumping officials. Imports commanding less than 3% market share or below in a 12-month period are regarded by US antidumping laws as "negligible imports" not worthy of investigation.[42] Thus, foreign firms not crossing such a "red line" would be safe.

Second, managers need to strengthen capabilities that more effectively compete and/or cooperate. In attacks and counterattacks, subtlety, frequency, complexity, and unpredictability are helpful. In cooperation, market similarity and mutual forbearance may be better. As Sun Tzu advised a long time ago, you, as a manager, need to "know yourself"—including your unit, your firm, and your industry.

Finally, savvy managers also need to know their "opponents" by developing skills in competitor analysis (see Figure 11.3). Managers need to develop skills and instinct to think like their opponents who are eager to collect competitive intelligence (Table 11.4). Overall, since business is simultaneously war *and* peace, a winning formula, as in war and chess, is "Look ahead, reason back."

TABLE 11.4 TIPS ON COMPETITIVE INTELLIGENCE AND COUNTERINTELLIGENCE

- If you are bidding against a major local rival in a foreign country, expect aggressive efforts to gather your information. If you leave your laptop in a hotel room, expect the hard drive to be copied.
- Be careful about cell (mobile) phones, whose signals can be intercepted. If you lose your cell phone for 30 seconds, your opponents may be able to put in a look-alike battery with a chip that will record and transmit your calls. This chip can also secretly turn your phone on as a microphone, without your knowledge.
- Be careful about the high-speed Internet service at your hotel. Go to the office of your local subsidiary. If there isn't such a safe local office, a random WiFi spot may be safer than the hotel Internet service.
- If your negotiation counterparts offer to book you into a luxurious suite or hotel, turn it down. Book your own.

Source: Based on text in G. Morse, 2005, H. Keith Melton on corporate espionage, *Harvard Business Review*, November: 26. Note this is an interesting but extremely cautious view.

CHAPTER SUMMARY

1. Understand the industry conditions conducive to cooperation and collusion
   - Industries primed for collusion tend to have (1) a smaller number of rivals, (2) a price leader, (3) homogeneous products, (4) high entry barriers, and (5) high market commonality (mutual forbearance).
2. Outline how antitrust and antidumping laws affect domestic competition and international competition
   - Domestically, antitrust laws focus on collusion and predatory pricing.
   - Internationally, antidumping laws discriminate against foreign firms and protect domestic firms.
3. Articulate how resources and capabilities influence competitive dynamics
   - Resource similarity and market commonality can yield a powerful framework for competitor analysis.
4. Identify the drivers for attacks, counterattacks, and signaling
   - There are three main types of attacks: (1) thrust, (2) feint, and (3) gambit. Counterattacks are driven by (1) awareness, (2) motivation, and (3) capability.
   - Without talking directly to competitors, firms can signal to rivals by various means.
5. Discuss how local firms fight MNEs
   - When confronting MNEs, local firms can choose a variety of strategic choices: (1) defender, (2) extender, (3) dodger, and (4) contender. They may not be as weak as many people believe.
6. Participate in two leading debates concerning competitive dynamics
   - They are (1) competition versus antidumping and (2) managers versus antitrust policymakers.
7. Draw implications for action
   - Managers need to understand the rules of the game, particularly the laws, governing domestic and international competition around the world.
   - Savvy managers know themselves and their opponents and will develop the skills and knowledge necessary to effectively analyze their competitors.

KEY TERMS

Antitrust laws 305
Antitrust policy 309
Attack 314
Capacity to punish 307
Cartel 305
Collusion 305
Collusive price setting 310
Competition policy 309
Competitive dynamics 304
Competitor analysis 304
Concentration ratio 307
Contender strategy 318
Counterattack 314
Cross-market retaliation 308
Defender strategy 317
Dodger strategy 318
Dumping 310
Explicit collusion 305
Extender strategy 317
Feint 315
Gambit 315
Game theory 305
Market commonality 308
Multimarket competition 308
Mutual forbearance 308
Predatory pricing 310
Price leader 307
Prisoners' dilemma 305
Resource similarity 313
Tacit collusion 305
Thrust 314

REVIEW QUESTIONS

1. Explain the differences between tacit collusion and explicit collusion.
2. How does a prisoners' dilemma play out in a business setting?
3. Name and describe the five factors that make an industry particularly conducive to collusion.
4. Some countries' competition/antitrust policy is procompetition and proconsumer, whereas other countries' policy is proincumbent and proproducer. How do they differ?
5. What is the difference between collusive price setting and predatory pricing?
6. Why is predatory pricing (in essence, domestic dumping) considered "anticompetitive" and cross-border dumping considered "unfair"?
7. Use your own examples to identify how the VRIO aspects of resources and capabilities affect competitive dynamics.
8. How does a firm's corporate culture and organization affect its ability to engage in competitive actions?
9. Name and describe the three main types of attack in business.
10. Name and describe three drivers for counterattacks.
11. Describe at least three ways a firm might signal its intention to cooperate with a competitor.
12. Under what conditions might a firm undertake a defender strategy?
13. Under what conditions might a firm adopt an extender strategy?
14. What criteria might induce a firm to choose a dodger strategy over a contender strategy, and vice versa?
15. Do you support or oppose antidumping restrictions? Explain your answer.
16. Using the United States as a case study, describe four arguments that managers might make regarding antitrust laws.
17. Devise your own example of a business-related statement, and express it using legal, competitive language and illegal (or overly aggressive) language based on your understanding of the US legal vocabulary.
18. What are some qualities you could develop in yourself to strengthen your capabilities for engaging in competitive dynamics?

CRITICAL DISCUSSION QUESTIONS

1. ON ETHICS: As CEO of a US firm, you feel the price war in your industry is killing profits for all firms. However, you have been warned by corporate lawyers not to openly discuss pricing with rivals, who you know personally (you went to school with them). How would you signal your intentions?
2. ON ETHICS: As a CEO, you are concerned that your firm and your industry in the United States are being devastated by foreign imports. Trade lawyers suggest filing an antidumping case against leading foreign rivals in China and assure you a win. Would you file an antidumping case or not? Why?

3. ON ETHICS: As part of a feint attack, your firm (firm A) announces that in the next year, it intends to enter country X, where the competitor (firm B) is very strong. Your firm's real intention is to march into country Y, where B is very weak. There is actually *no* plan to enter X. However, in the process of trying to "fool" B, customers, suppliers, investors, and the media are also being intentionally misled. What are the ethical dilemmas here? Do the pros of this action outweigh its cons?

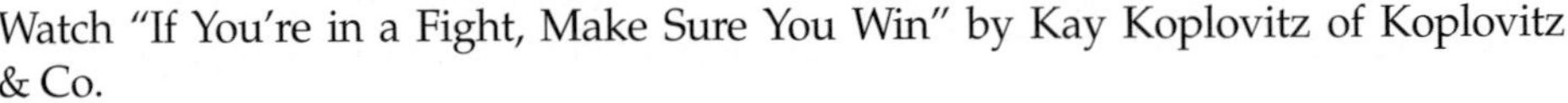

VIDEO CASE

Watch "If You're in a Fight, Make Sure You Win" by Kay Koplovitz of Koplovitz & Co.

1. What type of attack did Kay Koplovitz encounter? Would it have made any difference if the attack came in the US from a company based overseas?
2. What resource did Ms. Koplovitz use, and why did she choose that resource? Would there be any problem using that resource if the attack came from an overseas rival?
3. Was Ms. Koplovitz in an industry that could have been conducive to collusion? What led to the very opposite of collusion? If Ms. Koplovitz was part of an MNE under attack by another MNE, what other options might she have used?
4. What do you think of Ms. Koplovitz taking what might be viewed as hostile action against a customer? Would it have made any difference if that had been an overseas customer?
5. Do you think Ms. Koplovitz's tactics would deter similar future attacks? Is legal action the solution to her problem?

CLOSING CASE

Cisco versus Huawei: War and Peace

Founded in 1986, Cisco is a worldwide leader in networking for the Internet. Numerous rivals challenged Cisco, but none was threatening enough—until the rise of Huawei. Founded in 1987, Huawei distinguished itself as an aggressive company that led the telecommunications equipment market in China. It is remarkable that Huawei, despite being a nonstate-owned company, was able to not only beat all state-owned rivals but also a series of multinationals in China. In 1999, Huawei launched an overseas drive. Starting with $50 million sales (4% of overall sales) in international markets in 1999, Huawei's sales outside China reached $11 billion (65% of overall sales) in 2006. What is Huawei's secret weapon? Relative to offerings from competitors such as Cisco, Lucent, Nokia, and Siemens, Huawei's products offer comparable performance at 30% lower price. This is music to the ears of telecom operators. As a result, Huawei not only penetrated many emerging economies but also achieved significant breakthroughs in developed markets such as Japan and Western Europe. As of 2007, Huawei served 31 of the world's top 50 telecom operators, including Vodafone, Telefonica, KPN, FT/Orange, and Italia Telecom. Yet, North America remained the toughest nut to crack.

In 2002, Huawei turned its guns on North America—Cisco's stronghold. In Supercomm 2002 (a trade show) in Atlanta, Huawei's debut in North America, two guests visited the Huawei booth and asked detailed questions for 20 minutes. Only after the two guests left did one of Huawei's executives recognize that one of the guests was John Chambers, Cisco's CEO. Chambers thus personally experienced the aggressive arrival of his archrival from China. Thanks to Huawei, Cisco's sales in China peaked in 2001 at $1 billion and then never reached anything above $600 million. Correspondingly, Cisco's share in the Chinese router market went from 80% to 50%. In North America, facing suspicious buyers, Huawei offered "blind" performance tests on Huawei and Cisco machines whose logos were removed. Buyers often found that the only difference was price.

© Zhou Junxiang / Imagine China Photos/ Newscom

Cisco's response was both audacious and unexpected. On January 22, 2003, Cisco filed a lawsuit in Texas, alleging that Huawei unlawfully copied and misappropriated Cisco's software and documentation. Cisco's actions caught Huawei totally off guard—the first time it was sued by a foreign rival. Even the day of the attack was deliberately chosen. It was right before the Spring Festival, the main annual holiday in China. Thus, none of the Huawei top executives was able to spend a day with their family in the next few weeks. The media noted that this lawsuit squarely put Huawei "on the map" as Cisco's acknowledged enemy number one.

Huawei's response was also interesting. Huawei noted that as a firm that consistently invested at least 10% of its sales on R&D, it had always respected intellectual property rights (IPRs). In addition to hiring top American lawyers, Huawei also announced a joint venture with Cisco's rival 3Com several days before the court hearing in March 2003. Consequently, 3Com's CEO, Bruce Claflin, provided testimony supporting Huawei. By using an American CEO to fight off another American firm, Huawei thus skillfully eroded the "us versus them" feeling permeating this case at a time when China bashing was in the air.

While both Cisco and Huawei fought in court, negotiations between them, often involving American and Chinese officials, also intensified. In July 2004, Cisco dropped the case. Although the details of the settlement were confidential, *both* Cisco and Huawei declared victory. Huawei agreed to change the software and documentation in question, thus partially meeting Cisco's goals. More important, Cisco delayed Huawai's North America offensive by one and a half years. Huawei not only refuted most of Cisco's accusations but also showcased its technological muscle under intense media spotlight for which it did not have to spend a penny. In part thanks to this high-profile case, Huawei's international sales *doubled*—from approximately $1 billion in 2003 to $2 billion in 2004. Clearly, Huawei rapidly became a force to be reckoned with. In December 2005, Chambers visited Huawei and for the first time met its CEO Ren Zhengfei. The former plaintiff and the former defendant shook hands and had friendly discussions like pals, as if nothing had happened between them.

Case Discussion Questions

1. In retrospect, could Huawei have done something differently to avoid provoking Cisco to sue?
2. In retrospect, could Cisco have done something differently other than filing the lawsuit?
3. How would you characterize Cisco's attack? How about Huawei's counterattack?
4. What would be the likely content of the discussion between Chambers and Ren in December 2005?

Sources: I thank Sunny Li Sun (University of Texas at Dallas) for his assistance. Based on (1) http://www.cisco.com; (2) *Cisco Systems, Inc. et al. v. Huawei Technologies, Co., Ltd. et al.*, Civil Action No. 2:03-CV-027, Marshall, TX: US District Court for the Eastern District of Texas; (3) http://www.huawei.com; (4) J. Wu & Y. Ji (2006), *Huawei's World*, Beijing: China CITIC Press.

NOTES

Journal acronyms: **AME** – *Academy of Management Executive;* **AMJ** – *Academy of Management Journal;* **AMR** – *Academy of Management Review;* **APJM** – *Asia Pacific Journal of Management;* **BW** – *Business Week;* **CJE** – *Canadian Journal of Economics;* **HBR** – *Harvard Business Review;* **IE** – *International Economy;* **JEP** – *Journal of Economic Perspectives;* **JIBS** – *Journal of International Business Studies;* **JM** – *Journal of Management;* **JMS** – *Journal of Management Studies;* **JWB** – *Journal of World Business;* **LRP** – *Long Range Planning;* **OSc** – *Organization Science;* **OSt** – *Organization Studies;* **SMJ** – *Strategic Management Journal*

[1] D. Ketchen, C. Snow, & V. Hoover, 2004, Research on competitive dynamics, *JM*, 30: 779–804; N. Kumar, 2006, Strategies to fight low-cost rivals, *HBR*, December: 104–112.

[2] V. Rindova, M. Becerra, & I. Contardo, 2004, Enacting competitive wars, *AMR*, 29: 670–686.

[3] A. Brandenburger & B. Nalebuff, 1996, *Co-opetition* (p. 4), New York: Currency Doubleday.

[4] S. Evenett, M. Levenstein, & V. Suslow, 2001, International cartel enforcement, *IE*, 24: 1221–1245.

[5] A. Mainkar, M. Lubatkin, & W. Schulze, 2006, Toward a product-proliferation theory of entry barriers, *AMR*, 31: 1062–1075.

[6] C. Christensen, 1997, *The Innovator's Dilemma*, Boston: Harvard Business School Press.

[7] J. Barney, 2002, *Gaining and Sustaining Competitive Advantage* (p. 359), Upper Saddle River, NJ: Prentice Hall.

[8] M. Chen, 1996, Competitor analysis and interfirm rivalry (p. 106), *AMR*, 21: 100–134.

[9] F. Smith & R. Wilson, 1995, The predictive validity of the Karnani and Wernerfelt model of multipoint competition, *SMJ*, 16: 143–160; M. Semadeni, 2006, Minding your distance, *SMJ*, 27: 169–187.

[10] E. Graham & D. Richardson, 1997, Issue overview (p. 5), in E. Graham & D. Richardson (eds.), *Global Competition Policy* (pp. 3–46), Washington, DC: Institute for International Economics.

[11] J. Clougherty, 2005, Antitrust holdup source, cross-national institutional variation, and corporate political strategy implications for domestic mergers in a global context, *SMJ*, 26: 769–790.

[12] R. Lipstein, 1997, Using antitrust principles to reform antidumping law (p. 408, original italics), in E. Graham & D. Richardson (eds.), *Global Competition Policy* (pp. 405–438), Washington, DC: Institute for International Economics.

[13] OECD, 1996, *Trade and Competition: Frictions after the Uruguay Round* (p. 18), Paris: OECD.

[14] T. Prusa, 2001, On the spread and impact of antidumping (p. 598), *CJE*, 34: 591–611.

[15] S. Marsh, 1998, Creating barriers for foreign competitors, *SMJ*, 19: 25–37.

[16] M. Finger, F. Ng, & S. Wangchuk, 2001, Antidumping as safeguard policy (p. 6), Working paper, World Bank.

[17] J. R. Baum & S. Wally, 2003, Strategic decision speed and firm performance, *SMJ*, 24: 1107–1129; V. Terpstra & C. Yu, 1988, Determinants of foreign investment of US advertising agencies, *JIBS*, 19: 33–55.

[18] This paragraph draws heavily on *Economist*, 2005, A market for ideas, October 22: 1–18.

[19] W. Ferrier, K. Smith, & C. Grimm, 1999, The role of competitive action in market share erosion and industry dethronement, *AMJ*, 42: 372–388.

[20] D. Basdeo, K. Smith, C. Grimm, V. Rindova, & P. Derfus, 2006, The impact of market actions on firm reputation, *SMJ*, 27: 1205–1219.

[21] C. Pegels, Y. Song, & B. Yang, 2000, Management heterogeneity, competitive interaction groups, and firm performance, *SMJ*, 21: 911–923.

[22] B. Golden & H. Ma, 2003, Mutual forbearance, *AMR*, 28: 479–493; A. Kalnins, 2004, Divisional multimarket contact within and between multiunit organizations, *AMJ*, 47: 117–128.

[23] Chen, 1996, Competitor analysis and interfirm rivalry (p. 107). See also W. Desarbo, R. Grewal, & J. Wind, 2006, Who competes with whom? *SMJ*, 27: 101–129; L. Fuentelsaz & J. Gomez, 2006, Multipoint competition, strategic similarity, and entry into geographic markets, *SMJ*, 27: 477–499.

[24] This section draws heavily on R. McGrath, M. Chen, & I. MacMillan, 1998, Multimarket maneuvering in uncertain spheres of influence, *AMR*, 23: 724–740.

[25] W. Boeker, J. Goodstein, J. Stephen, & J. Murmann, 1997, Competition in a multimarket environment, *OSc*, 8: 126–142; M. Chen & I. MacMillan, 1992, Nonresponse and delayed response to competitive moves, *AMJ*, 35: 359–370.

[26] D. Yoffie & M. Kwak, 2001, *Judo Strategy* (p. 193), Boston: Harvard Business School Press.

[27] G. Stalk, 2006, Curveball: Strategies to fool the competition, *HBR*, September: 115–122.

[28] I. MacMillan, A. van Putten, & R. McGrath, 2003, Global gamesmanship, *HBR*, May: 62–71.

[29] W. C. Kim & R. Mauborgne, 2005, *Blue Ocean Strategy*, Boston: Harvard Business School Press.

[30] M. Cusumano & D. Yoffie, 1998, *Competing on Internet Time*, New York: Free Press.

[31] J. Anand & B. Kogut, 1997, Technological capabilities of countries, firm rivalry, and foreign direct investment, *JIBS*, 28: 445–465; J. Gimeno, 1999, Reciprocal threats in multimarket rivalry, *SMJ*, 20: 101–128; J. Hennart & Y. Park, 1994, Location, governance, and strategic determinants of Japanese manufacturing investment in the United States, *SMJ*, 15: 419–436; G. McNamara & P. Vaaler, 2000, The influence of competitive positioning and rivalry in emerging market risk assessment, *JIBS*, 31: 337–347; K. Ito & E. Rose, 2002, Foreign direct investment location strategies in the tire industry, *JIBS*, 33: 593–602; F. Knickerbocker, 1973, *Oligopolistic Reaction and Multinational Enterprise*, Boston: Harvard Business School Press; L. Thomas & K. Weigelt, 2000, Product location choice and firm capabilities, *SMJ*, 21: 897–909.

[32] J. Baum & H. Korn, 1996, Competitive dynamics of interfirm rivalry, *AMJ*, 39: 255–291.

[33] *USA Today*, 2005, Price remarks by Toyota chief could be illegal, June 10: 5B.

[34] This section draws heavily on N. Dawar & T. Frost, 1999, Competing with giants, *HBR*, March–April: 119–129.

[35] D. Lavie & A. Fiegenbaum, 2000, Strategic reaction of domestic firms to foreign MNC dominance, *LRP*, 33: 651–672.

[36] J. Mathews, 2006, Dragon multinationals, *APJM*, 23: 5–27.

[37] D. Xu, Y. Pan, C. Wu, & B. Yim, 2006, Performance of domestic and foreign-invested enterprises in China, *JWB*, 41: 261–274.

[38] R. Griffin & M. Pustay, 2003, *International Business*, 3rd ed. (p. 241), Upper Saddle River, NJ: Prentice Hall.

[39] J. Stiglitz, 2002, *Globalization and Its Discontent* (pp. 172–173), New York: Norton.

[40] R. D'Aveni, 1994, *Hypercompetition*, New York: Free Press.

[41] C. Fishman, 2006, *The Wal-Mart Effect*, New York: Penguin.

[42] M. Czinkota & M. Kotabe, 1997, A marketing perspective of the US International Trade Commission's antidumping actions (p. 183), *JWB*, 32: 169–187.

Making Alliances and Acquisitions Work

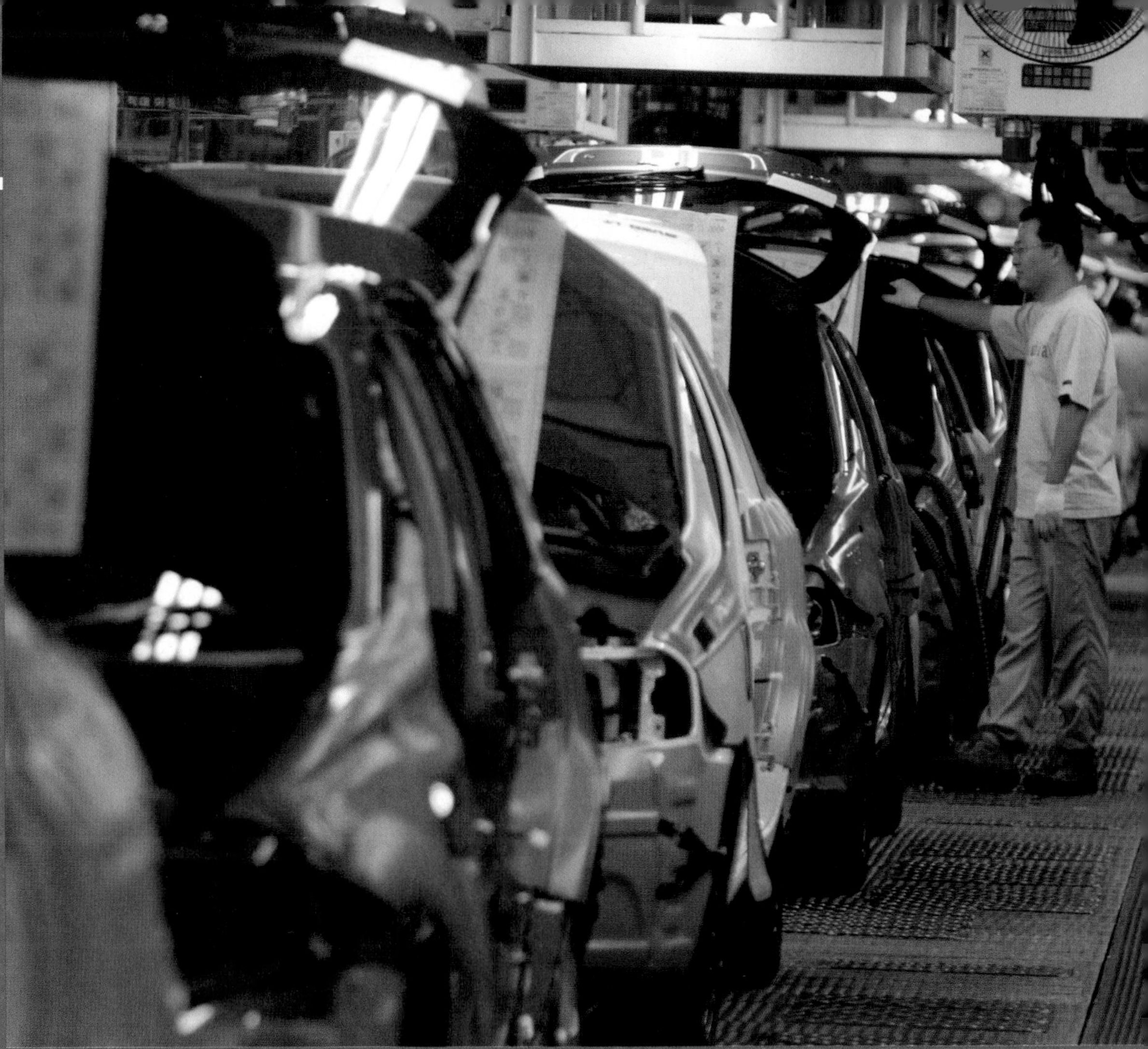

General Motors and Daewoo: From Alliance to Acquisition

In 1984, General Motors (GM) and Daewoo formed a 50/50 joint venture (JV), named the Daewoo Motor Company, each contributing $100 million equity. The JV would produce the Pontiac LeMans, based on GM's popular Opel Kadett model developed by GM's wholly owned German subsidiary Opel. Commentators hailed the alliance as a brilliant outcome of a corporate "marriage" of German technology and Korean labor (whose cost was low at that time). As a win-win combination, GM would tackle the small-car market in North America and eventually expand into Asia, whereas Daewoo would gain access to superior technology.

Unfortunately, the alliance was problematic. By the late 1980s, Korean workers at the JV launched a series of bitter strikes to demand better pay. Ultimately, the JV had to more than double their wages, wiping out the low-cost advantage. Equally problematic was the poor quality of the LeMans. Electrical systems and brakes often failed. US sales plummeted to 37,000 vehicles in 1991, down 86% from the 1988 high.

However, Daewoo argued that the poor sales were not primarily due to quality problems but due to GM's poor marketing efforts that had not treated the LeMans as one of GM's own models. Further, Daewoo was deeply frustrated by GM's determination to block its efforts to export cars to Eastern Europe, which Daewoo saw as its ideal market. GM's reasoning was that Eastern Europe was Opel's territory.

Gradually, Daewoo secretly developed independent car models, and GM initially was unaware of these activities. Once Daewoo launched competing car models, the troubles associated with this JV, long rumored by the media, became strikingly evident. The picture of an "ideal couple" with a "perfect kid" (the JV) was now replaced by the image of a dysfunctional family in which everybody was pointing fingers at each other.

In 1992, GM and Daewoo divorced, with Daewoo buying out GM's equity for $170 million. When GM exited the problematic JV, it was left without a manufacturing base in Korea. Daewoo, on the other hand, embarked upon one of the most ambitious marches into emerging economies, building a dozen auto plants in Indonesia, Iran, Poland, Ukraine, Vietnam, and Uzbekistan. In the process, Daewoo borrowed an astounding $20 billion, leading to its collapse during the 1997 Asian economic crisis.

In an interesting turn of events, GM and Daewoo joined hands again. Despite its bankruptcy, Daewoo attempted to avoid GM and strongly preferred a takeover by Ford. But Ford took a pass. Then GM entered the negotiations, eventually forming a new JV, called GM Daewoo Auto and Technology Company, with Daewoo's Korean creditors in 2001. The terms of this marriage were quite different from the previous one. Instead of a 50/50 split, GM was now in the driver's seat, commanding a 67% stake (with a bargain-basement price of $400 million)—in essence, a GM acquisition in disguise.

This time, GM has fully integrated GM Daewoo into its global strategy because GM now has uncontested control. GM Daewoo makes cars in South Korea and Vietnam and exports them to more than 140 countries. One of the most decisive moves is to phase out the Daewoo brand tarnished by quality problems and financial turbulence, except in South Korea and Vietnam. GM has labeled a vast majority of cars built by GM Daewoo as Chevrolet, a brand that GM usually pitches as more American than the Stars and Stripes. In the United States, Latin America, and Eastern Europe, the GM Daewoo-built Chevrolet Aveo has become one of the best-selling compact

LEARNING OBJECTIVES

After studying this chapter, you should be able to

1. articulate how institutions and resources affect alliances and acquisitions
2. gain insights into the formation, evolution, and performance of alliances
3. understand the motives and performance of acquisitions
4. participate in two leading debates on alliances and acquisitions
5. draw implications for action

cars, beating the Toyota Echo and the Hyundai Excel. In addition to finished cars, GM Daewoo also makes kits to be assembled by local factories in China, Colombia, India, Thailand, and Venezuela. In three years, GM Daewoo's worldwide sales of cars and kits reached one million, up from 400,000 when GM took over. That makes GM Daewoo one of the best-performing units of the troubled Detroit automaker.

Sources: I thank Professor Oded Shenkar (Ohio State University) for collaborating with me on related research cited in source (3). Adapted from (1) *Business Week*, 2004, Daewoo: GM's hot new engine, November 29: 52–53; (2) *Business Week*, 2005, Made in Korea, assembled in China, August 1: 48; (3) M. W. Peng & O. Shenkar, 2002. Joint venture dissolution as corporate divorce, *Academy of Management Executive*, 16: 92–105; (5) Wikipedia, 2007, GM Daewoo, http://en.wikipedia.org.

Why did GM and Daewoo form strategic alliances? Among many forms of alliances, why did they choose a JV form both times? Why did one JV fail but the second JV (essentially an acquisition) succeed? These are some of the key questions we address in this chapter. Alliances and acquisitions are two major strategies for the growth of the firm around the world, thus necessitating our attention. This chapter first defines alliances and acquisitions, followed by a discussion of how institution- and resource-based views shed light on these topics. We then discuss the formation, evolution, and performance of alliances and acquisitions. Debates and extensions follow.

LEARNING OBJECTIVE 1

articulate how institutions and resources affect alliances and acquisitions

strategic alliances
Voluntary agreements between firms involving exchange, sharing, or co-developing of products, technologies, or services.

contractual (nonequity-based) alliances
Alliances that are based on contracts and that do not involve the sharing of equity.

DEFINING ALLIANCES AND ACQUISITIONS

Strategic alliances are "voluntary agreements between firms involving exchange, sharing, or co-developing of products, technologies, or services."[1] As noted in Chapter 10, the dotted area in Figure 10.3 consisting of nonequity-based contractual agreements and equity-based JVs can all be broadly considered strategic alliances. Figure 12.1 illustrates this further, visualizing alliances as a *compromise* between pure market transactions and acquisitions. **Contractual (nonequity-based) alliances** include co-marketing, research and development (R&D) contracts, turnkey projects, strategic suppliers, strategic distributors, and licensing/franchising. **Equity-based alliances** include **strategic investment** (one partner invests in another) and **cross-shareholding** (both partners invest in each other). JV is one form of equity-based alliance. It involves the establishment of a new legally independent entity (in other words, a new firm) whose equity is provided by two (or more) partners.

FIGURE 12.1 THE VARIETY OF STRATEGIC ALLIANCES

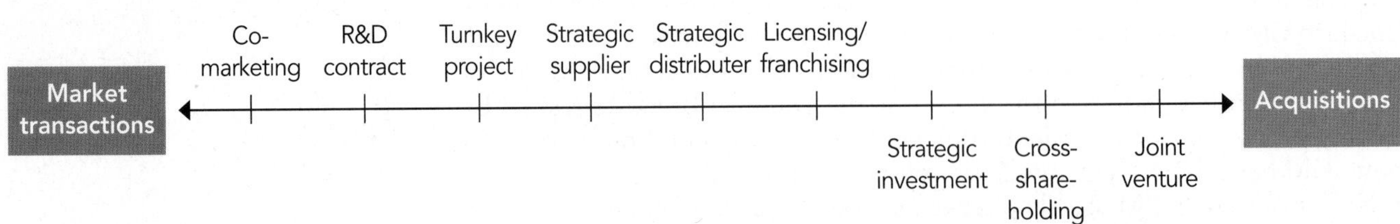

Although JVs are often used as examples of alliances (see Opening Case), *not* all alliances are JVs. A JV, such as Sony Ericsson, is a "corporate child" produced by two (or more) parent firms. A non-JV, equity-based alliance can be regarded as two firms getting married but not having children. For example, Renault is a strategic investor in Nissan, but both automakers still operate independently, and they have *not* given birth to a new car company (which would be a JV if they did).

Although the term **mergers and acquisitions (M&As)** is often used, in reality, acquisitions dominate the scene. An **acquisition** is transfer of the control of operations and management from one firm (target) to another (acquirer), the former becoming a unit of the latter. For example, Compaq is now a unit of HP. A **merger** is the combination of operations and management of two firms to establish a new legal entity. For instance, the merger between South African Breweries and Miller Beer resulted in SABMiller. Only 3% of M&As are mergers. Even many so-called "mergers of equals" turn out to be one firm taking over another (such as DaimlerChrysler). A recent *World Investment Report* opines that "The number of 'real' mergers is so low that, for practical purposes, 'M&As' basically mean 'acquisitions'."[2] Consequently, we will use "M&As" and "acquisitions" interchangeably.

Specifically, we focus on cross-border (international) M&As (Figure 12.2). This is not only because of our global interest but also because of (1) the high percentage of international deals among all M&As and (2) the high percentage of M&As among foreign direct investment (FDI) flows.[3] Globally, cross-border activities represent approximately 30% of all M&As. In 2006 (a record year), cross-border deals were worth $1.3 trillion, and the value of M&A deals topped $4 trillion for the first time.[4] In some countries (such as Australia), cross-border M&As exceed domestic M&As.[5] M&As represent the largest proportion of FDI flows, reaching approximately 70% of worldwide FDI.

What drives alliances? What drives acquisitions? The next section draws on institution- and resource-based views to shed light on these important questions.

equity-based alliances
Alliances that involve the use of equity.

strategic investment
One firm invests in another as a strategic investor.

cross-shareholding
Both firms invest in each other to become cross-shareholders.

acquisition
The transfer of the control of operations and management from one firm (target) to another (acquirer), the former becoming a unit of the latter.

merger
The combination of operations and management of two firms to establish a new legal entity.

FIGURE 12.2 THE VARIETY OF CROSS-BORDER MERGERS AND ACQUISITIONS

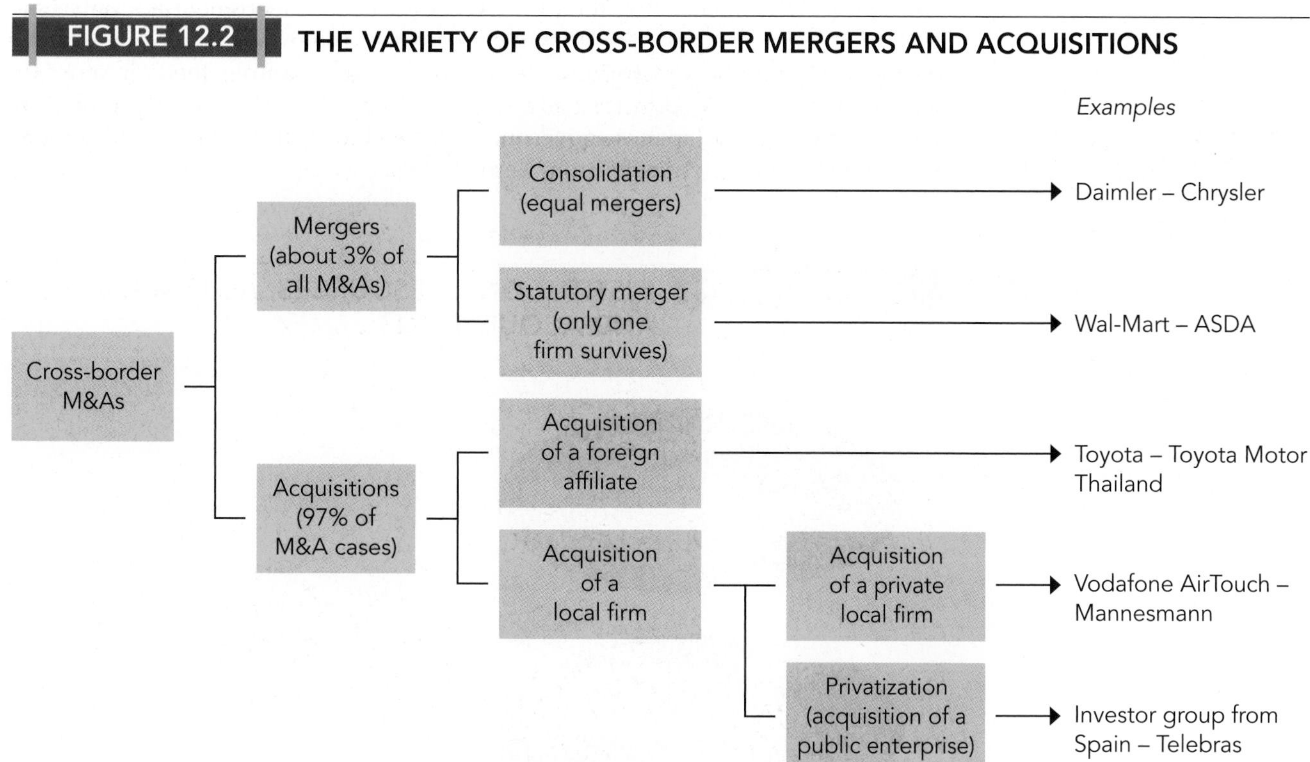

Source: Adapted from United Nations, 2000, *World Investment Report 2000* (p. 100), New York: UNCTAD.

HOW INSTITUTIONS AND RESOURCES AFFECT ALLIANCES AND ACQUISITIONS

The institution-based view suggests that as rules of the game, institutions affect how firms make strategic choices of alliances versus acquisitions. However, rules are not made for only one firm. The resource-based view argues that among a number of firms governed by the same set of rules, some excel more than others because of the differences in firm-specific capabilities that make alliances and acquisitions work (see Figure 12.3). This section examines why this is the case.

Institutions, Alliances, and Acquisitions

Formal Institutions Alliances function within a set of formal legal and regulatory frameworks. The impact of these *formal* institutions can be found along two dimensions: (1) antitrust concerns and (2) entry mode requirements. First, many firms establish alliances with competitors. For instance, Siemens and Bosch compete in automotive components and collaborate in white goods. Cooperation between competitors is usually suspected of at least some tacit collusion by antitrust authorities (see Chapter 11). However, because integration within alliances is usually not as tight as acquisitions (which would eliminate one competitor), antitrust authorities have a higher likelihood of approving alliances than acquisitions.[6] For example, the proposed merger between American Airlines and British Airways was blocked by both US and UK antitrust authorities. However, they have been allowed to form an alliance that has eventually grown to become the multipartner One World.

Second, another way formal institutions affect alliances and acquisitions is through formal requirements on market entry modes. In many countries, governments discourage or ban acquisitions to establish wholly owned subsidiaries (WOS), thereby leaving some sort of alliances with local firms to be the only entry choice for FDI. For instance, the pre-NAFTA Mexican government not only limited multinationals' entries to JVs but also dictated the maximum ceiling of their equity position to be 49% (prior to 1994). For another example, the Fuji Xerox JV was originally proposed in 1962 as a sales company to market Xerox products in Japan. However, the Japanese government refused to approve the JV unless there was some technology transfer from Xerox to Fuji.

FIGURE 12.3 INSTITUTIONS, RESOURCES, ALLIANCES, AND ACQUISITIONS

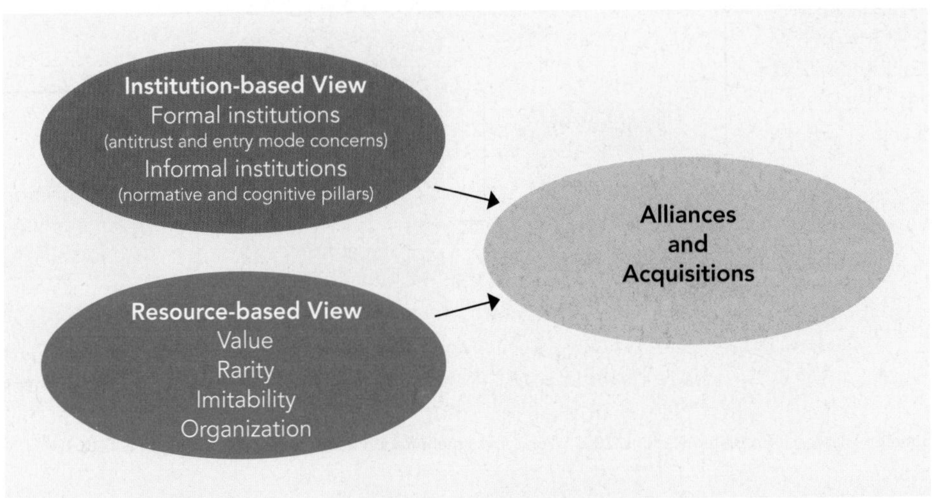

Recently, there are two characteristics concerning formal government policies on entry mode requirements. First, there is a general trend toward more liberal policies. Many governments (such as those in Mexico and South Korea) that historically only approved JVs have now allowed WOS as an entry mode. As a result, there is now a noticeable decline of JVs and a corresponding rise of acquisitions in emerging economies.[7] A second characteristic is that despite such general movement toward more liberal policies, many governments still impose considerable requirements, especially when foreign firms acquire domestic assets. Only JVs are permitted in the strategically important Chinese automobile assembly industry and the Russian oil industry, thus eliminating acquisitions as a choice. US regulations only permit up to 25% of the equity of any US airline to be held by foreign carriers, and EU regulations limit non-EU ownership to 49% of EU-based airlines.

Informal Institutions The first set of informal institutions centers on collective norms supported by a normative pillar. A core idea of the institution-based view is that because firms act to enhance or protect their legitimacy, copying what other reputable organizations are doing—even without knowing the direct performance benefits of doing so—may be a low-cost way to gain legitimacy. Therefore, when competitors are setting up alliances, jumping on the alliance bandwagon may be cool as opposed to ignoring industry trends. When M&As are in the air, managers who may have second thoughts about the wisdom behind M&As may nevertheless be tempted to hunt for acquisition targets. Although not every alliance/acquisition decision is driven by imitation, this motivation seems to explain a lot of these activities.[8] The flip side is that many firms rush into alliances and acquisitions without adequate due diligence and then get burned.[9]

A second set of informal institutions stresses the cognitive pillar centered on the internalized, taken-for-granted values and beliefs that guide alliances and acquisitions. Britain's BAE Systems, for instance, announced in the 1990s that *all* its future aircraft development programs would involve alliances. General Electric (GE) has 230 full-time staff members devoted to acquisitions. Many managers believe that such alliances and acquisitions are the right (and sometimes the only) thing to do.

Resources and Alliances

This section focuses on the VRIO framework within an alliance context.

Value Alliances must create value.[10] The three global airline alliance networks—One World, Sky Team, and Star Alliance—create value by reducing 18% to 28% ticket costs booked on two-stage flights compared with separate flights on the same route if these airlines were not allied.[11] Table 12.1 identifies three broad categories of value creation in terms of how advantages outweigh disadvantages. First, alliances may reduce costs, risks, and uncertainties.[12] As Google rises to preeminence,

TABLE 12.1 STRATEGIC ALLIANCES: ADVANTAGES AND DISADVANTAGES

Advantages	Disadvantages
Reducing costs, risks, and uncertainties	Choosing wrong partners
Accessing complementary assets and learning opportunities	Potential partner opportunism
Possibilities to use alliances as real options	Risks of helping nurture competitors (learning race)

former rivals, such as eBay, Yahoo!, and Microsoft (MSN), are now exploring alliances to counter its influence while not taking on excessive risks. Second, alliances allow firms to tap into complementary assets of partners and facilitate learning,[13] as evidenced by NUMMI, the GM-Toyota JV.

Finally, an important advantage of alliances lies in their value as *real options*. Conceptually, an option is the right, but not obligation, to take some action in the future. Technically, a financial option is an investment instrument permitting its holder, having paid for a small fraction of an asset, the right to increase investment to eventually acquire it if necessary. A **real option** is an investment in real operations as opposed to financial capital.[14] A real options view suggests two propositions:

real option
An investment in real operations as opposed to financial capital.

- In the first phase, an investor makes a small initial investment to buy an option, which leads to the right to future investment without being obligated to do so.
- The investor then holds the option until a decision point arrives in the second phase and then decides between exercising the option or abandoning it.

For firms interested in eventually acquiring other companies but unsure about such moves, working together in alliances thus affords an insider view to evaluate the capabilities of these partners. This is similar to trying new shoes on to see if they fit before buying them. Since acquisitions are not only costly but also very likely to fail, alliances permit firms to *sequentially* increase their investment should they decide to pursue acquisitions. On the other hand, after working together as partners, if firms find that acquisitions are not a good idea, there is no obligation to pursue them. Overall, alliances have emerged as great instruments of real options because of their flexibility to sequentially scale *up* or scale *down* the investment.[15]

On the other hand, alliances have a number of nontrivial drawbacks. First, there is always a possibility of being stuck with the wrong partner(s). Firms are advised to choose a prospective mate with caution, preferably a known entity. Yet, the mate should also be sufficiently differentiated to provide some complementary (nonoverlapping) capabilities. Just as many individuals have a hard time figuring out the true qualities of their spouses before they get married, many firms find it difficult to evaluate the true intentions and capabilities of their prospective partners until it is too late.

learning race
A situation in which alliance partners aim to outrun each other by learning the "tricks" from the other side as fast as possible.

A second disadvantage is potential partner opportunism. Although opportunism is likely in any kind of economic relationship, the alliance setting may provide especially strong incentives for some (but not all) partners to be opportunistic. This is because cooperative relationships always entail some elements of trust, which may be easily abused.[16] In an alliance with Britain's Rover, Honda shared a great deal of proprietary technology beyond what was contractually called for. Honda was stunned when informed by Rover's parent firm that Rover would be sold to BMW and that Honda would be literally kicked out. Unfortunately, such an example is not an isolated incident.

What conditions must be present to make a joint venture, such as Fujian Daimler Automotive Co., Ltd, work?

Finally, alliances, especially those between rivals, can be dangerous because they may help competitors. By opening their doors to outsiders, alliances make it *easier* to observe and imitate firm-specific capabilities. In alliances between competitors, there is a potential **learning race** in which partners aim to outrun each other by learning the "tricks" from the other side as fast as possible.[17] For example, the alliance between

GE and Rolls-Royce to jointly develop jet engines collapsed because both firms could not solve issues raised by their long-standing rivalry.[18]

Rarity The abilities to successfully manage interfirm relationships—often called **relational** (or **collaborative**) **capabilities**—may be rare. Managers involved in alliances require relationship skills rarely covered in the traditional business school curriculum that emphasizes competition as opposed to collaboration. To truly derive benefits from alliances, managers need to foster trust with partners, while at the same time being on guard against opportunism.[19]

relational (or **collaborative**) **capability**
Capability to successfully manage interfirm relationships.

As much as alliances represent a strategic and economic arrangement, they also constitute a social, psychological, and emotional phenomenon: Words such as *courtship*, *marriage*, and *divorce* often surface. Given that the interests of partner firms do not fully overlap and are often in conflict, managers involved in alliances live a precarious existence, trying to represent the interests of their respective firms while attempting to make the complex relationship work. Given the general shortage of good relationship management skills in the human population (remember, for example, 50% of marriages in the United States fail), it is not surprising that sound relational capabilities to successfully manage alliances are in short supply.[20]

Imitability The issue of imitability pertains to two levels: (1) firm level and (2) alliance level. First, as noted earlier, one firm's resources and capabilities may be imitated by partners. For instance, in the late 1980s, McDonald's set up a JV with the Moscow municipality government that helped it enter Russia. However, during the 1990s, the Moscow mayor set up a rival fast-food chain, The Bistro. The Bistro tried to eat McDonald's lunch by replicating numerous products and practices. There was very little that McDonald's could do because nobody sues the mayor in Moscow and hopes to win.

Another imitability issue refers to the trust and understanding among partners in successful alliances. Firms without good "chemistry" may have a hard time imitating such activities. CFM International, a JV set up by GE and Snecma to produce jet engines in France, has successfully operated for over 30 years. Rivals would have a hard time imitating such a successful relationship.

Organization Some alliance relationships are organized in a way that makes it difficult for others to replicate. There is much truth behind Tolstoy's opening statement in *Anna Karenina*: "All happy families are like one another; each unhappy family is unhappy in its own way." Given the difficulty for individuals in unhappy marriages to improve their relationship (despite an army of professional marriage counselors, social workers, and friends and families), it is not surprising that firms in unsuccessful alliances (for whatever reason) often find it exceedingly challenging, if not impossible, to organize and manage their interfirm relationships better.

Resources and Acquisitions

Value Do acquisitions create value?[21] Overall, their performance record is sobering. As many as 70% of acquisitions reportedly fail. On average, acquiring firms' performance does not improve after acquisitions.[22] Target firms, after being acquired and becoming internal units, often perform worse than when they were independent, stand-alone firms. The only identifiable group of winners is shareholders of target firms, who may experience on average a 24% increase in their stock value during the period of the transaction—thanks to the **acquisition premium** (the difference between the acquisition price and the market value of target firms). Shareholders of acquiring firms experience a 4% loss of their stock value during the same period. The combined wealth of shareholders of both acquiring and target firms is marginally positive, less than 2%.[23] Although these findings are

acquisition premium
The difference between the acquisition price and the market value of target firms.

mostly from three decades of M&A data in the United States (where half of the worldwide M&As take place and most of the M&A research is done), they probably also apply to cross-border acquisitions.[24] Consider DaimlerChrysler. In 1998, Daimler paid $35 billion for Chrysler. In 2007, Chrysler was sold to Cerberus Capital, a private equity firm, for $7.4 billion, one-fifth of what Daimler paid.

Rarity For acquisitions to add value, firms must have unique skills to execute such a strategy. In 2004, an executive team at Lenovo, China's leading PC maker, planned to acquire IBM's PC division. The team confronted Lenovo's suspicious board that raised a crucial question: If a venerable American technology company had failed to profit from the PC business, did Lenovo have what it takes to do better when managing such a complex global business? The answer was actually no. The board only gave its blessing to the plan when the acquisition team agreed not only to acquire the business but also to recruit top American executives (see Closing Case).

Imitability Although many firms undertake acquisitions, a much smaller number have mastered the art of postacquisition integration.[25] Consequently, firms that excel in integration possess *hard-to-imitate* capabilities. For example, at Northrop, integrating acquired businesses is down to a "science." Each must conform to a carefully orchestrated plan listing nearly 400 items, from how to issue press releases to which accounting software to use. Unlike its bigger defense rivals such as Boeing and Raytheon, Northrop thus far has not stumbled with any acquisitions.

strategic fit
The effective matching of complementary strategic capabilities.

organizational fit
The similarity in cultures, systems, and structures.

Organization Fundamentally, whether acquisitions add value boils down to how merged firms are organized to take advantage of the benefits while minimizing the costs. Preacquisition analysis often focuses on **strategic fit**, which is about the effective matching of complementary strategic capabilities. Yet, many firms do not pay adequate attention to **organizational fit**, which is the similarity in cultures, systems, and structures. On paper, Daimler and Chrysler had great strategic fit in terms of complementary product lines and geographic scope, but there was very little organizational fit. Despite the official proclamation of a "merger of equals," the American unit in DaimlerChrysler became "Occupied Chrysler." American managers resented the dominance of German managers, and Germans disliked being paid two-thirds less than their Chrysler colleagues. These clashes led to a mass exodus of American managers from Chrysler—a common phenomenon in acquired firms.[26]

Overall, institutions and resources significantly affect alliances and acquisitions. In Focus 12.1 outlines how Brazil's Embraer engages in alliances and acquisitions, and In Focus 12.2 sheds light on how to enhance the odds for M&A success in China. The next few sections discuss in some detail the formation, evolution, and performance of alliances and acquisitions.

IN FOCUS 12.1 Embraer's Alliances and Acquisitions

Embraer is a Brazilian manufacturer of small commercial and military aircraft. It was established in 1960 as a state-owned enterprise but was privatized in 1994 with 60% of shares owned by private Brazilian interests (though the government retains a controlling "golden share"). It invested overseas prior to privatization (the United States in 1979, Europe in 1988) primarily to offer sales and technical support to customers in developed markets. However, after 1994—and especially in 1999—it entered into a series of strategic alliances with European groups such as EADS and Thales (France) in order to gain technology (and to reduce risk by pooling resources). Later it made acquisitions to ensure brand recognition in specialist aerospace markets. In 2004, it established a manufacturing affiliate in China (in which it owns a 51% stake), which assembles final aircraft for the Chinese and regional market. With 90% of its global sales overseas, Embraer can be regarded as one of Brazil's (indeed Latin America's) few truly global players.

Source: Excerpts from United Nations, 2006, *World Investment Report 2006: FDI from Developing and Transition Economies* (p. 159), New York and Geneva: United Nations/UN Conference on Trade and Development (UNCTAD). © United Nations, 2006.

IN FOCUS 12.2 Making M&As Fly in China—Mike W. Peng

The first wave of foreign direct investment (FDI) in China, in the 1980s, mostly took the form of joint ventures (JVs). A second wave followed in the 1990s in the form of wholly foreign-owned enterprises (WFOEs). Now a third wave of FDI—cross-board mergers and acquisitions (M&As)—is gaining strength.

Consider the forces driving this third wave. China has a massive appetite for FDI; it is one of the world's largest FDI recipients. Yet, M&As account for only 10% to 15% of FDI flowing into China, compared with approximately 70% of FDI outside China that takes the form of M&As. One reason for this disparity is that, until China joined the World Trade Organization in 2001, national regulations often encouraged (or required) foreign entrants to form JVs or set up WFOEs, while explicitly discouraging M&As. But China has since gradually loosened the regulations that govern foreign takeovers of Chinese assets, especially state-owned enterprises (SOEs), and has made explicit moves to attract foreign M&As. In many industries, including financial services and manufacturing, constraints on M&As are just now being lifted. At the same time, Chinese firms are increasingly engaging in cross-border M&As of their own, as evidenced by their recent bids for Unocal, Maytag, and IBM's personal computer division (see Closing Case). To the extent that the Chinese government supports the outbound M&As, it must in most cases clear the path for inbound M&As, according to international norms of reciprocity.

Given the environment, how should foreign companies proceed? In many ways, strategies for M&As in China overlap those for M&As elsewhere. But my recent research has uncovered some idiosyncrasies that are specific to acquisitions in China.

First, Chinese SOEs are rife with organizational slack. Government agencies have restructured some SOEs to reduce underutilized resources and to make the SOEs more attractive M&A targets for foreign firms. Although slack usually indicates inefficiency, in certain firms, some slack—such as unabsorbed cash flow in the form of depreciation funds, reserve funds, and retained earnings—may indicate the potential for increased performance, actually enhancing targets' attractiveness.

Second, it is well known that many Chinese SOEs maintain three sets of books: one set that exaggerates performance, to brag to administrative superiors; one that underreports performance, for tax purposes; and one that is fairly accurate, for managers themselves. Acquisition targets are likely to show foreign negotiators the bragging books initially. As a result, foreign firms need to be aggressive in conducting due diligence to uncover an accurate picture of targets' assets and resources. This is particularly relevant when investigating slack.

Finally, most Western firms launching JVs and WFOEs in China have believed that ethnic Chinese managers—those from overseas Chinese economies, such as Hong Kong and Taiwan, who are well versed in the local language—were the best choice for running their operations in China. Meanwhile, they have presumed that Western managers would be less effective because of language and cultural barriers. But evidence from my own research and others' suggests the *opposite*: Using surveys, interviews, and other tools, researchers are finding that ethnic Chinese managers hired by Western companies to run these businesses are, on average, *less* effective than their non-Chinese counterparts, as measured by the length of their tenures and attainment of performance goals. How could this be?

One reason appears to be that ethnic Chinese managers often struggle with an ambiguous managerial identity: Western corporate headquarters views them as "us," and local Chinese employees also expect them to be "us." When these managers favor headquarters on issues where headquarters and locals conflict—such as whether Western employees and locals should receive equal compensation or whether chopsticks or forks should be used at company banquets—local employees may regard them as traitors of sorts. That corrodes employees' trust, ultimately undermining ethnic Chinese managers' performance. On the other hand, employees give Western managers the benefit of the doubt. They expect these managers to behave differently, to commit cultural errors, and to show allegiance to the parent firm. This tolerance by local employees of Western managers' differences can enhance these managers' confidence and performance.

Of course, not every non-Chinese manager outperforms every ethnic Chinese manager. It is clear, however, that managerial effectiveness in China does not depend on one's ability to use chopsticks. This point is crucial as more M&As flow into China and more acquiring companies staff their target firms' management.

Source: Adapted from M. W. Peng, 2006, Making M&A fly in China, *Harvard Business Review*, March: 26–27.

ALLIANCES AND ACQUISITIONS

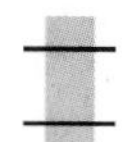

Holding institutions constant, how do firms choose between alliances and acquisitions?[27] Shown in Table 12.2, alliances, which tend to be loosely coordinated among partners, cannot work in a setting that requires a high degree of integration. Such a setting calls for acquisitions. Alliances work well when the ratio of soft to hard assets is relatively high (such as a heavy concentration of tacit knowledge),

TABLE 12.2 ALLIANCES VERSUS ACQUISITIONS

	Alliances	Acquisitions
Resource interdependence	Low	High
Ratio of soft to hard assets	High	Low
Primary source of value creation	Combining complementary resources	Eliminating redundant resources
Level of uncertainty	High	Low

Source: Based on text in J. Dyer, P. Kale, & H. Singh, 2004, When to ally and when to acquire? *Harvard Business Review*, July–August: 109–115.

whereas acquisitions may be preferred when such a ratio is low. Alliances create value primarily by combining complementary resources, whereas acquisitions derive most value by eliminating redundant resources. Finally, alliances, as real options, may be more suitable under a high level of uncertainty, and acquisitions are preferable when the level of uncertainty is low.[28]

While these rules are not exactly "rocket science," "few companies are disciplined to adhere to them."[29] Consider the 50/50 JV between Coca-Cola (Coke) and Procter and Gamble (P&G) that combined their fruit drinks businesses (such as Coke's Minute Maid and P&G's Sunny Delight) in 2001. The goal was to combine Coke's distribution system with P&G's R&D capabilities in consumer products. However, the stock market sent a mixed signal by pushing P&G's stock 2% *higher* and Coke's 6% *lower* on the day of the announcement. For three reasons, Coke probably could have done better by acquiring P&G's fruit drinks business. First, a higher degree of integration would be necessary to derive the proposed synergies. Second, because Coke's distribution assets were relatively easy-to-value hard assets whereas P&G's R&D capabilities were hard-to-value soft assets, the risk was higher for Coke. Finally, there was little uncertainty regarding the popularity of fruit drinks, and investors found it difficult to understand why Coke would share 50% of this fast-growing business with P&G, a laggard in this industry. Not surprisingly, the JV was quickly terminated within six months.

LEARNING OBJECTIVE 2

gain insights into the formation, evolution, and performance of alliances

FORMATION OF ALLIANCES

How are alliances formed? Figure 12.4 illustrates a three-stage model to address this question.[30]

Stage One: To Cooperate or Not to Cooperate?

In Stage One, a decision is made on whether to form alliances as opposed to relying on pure market transactions or acquisitions.[31] To grow by pure market transactions, the firm has to independently confront competitive challenges. This is very demanding, even for resource-rich multinationals.[32] As noted earlier in the chapter, acquisitions have some unique drawbacks. Thus, many managers conclude that alliances are the way to go.

FIGURE 12.4 ALLIANCE FORMATION

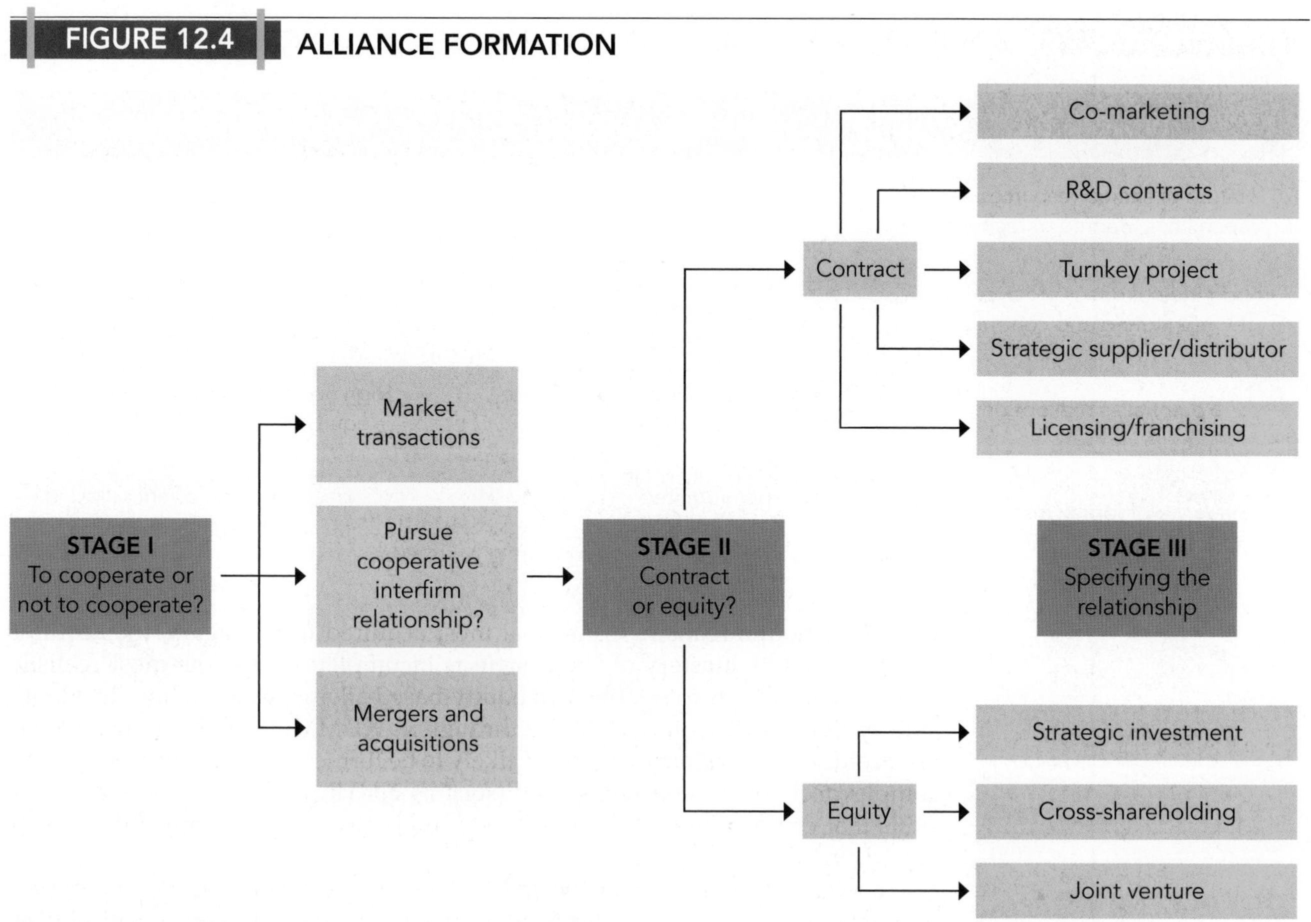

Source: Adapted from S. Tallman & O. Shenkar, 1994, A managerial decision model of international cooperative venture formation (p. 101), *Journal of International Business Studies*, 25 (1): 91–113.

Stage Two: Contract or Equity?

As noted in Chapters 6 and 10, the choice between contract and equity is crucial.[33] Table 12.3 identifies four driving forces. First, the key is the character of shared capabilities. The more tacit (that is, hard to describe and codify) they are, the more likely equity involvement would be preferred. Although not the only source of learning, **learning by doing** is perhaps the most effective way to learn *complex* know-how. Just as individuals learning how to cook will not get the job done by reading cookbooks alone, firms learning how to produce new cars will find that learning from books and reports that disseminate codified knowledge is not enough.[34] There is a lot of tacit knowledge that can only be acquired via learning by doing, preferably with experts as alliance partners.

learning by doing
An effective way to learn complex tasks.

A lot of tacit knowledge dealing with complex skills and know-how is embedded in specific organizational settings and is "sticky" (that is, hard to isolate from the particular firm that possesses the knowledge).[35] Hypothetically, assuming Toyota is able to codify all the tacit knowledge associated with the legendary Toyota production system (TPS)—of course, impossible to do in reality—and sell it, the buyer will probably find that no matter how hard it tries, it is simply unable to completely replicate TPS. This is because TPS is, by definition, firm-specific and has a high degree of stickiness associated with Toyota. Short of completely acquiring Toyota (an extremely costly proposition), no other firm can hope to totally master this system. Further, if many Toyota employees leave after

TABLE 12.3 EQUITY-BASED VERSUS NONEQUITY-BASED ALLIANCES

Driving forces	Equity-based alliances	Nonequity-based alliances
Nature of shared resources and capabilities (degree of tacitness)	High	Low
Importance of direct organizational monitoring and control	High	Low
Potential as real options	High (for possible upgrading to M&As)	High (for possible upgrading to equity-based relationships)
Influence of formal institutions	High (when required or encouraged by regulations)	High (when required or encouraged by regulations)

the acquisition (a realistic scenario at most acquired firms), again, the acquirer will find that its mastery of the system is incomplete. Thus, the most realistic way to access TPS is to establish an equity-based alliance to learn how to "do it" side by side with Toyota, as GM did through its NUMMI JV with Toyota. In general, equity-based alliances are more likely to be formed when dealing with more complex technology and know-how (such as NUMMI) than with less complex skills that can be more efficiently transferred between two organizations (such as McDonald's franchising).

A second driving force is the importance of direct monitoring and control. Equity relationships allow firms to have at least some partial direct control over joint activities on a continuing basis, whereas contractual relationships usually do not.[36] In general, firms prefer equity alliances (and a higher level of equity) if they fear that their intellectual property may be expropriated. This, for example, explains why there are so many JVs but so few licensing/franchising agreements in China.

A third driver is real options thinking. Some firms prefer to first establish contractual relationships, which can be viewed as real options (or stepping stones) for possible upgrading into equity alliances should the interactions turn out to be mutually satisfactory. For instance, the Airbus consortium (originally consisting of two partners, France's Aerospatiale and Germany's Deutsche Aerospace in the 1960s) first initiated contractual relationships with Spain's CASA and the UK's British Aerospace, which proved satisfactory. Later, CASA and British Aerospace became full-fledged equity members of the Airbus consortium in the 1970s.

Finally, the choice between contract and equity also boils down to institutional constraints.[37] Some governments in emerging economies eager to help domestic firms climb the technology ladder either require or actively encourage the formation of JVs between foreign and domestic firms. The Chinese auto industry is a case in point.

Stage Three: Specifying the Relationship

Eventually, firms need to choose a specific format among the family of equity-based or contractual (nonequity-based) alliances illustrated in Figure 12.4. Since Chapter 10 has already covered this topic as part of the discussion on entry modes, we do not repeat it here.

EVOLUTION OF ALLIANCES

All relationships evolve—some grow; others fail.[38] This section deals with two aspects of such evolution: (1) combating opportunism and (2) evolving from corporate marriage to divorce.

Combating Opportunism

The threat of opportunism looms large on the horizon. Most firms want to make their relationship work but also want to protect themselves in case the other side is opportunistic.[39] Although it is difficult to completely eliminate opportunism, it is possible to minimize its threat by (1) walling off critical capabilities or (2) swapping critical capabilities through credible commitments.

First, both sides can contractually agree to wall off critical skills and technologies not meant to be shared. For example, GE and Snecma cooperated to build jet engines, yet GE was not willing to share its proprietary technology fully with Snecma. GE thus presented several sealed "black box" components, the inside of which Snecma had no access to, while permitting Snecma access to final assembly. This type of relationship, in human marriage terms, is like married couples whose premarital assets are protected by prenuptial agreements. As long as both sides are willing to live with these agreements designed to minimize the threat of opportunism, these relationships can prosper.

The second approach, swapping skills and technologies, is the exact *opposite* of the first approach. Both sides not only agree not to hold critical skills and technologies back but also make credible commitments to hold each other as a "hostage."[40] Motorola, for instance, licensed its microprocessor technology to Toshiba, which in turn licensed its memory chip technology to Motorola. Setting up a parallel and reciprocal relationship may increase the incentives for both partners to cooperate. For example, the agreement between France's Pernod-Ricard and America's Heublein to distribute Heublein's Smirnoff vodka in Europe was balanced by another agreement in which Heublein agreed to distribute Pernod-Ricard's Wild Turkey bourbon in the United States. In a nutshell, such mutual "hostage taking" reduces the threat of opportunism.

In human marriage terms, mutual hostage taking is similar to the following commitment: "Honey, I will love you forever. If you dare to betray me, I'll kill you. If I betray you, feel free to cut my head off!" To think slightly outside the box, the precarious peace during the Cold War can be regarded as a case of mutual hostage taking that worked. Because both the United States and Soviet Union held each other as a hostage, nobody dared to launch a first nuclear strike. As long as the victim of the first strike had only *one* nuclear ballistic missile submarine (such as the American Ohio class or the Soviet Typhoon class) left, this single submarine would have enough retaliatory firepower to wipe the top 20 US or Soviet cities off the surface of earth, an outcome that neither of the two superpowers found acceptable (see the movie *The Hunt for Red October*). The Cold War did not turn hot in part because of such "mutually assured destruction" (MAD!)—a real jargon used in the military.

Both of these approaches help minimize the threat of opportunism in alliances. Unfortunately, sometimes none of these approaches works, and the relationship deteriorates, as shown next.

From Corporate Marriage to Divorce[41]

Alliances are often described as "corporate marriages" and, when terminated, "corporate divorces."[42] Figure 12.5 portrays an alliance dissolution model. To apply the metaphor of human divorce, we focus on the two-partner alliance.

FIGURE 12.5 ALLIANCE DISSOLUTION

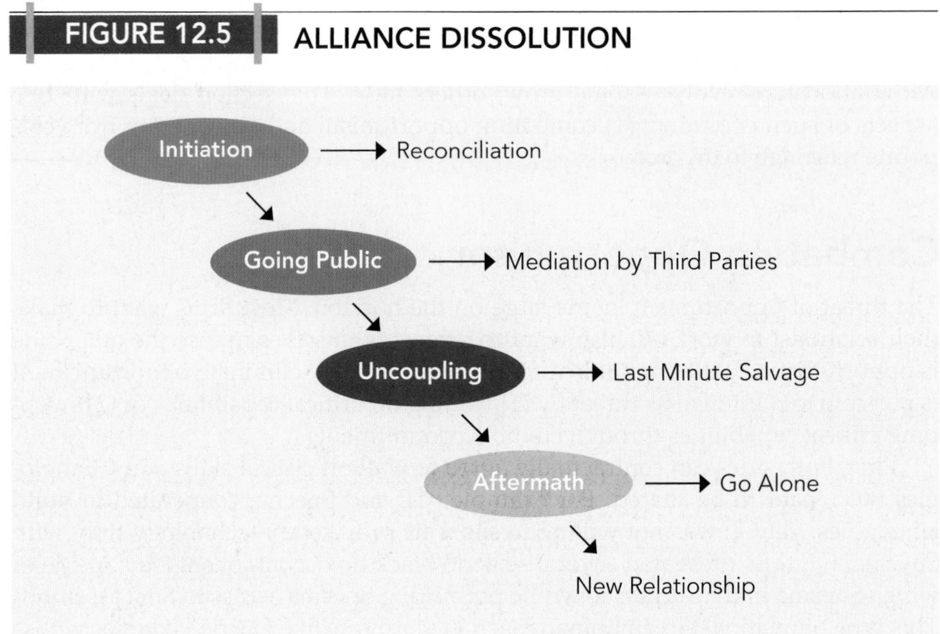

Source: M. W. Peng & O. Shenkar, 2002, Joint venture dissolution as corporate divorce (p. 95), *Academy of Management Executive*, 16 (2): 92–105.

Following the convention in human divorce research, the party that is the first to seek to exit is labeled the "initiator," and the other party is termed the "partner"—for lack of a better word. We will draw on our Opening Case to explain this process.

The first phase is initiation. The process begins when the initiator starts feeling uncomfortable with the alliance (for whatever reason). Wavering begins as a quiet, unilateral process by the initiator, which was Daewoo in the *first* JV with GM. After repeated demands to modify GM's behavior failed, Daewoo began to sense that the alliance is probably unsalvageable. At this point, the display of discontent became bolder. Initially, GM, the partner, might simply not "get it." The initiator's "sudden" dissatisfaction might confuse the partner. Sometimes, the partner responds by committing some grievous error, of the sort that GM seemingly made when flatly denying Daewoo's request to extend the JV's product line and market coverage. As a result, initiation tends to escalate.

The second phase is going public. The party that breaks the news has a first-mover advantage. By presenting a socially acceptable reason in favor of its cause, this party is able to win sympathy from key stakeholders, such as parent company executives, investors, and journalists. Not surprisingly, the initiator is likely to go public first, blaming the failure on the partner. Alternatively, the partner may preempt by blaming the initiator and establishing the righteousness of its position.

The third phase is uncoupling. Like human divorce, alliance dissolution can be friendly or hostile. In uncontested divorces, both sides attribute the separation more on, say, a change in circumstances. For example, Eli Lilly and Ranbaxy phased out their JV in India and remained friendly with each other. In contrast, contested divorces involve a party that accuses another. The worst scenario is "death by a thousand cuts" inflicted by one party at every turn.

The last phase is aftermath. Like most divorced individuals, most (but not all) "divorced" firms are likely to search for new partners. Understandably, the new alliance (such as the *second* GM-Daewoo JV) is often negotiated more extensively.[43] One Italian executive reportedly signed *each* of the 2,000 pages (!) of an alliance contract.[44] However, excessive formalization may signal a lack of trust—in the same way that prenuptials may scare away some prospective human marriage partners.

PERFORMANCE OF ALLIANCES

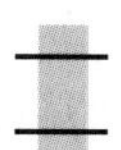

Although managers naturally focus on alliance performance,[45] there has been no consensus on what constitutes alliance performance.[46] A combination of objective measures (such as profit and market share) and subjective measures (such as managerial satisfaction) can be used. Figure 12.6 shows four factors that may influence alliance performance: (1) equity, (2) learning and experience, (3) nationality, and (4) relational capabilities. However, none of these is able to assert an unambiguous, direct impact on performance.[47] What has been found is that they may have some *correlations* with performance. First, the level of equity may be crucial. A higher level of equity stake is indicative of a firm's stronger commitment that is likely to result in higher performance.[48]

Second, whether firms have successfully learned from partners features prominently when assessing alliance performance.[49] Because learning is abstract, experience, which is relatively easy to measure, is often used as a proxy.[50] While experience certainly helps, its impact on performance is not linear. There is a limit beyond which further increase in experience may not enhance performance.[51]

Third, nationality may affect performance. For the same reason that human marriages between parties of dissimilar backgrounds are less stable than those with similar backgrounds, dissimilarities in national culture may create strains in alliances.[52] Not surprisingly, international alliances tend to have more problems than domestic ones.[53] When disputes and conflicts arise, it is often difficult to ascertain whether the other side is deliberately being opportunistic or is simply being (culturally) different.

Finally, alliance performance may fundamentally boil down to "soft," hard-to-measure relational capabilities. The art of relational capabilities, which is firm-specific and difficult to codify and transfer, may make or break alliances.[54] Overall, it would be naive to think that any of these single factors such as equity, learning, nationality, and relational capabilities would guarantee success. It is their *combination* that jointly increases the odds for the success of strategic alliances.

FIGURE 12.6 WHAT IS BEHIND ALLIANCE PERFORMANCE?

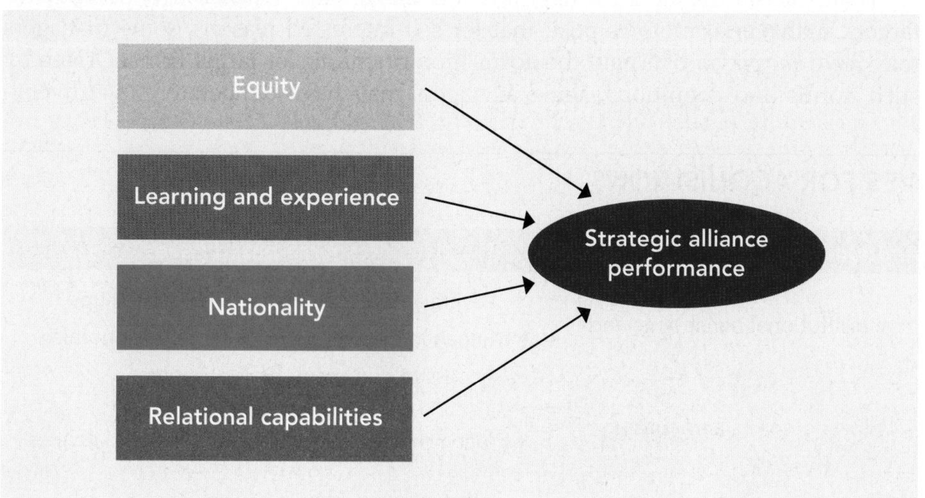

LEARNING OBJECTIVE 3

understand the motives and performance of acquisitions

MOTIVES FOR ACQUISITIONS

What drives acquisitions? Table 12.4 shows three drivers: (1) synergistic, (2) hubris, and (3) managerial motives, which can be illustrated by the institution- and resource-based views.[55] In terms of synergistic motives, from an institution-based view, acquisitions are often a response to formal institutional constraints and transitions in search of synergy.[56] It is not a coincidence that the number of cross-border acquisitions has skyrocketed in the last two decades. This is the same period during which trade and investment barriers have gone down and FDI has risen (see In Focus 12.1 and 12.2).[57]

From a resource-based standpoint, the most important synergistic rationale is to leverage superior resources.[58] Lufthansa recently acquired Air Dolomiti, an award-winning regional airline in northern Italy. At a time many small airlines drop out, Lufthansa's willingness to leverage its superior resources helps ensure Air Dolomiti's presence in the skies (despite its loss of independence). Another M&A driver is to enhance market power.[59] After a series of M&As in three years (such as Daimler/Chrysler, Renault/Nissan, and Ford/Jaguar), the top-10 automakers increased their global market share from 69% in 1996 to 80% in 1999.[60] Such M&As not only eliminate rivals but also reduce redundant assets. Finally, another motive is to gain access to complementary resources, as evidenced by Lenovo's interest in IBM's worldwide client base (see Closing Case).

hubris
A manager's overconfidence in his or her capabilities.

While all the synergistic motives, in theory, add value, hubris and managerial motives reduce value. **Hubris** refers to managers' overconfidence in their capabilities.[61] Managers of acquiring firms make two very strong statements.[62] The first is, "We can manage *your* assets better than you [target firm managers] can!" The second statement is even bolder. Given that acquirers of publicly listed firms always have to pay an acquisition premium, this is essentially saying: "We are smarter than the market!" To the extent that the capital market is (relatively) efficient and that the market price of target firms reflects their intrinsic value, there is simply no hope to profit from such acquisitions. Even when we assume the capital market to be inefficient, it is still apparent that when the premium is too high, acquiring firms must have overpaid.[63] This is especially true when there are multiple firms bidding for the same target; the winning acquirer may suffer from the "winner's curse" from auctions—the winner has overpaid. From an institution-based view, many managers join the acquisition bandwagon after some first-mover firms start doing some deals in an industry. The fact that M&As come in "waves" speaks volumes about such herd behavior.[64] Eager to catch up, many late movers in such waves may rush in, prompted by a "Wow! Get it!" mentality. Not surprisingly, many deals turn out to be bust.

While the hubris motives suggest that managers may *unknowingly* overpay for targets, managerial motives posit that for self-interested reasons, some managers may have *knowingly* overpaid the acquisition premium for target firms. Driven by such norms and cognitions, some managers may have deliberately overdiversi-

TABLE 12.4 MOTIVES FOR ACQUISITIONS

	Institution-based issues	Resource-based issues
Synergistic motives	• Respond to formal institutional constraints and transitions	• Leverage superior managerial capabilities • Enhance market power and scale economies • Access to complementary resources
Hubris motives	• Herd behavior—following norms and chasing fads of M&As	• Managers' overconfidence in their capabilities
Managerial motives	• Self-interested actions such as empire building guided by informal norms and cognitions	

fied their firms through M&As in their quest for more power, prestige, and money; these are known as agency problems (see Chapter 16 for details).

© JEWEL SAMAD / AFP / Getty Images

Why do you think Google agreed to pay $1.6 billion to acquire YouTube in 2006?

PERFORMANCE OF ACQUISITIONS

Why do as many as 70% of acquisitions reportedly fail? Problems can be identified in both pre- and postacquisition phases (Table 12.5). During the preacquisition phase, because of executive hubris and/or managerial motives, acquiring firms may overpay targets and fall into a "synergy trap."[65] In 1998, Daimler paid $35 billion, a 40% premium over market value, to acquire Chrysler. Such a high premium was indicative of (1) strong capabilities to derive synergy, (2) high levels of hubris, (3) significant managerial self-interests, or (4) *all of the above*. In 2007, four-fifths of the value had been destroyed, as Chrysler, when sold to its new owners, only commanded one-fifth of the purchase price that Daimler had paid. For another example, in 2006, Google paid $1.6 billion to acquire YouTube, a 20-month-old video-sharing site with *zero* profits. Microsoft CEO Steven Ballmer commented that "there's no business model for YouTube that would justify $1.6 billion."[66]

Another primary preacquisition problem is inadequate screening and failure to achieve strategic fit. For example, the $35 billion acquisition (claimed as a "merger") of Sweden's Astra by Britain's Zeneca, both in the pharmaceutical industry, in 1999 might lack strategic fit. Although the combined firm had greater scale economies, both had a large number of soon-to-expire patents and not enough longer lasting patents to fend off generic drug makers.[67]

Internationally, because of greater institutional and cultural distances, the preacquisition problems can be even worse. Nationalistic concerns against foreign acquisitions may erupt. When Japanese firms acquired Rockefeller Center and movie studios in the 1980s and 1990s, the US media reacted with indignation. More recently, when DP World from the United Arab Emirates and CNOOC from China attempted to acquire US assets, they had to back off due to political backlash.

During the postacquisition phase, numerous integration problems may pop up. In addition to strategic fit, organizational fit is also important.[68] One study reports that a striking 80% of acquiring firms do *not* analyze organizational fit with targets.[69] Another issue is the failure to address multiple stakeholders' concerns, which involves job losses and diminished power. Figure 12.7 illustrates the substantial concerns among a variety of stakeholders at all levels, and Figure 12.8 humorously portrays one particular challenge. Most firms focus on task issues

TABLE 12.5 SYMPTOMS OF ACQUISITION FAILURES

	Problems for all M&As	Particular problems for cross-border M&As
Preacquisition: Overpayment for targets	• Managers overestimate their ability to create value • Inadequate preacquisition screening • Poor strategic fit	• Lack of familiarity with foreign cultures, institutions, and business systems • Nationalistic concerns against foreign takeovers (political and media levels)
Postacquisition: Failure in integration	• Poor organizational fit • Failure to address multiple stakeholder groups' concerns	• Clashes of organizational cultures compounded by clashes of national cultures • Nationalistic concerns against foreign takeovers (firm and employee levels)

FIGURE 12.7 STAKEHOLDER CONCERNS DURING MERGERS AND ACQUISITIONS

Investors	Will synergy benefits be downscaled?	Optimistic view of return on investment?	Will efficiency & short-term revenues fall?
Top management	Synergies difficult to attain	Internal conflicts: fractious management groups, key staff leave	Unrealistic euphoria
Middle management	Concern over job security	Expect to do M&A + day jobs at the same time	Overwelmed by scale and scope
Front-line employees	What should I tell my customers?	When do lay-offs begin?	Who is setting my priorities and objectives?
Customers	So what?	Service quality dips, relationship suffers	No one is listening to me. Do I still matter?

FIGURE 12.8 A CHALLENGE IN POSTACQUISITION INTEGRATION

" As you know, some details of the new merger have yet to be resolved. "

Source: *Harvard Business Review*, February 2005, p. 102. Reprinted with permission.

(such as standardizing reporting) first and pay inadequate attention to people issues, resulting in low morale and high turnover.[70]

In cross-border M&As, integration difficulties may be much worse because clashes of organizational cultures are compounded by clashes of national cultures.[71] When Four Seasons acquired a hotel in Paris, the simple "American" request that employees smile at customers was resisted by French employees and laughed at by the local media as "la culture Mickey Mouse."[72]

Although acquisitions are often the largest capital expenditures most firms ever make, they are frequently the worst planned and executed activities. Unfortunately, when merging firms sort out the mess, competitors are likely to launch aggressive attacks. In 1996, while Boeing struggled in near total chaos with its acquisition of McDonnell Douglas (including a complete production halt), Airbus quickly increased its share from one-third to one-half of the global market. Likewise, when HP was distracted by its highly controversial acquisition of Compaq during 2002–2003, Dell invaded HP's stronghold in printers and unleashed a price war. Adding all of the above together, it is hardly surprising that most M&As fail.

DEBATES AND EXTENSIONS

LEARNING OBJECTIVE 4

participate in two leading debates on alliances and acquisitions

This chapter has introduced a number of debates (such as the merits of acquisitions), and this section discusses two leading debates: (1) M&As + alliances and (2) majority JVs versus minority JVs.

M&As + Alliances

Although alliances and acquisitions are alternatives, many firms seem to have plunged straight into merger mania. During 2004–2006, IBM and Oracle swallowed 30 and 14 firms, respectively. In many firms, an M&A group reports to the CFO, and a separate unit, headed by the VP or director for business development, deals with alliances. M&As and alliances are thus often undertaken in isolation.[73] A smaller number of firms, such as Eli Lilly, have a separate "office of alliance management." Few firms have established a combined "mergers, acquisitions, *and* alliance" function.[74] In practice, it may be advisable to explicitly compare and contrast acquisitions vis-à-vis alliances, as Cisco has successfully done (see Figure 12.4 and Table 12.2).[75]

Compared with acquisitions, alliances, despite their own problems, cost less and allow for opportunities to learn from working with each other before engaging in full-blown acquisitions.[76] While alliances do not preclude acquisitions and in fact may lead to acquisitions, acquisitions are often one-off deals swallowing both the excellent capabilities and mediocre units of target firms, leading to "indigestion" problems. Many acquisitions (such as DaimlerChrysler) probably would have been better off had firms pursued alliances first. Given the high rates of M&A failures, it seems imperative that firms seriously and thoroughly investigate alliances as an alternative before embarking on acquisitions.

Majority JVs as Control Mechanisms versus Minority JVs as Real Options

A long-standing debate focuses on the appropriate level of equity in JVs. Although the logic of having a higher level of equity control in majority JVs is straightforward, its actual implementation is often problematic. Asserting one party's control rights, even when justified based on a majority equity position, may irritate the other party. Local partners in JVs in emerging economies especially resent the dominance of Western multinationals. Despite the obvious needs for foreign capital, technology, and management, Russian managers often refuse to acknowledge that their country, which in their view is still a superpower, is an emerging, let alone developing, country.[77] Consequently, some authors advocate a 50/50 share of management control even when the MNE has majority equity.[78]

As alluded to earlier, a key benefit associated with minority JVs is their value as real options. In general, the more uncertain the conditions, the higher the value of real options. In highly uncertain but potentially promising industries and countries, M&As or majority JVs may be inadvisable because the cost of failure may be tremendous. Thus, minority JVs are recommended *toehold* investments as possible stepping stones for future scaling up, if necessary, while not exposing too heavily to the risks. Anheuser-Busch successfully followed this strategy in emerging economies such as Brazil, China, Mexico, and the Philippines in the 1990s. More recently, Anheuser-Busch seemed no longer interested in being a minority partner, as evidenced by its efforts to outbid SABMiller in a bidding war in China (In Focus 12.3). Whether this more aggressive strategy is justified remains to be seen.

IN FOCUS 12.3 ETHICAL DILEMMA: Anheuser-Busch: From Minority Shareholder to Aggressive Bidder

Anheuser-Busch (A-B) is the leader in the US beer market with a 49% market share and the world's third largest brewer with an 11% world market share (after InBev and SABMiller). Since domestic market growth is slow, A-B has been expanding overseas, especially in emerging economies. It has focused on establishing minority JVs with local brewers (with equity ranging from 5% to 50%) in emerging economies with uncertain, albeit fast-growing, demand for beer. These involve such prominent players as Grupo Modelo in Mexico, AmBev in Brazil, Asia Brewery in the Philippines, and Tsingtao in China. These small equity stakes represent tremendous opportunities to expand should demand in these countries grow favorably in the future, yet help limit A-B's downside risk if positive developments do not materialize.

However, one recent high-profile case indicates that A-B may have decided to become more aggressive. In March 2004, it offered to pay $139 million for a 29% stake in China's fourth largest beer maker, Harbin, the maker of Hapi beer. However, 29% of Harbin was owned by SABMiller, the world's second largest brewer headquartered in London after a merger between South African Breweries and Miller Beer of the United States. A-B's move was indeed designed to complicate SABMiller's expansion strategy in China. To fend off A-B, SABMiller tabled a hostile takeover bid of Harbin with $550 million—the first of its kind by a foreign firm in China. Although SABMiller became a strategic investor in Harbin starting in 2003, their relationship was very bad. This was in part because SABMiller also controlled 49% of Harbin's archrival, China Resources Breweries (CRB), and SABMiller failed to persuade CRB to give up a price war it had waged with Harbin. Encouraged by Harbin's management, A-B within one week made a $720 million counteroffer, representing a 30% premium over SABMiller's bid. In response, SABMiller dropped out, and let A-B win the bidding war in July 2004.

Although China is the world's largest beer market by volume, it is also one of the *least* profitable. At 50 times Harbin's 2003 earnings and 35 times 2004 forecast earnings, the *Economist* called A-B's offer "irrational" and "more about ego than sense." At that time in China, A-B already operated a Budweiser plant in Wuhan and owned 10% of Tsingtao, China's largest beer maker with a 13% market share. In 2005, A-B increased its equity stake in Tsingtao to 27%. However, there are no obvious synergies and no announced plan to combine Harbin with Tsingtao or Wuhan. Overall, it remains to be seen whether A-B's strategy to act as a minority shareholder has changed or the Harbin bidding war was an isolated episode in its overseas forays. From an ethical standpoint, one can certainly ask whether A-B's managers are using shareholders' money to build market or build empire.

Source: Based on (1) Anheuser-Busch, 2006, Key performance facts, http://anheuser-busch.com (accessed March 4, 2007), (2) Anheuser-Busch, 2004, Daily business brief, May 4; (3) *Economist*, 2004, The beers are on Anheuser, January 5: 60; (4) T. Tong, 2006, How Anheuser-Busch creates shareholder wealth through alliances, in M. W. Peng, *Global Strategy* (p. 277), Cincinnati, OH: Cengage South-Western; (5) Wikipedia, 2007, Anheuser-Busch, http://en.wikipedia.com (accessed March 4, 2007).

MANAGEMENT SAVVY

LEARNING OBJECTIVE 5

draw implications for action

What determines the success and failure in alliances and acquisitions around the globe? Our two core perspectives shed light on this "big question." The institution-based view argues that thorough understanding and skillful manipulation of the rules of the game governing alliances and acquisitions—of the sort exemplified by Lenovo and IBM (see Closing Case)—are often behind the fate of alliances and acquisitions. The resource-based view calls for the development of firm-specific capabilities to make a difference in enhancing alliance and acquisition performance.

Consequently, three clear implications for action emerge (Tables 12.6, 12.7, and 12.8). First, managers need to understand and master the rules of the game—both formal and informal—governing alliances and acquisitions around the world. Lenovo clearly understood and tapped into the Chinese government's support for homegrown multinationals. IBM likewise had a better understanding of the necessity for the new Lenovo to maintain an American image by persuading Lenovo

TABLE 12.6 IMPLICATIONS FOR ACTION

- Understand and master the rules of the game governing alliances and acquisitions around the world
- When managing alliances, pay attention to the "soft" relationship aspects
- When managing acquisitions, do not overpay, focus on both strategic and organizational fit, and thoroughly address integration concerns

TABLE 12.7 IMPROVING THE ODDS FOR ALLIANCE SUCCESS

Areas	Do's and don'ts
Contract versus "chemistry"	No contract can cover all elements of the relationship. Relying on a detailed contract does not guarantee a successful relationship. It may indicate a lack of trust.
Warning signs	Identify symptoms of frequent criticism, defensiveness (always blaming others for problems), and stonewalling (withdrawal during a fight).
Invest in the relationship	Like married individuals working hard to invigorate their ties, alliances require continuous nurturing. Once a party starts to waver, it is difficult to turn back the dissolution process.
Conflict resolution mechanisms	Good married couples also fight. Their secret weapon is to find mechanisms to avoid unwarranted escalation of conflicts. Managers need to handle conflicts—inevitable in any alliance—in a credible, responsible, and controlled fashion.

Source: Based on text in M. W. Peng & O. Shenkar, 2002, Joint venture dissolution as corporate divorce (pp. 101–102), *Academy of Management Executive*, 16 (2): 92–105.

TABLE 12.8 IMPROVING THE ODDS FOR ACQUISITION SUCCESS

Areas	Do's and don'ts
Preacquisition	• Do not overpay for targets and avoid a bidding war when premiums are too high • Engage in thorough due diligence concerning both strategic and organizational fit
Postacquisition	• Address the concerns of multiple stakeholders and try to keep the best talents • Be prepared to deal with roadblocks thrown out by people whose jobs and power may be jeopardized

to give up the idea of having dual headquarters in Beijing and New York and to set up its world headquarters in New York. This highly symbolic action made it easier to win approval from the US government in 2005. In contrast, in 2001, GE and Honeywell, two US-headquartered firms, proposed to merge and cleared US antitrust scrutiny. Yet, they failed to anticipate the incentive and power of the EU antitrust authorities to torpedo the deal. The upshot is that in addition to the economics of alliances and acquisitions, managers need to pay attention to the politics behind such high-stakes strategic moves.

Second, when managing alliances, managers need to pay attention to the "soft" relational capabilities that often make or break relationships (see Table 12.7). To the extent that business schools usually provide a good training on hard number-crunching skills, it is time for all of us to beef up on soft but equally important (and perhaps more important) relational capabilities.

Finally, when managing acquisitions, managers are advised to follow the suggestions outlined in Table 12.8, such as do not overpay for targets and focus on both strategic and organizational fit.[79] At GE, acquisition management is a full-time job involving 230 employees. However, at P&G, only the CEO and the CFO reportedly work on M&As. Some firms deploy ad hoc teams when needed. During the HP-Compaq merger, the integration team numbered more than 1,500.[80] Although approaches vary, no firm can afford to take acquisitions, especially the integration phase, lightly.

CHAPTER SUMMARY

1. Articulate how institutions and resources affect alliances and acquisitions
   - Formal institutions influence alliances and acquisitions through antitrust and entry mode concerns.
   - Informal institutions affect alliances and acquisitions through normative and cognitive pillars.
   - The impact of resources on alliances and acquisitions is illustrated by the VRIO framework.
2. Gain insights into the formation, evolution, and performance of alliances
   - Alliances are typically formed when managers go through a three-stage decision process.
   - Managers need to combat opportunism and, if necessary, manage the dissolution process.

- (1) Equity, (2) learning, (3) nationality, and (4) relational capabilities may affect alliance performance.

3. Understand the motives and performance of acquisitions
   - Acquisitions are often driven by synergistic, hubris, and managerial motives.
   - Many acquisitions fail because managers do not address pre- and postacquisition problems.
4. Participate in two leading debates on alliances and acquisitions
   - They are (1) M&As + alliances and (2) majority versus minority JVs.
5. Draw implications for action
   - Managers need to understand and master the rules of the game governing alliances and acquisitions around the world.
   - When managing alliances, managers must pay attention to the "soft" relationship aspects.
   - When managing acquisitions, the savvy manager should focus on both strategic and organizational fit.

KEY TERMS

Acquisition 331
Acquisition premium 335
Contractual (nonequity-based) alliances 330
Cross-shareholding 331
Equity-based alliances 331
Hubris 344
Learning by doing 339
Learning race 334
Merger 331
Merger and acquisition (M&A) 331
Organizational fit 336
Real option 334
Relational (collaborative) capability 334
Strategic alliances 330
Strategic fit 336
Strategic investment 331

REVIEW QUESTIONS

1. List several examples of contractual alliances and several examples of equity-based alliances.
2. Are mergers or acquisitions more common? Why?
3. In what two primary areas do formal institutions affect alliances? Briefly explain the two areas.
4. Describe at least one norm (or collective assumption) and how it would affect a firm's perspective on creating an alliance.
5. Use the VRIO framework to describe the difference between an alliance and an acquisition.
6. Explain the meaning of the term *real option*.
7. Referring to Figure 12.4 as needed, explain the three stages in the formation of an alliance.
8. Of the two methods allied firms can use to combat opportunism, which one do you think is better? Why?

9. What happens when an alliance fails and must be terminated? Summarize the process.
10. Of the four factors that may influence alliance performance shown in Figure 12.6, which do you think is the most important and which the least important? Explain your answer.
11. Describe the three most common motives for acquisition.
12. What are some criteria managers should consider to avoid preacquisition and postacquisition problems?
13. If you were part of a firm's leadership, under what conditions would you choose an acquisition over an alliance, and vice versa?
14. When does a majority JV seem more appropriate, and when does a minority JV hold more appeal?
15. Is it necessary for managers to pay attention to the politics behind alliances and acquisitions? Why?
16. Based on Table 12.7 and Table 12.8, assemble a list of soft, relational capabilities you think a savvy manager should possess.

CRITICAL DISCUSSION QUESTIONS

1. ON ETHICS: Some argue that in alliance management, engaging in a learning race is unethical. Others contend that a learning race is part and parcel of alliance relationships. What do you think?
2. ON ETHICS: During the courtship and negotiation stages, managers often emphasize equal partnerships and do not reveal (or try to hide) their true intentions. What are the ethical dilemmas here?
3. ON ETHICS: As a CEO, you are trying to acquire a foreign firm. The size of your firm will double, and it will become the largest in your industry. On the one hand, you are excited about the opportunity to be a leading captain of industry and the associated power, prestige, and income (you expect your salary, bonus, and stock option to double next year). On the other hand, you have just read this chapter and are troubled by the fact that 70% of M&As reportedly fail. How would you proceed?

VIDEO CASE

Watch "Acquisition and Execution" by Sir George Mathewson of the Royal Bank of Scotland

1. Sir George Mathewson discussed the success of an acquisition not just in regard to accomplishing the acquisition but also in terms of what followed the takeover. How does that illustrate Learning Objective 3: "Understand the motives and performance of acquisitions"?
2. The bidding for the takeover target was actually initiated by a competitor to which the Royal Bank of Scotland (RBS) responded. However, what did RBS do that enabled its response to beat the competitor?

3. Sir Mathewson felt that speed is essential in successful acquisitions. Why?
4. Why did he feel that acquisitions are superior to mergers?
5. To what extent would the RBS approach be of value in future acquisition attempts? What are the implications for global expansion?

CLOSING CASE

Lenovo and IBM: An Acquisition and an Alliance

In 2004, when Lenovo announced that it would acquire IBM's Personal Computing Division (PCD) for $1.75 billion, most people outside China, having never heard of Lenovo, reacted: IBM's PCD was acquired by *what*? Lenovo was the leading PC maker in China, controlling 25% of the market. Yet, its annual sales were only $3 billion, and the $10 billion-a-year PCD alone was three times the size of Lenovo—IBM's total sales would be $90 billion. This story of a start-up buying an icon thus grabbed global media attention.

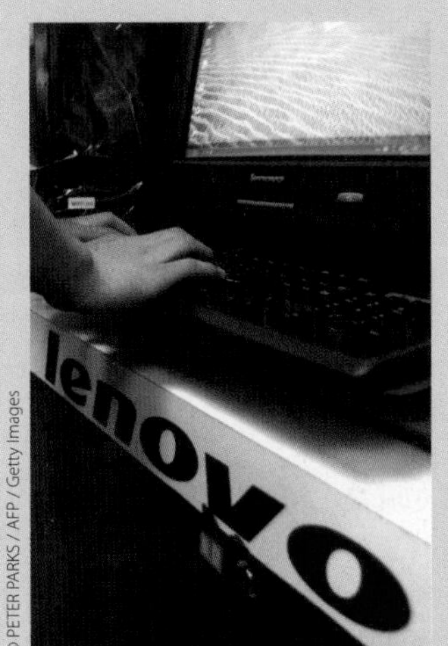

© PETER PARKS / AFP / Getty Images

In retrospect, the deal offered a compelling strategic fit. Although IBM added the P (personal) in front the C (computer) in the early 1980s, PCD, under relentless pressure from Dell and HP, had been barely profitable recently. As IBM moved toward higher value services, finding a buyer to offload its PCD was natural.

Founded in Beijing in 1984 on a shoestring budget of $25,000 as an investment from the Chinese Academy of Sciences (a government institute), Legend (as Lenovo had been called until 2003) was set up by 11 entrepreneurs. By 1994, Legend was trading on the Hong Kong Stock Exchange. Under attack by Dell, HP, and IBM, Legend sought to go global. "If we just focus on China," its CFO admitted, "we cannot generate returns for our shareholders." Yet, the road to go global was arduous. The Legend brand had already been registered by other firms elsewhere, and Legend thus had to change its name. In 2003, it changed its name to Lenovo, taking the *Le* from Legend and adding *novo*, the Latin word for "new," to reflect its spirit of innovation.

Now, how would you market a one-year-old brand that nobody knew? The solution was both ingenious and audacious: Acquire an icon like IBM (!). Obstacles were tremendous. From a resource-based standpoint, did Lenovo have what it takes to do better if a venerable American technology company had failed to profit from the PC business? This was the question that Lenovo's board raised when examining the acquisition plan in April 2004. Given Lenovo's lack of global experience (all of its executives were mainland Chinese), the answer, after three days of relentless questioning, was no. The board only gave its blessing to the acquisition plan when the acquisition team agreed to not only acquire the business but also to recruit top American executives.

IBM and Lenovo structured the deal as a part of a larger strategic alliance. IBM decided to keep a 13% stake in the combined company and contributed top IBMers, led by Steve Ward, former head of PCD, to help run it. In essence, IBM outsourced its PC business to Lenovo, and Lenovo outsourced much of its management and sales to IBM. Beyond PCs, Lenovo agreed to help IBM tackle the China market and elsewhere.

From an institution-based standpoint, although the Chinese government was understandably supportive, the biggest hurdles were on the American side. The Homeland Security Department and FBI expressed national security concerns, and several congressmen threatened to torpedo the deal. In the end, the US government concluded that the PC technology was mature with no real cutting-edge military use and approved the deal.

As a result, a $13 billion global PC company, the new Lenovo, was born in May 2005. One-third of the shares were owned by public shareholders, 28% by Legend Holdings (parent), 15% by the Chinese Academy of Sciences, and 13% by IBM. Headquartered in New York, Lenovo's principal operations are based in Beijing and Raleigh, North Carolina, near PCD's former home. It runs R&D centers in China, Japan, and the United States and operates facilities in Australia, Brazil, China, Hungary, India, Japan, Korea, Malaysia, Mexico, Slovakia, the United Kingdom, and the United States. In China, Lenovo now commands one-third of the PC market. Worldwide, Lenovo is the third largest PC maker (behind Dell and HP) with 27,000 employees and a 5% market share.

Whether this deal will eventually work also depends on organizational fit. On the surface, cultural and language differences are evident. Ward, the first CEO of the merged firm, convinced chairman Yang Yuanqing to give up the idea of having dual headquarters in Beijing and New York and to set up world headquarters in New York as an unambiguous signal of Lenovo's global outlook. Having an American CEO and a major US presence adds legitimacy to Lenovo. Instead of being a sideline to IBM, "PCs are our core business," proclaimed Yang, "we're focused on PCs to build our company as the strongest PC player in the world."

It is too early to tell whether this claim can materialize. Although American tech-buying experts noted that "we can still buy [IBM] ThinkPads with confidence," politically sensitive buyers are not so sure. In 2005, GE dropped Lenovo and went with Dell. In 2006, the US State Department changed the way it used some of its 14,000 PCs ordered from Lenovo, in fear that Chinese government snooping technology was tucked into the machines. In short, Lenovo, despite its inheritance of the IBM brand, faced tremendous liability of foreignness. Internally, the honeymoon was long over. Within a year, Ward was pushed out by the board, in part because he was too slow to cut costs. Since January 2006, the new CEO was William Amelio, who formerly ran Dell's Asian operations. Amelio brought a team of former Dell colleagues. In essence, Lenovo was trying to blend two national cultures and, to add to the stress, three corporate ones (Lenovo, IBM, and Dell). The $13 billion giant only made $22 million profits in 2006. Every step of the way, Lenovo is making history. So stay tuned . . .

Case Discussion Questions

1. From an institution-based view, why was there so much uncertainty?
2. From a resource-based view, does the new Lenovo have what it takes to make the deal work?
3. If you were in charge of Lenovo's postacquisition integration, what would be your top challenges?
4. How does IBM benefit from this alliance with Lenovo?

Sources: Based on (1) *Business Week*, 2005, East meets West, May 9: 74–78; (2) *Business Week*, 2005, Will ThinkPads still be ThinkPads? January 17: 22; (3) *Business Week*, 2006, China's first global capitalist, December 11: 52–58; (4) *Economist*, 2007, Bold fusion, February 17: 70; (5) http://www.lenovo.com; (6) http://www.ibm.com.

NOTES

Journal acronyms: **AME** – *Academy of Management Executive;* **AMJ** – *Academy of Management Journal;* **AMR** – *Academy of Management Review;* **APJM** – *Asia Pacific Journal of Management;* **ASQ** – *Administrative Science Quarterly;* **BW** – *Business Week;* **CMR** – *California Management Review;* **HBR** – *Harvard Business Review;* **IBR** – *International Business Review;* **JB** – *Journal of Business;* **JEP** – *Journal of Economic Perspectives;* **JFE** – *Journal of Financial Economics;* **JIBS** – *Journal of International Business Studies;* **JIM** – *Journal of International Management;* **JM** – *Journal of Management;* **JMS** – *Journal of Management Studies;* **MIR** – *Management International Review;* **MS** – *Management Science;* **OSc** – *Organization Science;* **SMJ** – *Strategic Management Journal;* **WSJ** – *Wall Street Journal*

[1] R. Gulati, 1998, Alliances and networks (p. 293), *SMJ*, 19: 293–317.

[2] United Nations, 2000, *World Investment Report 2000* (p. 99), New York: United Nations.

[3] H. Barkema & F. Vermeulen, 1998, International expansion through start-up or acquisition, *AMJ*, 41: 7–27; K. Brouthers & L. Brouthers, 2000, Acquisition or green-field start-up? *SMJ*, 21: 89–

98; A. Harzing, 2002, Acquisitions versus greenfield investments, *SMJ*, 23: 211–228; H. D. Hopkins, 1999, Cross-board M&As, *JIM*, 5: 207–239; K. Shimizu, M. Hitt, D. Vaidyanath, & V. Pisano, 2004, Theoretical foundations of cross-border M&As, *JIM*, 10: 307–353.

[4] *Economist*, 2007, Mergers and acquisitions, January 13: 90.

[5] A. Arikan, 2004, Cross-border M&As (p. 239), in B. Punnett & O. Shenkar (eds.), *Handbook for International Management Research* (pp. 239–264), Ann Arbor: University of Michigan Press.

[6] Federal Trade Commission & US Department of Justice, 2000, *Antitrust Guidelines for Collaborations among Competitors*, Washington, DC: FTC & DOJ.

[7] M. W. Peng, 2006, Making M&As fly in China, *HBR*, March: 26–27. See also M. Desai, C. F. Foley, & J. Hines, 2004, The costs of shared ownership, *JFE*, 73: 323–374; P. Kale & J. Anand, 2006, The decline of emerging economy JVs, *CMR*, 48: 62–76; S. Rossi & P. Volpin, 2004, Cross-country determinants of M&As, *JFE*, 74: 277–304; H. K. Steensma, L. Tihanyi, M. Lyles, & C. Dhanaraj, 2005, The evolving value of foreign partnerships in transitioning economies, *AMJ*, 48: 213–235.

[8] L. Alcantara, H. Mitsuhashi, & Y. Hoshino, 2006, Legitimacy in IJVs, *JIM*, 12: 389–407; M. T. Dacin, C. Oliver, & J. Roy, 2007, The legitimacy of strategic alliances, *SMJ*, 28: 169–187.

[9] M. Hayward & K. Shimizu, 2006, De-commitment to losing strategic action, *SMJ*, 27: 541–557; J. Reuer & R. Ragozzino, 2006, Agency hazards and alliance portfolios, *SMJ*, 27: 27–43.

[10] S. Lazzarini, 2007, The impact of membership in competing alliance constellations, *SMJ*, 28: 345–367; J. Dyer & N. Hatch, 2006, Relation-specific capabilities and barriers to knowledge transfers, *SMJ*, 27: 701–719; A. Madhok & S. Tallman, 1998, Resources, transactions, and rents, *OSc*, 9: 326–339; N. Park, J. Mezias, & J. Song, 2004, A resource-based view of strategic alliances and firm value in the electronic marketplace, *JM*, 30: 7–27.

[11] *Economist*, 2003, Open skies and flights of fancy (p. 67), October 4: 65–67.

[12] R. R. Sampson, 2007, R&D alliances and firm performance, *AMJ*, 50: 364–386.

[13] B. Bourdeau, J. Cronin, & C. Voorhees, 2007, Modeling service alliances, *SMJ*, 28: 609–622; A. Tiwana & M. Keil, 2007, Does peripheral knowledge complement control? *SMJ*, 28: 623–634.

[14] T. Chi, 2000, Option to acquire or divest a JV, *SMJ*, 21: 665–687; B. Kogut, 1991, JVs and the option to expand and acquire, *MS*, 37: 19–33; T. Tong, J. Reuer, & M. W. Peng, 2008, International joint ventures and the value of growth options, *AMJ* (in press).

[15] T. Folta & K. Miller, 2002, Real options in equity partnerships, *SMJ*, 23: 77–88; S. Rangan, 1998, Do multinationals operate flexibly? *JIBS*, 29: 217–237; M. Santoro & J. McGill, 2005, The effect of uncertainty and asset co-specialization on governance in biotechnology alliances, *SMJ*, 26: 1261–1269.

[16] P. Aulakh, M. Kotabe, & A. Sahay, 1996, Trust and performance in cross-border marketing partnerships, *JIBS*, 27: 1005–1032; S. Currall & A. Inkpen, 2002, A multilevel approach to trust in JVs, *JIBS*, 33: 479–495; T. Das & B. Teng, 1998, Between trust and control, *AMR*, 23: 491–512; J. Johnson, J. Cullen, T. Sakano, & H. Takenouchi, 1996, Setting the stage for trust and strategic integration in Japanese-US cooperative alliances, *JIBS*, 27: 981–1004; B. Nooteboom, H. Berger, & N. Noorderhaven, 1997, Effects of trust and governance on relational risk, *AMJ*, 40: 308–338.

[17] G. Hamel, 1991, Competition for competence and inter-partner learning within strategic alliances, *SMJ*, 12: 83–103; J. Hennart, T. Roehl, & D. Zietlow, 1999, "Trojan horse" or "workhorse"? *SMJ*, 20: 15–29; P. Kale, H. Singh, & H. Perlmutter, 2000, Learning and protection of proprietary assets in alliances, *SMJ*, 21: 217–237.

[18] J. Lampel & J. Shamsie, 2000, Probing the unobtrusive link (p. 593), *SMJ*, 21: 590–602.

[19] R. Kashlak, R. Chandran, & A. Benedetto, 1998, Reciprocity in international business, *JIBS*, 29: 281–304; L. Mesquita, 2007, Starting over when the bickering never ends, *AMR*, 32: 72–91.

[20] G. Lorenzoni & A. Lipparini, 1999, The leveraging of interfirm relationships, *SMJ*, 20: 317–338.

[21] K. Uhlenbruck, M. Hitt, & M. Semadeni, 2006, Market value effects of acquisitions involving Internet firms, *SMJ*, 27: 899–913.

[22] D. King, D. Dalton, C. Daily, & J. Covin, 2004, Meta-analyses of post-acquisition performance, *SMJ*, 25: 187–200.

[23] G. Andrade, M. Mitchell, & E. Stafford, 2001, New evidence and perspectives on mergers, *JEP*, 15: 103–120.

[24] J. Doukas & O. Kan, 2006, Does global diversification destroy firm value? *JIBS*, 37: 352–371.

[25] J. Haleblian, J. Kim, & N. Rajagopalan, 2006, The influence of acquisition experience and performance on acquisition behavior, *AMJ*, 49: 357–370.

[26] A. Buchholtz, B. Ribbens, & I. Houle, 2003, The role of human capital in postacquisition CEO departure, *AMJ*, 46: 506–514; R. Davis & A. Nair, 2003, A note on top management turnover in international acquisitions, *MIR*, 43: 171–183; J. Krug & W. H. Hegarty, 2001, Predicting who stays and leaves after an acquisition, *SMJ*, 22: 185–196.

[27] X. Yin & M. Shanley, 2007, Industry determinants of the "merger versus alliance" decision, *AMR* (in press).

[28] T. Tong & J. Reuer, 2007, Real options in MNCs, *JIBS*, 38: 215–230.

[29] J. Dyer, P. Kale, & H. Singh, 2004, When to ally and when to acquire, *HBR* (p. 113), July–August: 109–115.

[30] This section draws heavily on S. Tallman & O. Shenkar, 1994, A managerial decision model of international cooperative venture formation, *JIBS*, 25: 91–113.

[31] J. Hagedoorn & G. Duysters, 2002, External sources of innovative capabilities, *JMS*, 39: 167–188.

[32] S. Park, R. Chen, & S. Gallagher, 2002, Firm resources as moderators of the relationship between market growth and strategic alliances in semiconductor start-ups, *AMJ*, 45: 527–545.

[33] Y. Wang & S. Nicholas, 2007, The formation and evolution of non-equity alliances in China, *APJM*, 24: 131–150.

[34] M. Colombo, 2003, Alliance form, *SMJ*, 24: 1209–1229; A. Inkpen & A. Dinur, 1998, Knowledge management processes and IJVs, *OSc*, 9: 454–468; B. Kogut & U. Zander, 1993, Knowledge of the firm and the evolutionary theory of the multinational corporation, *JIBS*, 24: 625–645.

[35] R. Jensen & G. Szulanski, 2004, Stickiness and the adaptation of organizational practices in cross-border knowledge transfers, *JIBS*, 35: 508–523; B. Simonin, 2004, An empirical investigation of the process of knowledge transfer in international strategic alliances, *JIBS*, 35: 407–427.

[36] H. Mjoen & S. Tallman, 1997, Control and performance in IJVs, *OSc*, 8: 257–274; Y. Pan & X. Li, 2000, JV formation of very large multinational firms, *JIBS*, 31: 179–189.

[37] J. Hagedoorn, D. Cloodt, & H. van Kranenburg, 2005, Intellectual property rights and the governance of international R&D partnerships, *JIBS*, 36: 175–186.

[38] Y. Doz, 1996, The evolution of cooperation in strategic alliances, *SMJ*, 17: 55–83; M. Koza & A. Lewin, 1998, The co-evolution of strategic alliances, *OSc*, 9: 255–264; J. Reuer, M. Zollo, & H. Singh, 2002, Post-formation dynamics in strategic alliances, *SMJ*, 23: 135–152; J. Robins, S. Tallman, & K. Fladmoe-Lindquist, 2002, Autonomy and dependence of international cooperative ventures, *SMJ*, 23: 881–901.

[39] Y. Luo, 2007, Are JV partners more opportunistic in a more volatile environment? *SMJ*, 28: 39–60; S. White & S. Lui, 2005, Distinguishing costs of cooperation and control in alliances, *SMJ*, 26: 913–932.

[40] Y. Zhang & N. Rajagopalan, 2002, Inter-partner credible threat in IJVs, *JIBS*, 33: 457–478.

[41] This section draws heavily on M. W. Peng & O. Shenkar, 2002, JV dissolution as corporate divorce, *AME*, 16: 92–105.

[42] M. Serapio & W. Cascio, 1996, End-games in international alliances, *AME*, 10: 62–73.

[43] J. Reuer & A. Arino, 2007, Strategic alliance contracts, *SMJ*, 28: 313–330.

[44] A. Arino & J. Reuer, 2004, Designing and renegotiating strategic alliance contracts (p. 44), *AME*, 18: 37–48.

[45] J. Child & Y. Yan, 2003, Predicting the performance of IJVs, *JMS*, 40: 284–320; A. Goerzen, 2007, Alliance networks and firm performance, *SMJ*, 28: 487–509; D. Jolly, 2005, The exogamic nature of Sino-foreign JVs, *APJM*, 22: 285–306; R. Pearce, 1997, Toward understanding JV performance and survival, *AMR*, 22: 203–225.

[46] A. Arino, 2003, Measures of strategic alliance performance, *JIBS*, 34: 66–79; A. Goerzen & P. Beamish, 2005, The effect of alliance network diversity on MNE performance, *SMJ*, 26: 333–354; X. Lin & R. Germain 1998, Sustaining satisfactory JV relationships, *JIBS*, 29: 179–196; J. Lu & D. Xu, 2006, Growth and survival of IJVs, *JM*, 32: 426–448; P. Meschi, 2005, Stock market valuation of JV sell-offs, *JIBS*, 36: 688–700; A. Mohr, 2006, A multiple constituency approach to IJV performance measurement, *JWB*, 41: 247–260; A. Shipilov, 2006, Network strategy and performance of Canadian investment banks, *AMJ*, 49: 590–604; A. Yan & M. Zeng, 1999, IJV instability, *JIBS*, 30: 397–414.

[47] A. Gaur & J. Lu, 2007, Ownership strategies and survival of foreign subsidiaries, *JM*, 33: 84–110; A. Madhok, 2006, How much does ownership really matter? *JIBS*, 37: 4–11; T. Reus & W. Ritchie, 2004, Interpartner, parent, and environmental factors influencing the operation of IJVs, *MIR*, 44: 369–395.

[48] J. Barden, H. K. Steensma, & M. Lyles, 2005, The influence of parent control structure on parent conflict in Vietnamese IJVs, *JIBS*, 36: 156–174; C. Dhanaraj & P. Beamish, 2004, Effect of equity ownership on the survival of IJVs, *SMJ*, 25: 295–305; W. Newburry, Y. Zeira, & O. Yeheskel, 2003, Autonomy and effectiveness of equity IJVs in China, *IBR*, 12: 395–419.

[49] R. Aguilera, 2007, Translating theoretical logics across borders, *JIBS*, 38: 38–46; P. Lane, J. Salk, & M. Lyles, 2001, Absorptive capacity, learning, and performance in IJVs, *SMJ*, 22: 1139–1161; M. Lyles & J. Salk, 1996, Knowledge acquisition from foreign parents in IJVs, *JIBS*, 27: 877–903; K. Meyer, 2007, Contextualizing organizational learning, *JIBS*, 38: 27–37; E. Tsang, 2002, Acquiring knowledge by foreign partners from IJVs in a transition economy, *SMJ*, 23: 835–854.

[50] R. Sampson, 2005, Experience effects and collaborative returns in R&D alliances, *SMJ*, 26: 1009–1031.

[51] Y. Luo & M. W. Peng, 1999, Learning to compete in a transition economy, *JIBS*, 30: 269–296.

[52] V. Pothukuchi, F. Damanpour, J. Choi, C. Chen, & S. Park, 2002, National and organizational culture differences and IJV performance, *JIBS*, 33: 243–265; J. Salk & O. Shenkar, 2001, Social identity in an IJV, *OSc*, 12: 161–178; D. Sirmon & P. Lane, 2004, A model of cultural differences and international alliance performance, *JIBS*, 35: 306–319.

[53] D. Hambrick, J. Li, K. Xin, & A. Tsui, 2001, Compositional gaps and downward spirals in IJV management groups, *SMJ*, 22: 1033–1053; A. Inkpen & P. Beamish, 1997, Knowledge, bargaining power, and the instability of IJVs, *AMR*, 22: 177–202; S. Park & G. Ungson, 1997, The effect of national culture, organizational complementarity, and economic motivation on JV dissolution, *AMJ*, 40: 279–307.

[54] K. Brouthers & G. Mamossy, 2006, Post-formation processes in Eastern and Western European JVs, *JMS*, 43: 203–229; C. Fey & P. Beamish, 2000, Joint venture conflict, *IBR*, 9: 139–162; R. Krishnan, X. Martin, & N. Noorderhaven, 2006, When does trust matter to alliance performance? *AMJ*, 49: 894–917.

[55] K. Brouthers, P. van Hastenburg, & J. van den Ven, 1998, If most mergers fail why are they so popular? *LRP*, 31: 347–353; A. Seth, K. Song, & R. Pettit, 2000, Synergy, managerialism, or hubris? *JIBS*, 31: 387–405.

[56] W. Schneper & M. Guillen, 2004, Stakeholder rights and corporate governance, *ASQ*, 49: 263–295.

[57] J. Doh, 2000, Entrepreneurial privatization strategies, *AMR*, 25: 551–571; K. Meyer & S. Estrin, 2007, *Acquisition Strategies in European Emerging Markets*, London: Palgrave; K. Uhlenbruck & J. De Castro, 2000, Foreign acquisitions in Central and Eastern Europe, *AMJ*, 43: 381–402.

[58] J. Anand & A. Delios, 2002, Absolute and relative resources as determinants of international acquisitions, *SMJ*, 23: 119–134; D. Loree, C. Chen, & S. Guisinger, 2000, International acquisitions, *JWB*, 35: 300–315; T. Saxton & M. Dollinger, 2004, Target reputation and appropriability, *JM*, 30: 123–147; D. Schweiger & P. Very, 2001, International M&As special issue, *JWB*, 36: 1–2.

[59] A. Ranft & M. Lord, 2002, Acquiring new technologies and capabilities, *OSc*, 13: 420–441.

[60] *World Investment Report 2000* (p. 128).

[61] R. Roll, 1986, The hubris hypothesis of corporate takeovers, *JB*, 59: 197–216.

[62] P. Buckley & P. Ghauri, 2002, *International Mergers and Acquisitions* (p. 2), London: Thomson.

[63] P. Haunschild, A. Davis-Blake, & M. Fichman, 1994, Managerial overcommitment in corporate acquisition processes, *OSc*, 5: 528–540; S. Moeller, F. Schlingemann, & R. Stulz, 2004, Firm size and the gains from acquisitions, *JFE*, 73: 201–228.

[64] D. Angwin, 2001, M&As across European borders, *JWB*, 36: 32–57.

[65] M. Sirower, 1997, *The Synergy Trap*, New York: Free Press; J. M. Shaver, 2006, A paradox of synergy, *AMR*, 31: 962–976.

[66] *BW*, 2006, Ballmer: They paid how much for that? October 23: 37.

[67] M. Hitt, J. Harrison, & R. D. Ireland, 2001, *Mergers and Acquisitions* (p. 89), New York: Oxford University Press.

[68] C. Homburg & M. Bucerius, 2006, Is speed of integration really a success factor of M&As? *SMJ*, 27: 347–367; P. Puranam, H. Singh, & M. Zollo, 2006, Organizing for innovation, *AMJ*, 49: 263–280.

[69] T. Grubb & R. Lamb, 2000, *Capitalize on Merger Chaos* (p. 14), New York: Free Press.

[70] J. Birkinshaw, H. Bresman, & L. Hakanson, 2000, Managing the post-acquisition integration process, *JMS*, 37: 395–425; F. Gandolf, 2006, *Corporate Downsizing Demystified*, Hyderabad: ICFAI Press; A. Risberg, 2001, Employee experiences of acquisition processes, *JWB*, 36: 58–84; E. Vaara, 2003, Post-acquisition integration as sensemaking, *JMS*, 40: 859–894.

[71] J. Child, D. Faulkner, & R. Pitkethly, 2001, *The Management of International Acquisitions*, Oxford, UK: Oxford University Press; K. Meyer & E. Lieb-Doczy, 2003, Post-acquisition restructuring as evolutionary process, *JMS*, 40: 459–482; P. Morosini, S. Shane, & H. Singh, 1998, National cultural distance and cross-border acquisition performance, *JIBS*, 29: 137–158; A. Slangen, 2006, National cultural distance and initial foreign acquisition performance, *JWB*, 41: 161–170; K. Uhlenbruck, 2004, Developing acquired foreign subsidiaries, *JIBS*, 35: 109–123.

[72] R. Hallowell, D. Bowen, & C. Knoop, 2002, Four Seasons goes to Paris (p. 19), *AME*, 16: 7–24.

[73] J. Hagedoorn & B. Sadowski, 1999, The transition from strategic alliances to M&As, *JMS*, 36: 87–107.

[74] A. Goerzen, 2005, Managing alliance networks, *AME*, 19: 94–107.

[75] J. Hennart & S. Reddy, 1997, The choice between M&As and JVs, *SMJ*, 18: 1–12; D. Yiu & S. Makino, 2002, The choice between JV and wholly owned subsidiary, *OSc*, 13: 667–683.

[76] P. Porrini, 2004, Can a previous alliance between an acquirer and a target affect acquisition performance? *JM*, 30: 545–562.

[77] J. Barnes, M. Cook, T. Koybaeva, & E. Stafford, 1997, Why our Russian alliances fail, *LRP*, 30: 540–550; N. Napier & D. Thomas, 2004, *Managing Relationships in Transition Economies*, New York: Praeger; S. Puffer, D. McCarthy, & N. Alexander, 2000, *The Russian Capitalist Experiment*, Cheltenham, UK: Edward Elgar.

[78] C. Choi & P. Beamish, 2004, Split management control and IJV performance, *JIBS*, 35: 201–215; H. K. Steensma & M. Lyles, 2000, Explaining IJV survival in a transition economy, *SMJ*, 21: 831–851.

[79] H. Bresman, J. Birkinshaw, & R. Nobel, 1999, Knowledge transfer in international acquisitions, *JIBS*, 30: 439–469; L. Capron & N. Pistre, 2002, When do acquirers earn abnormal returns? *SMJ*, 23: 781–795; R. Larsson & S. Finkelstein, 1999, Integrating strategic, organizational, and human resource perspectives on M&As, *OSc*, 10: 1–26; J. Reuer, O. Shenkar, & R. Ragozzino, 2004, Mitigating risk in international M&As, *JIBS*, 35: 19–32; F. Vermeulen & H. Barkema, 2001, Learning through acquisitions, *AMJ*, 44: 457–477.

[80] R. Burgelman & W. McKinney, 2006, Managing the strategic dynamics of acquisition integration, *CMR*, 48: 6–27.

CHAPTER 13

Strategizing, Structuring, and Learning around the World

OPENING CASE

The Ups and Downs at Ford

Ford Motor Company was always more international than its two Detroit rivals, General Motors (GM) and Chrysler (before its acquisition by Daimler). In the 1960s, Ford of Europe was set up to consolidate independent operations in Britain and Germany. This structure was ahead of its time and was imitated by rivals. While the top brass at GM all featured American guys, Ford's top management ranks have routinely featured executives from Argentina, Australia, Britain, and Germany.

In 1993, the rise of Alex Trotman, a Scot who had worked for Ford since 1955, as Ford's chairman and CEO personified Ford's international character. In the 1960s, while working for Ford of Europe, Trotman wrote a proposal on global consolidation that, although not implemented, would prove prophetic. It advocated many of the tenets that would later be incorporated in Ford's global restructuring of the mid-1990s—under Trotman's leadership. Known as Ford 2000, the restructuring transformed Ford from several regional groups (Asia Pacific, Europe, North America, and South America) into one presumably seamless global organization with factories and sales companies reporting instantly across oceans spanned by broadband links. Ford 2000 drained power from the regions back to Dearborn (a Detroit suburb where Ford is headquartered). However, the end result, exemplified by a "world car," the Ford Mondeo, proved disappointing. The Mondeo was a hit in Europe where drivers preferred more engine performance, but it flopped as the Ford Contour and Mercury Mystique in America where rider comfort was preferred. Powerful regional managers and country heads naturally resented the loss of power. It simply did not make any sense for a factory manager in Cologne, Germany, to report to a global chief of manufacturing 3,000 miles away in Dearborn. However, few dared to declare the emperor naked.

In 1999, Trotman passed the baton to the next CEO, Jacques Nasser, a Lebanese-born executive who grew up in Australia. Recognizing the problems associated with the restructuring, Nasser quickly reversed large parts of Ford 2000. Europe and South America regained regional power. Nasser went on a shopping spree, acquiring Volvo Cars from Volvo and Range Rover from BMW and consolidating Mazda within the Ford portfolio. Unfortunately, Nasser's tenure was full of upheaval not only associated with Ford 2000 and the serial acquisitions but also with the faulty Bridgestone/Firestone tires that caused numerous Ford Explorer sport utility vehicles (SUVs) to accidentally roll over. Such upheaval caused Ford to take its eye off the ball. At the same time, Asian and European rivals turned up the heat by challenging Ford even in its stronghold markets for large SUVs and light trucks, where Ford made most of its profits in the 1990s. As an executive, Nasser was widely viewed as too abrasive, alienating managers, employees, suppliers, and eventually, the Ford family that still controlled 40% equity. By 2001, Nasser was forced by chairman Bill Ford (the original Henry Ford's great-grandson) to resign.

During 2001–2006, Bill Ford acted both as chairman and CEO, but he failed to turn around the company. Instead, the automaker continued its downward spiral, and its US market share reached a historical low of 18%. In 2006, Bill Ford hired Alan Mullaly as the new CEO. Mullaly used to head Boeing's fabled commercial plane division. All eyes are now on Mullaly to see how Boeing's best pilot can pull Ford out of a hard landing.

Sources: Based on (1) *Business Week*, 2006, Ford's new top gun, September 18: 30–34; (2) *Economist*, 2005, A hard lesson in globalization, April 30: 63; (3) http://en.wikipedia.org.

LEARNING OBJECTIVES

After studying this chapter, you should be able to

1. articulate the relationship between multinational strategy and structure
2. understand how institutions and resources affect strategy, structure, and learning
3. outline the challenges associated with learning, innovation, and knowledge management
4. participate in two leading debates on multinational strategy, structure, and learning
5. draw implications for action

How can multinational enterprises (MNEs) such as Ford be appropriately structured so that they can be successful both locally and internationally? How can they learn country tastes, global trends, and market transitions that would call for structural changes? How can they improve the odds for better innovation? These are some of the key questions we address in this chapter. The focus here is on relatively large MNEs with significant internationalization.

We start by discussing the crucial relationship between four strategies and four structures. Next, the institution- and resource-based views shed light on these issues. Then, we discuss worldwide learning, innovation, and knowledge management. Debates and extensions follow.

LEARNING OBJECTIVE 1

articulate the relationship between multinational strategy and structure

MULTINATIONAL STRATEGIES AND STRUCTURES

This section first introduces an integration-responsiveness framework centered on the pressures for cost reductions and local responsiveness. We then outline the four strategic choices and the four corresponding organizational structures that MNEs typically adopt.

Pressures for Cost Reductions and Local Responsiveness

integration-responsiveness framework
A framework of MNE management on how to simultaneously deal with two sets of pressures for global integration and local responsiveness.

local responsiveness
The necessity to be responsive to different customer preferences around the world.

MNEs primarily confront two sets of pressures: those for cost reductions and local responsiveness. The framework that deals with these two sets of pressures is called the **integration-responsiveness framework** because cost pressures often call for global integration, and local responsiveness urges MNEs to adapt locally.[1] In both domestic and international competition, pressures for cost reductions are almost universal. What is unique in international competition is the pressures for **local responsiveness**, which are reflected in different consumer preferences and host country demands. Consumer preferences vary tremendously around the world. For example, beef-based hamburgers brought by McDonald's obviously would find few (or no) costumers in India, a land where cows are sacred. Host country demands and expectations add to the pressures for local responsiveness. Throughout Europe, Canadian firm Bombardier manufactures an Austrian version of railcars in Austria, a Belgian version in Belgium, and so on. Bombardier believes that such local responsiveness, although not required, is essential for making sales to railway operators in Europe, which tend to be state-owned.

Taken together, being locally responsive certainly makes local customers and governments happy, but these actions unfortunately increase cost. Given the universal interest in lowering cost, a natural tendency is to downplay (or ignore) the different needs and wants of various local markets and to market a "global" version of products and services—ranging from the world car to the global song. The intellectual underpinning of the movement to globalize offerings can be traced to a 1983 article published by Theodore Levitt, with a self-explanatory title: "The Globalization of Markets."[2] Levitt argued that there is a worldwide convergence of consumer tastes. As evidence, Levitt pointed out Coke Classic, Levi Strauss jeans, and Sony color TVs, which were successful on a worldwide basis. Levitt predicted that such convergence would characterize most product markets in the future.

Levitt's article has often been used as the intellectual underpinning propelling many MNEs to globally integrate their products while minimizing local adaptation. Ford experimented with world car designs. MTV pushed ahead with the belief that viewers would flock to "global" (essentially American) programming. Unfortunately, most of these experiments have not been successful. Ford finds that there are wide-ranging differences among consumer tastes around the globe (see Opening Case). The Toyota Camry, for instance, is the best-selling car in the United States but a poor seller in its home country, Japan. MTV has eventually realized that there is no global song. In a nutshell, one size does not fit all.[3] Next, we discuss how MNEs can pay attention to *both* dimensions of cost reductions and local responsiveness.

Four Strategic Choices

Based on the integration-responsiveness framework, Figure 13.1 plots the four strategic choices for MNEs: (1) home replication, (2) localization, (3) global standardization, and (4) transnational strategy.[4] Each strategy has a set of pros and cons outlined in Table 13.1 (their corresponding structures, shown in Figure 13.1, are discussed in the next section).

Home replication strategy, often known as "international" (or "export") strategy, emphasizes international replication of home country-based competencies such as production scales, distribution efficiencies, and brand power. In manufacturing, this is usually manifested in an export strategy. In services, this is often done through licensing and franchising. This strategy is relatively easy to implement and usually the first one adopted when firms venture abroad.

home replication strategy
A strategy that emphasizes international replication of home country-based competencies such as production scales, distribution efficiencies, and brand power.

On the disadvantage side, this strategy suffers from a lack of local responsiveness because it focuses on the home country. This makes sense when the majority

FIGURE 13.1 MULTINATIONAL STRATEGIES AND STRUCTURES: THE INTEGRATION-RESPONSIVENESS FRAMEWORK

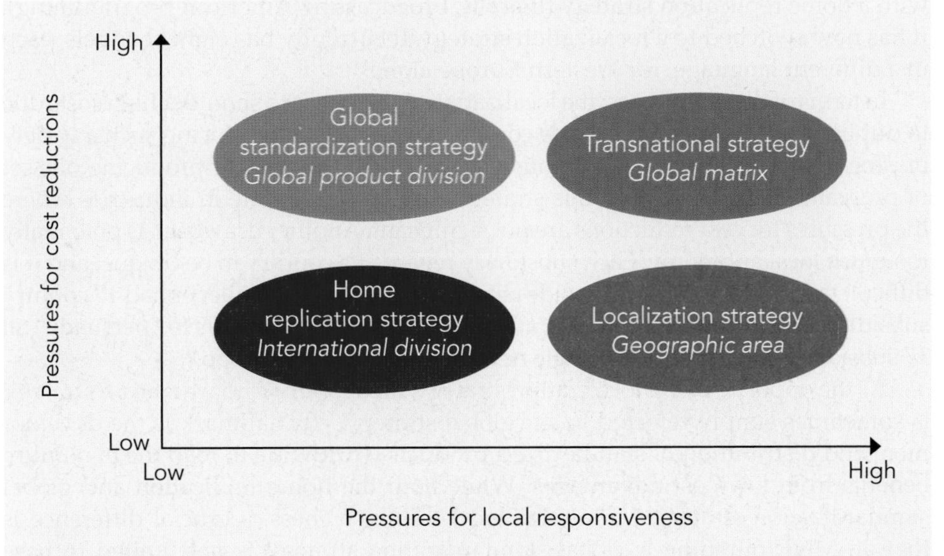

Note: In some other textbooks, "home replication" may be referred to as "international" or "export" strategy, "localization" as "multidomestic" strategy, and "global standardization" as "global" strategy. Some of these labels are confusing because one can argue that all four strategies here are "international" or "global," thus resulting in some confusion if we label one of these strategies as "international" and another as "global." The present set of labels is more descriptive and less confusing.

TABLE 13.1 FOUR STRATEGIC CHOICES FOR MULTINATIONAL ENTERPRISES

	Advantages	Disadvantages
Home replication	• Leverages home country-based advantages • Relatively easy to implement	• Lack of local responsiveness • May result in foreign customer alienation
Localization	• Maximizes local responsiveness	• High costs due to duplication of efforts in multiple countries • Too much local autonomy
Global standardization	• Leverages low-cost advantages	• Lack of local responsiveness • Too much centralized control
Transnational	• Cost efficient while being locally responsive • Engages in global learning and diffusion of innovations	• Organizationally complex • Difficult to implement

of a firm's customers are domestic. However, when the firm aspires to broaden its international scope to reach more foreign customers, failing to be mindful of foreign customers' needs and wants may result in their alienation. For instance, Wal-Mart, when entering Brazil, set up an exact copy of its stores in the United States, with a large number of *American* footballs. Unfortunately, in Brazil, the land of soccer that won five World Cups, nobody (perhaps other than a few homesick American expatriates in their spare time) plays American football.

localization (multidomestic) strategy
A strategy that focuses on a number of foreign countries/regions, each of which is regarded as a stand-alone "local" (domestic) market worthy of significant attention and adaptation.

Localization (multidomestic) strategy is an extension of the home replication strategy. Localization strategy focuses on a number of foreign countries/regions, each of which is regarded as a stand-alone "local" market worthy of significant attention and adaptation. Although sacrificing global efficiencies, this strategy is effective when there are clear differences among national and regional markets and low pressures for cost reductions. When first venturing overseas, MTV started with a home replication strategy (literally, broadcasting American programming). It has now switched to a localization strategy. It currently has eight channels, each in a different language, for Western Europe alone.

In terms of disadvantages, the localization strategy has to shoulder high costs due to duplication of efforts in multiple countries. The costs of producing such a variety of programming at MTV are obviously greater than the costs of producing one set of programming. As a result, this strategy is only appropriate in industries where the pressures for cost reductions are not significant. Another drawback is potentially too much local autonomy. Each subsidiary regards its country to be unique, and it is difficult to introduce corporate-wide changes. For example, Unilever had 17 country subsidiaries in Europe in the 1980s, and it took as long as four *years* to "persuade" all 17 subsidiaries to introduce a single new detergent across Europe.

global standardization strategy
A strategy that relies on the development and distribution of standardized products worldwide to reap the maximum benefits from low-cost advantages.

center of excellence
An MNE subsidiary explicitly recognized as a source of important capabilities, with the intention that these capabilities be leveraged by and/or disseminated to other subsidiaries.

worldwide (or global) mandate
The charter to be responsible for one MNE function throughout the world.

As the opposite of the localization strategy, the **global standardization strategy** is sometimes simply referred to as "global strategy." Its hallmark is the development and distribution of standardized products worldwide to reap the maximum benefits from low-cost advantages. While both the home replication and global standardization strategies minimize local responsiveness, a crucial difference is that an MNE pursuing a global standardization strategy is not limited to base its major operations at home. In a number of countries, the MNE may designate **centers of excellence**, defined as subsidiaries explicitly recognized as a source of important capabilities, with the intention that these capabilities be leveraged by and/or disseminated to other subsidiaries.[5] For example, Merck Frosst Canada, the Canadian subsidiary of Merck, is a center of excellence in R&D. Centers of excellence are often given a **worldwide (or global) mandate**—namely, the charter to be responsible for one MNE function throughout the world. HP's Singapore subsidiary, for instance, has a worldwide mandate to develop, produce, and market all HP handheld products.

In terms of disadvantages, a global standardization strategy obviously sacrifices local responsiveness. This strategy makes great sense in industries where pressures for cost reductions are paramount and pressures for local responsiveness are relatively minor (in such commodity industries as semiconductors and tires). However, as noted earlier, in numerous industries, ranging from automobiles to consumer products, a one-size-fits-all strategy may be inappropriate. Consequently, arguments such as "all industries are becoming global" and "all firms need to pursue a global (standardization) strategy" are potentially misleading.

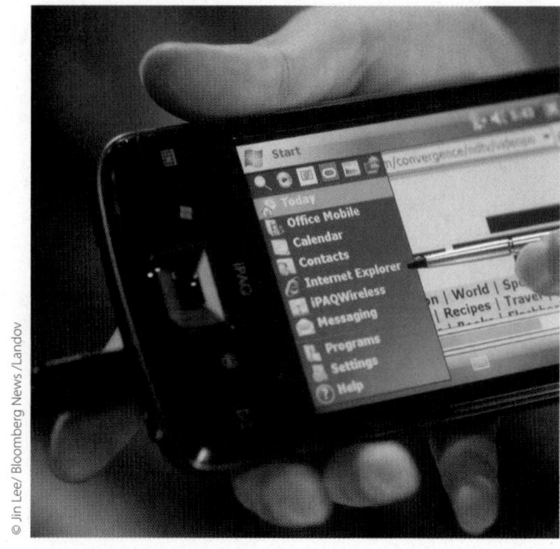

© Jin Lee/ Bloomberg News /Landov

Why do you think HP has issued a mandate to its Singapore subsidiary to develop, produce, and market all of HP's handheld products?

Transnational strategy aims to capture the best of both worlds by endeavoring to be cost efficient and locally responsive.[6] In addition to cost efficiency and local responsiveness, a third hallmark of this strategy is global learning and diffusion of innovations. Traditionally, the diffusion of innovations in MNEs is a one-way flow from the home country to various host countries—the label "home replication" says it all (!). Underpinning such a one-way flow is the assumption that the home country is the best location for generating innovations, an assumption that is increasingly challenged by critics, who make two points. First, given that innovations are inherently risky and uncertain, there is no guarantee that the home country will generate the highest quality innovations.[7] Second, for many large MNEs, their subsidiaries have acquired a variety of innovation capabilities, some of which may have the potential for wider applications elsewhere.[8] GM has ownership stakes in Daewoo, Opel, Saab, Subaru, and Suzuki as well as the Shanghai GM joint venture with China's SAIC. Historically, GM employed a localization strategy, and each subsidiary could decide what cars to produce by themselves. Consequently, some of these subsidiaries developed locally formidable but globally underutilized innovation capabilities. It makes sense for GM to tap into some of these local capabilities (such as Daewoo's prowess in small cars) for wider applications (see Chapter 12 Opening Case).

transnational strategy
A strategy that endeavors to be cost efficient, locally responsive, and learning driven simultaneously around the world.

Taking these two points together, MNEs that engage in a transnational strategy promote global learning and diffusion of innovations in multiple ways. Innovations not only flow from the home country to host countries (which is the traditional flow) but also from host countries to the home country and among subsidiaries in multiple host countries.[9]

On the disadvantage side, a transnational strategy is organizationally complex and difficult to implement. The large amount of knowledge sharing and coordination may slow down decision speed. Simultaneously trying to achieve cost efficiencies, local responsiveness, and global learning places contradictory demands on MNEs (discussed in the next section).

Overall, it is important to note that given the various pros and cons, there is no optimal strategy. The new trend in favor of a transnational strategy needs to be qualified with an understanding of its significant organizational challenges. This point leads to our next topic.

Four Organizational Structures

Also shown in Figure 13.1, there are four organizational structures that are appropriate for the four strategic choices just outlined: (1) international division structure, (2) geographic area structure, (3) global product division structure, and (4) global matrix structure.

International division is typically set up when firms initially expand abroad, often engaging in a home replication strategy. For example, Figure 13.2 shows Cardinal Health's new addition of an international division, in addition to its four

international division
A structure that is typically set up when firms initially expand abroad, often engaging in a home replication strategy.

FIGURE 13.2 INTERNATIONAL DIVISION STRUCTURE AT CARDINAL HEALTH

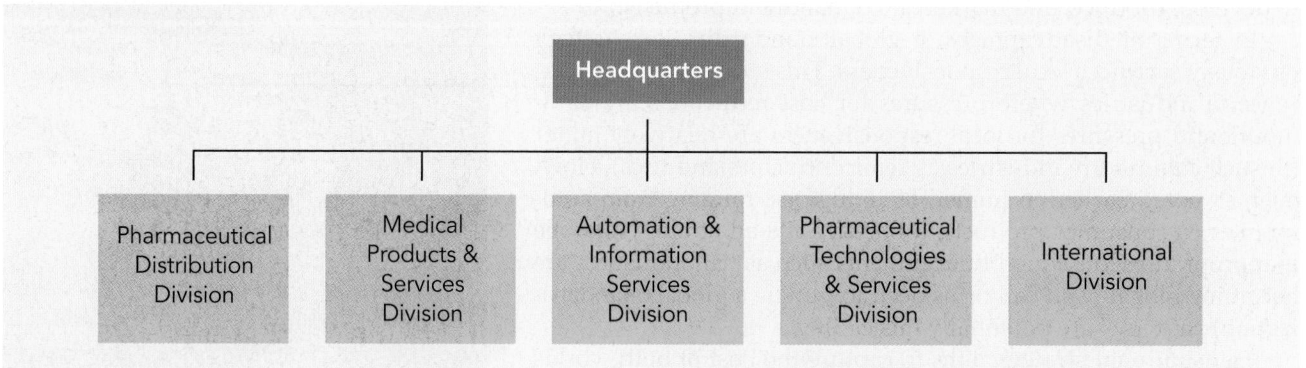

Source: Based on author's interview and http://www.cardinal.com. Headquarted in Dublin, Ohio (a suburb of Columbus), Cardinal Health is a Fortune 20 company.

product divisions that focus on the US healthcare markets. Although this structure is intuitively appealing, it often leads to two problems. First, foreign subsidiary managers, whose input is channeled through the international division, are not given sufficient voice relative to the heads of domestic divisions.[10] Second, by design, the international division serves as a "silo" whose activities are not coordinated with the rest of the firm that focuses on domestic activities. Consequently, many firms phase out this structure after their initial stage of overseas expansion.

geographic area structure
An organizational structure that organizes the MNE according to different countries and regions.

country or **regional manager**
The business leader of a specific geographic area or region.

global product division
An organizational structure that assigns global responsibilities to each product division.

Geographic area structure organizes the MNE according to different geographic areas (countries and regions). It is the most appropriate structure for a localization strategy. Figure 13.3 illustrates such a structure for Mittal Steel. A geographic area can be a country or a region, led by a **country** or **regional manager**. Each area is largely stand-alone. In contrast to the limited voice of subsidiary managers in the international division structure, country and regional managers carry a great deal of weight in a geographic area structure. Interestingly and paradoxically, *both* the strengths and weaknesses of this structure lie in its local responsiveness. Although being locally responsive can be a virtue, it also encourages the fragmentation of the MNE into highly autonomous, hard-to-control "fiefdoms."[11]

Global product division structure, which is the opposite of the geographic area structure, supports the global standardization strategy. Figure 13.4 shows such an example from EADS, whose most famous unit is Airbus. This structure treats each product division as a stand-alone entity with full worldwide—as opposed

FIGURE 13.3 GEOGRAPHIC AREA STRUCTURE AT MITTAL STEEL

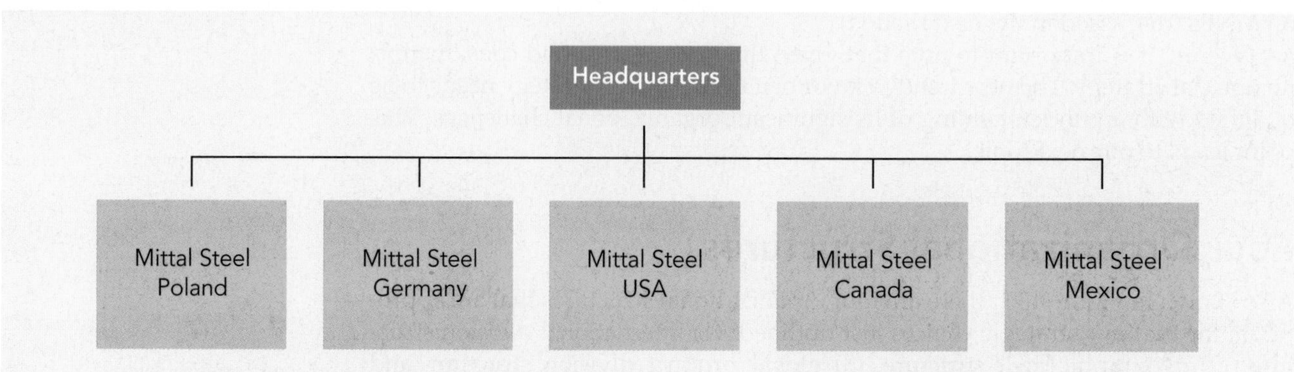

Source: Adapated from http://www.mittalsteel.com (accessed March 20, 2007). Headquartered in London, United Kingdom, Mittal Steel is the world's largest steelmaker. It has recently merged with Arcelor to form ArcelorMittal, and the postmerger structure may change

FIGURE 13.4 GLOBAL PRODUCT DIVISION STRUCTURE AT EUROPEAN AERONAUTIC DEFENSE AND SPACE COMPANY (EADS)

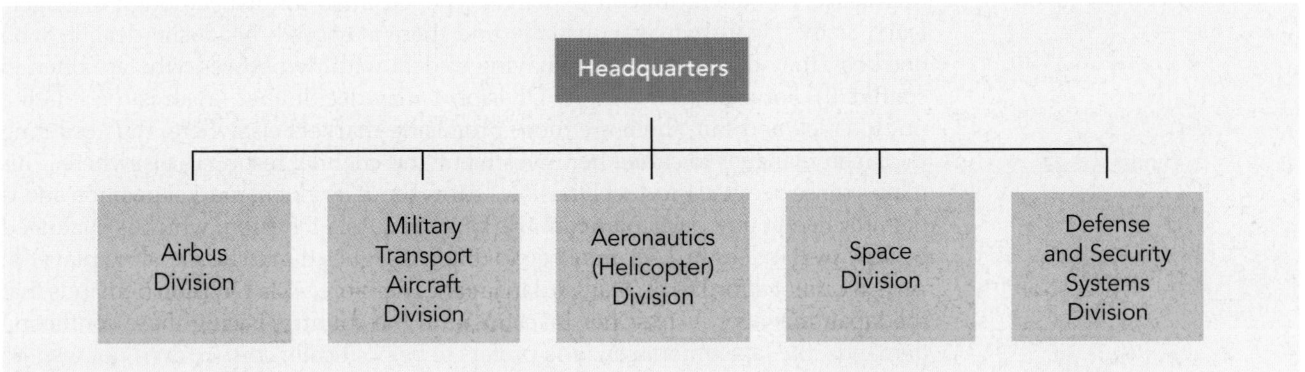

Source: Adapated from http://eads.com. Headquartered in Munich, Germany, and Paris, France, EADS is the largest commercial aircraft maker and the largest defense contractor in Europe.

to domestic—responsibilities. This structure greatly facilitates attention to pressures for cost efficiencies because it allows for consolidation on a worldwide (or at least regional) basis and reduces inefficient duplication in multiple countries. For example, Unilever reduced the number of soap-producing factories in Europe from ten to two after adopting this structure. Recently, because of the popularity of the global standardization strategy (noted earlier), the global product division structure is on the rise. Ford has phased out the geographic area structure in favor of the global product division structure, although its noticeable drawback is that local responsiveness suffers (see Opening Case).

global matrix
An organizational structure often used to alleviate the disadvantages associated with both geographic area and global product division structures, especially for MNEs adopting a transnational strategy.

Global matrix alleviates the disadvantages associated with both geographic area and global product division structures, especially for MNEs adopting a transnational strategy. Shown in Figure 13.5, its hallmark is the sharing and coordination of responsibilities between product divisions and geographic areas to be both cost efficient and locally responsive. In this hypothetical example, the country manager

FIGURE 13.5 A HYPOTHETICAL GLOBAL MATRIX STRUCTURE

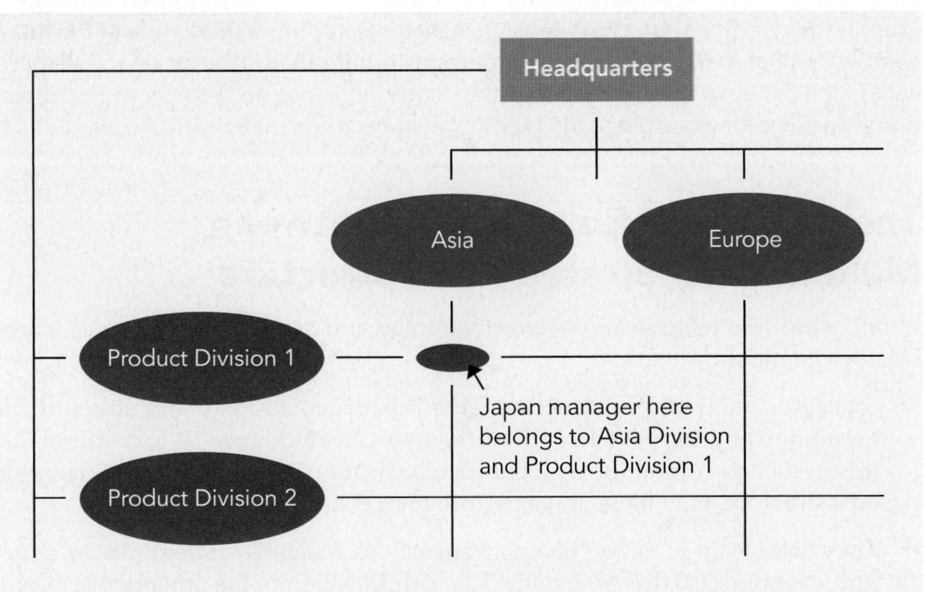

in charge of Japan—in short, the Japan manager—reports to Product Division 1 and Asia Division, both of which have equal power.

While this structure in theory supports the goals of the transnational strategy, in practice, it is often difficult to deliver. The reason is simple: Although managers (such as the Japan manager) usually find there is enough headache dealing with one boss, they do not appreciate having to deal with two bosses, who are often in conflict (!). For example, Product Division 1 may decide that Japan is too tough a nut to crack and that there are more promising markets elsewhere, thus ordering the Japan manager to *curtail* her investment and channel resources elsewhere. This makes sense because Product Division 1 cares about its global market position and is not attached to any particular country. However, Asia Division, which is evaluated by how well it does in Asia, may beg to differ. It argues that to be a leading player in Asia, it cannot afford to be a laggard in Japan. Therefore, Asia Division demands that the Japan manager *increase* her investment in the country. Facing these conflicting demands, the Japan manager, who prefers to be politically correct, does not want to make any move before consulting corporate headquarters. Eventually, headquarters may provide a resolution. However, in the process, crucial time may be lost, and important windows of opportunity for competitive actions may be missed.

Taken together, the global matrix structure, despite its merits on paper, may add layers of management, slow down decision speed, and increase cost while not showing significant performance improvement. There is no conclusive evidence for the superiority of the matrix structure.[12] Having experimented with the matrix structure, a number of MNEs, such as the highly visible Swiss-Swedish conglomerate ABB, have now moved back to the simpler and easier to manage global product structure. Even when the matrix structure is still in place, global product divisions are often given more power than geographic area divisions. The following quote from the then CEO of an early adopter of the matrix structure, Dow Chemical, is sobering:

> We were an organization that was matrixed and depended on teamwork, but there was no one in charge. When things went well, we didn't know whom to reward; and when things went poorly, we didn't know whom to blame. So we created a global product division structure, and cut out layers of management. There used to be 11 layers of management between me and the lowest level employees, now there are five.[13]

Overall, the positioning of the four structures in Figure 13.1 is not random. They evolve from the relatively simple international division through either geographic area or global product division structures and may finally reach the more complex global matrix stage. It is important to note that not every MNE experiences all these structural stages, and the evolution is not necessarily in one direction (consider, for example, ABB's withdrawal from the matrix structure).

The Reciprocal Relationship between Multinational Strategy and Structure

In one word, the relationship between strategy and structure is *reciprocal*. Three key ideas stand out.

- Strategy usually drives structure. The fit between strategy and structure, as exemplified by the *pairs* in each of the four cells in Figure 13.1, is crucial.[14] A misfit, such as combining a global standardization strategy with a geographic area structure, may have grave performance consequences.
- The relationship is not a "one-way street." As much as strategy drives structure, structure also drives strategy. The withdrawal from the unworkable matrix structure has called into question the wisdom of the transnational strategy.

- Neither strategies nor structures are static. It is often necessary to change strategy, structure, or both.[15] In Europe, many MNEs traditionally pursued a localization strategy supported by the geographic area structure (such as the 17 European subsidiaries for Unilever). However, significant integration within the European Union has made such a formerly value-adding strategy/structure match obsolete. Consequently, many MNEs have now moved toward a pan-European strategy (a miniversion of the global standardization strategy) with a regionwide structure. Unilever, for instance, created a Lever Europe group to consolidate the 17 subsidiaries.

HOW INSTITUTIONS AND RESOURCES AFFECT MULTINATIONAL STRATEGY, STRUCTURE, AND LEARNING

LEARNING OBJECTIVE 2

understand how institutions and resources affect strategy, structure, and learning

Having outlined the basic strategy/structure configurations, let us now introduce how the institution- and resource-based views shed light on these issues (Figure 13.6).

Institution-Based Considerations

MNEs face two sets of rules of the game: formal and informal institutions governing (1) *external* relationships and (2) *internal* relationships. Each is discussed in turn.

Formal and Informal External Institutions Externally, MNEs are subject to the formal institutional frameworks erected by various home and host country governments.[16] For instance, to protect domestic employment, the British government taxes British MNEs' foreign earnings at a higher rate than their domestic earnings. For another example, home country governments may for political reasons discourage or ban MNEs from structuring certain operations in "sensitive" countries. After the Cold War, US defense firms such as Boeing and

FIGURE 13.6 HOW INSTITUTIONS AND RESOURCES AFFECT MULTINATIONAL STRUCTURE, LEARNING, AND INNOVATION

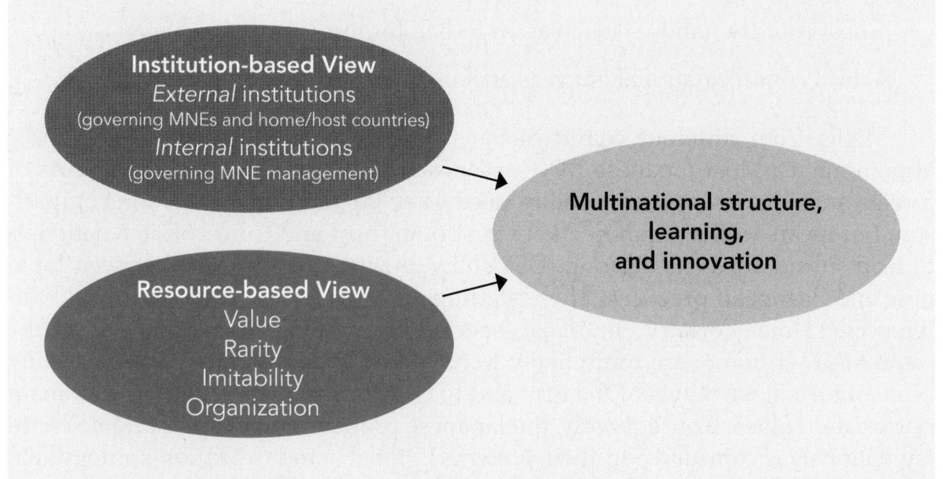

Lockheed Martin were eager to set up R&D subsidiaries in Russia, whose rocket scientists were some of the best (and certainly cheapest!) in the world. These firms were warned by the US government not to perform any mission-critical R&D there.

Host country governments, on the other hand, often attract, encourage, or coerce MNEs into undertaking activities that they may otherwise abdicate. For example, basic manufacturing generates low-paying jobs, does not provide sufficient technology spillovers (foreign technology being diffused domestically), and carries little prestige. Advanced manufacturing, R&D, and regional headquarters, on the other hand, generate higher paying (and better) jobs, provide more technology spillovers, and lead to greater prestige.[17] Therefore, host country governments (such as those in China, Hungary, and Singapore) often use a combination of "carrots" (such as tax incentives and free infrastructure upgrades) and "sticks" (such as threats to block market access) to attract MNE investments in higher value added areas (see Chapter 6).

In addition to formal institutions, MNEs also confront a series of informal institutions governing their relationships with *home* countries.[18] In the United States, despite heated media debates, there are few laws banning MNEs from aggressively setting up overseas subsidiaries. However, managers contemplating such moves have to weigh the informal but vocal backlash against such activities that often results in domestic job losses.

There are also numerous elements of informal institutions when dealing with *host* countries. For instance, Airbus spends 40% of its procurement budget with US suppliers in more than 40 states. While there is no formal requirement for Airbus to "farm out" supply contracts, its sourcing decisions are guided by the informal norm of reciprocity: If one country's suppliers are involved with Airbus, airlines based in that country are more likely to buy Airbus aircraft.

Formal and Informal *Internal* Institutions How MNEs are governed internally is determined by various formal and informal rules of the game. Formally, the organizational charts in Figures 13.2–13.5 specify the scope of responsibilities of various parties.[19] Most MNEs have systems of evaluation, reward, and punishment in place based on these formal rules.

What the formal organizational charts do not reveal is the informal rules of the game, such as organizational norms, values, and networks. The nationality of the head of foreign subsidiaries is such an example.20 Given the lack of formal regulations, MNEs essentially can have three choices when appointing a head of a subsidiary:

- A home country national as the head of a subsidiary (such as an American for a subsidiary of a US-headquartered MNE in India)
- A host country national (such as an Indian for the same subsidiary)
- A third country national (such as an Australian for the same subsidiary)

MNEs from different countries have different norms when making these appointments. Most Japanese MNEs seem to follow an informal rule: Heads of foreign subsidiaries, at least initially, need to be Japanese nationals.[21] In comparison, European MNEs are more likely to appoint host and third country nationals to lead subsidiaries. As a group, US MNEs' practices seem to be between Japanese and European practices. These staffing approaches may reflect strategic differences.[22] Home country nationals, especially those long-time employees of the same MNE at home, are more likely to have developed a better understanding of the informal workings of the firm and to be better socialized into its dominant norms and values. Consequently, the Japanese propensity to appoint home country nationals is conducive to their preferred global standardization strategy that values globally coordinated and controlled actions.[23] Conversely, the European comfort in appointing host and third country nationals is indicative of European MNEs' (traditional) preference for a localization strategy.

Beyond the nationality of subsidiary heads, the nationality of top executives at the highest level (such as board chair, CEO, and board members) seems to follow another informal rule: They are (almost always) home country nationals. To the extent that top executives are ambassadors of the firm and that the MNE headquarters' country of origin is a source of differentiation (for example, a German MNE is often perceived to be different from an Italian MNE),[24] home country nationals would seem to be the most natural candidates for top positions.

However, in the eyes of stakeholders such as employees and governments around the world, a top echelon consisting of largely one nationality does not bode well for an MNE aspiring to globalize everything it does. Some critics even argue that this "glass ceiling" reflects "corporate imperialism."[25] Consequently, such leading MNEs as GSK, Nissan, PepsiCo, and Sony have appointed foreign-born bosses to top posts (see In Focus 13.1). Such foreign-born bosses bring substantial diversity to the organization, which may be a plus. However, such diversity puts an enormous burden on these nonnative top executives to clearly articulate the values and exhibit behaviors expected of senior managers of an MNE associated with a particular country.[26] Procter & Gamble (P&G), for example, appointed Durk Jager, a native of the Netherlands, to be its chairman and CEO in 1999. Unfortunately, Jager's numerous change initiatives almost brought the venerable company to a grinding halt, and he was quickly forced to resign in 2000. Since then, the old rule is back: P&G has been led by an American executive.[27]

Overall, formal internal rules on how the MNE is governed may reflect conscientious strategic choices, but informal internal rules are often taken for granted and deeply embedded in administrative heritages, thus making them difficult to change.

IN FOCUS 13.1 Foreign-born Bosses

An increasingly large number of foreign-born bosses are now running the show at some of the world's largest and most visible MNEs. Since 1999, Nissan's CEO has been Carlos Ghosn, who more recently has also become CEO of Renault (since 2005). Born in Brazil to Lebanese immigrants, Ghosn was educated in France and rose to the ranks in French MNEs Michelin and Renault. Soon after Ghosn took over Nissan, he was receiving hate mail from Japanese employees slated to lose their jobs. Now he is revered in Japan and considered a national hero for his efforts to have successfully turned around Nissan.

Because of Renault's acquisition of a chunk of Nissan's equity, Ghosn was appointed to Nissan as an outsider. However, at many other MNEs, foreign-born CEOs were promoted from within. In 1993, Scottish-born Alex Trotman took over as Ford's chairman and CEO, who then in 1999 promoted the Lebanese-born Australian Jacques Nasser as his successor (see Opening Case). In 2004, Coca-Cola named Irish-born Neville Isdell its chairman and CEO. In 2005, Sony appointed Welsh-born American Howard Stringer as its CEO. In 2006, Pepsi promoted Indian-born Indra Nooyi to be its CEO. In all these cases, while the birthplaces of these executives were not in the home country of the MNEs, they have, respectively, worked at Ford, Coca-Cola, Sony, and PepsiCo for a long time. As a group, foreign-born bosses head up more of British MNEs. A total of 17 of the top-50 British firms are run by foreigners—compared with five in America and Germany and three in France. For example, GSK is run by a Frenchman, and Cadbury Schweppes is headed by an American. Every step of the way, these foreign-born bosses are breaking a piece of the "glass ceiling" that top jobs are off limits for nonnative-born talents. However, foreign-born bosses are often under tremendous stress and media scrutiny. So stay tuned . . .

Sources: Based on (1) *Business Week*, 2004, Nissan's boss, October 4: 50–60; (2) *Business Week*, 2006, Smoothest handover, December 18: 62; (3) *Economist*, 2005, Outside in, January 1: 42; (4) *Economist*, 2006, The Pepsi challenge, August 19: 51; (5) http://www.pepsico.com; (6) http://www.thecoca-colacompany.com.

Resource-Based Considerations

Shown in Figure 13.6, the resource-based view—exemplified by the VRIO framework—adds a number of insights.[28] First, the question of value needs to be confronted. As noted earlier, when making structural changes, whether the new structure (such as matrix) adds concrete value is crucial. Another example is the value of innovation.[29] A vast majority of innovations fail to reach market, and most new products that do reach market end up being financial failures. There is a crucial difference between an innovator and a *profitable* innovator. The latter not only has plenty of good ideas but also lots of complementary assets (such as appropriate organizational structures and marketing muscles) to add value to innovation (see Chapter 4). Philips, for example, is a great innovator, having invented rotary shavers, videocassettes, and compact discs (CDs). However, its abilities to profit from these innovations lag behind those of Sony and Matsushita, which have much stronger complementary assets.

A second question is rarity. Certain strategies or structures may be in vogue at one point in time. When rivals all move toward a global standardization strategy, this strategy cannot become a source of differentiation. To improve global coordination, many MNEs spend millions of dollars to equip themselves with enterprise resource planning (ERP) packages provided by SAP and Oracle. However, such packages are designed for broad appeal implementation, thus providing no firm-specific advantage for the adopting firm.

Even when capabilities are valuable and rare, they have to pass a third hurdle, namely, imitability. Formal structures are easier to observe and imitate than informal structures. This is one of the reasons the informal, flexible matrix is in vogue now. The informal, flexible matrix "is less a structural classification than a broad organizational concept or philosophy, manifested in organizational capability and management mentality."[30] It is obviously a lot harder, if not impossible, to imitate an intangible mentality than to imitate a tangible structure.

The last hurdle is organization—namely, how MNEs are organized, both formally and informally, around the world. As discussed earlier, if MNEs are able to derive the organizational benefits of the matrix without being burdened by a formal matrix structure (that is, building an informal, flexible, invisible matrix), they are likely to outperform rivals.

Having outlined how institutions and resources affect multinationals, let us next devote our attention to the crucial issue of learning, innovation, and knowledge management.

LEARNING OBJECTIVE 3

outline the challenges associated with learning, innovation, and knowledge management

THE CHALLENGE OF MANAGING LEARNING, INNOVATION, AND KNOWLEDGEMENT WORLDWIDE

Knowledge Management

knowledge management
The structures, processes, and systems that actively develop, leverage, and transfer knowledge.

Underpinning the recent emphasis on worldwide learning and innovation is the emerging interest in knowledge management. **Knowledge management** can be defined as the structures, processes, and systems that actively develop, leverage, and transfer knowledge. Some scholars argue that knowledge management is *the* defining feature of MNEs.[31]

Many managers regard knowledge management as simply information management. Taken to an extreme, "such a perspective can result in a profoundly mistaken belief that the installation of sophisticated information technology (IT) infrastructure is the be-all and end-all of knowledge management."[32] Knowledge management not only depends on IT but also more broadly on informal social relationships within the MNE. This is because there are two categories of knowledge: (1) explicit knowledge and (2) tacit knowledge. **Explicit knowledge** is codifiable (that is, can be written down and transferred with little loss of its richness). Virtually all the knowledge captured, stored, and transmitted by IT is explicit. **Tacit knowledge** is noncodifiable and its acquisition and transfer require hands-on practice.[33] For instance, mastering a driving manual (containing a ton of explicit knowledge) without any road practice does not make you a good driver. Tacit knowledge is evidently more important and harder to transfer and learn; it can only be acquired through learning by doing (driving, in this case). Consequently, from a resource-based view, explicit knowledge captured by IT may be strategically *less* important. What counts is the hard-to-codify and hard-to-transfer tacit knowledge.

explicit knowledge
Knowledge that is codifiable (that is, can be written down and transferred with little loss of its richness).

tacit knowledge
Knowledge that is noncodifiable and its acquisition and transfer require hands-on practice.

Knowledge Management in Four Types of MNEs

Differences in knowledge management among the four types of MNEs in Figure 13.1 fundamentally stem from the interdependence (1) between the headquarters and foreign subsidiaries and (2) among various subsidiaries (Table 13.2).[34] In MNEs pursuing a home replication strategy, such interdependence is moderate, and the role of subsidiaries is largely to adapt and leverage parent company competencies. Thus, knowledge about new products and technologies is mostly developed at the center and flowed to subsidiaries, representing the traditional one-way flow. Starbucks, for instance, insists on replicating around the world its US coffee shop concept, down to the elusive "atmosphere."

In MNEs adopting a localization strategy, the interdependence is low. Knowledge management centers on developing knowledge that can best tackle local markets. Ford of Europe used to develop cars for Europe with limited flow of knowledge from and toward headquarters.

TABLE 13.2 KNOWLEDGE MANAGEMENT IN FOUR TYPES OF MULTINATIONAL ENTERPRISES

Strategy	Home replication	Localization	Global standardization	Transnational
Interdependence	Moderate	Low	Moderate	High
Role of foreign subsidiaries	Adapting and leveraging parent company competencies	Sensing and exploiting local opportunities	Implementing parent company initiatives	Differentiated contributions by subsidiaries to integrate worldwide operations
Development and diffusion of knowledge	Knowledge developed at the center and transferred to subsidiaries	Knowledge developed and retained within each subsidiary	Knowledge mostly developed and retained at the center and key locations	Knowledge developed jointly and shared worldwide
Flow of knowledge	Extensive flow of knowledge and people from headquarters to subsidiaries	Limited flow of knowledge and people in both directions (to and from the center)	Extensive flow of knowledge and people from center and key locations to subsidiaries	Extensive flow of knowledge and people in multiple directions

Sources: Adapted from (1) C. Bartlett & S. Ghoshal, 1989, Managing across Borders: The Transnational Solution (p. 65), Boston: *Harvard Business School Press*; (2) T. Kostova & K. Roth, 2003, Social capital in multinational corporations and a micro-macro model of its formation (p. 299), *Academy of Management Review*, 28 (2): 297–317.

In MNEs pursuing a global standardization strategy, the interdependence is increased. Knowledge is developed and retained at the center and a few centers of excellence. Consequently, there is an extensive flow of knowledge and people from headquarters and these centers to other subsidiaries. For example, Yokogawa Hewlett-Packard, HP's subsidiary in Japan, won a coveted Japanese Deming Award for quality. The subsidiary was then charged with transferring such knowledge to the rest of the HP family that resulted in a tenfold improvement in *corporate-wide* quality in ten years.[35]

A hallmark of transnational MNEs is a high degree of interdependence and extensive and bidirectional flows of knowledge.[36] For example, extending a popular ice cream developed in Argentina based on a locally popular caramelized milk dessert, Häagen-Dazs introduced this flavor, Dulce de Leche, throughout the United States and Europe. Within one year, it became the second most popular Häagen-Dazs ice cream (next only to vanilla).[37] Particularly fundamental to transnational MNEs is knowledge flows among dispersed subsidiaries. Instead of a top-down hierarchy, the MNE thus can be conceptualized as an integrated network of subsidiaries (sometimes called the "N-form"), each not only developing locally relevant knowledge but also aspiring to contribute globally beneficial knowledge that enhances corporate-wide competitiveness of the MNE as a whole (see Siemens' ShareNet in Closing Case).

Globalizing Research and Development

R&D represents an especially crucial arena for knowledge management. Relative to production and marketing, only more recently has R&D emerged as an important function to be internationalized—often known as innovation-seeking investment.[38] For instance, Motorola has R&D units around the world (Figure 13.7).

The intensification of competition for innovation drives the globalization of R&D. Such R&D provides a vehicle to access a foreign country's local talents and expertise.[39] Recall earlier discussions in Chapters 6 and 10 on the importance of *agglomeration* of high caliber, innovative firms within a country or region. For foreign firms, a most effective way to access such a cluster is to be there through FDI—as Shiseido did in France (see In Focus 13.2).

IN FOCUS 13.2 Shiseido Smells at Innovations in France

France is the undisputed global innovation leader in perfumes. Blending ancient art with modern R&D, the knowledge about how to make fragrant perfumes is tacit and hard to codify. Non-French firms, such as Japan's Shiseido, face the significant challenge of how to access—or "plug into"—and manage such knowledge efficiently. In 1984, Shiseido established its Europe TechnoCentre in France, led by Japanese expatriates, to gather and transfer intelligence for the head office in Japan, which would then process and digest such knowledge. However, Shiseido perfumes developed in Japan initially failed in France.

© YOSHIKAZU TSUNO / AFP / Getty Images

In 1990, Shiseido realized that to plug into the fragrance knowledge in France, it had to have some of its people work side by side with the French masters of the trade. Consequently, it established a new subsidiary, Beauté Prestige International (BPI), aiming at the top end of the French market. In a very unusual step for a Japanese MNE, Shiseido hired a reputable French female CEO, who leveraged her social capital to recruit a staff of top-notch French perfume developers. Despite some cultural conflicts, the Japanese let the French "run the show" in R&D, planning, and marketing, whereas Japanese expatriates learned by close observation, interaction, and simply "smelling." Then, Shiseido opened its own plant in Gien in the heart of the French perfume "cluster." In 1992, Shiseido successfully launched two designer brand perfumes in France: Eau d'Issey and Jean Paul Gaultier. Since then, Shiseido has transferred such knowledge to Japan and elsewhere. At present, Shiseido is the world's fourth largest cosmetics firm.

Sources: Based on (1) Y. Doz, J. Santos, & P. Williamson, 2001, *From Global to Metanational* (pp. 66–67), Boston: Harvard Business School Press; (2) http://www.shiseido-europe.com.

FIGURE 13.7 MOTOROLA'S GLOBAL R&D NETWORK

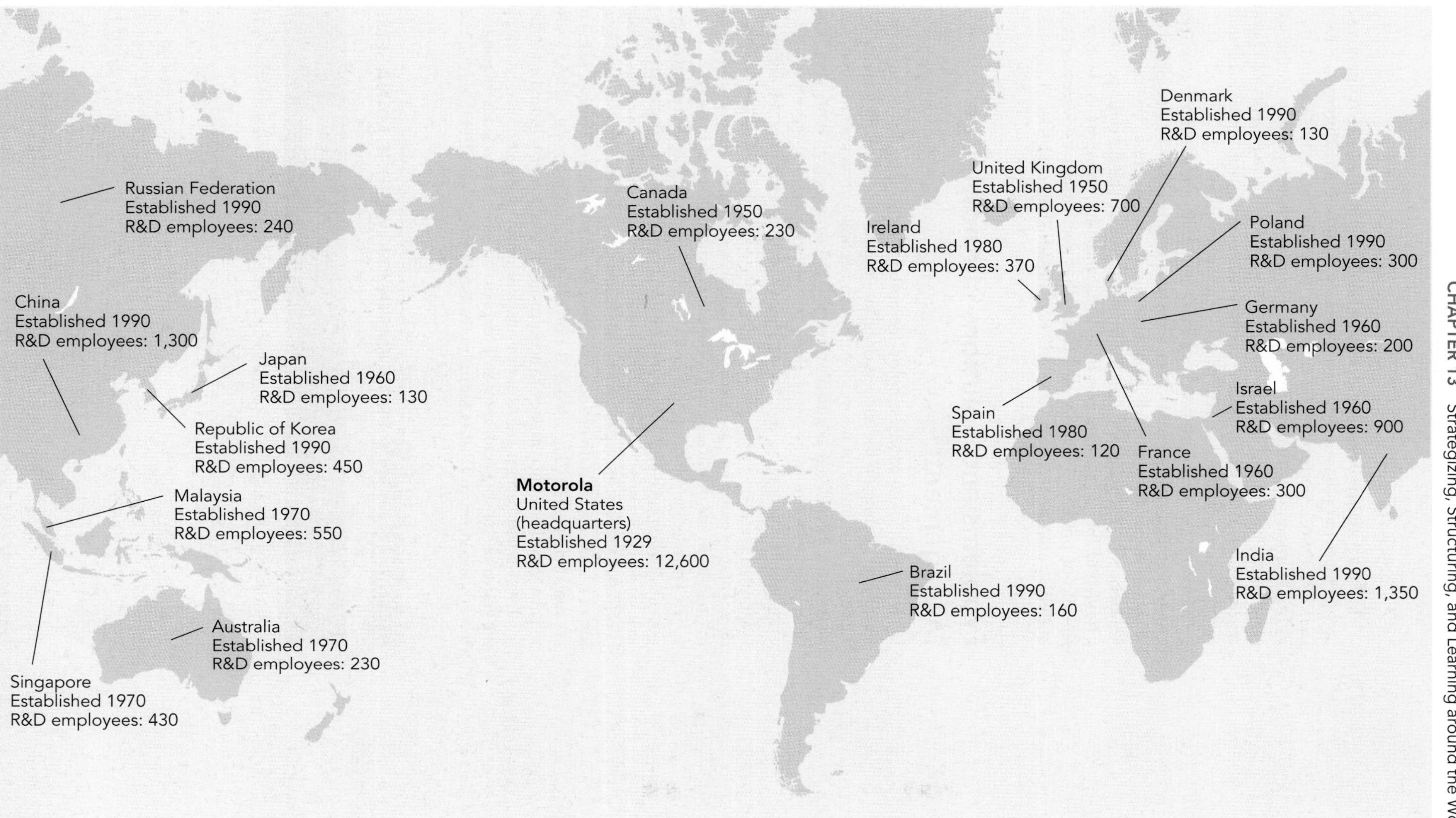

Source: UNCTAD, 2005, *World Investment Report 2005: Transnational Corporations and the Internationalization of R&D* (p. 144), New York and Geneva: United Nations/UNCATD.

From a resource-based standpoint, a fundamental basis for competitive advantage is innovation-based firm heterogeneity (that is, being different).[40] Decentralized R&D work performed by different locations and teams around the world virtually guarantees that there will be persistent heterogeneity in the solutions generated.[41] Britain's GSK, for example, has aggressively spun off R&D units as it becomes clear that simply adding more researchers in centralized R&D units does not necessarily enhance global learning and innovation.

Overall, the scale and scope of R&D by MNE units in host countries have grown significantly in recent years. On a worldwide basis, 16% of global business R&D is now conducted by MNEs in host countries. Of course, this percentage varies, between 72% in Ireland and 2% in South Korea. The percentage for Hungary, China, and the United States is 63%, 24%, and 14%, respectively.[42] Given such a significant presence, it is not surprising that host country governments increasingly pay attention to such "foreign" R&D inside their countries.

Problems and Solutions in Knowledge Management[43]

Institutionally, how MNEs employ formal and informal rules of the game has a significant bearing on the success or failure of knowledge management. Shown in Table 13.3, a number of informal rules can become problems in knowledge management. In knowledge acquisition, many MNEs prefer to invent everything internally. However, for large firms, there are actually *diminishing* returns for R&D.[44] Consequently, a new model, "open innovation," is emerging.[45] It relies on more collaborative research among various internal units, external firms, and university labs. There is evidence that firms that skillfully share research (including publishing results in the public domain) outperform those that fail to do so.[46]

In knowledge retention, the usual problems of employee turnover are compounded when such employees are key R&D personnel, whose departure will lead to knowledge leakage.[47] In knowledge outflow, there is the "how does it help me?" syndrome. Specifically, managers of the source subsidiary may view outbound sharing of knowledge as a diversion of scarce time and resources. Further, some managers may believe that "knowledge is power," and monopolizing certain knowledge may be viewed as the currency to acquire and retain power within the MNE.[48]

global virtual team
A team whose members are physically dispersed in multiple locations in the world. They operate on a virtual basis.

Even when certain subsidiaries are willing to share knowledge, inappropriate transmission channels may still torpedo effective knowledge sharing.[49] Given the advancement in IT, it is tempting to establish **global virtual teams**, which do

TABLE 13.3 PROBLEMS IN KNOWLEDGE MANAGEMENT

Elements of knowledge management	Common problems
Knowledge acquisition	Failure to share and integrate external knowledge
Knowledge retention	Employee turnover and knowledge leakage
Knowledge outflow	"How does it help me?" syndrome and "knowledge is power" mentality
Knowledge transmission	Inappropriate channels
Knowledge inflow	"Not invented here" syndrome and absorptive capacity

Source: Adapted from A. Gupta & V. Govindarajan, 2004, *Global Strategy and Organization* (p. 109), New York: Wiley.

not meet face to face, to transfer knowledge. Unfortunately, such teams often have to confront tremendous communication and relationship barriers.[50] For example, videoconferences can hardly show body language, and Skype often breaks down. As a result, face-to-face meetings are still often necessary.

Describe various ways global virtual team members can effectively communicate knowledge among themselves.

Finally, recipient subsidiaries may present two problems that block successful knowledge inflows. First, the "not invented here" syndrome causes some managers to resist accepting ideas from other units. Second, recipient subsidiaries may have limited **absorptive capacity**—"ability to recognize the value of new information, assimilate it, and apply it."[51]

As solutions to combat these problems, corporate headquarters can manipulate the formal rules of the game, such as (1) tying bonuses with measurable knowledge outflows and inflows, (2) using high-powered, corporate- or business-unit-based incentives (as opposed to individual- and single-subsidiary-based incentives), and (3) investing in codifying tacit knowledge. Siemens used some of these measures when promoting its ShareNet (Closing Case). However, these formal policies fundamentally boil down to the very challenging (if not impossible) task of how to accurately measure inflows and outflows of tacit knowledge. The nature of tacit knowledge simply resists such formal bureaucratic practices. Consequently, MNEs often have to rely on a great deal of informal integrating mechanisms, such as (1) facilitating management and R&D personnel networks among various subsidiaries through joint teamwork, training, and conferences and (2) promoting strong organizational (that is, MNE-specific) cultures and shared values and norms for cooperation among subsidiaries.[52]

absorptive capacity
The ability to recognize the value of new information, assimilate it, and apply it.

The key idea is that instead of using traditional, formal command-and-control structures that are often ineffective, knowledge management is best facilitated by informal **social capital**, which refers to the informal benefits individuals and organizations derive from their social structures and networks.[53] Because of the existence of social capital, individuals are more likely to go out of their way to help friends and acquaintances. Consequently, managers of the China subsidiary are more likely to help managers of the Chile subsidiary with needed knowledge if they know each other and have some social relationship. Otherwise, managers of the China subsidiary may not be as enthusiastic to provide such help if the call for help comes from managers of the Cameroon subsidiary, with whom there is no social relationship. Overall, the micro, informal interpersonal relationships among managers of different units may greatly facilitate macro, intersubsidiary cooperation among various units—in short, a **micro-macro link**.[54]

social capital
The informal benefits individuals and organizations derive from their social structures and networks.

micro-macro link
The informal interpersonal relationships (micro) among managers of different units that may greatly facilitate intersubsidiary cooperation (macro) among various units.

DEBATES AND EXTENSIONS

LEARNING OBJECTIVE **4**
participate in two leading debates on multinational strategy, structure, and learning

The question of how to manage complex MNEs has led to numerous debates, some of which have been discussed earlier (such as the debate on the matrix structure). Here, we outline two of the leading debates not previously discussed: (1) corporate controls versus subsidiary initiatives and (2) customer-focused dimensions versus integration, responsiveness, and learning.

Corporate Controls versus Subsidiary Initiatives

One of the leading debates on how to manage large firms is centralization versus decentralization. In an MNE setting, the debate boils down to central controls versus subsidiary initiatives. A starting point is that subsidiaries are not necessarily at the receiving end of commands from headquarters. When headquarters require that certain practices (such as quality circles) be adopted, some subsidiaries may be in full compliance, others may pay lip service, and still others may simply refuse to adopt, citing local differences.[55]

In addition to reacting to headquarters' demands differently, some subsidiaries may actively pursue their own *subsidiary*-level strategies and agendas.[56] These activities are known as **subsidiary initiatives**, defined as the proactive and deliberate pursuit of new opportunities by a subsidiary to expand its scope of responsibility.[57] For example, Honeywell Canada requested that headquarters designate itself as a global center for excellence for certain product lines (In Focus 13.3). Many authors argue that such initiatives may inject a much needed spirit of entrepreneurship throughout the larger, more bureaucratic corporation.

subsidiary initiative
The proactive and deliberate pursuit of new opportunities by a subsidiary to expand its scope of responsibility.

However, from the perspective of corporate headquarters, it is hard to distinguish between good-faith subsidiary initiatives and opportunistic "empire building." For instance, a lot is at stake when determining which subsidiaries become centers of excellence with worldwide mandates.[58] Subsidiaries that fail to attain this status may see their roles marginalized and, in the worst case, their facilities closed. Subsidiary managers are often host country nationals (such as Canadian managers at Honeywell Canada in In Focus 13.3), who would naturally prefer to strengthen their subsidiary—if only to protect local (and their own!) employment and not necessarily to be patriotic. However, these tendencies, although very natural and legitimate, are not necessarily consistent with the MNE's corporate-wide goals. These tendencies, if not checked and controlled, can surely lead to chaos.

Customer-Focused Dimensions versus Integration, Responsiveness, and Learning[59]

As discussed earlier, juggling the three dimensions of integration, responsiveness, and learning has often made the global matrix structure so complex that it is often unworkable. However, instead of simplifying, many MNEs have added new dimensions that make their structure *more* complex. Often, new customer-focused dimensions of structure are placed on top of an existing structure, resulting in a four- or five-dimension matrix.

IN FOCUS 13.3 ETHICAL DILEMMA: A Subsidiary Initiative at Honeywell Canada

Honeywell Limited is a wholly owned Canadian subsidiary—hereafter Honeywell Canada—of the Minneapolis-based Honeywell, Inc. that produces a variety of consumer products and engineering systems. Until the mid-1980s, Honeywell Canada was a traditional branch plant that mainly produced for the Canadian market in volumes approximately one-tenth of those of the main manufacturing operations in Minneapolis. By the late 1980s, the winds of change unleashed by the US-Canadian Free Trade Agreement (later to become NAFTA in the 1990s) threatened the very survival of Honeywell Canada, whose inefficient (suboptimal scale) operations could face closure when the high tariffs came down and Made-in-USA products could enter Canada duty-free. Canadian managers in the subsidiary entrepreneurially proposed to the US headquarters that their plant be given the mandate in certain product lines to produce for the entire North America. In exchange, they agreed to shut down some inefficient lines. Although some US managers were understandably negative, the head of the homes division was open-minded. Negotiations followed and the Canadian proposal was eventually adopted. Consequently, Honeywell Canada was designated as a Honeywell center of excellence for valves and actuators. At present, Honeywell Canada is Canada's leading controls company.

Although this is a successful case of subsidiary initiative, a potential ethical problem is that from a corporate headquarters' standpoint, it is often difficult to ascertain whether the subsidiary is making good-faith efforts acting in the best interest of the MNE or the subsidiary managers are primarily promoting their self-interest such as power, prestige, and their own jobs. How corporate headquarters can differentiate good-faith efforts from more opportunistic maneuvers remains a challenge.

Sources: Based on (1) J. Birkinshaw, 2000, *Entrepreneurship in the Global Firm* (p. 26), London: Sage; (2) http://www.honeywell.ca; (3) http://www.honeywell.com.

There are two primary customer-focused dimensions. The first is a **global account structure** to supply customers (often other MNEs) in a coordinated and consistent way across various countries. Most original equipment manufacturers (OEMs)—namely, contract manufacturers that produce goods *not* carrying their own brands (such as the makers of Nike shoes and Microsoft Xbox)—use this structure. Singapore's Flextronics, the world's largest electronics OEM, has dedicated global accounts for Dell, Palm, and Sony Ericsson. Second, a **solutions-based structure** is often used. As a "customer solution" provider, IBM would sell whatever combination of hardware, software, and services that customers prefer, whether that means selling IBM products or selling rivals' offerings.

global account structure
A customer-focused dimension that supplies customers (often other MNEs) in a coordinated and consistent way across various countries.

solutions-based structure
A customer-oriented solution in which a provider sells whatever combination of goods and services the customer prefers, including a rival's offerings.

The typical starting point is to put in place informal or temporary solutions rather than create new layers or units. However, this ad hoc approach can quickly run out of control, resulting in subsidiary managers' additional duties to report to three or four "informal bosses" (acting as global account managers) on top of their "day jobs." Eventually, new formal structures may be called for, resulting in inevitable bureaucracy.

So what is the solution when confronting the value-added potential of customer-focused dimensions and their associated complexity and cost? One solution is to *simplify*. For instance, in 2003, ABB, when facing grave performance problems, transformed its sprawling "Byzantine" matrix structure to a mere two global product divisions, power technology and automation.

MANAGEMENT SAVVY

LEARNING OBJECTIVE **5**
draw implications for action

MNEs are the ultimate large, complex, and geographically dispersed business organizations. What determines the success and failure of multinational strategy, structure, and learning? The answer boils down to the institution- and resource-based dimensions. The institution-based view calls for thorough understanding and skillful manipulation of the rules of the game both at home and abroad. The resource-based view focuses on the development and deployment of firm-specific capabilities to enhance the odds for successful MNE management.

Consequently, three clear implications emerge for savvy managers (Table 13.4). First, understanding and mastering the external rules of the game governing MNEs and home/host country environments become a must. In 2000, Philips took advantage of home country rules concerning antidumping (see Chapter 11) by suing Chinese lamp makers for dumping in the EU. However, after Philips upset the Chinese government, its sales in China, its second largest market after the United States, immediately dropped by 10% (from \$5.5 billion in 2000 to \$5 billion in 2001). Trying to repair the damage, in 2003, Philips's board held its first-ever meeting outside Amsterdam in Beijing and visited Chinese officials in central and local governments. It also moved Asia headquarters from Hong Kong to

TABLE 13.4 IMPLICATIONS FOR ACTION

- Understand and master the external rules of the game governing MNEs and home/host country environments
- Understand and be prepared to change the internal rules of the game governing MNE management
- Develop learning and innovation capabilities to leverage multinational presence as an asset—"act local, think global"

Shanghai, set up R&D units in Xian, and responded to government incentives to invest in China's economically failing Northeast region.

Second, managers need to understand and be prepared to change the internal rules of the game governing MNE management. Different strategies and structures call for different internal rules of the game. Some facilitate and others constrain MNE actions. It is impossible for a home replication firm to entertain having a foreigner as its CEO. Yet, as an MNE becomes more global in its operations, its managerial outlook needs to be broadened as well. Although not every MNE needs to appoint a foreigner as its head, the foreign-born bosses at Coca-Cola, Nissan, and Sony represent one of the strongest signals about these firms' global outlook (see In Focus 13.1).

Finally, managers need to actively develop learning and innovation capabilities to leverage multinational presence, as Siemens' ShareNet has done (Closing Case). A winning formula is "act local, think global." Failing to do so may be costly. During 1999–2000, many Ford Explorer SUVs accidentally rolled over and killed many people in the United States. Most of these accidents were caused by faulty tires made by Japan's Bridgestone and its US subsidiary Firestone. Before the number of US accidents skyrocketed, an alarming number of accidents had already taken place in warmer weather countries such as Brazil and Saudi Arabia, and local managers dutifully reported them to headquarters in Japan and the United States. Unfortunately, these reports were dismissed by the higher-up as "driver error" or "road condition." Bridgestone/Firestone thus failed to leverage its multinational presence as an asset; it should have learned from these reports and proactively probed into the potential for similar accidents in cooler weather countries (tires depreciate faster in warmer weather). In the end, a lot more lives were lost, and Bridgestone/Firestone as a brand was abandoned by many informed car (and tire) buyers.

CHAPTER SUMMARY

1. Articulate the relationship between multinational strategy and structure
   - Governing multinational strategy and structure is an integration-responsiveness framework.
   - There are four strategy/structure pairs: (1) home replication strategy/international division structure, (2) localization strategy/geographic area structure, (3) global standardization strategy/global product division structure, and (4) transnational strategy/global matrix structure.
2. Understand how institutions and resources affect strategy, structure, and learning.
   - MNEs are governed by external and internal rules of the game around the world.
   - Management of MNE structure, learning, and innovation needs to take VRIO into account.
3. Outline the challenges associated with learning, innovation, and knowledge management
   - Knowledge management primarily focuses on tacit knowledge.
   - Globalization of R&D calls for capabilities to combat a number of problems associated with knowledge creation, retention, outflow, transmission, and inflow.

4. Participate in two leading debates on multinational strategy, structure, and learning
   - The debates are (1) corporate controls versus subsidiary initiatives and (2) customer-focused dimensions versus integration, responsiveness, and learning.
5. Draw implications for action
   - Savvy managers must understand and master the external rules of the game and be prepared to change the internal rules governing MNEs.
   - "Act local, think global" means developing learning and innovation capabilities around the world.

KEY TERMS

Absorptive capacity 375
Center of excellence 362
Country (regional) manager 364
Explicit knowledge 371
Geographic area structure 364
Global account structure 377
Global matrix 365
Global product division 364
Global standardization strategy 362
Global virtual team 374
Home replication strategy 361
Integration-responsiveness framework 360
International division 363
Knowledge management 370
Local responsiveness 360
Localization (multidomestic) strategy 362
Micro-macro link 375
Social capital 375
Solutions-based structure 377
Subsidiary initiative 376
Tacit knowledge 371
Transnational strategy 363
Worldwide (global) mandate 362

REVIEW QUESTIONS

1. The pressure to reduce costs is common to both domestic and international competition, but what additional kind of pressure is unique to international competition? Explain your answer.
2. Referring to Figure 13.1 as needed, describe the four strategic choices in the integration-responsiveness framework.
3. Still referring to Figure 13.1 as needed, describe the four corresponding organizational structures in the integration-responsiveness framework.
4. What are three key lessons derived from an understanding of the reciprocal nature of the relationship between strategy and structure?
5. List three examples of how formal and informal external institutions affect MNEs.
6. Describe some of the informal rules of the game that govern what type of individual an MNE can appoint to be the head of a foreign subsidiary.
7. Summarize the insights revealed by using a VRIO framework to analyze a potential structural change.
8. How would you characterize the two types of knowledge found in an MNE?

9. Referring to Table 13.2 as needed, summarize how knowledge is developed and disseminated in each of the four types of MNEs.
10. What are some of the problems inherent in the functioning of a global virtual team?
11. What are some of the actions that MNEs can take to combat common problems in knowledge management?
12. Which do you think would be more integral to a firm's success: corporate controls or subsidiary-level strategies and agendas?
13. Describe the two primary customer-focused dimensions that many MNEs add to their global matrix structures.
14. From time to time, a manager may be faced with the need to change the internal rules of the game within his or her MNE. What skills and capabilities might be useful in achieving this?
15. What is your interpretation of the phrase "act local, think global"?

CRITICAL DISCUSSION QUESTIONS

1. In this age of globalization, some gurus argue that all industries are becoming global and that all firms need to adopt a global standardization strategy. Do you agree? Why or why not?
2. ON ETHICS: You are the manager of the best-performing subsidiary in an MNE. Because bonus is tied to subsidiary performance, your bonus is the highest among managers of all subsidiaries. Now headquarters is organizing managers from other subsidiaries to visit and learn from your subsidiary. You worry that if your subsidiary is no longer the star unit when other subsidiaries' performance catches up, your bonus will go down. What are you going to do?
3. ON ETHICS: You are a corporate R&D manager at Boeing and are thinking about transferring some R&D work to China, India, and Russia, where the work performed by a $70,000 US engineer reportedly can be done by an engineer in one of these countries for less than $7,000. However, US engineers at Boeing have staged protests against such moves. US politicians are similarly vocal concerning job losses and national security hazards. What are you going to do?

VIDEO CASE

Watch "Seek Out Ways to Share Best Practice" by J. W. Marriott, Jr. of Marriott International, Inc.

1. Regarding the relationship between multinational strategy and structure, how does Marriott's approach involve both localization and global standardization?
2. How does Marriott create knowledge? What international considerations should be part of the process?
3. Another source of knowledge for Marriott is suppliers. In a global corporation with global suppliers, how can that approach pay off?

4. How does his story about the desk in a room provide a perspective regarding focusing on customer needs with a limited resource?
5. Marriott's approach to learning, innovation, and knowledge management was directed toward improving operations and customer satisfaction. However, could there be relationship benefits as well?

CLOSING CASE

Siemens' ShareNet: A Knowledge Management System

Founded in 1847, Siemens, headquartered in Munich and Berlin, is an engineering conglomerate that produces power generation equipment, transportation systems, medical devices, and numerous other industrial products. In 1992, Siemens, in the words of its then CEO, was "an introverted, some would say arrogant, company, particularly in Germany, where 50% of our business and more than 50% of the people were still located at that time." Today, Siemens has 80% of sales, 70% of factories, and 66% of its 475,000 work force outside Germany. In 2005, the United States became its largest market, overtaking Germany. In 2006, Siemens had revenues of €87 billion.

© AP IMAGES

As Siemens significantly expands around the world, how to tap into and rejuvenate its employees' comprehensive knowledge and expertise that is geographically dispersed in 190 countries (!) remains a leading challenge. In response, since 1998, Siemens has developed a knowledge management (KM) system, ShareNet, that endeavors to put its employees' combined knowledge to work.

The ShareNet initiative has gone through four steps. The first step was concept definition. ShareNet was envisioned not only to handle explicit knowledge but also tacit knowledge. To overcome the drawbacks of traditional, repository-based KM systems, the new system had to integrate interactive components such as a forum for urgent requests and a platform for sharing rich knowledge. Pilot tests were carried out in Australia, China, Malaysia, and Portugal in early 1999 to gain cross-cultural insights from users far from Munich. The ShareNet team wanted to avoid the usual Siemens practice of rolling out initiatives from Munich to the rest of the MNE across the globe because such a practice often backfired.

The second step was the global rollout for 39 countries in late 1999. Siemens addressed the bias of both global integration and local responsiveness by adopting a "glocal" approach. While strategic direction was maintained in Munich, ShareNet managers were appointed to local subsidiaries. Importantly, these ShareNet managers were not expats from the headquarters but rather people from the local subsidiaries assigned to become the nucleus in their regions. This international group of ShareNet managers was a major cornerstone for leveraging the KM idea globally. To jump-start the system, ShareNet managers held local workshops and encouraged participants to post an unsolved problem as an urgent request that would be sent to all users worldwide. Without exception, by the end of the day, the posting would get at least one reply, and inevitably, the person who had posted it would be "stunned." Not surprisingly, every local workshop was followed by an increase in urgent requests from that country.

To be sure, resistance was extensive. In Germany, attitude toward the English-only ShareNet was negative initially. Some employees thought that a Germany-based firm should use German. Although the English proficiency of German employees was relatively high, many employees still dared not post a question in a forum where thousands of people could see their grammatical or spelling errors. Over time, such resistance was gradually overcome as users personally saw the benefits of using the system.

The third step was generating momentum. Many people said: "I don't have time for this." Others put it more bluntly: "Why do I have to share?" In 2000, Siemens provided incentives for local country managers and rewarded a country's overall participation. For a successful sale resulting from ShareNet collaboration, a bonus was given to both the country that had contributed the knowledge and the country that used it. Individual contributors were rewarded with various gifts and prizes, such as Siemens mobile phones, books, and even trips to visit knowledge exchange partners. Interesting patterns emerged. Contrary to expectations, Chinese employees were not shy. During 2000–2001, the average number of contributed knowledge pieces per contributor in China (16.67) was much higher than that in the United States (3.29). Indian employees were also enthusiastic. The ShareNet team suspected that this was in part because rewards were more attractive to Chinese and Indian employees (who were usually paid less) than to US employees. In India, some employees became overzealous, made low-quality contributions, and even neglected their "day jobs." The ShareNet team consequently adjusted rewards to less expensive goods such as books. But in general, the surge in participation was heartening and suggested that many employees felt good about establishing themselves as experts in the eyes of their peers around the world.

The fourth step was consolidating and sustaining performance. By 2002, ShareNet had 19,000 users in more than 80 countries, supported by 53 ShareNet managers in different countries. Yet, not everything was rosy. The post-9/11 downturn in the telecommunications sector forced corporate-wide layoffs, and the ShareNet team could not escape. After restructuring, the ShareNet team was trimmed to fewer than ten members worldwide. User behavior also changed dramatically. There was a noticeable decline in knowledge contribution, although the level of urgent requests was maintained. The rationale was simple: An urgent request could directly help solve an immediate problem in a tough time, whereas knowledge contribution did not yield an immediate payoff to the contributor. To demonstrate value added, the ShareNet team documented €5 million direct profits that had been generated by the KM system. To avoid ambiguity, the €5 million figure did not include the indirect but hard-to-quantify benefits associated with an expanded tacit knowledge base. On balance, ShareNet was considered a huge success. Siemens is currently building a larger and more powerful PeopleShareNet.

Case Discussion Questions

1. Does ShareNet satisfy the VRIO criteria? Is this KM system a firm-specific resource?
2. What are some of the problems associated with KM that the ShareNet team has to overcome?
3. How does this KM system support Siemens' strategy?

Sources: Based on (1) *Economist*, 2007, Home and abroad, February 10: 7–8; (2) http://www.siemens.com; (3) T. Stewart & L. O'Brien, 2005, Transforming an industrial giant, *Harvard Business Review*, February: 115–122; (4) S. Voelpel, M. Dous, & T. Davenport, 2005, Five steps to creating a global knowledge-sharing system: Siemens' ShareNet, *Academy of Management Executive*, 19: 9–23.

NOTES

Journal acronyms: **AME** – *Academy of Management Executive;* **AMJ** – *Academy of Management Journal;* **AMR** – *Academy of Management Review;* **APJM** – *Asia Pacific Journal of Management;* **ASQ** – *Administrative Science Quarterly;* **BW** – *Business Week;* **CMR** – *California Management Review;* **HBR** – *Harvard Business Review;* **IBR** – *International Business Review;* **JIBS** – *Journal of International Business Studies;* **JIM** – *Journal of International Management;* **JM** – *Journal of Management;* **JMS** – *Journal of Management Studies;* **MIR** – *Management International Review;* **OSc** – *Organization Science;* **SMJ** – *Strategic Management Journal*

[1] J. Birkinshaw, S. Ghoshal, C. Markides, J. Stopford, & G. Yip (eds.), 2003, *The Future of the Multinational Company*, London: Wiley; C. K. Prahalad & Y. Doz, 1987, *The Multinational Mission*, New York: Free Press; J. Stopford & L. Wells, 1972, *Managing the Multinational Enterprise*, New York: Basic Books.

[2] T. Levitt, 1983, The globalization of markets, *HBR*, May–June: 92–102.

[3] C. Baden-Fuller & J. Stopford, 1991, Globalization frustrated, *SMJ*, 12: 493–507; A. Rugman, 2001, *The End of Globalization*, New York: AMACOM.

[4] A. Harzing, 2000, An empirical analysis and extension of the Bartlett and Ghoshal typology of MNCs, *JIBS*, 31: 101–120.

[5] T. Frost, J. Birkinshaw, & P. Ensign, 2002, Centers of excellence in MNCs (p. 997), *SMJ*, 23: 997–1018. See also U. Andersson & M. Forsgren, 2000, In search of centers of excellence, *MIR*, 40: 329–350; G. Reger, 2004, Coordinating globally dispersed research centers of excellence, *JIM*, 10: 51–76.

[6] C. Bartlett & S. Ghoshal, 1989, *Managing across Borders*, Boston: Harvard Business School Press.

[7] N. Anand, H. Gardner, & T. Orris, 2007, Knowledge-based innovation, *AMJ*, 50: 406–428; H. Berry, 2006, Leaders, laggards, and the pursuit of foreign knowledge, *SMJ*, 27: 151–168; J. Cantwell, J. Dunning, & O. Janne, 2004, Towards a technology-seeking explanation of US direct investment in the United Kingdom, *JIM*, 10: 5–20; W. Chen & K. Miller, 2007, Situational and institutional determinants of firms' R&D search intensity, *SMJ*, 28: 369–381.

[8] J. Birkinshaw & N. Hood, 1998, Multinational subsidiary evolution, *AMR*, 23: 773–796; J. Manea & R. Pearce, 2006, MNEs' strategies in Central and Eastern Europe, *MIR*, 46: 235–255; A. Rugman & A. Verbeke, 2001, Subsidiary-specific advantages in MNEs, *SMJ*, 22: 237–250.

[9] J. Cantwell & R. Mudambi, 2005, MNE competence-creating subsidiary mandates, *SMJ*, 26: 1109–1128; K. Ruckman, 2005, Technology sourcing through acquisitions, *JIBS*, 36: 89–103.

[10] B. Lamont, V. Sambamurthy, K. Ellis, & P. Simmonds, 2000, The influence of organizational structure on the information received by corporate strategies of MNEs, *MIR*, 40: 231–252; Y. Ling, S. Floyd, & D. Baldrige, 2005, Toward a model of issue-selling by subsidiary managers in MNCs, *JIBS*, 36: 637–654.

[11] R. Edwards, A. Ahmad, & S. Ross, 2002, Subsidiary autonomy, *JIBS*, 33: 183–191; S. Miller & L. Eden, 2006, Local density and foreign subsidiary performance, *AMJ*, 49: 341–355.

[12] L. Burns & D. Wholey, 1993, Adoption and abandonment of matrix management programs, *AMJ*, 36: 106–139; T. Devinney, D. Midgley, & S. Venaik, 2000, The optimal performance of the global firm, *OSc*, 11: 674–695; J. Johnson, 1995, An empirical analysis of the integration-responsiveness framework, *JIBS*, 26: 621–635.

[13] R. Hodgetts, 1999, Dow Chemical CEO William Stavropoulos on structure (p. 30), *AME*, 13: 29–35.

[14] J. Wolf & W. Egelhoff, 2002, A reexamination and extension of international strategy-structure theory, *SMJ*, 23: 181–189.

[15] G. Benito, B. Grogaard, & R. Narula, 2003, Environmental influences on MNE subsidiary roles, *JIBS*, 34: 443–456; T. Malnight, 2001, Emerging structural patterns within MNCs, *AMJ*, 44: 1187–1210; T. Murtha, S. Lenway, & R. Bagozzi, 1998, Global mind-sets and cognitive shift in a complex MNC, *SMJ*, 19: 97–114; S. Venaik, D. Midgley, & T. Devinney, 2005, Dual paths to performance, *JIBS*, 36: 655–675; R. Whitley, G. Morgan, W. Kelley, & D. Sharpe, 2003, The changing Japanese multinational, *JMS*, 40: 643–672.

[16] A. Hillman & W. Wan, 2005, The determinants of MNE subsidiaries' political strategies, *JIBS*, 36: 322–340; T. Murtha & S. Lenway, 1994, Country capabilities and the strategic state, *SMJ*, 15: 113–130.

[17] Y. Akbar & J. McBride, 2004, MNE strategy, FDI, and economic development, *JWB*, 39: 89–105; W. Hejazi & A. E. Safarian, 1999, Trade, FDI, and R&D spillovers, *JIBS*, 30: 491–511; X. Liu, P. Siler, C. Wang, & Y. Wei, 2000, Productivity spillovers from FDI, *JIBS*, 31: 407–425; M. Wright, I. Filatotchev, T. Buck, & K. Bishop, 2002, Foreign partners in the former Soviet Union, *JWB*, 37: 165–179.

[18] T. Blumentritt & D. Nigh, 2002, The integration of subsidiary political activities in MNCs, *JIBS*, 33: 57–77; J. Laurila & M. Ropponen, 2003, Institutional conditioning of foreign expansion, *JMS*, 40: 725–751; T. Kostova & S. Zaheer, 1999, Organizational legitimacy under conditions of complexity, *AMR*, 24: 64–81; R. Ramamurti, 2004, Developing countries and MNEs, *JIBS*, 35: 277–283.

[19] W. Sine, H. Mitsuhashi, & D. Kirsch, 2006, Revisiting Burns and Stalker, *AMJ*, 49: 121–132.

[20] N. Noorderhaven & A. Harzing, 2003, The "country-of-origin effect" in MNCs, *MIR*, 43: 47–66.

[21] P. Beamish & A. Inkpen, 1998, Japanese firms and the decline of the Japanese expatriate, *JWB*, 33: 35–50; R. Belderbos & M. Heijltjes, 2005, The determinants of expatriate staffing by Japanese multinationals in Asia, *JIBS*, 36: 341–354.

[22] Y. Paik & J. Sohn, 2004, Expatriate managers and MNCs' ability to control international subsidiaries, *JWB*, 39: 61–71; R. Peterson, J. Sargent, N. Napier, & W. Shim, 1996, Corporate expatriate HRM policies, internationalization, and performance in the world's largest MNCs, *MIR*, 36: 215–230.

[23] J. Johansson & G. Yip, 1994, Exploiting globalization potential, *SMJ*, 15: 579–601; J. Sohn, 1994, Social knowledge as a control system, *JIBS*, 25: 295–325.

[24] J. Birkinshaw, P. Braunerhjelm, U. Holm, & S. Terjesen, 2006, Why do some MNCs relocate their headquarters overseas? *SMJ*, 27: 681–700.

[25] C. K. Prahalad & K. Lieberthal, 1998, The end of corporate imperialism, *HBR*, 76 (4): 68–79.

[26] L. Palich & L. Gomez-Mejia, 1999, A theory of global strategy and firm efficiency, *JM*, 25: 587–606; O. Richard, T. Barnett, S. Dwyer, & K. Chadwick, 2004, Cultural diversity in management, firm performance, and the moderating role of entrepreneurial orientation, *AMJ*, 47: 227–240.

[27] R. Berner, 2003, P&G: New and improved, *BW*, July 7: 52–63.

[28] P. Cloninger, 2004, The effect of service intangibility on revenue from foreign markets, *JIM*, 10: 125–146; A. Delios & P. Beamish, 2001, Survival and profitability, *AMJ*, 44: 1028–1039; E. Danneels, 2002, The dynamics of product innovation and firm competences, *SMJ*, 23: 1095–1122; S. Tallman, 1991, Strategic management models and resource-based strategies among MNEs in a host country, *SMJ*, 12: 69–82.

[29] K. Ojah & L. Monplaisir, 2003, Investors' valuation of global product R&D, *JIBS*, 34: 457–472.

[30] Bartlett & Ghoshal, 1989, *Managing across Borders* (p. 209).

[31] H. Bresman, J. Birkinshaw, & R. Nobel, 1999, Knowledge transfer in international acquisitions, *JIBS*, 30: 439–462; M. Crossan & I. Berdrow, 2003, Organizational learning and strategic renewal, *SMJ*, 24: 1087–1105; N. Foss & T. Pedersen, 2005, Organizing knowledge processes in the MNC, *JIBS*, 35: 340–349; R. Grant, 1996, Toward a knowledge-based theory of the firm, *SMJ*, 17: 109–122; B. Kogut & U. Zander, 1993, Knowledge of the firm and the evolutionary theory of the multinational corporation, *JIBS*, 24: 625–645; G. Szulanski & R. Jensen, 2006, Presumptive adaptation and the effectiveness of knowledge transfer, *SMJ*, 27: 937–957.

[32] A. Gupta & V. Govindarajan, 2004, *Global Strategy and Organization* (p. 104), New York: Wiley.

[33] R. Coff, D. Coff, & R. Eastvold, 2006, The knowledge-leveraging paradox, *AMR*, 31: 452–465; T. Felin & W. Hesterly, 2007, The knowledge-based view, *AMR*, 32: 195–218; X. Martin & R. Salomon, 2003, Knowledge transfer capacity and its implications for the theory of the MNE, *JIBS*, 34: 356–373; U. Schultze & C. Stabell, 2004, Knowing what you don't know? *JMS*, 41: 549–573.

[34] K. Hewett, M. Roth, & K. Roth, 2003, Conditions influencing headquarters and foreign subsidiary roles in marketing activities and their effects on performance, *JIBS*, 34: 567–585; M. Kotabe, D. Dunlap-Hinkler, R. Parente, & H. Mishra, 2007, Determinants of cross-national knowledge transfer and its effect on firm innovation, *JIBS*, 38: 259–282; S. Kumar & A. Seth, 1998, The design of coordination and control mechanisms for managing JV-parent relationships, *SMJ*, 19: 579–599; Y. Luo & H. Zhao, 2004, Corporate link and competitive strategy in MNEs, *JIM*, 10: 77–105.

[35] M. Porter, H. Takeuchi, & M. Sakakibara, 2000, *Can Japan Compete?* (p. 80), Cambridge, MA: Perseus.

[36] T. Frost & C. Zhou, 2005, R&D co-practice and "reverse" knowledge integration in MNCs, *JIBS*, 36: 676–687; Y. Luo & M. W. Peng, 1999, Learning to compete in a transition economy, *JIBS*, 30: 269–296.

[37] Y. Doz, J. Santos, & P. Williamson, 2001, *From Global to Metanational*, Boston: Harvard Business School Press.

[38] P. Almeida, 1996, Knowledge sourcing by foreign multinationals, *SMJ*, 17: 155–166; K. Asakawa & M. Lehrer, 2003, Managing local knowledge assets globally, *JWB*, 38: 31–42; R. Belderbos, 2003, Entry mode, organizational learning, and R&D in foreign affiliates, *SMJ*, 24: 235–255; W. Kuemmerle, 1999, The drivers of FDI into R&D, *JIBS*, 30: 1–24; M. Zedtwitz, O. Gassman, & R. Boutellier, 2004, Organizing global R&D, *JIM*, 10: 21–49.

[39] M. W. Peng & D. Wang, 2000, Innovation capability and foreign direct investment, *MIR*, 40: 79–83; J. Penner-Hahn & J. M. Shaver, 2005, Does international R&D increase patent output? *SMJ*, 26: 121–140.

[40] M. Sakakibara, 1997, Heterogeneity of firm capabilities and cooperative R&D, *SMJ*, 18: 143–164; G. Vegt, E. Vliert, & X. Huang, 2005, Location-level links between diversity and innovative climate depend on national power distance *AMJ*, 48: 1171–1182; G. Verona, 1999, A resource-based view of product development, *AMR*, 24: 132–142.

[41] F. Sanna-Randaccio & R. Veugelers, 2007, Multinational knowledge spillovers with decentralized R&D, *JIBS*, 38: 47–63.

[42] UNCTAD, 2005, *World Investment Report 2005* (p. 136), New York and Geneva: United Nations/UNCTAD.

[43] This section draws heavily on Gupta & Govindarajan, 2004, *Global Strategy and Organization*.

[44] H. Greve, 2003, A behavioral theory of R&D expenditures and innovations, *AMJ*, 46: 685–702.

[45] U. Andersson, M. Forsgren, & U. Holm, 2002, The strategic impact of external networks, *SMJ*, 23: 979–996; D. Gerwin & J. Ferris, 2004, Organizing new product development projects in strategic alliances, *OSc*, 15: 22–37; J. Hagedoorn & G. Duysters, 2002, External sources of innovative capabilities, *JMS*, 39: 167–188; A. Lam, 2003, Organizational learning in multinationals, *JMS*, 40: 673–703; W. McCutchen, P. Swamida, & B. Teng, 2004, R&D risk-taking in strategic alliances, *MIR*, 44: 53–67; M. Mol, P. Pauwels, P. Matthyssens, & L. Quintens, 2004, A technological contingency perspective on the depth and scope of international outsourcing, *JIM*, 10: 287–305; R. Narula & G. Duysters, 2004, Globalization and trends in international R&D alliances, *JIM*, 10: 199–218; R. Reagans & B. McEvily, 2003, Network structure and knowledge transfer, *ASQ*, 48: 240–267; F. Rothaermel & D. Deeds, 2004, Exploration and exploitation alliances in biotechnology, *SMJ*, 25: 201–221; W. Shermata, 2004, Competing through innovation in network markets, *AMR*, 29: 359–377.

[46] J. Spencer, 2003, Firms' knowledge-sharing strategies in the global innovation system, *SMJ*, 24: 217–233; K. Laursen & A. Salter, 2006. Open for innovation, *SMJ*, 27: 131–150; M. Yamin & J. Otto, 2004, Patterns of knowledge flows and MNE innovative performance, *JIM*, 10: 239–258.

[47] K. Asakawa & A. Som, 2008, Internationalizing R&D in China and India, *APJM*, 25 (in press); Q. Yang & C. Jiang, 2007, Location advantages and subsidiaries' R&D activities, *APJM*, 24: 341–358.

[48] I. Bjorkman, W. Barner-Rasmussen, & L. Li, 2004, Managing knowledge transfer in MNCs, *JIBS*, 35: 443–455; R. Mudambi & P. Navarra, 2004, Is knowledge power? *JIBS*, 35: 385–406.

[49] G. Szulanski & R. Jensen, 2006, Presumptive adaptation and the effectiveness of knowledge transfer, *SMJ*, 27: 937–957; R. Nobel & J. Birkinshaw, 1998, Innovation in MNCs, *SMJ*, 19: 479–496.

[50] T. Atamer & D. Schweiger, 2003, Transnational horizontal project teams, *JWB*, 38: 81–83; S. Chevrier, 2003, Cross-cultural management in multinational project groups, *JWB*, 38: 141–149; K. Goodall & J. Roberts, 2003, Only connect, *JWB*, 38: 150–160; K. Lagerstrom & M. Andersson, 2003, Creating and sharing knowledge within a transnational team, *JWB*, 38: 84–95; R. Lunnan & T. Barth, 2003, Managing the exploration vs. exploitation dilemma in transnational "bridging teams," *JWB*, 38: 110–126; M. Maznevski & K. Chudoba, 2000, Building space over time, *OSc*, 11: 473–492; A. Mendez, 2003, The coordination of globalized R&D activities through project teams organization, *JWB*, 38: 96–109; J. Salk & M. Brannen, 2000, National culture, networks, and individual performance in a multinational management team, *AMJ*, 43: 191–202; D. Schweiger, T. Atamer, & R. Calori, 2003, Transnational project teams and networks, *JWB*, 38: 127–140; M. Zellmer-Bruhn & C. Gibson, 2006, Multinational organization context, *AMJ*, 49: 501–518.

[51] W. Cohen & D. Levinthal, 1990, Absorptive capacity, *ASQ*, 35: 128–152; J. Hong, R. Snell, & M. Easterby-Smith, 2006, Cross-cultural influences on organizational learning in MNCs, *JIM*, 12: 408–429; J. Jansen, F. Bosch, & H. Volberda, 2005, Managing potential and realized absorptive capacity, *AMJ*, 48: 999–1015; P. Lane, B. Koka, & S. Pathak, 2006, The reification of absorptive capacity, *AMR*, 31: 833–863; D. Minbaeva, T. Pedersen, I. Bjorkman, C. Fey, & H. Park, 2003, MNC knowledge transfer, subsidiary absorptive capacity, and HRM, *JIBS*, 34: 586–599.

[52] P. Ensign, 2002, Reputation and technological knowledge sharing among R&D scientists in the multidivisional, multinational firm, PhD dissertation, University of Montreal; H. Kim, J. Park, & J. Prescott, 2003, The global integration of business functions, *JIBS*, 34: 327–344; I. Manev & W. Stevenson, 2001, Nationality, cultural distance, and expatriate status, *JIBS*, 32: 285–304; S. O'Donnell, 2000, Managing foreign subsidiaries, *SMJ*, 21: 525–548; M. Subramaniam & N. Venkatraman, 2001, Determinants of transnational new product development capability, *SMJ*, 22: 359–378.

[53] A. Inkpen & E. Tsang, 2005, Social capital, networks, and knowledge transfer, *AMR*, 30: 146–165; T. Kostova & K. Roth, 2003, Social capital in multinational corporations and a micro-macro model of its formation, *AMR*, 28: 297–317; M. Subramanian & M. Youndt, 2005, The influence of intellectual capital on the types of innovation capabilities, *AMJ*, 48: 450–463.

[54] M. W. Peng & Y. Luo, 2000, Managerial ties and firm performance in a transition economy, *AMJ*, 43: 486–501.

[55] R. Edwards, A. Ahmad, & S. Moss, 2002, Subsidiary autonomy, *JIBS*, 33: 183–192; T. Kostova & K. Roth, 2002, Adoption of an organizational practice by subsidiaries of multinational corporations, *AMJ*, 45: 215–233.

[56] B. Ambos & B. Schlegelmilch, 2007, Innovation and control in the MNC, *SMJ*, 28: 473–486; B. Allred & K. S. Swan, 2004, Contextual influences on international subsidiaries' product technology strategy, *JIM*, 10: 259–286; M. Geppert, K. Williams, & D. Matten, 2003, The social construction of contextual rationalities in MNCs, *JMS*, 40: 617–641; J. Medcof, 2001, Resource-based strategy and managerial power in networks of internationally dispersed technology units, *SMJ*, 22: 999–1012; K. Moore, 2001, A strategy for subsidiaries, *MIR*, 41: 275–290; W. Newburry, 2001, MNC interdependence and local embeddedness influences on perception of career benefits from global integration, *JIBS*, 32: 497–507; J. Taggart, 1998, Strategy shifts in MNC subsidiaries, *SMJ*, 19: 663–681.

[57] J. Birkinshaw, 2000, *Entrepreneurship in the Global Firm* (p. 8), London: Sage.

[58] S. Feinberg, 2000, Do world product mandates really matter? *JIBS*, 31: 155–167.

[59] This section draws heavily on J. Birkinshaw & S. Terjesen, 2003, The customer-focused multinational, in Birkinshaw et al. (eds.), *The Future of the Multinational Company* (pp. 115–127).

INTEGRATIVE CASE 3.1

DENTEK'S UK DECISION

Anne D. Smith and Amber Galbraith Quinn
University of Tennessee

On a lovely spring day in 2003, John Jansheski, CEO of DenTek (http://www.dentekoralcare.com), hung up the phone after a conversation with the distributor of his dental products in the United Kingdom. The distributor had given Jansheski (known as "J. J.") a choice: a formal joint venture (JV) or potential termination of their annual distribution agreement. J. J. leaned back in his chair and thought about the past 21 years with the company he had created. J. J. realized that his domestic strategy was in place, growing at a 30% annual rate (1986–2003) and yielding over $50 million in retail sales. DenTek and J. J. had faced large consumer products firms and lawsuits to build significant shelf space in major US discount and drugstore retailers. DenTek had continued to create a steady stream of new dental product innovations for consumers. However, J. J. was at a crossroads in his global strategy; specifically, should he enter into a JV with his UK distributor or not?

Background

Dr. Jansheski, J. J.'s father, was a successful dentist in northern California. He had developed an innovative design for a metal tartar removal device, called the Dental Pik. His patients had been asking for scalers to clean their teeth at home. Dr. Jansheski thought this product could be sold through dental offices and drugstores. J. J.'s older brother developed a business plan for manufacturing and marketing this product. Soon after, J. J.'s brother had the Dental Pik manufactured in the United States. With costs of about $2 per pick and a sales price to retailers of $4, consumers paid around $8 for the metal pick product. The largest retail contract was with Long's Drug Store for 13 of its Arizona stores. Yet, the business was floundering with limited end-user sales and significant business overhead. J. J.'s brother only generated $13,000 in sales, with no reorders from the drug chain. He eventually walked away from the business.

J. J. had undertaken a variety of endeavors while attending College of Marin, such as being a disc jockey, cleaning boats, and distributing HerbaLife. When his father asked him to take over the family business, J. J. requested 50% equity holdings and was given a 25% interest. "In 1985, I decided to give it a go . . . but I did not know much about running a business."[1] J. J. took over management of DenTek with $150,000 of debt and a product design (with no patent) that he believed needed a change. At this time, J. J.'s office consisted of two 6-foot-by-9-foot storage units, which he referred to as a "doublewide." He still recalls entering the "office" for the first time, full of fear.

With no sales during J. J.'s first six months, he quickly realized that the metal instrument "was a scary-looking product." Facing skeptical distributors, J. J. set out to design a plastic version of the Dental Pik. He moved the manufacturing to China before the launch of a national ad campaign. However, he was working with only a $30,000 line of credit, which funded developing a mold for the Dental Pik plastic handle, buying out a DenTek partner,[2] building inventory, launching

This case was written by Professor Anne D. Smith and graduate student Amber Galbraith Quinn (University of Tennessee). The purpose of the case is to serve as a basis for classroom discussion rather than to illustrate the effective or ineffective management of issues related to a medium-sized entrepreneurial firm and its international expansion.

an advertising campaign, and traveling to Asia to set up manufacturing. Back in the States, Jansheski developed low-cost advertising with product ads featuring his girlfriend in the *National Enquirer* magazine. Over time, his marketing and new product efforts led to the allocation of more drugstore shelf space to DenTek's products. By the late 1980s, retail sales approached $2 million.

Throughout the late 1980s and the 1990s, J. J. continued to develop new products (Table 1) and expand into new US retail outlets. His most popular product was the plastic disposable flosser. Yet, his successes were somewhat tempered by lawsuits from larger consumer products firms. Around 1995, DenTek faced a lawsuit from Butler, a leading firm that marketed a "G-U-M" product related to DenTek's Gingibrush electric toothbrush. J. J. described this experience:

> We were about $3 million in sales . . . If we had lost, it would have bankrupted us . . . We settled, after a $75,000 legal bill, and agreed not to trademark or contest the suit . . . after all, Butler was part of a multibillion dollar global consumer products firm.

After the Butler lawsuit, Jansheski faced a lawsuit from Johnson & Johnson in 1999, which alleged trademark infringement by a new DenTek product called Temparol. Temparol was a dental repair product that a consumer placed into a missing filling until a dentist could be seen. J. J. recounted to a business class in 2006, "After $150,000 in legal fees, we settled . . . we were spanked." DenTek renamed the product Temparin.[3]

In 1999, J. J. decided to relocate his company from Petaluma, California, to Maryville, Tennessee. The decision to move to the East Coast "was a no-brainer,"

TABLE 1 TIME LINE OF DENTEK PRODUCT DEVELOPMENT

Year Introduced	Product Name	Product Description
1984	Dental Pik	Consumers clean tartar between teeth
1990–1996	Temparin, Tempanol, and Gingibrush	Temporary filling material; electric toothbrush
1997	Floss Picks	Plastic flossers for consumers; in bags of 30 or 60
1999	Breath Remedy	Line of products to address the source of bad breath; includes mouth rinse, tongue sprays, tongue drops, and tongue cleaners
1999	Dental First Aid	Complete tooth pain and repair products for emergencies and the medicine cabinet
2000	Thin Set	First temporary cap and crown cement for consumers
2001	Explorer	Interdental pick for removing food between teeth
2002	Silk Floss Picks	For consumers with tight teeth, a hassle-free flossing experience
2002	Maximum Hold Temparin	10 times stronger hold than Temparin product
Products under development in 2003		
	Silk Easy Angle Floss Picks	For hard-to-reach back teeth
	Individually wrapped Silk Floss Picks	Easy on-the-go flossing
	Fun Flossers	With fluoride, for children
	evo Flossers	Longer reach flossers
	Narrow Brush Picks	Flossing made easier
	Wide Brush Picks	Cleaning around braces and bridges easier

according to J. J. "With 80% of our shipments heading east of the Mississippi, we needed to be closer to this base to reduce our distribution costs . . . We have saved at least $1 million in distribution by relocating to Tennessee." DenTek's facility includes a warehouse, a small assembly area, and offices for design staff, training, and executives. Its location in Maryville, Tennessee, puts DenTek in close proximity to major Interstate freeways and customers on the East Coast. "It was the most important financial decision we've ever made," even though J. J. had to replace most of his 40 employees from California.[4] With cheaper rent, taxes, and shipping costs, "we are putting all that money back into the company, and as a result, sales are now twice what they were. . . . It's helped us double the size of the company."[5] Construction had just been completed on a $1.7 million, 22,000 square foot addition that doubled the size of DenTek's Maryville facility, and plans were on the table for another 26,000 square foot addition.[6]

One consequence of the relocation was that J. J. lost or replaced all but one of his California executive team members, who had been primarily comprised of friends. As J. J. recounted, "Around 2001, I began to build a more professional management team, which was needed at this point."

Also in 1999, a serendipitous encounter at the National Association of Chain Drug Store trade show led to DenTek's early international expansion. There, J. J. met Dr. D.,[7] the owner of a British distributor of consumer products. Dr. D. was a successful plastic surgeon who also distributed his own line of facial products. After a year of conversations, visits, and negotiations, J. J. signed an agreement for Dr. D. to distribute DenTek products in the United Kingdom. By 2003, the distributor had built market presence for DenTek products at Boots, one of the largest drugstore chains in the UK. Dr. D. was a colorful character who J. J. stated "had a different perception of money . . . with many high-end sports cars to choose from in Beverly Hills." J. J. told a story about when Dr. D. chartered a jet to take Boots salespersons to see the Rockettes in Nashville. "This relationship over the past few years had gone swimmingly well . . . then he decided to push us to JV with him."

In 2001, J. J. hired an "aggressive" vice president (VP) of international sales. J. J. explained what happened during this part of DenTek's international push:

> The VP proceeded to open offices in Brazil, Mexico, and Germany in order to build a retail presence. We got greedy to go direct and boost our margins. We decided to bypass distribution to build retail. This was one of the dumbest decisions I've made. We lost over $1 million in three markets in two years. We had no sales in Mexico or Brazil, and I felt like every government official had their hand out to be greased. Germany was not a total loss; we still do some business there . . . but it is difficult.

By 2003, the VP and J. J. were both unhappy and decided to part ways.

Nature of Competition

DenTek faced formidable competitors both at home and abroad. As J. J. explained, "The US is the most difficult and competitive market for consumer packaged goods." This $4 billion market is the battleground of large multinational firms such as Johnson & Johnson, Butler, Listerine, and Procter & Gamble with Oral B.[8] These companies had deep pockets and were fierce competitors. J. J. was keenly watching the lawsuit between Johnson & Johnson and Listerine; Johnson & Johnson questioned Listerine's claim that its mouthwash was as effective in fighting gum disease as flossing. Jansheski was certainly aware that these consumer products firms were capable of targeting his products with versions of their own. The large companies' ability to quickly replicate products and to support them with large marketing budgets was one reason J. J. continued to innovate.

Despite the threat from large companies, J. J. stated that he was most worried about "the smaller scrappy passionate companies . . . The large multinationals, however . . . are not going to get down and fight." He continued, "I can predict the price that Johnson & Johnson is going to offer on their dental products, they own certain segments . . . The smaller scrappy ones are more unpredictable . . . [yet] even though we are aware of others, we focus on our show."

DenTek had a leading market share in many dental accessories and sold its products through Wal-Mart, Target, Walgreens, Rite Aid, Kmart, CVS, and other retail chains. DenTek was the category leader in disposable flossers, with over 500 million units packaged and sold and an estimated 32% US market share (see Table 2). Because many of these major retailers prefer not to deal with multiple suppliers, DenTek helps manage the category of dental accessories for several large retail chains.

One benefit to competing in the dental accessories industry is the positive growth trends due to Baby Boomer demographics. Sales of commodity dental products were flat, but "specialty segments"—particularly high-end products that offer increased cosmetic and therapeutic benefits—are driving category growth overall. "As Baby Boomers come into mid-life, they are at the prime age for periodontal disease, expanding the market for products that address this condition."[9]

Current Dilemma

In 2003, Jansheski was faced with a difficult decision related to his UK distributor. "Right now I make, let's say, 25 cents on each product that I sell to my distributor. He in turn buys the product from me for 50 cents and sells for $1 to Boots, who then retails for $2." This

TABLE 2 MASS MARKET SALES (EXCLUDING WAL-MART): DENTAL ACCESSORIES CATEGORY

Top Brands	2003 Dollar Sales (in millions)	2003 Unit Volume (in millions)
DenTek (flossers only)	13.1	4.8
Water Pik	8.6	0.3
Oral-B	7.7	2.8
Doctor's Nightguard	6.1	0.3
Glide	5.8	1.2
Butler G-U-M	5.3	1.9
Stim-U-Dent	4.7	2.0
Oral B super floss	4.6	1.4
Butler Proxabush	3.9	1.3
Butler G-U-M Proxabrush	3.6	1.4

Source: *Chain Drug Review*, 2003, 25 (10), June 6: 223.

arrangement had worked well for many years. Yet, Dr. D. was adamant that their short-term yearly distribution arrangement was to end in a few months unless they could work out a JV. Additionally, Dr. D. wanted the rights to distribute to the entire EU. J. J. pulled a legal pad out of his desk and began to consider aspects of this important decision that he would discuss with his president at tomorrow's meeting.

Case Discussion Questions

1. Should DenTek abandon global expansion efforts right now to more fully concentrate on new product innovations against marketing powerhouses in the United States? Is now the right time in DenTek's growth to build market share outside the United States?

2. What caused DenTek's independent international expansion (2001–2003) into Brazil, Mexico, and Germany to fail? If J. J. decides to pursue overseas opportunities again, what type of structure or safeguards should he put in place to ensure that it is not a repeat of its previous failed effort?

3. What are the pros and cons of entering into a JV with Dr. D.'s company? What are the risks associated with a 50/50 JV, a majority JV (in which DenTek has majority equity interest), or a minority JV (in which DenTek has minority equity interest)? What aspects are critical to include in JV legal documentation? What are the risks associated with passing on this JV proposal?

4. Which of the abovementioned options related to international expansion would enhance DenTek's attractiveness to a potential buyer (acquirer)? Why?

[1] Quotes without a linked publication are from interviews with or lectures by John Jansheski during 2006 and 2007.

[2] During the 1980s, J. J. bought out all previous partners in the DenTek business, including his father. He has not had outside investors since that time.

[3] DenTek currently markets a temporary filling product, launched in 1996. See Table 1 for DenTek's product innovation time line.

[4] From http://www.entrepreneur.com/magazine/entrepreneur/2005/september/79358.html.

[5] From http://www.entrepreneur.com/magazine/entrepreneur/2005/september/79358.html.

[6] J. Stiles, 2003, New product helps DenTek expand plant, add jobs, *Knoxville News Sentinel*, June 5: C1.

[7] Name disguised.

[8] In January 2005, Gillette (and its Oral B brand) was purchased by Procter & Gamble.

[9] *Drug Store News*, October 8, 2001.

INTEGRATIVE CASE 3.2

THE LG-NORTEL JOINT VENTURE

Bill Turner, Joe Bentz, Steve Caudill, Christine Pepermintwalla, and Ken Williamson
University of Texas at Dallas

Peter MacKinnon, chairman of the recently formed LG-Nortel joint venture (JV), is back in his Dallas office after two hard weeks in South Korea (hereafter Korea). Next week, he is off to Europe for a well-deserved vacation with his family. In his office, MacKinnon surrounds himself with family photos, awards, and souvenirs from around the world. He is highly dedicated to the LG-Nortel JV and currently spends two weeks each month in Korea. When in Dallas, he leaves the headquarters in Korea in the capable hands of LG-Nortel JV CEO Jae Ryung Lee.

MacKinnon tackles his work and personal challenges with 100% dedication, as shown in his drive to make the LG-Nortel JV a success. He has a passion for life and is one of those executives who "works hard and plays hard." This is evident by the ice hockey stick sitting an arm's-length from his desk chair and the fact that he plays in three hockey leagues when visiting Korea. Finding a balance between work and personal life remains a challenge with the current heavy workload and extended travel to Korea each month.

Having traveled around the globe and having been an expatriate in Europe previously, MacKinnon is no stranger to international travel. He describes some interesting cultural aspects of doing business in Korea and highlights "respect" and "knowledge for the cultural differences" as important. He is keenly aware of the dynamics of the corporate culture in Korea and its implications on the success of the JV, given the mixed management of Koreans and a few North Americans living in Korea.

With MacKinnon's new boss, Nortel CEO Mike Zafirovski (Mike Z.), driving for management excellence, there is little room for missteps. MacKinnon is currently a very hands-on full-time chairman as demanded by Mike Z. The LG-Nortel JV must satisfy the needs of both the corporate parents (Nortel and LG) as the conduit for their telecom products and also be Nortel's gateway to the Korean telecom market. In addition, MacKinnon must lead and leverage a highly capable and innovative group of Korean engineers to develop new products for the advanced Korean and worldwide telecom markets.

This is MacKinnon's first time chairing a board of directors (see his bio in Figure 1). Managing this new JV, with a multicultural management, is presenting a number of challenges. For the first six months since the JV was established, MacKinnon has been spending 16-hour days tackling a number of "start-up" problems. He has been driving this mixed cultural team to resolve the recent tactical and operational issues and is working to resolve cross-cultural and management tension. Lately, he has been contemplating how and when to shift to become more strategic and start to be a part-time chairman. His main challenge is how to establish the JV for success in the future and be the strategic part-time chairman that he wants and needs to be.

LG Electronics Background

LG (Korea Stock Exchange: 6657.KS) was established in Korea as a private company in 1958 as GoldStar. As a global leader in home appliances, digital media devices, and display and information and communications products, LG has more than 64,000 employees globally and its 2005 revenues reached over $16.9 billion (unconsolidated). It is comprised of 30 companies with about 130 overseas subsidiaries. As part of the LG corporate conglomerate, LG Electronics's goal is to enable the intelligent networking of digital products that will make consumers' lives better than ever.[1]

Nortel Background

Nortel (NYSE: NT; Toronto TSX: NT) is a 110-year-old Canadian company doing business in more than 150 countries with 2005 revenues of $10.52 billion. Nortel's portfolio of solutions for telecommunications network providers, government, and enterprises includes end-

This case was written by Bill Turner, Joe Bentz, Steve Caudill, Christine Pepermintwalla, and Ken Williamson (University of Texas at Dallas, EMBA 2007) under the supervision of Professor Mike Peng. The purpose of the case is to serve as a basis for classroom discussion rather than to illustrate the effective or ineffective handling of an administrative situation. The authors thank Mr. Peter MacKinnon for his time and for sharing his expertise and experiences. The views expressed are those of the authors (in their private capacity as EMBA students) and do not necessarily reflect those of the individuals and organizations mentioned.

FIGURE 1 PETER MACKINNON BIO

Peter MacKinnon is chairman, LG-Nortel JV and president, LG-Nortel Business Unit—a joint venture between Nortel and LG Electronics. In these roles, MacKinnon is responsible for magnifying the success of the joint venture by scaling its products into Nortel's global channels as well as coordinating the LG-Nortel and Nortel portfolios across Nortel's various business units. The portfolio includes Enterprise products, with a renewed focus on SMB, UMTS evolution to LTE, WiBro/WiMAX, and Wireline/IPTV.

Prior to this position MacKinnon was president, GSM/UMTS Networks for Nortel. With a global customer base in more than 100 countries, he was responsible for R&D, product management, sales, marketing, and customer support.

MacKinnon's previous roles at Nortel include: senior vice president, Wireless Networks Americas; vice-president and general manager of the Asia-Pacific wireless business unit and global responsibility for the product management and marketing efforts of Nortel's GSM networks business. He has also held positions in the North American SONET Transport Group—in product management, marketing, operations, and design.

MacKinnon is a director on the board of Guangdong Nortel Telecommunications Equipment Ltd (GDNT) in China.

MacKinnon earned an MBA as well as a BS degree in electrical engineering from McGill University in Montreal, Canada. He is fluent in English and French and enjoys experiencing different cultures. He also plays golf, ice hockey, and tennis. Mr. MacKinnon is married and has two daughters and a son.

Source: http://www.nortel.com/corporate/exec/mackinnon.html (accessed July 5, 2006).

to-end broadband (packet and optical), Voice over IP, multimedia services/applications, wireless networks, and wireless broadband networks.[2]

Nortel's Experience in New Markets

Expanding into new global markets, Nortel has had its share of successes and failures. Some expansions were accomplished through acquisition of wholly owned subsidiaries such as the acquisition of Matra in France and others through JVs. MacKinnon discussed one particular learning experience where Nortel entered into a 50-50 JV. Unfortunately, voting was deadlocked; the JV became ineffective and had to be shut down.

In 1998, with a presence in North America and Europe, Nortel entered into the rapidly expanding South Korean telecom market. This soon turned into a valuable lesson on how *not* to do business in Asia (through an understanding of the local culture but not of the "business culture"). Nortel assumed that to do business in Korea, all you needed was a few local Korean employees in a local office. This was a vital misunderstanding. MacKinnon summed up the challenge by saying, "You can't just hire a few Koreans and call yourself a Korean company; it's all about relationships." This first attempt was not successful, and Nortel backed out of South Korea.

Telecom in South Korea: An Industry Overview

South Korea has the 10th largest economy in the world and has one of the leading telecommunications infrastructures in the world. This was not true just a mere 30 years ago. In the late 1970s, with a population of 40 million, there was barely one phone line to every 160 persons. Today, there is nearly one phone line to every two persons. However, the demand for phone line service is in decline as more advanced services eliminate the need for basic phone lines. Mobile technology has advanced rapidly, and the subscriber base has grown to nearly 40 million with an increasing number of these subscribers using their service for wireless digital transfer.

Wireless Today in South Korea: An Accelerating Industry

South Korea's CDMA Network is the largest EVDO wireless network deployment in the world and has the most advanced early adopters with 75% user penetration. As of 2004, Korea already had 11 million subscribers using EVDO. Korea also boasts the most advanced data applications in the world, estimated to be two years ahead of North America. The government originally mandated CDMA wireless technology to be used in South Korea. However, recent mandates to the more widely adopted UMTS technology represent a major technology shift for the country and local equipment providers like LG.

The LG-Nortel Joint Venture

With the policy shift toward UMTS, LG was not prepared and did not have products for UMTS to meet these new government requirements. LG now found itself in need of a partner for UMTS products. Nortel had no footprint in the heavily competitive South Korean market since the 1998 retreat, and it needed a way to reenter South Korea. LGE was the leader of the Korean consumer electronics market. It also was a major global force in electronics, information, and communications products. Due to LGE's demonstrated innovative technology leadership position in Korea and Nortel's proven UMTS portfolio and worldwide reach, the mutual attraction was inevitable.

On August 17, 2005, LG and Nortel signed a definitive JV agreement with a contract closure target date of November 1, 2005. Nortel entered into the JV with a $145 million investment. For this investment, Nortel would receive ownership of 50% plus one share of the company and control a majority of positions on the board. Gaining 50% plus one share was a "deal breaker" for Nortel given the past experiences on 50-50 partnerships. MacKinnon was named chairman and Jae Ryung Lee would become CEO. Other key positions were filled accordingly with Nortel and LG executives (see Figure 2). The JV had over $500 million in sales in the first six months, but not without organizational and cultural issues to deal with.

Issues within the First Six Months

Of the 1,400 LG-Nortel JV employees, 1,350 are South Korean and 50 are American and Canadian. While building the JV organization, cultural differences surfaced immediately. A higher than normal attrition rate was seen in part as the result of placement of younger former Nortel employees over older former LG employees. This is not acceptable in Korean corporate culture, and thus, many Korean employees left. MacKinnon had also seen the cultural divide when a Korean male employee started holding his hand and confiding in him about some issues the Korean male employee was having. MacKinnon never pulled his hand away, heard the employee's message, and knew immediately that this kind of cultural exchange might happen to Americans and Canadians unaware or less tolerant of these differences in the future.

The burdens of implementing both US GAAP and Korean GAAP have taken their toll and created additional process and stress on the organization. In one instance, contract template issues caused revenue recognition problems, which in turn created a (financially) reported order backlog. The contract template issues were identified, and a plan to correct them was developed. Two contract templates accounted for 60% of the revenue with another 15 more accounting for the other 40% to be corrected. The implementation was now critical to finally recognizing the revenue needed to prove the JV was already a success to both parents, LG and Nortel.

Pre-JV, LGE had been mainly focused on Korea, concentrating on the requirements of the demanding high-growth and innovative local market. Now these highly qualified engineers needed to take a broader worldwide view of product development so products could be funneled back through Nortel's non-Korean markets.

Nortel canceled a major project within the JV as the project was just ramping up its development. This decision was made after the most recent planning and forecasting exercises used by Nortel had shown that the business case and market outlook would not provide the returns required by Nortel. Regardless of sunk costs for development by the JV, the project was canceled. The shock and awe felt by the Korean members of the JV were hard. They did not agree with this decision and could not understand why this first major project would be killed so soon into development. This caused major tension in the relationships with the LG and Nortel counterparts and with the Nortel corporate parent. CEO Lee started asking direct questions, such as "How could you do this?" and "Now why are we working together?"

With tensions mounting, small internal conflicts were happening in private. Then one day, in a public meeting, CEO Lee had a very emotional reaction and vented upon MacKinnon many of Lee's frustrations of working with a North American company. Understanding this was not the norm for a Korean executive, MacKinnon listened intently to everything Lee had to say. Once Lee finished, MacKinnon recognized that he must respond and struck back with a ten-minute speech directed at Lee. Afterward, the Korean managers at the meeting asked MacKinnon to go for drinks, but he declined. Seeing that MacKinnon had his hockey equipment with him when leaving, they realized that he had other plans that evening. In fact, MacKinnon had not taken up their offer to go drinking on a number of other occasions and was always sure to have other plans.

FIGURE 2 LG-NORTEL JV LEADERSHIP TEAM

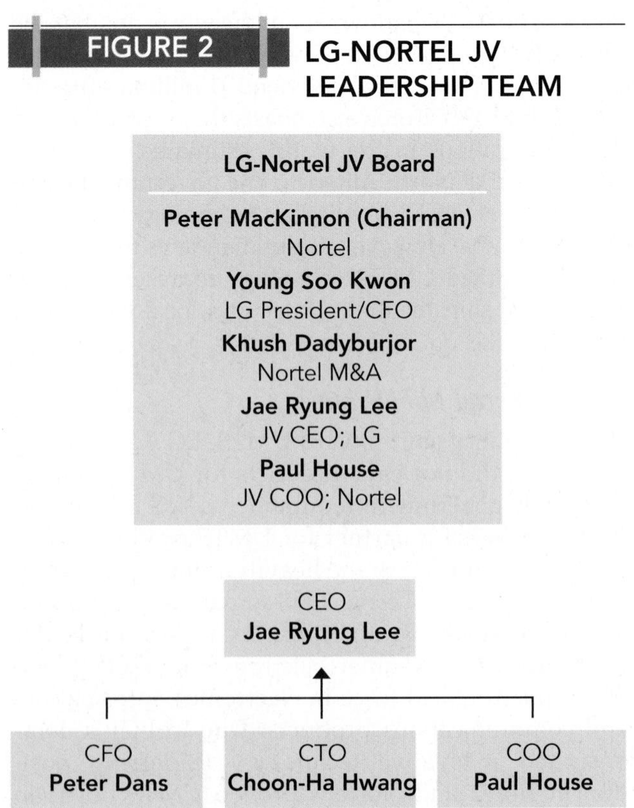

Source: JV IR Webcast May 17 v16.ppt, LG-Nortel, May 2006.

The Future Challenge of the LG-Nortel JV

MacKinnon is currently a full-time chairman as directed by Nortel CEO Mike Z. However, Mike Z. is also concerned about the possibility that MacKinnon might be burned out. MacKinnon himself fully recognizes that eventually he needs to gracefully retreat, become more strategic, and become a part-time chairman. To do this, he ponders how to set up the organization, processes, and people to be most effective. In addition, he must ensure success before trade talks among Korea, the United States, and Canada conclude, which would lower trade barriers and allow greater competition.[3] The big challenge for MacKinnon is: How can LG-Nortel be self-sustaining, and how can he pull away from the day-to-day operations of the JV?

Case Discussion Questions

1. Did Nortel make the right decision by (re)entering South Korea through a JV? What other market entry alternatives did Nortel have?
2. Discuss the advantages and disadvantages of having a strategic alliance such as the LG-Nortel JV. What are the unique advantages of controlling 50% equity plus one share?
3. What are the skills and attributes that successful JV managers would ideally possess? Does MacKinnon possess these skills and attributes?
4. What can MacKinnon do to reduce cross-cultural conflicts within the JV?
5. What can Nortel and LG do to improve the odds for the success of this JV?

[1] LGE website: http://us.lge.com/about/company/c_profile.jsp.

[2] Nortel website: http://www.nortel.com/corporate/index.html.

[3] E. Ramstad, 2006, In US-Korea free-trade talks, tense mood highlights the stakes, *Wall Street Journal*, July 11: A6.

INTEGRATIVE CASE 3.3

OCEAN PARK CONFRONTS HONG KONG DISNEYLAND

Donald Liu
University of Washington

Michael N. Young
Hong Kong Baptist University

In 2006, Thomas Mehrmann, CEO of Ocean Park, Hong Kong's 28-year-old, homegrown amusement park, faced a series of challenges. In September 2005, the Walt Disney Company had opened Hong Kong Disneyland—the third Disneyland to ever open outside the United States. Until then, Ocean Park had been the only amusement park in Hong Kong and had operated under monopoly conditions. Now it faced a competitor with very deep pockets that was legendary for its world-renowned innovation, unparalleled service, and ruthless competitiveness.

The dazzling commencement ceremony of Hong Kong Disneyland had taken place on September 12, 2005. Pundits had begun speculating as to what the "Disney effect" would be for Ocean Park. Several of Disney's characters, like Mickey Mouse, Donald Duck, and Winnie the Pooh, were household names all over the world, including Hong Kong. With Disney's legendary "imagineering," the company was cranking out amazing new animated characters that debuted in movies, making them well known by the time visitors encountered them in the parks. All of this made Ocean Park's mascot, "Mr. Whiskers" (Figure 1), look relatively tired and wimpy by comparison.

It was not that Ocean Park did not have support, as it was clearly the hometown favorite. Many local people were sympathetic to Ocean Park's position, as it seemed like a classic David versus Goliath competition. Ocean

This case was written by Donald Liu (University of Washington) and Michael N. Young (Hong Kong Baptist University). The initial research and an initial draft of this case were completed by Derek Au, Karen Hung, Crystal Wong, Marty Yam, and Olivia Yau as a course assignment at the Chinese University of Hong Kong under the direction of Professor Michael Young. The purpose of the case is to serve as a basis for classroom discussion rather than to illustrate either effective or ineffective handling of an administrative situation. We wish to acknowledge the help of Mr. Thomas Mehrmann, CEO of Ocean Park, for contributing his valuable time to give this case nuances that otherwise would be lacking.

FIGURE 1 OCEAN PARK'S MR. WHISKERS DURING THE SARS OUTBREAK

© Christian Keenan/ Stringer/ Getty Images

Park had been a long-time favorite of several generations of Hong Kong parents and children. Ocean Park, the clear underdog in the upcoming battle, had become a fixture of Hong Kong's cultural heritage. Disneyland, playing the part of Goliath, represented the quintessential faceless corporate chain set out to destroy the local cultural icon. But the fact was that, by 2006, Ocean Park was beginning to look and feel tired and shabby, and its attractions paled when compared with the glitz and glamour of Disney with its cosmopolitan appeal and reputation for creating magical experiences.

Would Ocean Park be able to survive intense competition with Disneyland? Mehrmann and the management team knew that they faced severe challenges. How should they attempt to compete against this potentially devastating rival? Were there opportunities that the management team was overlooking?

Ocean Park's History at a Glance

Ocean Park opened in 1977 with thrill rides and an aquarium. Its construction was funded by the Hong Kong Jockey Club with profits earned from horse racing. The land for Ocean Park was provided by the colonial government. The park was situated on the southern side of Hong Kong Island, not far from the central business district. By 2006, the park was a major tourist attraction in Hong Kong and one of the world's leading amusement parks and oceanariums. Its vision was to be the world leader in providing excellent guest experiences in an amusement park environment connecting people with nature.[1]

By 1987, Ocean Park ended its relationship with the Hong Kong Jockey Club and became an independent statutory body with a board of directors appointed by the Hong Kong government. Since then, as a nonprofit but financially self-sustaining entity, Ocean Park had been owned by the Hong Kong government, supported by the Home Affairs Bureau and the Tourism Board, and managed by the Ocean Park Corporation. In June 2005, the park achieved the highest recorded attendance in its history and welcomed the four millionth visitor in a year. Compared to the prior year, overall visitor attendance increased by 9% in 2004–2005, topping 4.03 million. Gross revenues grew 12% year on year and were HK$684 million in 2005, giving the park a surplus of HK$119.5 million and making it the highest surplus on record for the park.[2] By 2006, more than 60 million people had visited the park since its inception.

Past Challenges

It had not always been easy sailing for Ocean Park. The Asian financial crisis contributed to four consecutive years of losses from 1999 to 2002. In 2002, Ocean Park lost HK$80 million. This was a difficult period, and there was even some talk of closing it down. To make matters worse, the outbreak of Severe Acute Respiratory Syndrome (SARS) in 2003 greatly affected tourism in Hong Kong. Ocean Park lost an additional HK$60 million during a three-month period in 2003 because of SARS. (Kids in Figure 1 wore masks in fear of SARS.)

The park's poor performance was not due entirely to external factors. The park had failed to innovate, and the characters, rides, and marine exhibits were beginning to look dated and shabby. With near monopoly conditions, the management at the time had become content with the status quo. Paul Pei, the sales and marketing director of Ocean Park in 2006, said of the park before the reengineering that "customers did not understand and did not like what they were paying for." Nor did the park establish a winning brand image or corporate logo. Human resource management (HRM) practices had also failed to keep up with the times. Most staff members at the park were unskilled workers with long hours, low pay, and monotonous jobs that made turnover a problem. In Hong Kong, tourism workers were highly mobile. As sales continued to slide, management became increasingly aware of the need for a renovation of the park's brand image, HRM, and operations.

Brand Repositioning

In 2000, Ocean Park took on a program of reengineering, which consisted of brand repositioning and product updates. By 2005, the park turned the corner from deficit to surplus.

In Asia, a lack of strong brand image often allows firms to move quickly from one industry to another. However, this can be a hindrance to higher value added, fast growth firms.[3] One of the biggest problems of Ocean Park was the unattractive brand image, symbolized by the Seahorse logo. The nonsmiling seahorse was far from warm and cuddly to the impressionable younger customers of Ocean Park—it was hard for children to imagine snuggling with a seahorse. The logo did not cater to the park's visitors, among whom 35% were families who came to Ocean Park to entertain children. In addition, the seahorse was too small to strengthen the visitors' impression of Ocean Park. As Pei commented: "You could say that we had no brand image at all at that time."

Ocean Park set out to search for a new icon from all the animals available in the park. The sea lion got a nod from virtually everyone involved in the search. It always has a smile on its face, it is always waving a warm welcome with its flippers, and youngsters tend to have a favorable response to it. As a result, Ocean Park introduced a sea lion (named "Whiskers") as the park's mascot (see Figure 1). Whiskers was significantly different from the seahorse. Whiskers was cute with a smile, triggering a much warmer and easily approachable feeling to customers. Whiskers was also an animated character, which was more appealing to children. Sea lions are bigger and more common than seahorses, which further added to their appeal. For these reasons, customers could more readily recall Whiskers, and he left a deeper impression on visitors. Soon after Whiskers was introduced to the park in 2000, he became a household name in Hong Kong, particularly with children and families.

Revamping the Product Line

In addition to brand repositioning, the reengineering effort also revamped product line to better support the new brand image. The park brought in new attractions, such as the Abyss Turbo Drop thrill ride, which cost approximately HK$70 million. The park also began having festival events and activities to vary the atmosphere throughout the year. There were five seasonal holiday themes: Chinese New Year, Easter Holiday, Summer Holiday, Halloween, and Christmas. For example, during the Easter Holiday of 2005, Ocean Park organized an anniversary party for the pandas. Translated from Chinese, the party was called "Lovely Giant Panda Party." This event also served as a fund-raising event for the Hong Kong Society for Panda Conservation. By launching this party, Ocean Park hoped to further its image of social responsibility. During the hot Hong Kong summer, the park targeted teenagers by organizing several popular water-related activities, such as Water-war and Water-bomb. Around Halloween, the park put on horror shows and opened haunted houses. Of these events and activities, Halloween was the most successful. Since it was introduced, the number of visitors attending during the Halloween festival had increased from 54,000 to 120,000 by 2005.

By 2006, Ocean Park had also introduced a variety of interactive activities with animals, such as having meals with pandas and sea lions. In addition, "edutainment" programs gave visitors a chance to learn more about the animals and have fun at the same time. Examples included Honorary Giant Panda Keeper, Dolphin Encounter, Animal Meet and Greet, Animal Academy, and Panda Time Theatre. All of these carefully focused special events and seasonal promotions have encouraged customers to visit more often and stay longer with each visit, allowing the park to sell additional souvenirs and refreshments.

By attempting to provide high value for money, Ocean Park did not engage in glitzy, high-profile advertising and publicity stunts. Instead, the park tended to rely more on word of mouth to generate additional business. As Pei stated, "If customers believe that going to Ocean Park is worth their money and their time, then they would visit again with friends and family."

Employee Resistance to Change

After 28 years of operation, the work culture and practice among employees at Ocean Park had become entrenched. The reengineering program necessitated changing the remuneration system and other HRM policies. As is always the case, employees resisted the changes as they were naturally worried, anxious, and reluctant to face the new challenges. Nevertheless, management believed that all of these changes were vital. Thus, management had attempted to alter the corporate culture and secure employee buy-in through various reward policies. New incentive compensation was introduced that linked employee compensation to the financial performance of the park. Of course, if the park was forced to shut down, the employees would be out of a job. Given the four years (1999–2003) of deficits, this was a real enough possibility to motivate long-term employees to push for successful outcomes of the reengineering.

Management also tried to implement a culture of innovation. It was believed that continually adding new features and attractions would encourage visitors to return to the park. This was difficult because of the short life cycle of new fixed-asset attractions. For example, the new HK$70 million Abyss Turbo Drop thrill ride was initially a big success, but it was difficult to come up with an encore. As one visitor stated, "It is really exciting and attractive to try that new Abyss Turbo ride, however not for the second time." Ocean Park lacked the budget or space to provide a continuous supply of big-ticket thrill rides. Thus, management tried to find alternatives to attract repeat customers. It appeared that seasonal and special events were in a better position to provide novelty to get repeat visits.

Hong Kong Disneyland

Hong Kong Disneyland was set up as a joint venture between the Walt Disney Company and the Hong Kong SAR government. Located on Lantau Island, Disneyland could be reached in just 10 minutes from the new airport and in just 30 minutes from downtown Hong Kong. The Hong Kong park was based on other Disneyland parks and was divided into four parts, including Main Street USA, Fantasyland, Adventureland, and Tomorrowland. Guests visiting a Disneyland park could disengage from the real world and enter into a fairytale kingdom and the world of tomorrow in a flavor of adventure. In addition, two hotels were constructed to provide on-site lodging. At least 5.6 million people were expected to visit Hong Kong Disneyland during its first year of operation. The admission price was set at HK$295 during the week and HK$350 on weekends and peak days. This was acclaimed to be the least expensive among the five Disney parks around the world.[4] The construction of a second amusement park of Disney was scheduled to begin soon at the same resort. This was designed to upgrade Disneyland into a multiday destination to generate additional revenue from the hotels and restaurants as well as ticket sales.[5]

Competition between the Parks

Immediately after the inception, Disneyland captivated Hong Kong. Ocean Park was forced to devise a strategy to respond. There was the real possibility that Ocean Park would come up short in face-to-face competition. Yet, when comparing the two parks, one would be struck by the unique and different resources and competencies (Table 1). While Ocean Park did have thrill rides, its primary focus was on nature and wildlife with many animal-related activities. It had an Ocean Theatre that staged dolphin and sea lion shows every day. Furthermore, the world-class Atoll Reef, Shark Aquarium, Bird Aviary, and Pacific Pier gave visitors opportunities to view wild animals and beautiful scenery up close—a real rarity in urban Hong Kong. What's more, Ocean Park had distinct Chinese characteristics that reflected its roots in Hong Kong, a quintessentially Chinese city.

TABLE 1 OCEAN PARK VERSUS HONG KONG DISNEYLAND *

	Ocean Park	Hong Kong Disneyland
Date of Opening	January 1977	September 2005
Selling points	Sea world, marine life, and real animals: 35 rides and attractions	Disney cartoon characters, fantastic world, and famous American brand: 23 rides and attractions
Admission fee	Adult: HK$185 Child: HK$95	Adult: HK$295 (weekday), HK$350 (holiday) Child: HK$210 (weekday), HK$250 (holiday)
Area	215 acres	310 acres
Annual attendance	5 million	5.6 million expected
Daily maximum capacity	35,000 people	30,000 people
Number of jobs created	37,100	18,000
Economic contribution	HK$145 billion	HK$148 billion
Investment	HK$5.6 billion	HK$22.4 billion
Hotel	3 hotels	2 hotels

* In 2006, US$1 = HK$7.8.

On the other hand, Disneyland's core competence stems from its pioneering efforts in animation with the first widely appealing animated cartoon character (Mickey Mouse) and the first full-length animated movie (*Snow White and the Seven Dwarfs*). All of these gave Disney the ability to create fantasy and virtual situations, which center around the personalities of its numerous characters. Disney called this process "imagineering," and it attempted to leverage the benefits of animation into movies, TV shows, toys, and merchandise as well as amusement parks. Hong Kong Disneyland, like the other two Disney parks in Tokyo and Paris, allowed Disney to further leverage its core competence to international markets. Almost all of the Hong Kong Disneyland attractions build off of Disney's library of animated characters and movies. Buzz Lightyear inhabits Tomorrowland; Winnie the Pooh, Mickey Mouse, and Snow White inhabit Fantasyland; and Tarzan and Lion King inhabit Adventureland. These features of Disneyland target the same demographic set and customer base in Hong Kong as Ocean Park.

Ocean Park's Initial Reaction

In response to Disney's onslaught, Ocean Park proposed spending HK$5.55 billion, obtained from private and government loans, to revamp its well-worn product line. "We are receiving challenges from a formidable giant, and we need to survive," stated Allan Zeman, Ocean Park's board chairman. "The only way we can survive is to make our park world class," he added. Ocean Park's management was convinced that hesitation would be lethal in the increasingly competitive and globalized tourism market.

The ambitious HK$5.55 billion master plan included a new roller coaster, a subzero Ice Palace, and a 7.6 million liter aquarium with an underwater restaurant. An extra 33 animal species were to be brought in, and the number of rides was to double to 70. The redevelopment plan of Ocean Park also called for a two- or three-star hotel at the Mass Transit Railway (MTR) subway station and a five-star "boutique, spa-type" hotel atop the hillside with a 360-degree view of the surrounding sea and mountains. This would be head-on confrontation with Disney, which traditionally offered accommodations within its amusement parks. These improvements were planned on the assumption that the government would build a new MTR station near the amusement park. Zeman believed that an underground transport link to Ocean Park would help it compete with Disney, which had its own MTR station. According to the ambitious plan, Ocean Park was to have a new look to be divided into two major areas—Waterfront and Summit—which together would boast more than 70 distinctive attractions.

The management of Ocean Park hoped that the overhaul project would boost the number of annual visitors from 4.3 million in 2004 to 5 million by 2010. They also hoped that this would help to jump-start the government's plan to transform the nearby Aberdeen area into a Fisherman's Wharf attraction. Half the visitors were expected to be from mainland China, and 40% were predicted to be local visitors, with the rest coming from other areas. As to local economic benefits, Ocean Park's management hoped that the park would make a 0.5% contribution to Hong Kong's GDP in 2010.

Just as its name designated, Ocean Park hoped to position itself as a world-class marine-based attraction with real animals in this ambitious overhaul. The park would also continue in its efforts of wildlife conservation and would continue to supply visitors with experiences that combined entertainment and education. Ocean Park's management hoped that the redevelopment of the park would further strengthen its core competence in "real" nature in contrast to Disney's strengths in cartoon characters, castles, virtual reality, and fantasy. It was hoped that in this way, Ocean Park could differentiate itself more clearly from Disneyland.

Accordingly, the plan called for more animal species to be introduced to Ocean Park, and the lower area would be renamed the Waterfront. Three themed zones in the park would be Aqua City aquarium, Birds of Paradise aviary, and Whiskers Harbor family area. Ocean Park would be transformed into a spectacular, marine-based theme park with 33 amazing new species of animals, including whales, polar bears, and penguins. In addition to enhanced promotional activities in Hong Kong, the park planned to open offices in the major affluent urban areas of Guangzhou, Beijing, and Shanghai to attract more mainland visitors, who, it was hoped, would make up an ever larger portion of the park's clientele.

HRM Policy

Ocean Park had always experienced a shortage of service personnel. In Hong Kong, hotels, resorts, and amusement parks compete intensely for young, talented, educated employees. The situation is exacerbated because of the traditional gap in compensation between tourism and the more lucrative industries in Hong Kong such as banking and finance. Although tourism is a major industry and employer, many of the brightest university students hope to work in Hong Kong's financial markets. As Brian Ho, the HR manager of Ocean Park in 2005, stated, "Why, when they could be working in air-conditioned offices, would kids want to work outside on a hot Hong Kong day, dealing with mainland tourists?"[6]

In addition to competing with Ocean Park for customers, Disney would now be competing with Ocean Park for the best and brightest employees. Disney had hired 5,000 people, who were just the type of employees that Ocean Park desperately needed. Quite possibly, prospective employees would be lured to work in Disney, as it had the glitz and glamour of a large multinational corporation with better promotion opportunities and higher compensation. Thus, to add insult to injury, in addition to potentially grabbing its customers, Disney was poaching Ocean Park's best workers (!). As Hong Kong's tourism industry continued to rebound from the Asian financial crisis and the SARS scare, this fierce competition for talent was projected to increase in the foreseeable future.

To address this problem, Ocean Park had begun implementing a project of succession planning. Succession planning involved the whole process of recruiting employees, developing their skills and abilities, preparing them for different work roles, and motivating them to peak performance. In short, succession planning was hoped to enhance employee loyalty while helping them achieve personal growth. The park planned to begin hiring staff at three different levels; as the first tier experienced attrition, it was hoped the second tier and then the third tier could promptly fill in. Management believed that succession planning could play a significant role in realizing Ocean Park's future development goals because it would ensure that the park would be able to acquire the human resources needed to stay competitive.

Pricing Strategy

Although the proposed plan would be expensive, management hoped that Ocean Park could maintain its current ticket prices. "In particular, visitors from mainland China are very price sensitive but they represent a major source of Ocean Park's income," said Mehrmann. Management planned to keep Ocean Park's admission fee at HK$185 for an adult compared to Disney's price of HK$295 on weekdays and HK$350 on special days. "It is premature to discuss whether the price will increase or drop in 2010," said Mehrmann. "But it must be lower than Disneyland's."

Moreover, to boost the attendance frequency of local visitors, Ocean Park planned to introduce a unique SmartFun Annual Pass program, which entitled annual pass holders to unlimited admission for an entire year. There would be three different types of SmartFun Annual Passes: gold pass (HK$495 for adults and HK$250 for children aged 3 to 11), silver pass (HK$375 for adult and HK$188 for children aged 3 to 11), and full-time student pass (HK$295). It was hoped that this program would encourage annual pass holders to visit the park many more times. Ideally, annual pass holders would also bring along other visitors. It was hoped that both the lower price and SmartFun Annual Pass program could draw larger crowds in the face of Disneyland's growing popularity. The low-price policy, on the other had, was designed to immediately address the threat in the increasingly competitive tourism industry.

Potential Obstacles

The pending overhaul plan would have a decisive influence on Ocean Park's future. Still, as with any major reorientation of strategy, the ultimate outcomes were uncertain. A major factor in success would depend on implementation. Moreover, the new MTR station would be crucial for the plan, and its completion was not a foregone conclusion. While Ocean Park's location was quite convenient, the proposed MTR line extending to the southern region of Hong Kong island would be of immense benefit. The proposal for the new MTR station had to be approved by Hong Kong's legislative council, and the proposal faced opposition from the bus companies and taxi drivers. If the MTR station failed to get approval, Ocean Park might have to delay or even abort its overhaul plan.

In addition, the huge HK$5.55 billion investment would put a severe financial burden on Ocean Park, as half of the investment would come from bank loans. Ocean Park's profit in 2005 was only HK$119.5 million. It would be difficult to service the loans from ticket receipts and consumption in the park. Management was counting on the hotels to generate sufficient operating income for Ocean Park. The construction of the hotels required the approval of the Town Planning Board as well.

Finally, some environmental groups and animal rights activists were opposed to the importation of wild animals. Some of the park's favorite animals, including killer whales, penguins, and polar bears, do not do well in captivity in Hong Kong's hot and humid tropical climate. The life span of killer whales will be reduced by more than one-tenth, and polar bears often get infectious skin diseases. Bad publicity and feasibility problems in importing more animals could further thwart Ocean Park's ambitious plans.

Strategic Challenges Ahead

After 28 years of continuous operation, Ocean Park was becoming dated, and its appeal to tourists was dwindling. Regardless of Disney's threat, the park was in need of a revamp, whereas the outcome of this revamp was long term and potentially risky. As Mehrmann contemplated all of these factors, he could not help but feel somewhat frustrated. Ocean Park had finally turned the corner on four years of disastrous losses. But just when it appeared that the park's reengineering efforts were finally beginning to turn the corner, the park faced a new and unprecedented threat from Disneyland. As one analyst mused, "The hammerhead sharks [of Ocean Park] are now facing a fierce new competitor: Mickey Mouse [of Disneyland]." Despite some initial glitches and a less than perfect beginning, the new Disneyland loomed large over Hong Kong by 2006.

As of now, Ocean Park was able to hold its own. However, it was not clear what the long-term impact of this giant competitor would be. Ocean Park had become complacent in its position as the only amusement park in Hong Kong, but now it appeared drab and low tech in comparison with Disneyland. Disney had a proven 50-year track record. It created a magic world of cartoons and castles, backed by large merchandising and gigantic larger-than-life cartoon personalities. Initially after its opening, Ocean Park sat back and watched Disney grab its customers, as Ocean Park's attendance continued to drop. Furthermore, these two parks were competing for talent from the same HR pool; many former staff members of Ocean Park had already quit to join Disneyland.

Still, Ocean Park was not going to give up without a fight. As the industry was undergoing a far-reaching transformation, Hong Kong tourism was becoming more challenging and dynamic. Zeman, Mehrmann, and the other members of Ocean Park's management team were convinced that to remain competitive, Ocean Park could not be complacent. Still they were unsure about how to proceed. Was there enough room in Hong Kong for two large-scale amusement parks? What impact would the increasing number of mainland Chinese visitors have on Hong Kong's tourism industry? To what extent should Ocean Park imitate Disney and to what extent should the park attempt to complement Disney? Is it possible that a win-win situation could be achieved by the two parties? Whatever strategy the management team developed, Ocean Park was sure to face challenges.

Case Discussion Questions

1. When confronting multinationals (such as Disney), are local companies (such as Ocean Park) doomed?
2. In which cell in Chapter 11's Figure 11.4 would you put Ocean Park?
3. How does the influx of mainland Chinese tourists resulting from Disneyland affect the tourism industry in Hong Kong? Can Ocean Park capitalize on this new phenomenon? (Hint: Check out how other parks surrounding Disney, such as Sea World and Universal Studios, survive in Anaheim and Orlando.)
4. Should Ocean Park intensify or reduce head-on competition with Hong Kong Disneyland?
5. For whatever action Ocean Park chooses, how should Hong Kong Disneyland react?

[1] Information is partly from Ocean Park website at http://www.oceanpark.com.hk/eng/main/index.html.

[2] Information is partly from Ocean Park Annual Report 2004–2005. In 2006, the exchange rate was US$1 = HK$7.8.

[3] D. Ahlstrom, M. Young, E. S. Chan, & G. Bruton, 2004. Facing constraints to growth? Overseas Chinese entrepreneurs and traditional business practices in East Asia, *Asia Pacific Journal of Management*, 18: 263–273.

[4] D. Lee & K. Christensen, 2005, Translating Anaheim for Asia, *Los Angeles Times*, September 6: C1.

[5] The Disney report. Hong Kong Disneyland Resort to build second theme park (September 14, 2005) at http://www.disneylandreport.com/disneynews.html.

[6] J. Landreth, 2005, Hong Kong Disneyland opens with wealth of challenges, *Hollywood Reporter*, August 31.

INTEGRATIVE CASE 3.4

GLOBAL KNOWLEDGE MANAGEMENT AT ACCENTURE

Yongsun Paik and David Y. Choi
Loyola Marymount University

Accenture is one of the leading global management consulting firms. It is the largest of the pure consultancies with 75,000 consultants in 48 countries and net revenues of $11.8 billion.[1] Accenture is a particularly interesting company because, like other leading consulting companies, it considers knowledge, especially management knowledge, to be a core capability for achieving competitive advantage.[2]

Accenture has been a pioneer in knowledge management (KM): It was among the first companies to invest in KM on a global scale to collect past experiences and knowledge of its consultants. Competing directly with behemoths such as McKinsey & Company in strategic management and IBM in IT system implementation, Accenture's professionals needed a KM system that could help deliver high-quality solutions in a timely manner. Starting in the early 1990s, Accenture has spent more than $500 million on IT and people to support its overall KM strategy.[3] It continues to spend $250 million on R&D annually, which includes the payroll for its 500 KM staff.[4] As a result of the scale of its investments as well as its early achievements, Accenture has been perceived as a KM leader in its industry.

Knowledge Exchange (KX): Push for a Global Standardized KM Practice

At the heart of Accenture's corporate KM efforts was a sophisticated electronic repository system called the Knowledge Exchange (KX). KX housed approximately 7,000 individual databases grouped by industries and topics. KX's primary purpose was to store internally generated knowledge—i.e., client presentations, methodologies, best practices, and past proposals—that could be accessed by its employees using Lotus Notes and the Internet. The KM efforts were managed and promoted by 500 KM staff members around the globe. About 150 knowledge managers focused on the actual database administration at any one time. They synthesized, repackaged, and organized the content to be utilized by consultants.

KX was essential to a consultant's daily work. It was common for a consultant to access more than ten different databases on a particular day. Most new client projects began with a search of the KX for past experiences on similar projects. Strategy consultants reviewed analyses performed on similar projects to employ a similar methodology or even reproduce market research data. IT consultants looked for relevant methodologies and procedural templates to follow. Project managers often found best-in-class project plans for managing large engineering teams. Such past analyses, presentations, and project plans helped reduce planning time, minimize risk, and improve quality of the client deliverable. Our interviewees agreed that KX was the single most important knowledge capturing and transferring tool at Accenture.

Nevertheless, Accenture was unable to truly harness and transfer management knowledge across its global organization. What we found repeatedly in the organization were inconsistent and uneven levels of participation by its consultants. Post-project KX contributions, which had been made "mandatory" by the organization, were exceptionally low in East Asia compared to other regions including the US. Furthermore, the quality of submitted knowledge, which was often at the discretion of the consultant, was highly inconsistent in Asia.

The problems that Accenture's KM practice faced had little to do with technology, people, or the overall vision. Most had to do with a few very critical elements in the KM plan that Accenture appeared to have overlooked—probably because of its failure to fully appreciate the complexities and intricacies associated with knowledge management in a global context. Three major shortcomings in Accenture's global KM practice are outlined below.

Lack of Appreciation for Regional Knowledge

East Asian consultants were not as motivated as their US counterparts to make KX submissions. Some of the consultants and KM staff members in the East Asian region thought that their knowledge was not valued or appreciated by their colleagues in other regions. This per-

This case was written by Yongsun Paik and David Y. Choi (both at Loyola Marymount University, Los Angeles, California). It was adapted from Yongsun Paik and David Y. Choi, 2005, The shortcomings of a standardized global knowledge management system: The case study of Accenture, *Academy of Management Executive*, 19 (2): 81–84. © Academy of Management.

ception was troubling since most consultants we interviewed agreed that effective knowledge management was a cornerstone for Accenture in reaching its vision of becoming "one global firm." As one of the Asian managers effectively articulated: "Knowledge management is a symbol of being one global firm . . . If Accenture is 'one global firm,' it would be represented in how we share our knowledge across offices and regions . . . Otherwise, we are not a global company." However, while Asian consultants were active users of KX, they did not share their knowledge with the organization. The lack of KM submissions by Asian consultants and the unilateral flow of knowledge from the US or Europe to East Asia were hardly any indication of the effective global organization that Accenture was envisioning.

In fact, there was more to the one-sided flow of knowledge. It appeared to represent an underlying assumption in the organization—that good management knowledge came exclusively from the West. Several Asian interviewees expressed their view that Accenture as an organization was not interested in their expertise. Indeed, very few US consultants intentionally sought out management experiences from Asia. Our interviews confirmed that most US consultants were not aware of projects in Asia. Given the relatively smaller KM staff in Asia and little inquiry for their knowledge, many Asian consultants doubted that their knowledge was being sought or appreciated. The ones who submitted knowledge received no feedback that their input was being utilized by anyone.

To make matters worse, at Accenture, not unlike other large consulting firms, the East Asian offices felt somewhat isolated from the rest of the company. A wide range of factors limited direct interaction with headquarters, such as brief history of presence in Asia, lower salary structure among Asian employees relative to those of other regions, and small number of Asians in a position of seniority. Consequently, there was no clear conviction among the consultants in the region that Accenture was indeed "one global firm." Without a strong shared sense of ownership, few Asian consultants felt motivated to share their knowledge for the common good of the company.

This was an unfortunate situation. Asian consultants had valuable knowledge that could be shared with the rest of the organization. For example, there was little doubt that Japanese and Korean experiences with wireless communications could provide interesting marketing and new product knowledge to consultants in the US and Europe. Some project teams in the US would have benefited from the various market data collected in Asia. Accenture could have prevented the situation by showing more interest in or promoting the work of all regions, including East Asia. Furthermore, the company should have considered implementing a positive feedback mechanism to track how submitted knowledge was being used by the organization.

Inadequate Support for Challenges at the Local Offices

Most indications were that Accenture's global KM did not provide adequate support or resources for dealing with local and cross-cultural challenges. One clear, practical impediment to knowledge sharing was the language barrier. We observed Accenture's inability or unwillingness to address a fundamental issue with language—that most Asian documents had to be translated from the local language to English, the official company language, before submission to KX. Most consultants in Taipei, Beijing, Seoul, or Tokyo, while conversant in English, were not proficient in translating professional documents accurately in a timely manner. In addition, submissions required a consultant to fill out a standardized form and write an abstract in English.

As consultants were already hard-pressed for time during and between projects, they were reluctant to write or translate a lengthy document in an unfamiliar language upon completion of a demanding project. Consultants in the business areas (versus technology) found submissions particularly challenging as their materials (e.g., market analyses) tended to be more language intensive (than, e.g., software codes). When a KM staff member urged a consultant in Asia to submit a KM piece, a common response was, "Sorry, but my English is not very good." Without anyone helping them with the time-consuming work of translation, Asian consultants were apprehensive that their contributions with less than perfect English would not be appreciated or would even be used to their detriment. However, neither Accenture's headquarters nor the local offices took adequate action to have the translations resources available.

Accenture also faced cultural complexities that affected motivation for knowledge sharing in Asia in unexpected ways. For instance, in Japan, employees preferred to wait until instructed directly to make their own knowledge contributions, as submissions to the KX were associated with self-promotion. On the other hand, the situation was very different in China, where many of the consultants were puzzled about how knowledge sharing had any direct benefit to them personally. "Perhaps the consultants in the US are more interested in contributing," one interviewee in China suggested. "Chinese are in general not so interested in doing something that does not have direct benefit for themselves." As one Chinese KM officer remarked, "It is less common for Asians to write something and submit to KX on a voluntary basis." Again, Accenture provided little consideration or support for dealing with such local or cross-cultural challenges.

As an alternative to the existing process, Accenture could have shifted the KM responsibilities to consultants themselves.[5] Thus, the push for submission would have come not from corporate KM staff but from fellow consultants whom they might end up working with. In this manner, the organization could have reinforced the feeling through positive feedback that their knowledge was of use to their peers and would not be used to their detriment. This arrangement could have helped increase the level of trust and camaraderie among consultants so that they were willing to share their knowledge. However, this still would have required more local resources for such activities as translation.

Insufficient Allowances for Local Control

In its vision for creating "one global firm," Accenture pursued a uniform global KM policy throughout the organization with the hope of reaching similar results in all regions. It assumed, for instance, that employees would be similarly motivated to contribute to knowledge and that they would respond promptly to the demands by KM staff. Nevertheless, due to the language and cultural issues mentioned above, Asian consultants faced special challenges overlooked by the company's one-size-fits-all policy. East Asian offices should have been allowed, if not actively encouraged, to customize their own incentive programs. For example, Japan should have been urged to develop a practice of encouraging submission from the top level. China could have considered implementing an extrinsic, financial reward system.

The need for local control was evident also in other areas. Since KX required all documents to be in English, several Asian offices (including Seoul and Tokyo) took it onto themselves to create their own regional mini-KX system in their local language. Employees in these offices regularly contributed to their local databases and favored them over KX. Submissions in Japan had increased significantly over the previous year with an upgrade of the Japanese language database. The regional databases were viewed as being more useful and user-friendly than the standard KX. In fact, one KM manager from the Hong Kong office wished that Accenture's KX would allow more flexibility at the local level, e.g., in terms of language choice and document formats, as the regional databases did.

Interestingly, despite corporate-wide communication, there was some ambiguity in East Asia as to whether a post-project KM contribution was indeed "mandatory" or not: Several consultants interviewed in Asian offices thought that the mandatory requirement did not apply to them. It did not make sense to them that all documents needed to be submitted to KX because some projects were very local in nature and unlikely to be of interest to others. However, there were no clear instructions from the headquarters or from the regional offices on which or what types of projects had to be captured. Without specific local instructions, corporate KM policies were not fully internalized in the Asian offices.

Balancing Global Integration and Local Responsiveness

Overall, it has become evident from this case that a standardized global system of codified knowledge could run the danger of not making sufficient allowance for important local and regional needs. As the case illustrates, a global company like Accenture can face various regional or local needs that cannot be neglected. While the pursuit of "one global firm" by Accenture is admirable and probably necessary, a one-size-fits-all approach without allowance or encouragement for local adjustments is unlikely to produce the desired results. Creating a successful global KM practice, like other kinds of globalization activities, requires a balancing act between global integration and local responsiveness.

Case Discussion Questions

1. Why does Accenture consider knowledge and knowledge management to be its primary source of competitive advantage?
2. What problems in knowledge management has KX exhibited?
3. From an institution-based standpoint, what norms and values have inhibited the more effective flow of knowledge through KX?
4. How would you address the knowledge management problems at Accenture?

[1] For example, IBM or HP would not be considered a "pure consultancy" because they develop and market their hardware and software. Accenture annual statement for the fiscal year ending August 31, 2003.

[2] See A. M. Chard, 1997, Knowledge management at Ernst & Young, Case S-M-291, Graduate School of Business, Stanford University.

[3] The amount to date is expected to be substantially larger. The $500 million is based on M. T. Hansen, N. Nohria, & T. Tierney, 1999, What's your strategy for managing knowledge? *Harvard Business Review*, March–April.

[4] A. Lam, 2000, Tacit knowledge, organizational learning and societal institutions: An integrated framework, *Organization Studies*, 21 (3).

[5] For example, at DiamondCluster International, consultants head up each KM area and are proactive in motivating others to make submissions.

INTEGRATIVE CASE 3.5

DHL BANGLADESH

Hemant Merchant
Florida Atlantic University

Masud Chand
Simon Fraser University

Late in October 2001, Nurul Rahman, special assistant to vice president—human resources (VP-HR) at DHL Bangladesh (DHLB), contemplated his options regarding adoption of a Human Resource Information System (HRIS) that the firm's regional headquarters (HQ) in Singapore had proposed. The HRIS would computerize various human resource management (HRM) routines and provide much needed infrastructure to DHLB's HR department, which had difficulty coping with the organization's rapid growth. Yet, the proposed HRIS was an expensive initiative that DHLB seemed reluctant to adopt not only due to its uncertain payoffs but also because its implementation would solely be DHLB's responsibility. The charge of making an initial recommendation fell on Nurul, who knew his counsel would be heeded by his boss, Mr. Jahar Saha, VP-HR and a DHLB veteran. Mr. Saha would almost certainly endorse Nurul's recommendation to the board. Nurul was also aware of the likely political fallout of a wrong choice.

In reaching a decision, Nurul had to balance the claims of various stakeholders, particularly DHLB and its regional HQ (in Singapore) that had often expressed a strong preference for streamlining HR systems across its Asian subsidiaries. Was the HRIS recommended by Singapore appropriate for DHLB? If so, where could DHLB find resources for the initiative's adoption? If not, what modifications would be needed to augment HRIS's suitability for DHLB? Nurul had less than a week to make a recommendation.

This is the condensed version of "DHL Bangladesh: Managing HQ-Subsidiary Relations," published in *Thunderbird International Business Review*, 2008 (in press). The award-winning case was written by Dr. Hemant Merchant (Florida Atlantic University) with assistance from Masud Chand (Simon Fraser University) solely to provide material for class discussion. The authors do not intend to illustrate either effective or ineffective handling of a managerial situation and may have disguised certain names and other identifying information to protect confidentiality. However, all essential facts and relationships remain unchanged.

DHL Bangladesh

A subsidiary of the privately held DHL Worldwide Express, DHLB was a pioneer and the acknowledged market leader in the air express industry in Bangladesh. DHLB's principal business consisted of delivering time-sensitive documents and parcels worldwide to and from Bangladesh. Created in 1979, DHLB had grown into a US$10 million business by 2002. During this period, DHLB's employee base had increased from five to almost 300. Most of them were based in Dhaka, Bangladesh's capital, where the bulk of DHLB's clientele had their offices.

The rapid economic growth in Bangladesh created opportunities as well as challenges for DHLB. On the one hand, it allowed DHLB to increase its revenues and profitability and to achieve greater visibility within the DHL Worldwide network. On the other hand, this growth significantly increased workload for DHLB employees, who were overworked and stressed.

Although DHLB's organizational structure enabled the firm to grow with Bangladesh's anticipated expansion, the company's various departments had not grown evenly. Nurul recalled:

> In 2000, DHL Asia had implemented a region-wide cost management program. An important aspect of that program was to reduce back-line costs. Consequently, recruitment for back-line departments [such as HR] was frozen, and any new hiring for these departments had to be approved by the regional HQ. In fact, the cost-reduction initiative was so vital that DHL subsidiaries needed regional approval even if they wanted to fill vacancies created by retirements or turnover. There had been instances where such replacement hiring had not been approved by the regional HQ.

The lopsided growth in DHLB's organizational structure created a bottleneck. Nowhere was this bottleneck more evident than in the HR department, which had been operating with just three employees since 1994, when DHLB had 150 employees. This situation presented a major constraint because DHLB considered people to be its principal resource. This made it imperative that all DHLB employees were well trained and highly motivated. Thus—despite being widely viewed as a "support" function—HR, in fact, played a vital role in DHLB's growth.

HR Department in DHLB

Despite its small size, the HR department in DHLB performed multiple functions whose discharge strained the two executives who were involved in its day-to-day functioning. A key priority for DHLB was employee recruitment at various levels. The bulk of this hiring was at the entry level, where demands upon the HR department were the greatest.

Over the past three years, these HR responsibilities not only had increased greatly because of employee hiring in various departments but also focused on development of generalist skills in the long term. There was also a sharp increase in the training and development of senior executives who were sent abroad for skills-enhancement workshops. Keeping track of these activities and ensuring a structure in which employees could perform multiple tasks increased the demands on the HR department significantly more than it had done at any other period in DHLB's history.

Perhaps the fastest growing HR function was the administration of compensation and benefits. Until 1998, employee benefits were decided on a companywide basis, and salary increments were based on recommendations of individual department managers. Over the last four years, this policy had changed drastically. Now, all nonsalary benefits were being streamlined to DHL's standards for its Asia-Pacific region.

Likewise, salary increments were now being modeled on the latest techniques, and merit matrices were being implemented across all levels of DHLB. The "new" protocols for administering benefits and compensation created significant pressure on the two HR executives, who were already struggling with keeping up with their other HR obligations.

HRIS Requirements at DHLB

Currently, the core HR functions were managed with nonspecialized software, usually Microsoft's Excel spreadsheet. This software solution had served DHLB well even though it limited ways in which HR data could be manipulated or viewed. With the recent growth in DHLB staff, the HR department found it increasingly difficult to rely on a system that now seemed both "primitive and increasingly unwieldy" to manage. Sensing the imperative for better computerization within the HR department, DHLB management had (in November 2000) approved the acquisition of an HRIS that met the growing company's needs.

After consulting various DHLB stakeholders, the HR department had identified five criteria for selecting an HRIS: (1) ability to automate multiple HR functions, (2) ability to link various HR databases, (3) user friendliness, (4) adaptability to current and anticipated needs, and (5) initial purchase price and operating costs. By December 2000, HR had begun evaluating systems that were offered by local vendors. Although none of the vendors had an existing software application that exactly matched DHLB's needs, most vendors assured DHLB they would be able to develop a satisfactory solution within a reasonable period. All vendors offered DHLB free long-term technical support. Once DHLB decided on a vendor, it would take the vendor about two or three months to customize the solution to the subsidiary's requirements. If all went well, DHLB was expected to have an HRIS operating in approximately six months from the time DHLB placed its order. The system would adequately meet DHLB's needs for the foreseeable future.

Despite their merits, a major limitation of HRIS vendors was that their proposed software solutions would not be compatible with their counterparts in other DHL subsidiaries in the region. This did not seem to matter to some DHLB executives, who simply viewed HRIS as an instrument to ease the increasing HR burden on their subsidiary. Such sentiments were not endemic to DHLB. Other DHL subsidiaries in the region, including those in Pakistan, Nepal, and Sri Lanka, were also considering solutions that suited their unique needs. On various occasions, these subsidiaries had informed regional HQ of their desire to develop customized systems. Indeed, in 2000, DHL's Pakistan subsidiary had already developed an HRIS that it had customized to its own needs. Eager to assist other DHL subsidiaries, and perhaps to share some of its developmental costs, Pakistan had been keen to recommend its own system to other DHL units.

Regional HQ and HRIS

The fungibility of Pakistan HRIS appealed to regional HQ that seriously considered it for the entire region. The regional HQs played multiple roles within the DHL Worldwide network. Regional HQ was also responsible for the overall well-being of DHL's regional operations.

In the latter role, one of the main functions of regional HQ was to take data from its individual Asian subsidiaries and combine them into regionwide reports to facilitate subsidiary management and control. The HR function did not lend itself well to such regionwide analysis. Due to country-specific differences in HR practices, subsidiaries in each country where DHL operated used different types of information and reporting systems. This diversity had strained the regional HQ's personnel in their efforts to consolidate and analyze HR data from DHL Asian subsidiaries. As such, regional HQ always had an interest in standardizing the HR reporting practices across countries. Pakistan's proposal seemed to be just the tool regional HQ was looking for to reduce differences in the functional and reporting styles of DHL subsidiaries across Asia. Nurul recalled:

> From the regional HQ's viewpoint, a single HRIS that worked across different countries made perfect sense. It would considerably reduce the work of regional HR staff as they would no longer need to spend time consolidating and analyzing data from different countries. Besides, standardizing processes across the region was one of regional HQ's main functions. However, differences in reporting styles across countries were not merely cosmetic; they were the products of inherently different HR systems which reflected distinct corporate and legal environments of each country.

In December 2000, the regional HQ asked DHLB to suspend evaluating local vendors and consider DHL Pakistan's offer. In response, the HR manager at DHLB asked for an opportunity to acquaint himself with the Pakistan HRIS system. As he would later learn, the HR managers in DHL Nepal and DHL Sri Lanka had also made similar requests, to which the regional HQ had replied favorably. The meeting to evaluate Pakistan HRIS was scheduled in late February 2001 in Karachi, Pakistan, where DHL Pakistan was headquartered. It was expected that the meeting would be attended by senior HR managers of DHL Bangladesh and DHL Sri Lanka, the country manager of DHL Nepal, and Bruce Newton, the regional VP-HR. The responsibility of representing DHLB at the Karachi meeting had fallen on Nurul because of a scheduling conflict involving Mr. Saha, the VP-HR at DHLB, who would normally have represented his country.

HRIS Search at DHLB

Nurul had joined DHLB relatively recently and was one of the newest and youngest members of the DHLB team. He had graduated from the country's premier business school, which was affiliated with the University of Dhaka. Nurul's ability to deliver "quality" on special HR projects had earned him the respect of his colleagues and brought him to the attention of DHLB's senior management. Nurul had moved up through DHLB's ranks quickly and had earned the trust of Mr. Saha, who had often assigned him to work on key HR projects under his personal supervision. One such project was the search for a suitable HRIS vendor—that is, until the regional HQ put a stop to that search with its own suggestion.

After an extensive analysis, Nurul had shortlisted two local vendors that could easily demonstrate their solutions within a week of being told to do so. Now Nurul had to consider a third option that regional HQ had proposed: the Pakistan HRIS. Doing so would not only significantly delay DHLB's decision about adopting a customized HRIS but also require a very careful scrutiny of the broader context in which the HRIS acquisition decision was situated. Mr. Saha had been informed that regional HQ had now set a date for the HRIS project meeting during which DHL Pakistan would demonstrate its HRIS to the regional HQ and other subsidiary managers. DHL Pakistan hoped to persuade other subsidiaries that its own HRIS was the right software solution to their individual needs.

The Karachi Meeting

The Karachi meeting was as "interesting" as Nurul had expected. During the three-day meeting, DHL Pakistan managers briefed other DHL participants on the HRIS system currently used in Pakistan and acquainted them with the system. The hosts also gave the visitors short user training related to different functionalities of the Pakistan HRIS. Nurul recalled:

> The Pakistan HRIS was a complicated software solution that required a lot of familiarization to become comfortable with. Although the HR employees at DHL Pakistan appeared to be comfortable with its use, it was clear that this software required a lot of first hand involvement to attain proficiency using it. Despite this, I was surprised that Pakistan had not yet developed any user- or technical-training manuals. While the Pakistan system brought all HR functions together under a comprehensive database, it would require a great deal of customization to be brought up to DHL Bangladesh's requirements. DHL Bangladesh and DHL Pakistan were very different in terms of their operations and size, and the two countries' HRIS requirements reflected that divergence.

DHL Pakistan was roughly twice the size of DHL Bangladesh, both in terms of revenue and personnel. The Pakistan subsidiary's operations were also much more geographically widespread. Moreover, the roles of HR departments in the two countries were generally different. Indeed, the demonstrated HRIS was primarily designed to meet the Pakistan subsidiary's needs—many of them quite different from those of the Bangladesh subsidiary.

The differences in HR practices manifested themselves in the expectations of the HRIS in each DHL subsidiary. For example, there were variances in the process of calculating gross salary for personnel. Although the calculation algorithm itself was easy to amend, the routine was hardwired into the system so that users could not change the settings from their side. To convert the system to do things in the DHLB style would require changes from the technical side—that is, from the original designers of the system. The DHL Pakistan staff could make these changes before the system was operational in Bangladesh. However, if there were any further changes—even minor ones—based on DHL Bangladesh's methods, or if there were any changes in industrial laws brought about by the government of Bangladesh, the system would have to be reconfigured from the technical side by its designers.

Another major difference was that DHLB often recruited temporary employees who were not eligible for many company benefits, whereas Pakistan regulations required DHL there to treat all employees as regular employees. Such adjustments would further complicate the Pakistan HRIS.

Yet another difference pertained to training records. DHLB maintained a database on training imparted to all employees. In contrast, DHL Pakistan maintained training records only for the last three years. Because these recordkeeping protocols were hardwired into the Pakistan HRIS, they could be not be modified by the user. This meant the existing HRIS software would have to be rewritten by engineers before it could become useful to DHLB. All this suggested DHLB not only would incur significant financial and nonfinancial costs if it adopted the Pakistani HRIS, but it ran the additional risk of downtime and operational dependence on another subsidiary.

Such concerns were downplayed by DHL Pakistan managers. In fact, they assured the visiting executives that their technical team could make country-specific customizations relatively quickly and at a reasonable price. Nurul believed if an application designed by Pakistan were adopted by DHL subsidiaries in the region, it would provide a major boost to DHL Pakistan's standing and influence. It would also raise the odds for Pakistan staff (especially from HR) to move upward to the regional level. Bruce Newton, the regional VP-HR, was highly impressed with the software and was confident of Pakistan HRIS's ability to be the platform for standardizing DHL's HR systems in the region. He let the executives know where he stood. Bruce said at the meeting:

> The Pakistan team has done a fine job of designing this software and I thank them for it. I can see they have put a great deal of thought and effort in designing it. Based on the demonstration we have viewed today, I am confident the Pakistan HRIS can be modified to meet the purposes of all DHL subsidiaries in the region. The only question I have is whether Pakistan can provide the level of technical support that might be needed by DHL's Asian subsidiaries.

The regional HQ's apparent liking for the Pakistan HRIS appeared to be driven by a variety of factors. First, the Pakistan HRIS not only was fully functional but also worked well in Pakistan. Second, the Pakistan HRIS was the quickest way for HQ to achieve its goal to standardize HR reporting systems across Asia. Third, the Pakistan team had assured Bruce that it could easily customize its HRIS to suit other DHL subsidiaries' requirements and that it also had the ability and willingness to provide technical assistance whenever needed. Given Pakistan's continued assurances of support, and perhaps because of Bruce's enthusiasm, the visiting DHL delegates also expressed confidence in the Pakistan HRIS.

Nurul, however, had reservations about the system he had just seen. Although he did not share his thoughts in Karachi, Nurul let his boss know about them when he returned to Dhaka. First, the financial burden of buying into the Pakistan HRIS would be five times that of finding a local solution. A locally developed solution would cost DHLB less than $5,000, whereas the Pakistan system (inclusive of ancillary expenses) would cost approximately $100,000, which would be split four ways among the three countries and the regional HQ. While DHLB management would probably approve this $25,000 expense, the monies would represent the HR department's biggest outlay for the year. Indeed, the outlay would constitute the largest HRIS investment in Bangladesh's air express industry.

Nurul's second reservation pertained to the variety of customized modules needed to make the demonstrated HRIS suitable for DHLB's needs. Nurul was particularly concerned about the range of these changes because they would have to be developed around the Pakistan HRIS architecture. Doing so was expected to needlessly complicate DHLB's system:

> The problems with the Pakistan HRIS suitability for DHLB were both short- and long-term. In the short-term, DHLB would inherit a system that was expensive (probably the single largest line item after salaries on our budget) and complicated. In the long-run, DHLB would have a system that not only was extremely inflexible from the user front, but also dependent on another DHL subsidiary on the technical front.

Nurul was also concerned about DHLB's technical dependence on the Pakistan subsidiary. He had noticed that DHL Pakistan had an IT specialist whose sole responsibility was to maintain the subsidiary's HRIS. This reinforced Nurul's suspicion that the demonstrated HRIS needed regular technical upkeep.

Although DHLB also had IT specialists on its staff, there were fewer of them. In that all software changes would be designed in Pakistan—over which Bangladesh had no authority—DHLB would be at the Pakistan subsidiary's mercy vis-à-vis any and all technical assistance. Seeking the regional HQ's intervention was not a sustainable solution and, moreover, would make DHLB staff "look bad" to the regional office. Additionally, software documentation on user as well as technical platforms was either inadequate or nonexistent. DHL Pakistan would have to provide this documentation before its reconfigured HRIS system could be implemented in Bangladesh.

DHLB and Its Regional HQ

Mr. Saha relayed these concerns to regional HQ, which had psychologically bought into what DHL Pakistan had to offer other DHL subsidiaries in the region. This was an important point that DLHB could not afford to ignore. DHLB reported directly to the Singapore-based regional HQ, which played an important strategic role in the DHL system.

The responsibility for fulfilling this role fell on the regional management team, which consisted of Asia-region VPs and some other top-level executives. This group had line authority over country-level top management and was ultimately responsible for the overall success of DHL in Asia. The regional VPs were important members of the group and served as principal advisers to the functional area VPs in individual countries: It was very rare that their "advice" was not heeded by subsidiary VPs. Although regional VPs did not have direct control over subsidiary VPs, the regional VPs had "very real power" and could significantly enhance or diminish the career prospects of subsidiary-level managers.

At the country level, all functional area VPs were in a quasi-matrix reporting structure (see Figure 1). A functional area VP reported directly to his country manager and also, indirectly, to the regional VP holding that particular functional portfolio. Thus, Mr. Saha also reported to Bruce Newton, the regional VP-HR. The regional VPs did not have line authority over their country-level counterparts and could not issue direct orders to subsidiary VPs. Rather, the regional VPs' role was to coach, guide, provide expert knowledge, and lead cross-national projects. At least on paper, the regional HQ played a paternal role.

In reality, however, the regional VPs often wielded significant influence over country-level VPs, as most major country-level decisions required regional approval. Subsidiary-initiated projects not supported by a regional VP were rarely approved at the country level. Thus, regional VPs were crucial individuals to get on board whenever any major country-level program was initiated. Their influence was further magnified by their role as functional advisers to the regional president, who had direct authority over country management teams.

DHL also followed a 360-degree feedback model for evaluating the performance of its senior managers worldwide. This process involved seeking feedback from an individual's immediate supervisor, peers, subordinates, and customers as well as the regional management team. Thus, a regional VP's feedback played a crucial role in the career progression of an individual senior manager—especially if a country-level VP had any regional-level aspirations. The regional VP's strong endorsement was absolutely essential for any move to the regional office. An ambitious and upwardly mobile VP at the country level would think long and hard before turning down any advice from the regional VP.

FIGURE 1 DHL BANGLADESH'S MATRIX STRUCTURE

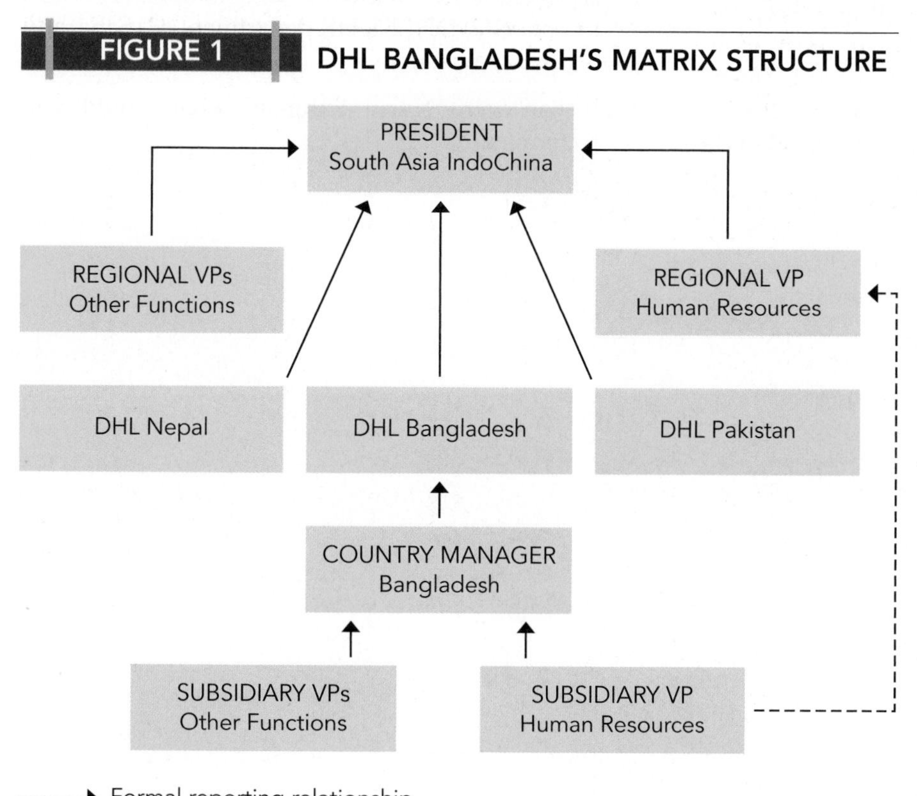

One written negative comment by a regional VP in a performance appraisal could easily be a career killer for the concerned country-level VP.

The HRIS Decision

Given the competing interests of various stakeholders, Nurul knew he had a tough recommendation to make. On the one hand, dropping the Pakistan HRIS customization idea was worth consideration. The modification might not live up to its potential in DHLB, and there still were Bangladeshi vendors willing to do the job for a fraction of the cost. On the other hand, DHLB had already spent considerable time and money on this project and could not afford further delays. The subsidiary's discussions with regional HQ and the Pakistan subsidiary managers had exhausted the HR department and, ironically, set it further behind in its day-to-day task completion. In any case, the regional HQ had constantly assured DHLB about Pakistan's commitment and technical support vis-à-vis the HRIS project. Would it not be better to continue with the Pakistan offer and solve potential problems when they arose? After all, the project had backing from the regional HQ.

Whatever Nurul recommended would have major ramifications at all levels. For DHLB, it was foremost a question about possessing the HRIS. Without it, there was no way the HR staff could stretch itself for much longer. It was also imperative to consider relations between the regional HQ and DHLB and between DHLB and other DHL subsidiaries in Asia. How might regional HQ view a deviation—even a "justified" one—from its position? Would it invite greater scrutiny in the future? Would it curtail the subsidiary's operational and strategic freedom? Would it be prudent for DHLB to accede to regional HQ's choice and save organizational energies for a "bigger battle" that might arise in the future? At an individual level, Nurul had to consider potential reprisals from a very powerful stakeholder. Indeed, how would his recommendation affect his own career at DHL? How might other HR staffers be affected? What about Mr. Saha himself? How would Saha view Nurul's integrity? These questions occupied Nurul's thoughts as he looked out of his office window: "What do I tell my boss three days from now? How—and how much—do I justify my recommendation?"

Case Discussion Questions

1. What advantages and disadvantages associated with a matrix structure does this case reveal?
2. For Nurul, identify the advantages and disadvantages for the three options: (1) proceeding with DHL Pakistan's HRIS, (2) proceeding with a local Bangladesh vendor, and (3) negotiating with regional HQ.
3. Rank order the factors in question 2 in terms of their (1) potential for solving DHLB's problems and (2) political importance from the viewpoint of DHLB and regional HQ. For a more detailed analysis, include the following stakeholders: (1) Nurul Rahman, (2) DHLB's HR department, (3) Saha, and (4) DHL Pakistan.
4. If you were Nurul Rahman, what would you recommend?

PART 4

Building Functional Excellence

CHAPTERS

14 Competing on Marketing and Supply Chain Management

15 Managing Human Resources Globally

16 Governing the Corporation around the World

17 Managing Corporate Social Responsibility Globally

CHAPTER 14

Competing on Marketing and Supply Chain Management

OPENING CASE

Zara: Rewriting Rules on Marketing and Supply Chain Management

Zara is one of the hottest fashion chains of the 21st century. Founded in 1975, Zara's parent, Inditex, has become one of the leading global apparel retailers. Since its initial public offering (IPO) in 2001, Inditex tripled its sales and profits and doubled the number of its stores of eight brands, of which Zara contributes two-thirds of total sales. Zara succeeds by breaking and then rewriting rules on marketing and supply chain management.

Rule number one: The country-of-origin of a fashion house usually carries some cachet. However, Zara does not hail from Italy or France—it is from Spain. Even within Spain, Zara is not based in a cosmopolitan city like Barcelona or Madrid. It is headquartered in Arteixo, a town of only 25,000 people in a remote corner of northwestern Spain that a majority of this book's readers would never have heard of. Yet, Zara is active in Europe, the Americas, Asia, and Africa. In 2006, Inditex launched 439 new stores—more than one per *day*. As of 2007, the total number of stores was over 3,100 in 64 countries (the three newest countries entered were China, Serbia, and Tunisia). Zara stores occupy some of the priciest top locations: Paris's Champs-Elysées, Tokyo's Ginza, New York's Fifth Avenue, and Dallas's Galleria.

Rule number two: Avoid stock-outs (a store running out of items in demand). Zara's answer? Occasional shortages contribute to an urge to buy now. With new items arriving at stores *twice* a week, experienced Zara shoppers know that "If you see something and don't buy it, you can forget about coming back for it because it will be gone." The small batch of merchandise during a short window of opportunity for purchasing motivates shoppers to visit Zara stores more frequently. In London, shoppers visit the average store four times a year but frequent Zara 17 times annually. There is a good reason to do so: Zara makes about 20,000 items a year, about triple what Gap does. As a result, "At Gap, everything is the same," according to a Zara fan, "and buying from Zara, you'll never end up looking like someone else."

Rule number three: Bombarding shoppers with ads is a must. Gap and H&M spend on average 3% to 4% of their sales on ads. Zara begs to differ: It devotes just 0.3% of its sales to ads. The high traffic in the stores alleviates some needs for advertising in the media, most of which only serves as a reminder to visit the stores.

Rule number four: Outsource. Gap and H&M do not own any production facilities. However, outsourcing production (mostly to Asia) requires a long lead time, usually several months. Again, Zara has decisively deviated from the norm. By concentrating (most of) its production in-house and in Spain, Zara has developed a super-responsive supply chain. It designs, produces, and delivers a new garment to its stores worldwide in a mere 15 *days*, a pace that is unheard of in the industry. The best speed the rivals can achieve is two *months*. Outsourcing may not necessarily be "low cost" because errors in prediction can easily lead to unsold inventory, forcing retailers to offer steep discounts. The industry average is to offer 40% discounts across all merchandise. In contrast, Zara sells more at full price, and when it discounts, it averages only 15%.

Rule number five: Strive for efficiency through large batches. In contrast, Zara intentionally deals with small batches. Because of its flexibility, Zara does not worry about "missing the boat" for a season. When new trends emerge, Zara can react quickly. More interesting, Zara runs its supply chain like clockwork with a fast but predictable rhythm: Every store places orders on Tuesday/Wednesday and Friday/Saturday. Trucks and cargo flights run on established schedules—like a bus service. From Spain, shipments reach

LEARNING OBJECTIVES

After studying this chapter, you should be able to

1. articulate three of the four Ps in marketing (product, price, and promotion) in a global context
2. explain how the fourth P in marketing (place) has evolved to be labeled supply chain management
3. outline the triple As in supply chain management (agility, adaptability, and alignment)
4. discuss how institutions and resources affect marketing and supply chain management
5. participate in two leading debates concerning marketing and supply chain management
6. draw implications for action

most European stores in 24 hours, US stores in 48 hours, and Asian stores in 72 hours. Not only does store staff know exactly when shipments will arrive, regular customers also know that too, thus motivating them to check out the new merchandise more frequently on those days.

Overall, marketing and supply chain management have become an integrated system that mutually reinforces each other and propels Zara's formidable rise to new heights around the globe. Gap is still bigger ($16 billion sales) than Inditex ($12 billion), but Zara's 16.5% margins beat Gap's 11%.

Sources: Based on (1) *Business Week*, 2006, Fashion conquistador, September 4: 38–39; (2) K. Ferdows, M. Lewis, & J. Machuca, 2004, Rapid-fire fulfillment, *Harvard Business Review*, November: 104–110; (3) http://www.zara.com.

How can firms such as Zara market themselves to attract customers? Having attracted customers, how can firms ensure a steady supply of products and services? This chapter deals with these and other important questions associated with marketing and supply chain management. **Marketing** refers to efforts to create, develop, and defend markets that satisfy the needs and wants of individual and business customers.[1] **Supply chain** is the flow of products, services, finances, and information that passes through a set of entities from a source to the customer.[2] **Supply chain management** refers to activities to plan, organize, lead, and control the supply chain.[3] In this chapter, instead of viewing marketing and supply chain as two separate functions, we view them as one integrated function that may make or break a firm.[4]

marketing
Efforts to create, develop, and defend markets that satisfy the needs and wants of individual and business customers.

supply chain
Flow of products, services, finances, and information that passes through a set of entities from a source to the customer.

supply chain management
Activities to plan, organize, lead, and control the supply chain.

We first outline major marketing and supply chain activities in global business. Then we discuss how the institution- and resource-based views enhance our understanding of the drivers behind marketing and supply chain management success. Finally, debates and extensions follow.

THREE OF THE FOUR Ps IN MARKETING

LEARNING OBJECTIVE 1
articulate three of the four Ps in marketing (product, price, and promotion) in a global context

Figure 14.1 shows the four Ps that collectively consist of the **marketing mix**: (1) product, (2) price, (3) promotion, and (4) place.[5] We start with the first three Ps. The last P—place (where the product is sourced, produced, and distributed)—will be discussed in the next section.

marketing mix
The four underlying components of marketing: product, price, promotion, and place.

FIGURE 14.1 THE FOUR Ps OF MARKETING MIX

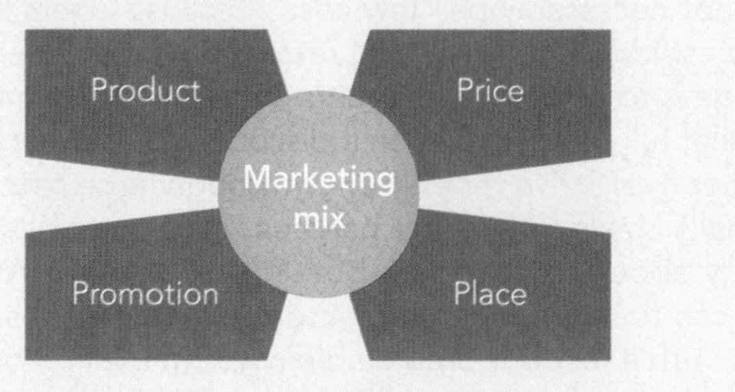

Product

product
The offerings that customers purchase.

Product refers to offerings that customers purchase. Although the word *product* originally referred to a physical product, its modern use has included services. To avoid confusion, we will use "products and services" in this chapter. This makes sense because broadly speaking, when a customer purchases a product, this product also embodies service elements (such as maintenance and upgrades).

Even for a single category (such as women's clothing or sports cars), product attributes vary tremendously. For firms interested in doing business around the world, the leading concern is standardization versus localization.[6] Localization is natural. McDonald's, for example, sells wine in France, beer in Germany, mutton pot pies in Australia, and Maharaja Mac and McCurry Pan in India. What is interesting is the rise of standardization, which is often attributed to Theodore Levitt's 1983 article, "The Globalization of Markets."[7] This article advocated globally standardized products and services, as evidenced by Hollywood movies and Coke Classic. However, numerous subsequent experiments such as Ford's world car and MTV's global (essentially American) programming backfired. Marketers thus face a dilemma: One size does not fit all, but most firms cannot afford to create products and services for just one group of customers. Thus, how much to standardize and how much to localize remain a challenge.[8]

As first noted in Chapter 13, localization is appealing (in the eyes of local consumers and governments) but expensive. A sensible solution is to have a product that *appears* locally adapted while deriving as much synergy (commonality) as possible in ways that customers cannot easily recognize. Consider the two global weekly business magazines, US-based *Business Week* and UK-based *Economist*.[9] In addition to its US edition, *Business Week* publishes two English (language) editions for Asia and Europe and a Chinese edition for China. Although these four editions share certain content, there is a lot of local edition-only material that is expensive to support and produce. In comparison, each issue of the *Economist* has the following regional sections: (1) the Americas (excluding the United States), (2) Asia, (3) Britain, (4) Europe (excluding Britain), (5) Middle East and Africa, and (6) United States. Although the content for each issue is identical, the order of appearance of the regional sections varies. For US subscribers, their *Economist*

Why does McDonald's offer localized products in its restaurants based outside the US?

starts with the United States section; for Asian subscribers, their magazine starts with the Asia section; and so forth. By doing that, the *Economist* appears to be responsive to readers with different regional interests without incurring the costs of running multiple editions for different regions, as *Business Week* does. Therefore, how many editions does one issue of the *Economist* have? We can say one—or six if we count the six different ways of stapling regional sections together.

market segmentation
A way to identify consumers who differ from others in purchasing behavior.

One of the major concerns for multinational enterprises (MNEs) is to decide whether to market global brands (such as Nestlé) or local brands in their portfolio (see Table 14.1). The key is **market segmentation**—identifying segments of consumers who differ from others in purchasing behavior.[10] There are limitless ways of segmenting the market (males versus females, college versus high school educated, urban dwellers versus rural residents, Africans versus Latin Americans). The million dollar question for marketers is: How does one generalize from such a wide variety of market segmentation in different countries to generate products that can cater to a few of these segments *around the world*?

One globally useful way of segmentation is to divide consumers in four categories:

- Global citizens (who are in favor of buying global brands that signal prestige and cachet)
- Global dreamers (who may not be able to afford, but nevertheless admire, global brands)
- Antiglobals (who are skeptical about whether global brands deliver higher quality goods)
- Global agnostics (who are most likely to lead antiglobalization demonstrations smashing McDonald's windows)

Figure 14.2 shows that the distribution of these different groups within each country is uneven. Interestingly, Brazil, China, and Indonesia have higher percentages of global citizens than the US and the UK, which correspondingly have higher percentages of global agnostics.[11]

The implications are clear. For the first two categories of global citizens and global dreamers (who total approximately 78% of the consumers surveyed), firms

TABLE 14.1 TOP-20 GLOBAL BRANDS

1	Coca-Cola (USA)	11	Citi (USA)
2	Microsoft (USA)	12	Hewlett-Packard (USA)
3	IBM (USA)	13	BMW (Germany)
4	GE (USA)	14	Marlboro (USA)
5	Nokia (Finland)	15	American Express (USA)
6	Toyota (Japan)	16	Gillette (USA)
7	Intel (USA)	17	Louis Vuitton (France)
8	McDonald's (USA)	18	Cisco (USA)
9	Disney (USA)	19	Honda (Japan)
10	Mercedes-Benz (Germany)	20	Google (USA)

Source: Adapted from *Business Week*, 2007, The 100 top brands (pp. 59–60), August 6: 58–64.

FIGURE 14.2 **SEGMENTATION OF CONSUMERS AS THEY RELATE TO GLOBAL BRANDS**

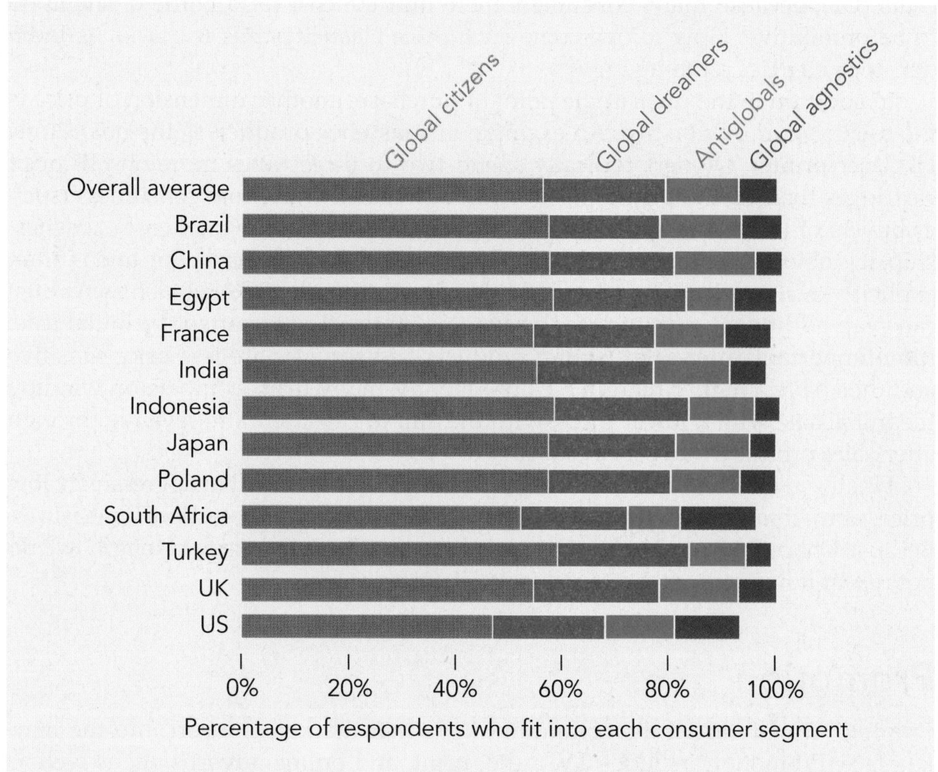

Source: D. Holt, J. Quelch, & E. Taylor, 2004, How global brands compete (p. 73), *Harvard Business Review*, September: 68–75. Results are based on a survey of 1,500 urban consumers between 20 and 35 years old in 41 countries.

are advised to leverage the global brands and their relatively more standardized products and services. "Global brands make us feel like citizens of the world," an Argentinean consumer observed. However, MNEs do not necessarily have to write off the antiglobals and global agnostics as lost customers because MNEs can market localized products and services under local brands. Nestlé, for example, owns 8,000 (!) brands around the world, most of which are local, country-specific (or region-specific) brands not marketed elsewhere.

Overall, Levitt may be *both* right and wrong. A large percentage of consumers around the world indeed have converging interests and preferences centered on global brands. However, a substantial percentage of them also resist globally standardized brands, products, and services. Armed with this knowledge, firms—both MNEs and locals—can better craft their products and services.

Price

Price refers to the expenditures that customers are willing to pay for a product. Most consumers are "price sensitive." The jargon is **price elasticity**—how demand changes when prices change. Basic economic theory of supply and demand suggests that when prices drop, consumers will buy more and generate stronger demand, which in turn will motivate firms to expand production to meet this demand. This theory, of course, underpins numerous firms' relentless drive around the world to cut costs and then prices. The question is *how* price sensitive consumers are. Holding the product (such as shampoo) constant, in general, the lower income

price
The expenditures that customers are willing to pay for a product.

price elasticity
How demand changes when prices change.

the consumers are, the more price sensitive they are. American, European, and Japanese consumers take it for granted that shampoo is sold by the bottle. But in India, shampoo is often sold in single-use packets, each costing about one to ten cents (US), because many consumers there find the cost for a bottle of shampoo to be prohibitive. How to overcome such price elasticity thus is crucial as India develops its mass retailing.

total cost of ownership
Total cost needed to own a product, consisting of initial purchase cost and follow-up maintenance/service cost.

In addition to the price at the point of purchase, another dimension of price is the **total cost of ownership**. An example in consumer products is the ubiquitous HP laser printer. Owners typically spend two to three times more on HP print cartridges than on the printer itself. Although many individual consumers (such as buyers of HP printers) do not pay explicit attention to the total cost of ownership, it is obviously more important in business-to-business marketing and is often explicitly evaluated prior to purchase decisions. Aircraft makers (such as Airbus) can reap additional revenues for as long as 20 to 30 years after the initial sale. More important, after-sales (spare) products and services are less price sensitive and thus have a higher margin.[12] Consequently, many firms compete on winning the initial sale with a lower price, with the aim to capture more revenue through after-sales products and services.

Finally, in international marketing, it is important to note that aggressively low prices abroad may be accused of dumping, thus triggering protectionist measures. Because Chapter 11 has already discussed the antidumping issue at length, we do not repeat it here other than to stress its importance.

Promotion

promotion
Communications that marketers insert into the marketplace.

Promotion refers to all the communications that marketers insert into the marketplace. Promotion includes TV, radio, print, and online advertising, as well as coupons, direct mail, billboards, direct marketing (personal selling), and public relations. Marketers face a strategic choice of whether to standardize or localize promotional efforts. Standardized promotion not only projects a globally consistent message (crucial for global brands) but can also save a lot of money. One large campaign may be more cost effective than 100 smaller campaigns.

However, there is a limit to the effectiveness of standardized promotion. In the 1990s, Coca-Cola ran a worldwide campaign featuring a cute polar bear cartoon character. Research later showed that viewers in warmer weather countries had a hard time relating to this ice-bound animal with which they had no direct experience. In response, Coca-Cola switched to more costly but more effective country-specific advertisements. For instance, the Indian subsidiary launched a campaign that equated Coke with *thanda*, the Hindi word for "cold." The German subsidiary developed commercials that showed a "hidden" kind of eroticism (!).[13] While this is merely one example, it does suggest that even some of the most global brands (such as Coca-Cola) can benefit from localized promotion.

Many firms promote products and services overseas without doing their "homework" and end up making blunders (huge mistakes). GM marketed its Chevrolet Nova in Latin America without realizing that *nova* means "no go" in Spanish. Coors Beer translated its successful slogan "Turn it loose" from English to Spanish as "Drink Coors, get diarrhea."[14] Table 14.2 outlines some blunders that are hilarious to readers but *painful* to marketers, some of whom were fired because of these huge mistakes.

country-of-origin effect
The positive or negative perception of firms and products from a certain country.

In international marketing, there is a **country-of-origin effect**, which refers to the positive or negative perception of firms and products from a certain country.[15] Marketers have to decide whether to enhance or downplay such an effect. This can be very tricky. Disneyland Tokyo became popular in Japan because it played up its American image. But Disneyland Paris received relentless negative press coverage in France because it insisted on its "wholesome American look."[16]

TABLE 14.2 SOME BLUNDERS IN INTERNATIONAL MARKETING

- One US toymaker received numerous complaints from American mothers because a talking doll told their children, "Kill mommy!" Made in Hong Kong, the dolls were shipped around the world. They carried messages in the language of the country of destination. A packing error sent some Spanish-speaking dolls to the United States. The message in Spanish "Quiero mommy!" means "I love mommy!" (This is also a supply chain blunder.)
- AT&T submitted a proposal to sell phone equipment in Thailand. Despite its excellent technology, the proposal was rejected out of hand by telecom authorities because Thailand required a 10-year warranty but AT&T only offered a five-year warranty—thanks to standardization on warranty imposed by US headquarters.
- To better adapt its products to Egypt, one Chinese shoe manufacturer placed Arabic characters on the soles of the shoes. Unfortunately, the designers did not know Arabic and merely copied words from elsewhere. The words they chose meant "God." China's ambassador to Egypt had to apologize for this blunder.
- Japan's Olympia tried to market a photocopier to Latin America under the name Roto. Sales were minimal. Why? *Roto* means "broken" in Spanish. (This happened after Chevrolet tried to sell its Nova car in the region—*no va* means "no go" in Spanish.)
- In their eagerness to export to the English-speaking world, Chinese firms have marketed the following products: White Elephant brand batteries, Sea Cucumber brand shirts, and Maxipuke brand poker cards (the two Chinese characters, *pu ke*, mean poker, and they should have been translated as Maxi brand poker cards—but its package said "Maxipuke").

Sources: Based on text in (1) T. Dalgic & R. Heijblom, 1996, International marketing blunders revisited—some lessons for managers, *Journal of International Marketing*, 4 (1): 81–91; (2) D. Ricks, 1999, *Blunders in International Business*, 3rd ed., Oxford, UK: Blackwell.

Singapore Airlines projects a "Singapore girl" image around the world. In contrast, Li Ning downplays its Chinese origin by using American NBA players in its commercials (see Closing Case). Giordano is an Italian-sounding brand of a clothing line made by a Hong Kong company that has no connection with Italy. Yet, Giordano figured that Italy has some positive country-of-origin effect from which it can benefit.

In addition to the traditional domestic versus international challenge, a new challenge lies in the pursuit of online versus offline (traditional) advertising. As the first cohort to grow up Internet savvy, today's teens and twenty-somethings in many countries flock to social networks such as Second Life, MySpace, Xanga, Facebook, and their equivalents around the world. These young people "do not buy stuff because they see a magazine ad," according to one expert; "they buy stuff because other kids tell them to online."[17] What is challenging is how marketers can reach such youth. Firms such as Apple and P&G experiment with a variety of formats, including sponsorships and blogs, with some hits, some misses, and lots of uncertainty. The basic threat to such social networks is the whim of their users, whose interest in certain topics and networks themselves may change or even evaporate overnight.

Overall, marketers need to experiment with a variety of configurations of the three Ps (product, price, and promotion) around the world to optimize the marketing mix. What has not yet been discussed is the fourth P, place, to which we turn in the next section.

LEARNING OBJECTIVE 2

explain how the fourth P in marketing (place) has evolved to be labeled supply chain management

place
The location where products and services are provided.

distribution channel
The set of firms that facilitates the movement of goods from producers to consumers.

FROM DISTRIBUTION CHANNEL TO SUPPLY CHAIN MANAGEMENT

As the fourth P in the marketing mix, **place** refers to the location where products and services are provided (which now, of course, includes the online marketplace). Technically, place is also often referred to as the **distribution channel**—the set of firms that facilitates the movement of goods from producers to consumers. Until the 1980s, a majority of producers made most goods in-house, and one of the key concerns was distribution. Since then, production outsourcing has grown significantly (see Chapter 4). Many producers (such as Nike) do not physically produce their branded products at all; they rely on contract manufacturers to get the job done. Other producers that still produce in-house rely on their suppliers to provide an increasingly higher percentage of the value added. Therefore, the new challenge is how to manage the longer distribution channel—more specifically, the distribution from suppliers (and contract manufacturers) all the way to consumers[18] (see Figure 14.3).

Consequently, a new term, *supply chain*, has been coined, and as jargon, it has now almost replaced the old-fashioned "distribution channel." To be sure, the focal firm has always dealt with suppliers. Strategy guru Michael Porter labels this function as "inbound logistics" (and the traditional distribution channel as "outbound logistics").[19] In a broad sense, the new term *supply chain* is almost synonymous with *value chain*, encompassing both inbound and outbound logistics (see Chapter 4). In the military, logistics is widely acknowledged as a contributor to wartime success. But no army recruitment material would brag about a glamorous career in logistics in the military to attract new soldiers. Similarly, traditional business logistics tends to be tactical and lacks prestige. However, if supply chain is value chain, then supply chain management essentially handles the entire process of value creation, which is the core mission of the firm. Consequently, supply chain management has now taken on new strategic importance and gained tremendous prestige.

One indication that supply chain management has gained traction is that instead of being obscure players, leading supply chain management firms, such as UPS and FedEx, have now become household names. On any given day, 2% of the world's GDP can be found in UPS trucks and planes. "FedEx" has become a verb, and even live *whales* have reportedly been "FedExed."[20] Modern supply chains aim to "get the right product to the right place at the right time—all the time."[21] Next, we discuss the triple As underpinning supply chains: (1) agility, (2) adaptability, and (3) alignment.[22]

FIGURE 14.3 SUPPLY CHAIN MANAGEMENT

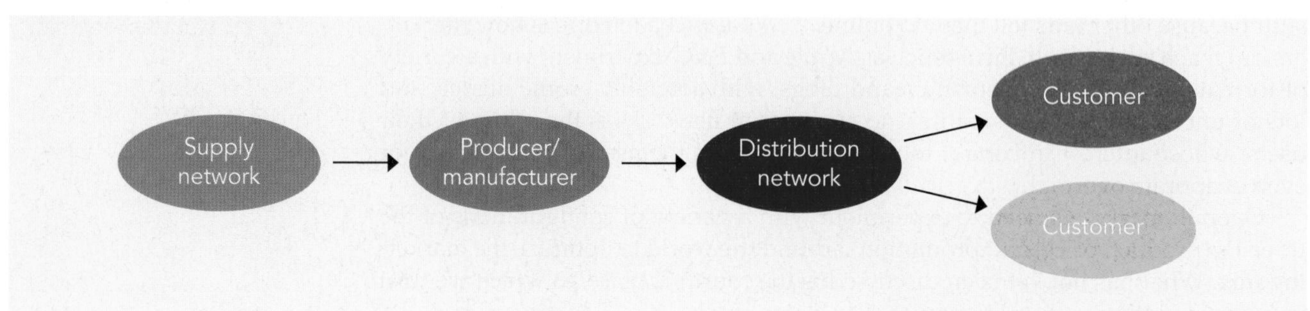

THE TRIPLE As IN SUPPLY CHAIN MANAGEMENT

LEARNING OBJECTIVE 3

outline the triple As in supply chain management (agility, adaptability, and alignment)

Agility

agility
The ability to quickly react to unexpected shifts in supply and demand.

Agility refers to the ability to quickly react to unexpected shifts in supply and demand. To reduce inventory, many firms now use the trucks, ships, and planes of their suppliers and carriers as their warehouse. In their quest for supply chain speed, cost, and efficiency, many firms fail to realize the cost they have to pay for disregarding agility. On the other hand, firms such as Zara thrive in large part because of the agility of their supply chain (see Opening Case). Zara's agility permeates throughout its entire operations, starting with design processes. As soon as designers spot certain trends, they create sketches and go ahead to order fabrics without finalizing designs. This speeds things up because fabric suppliers require a long lead time. Designs are finalized when reliable data from stores come. Production commences as soon as designs are complete. In addition, Zara's factories only run one shift, easily allowing for overtime production if demand calls for it. Its distribution centers are also highly efficient, allowing it to handle demand fluctuation without creating bottlenecks.

Agility may become more important in the 21st century because shocks to supply chains are now more frequent (due to terrorist attacks, Iraq, and SARS). Under shocks, an agile supply chain can rise to the challenge while a static one can pull a firm down.[23] In 2000, Nokia and Ericsson fought in the mobile handset market. Consider how Nokia and Ericsson reacted differently to a fire induced by a thunderstorm at a New Mexico factory of their handset chip supplier, Philips. The damage was minor, and Philips expected to resume production within a week. However, Nokia took no chances, and it quickly carried out design changes so that two other suppliers, one in Japan and another in the United States, could manufacture similar chips for Nokia (these were the only two suppliers in the world other than Philips that were capable of delivering similar chips). Nokia then quickly placed orders with these two suppliers. In contrast, Ericsson's supply chain had no such agility: It was set up to function exclusively with the damaged Philips plant in New Mexico—in other words, Ericsson had no plan B. Unfortunately, Philips later found out that the damage was larger than first reported, and production would be delayed for months. By that time, Ericsson scrambled to contact the other two suppliers, only to find out that Nokia had locked up all of their output for the next few months. The upshot? By 2001, Ericsson was driven out of the handset market as an independent player (it reentered the market with a joint venture with Sony called Sony Ericsson).[24]

Adaptability

While agility focuses on flexibility that can overcome short-term fluctuation in the supply chain, **adaptability** refers to the ability to change supply chain configurations in response to long-term changes in the environment and technology. Enhancing adaptability often entails making a series of **make-or-buy decisions** (see In Focus 14.1). This requires firms to *continuously* monitor major geopolitical, social, and technological trends in the world, make sense of them, and reconfigure the supply chain accordingly.[25] The damage for failing to do so may not be visible immediately or annually, but across a number of years, firms failing to do so may be selected out of market.

adaptability
The ability to change supply chain configurations in response to long-term changes in the environment and technology.

make-or-buy decision
The decision on whether to produce in-house or to outsource.

Consider Lucent, the American telecommunications equipment giant. In the mid-1990s, in response to competitive pressures from its rivals Siemens and Alcatel that benefited from low-cost, Asia-based production in switching systems, Lucent

IN FOCUS 14.1 Make-or-Buy Decisions in Making Luxury Cars

The term *make-or-buy decisions* is jargon that refers to decisions on whether to produce in-house (that is, make) or outsource (that is, buy). Conceptually, there is nothing new from our previous discussion on outsourcing (see Chapters 1, 4, and 6, especially Figure 4.4). In manufacturing, firms want to make if (1) the product contains a high level of proprietary technology, (2) it requires close coordination in the supply chain, and (3) suppliers are less capable. On the other hand, firms prefer to buy (or outsource) when (1) strategic flexibility is necessary, (2) suppliers lower cost, and (3) several capable suppliers vigorously compete. The make-or-buy jargon has also been expanded to services. For example, in export trade, *make* means one firm setting up its own export distribution channel, whereas *buy* refers to purchasing channel services from intermediaries such as third-party logistics (3PL) providers.

In luxury car making, believe it or not, Porsche, Mercedes, and BMW have all used contract manufacturers to make *entire* cars (not just components). How they do it is interesting. Porsche has used Finland's Valmet. However, such outsourcing does not involve Porsche's high-end 911, Cayenne, and Carrera models. Valmet makes the Boxster, a luxury car in the eyes of many that is nevertheless Porsche's *low*-end model. For another example, Austria's Magna Steyr has assembled the Mercedes-Benz M-class SUV and the BMW X3. This is similar to one electronics contract manufacturer making products for Philips and Sony side by side, except in the case of making luxury cars, a lot more proprietary technology is involved. Given the sensitive nature of such outsourcing, BMW's contract with Magna Steyr ran to more than 5,000 pages (!). Conflicts are still inevitable with contract manufacturers. To avoid overdependence on one contract manufacturer, Porsche has recently reclaimed one-third of the Boxster's production back to Germany.

Sources: Based on (1) B. Arrunada & X. Vazquez, 2006, When your contract manufacturer becomes your competitor, *Harvard Business Review*, September: 135–145; (2) T. Holcomb & M. Hitt, 2007, Toward a model of strategic outsourcing, *Journal of Operations Management*, 25: 464–481; (3) M. W. Peng, Y. Zhou, & A. York, 2006, Behind the make or buy decisions in export strategy, *Journal of World Business*, 41: 289–300.

successfully adapted its supply chain by phasing out more production in high-cost developed economies and setting up plants in China and Taiwan. However, Lucent then failed to adapt continuously. It concentrated its production in its own Asia-based plants, whereas rivals outsourced such manufacturing to Asian suppliers that became more capable of taking on more complex work. In other words, Lucent used foreign direct investment (FDI) to "make" whereas rivals adopted outsourcing to "buy." Ultimately, Lucent was stuck with its own relatively higher cost (although Asia-based) plants and was overwhelmed by rivals. By 2002, Lucent was forced to shut down its Taiwan factory and to create an outsourced supply chain. But it was too late. By 2006, Lucent lost its independence and was acquired by its archrival Alcatel.

Alignment

alignment
The alignment of interest of various players.

Alignment refers to the alignment of interests of various players involved in the supply chain. In a broad sense, each supply chain is a strategic alliance involving a variety of players, each of which is a profit-maximizing, stand-alone firm.[26] As a result, conflicts are natural. However, players associated with one supply chain must effectively coordinate to achieve desirable outcomes. Therefore, this is a crucial dilemma.[27] Supply chains that can better solve this dilemma may be able to outperform other supply chains. For example, for Boeing's 787 Dreamliner, some 40% of the $8 billion development cost is outsourced to suppliers: Mitsubishi makes the wings, Messier-Dowty provides the landing gear, and so forth.[28] Many suppliers are responsible for end-to-end design of whole subsections. Headed by a vice president for global partnerships, Boeing treats its suppliers as partners, has "partner councils" with regular meetings, and fosters long-term collaboration.

Conceptually, there are two key elements to achieve alignment: power and trust.[29] Not all players in a supply chain are equal, and more powerful players such as Boeing naturally exercise greater bargaining power.[30] Having a recognized leader exercising power, such as Toyota in its supply chain (known as the *keiretsu* in Japanese), facilitates legitimacy and efficiency of the whole supply chain. Otherwise, excessive negotiation and bargaining will have to be conducted among supply chain members of more or less equal standing.

Trust stems from perceived fairness and justice from all supply chain members.[31] Although supply chains have become ever more complex and extended, modern practices, such as low (or zero) inventory, frequent just-in-time (JIT) deliveries, and more geographic dispersion of production, have made all parties more vulnerable if the *weakest* link breaks down. Therefore, it is in the best interest of all parties to invest in trust-building mechanisms to foster more collaboration.

For instance, Seven-Eleven Japan exercised a great deal of power by dictating that vendors resupply its 9,000 stores at three *specific* times a day. If a truck is late by more than 30 minutes, the vendor has to pay a penalty equal to the gross margin of the products carried to the store. This may seem harsh, but it is necessary. This is because Seven-Eleven Japan staff reconfigures store shelves three times a day to cater to different consumers at different *hours*, such as commuters in the morning and school kids in the afternoon. Time literally means money. However, Seven-Eleven Japan softens the blow by trusting its vendors. It does not verify the contents of deliveries. This allows vendors to save time and money because after deliveries, truck drivers do not have to wait for verification and can immediately move on to their next stop. The alignment of interest of such a supply chain is legendary. Hours after the Kobe earthquake in January 1995, when relief trucks moved at two miles an hour (if they moved at all) on the damaged roads, Seven-Eleven Japan's vendors went the extra mile by deploying seven helicopters and 125 motorcycles to deliver 64,000 rice balls to the starving city.

Sometimes, introducing a neutral intermediary (middleman)—more specifically, **third-party logistics (3PL)** providers—may more effectively align the interests in the supply chain. In the case of outsourcing in Asia, buyers (importers) tend to be large Western MNEs such as Gap, Nike, and Marks & Spencer, and suppliers (exporters) are often smaller Asian manufacturers. Despite best intentions, both sides may still distrust each other. MNE buyers are not sure of the quality and timeliness of delivery. Further, MNE buyers are unable to control labor practices in supplier factories, some of which may be dubious (such as running "sweatshops"). In the 1990s, Nike's reputation took a severe hit due to alleged questionable labor practices at its supplier factories. However, suppliers may also be suspicious. Since most contracts for shoes, clothing, toys, and electronics are written several months ahead, suppliers are not confident about MNE buyers' ability to correctly forecast demand. Suppliers thus worry that in case of lower than anticipated demand, buyers may reject shipments to reduce excess inventory by citing excuses such as labor practices or quality issues.[32]

third-party logistics (3PL)
A neutral intermediary in the supply chain that provides logistics and other support services.

One solution lies in the involvement of 3PL intermediaries, such as the Hong Kong–based Li & Fung. Originating as a trading company, Li & Fung maintains a network of suppliers and factories throughout Asia.[33] By bargaining on behalf of the "small guys," Li & Fung enhances their bargaining power vis-à-vis MNE buyers. In exchange, Li & Fung enforces a code of conduct that prevents labor abuses and substandard quality. Suppliers found to violate this code are excluded from accessing Li & Fung's buyers. On the other hand, Li & Fung keeps MNE buyers honest. If they refuse shipments due to their own problems (such as faulty forecast), Li & Fung denies them future access to its supplier network. Of course, Li & Fung's buyers and suppliers pay a fee for its services, but the fee is lower than the transaction costs associated with the haggling, uncertainties, and headaches when buyers and suppliers bargain directly.[34] Overall, 3PL firms may add value by aligning the interests of all parties.

From humble roots of low-profile "logistics," supply chain management has now come of age. A huge logistics industry has grown (In Focus 14.2). Table 14.3 shows where BMW's Mini gets components. Speaking of the alignment of interests, Thomas Friedman in *The World Is Flat* offers an interesting "Dell theory" of world peace: No two countries that are both part of Dell's global supply chain will fight a war against each other.[35] First introduced in our Chapter 2 (see In Focus 2.1), this

IN FOCUS 14.2 Ocean Shipping: Maxing Out?

Compared with the high-profile FedEx and UPS jets, ships are slow—from Shanghai to Los Angeles in 12 to 13 days. Yet, it is the slow-moving ships that do the heavy lifting in modern supply chains. Every day, 15 million containers are moving around, accounting for 90% of the world's traded cargo by value. Today, there are some 4,000 container ships. However, there are signs that the global ocean shipping industry is maxing out.

First, with world merchandise trade growing by 15% and China's exports at nearly double that rate, there are simply not enough ships. The industry has recently ordered another 1,300 container ships. The mightiest is the *Emma Maersk* (pictured), which started to ferry toys from China to Europe by the end of 2006. This 150,000-ton ship can carry 11,000 twenty-foot containers (in the jargon, TEUs—twenty-foot equivalent units). A train carrying that load would be 44 miles (71 kilometers) long (!). In comparison, until 1988, the biggest container ship had only carried 5,000 TEUs, small enough to sail through the Panama Canal. Such ships are known as Panamax. The huge new container ships are labeled post-Panamax. They are far too big for the Canal.

Second, port facilities, especially those on the West Coast, cannot cope with the demand. From Asia, most Panamax ships now unload their cargo at one of the following ports (in descending order of volume): Los Angeles/Long Beach, Oakland, Seattle, Vancouver, Tacoma, and Portland. Port facilities in recent years have been growing at the rate of one Port of Vancouver a year, and there is very little room to further expand. In response, the 93-year-old Panama Canal is now embarking on a $5 billion project to widen itself in order to handle the Maersk monster. Discussions of all-new West Coast ports in Panama and Mexico have also surfaced.

© Kyodo /Landov

Sources: Based on (1) P. Barnes & R. Oloruntoba, 2005, Assurance of security in maritime supply chains, *Journal of International Management*, 11: 519–540; (2) *Economist*, 2002, When trade and security clash, April 6: 59–62; (3) *Economist*, 2007, Container ships, March 3: 71; (4) G. Stalk, 2006, The costly secret of China sourcing, *Harvard Business Review*, February: 64–66.

TABLE 14.3 WHERE DO COMPONENTS FOR BMW'S MINI-ASSEMBLY PLANT IN ENGLAND COME FROM?

Mini Car Part	Country of Origin
Grille	Germany
Hood	Netherlands
Windshield	Belgium
Headliner	UK
Outside Mirrors	Germany
Seats	UK
Gasoline Engine	Brazil
Diesel Engine	Japan
Front and Rear Bumpers	UK
Wheel Bearings	UK
Wheels	Italy and Germany
Exhaust System	UK

theory is of course offered with tongue in cheek: How can a "lowly" supply chain now become a guardian of world peace? The more serious point is that as various firms and countries are woven into a global supply chain that benefits all participants, which is symbolized by Dell, the cost of war may become prohibitive.

HOW INSITITUTIONS AND RESOURCES AFFECT MARKETING AND SUPPLY CHAIN MANAGEMENT

LEARNING OBJECTIVE 4

discuss how institutions and resources affect marketing and supply chain management

Having outlined the basic features of marketing and supply chain management, let us now use the institution- and resource-based views to shed additional light on these topics (Figure 14.4).

Institutions, Marketing, and Supply Chain Management

As an important form of institutions, formal rules of the game obviously have a significant impact. Most countries impose restrictions, ranging from taboos in advertising to constraints on the equity level held by foreign retailers and 3PL providers. Germany bans advertisement that portrays another product as inferior. Goodyear Tire exported a successful ad used in the United States to Germany, which showed that its tire cord could break a steel chain. Because the ad was viewed as insulting the German steel chain manufacturers, the German government banned it. In India, until 2006, FDI had not been allowed in the retail sector (see In Focus 14.3). Likewise, China forbids foreign retailers from operating wholly owned stores and only approves joint-venture stores. In China, France's Carrefour is the most aggressive foreign retailer with sales ahead of Wal-Mart. In some cities, Carrefour struck sweetheart deals with officials and operated wholly owned stores, which provoked Beijing's wrath. The upshot? Carrefour was forced

FIGURE 14.4 INSTITUTIONS, RESOURCES, MARKETING, AND SUPPLY CHAIN MANAGEMENT

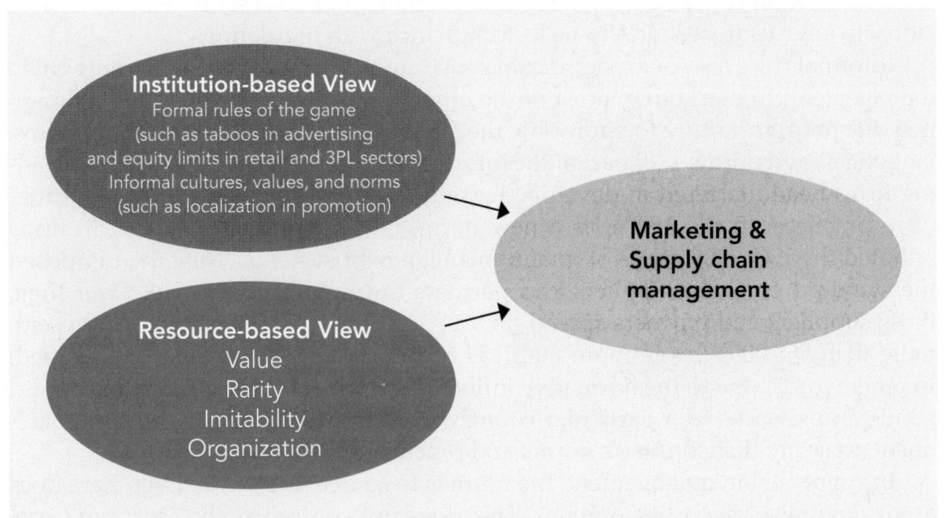

IN FOCUS 14.3 ETHICAL DILEMMA: India: Forthcoming Retail Revolution + Supply Chain Revolution?

India has the world's highest density of retail outlets of any country. It has more than 15 million retail outlets, compared with 900,000 in the United States, whose market (by revenue) is 13 times bigger. At present, 97% of retail sales in India are made in tiny mom-and-pop shops, mostly of less than 500 square feet (46 square meters). In Indian jargon, this is known, quite accurately, as the "unorganized" retail sector. The "organized" (more modern) retail sector commands only 3% of total sales, of which 96% is in the top-ten cities. The retail industry is the largest provider of jobs after agriculture, accounting for 6% to 7% of jobs and 10% of GDP.

With a booming economy and a fast-growing middle class, it is not surprising that foreign retailers, such as America's Wal-Mart, France's Carrefour, Germany's Metro, and Britain's Tesco, are knocking at the door trying to expand the organized retail sector. However, there is one catch: The door is still closed to foreign direct investment (FDI) in the retail sector, which remains one of the last large sectors that has yet to open up to FDI. Millions of shopkeepers, supported by leftist politicians and trade unionists, are worried about the onslaught of multinationals. Citing the controversial "Wal-Mart effect" being debated in the United States and elsewhere, one Indian union leader labeled Wal-Mart "one of the ten worst corporations in the world."

In response, the reformist government that has brought India to the global spotlight since 1991 delicately tries to balance the interests of various stakeholders. FDI is still officially banned in *mass* retailing. However, a side door is now open. Foreign firms can take up to 51% equity in *single-brand* shops that sell their own products, such as Nike, Nokia, and Starbucks shops. Further, FDI in the supply chain is now permitted. Foreign firms can set up wholesale and sourcing subsidiaries that supply local mass retail partners. The first to do this was Australia's Woolworths, which in 2006 started to supply Croma stores owned by Tata Group, India's second largest conglomerate. To better compete with multinational retailers that may eventually arrive, Reliance Group, India's largest conglomerate, is now making huge waves by investing $5.5 billion to build 1,000 hypermarkets and 2,000 supermarkets to blanket the country in the next five years.

On average, Indians are still poor. Only one in 50 households has a credit card; only one in six has a refrigerator. However, as in China 15 years ago, such statistics do not deter foreign entrants. Instead, these data suggest tremendous potential. Despite objections, Wal-Mart is visibly leading the foreign lobby. One of its arguments is that super efficient retail operations will enhance efficiency throughout the entire supply chain. For example, at present, 35% to 40% of fruits and vegetables in India rot while in transit. Food processing adds just 7% to the value of agricultural output, compared with 40% in China and 60% in Thailand, both of which embraced Wal-Mart. As local suppliers become more familiar with Wal-Mart's requirements, exports may naturally follow; Wal-Mart now accounts for 10% of China's exports to the United States. In sum, both a retail revolution and a supply chain revolution is underway in India as you read this case. A crucial ethical dilemma confronting Indian policy makers is whether they should allow well-endowed foreign retail giants to enter the country at the expense of numerous smaller retailers in the "unorganized" sectors, some of which will undoubtedly go out of business. So stay tuned . . .

Sources: Based on (1) *Economist*, 2006, Coming to market, April 15: 69–71; (2) *Economist*, 2006, Setting up shop, November 4: 73–74; (3) A. Mukherjee & N. Patel, 2005, *FDI in Retail Sector*, New Delhi: Department of Consumer Affairs.

to sell a portion of its equity to Chinese partners and convert its wholly owned stores to joint-venture stores to be in compliance with regulations.

Informal rules also place significant constraints on marketing and supply chain management. In marketing, most of the blunders documented in Table 14.2 happen due to firms' failure to appreciate the deep underlying differences in cultures, languages, and norms—all part of the informal institutions. In supply chains, leading firms headquartered in developed economies may be able to diffuse cutting-edge practices. In the 1990s, as a new norm, large numbers of European firms adopted the ISO 9000 series of quality management systems. They then imposed the standard on their suppliers and partners throughout the world. Over time, these suppliers and partners spread ISO 9000 to other domestic firms. At present, more than 560,000 sites in more than 150 countries have been ISO 9000 certified. In other words, due to the normative influence, suppliers and partners that export goods and services to a particular country in a supply chain may be simultaneously *importing* that country's norms and practices.[36]

In supply chain management, the norm is to source from Asia. Even Zara does a fair amount of such outsourcing. This does not contradict the Opening Case, which states that Zara concentrates *most* of its production in-house and in Spain. While Zara's in-house work focuses on fast-turnaround, high-margin merchandise, it has outsourced basic T-shirts whose demand is relatively stable and easy to predict to low-cost suppliers in Asia. Overall, a new trend is that procurement executives are trickling toward Asia to be closer to where the action is. In 2006, IBM's chief procurement officer and the global procurement office moved to Shenzhen, China. This is the first time IBM has based a *corporate*-wide function outside the United States. Asia accounts for a lion's share of IBM's supply base, so it makes sense to locate key supply chain managers in the region.

Resources, Marketing, and Supply Chain Management

As before, we can evaluate marketing and supply chain management activities based on the VRIO criteria[37] (see Figure 14.4). First, managers need to ask: Do these activities add *value*?[38] Marketers now increasingly scratch their heads, as traditional media are losing viewers, readers, and thus effectiveness, but marketers do not have a good handle of how advertising on the new online media adds value. This is especially unsettling in a cross-cultural context. Drivers for online value creation in a country with a very high Internet adoption rate such as South Korea (which leads the world on this dimension) may be very different from drivers of such value creation elsewhere.

Second, managers need to assess the *rarity* of marketing and supply chain activities. If all rival firms advertise in the *Economist* and use FedEx to manage logistics (all of which do add value), these activities, in themselves, are not rare. In supply chain management, first movers in radio frequency identification (RFID) tags may derive benefits because they are rare. Wal-Mart has been experimenting with RFID in 150 stores in the Dallas area and reaped some benefits (such as 16% reduction in out-of-stock items).[39] However, as RFID becomes more available, its rarity will drop.

Third, having identified valuable and rare capabilities, managers need to assess how likely it is for rivals and partners to *imitate*.[40] Although there is no need to waste more ink on the necessity to watch out for rivals, firms also need to be careful about partners in the supply chain. Let us discuss two scenarios. First, as more Western MNEs outsource production to suppliers (or using a new jargon, contract manufacturers), it is always possible that some of the aggressive contract manufacturers may bite the hand that feeds them by directly imitating and competing with Western MNEs. This is not necessarily "opportunism." It is natural for ambitious contract manufacturers to flex their muscle. Such muscle is often directly strengthened by the Western MNEs themselves that willingly transfer technology and share know-how, which is often known as supplier (or vendor) development.[41] China's Haier (household appliances), TCL (televisions), and Galanz (microwaves) have become global leaders in just that way. While it is possible to imitate and acquire world-class manufacturing capabilities, marketing prowess and brand power are more intangible and thus harder to imitate. Hence, Western MNEs often cope by (1) being careful about what they outsource and (2) strengthening customer loyalty to their brands, such as Nike, to fend off contract manufacturers.

A second scenario is the imitation of 3PL capabilities from both buyers and suppliers. 3PL specialists such as Li & Fung thrive by working with small and medium-sized client firms on *both* sides. When buyers such as IBM grow and expand their purchasing volume from Asia, they are likely to set up their own procurement channels in Asia directly.[42] Therefore, Li & Fung is bypassed. On the other hand, when suppliers such as Taiwan's BenQ become more successful overseas, their

© ALY SONG/Reuters /Landov

In a VRIO analysis of a manufacturer's supply chain, how might this activity give the firm a competitive advantage?

export volume justifies their investment to set up their own distribution channels in the West, again bypassing the likes of Li & Fung. Thus, 3PL firms, as intermediaries, live in a precarious world, constantly under the threat of imitation from both sides of their clients.[43] The solution is to make some of the 3PL capabilities *untouchable*. For Li & Fung, this entails constantly developing and leveraging its intimate knowledge about both sides as a hard-to-imitate strategic weapon.[44] Li & Fung often scouts for smaller and lower cost Asian manufacturers and for smaller Western buyers that would benefit from the wide selection and reliability that Li & Fung's network provides. For DHL, FedEx, and UPS, this calls for constantly enhancing the value and reliability (such as a money-back guarantee for late deliveries) that no clients in their right mind would want to think about imitating and competing with 3PL providers.

Finally, managers need to ask: Is our firm *organizationally* ready to accomplish our objectives? Oddly, in many firms, Marketing and Sales functions do not get along well—to avoid confusion, here we spell the two terms with a capital letter to refer to these functions. When revenues are disappointing, the blame game begins: Marketing blames Sales for failing to execute a brilliant plan, and Sales blames Marketing for setting the price too high and burning too much of the budget in high-flying but useless promotion. Marketing staff tend to be better educated, more analytical, and disappointed when certain initiatives fail. In contrast, Sales people are often "street smart," persuasive, and used to rejections all the time. It is not surprising that Marketing and Sales have a hard time working together.[45] Yet, work together they must. Some leading firms have disbanded Marketing and Sales as separate functions and have created an integrated function—called Channel Enablement at IBM. Clearly, an organization with warring functions will be dysfunctional.

LEARNING OBJECTIVE 5

participate in two leading debates concerning marketing and supply chain management

DEBATES AND EXTENSIONS

There are some long-standing debates in this field, such as the standardization versus localization debate discussed earlier. Here, we focus on two important debates not previously discussed: (1) manufacturing versus services and (2) market orientation versus relationship orientation.

Manufacturing versus Services

This debate deals with the nature of certain economic activities. Consider contract manufacturing service. Is it manufacturing? Service? Both? Does it matter? Our vocabulary evolves with—and is also trapped by—the history of economic development. As the first sector for organized economic activities, agriculture was usually seen as *primary*. Emerging in the Industrial Revolution in the 18th and 19th centuries, manufacturing was often the *secondary* sector (after agriculture). Consequently, the residual service activities were typically viewed as *tertiary* (third sector).

Throughout the first half of the 20th century, agriculture declined in importance, and "economic development" often meant industrialization centered on manufacturing. However, in the second half of the 20th century, it was services that occupied the commanding height.[46] In 2006, services accounted for 83% of US employment, whereas manufacturing accounted for only 10% of jobs.[47] The real jobs in manufacturing may be even fewer because in a so-called manufacturing firm or plant, 60% to 70% of employees provide internal services such as accounting and marketing.[48]

Despite the recent prominence of the service sector, it historically lacks prestige. History offers a clue as to why this is the case. Service has a much longer history than manufacturing. The word *service* originated from the Latin word *servus*, which means "slave" or "servant." Nothing could be lower than this. To "add salt to the injury," Adam Smith in *The Wealth of Nations* (1776) labeled service "nonproductive activities." Believing "real man makes stuff," the Soviet Union and China during the heyday of socialism had highly developed heavy manufacturing industries but a severely underdeveloped service sector. Thus, the Soviet Union and China were able to launch rockets to outer space but did not have enough decent mechanics to fix toilets (!).

Toward the end of the 20th century, as Russia and China "woke up" and looked at developed economies for inspiration, they found a highly developed service sector. In fact, it is innovations in services that drive much of economic growth now. Consider McDonald's. In the 1950s, McDonald's drew on the principle of the assembly line, a core manufacturing principle dating back to Henry Ford in the 1910s, to develop high-volume, fast, and standardized services—and the rest is history.

Although marketing and supply chain management would be regarded as services historically, this classification may not matter that much. Half-jokingly, we can ask: Does McDonald's manufacture hamburgers? Seriously, how much difference is there between McDonald's and Boeing? Both market new products, both make to order (finalize a product based on an order), and both extensively rely on powerful supply chain management systems around the world. As alluded to earlier, in the black-and-white world separating manufacturing and services, "contract manufacturing service" would be an oxymoron. Yet today, *integrating* manufacturing and services is both a reality and a necessity.

Market Orientation versus Relationship Orientation

Market orientation refers to a philosophy or way of thinking that places the highest priority on the creation of superior customer value in the marketplace.[49] Although it originated as a marketing concept, its impact permeates throughout a firm and involves not only the marketing function but also strategy, supply chain, IT, and numerous other functions.[50] A market-oriented firm genuinely listens to customer feedback and allocates resources accordingly to meet customer expectations. For example, Boeing used to be an engineering-driven firm with the attitude that its engineers would do airlines a favor by sharing technological wonders with them. Since the development of the 777 in the 1990s, Boeing has transformed itself by involving not only its customers (airlines) but also its suppliers in the conceptualization and design process. Thus, after a period of being outfoxed by Airbus, Boeing is now king of the hill in its domain again (see Chapter 11 Opening Case). The Boeing experience is not isolated. Many firms around

market orientation
A philosophy or way of thinking that places the highest priority on the creation of superior customer value in the marketplace.

the world have enjoyed better performance by being more market oriented. The debate centers on how firms benefit from market orientation *differently* around the world.

relationship orientation
A focus to establish, maintain, and enhance relationships with customers.

Another concept is **relationship orientation**, defined as a focus to establish, maintain, and enhance relationships with customers.[51] Relationship orientation also originates from marketing (often known as "relationship marketing"). Like market orientation, relationship orientation has more recently been expanded to touch many functions beyond marketing. Given the necessity for building trust and coordinating operations, supply chains certainly can benefit from a relationship orientation. Instead of selling engines and then waiting for customers to order spare parts, Rolls-Royce now builds deeper relationships with airlines by renting engines to them, providing 24/7 monitoring on every engine, carrying out full maintenance, and getting paid for every hour the engine is in flight.[52] Rolls-Royce can fix problems before they create damage, thus offering superior value for airlines.

Marketers have heavily debated whether a market orientation or a relationship orientation is more effective in global markets. Key to the debate is how firms benefit from market or relationship orientation differently around the world. Consider competition in China, where *guanxi* (relationship) reportedly is crucial. Firms have to allocate resources between building market-oriented capabilities (such as quality, pricing, and delivery) and relationship-oriented assets (such as wining and dining). China thus offers a strong test for the debate between market and relationship orientation. Researchers find two interesting results. First, relationship-oriented assets do add value. Second, for truly outstanding performance, relationships are necessary but not sufficient. Market-oriented capabilities contribute *more* toward performance.[53] These results make sense in light of China's increasingly market-driven competition that gradually reduces (but does not eliminate) the importance of *guanxi*.

Viewed globally, the strongest effect of market orientation on performance has been found in US firms, which operate in arguably the most developed market economy.[54] In weak market economies such as Russia and Ukraine, the returns from being market oriented are very limited.[55] In other words, firms there can "get away" from a minimal amount of market orientation. Viewed collectively, these findings support the *institution-based* view: By definition, market orientation functions more effectively in a market economy.[56] In a comparative test between mainland Chinese and Hong Kong firms, market orientation has a greater effect on performance than does relationship orientation for Hong Kong firms. However, the pattern is reversed for mainland Chinese firms.[57]

Finally, it is important to note that all these studies take a snapshot, but economies constantly evolve. Although it is always the *combination* of market and relationship orientation that differentiates winning firms from losers, the debate boils down to the relative distribution between the two. There is reason to believe that as China, Russia, and other emerging economies develop further and follow more global rules of the game, market orientation may play an increasingly important role.[58]

draw implications for action

MANAGEMENT SAVVY

What determines the success and failure in marketing and supply chain management around the globe? The institution-based view points out the impact of formal and informal rules of the game. In a nonmarket economy (think of North Korea), marketing would be irrelevant. In a world with high trade and investment barriers, globe-trotting FedEx jets would be unimaginable. The resource-based view argues that holding institutions constant, firms such as Zara and Li Ning that develop the best capabilities in marketing and supply chain management will emerge as winners (see Opening and Closing Cases).

Consequently, three implications for action emerge (Table 14.4). First, marketers and supply chain managers need to know the rules of the game inside and out in order to craft savvy responses. For instance, given the limitations of formal regulatory frameworks in prosecuting cross-border credit card crimes, some US e-commerce firms refuse to ship to overseas addresses. Legitimate overseas purchasers are in turn denied business. As online shopping became a more widespread informal norm, FedEx acquired Kinkos and UPS took over Mail Boxes Etc. (which became The UPS Store). E-commerce firms can now ship to the US addresses of Kinkos and The UPS Store, and FedEx and UPS can then forward products to the overseas purchasers from these stores. This is but one example of superb problem solving in the face of cumbersome formal rules and changing informal norms.

Second, in marketing, focus on the four Ps. This obviously is a cliché that you can get from every marketing textbook. However, in international marketing, managers need to do all it takes to avoid costly and embarrassing blunders (see Table 14.5). Remember: Despite their magnitude, blunders are *avoidable* mistakes. At the very least, international marketers should try very hard to avoid being written up as blunders in the next edition of this textbook.

Finally, in supply chain management, focus on the triple As. This is not cliché, as this idea was published only a few years ago, and few other textbooks share it. Not aware of the importance of the triple As, many firms would only deliver container loads to minimize the number of deliveries and freight costs. When demand

TABLE 14.4 IMPLICATIONS FOR ACTION

- Know the formal and informal rules of the game on marketing and supply chain management inside and out
- In marketing, focus on product, price, promotion, and place (the four Ps) and do all it takes to avoid blunders
- In supply chain management, focus on agility, adaptability, and alignment (the triple As)

TABLE 14.5 DO'S AND DON'TS TO AVOID BLUNDERS IN INTERNATIONAL MARKETING

Do's	Don'ts
• Avoid ethnocentrism. Be sensitive to nationalistic feelings of local consumers, employees, and governments. • Do your homework about the new market. Pay attention to details and nuances, especially those related to cultures, values, and norms. • Avoid the pushy sales representative approach. The pace of business may seem too slow in some countries, but impatience does not bring sales. • Act like a diplomat—build relationships.	• Don't be overconfident about the potential of your products or services—firms will be better off by continuously testing the "water" and experimenting. • Don't cut corners and save back-translation cost—always back-translate (after translating from English to Russian, get someone else to translate it from Russian to English to check accuracy). • Don't use jokes in international advertising. Humor is usually impossible to translate. What is viewed as funny by some may be offensive to others.

Sources: Based on text in (1) T. Dalgic & R. Heijblom, 1996, International marketing blunders revisited—some lessons for managers, *Journal of International Marketing*, 4 (1): 81–91; (2) D. Ricks, 1999, *Blunders in International Business*, 3rd ed., Oxford, UK: Blackwell.

for a particular product suddenly rises, these firms often fail to react quickly; they have to wait until the container (or sometimes even the container *ship*) is full. Such a "best" practice typically delays shipment by a week or more, forcing stock-outs in stores that disappoint consumers. When firms eventually ship container loads, they often result in excess inventory because most buyers do not need a full container load. To get rid of such inventory, as much as a third of the merchandise carried by department stores is sold at a discount. Such discounts not only destroy profits for every firm in the supply chain but also undermine brand equity by upsetting consumers who recently bought the discounted items at full price. In contrast, the triple As urge savvy supply chain managers to focus on agility, adaptability, and alignment of interests of the entire chain.

CHAPTER SUMMARY

1. Articulate three of the four Ps in marketing (product, price, and promotion) in a global context
   - In international marketing, the number-one concern on product is standardization versus localization.
   - Marketers care about price elasticity—how responsive purchasing behavior is when prices change.
   - In promotion, marketers need to decide whether to enhance or downplay the country-of-origin effect.
2. Explain how the fourth P in marketing (place) has evolved to be labeled supply chain management
   - Technically, place used to refer to distribution channel—the location where products are provided.
   - More recently, the term *distribution channel* has been replaced by *supply chain management* in response to more outsourcing to suppliers, contract manufacturers, and 3PL providers.
3. Outline the triple As in supply chain management (agility, adaptability, and alignment)
   - Agility deals with the ability to quickly react to unexpected shifts in supply and demand.
   - Adaptability refers to the ability to reconfigure supply chain in response to longer term external changes.
   - Alignment focuses on the alignment of interests of various players in the supply chain.
4. Discuss how institutions and resources affect marketing and supply chain management
   - Formal and informal rules of the game around the world significantly impact these two areas.
   - Managers need to assess marketing and supply chain management based on the VRIO criteria.
5. Participate in two leading debates concerning marketing and supply chain management
   - The debates are (1) manufacturing versus services and (2) market orientation versus relationship orientation.
6. Draw implications for action
   - Knowing the formal and informal rules of the game will enable savvy managers to answer challenges in marketing and supply chain management.

- To avoid marketing blunders, managers should focus on product, price, promotion, and place (the four Ps).
- Managers can enhance supply chain management by focusing on agility, adaptability, and alignment (the triple As).

KEY TERMS

Adaptability 419
Agility 419
Alignment 420
Country-of-origin effect 416
Distribution channel 418
Make-or-buy decision 419
Market orientation 427
Market segmentation 414
Marketing 412
Marketing mix 412
Place 418
Price 415
Price elasticity 415
Product 413
Promotion 416
Relationship orientation 428
Supply chain 412
Supply chain management 412
Third-party logistics (3PL) 421
Total cost of ownership 416

REVIEW QUESTIONS

1. Describe the four components of marketing mix.
2. Market segmentation can be used to divide consumers around the world into what four categories?
3. How much price elasticity would you say there is among consumers of cars, mobile phones, and rice in your home country?
4. Devise and explain your own example of a product that has a significant total cost of ownership.
5. Why does supply chain management now become an integral part of the "place" in the marketing mix?
6. Name and describe the triple As in supply chain management.
7. How might a make-or-buy decision relate to an alliance or an acquisition?
8. List two examples of how formal institutions affect marketing and/or supply chain management.
9. List two examples of how informal institutions affect marketing and/or supply chain management.
10. If a firm was using a VRIO framework to analyze its marketing mix, which of the four qualities do you think would be most significant? Why?
11. For firms that are both manufacturing and service oriented, which function do you think deserves more time and attention? Explain your answer.
12. Devise your own example of a common business situation, and explain how a market-oriented firm would handle it as opposed to a relationship-oriented firm.
13. If you were a manager of a firm that was planning to begin marketing its product internationally, what steps would you take to avoid marketing blunders?
14. How might a savvy manager use the triple As to enhance a firm's supply chain?

CRITICAL DISCUSSION QUESTIONS

1. Canada has an official animal: the beaver. In 2007, the Canadian prime minister suggested replacing it with the wolverine and stirred up a national debate. Does your country have an official animal? If you were hired as a marketing expert by the government of Canada (or of whatever country), how would you best market the country using an animal?
2. ON ETHICS: You are a supply chain manager at a UK firm. In 2003, SARS broke out in Asia, potentially affecting your supplier in the region. On the one hand, you are considering switching to a new supplier in Central Europe. On the other hand, you feel bad about abandoning your Asian supplier, with whom you have built a pleasant personal and business relationship, at this difficult moment. Yet, your tightly coordinated production cannot afford to miss one supply shipment. How do you proceed?
3. ON ETHICS: In Hollywood movies, it is common to have product placement (have products, such as cars, from sponsored companies appear in movies without telling viewers that these are commercials). As a marketer, you are concerned about the ethical implications of product placement via Hollywood, yet you know the effectiveness of traditional advertising is declining. How do you proceed?

VIDEO CASE

Watch "Supplier Relationships" by Lord Kalms of Dixons Groups.

1. How would Lord Kalms's approach to supplier relationships provide the agility to quickly react to unexpected shifts in supply and demand? What are the global implications?
2. What current controversy involving global trade was illustrated by Marks and Spencer's policy regarding its procurement?
3. In what ways did Marks and Spencer's harm itself as a result of its supplier relationships?
4. Lord Kalms felt that a company's suppliers have a different agenda than the company. Explain by giving both sides of that view.
5. On the one hand (based on the different agenda in question 4), Lord Kalms said that suppliers are his enemies, but on the other hand, he maintained a good relationship with those suppliers. Is that a contradiction? What are the strategic implications? Explain.

CLOSING CASE

Li Ning

Li Ning is China's leading sporting goods company. It was founded in 1989 by Li Ning, who captured three gold medals in gymnastics in the 1984 Los Angeles Olympic Games. Li Ning thus became a national hero in China at the age of 21, and he has enjoyed almost 100% recognition of his name in the country.

Li Ning (hereafter referring to the company, not the founder) positioned itself at an intermediate price/value range between international and local brands. In China, Nike and Adidas focus on the high end with footwear retail prices of $75 to $125 per pair, and most local rivals target the low end at $7 to $25 per pair. Li Ning is the only player with the midrange pricing of $25 to $60 per pair. There are more than 200 sporting goods brands in China. The top-three players—Nike, Adidas, and Li Ning (in that order)—have approximate market shares of 10%, 9.3%, and 8.7%, respectively. Li Ning thus is well within striking distance to surge ahead. It remains well ahead of local competitors (its closest local peer, Anta, has a 3% market share).

© AP IMAGES

Li Ning intensely benchmarks itself against the industry leader, Nike. Over time, as Li Ning grows, it has gained more self-confidence with a clearer identity. Li Ning has become a genuine upgrade, rather than a cheaper alternative, for China's emerging middle class.

Li Ning embarked on internationalization in 2001 by sponsoring Spain's men's and women's basketball teams. In 2005, it forged a strategic partnership with the (US) National Basketball Association (NBA), as part of its "Anything is Possible" marketing campaign. Since then, Li Ning signed agreements with three NBA stars: Shaq O'Neal of the Miami Heat (pictured), Damon Jones of the Cleveland Cavaliers, and Chuck Hayes of the Houston Rockets. Over the last few years, Li Ning has undergone visible brand-image and product-quality upgrades. It now brags about its global credentials as a sponsor of NBA superstars and the 2006 men's basketball world championship team, Spain.

In supply chain management, Li Ning outsourced production and franchised retail outlets. It has been investing heavily in advertising and R&D, both exceeding 18% and 2% of sales, respectively. This has allowed Li Ning to enjoy margin expansion as it turns from a local sportswear company into a global brand company.

All eyes are now on the 2008 Beijing Olympics. Although Li Ning has lost out to Adidas to be the official sponsor of the games, Li Ning has instead sponsored four Chinese teams with gold medal potential (gymnastics, diving, table tennis, and shooting), the Spanish men's and women's basketball teams, the Sudanese track and field team, the Argentinean basketball team, as well as the entire Swedish Olympic delegation. Li Ning hopes that the Beijing Olympics will mark its coming of age as one of the top-five global sporting goods brands.

Case Discussion Questions

1. What aspects of marketing distinguish Li Ning from both international brands and local rivals?
2. Relative to Nike and Adidas, does Li Ning have any advantage in marketing?
3. After the 2008 Beijing Olympics, is Li Ning likely to become one of the top-five global sporting goods brands?

Sources: This case was written by **Sunny Li Sun** (University of Texas at Dallas) under the supervision of Professor Mike W. Peng. It was based on (1) D. Chai & K. So, 2007, Li Ning Co. Ltd.: New NBA coup to strengthen brand appeal, *Merrill Lynch Research*, December 12; (2) A. Jenwipakul & P. McKenzie, 2006, *CLSA Research on Li Ning*, December 14; (3) Li Ning Company IPO and Annual Reports, 2004, 2005, 2006; (4) Y. Liu, 2006, Li Ning rebounding with Shaq? *Beijing Review*, December 21; (5) M. W. Peng, 2006, Li Ning: From Olympic gold medalist to star entrepreneur, in M. W. Peng, *Global Strategy* (pp. 205–206), Cincinnati, OH: Cengage South-Western.

NOTES

Journal acronyms: **AMJ** – *Academy of Management Journal;* **AMR** – *Academy of Management Review;* **APJM** – *Asia Pacific Journal of Management;* **BW** – *Business Week;* **EJM** – *European Journal of Marketing;* **HBR** – *Harvard Business Review;* **IMR** – *International Marketing Review;* **JAMS** – *Journal of the Academy of Marketing Science;* **JBR** – *Journal of Business Research;* **JIBS** – *Journal of International Business Studies;* **JIMktg** – *Journal of International Marketing;* **JMktg** – *Journal of Marketing;* **JMS** – *Journal of Management Studies;* **JOM** – *Journal of Operations Management;* **JWB** – *Journal of World Business;* **MIR** – *Management International Review;* **MSOM** – *Manufacturing and Service Operations Management;* **SMJ** – *Strategic Management Journal*

[1] In 2004, the American Marketing Association (AMA) formally defined marketing as "an organizational function and a set of processes for creating, communicating, and delivering value to customers and for managing customer relationships in ways that benefit the organization and its stakeholders," http://www.marketingpower.com (accessed April 25, 2007).

[2] M. Lejeune & N. Yakova, 2005, On characterizing the 4 C's in supply chain management, *JOM*, 23: 81–100.

[3] T. Choi & D. Krause, 2006, The supply base and its complexity, *JOM*, 24: 637–652; G. T. Hult, D. Ketchen, & S. Slater, 2004, Information processing, knowledge management, and strategic supply chain performance, *AMJ*, 47: 241–253.

[4] D. Ketchen & G. T. Hult, 2007, Bridging organization theory and supply chain management, *JOM*, 25: 573–580.

[5] P. Kotler & K. Keller, 2005, *Marketing Management*, 12th ed., Upper Saddle River, NJ: Prentice Hall.

[6] D. Dow, 2006, Adaptation and performance in foreign markets, *JIBS*, 37: 212–226; S. Jain (ed.), 2003, *Handbook of Research in International Marketing*, Cheltenham, UK: Edward Elgar; C. Katsikeas, S. Samiee, & M. Theodosiou, 2006, Strategy fit and performance consequences of international marketing standardization, *SMJ*, 27: 867–890; L. Lim, F. Acito, & A. Rusetski, 2006, Development of archetypes of international marketing strategy, *JIBS*, 37: 499–524.

[7] T. Levitt, 1983, The globalization of markets, *HBR*, May–June: 92–102.

[8] M. Harvey & M. Myers, 2000, Marketing in emerging and transition economies, *JWB*, 35: 111–113; B. Money & D. Colton, 2000, The response of the new consumer to promotion in the transition economies, *JWB*, 35: 189–205; D. Rigby & V. Vishwanath, 2006, Localization, *HBR*, April: 82–92; A. Schuh, 2000, Global standardization as a success formula for marketing in Central Eastern Europe? *JWB*, 35: 133–148.

[9] *Business Week* and *Economist* are two of the main sources of information for this book. Given this discussion, it is important to clarify that all page numbers cited in this book for these magazines are from their US editions. For the same articles cited, page numbers may be different in editions for other regions.

[10] D. Yankelovich & D. Meer, 2006, Rediscovering market segmentation, *HBR*, February: 122–131.

[11] D. Holt, J. Quelch, & E. Taylor, 2004, How global brands compete, *HBR*, September: 68–75.

[12] M. Cohen, N. Agrawal, & V. Agrawal, 2006, Winning in the aftermarket, *HBR*, May: 129–138.

[13] K. Macharzina, 2001, The end of pure global strategies? (p. 106), *MIR*, 41: 105–108.

[14] D. Ricks, 1999, *Blunders in International Business*, 3rd ed. (p. 88), Oxford: Blackwell.

[15] L. Brouthers & K. Xu, 2002, Product stereotypes, strategy, and performance satisfaction, *JIBS*, 33: 657–677; L. Brouthers, E. O'Connell, & J. Hadjimarcou, 2005, Generic product strategies for emerging market exports into Triad nation markets, *JMS*, 42: 225–245; J. Knight, D. Holdsworth, & D. Mather, 2007, Country-of-origin and choice of food imports, *JIBS*, 38: 107–125; S. Samiee, T. Shimps, & S. Sharma, 2005, Brand origin recognition accuracy, *JIBS*, 36: 379–397; P. Verlegh, 2007, Home country bias in product evaluation, *JIBS*, 38: 361–373.

[16] M. Brannen, 2004, When Mickey loses face, *AMR*, 29: 593–616.

[17] *BW*, 2005, The MySpace generation (p. 92), December 12: 86–96.

[18] E. Rabinovich, A. M. Knemeyer, & C. Mayer, 2007, Why do Internet commerce firms incorporate logistics service providers in their distribution channels? *JOM*, 25: 661–681.

[19] M. Porter, 1985, *Competitive Advantage*, New York: Free Press.

[20] *Economist*, 2006, The physical Internet, June 17: 3–4.

[21] R. Slone, 2004, Leading a supply chain turnaround (p. 116), *HBR*, October: 114–121.

[22] The following discussion draws heavily on H. Lee, 2004, The triple-A supply chain, *HBR*, October: 102–112.

[23] B. Avittathur & P. Swamidass, 2007, Matching plant flexibility and supplier flexibility, *JOM*, 25: 717–735; A. Muriel, A. Somasundaram, & Y. Zhang, 2006, Impact of partial manufacturing flexibility on production variability, *MSOM*, 8: 192–205; E. Prater & S. Ghosh, 2006, A comparative model of firm size and the global operational dynamics of US firms in Europe, *JOM*, 24: 511–529.

[24] *Economist*, 2006, When the chain breaks, June 17: 18–19.

[25] R. Belderbos & L. Sleuwaegen, 2005, Competitive drivers and international plant configuration strategies, *SMJ*, 26: 577–593; F. Rothaermel, M. Hitt, & L. Jobe, 2006, Balancing vertical integration and strategic outsourcing, *SMJ*, 27: 1033–1056.

[26] J. Murray, M. Kotabe, & J. Zhou, 2005, Strategic alliance-based sourcing and market performance, *JIBS*, 36: 187–208.

[27] M. McCarter & G. Northcraft, 2007, Happy together? *JOM*, 25: 498–511.

[28] C. Niezen & W. Weller, 2006, Procurement as strategy, *HBR*, September: 22–23.

[29] R. D. Ireland & J. Webb, 2007, A multi-theoretic perspective on trust and power in strategic supply chains, *JOM*, 25: 482–497.

[30] W. C. Benton & M. Maloni, 2005, The influence of power driven buyer/supplier relationships on supply chain satisfaction, *JOM*, 23: 1–22; T. R. Crook & J. Combs, 2007, Sources and consequences of bargaining power in supply chains, *JOM*, 25: 546–555.

[31] D. Krause, R. Handfield, & B. Tyler, 2007, The relationships between supplier development, commitment, social capital accumulation, and performance improvement, *JOM*, 25: 528–545; C. Rodriguez & D. Wilson, 2002, Relationship bonding and trust as a foundation for commitment in US-Mexican strategic alliances, *JIMKtg*, 10: 53–76.

[32] N. Morgan, A. Kaleka, & R. Gooner, 2007, Focal supplier opportunism in supermarket retailer category management, *JOM*, 25: 512–527.

[33] V. Narayanan & A. Raman, 2004, Aligning incentives in supply chains, *HBR*, November: 94–102.

[34] M. W. Peng, 1998, *Behind the Success and Failure of US Export Intermediaries*, Westport, CT: Quorum.

[35] T. Friedman, 2005, *The World Is Flat*, New York: Farrar, Straus and Giroux.

[36] C. Corbett, 2006, Global diffusion of ISO 9000 certification through supply chains, *MSOM*, 8: 330–350.

[37] M. W. Peng & A. York, 2001, Behind intermediary performance in export trade, *JIBS*, 32: 327–346. See also N. Morgan, A. Kaleka, & C. Katsikeas, 2004, Antecedents of export venture performance, *JMktg*, 68: 90–108.

[38] J. Anderson, J. Narus, & W. Rossum, 2006, Customer value propositions in business markets, *HBR*, March: 91–99; R. Priem, 2007, A consumer perspective on value creation, *AMR*, 32: 219–235.

[39] *Economist*, 2006, Chain reactions, June 17: 14–18.

[40] F. Pil & S. Cohen, 2006, Modularity: Implications for imitation, *AMR*, 31: 995–1011.

[41] S. Modi & V. Mabert, 2007, Supplier development, *JOM*, 25: 42–64; K. Rogers, L. Purdy, F. Safayeni, & P. R. Dimering, 2007, A supplier development program, *JOM*, 25: 556–572.

[42] H. F. Lau, 2008, Export channel structure in a newly industrialized economy, *APJM*, 26 (in press).

[43] M. W. Peng & A. Ilinitch, 1998, Export intermediary firms, *JIBS*, 29: 609–620.

[44] G. T. Hult, D. Ketchen, S. T. Cavusgil, & R. Calatone, 2006, Knowledge as a strategic resource in supply chains, *JOM*, 24: 458–475.

[45] P. Kotler, N. Rackham, & S. Krishnaswamy, 2006, Ending the war between sales and marketing, *HBR*, July: 68–78.

[46] J. Heineke & M. Davis, 2007, The emergence of service operations management as an academic discipline, *JOM*, 25: 364–374.

[47] R. Chase & U. Apte, 2007, A history of research in service operations, *JOM*, 25: 375–386.

[48] D. Quinn, 1992, *Intelligent Enterprise*, New York: Free Press.

[49] A. Kohli & B. Jaworski, 1990, Market orientation, *JMktg*, 54: 1–18; J. Narver & S. Slater, 1990, The effect of a market orientation on business profitability, *JMktg*, 54: 20–35; C. Nobel, R. Sinha, & A. Kumar, 2002, Market orientation and alternative strategic orientations, *JMktg*, 66: 25–39; K. Zhou, B. Yim, & D. Tse, 2005, The effects of strategic orientations on technology- and market-based breakthrough innovations, *JMktg*, 69: 42–60.

[50] T. Dalgic, 1998, Dissemination of market orientation in Europe, *IMR*, 15: 45–60; G. T. Hult, D. Ketchen, & S. Slater, 2005, Market orientation and performance, *SMJ*, 26: 1173–1181; S. Slater, E. Olsen, & G. T. Hult, 2006, The moderating influence of strategic orientation on the strategy formation capability-performance relationship, *SMJ*, 27: 1221–1231.

[51] L. Berry, 1995, Relationship marketing of services, *JAMS*, 23: 236–245; G. Hoetker, 2005, How much do you know versus how well I know you, *SMJ*, 26: 75–96.

[52] *BW*, 2005, Rolls-Royce, at your service, November 14: 92–93.

[53] M. W. Peng & Y. Luo, 2000, Managerial ties and firm performance in a transition economy, *AMJ*, 43: 486–501.

[54] P. Ellis, 2006, Market orientation and performance, *JMS*, 43: 1089–1107.

[55] I. Akimova, 2000, Development of market orientation and competitiveness of Ukrainian firms, *EJM*, 34: 1128–1148; P. Golden, P. Doney, D. Johnson, & J. Smith, 1995, The dynamics of marketing orientation in transition economies, *JIMktg*, 3: 29–49.

[56] J. Fahy, G. Hooley, T. Cox, J. Beracs, K. Fonfoara, & B. Snoj, 2000, The development and impact of marketing capabilities in Central Europe, *JIBS*, 31: 63–81; K. Zhou, J. Brown, C. Dev, & S. Agarwal, 2007, The effects of customer and competitor orientations on performance in global markets, *JIBS*, 38: 303–319.

[57] L. Sin, A. Tse, O. Yau, P. Chow, & J. Lee, 2005, Market orientation, relationship marketing orientation, and business performance, *JIMktg*, 13: 36–57.

[58] M. W. Peng, 2003, Institutional transitions and strategic choices, *AMR*, 28: 275–296; K. Zhou & C. Li, 2007, How does strategic orientation matter in Chinese firms? *APJM*, 24: 447–466.

CHAPTER 15

Managing Human Resources Globally

OPENING CASE

Portman Ritz-Carlton Hotel: The Best Employer in Asia

In China, many multinationals face a constant shortage of talent and high employee turnover. Yet, the five-star Portman Ritz-Carlton Hotel in Shanghai has been able to attract, develop, and retain high-quality talent to deliver excellent customer service and ensure profitable growth. Since 1998, it has been under the leadership of general manager Mark DeCocinis, a native of Italy who grew up in the United States. The Portman Ritz-Carlton has not only been named the "Best Employer in Asia" by Hewitt Associates three consecutive times, but has also been rated the highest in employee satisfaction among all of the Ritz-Carlton's 59 hotels worldwide for five consecutive years. How can DeCocinis and his leadership team achieve such remarkable results? DeCocinis shares his insights in an interview with a professor.

Question: *What's your secret to success in people management?*

Answer: The secret is consistency in execution. Our priority is taking care of our people. We're in the service business, and service comes only from people. It's about keeping our promise to our employees and making that an everyday priority. Our promise is to take care of them, trust them, develop them, and provide a happy place for them to work. The key is everyday execution.

Question: *What's the hiring process to ensure you've selected the right candidate?*

Answer: The general manager is involved in the interview process of all employees, to show the importance of the individual to the company. In 99% of the cases, I agree with the selection decision.

Question: *In most companies, the general manager is not involved in the selection of frontline employees. What do you ask during these interviews?*

Answer: I usually ask them about themselves and try to make a connection. But the important question is: Why do you want to join? Whatever they say, the most important notion needs to be "*I enjoy working with people*," not just using the phrase "I *like* people" . . . I really want to find out what motivates them. If the person smiles naturally, that's very important to us, because this is something you can't force. And if you're happy on the inside, you're happy on the outside. That makes others feel good.

Question: *You start with a philosophy that employee satisfaction leads to guest satisfaction, which in turn leads to good financial results. How do you know such a relationship really exists?*

Answer: Our employee satisfaction rate is 98%. In the last five years, it was 95%, 97%, and 98%. Our guest satisfaction is between 92% and 95%. Financially, our year-on-year growth has been 15% to 18%. If employee satisfaction were to decrease, I guarantee the other factors would decline. Let's say the employees are happy but the guests are not, that means we are not balanced.

Question: *How do you make sure employee satisfaction leads to customer satisfaction?*

Answer: All our performance goals are aligned with our company goal, and from the company to our hotel, and from the hotel to each division. This means that everyone is part of the whole. Each employee comes up with a plan to reach the goal for the next year, measured by guest satisfaction, financial performance, and employee satisfaction. The bonus at the end of the year is based on improvements.

Question: If the Ritz-Carlton worldwide adopts the same culture and philosophy, what makes the Portman Ritz-Carlton the best?

Answer: It's our priority every day to make sure we're walking the walk, starting with me and the people around me . . . People believe what they

LEARNING OBJECTIVES

After studying this chapter, you should be able to

1. explain staffing decisions with a focus on expatriates
2. identify training and development needs for expatriates and host country nationals
3. discuss compensation and performance appraisal issues
4. understand labor relations in both home and host countries
5. discuss how the institution- and resource-based views shed additional light on HRM
6. participate in three leading debates concerning HRM
7. draw implications for action

see, not what is said. I can say "I care about you," but when I look you in the eye and say it, you know I mean it.

Question: *You mentioned the importance of role modeling, starting from the top. Looking back at the last 7–8 years, are there any major incidents that really sent a powerful message to employees that you really care?*

Answer: During the 2003 SARS crisis, business started to deteriorate. By April, our occupancy rate, which should have been at 95%, dropped to 35% . . . The first step was for me and the executive team to take a 30% pay cut . . . Then it got worse. In May, the occupancy rate was 17%–18%. We reduced the workweek to four days, and people were asked to take their outstanding paid leave days. And then, when these reserves were getting used up, that's when everyone really pulled together. Employees who were single gave their shifts to colleagues who had families to support. Some employees were worried that their contracts would not be renewed given the low occupancy rates, we renewed them without a second thought . . . Our employee satisfaction rate that year was 99.9% . . . This was one of those negative things that turned out to be extremely positive.

Source: Excerpts from A. Yeung, 2006, Setting the people up for success: How the Portman Ritz-Carlton Hotel gets the best from its people, *Human Resource Management*, 45 (2): 267–275. Arthur Yeung is a human resource management professor at the University of Michigan and the China Europe International Business School in Shanghai. © Wiley Periodicals, Inc.

human resource management (HRM)
Activities that attract, select, and manage employees.

staffing
The HRM activities associated with hiring employees and filling positions.

host country nationals (HCN)
An individual from the host country who works for an MNE.

expatriate (expat)
A nonnative employee who works in a foreign country.

How can firms such as the Portman Ritz-Carlton select, retain, reward, and motivate the best employees that they can attract? How can they link the management of people with firm performance? These are some of the crucial questions we address in this chapter. This chapter is devoted to **human resource management (HRM)**—activities that attract, select, and manage employees.[1] As a function, HRM used to be called "personnel" and before that "records management." Few of you are experts in HRM, but everyone can appreciate its rising importance just by looking at the evolution of the terminology. The term "human resource management" clearly indicates that people are key resources of the firm to be actively managed and developed. In the last two decades, HRM has become even more important and often sports the word *strategic* to make it "strategic HRM."[2] From a lowly administrative support function, HRM has now increasingly been recognized as a strategic function (often known as a "business partner") that, together with other crucial functions such as finance and marketing, helps accomplish organizational effectiveness and financial performance.[3]

This chapter first reviews the four main areas of HRM: (1) staffing, (2) training and development, (3) compensation and performance appraisal, and (4) labor relations. Then, we use the institution- and resource-based views to shed light on these issues. Debates and extensions follow.

LEARNING OBJECTIVE 
explain staffing decisions with a focus on expatriates

STAFFING

Staffing refers to HRM activities associated with hiring employees and filling positions.[4] In multinational enterprises (MNEs), there are two types of employees: **host country nationals** (**HCNs**, often known as "locals") and **expatriates** (**expats** in short—nonnative employees who work in a foreign country). The general manager at the Portman Ritz-Carlton Hotel, Mark DeCocinis, is an expatriate, and all the Chinese employees he hired are HCNs. Among expatriates, there are two types: (1) **Parent (home) country nationals (PCNs)** come from the parent country of the multinational enterprise (MNE) and work at its local subsidiary. For the US-based Ritz-Carlton, PCNs would be Americans. (2) **Third country nationals (TCNs)** come from neither the parent country nor the host country. For the Portman Ritz-Carlton, TCNs can be from any country other than the United States and China.

parent (home) country national (PCN)
An employee who comes from the parent country of the MNE and works at its local subsidiary.

third country national (TCN)
An employee who comes from neither the parent country nor the host country.

The majority of an MNE's employees (that is, those in the lower and midranks) would be HCNs. For example, of HSBC's 28,400 employees worldwide, only a small cadre of 400 executives are expatriates, and another 1,600 employees are short-term assignees abroad.[5] A leading concern is how to staff the *top* executive positions abroad, such as the subsidiary CEO, country manager, and key functional heads (such as CFO and CIO). Of the three choices for top positions, PCNs, TCNs, and HCNs all have their pros and cons (Table 15.1). The staffing choices are not random and are often a reflection of the strategic posture of the MNE as discussed next.

Ethnocentric, Polycentric, and Geocentric Approaches to Staffing

There are three primary approaches when making staffing decisions for top positions at subsidiaries.[6] An **ethnocentric approach** emphasizes the norms and practices of the parent company (and the parent country of the MNE) by relying on PCNs. PCNs can not only ensure and facilitate control and coordination by headquarters, but they may also be the best qualified people for the job because of special skills and experience. A perceived lack of talent and skills of HCNs often necessitates an ethnocentric approach. In addition, a cadre of internationally mobile and experienced managers, who are often PCNs, can emerge to spearhead further expansion around the world.

ethnocentric approach
An emphasis on the norms and practices of the parent company (and the parent country of the MNE) by relying on PCNs.

The opposite of an ethnocentric approach, a **polycentric approach** focuses on the norms and practices of the host country. In short, "when in Rome, do as the Romans do." Who will be the best managers if we have an operation in Rome? Naturally, Roman (or Italian) managers—technically, HCNs. HCNs have no language and cultural barriers. Unlike PCNs who often pack their bags and move after several years, HCNs stay in their positions longer, thus providing more continuity of management. Further, placing HCNs in top subsidiary positions sends a morale-boosting signal to other HCNs who may feel that they, too, can reach the top (at least in that subsidiary).

polycentric approach
An emphasis on the norms and practices of the host country.

TABLE 15.1 PARENT, THIRD, AND HOST COUNTRY NATIONALS

	Advantages	Disadvantages
Parent country nationals (PCNs)	• Control by headquarters is facilitated • PCNs may be the most qualified people • Managers are given international experience	• Opportunities for HCNs are limited • Adaptation may take a long time • PCNs are usually very expensive
Third country nationals (TCNs)	• TCNs may bridge the gap between headquarters and the subsidiary (and between PCNs and HCNs) • TCNs may be less expensive than PCNs	• Host government and employees may resent TCNs • Similar to disadvantages for PCNs
Host country nationals (HCNs)	• Language and cultural barriers are eliminated • Continuity of management improves because HCNs stay longer in positions • Usually cheaper	• Control and coordination by headquarters may be impeded • HCNs may have limited career opportunities • International experience for PCNs is limited

Source: Adapted from P. Dowling & D. Welch, 2005, *International Human Resource Management*, 4th ed. (p. 63), Cincinnati, OH: Cengage South-Western.

geocentric approach
A focus on finding the most suitable managers, who can be PCNs, HCNs, or TCNs.

Disregarding nationality, a **geocentric approach** focuses on finding the most suitable managers, who can be PCNs, HCNs, or TCNs. In other words, a geocentric approach is "color-blind"—the color of a manager's passport does not matter (see In Focus 13.1). For a geographically dispersed MNE, a geocentric approach can facilitate the emergence of a corporate-wide culture and identity. This can reduce the typical "us versus them" feeling in firms that use either ethnocentric or polycentric approaches. On the other hand, molding managers from a variety of nationalities is a lot more complex than integrating individuals from two (parent and host) countries.

Overall, there is a systematic link between MNEs' strategic postures (see Chapter 13) and staffing approaches (Table 15.2). MNEs pursuing a home replication strategy usually pursue an ethnocentric approach, staffing subsidiaries with PCNs. MNEs interested in a localization strategy are typically polycentric in nature, placing HCNs to head subsidiaries. Global standardization or transnational strategies often necessitate a geocentric approach, resulting in a mix of HCNs, PCNs, and TCNs.

The Role of Expatriates

expatriation
The process of selecting, managing, and motivating expatriates to work abroad.

Expatriation is the process of selecting, managing, and motivating expatriates to work abroad. Shown in Figure 15.1, expatriates play four important roles:

- Expatriates are *strategists* representing the interests of the MNE's headquarters.[7] Expatriates, especially PCNs who have a long tenure with a particular MNE, may have internalized the parent firm's values and norms. They may not only enable headquarters to control subsidiaries, but also facilitate the socialization process to bring subsidiaries into an MNE's global "orbit."
- Expatriates act as *daily managers* to run operations and to build local capabilities. One of the reasons they are sent in the first place is often due to a lack of local management talent.
- Expatriates are also *ambassadors*.[8] Representing headquarter's interests, they build relationships with host country stakeholders such as local managers, employees, suppliers, customers, and government officials. Importantly, expatriates also serve as ambassadors representing the interests of the *subsidiaries* when interacting with headquarters.
- Finally, expatriates are *trainers* for their replacements. Over time, some localization in staffing is inevitable, calling for expatriates to train local employees.

TABLE 15.2 MULTINATIONAL STRATEGIES AND STAFFING APPROACHES

MNE strategies	Typical staffing approaches	Typical top managers at local subsidiaries
Home replication	Ethnocentric	Parent country nationals
Localization	Polycentric	Host country nationals
Global standardization	Geocentric	A mix of parent, host, and third country nationals
Transnational	Geocentric	A mix of parent, host, and third country nationals

FIGURE 15.1 THE ROLES OF EXPATRIATES

Expatriate Failure and Selection

Few expatriates can simultaneously play the challenging multidimensional roles effectively.[9] It is not surprising that expatriate failure rates are high. "Expatriate failure" can be defined differently, such as (1) premature (earlier than expected) return, (2) unmet business objectives, and (3) unfulfilled career development objectives. Using the relatively easy-to-observe measure of premature return, studies in the 1980s reported that 76% of US MNEs have more than 10% of expatriates failing, and 41% and 24% of European and Japanese MNEs, respectively, have a comparable number of failure cases.[10] More recent studies find that the failure rates may have declined a little.[11] However, given the much larger number of expatriates now (at present, 1.3 million from the United States alone), expatriate failure rates are still high enough to justify attention. Since expatriates typically are the most expensive group of managers, the cost of each failure is tremendous (between $250,000 and $1 million).

A variety of reasons can cause expatriate failure. Surveys of US and European MNEs find that the inability of the spouse and the family to adjust is the leading cause. In the case of Japanese MNEs, the leading cause is the inability to cope with the larger scope of responsibilities overseas. It usually is a *combination* of work-related and family-related problems that leads to expatriate failures.

Given the importance of expatriates and their reported high failure rates, how can firms enhance the odds for expatriate success? Figure 15.2 outlines a model for expatriate selection, with six underlying factors grouped along situation and individual dimensions. In terms of situation dimensions, both headquarters' and subsidiary's preferences are important (Table 15.2). In some Asian countries where seniority is highly respected,[12] younger expatriates may be ineffective. The subsidiary may have specific requests (such as "Send a more senior IT person"). Also, it is preferable for expatriates to have some command (or better yet, mastery) of the local language.

In terms of individual dimensions, both technical ability and cross-cultural adaptability are a must. Desirable attributes include a positive attitude, emotional stability, and previous international experience.[13] Last (but certainly not least), spouse and family preferences must enter the equation.[14] The accompanying spouse may have left behind a career and a social network. He or she has to find meaningful endeavors abroad (to protect local jobs, many countries do not permit the spouse to work). It is not surprising that frustration permeates many families, thus leading to expatriate failure.

What can expatriates do to prepare for an assignment and improve their chances of success?

FIGURE 15.2 FACTORS IN EXPATRIATE SELECTION

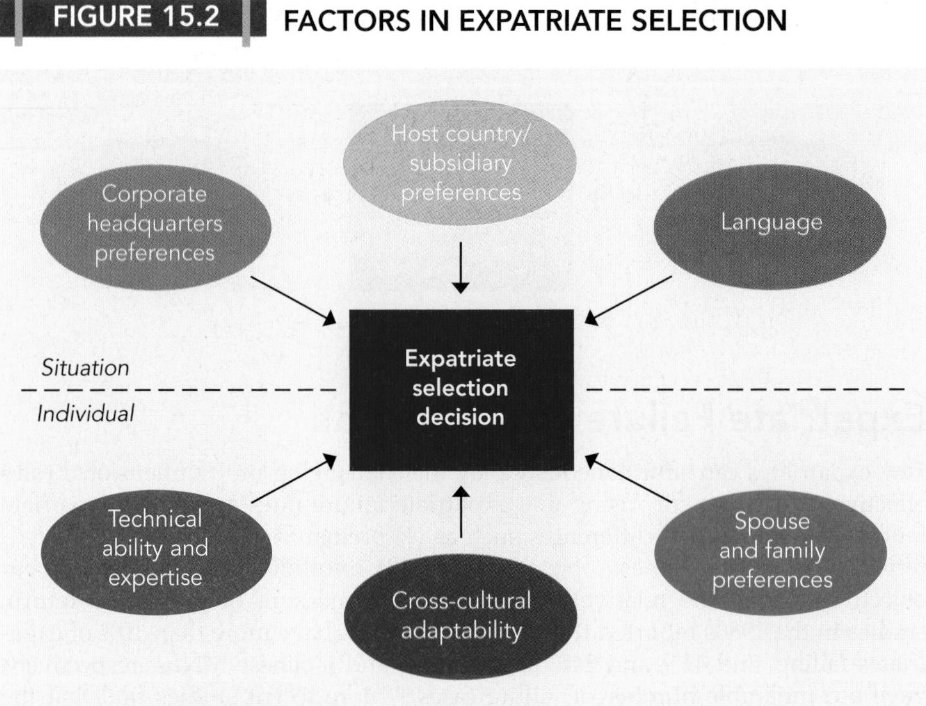

Source: Adapted from P. Dowling & D. Welch, 2005, *International Human Resource Management*, 4th ed. (p. 98), Cincinnati, OH: Cengage South-Western.

While expatriates, in general, are expensive and failure rates are high, middle-aged expatriates (forty-somethings) are the most expensive because the employer often has to provide heavy allowances for children's education. High-quality schools are very expensive. In places such as Manila, Mexico City, and Moscow, international or American schools cost $10,000 to $30,000 per year. Unfortunately, these expatriates also have the highest percentage of failure rates in part because of their family baggage. In response, many MNEs move to (1) select expatriates in their 50s, whose children may have left the home, and/or (2) promote younger expatriates in their late 20s and early 30s, who may not yet have a family (or children). The younger expatriates have no need for a large home and no school-age kids. The second preference has strong implications for students studying this book now: These overseas opportunities may come sooner than you expect—are *you* ready?

LEARNING OBJECTIVE 2

identify training and development needs for expatriates and host country nationals

TRAINING AND DEVELOPMENT NEEDS

Training is specific preparation to do a particular job. **Development** refers to longer term, broader preparation to improve managerial skills for a better career.[15] Training and development programs focus on two groups: (1) expatriates and (2) HCNs. Each is discussed in turn.

training
The specific preparation to do a particular job.

development
The longer term, broader preparation to improve managerial skills for a better career.

Training for Expatriates

The importance and cost of expatriates and their reported high failure rates necessitate training. Yet, about one-third of MNEs do not provide any predeparture training for expatriates—other than wishing them "good luck."[16] Even for firms that provide training, many offer short, one-day-type programs that are inadequate. Not surprisingly, many MNEs and expatriates are "burned" for such underinvestment in preparation for arguably some of the most challenging managerial assignments.

Ideally, training length and rigor should vary according to the length of stay for expatriates. For a short stay, training can be short and less rigorous. Sometimes, survival-level language training (such as "Where is the ladies' room?" and "I'd like a beer") would suffice. However, for a long stay of several years, it is imperative that longer length and more rigorous training be provided, especially for neophyte expatriates. This would entail more extensive language training and sensitivity training, preferably with an immersion approach (training conducted in a foreign language/culture environment). More enlightened firms now involve the spouse in expatriate training.

Development for Returning Expatriates (Repatriates)

Many expatriate assignments are not one-shot deals; instead, they are viewed as part of the accumulation of a manager's experience and expertise for long-term career development in the firm.[17] Although in theory this idea sounds good, in practice (see Table 15.3), many MNEs do a lousy job managing **repatriation**—the process of facilitating the return of expatriates.

repatriation
The process of facilitating the return of expatriates.

repatriate
Returning expatriate.

psychological contract
An informal understanding of expected delivery of benefits in the future for current services.

Chief among the problems is career anxiety experienced by **repatriates** (returning expatriates). A leading concern is "What kind of position will I have when I return?" Prior to departure, many expatriates are encouraged by their boss: "You should take (or volunteer for) this overseas assignment. It's a smart move for your career." Theoretically, this is known as a **psychological contract**—an informal understanding of expected delivery of benefits in the future for current services. However, a psychological contract is easy to violate. Bosses may have now changed their mind. Or they may have been replaced by new bosses. Violated psychological contracts naturally lead to disappointments.

Many returning expatriates experience painful adjustment at the workplace. Ethnocentrism continues to characterize many MNEs: Knowledge transfer is typically one way—from headquarters to subsidiaries via expatriates. However, few (or none) at headquarters seem interested in learning from expatriates' overseas experience and knowledge. Having been "big fish in a small pond" in subsidiaries, they often feel like "small fish in a big pond" at headquarters. Instead of being promoted, many end up taking a comparable (or lower level) position.

Returning expatriates may also experience a loss of status. Overseas, they are "big shots," rubbing shoulders with local politicians and visiting dignitaries. They often command lavish expatriate premiums, with chauffeured cars and maids. However, most of these perks disappear now.

Finally, the spouse and the children may also find it difficult to adjust back home. The feeling of being a part of a relatively high-class, close-knit expatriate community is gone. Instead, life at home may now seem lonely, dull, unexciting, and in some cases, dreadful. In the United States, some wives of Honda

TABLE 15.3 PROBLEMS ASSOCIATED WITH REPATRIATION

- Career anxiety—what kind of position will I have when I return (if I do have a position)?
- Work adjustment—from a big fish in a small pond (at the subsidiary) to a small fish in a big pond (at headquarters)
- Loss of status and pay—expatriate premiums are gone; chauffeured cars and maids are probably unavailable
- Difficult for the spouse and children to adjust—going home is not that easy

executives enjoy being Avon Ladies (direct selling). When the long anticipated repatriation notice comes, they are excited about expanding their business back to Japan. However, prior to returning home, all husbands receive a letter from headquarters, demanding that their wives quit direct selling. This is because direct selling is viewed as a low-prestige occupation not worthy for the spouses of executives at a prestigious firm such as Honda—doesn't Honda pay executives enough? The letter ends with a warning that if their wives are found to continue selling Avon cosmetics in Japan, their husbands will be *fired*.[18] Likewise, children, being out of touch with current slang, sports, and fashion, may struggle to regain acceptance into peer groups. Having been brought up overseas, (re)adjusting back to the home country educational system may be especially problematic. Some of the returning Japanese teenagers committed suicide after failing to make the grade back home.

Overall, repatriation, if not managed well, can be traumatic not only for expatriates and their families but also for the firm. Unhappy returning expatriates do not last very long.[19] Approximately one in four exits the firm within one year. Since a US MNE spends on average around $1 million on each expatriate over the duration of a foreign assignment, losing that individual can wipe out any return on investment.[20] Worse yet, the returnee may end up working for a rival firm.

The best way to reduce expatriate turnover is a career development plan.[21] A good plan also comes with a mentor (also known as a champion, sponsor, or "godfather").[22] The mentor helps alleviate the "out-of-sight, out-of-mind" feeling by ensuring that the expatriate is not forgotten at headquarters and by helping secure a challenging position for the expatriate upon return.

Overall, there are numerous "horror stories," but there are many high-profile cases of expatriate success as well. For example, Carlos Ghosn, after successfully turning around Nissan as a PCN, went on to become CEO of the parent company, Renault. To reach the top at most MNEs today, international experience is a must. Therefore, despite the drawbacks, aspiring managers should not be deterred. Who said being a manager was easy?

Training and Development for Host Country Nationals

Although most international HRM practice and research focus on expatriates, it is important to note that HCNs deserve significant attention for their training and development needs. In the ongoing "war for talent" in China, whether employers can provide better training and development opportunities often becomes a key determining factor on whether top talent is retained or not (In Focus 15.1). To stem the tide of turnover, many MNEs now have formal career development plans and processes for HCNs in China. Kodak, for example, strives for the "Four Greats": (1) great hires, (2) great moves (fast promotion), (3) great assignments, and (4) great feedback.

LEARNING OBJECTIVE 3

discuss compensation and performance appraisal issues

COMPENSATION AND PERFORMANCE APPRAISAL

compensation
The determination of salary and benefits.

As an HRM area, **compensation** refers to the determination of salary and benefits.[23] **Performance appraisal** entails the evaluation of employee performance for promotion, retention, or termination purposes. Three related issues are discussed here: (1) compensation for expatriates, (2) compensation for HCNs, and (3) performance appraisal.

IN FOCUS 15.1 Competing for Talent in China

This may be hard to believe, but the most populous country in the world has a shortage of people—managers. Chinese and foreign firms need 75,000 globally competitive executives in China. At present, only approximately 3,000 to 5,000 Chinese executives fit the profile. Thus, MNEs of all stripes are going after the same pool of talent, and the pickings are especially slim at the top. The war on talent is real in China.

Although the average pay raise has been 10% or more in recent years, for top talent, "you see title inflation and raises of 50% to 60% a year," says an HR professional. Top talent is often snatched, quickly promoted, and then, all too often, stolen away. One study finds that every year, 43% of executives in China voluntarily quit, compared with 5% in Singapore and 11% in Australia. Another study puts the average turnover at 14%. Although estimates vary, China probably now has the world's highest turnover rate for managers.

In a tight job market, money clearly matters. But beyond compensation, training and development are the new frontier for differentiation, with inpatriation in the MNE's parent country being one of the most highly sought-after prizes. At GE China, 60% of the salaried employees are under 35. Young managers take on responsibilities that twenty-something employees elsewhere can only dream about. A position that takes ten years to reach in Japan or five years to reach in the West often takes only three years to get in China; otherwise, the MNE risks losing such talent. GE finds that its executives are especially vulnerable after three years. This is a crucial point at which they have soaked up enough training and responsibility to make themselves attractive, but they are not yet really loyal to GE. In response, GE tries hard to make promising managers stimulated, recognized, and nurtured, and it manages to reduce its executive turnover to "only" 7%.

Both the shortage of talent and the rush of MNEs entering China for the first time with expats mean that the country now has more expats than ever with tremendous diversity. Kodak distinguishes among (1) full expats (from the US and EU), (2) regional expats (from Hong Kong, Taiwan, and Singapore), (3) local foreigners (hired locally, who do not command expat packages), and (4) fully local hires (HCNs). Kodak tries to pay each group according to the going rate in its home region. Most MNEs aim to eventually replace expats with Chinese nationals. Such localization is often fueled by a desire to reduce cost. However, trimming expats may not necessarily save money because compensation for HCNs has been skyrocketing recently.

Adding to the heat, Chinese firms have entered the fray. Alibaba, Gome, Haier, Huawei, Lenovo, Li Ning, and TCL have successfully raided the managerial ranks of Microsoft, Nokia, and other MNEs. This reflects a sea change. As recently as five years ago, no self-respecting executive would quit a *Fortune* 500 MNE to join a local outfit. Now such moves are considered very smart. Although Chinese firms do not necessarily outbid the MNEs in compensation, Chinese firms offer something that is hard to beat: no glass ceiling, no expats, and the sky is the limit. There will be no shortage of Chinese rivals eager to snatch away managers trained by MNEs.

Sources: Based on (1) author's interviews in China; (2) *Business Week*, 2006, Management grab, August 21: 88–90; (3) *Business Week*, 2005, Stealing managers from the big boys, September 26: 54–55; (4) V. Hulme, 2006, Short staffed, *China Business Review*, March–April: 18–23; (5) Y. Zhang, J. George, & T. Chan, 2006, The paradox of dueling identities: The case of local senior executives in MNC subsidiaries, *Journal of Management*, 32: 400–425.

Compensation for Expatriates

A leading issue in international HRM is how to properly compensate, motivate, and retain expatriates. There are two primary approaches: (1) going rate and (2) balance sheet (Table 15.4).

The **going rate approach** pays expatriates the going rate for comparable positions in a host country. When the new Lenovo sends Chinese expatriates to New York, it pays them the going rate for comparable positions for HCNs and other expatriates in New York. This approach fosters equality among PCNs, TCNs, and HCNs in the same subsidiary. It would be attractive for PCNs and TCNs to work in a location where pay is higher than in the home country. This approach excels in its simplicity. Expatriates also develop strong identification with the host country.

However, the going rate, for the same position, differs around the world, with the United States leading in managerial compensation. For example, the typical US CEO commands a total compensation package of over $2 million, whereas the British CEO receives less than $1 million, the Japanese CEO $500,000, and the Chinese CEO $200,000. According to the going rate approach, returning Lenovo expatriates, having been used to New York-level high salaries, will have a hard time accepting relatively lower Beijing-level salaries, thus triggering repatriation problems.

performance appraisal
The evaluation of employee performance for promotion, retention, or termination purposes.

going rate approach
A compensation approach that pays expatriates the prevailing (going) rate for comparable positions in a host country.

TABLE 15.4 GOING RATE VERSUS BALANCE SHEET APPROACH IN EXPATRIATE COMPENSATION

	Advantages	Disadvantages
Going rate	• Equality among parent, third, and host country nationals in the same location • Simplicity • Identification with host country	• Variation between assignments in different locations for the same employee • Reentry problem if the going rate of parent country is less than that of host country
Balance sheet	• Equity between assignments for the same employee • Facilitates expatriate reentry	• Costly and complex to administer • Great disparities between expatriates and host country nationals

balance sheet approach
A compensation approach that balances the cost of living differences based on parent country levels and adds a financial inducement to make the package attractive.

A second approach is the **balance sheet approach**, which balances the cost of living differences based on parent country levels and adds a financial inducement to make the package attractive. This is the most widely used method in expatriate compensation. There is a historical reason for this preference because, until recently, a majority of expatriates had come from higher pay developed economies going to lower pay locations. In this case, the going rate approach would not work because no expatriate from New York would accept the going rate in Beijing. The balance sheet approach essentially offers "New York Plus" for Beijing-bound expatriates. The "Plus" is nontrivial: additional financial inducement (premium), cost of living allowance (such as housing and children's education), and hardship allowance (although fewer companies now pay a hardship allowance for Beijing, many MNEs used to). Table 15.5 shows one hypothetical example. Adding housing and taxation that the MNE pays (not shown in the table), the total cost to the firm may reach $300,000 a year.

The balance sheet approach has two advantages (see Table 15.4). First, there is equity between assignments for the same employee, whose compensation is always anchored to the going rate in the parent country. Second, it also facilitates repatriation, with relatively little fluctuation between overseas and parent country pay despite the cost of living differences around the world (Figure 15.3)

However, there are three disadvantages. The first is cost. Using the example in Table 15.5, the cost can add up to $1 million for a three-year tour of duty. The second disadvantage is the great disparities between expatriates (especially PCNs) and HCNs. In the 1990s, a British MNE had an India-based operation of 300 employees, three of whom were British PCNs. About 80% of the total budget for compensation went to the three British PCNs. HCNs' resentment would be natural.

Finally, the balance sheet approach is organizationally complex to administer. For a US firm operating in South Africa, both the American PCNs and Australian TCNs are likely to be compensated more than the South African HCNs. The situation becomes more complicated when the US firm recruits South African MBAs before they finish business school training in the United States. Should they be paid as locally hired HCNs in South Africa or as expatriates from the United States? What about TCNs from Kenya, Morocco, and Nigeria who also finish US MBA training and are interested in going to work for the US MNE in South Africa? Ideally, firms pay for a position regardless of passport color. However, the market for expatriate compensation is not quite there yet.

Compensation for Host Country Nationals

At the bottom end of the compensation scale, low-level HCNs, especially those in developing countries, have relatively little bargaining power. The very reason that they have a job at the MNE subsidiaries is often because of their low labor cost—that

TABLE 15.5 A HYPOTHETICAL EXPATRIATE COMPENSATION PACKAGE USING THE BALANCE SHEET APPROACH

Items for a hypothetical US expatriate	Amount (US$)
Base salary	$150,000
Cost-of-living allowance (25%)	$37,500
Overseas premium (20%)	$30,000
Hardship allowance (20%)	$30,000
Housing deduction (–7%)	–$10,500
TOTAL (pretax)	**$237,000**

Note: The host country has a cost-of-living index of 150 relative to the United States. *Not* shown here are (1) the full cost of housing and (2) the cost to pay the difference between a higher income tax in a host country and a lower income tax in the parent country. Adding housing and taxation, the net cost on the MNE can reach $300,000 in this case.

is, they are willing to accept wage levels substantially lower than those in developed countries. To them, the benchmark groups are typically farmhands sweating in the fields making much less or unemployed taking home nothing to feed the family. Despite some social activist groups' accusations of "exploitation" by MNEs, MNEs typically pay *higher* wages relative to similar positions in developing countries.

On the other hand, HCNs in management and professional positions have increasing bargaining power. MNEs are rushing into Brazil, Russia, India, and China (BRIC), where local supply of top talent is limited. Wage inflation in India's IT sector is now 16% a year, with a 40% turnover.[24] It is not surprising that high-caliber HCNs, because of their scarcity, will fetch more pay (In Focus 15.1). The question is: How much more? Most MNEs aim to eventually replace even top-level expatriates with HCNs, in part to save cost. However, if HCNs occupying the same top-level positions are paid the same as expatriates, then there will be no cost savings. However,

FIGURE 15.3 DIFFERENCES IN COST OF LIVING FOR EXPATRIATES IN SELECTED CITIES (NEW YORK = 100)

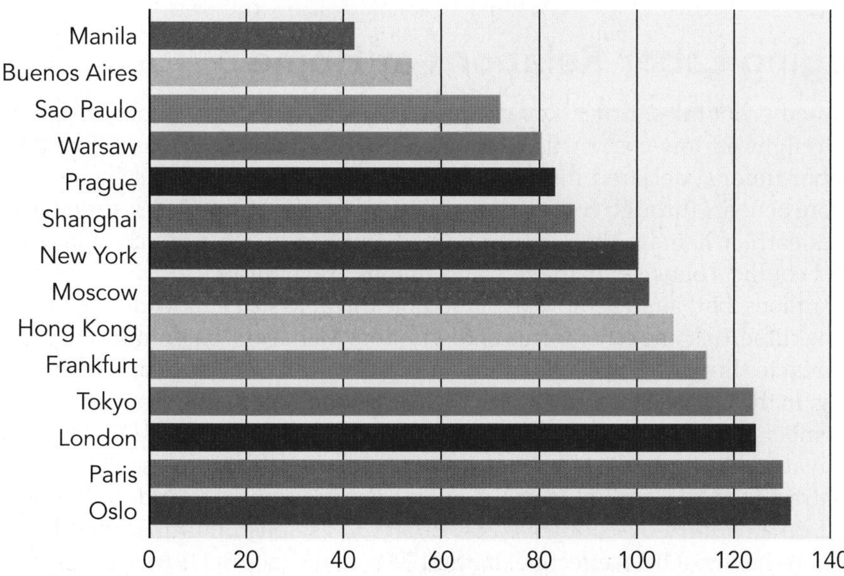

Source: Adapted from *Economist*, 2007, The cost of living, March 17: 105. All data are for March 2007.

MNEs unwilling to pay top local talent top dollar may end up losing such high-caliber HCNs to competitors that are willing to do so. The war for talent is essentially a bidding war for top HCNs.[25] Eventually, for qualified individuals in top positions, MNEs may have to pay international rates regardless of nationality.

Performance Appraisal

Although initial compensation is determined upon entering a firm, follow-up compensation usually depends on performance appraisal. It focuses on decision making (to determine pay and promotion), development, documentation, and subordinate expression. In our case, performance appraisal entails (1) how expatriates provide performance appraisal to HCNs and (2) how expatriates are evaluated.

When expatriates evaluate HCNs, cultural differences may create problems. Western MNEs emphasize an opportunity for subordinates to express themselves. However, high power-distance countries in Asia and Latin America would not foster such an expression, which would potentially undermine the power and status of supervisors. Employees themselves do not place a lot of importance on such an expression.[26] Thus, Western expatriates pushing HCNs in these cultures to express themselves in performance appraisal meetings would be viewed as indecisive and lacking integrity.

Expatriates need to be evaluated by their own supervisors. However, in some cases, expatriates are the top manager in a subsidiary (such as country manager), and their supervisors are more senior executives based at headquarters. Some of these off-site managers have no experience as expatriates themselves. They often evaluate expatriates based on hard numbers, such as productivity and market growth, some of which are beyond the control of expatriates (what about a currency crisis?). This is one of the reasons many expatriates feel that they are not evaluated fairly. The solution lies in (1) fostering more visits and exchange of views between on-site expatriates and off-site supervisors and (2) relying on former expatriates now based at headquarters to serve as off-site supervisors.

LEARNING OBJECTIVE 4

understand labor relations in both home and host countries

LABOR RELATIONS

Labor relations refer to firms' relations with organized labor (unions) in both home and host countries. Each is discussed in turn.

labor relations

A firm's relations with organized labor (unions) in both home and host countries.

Managing Labor Relations at Home

In developed economies, firms' key concern is to cut cost and enhance competitiveness to fight off low-cost rivals from emerging economies such as China and India. Labor unions' declared interest is to help workers earn higher wages and obtain more benefits through collective bargaining. In the United States, unionized employees earn 30% more than nonunionized employees. As a result, disagreements and conflicts between managers and unions are natural.

Labor unions' bargaining chip is their credible threat to strike, slow down, refuse to work overtime, or some other forms of disruption. Managers' bargaining chip lies in their threat to shut down operations and move jobs overseas. It is clear which side is winning. In the United States, there has been a 25-year slide in union membership. Union membership dropped from 20% of the US work force in 1983 to 12% now.[27] In the US private sector, only 7% of employees are union members at present.[28]

In contrast to MNEs' ability to move operations around the world, unions are organized on a country-by-country basis. Efforts to establish multinational labor organizations have not been effective. In the 1990s, in the face of US MNEs' aggressive efforts to move operations to Mexico to take advantage of NAFTA, AFL-CIO, the leading US union, contacted the Mexican government and requested that it be permitted to recruit members in Mexico. It was flatly rejected. In 2007, the House of Representatives passed a new Employee Free Choice Act, designed to make it easier to organize unions in the United States. It has provoked fierce debates and been criticized by GE's former CEO Jack Welch as an "insidious" blow to American competitiveness (see In Focus 15.2).

Managing Labor Relations Abroad

If given a choice, MNEs would prefer to deal with nonunionized work forces. For example, when Japanese and German automakers came to the United States, they avoided the Midwest, a union stronghold. Instead, these MNEs went to the rural South and set up nonunion plants in small towns in Alabama (Mercedes and

IN FOCUS 15.2 ETHICAL DILEMMA: The Unemployment Act —Jack Welch and Suzy Welch

Question: *Are you at all concerned about American competitiveness in the future?*

Yes . . . We are as worried as can be that American competitiveness is about to be whacked by something no one seems to be talking about: the Employee Free Choice Act, which is currently *[March 2007—editor]* weaving an insidious path through Congress toward becoming law. If it does, the long-thriving American economy will finally meet its match.

You didn't read wrong. We know it must sound strange to oppose legislation that promises "free choice." But the title of this bill is pure propaganda. It won't encourage liberty or self-determination in the workplace; more likely it will introduce intimidation and coercion by labor organizers, who after a long slide into near-oblivion, finally see a glorious new route to millions of dues-paying members. Their campaign could trigger a surge in unionization across US industry—and in time, a reversion to the bloated economy that brought America to its knees in the late 1970s and early '80s and that today cripples much of European business . . .

Make no mistake. We don't unilaterally oppose unions. Indeed, if a company is habitually unfair or unreasonable, it deserves what it gets from organized labor. But the problem with unions is that they make a sport out of killing productivity even when companies are providing good wages, benefits, and working conditions. It is not uncommon in a union shop to shut down production rather than allow a nonunion worker to flip a switch. Only a union or millwright electrician can do that job! Come on. Companies today can't afford such petty bureaucracy or the other excesses unions so often lead to, such as two people for every job and a litigious approach to even the smallest matters. Yes, managers and employees will sometimes disagree. But in the global economy, they have to work through these differences not as adversaries but as partners.

The Employee Free Choice Act undermines that. Here's how. Currently, when labor organizers want to launch a unionization effort, they ask each worker to sign a card as a show of support. If 30% or more employees do so, a federally supervised election can be called and conducted within one of the most revered mechanisms in democracy, the secret ballot. Thus, employees can vote their conscience, without fear of retribution from either union leaders or management.

By contrast, under the Employee Free Choice Act, organizers could start a union if 50% of employees, plus one more worker, sign cards. That's right—no more secret ballot. Instead, employees would likely get a phone call with a pointed solicitation, or worse, a home visit from a small team of organizers. You can just imagine the scenario. The organizers sit around the kitchen table and make their case, likely with a lot of passion. Then they slide a card in front of the employee with a pen. Who would say no? Who could?

Now, union supporters will tell you that they won't intimidate employees for votes, and regardless, management intimidates all the time by threatening to fire employees who vote union. But the system as it exists has safeguards, including heavy fines against companies that misbehave.

Still, the advance of the Employee Free Choice Act continues unabated. And so pretty soon, if enough business leaders and legislators don't stand up, it may well be: Hello again, unions. So long, American competitiveness. The change won't happen instantly. Companies will fight unions as if their lives depended on it, because they do. But given the logistics of the Employee Free Choice Act, any management campaign is hobbled. If you can't be at the kitchen table with the organizers and their hard stares, you probably can't win.

It's too bad. In fact, it's terrible. And ironic. First, because the ability to unionize already exists in America, thanks to the secret ballot. And second, because the Employee Free Choice Act ultimately only provides a free choice nobody would ever want: how to spend a government-issued unemployment check.

Source: Excerpts from J. Welch & S. Welch, 2007, The unemployment act, *Business Week*, March 12: 108. Jack Welch is the former chairman and CEO of GE, and Suzy Welch is the former editor of *Harvard Business Review*.

Hyundai), Kentucky (Toyota), and South Carolina (BMW). When MNEs have to deal with unions abroad, they often rely on experienced HCNs instead of locally inexperienced PCNs or TCNs.

Throughout many developing countries, governments welcome MNEs and at the same time silence unions. In China, the right to strike was removed from the constitution in 1982. Only 10% of the half a million foreign-invested firms in China have unions. A recent high-profile case is Wal-Mart's decision to allow its 31,000-strong Chinese work force to organize unions. The power of unions in developing countries certainly deserves some attention from MNE management.

LEARNING OBJECTIVE 5

discuss how the institution- and resource-based views shed additional light on HRM

HOW INSTITUTIONS AND RESOURCES AFFECT HUMAN RESOURCE MANAGEMENT

Having outlined the four basic areas of HRM, let us now turn to the institution- and resource-based views to see how they shed additional light (see Figure 15.4).

Institutions and Human Resource Management

HRM is significantly shaped by formal and informal rules of the game both at home and abroad.[29] Let us start with *formal* institutions. Every country has rules, laws, and regulations governing the do's and don'ts of HRM. Foreign firms ignoring such rules do so at their own peril. For instance, in Japan, firms routinely discriminate against women and minorities. However, when Japanese MNEs engage in such practices in the United States, they are often legally challenged. By the late 1980s, 60% of Japanese MNEs doing business in the United States faced possible equal employment opportunity (EEO) litigation.[30]

On the other hand, foreign firms well versed in local regulations may take advantage of them. In France, legal hurdles for firing full-time workers are legendary. HP got a phone call from (then) President Jacques Chirac who complained after HP announced a plan to lay off 1,200 employees.[31] Interestingly, France is a highly lucrative market for US-based Manpower. Manpower's expertise in providing part-time workers is highly valued by French firms unwilling to hire full-

FIGURE 15.4 INSTITUTIONS, RESOURCES, AND HUMAN RESOURCE MANAGEMENT

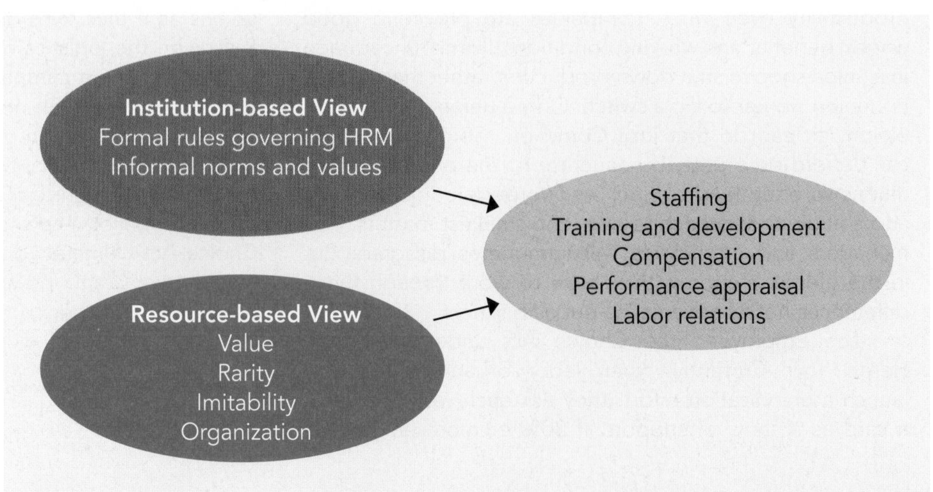

time employees. France is now Manpower's *largest* market, ahead of the United States (In Focus 15.3).

Informal rules of the game, embodied in cultures, norms, and values, also assert a powerful influence (see Table 15.6). MNEs from different countries have different norms in staffing. Most Japanese MNEs follow an informal rule: Heads of foreign subsidiaries, at least initially, need to be PCNs.[32] In comparison, European MNEs are more likely to appoint HCNs and TCNs to lead subsidiaries. There is a historical reason for such differences: Most European MNEs expanded globally before low-cost telephones, faxes, and e-mails were available. Thus, a localization strategy relying on HCNs and TCNs was necessary. Most Japanese MNEs went abroad in the 1980s, when modern communication technology enabled more centralized control from headquarters. In addition to technology, the Japanese cultural preference for low uncertainty also translated into a higher interest in headquarters' control. Thus, Japanese MNEs often implemented a home replication strategy that relied on PCNs who constantly communicated with headquarters.[33]

What are some formal and informal institutions that govern this woman's work experience?

Although informal cultures, norms, and values are important, HR managers need to avoid stereotyping and consider changes. In the area of compensation, one study hypothesizes that presumably collectivistic Chinese managers would prefer more equal compensation when compared with their individualistic US counterparts. The results turn out to be surprising: Chinese managers actually prefer more merit-based pay, whereas US managers behave exactly the opposite—in other words, the Chinese seem more "American" than Americans (!).[34] Further digging reveals that these are not average Chinese; they are HCNs working for some of the most competitive Western MNEs in China. The upshot? Naive adaptation to presumed local norms and values, often based on outdated stereotypes, may backfire. HR managers must do more "homework" to better understand their HCNs.

Consider expatriation, which has roots in colonialism. During the age of colonialism, hardship allowance was paid not only as an inducement but also as a path to riches. Before India's independence, British officers in the Indian Administrative

IN FOCUS 15.3 Manpower

Who is the largest employer in the world now? Surprise—it's Manpower, Inc. (NYSE: MAN)! Headquartered in Milwaukee, Wisconsin, Manpower is a world leader in the employment services industry. The $18 billion company has a network of 4,400 offices in 73 countries that "employ" 400,000 part-time workers. Manpower has 27,000 full-time employees. Its core capabilities consist of its ability to provide "flexible, ready-trained, on-demand, and enterprise-ready talent." In France, where the firing of full-time employees is difficult, Manpower has risen to the challenge by meeting the staffing needs of numerous firms that are afraid of being eventually stuck with unwanted full-time employees. As a result, France is now Manpower's largest market, contributing 33% of its revenues. In comparison, the United States only contributes 13% of its revenues.

Starting with the niche of providing part-time and temporary workers, Manpower is now a full-fledged employment services provider that also manages the recruitment of full-time staff for client organizations, conducts training for companies and governments, and provides outsourcing and consulting services. In Australia, the military has outsourced all of its recruitment (9,000 people every year) to Manpower, resulting in improved performance on recruiting goals and better retention rates. In Argentina, Manpower has partnered with the Ministry of Social Development to provide skill training to disadvantaged youth.

In a widely circulated white paper, "Confronting the Talent Crunch," Manpower cites 41% of employers worldwide that have difficulty filling positions. What is Manpower's advice for managers scratching their heads trying to confront the talent shortage? "Making a strategic partnership with a specialist provider of employment services can be an extremely savvy move," obviously implying that Manpower is it.

Sources: Based on (1) *Economist*, 2007, The world of work, January 6: 57–58; (2) Manpower, 2007, Confronting the talent crunch, White paper; (3) http://www.manpower.com.

TABLE 15.6 SOME BLUNDERS IN INTERNATIONAL HRM

- An American expatriate made a presentation to the prime minister of a small Caribbean country and his cabinet members by starting with "Honorable Mr. Tollis and esteemed members of the cabinet." The prime minister immediately interrupted him and asked him to start over. This went back and forth several times. Eventually, someone advised the bewildered and then embarrassed expatriate that Mr. Tollis was the *former* prime minister, who had been deposed by the current prime minister (the man sitting in front of the expatriate).
- A Spanish company sent to Saudi Arabia a team of expatriates, including a number of young, intelligent women dressed in the height of current style. Upon arrival, the Saudi immigration official took a look at their miniskirts and immediately sent the entire team on the next flight back to Spain. The expatriate team and the company belatedly learned that despite the heat, women in Saudi Arabia never show their bare legs in public.
- In Malaysia, an American expatriate was introduced to an important potential client he thought was named "Roger." He proceeded to call this person "Rog." Unfortunately, this person was a "Rajah," which is an important title of nobility. In this case, the American tendency to liberally use another person's first name—and to proactively shorten it—appeared disrespectful and insensitive. The Rajah walked away from the deal.
- A Japanese subsidiary CEO in New York, at a staff meeting consisting entirely of Americans (except him), informed everybody of the firm's grave financial losses and passed the request from headquarters in Japan that everybody redouble efforts. The staff immediately redoubled their efforts—by sending their résumés out to other employers.
- A female South Korean expatriate at a textile plant in Vietnam confronted a worker. She yelled in Korean "Move!" The Vietnamese worker did not move because he did not understand Korean. The South Korean expatriate then kicked and slapped him. According to the media, in South Korea, it is common for employers to scold or even beat employees if they make a big mistake. But in this case, ten Vietnamese colleagues retaliated by beating up the expatriate, who was wounded, hospitalized, and then deported. The workers went on to strike for four days and obtained 10% to 15% pay raises.

Sources: Based on text in (1) P. Dowling & D. Welch, 2005, *International Human Resource Management*, 4th ed. (p. 59), Cincinnati, OH: Cengage South-Western; (2) R. Linowes, 1993, The Japanese manager's traumatic entry into the United States, *Academy of Management Executive*, 7 (4): 21–38; (3) D. Ricks, 1999, *Blunders in International Business*, 3rd ed. (pp. 95–105), Oxford, UK: Blackwell.

Service that ran the colonial government in India were the *highest* paid civil servants in the world. At that time, HCNs were unlikely to view themselves as equals of PCNs.[35] In the 21st century, many well-educated Brazilians, Indians, and Chinese—often armed with degrees from Western universities—are as qualified as some Western expatriates. Such HCNs naturally resent being treated as second-class citizens. Thus, the stereotypical expatriate, leading a life of luxury to compensate for hardship overseas, may be increasingly rare.

Even for expatriates from the West, they now tend to be younger, may not qualify for the most senior positions overseas, and may be sent abroad to gain experience—often with more down-to-earth titles such as "assignees" or "secondees." Also, more expatriates are now being sent on short-term, commuter-type assignments for which they do not need to uproot their families.[36] They may work weekdays in Shanghai and Budapest and then fly home to Hong Kong and London, respectively, for the weekend. Overall, the norms and images associated with the expatriate are changing rapidly.

Resources and Human Resource Management

As HRM becomes more strategic, the VRIO dimensions are increasingly at center stage. To start, managers need to ask: Does a particular HR activity add *value*?[37] Consider two examples. First, labor-intensive chores, such as administering payroll, benefits, and basic training, may not add value. They can often be outsourced (see In Focus 15.3). Second, training is expensive. Does it really add value?[38] Results pooled from 397 studies find that, on average, training adds value by leading to approximately 20% performance improvement for that individual.[39] Thus, training is often justified.

Next, are particular HR activities *rare*? The relentless drive to learn, share, and adopt "best practices" may reduce their rarity and thus usefulness. If every MNE in China provides training to high-caliber HCNs, such training, which is valuable, will be taken for granted but not viewed as rare.

Further, how *imitable* are certain HR activities? It is relatively easy to imitate a single practice; however, it is much more difficult to imitate a complex HR *system* (or *architecture*) consisting of multiple, mutually reinforcing practices that work together.[40] Consider the Portman Ritz-Carlton (Opening Case). Its expatriate general manager personally interviews *every* new hire. It selects HCNs genuinely interested in helping guests. It deeply cares about employee satisfaction, which has led to superb guest satisfaction. Each single practice here may be imitable, and the Portman Ritz-Carlton has been meticulously studied by all rivals (and numerous nonrivals) in China and around the world. Yet, none has been able to successfully imitate its system. On the surface, every firm says, "We care about our people." But the reality at many firms is increasing underinvestment by both employers and employees with declining loyalty and commitment.[41] Studies find that firm performance is the best with a mutual investment approach, as exemplified by the Portman Ritz-Carlton.[42] However, it is very difficult to imitate a mutual investment approach that comes together as a system (or architecture).

Finally, do HR practices support *organizational capabilities* to help the firm accomplish its performance goals? Consider teamwork and diversity, especially multinational teams consisting of members from different subsidiaries. Although most firms promote some sort of teamwork and diversity, it is challenging to organizationally leverage such teamwork and diversity to enhance performance.[43] Too little or too much diversity may hurt performance.[44] In teamwork, certain disagreements may be helpful to promote learning. But obviously too many disagreements may lead to conflicts and torpedo team effectiveness.[45] However, few managers (and few firms) master the art of drawing the line before disagreements within a team get out of control.

DEBATES AND EXTENSIONS

LEARNING OBJECTIVE 6

participate in three leading debates concerning HRM

This chapter has already alluded to a number of HR debates, such as the value of expatriates. Here, we focus on three previously untouched debates: (1) best fit versus best practice, (2) expatriation versus inpatriation, and (3) across-the-board pay cut versus reduction in force.

Best Fit versus Best Practice

The "best fit" school argues that a firm needs to search for the best external and internal fit. Externally, HRM is shaped by national and industry contexts. Internally, HRM is driven by firm strategy. On the product dimension, a firm pursuing a differentiation strategy needs to reinforce the passion for higher quality, better service, and more sustained learning.[46] On the international dimension, a firm using a localization strategy needs to deploy more HCNs (Table 15.2). Moreover, the quest for the best fit is *continuous*. Even for the same MNE in the same country, a good fit now may not be good enough ten years later. In two words, the best fit school argues: It depends.[47]

The "best practice" school begs to differ. Proponents argue that firms should adopt best practices irrespective of context. Such best practices often include extensive training, high pay for high performance, and self-managed teams (emphasizing teamwork). While the list of best practices may vary, the underlying spirit seems to be the same around the world.[48]

Critics of the "best practice" school make two points. First, they point out that "there is overwhelming evidence against a universal set of HR practices based on national variations."[49] Second, they argue that from a resource-based view, if all firms adopt universal "best practices," such practices lose their value. To reconcile the debate, experts note that "it is not a question of either/or but a question of the appropriate balance."[50] They argue that during the next decade, most firms may still benefit from adopting some "best practices" because most firms are not at that frontier yet.

Expatriation versus Inpatriation

inpatriation
Relocating employees of a foreign subsidiary to the MNE's headquarters for the purposes of (1) filling skill shortages at headquarters and (2) developing a global mindset for such inpatriates.

Addressing the expatriation problem, one solution is **inpatriation**—relocating employees of a foreign subsidiary to the MNE's headquarters for the purposes of (1) filling skill shortages at headquarters and (2) developing a global mindset for such inpatriates. The term *inpatriation* of course is derived from *expatriation*, and most inpatriates are expected to eventually return to their home country to replace expatriates (see Closing Case). Examples would include IT inpatriates from India to work at IBM in the United States and telecom inpatriates from China to work at Alcatel in France. Technically, these inpatriates are expatriates from India and China, who will experience some of the problems associated with expatriation discussed earlier in this chapter.

In addition, some inpatriates, being paid by the going rate of their home (typically developing) countries, are upset after finding out the compensation level of colleagues at headquarters doing equivalent work; the cost of an Indian IT professional is approximately 10% to 12% that of an American one. Some inpatriates thus refuse to go back and find work in their host countries with much higher pay. Other inpatriates go back to their home countries but quit their sponsoring MNE and jump ship to rivals willing to pay more.

Even for inpatriates who return to assume leadership positions in subsidiaries in their home countries (as originally planned), unfortunately, many are ineffective. In China, inpatriated ethnic Chinese often struggle with an ambiguous identity: Western headquarters views them as "us" whereas HCNs also expect them to be "us." When these managers favor headquarters on issues where HQ and locals conflict (such as refusing to pay HCNs more), HCNs view them as traitors of sorts. These problems erupt in spite of these inpatriates' Chinese roots—or perhaps, *because* of their Chinese roots. Overall, one lesson we can draw is that there will be no panacea in international staffing. Inpatriates, just like expatriates, have their fair share of problems and headaches.

Across-the-Board Pay Cut versus Reduction in Force

Both HR and line managers often have to make tough decisions. One of the most challenging decisions is how to cope with a downturn. Reduction in force (RIF), a euphemism for mass layoffs, is often used in the United States and United Kingdom. However, outside the Anglo-American world, mass layoffs are often viewed as unethical. Some critics label mass layoffs as "corporate cannibalism." One alternative is for the entire firm to have an across-the-board pay cut while preserving all current jobs, as the Portman Ritz-Carlton in Shanghai did during the SARS crisis in 2003 (Opening Case). Which approach is better?

There is no doubt that a majority of Chinese HCNs at the Portman Ritz-Carlton supported the across-the-board pay cut, as evidenced by the 99.9% employee satisfaction in that year. However, when US firms experiment with an across-the-board pay cut, the results tend to be very *negative*. To avoid RIF, Applied Materials in the post-2001 downturn implemented an across-the-board pay cut in the United States: Executives took a 10% hit, managers and professionals 5%, and hourly production workers 3%. The pay cut lasted for 18 months. An HR executive at Applied Materials commented:

> This across-the-board pay cut has a longer lasting and far greater negative impact on morale than an RIF would have. RIFs are very hard on the impacted employees as well as the survivors. However, when managed correctly, impacted employees are able to separate from the company with dignity and in the case of Applied Materials, with a very generous financial package . . . I don't know of any surviving employees that appreciated having their paycheck impacted every two weeks for 18 months . . . Ultimately, pay levels were restored. However, employee memories are very long and this particular event was pointed to over and over again throughout multiple employee surveys as an indicator of poor leadership and a major cause of employee dissatisfaction.[51]

Applied Materials and other US firms that implement across-the-board pay cuts have lost numerous star performers who find "greener pastures" elsewhere. This raises serious concerns as to whether such large-scale sacrifice is worth it, at least in an individualistic culture.

MANAGEMENT SAVVY

LEARNING OBJECTIVE 7
draw implications for action

What determines the success and failure of HRM around the world? A simple answer is effectiveness of HR activities in areas such as staffing, training and development, compensation, and labor relations. A more interesting question is: How much is the impact of effective HRM on firm performance?[52] Results from 3,200 firms find that a change of one standard deviation in the HR system affects 10% to 20% of a firm's market value.[53] Findings from 92 studies suggest that an increase of one standard deviation in the use of effective HR system is associated with a 4.6% increase in return on assets (ROA).[54] These recent findings validate a long-held belief among HRM practitioners and scholars: HRM is indeed *strategic*, as it has become a direct answer to the fundamental question of our field: What determines the success and failure of firms around the world?

Consequently, we identify four implications for action (Table 15.7). Centered on the four Cs developed by Susan Meisinger, president of the Society for Human Resource Management, the first three implications are for HR managers,[55] and the last one is for non-HR managers. First, savvy HR managers need to be *curious*. They need to be well versed in the numerous formal and informal rules of the game governing HRM in worldwide operations. They must be curious about emerging trends of the world (such as the rise of outsourcing) and create people strategies to respond to these trends.

Second, HR managers must be *competent*. From its lowly roots as a lackluster administrative support function, HRM is now acknowledged to be a more strategic function that directly contributes to the bottom line. As a result, HR managers need to develop organizational capabilities that drive business success. This starts with enhancing the basic business competencies of HR managers, who may have been trained more narrowly and with a more micro (nonstrategic) focus. Now, HR managers not only must contribute to the strategy conversation but also need to take things off the CEO's desk as his or her full-fledged "business partners."

Third, HR managers must be *courageous* and *caring*. As guardians of talent, HR managers need to nurture and develop employees. This often means that as employee advocates, HR managers sometimes need to be courageous enough to

TABLE 15.7 IMPLICATIONS FOR ACTION

For HR managers: The four Cs

- Be *curious*—need to know formal and informal rules of the game governing HRM in all regions of operations
- Be *competent*—develop organizational capabilities that drive business success
- Be *courageous* and *caring*—as guardians of talent, HR managers need to nurture and develop people

For non-HR managers:

- Be proactive in managing your (international) career

disagree with the CEO and other line managers if necessary. GE's recently retired head of HR, William Conaty, is such an example. "If you just get closer to the CEO, you're dead," Conaty shared with a reporter. "I need to be independent. I need to be credible."[56] GE's CEO Jeff Immelt called Conaty "the first friend, the guy that could walk in my office and kick my butt when it needed to be"—exactly how a full-fledged business partner should behave.

Finally, non-HR managers need to have proactive career management to develop a global mindset.[57] Given that international experience is now a prerequisite for reaching the top at many firms, managers need to prepare by investing in their own technical expertise, cross-cultural adaptability, and language training. Some of these investments (such as language) are long term in nature, and just-in-time preparation will not cut it. This point thus has strategic implications for students who are studying this book *now*: Have you picked up a foreign language? Have you spent one semester or year abroad? Have you made some friends from abroad who are studying in this class together with you now? Imagine a scenario for expatriate selection five to ten years down the road: Wouldn't you hate it when your non-Chinese colleague who speaks Chinese is tapped to go to China as a high-profile expat, but you are passed over because you have never studied Chinese (you and your colleague were classmates in school and studied this book together)? The difference may be that your colleague started investing in learning Chinese five to ten years ago, and you didn't. To make yourself "China ready," you have to start now. The point of course is not just about China. It is about arming yourself with the knowledge now, making proper investments, and maneuvering yourself to be picked eventually. In the global economy, it is *your* career that is in your hands.

CHAPTER SUMMARY

1. Explain staffing decisions with a focus on expatriates
   - International staffing primarily relies on ethnocentric, polycentric, and geocentric approaches.
   - Expatriates (primarily PCNs and to a lesser extent TCNs) play multiple challenging roles and often have high failure rates. They need to be carefully selected, taking into account a variety of factors.
2. Identify training and development needs for expatriates and HCNs
   - Expatriates need to be properly trained and cared for both before departure and during repatriation.
   - Training and development of HCNs are now an area of differentiation among many MNEs.
3. Discuss compensation and performance appraisal issues
   - Expatriates are compensated using the going rate and balance sheet approaches.

- Top talent HCNs now increasingly command higher compensation.
- Performance appraisal needs to be carefully provided to achieve its intended purposes.

4. Understand labor relations in both home and host countries
   - Despite efforts to revive unions, the power of unions has been declining in developed countries.
   - The power of unions in most developing countries requires some attention but is mostly limited.
5. Discuss how the institution- and resource-based views shed additional light on HRM
   - HRM is significantly shaped by formal and informal rules of the game both at home and abroad.
   - As HRM becomes more strategic, VRIO dimensions are now more important.
6. Participate in three leading debates concerning HRM
   - These are (1) best fit versus best practice, (2) expatriation versus inpatriation, and (3) across-the-board pay cut versus reduction in force.
7. Draw implications for action
   - HR managers need to have the four Cs: being curious, competent, courageous, and caring about people.
   - Non-HR managers need to proactively develop an international career mindset.

KEY TERMS

Balance sheet approach 446
Compensation 444
Development 442
Ethnocentric approach 439
Expatriate (expat) 438
Expatriation 440
Geocentric approach 440
Going rate approach 445
Host country national (HCN) 438
Human resource management (HRM) 438
Inpatriation 454
Labor relations 448
Parent (home) country national (PCN) 439
Performance appraisal 444
Polycentric approach 439
Psychological contract 443
Repatriate 443
Repatriation 443
Staffing 438
Third country national (TCN) 439
Training 442

REVIEW QUESTIONS

1. Name and describe three types of staffing approaches.
2. Summarize the four roles that expatriates typically play.
3. What factors often lead to difficulties or failure of an expatriate on an overseas assignment?
4. Describe some of the problems experienced by repatriates and how training and development might alleviate them.
5. In what ways does a career development plan benefit an expatriate?
6. In terms of expatriate compensation, what is the difference between the going rate approach and the balance sheet approach?
7. What are some of the problems inherent in evaluating an expatriate's job performance?

8. Who is currently winning when labor unions and management bargain with each other and why?
9. Why do you think efforts to establish multinational labor organizations have been unsuccessful?
10. How can an understanding of informal institutions help an HR manager avoid problem-causing stereotypes?
11. Of the four dimensions in the VRIO analysis of HR activities, which one is most likely to give a firm a competitive edge?
12. What concept can be used to reconcile the best fit versus best practice debate, and how does it work?
13. What are the benefits of inpatriation?
14. How do HR managers benefit from the four Cs as described by Susan Meisinger?
15. What steps can you take to proactively develop a global mindset in your career?

CRITICAL DISCUSSION QUESTIONS

1. You have been offered a reasonably lucrative opportunity for an expatriate assignment for the next three years, and your boss will have a meeting with you next week. What would you discuss with your boss?
2. ON ETHICS: If you were an HCN, do you think pay should be equal between HCNs and expatriates in equivalent positions? If you were president of your subsidiary in a host country, as a PCN your pay is five times higher than the pay for the highest paid HCN (your vice president). What do you think?
3. ON ETHICS: As HR director for an oil company, you are responsible for selecting 15 expatriates to go to work in Iraq. However, you are personally concerned about their safety there. How do you proceed?

VIDEO CASE

Watch "Your Business Is the Training and Development of Your People" by William Pollard of ServiceMaster.

1. To what extent is the importance of the theme of the video affected by staffing decisions?
2. Given Mr. Pollard's focus on lifelong learning, to what extent does his organization have a clear distinction between training and development?
3. What are the risks and benefits of providing training and development to local nationals overseas?
4. How does a changing global environment impact on choosing between the training and development of HCNs versus PCNs?
5. Suppose you had job offers from two global corporations in which the pay, benefits, job security, and work environment were comparable. However, Company A paid just slightly more than Company B, but Company B had an extensive and far superior training and development program. Which job offer would you more likely accept? Why?

CLOSING CASE

Dallas versus Delhi

Prashant Sarkar is director for corporate development for the New Delhi, India, subsidiary of the US-based Dallas Instruments. Sarkar has an engineering degree from the Indian Institute of Technology and an MBA from the University of Texas at Dallas. After obtaining his MBA in 1990, he worked at a Dallas Instruments facility in Richardson, Texas (a suburb of Dallas), and picked up a green card (US permanent residence) while maintaining his Indian passport. In 2000, when Dallas Instruments opened its first Indian subsidiary in New Delhi, Sarkar was tapped to be one of the first managers sent from the United States. India of the early 21st century is certainly different from the India of the mid-1980s that Sarkar had left behind. Reform is now in the air, MNEs are coming left and right, and an exhilarating self-confidence permeates the country.

As a manager, Sarkar has shined in his native New Delhi. His wife and two children (born in 1995 and 1998 in the United States) are also happy. After all, curry in New Delhi is a lot more authentic and fresher than that in Indian grocery stores in Dallas. Grandparents, relatives, and friends are all happy to see the family back. In Dallas, Prashant's wife, Neeli, a teacher by training, taught on a part-time basis but couldn't secure a full-time teaching position because she didn't have a US degree. Now she is principal of a great school. The two children are enrolled in the elite New Delhi American School, the cost of which is paid for by the company. New Delhi is not perfect, but the Sarkars feel good about coming back.

"Prashant, I have great news for you!" the American CEO of the subsidiary tells Sarkar at the end of 2009, "Headquarters wants you to move back to Dallas. You'll be in charge of strategy development for *global* expansion, working directly under the group vice president. Isn't that exciting? They want someone with proven success. You are my best candidate. I don't know what design they have for you after this assignment, but I suspect it'll be highly promising. Don't quote me, but I'd say you may have a shot to eventually replace me or the next American CEO here. While I personally enjoy working here, my family sometimes still complains a bit about the curry smell. Or folks in Dallas may eventually want you to go somewhere else. Frankly, I don't know, but I'm just trying to help you speculate. I know it's a big decision. Talk to Neeli and the kids. But they lived in Dallas before, so they should be fine going back. Of course, I'll put you in touch with the folks in Dallas directly so that you can ask them all kinds of questions. Let me know what you think in a week."

Instead of calling his wife immediately, Sarkar has decided to wait until he gets home in the evening so that he can have a few hours to think about this. An avid reader, he has placed an order for a copy of Mike Peng's brand new *Global Business*. As a coincidence (or perhaps as an omen), the book arrives one hour after his meeting with the CEO. Instead of starting with Chapter 1, he immediately dives into Chapter 15 on HRM.

Case Discussion Questions

1. Going from Dallas to New Delhi, Sarkar, with his Indian passport, would be an HCN. With his green card, he could also be considered a US national and thus an expatriate. Now if he goes from New Delhi to Dallas, would he be an expatriate or inpatriate? What difference does that make?
2. What questions should Sarkar ask the people at headquarters in Dallas?
3. Will Neeli and the children be happy about this move? Why?
4. Should Sarkar accept or decline this opportunity? Why?

Sources: Based on the author's interviews. All individual and corporate names are fictitious.

NOTES

Journal acronyms: **AME** – *Academy of Management Executive;* **AMJ** – *Academy of Management Journal;* **AMR** – *Academy of Management Review;* **APJM** – *Asia Pacific Journal of Management;* **BW** – *Business Week;* **CJWB** – *Columbia Journal of World Business;* **CMR** – *California Management Review;* **HBR** – *Harvard Business Review;* **HRM** – *Human Resource Management;* **HRMR** – *Human Resource Management Review;* **IJCCM** – *International Journal of Cross Cultural Management;* **IJHRM** – *International Journal of Human Resource Management;* **IJMR** – *International Journal of Management Reviews;* **JAP** – *Journal of Applied Psychology;* **JIBS** – *Journal of International Business Studies;* **JM** – *Journal of Management;* **JMS** – *Journal of Management Studies;* **JOB** – *Journal of Organizational Behavior;* **JWB** – *Journal of World Business;* **MIR** – *Management International Review;* **PP** – *Personnel Psychology;* **SMJ** – *Strategic Management Journal*

[1] W. Newburry, N. Gardberg, & L. Belkin, 2006, Organizational attractiveness is in the eye of the beholder, *JIBS*, 37: 666–686.

[2] S. Taylor, S. Beechler, & N. Napier 1996, Toward an integrative model of strategic international HRM, *AMR*, 21: 959–985.

[3] D. Bowen, C. Galang, & R. Pillai, 2002, The role of HRM, *HRM*, 41: 103–122; W. Cascio, 2005, From business partner to driving business success, *HRM*, 44: 159–163; E Lawler, 2005, From HRM to organizational effectiveness, *HRM*, 44: 165–169.

[4] R. Ployhart, 2006, Staffing in the 21st century, *JM*, 32: 868–897.

[5] *Economist*, 2006, Traveling more lightly (p. 77), June 24: 77–79.

[6] H. Perlmutter, 1969, The tortuous evolution of the multinational corporation, *CJWB*, 4: 9–18.

[7] C. Chung & P. Beamish, 2005, Investment mode strategy and expatriate strategy during times of economic crisis, *JIM*, 11: 331–355; A. Goerzen & P. Beamish, 2007, The Penrose effect, *MIR*, 47: 221–239; D. Tan & J. Mahoney, 2006, Why a multinational firm chooses expatriates, *JMS*, 43: 457–484.

[8] M. Janssens, T. Cappellen, & P. Zanoni, 2006, Successful female expatriates as agents, *JWB*, 41: 133–148; A. Varma, S. Toh, & P. Budhwar, 2006, A new perspective on the female expatriate experience, *JWB*, 41: 112–120; D. Vora & T. Kostova, 2007, A model of dual organizational identification in the context of the multinational enterprise, *JOB*, 28: 327–350.

[9] P. Bhaskar-Shrinivas, D. Harrison, M. Shaffer, & D. Luk, 2005, Input-based and time-based models of international adjustment, *AMJ*, 48: 257–281; J. Black, M. Mendenhall, & G. Oddou, 1991, Toward a comprehensive model of international adjustment, *AMR*, 16: 291–317.

[10] R. L. Tung, 1982, Selection and training procedures for US, European, and Japanese multinationals, *CMR*, 25: 57–71. See also A. Harzing, 2002, Are our referencing errors undermining our scholarship and credibility? *JOB*, 23: 127–148.

[11] P. Dowling & D. Welch, 2005, *International Human Resource Management*, 4th ed. (p. 87), Cincinnati, OH: Thomson.

[12] G. Graen, R. Dharwadkar, R. Grewal, & M. Wakabayashi, 2006, Japanese career progress, *JIBS*, 37: 148–161; E. Pellegrini & T. Scandura, 2006. Leader-member exchange (LMX), paternalism, and delegation in the Turkish business culture, *JIBS*, 37: 264–279.

[13] P. Caligiuri, 2006, Developing global leaders, *HRMR*, 16: 219–228; A. Molinsky, 2007, Cross-cultural code-switching, *AMR*, 32: 622–640; S. Shin, F. Morgeson, & M. Campion, 2007, What you do depends on where you are, *JIBS*, 38: 64–83; R. Takeuchi, P. Tesluk, S. Yun, & D. Lepak, 2005, An integrative view of international experience, *AMJ*, 48: 85–100; A. Vianen, I. Pater, A. Kristof-Brown, & E. Johnson, 2004, Fitting in, *AMJ*, 47: 697–709.

[14] M. Shaffer & D. Harrison, 2001, Forgotten partners of international assignments, *JAP*, 86: 238–254.

[15] E. Drost, C. Frayne, K. Lowe, & J. M. Geringer, 2002, Benchmarking training and development practices, *HRM*, 41: 67–86.

[16] A major 2002 survey cited in Dowling & Welch, 2005, *International Human Resource Management* (p. 119).

[17] M. Lazarova & J. Cerdin, 2007, Revisiting repatriation concerns, *JIBS*, 38: 404–429.

[18] T. Amino, a retired Honda executive and a friend of the author, personal communication, May 2002.

[19] S. Fineman, 2006, On being positive, *AMR*, 31: 270–291.

[20] L. Bassi & D. McMurrer, 2007, Maximizing your return on people, *HBR*, March: 115–123.

[21] L. Stroh, 1995, Predicting turnover among repatriates, *IJHRM*, 6: 440–455.

[22] J. Mezias & T. Scandura, 2005, A needs-driven approach to expatriate adjustment and career development, *JIBS*, 36: 519–538.

[23] E. Chang, 2006, Individual pay for performance and commitment: HR practices in South Korea, *JWB*, 41: 368–381; J. DeVaro, 2006, Strategic promotion tournaments and worker performance, *SMJ*, 27: 721–740; K. Lowe, J. Milliman, H. De Cieri, & P. Dowling, 2002, International compensation practices, *HRM*, 41: 45–66; Y. Yanadori & J. Marler, 2006, Compensation strategy, *SMJ*, 27: 559–570.

[24] *Economist*, 2006, The world is our oyster, October 7: 9.

[25] T. Gardner, 2005, Interfirm competition for HR, *AMJ*, 48: 237–256.

[26] J. Milliman, S. Nason, C. Zhu, & H. De Cieri, 2002, An exploratory assessment of the purposes of performance appraisals in North and Central America and the Pacific Rim, *HRM*, 41: 87–102.

[27] AFL-CIO, 2007, Ten key facts for the Employee Free Choice Act, http://www.aflcio.org; Bureau of Labor Statistics, 2007, Union members in 2006, Washington, DC: Department of Labor, http://www.bls.gov.

[28] Bureau of Labor Statistics, 2007, Union member summary, Washington, DC: Department of Labor, http://www.bls.gov.

[29] I. Bjorkman, C. Fey, & H. Park, 2007, Institutional theory and MNC subsidiary HRM practices, *JIBS*, 38: 430–446.

[30] R. Schuler, P. Budhwar, & G. Florkowski, 2002, International HRM (p. 56), *IJMR*, 4: 51–70.

[31] *BW*, 2005, HP's French twist, October 10: 52–53.

[32] N. Ando, N. Park, & D. Rhee, 2008, Parent country nationals or local national for executive positions in foreign affiliates, *APJM*, 25 (in press); A. Delios & I. Bjorkman, 2000, Expatriate staffing in foreign subsidiaries of Japanese MNCs in the PRC and the US,

IJHRM, 11: 278–293; R. Belderbos & M. Heijltjes, 2005, The determinants of expatriate staffing by Japanese multinationals in Asia, *JIBS*, 36: 341–354.

[33] A. Bird & S. Beechler, 1995, Links between business strategy and HRM strategy in US-based Japanese subsidiaries, *JIBS*, 26: 23–46; Y. Paik & J. Sohn, 2004, Expatriate managers and MNCs' ability to control international subsidiaries, *JWB*, 39: 61–71; R. Peterson, J. Sargent, N. Napier, & W. Shim, 1996, Corporate expatriate HRM policies, internationalization, and performance in the world's largest MNCs, *MIR*, 36: 215–230.

[34] C. Chen, 1995, New trends in allocation preferences, *AMJ*, 38: 408–428.

[35] S. Toh & A. DeNisi, 2005, A local perspective to expatriate success, *AME*, 19: 132–146.

[36] D. Collings, H. Scullion, & M. Morley, 2007, Changing patterns of global staffing in the MNE, *JWB*, 42: 198–213.

[37] S. Kang, S. Morris, & S. Snell, 2007, Relational archetypes, organizational learning, and value creation, *AMR*, 32: 236–256; K. Law, D. Tse, & N. Zhou, 2003, Does HR matter in a transition economy? *JIBS*, 34: 255–265.

[38] J. Selmer, 2002, To train or not to train? *IJCCM*, 2: 37–51.

[39] W. Arthur, W. Bennett, P. Edens, & S. Bell, 2003, Effectiveness of training in organizations, *JAP*, 88: 234–245.

[40] J. Arthur & T. Boyles, 2007. Validating the HR system structure, *HRMR*, 12: 77–92; B. Colbert, 2004, The complex resource-based view, *AMR*, 28: 341–358; D. Lepak & S. Snell, 1999, The HR architecture, *AMR*, 24: 31–48.

[41] A. Tsui & J. Wu, 2005, The new employment relationship versus the mutual investment approach, *HRM*, 44: 115–121.

[42] J. Shaw, M. Dufy, J. Johnson, & D. Lockhart, 2005, Turnover, social capital losses, and performance, *AMJ*, 48: 594–606; A. Tsui, L. Pearce, L. Porter, & A. Tripoli, 1997, Alternative approaches to the employee-organization relationship, *AMJ*, 40: 1089–1121; D. Wang, A. Tsui, Y. Zhang, & L. Ma, 2003, Employment relationships and firm performance, *JOB*, 24: 511–535.

[43] C. Boone, W. Olffen, A. Witteloostujin, & B. Brabander, 2004, The genesis of top management team diversity, *AMJ*, 47: 633–656; O. Richard, B. Murthi, & K. Ismail, 2008, The impact of racial diversity on intermediate and long-term performance, *SMJ* (in press); Z. Simsek, J. Veiga, M. Lubatkin, & R. Dino, 2005, Modeling the multilevel determinants of top management team behavioral integration, *AMJ*, 48: 69–84.

[44] K. Dahlin, L. Weingart, & P. Hinds, 2005, Team diversity and information use, *AMJ*, 48: 1107–1123.

[45] J. Brett, K. Behfar, & M. Kern, 2006, Managing multicultural teams, *HBR*, November: 84–91; P. Balkundi & D. Harrison, 2006, Ties, leaders, and time in teams, *AMJ*, 49: 49–68; C. Collins & K. Smith, 2006, Knowledge exchange and combination, *AMJ*, 49: 544–560; M. Zellmer-Bruhn & C. Gibson, 2006, Multinational organization context, *AMJ*, 49: 501–518.

[46] R. Schuler & S. Jackson, 1987, Linking competitive strategies and HRM practices, *AME*, 1: 207–219.

[47] J. Delery & D. Doty, 1996, Modes of theorizing in strategic HRM, *AMJ*, 39: 802–835.

[48] J. M. Geringer, C. Frayne, & J. Milliman, 2002, In search of "best practices" in international HRM, *HRM*, 41: 5–30; M. von Glinow, E. Drost, & M. Teagarden, 2002, Converging on IHRM best practices, *HRM*, 41: 123–140.

[49] P. Boxall & J. Purcell, 2000, Strategic HRM (p. 190), *IJMR*, 2: 183–203. See A. Ferner, P. Almond, & T. Colling, 2005, Institutional theory and the cross-national transfer of employment policy, *JIBS*, 36: 304–321; J. Gamble, 2006, Introducing Western-style HRM practices to China, *JWB*, 41: 328–343; P. Huo, J. Huang, & N. Napier, 2002, Divergence or convergence, *HRM*, 41: 31–44; W. Newburry & N. Yakova, 2006, Standardization preferences, *JIBS*, 37: 44–60; O. Tregaski & C. Brewster, 2006, Converging or diverging? *JIBS*, 37: 111–126.

[50] B. Becker & M. Huselid, 2006, Strategic HRM (p. 905), *JM*, 32: 898–925.

[51] S. Parker, EMBA student in Professor M. W. Peng's class, individual assignment 1, University of Texas at Dallas, January 2007.

[52] S. Colakoglu, D. Lepak, & Y. Hong, 2006, Measuring HRM effectiveness, *HRMR*, 16: 209–218; D. Datta, J. Guthrie, & P. Wright, 2005, HRM and labor productivity, *AMJ*, 48: 135–145.

[53] Becker & Huselid, 2006, Strategic HRM (p. 907).

[54] J. Combs, D. Ketchen, A. Hall, & Y. Liu, 2006, Do high performance work practices matter? *PP*, 59: 501–528.

[55] S. Meisinger, 2005, The four Cs of the HR profession, *HRM*, 44: 189–194.

[56] *BW*, 2007, Secrets of an HR superstar (p. 66), April 19: 66–67.

[57] T. Cappellen & M. Janssens, 2005, Career paths for global managers, *JWB*, 40: 348–360; M. Dickman & H. Harris, 2005, Developing career capital for global careers, *JWB*, 40: 399–408; O. Levy, S. Beechler, S. Taylor, & N. Boyacigiller, 2007, What we talk about when we talk about "global mindset," *JIBS*, 38: 231–258; D. Thomas, M. Lazarova, & K. Inkson, 2005, Global careers, *JWB*, 40: 340–347; C. Vance, 2005, The personal quest for building global competence, *JWB*, 40: 374–385.

CHAPTER 16

Governing the Corporation around the World

OPENING CASE

List in New York? No, Thanks!

Not too long ago, listing in New York—either at the New York Stock Exchange (NYSE) for large firms or NASDAQ for small firms—was widely viewed as a rite of passage for ambitious non-US firms. Such listings not only offered direct access to the world's largest capital market but also an invaluable global cachet. In 2000, nine of the top-ten initial public offerings (IPOs) came to New York. New York's rivals, London and Hong Kong, did not seem to matter much: In 2000, NYSE and NASDAQ commanded 60% of worldwide IPO proceeds, London only took away 8%, and Hong Kong received 5%.

However, winds change. In 2006, New York was beaten by *both* London (London Stock Exchange [LSE] for large firms and the new Alternative Investment Market [AIM] for small firms) and Hong Kong. Many non-US firms are shying away from New York, which grabbed an embarrassingly low 17% of the worldwide IPO proceeds in 2006. In comparison, London took away 21% and Hong Kong 18%. Of the top-25 global IPOs in 2006, only one took place in New York. London is positioning itself as a natural home for firms from Europe, Russia, and Israel. Hong Kong benefits from the gush of Chinese listings. There is more at stake than simple bragging rights on who is bigger. If US exchanges fail to attract new overseas listings, they will lose out on the trading that follows—the lifeblood of capital markets. Wall Street's decline could also translate into lost American jobs and reduced economic growth. In 2006, New York's Mayor Michael Bloomberg published a high-profile article with an alarming title: "To Save New York, Learn from London."

So, what happened? As soul-searching debates rage throughout New York, scholars, practitioners, officials, and journalists suggest two broad reasons, one uncontrollable and one controllable. The uncontrollable reason is simply global competition among financial markets. Because of financial liberalization, New York, still the largest capital market, faces a lot more competitive heat than before.

Since little can be done on the uncontrollable development, most of the finger pointing is directed to a controllable root cause: the Sarbanes-Oxley (SarbOx) Act of 2002. Enacted in the wake of the Enron scandal, SarbOx was meant to enhance the protection of shareholders, a noble goal. However, in the rush to do something, lawmakers failed to account for compliance costs, which have skyrocketed. Regarded by executives as the corporate equivalent of a root canal, SarbOx compliance costs came with a tab of $2 million to $8 million per firm in the first year alone—billions of dollars across all US-listed firms. This burden is disproportionately heavy for smaller listed firms. Former Ohio Congressman Michael Oxley, who cosponsored SarbOx, admitted in a 2007 interview that the compliance costs "proved to be much more expensive than anticipated." However, listed US firms have no choice but to comply.

SarbOx has driven away many US firms that do have a choice. About 50 smaller US firms that might have listed on NASDAQ went to list instead on London's AIM, and hundreds of others are considering the same move. Many non-US firms are saying to New York: "No, thanks!" Listing in New York (or any foreign location) is never free. It always boils down to a cost-benefit analysis. The benefits are typically lower cost of capital and higher company valuation. The costs are typically reporting and compliance requirements and occasionally costs related to enforcement by securities authorities, civil lawsuits by shareholders, and even criminal prosecutions by state and federal authorities. SarbOx has dramatically increased these

LEARNING OBJECTIVES

After studying this chapter, you should be able to

1. Differentiate various ownership patterns around the world
2. Articulate the role of managers in both principal-agent and principal-principal conflicts
3. Explain the role of the board of directors
4. Identify voice- and exit-based governance mechanisms and their combination as a package
5. Acquire a global perspective on how governance mechanisms vary around the world
6. Articulate how institutions and resources affect corporate governance
7. Participate in two leading debates on corporate governance
8. Draw implications for action

costs and has emboldened American shareholders to sue foreign firms. This is not a theoretical possibility. Within *days* of listing in New York in 2003, China Life, an insurer, was sued by shareholders for its alleged failure to disclose old liabilities. Since then, China's big banks all chose to list first in friendlier Hong Kong.

However, defenders of SarbOx argue that New York, with or without SarbOx, has always demanded the highest level of corporate governance. There is a reason that, on average, only one in ten public firms from outside the United States would list in New York: The other nine may not be good enough. In other words, if shady Russian firms go to London, so be it! As an example, consider PartyGaming, an online gambling company headquartered in Gibraltar and listed on LSE since 2005. Until 2006, 90% of its revenues had come from US residents, although online gambling was illegal in the United States. PartyGaming's prospectus for LSE disclosed this risk, noting that it "takes comfort in an apparent unwillingness or inability" of US authorities to enforce the law. A firm with such a dubious business model obviously would not have qualified for a New York listing if it had applied. In October 2006, US authorities moved to ban money transfers to gambling sites such as PartyGaming. Its stock dropped 60% in 24 hours. SarbOx defenders suggest that firms such as PartyGaming are exactly the kind of shady outfits that SarbOx is designed to weed out from listing in New York. London may win the listings war, but London investors can get burned.

Sources: Based on (1) *Business Week*, 2006, London's freewheeling exchange, November 27: 40; (2) *Business Week*, 2007, Michael Oxley's next act, April 9: 104; (3) C. Doidge, A. Karolyi, & R. Stulz, 2004, Why are foreign firms listed in the US worth more? *Journal of Financial Economics*, 71: 205–238; (4) *Economist*, 2006, Down on the street, November 25: 69–71; (5) *Economist*, 2006, What's wrong with Wall Street, November 25: 11; (6) The Honorable Michael Oxley, 2007, The status of corporate governance in the first decade of the 21st century, keynote speech, "Balancing Stakeholder Interests" Conference, Institute for Excellence in Corporate Governance, University of Texas at Dallas, November 1 (http://www.utdallas.edu/news/archive/2007/11-01-001.html).

Why are there differences in the rules governing firms listed in New York, London, and Hong Kong? Why has SarbOx deterred many foreign firms from listing in New York? How can investors in New York (and elsewhere) assure themselves that they are investing in credible firms whose business will not collapse overnight? These are some of the key questions addressed in this chapter, which focuses on how to govern the corporation around the world. **Corporate governance** is "the relationship among various participants in determining the direction and performance of corporations."[1] The primary participants are (1) owners, (2) managers, and (3) boards of directors—collectively known as the "tripod" underpinning corporate governance (Figure 16.1).

corporate governance
The relationship among various participants in determining the direction and performance of corporations.

FIGURE 16.1 THE TRIPOD OF CORPORATE GOVERNANCE

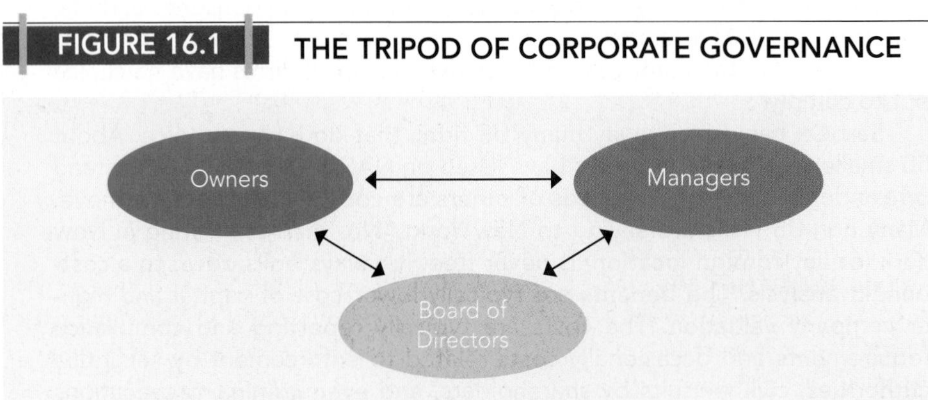

We start by discussing each of the three legs of the tripod. Next, we introduce internal and external governance mechanisms from a global perspective. Then, institution- and resource-based views on corporate governance are outlined. As before, debates and extensions follow.

OWNERS

LEARNING OBJECTIVE 1

Differentiate various ownership patterns around the world

Owners provide capital, bear risks, and own the firm. Three broad patterns exist: (1) concentrated versus diffused ownership, (2) family ownership, and (3) state ownership.

Concentrated versus Diffused Ownership

Founders usually start up firms and completely own and control them. This is referred to as **concentrated ownership and control**. However, at some point, if the firm aspires to grow and needs more capital, the owners' desire to keep the firm in family hands will have to accommodate the arrival of other shareholders. Approximately 80% listed US firms and 90% listed UK firms are now characterized by **diffused ownership**, with numerous small shareholders but none with a dominant level of control.[2] In such firms, there is a **separation of ownership and control** in that ownership is dispersed among many small shareholders and control is largely concentrated in the hands of salaried, professional managers who own little (or no) equity.

concentrated ownership and control
Founders start up firms and completely own and control them on an individual or family basis.

diffused ownership
Publicly traded corporations owned by numerous small shareholders but none with a dominant level of control.

separation of ownership and control
The dispersal of ownership among many small shareholders, in which control is largely concentrated in the hands of salaried, professional managers who own little (or no) equity.

If majority or dominant owners (such as founders) do not personally run the firm, they are naturally interested in keeping a close eye on how the firm is run. However, dispersed owners, each with a small stake, have neither incentives nor resources to do so. Most small shareholders do not bother to show up at annual shareholder meetings. They prefer to free ride and hope that other shareholders will properly monitor and discipline managers. If they are not happy, they will simply sell the stock and invest elsewhere. However, if all shareholders behaved in this manner, then no shareholder would care, and managers would end up acquiring significant de facto control power.

The rise of institutional investors, such as professionally managed mutual funds and pension pools, has significantly changed this picture.[3] Institutional investors have both incentives and resources to closely monitor and control managerial actions. The increased size of institutional holdings limits the ability of institutional investors to dump the stock because when one's stake is large enough, selling out depresses the share price and harms the seller.

Although the image of widely held corporations is a reasonably accurate description of most modern large US and UK firms, it is *not* the case in other parts of the world. Outside the Anglo-American world, there is relatively little separation of ownership and control. Most large firms are typically owned and controlled by families or the state.[4] Next, we turn our attention to such firms.

Family Ownership

The vast majority of large firms throughout continental Europe, Asia, Latin America, and Africa feature concentrated family ownership and control.[5] On the positive side, family ownership and control may provide better incentives for the firm to focus on long-run performance. It may also minimize the conflicts between owners and professional managers typically encountered in widely owned firms.[6] However, on the negative side, family ownership and control may lead to the selection of less qualified managers (who happen to be the sons, daughters, and relatives of founders), the destruction of value because of family conflicts, and the expropriation of minority shareholders (discussed later).[7] At present, there is no conclusive evidence on the positive or negative role of family ownership and control on the performance of large firms.[8]

State Ownership

Other than families, the state is another major owner of firms in many parts of the world. Since the 1980s, one country after another—ranging from Britain to Brazil to Belarus—has realized that their state-owned enterprises (SOEs) often perform poorly. SOEs suffer from an incentive problem. In theory, although all citizens (including employees) are owners, in practice, they have neither rights to enjoy dividends generated by SOEs (as shareholders would) nor rights to transfer or sell "their" property. SOEs are de facto owned and controlled by government agencies far removed from ordinary citizens and employees. Thus, there is little motivation for SOE managers and employees to improve performance, which they can hardly benefit from personally. In a most cynical fashion, SOE employees in the former Soviet Union described the situation well: "They pretend to pay us and we pretend to work." As a result, a wave of privatization has hit the world since the 1980s.[9] The SOE share has declined from more than 10% of global GDP in 1979 to 5% today.[10]

LEARNING OBJECTIVE 

Articulate the role of managers in both principal-agent and principal-principal conflicts

MANAGERS

Managers, especially executives on the **top management team (TMT)** led by the chief executive officer (CEO), represent another crucial leg of the corporate governance tripod.

top management team (TMT)
The team consisting of the highest level of executives of a firm led by the CEO.

agency relationship
The relationship between principals (such as shareholders) and agents (such as managers).

principal
A person (such as owner) delegating authority.

agent
A person (such as manager) to whom authority is delegated.

agency theory
A theory that focuses on principal-agent relationships (or in short, agency relationships).

principal-agent conflicts
Conflicts between principals and agents.

Principal-Agent Conflicts

The relationship between shareholders and professional managers is a relationship between principals and agents—in short, an **agency relationship**. **Principals** are persons (such as owners) delegating authority, and **agents** are persons (such as managers) to whom authority is delegated. **Agency theory** suggests a simple yet profound proposition: To the extent that the interests of principals and agents do not completely overlap, there will *inherently* be **principal-agent conflicts**. These conflicts result in **agency costs**, including (1) principals' costs of monitoring and controlling agents and (2) agents' costs of bonding (signaling that they are trustworthy).[11] In a corporate setting, when shareholders (principals) are interested in maximizing the long-term value of their stock, managers (agents) may be more interested in maximizing their own power, income, and perks.

Manifestations of agency problems include excessive executive compensation, on-the-job consumption (such as corporate jets), low-risk, short-term investments (such as maximizing current earnings while cutting long-term R&D), and empire building (such as value-destroying acquisitions). Consider executive compensation. In 1980, the average US CEO earned approximately 40 times what the average blue-collar worker earned. Today, the ratio is 400 times.[12] Despite some performance improvement, it seems difficult to argue that the average firm's CEO improved performance 10 times faster than the workers since 1980 and thus deserved a pay package worth 400 workers' salaries today.[13] In other words, one can "smell" some agency costs.

Directly measuring agency costs, however, is difficult. In one of the most innovative (and hair-raising) attempts to directly measure agency costs, one study finds

For whom are these managers working?

that some sudden CEO *deaths* (plane crashes or heart attacks) are accompanied by an increase in share prices of their firms.[14] These CEOs reduced agency costs that shareholders had to shoulder by dropping dead (!). Conversely, we could imagine how much value these CEOs destroyed when they were alive. The capital market, sadly (and some may even say cruelly), was pleased with such human tragedies.

agency costs
The costs associated with principal-agent relationships.

The primary reason agency problems persist is because of **information asymmetries** between principals and agents; that is, agents such as managers almost always know more about the property they manage than principals do. Although it is possible to reduce information asymmetries through governance mechanisms, it is not realistic to completely eliminate agency problems.

information asymmetries
Asymmetric distribution and possession of information between two sides.

Principal-Principal Conflicts

Since concentrated ownership and control by families is the norm in many parts of the world, different kinds of conflicts are at play. One of the leading indicators of concentrated family ownership and control is the appointment of family members as board chair, CEO, and other TMT members. In East Asia, approximately 57% of the corporations have board chairs and CEOs from the controlling families.[15] In continental Europe, the number is 68%.[16] The families are able to do so because they are controlling (although not necessarily majority) shareholders. For example, in 2003, 30-year-old James Murdoch became CEO of British Sky Broadcasting (BSkyB), Europe's biggest satellite broadcaster, in the face of loud minority shareholder resistance. The reason? James's father is Rupert Murdoch, who controlled 35% of BSkyB and chaired the board.

The BSkyB case is a classic example of the conflicts in family-owned and family-controlled firms. Instead of between principals (shareholders) and agents (professional managers), the primary conflicts are between two classes of principals: controlling shareholders and minority shareholders—in other words, **principal-principal conflicts**[17] (Figure 16.2 and Table 16.1). Family managers such as Rupert and James Murdoch, who represent (or are) controlling shareholders, may advance family interests at the expense of minority shareholders. Controlling shareholders' dominant position as *both* principals and agents (managers) may allow them to override traditional governance mechanisms designed to curtail principal-agent conflicts. For example, the board of directors will be ineffective when the CEO being evaluated is the son of the board chairman.

principal-principal conflicts
Conflicts between two classes of principals: controlling shareholders and minority shareholders.

The result of concentrated ownership by families is that family managers may engage in **expropriation** of minority shareholders, defined as activities that enrich controlling shareholders at the expense of minority shareholders. For example, managers from the controlling family may divert resources from the firm for personal or family use. This activity is vividly nicknamed **tunneling**—digging a tunnel to sneak out.[18] Although such tunneling (often known as "corporate theft") is

expropriation
The activities that enrich controlling shareholders at the expense of minority shareholders.

tunneling
A form of corporate theft that occurs when managers from the controlling family divert resources from the firm for personal or family use.

FIGURE 16.2 PRINCIPAL-AGENT CONFLICTS AND PRINCIPAL-PRINCIPAL CONFLICTS

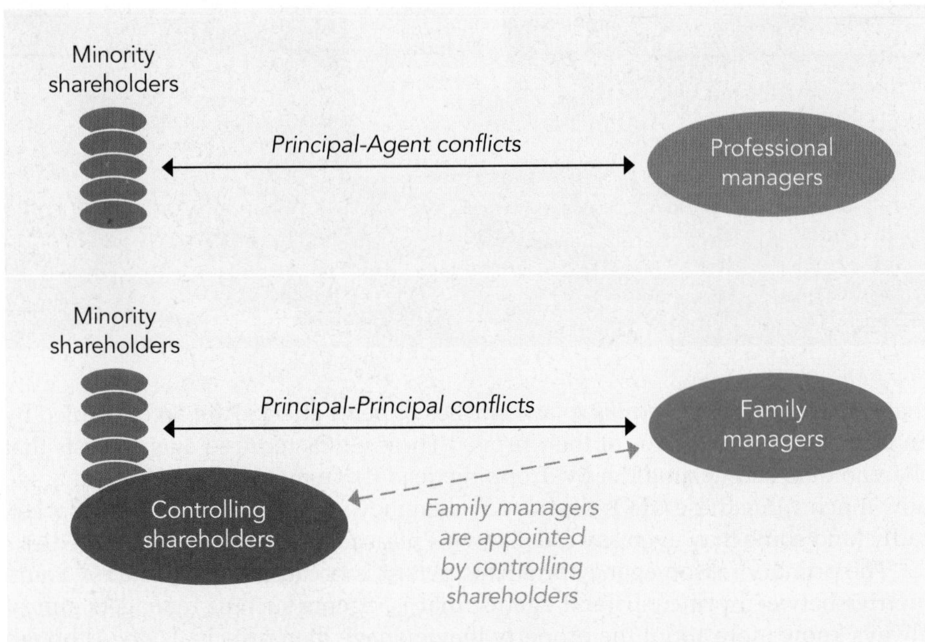

TABLE 16.1 PRINCIPAL-AGENT VERSUS PRINCIPAL-PRINCIPAL CONFLICTS

	Principal–Agent Conflicts	Principal–Principal Conflicts
Ownership pattern	Dispersed—shareholders holding 5% of equity are regarded as "blockholders"	Dominant—often greater than 50% of equity is controlled by the largest shareholders
Manifestations	Strategies that benefit entrenched managers at the expense of shareholders (such as shirking, excessive compensation, and empire building)	Strategies that benefit controlling shareholders at the expense of minority shareholders (such as minority shareholder expropriation and cronyism)
Institutional protection of minority shareholders	Formal constraints (such as courts) are more protective of shareholder rights; informal norms adhere to shareholder wealth maximization	Formal institutional protection is often lacking; informal norms are typically in favor of controlling shareholders
Market for corporate control	Active, at least in principle, as the "governance mechanism of last resort"	Inactive, even in principle; concentrated ownership thwarts notions of takeover

Source: Adapted from M. Young, M. W. Peng, D. Ahlstrom, G. Bruton, & Y. Jiang, 2008, Corporate governance in emerging economies: A review of the principal-principal perspective, *Journal of Management Studies* (in press).

related transaction
Controlling shareholders sell goods or firm's assets to another firm they own at below-market prices or spin off the most profitable part of a public firm and merge it with another private firm of theirs.

illegal, expropriation can be done legally through **related transactions**, whereby controlling shareholders sell firm's assets to another firm they own at below-market prices or spin off the most profitable part of a public firm and merge it with another private firm of theirs.[19]

Overall, while corporate governance practice and research traditionally focus on how to control professional managers because of the separation of ownership and control in US and UK firms, how to govern family managers in firms with concentrated ownership and control is of equal or probably higher importance around the world (see In Focus 16.1).

IN FOCUS 16.1 Family Ownership and Control

In mid-2005, few investors in Porsche would have guessed that only 18 months later their firm would be the dominant shareholder in Volkswagen. Then again, it is none of their business because they have little say over the sports-car maker's managers or strategy. The Porsche and Piëch families have total voting control over Porsche, despite owning only half of its equity. The publicly traded shares, providing the other half of Porsche's capital, have no right to vote.

Porsche is an extreme example of how a family can wield great power by harnessing large amounts of other people's money. But it is not unusual. In America, 6% by number and 8% by capitalization of quoted companies had dual-class shares in 2002. Only two-thirds of large European companies rigorously apply the principle that one share should command one vote.

Some of the best-known North American companies use dual-class shares. The Ford family may no longer own the company—it has a slender 3.75% of the shares—but nobody can doubt who is in control. When the firm went public in 1956, the family's shares were converted into a special class that is guaranteed 40% of the voting power, no matter how many ordinary shares are in issue.

Dual-class shares are no hangover from the past. When Google went public in 2004, its founders, Larry Page and Sergey Brin, insisted on a dual-class share structure. Google sold the public new A shares with one vote per share; its existing shares, mostly held by Mr. Page and Mr. Brin, became B shares with ten times as many votes per share. With around one-fifth of Google's total equity, the founders still command about three-fifths of votes and thus retain control.

Source: Excerpts from *Economist*, 2007, Our company right or wrong (pp. 75–76), March 17: 75–77. © The Economist Newspaper Group.

THE BOARD OF DIRECTORS

LEARNING OBJECTIVE 3

Explain the role of the board of directors

As an intermediary between owners and managers, the board of directors oversees and ratifies strategic decisions and evaluates, rewards, and if necessary penalizes top managers.

Key Features of the Board

These include (1) composition, (2) leadership structure, and (3) interlocks.

Board Composition Otherwise known as the insider/outsider mix, board composition has recently attracted significant attention. **Inside directors** are top executives of the firm. The trend around the world is to introduce more **outside directors**, defined as nonmanagement members of the board. Outside directors presumably are more independent and can better safeguard shareholder interests.[20] In the post-Enron era, many US firms have added outside directors.

inside director
A member of the board who is a top executive of the firm.

outside director
A nonmanagement member of the board.

Although there is a widely held belief in favor of a higher proportion of outside directors, academic research has *failed* to empirically establish a link between the outsider/insider ratio and firm performance.[21] Even "stellar" firms with a majority of outside directors on the board (on average 74% of outside directors at Enron, Global Crossing, and Tyco before their scandals erupted) can still be plagued by governance problems.[22] It is possible that some of these outside directors are *affiliated* directors who may have family, business, and/or professional relationships with the firm or firm management. In other words, such affiliated outside directors are not necessarily "independent." For example, outside directors on Japanese boards often come from banks, other member firms of the same *keiretsu*, and their parent firms.[23]

Leadership Structure Also important is whether the board is led by a separate chair or by the CEO who doubles as a board chair—a situation known as **CEO duality**. From an agency theory standpoint, if the board is to supervise agents such as the CEO, it seems imperative that the board is chaired by a separate individual. Otherwise, how can the CEO be evaluated by the body that he or she chairs? However, a corporation led by two top leaders (a board chair and a CEO) may lack a

CEO duality
The CEO serves as a board chair.

unity of command and experience top-level conflicts. Not surprisingly, there is significant divergence across countries. For instance, while a majority of the large UK firms separate the two top jobs, most large US firms combine them. A practical difficulty often cited by US boards is that it is very hard to recruit a capable CEO without the board chair title.

Around the world, both practices exist. Academic research is inconclusive on whether CEO duality (or nonduality) is more effective.[24] However, there are now pressures around the world for firms to split the two jobs to at least show that they are serious about controlling the CEO.

Board Interlocks Who the directors are and where they come from are also important. Directors tend to be economic and social elites who share a sense of camaraderie and reciprocity. When one person affiliated with one firm sits on the board of another firm, an **interlocking directorate** has been created. Firms often establish relationships through such board appointments. For instance, outside directors from financial institutions often facilitate financing. Outside directors experienced in acquisitions may help the focal firms engage in these practices.[25]

interlocking directorate
A situation whereby two or more firms share one director affiliated with one firm who serves on multiple boards.

In the United States, Frank Carlucci, a former secretary of defense and chairman of the Carlyle Group, served on 20 boards (!) at one time. In Hong Kong, the most heavily connected director, David Li, chairman of the Bank of East Asia, sat on nine boards.[26] Critics argue that "no one, however talented, can hope to sit on the boards of that many companies and effectively monitor the management of each."[27] In fact, one of the boards David Li served on was Enron's. In the post-Enron environment, such unusual practices are increasingly rare.

The Role of Boards of Directors

In a nutshell, boards of directors perform (1) control, (2) service, and (3) resource acquisition functions. Boards' effectiveness in serving the control function stems from their independence, deterrence, and norms.

- The ability to effectively control managers boils down to how independent directors are. Outside directors who are personally friendly and loyal to the CEO are unlikely to challenge managerial decisions. Exactly for this reason, CEOs often nominate family members, personal friends, and other independent but passive directors.[28]
- There is a lack of deterrence on the part of directors should they fail to protect shareholder interests. Courts usually will not second-guess board decisions in the absence of bad faith or insider dealing. Directors are often protected from the consequences of bad decisions.
- There is often a lack of norms for directors to challenge management. Directors who "stick their necks out" by confronting the CEO in meetings tend to be frozen out of board deliberations.[29] When they raise a point, nobody picks it up.

In addition to control, another important function of the board is service—primarily advising the CEO.[30] Finally, another crucial board function is resource acquisition for the focal firm, often through interlocking directorates. For example, in China, outside directors from buyers, suppliers, and alliance partners bring in more resources resulting in higher sales growth.[31]

Overall, until recently, many boards of directors simply "rubber stamped" (approve without scrutiny) managerial actions. Prior to the 1997 economic crisis, many South Korean boards did not bother to hold meetings, and board decisions would be literally rubber stamped—not even by directors themselves; corporate secretaries would stamp all the seals of directors that were kept in the corporate office. However, change is now in the air throughout the world. In South Korea, board meetings are now held regularly, and seals are personally stamped by directors themselves.

GOVERNANCE MECHANISMS AS A PACKAGE

LEARNING OBJECTIVE 4

Identify voice- and exit-based governance mechanisms and their combination as a package

Governance mechanisms can be classified as internal and external—otherwise known as voice-based and exit-based mechanisms, respectively. **Voice-based mechanisms** refer to shareholders' willingness to work with managers, usually through the board, by "voicing" their concerns. **Exit-based mechanisms** indicate that shareholders no longer have patience and are willing to "exit" by selling their shares. This section outlines these mechanisms.

voice-based mechanisms
Corporate governance mechanisms that focus on shareholders' willingness to work with managers, usually through the board, by "voicing" their concerns.

exit-based mechanisms
Corporate governance mechanisms that focus on exit, indicating that shareholders no longer have patience and are willing to "exit" by selling shares.

Internal (Voice-Based) Governance Mechanisms

The two internal governance mechanisms typically employed by boards can be characterized as (1) "carrots" and (2) "sticks." To better motivate managers, increasing executive compensation as "carrots" is often a must (see In Focus 16.2). Stock options that help align the interests of managers and shareholders have become increasingly popular.[32] The underlying idea is pay for performance, which seeks to link executive compensation with firm performance.[33] In principle, this idea is sound, but in practice, it has a number of drawbacks. If accounting-based measures (such as return on sales) are used, managers are often able to manipulate numbers to make them look better. If market-based measures (such as stock prices) are adopted, stock prices obviously are subject to too many forces beyond managers' control. Consequently, the pay-for-performance link in executive compensation is usually not very strong.[34]

In general, boards are likely to use "carrots" before considering "sticks." However, when facing continued performance failures, boards may have to dismiss the CEO.[35] Approximately 40% of all CEO changes in recent years are sackings for underachievement.[36] In brief, boards seem to be more "trigger-happy." Because top managers have to shoulder substantial firm-specific employment risk (a fired CEO is unlikely to run

IN FOCUS 16.2 Executive Compensation at SAP

Executive compensation is often criticized to have a weak (or no) link with performance. In an effort to provide powerful incentives to executives to scale new heights, SAP, the leading German enterprise software provider, announced in 2006 that it would pay $125 million in bonuses to the top-seven executives if they could double market capitalization—from a $57 billion starting point—by the end of 2010. This was considered not only out of character for SAP but also out of character for a German firm, whose executives are typically paid less than half as much as their American counterparts. SAP was immediately criticized by the German media. Doubling market capitalization would be a stretch goal for an industry leader such as SAP, whose room for growth was limited. SAP's price-earnings ratio of 39 was already way above that of rivals Oracle (24) and IBM (16). SAP's cofounder Hasso Plattner, architect of this bold initiative, argued: "If you want extraordinary growth, you want to have an extraordinary bonus scheme." It remains to be seen whether SAP can accomplish such growth and then pay its executives accordingly by 2010.

Sources: Based on (1) *Business Week*, 2006, SAP dangles a big, fat carrot, May 22: 66–68; (2) http://www.sap.com.

another publicly traded company), they naturally demand more generous compensation—a premium on the order of 30% or more—before taking on new CEO jobs. This in part explains the rapidly rising levels of executive compensation.[37]

External (Exit-Based) Governance Mechanisms

There are three external governance mechanisms: (1) market for product competition, (2) market for corporate control, and (3) market for private equity. Product market competition is a powerful force compelling managers to maximize profits and, in turn, shareholder value. However, from a corporate governance perspective, product market competition *complements* the market for corporate control and the market for private equity, each of which is outlined next.

The Market for Corporate Control This is the main external governance mechanism, otherwise known as the takeover market or the mergers and acquisitions (M&A) market (see Chapter 12). It is essentially an arena where different management teams contest for the control rights of corporate assets. As an external governance mechanism, the market for corporate control serves as a disciplining mechanism of last resort when internal governance mechanisms fail. The underlying logic is spelled out by agency theory, which suggests that when managers engage in self-interested actions and internal governance mechanisms fail, firm stock will be undervalued by investors. Under these circumstances, other management teams, which recognize an opportunity to reorganize or redeploy the firm's assets and hence to create new value, bid for the rights to manage the firm. The market for corporate control was relatively inactive prior to the 1980s. However, since the 1980s, a large wave of M&As and restructuring has emerged (see Chapter 12).

How effective is the market for corporate control? Three findings emerge:[38]

- On average, shareholders of target firms earn sizable acquisition premiums.
- Shareholders of acquiring firms experience slight but insignificant losses.
- There is a substantially higher level of top management turnover following M&As.

In summary, while internal mechanisms aim at fine-tuning, the market for corporate control enables the wholesale removal of entrenched managers. As a radical approach, the market for corporate control has its own limitations. It is very costly to wage such financial battles. In addition, a large number of M&As seem to be driven by acquirers' sheer hubris or empire building, and the long-run profitability of postmerger firms is not particularly impressive.

Nevertheless, the net impact, at least in the short run, seems to be positive because the threat of takeovers does limit managers' divergence from shareholder wealth maximization. In Japan, an increasingly credible threat of takeovers has been rising. For example, Minolta was recently taken over by HOYA. As a result, more and more Japanese managers are now paying attention to their firms' stock prices. Of course, the number of M&A cases in Japan is still small, but a rising threat itself is already having some effect on managerial behavior.

private equity
Equity capital invested in private companies that, by definition, are not publicly traded.

leveraged buyout (LBO)
A means by which private investors, often in partnership with incumbent managers, issue bonds and use the cash raised to buy the firm's stock.

The Market for Private Equity Instead of being taken over, a large number of publicly listed firms have gone private by tapping into **private equity**, primarily (but not always) through **leveraged buyouts (LBOs)**. In an LBO, private investors, often in partnership with incumbent managers, issue bonds and use the cash raised to buy the firm's stock—in essence replacing shareholders with bondholders and transforming the firm from a public to a private entity. As another external governance mechanism, private equity utilizes the bond market, as opposed to stock market, to discipline managers. LBO-based private equity transactions are associated with three major changes in corporate governance:

- LBOs change the incentives of managers by providing them with substantial equity stakes.
- The high amount of debt imposes strong financial discipline.
- LBO sponsors closely monitor the firms they have invested in.

Overall, evidence suggests that LBOs improve efficiency, at least in the short run.[39] However, the picture is less clear on the long run because LBOs may have forced managers to reduce investments in long-run R&D.[40] Around the world, private equity has grown by leaps and bounds in recent years, from 0.25% of world GDP in 2000 to 1.5% in 2007, now representing approximately 20% of all M&A activities (see Closing Case for more details).

© AP IMAGES

In what ways do the shareholders influence a corporation's governance?

Internal Mechanisms + External Mechanisms = Governance Package

Taken together, the internal and external mechanisms can be considered a "package."[41] Michael Jensen, a leading agency theorist, argues that in the United States, failures of internal governance mechanisms in the 1970s activated the market for corporate control in the 1980s.[42] Managers initially resisted. However, over time, many firms that are not takeover targets or that have successfully defended themselves against such attempts end up restructuring and downsizing—doing exactly what "raiders" would have done had these firms been taken over. In other words, the strengthened external mechanisms force firms to improve their internal mechanisms.

Overall, since the 1980s, American managers have become much more focused on stock prices, resulting in a new term, **shareholder capitalism**, that has been spreading around the world.[43] In Europe, executive stock options become popular and M&As more frequent.[44] In Russia, after the 1998 collapse, there are now some traces of modern corporate governance.[45]

shareholder capitalism
A view of capitalism that suggests that the most fundamental purpose for firms to exist is to serve the economic interests of shareholders (also known as capitalists).

A GLOBAL PERSPECTIVE ON GOVERNANCE MECHANISMS

LEARNING OBJECTIVE 5

Acquire a global perspective on how governance mechanisms vary around the world

Illustrated in Figure 16.3, different corporate ownership and control patterns around the world lead to a different mix of internal and external mechanisms. The most familiar type is cell 4, exemplified by most large US and UK firms. Although external governance mechanisms (M&As and private equity) are active, internal mechanisms are relatively weak due to the separation of ownership and control that gives managers significant de facto control power.

The opposite can be found in cell 1—namely, firms in continental Europe and Japan where the market for corporate control is relatively inactive (although there is more activity recently). Consequently, the primary governance mechanisms remain concentrated ownership and control.[46]

Overall, the Anglo-American and continental European-Japanese (otherwise known as German-Japanese) systems represent the two primary corporate governance families in the world, with a variety of labels (see Table 16.2). Given that both the United States and United Kingdom as a group and continental Europe and Japan as another group are highly developed, successful economies, it is difficult and probably not meaningful to argue whether the Anglo-American or German-Japanese system is better.[47] Evidently, each has different strengths and weaknesses.

FIGURE 16.3 INTERNAL AND EXTERNAL GOVERNANCE MECHANISMS: A GLOBAL PERSPECTIVE

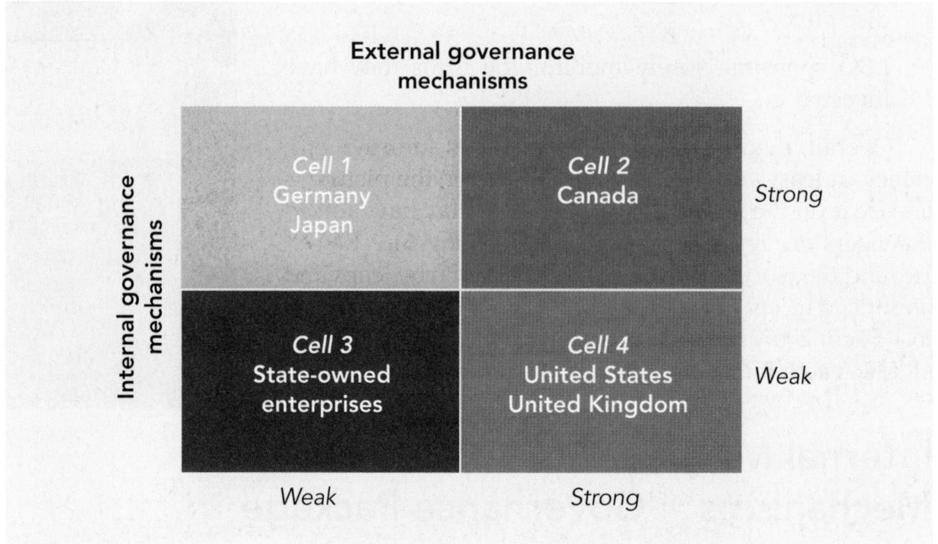

Source: Cells 1, 2, and 4 are adapted from E. R. Gedajlovic & D. M. Shapiro, 1998, Management and ownership effects: Evidence from five countries (p. 539), *Strategic Management Journal*, 19: 533–553. The label of cell 3 is suggested by the present author.

There are other systems that do not easily fit into such a dichotomous world. Placed in cell 2, Canada has *both* a relatively active market for corporate control and a large number of firms with concentrated ownership and control: More than 380 of the 400 largest Canadian firms are controlled by a single shareholder.[48] Canadian managers thus face powerful internal and external constraints.

Finally, SOEs (of all nationalities) are in an unfortunate position of both weak external and internal governance mechanisms (cell 3). Prereform SOEs in the former Soviet bloc and China serve as a case in point. Externally, the market for corporate control simply did not exist. Internally, managers were supervised by officials who acted as de facto "owners" with ineffective control.

Overall, firms around the world are governed by a combination of internal and external mechanisms. For firms in cells 1, 2, and 4, there is some partial substitution between internal and external mechanisms (for example, weak boards may be partially substituted by a strong market for corporate control). However, it is not viable to be stuck in cell 3 with both weak internal and external mechanisms in the long run. From a corporate governance standpoint, the global wave of privatization of SOEs is a movement to migrate out of the unfortunate cell 3 in Figure 16.3.[49]

TABLE 16.2 TWO PRIMARY FAMILIES OF CORPORATE GOVERNANCE SYSTEMS

Corporations in the United States and United Kingdom	Corporations in Continental Europe and Japan
Anglo-American corporate governance models	German-Japanese corporate governance models
Market-oriented, high-tension systems	Bank-oriented, network-based systems
Rely mostly on exit-based, external mechanisms	Rely mostly on voice-based, internal mechanisms
Shareholder capitalism	Stakeholder capitalism

HOW INSTITUTIONS AND RESOURCES AFFECT CORPORATE GOVERNANCE

LEARNING OBJECTIVE 6

Articulate how institutions and resources affect corporate governance

The institution-based view posits that differences around the world are affected by *formal* securities laws, corporate charters, and codes and *informal* conventions, norms, and values—collectively known as institutions (or rules of the game).[50] The resource-based view argues that among a number of firms governed by the same set of rules, some excel more than others because of differences in firm-specific capabilities (Figure 16.4). This section examines these views.

Institutions and Corporate Governance

Formal Institutional Frameworks A fundamental difference is between the separation of ownership and control in (most) Anglo-American firms and the concentration of ownership and control in the rest of the world. Although there are many explanations, a leading example for such a difference is an institutional one. In brief, better formal legal protection of shareholder rights, especially those held by *minority* shareholders, in the United States and United Kingdom encourages founding families to dilute their equity to attract minority shareholders and delegate day-to-day management to professional managers. Given reasonable investor protection, founding families themselves (such as the Rockefellers at ExxonMobil) may over time feel comfortable becoming minority shareholders of the firms they founded. On the other hand, when formal legal and regulatory institutions are dysfunctional, founding families *must* run their firms directly. In the absence of investor protection, bestowing management rights to outside professional managers may invite abuse and theft.[51]

There is strong evidence that the weaker the formal legal and regulatory institutions protecting shareholders, the more concentrated ownership and control rights become—in other words, there is some substitution between the two. Common-law countries (the United States, United Kingdom, and former British colonies) generally have the strongest legal protection of investors and lowest concentration of corporate ownership.[52] Among common-law countries, such ownership concentration is higher for firms in emerging economies (such as Hong Kong, India,

FIGURE 16.4 INSTITUTIONS, RESOURCES, AND CORPORATE GOVERNANCE

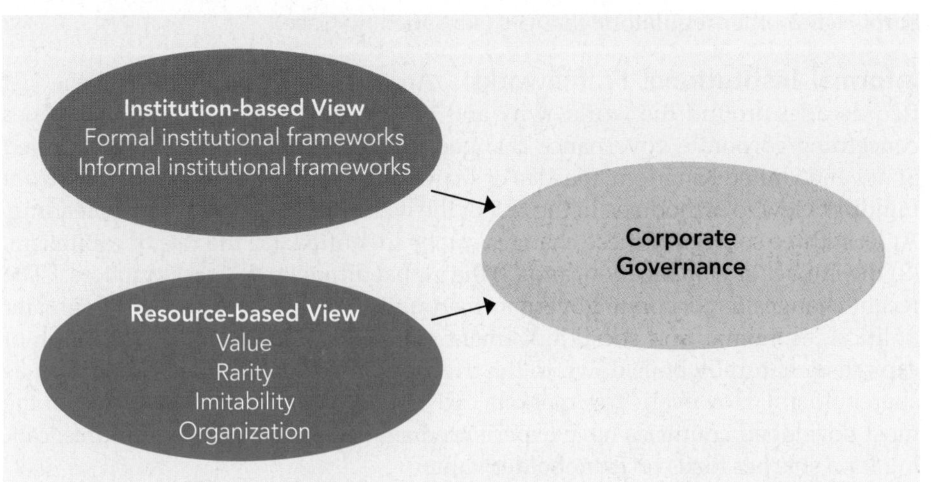

Israel, and South Africa) than developed economies (such as Australia, Canada, Ireland, and New Zealand). In short, concentrated ownership and control are an answer to potentially rampant principal-agent conflicts in the absence of sufficient legal protection of shareholder rights.

However, what is good for controlling shareholders is not necessarily good for minority shareholders and for an economy. As noted earlier, the minimization of principal-agent conflicts through concentration of ownership and control, unfortunately, introduces more principal-principal conflicts (see In Focus 16.1). Consequently, many potential minority shareholders may refuse to invest. "How to avoid being expropriated as a minority shareholder?" one popular saying in Asia suggests, "Don't be one!" If minority shareholders are informed enough to be aware of these possibilities and still decide to invest, they are likely to discount the shares floated by family owners, resulting in lower corporate valuations, fewer publicly traded firms, inactive and smaller capital markets, and in turn, lower levels of economic development in general.

Given that almost every country desires vibrant capital markets and economic development, it seems puzzling that the Anglo-American-style investor protection is not universally embraced. It is important to note that at its core, corporate governance ultimately is a choice about *political* governance. For largely historical reasons, most countries have made hard-to-reverse political choices. For example, the German practice of "codetermination" (employees control 50% of the votes on supervisory boards) is an outcome of political decisions made by postwar German governments.[53] If German firms were to have US/UK-style dispersed ownership and still allowed employees to control 50% of the votes on supervisory boards, these firms would end up becoming *employee*-dominated firms. Thus, concentrated ownership and control become a natural response.

Changing political choices, although not impossible, will encounter significant resistance, especially from incumbents (such as German labor unions or Asian families) who benefit from the present system.[54] In the nine countries of East Asia (excluding China), the top-15 families on average control approximately 53% of listed assets and 39% of GDP.[55] Some of the leading business families not only have great connections with the government; sometimes, they *are* the government. For example, two recent prime ministers of Italy and Thailand—Silvio Berlusconi and Thaksin Shinawatra, respectively—came from leading business families in these countries.[56]

Only when extraordinary events erupt would some politicians muster sufficient political will to initiate major corporate governance reforms. The spectacular corporate scandals in the United States (such as Enron) are an example of such extraordinary events prompting more serious political reforms in the form of SarbOx and other regulatory changes (see Opening Case).

Informal Institutional Frameworks An interesting question is: In the last two decades around the world, why and how have informal norms and values concerning corporate governance changed to such a great extent? In the United States and United Kingdom, the idea of shareholder capitalism has graduated from minority view to orthodoxy. In the rest of the world, this idea is rapidly spreading. At least three sources of these changes can be identified: (1) the rise of capitalism, (2) the impact of globalization, and (3) the global diffusion of "best practices." The recent changes in corporate governance around the world are part of the greater political, economic, and social movement embracing capitalism. The triumph of capitalism naturally boils down to the triumph of *capitalists* (otherwise known as shareholders). However, "free markets" are not necessarily free. Even some of the most developed countries have experienced significant governance failures, calling for a sharper focus on shareholder value.

At least three aspects of recent globalization have a bearing on corporate governance. First, thanks to more trade and investment, firms with different governance norms increasingly come into contact and expose their differences. Being aware of alternatives, shareholders as well as managers and policymakers are no longer easily persuaded that "our way" is the most natural and most efficient method of corporate governance.[57] Second, foreign portfolio investment (FPI)—foreigners purchasing stocks and bonds (see Chapter 6)—has scaled new heights. These investors naturally demand better shareholder protection before committing their funds. Finally, the global thirst for capital has prompted many firms to pay attention to corporate governance. Many foreign firms, for example, have listed their stock on the New York and London Exchanges. In return for such privileges, they must be in compliance with US and UK listing requirements (Opening Case).

In addition, the changing norms and values are also directly promoted by the global diffusion of codes of "best practices."[58] Led by Britain's Cadbury Report in 1992, the global proliferation of such codes is striking (Table 16.3). A lot of these codes are advisory and not legally binding. However, there are strong pressures for firms to "voluntarily" adopt these codes. In Russia, although adopting the 2002 Code of Corporate Conduct is in theory voluntary, firms that opt not to adopt have to publicly explain why, essentially naming and shaming themselves.

In addition, the Organization for Economic Cooperation and Development (OECD) has spearheaded the efforts to globally diffuse best practices. In 1999, it published the *OECD Principles of Corporate Governance*, suggesting that the overriding objective of the corporation should be to optimize shareholder returns over time.[59] The *Principles* are nonbinding even for the 30 OECD member countries. Nevertheless, the global norms seem to be moving toward the *Principles*. For example, China and Taiwan—both are non-OECD members—have recently taken a page from the *Principles* and allowed for class-action lawsuits brought by shareholders.[60]

Slowly but surely, change is in the air in almost every country. Although some companies and countries may adopt such changes for "window dressing" purposes, over time, some of the new shapes and forms of corporate governance may indeed change deeply held cognitive beliefs.

Resources and Corporate Governance

From a corporate governance standpoint, the ability to successfully list on a high-profile exchange such as the NYSE and LSE is *v*aluable, *r*are, and hard-to-*i*mitate (the first three, VRI, in the VRIO framework). In 1997, the valuations of foreign firms listed in New York were 17% higher than their domestic counterparts in the same country that were either unable or unwilling to list abroad.[61] Now, despite hurdles such as SarbOx (see Opening Case), the select few that are able to list in New York are rewarded more handsomely: Their valuations are now 37% higher

TABLE 16.3 SELECTED CORPORATE GOVERNANCE (CG) CODES AROUND THE WORLD SINCE THE 1990s

Developed Economies	Emerging Economies
Cadbury Report (United Kingdom, 1992)	King Report (South Africa, 1994)
Dey Report (Canada, 1994)	Confederation of Indian Industry Code of CG (India, 1998)
Bosch Report (Australia, 1995)	Korean Stock Exchange Code of Best Practice (Korea, 1999)
CG Forum of Japan Code (Japan, 1998)	Mexican Code of CG (Mexico, 1999)
German Panel on CG Code (Germany, 2000)	Code of CG for Listed Companies (China, 2001)
Sarbanes-Oxley Act (United States, 2002)	Code of Corporate Conduct (Russia, 2002)

than comparable groups of domestic firms in the same country.[62] London-listed foreign firms do not enjoy such high valuations. This is classic resource-based logic at work: Precisely because it is much more challenging to list in New York in the SarbOx era, the small number of foreign firms that are able to do that are truly exceptional not only in product market capabilities but also in governance effectiveness. Therefore, they deserve much higher valuations.

managerial human capital The skills and abilities acquired by top managers.

Some of the most valuable, rare, and hard-to-imitate firm-specific resources are top managers and directors—often regarded as **managerial human capital**. Some of these resources, such as the social networks of these executives, are unique and likely to add value.[63] Also, top managerial talents are hard to imitate—unless they are hired away by competitor firms.

The last crucial component in the VRIO framework is O: organizational. It is within an organizational setting (in TMTs and boards) that managers and directors function.[64] Overall, the few people at the top of an organization can make a world of difference. Governance mechanisms need to properly motivate and discipline them to make sure they make a positive impact.

LEARNING OBJECTIVE 7

Participate in two leading debates on corporate governance

DEBATES AND EXTENSIONS

Recent changes in corporate governance are often driven by significant debates, some of which have already been discussed. This section discusses two other major debates: (1) opportunistic agents versus managerial stewards and (2) global convergence versus divergence.

Opportunistic Agents versus Managerial Stewards

Agency theory assumes managers to be agents who may engage in self-serving, opportunistic activities if left to their own devices. However, critics contend that most managers are likely to be honest and trustworthy. Managerial mistakes may be due to a lack of competence, information, or luck but not necessarily due to self-serving. Thus, it may not be fair to characterize all managers as opportunistic agents. Although very influential, agency theory has been criticized as an "anti-management theory of management."[65] A "pro-management" theory, **stewardship theory**, has emerged recently. It suggests that most managers can be viewed as owners' stewards.[66] Safeguarding shareholders' interests and advancing organizational goals, as opposed to one's own self-serving agenda, will maximize (most) managers' own utility functions.

stewardship theory A theory that suggests that most managers can be viewed as owners' stewards interested in safeguarding shareholders' interests and advancing organizational goals.

Stewardship theorists agree that agency theory is useful when describing a certain portion of managers and under certain circumstances (such as under siege during takeover battles).[67] However, if all principals view all managers as self-serving agents with control mechanisms to put managers on a "tight leash," some managers, who initially view themselves as stewards, may become so frustrated that they end up engaging in the very self-serving behavior agency theory seeks to minimize. In other words, as a self-fulfilling prophecy, agency theory may *induce* such behavior.[68]

Global Convergence versus Divergence

Another leading debate is whether corporate governance is converging or diverging globally. Convergence advocates argue that globalization unleashes a "survival-of-the-fittest" process by which firms will be forced to adopt globally best (essentially Anglo-American) practices.[69] Global investors are willing to pay a premium for stock in firms with Anglo-American-style governance, prompting other firms to follow. Most of the recent governance codes (Table 16.3) largely draw from core Anglo-American concepts. The OECD has been promoting these Anglo-American principles as the "gold" standard. As a result, shareholder activism, an unheard of phenomenon in many parts of the world, is now becoming more visible (see In Focus 16.3).

One interesting phenomenon often cited by convergence advocates is **cross-listing**, namely, listing shares on foreign stock exchanges (Opening Case). Such cross-listing is primarily driven by the desire to tap into larger pools of capital. Foreign firms thus have to comply with US and UK securities laws and adopt Anglo-American corporate governance norms. There is evidence, for instance, that Japanese firms listed in New York and London, compared with those listed at

cross-listing
Listing shares on foreign stock exchanges.

IN FOCUS 16.3 David Webb: A Shareholder Activist in Hong Kong

Although Hong Kong may have a reputation to house one of the world's most sophisticated financial markets, minority shareholders have a tradition of being abused by controlling shareholders. Hong Kong regulations were largely cut and pasted from British statutes, but the nature of Hong Kong's listed firms means that the laws leave gaping loopholes that are exploited by controlling shareholders. Since most listed British firms do not have controlling shareholders, the board is apt to reasonably reflect the interests of all shareholders. However, in Hong Kong, 32 of the 33 "blue chips" in the Hang Seng Index, except HSBC, have controlling shareholders—a single person or group of persons, typically from a family, who has the ability to control the board.

Crusading against such an Establishment, David Webb, who was one of the 50 "Stars of Asia" featured by *Business Week*, is a unique character in the emerging shareholder activism movement in Hong Kong. Webb, a native of England and an Oxford University graduate, moved to Hong Kong in 1991. He worked in investment banking and corporate finance until 1998 when he retired to become a full-time investor. His website (http://www.webb-site.com) now boasts 9,000 subscribers. He is an outspoken critic at many shareholder meetings and an advocate for minority shareholders. He says that over 90% of listed companies have a shareholder who owns more than 20% and has de facto control. He believes where either a family or a government controls most listed companies, minority shareholders tend to be abused. "He has been an important voice in promoting good corporate governance among listed companies," said David O'Rear, chief economist for the Hong Kong General Chamber of Commerce.

As it stands now, the families that control most Hong Kong companies simply appoint directors and railroad their elections through at shareholder meetings. After buying 10 shares in each of the 33 companies that make up the Hang Seng Index, Webb has been regularly attending shareholder meetings and demanding formal votes on *all* proposals. That does not win him many friends among the tycoon set accustomed to doing cozy deals without outside scrutiny. Webb recognizes that the primary problems in corporate governance in Hong Kong—and also across Asia—arise from the concentrated ownership and control of companies.

Webb has been using his website to help increase awareness of the problem. In 2006, he recommended minority shareholders of Herderson Investment Ltd. to vote against the buyout offer from its parent company, Henderson Land Development Co., because the controlling shareholders did not offer a fair price in such a related transaction. He was pleased to see that minority shareholders vetoed the buyout plan. In the "Hall of Shame" on his website, he lists the companies under investigation by the Hong Kong authorities and writes analyses exposing instances where shareholders seem to be cheated or overlooked.

One of Webb's key targets is often the government of the Hong Kong Special Administrative Region, itself a major investor in the local market, even though the government has also turned to him for advice. Webb has been invited to serve on a number of corporate governance reform committees. In 2007, he was reappointed to Takeovers Panel and Takeovers Appeal Committee in the Hong Kong Securities and Futures Commission. Webb opined: "There is a reform process here, but it is incredibly slow. I take the position that it's better to lobby from the inside rather than the outside . . . You can't rock the boat if you are swimming around outside it."

Sources: This case was written by **Yi Jiang** (California State University, East Bay). It is based on (1) G. Wehrfritz, 2005, Safe haven? The slippery slope: Market watcher David Webb says shady China deals threaten Hong Kong's once sterling reputation, *Newsweek International Edition*, May 2 (online); (2) V. England, 2005, Spotlight: A crusader in Hong Kong, *International Herald Tribune*, August 20 (online); (3) H. Wan, 2006, Henderson Investment slumps on rejected buyout offer, *Bloomberg*, January 23 (online); (4) SFC appoints takeovers panel and takeovers appeal committee members, http://www.sfc.hk, March 30, 2007; (5) M. Young, M. W. Peng, D. Ahlstrom, G. Bruton, & Y. Jiang, 2008, Corporate governance in emerging economies: A review of the principal-principal perspective, *Journal of Management Studies* (in press); (6) http://www.webb-site.com.

home, are relatively more concerned about shareholder value.[70] A US or UK listing can be viewed as a signal of the firm's commitment to strengthen shareholder value, resulting in higher valuations.[71]

Critics contend that governance practices will continue to diverge throughout the world.[72] For example, promoting more concentrated ownership and control is often recommended as a solution to combat principal-agent conflicts in US and UK firms. However, making the same recommendation to reform firms in continental Europe, Asia, and Latin America may be counterproductive or even disastrous. This is because the main problem there is that controlling shareholders typically already have too much ownership and control.[73] Finally, US and UK practices differ. In addition to the split on CEO duality (the UK against, the US for) discussed earlier, none of the US antitakeover defenses (such as "poison pills") is legal in the UK.

In the case of cross-listed firms, divergence advocates make two points. First, compared to US firms, these foreign firms have significantly larger boards, more inside directors, lower institutional ownership, and more concentrated ownership.[74] In other words, cross-listed foreign firms do not necessarily adopt US governance practices before or after listing. Second, despite the popular belief that US and UK securities laws would apply to cross-listed foreign firms, in practice, these laws have rarely been effectively enforced against foreign firms' "tunneling."[75]

At present, complete divergence is probably unrealistic, especially for large firms in search of capital from global investors. Complete convergence also seems unlikely. What is more likely is "cross-vergence," balancing the expectations of global investors and those of local stakeholders.

LEARNING OBJECTIVE 8

Draw implications for action

MANAGEMENT SAVVY

From the institution- and resource-based views, two straightforward implications for action emerge (Table 16.4). First, savvy managers need to understand the rules, anticipate changes, and be aware of differences, especially when doing business abroad. Consider the two examples in the Opening Case. While PartyGaming, until 2006, had an excellent understanding of the rules (the nonenforcement of the US ban on online gambling), it had failed to anticipate the swift regulatory changes that brought down its business almost overnight (the enforcement to ban money transfers to gambling sites since October 2006). In retrospect, PartyGaming made at least one wise decision—not trying to list in New York, where its disclosure that 90% of its revenues came from illegal online gambling by US residents would have failed to pass regulatory screening. In contrast, China Life made a huge mistake by coming to New York and failing to understand American investor sentiments. It thought it could have it both ways: tapping into the vast US investor pool and hiding some liabilities without full disclosure (evidently a common practice at home). Unfortunately, some American shareholders dragged China Life to court in New York within *days* of its listing.

Second, managers need to develop firm-specific capabilities to differentiate on governance dimensions. In Japan, Sony stands out. In 1970, it became the

TABLE 16.4 IMPLICATIONS FOR ACTION

- Understand the rules affecting corporate governance, anticipate changes, and be aware of differences
- Develop firm-specific capabilities to differentiate a firm on corporate governance dimensions

first Japanese firm to list in New York, London, and Amsterdam. In the 1990s, it reduced the number of directors from 39 to a more manageable ten. In 2002, its board became dominated by outsiders.[76] From 15% in 1990, Sony's foreign equity ownership increased to 45% in 2000. In contrast, the ratio for all listed Japanese firms only increased from 4% in 1990 to 13% in 2000. Sony thus reaps significant benefits from more foreign investment and thus a lower cost of capital.

In India, Infosys has emerged as an exemplar.[77] It leads the pack by being the first Indian firm to follow US generally accepted accounting principles (GAAP), the first to offer stock options to all employees, and one of the first to introduce outside directors. Since its listings in Bombay in 1993 and NASDAQ in 1999, it has gone far beyond disclosure requirements mandated by both Indian and US standards. On NASDAQ, Infosys *voluntarily* behaves like a US domestic issuer rather than subjecting itself to the less stringent standards of a foreign issuer. In interviews, Infosys executives dismiss the idea that its governance practices are fueled by its interest in attracting capital, of which it has plenty. Instead, the primary reason cited is to gain credibility with Western customers in the rough-and-tumble software product market. In other words, excellent governance practices make Infosys stand out in the product market. In conclusion, for any manager in doubt about whether sound governance practices are merely window dressing to appease regulators and shareholders, Sony and Infosys offer two shining examples of how to differentiate from the rest of the competition on corporate governance dimensions and to contribute to product market success.

CHAPTER SUMMARY

1. Differentiate various ownership patterns (concentrated/diffused, family, and state ownership) around the world
   - Owners represent the first leg in the "tripod" for corporate governance.
   - In the US and UK, firms with separation of ownership and control dominate. Elsewhere, firms with concentrated ownership and control in the hands of families or governments are predominant.
2. Articulate the role of managers in both principal-agent and principal-principal conflicts
   - In firms with separation of ownership and control, the primary conflicts are principal-agent conflicts.
   - In firms with concentrated ownership, principal-principal conflicts prevail.
3. Explain the role of the board of directors
   - The board of directors performs (1) control, (2) service, and (3) resource acquisition functions.
   - Around the world, boards differ in composition, leadership structure, and interlocks.
4. Identify voice- and exit-based governance mechanisms and their combination as a package
   - Internal, voice-based mechanisms and external, exit-based mechanisms combine as a package to determine corporate governance effectiveness. The market for corporate control and the market for private equity are two primary means of external mechanisms.
5. Acquire a global perspective on how governance mechanisms vary around the world
   - Different combinations of internal and external governance mechanisms lead to four main groups.
   - Privatization around the world represents efforts to enhance governance effectiveness.

6. Articulate how institutions and resources affect corporate governance
   - Institution- and resource-based views shed considerable light on governance issues.
7. Participate in two leading debates on corporate governance
   - These are (1) opportunistic agents versus managerial stewards and (2) global convergence versus divergence.
8. Draw implications for action
   - Understanding the rules affecting corporate governance, anticipating changes, and being aware of differences are all hallmarks of savvy managers.
   - Savvy managers must learn to develop firm-specific capabilities to differentiate on corporate governance dimensions.

KEY TERMS

Agency cost 466
Agency relationship 466
Agency theory 466
Agent 466
CEO duality 469
Concentrated ownership control 465
Corporate governance 464
Cross-listing 479
Diffused ownership 465
Exit-based mechanism 471
Expropriation 467
Information asymmetry 467
Inside director 469
Interlocking directorate 470
Leveraged buyout (LBO) 472
Managerial human capital 478
Outside director 469
Principal 466
Principal-agent conflict 466
Principal-principal conflict 467
Private equity 472
Related transaction 468
Separation of ownership and control 465
Shareholder capitalism 473
Stewardship theory 478
Top management team (TMT) 466
Tunneling 467
Voice-based mechanism 471

REVIEW QUESTIONS

1. How would you characterize a corporation with diffused ownership?
2. What are some of the pros and cons of family ownership?
3. How do you explain the decline in SOEs?
4. Describe the costs involved in principal-agent conflicts.
5. Define the concept of expropriation of minority shareholders.
6. What do inside directors bring to a board of directors? What do outside directors have to offer?
7. What are the advantages and disadvantages of having the positions of board chair and CEO to be held by two different individuals (as opposed to combining these two positions)?
8. Why would firms want to create an interlocking directorate?
9. Explain how independence, deterrence, and norms allow a board of directors to effectively control a corporation.

10. Name and describe the two internal governance mechanisms typically employed by boards.
11. Briefly summarize the three external governance mechanisms.
12. How does the typical ownership structure found in a Canadian firm differ from one in the US, Europe, or Japan?
13. Why do most SOEs suffer from weak external and internal governance mechanisms?
14. What are some of the formal institutions that affect corporate governance?
15. Explain how three aspects of recent globalization have influenced corporate governance.
16. Where does managerial human capital fit into a VRIO framework?
17. How would you explain stewardship theory?
18. Given the arguments for converging or diverging corporate governance around the world, which do you think is more likely to occur and why?
19. Devise your own example of how a firm might differentiate itself in terms of corporate governance.

CRITICAL DISCUSSION QUESTIONS

1. Some argue that the Anglo-American-style separation of ownership and control is an inevitable outcome. Others contend that this is one variant (among several) of how large firms can be effectively governed and that it is not necessarily the most efficient form. What do you think?
2. Recent corporate governance reforms in various countries urge (and often require) firms to add more outside directors to their boards and separate the jobs of board chair and CEO. Yet, academic research has not been able to conclusively confirm the merits of both practices. Why?
3. ON ETHICS: As a board chair/CEO, you are choosing two candidates for one outside independent director position on your board. One is another CEO, a long-time friend whose board you have served on for many years. The other is a known shareholder activist whose tag line is, "No need to make fat cats fatter." Placing him on the board will earn you kudos among analysts and journalists for inviting a leading critic to scrutinize your work. But he may try to prove his theory that CEOs are overpaid; in other words, your compensation might be on the line. Who would you choose?

VIDEO CASE

Watch "Effective Corporate Governance" by Paul Skinner of Rio Tinto.

1. One of this chapter's Learning Objectives is to be able to "Explain the role of the board of directors." How did Paul Skinner seek to do that at Rio Tinto?
2. Prior to the change discussed by Skinner, the CEO and the Chairman were one and the same—that is, CEO duality. How might that have been beneficial in a truly global corporation such as Rio Tinto?

3. Rio Tinto was a successful giant global corporation under its CEO duality. What did the board do to make sure that its changes would represent an improvement?
4. How might Paul Skinner's background prior to becoming Chairman of Rio Tinto contribute to his success in that role?
5. How might Paul Skinner's role as Chairman be affected if a majority of the board consisted of inside directors? Who would really dominate the board in such a case?

CLOSING CASE

ETHICAL DILEMMA: The Private Equity Challenge

Leading private equity firms include Apax Partners, Blackstone Group, Carlyle Group, Kohlberg Kravis Roberts (KKR), and Texas Pacific. They often take an underperforming publicly listed firm off the stock exchange, add some heavy dose of debt, throw in sweet "carrots" to incumbent managers, and trim all the "fat" (typically through layoffs). Private equity firms get paid by (1) the fees and (2) the profits to reap when they take the private firms public again through a new initial public offering (IPO). Annual returns of 20% are commonplace. Windfalls are expected.

© Bill Pugliano / Stringer / Getty Images

Private equity first emerged on a large scale in the 1980s, with a stream of deals peaked by KKR's $25 billion takeover of RJR Nabisco in 1988—then the highest price paid for a public firm. While KKR disciplined deadwood managers who destroyed shareholder value, it received a ton of bad press, cemented in a best-selling book *Barbarians at the Gate* that portrayed KKR as a greedy and ruthless raider.

After the RJR Nabisco deal, the industry stagnated during the 1990s. However, in the 2000s, private equity scaled new heights, growing from 0.25% of world GDP in 2000 to 1.5% in 2007. In 1991, just 57 private equity firms existed. In 2007, close to 700 were in the chase. Helped by low interest rates, the $430 billion private equity funds raised in 2006 alone were more than the total sum of such funds in the entire 1990s. Since 2005, Europe has had more actions (measured by transaction values) than the United States. Overall, private equity buyouts now represent about 20% of global M&As. In 2007, Cerberus Capital Management, a private equity firm, purchased Chrysler from DaimlerChrysler for $7.4 billion. Apax Partners, another private equity shop, spent $7.75 billion to take over Thomson Learning from The Thomson Corporation listed both in New York (NYSE: TOC) and Toronto (TSX: TOC)—the publisher of *this book*.

Private equity has always been controversial. Proponents argue that private equity is a response to the corporate governance deficiency of the public firm. Private equity excels in four ways:

- Private owners, unlike dispersed individual shareholders, care deeply about the return on investment. Private equity firms always send experts to sit on the board and are hands on in managing.
- A high level of debt imposes strong financial discipline to minimize waste.
- Private equity turns managers from agents to principals with substantial equity, thus providing a powerful incentive. Private equity firms pay managers more generously but also punish failure more heavily. Managers' compensation at companies under private ownership, according to a leading agency theorist, Michael Jensen, is *20 times* more sensitive to performance than at companies listed publicly. A manager in a really successful deal may earn $50 million to $70 million. One Norwegian manager earned ten times as much in private equity as he had been getting in his listed firm. On average, private equity

makes the *same* managers, managing the *same* assets, perform much more effectively.

- Finally, privacy is fabulous. For managers, no more short-term burden to "meet the numbers" for Wall Street, no more burdensome paperwork from regulators (an especially crushing load thanks to SarbOx), and better yet, no more disclosure in excruciating detail of how much they are paid (an inevitable invitation to be labeled "fat cats"). Top managers under private ownership are indeed *fatter* cats. It is not surprising that more managers prefer a quieter but far more lucrative life.

All of the above, according to critics, are exactly what is wrong with private equity. Other than "barbarians," private equity has also been labeled "asset strippers" and "locusts." As high executive compensation at public firms has already become a huge controversy, private equity has further increased the income inequality between the high financiers and top managers as one group and the rest of us as another group. Private equity has rapidly proliferated around the world. Some of the fuss reflects the shock in countries suddenly facing the full rigor of Anglo-American private equity. In South Korea, Lone Star Funds of Dallas was initially hailed in 2003 as a brave outsider willing to invest in troubled Korean firms. However, in 2006, when Lone Star tried to cash out by selling its 51% equity of Korea Exchange Bank, unions took to the street to protest, and prosecutors issued a warrant to arrest its cofounder for alleged financial manipulation.

The recent surge of private equity around the world coincides with rising criticisms. Unions guard jobs. Regulators worry about overleveraging and massive bankruptcies. Nationalists resent foreign private equity takeovers. And everybody hates fat cats. Leading private equity practitioners concede that instead of talking about economic value added, too often they brag about how much money they make. To be sure, private equity results in job cuts, but the same would happen if targets were acquired by public firms. Private buyers do not intentionally set out to destroy their prize. Their record as corporate citizens is no more barbaric than that of public firms. In a record-breaking $45 billion buyout in 2007, Texas Pacific and KKR jointly took over a Texas utility TXU (NYSE: TXU). Private owners paid shareholders a 25% premium, gave retail customers a 10% price cut, and forced TXU to jettison plans to build eight dirty coal-fired power plants—hailed by environmentalists as a major victory. While these actions were not necessarily fueled by altruism, they significantly benefited TXU shareholders and customers and made the earth a little cleaner.

Case Discussion Questions

1. If you were a private equity specialist, what kind of target firms would you look for?
2. If you were CEO of a publicly traded firm and were approached by a private equity firm for a possible LBO, how would you proceed with the negotiations?
3. As a regulator in South Korea, how concerned should you be when US private equity firms arrive?

Sources: Based on (1) *Business Week*, 2006, Public score for private equity, December 4: 48; (2) *Economist*, 2006, In the shadows of debt, September 23: 79–81; (3) *Economist*, 2006, The benefits of privacy, March 18: 65; (4) *Economist*, 2007, Barbarians in dock, March 3: 12; (5) *Economist*, 2007, Better pay for all, January 20: 18–19; (6) *Economist*, 2007, Caveat investor, February 10: 12–13; (7) *Economist*, 2007, The uneasy crown, February 10: 74–76; (8) M. Jensen, 1989, Eclipse of the public corporation, *Harvard Business Review*, September: 61–74; (9) TXU, 2007, News release, February 26.

NOTES

Journal acronyms: **AER** – *American Economic Review;* **AME** – *Academy of Management Executive;* **AMJ** – *Academy of Management Journal;* **AMR** – *Academy of Management Review;* **APJM** – *Asia Pacific Journal of Management;* **ASQ** – *Administrative Science Quarterly;* **BW** – *Business Week;* **JAE** – *Journal of Accounting and Economics;* **JEL** – *Journal of Economic Literature;* **JEP** – *Journal of Economic Perspectives;* **JF** – *Journal of Finance;* **JFE** – *Journal of Financial Economics;* **JIBS** – *Journal of International Business Studies;* **JLE** – *Journal of Law and Economics;* **JM** – *Journal of Management;* **JMS** – *Journal of Management Studies;* **JPE** – *Journal of Political Economy;* **JWB** – *Journal of World Business;* **MIR** – *Management International Review;* **MOR** – *Management and Organization Review;* **OSc** – *Organization Science;* **OSt** – *Organization Studies;* **SMJ** – *Strategic Management Journal*

[1] R. Monks & N. Minow, 2001, *Corporate Governance* (p. 1), Oxford, UK: Blackwell. See also M. Benz & B. Frey, 2007, Corporate governance, *AMR*, 32: 92–104.

[2] R. Stulz, 2005, The limits of financial globalization (p. 1618), *JF*, 60: 1595–1638.

[3] L. Tihanyi, R. Johnson, R. Hoskisson, & M. Hitt, 2003, Institutional ownership differences and international diversification, *AMJ*, 46: 195–211.

[4] R. La Porta, F. Lopez-de-Silanes, & A. Shleifer, 1999, Corporate ownership around the world, *JF*, 54: 471–517.

[5] M. Carney & E. Gedajlovic, 2002, The coupling of ownership and control and the allocation of financial resources, *JMS*, 39: 123–146; S. Thomson & T. Pederson, 2000, Ownership structure and economic performance in the largest European companies, *SMJ*, 21: 689–705.

[6] R. Anderson & D. Reeb, 2003, Founding-family ownership and firm performance, *JF*, 58: 1301–1328.

[7] S. Chang, 2003, Ownership structure, expropriation, and performance of group-affiliated companies in Korea, *AMJ*, 46: 238–254; L. Gomez-Mejia, M. Nunez-Nickel, & I. Gutierrez, 2001, The role of family ties in agency contracts, *AMJ*, 44: 81–95; W. Schulze, M. Lubatkin, R. Dino, & A. Buchholtz, 2001, Agency relationships in family firms, *OSc*, 12: 99–116.

[8] M. W. Peng & Y. Jiang, 2008, Family ownership and control of large corporations: The good, the bad, the irrelevant—and why, Working paper, University of Texas at Dallas.

[9] M. W. Peng, T. Buck, & I. Filatotchev, 2003, Do outside directors and new managers help improve firm performance? An exploratory study in Russian privatization, *JWB*, 38: 348–360.

[10] J. De Castro & K. Uhlenbruck, 1997, Characteristics of privatization, *JIBS*, 28: 123–143; W. Megginson & J. Netter, 2001, From state to market, *JEL*, 39: 321–389.

[11] M. Jensen & W. Meckling, 1976, Theory of the firm, *JFE*, 3: 305–360.

[12] *BW*, 2002, How to fix corporate governance, May 6: 69–78.

[13] J. Combs & M. Skill, 2003, Managerialist and human capital explanations for key executive pay premiums, *AMJ*, 46: 63–77.

[14] W. Johnson, R. Magee, N. Nagarajan, & H. Newman, 1985, An analysis of the stock price reaction to sudden executive deaths, *JAE*, 7: 151–174.

[15] S. Claessens, S. Djankov, & L. Lang, 2000, The separation of ownership and control in East Asian corporations, *JFE*, 58: 81–112.

[16] M. Faccio & L. Lang, 2002, The ultimate ownership of Western European corporations, *JFE*, 65: 365–395.

[17] M. Young, M. W. Peng, D. Ahlstrom, G. Bruton, & Y. Jiang, 2008, Corporate governance in emerging economies: A review of the principal-principal perspective, *JMS* (in press).

[18] S. Johnson, R. La Porta, F. Lopez-de-Silanes, & A. Shleifer, 2000, Tunneling, *AER*, 90: 22–27.

[19] S. Chang & J. Hong, 2000, Economic performance of group-affiliated companies in Korea, *AMJ*, 43: 429–448.

[20] A. Ellstrand, L. Tihanyi, & J. Johnson, 2002, Board structure and international political risk, *AMJ*, 45: 769–777; S. T. Certo, 2003, Influencing initial public offering investors with prestige, *AMR*, 28: 432–446.

[21] D. Dalton, C. Daily, A. Ellstrand, & J. Johnson, 1998, Meta-analytic reviews of board composition, leadership structure, and financial performance, *SMJ*, 19: 269–290; Y. Kor, 2006, Direct and interaction effects of top management team and board compositions on R&D investment strategy, *SMJ*, 27: 1081–1099.

[22] S. Finkelstein & A. Mooney, 2003, Not the usual suspects, *AME*, 17: 101–113.

[23] E. Gedajlovic & D. Shapiro, 2002, Ownership structure and firm profitability in Japan, *AMJ*, 45: 565–575; T. Yoshikawa & J. McGuire, 2008, Change and continuity in Japanese corporate governance, *APJM*, 25 (in press).

[24] B. R. Baliga, R. C. Moyer, & R. Rao, 1996, CEO duality and firm performance, *SMJ*, 17: 41–53; M. W. Peng, S. Zhang, & X. Li, 2007, CEO duality and firm performance during China's institutional transitions, *MOR*, 3: 205–225.

[25] R. Gulati & J. Westphal, 1999, Cooperative or controlling? *ASQ*, 44: 473–506.

[26] K. Au, M. W. Peng, & D. Wang, 2000, Interlocking directorates, firm strategies, and performance in Hong Kong (p. 32), *APJM*, 17: 29–47.

[27] Monks & Minow, 2001, *Corporate Governance* (p. 188).

[28] T. Pollock, H. Fischer, & J. Wade, 2002, The role of power and politics in the repricing of executive options, *AMJ*, 45: 1172–1183; J. Westphal & I. Stern, 2007, Flattery will get you everywhere, *AMJ*, 50: 267–288.

[29] J. Westphal & P. Khanna, 2004, Keeping directors in line, *ASQ*, 48: 361–399.

[30] N. Athanassiou & D. Nigh, 1999, The impact of US company internationalization on top management team advice networks, *SMJ*, 20: 93–99; M. Carpenter & J. Westphal, 2001, The strategic context of external network ties, *AMJ*, 44: 639–660; J. Westphal & J. Fredrickson, 2001, Who directs strategic change? *SMJ*, 22: 1113–1137.

[31] M. W. Peng, 2004, Outside directors and firm performance during institutional transitions, *SMJ*, 25: 453–471.

[32] C. Devers, R. Wiseman, & R. M. Holmes, 2007, The effects of endowment and loss aversion in managerial stock option valuation, *AMJ*, 50: 191–208; T. Eisenmann, 2002, The effects of CEO equity ownership and firm diversification on risk taking, *SMJ*, 23: 513–534; M. Goranova, T. Alessandri, P. Brandes, & R. Dharwadkar, 2007, Managerial ownership and corporate diversification, *SMJ*, 28: 211–225; J. McGuire & E. Matta, 2003, CEO stock options, *AMJ*, 46: 255–265; J. O'Conner, R. Priem, J. Coombs, & K. M. Gilley, 2006, Do CEO stock options prevent or promote fraudulent financial reporting? *AMJ*, 49: 483–500.

[33] A. Bruce, T. Buck, & B. Main, 2005, Top executive remuneration, *JMS*, 42: 1493–1506; C. Cadsby, F. Song, & F. Tapon, 2007, Sorting and incentive effects of pay for performance, *AMJ*, 50: 387–405; M. Carpenter & W. G. Sanders, 2002, Top management team compensation, *SMJ*, 23: 367–375; P. Fiss, 2006, Social influence effects and managerial compensation: Evidence from Germany, *SMJ*, 27: 1013–1031; L. Gomez-Mejia, R. Wiseman, & B. Dykes, 2005, Agency problems in diverse contexts, *JMS*, 42: 1507–1517; M. Makri, P. Lane, & L. Gomez-Mejia, 2006, CEO incentives, innovation, and performance in technology-intensive firms, *SMJ*, 27: 1057–1080; P. Wright, M. Kroll, J. Krug, & M. Pettus, 2007, Influences of top management team incentives on firm risk taking, *SMJ*, 28: 81–89.

[34] L. Bebchuk & J. Fried, 2004, *Pay without Performance*, Cambridge, MA: Harvard University Press; M. Jensen & K. Murphy, 1990, Performance pay and top management incentives, *JPE*, 98: 225–263; J. Wade, J. Porac, T. Pollock, & S. Graffin, 2006, The burden of celebrity, *AMJ*, 49: 643–660.

[35] W. Shen & T. Cho, 2005, Exploring involuntary executive turnover through a managerial discretion framework, *AMR*, 30: 843–854; Y. Zhang & N. Rajagopalan, 2004, When the known devil is better than an unknown god, *AMJ*, 47: 483–500.

[36] *Economist*, 2003, Coming and going, October 25: 12–14.

[37] M. Ezzamel & R. Watson, 1998, Market comparison earning and the bidding up of executive cash compensation, *AMJ*, 41: 221–232.

[38] G. Jarrell, J. Brickley, & J. Netter, 1988, The market for corporate control, *JEP*, 2: 49–68; J. Krug & W. Hegarty, 1997, Postacquisition turnover among US top management teams, *SMJ*, 18: 667–675.

[39] P. Phan & C. Hill, 1995, Organizational restructuring and economic performance in leveraged buyouts, *AMJ*, 38: 704–739.

[40] W. Long & D. Ravenscraft, 1993, LBOs, debt, and R&D intensity, *SMJ*, 14: 119–136.

[41] K. Rediker & A. Seth, 1995, Boards of directors and substitution effects of governance mechanisms, *SMJ*, 16: 85–99.

[42] M. Jensen, 1993, The modern industrial revolution, exit, and failure of internal control systems, *JF*, 48: 831–880.

[43] P. Fiss & E. Zajac, 2004, The diffusion of ideas over contested terrain, *ASQ*, 49: 501–534; W. Schneper & M. Guillen, 2004, Stakeholder rights and corporate governance, *ASQ*, 49: 263–295.

[44] A. Tuschke & W. G. Sanders, 2003, Antecedents and consequences of corporate governance reform, *SMJ* 24: 631–649.

[45] T. Buck, 2003, Modern Russian corporate governance, *JWB*, 38: 299–313; W. Judge, I. Naoumova, & N. Koutzevol, 2003, Corporate governance and firm performance in Russia, *JWB*, 38: 397–415; D. McCarthy & S. Puffer, 2003, Corporate governance in Russia, *JWB*, 38: 397–415.

[46] T. Pederson & S. Thomsen, 1997, European patterns of corporate ownership, *JIBS*, 28: 759–778.

[47] A. Shleifer & R. Vishny, 1997, A survey of corporate governance (p. 774), *JF*, 52: 737–783.

[48] E. Gedajlovic & D. Shapiro, 1998, Management and ownership effects (p. 536), *SMJ*, 19: 533–553.

[49] A. Cuervo, 2000, Explaining the variation in the performance effects of privatization, *AMR*, 25: 581–591; I. Filatotchev, T. Buck, & V. Zhukov, 2000, Downsizing privatized firms in Russia, Ukraine, and Belarus, *AMJ*, 43: 286–304; P. Mar & M. Young, 2001, Corporate governance in transition economies, *JWB*, 36: 280–302; R. Ramamurti, 2000, A multilevel model of privatization in emerging economies, *AMR*, 25: 525–551.

[50] C. Kwok & S. Tadesse, 2006, National culture and financial systems, *JIBS*, 37: 227–247.

[51] M. Burkart, F. Panunzi, & A. Shleifer, 2003, Family firms, *JF*, 58: 2167–2201.

[52] R. La Porta, F. Lopez-de-Silanes, A. Shleifer, & R. Vishny, 1998, Law and finance, *JPE*, 106: 1113–1155.

[53] T. Buck & A. Shahrim, 2005, The translation of corporate governance changes across national cultures, *JIBS*, 36: 42–61.

[54] R. Rajan & L. Zingales, 2003, The great reversals, *JFE*, 69: 5–50.

[55] Claessens, Djankov, & Lang, 2000, The separation of ownership and control in East Asian corporations (p. 108).

[56] S. White, 2004, Stakeholders, structure, and the failure of corporate governance reform initiatives in post-crisis Thailand, *APJM*, 21: 103–122.

[57] P. David, T. Yoshikawa, M. Chari, & A. Rasheed, 2006, Strategic investments in Japanese corporations, *SMJ*, 27: 591–600; A. Hassel, M. Hopner, A. Kurdelbusch, B. Rehder, & R. Zugehor, 2003, Two dimensions of the internationalization of firms, *JMS*, 40: 705–723; L. Oxelheim & T. Randoy, 2005, The Anglo-American financial minfluence on CEO compensation in non-Anglo-American firms, *JIBS*, 36: 470–483; T. Yoshikawa, P. Phan, & P. David, 2005, The impact of ownership structure on wage intensity in Japanese corporations, *JM*, 31: 278–300.

[58] R. Aguilera & A. Cuervo-Cazurra, 2004, Codes of good governance worldwide, *OSt*, 25: 415–443.

[59] OECD, 1999, *OECD Principles of Corporate Governance*, Paris: OECD.

[60] OECD, 2003, *Experiences from the Regional Corporate Governance Roundtables* (p. 23), Paris: OECD.

[61] C. Doidge, A. Karolyi, & R. Stulz, 2004, Why are foreign firms listed in the US worth more? *JFE*, 71: 205–238.

[62] *Economist*, 2007, Down on the street (p. 70), November 25: 69–71.

[63] M. W. Peng & Y. Luo, 2000, Managerial ties and firm performance in a transition economy, *AMJ*, 43: 486–501. See also C. Collins & K. Clark, 2003, Strategic human resource practices, top management team social networks, and firm performance, *AMJ*, 46: 740–751.

[64] Z. Simsek, 2007, CEO tenure and organizational performance, *SMJ*, 28: 653–662.

[65] L. Donaldson, 1995, *American Anti-management Theories of Management*, Cambridge, UK: Cambridge University Press.

[66] J. Davis, F. D. Schoorman, & L. Donaldson, 1997, Toward a stewardship theory of management, *AMR*, 22: 20–47; P. Lee & H. O'Neill, 2003, Ownership structure and R&D investments of US and Japanese firms, *AMJ*, 46: 212–225.

[67] P. Lane, A. Cannella, & M. Lubatkin, 1998, Agency problems as antecedents to unrelated mergers and diversification, *SMJ*, 19: 555–578.

[68] S. Ghoshal & P. Moran, 1996, Bad for practice, *AMR*, 21: 31–47.

[69] M. Rubach & T. Sebora, 1998, Comparative corporate governance, *JWB*, 33: 167–184; P. Witt, 2004, The competition of international corporate governance systems, *MIR*, 44: 309–333.

[70] T. Yoshikawa & E. Gedajlovic, 2002, The impact of global capital market exposure and stable ownership on investor relations practices and performance of Japanese firms, *APJM*, 19: 525–540.

[71] P. Vaaler & B. Schrage, 2006, Legal systems and rule of law effects on US cross-listing to bond by emerging-market firms, Working paper no. 06-0126, University of Illinois at Urbana–Champaign.

[72] R. Aguilera & G. Jackson, 2003, The cross-national diversity of corporate governance, *AMR*, 28: 447–465.

[73] G. Bruton, D. Ahlstrom, & J. Wan, 2003, Turnaround in East Asian firms, *SMJ*, 24: 519–540; M. Carney & E. Gedajlovic, 2001, Corporate governance and firm capabilities, *APJM*, 18: 335–354.

[74] G. Davis & C. Marquis, 2003, The globalization of stock markets and convergence in corporate governance, in R. Swedberg (eds.), *Economic Sociology of Capitalist Institutions*, Cambridge, UK: Cambridge University Press.

[75] J. Siegel, 2003, Can foreign firms bond themselves effectively by renting US securities laws? *JFE*, 75: 319–359.

[76] T. Yoshikawa, L. Tsui-Auch, & J. McGuire, 2008, Corporate governance reform as institutional innovation, *OSc* (in press).

[77] T. Khanna & K. Palepu, 2004, Globalization and convergence in corporate governance, *JIBS*, 35: 484–507.

CHAPTER 17

Managing Corporate Social Responsibility Globally

OPENING CASE

Starbucks and Corporate Social Responsibility

Founded in 1971, Starbucks took off in 1987 after being purchased by Howard Schultz, who is its present chairman. From a single store in 1971, Starbucks now has 13,500 stores in 40 countries with annual revenues of $7.8 billion. The goal is to reach 40,000 stores with $23 billion annual sales by 2012.

Since its 1987 (re)birth, Starbucks is known as a company that, in the words of Schultz, "puts people first and profits last." In the 1990s, Starbucks developed an environmental mission statement, created a corporate social responsibility (CSR) department, named a senior vice president for CSR, and began working with nongovernment organizations (NGOs) on CSR issues. Unfortunately, by 2000, Starbucks was singled out by a leading NGO, Global Exchange, for not doing enough.

Not an average NGO, Global Exchange was a leader in the campaign against Nike in the 1990s. One of its current efforts is "Fair Trade." Despite market fluctuation of coffee price, the Fair Trade movement advocated a minimum "fair" price of $1.26 per pound to ensure a "living wage" for coffee producers—regardless of market price, which was only 64 cents per pound in 2000. In early 1999, TransFair USA, a third-party licensing organization, launched a Fair Trade Certified label. In November 1999, TransFair and Starbucks met to discuss Fair Trade coffee. Before Starbucks responded, Global Exchange suddenly turned up the heat on Starbucks in February 2000 by demonstrating in front of a San Francisco store after a local TV station aired a clip on child labor on Guatemalan coffee farms. A few days later, during the open forum portion of the Starbucks shareholders meeting, Global Exchange activists took the microphone and demanded that Starbucks offer Fair Trade coffee. Things got heated and these activists were physically removed from the meeting. Afterward, they met with Starbucks officials and threatened that if Starbucks did not offer Fair Trade coffee by mid-April, they would launch a nationwide campaign.

Given Global Exchange's unrelenting campaign against Nike, it clearly presented a credible threat to Starbucks. Customers flocked to Starbucks for a high-quality experience. Nationwide protests would not only damage Starbucks' image but would also make it *physically* difficult for customers to enter and leave stores. Financially, buying Fair Trade coffee ($1.26 per pound) would not be prohibitively expensive, since Starbucks was already paying a premium price of $1.20 per pound. However, Starbucks was not sure whether Fair Trade growers would meet its stringent quality standards.

Starbucks' choices ranged from ignoring Global Exchange, to fighting back, to capitulation. Ignoring the NGO or fighting back might energize the opponent, given its tenacity. Capitulation had a major drawback of being an "easy target" and inviting other activists to launch attacks. Eventually, Starbucks chose a middle ground. It agreed to sell Fair Trade coffee in its domestic company-owned stores, with an understanding that this decision would be evaluated in a year on whether to continue or not.

Starbucks soon became the largest US purchaser of Fair Trade coffee, increasing its purchase from 653,000 pounds in 2001 to 1.1 million pounds in 2003. Most of it was also cocertified as organic and shade grown. But the overall demand was low. At present, Fair Trade coffee has a US market share of less than 1%. Of the 235 million pounds of coffee produced by Fair Trade producers, only 20% was marketed as Fair Trade coffee, and the rest had to be sold at the lower, world market price due to lack of demand. Also, many Fair Trade co-ops did not have the consistent volume or quality required by Starbucks.

LEARNING OBJECTIVES

After studying this chapter, you should be able to

1. articulate a stakeholder view of the firm
2. apply the institution-based view to analyze corporate social responsibility
3. use the resource-based view to better understand corporate social responsibility
4. participate in three leading debates concerning corporate social responsibility
5. draw implications for action

In addition to purchasing Fair Trade coffee, Starbucks since 2001 has launched its own Coffee and Farmer Equity (CAFE) guidelines to "ensure the sustainable supply of high quality coffee, achieve economic accountability, promote social responsibility within the coffee supply chain, and protect the environment." By 2006, Starbucks had 143 trained CAFE practices "verifiers" (inspectors) and purchased more than 50% of its total volume of 294 million pounds of coffee from CAFE practices suppliers.

Since 2001, Starbucks has been publishing a *Corporate Social Responsibility Annual Report*, starting with a letter from Schultz to "dear stakeholders." Available in six languages, the printed *abridged* version for the 2006 report was 24 pages long (the whole report was online). Interestingly, Starbucks placed all discussion of Fair Trade coffee online and did not include it in the printed abridged version. Global Exchange continues to be unhappy, demanding that Starbucks serve Fair Trade coffee once a *week* instead of once a *month* (the current practice). Although Global Exchange's website acknowledges CAFE to be a "launching point for improvements," it "in no way reduces our initial and still unmet demands." Following Global Exchange's lead, other NGOs, such as Co-op America, Organic Consumers Association, and TransFair USA, have made Starbucks a perpetual NGO target.

Sources: Based on (1) P. Argenti, 2004, Collaborating with activists, *California Management Review*, 47: 91–116; (2) *Business Week*, 2007, Saving Starbucks' soul, April 9: 56–61; (3) Starbucks, 2006, *Corporate Social Responsibility Annual Report* (abridged version), http://www.starbucks.com; (4) D. Vogel, 2005, The low value of virtue, *Harvard Business Review*, June: 26; (5) http://www.globalexchange.org.

Although Starbucks is widely regarded as one of the most socially responsible firms, the Opening Case raises two crucial questions: Can a firm ever be socially responsible enough? When a firm pursues a social mission, is it setting itself up to be a target?[1] Obviously, there are no easy answers to these questions. This chapter helps you answer these and other questions concerning **corporate social responsibility (CSR)**—"consideration of, and response to, issues beyond the narrow economic, technical, and legal requirements of the firm to accomplish social benefits along with the traditional economic gains which the firm seeks."[2] Historically, issues concerning CSR have been on the "backburner" of management discussions, but these issues are now increasingly brought to the forefront of corporate agendas.[3] Although this chapter is the last in this book, by no means do we suggest that CSR is the least important topic. Instead, we believe that this chapter is one of the best ways to *integrate* all previous chapters concerning international trade, investment, strategy, supply chain, human resources, and corporate governance.[4] The comprehensive nature of CSR is evident in our Opening Case on Starbucks.

corporate social responsibility (CSR)
The consideration of, and response to, issues beyond the narrow economic, technical, and legal requirements of the firm to accomplish social benefits along with the traditional economic gains which the firm seeks.

At the heart of CSR is the concept of **stakeholder**, which is "any group or individual who can affect or is affected by the achievement of the organization's objectives."[5] Shown in Figure 17.1, while shareholders certainly are an important group of stakeholders, other stakeholders include managers, nonmanagerial employees (hereafter "employees"), suppliers, customers, communities, governments, and social and environmental groups. Since Chapter 16 has already dealt with shareholders at length, this chapter focuses on *nonshareholder stakeholders*, which we term *stakeholders* here for compositional simplicity. A leading debate

stakeholder
Any group or individual who can affect or is affected by the achievement of the organization's objectives.

on CSR is whether managers' efforts to promote the interests of these stakeholders are at odds with their fiduciary duty to safeguard shareholder interests.[6] To the extent that firms are not social agencies and that their primary function is to serve as economic enterprises, it is certainly true that firms should not (and are unable to) take on all the social problems of the world. Yet on the other hand, failing to heed certain CSR imperatives may be self-defeating in the long run. Therefore, the key is how to prioritize, which is a crucial task.

The remainder of this chapter first introduces a stakeholder view of the firm. Then we discuss how the institution- and resource-based views inform the CSR discussion. As before, debates and extensions follow.

A STAKEHOLDER VIEW OF THE FIRM

LEARNING OBJECTIVE 1

articulate a stakeholder view of the firm

A Big Picture Perspective

A stakeholder view of the firm, with a quest for global sustainability, represents a "big picture." A key goal for CSR is **global sustainability**, which is defined as the ability "to meet the needs of the present without compromising the ability of future generations to meet their needs."[7] It not only refers to a sustainable social and natural environment but also sustainable capitalism.[8] Globally, at least three sets of drivers are related to the urgency of sustainability in the 21st century.[9] First, rising levels of population, poverty, and inequity associated with globalization call for new solutions. The repeated protests staged around the world since the Seattle protests in 1999 (see Chapter 1) are but tips of an iceberg of antiglobalization sentiments. Second, compared with the relatively eroded power of national governments in the wake of globalization, nongovernment organizations (NGOs)

global sustainability
The ability to meet the needs of the present without compromising the ability of future generations to meet their needs around the world.

FIGURE 17.1 A STAKEHOLDER VIEW OF THE FIRM

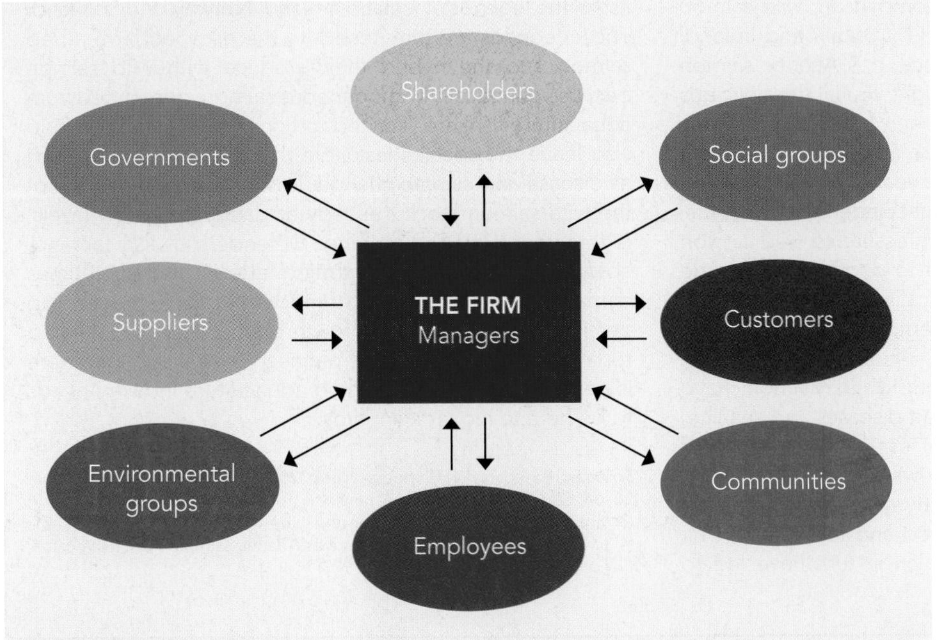

Source: Adapted from T. Donaldson & L. Preston, 1995, The stakeholder theory of the corporation: Concepts, evidence, and implications (p. 69), *Academy of Management Review*, 20: 65–91.

and other civil society stakeholders, such as Global Exchange (see Opening Case), have increasingly assumed the role of monitor and in some cases enforcer of social and environmental standards.[10] Finally, industrialization has created some irreversible effects on the environment.[11] Global warming, air and water pollution, soil erosion, deforestation, and overfishing have become problems demanding solutions (see In Focus 17.1 and Closing Case). Because firms contribute to many of these problems, many citizens believe that firms should also take on at least some responsibility for solving them.

Drivers underpinning global sustainability are complex and multidimensional. For multinational enterprises (MNEs) with operations spanning the globe, their CSR areas, shown in Table 17.1, seem mind-boggling. This bewilderingly complex big picture forces managers to *prioritize*.[12] To be able to do that, primary and secondary stakeholders must be identified.[13]

IN FOCUS 17.1 Salmon: Chicken of the Sea

There is an explosion in the global supply of salmon recently. This rising supply is not due to any increase of wild salmon catch, which has been in steady decline for decades because of dams, pollution, and overfishing. As the wild Atlantic salmon disappear (wild Pacific salmon are still relatively safe), salmon farming (aquaculture) has been on the rise.

Starting in Norway as a cottage industry in the late 1960s, salmon farming quickly spread to Britain, Canada, Iceland, and Ireland in the 1970s, the United States in the 1980s, and Chile in the 1990s. Farm-raised salmon live in sea cages. They are fed pellets to speed their growth (twice as fast as in the wild), pigments to replicate the pink wild salmon flesh, and pesticides to kill the lice that go hand in hand with an industrial feedlot. Atlantic salmon farming (still dominated by Norwegian firms and followed by Chilean companies) has exploded into a $2 billion a year global business that produces approximately 700,000 tons of fish annually. In comparison, wild salmon catch in the Atlantic (only allowed by Britain and Ireland) is only 3,000 tons a year. In essence, it is Atlantic salmon farming companies that have brought you all the delicious and nutritious salmon, which has been transformed from a rare, expensive seasonal delicacy to a common chicken of the sea to be enjoyed by everyone year round. In addition, Atlantic salmon farming has brought undeniable benefits, such as taking commercial fishing pressure off wild salmon stocks and providing employment to depressed maritime regions. For example, in economically depressed western Scotland, salmon aquaculture employs approximately 6,400 workers.

But here is the catch: Farm-raised salmon have (1) fouled the nearby sea, (2) spread diseases and sea lice, and (3) led to a large number of escaped fish. Each of these problems has become a growing controversy. First, heavy concentration of fish in a tiny area—up to 800,000 in one floating cage—leads to food and fecal waste that promotes toxic algae blooms, which in turn have led to closure of shellfishing in nearby waters. Second, sea lice outbreaks at fish farms in Ireland, Norway, and Scotland have devastating effects on wild salmon and other fish. In Cobscook Bay, the aquaculture center of Maine, 2.1 million tainted fish had to be slaughtered recently. The third and probably most serious problem is the escaped salmon. Many salmon have escaped when seals chewed through pens, storms demolished cages, or fish were spilled during handling. In Scotland, for example, nearly 300,000 farmed fish escaped in 2002. Research has found that escaped salmon interbreed with wild salmon. In Norwegian rivers that are salmon spawning grounds, 10% to 35% of the "wild" fish are found to be escaped salmon.

Wild salmon are an amazing species, genetically programmed to find their spawning grounds in rivers after years of wandering in the sea. Although at present, only one egg of every 4,000, after maturing to become a fish, is likely to complete such an epic journey, salmon have been magical fish in the legends of Iceland, Ireland, Norway, and Scotland. These legends are threatened by the escaped farm-raised salmon and the hybrid they produce with wild salmon because genetically homogeneous salmon, descended from aquaculture fish, are ill suited to find these rivers and could also leave the species less able to cope with threats such as disease and climate change. In short, the biodiversity of the wild salmon stocks, already at dangerously low levels, is threatened by fish farming. Defenders of fish farming, however, argue that *all* farming alters, and sometimes damages, the environment. If modern agriculture featuring pesticides, fertilizers, and growth hormones were invented today, it probably would be banned. They argue that there is no reason that the emerging aquaculture industry needs to be held to higher standards.

Sources: Based on (1) *Business Week*, 2006, Fished out, September 4: 56–64; (2) *Economist*, 2003, A new way to feed the world, August 9: 9; (3) *Economist*, 2003, The promise of a blue revolution, August 9: 19–21; (4) F. Montaigne, 2003, Everybody loves Atlantic salmon: Here's the catch, *National Geographic*, 204 (1): 100–123.

TABLE 17.1 CORPORATE SOCIAL RESPONSIBILITIES FOR MULTINATIONAL ENTERPRISES (MNEs) RECOMMENDED BY INTERNATIONAL ORGANIZATIONS

MNEs and Host Governments
• Should not interfere in the internal political affairs of the host country (OECD, UN) • Should consult government authorities and national employers' and workers' organizations to ensure that their investments conform to the economic and social development policies of the host country (ICC, ILO, OECD, UN) • Should reinvest some profits in the host country (ICC)
MNEs and Laws, Regulations, and Politics
• Should respect the right of every country to exercise control over its natural resources (UN) • Should refrain from improper or illegal involvement in local politics (OECD) • Should not pay bribes or render improper benefits to public servants (OECD, UN)
MNEs and Technology Transfer
• Should develop and adapt technologies to the needs of host countries (ICC, ILO, OECD) • Should provide reasonable terms and conditions when granting licenses for industrial property rights (ICC, OECD)
MNEs and Environmental Protection
• Should respect the host country laws and regulations concerning environmental protection (OECD, UN) • Should supply to host governments information concerning the environmental impact of MNE activities (ICC, UN)
MNEs and Consumer Protection
• Should preserve the safety and health of consumers by disclosing appropriate information, labeling correctly, and advertising accurately (UN)
MNEs and Employment Practices
• Should cooperate with host governments to create jobs in certain locations (ICC) • Should give advance notice of plant closures and mitigate the adverse effects (ICC, OECD) • Should respect the rights for employees to engage in collective bargaining (ILO, OECD)
MNEs and Human Rights
• Should respect human rights and fundamental freedoms in host countries (UN)

Sources: Based on (1) ICC: *The International Chamber of Commerce Guidelines for International Investment*, http://www.iccwbo.org; (2) ILO: *The International Labor Office Tripartite Declarations of Principles Concerning Multinational Enterprises and Social Policy*, http://www.ilo.org; (3) OECD: *The Organization for Economic Cooperation and Development Guidelines for Multinational Enterprises*, http://www.oecd.org; (4) UN: *The United Nations Code of Conduct on Transnational Corporations*, http://www.un.org.

Primary and Secondary Stakeholder Groups

primary stakeholder groups
The constituents on which the firm relies for its continuous survival and prosperity.

secondary stakeholder groups
Those who influence or affect, or are influenced or affected by, the corporation, but they are not engaged in transactions with the corporation and are not essential for its survival.

triple bottom line
The economic, social, and environmental performance that simultaneously satisfies the demands of all stakeholder groups.

Primary stakeholder groups are constituents on which the firm relies for its continuous survival and prosperity.[14] Shareholders, managers, employees, suppliers, customers—together with governments and communities whose laws and regulations must be obeyed and to whom taxes and other obligations may be due—are typically considered primary stakeholders.

Secondary stakeholder groups are defined as "those who influence or affect, or are influenced or affected by, the corporation, but they are not engaged in transactions with the corporation and are not essential for its survival."[15] Environmental groups (such as Greenpeace) often take it upon themselves to promote pollution-reduction technologies. Fair labor practice groups (such as the Fair Labor Association) frequently challenge firms that allegedly fail to provide decent labor conditions for employees at home and abroad. Although the firm does not depend on secondary stakeholder groups for its survival, such groups may have the potential to cause significant embarrassment and damage to a firm—think of Nike in the 1990s.

A key proposition of the stakeholder view of the firm is that instead of only pursuing an economic bottom line such as profits and shareholder returns, firms should pursue a more balanced **triple bottom line**, consisting of *economic, social,* and *environmental* performance, by simultaneously satisfying the demands of all stakeholder groups.[16] To the extent that some competing demands obviously exist, it seems evident that the CSR proposition represents a dilemma. In fact, it has provoked a fundamental debate, which is introduced next.

A Fundamental Debate

The CSR debate centers on the nature of the firm in society. Why does the firm exist?[17] Most people would intuitively answer "to make money." Milton Friedman, a former University of Chicago economist and Nobel laureate who passed away in 2006, had eloquently suggested: "The business of business is business."[18] The idea that the firm is an economic enterprise seems to be uncontroversial. At issue is whether the firm is *only* an economic enterprise.

One side of the debate argues that "the social responsibility of business is to increase its profits," which is the title of Friedman's influential article mentioned earlier that was published in 1970. This free market school of thought draws upon Adam Smith's idea that pursuit of economic self-interest (within legal and ethical bounds) leads to efficient markets. Free market advocates believe that the first and foremost stakeholder group is shareholders, whose interests managers have a fiduciary duty (required by law) to look after. To the extent that the hallmark of our economic system remains capitalism, the providers of capital—namely, capitalists or shareholders—deserve a commanding height in managerial attention. In fact, since the 1980s, a term that explicitly places shareholders as the single most important stakeholder group, namely, *shareholder capitalism*, has become increasingly influential around the world (see Chapter 16).

Free market advocates argue that if firms attempt to attain social goals, such as providing employment and social welfare, managers will lose their focus on profit maximization (and its derivative, shareholder value maximization).[19] Consequently, firms may lose their character as capitalistic enterprises and become *socialist* organizations. This perception of socialist organization is not a pure argumentative point but an accurate characterization of numerous state-owned enterprises (SOEs) throughout the prereform Soviet Union, Central and Eastern Europe, and China as well as other developing countries in Africa, Asia, and Latin America. Privatization, in essence, is to remove the social function of these firms and restore their economic focus through private ownership. Overall, the free market school is increasingly influential around the world. It has also provided much of the intellectual underpinning for globalization spearheaded by MNEs.

It is against such a formidable and influential school of thought that the CSR movement has emerged.[20] CSR advocates argue that a free market system that takes the pursuit of self-interest and profit as its guiding light—although in theory constrained by rules, contracts, and property rights—may in practice fail to constrain itself, thus often breeding greed, excesses, and abuses.[21] Firms and managers, if left to their own devices, may choose self-interest over public interest. While not denying that shareholders are important stakeholders, CSR advocates argue that all stakeholders have an *equal* right to bargain for a "fair deal."[22] Given stakeholders' often conflicting demands, the very purpose of the firm, instead of being a profit-maximizing entity, is to serve as a vehicle for coordinating their interests. Of course, a very thorny issue in the debate is whether all stakeholders indeed have an equal right and how to manage their (sometimes inevitable) conflicts.

© AP IMAGES

If you had the power to create employment laws to which domestic and foreign companies must adhere, what would you do to protect child laborers?

Starting in the 1970s as a peripheral voice in an ocean of free market believers, the CSR school of thought has slowly but surely made progress in becoming a more central part of management discussions. There are two driving forces. First, even as free markets march around the world, the gap between the haves and have-nots has *widened*. Although many emerging economies have been growing by leaps and bounds, the per capita income gap between developed economies and much of Africa, Asia (except the Four Tigers), and Latin America has widened. While 2% of the world's children living in America enjoy 50% of the world's toys, 25% of the children in Bangladesh and Nigeria are in their countries' work force.[23] Even within developed economies such as the United States, the income gap between the upper and lower echelons of society has widened. In 1980, the average American CEO was paid 40 times more than the average worker. The ratio is now above 400. Although American society accepts greater income inequality than many others do, aggregate data of such widening inequality, which both inform and numb, often serve as a stimulus for reforming the "leaner and meaner" capitalism. However, the response from free market advocates is that to the extent there is competition, there will always be *both* winners and losers. What CSR critics describe as "greed" is often translated as "incentive" in the vocabulary of free market advocates.

A second reason behind the rise of the CSR movement seems to be waves of disasters and scandals. For example, in 1984, a toxic accident at Union Carbide's Bhopal, India, plant killed over 3,000 people and injured another 300,000. In 1989, the oil tanker *Exxon Valdez* spilled a tanker load of oil in the pristine waters of Alaska. In 2001–2002, corporate scandals of Enron, WorldCom, Royal Ahold, and Parmalat rocked the world. Not surprisingly, new disasters and scandals often propel CSR to the forefront of public policy and management discussions. For example, the rise of the CSR movement in China can be directly attributed to the worsening environmental problems that are unfolding during the reform era (see In Focus 17.2).

Overall, managers as a stakeholder group are unique in that they are the only group that is positioned at the center of all these relationships. It is important to understand how they make decisions concerning CSR, as illustrated next.

IN FOCUS 17.2 Dow Chemical Company in China

Dow Chemical Company is a leading US-based MNE that has presence in more than 175 countries. It has paid considerable attention to CSR. Since 1999, Dow has advocated the Guiding Principles of Responsible Care, a voluntary initiative within the global chemical industry to safely handle its products from inception to ultimate disposal.

China naturally has become an increasingly important market for Dow. However, beyond Dow's immediate market reach, the general deteriora-tion of the environment in China, an unfortunate byproduct of the strong economic growth, is visible and getting worse. For example, on a sunny day, pedestrians in Beijing have a hard time seeing through the smog and actually seeing the sun. As a result, China's leadership is putting increasing focus on environmental sustainability as a key national policy.

Courtesy of Dow Chemical Company

Aspiring to serve as a multinational role model fully aligned with Dow's own CSR commitment and with the government's concern to reduce pollution, Dow partnered with the State Environmental Protection Administration (SEPA) of China to launch a SEPA-Dow National Cleaner Production Pilot Project in 2005. Dow agreed to contribute $750,000 over the first three years. Cleaner Production is the continuous application of an integrated preventive environmental strategy to processes, products, and services to increase efficiency and reduce risks and possible damage to humans and the environment. The pilot project has focused on training local environmental protection agencies and officials as well as managers at small and medium-sized enterprises (SMEs), a category of firms in China that, on average, tends to be less professional and more reckless in environmental management.

In the pilot project's first year, 19 SMEs from seven provinces in the chemical, dyeing, electronics, brewery, and food industries participated. The project generated a combined reduction of wastewater by 3.3 million cubic meters, of exhaust gas emission by 554 tons, and of solid waste by 487 tons. This resulted in 538 cleaner production measures and an annual economic profit of approximately $130,000 for the 19 participating firms. Overall, these achievements, in Dow's own words, "confirm Dow's belief that Cleaner Production not only reduces waste in the production processes, it also increases the efficiency of energy resources and ultimately improves competitiveness of enterprises." Fur-ther, through environmental audits, case studies, and further dissemination, Dow intends to diffuse such best practices to more firms in China and beyond.

Sources: Based on (1) *China Business Review*, 2007, Dow partners with China's SEPA, May–June: 17; (2) Dow, 2006, SEPA-Dow Cleaner Production National Pilot Project achieves strong start and outstanding results, http://news.dow.com (accessed June 3, 2007); (3) M. W. Peng, 2006, Dow Chemical in America and China, in M. W. Peng, *Global Strategy* (pp. 511–512), Cincinnati, OH: Cengage South-Western.

LEARNING OBJECTIVE 2

apply the institution-based view to analyze corporate social responsibility

INSTITUTIONS AND CORPORATE SOCIAL RESPONSIBILITY

Although some people view that CSR is not an integral part of global business, Figure 17.2 shows that the two traditional perspectives that we have used to illustrate every traditional topic (ranging from strategy to supply chain) thus far can inform CSR discussions with relatively little adaptation. This section articulates why this is the case from an institution-based view.

The institution-based view sheds considerable light on the gradual diffusion of the CSR movement and the strategic responses of firms.[24] At the most fundamental level, regulatory pressures underpin *formal* institutions, whereas normative and cognitive pressures support *informal* institutions. The strategic response framework consisting of (1) reactive, (2) defensive, (3) accommodative, and (4) proactive strategies, first introduced in Chapter 3 (see Table 3.5), can be extended to explore how firms make CSR decisions—as illustrated in Table 17.2.

FIGURE 17.2 INSTITUTIONS, RESOURCES, AND CORPORATE SOCIAL RESPONSIBILITY

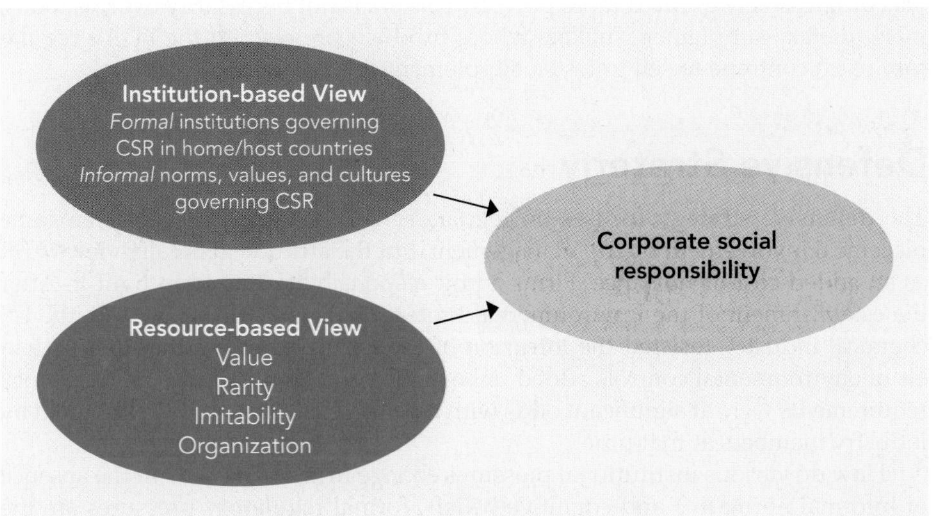

Reactive Strategy

The **reactive strategy** is indicated by relatively little or no support of top management to CSR causes.[25] Firms do not feel compelled to act in the absence of disasters and outcries. Even when problems arise, denial is usually the first line of defense. Put another way, the need to accept some CSR is neither internalized through cognitive beliefs, nor does it result in any norms in practice. That only leaves formal regulatory pressures to compel firms to be in compliance. For example, in America, food and drug safety standards that we take for granted today were fought by food and drug companies in the early half of the 20th century. The very basic

reactive strategy
A strategy that would only respond to CSR causes when disasters and outcries break out.

TABLE 17.2 THE US CHEMICAL INDUSTRY RESPONDS TO ENVIRONMENTAL PRESSURES

Phase	Primary strategy	Representative statements from the industry's trade journal, *Chemical Week*
1. 1962–1970	Reactive	Denied the severity of environmental problems and argued that these problems could be solved independently through the industry's technological prowess.
2. 1971–1982	Defensive	"Congress seems determined to add one more regulation to the already 27 health and safety regulations we must answer to. This will make EPA [Environmental Protection Agency] a chemical czar. No agency in a democracy should have that authority" (1975).
3. 1983–1988	Accommodative	"EPA has been criticized for going too slow . . . Still, we think that it is doing a good job" (1982). "Critics expect overnight fix. EPA deserves credit for its pace and accomplishments" (1982).
4. 1989–present	Proactive	"Green line equals bottom line—The Clean Air Act equals efficiency. Everything you hear about the 'costs' of complying with CAA [Clean Air Act] is probably wrong . . . Wiser competitors will rush to exploit the Green Revolution" (1990).

Sources: Adapted from A. Hoffman, 1999, Institutional evolution and change: Environmentalism and the US chemical industry, *Academy of Management Journal*, 42: 351–371, for the phases and statements. Hoffman's last phase ended in 1993; its extension to the present is done by the present author.

idea that food and drugs should be tested before they could be sold to customers and patients was bitterly contested. Thousands of people ended up dying because of unsafe foods and drugs. As a result, the Food and Drug Administration (FDA) was progressively granted more powers. This era is not necessarily over, as today, many dietary-supplement makers whose products are beyond the FDA's regulatory reach continue to sell untested supplements and deny responsibility.[26]

Defensive Strategy

defensive strategy
A strategy that focuses on regulatory compliance with little top management commitment to CSR causes.

The **defensive strategy** focuses on regulatory compliance. There may be some piecemeal involvement by top management, but the attitude generally views CSR as an added cost or nuisance. Firms admit responsibility but often fight it. After the establishment of the Environmental Protection Agency (EPA) in 1970, the US chemical industry resisted the intrusion of the EPA by arguing that greater levels of environmental controls added unbearable costs (Table 17.2). The regulatory requirements were at significant odds with the norms and cognitive beliefs held by industry members at that time.

How do various institutional pressures change firms' behavior? In the absence of informal normative and cognitive beliefs, formal regulatory pressures are the only feasible way to push firms ahead. A key insight of the institution-based view is that individuals and organizations make *rational* choices given the right kind of incentives. For example, one efficient way to control pollution is to make polluters pay some "green" taxes. These can range from gasoline retail taxes to landfill charges on waste disposal. However, how demanding these regulatory pressures should be remains controversial. One side of the debate argues that tough environmental regulations may lead to higher costs and reduced competitiveness, especially when competing with foreign rivals not subject to such demanding regulations.[27] In other words, there is no "free environmental lunch."[28]

However, CSR advocates, endorsed by former Vice President Al Gore and strategy guru Michael Porter, argue that stringent environmental regulation may force firms to innovate, however reluctantly, thus benefiting the competitiveness of an industry and a country.[29] For instance, a 1991 Japanese law set standards to make products easier to disassemble. In response, Hitachi, which initially resisted this law, redesigned products to simplify disassembly by reducing the number of parts in a washing machine by 16% and the number of parts in a vacuum cleaner by 30%. The products became not only easier to disassemble but also easier and cheaper to *assemble* in the first place, thus providing Hitachi with a significant cost advantage.[30]

Accommodative Strategy

accommodative strategy
A strategy that is characterized by some support from top managers, who may increasingly view CSR as a worthwhile endeavor.

The **accommodative strategy** is characterized by some support from top managers, who may increasingly view CSR as a worthwhile endeavor. Since formal regulations may be in place and informal social and environmental pressures on the rise, the CSR concern may be shared by a number of firms, thus leading to the emergence of some new industry norms. Further, some new managers passionate about or sympathetic toward CSR causes may have joined the organization, whereas some traditional managers may change their outlook, leading to increasingly strong cognitive beliefs that CSR is the right thing to do. In other words, from both normative and cognitive standpoints, it becomes legitimate, a matter of social obligation, to accept responsibility and do all that is required.[31] For example, in the US chemical industry, such a transformation probably took place in the early 1980s (see Table 17.2).

One tangible action firms often take to indicate their willingness to accept CSR is to adopt **codes of conduct** (sometimes called **codes of ethics**). Firms under the most intense CSR criticisms, such as those in the sportswear industry, often actively engage in these activities. Interestingly (but not surprisingly), the content of these codes varies by individual firm, industry, and country.[32] US codes of conduct tend to pay less attention to immediate production concerns and more attention to secondary stakeholder issues, such as welfare of the community and environmental protection. European codes concentrate more on production activities, such as quality management and limiting the environmental footprint of activities. Hong Kong codes tend to focus narrowly on corruption prevention but pay less attention to broader CSR issues.

code of conduct (code of ethics)
Written policies and standards for corporate conduct and ethics.

There is an intense debate regarding the diffusion of codes of conduct. First, some argue that firms may not necessarily be sincere. This *negative* view suggests that given the rising interest in CSR, firms may be compelled to appear sensitive to CSR by "window dressing."[33] Many firms may chase fads by following what others are doing without having truly internalized the need to genuinely address CSR concerns. Second, an *instrumental* view suggests that CSR activities simply represent a useful instrument to make good profits. Firms are not necessarily becoming more "ethical." Finally, a *positive* view believes that (at least some) firms may be self-motivated to "do it right" regardless of social pressures. Codes of conduct tangibly express values that organizational members view as central and enduring.[34]

The institution-based view suggests that all three perspectives are probably valid. This is to be expected given how institutional pressures work to instill value. Regardless of actual motive, the fact that firms are embarking on some tangible CSR journey is encouraging, indicative of the rising *legitimacy* of CSR on the management agenda.[35] Even for firms adopting codes of conduct only for window dressing purposes, publicizing a set of CSR criteria against which they can be judged opens doors for more scrutiny by concerned stakeholders. These pressures are likely to encourage these firms' internal transformation to become more self-motivated, better corporate citizens. For example, it probably is fair to say that Nike is a more responsible corporate citizen in 2010 than what it was in 1990.

Proactive Strategy

From a CSR perspective, the best firms engage in a **proactive strategy**, constantly anticipating responsibility and endeavoring to do more than is required. Top management not only supports and champions CSR activities but also views CSR as a source of differentiation.[36] For example, in 1990, BMW anticipated its emerging responsibility associated with the German government's proposed "take-back" policy. It not only designed easier-to-disassemble cars but also signed up the few high-quality dismantler firms as part of an exclusive recycling infrastructure. Further, BMW actively participated in public discussions and succeeded in establishing the BMW approach as the German national standard for automobile disassembly. Other car companies were thus required to follow BMW's lead. However, they were left to fight over smaller, lower quality dismantlers or develop in-house dismantling infrastructure from scratch, both of which cost more, whereas BMW scored points on the triple bottom line.[37]

proactive strategy
A strategy that endeavors to do more than is required in CSR.

Proactive firms often engage in three areas of activities. First, like BMW, they actively participate in regional, national, and international policy discussions. To the extent that policy discussions today may become regulations in the future, it seems better to get involved early and (ideally) steer the course toward a favorable direction. Otherwise, relatively passive firms are likely to see regulations to which they have little input being imposed on them.[38] In short, "if you're not at the table, you're on the menu."[39]

Second, proactive firms often build alliances with stakeholder groups.[40] For example, many firms collaborate with NGOs. Because of historical tension and distrust, these "sleeping-with-the-enemy" alliances are not easy to handle. The key lies in identifying relatively short-term, manageable projects of mutual interest. For instance, UPS collaborated with the Alliance for Environmental Innovation to help packaging material suppliers reduce almost 50% air pollution and 12% energy use.[41]

Third, proactive firms often engage in *voluntary* activities that go beyond what is required by regulations.[42] While there are numerous examples of industry-specific self-regulation,[43] an area of intense global interest is the pursuit of the International Organization for Standardization (ISO) 14001 certification of environment management system (EMS). Headquartered in Switzerland, ISO is an influential NGO consisting of national standards bodies of 111 countries. Launched in 1996, the ISO 14001 EMS has become the gold standard for CSR-conscious firms.[44] Although not required by law, many MNEs, such as Ford, IBM, and Skanska, have adopted ISO 14001 standards in all their facilities worldwide. Firms such as GM, Toyota, and Siemens have demanded that all of their top-tier suppliers be ISO 14001 certified.

From an institutional perspective, these areas of proactive activities are indicative of the normative and cognitive beliefs held by many managers on the importance of doing the right thing. Although there is probably a certain element of window dressing and a quest for better profits, it is obvious that these efforts provide some tangible social and environmental benefits.

LEARNING OBJECTIVE 3

use the resource-based view to better understand corporate social responsibility

RESOURCES AND CORPORATE SOCIAL RESPONSIBILITY

CSR-related resources can include (1) *tangible* technologies and processes and (2) *intangible* skills and attitudes.[45] The VRIO framework can shed considerable light on CSR.

Value

Do a firm's CSR-related resources and capabilities add value? For many large firms, especially MNEs, their arsenal of financial, technological, and human resources can be applied toward a variety of CSR causes. For example, firms can choose to appease antinuclear groups by refusing to purchase energy from nuclear power plants or to respond to human rights groups by not doing business in (or with) countries accused of human rights violations. These activities can be categorized as **social issue participation** not directly related to the management of primary stakeholders. Research suggests that these activities may actually *reduce* shareholder value.[46] Overall, although social issue participation may create some remote social and environmental value, to the extent that one of the legs of the tripod of triple bottom line is economic, these abilities do not qualify as value-adding firm resources and capabilities.

social issue participation
Firms' participation in social causes not directly related to the management of primary stakeholders.

In contrast, expertise, techniques, and processes associated with the direct management of primary stakeholder groups are likely to add value.[47] For example, US companies excelling in diversity programs may gain a leg up when dealing with two primary stakeholder groups: employees and customers. Between 2000 and 2020, the number of Hispanics, African, Asian, and Native Americans will reportedly grow by 42 million, whereas Caucasians will rise by a mere 10 million.[48] Many companies compete on diversity via internships, scholarships, ad campaigns, and aggressive recruiting of minority candidates. Firms most sought after by minority employees and customers will possess some very valuable resources and capabilities in the competition for the hearts and minds (and wallets) of the future.[49]

Rarity

If competitors also possess certain valuable resources, then the focal firm is not likely to gain a significant advantage by having them. For example, both Home Depot and Lowe's have their suppliers in Brazil, Indonesia, and Malaysia certify—via external verification by NGOs such as the Forest Stewardship Council—that their sources of wood are from renewable forests. These complex processes require strong management capabilities, such as negotiating with local suppliers, undertaking internal verification, coordinating with NGOs for external verification, and disseminating such information to stakeholders. Since both competitors possess capabilities to manage these processes, they become valuable but common (not rare) resources.

Imitability

Although valuable and rare resources may provide some competitive advantage, such an advantage will only be temporary if competitors are able to imitate.[50] Only resources that are not just valuable and rare but also hard to imitate can give firms some sustainable (not merely temporary) competitive advantage. For example, pollution-*prevention* technologies may provide firms with a significant advantage, whereas pollution-*reduction* technologies may offer no such advantage. This is because the relatively simple, "end-of-pipe" pollution-reduction technologies can be more easily imitated. On the other hand, pollution-prevention technologies are more complex and more integrated with the entire chain of production (In Focus 17.2). Rivals often have a harder time imitating such complex capabilities.

In addition, at some firms, CSR-related capabilities are deeply embedded in very idiosyncratic managerial and employee skills, attitudes, and interpretations.[51] The socially complex way of channeling these people's energy and conviction toward CSR cannot be easily imitated. For example, the enthusiasm and energy that Starbucks devotes to CSR are very difficult to imitate (see Opening Case). Although Starbucks may not please every NGO, it is difficult to argue that Starbucks is "faking"—just consider all the expenses devoted to purchasing a large quantity of Fair Trade coffee, supporting 143 CAFE verifiers, and preparing both the abridged and full versions of its CSR annual report in six languages.

Organization

Is the firm organized to exploit the full potential of CSR?[52] Numerous components within a firm may be relevant, such as formal management control systems and informal relationships between managers and employees. These components are often called complementary assets (see Chapter 4) because, by themselves, they have difficulty generating advantage. However, these complementary assets, when combined with valuable, rare, and hard-to-imitate capabilities, may enable a firm to fully utilize its CSR potential.

For example, assume Firm A is able to overcome the three previously mentioned hurdles (V, R, and I) by achieving a comprehensive understanding of some competitors' "best practices" in pollution prevention. Although Firm A has every intention to implement such best practices, chances are that they may not work unless Firm A also possesses a number of complementary assets. This is because process-focused best practices of pollution prevention are not in isolation and are often difficult to separate from a firm's other organizational activities. These best practices require a number of complementary assets, such as a continuous emphasis on process innovation, an uncompromising quest to reduce costs, and a dedicated work force. These complementary assets are not developed as part of new environmental strategies; rather, these assets are grown from more general business strategies (such as differentiation).[53] If such complementary assets are already in place, they are available to be leveraged in the new pursuit of best environmental practices. Otherwise, single-minded imitation is not likely to be effective.[54]

The CSR-Economic Performance Puzzle

The resource-based view helps solve a major puzzle in the CSR debate since the 1970s. The puzzle—and a source of frustration to CSR advocates—is why there is no conclusive evidence on a direct, positive link between CSR and *economic* performance such as profits and shareholder returns.[55] Although some studies indeed report a *positive* relationship,[56] others find a *negative* relationship[57] or *no* relationship.[58] There can be a number of explanations for this intriguing mess, but a resource-based explanation suggests that because of capability constraints discussed earlier, many firms are not cut out for a CSR-intensive (differentiation) strategy. Since all studies have some sampling bias (no study is "perfect"), studies oversampling firms not ready for a high level of CSR activities are likely to report a negative relationship between CSR and economic performance, and studies oversampling firms ready for CSR may find a positive relationship. Also, studies with more balanced (more random) samples may fail to find any statistically significant relationship. In summary, because each firm is different (a basic assumption of the resource-based view), not every firm's economic performance is likely to benefit from CSR.

LEARNING OBJECTIVE 4

participate in three leading debates concerning corporate social responsibility

DEBATES AND EXTENSIONS

Without exaggeration, the entire subject of CSR is about debates. Some may even debate whether CSR belongs to a global business text. *None* of the other global (or international) business textbooks has a full chapter devoted to CSR in addition to another full chapter on ethics, cultures, and institutions (see Chapter 3). Here, we discuss three recent, previously unexplored debates particularly relevant for international operations: (1) domestic versus overseas social responsibility, (2) race to the bottom ("pollution haven") versus race to the top, and (3) active versus inactive CSR engagement overseas.

Domestic versus Overseas Social Responsibility

Given that corporate resources are limited, resources devoted to overseas CSR, unfortunately, often mean fewer resources devoted to domestic CSR. Consider two *primary* stakeholder groups: domestic employees and communities. Expanding overseas, especially toward emerging economies, may not only increase corporate profits and shareholder returns but also provide employment to host countries and develop these economies at the "base of the pyramid," all of which have noble CSR dimensions (see Chapter 1 Closing Case and In Focus 17.2). However, this is often done at the expense of domestic employees and communities. One can vividly appreciate the devastation of job losses on such employees and communities by watching the movie *The Full Monty*, which took place in Sheffield, England, the former steel capital of Europe and the world. Laid-off steel mill workers ended up taking an "alternative" line of work (male strip dancing). To prevent such a possible fate, in 2004, DaimlerChrysler's German unions had to scrap a 3% pay raise and endure a 11% increase of work hours (from 35 to 39 hours) with no extra pay in exchange for promises that 6,000 jobs would be kept in Germany for eight years. Otherwise, their jobs would go to the Czech Republic, Poland, and South Africa. However, such labor deals will probably only slow down but not stop the outgoing tide of jobs in developed economies. The wage differentials are just too great. "When we find a certain product can be made with a 50% decrease in salary costs in another country," argued a German executive, "we cannot avoid that if we want to stay competitive."[59]

To the extent that few (or no) laid-off German employees would move to the neighboring Czech Republic and Poland to seek work (and forget about moving to South Africa), most of them will end up being social welfare recipients in Germany. Thus, one may argue that MNEs' actions shirk their CSR by increasing the social burdens of their home countries. Executives making these decisions are often criticized by the media, unions, and politicians. However, from a corporate governance perspective—especially the "shareholder capitalism" variant—MNEs are doing nothing wrong by maximizing shareholder returns (see Chapter 16).

Although framed in a domestic versus overseas context, the heart of this debate boils down to a fundamental point that frustrates CSR advocates: In a capitalist society, it is shareholders (otherwise known as *capitalists*) who matter at the end of the day.[60] According to Jack Welch, GE's former chairman and CEO:

> Unions, politicians, activists—companies face a Babel of interests. But there's only one owner. A company is for its shareholders. They own it. They control it. That's the way it is, and the way it should be.[61]

When companies have enough resources, it would be nice to take care of domestic employees and communities. However, when confronted with relentless pressures for cost cutting and restructuring, managers have to prioritize.[62] Paradoxically, in this age of globalization, while the CSR movement is on the rise, the great migration of jobs away from developed economies is also accelerating. While people and countries at the base of the global pyramid welcome such migration, domestic employees and communities in developed economies as well as unions and politicians frankly hate it. Given the lack of a clear solution, this politically explosive debate is likely to heat up in the years to come.

Race to the Bottom ("Pollution Haven") versus Race to the Top

In global business, there is a controversial "pollution haven" debate. One side of the debate argues that because of heavier environmental regulation in developed economies, MNEs may have an incentive to shift pollution-intensive production to developing countries, where environmental standards may be lower. To attract investment, developing countries may enter a "race to the bottom" by lowering (or at least not tightening) environmental standards, and some may become "pollution havens."[63]

The other side argues that globalization does not necessarily have negative effects on the environment in developing countries to the extent suggested by the pollution haven hypothesis. This is largely due to many MNEs' *voluntary* adherence to environmental standards higher than those required by host countries.[64] One study finds that US capital markets significantly reward these practices, thus refuting the perspective that being green constitutes a liability that depresses market value.[65] In general, most MNEs reportedly outperform local firms in environmental management.[66] The underlying motivations behind MNEs' voluntary "green practices" can be attributed to (1) worldwide CSR

Do you think a firm that locates its pollution-heavy manufacturing in a developing country is acting responsibly?

pressures in general, (2) CSR demands made by customers in developed economies, and (3) requirements of MNE headquarters for worldwide compliance of higher CSR standards (such as ISO 14001). Although it is difficult to suggest that the race to the bottom does not exist, MNEs as a group do not necessarily add to the environmental burden in developing countries. Some MNEs, such as Dow, may facilitate the diffusion of better environmental technologies and standards to these countries (In Focus 17.2).

Active versus Inactive CSR Engagement Overseas

Active CSR engagement is now increasingly expected of MNEs.[67] MNEs that fail to do so are often criticized by NGOs. In the 1990s, Shell was harshly criticized for "not lifting a finger" when the Nigerian government brutally cracked down on rebels in the Ogoni region in which Shell operated. However, such well-intentioned calls for greater CSR engagement are in direct conflict with a long-standing principle governing the relationship between MNEs and host countries: nonintervention in local affairs (see the *first* bulleted point in Table 17.1).

The nonintervention principle originated from concerns that MNEs might engage in political activities against the national interests of the host country. Chile in the 1970s serves as a case in point. After the democratically elected socialist President Salvador Allende had threatened to expropriate the assets of ITT (a US-based MNE) and other MNEs, ITT, allegedly in connection with the Central Intelligence Agency (CIA), promoted a coup that killed President Allende. Consequently, the idea that MNEs should not interfere in the domestic political affairs of the host country has been enshrined in a number of codes of MNE conduct (see Table 17.1).

However, CSR advocates have been emboldened by some MNEs' actions during the apartheid era in South Africa, when local laws required racial segregation of the work force. Although many MNEs withdrew, those that remained were encouraged by the Sullivan Principles to challenge, breach, and seek to dismantle the apartheid system undermining the government's base of power. BP, for example, desegregated its employees. Emboldened by the successful removal of the apartheid regime in South Africa in 1994, CSR advocates have unleashed a new campaign, stressing the necessity for MNEs to engage in actions that often constitute political activity, in particular, in the human rights area. Shell, after its widely criticized (lack of) action in Nigeria, has explicitly endorsed the United Nations Declaration on Human Rights and supported the exercise of such rights "within the legitimate role of business" since 1996.

But what exactly is the "legitimate role" of CSR initiatives in host countries? In almost every country, there are local laws and norms that some foreign MNEs may find objectionable. In Malaysia, ethnic Chinese are discriminated against by law. In Estonia, ethnic Russians have a hard time. In many Arab countries, women do not have equal legal rights as men do. In the United States, a number of groups (ranging from Native Americans to homosexuals) claim to be discriminated against. At the heart of this debate is whether foreign MNEs should spearhead efforts to remove some of these discriminatory practices or should remain politically neutral by conforming to current host country laws and norms. This obviously is a nontrivial challenge.

MANAGEMENT SAVVY

LEARNING OBJECTIVE 5
draw implications for action

Concerning CSR, the institution- and resource-based views suggest three clear implications for action (Table 17.3). First, savvy managers need to understand the formal and informal rules of the game, anticipate changes, and seek to shape such changes. In the case of carbon offsetting, although the US government has refused to ratify the Kyoto Protocol, many farsighted US managers realize that as more countries around the world join Kyoto, competitors based in these countries may gain a strong "green" advantage.[68] Therefore, many US firms voluntarily participate in CSR activities not (yet) mandated by law in anticipation of more stringent environmental requirements down the road (see Closing Case).

Second, savvy managers need to pick CSR battles carefully. The resource-based view suggests an important lesson, which is captured by Sun Tzu's timeless teaching: "Know yourself, know your opponents." Although your opponents may engage in high-profile CSR activities allowing them to earn a lot of bragging rights while contributing to their triple bottom line, blindly imitating these practices, while not knowing enough about yourself (you as a manager and the firm/unit you lead) may lead to some disappointment. Instead of always chasing the newest best practices, firms are advised to select CSR practices that fit with their *existing* resources, capabilities, and especially, complementary assets.[69]

Third, given the increasingly inescapable responsibility to be good corporate citizens, managers may want to integrate CSR as part of the core activities and processes of the firm—instead of "faking it" and making cosmetic changes.[70] For example, instead of treating NGOs as threats, Home Depot, Lowe's, and Unilever have their sourcing policies certified by NGOs. Dow Chemical has established community advisory panels in most of its locations worldwide. Many managers traditionally treat CSR as a nuisance, involving regulation, added costs, and liability. Such an attitude may underestimate potential business opportunities associated with CSR.

What determines the success and failure of firms around the world? No doubt, CSR will increasingly become an important part of the answer. The best performing firms are likely to be those that can integrate CSR activities into the core economic functions of the firm while addressing social and environmental concerns.[71] The globally ambiguous and different CSR standards, norms, and expectations make many managers uncomfortable. As a result, many managers continue to relegate CSR to the backburner. However, this does not seem to be the right attitude for current and would-be managers who are studying this book—that is, *you*. It is important to note that we live in a dangerous period of global capitalism. In the *post-Seattle, post-9/11, and post-Enron* world (see Chapter 1), managers, as a unique group of stakeholders, have an important and challenging responsibility to safeguard and advance capitalism. From a CSR standpoint, this means building more humane, more inclusive, and fairer firms that not only generate wealth and develop economies but also respond to changing societal expectations concerning CSR around the world.[72]

TABLE 17.3 IMPLICATIONS FOR ACTION

- Understand the rules of the game, anticipate changes, and seek to shape and influence such changes
- Pick your CSR battles carefully; don't blindly imitate other firms' CSR activities
- Integrate CSR as part of the core activities and processes of the firm; faking it doesn't last very long

CHAPTER SUMMARY

1. Articulate a stakeholder view of the firm
   - A stakeholder view of the firm urges companies to pursue a more balanced set of triple bottom lines, consisting of economic, social, and environmental performance.
   - Despite the fierce defense of the free market school, especially its shareholder capitalism variant, the CSR movement has now become a more central part of management discussions.
2. Apply the institution-based view to analyze corporate social responsibility
   - The institution-based view suggests that when confronting CSR pressures, firms may employ (1) reactive, (2) defensive, (3) accommodative, and (4) proactive strategies.
3. Use the resource-based view to better understand corporate social responsibility
   - The resource-based view suggests that not all CSR activities satisfy the VRIO requirements.
4. Participate in three leading debates concerning corporate social responsibility
   - These are: (1) domestic versus overseas social responsibility, (2) race to the bottom versus race to the top, and (3) active versus inactive CSR engagement overseas.
5. Draw implications for action
   - Savvy managers must understand the rules of the game concerning CSR, anticipate changes, and seek to influence such changes.
   - CSR battles should be chosen carefully, not simply as an effort to imitate other firms' CSR activities.
   - CSR should be an integral part of the core activities and processes of a firm.

KEY TERMS

Accommodative strategy 498
Code of conduct (code of ethics) 499
Corporate social responsibility (CSR) 490
Defensive strategy 498
Global sustainability 491
Primary stakeholder groups 494
Proactive strategy 499
Reactive strategy 497
Secondary stakeholder groups 494
Social issue participation 500
Stakeholder 490
Triple bottom line 494

REVIEW QUESTIONS

1. Give an example of global sustainability that demonstrates your understanding of the concept.
2. How do the concerns of a primary stakeholder differ from those of a secondary stakeholder?
3. What does it mean for a corporation to have a triple bottom line?
4. Using Table 17.2, summarize the four types of strategies that can be used to make CSR decisions.

5. Describe at least three topics or issues you would expect to see addressed in a code of conduct by a corporation from *your home country*.
6. Devise two examples: one in which a corporation's participation in a social issue adds value to the firm and one in which it decreases value in the eyes of the stakeholders.
7. Using a resource-based view, explain why some firms improve their economic performance by adopting a CSR strategy, whereas others achieve no or damaging results.
8. Many have criticized offshoring, but how might this activity be seen as part of an overseas CSR strategy?
9. Do you think "green practices" should be voluntary or mandatory for businesses? Explain your answer.
10. In your opinion, do you think an MNE should remain politically neutral and adopt practices and laws of the host country?
11. As a manager, what are some of the considerations you would take into account before adopting any CSR-related policy?

CRITICAL DISCUSSION QUESTIONS

1. In the landmark *Dodge v. Ford* case in 1919, the Michigan State Supreme Court determined whether or not Henry Ford could withhold dividends from the Dodge brothers (and other shareholders of the Ford Motor Company) to engage in what today would be called CSR activities. With a resounding no, the court opined, "A business organization is organized and carried on primarily for the profits of the stockholders." If the court in your country were to decide on this case this year (or in 2019), what do you think would be the likely outcome?
2. ON ETHICS: Some argue that investing in emerging economies greatly increases the economic development and standard of living of the base of the global economic pyramid. Others contend that moving jobs to low-cost countries not only abandons CSR for domestic employees and communities in developed economies but also exploits the poor in these countries and destroys the environment. How would you participate in this debate if you were (1) CEO of an MNE headquartered in a developed economy moving production to a low-cost country, (2) the leader of a labor union in the home country of the MNE that is losing lots of jobs, or (3) the leader of an environmental NGO in the low-cost country in which the MNE invests?
3. ON ETHICS: Hypothetically, your MNE is the largest foreign investor in (1) Vietnam where religious leaders are reportedly being prosecuted or (2) Estonia where ethnic Russian citizens are being discriminated against by law. As the country manager there, you understand that the MNE is being pressured by NGOs of all stripes to help the oppressed groups in these countries. But you also understand that the host government could be upset if your firm is found to engage in local political activities deemed inappropriate. These alleged activities, which you personally find distasteful, are not directly related to your operations. How would you proceed?

VIDEO CASE

Watch "The Need to Measure and Explain CSR" by Julia Cleverdon of Business in the Community.

1. How does the "trust bank" affect a corporation's CSR?
2. Why isn't simply "doing the right thing" enough to solve the trust bank problem?
3. How can a company's open public acknowledgment of its CSR challenges be helpful in building public trust? What needs to accompany that acknowledgment?
4. Why must a company be careful in regards to following the industry leader in CSR?
5. What particular CSR problems might a global corporation have to confront?

CLOSING CASE

ETHICAL DILEMMA: Have You Offset Your Carbon Emission?

No longer only referring to a Japanese city, Kyoto has now become a new buzzword. The 1997 Kyoto Protocol (hereafter Kyoto in short) was a global initiative to reduce emissions of greenhouse gases linked to global warming. Kyoto was a hard-fought attempt to do something immensely difficult: create a worldwide mechanism for solving a long-term problem. Under Kyoto, developed countries pledge to cut emissions by 6% from 1990 levels by 2012. Each country is permitted to emit a certain quantity of carbon dioxide. Governments issue emission "allowances" (permits) to polluting firms within their borders, and such allowances (essentially rights to pollute) can be bought and sold by firms worldwide. Through this carbon trading system, polluting firms in developed countries can pay someone else (at home or abroad) to cut emission and claim credit.

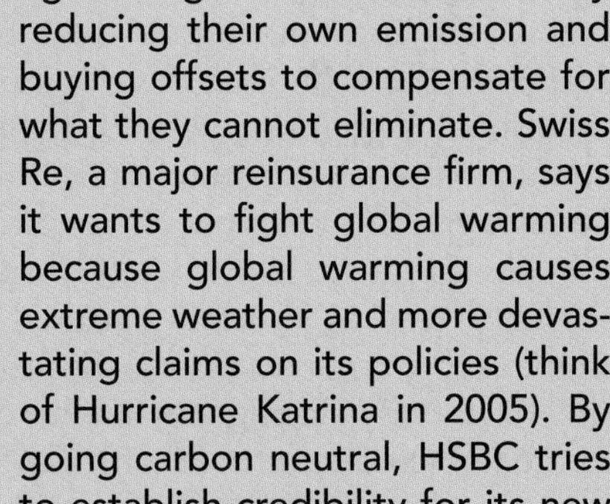
© GARY HERSHORN/Reuters /Landov

The EU has taken Kyoto most seriously. The British economy grew by 36% between 1990 and 2002 while greenhouse emission fell by 15%, thus already exceeding Kyoto. In comparison, the United States and Australia did not ratify Kyoto. Canada and Japan, both at present running at 25% *above* 1990 levels, may fail to comply. China, India, and many developing countries essentially argue: "Sorry, we have to develop our economy first—and have to forget about Kyoto now."

Effective as of February 2005, the market for emission allowances has soared. Most of the action takes place on the Amsterdam-based European Climate Exchange (ECX). Such trading is literally "selling hot air." The British government, Bank of Tokyo-Mitsubishi, Swiss Re, HSBC, and many others have pledged to go "carbon neutral" by reducing their own emission and buying offsets to compensate for what they cannot eliminate. Swiss Re, a major reinsurance firm, says it wants to fight global warming because global warming causes extreme weather and more devastating claims on its policies (think of Hurricane Katrina in 2005). By going carbon neutral, HSBC tries to establish credibility for its new carbon-finance business.

Interestingly, while the US federal government has refused to ratify Kyoto, numerous states, industries, firms, and NGOs have joined forces to combat climate change. America's leading Kyoto crusader is Al Gore, the former vice president turned alarmist film maker. His documentary film on global warming, *An Inconvenient Truth*, won an Oscar in 2007. Al Gore flies commercial most of the time to generate less CO_2 and purchases offsets to maintain a carbon-neutral life. Although he drives an SUV, it is a Mercury hybrid. In part due to Gore's campaign, a dozen or so states—in the absence of federal action—have moved to restrict CO_2 emission. More encouragingly, the Chicago Climate Exchange (CCX) was set up in 2003, with its membership growing from an initial 23 firms to over 200 now, including DuPont, Ford, and Motorola.

CSR advocates argue that voluntary offsets, while small at the moment, can in time help slow global warming. However, close scrutiny by *Business Week* revealed some deals amounted to little more than "feel-good hype." For instance, in 2005, Seattle City Light made an astounding announcement that it eliminated its share to contribute to global warming. Of course, it still puffed out some 200,000 tons of greenhouse gases annually. But Seattle City Light claimed to have paid other organizations to reduce more than 200,000 tons of emissions. Such buying and selling offsets have now gone global. The sellers are often developing countries; China may soon beat the United States and become the largest greenhouse gas emitter by 2015. At the Carbon Fair in Cologne, Germany, organized by the World Bank, the Chinese state planning committee distributed a glossy 200-page book crammed with projects. Since developed countries that ratified Kyoto are expected to produce 3.5 billion tons of carbon above their targets by 2012, the sellers have excellent prospects. While paying someone else to do the (less) dirty work is nice, it reduces the incentive for firms in developed countries to bite off the more challenging task of reducing their own emissions.

Another issue is the lack of standards and oversight. Buying and selling offsets have rapidly become an industry of its own, with a number of for-profit intermediaries. For example, the for-profit, two-year-old TerraPass issued every 2007 Oscar performer and presenter (including Gore) a "carbon-neutral" certificate, by using funds from the Oscar organizers to pay for emission-reduction projects, primarily at Waste Management landfill facilities in Arkansas. However, *Business Week* found that the Waste Management projects in Arkansas had been launched long *before* any carbon-offsets deals. In other words, the offsets had nothing to do with emission reduction at the particular facilities. The main effects of the offsets were "to salve guilty celebrity consciences and provide Waste Management, a $13 billion company, with some extra revenue." According to *Business Week*, this was another "inconvenient truth." Overall, Kyoto may be flawed, but it seems better than nothing.

Case Discussion Questions

1. From an institution-based view, explain why some firms in countries such as the United States whose governments did *not* ratify Kyoto are interested in participating in carbon offsets?
2. From a resource-based view, identify potential first-mover advantages in carbon offsets.
3. As CEO of a coal-fired utility in Canada, how can your firm reduce greenhouse gas emissions? As CEO of a similar utility in China, what are your options?

Sources: Based on (1) T. Blair, 2005, A year of huge challenges, *Economist*, January 1: 44–46; (2) *Business Week*, 2007, Another inconvenient truth, March 26: 96–102; (3) *Economist*, 2006, Upset about offsets, August 5: 53–54; (4) *Economist*, 2007, Selling hot air, September 17-18; (5) A. Gore, 1992, *Earth in the Balance*, New York: Harper & Row; (6) *Time*, 2007.

NOTES

Journal acronyms: **AME** – *Academy of Management Executive;* **AMJ** – *Academy of Management Journal;* **AMR** – *Academy of Management Review;* **APJM** – *Asia Pacific Journal of Management;* **ASQ** – *Administrative Science Quarterly;* **BEQ** – *Business Ethics Quarterly;* **BW** – *Business Week;* **CMR** – *California Management Review;* **HBR** – *Harvard Business Review;* **JBE** – *Journal of Business Ethics;* **JIBS** – *Journal of International Business Studies;* **JIM** – *Journal of International Management;* **JM** – *Journal of Management;* **JMS** – *Journal of Management Studies;* **JWB** – *Journal of World Business;* **MS** – *Management Science;* **NYTM** – *New York Times Magazine;* **OSc** – *Organization Science;* **SMJ** – *Strategic Management Journal;* **SMR** – *Sloan Management Review;* **TC** – *Transnational Corporations*

1 P. Argenti, 2004, Collaborating with activists (p. 106), *CMR*, 47: 91–116.

2 K. Davis, 1973, The case for and against business assumption of social responsibilities (p. 312), *AMJ*, 16: 312–322. See also A. McWilliams, D. Siegel, & P. Wright, 2006, Corporate social responsibility, *JMS*, 43: 1–18.

3 P. Godfrey, 2005, The relationship between corporate philanthropy and shareholder wealth, *AMR*, 30: 777–798; T. Jones, W. Felps, & G. Bigley, 2007, Ethical theory and stakeholder-related decisions, *AMR*, 32: 137–155; J. Post, L. Preston, & S. Sachs, 2002, *Redefining the Corporation*, Stanford, CA: Stanford University Press.

[4] Y. He, Z. Tian, & Y. Chen, 2007, Performance implications of nonmarket strategy in China, *APJM*, 24: 151–169; K. O'Shaughnessy, E. Gedajlovic, & P. Reinmoeller, 2007, The influence of firm, industry, and network on the corporate social performance of Japanese firms, *APJM*, 24: 283–304.

[5] E. Freeman, 1984, *Strategic Management: A Stakeholder Approach* (p. 46), Boston: Pitman.

[6] P. David, M. Bloom, & A. Hillman, 2007, Investor activism, managerial responsiveness, and corporate social performance, *SMJ*, 28: 91–100.

[7] World Commission on Environment and Development, 1987, *Our Common Future* (p. 8), Oxford: Oxford University Press. See also P. Bansal, 2005, Evolving sustainably, *SMJ*, 26: 187–218.

[8] S. Hart, 2005, *Capitalism at the Crossroads*, Philadelphia: Wharton School Publishing; R. Rajan & L. Zingales, 2003, *Saving Capitalism from the Capitalists*, New York: Crown.

[9] S. Hart & M. Milstein, 2003, Creating sustainable value, *AME*, 17: 56–67; P. Shrivastava, 1995, The role of corporations in achieving ecological sustainability, *AMR*, 20: 936–960.

[10] J. Doh & T. Guay, 2006, CSR, public policy, and NGO activism in Europe and the United States, *JMS*, 43: 47–73; H. Teegen, 2003, International NGOs as global institutions, *JIM*, 9: 271–285.

[11] P. Romilly, 2007, Business and climate change risk, *JIBS*, 38: 474–480.

[12] J. Coombs & K. M. Gilley, 2005, Stakeholder management as a predictor of CEO compensation, *SMJ*, 26: 827–840; B. Husted & D. Allen, 2006, CSR in the MNE, *JIBS*, 37: 838–849; G. Kassinis & N. Vafeas, 2006, Stakeholder pressures and environmental performance, *AMJ*, 49: 145–159; S. Sharma & I. Henriques, 2005, Stakeholder influences on sustainability practices in the Canadian forest products industry, *SMJ*, 26: 159–180.

[13] C. Eesley & M. Lenox, 2006, Firm responses to secondary stakeholder action, *SMJ*, 27: 765–781; R. Mitchell, B. Agle, & D. Wood, 1997, Toward a theory of stakeholder identification and salience, *AMR*, 22: 853–886.

[14] T. Kochan & S. Rubinstein, 2000, Toward a stakeholder theory of the firm, *OSc*, 11: 367–386; R. Wolfe & D. Putler, 2002, How tight are the ties that bind stakeholder groups? *OSc*, 13: 64–80.

[15] M. Clarkson, 1995, A stakeholder framework for analyzing and evaluating corporate social performance (p. 107), *AMR*, 20: 92–117.

[16] T. Donaldson & L. Preston, 1995, The stakeholder theory of the corporation, *AMR*, 20: 65–91; J. Elkington, 1997, *Cannibals with Forks: The Triple Bottom Line of 21st Century Business*, New York: Wiley.

[17] O. Williamson, 1985, *The Economic Institutions of Capitalism*, New York: Free Press.

[18] M. Friedman, 1970, The social responsibility of business is to increase its profits, *NYTM*, September 13: 32–33.

[19] M. Jensen, 2002, Value maximization, stakeholder theory, and the corporate objective function, *BEQ* 12: 235–256.

[20] H. Mintzberg, R. Simons, & K. Basu, 2002, Beyond selfishness, *SMR*, Fall: 67–74.

[21] C. Nielsen, 2005, Competition within the US national security regime, *JIM*, 11: 497–517.

[22] R. Buchholz, 2004, The natural environment, *AME*, 18: 130–133; O. Ferrell, 2004, Business ethics and customer stakeholders, *AME*, 18: 126–129.

[23] J. Margolis & J. Walsh, 2003, Misery loves companies, *ASQ*, 48: 268–305.

[24] P. Christmann, 2004, Multinational companies and the natural environment, *AMJ*, 47: 747–760; D. Waldman et al., 2006, Cultural and leadership predictions of CSR values of top management, *JIBS*, 37: 823–837.

[25] I. Henriques & P. Sadorsky, 1999, The relationship between environmental commitment and managerial perceptions of stakeholder importance, *AMJ*, 42: 87–99.

[26] P. Hilts, 2003, *Protecting America's Health*, New York: Knopf.

[27] T. Newton & G. Harte, 1996, Green business, *JMS*, 34: 75–98.

[28] L. Amine, 2003, An integrated micro- and macrolevel discussion of global green issues, *JIM*, 9: 373–393.

[29] A. Gore, 1992, *Earth in the Balance*, New York: Harper & Row; M. Porter & M. Kramer, 2006, Strategy and society, *HBR*, December: 78–92.

[30] M. Porter & C. van der Linde, 1995, Green and competitive, *HBR*, 73 (5): 120–134. For counterarguments and evidence, see A. King & J. M. Shaver, 2001, Are aliens green? *SMJ*, 22: 1069–1085; A. Rugman & A. Verbeke, 1998, Corporate strategies and environmental regulations, *SMJ*, 19: 363–375.

[31] S. Banerjee, 2001, Managerial perceptions of corporate environmentalism, *JMS*, 38: 489–513; D. Matten & A. Crane, 2005, Corporate citizenship, *AMR*, 30: 166–179.

[32] A. Kolk & R. Vam Tulder, 2004, Ethics in international business, *JWB*, 39: 49–60; I. Maignan & D. Ralston, 2002, CSR in Europe and the US, *JIBS*, 33: 497–514; G. Weaver, 2001, Ethics programs in global businesses, *JBE*, 30: 3–15.

[33] P. Bansal & I. Clelland, 2004, Talking trash, *AMJ*, 47: 93–103.

[34] C. Robertson & W. Crittenden, 2003, Mapping moral philosophies, *SMJ*, 24: 385–392; J. van Oosterhout, P. Heugens, & M. Kaptein, 2006, The internal morality of contracting, *AMR*, 31: 521–539.

[35] J. Howard-Grenville & A. Hoffman, 2003, The importance of cultural framing to the success of social initiatives in business, *AME*, 17: 70–84.

[36] O. Branzei, T. Ursacki-Bryant, I. Vertinsky, & W. Zhang, 2004, The formation of green strategies in Chinese firms, *SMJ*, 25: 1075–1095.

[37] Hart, 2005, *Capitalism at the Crossroads*.

[38] D. Schuler, K. Rehbein, & R. Cramer, 2002, Pursuing strategic advantage through political means, *AMJ*, 45: 659–672.

[39] *Economist*, 2007, Everybody's green now (p. 6), June 2: 6.

[40] B. Arya & J. Salk, 2006, Cross-sector alliance learning and effectiveness of voluntary codes of CSR, *BEQ*, 16: 211–234; C. Hardy, T. Lawrence, & D. Grant, 2005, Discourse and collaboration, *AMR*, 30: 58–77; J. Selsky & B. Parker, 2005, Cross-sector partnerships to address social issues, *JM*, 31: 849–873.

[41] D. Rondinelli & T. London, 2003, How corporations and environmental groups cooperate, *AME*, 17: 61–76.

[42] P. Bansal & K. Roth, 2000, Why companies go green, *AMJ*, 43: 717–737.

[43] A. King & M. Lenox, 2000, Industry self-regulation without sanctions, *AMJ*, 43: 698–716.

[44] R. Jiang & P. Bansal, 2003, Seeing the need for ISO 14001, *JMS*, 40: 1047–1067; A. King, M. Lenox, & A. Terlaak, 2005, The strategic use of decentralized institutions, *AMJ*, 48: 1091–1106.

[45] R. Chan, 2005, Does the natural-resource-based view of the firm apply in an emerging economy? *JMS*, 42: 625–675; J. A. Aragon-Correa & S. Sharma, 2003, A contingent resource-based view of proactive corporate environmental strategy, *AMR*, 28: 71–88; A. Marcus & M. Anderson, 2006, A general dynamic capability, *JMS*, 43: 19–46; C. Neht, 1998, Maintainability of first mover advantages when environmental regulations differ between countries, *AMR*, 23: 77–97.

[46] A. Hillman & G. Keim, 2001, Shareholder value, stakeholder management, and social issues, *SMJ*, 22: 125–139; M. Meznar, D. Nigh, & C. Kwok, 1998, Announcements of withdrawal from South Africa revisited, *AMJ*, 41: 715–730; P. Wright & S. Ferris, 1997, Agency conflict and corporate strategy, *SMJ*, 18: 77–93.

[47] W. Judge & T. Douglas, 1998, Performance implications of incorporating natural environmental issue into the strategic planning process, *JMS*, 35: 241–262; R. Klassen & C. McLaughlin, 1996, The impact of environmental management on firm performance, *MS*, 42: 1199–1214.

[48] *BW*, 2003, Diversity is about to get more elusive, not less, July 7: 30–31.

[49] D. Turban & D. Greening, 1996, Corporate social performance and organizational attractiveness to prospective employees, *AMJ*, 40: 658–672.

[50] S. Sharma & H. Vredenburg, 1998, Proactive corporate environmental strategy and the development of competitively valuable organizational capabilities, *SMJ*, 19: 729–754.

[51] L. Andersson & T. Bateman, 2000, Individual environmental initiative, *AMJ*, 43: 548–570; M. Cordano & I. Frieze, 2000, Pollution reduction preferences of US environmental managers, *AMJ*, 43: 627–641; C. Egri & S. Herman, 2000, Leadership in the North American environmental sector, *AMJ*, 43: 571–604; C. Ramus & U. Steger, 2000, The roles of supervisory support behaviors and environmental policy in employee "ecoinitiatives" at leading-edge European companies, *AMJ*, 43: 605–626.

[52] N. Darnall & D. Edwards, 2006, Predicting the cost of environmental management system adoption, *SMJ*, 27: 301–320; M. Russo & N. Harrison, 2005, Organizational design and environmental performance, *AMJ*, 48: 582–593.

[53] M. Delmas, M. Russo, & M. Montes-Sancho, 2007, Deregulation and environmental differentiation in the electric utility industry, *SMJ*, 28: 189–209.

[54] P. Christmann, 2000, Effects of best practices of environmental management on cost advantage, *AMJ* 43: 663–680.

[55] M. Barnett & R. Salomon, 2006, Beyond dichotomy, *SMJ*, 27: 1101–1122; J. Harrison & R. E. Freeman, 1999, Stakeholders, social responsibility, and performance, *AMJ*, 42: 479–487; A. Lockett, J. Moon, & W. Visser, 2006, CSR in management research, *JMS*, 43: 115–136; D. Schuler & M. Cording, 2006, A corporate social performance-corporate financial performance behavioral model for consumers, *AMR*, 31: 540–558; V. Strike, J. Gao, & P. Bansal, 2006, Being good while being bad, *JIBS*, 37: 850–862.

[56] S. Berman, A. Wicks, S. Kotha, & T. Jones, 1999, Does stakeholder orientation matter? *AMJ*, 42: 488–506; B. Lev, C. Petrovits, & S. Radhakrishnan, 2006, Is doing good good for your? Working paper, University of Texas at Dallas; M. Russo & P. Fouts, 1997, A resource-based perspective on corporate environmental performance and profitability, *AMJ*, 40: 534–559; S. Waddock & S. Graves, 1997, The corporate social performance-financial performance link, *SMJ*, 18 303–319.

[57] D. Vogel, 2005, The low value of virtue, *HBR*, June: 26.

[58] B. Agle, R. Mitchell, & J. Sonnenfeld, 1999, What matters to CEOs? *AMJ*, 42: 507–525; A. McWilliams & D. Siegel, 2000, CSR and financial performance, *SMJ*, 21: 603–609.

[59] *BW*, 2004, European workers' losing battle (p. 41), August 9: 41.

[60] R. E. Freeman, A. Wicks, & B. Parmar, 2004, Stakeholder theory and "The Corporate Objective Revisited," *OSc*, 15: 364–369.

[61] J. Welch & S. Welch, 2006, Whose company is it anyway? *BW*, October 9: 122.

[62] A. Sundaram & A. Inkpen, 2004, The corporate objective revisited, *OSc*, 15: 350–363.

[63] H. J. Leonard, 1988, *Pollution and the Struggle for a World Product*, Cambridge, UK: Cambridge University Press.

[64] P. Christmann & G. Taylor, 2006, Firm self-regulation through international certifiable standards, *JIBS*, 37: 863–878; A. Rugman & A. Verbeke, 1998, Corporate strategy and international environmental policy, *JIBS*, 29: 819–833.

[65] G. Dowell, S. Hart, & B. Yeung, 2000, Do corporate global environmental standards create or destroy market value? *MS*, 46: 1059–1074.

[66] J. Child & T. Tsai, 2005, The dynamic between MNC strategy and institutional constraints in emerging economies, *JMS*, 42: 95–126; M. Hansen, 2003, Managing the environment across borders, *TC*, 12: 27–52.

[67] J. Kline, 2003, Political activities by transnational corporations, *TC*, 12: 1–26.

[68] J. Lash & F. Wellington, 2007, Competitive advantage on a warming planet, *HBR*, March: 95–102.

[69] A. McWilliams & D. Siegel, 2001, Corporate social responsibility, *AMR*, 26: 117–127.

[70] S. Sharma, 2000, Managerial interpretations and organizational context as predictors of corporate choice of environmental strategy, *AMJ*, 43: 681–697.

[71] B. Husted & J. Salazar, 2006, Taking Friedman seriously, *JMS*, 43: 75–91.

[72] N. Gardberg & C. Fombrun, 2006, Corporate citizenship, *AMR*, 31: 329–346; A. Peredo & J. Chrisman, 2006, Toward a theory of community-based enterprise, *AMR*, 31: 309–328; P. Sethi, 1995, Societal expectations and corporate performance, *AMR*, 20: 18–21.

INTEGRATIVE CASE 4.1

SHAKIRA: THE DILEMMA OF GOING GLOBAL

The Economist

To sing in Spanish or in English? That was the tricky choice facing Shakira and her record company, Sony BMG, as they pondered how to follow the Colombian pop star's 2001 global chart-topping, 13 million-selling album, "Laundry Service." That album, Shakira's first (mostly) in English, was a dramatic entry into the lucrative English-language pop market for a singer who had sold some 12 million of her four previous albums, all in Spanish. Having penned her first song at the age of eight and released her first album aged 13, earning an estimated $30 million even before "Laundry Service," Shakira found herself described as Latin America's biggest star and, by some wags, Colombia's greatest legal export.

"Laundry Service" put Shakira's commercial achievements on a par with—perhaps even ahead of—those of other leading pop stars who have lately crossed over from Spanish to English, such as Ricky Martin, Enrique Iglesias, and Gloria Estefan. But how to build on that triumph? "The industry would have liked me to put out another English album six months after 'Laundry Service,'" says Shakira, now 28. "But I can't make music like hamburgers." Sony had little choice but to wait for her to deliver in her own time—and in the language, or, as it turned out, languages, of her choice. This year [*2005—Editor*], several years late, from the industry's point of view, Shakira is releasing not one but two new albums. And, even more contrary to industry conventional wisdom, the first, just out, is in Spanish—"Fijación Oral volumen 1"—with an English-language album, "Oral Fixation volume 2," held back until November.

This strategy, Shakira concedes, is a gamble, albeit one for which she is happy to accept responsibility. "I like risk and challenges . . . If it goes wrong, I'm to blame." In an industry in which established artists are steadily grabbing power from the big corporations (whose main defense is to try to "manufacture" a stream of easy-to-manage identikit boy and girl bands, or turn many a non-entity into a "Pop Idol"), Shakira is said to exercise tighter than average control over all aspects of her career. In interviews she may attribute her decisions to "irrational impulses" and "feminine intuition," but industry insiders say she has an impressive grasp of business logic. As her career approached a crucial stage in the mid-1990s, for example, she teamed up with Emilio Estefan (husband of Gloria), the Miami-based king- (and queen-) maker of Latin pop. She has always written her own material: when she decided to enter the English-language market, she learned English well enough to write songs in it, and thereby ensured that she retained control over her music. She also changed her image ahead of the launch of "Laun-

This case was first published as "The Crossover Queen," in *The Economist*, July 23, 2005, p. 62, © Economist Newspaper Group. Reprinted with permission. Case discussion questions were added by Mike Peng.

dry Service," with a striking new blonde look—though, typically, she denies this had any business motive, saying instead that it was simply the result of her natural brown hair having become "like a jail . . . I didn't want to be buried with it."

So what is the business logic behind this year's belated two-album release strategy? After all, there was a high price to pay for taking so long to launch a new album. The momentum created by "Laundry Service" has been largely lost, says one Sony executive, so when it came to market her new work the firm had "to assume it was starting from scratch again." On the other hand, he concedes, "you can't rush an act like Shakira"—whose work has even been praised for its "innocent sensuality" in an essay by the novelist Gabriel García Márquez (a fellow Colombian).

Releasing the Spanish album first had two main goals. One was to re-establish her roots in the Latin marketplace. "When Hispanics heard I was writing in English, they probably thought I was leaving forever," she says. Certainly, back home her fellow Colombians grumble about Shakira having "abandoned" her middle-class origins for the Latin elite based around Miami and the Bahamas—she has homes in both—and "speaking Spanish with an Argentine accent" since she started to date Antonio de la Rua, the son of a former Argentine president. Two English albums in a row might have been too many, not just in Colombia.

Yet, Shakira points out, economic woes, social inequality and bureaucratic governments (among other constraints) mean that many Latinos have to go abroad to make it big. For a global pop star who is often touring, the transport links out of Miami are far better than those from Colombia. But, she says, "I have always been patriotic," visiting Colombia often and involving herself in its social problems. She is extremely active in the foundation she started when she was 18, Pies Descalzos ("Bare Feet")—named after her third album—which helps children affected by the violence and war on drugs that have displaced some two million Colombians. She has even harmonized her commercial endorsement strategy with her social activism. Having initially followed the likes of Madonna and Michael Jackson by becoming a face of Pepsi—which "gave me exposure at a time I needed it"—she has since moved on to Reebok which, she says, is interested in human rights and donated 50,000 pairs of shoes via her foundation, because "we realized we could achieve a lot together."

The Spanish-language market extends far beyond Latin America, of course, and is booming both in America, where Hispanics already account for 14% of the population, and Spain (Shakira performed in a concert promoting Madrid's bid to host the 2012 Olympics)—so it is well worth reconnecting with. But, more ambitiously, Shakira has also decided to market her new Spanish album to non-Spanish-speaking fans. Globalization, she says, has "made frontiers between cultures very blurry," and "I wanted to integrate my two audiences." So far, the gamble is paying off. Sales of "Fijación Oral volumen 1" have already topped two million. It is in the top five in such non-traditional Latin markets as Germany and Finland, and the top ten in France. Perhaps she should re-record volume two in Spanish.

Case Discussion Questions

1. A leading concern in international marketing is localization versus standardization, which, in this case, is singing in Spanish versus in English. Discuss the pros and cons of each approach.
2. From a resource-based view, explain what is behind Shakira's phenomenal success.
3. From an institution-based view, discuss the informal norms constraining Shakira's choices. For example, even if she so chooses, can she sing 100% in English? Can she afford to be perceived as having "abandoned" her Colombian middle-class origins for the Latin elite based around Miami and the Bahamas?
4. Does her manifestation in social responsibility play a role in facilitating her commercial success?
5. In what language should Shakira release her next album?

INTEGRATIVE CASE 4.2

KALASHNIKOV: SWORDS INTO VODKA

John Ness
Newsweek

If he had designed an athletic shoe, Lt. Gen. Mikhail Kalashnikov wouldn't have to be hustling so hard at his age. Kalashnikov's gift for guns made him a hero of the Soviet Union many times over, and his 85th birthday was feted by nostalgic Russians last week [*in November 2004—Editor*]. But his legendary AK-47 is so sturdy that old models have created a permanent glut, contributing to a worldwide decline in the sale of new small arms. That, in turn, is forcing gun makers into new lines. Kalashnikov [*who is the "K" in AK-47, which stands for "automatic Kalashnikov first made in the year 1947"—Editor*] has lent his name to umbrellas, penknives, watches, golf tees, and two different vodkas. One is Russian, and Kalashnikov was recently in London to unveil a British version. "What can you do?" says Kalashnikov, a reluctant entrepreneur in an aging uniform, speaking in his gritty hometown of Izhevsk. "These are our times now."

Since the end of the cold war, small-arms makers around the world have felt the pinch. While sales of high-tech military hardware are soaring, the world's estimated $7.4 billion market for small arms—rifles and handguns—remains flat, largely immune to innovation, yet fought over by a growing number of increasingly desperate competitors. The Geneva-based Small Arms Survey reported in its 2004 survey that the world market is in decline. Romanian gun maker Romarm recently began making washing and sewing machines. Izhmash, the Russian company that made the Kalashnikov, now sells machine tools. The world's leading handgun company, Smith & Wesson, last year launched a decidedly feminine line of bedding featuring pillows with cowgirl patterns on them. It lasted only a few months.

Kalashnikov is the most poignant symbol of the decline. When the Soviet Union began to crumble in 1989, the legendary gun maker was 70 years old, rich in official honors and titles, but ill prepared for the market forces about to sweep Russia.

Kalashnikov makes nothing from his gun designs. The Soviet Union had licensed more than a dozen countries to manufacture his weapons. After 1991 post-communist middlemen began selling stock out of old Soviet armories, and today there are an estimated 100 million AK-47s in circulation. The rifle is featured on the flags of Mozambique and numerous jihadist groups. Knockoffs are everywhere; General Kalashnikov and Izhmash accused the United States this summer of buying pirate AK-47s for the Iraqi police force. And authentic AK-47s remain dirt cheap. "Militarily, the guys who are buying are poor and they're insurgents and they're just going to buy AK-47s," says Old Dominion University professor and small-arms expert Aaron Karp. "They'd be foolish not to."

Kalashnikov knows it's too late to re-establish control over his gun designs, so he has moved on. In 2003, he received a 33% stake in the MMI Co. in Germany, which turns out the Kalashnikov umbrellas, watches, penknives, and golf tees. Kalashnikov says he has not seen "a single kopeck" [*the Russian monetary unit below the ruble, similar to the penny below the dollar—Editor*].

This case was written by John Ness (*Newsweek*) and first published as "Swords into Vodka" in *Newsweek*, November 22, 2004, p. 46. © Newsweek. Reprinted with permission. Case discussion questions were added by Mike Peng.

MMI says he will, once the start-up costs are paid, if the line sells.

Kalashnikov describes his new role as a "distinguished representative" for quality products. His first venture in distilling was a unique formula including salt, sugar, vanilla and glycerin. Sales of "Vodka Kalashnikov" were mediocre. Enter John Florey, 34, a British entrepreneur who brought in top-shelf marketing and rolled out a premium British "Kalashnikov Vodka" in September. Florey won't disclose sales but says the new line will launch in continental Europe and America next year.

In the United States, gun makers face a steadily dropping crime rate—historically a killer for handgun sales—and the rise of cheap competition from Brazil and Israel. One answer is consolidation: Germany's Heckler & Koch, Belgium's FN Herstal, France's Giat, Switzerland's RUAG and the United States' Alliant Techsystems have begun cooperating on design and production. Russia is absorbing its small-arms producers into two state companies.

Another answer is new products. Even as the company was launching its cowgirl prints, Smith & Wesson unveiled the Five Hundred, a supersize .50-caliber handgun that sells for $1,000 and has since helped boost overall sales by 50%, to $120 million. Its customers are "the guys and gals that like to have the biggest cars and the biggest tires," says Roy Cuny, who stepped down as Smith & Wesson CEO November 3. Karp calls the weapon "totally useless" but symbolic of where the industry's future lies: "technologically nothing new, but very romantic."

The romance is gone for Kalashnikov. He says he has been very careful about lending his name only to honorable products, but less so about the financial details. "I haven't become a billionaire. I haven't become a millionaire," he says. "And I think it's unlikely I ever will."

Case Discussion Questions

1. In international marketing, there is a well-known country-of-origin effect. How does this affect products and companies out of Russia in general?
2. This case deals with two of the arguably strongest "brand images" (if not strict brands per se) out of Russia: Kalashnikov and vodka. Essentially, in the new Russia, General Kalashnikov is becoming an entrepreneur by leveraging his brand to enter the vodka (and other) business. From a resource-based view, predict whether his new vodka venture is likely to succeed.
3. What are the ideal marketing and supply chain capabilities for the small-arms business? What are the ideal marketing and supply chain capabilities for the vodka business?
4. From an institution-based view, explain why Kalashnikov, now 85, is still interested in making money.
5. What does the future hold for the small-arms industry?

INTEGRATIVE CASE 4.3

COMPUTIME

Bee-Leng Chua
Hawaii Pacific University

Michael N. Young
Hong Kong Baptist University

Xi Zou
Columbia University

In the spring of 2003, Bernard Auyang, CEO of Computime, Limited, sat in his office in Hong Kong, pondering his company's future. Over the past ten years, Computime had grown to become one of the world's largest original equipment manufacturers (OEMs) of electronic equipment. The company manufactured primarily in Shenzhen across the border from Hong Kong. Computime was experiencing dramatic growth, along with the rest of southern China. Computime had successfully made the transition from a local, Asian family business to a global player. Now it seemed that the company structure was becoming unwieldy and difficult to manage. Bernard believed that the company needed to be restructured to achieve the goals that he had set for it. He had developed a plan for restructuring that would provide more flexibility. Yet, Computime's board of directors was skeptical, and many members had brought up serious objections. Bernard appreciated his board's concerns, and although he and his father were the dominant owners of the organization, he encouraged the board's independence. He knew that the board was raising some valid points. This added to his quandary because deep inside he was convinced that something needed to change.

A Second Generation Family Business

Computime was founded in 1974 in Hong Kong by Ho Auyang, Bernard's father. The company was one of Asia's leading providers of electronic design and manufacturing services, and it had clients worldwide. Computime offered end-to-end solutions in consumer and industrial electronics, including product engineering and design, testing, supply chain management, contract manufacturing, and logistics services. The company was particularly adept in electronic controls, an area in which it was a world leader. With over 3,000 employees worldwide, Computime operated more than a dozen design, manufacturing, and sales facilities in Asia, Europe, and North America. The company's total revenue was US$135 million in 2002.

Bernard Auyang had taken over as CEO from his father. He had graduated from Harvard University with a degree in economics and Asian studies. Before joining the family firm, he worked at the Board of Trade in Chicago. Bernard enjoyed building things, so his first job with Computime was on the production line. He then moved on to the warehouse, accounting, and then sales and marketing. Eventually, he took over as CEO in 1998 after working in the family business for ten years.

By 2003, Bernard joked that his father was more interested in playing with the grandchildren than worrying about the company. Still, Bernard sometimes felt that he was working in his father's shadow even though he had been CEO for five years. Despite Mr. Auyang Sr.'s retirement, he still had a strong influence on major investment decisions, and it was clear that he had had a formative impact on Bernard's business philosophy. For example, Bernard remembered a situation when he was involved in negotiating an acquisition. His father told him: "In any project, even if you have 20 reasons to invest and only one reason not to invest, you should walk away." Bernard did indeed walk away from that particular project, and he had not regretted the decision. So far, Mr. Auyang Sr. had not raised specific objections to Bernard's ideas for restructuring, but he wanted to see how Bernard responded to the questions raised by the board. To that end, his father reminded him of constant self-reflection when the board raised issues that he had not anticipated.

This is the condensed version of "Computime, Limited: China's Boom Times Cause Growing Pains," published in the *Asian Case Research Journal*, 8 (2): 241–263. This case was written by Bee-Leng Chua (Hawaii Pacific University), Michael N. Young (Hong Kong Baptist University), and Xi Zou (Columbia University). The purpose of the case is to serve as a basis for classroom discussion rather than to illustrate either effective or ineffective handling of an administrative situation. The authors wish to acknowledge the help of Mr. Bernard Auyang, CEO of Computime, Ltd., for providing access to company strategy and records and other helpful insights and suggestions. The company website is http://www.computime.com.

The Booming Pearl River Delta in Southern China

In 2003, while the rest of the world was mired in recession, China went against the trend with rapid growth rates of approximately 8%. Within China, development was uneven. The Pearl River Delta (including Guangzhou and Shenzhen) was experiencing unprecedented economic boom times as China assumed the role of the "workshop of the world." Over the past 25 years, the delta had been transformed from an agricultural backwater in one of Asia's poorest economies into one of the world's leading manufacturing locations.

From 1980 to 2000, the region's economy grew at a rate of 16.9%, compared with 13.8% for Guangdong Province and 9.6% for China as a whole. Over the period of China's reforms, the delta was the fastest growing part of the fastest growing province in the fastest growing large economy in the world. In 2001, the delta accounted for about 3% of the population of mainland China, but 9% of gross domestic product, 25% of foreign direct investment (FDI), and 34% of exports.

The delta benefited from its proximity to Hong Kong, which supplied capital, management, technology, market knowledge, and access to international markets. Hong Kong was the source of more than 70% of FDI in the region since 1979. Hong Kong linked the region to the rest of the world, handling 70% to 80% of the delta's exports.

Many multinationals were also operating successfully in the region. Wal-Mart sourced about US$11 billion in goods from the mainland—most of it through the delta. Other success stories included Procter & Gamble, Whirlpool, IBM, and Honda. Indigenous companies from the delta, such as Huawei and TCL, were emerging in international markets. The region had also attracted facilities of some leading companies from other parts of China, such as computer makers Lenovo and Founder.

Further, the Pearl River Delta region was poised to foster substantial business opportunities in the future. Its economy was forecasted to grow by 12% a year through 2005. Its light industrial, electrical, and electronics industries were likely to further develop as more local suppliers of components and capital goods emerged. All of these frenetic activities had been part of Computime's environment. The company could not help but feel the world was changing around it.

Three Main Operational Areas

Computime's product mix is shown in Figure 1. Its operations center on (1) design and engineering, (2) manufacturing, and (3) research and development (R&D). In design and engineering, Computime had over 100 design engineers, and the design and engineering services were an integral part of the company's strategy. This division worked in conjunction with the customers' product development team to achieve synergy. Computime could provide turnkey product design services in the area of company's core technologies, including systems, software, electrical, mechanical, and packaging capabilities. The design group's expertise included power supplies, programmable controls, logic technology, wireless controls, and motion-sensing technologies, as well as experience in designing products including microprocessors, backlit LCD, environmental control, rolling code remote control, infrared/radio frequency devices, touch screen, and voice input technologies. Computime was particularly strong in designing and manufacturing electronic control devices for residential, commercial, and industrial applications. The company designed and built world-class, end-to-end control systems for home appliances, wireless applications, heat ventilation and air conditioning (HVAC) systems, and home comfort appliances.

In manufacturing, Computime's principal plant was located in Shenzhen. It employed approximately 2,800 people, with over 350,000 square feet (33,000 square meters) of manufacturing space. The plant was vertically integrated and strived for zero defects. Manufacturing was certified to the Six-Sigma standard, and the company attempted to control quality and cost over every aspect of manufacturing process. In addition, Computime's vertically integrated plant lowered manufacturing costs and improved the quality of a range of manufactured products.

R&D was indispensable. However, facing strong competition, Bernard was thinking of outsourcing the R&D arm. Currently, Computime had a technology center in Louisville, Kentucky. Bernard planned to buy part of a company at a university-sponsored technology center in Hong Kong that was developing technology that could enhance Computime's business. By doing so, Computime obtained the right to obtain more cutting-edge technology without the cost and risk of in-house R&D. Bernard considered that such a strategy fitted well with the firm's scale, especially when much resource would be locked into new investments for the reorganization.

Bernard's strategy of acquiring innovation was not the common practice in Hong Kong.[1] In addition, there was always the risk that little would come out from the acquisition. But this did not discourage Bernard as he believed that he had to take the chance after conducting his own due diligence on the efficacy of the technology being developed.

Customer Focus

By 2003, Computime's OEM customer base had expanded to include some of the most demanding companies in the world, such as Electrolux, GE, Honeywell, Siemens, and Whirlpool. For each large customer, Computime provided a single point of contact and a dedicated team. Computime managers had a saying that customers should be able to write what they wanted on the back of a napkin. Then, Computime would design, engineer, and manufacture a viable solution from scratch.

The unique quality of Computime's OEM customer base provided the company with a "global footprint" and access to a network of component suppliers. Computime's international presence in North America, Europe, and Asia allowed rapid customer response, independent of time zones. Bernard saw the demanding customer base as an asset. This provided quality feedback that forced the company to constantly push for improvement.

Also to push the company even harder, Bernard insisted that Computime benchmark its engineering, manufacturing, testing, and supply chain management against the best global practices. Stringent process management and control systems were a part of Computime's objective of exceeding customers' quality standards. To reach that goal, Computime attempted to empower every employee with the responsibility for identifying and preventing quality problems.

Vendors

Computime was ISO 9001/9002 and QS 9000 certified. The company's commitment to total quality management (TQM) made quality the primary focus of every phase of the product life cycle. The new product introduction (NPI) process assured that every product was built to the quality and design expectations of its customers. The company's approved and preferred vendor base included suppliers in Asia and

FIGURE 1 COMPUTIME'S BUSINESS MIX

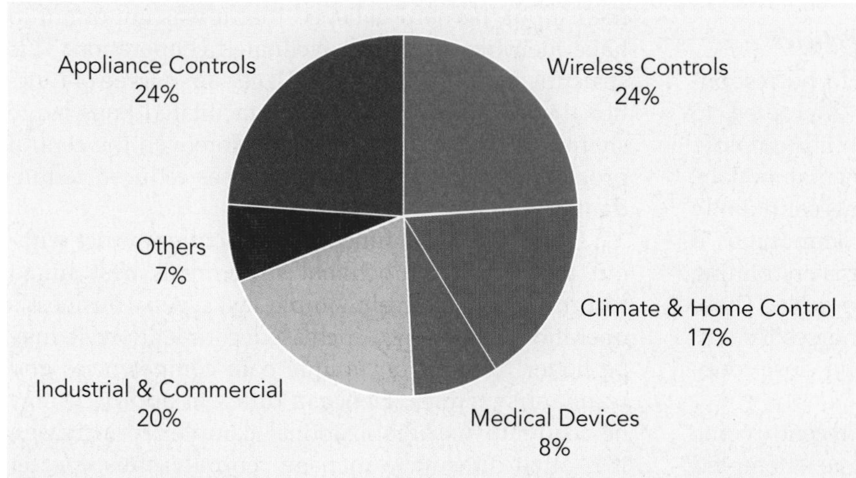

Source: Company records.

North America, and the company also maintained partnerships with leading technology developers in Japan and Hong Kong.

To become an "approved vendor," a component supplier had to undergo a thorough quality audit. The company then continuously tracked the quality and delivery performance of suppliers. In addition, Computime was determined to utilize the Six-Sigma program throughout the company. Employees were formally trained in Six-Sigma protocol and were encouraged to apply it.

Although Computime was shortening the time required for delivery from its suppliers, Computime's customers were, in turn, shortening the time required for delivery from it. For example, one of the multinationals that used to give 12-week forecasts now would only commit to 4. However, the vendors still delivered in 12 weeks, which was out of Computime's control. If the supply chain was mismanaged or Computime was not agile, it would be forced to reconcile the two deadlines.

Human Resource Management (HRM)

HR was managed under a three-layer structure. The first layer was the benefits and compensation committee chaired by Bernard. The second layer was the HR department, which was under the supervision of the chief financial officer. Under the HR department, there were two divisions that managed daily operation in Hong Kong and mainland China, respectively. At Computime, HR decisions tended to be based on financial objectives rather than strategic objectives, which reflected the weak role that HRM played in the organization. Bernard envisioned that the passive administrative role of carrying out instructions would be transformed to an empowered, proactive, and strategic role in helping the company achieve its corporate and business goals. Yet, this type of policy faced obstacles in its operations in China, where the culture did not naturally support the idea of employee empowerment.[2]

Social, Employee, and Environmental Policies

Bernard always advocated: "We want to be responsive to the community." Computime attempted to be a good corporate citizen, adhering to fair employment practices and minimal environmental impact. In the area of social policy, Computime continually strived to strengthen its ties with the communities it was operating in, with particular emphasis on training and opportunity programs for young people. These included internships and cooperative courses for students, ongoing scholarship assistance, and close cooperation with local universities.

Whereas labor policies in China had recently come under international scrutiny, Computime attempted to look after employee well-being and satisfaction. In particular, it strived for a safe and nonharmful working environment, providing its employees with safety training, regular medical exams, and a health insurance plan. To further individual development, the company sponsored "Employee Learning Circles" and a broad range of recreational activities. Bernard did not foresee any of this changing as a result of his envisioned restructuring.

Computime was also proactive in environmental protection. It carried on a program of conservation, preventing pollution, recycling reusable materials, and eliminating harmful chemicals from the manufacturing. These policies set it far above the average Pearl River Delta company.

Management Philosophy

Computime believed that the most valuable resources were its people and that they were important to the company's success. The company emphasized employee training and supported continuous learning and career development. Bernard said, "I truly believe in training . . . wish I could share with you how much money and time I spent in training." Bernard believed that people were not solely motivated by a paycheck and thus could not be "purchased." They aspired for learning and development. At Computime, management was striving to create an innovative, flexible, team-driven culture in which employees could realize their full potential.

Organizational Structure

By 2003, Computime had outgrown the simple structure of a family firm, and a two-tier management team had evolved. It consisted of a "core" team with five people and the remainder of the team, with approximately 14 members, who managed the individual organizational functions. The functional line managers led the management teams in dominant organizational areas, namely, manufacturing, marketing, and accounting. When major decisions were made, functional management teams were included to provide their input. Bernard believed that it was important to have their buy-in, which facilitated cooperation. This structure not only allowed for a certain degree of functional specialization, but it also facilitated knowledge sharing and idea development. Moreover, the central procurement and material purchases reduced redundant personnel.

However, such a functional structure was not without problems. A functional structure is best suited to firms with relatively simple tasks. As a business's operations experience increased competition, it may be better to focus on unique core competencies and resultant synergies. Hence, a different approach may be required. As organizational complexity increases, it is often difficult to manage centrally; thus, greater decentralization and specialization may be required. A functional structure may be unable to coordinate the numerous functions and organizational levels, which in turn could stifle efficiency.

This is where Bernard saw the need for change. He believed that the disadvantages of centralization had begun to outweigh the advantages. The organizational structure was increasingly becoming bureaucratic, which slowed responses to customers. According to Bernard, this put the company at a disadvantage in the increasingly hypercompetitive electronic OEM business. Bernard stated: "we are growing, not necessarily too big, however we are beginning to see red tape and slower response in the organization . . . the functional guys are saying 'we can't do this because we have to fill in three more forms . . . we need to get ten signatures' and so on. This slows things down."

Competition in the Electronics OEM Industry

While Computime was in a relatively good position, it faced intense competition in its core electronic manufacturing services (EMS) business at both the regional and global levels. The global competitors consisted of companies such as Solectron (operating in more than 20 countries, including three manufacturing sites in China) and Flextronics (with revenues of $13.1 billion in 2002 and approximately 95,000 employees). Recently, Sanmina had acquired SCI Systems to become Sanmina-SCI, the world's second largest EMS player—behind Flextronics. Similar to Computime, these organizations provided design, manufacturing, and supply chain management to their customers. Yet, they were all larger. Moreover, global EMS companies were in the process of shifting manufacturing to China in response to its recent WTO entry. While Computime focused on the control business, many of these larger organizations were focusing on telecom, computer, and communications.

In addition to the global competitors, Computime also faced local competitors, such as Wong's Electronics and WKK Electronics based in Hong Kong and PCI Electronics Manufacturing Services in Singapore. In recent years, these local companies had put increasing emphasis on product diversification and the new market penetration. Many of these companies had also started as traditional Asian family businesses. They had already gone through major reorganization or even been publicly listed. Bernard believed that the local Chinese companies would become a formidable group of competitors. For this reason, he monitored the local competitors closely.

Bernard's Ideas for Restructuring Computime

When Bernard's father began manufacturing electronic products in 1974, the company only had a small domestic market. To survive, Mr. Auyang Sr. decided to enter the US market. After some years of modest success, the company's market share in the US was threatened by the entry of larger competitors, so in the 1990s, the company embarked on a program of geographic diversification and began operations in Japan and Europe. By 2003, it had three locations around the world, and the business had successfully diversified geographically with 40% of its overseas market outside the United States. Rapid expansion and diversification were keys to success. Bernard believed that competition, locally as well as globally, would become more intense. Turning down acquisition proposals from competitors, Bernard not only met challenges that were coming his way but also set out a plan to transform his family business.

Bernard was determined to make his own mark on the company; he hoped to increase sales by threefold and increase the profit margin by 2.5% by 2007. In addition to the financial performance, he also planned to set up a new factory. In five years, Bernard projected that Computime would encounter capacity issues—running out of space. To handle more diversified business and the specification trend, he was determined to decentralize and expand the manufacturing scale. In Bernard's words: "Selling globally is no longer a dream for small firms, but a matter of survival. Thus, Computime will look at how to achieve that and become an active global player."

Bernard called this a "3 by 5" plan, which was to be implemented by a three-step strategy. Stage 1 would be the Focus Stage where the top management team would identify the company's core competencies, formulate internal teams, and establish a structure to best leverage those competencies. Stage 2 would be the Specialize Stage in which the organization would identify optimal strategies, build the needed skill sets, and establish systems needed for implementation. Finally, Stage 3 was to be the Expansion Stage, whereby the company would set up the entities needed for expansion of the company's capabilities, revenues, and profit margins.

This was an ambitious plan. Bernard was convinced that the company would have to further restructure into specific divisions to handle this type of growth. Otherwise, he was afraid that the organization would become too unwieldy and inflexible. Computime's organizational structure in 2003 is contrasted with Bernard's proposed restructuring in Figure 2.

Phases of the Restructuring

The planned reorganization would be done in two steps. In the first step, the previous centralized manufacturing function would be divided and merged with the existing two strategic business units (SBUs), namely, Total Solution Provider (TSP) business and Advanced Control Technologies (ACT) business. The quality function would remain centralized, as would be the corporate function. A COO would be hired to manage the centralized quality control function. At the same time, each SBU would have its own marketing,

FIGURE 2 CURRENT STRUCTURE

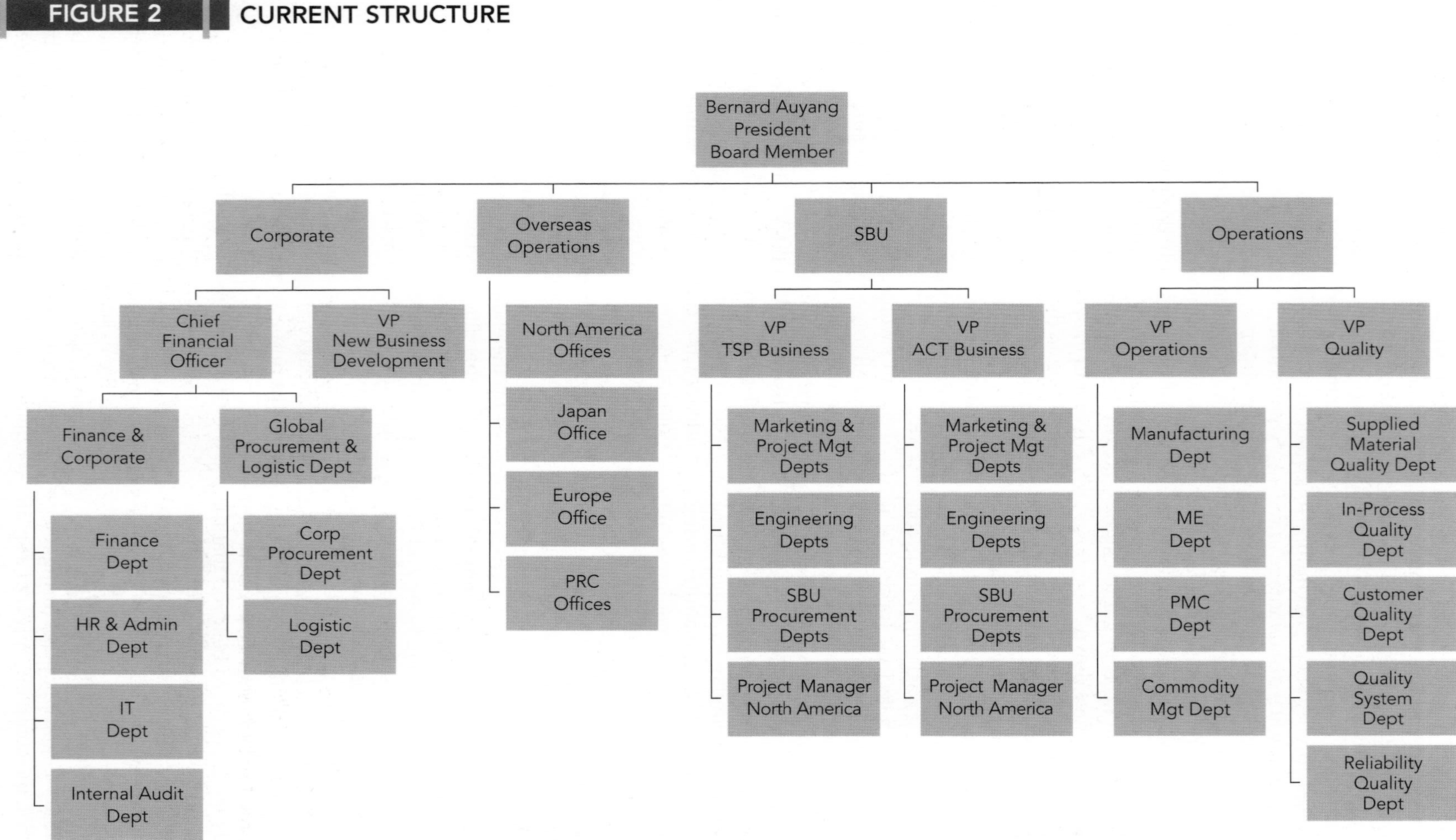

BERNARD'S PROPOSED STRUCTURE AFTER REORGANIZATION

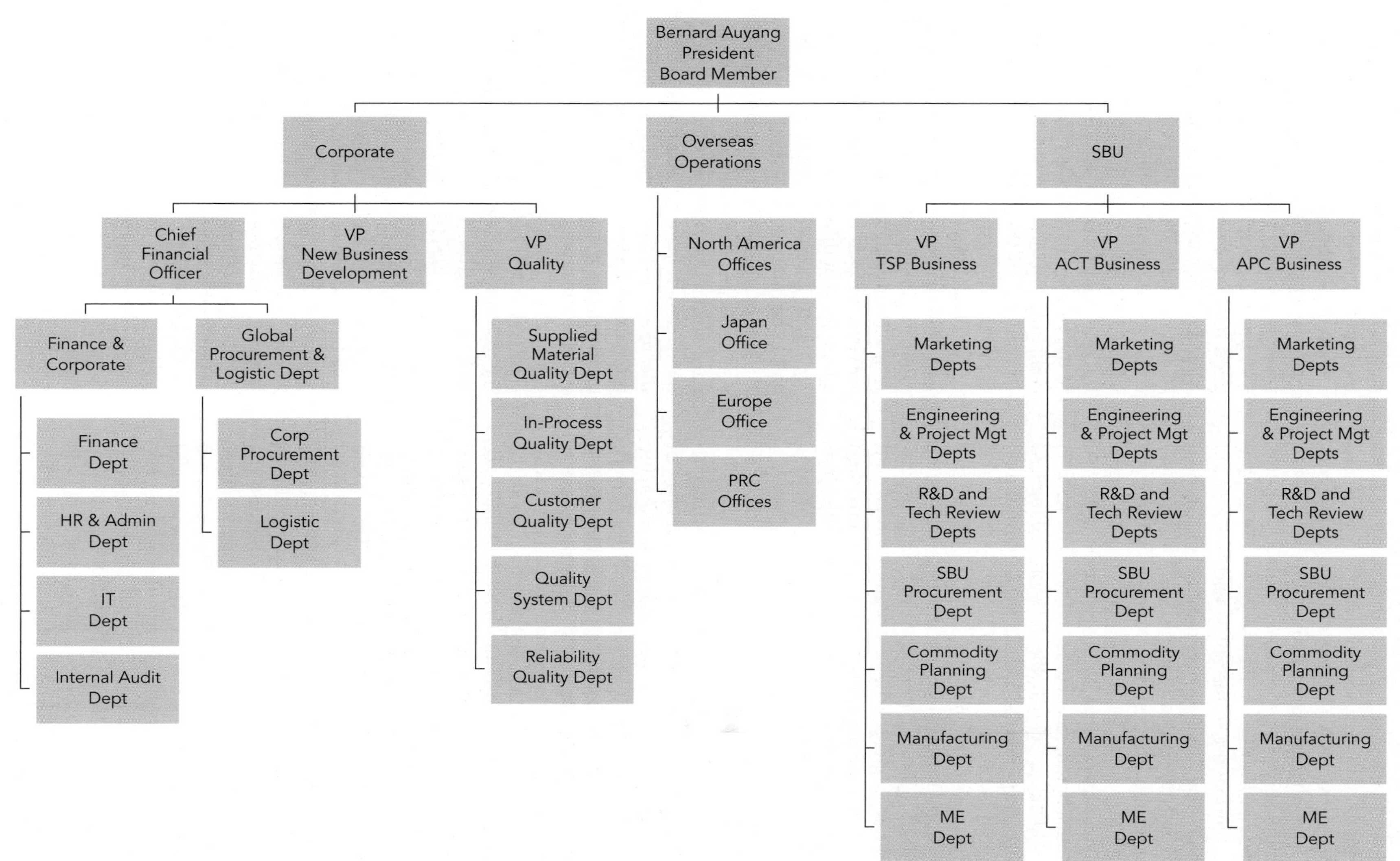

Source: Company records; SBU—Strategic Business Unit; TSP—Total Solution Provider; ACT—Advanced Control Technologies; APC—Appliance Control.

engineering, procurement, manufacturing, and R&D departments. As the existing SBUs became more independent, the second step was to create a new SBU—Appliance Control (APC) business. In short, the product lines were changed from two to three, with each SBU focusing on its own specialized business.

The decentralization would also give more responsibility and autonomy to the SBUs. Each SBU would be required to make its own decisions and hire its own executives and consequently would be held responsible for the results. The resulting structure within each individual SBU would be flatter, giving the managers more opportunity to focus on their specific tasks and train specialists in the needed disciplines. The restructuring would also accelerate the decision-making and implementation processes. Ultimately, Bernard hoped that this would improve organizational flexibility and provide the impetus to grow.

Bernard had learned from his business studies the importance of having an organizational structure that supports strategic goals. When the organization would grow, structure may experience "growing pains" and need to evolve to facilitate implementation of the strategies. To this end, Bernard believed that reorganization could help Computime achieve his objectives.

Making the Reorganization Happen

There is a Chinese saying that "a task that is well begun is half done." But even before the commencement of the reorganization, Bernard knew that he faced many challenges. Sitting in the office, he pondered how he could get the board of directors' approval. He was also concerned as to whether the employees would support this major restructuring, as human nature is such to avoid change. If he moved too fast, he might make the organizational members uncomfortable with the pace of change. However, if he moved too slowly, the board and other members might lose patience, or the organization could become bogged down in a state of limbo.

The immediate challenge facing Bernard was convincing the board of the merits of the plan. This would be difficult, as many members openly expressed their reservations. Although Computime was still a family business, the board was rather independent. It was composed of people who had expertise in the industry, including manufacturing specialists, engineers, business people, lawyers, and accountants. They believed that the firm should strengthen the R&D development and grow through consolidation and merging current units. Yet, Bernard's plan was to split up the organization. In his words, "If we collectively decide that investing R&D in certain areas is more important than investing in our manufacturing facility in that area, [we] need to be small enough to understand the implications of that." Bernard's vision differed from that of some of the board members. He believed that the path to growth was to have his professionals run smaller business units with focused business objectives.

Of course, this major reorganization would demand additional capital and HR that could be used for other possibly more productive purposes. Bernard believed that financing would not be an issue. Computime had good retained earnings, and the company maintained a good relationship with the local banking community. In that respect, Bernard believed that the company could make a small acquisition or even a major acquisition with few problems. However, HRM continued to be a major concern for several reasons. First, half of the employees who were in the "back room" of the company did not support the reorganization. They were afraid of the possible turmoil, especially when the external labor market was tight and restructuring could result in some employees being laid off. Bernard said the biggest challenge was to change people's mindset. To gauge the general attitude toward the restructuring, the company was carrying out monthly surveys. Bernard also wanted the workers to maintain a high level of diligence on tasks with high repeatability. Yet, maintaining stability during the reorganization would be difficult.

This is where HR could take a proactive stance—to communicate and justify what is going to happen. Bernard was also concerned that the company might not have enough talented managers to fulfill the needs of the reorganization. The decentralized SBUs wanted more experienced managers to be individual department heads, and each SBU needed to develop new job specifications, pay and benefits packages, and retraining. The company did not have enough experienced managers to fill these positions. In this sense, the restructuring would demand tough administrative tasks from HRM.

Thus far, the HR manager had failed to play an active role in the strategic planning process and did not display the forward-looking vision to help transform the company into a global player. Yet, Bernard thought that this lack of initiative was due to the simple and hierarchical tradition of the existing organizational structure. It took time for the current HR manager to adjust herself to the dramatically altered role expected under the reorganization. Bernard once said, "I would likely to do what is necessary to develop my managers." But on the other hand, if the current HR manager was not able to be up to the challenges and leverage her experience with Computime into the restructuring process, Bernard would consider hiring a professional manager from outside the company. Overall, the reorganization would be a highly risky strategy. In Bernard's words, unless the plan was well thought out and implemented, Computime could face "a disaster."

Strategic Challenges

The restructuring Bernard was contemplating, like every strategic decision, involved costs and benefits, and the ultimate outcome was uncertain. Board members were concerned that the functional expertise would diminish as the best functional heads were removed to lead the new divisions. Board members were also afraid that they could not obtain enough competent leaders and supporting staff to facilitate the consolidation. Furthermore, they were afraid that dividing the company would reduce economies of scale and could create three distinct cultures. On the whole, as the board members said, they felt comfortable about the financial side and the balance sheet and knew that they needed to reinvest in the company. What they wanted to know was whether the reorganization was the right way to reinvest rather than whether they could afford it.

With the passage of time, Computime's employee base had increased along with its explosive growth. In preparing the reorganization plan for the board, Bernard had thought long and hard about Computime's strengths and weaknesses. His analysis showed that the role of HRM had not kept up with the increasing complexity that came with a larger, more complex organization. Yet, with the impending restructuring, Bernard needed his HR staff to help him plan and carry out the changes with minimal negative impact. Computime also needed high-caliber managers who could perform in conditions marked by growth and fast advancing technology in a highly competitive business. Bernard had doubts about his managers' readiness and ability. Already, the changes were having an impact among the lower level staff. The uncertainty and ambiguity inherent in a situation of growth and change had resulted in the employees bickering over "territorial" issues of "who should be doing what." All these required HR to take a larger role in employee matters.

As Bernard sat at his desk thinking about the points raised by his board of directors, he realized that they were probably correct on a lot of the issues that they raised. Should he scale back his ambitions? How would the corporate office be financially supported after the reorganization of Computime into SBUs? Would it be perceived as a cost center? What needs to be done to build up the HR function and have it play its critical role? Should the firm hire a professional HR manager? Whatever direction he took to build his family business, Bernard was certain to face challenges.

Case Discussion Questions

1. What is the general environmental situation faced by Computime?
2. What is the rationale behind Bernard's reorganization idea? How can Bernard expand the business?
3. If you were an employee of Computime, would you welcome the restructuring plan? Why or why not? What steps can Bernard take to get organizational members to accept the reorganization and to make the transition go smoothly?
4. What are the major challenges facing Bernard in the course of the restructuring? How should he address those challenges?
5. Why does the board of directors have reservations regarding the reorganization plan? Are the reservations valid? What can Bernard do to win them over to his plan?
6. To carry out restructuring successfully, what are some of the HRM issues that Bernard should address? If you were the HR manager, what would you do?

[1] Source: http://www.gemconsortium.org. See *The Global Entrepreneurship Monitor (GEM) Hong Kong 2002 Report* (p. 50).

[2] See D. Ahlstrom, S. Foley, M. Young, and E. Chan, 2005, Human resource strategies for achieving competitive advantage in post WTO China. *Thunderbird International Business Review,* 47 (3): 263–285. A condensed version of this article was published by the German Chamber of Commerce in China in *Business Forum China,* March–April 2006: 13–17.

INTEGRATIVE CASE 4.4

SHAKTI: UNILEVER COLLABORATES WITH WOMEN ENTREPRENEURS IN RURAL INDIA

Ted London
University of Michigan

Maulin Vakil
University of North Carolina at Chapel Hill

Unilever in India

From ice cream to washing powder, the Anglo-Dutch group Unilever is one of the world's biggest makers of fast-moving consumer goods (FMCGs). The company grew out of a merger in 1930 between Dutch company Margarine Unie and British soap maker Lever Brothers. Today, Unilever markets renowned household names such as Pond's, Dove, Hellman's, Surf, Lipton, Axe, Bertolli, and numerous others and operates in over 100 countries. The company is a leader in several product categories in North America and Europe, such as frozen foods, margarines, olive oil, detergents, and tea.

Unilever products made their first appearance in India in 1888, when India was still a British colony. In 1956, the company merged its Indian operations to form Hindustan Lever Limited (HLL). HLL offered 10% of its equity to the Indian public, being the first among international companies in India to do so. Unilever, which has gradually divested its stake in HLL (also known as Unilever India), now holds 52% equity in HLL. The rest of the shares are distributed among about 380,000 individual shareholders and financial institutions.[1]

Today, India contributes approximately $2.5 billion of Unilever's nearly $40 billion sales revenues. HLL is comprised of two operating divisions: Home and Personal Products (HPC) (consisting of its detergents, soaps, and personal care lines of products) and Foods (consisting of staple foods, bakery, confectionary, beverages, and frozen foods). In past years, leading national and international publications like *The Economic Times, Business World, Far Eastern Economic Review,* and *Business Today* have frequently rated HLL as one of India's best managed and most admired companies and commended its achievements at enhancing value for its shareholders.

Selling to the Wealthy: A Strategy Rooted in Consumer Marketing and Distribution

HLL brought a scientific, consumer-oriented approach and competitive acumen to its business in India. Early on, the company became known and recognized for its various products that had slowly but steadily appeared on virtually every shop shelf across urban and semiurban India.

The company's philosophy as a maker of high-quality, mostly premium-priced products strongly influenced its marketing strategy. In the 1970s, HLL emerged as a prominent advertiser on the radio, magazines, and daily press, as well as billboards across the country, and spent as much as 10% of its annual turnover on advertising and media. Its brands quickly captured the imagination of the wealthy and middle class with the clever use of characters such as the Liril waterfall girl and leading Indian cinema celebrities who endorsed Lux bath soap.

At the same time, HLL invested in an extensive distribution system in India that eventually became a source of its competitive advantage. By focusing on efficiencies, reach, and visibility, it was able to stitch together a vast network of retail outlets that were connected seamlessly by the country's most sophisticated distribution chain. These retailers were loyal because a large portion of revenues typically was comprised of Unilever products. Using this distribution chain, HLL could efficiently provide its products to consumers in a convenient fashion, offering the company an advantage that was the envy of its competitors.

Yet, even HLL's large network was insufficient to cater to a majority of Indian people who lived in remote villages, where supplying and selling everyday products were not amenable to the company's existing distribution methods. Indeed, its vaunted distribution network failed to serve more than 500,000 rural villages, meaning that the company was ignoring more than 500 million potential customers (nearly half of the country's population) located at the base of the economic pyramid.[2] With this gap in distribution, HLL had little access to market knowledge about how the less affluent purchased and used personal care and food products that were the staple of the company's product line.

A New Challenge: Slowdown in Growth

The 1980s and 1990s proved to be outstanding years for HLL. It systematically outcompeted global giants such as Procter & Gamble and Colgate Palmolive, as well as local rivals such as Tata and Godrej. It took up leadership positions in several categories within the consumer packaged goods space. But after nearly two decades of

Research Assistant Maulin Vakil and Professor Ted London at the William Davidson Institute and the Ross School of Business at the University of Michigan prepared this case as a basis for class discussion. It is not intended to serve as an endorsement, sources of primary data, or illustration of effective or ineffective management.

heady expansion, HLL seemingly stopped growing in 1999. During 1993–1999, sales surged fivefold to $2.3 billion. But since 1999, growth had stagnated, and the company closed calendar year 2004 at $2.33 billion.[3] HLL's series of mergers had added market clout and created opportunities for efficiencies but had also made it difficult to maintain growth momentum.

Analysts highlighted some obvious areas of concern: a high margin structure, large overheads relative to those of its local competitors, and a lack of genuine product and business model innovation.[4] With a lack of growth, increasing attention was placed on HLL's Millennium Plan—an ambitious blueprint outlining the company's growth strategies for the 21st century.

HLL's Millennium Plan

> *Rural demand and consumption of consumer products is set to explode. The challenge for most companies is to be able to offer appropriate products in an affordable way in relatively remote locations. It is our view that India will soon see an Inflexion Point in rural consumption.*
>
> – Excerpted from Hindustan Lever Limited Chairman Mr. K. B. Dadiseth's address 7at the annual shareholders meeting held on April 25, 2000

On April 25, 2000, at the annual shareholders meeting, then Chairman K. B. Dadiseth (who has since retired) unveiled the much discussed Millennium Plan—a strategic blueprint for the company that had been prepared with external consultants. Ideas for growth were extensively debated, and the team of consultants and company managers identified nine ventures to further explore. These ventures were selected based on an assessment of the changing business environment in India, HLL's existing resources, and the company's ability to build new capabilities over time. A New Ventures Group was formed within the company to implement these new growth opportunities.

Among those that were selected was an idea that would later be dubbed Shakti, an initiative to increase HLL's penetration into rural India. The centerpiece of this initiative was a fundamentally different rural distribution system based on self-help groups (SHG), such as those used by Grameen Bank in Bangladesh.[5]

Rural India: Challenges and Opportunities

Approximately one-tenth of the world's population (and approximately three-quarters of India's) live in rural Indian villages. India's nearly 639,000 villages are spread over 128 million households and have a rural population of 742 million.[6] The Indian rural population is substantially poorer, with a per capita annual income below Rs.10,000 ($227),[7] compared to the national average of approximately Rs.21,000 ($477).[8] Table 1 shows the dispersion of rural income by household.

Due to the sheer size of rural India's population, HLL saw this as a potentially lucrative market for its consumer products. Indeed, rural India's consumption has also been growing steadily since the 1980s and is now bigger than the urban market for both FMCGs (53% share of the total market) and consumer durables (59%). More than half of HLL's products were bought by rural consumers. Yet when HLL considered that its products were currently available in less than 15% of the villages, the company recognized the vast untapped potential in rural India.

TABLE 1 DISTRIBUTION OF RURAL INCOME BY HOUSEHOLD

Consumer class	Annual income	Distribution by percentage of total population 1995–1996	Distribution by percentage of total population 2006–2007 (estimates)
Very Rich	Above Indian Rupees 215,000	0.3	0.9
Consuming Class	Indian Rupees 45,001– 215,000	13.5	25.0
Climber	Indian Rupees 22,001–45,000	31.6	49.0
Aspirant	Indian Rupees 16,001–22,000	31.2	14.0
Destitute	Indian Rupees 16,000 & Below	23.4	11.1
Total		**100.0**	**100.0**

Note: In December 1995, the exchange rate was US$1 = 35.2 Indian rupees; in May 2005, it was US$1 = 44 Indian rupees.

Source: National Council for Applied Economic Research. The NCAER study is based on the population data provided by the Census of India, which is conducted every 10 years. In 2001 (most recent data), the ratio of rural to urban population in India was 742 million to 285 million. The same ratio was 628 million to 217 million in 1991.

For HLL and other consumer products companies, several infrastructural and economic challenges make the task of reaching these small, dispersed markets extremely daunting. First, villages do not have the same infrastructure connectivity as large towns, making flow of goods difficult. For example, in the last 50 years, only 40% of villages have been connected by paved, "permanent" roads.[9]

Second, the majority of the 638,691 villages are highly scattered with relatively small populations (see Table 2). HLL, with the most extensive distribution network in the country, was able to reach only 100,000 of these directly. This geographic dispersion, coupled with low per capita volume demand, means that these markets are less cost effective to distribute into using traditional approaches due to the distribution challenges and high capital and operating expenditures.

Third, these villages have poor literacy levels and limited availability of electricity, resulting in low reach of traditional media such as print and television. And finally, there was the question of the need for consumer awareness to influence rural consumers into trying nonlocal alternatives for hygiene, personal care, and diet.

A Need for a New System

In the past, HLL had tried traditional approaches to expand reach, such as appointing new distributors and wholesalers. However, these projects were limited in their ability to solve the entire problem. To begin with, these projects required setting up an expensive distribution system in small markets. In addition, these efforts were unable to stimulate demand in villages where there was low awareness of Unilever products. They also failed to overcome logistical challenges such as getting products into markets without good roads or telephone networks. In the end, these efforts yielded only limited results, and what the company was looking for was a fundamentally different approach that overcame these distribution and marketing challenges.

Indeed, Shakti (which means "strength" or "empowerment" in many of the local Indian languages) was different from other rural expansion efforts by HLL, as well as by other consumer products companies in India, for two key reasons. First, it was designed to overcome most, if not all, of the hurdles encountered in prior rural forays while still maintaining channel control and cost efficiency. Second, the Shakti mindset provided the company an opportunity to participate in social and economic development of rural areas, a significant shift in the selling-only model that previously dictated MNC activities in rural markets.

How Shakti Works

The team at HLL manages three separate initiatives under the Shakti umbrella: (1) the Shakti Entrepreneur Program, (2) the Shakti Vani Program, and (3) the I-Shakti community portal. Shakti leverages the network of self-help groups that had been created by the federal and state governments across villages in India. These self-help groups were development initiatives targeted at enhancing local savings and industry (such as handicrafts) and creating a stronger social system within rural villages.

A typical self-help group consisted of 8 to 20 members, and activities included learning new vocational skills, airing grievances, and resolving local disputes. Moreover, these groups also acted as savings cooperatives. Daily contributions by the members are invested in a joint account and then loaned internally to members according to their needs. Based on savings, these groups also gained access to institutions engaged in microcredit lending activities, many of them supported by the government or local or international nonprofits.

However, the limited number of opportunities to use microcredit in developing new ventures was a continuing gap in the rural economy and hindered the development of self-help groups. Most microenterprises usually consisted of small

TABLE 2 DISTRIBUTION OF RURAL POPULATION

Size of population	No. of villages	% of total villages
Fewer than 200	92,541	15.6
200–500	127,054	21.4
501–1,000	144,817	24.4
1,001–2000	129,662	21.9
2,001–5,000	80,313	13.5
5,001–10,000	18,758	3.2
Total no. of villages	**593,154***	**100.0**

*Total inhabited villages are 638,691.
Source: Census of India, 2001.

ventures such as basket weaving, local handicrafts, and agriculture projects that produced outputs sold within the same community. The managers at HLL recognized the opportunity to create a new type of profitable venture by applying microfinance to building a local business that had long-term profit and growth potential for the entrepreneur.

Shakti Entrepreneur Program

As the longest running and most successful Shakti initiative, the Shakti Entrepreneur Program seeks to expand HLL's reach by involving the village communities, specifically rural women, into its business venture. Leveraging the participants of existing self-help groups, HLL invites one woman (or sometimes more depending on the size of the area to be served) from a target village to become a Shakti entrepreneur or Shakti-amma[10] to promote and distribute Unilever products within of a group of four to six neighboring communities. Often in collaboration with local partners, the Shakti team holds a local Concept Selling Meeting in which prospective entrepreneurs are screened on a range of criteria. These include support extended to the entrepreneur from her family and community, access to funds and current sources of income, ability to devote time and energy to Shakti, and ability to manage the business without ongoing active supervision.

Initially, Shakti entrepreneurs are expected to invest around Rs.10,000 ($227, which is approximately equal to the annual per capita income in rural India) to buy the necessary inventory of Unilever products. These funds are usually made available via micro-credit loans through self-help groups because perspective rural entrepreneurs may not have access to traditional means of credit. Sometimes, though, bank loans may be obtained against collateral such as cattle and livestock. Unilever products such as soaps, laundry detergent, oral and skin care products, hair oil and shampoos, flour, tea, and salt are provided in affordable, small, "daily-use" sizes (e.g., sachets), each costing between Rs.2 to Rs.18 ($0.04 to $0.38). The entrepreneur is supported by an HLL team member, the rural sales promoter (RSP), who is responsible for training each Shakti entrepreneur in the skills required to be a distributor.

Shakti entrepreneurs are encouraged to sell to the village community as well as to small local retailers (Figure 1). They sell to consumers at the retail prices and to retailers at the trade price, earning 11% to 13% on consumer sales and 3% on trade sales. Monthly turnover is expected to be approximately equivalent to the initial inventory of Rs.10,000 ($227), although in the case of mature entrepreneurs, it is known to exceed Rs.25,000 ($568). For the typical entrepreneur, this

FIGURE 1 A SHAKTI ENTREPRENEUR

Photo by Maulin Vakil

leaves her with a net monthly profit of Rs.700–1,200 ($16–$27), which is equal to or exceeds the average monthly income in rural India. Moreover, for most Shakti entrepreneurs, these business activities are designed to be supplemental in nature, leaving sufficient time for existing local activities.

Entrepreneurs are known to apply ingenuity in overcoming the infrastructural challenges faced in rural India. For example, an entrepreneur in Nalgonda district was able to expand her market reach by contracting the back-hauling services of an auto-rickshaw that plied between neighboring villages. Others are known to hire relatives and friends in surrounding villages to act as salespersons. HLL's RSPs also assist the entrepreneur in creating sales promotions and special events, such as a health day,[11] which brings a doctor to the village to disseminate information about health and hygiene, and Shakti day, which creates a village fair atmosphere with games, songs, and product giveaways.

Shakti Vani Program

The second initiative in Shakti is a communication-led program called Shakti *Vani* (Sanskrit for "speech"). Vani is a socially led communication effort that involves a Vani (speaker), appointed from the community, to spread information and awareness on important issues such as health, hygiene, sanitation, and personal care. The objective for this program is to be an advertising medium within the rural markets for both health challenges and company solutions. Hence, Vani helps create awareness of not only the problems but also how HLL's products offer ways to overcome them.

The Vani is appointed from the self-help group and, after a training program, travels from village to village spreading information about Unilever products at gatherings such as village events, local schools, and self-help group meetings. The Vani earns a daily salary based on the route and villages covered. The program does not generate any direct revenues for HLL. Rather, it is designed to be a cost-effective approach to promoting company brands. The program covered 10,000 villages in 2004 and targeted 50,000 more in 2005. It was expected to cost around Rs.9,000–11,000 per village per year.

Shakti Community Portal

A recent addition to Shakti is the I-Shakti community-based portal (Figure 2). I-Shakti makes available Internet connectivity, relevant information, and education services to rural areas. Currently, the project has been rolled out in Andhra Pradesh in south-central India in cooperation with the local government, which has set up computer kiosks in local villages. The portal has modules covering important information such as health, sanitation, agriculture, and animal husbandry and has also linked to the Internet via a once-daily dial-up connection. For villages poorly connected with road transport, this results in a significant advantage when compared with the need to travel to towns for basic information about prices of agricultural outputs, local weather forecasts, and medical queries.

Although the I-Shakti program was designed primarily as a resource for the local community, the company can also use this as a medium to convey its brand messages. In an area that was not conducive to traditional advertising methods, these community-based portals provided a useful marketing tool. By building brand messages into the software package, HLL's I-Shakti portal can help the company market to areas with limited media coverage and low literacy. To scale up the program to other regions, the cost was estimated to be approximately Rs.29,000 (US$648) per portal.

FIGURE 2 AN I-SHAKTI

Photo by Maulin Vakil

Shakti Today

Since its inception in 2001, Shakti has expanded its network to cover 80,000 villages through 25,000 Shakti entrepreneurs in 12 of 28 states of India. What makes the project especially intriguing is that it offers a model for generating economic benefits for the company while also producing social benefits for rural communities.

Economically, HLL sees considerable advantages from the Shakti model as an entrepreneurial approach to entering new markets in rural India. First, it leads to greater reach without having to augment an expensive distribution chain built around large volumes. Second, it creates goodwill and awareness for the company and its products by using local talent to act as spokespersons in areas where traditional advertising media cannot reach. In this environment, word of mouth is an effective source of influence and persuasion. Third and finally, it creates a stake in the communities within which Shakti operates, creating a first-mover advantage over rival FMCG companies as well as countering the future growth of possible imitation products.

An important component of the local social impact of Shakti comes from its focus on women entrepreneurs. As other microcredit initiatives serving the rural poor have shown, women on average are better borrowers than men. Women have better repayment rates and are more likely to invest profits in opportunities to improve their families' condition.

Furthermore, HLL also believed that improving the condition of women could positively impact their status in the family and in the community. Gaining control over some portion of household income can empower women and help alleviate some of the gender inequality that exists in families in rural India. Additionally, being a Shakti entrepreneur can generate newfound respect for these women by others in the community. To quote a Shakti entrepreneur, "Now, when I go out of the house, everyone immediately recognizes me and calls out 'Shakti-amma' . . . I want my children to have even greater opportunities and I think that this can only happen with education."

Shakti: The Challenges Ahead

The Shakti model took some time to develop before it was ready for large-scale implementation. The project was approved within HLL in 2000, and by the end of 2003, there were fewer than 3,000 entrepreneurs. By mid-2005, scale-up was beginning to occur, and the Shakti team was looking to extend its reach to 100,000 villages and 30,000 entrepreneurs by the end of 2006. HLL, however, is still looking to refine its model. The Shakti management team is exploring ways to increase the income of the individual Shakti entrepreneurs, which they feel will help manage the dropout rates. They also recognize that additional training is crucial for the entrepreneur to improve her earning capabilities. Although dropout rates are declining, they are still around 5% to 7% per quarter.

The sheer size of operations as the initiative scales up has also brought challenges. Shakti began as a two-member team at HLL with ambitious goals. Today, the project has relationships with over 350 nonprofit organizations and other nontraditional partners. For Shakti, local and international nonprofits play a vital role in providing an understanding of local communities. Moreover, they act as aggregators of the local communities through the self-help groups that they run and offer Shakti local credibility due to the goodwill established in rural villages. To help manage these new partnerships, the Shakti team has grown to 45 at HLL. Collaborating with such a diverse and growing group of partners, however, brings out a set of challenges around relationship management and social performance expectations that are new for HLL.

Is Shakti a Solution to the Growth Crisis at HLL?

By the end of 2006, Shakti was poised to reach 100,000 villages and 30,000 entrepreneurs. As a result, the Shakti model has been extensively studied by other Unilever subsidiaries, journalists, and students as well as competitors. Currently, Shakti-inspired models are being implemented in Unilever Bangladesh and Unilever Sri Lanka. Yet, crucial questions remain: Will Shakti and the base-of-the-pyramid markets it targets deliver to HLL much needed long-term growth and become a key source of future profitability? If other competitors introduce similar distribution approaches, will Shakti need to modify its business model? And can HLL convert this ambitious new rural thrust into a source of sustainable competitive advantage?

Case Discussion Questions

1. From a resource-based view, what were HLL's competitive advantages prior to launching Shakti?
2. From an institution-based view, what are the barriers against ventures such as Shakti?
3. Why is HLL pursuing Shakti? Is Shakti successful?
4. From the perspective of those at the base of the pyramid, what is the impact of Shakti's activities on poverty alleviation?
5. What metrics can Shakti use to measure its impact?
6. What should Shakti do to enhance its poverty alleviation impact?

[1] Hindustan Lever Limited Corporate Profile, http://www.hll.com.

[2] C. K. Prahalad & S. L. Hart, 2002, The fortune at the bottom of the pyramid. *Strategy + Business*, 26, First Quarter: 2–14.

[3] For a new improved HLL, see http://wwwrediff.com.

[4] A premium future for HLL, *Economic Times*, September 4, 2004.

[5] Grameen Bank was a pioneering microcredit organization started in 1976 in Bangladesh by economics professor Mohammad Yunus. The bank defied conventional banking rules by lending to the poor with no collateral and relied on self-help groups as a means to ensure accountability of borrowers. As of 2005, Grameen Bank had made cumulative loans of over US$5 billion and maintained a repayment rate of 96%, higher than that of traditional commercial banks. Widely admired by the development community, Grameen's model has been replicated in a number of other emerging economies.

[6] Census of India, 2001.

[7] Census of India, 2001; US$1 = Indian Rs.44, as per foreign exchange rate in May 2005.

[8] National Council for Applied Economic Research.

[9] Issues in Rural Markets, Pradeep Kashyap.

[10] *-amma*: literally, mother but also a general term for elder women in India.

[11] C. K. Prahalad, 2004, *The Fortune at the Bottom of the Pyramid: Eradicating Poverty through Profits*, Philadelphia, PA: Wharton School Publishing.

GLOSSARY

absolute advantage The economic advantage one nation enjoys that is absolutely superior to other nations.

absorptive capacity The ability to recognize the value of new information, assimilate it, and apply it.

accommodative strategy A strategy that is characterized by some support from top managers, who may increasingly view CSR as a worthwhile endeavor.

acquisition The transfer of the control of operations and management from one firm (target) to another (acquirer), the former becoming a unit of the latter.

acquisition premium The difference between the acquisition price and the market value of target firms.

adaptability The ability to change supply chain configurations in response to long-term changes in the environment and technology.

administrative policy Bureaucratic rules that make it harder to import foreign goods.

agency costs The costs associated with principal-agent relationships.

agency relationship The relationship between principals (such as shareholders) and agents (such as managers).

agency theory A theory that focuses on principal-agent relationships (or in short, agency relationships).

agent A person (such as manager) to whom authority is delegated.

agglomeration The location advantages that arise from the clustering of economic activities in certain locations.

agility The ability to quickly react to unexpected shifts in supply and demand.

alignment The alignment of interest of various players.

Andean Community A customs union in South America that was launched in 1969.

antidumping duty Pentalties levied on imports that have been "dumped" (selling below costs to "unfairly" drive domestic firms out of business).

antitrust laws Laws that attempt to curtail anticompetitive business practices.

antitrust policy Laws designed to combat monopolies and cartels.

Asia-Pacific Economic Cooperation (APEC) The official title for regional economic integration involving 21 member economies around the Pacific.

Association of Southeast Asian Nations (ASEAN) The organization underpinning regional economic integration in Southeast Asia.

attack An initial set of actions to gain competitive advantage.

balance of payments A country's international transaction statement, including merchandise trade, service trade, and capital movement

balance of trade The aggregation of importing and exporting that leads to the country-level trade surplus or deficit.

balance sheet approach An expatriate compensation approach that balances the cost of living differences based on parent country levels and adds a financial inducement to make the package attractive.

bandwagon effect The result of investors moving as a herd in the same direction at the same time.

bargaining power The ability to extract a favorable outcome from negotiations due to one party's strengths.

base of the pyramid The vast majority of humanity, about four billion people, who make less than $2,000 a year.

benchmarking An examination as to whether a firm has resources and capabilities to perform a particular activity in a manner superior to competitors.

bid rate The price offered to buy a currency.

born global Start-up companies that attempt to do business abroad from inception.

Bretton Woods system A system in which all currencies were pegged at a fixed rate to the US dollar.

BRIC A newly coined acronym for the emerging economies of Brazil, Russia, India, and China.

build-operate-transfer (BOT) agreement A nonequity mode of entry used to build a longer term presence.

capability The tangible and intangible assets a firm uses to choose and implement its strategies.

capacity to punish Sufficient resources possessed by a price leader to deter and combat defection.

capital flight A phenomenon in which a large number of individuals and companies exchange domestic currencies for a foreign currency.

captive sourcing Setting up subsidiaries abroad—the work done is in-house but the location is foreign. Conceptually, this is also known as foreign direct investment (FDI).

cartel An entity that engages in output- and price-fixing, involving multiple competitors.

causal ambiguity The difficulty of identifying the causal determinants of successful firm performance.

center of excellence An MNE subsidiary explicitly recognized as a source of important capabilities, with the intention that these capabilities be leveraged by and/or disseminated to other subsidiaries.

CEO duality The CEO serves as a board chair.

civilization The highest cultural grouping of people and the broadest level of cultural identity people have.

civil law A legal tradition that uses comprehensive statutes and codes as a primary means to form legal judgments.

classical trade theories The major theories of international trade that were advanced before the 20th century, which consist of mercantilism, absolute advantage, and comparative advantage.

clean (or **free**) **float** A pure market solution to determine exchange rates.

cluster Countries that share similar cultures together.

code of conduct A set of guidelines for making ethical decisions.

code of conduct (code of ethics) Written policies and standards for corporate conduct and ethics.

cognitive pillar The internalized, taken-for-granted values and beliefs that guide individual and firm behavior.

collectivism The idea that the identity of an individual is primarily based on the identity of his or her collective group.

collusion Collective attempts between competing firms to reduce competition.

collusive price setting Price setting by monopolists or collusion parties at a higher than competitive level.

co-marketing Efforts among a number of firms to jointly market their products and services.

command economy An economy in which all factors of production are government- or state-owned and controlled, and all supply, demand, and pricing are planned by the government.

commoditization A process of market competition through which unique products that command high prices and high margins gradually lose their ability to do so—these products thus become "commodities."

common law A legal tradition that is shaped by precedents and traditions from previous judicial decisions.

common market Combining everything a customs union has, a common market, in addition, permits the free movement of goods and people.

comparative advantage Relative (not absolute) advantage in one economic activity that one nation enjoys in comparison with other nations.

compensation The determination of salary and benefits.

competition policy Policy governing the rules of the game in competition in a country.

competitive dynamics The actions and responses undertaken by competing firms.

competitor analysis The process of anticipating a rivals' actions in order to both revise a firm's plan and prepare to deal with rivals' responses.

complementary assets The combination of numerous resources and assets that enable a firm to gain a competitive advantage.

concentrated ownership and control Founders start up firms and completely own and control them on an individual or family basis.

concentration ratio The percentage of total industry sales accounted for by the top four, eight, or twenty firms.

contender strategy This strategy centers on a firm engaging in rapid learning and then expanding overseas.

context The underlying background upon which interaction takes place.

contractual (nonequity-based) alliances Alliances that are based on contracts and that do not involve the sharing of equity.

copyrights Exclusive legal rights of authors and publishers to publish and disseminate their work.

corporate governance The relationship among various participants in determining the direction and performance of corporations.

corporate social responsibility (CSR) The consideration of, and response to, issues beyond the narrow economic, technical, and legal requirements of the firm to accomplish social benefits along with the traditional economic gains which the firm seeks.

corruption The abuse of public power for private benefits, usually in the form of bribery.

counterattack A set of actions in response to an attack.

country-of-origin effect The positive or negative perception of firms and products from a certain country.

country or regional manager The business leader of a specific geographic area or region.

cross-listing Listing shares on foreign stock exchanges.

cross-market retaliation The ability of a firm to expand in a competitor's market if the competitor attacks in its original market.

cross-shareholding Both firms invest in each other to become cross-shareholders.

cultural distance The difference between two cultures along some identifiable dimensions (such as individualism).

cultural intelligence An individual's ability to understand and adjust to new cultures.

culture The collective programming of the mind that distinguishes the members of one group or category of people from another.

currency board A monetary authority that issues notes and coins convertible into a key foreign currency at a fixed exchange rate.

currency hedging A transaction that protects traders and investors from exposure to the fluctuations of the spot rate.

currency risk The fluctuations of the foreign exchange market.

currency swap A foreign exchange transaction between two firms in which one currency is converted into another in Time 1, with an agreement to revert it back to the original currency at a specific Time 2 in the future.

customs union One step beyond a free trade area (FTA), a customs union imposes common external policies on nonparticipating countries.

deadweight costs Net losses that occur in an economy as the result of tariffs.

defender strategy This strategy centers on leveraging local assets in areas in which MNEs are weak.

defensive strategy A strategy that focuses on regulatory compliance with little top management commitment to CSR causes.

democracy A political system in which citizens elect representatives to govern the country on their behalf.

demonstration effect (**contagion** or **imitation effect**) The reaction of local firms to rise to the challenge demonstrated by MNEs through learning and imitation.

development The longer term, broader preparation to improve managerial skills for a better career.

diffused ownership Publicly traded corporations owned by numerous small shareholders but none with a dominant level of control.

direct export The sale of products made by firms in their home country to customers in other countries.

dirty (or **managed**) **float** The common practice of determining exchange rates through selective government intervention.

dissemination risks The risks associated with unauthorized diffusion of firm-specific know-how.

distribution channel The set of firms that facilitates the movement of goods from producers to consumers.

dodger strategy A strategy that centers on cooperating through joint ventures (JVs) with MNEs and sell-offs to MNEs.

downstream vertical FDI A type of vertical FDI in which a firm engages in a downstream stage of the value chain in two different countries.

dumping An exporter selling below cost abroad and planning to raise prices after eliminating local rivals.

economic system Rules of the game on how a country is governed economically.

economic union In addition to having all the features of a common market, members of an economic union coordinate and harmonize economic policies.

efficiency seeking Firms' quest to single out the most efficient locations featuring a combination of scale economies and low-cost factors.

emerging economies A term that has gradually replaced the term *developing* countries since the 1990s. Another often used term is **emerging markets**.

entrepreneurs Those who may be founders and owners of new businesses or managers of existing firms.

entrepreneurship The identification and exploitation of previously unexplored opportunities.

equity-based alliances Alliances that involve the use of equity

equity mode A mode of entry (JVs and wholly owned subsidiaries) that is indicative of relatively larger, harder to reverse commitments.

ethical imperialism The absolute belief that "there is only one set of Ethics (with the capital E), and we have it."

ethical relativism A perspective that suggests that all ethical standards are relative.

ethics The principles, standards, and norms of conduct governing individual and firm behavior.

ethnocentric approach An emphasis on the norms and practices of the parent company (and the parent country of the MNE) by relying on PCNs.

ethnocentrism A self-centered mentality by a group of people who perceive their own culture, ethics, and norms as natural, rational, and morally right.

euro The currency currently used in 12 EU countries.

euro zone The 12 EU countries that currently use the euro as the official currency.

European Union (EU) The official title of European economic integration since 1993.

exit-based mechanisms Corporate governance mechanisms that focus on exit, indicating that shareholders no longer have patience and are willing to "exit" by selling shares.

expatriate (expat) A nonnative employee who works in a foreign country.

expatriate manager A manager who works abroad (expat in short).

expatriation The process of selecting, managing, and motivating expatriates to work abroad.

explicit collusion Firms directly negotiate output, fix pricing, and divide markets.

explicit knowledge Knowledge that is codifiable (that is, can be written down and transferred with little loss of its richness).

exporting Selling abroad.

export intermediary A firm that performs an important "middleman" function by linking sellers and buyers overseas that otherwise would not have been connected.

expropriation (1) Government's confiscation of foreign assets; (2) the activities that enrich controlling shareholders at the expense of minority shareholders.

extender strategy This strategy centers on leveraging homegrown competencies abroad.

factor endowments The extent to which different countries possess various factors, such as labor, land, and technology.

factor endowment theory (or **Heckscher-Ohlin theory**) A theory that suggests that nations will develop comparative advantage based on their locally abundant factors.

FDI flow The amount of FDI moving in a given period (usually a year) in a certain direction.

FDI inflow Inbound FDI moving into a country in a year.

FDI outflow Outbound FDI moving out of a country in a year.

FDI stock The total accumulation of inbound FDI in a country or outbound FDI from a country across a given period of time (usually several years).

feint A firm's attack on a focal arena important to a competitor but not the attacker's true target area.

femininity A relatively weak form of societal-level sex-role differentiation whereby more women occupy positions that reward assertiveness and more men work in caring professions.

first-mover advantage Advantage that first entrants enjoy and do not share with late entrants.

fixed exchange rate policy A policy that fixes the exchange rate of a currency relative to other currencies.

floating (or **flexible**) **exchange rate policy** The willingness of a government to let the demand and supply conditions determine exchange rates.

Foreign Corrupt Practices Act (FCPA) A US law enacted in 1977 that bans bribery to foreign officials.

foreign direct investment Investments in, controlling, and managing value-added activities in other countries.

foreign exchange market A market where individuals, firms, governments, and banks buy and sell foreign currencies.

foreign exchange rate The price of one currency in terms of another.

foreign portfolio investment Investment in a portfolio of foreign securities such as stocks and bonds.

formal institutions Institutions represented by laws, regulations, and rules

forward discount A condition under which the forward rate of one currency relative to another currency is higher than the spot rate.

forward premium A condition under which the forward rate of one currency relative to another currency is lower than the spot rate.

forward transaction A foreign exchange transaction in which participants buy and sell currencies now for future delivery, typically in 30, 90, or 180 days, after the date of the transaction.

franchising Firm A's agreement to give Firm B the rights to use A's proprietary assets for a royalty fee paid to A by B. This is typically done in service industries.

free market view on FDI A political view that suggests that FDI, unrestricted by government intervention, will enable countries to tap into their absolute or comparative advantages by specializing in the production of certain goods and services.

free trade A theory that suggests that under free trade, each nation gains by specializing in economic activities in which it has absolute advantage.

free trade area (FTA) A group of countries that remove trade barriers among themselves.

Free Trade Area of the Americas (FTAA) A proposed free trade area for the entire Western Hemisphere.

gambit Withdrawal from a low-value market to attract rivals to divert resources into it and then to capture a high-value market.

game theory A theory that studies the interactions between two parties that compete and/or cooperate with each other.

General Agreement on Tariffs and Trade (GATT) A multilateral agreement governing the international trade of goods (merchandise).

General Agreement on Trade in Services (GATS) A WTO agreement governing the international trade of services.

geocentric approach A focus on finding the most suitable managers, who can be PCNs, HCNs, or TCNs.

geographic area structure An organizational structure that organizes the MNE according to different countries and regions.

global account structure A customer-focused dimension that supplies customers (often other MNEs) in a coordinated and consistent way across various countries.

global business Business around the globe

global economic integration Efforts to reduce trade and investment barriers around the globe.

globalization The close integration of countries and peoples of the world.

global matrix An organizational structure often used to alleviate the disadvantages associated with both geographic area and global product division structures, especially for MNEs adopting a transnational strategy.

global product division An organizational structure that assigns global responsibilities to each product division.

global standardization strategy A strategy that relies on the development and distribution of standardized products worldwide to reap the maximum benefits from low-cost advantages.

global sustainability The ability to meet the needs of the present without compromising the ability of future generations to meet their needs around the world.

global virtual team A team whose members are physically dispersed in multiple locations in the world. They operate on a virtual basis.

going rate approach A compensation approach that pays expatriates the prevailing (going) rate for comparable positions in a host country.

gold standard A system in which the value of most major currencies was maintained by fixing their prices in terms of gold, which served as the common denominator.

green-field operation Building factories and offices from scratch (on a proverbial piece of "green field" formerly used for agricultural purposes).

gross domestic product (GDP) The sum of value added by resident firms, households, and governments operating in an economy.

gross national income (GNI) GDP plus income from nonresident sources abroad. GNI is the term used by the World Bank and other international organizations to supersede the term GNP.

gross national product (GNP) Gross domestic product plus income from nonresident sources abroad.

herd mentality A behavior influenced by the movement of the crowd (or the herd) with little independent judgment.

high-context culture A culture in which communication relies a lot on the underlying unspoken context, which is as important as the words used.

home replication strategy A strategy that emphasizes international replication of home country-based competencies such as production scales, distribution efficiencies, and brand power.

horizontal FDI A type of FDI in which a firm duplicates its home country-based activities at the same value chain stage in a host country.

host country national (HCN) An individual from the host country who works for an MNE.

hubris A manager's overconfidence in his or her capabilities.

human resource management (HRM) Activities that attract, select, and manage employees.

importing Buying from abroad.

import quota Restrictions on the quantity of imports.

import tariff A tax imposed on imports.

indirect exports A way for SMEs to reach overseas customers by exporting through domestic-based export intermediaries.

individualism The perspective that the identity of an individual is fundamentally his or her own.

infant industry argument The argument that if domestic firms are as young as "infants," in the absence of government intervention, they stand no chance of surviving and will be crushed by mature foreign rivals.

informal institutions Institutions represented by cultures, ethics, and norms.

information asymmetries Asymmetric distribution and possession of information between two sides.

in-group Individuals and firms regarded as part of "us."

innovation seeking Firms target countries and regions renowned for generating world-class innovations.

inpatriation Relocating employees of a foreign subsidiary to the MNE's headquarters for the purposes of (1) filling skill shortages at headquarters and (2) developing a global mindset for such inpatriates.

inshoring Outsourcing to a domestic firm.

inside director A member of the board who is a top executive of the firm.

institutional distance The extent of similarity or dissimilarity between the regulatory, normative, and cognitive institutions of two countries.

institutional framework Formal and informal institutions governing individual and firm behavior.

institutional transitions Fundamental and comprehensive changes introduced to the formal and informal rules of the game that affect organizations as players.

institutions Formal and informal rules of the game.

institution-based view A leading perspective in global business that suggests that firm performance is, at least in part, determined by the institutional frameworks governing firm behavior around the world.

intangible resources and capabilities Assets that are hard to observe and difficult (or sometimes impossible) to quantify.

integration-responsiveness framework A framework of MNE management on how to simultaneously deal with two sets of pressures for global integration and local responsiveness.

intellectual property Intangible property that results from intellectual activity (such as books, videos, and websites).

intellectual property rights Rights associated with the ownership of intellectual property.

interlocking directorate A situation whereby two or more firms share one director affiliated with one firm who serves on multiple boards.

internalization The replacement of cross-border markets (such as exporting and importing) with one firm (the MNE) locating in two or more countries—essentially internalizing the external market transaction and turning it in-house.

international business (1) A business (firm) that engages in international (cross-border) economic activities and/or (2) the action of doing business abroad.

international division A structure that is typically set up when firms initially expand abroad, often engaging in a home replication strategy.

international entrepreneurship A combination of innovative, proactive, and risk-seeking behavior that crosses national borders and is intended to create wealth in organizations.

International Monetary Fund (IMF) An international organization that was established to promote international monetary cooperation, exchange stability, and orderly exchange arrangements.

international premium A significant pay raise commanded by expats when working overseas.

intrafirm trade International trade between two subsidiaries in two countries controlled by the same MNE.

joint venture (JV) A new corporate entity given birth and jointly owned by two or more parent companies.

knowledge management The structures, processes, and systems that actively develop, leverage, and transfer knowledge.

knowledge spillover Knowledge diffused from one firm to others among closely located firms.

labor relations A firm's relations with organized labor (unions) in both home and host countries.

late-mover advantages Advantages that late movers obtain and that first movers do not enjoy.

learning by doing An effective way to learn complex tasks.

learning race A situation in which alliance partners aim to outrun each other by learning the "tricks" from the other side as fast as possible.

legal system The rules of the game on how a country's laws are enacted and enforced.

letter of credit (L/C) A financial contract that states that the importer's bank will pay a specific sum of money to the exporter upon delivery of the merchandise.

leveraged buyout (LBO) A means by which private investors, often in partnership with incumbent managers, issue bonds and use the cash raised to buy the firm's stock.

liability of foreignness The inherent disadvantage that foreign firms experience in host countries because of their nonnative status.

licensing Firm A's agreement to give Firm B the rights to use A's proprietary technology (such as a patent) or trademark (such as a corporate logo) for a royalty fee paid to A by B. This is typically done in manufacturing industries.

lingua franca The dominance of one language as a global business language.

local content requirement A requirement that a certain proportion of the value of the goods made in one country originate from that country.

localization (multidomestic) strategy A strategy that focuses on a number of foreign countries/regions, each of which is regarded as a stand-alone "local" (domestic) market worthy of significant attention and adaptation.

local responsiveness The necessity to be responsive to different customer preferences around the world.

location Advantages enjoyed by firms operating in certain locations.

location-specific advantages Favorable locations in certain countries may give firms operating there an advantage.

long-term orientation A perspective that emphasizes perseverance and savings for future betterment.

low-context culture A culture in which communication is usually taken at face value without much reliance on unspoken context.

make-or-buy decision The decision on whether to produce in-house or to outsource.

management control rights The rights to appoint key managers and establish control mechanisms.

managerial human capital The skills and abilities acquired by top managers.

market commonality The overlap between two rivals' markets.

market economy An economy that is characterized by the "invisible hand" of market forces.

market imperfections (or **market failure**) The imperfect rules governing international transactions.

marketing Efforts to create, develop, and defend markets that satisfy the needs and wants of individual and business customers.

marketing mix The four underlying components of marketing: product, price, promotion, and place.

market orientation A philosophy or way of thinking that places the highest priority on the creation of superior customer value in the marketplace.

market seeking Firms' quest to go after countries that offer strong demand for their products and services.

market segmentation A way to identify consumers who differ from others in purchasing behavior.

market transition debate The debate about how to make the transition to a market economy work in the most effective and least disruptive way.

masculinity A relatively strong form of societal-level sex-role differentiation whereby men tend to have occupations that reward assertiveness and women tend to work in caring professions.

merchandise Tangible products being traded.

Mercosur A customs union in South America that was launched in 1991.

merger The combination of operations and management of two firms to establish a new legal entity.

microfinance Lending institutions provide tiny loans ($50–$300) to entrepreneurs in developing countries that would lift them out of poverty.

micro-macro link The informal interpersonal relationships (micro) among managers of different units that may greatly facilitate intersubsidiary cooperation (macro) among various units.

mixed economy An economy that has elements of both a market economy and a command economy.

modern trade theories The major theories of international trade that were advanced in the 20th century, which consist of product life cycle, strategic trade, and national competitive advantage.

mode of entry The format of foreign market entry.

monetary union A group of countries that use a common currency.

moral hazard Recklessness when people and organizations (including governments) do not have to face the full consequences of their actions.

multilateral trading system The global system that governs international trade among countries—otherwise known as the GATT/WTO system.

multimarket competition Firms engage the same rivals in multiple markets.

multinational enterprise A firm that engages in foreign direct investment and operates in multiple countries.

mutual forbearance Multimarket firms respect their rivals' spheres of influence in certain markets, and their rivals reciprocate, leading to tacit collusion.

natural resource seeking Firms' quest to pursue natural resources in certain locations.

nondiscrimination A principle that a country cannot discriminate among its trading partners (a concession given to one country needs to be made available to all other GATT/WTO members).

nonequity mode A mode of entry (exports and contractual agreements) that tends to reflect relatively smaller commitments to overseas markets.

nongovernment organizations (NGOs) Organizations, such as environmentalists, human rights activists, and consumer groups, that are not affiliated with governments.

nontariff barrier (NTB) Trade barriers that rely on nontariff means to discourage imports.

normative pillar The mechanism through which norms influence individual and firm behavior.

norms The prevailing practices of relevant players that affect the focal individuals and firms.

North American Free Trade Agreement (NAFTA) A free trade agreement among Canada, Mexico, and the United States.

obsolescing bargain The deal struck by MNEs and host governments, which may change their requirements after the initial FDI entry and make the original deal obsolete.

offer rate The price offered to sell a currency.

offshoring Outsourcing to an international or foreign firm.

OLI advantages A firm's quest for ownership (O) advantages, location (L) advantages, and internalization (I) advantages via FDI.

oligopoly Industries populated by a small number of players.

opportunism Self-interest seeking with guile.

opportunity cost Given the alternatives (opportunities), the cost of pursuing one activity at the expense of another activity.

organizational fit The similarity in cultures, systems, and structures.

original brand manufacturer (OBM) A firm that designs, manufactures, and markets branded products.

original design manufacturer (ODM) A firm that designs and manufactures products.

original equipment manufacturer (OEM) A firm that executes the design blueprints provided by other firms and manufactures such products.

out-group Individuals and firms not regarded as part of "us."

outside director A nonmanagement member of the board.

outsourcing Turning over an organizational activity to an outside supplier that will perform it on behalf of the focal firm.

ownership The MNEs' possession and leveraging of certain valuable, rare, hard-to-imitate, and organizationally embedded (VRIO) assets overseas in the context of FDI.

parent (home) country national (PCN) An employee who comes from the parent country of the MNE and works at its local subsidiary.

patents Legal rights awarded by government authorities to inventors of new products or processes, who are given exclusive (monopoly) rights to derive income from such inventions through activities such as manufacturing, licensing, or selling.

path dependency The present choices of countries, firms, and individuals are constrained by the choices made previously.

peg A stabilizing policy of linking a developing country's currency to a key currency.

performance appraisal The evaluation of employee performance for promotion, retention, or termination purposes.

piracy The unauthorized use of intellectual property rights.

place The location where products and services are provided.

political risk Risk associated with political changes that may negatively impact domestic and foreign firms.

political system A system of the rules of the game on how a country is governed politically.

political union The integration of political and economic affairs of a region.

polycentric approach An emphasis on the norms and practices of the host country.

post–Bretton Woods system A system of flexible exchange rate regimes with no official common denominator.

power distance The extent to which less powerful members within a country expect and accept that power is distributed unequally.

pragmatic nationalism A political view that approves FDI only when its benefits outweigh its costs.

predatory pricing An attempt to monopolize a market by setting prices below cost and intending to raise prices to cover losses in the long run after eliminating rivals.

price The expenditures that customers are willing to pay for a product.

price elasticity How demand changes when prices change.

price leader A firm that has a dominant market share and sets "acceptable" prices and margins in the industry.

primary stakeholder groups The constituents on which the firm relies for its continuous survival and prosperity.

principal A person (such as owner) delegating authority.

principal-agent conflicts Conflicts between principals and agents.

principal-principal conflicts Conflicts between two classes of principals: controlling shareholders and minority shareholders.

prisoners' dilemma In game theory, a type of game in which the outcome depends on two parties deciding whether to cooperate or to defect.

private equity Equity capital invested in private companies that, by definition, are not publicly traded.

proactive strategy A strategy that endeavors to do more than is required in CSR.

product The offerings that customers purchase.

product life cycle theory A theory that accounts for changes in the patterns of trade over time by focusing on product life cycles.

promotion Communications that marketers insert into the marketplace.

property rights The legal rights to use an economic property (resource) and to derive income and benefits from it.

protectionism The idea that governments should actively protect domestic industries from imports and vigorously promote exports.

psychological contract An informal understanding of expected delivery of benefits in the future for current services.

purchasing power parity A conversion that determines the equivalent amount of goods and services different currencies can purchase. This conversion is usually used to capture the differences in cost of living in different countries.

R&D contract Outsourcing agreements in R&D between firms.

radical view on FDI A political view that is hostile to FDI.

reactive strategy A strategy that would only respond to CSR causes when disasters and outcries break out.

real option An investment in real operations as opposed to financial capital.

regional economic integration Efforts to reduce trade and investment barriers within one region.

regulatory pillar The coercive power of governments.

related transaction Controlling shareholders sell goods or firm's assets to another firm they own at below-market prices or spin off the most profitable part of a public firm and merge it with another private firm of theirs.

relational (or **collaborative**) **capability** Capability to successfully manage interfirm relationships.

relationship orientation A focus to establish, maintain, and enhance relationships with customers.

repatriate Returning expatriate.

repatriation The process of facilitating the return of expatriates.

resource-based view A leading perspective in global business that posits that firm performance is fundamentally driven by differences in firm-specific resources and capabilities.

resource mobility The assumption that a resource removed from one industry can be moved to another.

resources The tangible and intangible assets a firm uses to choose and implement its strategies.

resource similarity The extent to which a given competitor possesses strategic endowments comparable, in terms of both type and amount, to those of the focal firm.

scale of entry The amount of resources committed to foreign market entry.

Schengen A passport-free travel zone within the EU.

secondary stakeholder groups Those who influence or affect, or are influenced or affected by, the corporation, but they are not engaged in transactions with the corporation and are not essential for its survival.

semiglobalization A perspective that suggests that barriers to market integration at borders are high but not high enough to completely insulate countries from each other.

separation of ownership and control The dispersal of ownership among many small shareholders, in which control is largely concentrated in the hands of salaried, professional managers who own little (or no) equity.

services Intangible services being traded.

shareholder capitalism A view of capitalism that suggests that the most fundamental purpose for firms to exist is to serve the economic interests of shareholders (also known as capitalists).

small and medium-sized enterprises (SMEs) Firms with fewer than 500 employees.

social capital The informal benefits individuals and organizations derive from their social structures and networks.

social complexity The socially complex ways of organizing typical of many firms.

social issue participation Firms' participation in social causes not directly related to the management of primary stakeholders.

solutions-based structure A customer-oriented solution in which a provider sells whatever combination of goods and services the customer prefers, including a rival's offerings.

sporadic (or **passive**) **exporting** The sale of products prompted by unsolicited inquiries from abroad.

spot transaction The classic single-shot exchange of one currency for another.

spread The difference between the offered price and the bid price.

staffing The HRM activities associated with hiring employees and filling positions.

stage models Models of internationalization that portray the slow step-by-step (stage-by-stage) process an SME must go through to internationalize its business.

stakeholder Any group or individual who can affect or is affected by the achievement of the organization's objectives.

stewardship theory A theory that suggests that most managers can be viewed as owners' stewards interested in safeguarding shareholders' interests and advancing organizational goals.

strategic alliances Voluntary agreements between firms involving exchange, sharing, or co-developing of products, technologies, or services.

strategic fit The effective matching of complementary strategic capabilities.

strategic hedging Spreading out activities in a number of countries in different currency zones to offset the currency losses in certain regions through gains in other regions.

strategic investment One firm invests in another as a strategic investor.

strategic trade policy A policy informed by strategic trade theory that advocates economic policies to provide companies a strategic advantage through government subsidies.

strategic trade theory A theory that suggests that strategic intervention by governments in certain industries can enhance their odds for international success.

subsidiary initiative The proactive and deliberate pursuit of new opportunities by a subsidiary to expand its scope of responsibility.

subsidy Government payments to domestic firms.

sunk cost Cost that a firm has to endure even when its investment turns out to be unsatisfactory.

supply chain Flow of products, services, finances, and information that passes through a set of entities from a source to the customer.

supply chain management Activities to plan, organize, lead, and control the supply chain.

SWOT analysis An analytical tool for delineating one firm's strengths (S), weaknesses (W), opportunities (O), and threats (T).

tacit collusion Firms indirectly coordinate actions by signaling their intention to reduce output and maintain pricing above competitive levels.

tacit knowledge Knowledge that is noncodifiable and its acquisition and transfer require hands-on practice.

tangible resources and capabilities A policy of limited intervention, occurring only when assets that are observable and easily quantified.

target exchange rates (or **crawling bands**) A limited policy of intervention, occurring only when the exchange rate moves out of the specified upper or lower bounds.

tariff barrier Trade barrier that relies on tariffs to discourage imports.

technology spillover Foreign technology diffused domestically that benefits domestic firms and industries.

The Doha Round A round of WTO negotiations to reduce agricultural subsidies, slash tariffs, and strengthen intellectual property protection that started in Doha, Qatar, in 2001—officially known as the "Doha Development Agenda." It was suspended in 2006 due to disagreements.

theocratic law A legal system based on religious teachings.

theory of absolute advantage A theory that suggests that under free trade, each nation gains by specializing in economic activities in which it has absolute advantage.

theory of comparative advantage A theory that focuses on the relative (not absolute) advantage in one economic activity that one nation enjoys in comparison with other nations.

theory of mercantilism A theory that holds that the wealth of the world (measured in gold and silver) is fixed and that a nation that exports more and imports less would enjoy the net inflows of gold and silver and thus become richer.

theory of national competitive advantage of industries (or **diamond theory**) A theory that suggests that the competitive advantage of certain industries in different nations depends on four aspects that form a "diamond."

third-party logistics (3PL) A neutral intermediary in the supply chain that provides logistics and other support services.

third country national (TCN) An employee who comes from neither the parent country nor the host country.

thrust The classic frontal attack with brute force.

top management team (TMT) The team consisting of the highest level of executives of a firm led by the CEO.

total cost of ownership Total cost needed to own a product, consisting of initial purchase cost and follow-up maintenance/service cost.

totalitarianism (or **dictatorship**) A political system in which one person or party exercises absolute political control over the population.

trade deficit An economic condition in which a nation imports more than it exports.

trade embargo Politically motivated trade sanctions against foreign countries to signal displeasure.

trademarks Exclusive legal rights of firms to use specific names, brands, and designs to differentiate their products from others.

Trade-Related Aspects of Intellectual Property Rights (TRIPS) A WTO agreement governing intellectual property rights.

trade surplus An economic condition in which a nation exports more than it imports.

training The specific preparation to do a particular job.

transaction costs The costs associated with economic transactions—or more broadly, costs of doing business.

transnational strategy A strategy that endeavors to be cost efficient, locally responsive, and learning driven simultaneously around the world.

Triad Three regions of developed economies (North America, Western Europe, and Japan).

triple bottom line The economic, social, and environmental performance that simultaneously satisfies the demands of all stakeholder groups.

tunneling A form of corporate theft that occurs when managers from the controlling family divert resources from the firm for personal or family use.

turnkey project A project in which clients pay contractors to design and construct new facilities and train personnel.

uncertainty avoidance The extent to which members in different cultures accept ambiguous situations and tolerate uncertainty.

United States-Dominican Republic-Central America Free Trade Agreement (CAFTA) A free trade agreement between the United States and five Central American countries and Dominican Republic.

upstream vertical FDI A type of vertical FDI in which a firm engages in an upstream stage of the value.

value chain A chain of vertical activities used in the production of goods and services that add value.

vertical FDI A type of FDI in which a firm moves upstream or downstream in different value chain stages in a host country.

voice-based mechanisms Corporate governance mechanisms that focus on shareholders' willingness to work with managers, usually through the board, by "voicing" their concerns.

voluntary export restraint An international agreement that shows that exporting countries voluntarily agree to restrict their exports.

VRIO framework The resource-based framework that focuses on the value (V), rarity (R), imitability (I), and organizational (O) aspects of resources and capabilities.

wholly owned subsidiary (WOS) A subsidiary located in a foreign country that is entirely owned by the parent multinational.

World Trade Organization (WTO) The official title of the multilateral trading system and the organization underpinning this system since 2005.

worldwide (or **global**) **mandate** The charter to be responsible for one MNE function throughout the world.

NAME INDEX

A

Abele, J., 81
Acedo, F., 108n3
Acemoglu, D., 53n29
Acito, F., 434n6
Acs, Z., 274nn4,22
Adner, R., 108n24, 275n51
AFL-CIO, 460n27
Agarwal, S., 108n21, 435n56
Agle, B., 510n13, 511n58
Agmon, T., 169, 178n39
Agrawal, N., 434n12
Agrawal, V., 434n12
Aguilera, R., 356n49, 487nn58,72
Ahlstrom, D., 274n25, 399n3, 468, 479, 486n17, 487n73, 523n2
Ahmad, A., 383n11, 385n55
Aitken, B., 178n27
Akbar, Y., 383n17
Akimova, I., 435n55
Akpatou, F. S., 273
Alcantara, L., 355n8
Alessandri, T., 486n32
Alexander, N., 357n77
Al-Issawi, T., 115n7,8
Allegretti, P., 208
Allen, D., 510n12
Allende, S., 504
Allred, B., 108n11, 385n56
Almeida, J., 275n46
Almeida, P., 384n38
Almond, P., 461n49
Ambos, B., 385n56
Amelio, W., 354
Amine, L., 510n28
Amino, T., 460n18
Anand, J., 108n21, 326n31, 355n7, 356n58
Anand, N., 383n7
Anderson, J., 108n24, 435n38
Anderson, M., 511n45
Anderson, R., 486n6
Andersson, L., 511n51
Andersson, M., 384n50
Andersson, U., 383n5, 384n45
Ando, N., 460–461n32
Andrade, G., 355n23
Ang, S., 77
Angwin, D., 356n64
Apte, U., 435n47
Apud, S., 85n68
Aragon-Correa, J. A., 511n45
Ardichvili, A., 84n58
Argenti, P., 490, 509n1
Arikan, A., 355n5
Arino, A., 356nn43,44,46
Armington, C., 274n4
Arnold, W., 250
Arora, A., 300n38
Arrunada, B., 420
Arthur, J., 461n40
Arthur, W., 461n39
Arya, B., 510n40
Asaba, S., 109n35
Asakawa, K., 384nn38,47
ASEAN Secretariat, 235n38–40
Aswicahyono, H., 178n39
Atamer, T., 384n50
Athanassiou, N., 486n30
Au, D., 393
Au, K., 83n6, 274n5, 486n26
Audretsch, D., 274nn13,22
Augier, M., 298–299n4
Aulakh, P., 25, 26n33, 300n38, 355n16
Autio, E., 260, 275nn43,46
Auyang, B., 515–519, 522–523
Auyang, H., 515, 516, 519
Avittathur, B., 434n23
Aycan, Z., 83–84n32
Azcárraga, E., 278
Aziaka, Y., 272

B

Baden-Fuller, C., 382n3
Bae, Z., 274n14
Baetz, M., 275n30
Baggs, J., 150, 151n1
Bagozzi, R., 383n15
Bailey, W., 84n38
Balabanis, G., 300n34
Baldrige, D., 383n10
Baliga, B. R., 486n24
Balkundi, P., 461n45
Ballmer, S., 345
Banerjee, S., 510n31
Banga, R., 178n27
Bansal, P., 510nn7,33,42, 511nn44,55
Barden, J., 52n8, 356n48
Barham, M., 208
Barham, T., 208
Barkema, H., 299n17, 300n40, 354n3, 357n79
Barner-Rasmussen, W., 384n48
Barnes, J., 357n77
Barnes, P., 27n36, 422
Barnett, M., 511n55
Barnett, T., 383n26
Barnett, W., 274n23
Barney, J., 26n13, 90, 96, 108nn1,5,7,23, 109nn31,40, 274n12, 275n52, 326n7
Barringer, B., 275n40
Barro, R., 53n29
Barroso, C., 108n3
Barry, F., 178n31
Barth, T., 384n50
Barthelemy, J., 108n16
Bartlett, C., 83n29, 371, 383nn6,30
Basdeo, D., 326n20
Bassi, L., 460n20
Bastiat, F., 141, 151n16
Basu, K., 510n20
Bateman, T., 511n51
Bates, K., 109n31
Baum, J., 274n13, 326n32
Baum, J. R., 326n17
Baumol, W., 274n9
Bayh, E., 177
Beal, B., 298n3
Beamish, P., 53n36, 82–83n4, 108n4, 109n41, 275n31, 356nn46,48,53,54, 357n78, 383nn21,28, 460n7
Bearpark, A., 120
Beaulieu, M., 53n18
Bebchuk, L., 486n34
Becerra, M., 326n2
Becker, B., 461nn50,53
Beechler, S., 460n2, 461nn33,57
Beemer, B., 236
Begley, T., 83n25, 84n42, 274n9
Behfar, K., 461n45
Behrman, J., 178n32
Belderbos, R., 299n6, 383n21, 384n38, 434n25, 460–461n32
Belkin, L., 460n1
Bell, J., 275n38, 299n17
Bell, S., 461n39
Benedetto, A., 355n19
Benito, G., 383n15
Bennett, W., 461n39
Benton, W. C., 434n30
Bentz, J., 390
Benz, M., 485n1
Beracs, J., 109n43, 435n56
Berdrow, I., 383n31
Berg, D., 299n8
Berger, H., 355n16
Bergh, R., 53n14
Berman, P., 316
Berman, S., 511n56
Berner, R., 383n27
Bernhofen, D., 151n10
Berns, S., 84n43
Bernstein, A., 20
Berry, H., 299n5, 383n7
Berry, L., 435n51
Bestor, T., 75
Bevan, A., 178n37
Bhagat, R., 67, 83n19
Bhagwati, J., 27n34, 145–146, 151nn12,26,27, 229, 235n42
Bhaskar-Shrinivas, P., 460n9
Biggart, N., 52n11
Bigley, G., 26n14, 509n3
Bilkey, T., 114
Bird, A., 27n38, 83n24, 83–84n32, 461n33
Birkinshaw, J., 108n11, 109n41, 300n44, 357nn70,79, 376, 382n1, 383nn5,8,24,31, 384n49, 385nn57,59
Bishop, K., 383n17
Biswas, Mr., 116, 118
Björk, 58, 107
Bjorkman, I., 83n23, 384nn48,51, 460n29, 460–461n32
Black, J., 460n9
Blair, T., 509
Block, S., 53n33
Bloom, M., 510n6
Bloomberg, M., 463
Blume, C., 244
Blumentritt, T., 383n18
Boddewyn, J., 25–26n2, 53n14, 109n45, 178n38
Boeker, J., 326n25
Bon Jovi, 106
Bonardi, J., 53n14
Bond, M., 84n52
Boone, C., 461n43
Bosch, F., 384n51
Boter, H., 275n30
Bourdeau, B., 355n13
Boush, D., 83n21

Boutellier, R., 384n38
Bowen, D., 357n72, 460n3
Boxall, P., 461n49
Boyacigiller, N., 461n57
Boyd, N., 109n36
Boyles, T., 461n40
Brabander, B., 461n43
Brand Week, 91
Brandenburger, A., 326n3
Brander, J., 137, 150, 151nn1,5
Brandes, P., 486n32
Brannen, M., 82n1, 384n50, 434n16
Branzei, O., 510n36
Braunerhjelm, P., 178n33, 300n44, 383n24
Bresman, H., 357nn70,79, 383n31
Brett, J., 461n45
Brewer, T., 53nn14,15, 177n5, 178n38, 179n41
Brewster, C., 461n49
Brickley, J., 487n38
Bridis, T., 115n4
Brin, S., 469
Brock, D., 298–299n4
Brouthers, K., 83n21, 299n32, 354–355n3, 356nn54,55
Brouthers, L., 25, 83n21, 178nn25,30, 299n32, 300n42, 354–355n3, 434n15
Brown, J., 151n10, 435n56
Browne, A., 56
Bruce, A., 486n33
Bruton, G., 26n33, 178n15, 274nn15,25, 399n3, 468, 479, 486n17, 487n73
Bryce, D., 109n31
Bucerius, M., 357n68
Buchan, N., 67, 83n19
Buchholtz, A., 355n26, 486n7, 510n22
Buck, T., 383n17, 486nn9,33, 487nn45,49,53
Buckley, P., 108n4, 178nn16,21,27, 356n62
Budhwar, P., 82n1, 460nn8,30
Burbridge, J., 84n43
Bureau of Labor Statistics, 460n28
Burgelman, R., 357n80
Burgess, S., 30, 280
Burkart, M., 487n51
Burns, L., 383n12
Busenitz, L., 82–83n4, 274nn9,12,41
Bush, D., 306
Bush, G. W., 55, 114, 115, 139
Business Today, 524
Business Week (BW), 7, 26n10, 40, 75, 82, 94, 97, 108n17, 109n32, 120, 123, 145, 151nn19,29, 154, 177, 178n19, 179n44, 182, 204n13, 213, 235nn25,27,29,30,33,34, 261, 274n18, 282, 298n2, 300n48, 304, 314, 330, 354, 357n66, 359, 369, 412, 413, 414, 434nn9,17, 435n52, 445, 460n31, 461n56, 464, 471, 479, 485, 486n12, 490, 492, 509, 511nn48,59
Business World, 524
Butler, K., 53n15
Bygrave, W., 260
Bynke, H., 207

C

Cadsby, C., 486n33
Calatone, R., 435n44
Calhoun, M., 53n31
Caligiuri, P., 460n13
Calori, R., 384n50
Camiah, N., 178n29
Camp, S. M., 274n1
Campa, J., 178n21
Campion, M., 460n13
Canina, L., 299n7
Cannella, A., 487n67
Cannice, M., 178n13
Cannon, J., 84n63
Cantwell, J., 383nn7,9
Cao, S. R., 88
Capell, K., 208
Cappellen, T., 460n8, 461n57
Capron, L., 357n79
Carafano, J., 19
Carbaugh, R., 197, 198, 204, 204nn8,17, 214, 234, 235n6
Carey, M., 106
Caringal, C., 109n33
Carlucci, F., 470
Carmeli, A., 108n9
Carney, M., 486n5, 487n73
Carpenter, M., 486nn30,33
Carr, C., 84n59
Carr, N., 109n28
Carrieri, F., 204n9
Cascio, W., 356n42, 460n3
Casson, M., 108n4, 178n21
Caudill, S., 390
Caves, R., 25n1, 177n1
Cavusgil, S. T., 274n26, 300nn36–38, 435n44
Cerdin, J., 460n17
Certo, S. T., 486n20
Chadwick, K., 383n26
Chai, D., 433
Chain Drug Review, 389
Chakravarthy, B., 109n43
Chambers, J., 325
Chan, C., 298n3
Chan, E., 523n2
Chan, E. S., 399n3
Chan, K., 274n20
Chan, R., 511n45
Chan, T., 445
Chand, M., 403
Chandran, R., 355n19
Chang, E., 460n23
Chang, S., 298–299n4, 486nn7,19
Chard, A. M., 402n2
Chari, M., 298–299n4, 487n57
Charlton, A., 235nn3,32
Chase, R., 435n47
Chattopadhyay, A., 25
Chattopadhyay, P., 52n8
Chavez, H., 172, 225
Chen, C., 83n21, 356nn52,58, 461n34
Chen, M., 88, 274n17, 313, 326nn8,23,24
Chen, R., 178n13, 275n28, 355n32
Chen, S., 299n31, 300nn39,46
Chen, W., 383n7
Chen, X., 83–84n32
Chen, Y., 510n4
Chetty, S., 275n35
Cheung, G., 83n6
Cheung, J., 106
Cheung, M., 299n17
Chevrier, S., 384n50
Chi, S., 83–84n32
Chi, T., 355n14
Child, J., 52n6, 83n31, 356n45, 357n71, 511n66
China Business Review, 496
Chirac, J., 55, 450
Cho, H., 108n11
Cho, K., 299n29
Cho, T., 486n35
Choe, S., 83n21
Choi, C., 300n46, 357n78
Choi, D. Y., 400
Choi, J., 83n21, 356n52
Choi, T., 109n49, 434n3
Chow, I., 83n6
Chow, P., 435n57
Chowdhury, S., 83n8
Chrisman, J., 27n41, 511n72
Christensen, C., 274n21, 326n6
Christensen, K., 399n4
Christmann, P., 510n24, 511nn54,64
Chua, B.-L., 515, 516
Chudoba, K., 384n50
Chung, C., 460n7
Chung, W., 178nn17,18, 299n12
CIA World Factbook, 60, 123, 220
Citigroup 2004 Annual Report, 82
Claessens, S., 486n15, 487n55
Claflin, B., 325
Clark, D., 40
Clark, K., 108n11, 487n63
Clark, T., 26n17
Clarkson, M., 510n15
Clegg, J., 178n27
Clelland, I., 510n33
Cleverdon, J., 508
Click, R., 53n16
Clinton, H., 113, 172
Cloninger, P., 383n28
Cloodt, D., 356n37
Clougherty, J., 326n11
Cochran, P., 84n35
Coff, D., 384n33
Coff, R., 384n33
Cohen, M., 434n12
Cohen, S., 435n40
Cohen, W., 384n51
Colakoglu, S., 461n52
Colbert, B., 461n40
Colbert, J.-B., 127, 137
Colling, T., 461n49
Collings, D., 461n36
Collins, C., 108n11, 461n45, 487n63
Collins, J., 84n43, 299n32
Colombo, M., 355n34
Colton, D., 434n8

Combs, J., 275n29, 434n30, 461n54, 486n13
Conaty, W., 456
Confucius, 74
Connelly, B., 298–299n4
Contardo, I., 326n2
Conyers, J., Jr., 177
Cook, M., 357n77
Coombs, J., 486n32, 510n12
Coon, H., 83n20
Corbett, C., 435n36
Cordano, M., 511n51
Cording, M., 511n55
Cort, K., 84n43
Cory, K., 53n13
Cosset, J., 53n18
Coviello, N., 275n35
Covin, J., 355n22
Cox, T., 435n56
Cramer, R., 53n13, 510n38
Crane, A., 510n31
Crawford, R., 162
Crittenden, W., 27n41, 510n34
Cronin, J., 355n13
Crook, T. R., 434n30
Crossan, M., 383n31
Cuervo, A., 487n49
Cuervo-Cazurra, A., 26n33, 84n42, 487n58
Cullen, J., 84nn38,64, 355n16
Cummings, J., 84n55
Cuny, R., 515
Currall, S., 355n16
Custy, M., 30
Cusumano, M., 326n30
Czinkota, M., 27n36, 327n42

D

Dacin, M. T., 355n8
Dadiseth, K. B., 525
Dadyburjor, K., 392
Dahlin, K., 461n44
Dahmer, W., 30
Daily, C., 355n22, 486n21
Dalgic, T., 275n32, 417, 429, 435n50
Dalton, D., 355n22, 486n21
Damanpour, F., 83n21, 356n52
Dana, L., 274n3
Daniels, J., 178n13
Danis, W., 178n29
Danneels, E., 108n8, 383n28
Dans, P., 392
Darnall, N., 511n52
Das, J., 84n43
Das, T., 355n16
Datta, D., 461n52
D'Aunno, T., 26n14
D'Aveni, R., 327n40
Davenport, T., 382
David, P., 298–299n4, 487n57, 510n6
Davies, H., 151n8
Davis, G., 487n74
Davis, J., 487n66
Davis, K., 509n2
Davis, M., 435n46
Davis, R., 355n26
Davis-Blake, A., 356n63
Dawar, N., 25, 318, 327n34
De Castro, J., 109n26, 356n57, 486n10
De Cieri, H., 460nn23,26
de Soto, H., 37, 53n21
DeCocinis, M., 437–439
Deeds, D., 275n42, 384n45
Delbridge, R., 52n11
Delegation of the European Commission to the USA, 235n10
Delery, J., 461n47
Delios, A., 26n33, 53nn34,36, 108n21, 109n41, 116, 299n29, 356n58, 383n28, 460–461n32
Delmas, M., 511n53
Dembovsky, M., 298–299n4
Denekamp, J., 178n13
DeNisi, A., 461n35
Derfus, P., 326n20
Desai, M., 355n7
DeSarbo, W., 109n50, 326n23
DeSilva, D., 161
Dess, G., 108n2, 274n19
Dev, C., 435n56
Devaraj, S., 298–299n4
DeVaro, J., 460n23
Devers, C., 486n32
Devinney, T., 383nn12,15
Dhanaraj, C., 355n7, 356n48
Dharwadkar, R., 460n12, 486n32
Dibrell, C., 83n30
Dickman, M., 461n57
Dimering, P. R., 435n41
Dimitratos, P., 274n3
Dino, R., 461n43, 486n7
Dinur, A., 355n34
Dion, C., 153
Dirienzo, C., 84n43
Djankov, S., 257, 274n8, 486n15, 487n55
Dobbs, L., 113, 151n21
Dobrev, S., 274n23
Doern, R., 274n11
Doh, J., 27n39, 84n43, 109n46, 179n42, 299n32, 356n57, 510n10
Doidge, C., 464, 487n61
Dollinger, M., 356n58
Donaldson, L., 487nn65,66
Donaldson, T., 69, 70, 84n39, 491, 510n16
Doney, P., 84n63, 435n55
Dorfman, R., 63, 67, 83n14
Doty, D., 461n47
Douglas, T., 511n47
Doukas, J., 355n24
Dous, M., 382
Dow, D., 83n20, 299n32, 434n6
Dow (data source), 496
Dowell, G., 299n22, 511n65
Dowling, G., 108n13
Dowling, P., 439, 442, 452, 460nn11,16,23
Doyle, J., 238
Doz, Y., 107, 356n38, 372, 382n1, 384n37
Driffield, N., 299n12
Droge, C., 299n17
Drost, E., 460n15, 461n48
Drucker, P., 177n6
Drug Store News, 386, 389n9
Drummond, A., 82–83n4
Du, J., 84n43
Duckett, M., 253, 264
Dufy, M., 461n42
Dunbar, R., 83n24
Duncan, W., 238
Dunfee, T., 84n38
Dunlap-Hinkler, D., 384n34
Dunning, J., 25n1, 151n8, 158, 178nn9,16, 299n6, 383n7
Durand, R., 84n35
Dutta, S., 108n9
Duysters, G., 355n31, 384n45
Dwyer, S., 383n26
Dyer, J., 108n10, 338, 355nn10,29
Dykes, B., 486n33

E

Earley, P. C., 77, 84n33, 85n68
Easterby-Smith, M., 384n51
Eastvold, R., 384n33
Ebben, J., 274n17
Economic Times, 524, 529n4
Economist, 5, 6, 7, 26n4, 30, 40, 52, 52n9, 53n27, 56, 57, 70, 82, 84n41, 88, 91, 109nn29,30,34,51, 120, 145, 150, 151nn11,13, 15,22,30, 154, 171, 179nn43,45, 185, 197, 199, 204nn3,7,12,16, 215, 230, 235nn7,9,13–17,19–24, 33,34,36,44, 250, 258, 259, 280, 282, 284, 299n19, 300n43, 304, 326n18, 348, 354, 355nn4,11, 359, 369, 382, 413–414, 422, 424, 425, 434nn9,20,24, 435n39, 447, 451, 460nn5,24, 464, 469, 485, 487nn36,62, 492, 509, 510n39, 512
Economist Atlas, 58
Economist Intelligence Unit, 25, 26n6, 44, 299n9
Eden, L., 26nn5,14,28, 84nn42,43, 178n22, 299n32, 383n11
Edens, P., 461n39
Edmondson, G., 250
Edwards, D., 511n52
Edwards, R., 383n11, 385n55
Eesley, C., 510n13
Egelhoff, W., 383n14
Egri, C., 511n51
Egri, S., 84n58
Eisenhardt, K., 108n11
Eisenmann, T., 486n32
Eisner, M., 108n2
Elango, B., 26n33, 178n15
Elbanna, S., 52n6
Elenkov, D., 52n6
Elkington, J., 510n16
Ellis, K., 383n10
Ellis, P., 151n8, 435n54
Ellstrand, A., 486nn20,21
Engelhard, J., 178n29
England, V., 479
Enright, M., 26n30
Ensign, P., 383n5, 384n52
Enz, C., 299n7
Erez, M., 67, 83n19

Eriksson, K., 275n35
Erramilli, M. K., 83n22, 108n21
Essaddam, N., 53n18
Estfan, E., 512
Estfan, G., 512
Estrin, S., 178n37, 299n32, 356n57
Etemad, H., 274n4
Ethiraj, S., 109n30
Euromoney, 44, 45, 46
European Commission, 304
Evans, J., 83n21, 299n20
Evans, P., 178n35
Evenett, S., 326n4
Expression, 88
Ezzamel, M., 487n37

F

Faccio, M., 486n16
Fadahunsi, A., 274n7
Faff, R., 204n14
Fahy, J., 109n43, 435n56
Fang, T., 67
Far Eastern Economic Review, 524
Farashahi, M., 26n5
Farnstrand, E., 244
Farrell, D., 100, 109n47
Faulkner, D., 83n31, 357n71
Feinberg, S., 178n26, 385n58
Felin, T., 384n33
Felps, W., 509n3
Ferdows, K., 412
Fernandez, Z., 275n35
Ferner, A., 461n49
Ferreira, M., 27n36
Ferrell, O., 510n22
Ferrier, W., 326n19
Ferris, J., 384n45
Ferris, S., 511n46
Fey, C., 83n23, 274n11, 356n54, 384n51, 460n29
Fichman, M., 356n63
Fiegenbaum, A., 327n35
Filatotchev, I., 25, 26nn5,33, 178n22, 383n17, 486n9, 487n49
Financial Services Agency, 82
Fineman, S., 460n19
Finger, M., 326n16
Finkelstein, S., 357n79, 486n22
Fischer, E., 275n35
Fischer, H., 486n28
Fishman, C., 182, 327n41
Fiss, P., 486n33, 487n43
Fjeldstad, O., 108n14
Fladmoe-Lindquist, K., 108n8, 274n20, 356n38
Flannery, J., 272–273
Flannery, M., 272–273
Florey, J., 515
Florida, R., 151n28
Florkowski, G., 460n30
Floyd, S., 383n10
Flyer, F., 178n17, 299n12
Foley, C. F., 355n7
Foley, S., 523n2
Folta, T., 355n15
Fombrun, C., 84n37, 108n12, 511n72
Fonfara, K., 109n43
Fonfoara, K., 435n56
Fong, C., 27n42
Ford, B., 359
Ford, H., 427
Forsgren, M., 383n5, 384n45
Fortune, 15, 16, 17, 18, 26n27, 240, 282, 291, 292
Fosfuri, A., 275n29, 300n38
Foss, N., 383n31
Fouts, P., 511n56
Frank, D., 237
Franke, R., 84n52
Franklin, V., 82–83n4
Frayne, C., 460n15, 461n48
Frazao, J., 273
Fredrickson, J., 486n30
Freeman, E., 510n5
Freeman, R. E., 84n37, 182, 511nn55,60
Frey, B., 485n1
Fried, J., 486n34
Friedman, M., 494, 510n18
Friedman, R., 83–84n32
Friedman, T., 23, 27n37, 36, 104, 109n53, 421, 435n35
Frieze, I., 511n51
Frost, T., 318, 327n34, 383n5, 384n36
Frynas, J. G., 299n22
Fuentelsaz, L., 299n25, 326n23
Fukuyama, F., 84n65

G

Gaba, V., 299n26
Gabrijan, V., 109n43
Galan, J., 108n3, 178n23, 299n31
Galang, C., 460n3
Gallagher, S., 355n32
Gamble, J., 461n49
Gandolf, F., 357n70
Gao, J., 511n55
García Márquez, G., 513
Gardberg, N., 108n12, 460n1, 511n72
Gardner, H., 383n7
Gardner, T., 460n25
Garg, A., 26n33
Garten, J., 235n28
Gasparishvili, A., 84n58
Gassman, O., 384n38
Gaur, A., 356n47
Gedajlovic, E., 474, 486nn5,23, 487nn48,70,73, 510n4
Gelbuda, M., 299nn15,18
George, E., 52n8
George, G., 274n17, 275n43
George, J., 445
Geppert, M., 385n56
Geringer, J. M., 460n15, 461n48
Germain, R., 356n46
Gerwin, D., 384n45
Gettelfinger, R., 237
Ghauri, P., 356n62
Ghemawat, P., 26nn29,30
Ghosh, E., 434n23
Ghoshal, S., 52n11, 83n29, 84n62, 371, 382n1, 383nn6,30, 487n68
Ghosn, C., 369, 444
Gibson, C., 67, 83n19, 384n50, 461n45
Giddens, A., 26n18
Gilbert, B., 274n13
Gillespie, K., 299n15
Gilley, K. M., 486n32, 510n12
Gimeno, J., 298n3, 313, 326n31
Gioia, D., 84n49
GLOBE, 63, 64
Globerman, S., 84n44
Godfrey, P., 509n3
Goerzen, A., 108n4, 356nn45,46, 357n74, 460n7
Golden, B., 326n22
Golden, P., 435n55
Goldman, L., 316
Goldstein, J., 235n45
Gomez, C., 82–83n4, 275n41
Gomez, J., 299n25, 326n23
Gomez-Mejia, L., 383n26, 486nn7,33
Gonzalez-Benito, J., 178n23, 299n31
Goodall, K., 384n50
Goodstein, J., 326n25
Gooner, R., 435n32
Gopinath, C., 111, 112
Goranova, M., 486n32
Gore, A., 498, 508–509, 510n29
Gorg, H., 178n26
Goteman, I., 275n45
Gottfredson, M., 109n48
Govindarajan, V., 275n44, 374, 384nn32,43
Graddol, D., 58, 83n7
Graen, G., 460n12
Graffin, S., 486n34
Graham, E., 326nn10,12
Graham, J., 83n21, 83–84n32, 85n67
Graham, L., 113
Grant, D., 510n40
Grant, R., 383n31
Graves, S., 511n56
Greening, D., 511n49
Greenspan, A., 144
Greenwald, B., 109n44
Greenwood, R., 52n11
Greve, H., 384n44
Grewal, R., 326n23, 460n12
Griffin, D., 274n5
Griffin, R., 83n28, 327n38
Griffith, D., 83–84n32, 85n70
Grimm, C., 274n20, 326nn19,20
Grogaard, B., 383n15
Grosse, R., 27n36, 178n16, 300n46
Grove, A., 259
Grubb, T., 357n69
Guardian, 306
Guay, T., 510n10
Guillen, M., 26n31, 52n4, 53n17, 178n21, 356n56, 487n43
Guisinger, S., 84n44, 299n8, 356n58
Gulati, R., 354n1, 486n25
Gunter, F., 197
Gupta, A., 275n44, 374, 384nn32,43
Gupta, V., 63, 83n14
Guriev, S., 52
Guthrie, J., 461n52
Gutierrez, I., 486n7

H

Habib, M., 84n46
Hadjimarcou, J., 25, 300n42, 434n15
Hagedoorn, J., 300n41, 355n31, 356n37, 357n73, 384n45
Hakanson, L., 357n70
Haleblian, J., 355n25
Haley, U., 52n11
Hall, A., 461n54
Hall, C., 208
Hall, D., 26n8
Hall, E., 83n12
Hall, M., 83n12
Hall, R., 90
Hallowell, R., 357n72
Hambrick, D., 274n17, 356n53
Hamel, G., 96, 109nn27,52, 355n17
Hammond, A., 7
Hanafi, M., 178n28
Handfield, R., 434n31
Hanges, P., 63, 67, 83n14
Hansen, M., 511n66
Hansen, M. T., 402n3
Hardy, C., 510n40
Harris, H., 461n57
Harrison, A., 178n27
Harrison, D., 84n35, 460nn9,14, 461n45
Harrison, J., 84n37, 299n7, 357n67, 511n55
Harrison, N., 511n52
Hart, S., 6, 7, 25, 26nn7,30, 27n40, 37, 84n50, 510nn8, 9,37, 511n65, 529n2
Harte, G., 510n27
Harvard Business Review, 346
Harvey, M., 434n8
Harzing, A., 300n40, 354–355n3, 383nn4,20, 460n10
Hasfi, T., 26n5
Hashai, N., 178n16
Hassel, A., 487n57
Hatch, N., 108n10, 355n10
Hatchuel, A., 27n42
Hatem, T., 83n23
Haunschild, P., 356n63
Hayek, F., 111
Hayes, C., 433
Hayward, M., 108n12, 274n5, 355n9
He, Y., 510n4
Heath, P., 108n4
Heckscher, E., 131, 137
Hegarty, W., 355n26, 487n38
Heijblom, R., 417, 429
Heijltjes, M., 383n21, 460–461n32
Heine, K., 109n38, 274n20
Heineke, J., 435n46
Hejazi, W., 178n33, 383n17
Helfat, C., 108n6
Hellman, J., 84n47
Henisz, W., 26n14, 45, 53nn32,34, 299n29
Hennart, J., 83n21, 300n39, 326n31, 355n17, 357n75
Henriques, I., 510nn12,25
Henry, N., 178n18, 299n7
Heritage Foundation, 53n25
Herman, S., 511n51
Hesterly, W., 384n33
Heuer, M., 84n55
Heugens, P., 510n34
Hewett, K., 384n34
Hickson, P., 275n41
Hill, C., 40, 53n22, 63, 178n11, 204n10, 275n56, 299n30, 487n39
Hill, H., 178n39
Hillman, A., 53n13, 84n43, 383n16, 510n6, 511n46
Hilts, P., 510n26
Hinds, P., 461n44
Hines, J., 355n7
Hitt, G., 115n7
Hitt, M., 82–83n4, 84n37, 96, 108nn3,16,24, 274n1, 275n31, 298–299n4, 354–355n3, 355n21, 357n67, 420, 434n25, 486n3
Ho, B., 397
Ho, Y., 84n38
Hobbs, C., 306
Hodgetts, R., 383n13
Hoegl, M., 84n64
Hoetker, G., 109n37, 435n51
Hoffman, A., 497, 510n35
Hofstede, G., 57, 65–67, 82n2, 83nn5,26, 84n52, 85n69
Holburn, G., 53n14
Holcomb, T., 108n24, 420
Holdsworth, D., 300n42, 434n15
Hollinshead, G., 178n29
Holm, U., 300n44, 383n24, 384n45
Holmes, R. M., 486n32
Holmquist, C., 275n30
Holt, D., 84n59, 415, 434n11
Homburg, C., 357n68
Hong, J., 486n19
Hong, Y., 461n52
Hood, N., 109n41, 383n8
Hooley, G., 109n43, 435n56
Hoover, V., 326n1
Hopkins, H. D., 354–355n3
Hopner, M., 487n57
Hoshino, Y., 355n8
Hoskisson, R., 25, 26n5, 96, 298n3, 486n3
Houle, I., 355n26
House, P., 392
House, R., 62, 63, 67, 83nn14,19
Howard-Grenville, J., 510n35
Hu, M., 83–84n32
Hua, Y., 57
Huang, H., 250
Huang, J., 461n49
Huang, X., 83–84n32, 384n40
Hulme, V., 445
Hult, G. T., 109n50, 434nn3,4, 435nn44,50
Hung, K., 393
Huntington, S., 58, 62–63, 83n15
Huo, P., 461n49
Huselid, M., 461nn50,53
Husted, B., 26n19, 510n12, 511n71
Hutabarat, W., 84n55
Hwang, C.-H., 392
Hwang, P., 178n11, 299n30
Hymer, S., 298n1

I

Iankova, E., 179n46
Ibrayeva, E., 274n7
Ilinitch, A., 275n36, 435n43
Illy, A., 259
Immelt, J., 456
Inkpen, A., 355nn16,34, 356n53, 383n21, 385n53, 511n62
Inkson, K., 461n57
International Monetary Fund, 191, 204n1
Ireland, R. D., 96, 108n3, 274n1, 275n31, 357n67, 434n29
Isdell, N., 369
Ismail, K., 461n43
Isobe, T., 298n3, 299n24
Itami, H., 108n9
Ito, K., 178n20, 326n31

J

Jackson, G., 487n72
Jackson, M., 513
Jackson, P., 146
Jackson, S., 461n46
Jacobides, M., 108n18
Jacque, L., 204n9
Jager, D., 369
Jain, S., 434n6
James, L., 83n11
Janne, O., 383n7
Jansen, J., 109n40, 384n51
Jansheski, J., 386–389, 389nn1,2
Janssens, M., 460n8, 461n57
Jarrell, G., 487n38
Javidan, M., 63, 67, 83n14
Javorcik, B., 178n27
Jaworski, B., 435n49
Jenkins, M., 178n18, 299n7
Jensen, M., 473, 484, 486nn11,34, 487n42, 510n19
Jensen, R., 355n35, 383n31, 384n49
Jenwipakul, A., 433
Ji, Y., 325
Jiang, C., 384n47
Jiang, R., 511n44
Jiang, Y., 26n12, 52n1, 468, 479, 486nn8,17
Joaquin, D., 53n15
Jobe, L., 108n16, 434n25
Johanson, J., 275n32, 299n18
Johansson, J., 299n15, 383n23
Johnson, A., 274n17
Johnson, D., 435n55
Johnson, E., 460n13
Johnson, G., 108n15
Johnson, J., 85n68, 355n16, 383n12, 461n42, 486nn20,21
Johnson, L., 190, 282
Johnson, N., 486n14
Johnson, R., 486n3
Johnson, S., 53n29, 486n18
Jolly, D., 356n45
Jones, D., 433
Jones, F., 275n40
Jones, G., 84n47
Jones, M., 275n31

Jones, T., 84n36, 509n3, 511n56
Juarez, L., 178n22
Judge, W., 487n45, 511n47
Junttila, M., 109n31
Juste, C., 55

K

Kahn, J., 109n44
Kalashnikov, M., 514–515
Kale, P., 109n30, 338, 355nn7,17,29
Kaleka, A., 435nn32,37
Kalms, L., 432
Kalnins, A., 178nn17,18, 299n12
Kan, O., 355n24
Kang, S., 461n37
Kaptein, M., 510n34
Kapur, D., 151n9
Karolyi, A., 464, 487n61
Karp, A., 514–515
Karunaratna, A., 83n20
Kashlak, R., 355n19
Kashyap, P., 529n9
Kassinis, G., 510n12
Katila, R., 274n19
Katsikeas, C., 300nn33,36, 434n6, 435n37
Katz, J., 179n46
Kaufmann, D., 84n47
Kearney, C., 178n31
Kedia, B., 27n43
Keil, M., 355n13
Keim, G., 511n46
Keller, K., 434n5
Kelley, W., 383n15
Kemmelmeier, M., 83n20
Kern, M., 461n45
Ketcheb, D., 275n29
Ketchen, D., 109n50, 326n1, 434nn3,4, 435nn44,50, 461n54
Keummerle, W., 109n40
Khan, O., 273
Khanna, P., 486n29
Khanna, T., 26n14, 487n77
Khatri, N., 84n42
Khoury, T. A., 39
Kim, B., 26n14, 123
Kim, C., 178n11
Kim, H., 384n52
Kim, J., 355n25
Kim, S., 84n43, 108n21, 123
Kim, U., 83n16
Kim, W. C., 299n30, 326n29
Kindleberger, C., 209
King, A., 84n51, 109n33, 384n39, 510n30, 511nn43,44
King, D., 355n22
King, N., Jr., 115n12
Kirkman, B., 83n19
Kirkman, K., 67
Kirsch, D., 274n16, 383n19
Kirton, J., 235n26
Klassen, R., 511n47
Klein, A., 26n33
Kline, J., 511n67
Kling, K., 275n45
Knemeyer, A. M., 434n18
Knickerbocker, F., 178n20, 326n31
Knight, G., 27n36, 274nn4,26, 275n48
Knight, J., 300n42, 434n15
Knoop, C., 357n72
Knott, A., 109n31, 275n55
Knowles, L., 26n17
Kobrin, S., 293
Kochan, T., 510n14
Kogut, B., 83n21, 178n15, 204n11, 299n13, 326n31, 355nn14,34, 383n31
Kohli, A., 435n49
Koka, B., 384n51
Kolk, A., 84n35, 510n32
Kong Fu Zi, 74
Koplovitz, K., 324
Kor, Y., 109n40, 486n21
Korn, H., 326n32
Kostova, T., 82–83n4, 109nn40,42, 371, 383n18, 385nn53–55, 460n8
Kotabe, M., 27n35, 52n11, 109n37, 327n42, 355n16, 384n34, 434n26
Kotha, S., 83n24, 275n34, 511n56
Kotler, P., 434n5, 435n45
Koutzevol, N., 487n45
Koybaeva, T., 357n77
Koza, M., 356n38
Kramer, M., 510nn29,30
Krause, D., 434nn3,31
Kreinin, M., 151n17, 204n4
Krishnan, R., 356n54
Krishnana, M., 109n30
Krishnaswamy, S., 435n45
Kristof-Brown, A., 460n13
Kroll, M., 109n36, 486n33
Krug, J., 355n26, 486n33, 487n38
Krugman, P., 137, 143, 151nn5,6,20
Kshetri, N., 27n36
Kuemmerle, W., 384n38
Kulatilaka, N., 204n11
Kumar, A., 435n49
Kumar, N., 326n1
Kumar, S., 384n34
Kuperman, J., 299n25
Kurdelbusch, A., 487n57
Kwak, M., 326n26
Kwok, C., 84n48, 487n50, 511n46
Kwon, Y. S., 392

L

La Porta, R., 53n19, 257, 274n8, 486nn4,18, 487n52
Lado, A., 109n36
Lagerstrom, K., 384n50
Lai, X. C., 116, 117–118
Lam, A., 384n45, 402n4
Lam, K., 83n21
Lam, N., 85n67
Lamb, R., 357n69
Lamont, B., 383n10
Lampel, J., 355n18
Landreth, J., 399n6
Lane, H., 83n21, 299n20
Lane, P., 356nn49,52, 384n51, 486n33, 487n67
Lang, L., 486nn15,16, 487n55
Lanzolla, G., 299n27
Larimo, J., 83n21, 83–84n32
Larsson, R., 357n79
Lash, J., 511n68
Lasserre, P., 293, 300n47
Lau, C., 26nn5,33, 178n15, 274n9
Lau, H., 300n36
Lau, H. F., 435n42
Lau, T., 274n20
Lau, V., 274n5
Laurila, J., 383n18
Laursen, K., 384n46
Laux, P., 204n12
Laverty, K., 83n31
Lavie, D., 109n26, 327n35
Law, K., 461n37
Lawler, E., 460n3
Lawrence, J., 83n20
Lawrence, T., 510n40
Lazarova, M., 460n17, 461n57
Lazzarini, S., 355n10
Lecraw, D., 178n34
Lee, A., 58
Lee, D., 399n4
Lee, H., 274n20, 434n22
Lee, J., 26n33, 83n21, 435n57
Lee, J. R., 390, 392
Lee, K., 83–84n32, 84n38, 123
Lee, M., 84n66
Lee, P., 108n13, 487n66
Lee, S., 26n13, 84n42, 275nn52,55, 299n23
Lee, S. M., 116, 117, 118
Lehrer, M., 384n38
Lejeune, M., 434n2
Lenartowicz, T., 85n68
Lenin, 39
Lenox, M., 84n51, 510n13, 511nn43–44
Lenway, S., 26n28, 52n6, 151n18, 178n34, 383nn15,16
Leonard, H. J., 511n63
Leonard-Barton, D., 109n25
Leong, J., 88
Leonidou, L., 300n33
Lepak, D., 274n11, 460n13, 461nn40,52
Leung, K., 67, 83n19, 84n66
Lev, B., 511n56
Levenstein, M., 326n4
Leviev, L., 316
Levinthal, D., 384n51
Levitt, T., 84n56, 360, 361, 382n2, 413, 434n7
Levy, D., 108n22
Levy, M., 149
Levy, O., 461n57
Lewin, A., 356n38
Lewis, D., 26n20, 177n4, 237
Lewis, M., 412
Li, C., 435n58
Li, D., 88, 178n22, 275n32, 470
Li, J., 83n21, 356n53
Li, L., 274n22, 275n32, 300nn36,46, 384n48
Li, P., 26n33
Li, S., 27n36, 83–84n32
Li, X., 356n36, 486n24
Lieb-Doczy, E., 357n71
Lieberman, M., 109n35, 299n22
Lieberthal, K., 213, 383n25

Lien, Y., 26n33, 178n22
Liesch, P., 27n36, 108n4, 275n48, 299n18
Lim, K., 84n66
Lim, L., 434n6
Lin, X., 356n46
Lindbergh, J., 275n35
Lindblom, C., 178n36
Ling, Y., 383n10
Linowes, R., 452
Lipparini, A., 355n20
Lippman, S., 108n24
Lipstein, R., 326n12
Liu, D., 393
Liu, L., 83–84n32
Liu, X., 178n26, 383n17
Liu, Y., 433, 461n54
Locke, E., 274n13
Lockett, A., 511n55
Lockhart, D., 461n42
London, T., 25, 26n7, 27n40, 510n41, 524
Long, W., 487n40
Lopez-de-Silanes, F., 53n19, 257, 274n8, 486nn4,18, 487n52
Lord, M., 53n13, 108n19, 299n28, 356n59
Loree, D., 84n44, 356n58
Lorenzoni, G., 355n20
Lounsbury, M., 82–83n4
Lovallo, D., 109n33
Lowe, K., 67, 83n19, 460nn15,23
Lowe, R., 274n5
Lu, J., 52n4, 275n31, 356nn46,47
Lubatkin, M., 326n5, 461n43, 486n7, 487n67
Lucas, G., 146
Luehrmann, J., 236, 238
Lui, S., 356n39
Luk, D., 460n9
Lumpkin, G., 274n19
Lumpkin, T., 108n2
Lunnan, R., 384n50
Luo, Y., 26n33, 299nn21,28, 32, 356nn39,51, 384nn34,36, 385n54, 435n53, 487n63
Luque, M., 67
Luthans, F., 274n7
Lyles, M., 275n50, 355n7, 356nn48,49, 357n78
Lyons, R., 189, 204n5

M

Ma, H., 326n22
Ma, L., 461n42
Mabert, V., 435n41
Machalaba, D., 115n2
Macharzina, K., 434n13
Macher, J., 53n34
Machuca, J., 412
MacKinnon, P., 390, 391–393
MacMillan, I., 274n19, 326nn24,25,28
Madam Tien/Ten, 117
Madhok, A., 108n21, 177n8, 298n1, 355n10, 356n47
Madonna, 253, 513
Magee, R., 486n14
Mahmood, I., 26n14
Mahoney, J., 108n4, 109n40, 299n5, 460n7
Maignan, I., 84n35, 510n32
Main, B., 486n33
Mainkar, A., 326n5
Maitland, E., 178n17, 299n7
Majerbi, B., 204n9
Majumdar, S., 178n26
Makadok, R., 108n20
Makino, S., 83–84n32, 298n3, 299n24, 357n75
Makri, M., 486n33
Malnight, T., 383n15
Maloni, M., 434n30
Mamossy, G., 356n54
Man, T., 274n20
Mandela, N., 29
Manea, J., 383n8
Manev, I., 384n52
Mann, C., 151n23
Mar, P., 487n49
Marcus, A., 511n45
Margolis, J., 510n23
Marihart, J., 242–243, 244
Marino, L., 275n41
Markides, C., 382n1
Marler, J., 460n23
Marquis, C., 487n74
Marriott, J. W., 380
Marsden, D., 207
Marsh, L., 108n8, 274n20
Marsh, S., 326n15
Marshall, A., 204n14, 280
Marshall, R. S., 83n21
Martin, G., 236
Martin, M., 275n28
Martin, P., 150
Martin, X., 178n14, 356n54, 384n33
Martinez, Z., 25–26n2, 109n45
Mather, D., 300n42, 434n15
Mathews, J., 25, 26n33, 275n47, 327n36
Mathewson, G., 352
Matta, E., 486n32
Matten, D., 385n56, 510n31
Matthews, L., 235n31
Matthyssens, P., 384n45
Mauborgne, R., 326n29
Mavondo, F., 83n21, 299n20
Mayer, C., 434n18
Mayer, K., 108n12
Maznevski, M., 384n50
McAlinden, S., 176, 177
McBride, J., 383n17
McCarter, M., 434n27
McCarthy, D., 52, 53n12, 84n38, 357n77, 487n45
McCarthy, W., 237
McCutchen, W., 384n45
McDougall, P., 274n13, 274nn3,26, 275nn33,49
McEvily, B., 384n45
McEvily, S., 108n11, 109n43
McGarvie, B., 202
McGill, J., 355n15
McGrath, R., 274n19, 275n53, 326nn24,28
McGuire, J., 486nn23,32, 487n76
McKenzie, P., 433
McKinney, W., 357n80
McLaughlin, C., 511n47
McMullen, J., 274n1
McMurrer, D., 460n20
McNamara, G., 326n31
McNaughton, R., 275n38
McSweeney, B., 67
McWilliams, A., 53n13, 509n2, 511nn58,69
Meckling, W., 486n11
Medcof, J., 385n56
Meer, D., 434n10
Megginson, W., 486n10
Mehrmann, T., 393, 394, 398, 399
Meisinger, S., 455, 461n55
Melin, L., 108n15
Mellahi, K., 299n22
Melton, H. K., 321
Mendel, J., 237
Mendenhall, M., 460n9
Mendez, A., 384n50
Merchant, H., 403
Merret, N., 244
Meschi, P., 356n46
Mesquita, L., 355n19
Metcalf, L., 83–84n32
Meyer, G. D., 274n24
Meyer, K., 26n5, 56, 57, 178nn28,37, 235nn18,48, 299nn15,18,32, 356nn49,57, 357n71
Mezias, J., 26n16, 298n1, 355n10, 460n22
Meznar, M., 511n46
Michaels, S., 275n29
Michailova, S., 82n3, 178n29
Midgley, D., 383nn12,15
Miles, G., 275n30
Miller, C., 300n46
Miller, D., 109nn31,39, 204n9
Miller, K., 355n15, 383n7
Miller, R. S., Jr., 176–177
Miller, S., 26n16, 298n1, 298–299n4, 383n11
Miller, T., 298–299n4
Milliman, J., 460nn23,26, 461n48
Milstein, M., 27n40, 510n9
Minbaeva, D., 384n51
Minniti, M., 260
Minow, N., 485n1, 486n27
Mintzberg, H., 510n20
Mishina, Y., 109n40
Mishra, H., 384n34
Mitchell, M., 355n23
Mitchell, R., 275n41, 510n13, 511n58
Mitsuhashi, H., 274n16, 355n8, 383n19
Mjoen, H., 356n36
Modi, S., 435n41
Moeller, S., 356n63
Mohr, A., 356n46
Mol, M., 384n45
Molinsky, A., 460n13
Money, B., 434n8
Monin, P., 84n35
Monks, R., 485n1, 486n27
Monplaisir, L., 383n29
Montaigne, F., 492
Montes-Sancho, M., 511n53
Montgomery, D., 299nn22,24

Moon, H., 151n8
Moon, J., 511n55
Mooney, A., 486n22
Moore, K., 26n20, 177n4, 385n56
Morales, E., 172
Moran, P., 52n11, 84n62, 109n42, 487n68
Morck, R., 151n18
Morgan, G., 383n15
Morgan, N., 435nn32,37
Morgeson, F., 460n13
Morley, M., 461n36
Morosini, P., 83n21, 299n20, 357n71
Morris, S., 461n37
Morrison, J., 253
Morrow, J., 108n24
Morse, E., 275n41
Morse, G., 321
Mosakowski, E., 77, 84n33, 85n68, 274n11
Moss, S., 385n55
Moyer, R. C., 486n24
Mudambi, R., 52n11, 274n6, 383n9, 384n48
Mueller, S., 83n25, 274n10
Muhammad, 37, 55
Muhanna, W., 109n31
Mukherjee, A., 424
Mukherji, A., 27n43
Muldoon, J., 113
Mullaly, A., 359
Mullen, M., 84n63
Munday, M., 299n12
Murdoch, J., 467
Murdoch, R., 278, 314, 467
Muriel, A., 434n23
Murmann, J., 326n25
Murphy, K., 486n34
Murray, J., 109n37, 434n26
Murtha, T., 52n6, 178n34, 383nn15,16
Murthi, B., 461n43
Myers, M., 299n17, 434n8

N

Nachum, L., 109n45, 178n18, 298–299n4, 299n7
Nadkarni, S., 275n47
Nagarajan, W., 486n14
Nagele, J., 178n29
Nair, A., 355n26
Nakata, C., 83n17
Nalebuff, B., 326n3
Naoumova, I., 487n45
Napier, N., 357n77, 383n22, 461nn33,49
Napier, S., 57, 460n2
Narasimhan, O., 108n9
Narayanan, V., 435n33
Narula, R., 383n15, 384n45
Narus, J., 108n24, 435n38
Narver, J., 435n49
Nason, S., 460n26
Nasser, J., 359, 369
National Commission on Terrorist Attacks on the United States, 84n57
Navarra, P., 384n48
Neht, C., 511n45
Nelson, K., 84n34
Nelson, T., 274n14
Nendetto, C., 109n50
Ness, J., 514
Netter, J., 486n10, 487n38
Neubaum, D., 275n40
Neupert, K., 83–84n32
New York Times, 115n9
Newbert, S., 108n3
Newburry, W., 26n9, 83–84n32, 356n48, 385n56, 460n1, 461n49
Newman, H., 486n14
Newsweek, 120, 514
Newton, B., 405, 406, 407
Newton, T., 510n27
Ng, F., 326n16
Nguyen, H., 57
Nicholas, S., 178n17, 299n7, 355n33
Nicholls-Nixon, C., 274n16
Nielsen, A., 109n43
Nielsen, C., 510n21
Nieto, M., 275n35
Niezen, C., 434n28
Nigh, D., 383n18, 486n30, 511n46
Ning, L., 433
Nobel, C., 435n49
Nobel, R., 108n11, 357n79, 383n31, 384n49
Nohria, N., 402n3
Nooderhaven, N., 355n16, 383n20
Noorderhaven, N., 356n54
Nooteboom, B., 355n16
Nooyi, I., 369
Nordas, H., 151n14
North, D., 31, 43, 46, 52n2, 53nn26,28,29,35, 110
Northcraft, G., 434n27
Nunez-Nickel, M., 486n7

O

O'Brien, L., 382
O'Connell, E., 300n42, 434n15
O'Conner, J., 486n32
Oddou, G., 460n9
O'Donnell, E., 25
O'Donnell, S., 384n52
OECD Principles of Corporate Governance, 477
Office of the US Trade Representative, 304
O'Grady, S., 83n21, 299n20
Oh, K., 84n42
Oh, K. K., 123
Ohlin, B., 131, 137, 151n3
Ojah, K., 383n29
O'Leary, M., 207
Olffen, W., 461n43
Oliver, C., 355n8
Oloruntoba, R., 27n36, 422
Olsen, E., 435n50
O'Neal, S., 433
O'Neill, H., 487n66
O'Neill, P., 143
O'Rear, D., 479
Orris, T., 383n7
Ortiz, C., 120
Osegowitsch, T., 108n21
O'Shaughnessy, K., 510n4
Otto, J., 384n46
Overby, P., 115n3
Oviatt, B., 274nn3,26, 275nn33,49
Oxelheim, L., 178n33, 487n57
Oxley, J., 26n26, 275n41
Oxley, M., 463, 464
Oyserman, D., 83n20
Ozawa, T., 52n11

P

Padmansbhan, P., 299n29
Page, L., 469
Paik, Y., 383n22, 400, 461n33
Paine, L., 162
Pak, Y., 178n10
Palepu, K., 487n77
Palich, L., 383n26
Pan, Y., 82–83n4, 235n5, 288, 299nn26,30, 327n37, 356n36
Panagariya, A., 151nn26,27
Pantzalis, C., 204n12
Panunzi, F., 487n51
Parboteeah, B., 84n64
Parboteeah, K., 84n38
Parente, R., 109n37, 384n34
Park, H., 384n51, 460n29
Park, J., 384n52
Park, N., 355n10, 460–461n32
Park, S., 83n21, 274n14, 355n32, 356nn52,53
Park, Y., 178n10, 326n31
Parker, B., 510n40
Parker, S., 461n51
Parkes, C., 82n1
Parkhe, A., 26n16, 52n11, 298n1
Parmar, B., 511n60
Parmigiani, A., 108n15
Parnell, J., 83n23
Patel, N., 424
Pater, I., 460n13
Pathak, S., 384n51
Pattnaik, C., 26n33, 178n15
Paul, C., 52n11
Paul, L., 296
Pauly, P., 178n33
Pauwels, P., 384n45
PBS/Frontline, 182
Pearce, L., 461n42
Pearce, R., 356n45, 383n8
Pedersen, T., 298–299n4, 383n31, 384n51
Pederson, T., 486n5, 487n46
Pegels, C., 326n21
Pei, P., 394–395
Pellegrini, E., 83n23, 460n12
Peng, M. W., 4, 20, 25, 26nn3,5,11,12,13,15, 39, 40, 52, 52nn1,5,8,10, 53nn12,20,23, 57, 58, 59, 63, 84nn54,60, 107, 108nn1,4, 109nn45,53, 110, 118, 119, 123, 151n2, 179n40, 197, 234, 235nn18,48, 238, 241, 244, 250, 265, 275nn36,37,42,52,55–56, 288, 298–299n4, 299nn11,21,23,27,28, 300n35, 316, 330,

337, 342, 348, 349, 355nn7,14, 356nn41,51, 364, 384nn36,39, 385n54, 390, 420, 433, 435nn34,37,43,53,58, 445, 459, 468, 474, 479, 486nn8,9,17,24,26,31, 487n63, 496, 497, 512, 514
Penner-Hahn, J., 384n39
Pennings, J., 299n17
Penrose, E., 108n4
Pepermintwalla, C., 390
Peredo, A., 27n41, 511n72
Perez, P., 275n47
Perlmutter, H., 355n17, 460n6
Perot, H. R., 223
Peteraf, M., 108n6
Petersen, B., 298–299n4
Peterson, B., 300n41
Peterson, M., 83n27
Peterson, R., 83n30, 383n22, 461n33
Petrovits, C., 511n56
Pett, T., 83n30
Pettit, R., 356n55
Pettus, M., 108n4, 486n33
Pfanner, E., 56
Pfeffer, J., 27n42
Phan, P., 487nn39,57
Phelan, S., 299n8
Phelps, C., 299n25
Phene, A., 108n8, 274n20
Phillips, S., 109n48
Piesse, J., 26n33, 178n22
Pigman, G., 299n22
Pil, F., 435n40
Pillai, R., 460n3
Pinch, S., 178n18, 299n7
Pisano, G., 108n6
Pisano, V., 354–355n3
Pistre, N., 357n79
Pitelis, C., 108n4
Pitkethly, R., 83n31, 357n71
Pitman, S., 91
Plattner, H., 471
Pleggenkuhle-Miles, E., 238, 241
Ployhart, R., 460n4
Pollard, W., 458
Pollock, T., 108n12, 109n40, 486nn28,34
Polo, Y., 299n25
Porac, J., 109n40, 486n34
Porrini, P., 357n76
Porter, L., 461n42
Porter, M., 108n14, 135–136, 137, 151n7, 178n18, 384n35, 418, 434n19, 498
Posen, H., 109n31, 275n55
Post, J., 509n3
Pothukuchi, V., 83n21, 356n52
Pouder, R., 178n18
Powell, T., 109n33
Poynter, T., 178n24
Prahalad, C. K., 6, 7, 26n7, 109n52, 382n1, 383n25, 529nn2,11
Prater, S., 434n23
Pratt, M., 273
Preece, S., 275n30
Prescott, J., 26n14, 108n11, 384n52
Presley, E., 153
Preston, L., 491, 509n3, 510n16
Priem, R., 435n38, 486n32
Prince, C., 82
Prunnett, B., 355n5
Prusa, T., 326n14
Pucik, V., 108n11
Puffer, S., 52, 53n12, 84n38, 357n77, 487n45
Puranam, P., 357n68
Purcell, J., 461n49
Purcell, W., 178n17
Purdy, L., 435n41
Puryear, R., 109n48
Pustay, M., 83n28, 327n38
Putin, V., 50–51, 316
Putler, D., 510n14

Q

Qian, G., 83n21, 84n38, 274n22
Quelch, J., 415, 434n11
Quinn, A. G., 386
Quinn, D., 435n48
Quintens, L., 384n45

R

Rabinovich, E., 434n18
Rachinsky, A., 52
Rackham, N., 435n45
Radhakrishnan, S., 511n56
Ragozzino, R., 355n9, 357n79
Rahman, N., 403, 405, 406, 408
Rajagopalan, N., 355n25, 356n40, 486n35
Rajan, R., 27n34, 487n54
Rajiv, S., 108n9
Ralston, D., 57, 84nn35,58,59, 510n32
Ramamurti, R., 26n5, 52n6, 151n9, 179n42, 383n18, 487n49
Raman, A., 435n33
Ramsey, F., 273
Ramstad, E., 393n3
Ramus, C., 511n51
Randoy, T., 487n57
Ranft, A., 108n19, 299n28, 356n59
Rangan, S., 82–83n4, 275n51, 355n15
Rao, H., 84n35
Rao, R., 486n24
Rasheed, A., 487n57
Ravenscraft, D., 487n40
Ray, G., 109n31
Rayasam, R., 253
Reagans, R., 384n45
Redding, G., 84n65
Reddy, S., 300n39, 357n75
Rediker, K., 487n41
Reeb, D., 486n6
Reger, G., 383n5
Rehbein, K., 53n13, 510n38
Rehder, B., 487n57
Reid, B., 23
Reinmoeller, P., 510n4
Ren, Z., 325
Reuber, A. B., 275n35
Reuer, J., 204n9, 355nn9,14,28, 356nn38,43,44, 357n79
Reus, T., 356n47
Reynolds, P., 56
Reynolds, S., 84n34
Rhee, D., 460–461n32
Rhee, S., 178n28
Ribbens, B., 355n26
Ricardo, D., 129, 137, 138, 142, 166
Ricart, J., 26n30
Rice, C., 150
Richard, O., 383n26, 461n43
Richards, M., 298–299n4
Richardson, D., 326nn10,12
Ricks, D., 27n43, 83nn9,10, 429, 434n14, 452
Ridderstrale, J., 108n11
Riddle, L., 299n15
Rigby, D., 434n8
Rindova, V., 108n12, 275n34, 326nn2,20
Ring, P., 26n14
Risberg, A., 357n70
Ritchie, W., 356n47
Rivers, D., 235n45
Roath, A., 300nn36,37
Roberts, D., 250
Roberts, J., 384n50
Roberts, P., 108n13, 274n20
Robertson, C., 27n41, 75, 84n43, 510n34
Robins, J., 356n38
Robinson, J., 53n29
Roddick, A., 91, 272
Rodriguez, C., 434n31
Rodriguez, P., 26n14, 84nn42,43, 178n22, 299n32
Roehl, T., 83n21, 108n9, 355n17
Rogers, F., 435n41
Roland, G., 53n29
Roll, R., 356n61
Romilly, P., 510n11
Rondinelli, D., 27n40, 510n41
Ronen, S., 62, 63, 64, 83n13
Ropponen, M., 383n18
Rosa, P., 274n7
Rose, A., 230, 235n43
Rose, E., 299n7, 326n31
Rosenzweig, P., 83n8, 298–299n4
Ross, S., 383n11
Rossetti, C., 109n49
Rossi, S., 355n7
Rossum, W., 435n38
Roth, K., 109nn40,42, 371, 384n34, 385nn53–55, 510n42
Roth, M., 384n34
Rothaermel, F., 108n16, 275n34, 384n45, 434n25
Rowe, G., 274n16
Roy, J., 355n8
Rubach, M., 487n69
Rubanik, Y., 274n15
Rubinstein, S., 510n14
Ruckman, K., 383n9
Rufin, C., 26n14
Rugman, A., 26n30, 109n41, 151n8, 177n5, 235nn26, 46–47, 291, 292, 300n45, 382n3, 383n8, 510n30, 511n64
Rumelt, R., 108n24
Rusetski, A., 434n6
Russell, C., 85n70

Russo, M., 511nn52,53,56
Ryans, J., 83–84n32

S

Sachs, J., 193
Sachs, S., 509n3
Sadorsky, P., 510n25
Sadowski, B., 300n41, 357n73
Safarian, A. E., 383n17
Safayeni, K., 435n41
Saha, J., 403, 405, 407, 408
Sahay, A., 355n16
St. John, C., 178n18
Sakakibara, M., 384nn35,40
Sakano, T., 84n38, 355n16
Sala-i-Martin, X., 53n29
Salazar, J., 511n71
Salk, J., 82n1, 356nn49,52, 384n50, 510n40
Salomon, R., 178n14, 300n33, 384n33, 511n55
Salter, A., 384n46
Sambamurthy, V., 383n10
Samiee, S., 300n42, 434nn6,15
Sampson, R., 356n50
Sampson, R. R., 355n12
Samuelson, P., 143–144, 145, 151nn24,25
Sanders, W. G., 486n33, 487n44
Sanger, D. E., 115n5
Sanna-Randaccio, F., 384n41
Santoro, M., 355n15
Santos, J., 107, 372, 384n37
Saparito, P., 84nn54,60
Sapienza, H., 275nn43,46
Sargent, F., 208
Sargent, J., 235n31, 383n22, 461n33
Sarkar, M., 300n38
Sarkar, N., 459
Sarkar, P., 459
Sawyerr, O., 52n6
Saxton, T., 275n50, 356n58
Sayre, E., 299n15
Scandura, T., 83n23, 460nn12,22
Scheele, N., 176
Schlegelmilch, B., 300n36, 385n56
Schlingemann, F., 356n63
Schneper, W., 356n56, 487n43
Schnietz, K., 26n26
Schomburg, A., 274n20
Schoorman, F. D., 487n66
Schrage, B., 53n33, 487n71
Schroeder, R., 109n31
Schuh, A., 434n8
Schuler, D., 53n13, 510n38, 511n55
Schuler, R., 460n30, 461n46
Schultz, H., 489
Schultze, U., 384n33
Schulz, S., 120
Schulze, W., 326n5, 486n7
Schumer, C., 113
Schumpeter, J., 269
Schwab, S., 213
Schwartz, S., 83n16
Schweiger, D., 356n58, 384n50
Scott, R., 31
Scott, W. R., 52n3
Scullion, H., 461n36
Seawright, K., 275n41
Sebora, T., 487n69
Selmer, J., 461n38
Selsky, J., 510n40
Semadeni, M., 326n9, 355n21
Serapio, M., 356n42
Seth, A., 356n55, 384n34, 487n41
Sethi, D., 299n8
Sethi, P., 511n72
Sexton, D., 274n1
Shaffer, M., 274n5, 460nn9,14
Shahrim, A., 487n53
Shakira, 58, 512–513
Shamsie, J., 109n39, 299n25, 355n18
Shane, S., 83n21, 274nn2,3,19, 275n33, 299n20, 357n71
Shankarmahesh, M., 83–84n32
Shanley, M., 355n27
Shapiro, D., 84n44, 486n23, 487n48
Shapiro, D. M., 474
Sharma, S., 300n42, 434n15, 510n12, 511n45,50,70
Sharpe, D., 383n15
Shaver, J. M., 178n17, 299n12, 300n33, 357n65, 384n39, 510n30
Shaw, J., 461n42
Shen, W., 486n35
Shenkar, O., 25n1, 62, 63, 64, 82–83n4, 83n13, 85n70, 145, 151n21, 299n14, 330, 339, 342, 349, 355nn5,30, 356nn41,52, 357n79
Shepherd, D., 274nn1,5, 275n54
Sheremata, W., 384n45
Shim, W., 383n22, 461n33
Shimizu, K., 354–355n3, 355n9
Shimps, T., 300n42, 434n15
Shin, H., 20
Shin, S., 460n13
Shipilov, A., 356n46
Shleifer, A., 52, 53n19, 257, 274n8, 486nn4,18, 487nn47,51,52
Shrivastava, P., 510n9
Shuen, A., 108n6
Sia, C., 84n66
Siegel, D., 84n43, 509n2, 511nn58,69
Siegel, J., 487n75
Siggelkow, N., 109n26
Siler, P., 178n26, 383n17
Silvers, S., 91
Simkins, B., 204n12
Simmonds, P., 383n10
Simone, J., 53n24
Simonin, B., 355n35
Simons, R., 510n20
Simsek, Z., 461n43, 487n64
Sin, L., 435n57
Sine, W., 274n16, 383n19
Singer, P., 120
Singh, H., 83n21, 109n30, 299nn13,20, 338, 355nn17,29, 356n38, 357nn68,71
Singh, J., 109n30
Singh, K., 85n70
Sinha, I., 109n50
Sinha, R., 435n49
Sinkovics, R., 300n37
Sirmon, D., 108nn3,24, 356n52
Sirower, M., 357n65
Sitkin, S., 52n8
Sivakumar, K., 83n17
Skaggs, B., 109n31
Skarmeas, D., 300n36
Skill, M., 486n13
Skinner, P., 50, 483
Slangen, A., 357n71
Slater, J., 26n33
Slater, S., 109n50, 434n3, 435nn49,50
Sleuwaegen, L., 299n6, 434n25
Slone, R., 434n21
Smith, A., 39, 40, 41, 42, 111, 127–128, 129, 131, 132, 137, 138, 142, 166, 305, 427, 494
Smith, A. D., 386
Smith, B., 275n41
Smith, F., 326n9
Smith, G., 299n10
Smith, J., 435n55
Smith, K., 108n11, 274nn11,13,20, 326nn19,20, 461n45
Smith, P., 67, 83n27
Smith, T., 178n17
Snell, R., 384n51
Snell, S., 461nn37,40
Snoj, B., 435n56
Snow, C., 326n1
So, K., 433
Soekarnoputri, M., 117
Sohn, J., 383nn22,23, 461n33
Som, A., 384n47
Somasundaram, A., 434n23
Song, F., 486n33
Song, J., 355n10
Song, K., 356n55
Song, M., 109n50
Song, Y., 326n21
Sonnenfeld, J., 511n58
Sorensen, J., 275n29
Soros, G., 88, 89
Sorrell, M., 233
South China Morning Post, 145, 182
Spencer, B., 137, 151n5
Spencer, J., 82–83n4, 275n41, 384n46
Spicer, A., 84n38
Spich, R., 27n36
Spinella, A., 237
Sribivasan, T., 151n26
Stabell, C., 108n14, 384n33
Stafford, E., 355n23, 357n77
Stalk, G., 326n27, 422
Stanbury, W., 26n31
Stanislaw, J., 26nn21,23
Starkey, K., 27n42
Steen, J., 27n36, 108n4, 299n18
Steensma, H. K., 84n35, 108n11, 275n41, 355n7, 356n48, 357n78
Steger, U., 511n51
Stephen, W., 326n25
Stern, I., 486n28
Stevens, C., 298
Stevens, J., 84n35

Stevens, M., 27n38
Stevenson, W., 384n52
Stewart, S., 84n58
Stewart, T., 382
Stieglitz, N., 109n38, 274n20
Stiglitz, J., 26nn22,25, 193, 235nn3,32, 319, 327n39
Stiles, J., 389n6
Sting, 106, 253
Stopford, J., 382nn1,3
Strang, N., 244
Strange, R., 26n33, 178n22
Strange, S., 26n18
Straw, J., 55
Strike, V., 511n55
Stringer, H., 369
Strobl, E., 178n26
Stroh, L., 460n21
Stulz, R., 356n63, 464, 485n2, 487n61
Sturges, D., 299n15
Suarez, F., 299n27
Subramanian, A., 235n45
Subramanian, M., 108n11, 384n52, 385n53
Suddaby, R., 52n11
Suh, T., 299n32
Suharto, 117
Sun, S. L., 88, 325, 433
Sun Tzu, 305, 321
Sundaram, A., 511n62
Suslow, V., 326n4
Swamidass, P., 384n45, 434n23
Swaminathan, A., 299n22
Swan, K. S., 385n56
Szulanski, G., 355n35, 383n31, 384n49

T

Tadesse, S., 84n48, 487n50
Taggart, J., 385n56
Takenouchi, H., 355n16
Takeuchi, H., 384n35
Takeuchi, R., 460n13
Tallman, S., 27n36, 109n41, 178n18, 299n7, 339, 355nn10,30, 356nn36,38, 383n28
Tam, A., 106
Tan, B., 299n24
Tan, D., 108n4, 299n5, 460n7
Tan, J., 299n23
Tan, W., 274n9
Tao, Q., 245, 250
Tapon, F., 486n33
Tasker, R., 178n12
Taylor, A., 204n2
Taylor, E., 415, 434n11
Taylor, G., 511n64
Taylor, M., 204n2
Taylor, M. S., 274n11
Taylor, S., 460n2, 461n57
Teagarden, M., 461n48
Teece, D., 108n6, 298–299n4
Teegen, H., 27n39, 510n10
Tempest, S., 27n42
Teng, B., 355n16, 384n45
Terjesen, S., 300n44, 383n24, 385n59
Terlaak, A., 84n51, 511n44
Terpstra, R., 84nn58,59
Terpstra, V., 326n17
Tesker, R., 275n39
Tesluk, P., 460n13
Theodosiou, M., 434n6
Thomas, A., 83n25, 274n10
Thomas, D., 357n77, 461n57
Thomas, L., 83n30, 326n31
Thomke, S., 109n40
Thomsen, S., 487n46
Thomson, S., 486n5
Thulin, P., 178n33
Thun, E., 250
Tian, W., 83n25
Tian, Z., 510n4
Tierney, T., 402n3
Tiessen, J., 275n34
Tihanyi, L., 85n70, 298–299n4, 355n7, 486nn3,20
Time, 509
Timmons, J., 274n6
Tishler, A., 108n9
Tiwana, A., 355n13
Toh, S., 460n8, 461n35
Tolstoy, L., 335
Tomz, M., 235n45
Tong, T., 348, 355nn14,28
Toyne, B., 25–26n2, 109n45
Trabold, H., 275n36, 300n35
Trainer, T., 40
Transparency International Corruption Perceptions Index, 71
Tregaski, O., 461n49
Treisman, D., 52
Trevino, L., 84n34, 178n16
Tripoli, A., 461n42
Trompenaars, F., 83n16
Trotman, A., 359, 369
Tsai, T., 511n66
Tsang, E., 75, 84n42, 299n16, 356n49, 385n53
Tse, A., 435n57
Tse, D., 288, 299n30, 435n49, 461n37
Tsui, A., 356n53, 461nn41,42
Tsui-Auch, L., 487n76
Tulder, R., 84n35
Tung, R., 26n33, 460n10
Turban, D., 511n49
Turner, B., 390
Turner, I., 275n34
Turner, T., 314
Tuschke, A., 487n44
Twain, S., 106
Tyler, B., 434n31
Tyson, L., 144, 145, 235n22

U

Ucbasaran, D., 275n35
Uhlenbruck, K., 26n14, 84nn42,43, 299n32, 355n21, 356n57, 357n71, 486n10
Ungson, G., 299n26, 356n53
United Nations, 19, 26nn24,32, 177nn3,7, 235n35, 331, 336, 354n2
United Nations Conference on Trade and Development (UNCTAD), 157, 166, 373, 384n42
Urbano, J., 237
Ursacki-Bryant, T., 510n36
US Census Bureau, 177n2
US Department of Commerce, Bureau of Economic Analysis, 187
US Department of Justice, 306
US Trade Representative, 235n37
USA Today, 236, 237, 326n33

V

Vaaler, P., 53n33, 204n9, 326n31, 487n71
Vaara, E., 357n70
Vachani, S., 27n39
Vafeas, N., 510n12
Vahlne, J., 275n32, 299nn15,18
Vaidyanath, D., 354–355n3
Vakil, M., 524
Valdelamar, D., 83–84n32
Vam Tulder, R., 510n32
van Agtmael, A., 26n23
Van de Vliert, E., 83–84n32
Van den Bosch, F., 109n40
van den Ven, J., 356n55
van der Linde, C., 510n30
Van der Vegt, G., 83–84n32
van Fleet, D., 53n13
van Hastenburg, P., 356n55
van Kranenburg, H., 356n37
van Oosterhout, J., 510n34
van Putten, A., 326n28
Van Rossum, W., 108n24
van Wyk, J., 30
Vance, C., 461n57
Varma, A., 460n8
Vazquez, X., 420
Vegt, E., 83–84n32
Vegt, G., 384n40
Veiga, J., 461n43
Venaik, S., 383nn12,15
Venkataraman, S., 274n2
Venkatraman, N., 384n52
Verbeke, A., 26n30, 108n4, 109n41, 151n8, 235n47, 291, 292, 299n5, 300n45, 383n8, 510n30, 511n64
Verlegh, P., 300n42, 434n15
Vermeulen, F., 300n40, 354n3
Vermulen, F., 357n79
Vernon, R., 132, 137, 151n4, 178n24
Verona, G., 384n40
Vertinsky, I., 26n31, 299n24, 510n36
Very, P., 356n58
Veugelers, R., 384n41
Vianen, A., 460n13
Victor, B., 84n38
Vishny, R., 53n19, 487nn47,52
Vishwanath, V., 434n8
Visser, W., 511n55
Vliert, E., 384n40
Voelpel, S., 382
Vogel, D., 84n40, 490, 511n57
Volberda, H., 109n40, 384n51
Volpin, P., 355n7
von Glinow, M., 461n48
Voorhees, C., 355n13
Vora, D., 460n8
Voss, M., 237
Vredenburg, H., 511n50

W

Waddock, S., 511n56
Wade, J., 486nn28,34
Wakabayashi, M., 460n12
Waldman, D., 510n24
Wall, H., 216
Wall Street Journal, 115nn1, 11, 183
Wally, S., 326n17
Walsh, J., 510n23
Wan, H., 479
Wan, J., 487n73
Wan, W., 53n13, 298n3, 383n16
Wang, C., 178nn26,27, 383n17
Wang, D., 26n12, 39, 52n1, 63, 275n56, 299n11, 384n39, 461n42, 486n26
Wang, Y., 213, 355n33
Wang, Z., 83n27
Wangchuk, S., 326n16
Ward, S., 353, 354
Waring, G., 83n30
Warner, J., 114
Warsi, P., 106
Watson, A., 84n43
Watson, K., 275n50
Watson, R., 487n37
Weaver, G., 84n34, 510n32
Weaver, M., 275n41
Webb, D., 479
Webb, J., 434n29
Weber, M., 41, 73
Wehrfritz, G., 479
Wei, S., 84n45, 235n45
Wei, Y., 178n26, 238, 383n17
Weigelt, K., 326n31
Weiner, R., 204n14
Weingart, L., 461n44
Weiss, J., 69
Weitzel, U., 84n43
Welch, D., 177, 250, 300n41, 439, 442, 452, 460nn11,16
Welch, J., 449, 503, 511n61
Welch, L., 300n41
Welch, S., 449, 511n61
Weller, W., 434n28
Wellington, F., 511n68
Wells, L., 382n1
Werner, S., 178n25, 299n32
Wernerfelt, B., 108n1
West, G. P., 109n26
West, J., 83n21
Westhead, P., 275n35
Westphal, J., 486nn25,28–30
White, S., 356n39, 487n56
Whitley, R., 383n15
Whittington, R., 108n15
Wholey, D., 383n12
Whyman, P., 235n12
Whyte, R., 161
Wicks, A., 511nn56,60
Wilkins, M., 177n5
Wilkinson, T., 178nn25,30
Williams, K., 385n56
Williamson, K., 390
Williamson, O., 32, 52n7, 84n61, 107, 510n17
Williamson, P., 162, 372, 384n37
Wilson, D., 434n31
Wilson, K., 207
Wilson, R., 326n9
Wind, J., 326n23
Winter, S., 108n18
Wiseman, R., 486nn32,33
Witt, P., 487n69
Witteloostujin, A., 461n43
Woldu, H., 82n1
Wolf, J., 383n14
Wolfe, R., 510n14
Wong, C., 393
Woo, C. Y., 313
Wood, D., 510n13
Woodyard, C., 236
Wooster, R., 25
Worcke, S., 26n33
World Bank, 6, 15, 42, 53n30, 59, 83n18, 84n53
World Development Report, 42
World Investment Report, 19, 26nn24,32, 157, 166, 177nn3,7, 235n35, 331, 336, 354n2, 356n60, 373, 384n42
World Trade Organization, 125, 126, 150, 212, 213, 214, 235nn1–4,8,41, 304
Wright, M., 25, 26n5, 274n25, 275n35, 383n17
Wright, P., 109n36, 461n52, 486n33, 509n2, 511n46
Wright, R., 274n4, 275n34
Wu, C., 235n5, 327n37
Wu, F., 300n37
Wu, J., 325, 461n41
Wymbs, C., 299n7
Wysocki, B., 162

X

Xin, K., 356n53
Xu, D., 82–83n4, 235n5, 299n14, 327n37, 356n46
Xu, K., 434n15

Y

Yaffe, T., 298–299n4
Yakova, N., 83–84n32, 434n2, 461n49
Yam, M., 393
Yamakawa, Y., 82, 275nn42,55
Yamin, M., 384n46
Yan, A., 26n8, 356n46
Yan, Y., 356n45
Yanadori, Y., 460n23
Yang, B., 326n21
Yang, G., 83–84n32
Yang, Q., 384n47
Yankelovich, D., 434n10
Yarbrough, B., 204n15, 216
Yarbrough, B. V., 141, 150
Yarbrough, R., 204n15, 216
Yarbrough, R. M., 141, 150
Yau, O., 393, 435n57
Yearbook of China's Automobile Industry, 245
Yeh, K., 274n25
Yeh, R., 83n20
Yeheskel, O., 356n48
Yeltsin, B., 50, 51, 316
Yeoh, P., 109n40
Yergin, D., 26nn21,23
Yeung, A., 438
Yeung, B., 151n18, 275n41, 511n65
Yeung, H., 275n41
Yi, L., 238
Yim, B., 235n5, 327n37, 435n49
Yin, E., 300n46
Yin, X., 355n27
Yip, G., 382n1, 383n23
Yip, P., 299n16
Yiu, D., 26n33, 178n15, 357n75
Yoffie, D., 326nn26,30
York, A., 275n37, 300n35, 420, 435n37
Yoshikawa, T., 486n23, 487nn57,70,76
Youndt, M., 108n11, 109n31, 385n53
Young, M., 393, 399n3, 479, 486n17, 487n49, 515, 523n2
Young, P., 253
Young, S., 274n3, 275n38
Yu, C., 326n17
Yu, J., 84n38, 178n20
Yu, K., 84nn58,59
Yuan, W., 108n4, 299n5
Yuanqing, Y., 354
Yun, S., 460n13
Yunus, M., 261, 529n5

Z

Zacharakis, A., 274n24, 275n27
Zafirovski, M., 390, 393
Zaheer, S., 26n16, 82–83n4, 298n1, 383n18
Zahra, S., 109n43, 274n6, 275nn31,43
Zajac, E., 487n43
Zander, I., 275n47
Zander, U., 178n15, 355n34, 383n31
Zanoni, P., 460n8
Zdinakova, T., 208
Zedtwitz, M., 384n38
Zeira, Y., 356n48
Zellmer-Bruhn, M., 384n50, 461n45
Zelner, B., 26n14, 53n32
Zeman, A., 397, 399
Zemsky, P., 108n24
Zeng, G., 250
Zeng, M., 162, 356n46
Zestos, G., 235n11
Zhang, C., 300n36
Zhang, S., 486n24
Zhang, W., 510n36
Zhang, Y., 356n40, 434n23, 445, 461n42, 486n35
Zhao, H., 384n34
Zhao, J. H., 84n43
Zhao, L., 299n32
Zhou, C., 384n36
Zhou, J., 434n26
Zhou, K., 435nn49,56,58
Zhou, N., 461n37
Zhou, Y., 275n37, 300n35, 420
Zhu, C., 460n26
Zhu, G., 26n8
Zhu, H., 82–83n4
Zhukov, V., 487n49
Ziedonis, A., 274n5
Zietlow, D., 355n17
Zingales, L., 27n34, 487n54
Zollo, M., 356n38, 357n68
Zou, X., 515, 516
Zuchowski, D., 97
Zugehor, R., 487n57
Zurawicki, L., 84n46

ORGANIZATION INDEX

A

A-B (Anheuser-Busch), 25, 348
ABB, 366, 377
ABC, 314
ABN AMRO, 281, 286
ABSA, 280
Academy of Agricultural Sciences, 240
Accenture, 19, 400–402, 402n1
Adidas, 433
ADM (Archer Daniels Midland), 240, 241
Advansys, 207, 208
Aerospatiale, 303, 340
AFL-CIO, 448, 460n27
African Management Services Company (AMSCO), 258
AGRANA, 241–44
Ahava, 317
AIG, 15, 29
Air Baltic, 207, 208
Airbus, 87, 96, 130, 134–35, 136, 141, 161, 162, 278, 303–4, 320, 340, 347, 364, 365, 368, 416, 427
Air Dolomiti, 344
Air France, 208
Alcan, 19, 292
Alcoa, 19
Alliant Techsystems (ATK), 258
Allianz, 15
Alrosa, 316
Alstom, 292
Aluminum Corp. of China, 19
AMA (American Marketing Association), 434n1
Amanah, 286
Amazon, 89, 257, 297–98
AmBev, 348
AMD, 317
American Airlines, 311, 313, 332
American Aviation, 88
American Express, 414
American Marketing Association (AMA), 434n1
American Motors, 246, 248, 250n1
America's Research Group, 236
AMSCO (African Management Services Company), 258
AngloGold, 29
Anglo Selling Corporation, 316
Anheuser-Busch (A-B), 25, 348
Anhui Chery, 247, 249, 250n2
Apax Partners, 3, 5, 484
APL, 19
A.P. Moller-Maersk, 19, 56, 114
Apple, 417
Applied Materials, 455
Arcelor Mittal, 19
Archer Daniels Midland (ADM), 240, 241
Arla Foods, 55
ASDA, 331
Asia Brewery, 348
Asian Paints, 318
Asia Trade, 265
Assicurazioni Generali, 15
Astra, 345
AstraZeneca, 292
ATK (Alliant Techsystems), 258
Atys Group, 243
Audi, 237, 247, 282
Aventis, 292, 306
Avon, 46, 444
AXA, 15
Axe, 524

B

BA (British Airways), 208, 332
BAE Systems, 291, 292
Baidu, 266–267
Bank of America, 15, 281
Bank of China, 263
Bank of East Asia, 470
Bank of New York, 281
Bank of Scotland, 281
Bank of Tokyo-Mitsubishi, 508
Baogang Seed-Oil Corporation, 240
Baosteel, 19
BAPSC (British Association of Private Security Companies), 118, 120
Barclays, 281
Bare Feet (Pies Descalzos), 513
Barnes & Noble, 297
Bath & Body Works, 99
Bayer, 292
Beauté Prestige International (BPI), 372
Beauty in Prague, 208
Beijing Auto Group, 246
Beijing Auto Works, 246
Beijing Benz-DaimlerChrysler Automotive Co., Ltd., 250n1
Beijing Hyundai, 246, 247
Beijing Jeep Corporation, 245, 246, 247, 248, 250n1
BenQ, 101, 425
Berkshire Hathaway, 15
Bertelsmann, 99
Bertolli, 524
BHP Billiton, 19
Bill Currie Ford, 237
Bird, 318
The Bistro, 335
BISYS, 281
Blackstone Group, 484
Blackwater, 119, 120
BMW, 153, 155, 156, 157, 158, 249, 283, 334, 359, 414, 420, 421, 422, 450, 499
BNP Paribas, 15, 281
The Body Shop, 89, 91
The Body Shop International, 272
Boeing, 96, 134–35, 141, 161, 195, 258, 285, 303–4, 336, 340, 359, 367–68, 427
Bollinger/Incat USA, 277, 290
Bollinger Shipyards, 277, 278
Bombardier Aerospace/Leerjet, 161, 360
Boots, 388
Borders, 297
BP Amoco, 292
BPI (Beauté Prestige International), 372
Bridgestone, 292, 378
Bridgestone/Firestone, 359, 378
British Aerospace, 291, 340
British Airways (BA), 208, 332
British Association of Private Security Companies (BAPSC), 118, 120
British Petroleum (BP), 14, 19, 163–64
BSkyB, 467
Budweiser, 348
Bunge, 240
Bureau of Labor Statistics, 460nn27–28
Business in the Community, 508
Butler, 387, 388, 389

C

CAAC (Civil Aviation Administration of China), 87
Cadbury Schweppes, 369
Canon, 89, 136, 292
The Caparo Group, 296
Cape Diving & Salvage of South Africa, 30
Cardinal Health, 364
Cargill, 240
Carlsberg, 25, 55
Carlyle Group, 470, 484
Carrefour, 15, 55, 56, 99, 423, 424
CASA, 340
CBS, 314
CBS News, 114
Cengage Learning, 4
Census of India, 526, 529n6–7
Cerberus Capital Management, 336, 484
Cessna Aircraft, 161
CFIUS (US Committee on Foreign Investment), 112, 113
CFM International, 335
Changan Auto Motors, 246
Changan Ford, 246, 247
Chevron, 14, 19, 172
China Life, 480
China National Petroleum, 15
China Resources Breweries (CRB), 348
China Shipping, 19
Chinese Academy of Sciences, 353
Chrysler, 246, 250n1, 285, 308, 331, 336, 344, 345, 359, 484
Chrysler Group, 236, 237
CIGNA HealthCare, 281
Cisco, 324–25, 347, 414
Citco, 281
Citi, 414
Citibank Islamic Bank, 286
Citigroup, 15, 57, 68, 81–82, 194, 281
Citroën, 245, 246, 247
Civil Aviation Administration of China (CAAC), 87
CMA CGM, 19
CNN, 314
CNOOC, 345
CNPC, 19
CNW Marketing Research, 237
Coca-Cola, 168, 241, 278, 292, 317, 338, 360, 369, 413, 414, 416

Colgate Palmolive, 524
Commercial Metals, 19
Compal, 101
Compaq, 347
Computine Limited, 515–23
ConAgra, 241
Congressional Research Service, 237
ConocoPhillips, 15, 19
Continental (tires), 153
Co-op America, 490
Coors Beer, 58, 416
Corus, 19
COSCO, 19
Costco, 25, 181
CRB (China Resources Breweries), 348
Crédit Agricole, 15
Credit Suisse, 15
Croma, 424
CVS, 388

D

Daewoo Motor Company, 329–30, 342, 363
Daimler, 250n1, 336, 344, 345, 359
Daimler-Benz, 248
DaimlerChrysler, 15, 236, 245, 250n1, 292, 303, 331, 336, 347, 484, 503
Danone, 241
De Beers, 280, 314, 316
DeCare Dental, 281
Deere, 199
de Haviland, 285
Delegation of the European Commission to the USA, 235n10
Delhaize "Le Lion," 292
Dell, 36, 94, 95, 102, 347, 353, 354, 377, 421
Delphi Corporation, 168, 176–77
Delta, 87
DenTek, 386–89, 389nn2–3
Deutsche Aerospace, 340
Deutsche Bank, 15, 194, 281
Dexia Group, 15
DHL, 94, 403–8, 426
DHL Bangladesh (DHLB), 403–8
DHL Nepal, 405, 407
DHL Pakistan, 405, 406, 407, 408
DHL Sri Lanka, 405
DHL Worldwide Express, 403, 404
Diageo, 292
DiamondCluster International, 402n5
Dimension Data (Didata), 280
Dirafrost, 243
Disney, 99, 393, 396, 414
Disneyland Hong Kong, 291, 393–99
Disneyland Paris, 291, 416
Disneyland Tokyo, 291, 416
Dixons Group, 432
Dodge, 19, 236, 249, 507
Dove, 524
Dow Chemical Company, 496, 504, 505
DP (Dubai Ports) World, 345
Dubai Ports (DP) World, 111–15, 171–72
DuPont, 509
DynCorp, 119

E

EADS (European Aeronautic Defense and Space Company), 278, 292, 336, 365
Eastman Kodak, 101, 102, 199
easyJet, 208
eBay Inc., 273, 297, 334
EDS, 94, 101
Electrolux, 292, 517
Eli Lilly, 342, 347
Eller & Co., 113
Embraer, 336
EMI, 106, 107, 285
Emma Maersk, 422
ENI, 15, 19
Enron, 469, 470, 476, 495
Environmental Protection Agency (EPA), 498
Epson, 285
Ericsson, 94, 292, 419
Eurogate, 114
European Aeronautic Defense and Space Company (EADS), 278, 292, 336, 365
European Union (EU), 31
Evergreen, 19
Exporters Association, 253
ExxonMobil, 14, 19, 69, 199, 475, 495

F

Facebook, 417
Fairchild Semiconductor, 259
Fair Labor Association, 494
FAW VW (First Auto Works Volkswagon), 246, 247
FDA (Food and Drug Administration), 498
Federal Bureau of Investigation (FBI), 353–54
Federal Trade Commission, 355n6
FedEx, 422, 426, 429
Fiat, 282
Fiat-Iveco, 245
Financial Services Agency, 82
Firestone, 378
First Auto Works Volkswagon (FAW VW), 246, 247
Flextronics, 94, 101, 292, 377
FMCG, 528
FN Herstal, 515
Food and Drug Administration (FDA), 498
Ford Motor Company, 15, 59, 72, 73, 92, 157, 176, 236, 237, 245, 246, 247, 282, 308, 320, 329, 344, 359, 360, 361, 365, 369, 371, 378, 413, 427, 469, 500, 507, 509
Forest Stewardship Council, 501
Fortis, 15, 281
Founder, 516
Four Seasons, 347
Fox News Channel, 314
FT/Orange, 324
Fujian Daimler Automotive Co., Ltd, 334
Fuji Xerox, 332
Furukawa, 19

G

Galanz, 425
Gap, 411, 412
General Electric (GE), 15, 25, 333, 335, 341, 350, 354, 414, 445, 503, 517
General Motors (GM), 14, 25, 92, 162, 236, 237, 245, 246, 247, 248, 250n2, 285, 320, 329–30, 340, 342, 359, 363, 416, 500
Giat, 515
Gillette, 389n8, 414
Giordano, 417
GlaxoSmithKline (GSK), 292
Global Crossing, 469
Global Exchange, 489, 490, 492
GM. *See* General Motors (GM)
Godrej, 524
GoldStar, 390
Goodyear Tire, 423
Google, 257, 259, 345, 469
Grameen Bank, 525, 529n5
Greenpeace, 494
Grupo Mexico, 283
Grupo Modelo, 348
Grupo Televista, 278
GSK (GlaxoSmithKline), 369, 374
Guangzhou Auto Group, 246, 248
Guangzhou Honda, 245, 246, 247, 248
Guangzhou Peugeot, 246, 247, 248
GUCCI, 99

H

Häagen-Dazs, 372
Haier, 89, 162, 425
Hainan Airlines, 87–88, 96, 102
Halliburton, 119
Hanjin, 19
Hapag-Lloyd, 19
Harbin, 348
The Hartford, 281
Heckler & Koch, 515
Heineken, 25
Hellman's, 524
Henderson Land Development Co., 479
HerbaLife, 386
Heritage Foundation, 53n25
Hershey Foods, 241
Heublein, 341
Hewitt Associates, 94, 437
Hewlett-Packard (HP), 15, 102, 347, 353, 354, 363, 372, 402n1, 414
Hindustan Lever Limited Corporate (HLL), 524–29
Hitachi, 19, 498
H&M, 411
Home Depot, 15, 181, 501, 505

Honda Motor Company, 15, 25, 89, 97, 98, 195–96, 236, 237, 245, 246, 247, 248, 249, 285, 292, 320, 330, 334, 414, 444, 516
Honeywell, 350, 376, 517
Honeywell Canada, 376
Honeywell Limited, 376
Hong Kong Jockey Club, 394
Hong Kong Society for Panda Conservation, 395
Hon Hai, 94, 101
HOYA, 472
HP. *See* Hewlett-Packard
HP-Compaq, 350
HSBC, 15, 281, 286, 479, 508
HTC, 101
Huawei, 101, 318, 324–25, 516
Huggies, 284
Hundustan Lever Limited (HLL), 524
Hungarian Dental Travel Ltd., 208
Hutchison Whampoa, 114, 285
Hyundai, 97, 245, 246, 247, 248, 249, 282, 285, 294, 450

I

IBM, 15, 29, 95, 96, 101, 103, 199, 285, 292, 336, 337, 347, 349, 353–54, 377, 402n1, 414, 425, 454, 471, 516
IDA Ireland, 281
IFS International Fund Services, 281
IKEA, 32, 57, 99, 267, 268, 290
Illycaffé, 259
IMF. *See* International Monetary Fund
Incat, 277
Inco, 19
Infosys, 94, 481
ING Group, 15, 286, 292
Intel, 169, 259, 292, 317, 414
International Chamber of Commerce (ICC), 493
International Labor Office (ILO), 493
International Monetary Fund (IMF), 13, 31, 144
International Peace Operations Association (IPOA), 118, 120
Italia Telecom, 324
ITT, 504

J

J. D. Power and Associates, 237
J. P. Morgan Chase, 15
Jaguar, 344
Japan Airlines (JAL), 195
Japan Automobile Manufacturers Association, 238
JetBlue, 11
JFE Steel, 19
Johnson & Johnson, 387, 388

K

Kalms, Lord, 432
Kia, 245, 282
Kinkos, 429
Kiva, 272–73
Kmart, 181, 388
Kodak, 292
Kohlberg Kravis Roberts (KKR), 484, 485
Komatsu, 320
Kong Fu Zi, 74
Koplovitz & Co., 324
Korea Exchange Bank, 485
KPN, 324
Kroger, 181
Kwok Brothers Corporation, 240

L

Lafarge, 292
Legend, 353
Legend Holdings, 354
Lego, 55, 99
Lenovo, 25, 95, 349–50, 353–54, 445, 516
Lever Brothers, 524
Levi Strauss, 74, 360
LG Electronics (LGE), 7, 19, 390, 391
LG-Nortel, 390–93
Li & Fung, 421, 425, 426
The Limited, 99
The Limited Brands, 99
Li Ning, 417, 428–29, 433
Lipton, 524
Listerine, 388
Lockheed Martin, 368
Lone Star Funds of Dallas, 485
Long's Drug Store, 386
L'Oreal, 89, 91, 292
Louis Dreyfus, 240
Louis Vuitton, 414
Lowe's, 501, 505
Lucent, 324
Lufthansa, 208
LukOil, 164, 165
LVMH, 99, 292

M

Madonna, 253, 513
Maersk, 19, 56, 114
Magna Steyr, 420
Mail Boxes Etc., 429
Mannesmann, 331
Manpower, Inc., 94, 292, 450–51
Margarine Unie, 524
Markel Corporation, 200, 203–4
Marks & Spencer, 421
Marlboro, 215, 414
Marriott International, Inc., 380
Maruzen, 297
Mary Kay, 46
Matsushita, 19, 68, 285, 370
Maytag, 337
Mazda, 237, 359
McDonald's, 13, 25, 36, 185–86, 264, 289, 292, 335, 340, 360, 413, 414, 427
McDonnell Douglas, 303, 347
McGraw-Hill, 3, 5
McKesson, 15
McKinsey & Company, 400
McKinsey Global Institute, 100
Mediterranean, 19
Mercedes, 153, 283, 420, 449
Mercedes-Benz, 414, 420
Merck Frosst Canada, 362
Merrill Lynch, 281
Messier-Dowty, 420
Metro, 424
Michelin, 292, 369
Microsoft, 11, 40, 94, 96, 285, 314, 315, 320, 334, 345, 377, 404, 414, 445
Military Professional Resources, Inc., 119
Miller Beer, 331, 348
Minolta, 472
Minor Group, 266
Mitsubishi, 420
Mitsubishi Electric, 19
Mitsubishi Motors, 68
Mittal Steel, 364
Moeller Maersk, 19
Monster.com, 8
Motorola, 7, 285, 292, 318, 341, 372, 509
MSGM Masuku Jeena, 30
MSNBC, 314
MTN, 280
MTV, 74, 361, 362, 413
MySpace, 417

N

National Association of Chain Drug Stores, 388
National Basketball Association (NBA), 417, 433
National Commission on Terrorist Attacks on the United States, 84n57
National Council for Applied Economic Research, 525, 529n8
National Enquirer, 387
NBC, 314
NEC, 285, 290
Nestlé, 195, 241, 414
Neumann, 153
New Delhi American School, 459
New York Post, 314
News Corporation, 99, 278, 292, 314
Nigerian National Petroleum Corporation (NNPC), 163–64
Nike, 72, 92, 377, 418, 421, 424, 425, 433, 489, 494, 499
Nintendo, 96
Nippon Steel, 19
Nissan Motor, 15, 90, 98, 237, 245, 247, 249, 292, 331, 344, 369, 378, 444
Nokia, 7, 102, 167, 292, 318, 324, 414, 419, 424, 445
Noriba, 286
Nortel, 102, 390–91, 392, 393
Northern Trust, 281
Northrop, 336
Novo Nordisk, 55
NTT, 15
Nucor, 19
No. 93 Seed-Oil Corporation, 239, 240
NUMMI, 334, 340
NYK, 19

O

Occidental Petroleum, 172
Ocean Park, 393–99
OECD. *See* Organization for Economic Cooperation and Development (OECD)
Old Mutual, 280
OMERS Partners, 3, 5
One World, 332, 333
Onex Corporation, 161
Opel, 248, 282, 329, 363
Oracle, 347, 370, 471
Oral B, 388, 389
Organic Consumers Association, 490
Organization for Economic Cooperation and Development (OECD), 70, 71, 123, 239, 254, 309, 310, 326n13, 477, 479, 487nn59–60, 493

P

PacifiCare International Ltd., 281
Palm, 377
PalmOne, 102
Pampers, 284
Parmalat, 495
PartyGaming, 464, 480
PayPal, 273
PBS, 181, 273
PCI Electronics Manufactureing Services, 519
Pearson, 5
Pemex, 15
Peninsular & Oriental Steam Navigation Co. (P&O), 111, 112, 113, 114, 171
PepsiCo, 11, 168, 241, 278, 317, 369, 513
Pernod-Ricard, 341
Peugeot, 246, 247, 248, 282, 285
PFPC, 281
P&G. *See* Procter & Gamble
Phelps, 19
Philip Morris, 315
Philips, 292, 370, 377, 419, 420
Piëch family, 469
Pies Descalzos (Bare Feet), 513
Pizza Company, 156, 266
Pizza Hut, 159, 289
PNC Financial Services Group, 203
PolyGram/Universal, 106–7
Pond's, 524
Porsche, 97, 237, 420, 469
Portman Ritz-Carlton Hotel, 437–38, 439, 453, 454–55
POSCO, 19
Pramerica Financial, 281
PricewaterhouseCoopers, 30
Procter and Gamble (P&G), 338, 350, 369, 388, 389n8, 417, 516, 524
PSA, 114
PSA Peugeot Citroën, 248, 282
Publicis Groupe, 149

Q

QDOS, 94
Qinghe Technology, Ltd., 240
Quantum Fund, 88

R

R. J. Reynolds (RJR), 315
Radio Corporation of America (RCA), 101
Rakuten, 297
Ranbaxy, 342
Range Rover, 334, 359
Raytheon/Beech Aircraft, 161, 258, 336
RCA (Radio Corporation of America), 101
Reebok, 513
Reliance Group, 424
Renault, 247, 282, 331, 344, 369, 444
Rhose-Poulenc Rorer, 70
Rio Tinto, 19, 50, 483
Rite Aid, 388
Riva, 19
RJR (R. J. Reynolds), 315
RJR Nabisco, 484
Roche, 292
Rockefeller Center, 345
Rockefeller family, 475
Rolls-Royce, 59, 335, 428
Royal Ahold, 292, 495
Royal Bank of Scotland, 352
Royal Dutch Shell, 14, 16, 172
Royal Philips, 19
RUAG, 515
Ryanair, 11, 96, 207, 208, 219, 231, 312

S

Saab, 363
SAB. *See* South African Breweries
SABMiller, 25, 280, 331, 348
Sabre Travel Network, 171
S&A Foods, 106
SAIC. *See* Shanghai Automotive Industrial Corporation (SAIC)
Sam's Club, 25
Samsung, 7, 75, 158, 317
Samsung Electronics, 15, 19, 90
Sanmina, 519
Sanmina-SCI, 519
Santander, 292
SAP, 370, 471
SAPPI, 29
Sasol, 29, 280
SCI Systems, 519
Sea Land, 113
Sears, 181
Seattle City Light, 509
Seattle Coffee, 266
Seattle Computer Products, 94
Second Auto Works, 246
Second Life, 417
SEPA (State Environmental Protection Administration), 496
ServiceMaster, 458
Seven-Eleven Japan, 421
Sew What? Inc., 253, 254, 264
Shanghai Automotive Industrial Corporation (SAIC), 246, 247, 248, 363
Shanghai General Motors, 246, 247, 248
Shanghai Volkswagen, 246, 247, 248
Sharp, 97
Shell, 19, 504
Sheraton, 57
Shiseido, 372
Siemens, 15, 19, 324, 378, 381–82, 500, 517
Sinopec, 15, 19
Skanska, 292
Skoda, 318
SkyEurope, 208
Sky Team, 333
Slovenian Properties, 208
Small Arms Survey, 514
Smith & Wesson, 514, 515
Snecma, 335, 341
Snow Patrol, 106
Sodexho Alliance, 292
Sony, 19, 75, 90, 94, 285, 292, 317, 360, 369, 370, 378, 419, 420, 480–81
Sony BMG, 512
Sony Ericsson, 7, 94, 331, 377, 419
Sony Music, 106, 107
South African Breweries (SAB), 25, 280, 331, 348
Southwest Airlines, 11, 87, 88, 96, 207, 312
Spearhead (TSV-1X), 277
Spirit AeroSystems, 161
Standard Bank, 280
Star Alliance, 289, 333
Starbucks, 99, 160, 259, 266, 290, 371, 424, 489–90, 501
State Environmental Protection Administration (SEPA), 496
State Grid, 15
State Street, 281
Steirerobst, 243
Subaru, 363
Sugar Traders Association, 244
Sun Life Financial, 281
Sun Microsystems, 292
Surf, 524
Suzuki, 237, 282, 363
Swissair, 87
Swiss Re, 508

T

Target, 162, 181, 388
Tata, 524
TCL, 89, 101, 318, 425, 516
Telebras, 331
Telefonica, 324
Telkom, 29
Tesco, 424
Texas Instruments (TI), 290
Texas Pacific, 484, 485
Textron, 161
Thales, 336
Thomson, 3, 4, 5, 101
Thomson Corporation, 3, 484
Thomson Learning, 3, 484
Thomson Learning South-Western, 3, 5
Thomson-Reuters, 3
3Com, 325
3M, 199, 200, 292

ThyssenKrupp, 19
TI (Texas Instruments), 290
Tianjin Toyota, 246, 247
Time Warner, 99, 314
Toshiba, 19, 290, 341
Total, 15, 19, 172
Toyota Motor Company, 11, 14, 16, 89, 90, 97–98, 102, 162, 167, 195, 236, 237, 238, 245, 246, 247, 249, 282, 285, 292, 317, 320, 330, 331, 339, 340, 361, 414, 420, 450, 500
TransFair USA, 489, 490
Tsavliris Salvage Group of Greece, 30
Tsingtao, 348
TXU, 485
Tyco, 19, 469
Tyson Foods, 241

U

Unilever, 292, 505, 524, 526
Union Bank of Switzerland (UBS), 15, 194
Union Carbide, 495
United Airlines, 87
United Auto Workers (UAW), 176, 177, 237
United Colors of Benetton, 99
United Nations, 19, 26nn24,32, 155, 177nn3,7, 235n35, 331, 336, 354n2, 493
United Nations Conference on Trade and Development (UNCTAD), 157, 166, 373, 384n42
Universal Music Group (UMG), 106, 107
Unocal, 337
UN Security Council, 119
UPS, 94, 418, 422, 426, 429, 500
The UPS Store, 429
US Census Bureau, 177n2
US Coast Guard, 114
US Committee on Foreign Investment (CFIUS), 112, 113
US Customs and Border Protection, 114
US Department of Commerce, Bureau of Economic Analysis, 187
US Department of Homeland Security, 115, 353–54
US Department of Justice, 306, 355n6
US Government Accountability Office, 114
US Steel, 19

V

Vale do Rio Doce, 19
Valero, 19
Valero Energy, 15
Vallø Saft, 243
Valmet, 420
Verizon, 15
Vesta, 281
Viacom, 99
Victoria's Secret, 99
Vivendi Universal, 99
Vodafone, 324
Vodafone Air Touch, 331
Volkswagen (VW), 15, 163, 237, 245, 246, 247, 248, 249, 250, 282, 285, 318, 469
Volvo Cars, 359

W

Walgreens, 388
Wal-Mart, 14, 99, 124, 145, 158, 160, 162, 181–82, 200, 294, 320, 331, 362, 388, 423, 424, 425, 450, 516
Walt Disney Company, 99, 393, 396, 414
Waste Management, 509
Wells Fargo & Co., 273
Wendy's, 264
Whirlpool, 516, 517
Wikipedia, 314, 330, 348
Wink Group, 243
Wipro, 96–97
WKK Electronics, 519
Wolseley, 292
Wong's Electronics, 519
Woolworths, 424
World Bank, 12, 44, 70, 110, 204n6, 255, 258, 319, 509
WorldCom, 495
World Commission on Encironment and Development, 510n7
World Trade Organization (WTO), 17, 31, 126n, 150, 212, 213, 214, 240, 245, 246
Wrigley, 141
Wuhan Shenlong Citroën, 246, 247, 248

X

Xanga, 417
Xianyang Andre Juice Co. Ltd., 243

Y

Yahoo!, 293, 297, 334
Yamaha, 320
Yokogawa Hewlett-Packard, 372
YouTube, 345

Z

Zara, 411–12, 419, 425, 428–29
Zeneca, 345
ZIM Integrated Shipping Services Ltd., 113

SUBJECT INDEX

A

absolute advantage, 127–29, 137
  defined, 127
absolute advantage theory, defined, 127
absorptive capacity, defined, 375
accommodative strategy
  CSR and, 498–99
  defined, 498
acquisition premium, defined, 335
"Acquisition and Execution" (video), 352
acquisitions. *See also* alliances and acquisitions
  acquisition premium, 335
  AGRANA integrative case, 241–44
  challenges in postacquisition integration, 346
  defined, 331
  Embraer small commercial and military aircraft case, 336
  hubris and, 344
  imitability and, 336
  improving odds for acquisition success, 350
  motives for, 344–45
  organizational fit and, 336
  organization and, 336
  performance of, 345–47
  rarity and, 336
  resources and, 335–36
  stakeholder concerns during M&As, 346
  symptoms of failures of, 345
  value and, 335–36
  variety of cross-border mergers and acquisitions, 331
actions and criticisms case, IMF's, 193
adaptability, defined, 419
administrative policy, defined, 140
Africa. *See also* South Africa
  beefing up management capabilities in, 258
  cotton farmers in West Africa and Mississippi case, 234
  regional economic integration in, 228, 229
  SMEs and, 258
African National Congress (ANC), 29, 34
agency costs, defined, 467
agency relationship, defined, 466
agency theory, defined, 466
agent, defined, 466
agglomeration
  defined, 161, 280
  of financial services firms in Ireland, 281
agility, defined, 419
AGRANA integrative case, 241–44
  acquisitions and, 243–44
  Central and Eastern Europe origins and expansion to worldwide industry and, 241–42
  diversifying into biofuel and, 244
  divisions, 242
  plant locations, 242, 243
  product-related diversification and, 242–43
airline industry
  air capital in Wichita, Kansas case, 161
  Boeing versus Airbus case, 303–4
  prisoners' dilemma for, 307
  Sabre Travel and FDI versus outsourcing case, 171
alignment defined, 420
  supply chain management and, 420–23
  3PL and, 420
alliances
  combating opportunism in evolution of, 341
  from corporate marriage to divorce in evolution of, 341–43
  dissolution of, 342
  equity-based versus nonequity-based, 340
  evolution of, 341–43
  factors constituting alliance performance, 343
  formation chart, 339
  formation of, 338–40
  imitability and, 335
  improving odds for alliance success, 349
  learning by doing and, 339
  M&As and, 347
  organization and, 335
  performance of, 343
  rarity and, 335
  relational capability and, 335
  resources and, 333–35
  stage one, to cooperate or not to cooperate in formation of, 338
  stage two, contract or equity in formation of, 339–40
  stage three, specifying relationship in formation of, 340
  value and, 333–35
alliances and acquisitions
  A-B goes from minority shareholder to aggressive bidder case, 348
  alliances versus acquisitions table, 338
  choosing between, 337–38
  contractual alliances, 331
  Daewoo and GM from alliance to acquisition case, 329–30
  equity-based alliances, 330, 331
  implications for actions of management and, 349
  institutions and resources and, 332–33
  Lenovo and IBM case, 353–54
  majority JVs as control mechanisms versus minority JVs as real options debate, 347–48
  management savvy and, 349–50
  M&As and, 331
  mergers and, 331
  strategic alliances, 330, 333
  strategic investment and, 330
  variety of cross-border mergers and acquisitions, 331
  variety of strategic alliances, 330
Amazon in Japan case, 297–98
American auto industry
  integrative case, 236–38
  automakers using American and Canadian parts, 237
  components and manufacture of American cars, 236
Americas. *See* North America; South America; specific countries
ANC (African National Congress), 29, 34
Andean Community, defined, 224
Anheuser-Busch, from minority shareholder to aggressive bidder case, 348
Anna Karenina (Tolstoy), 335
antidumping
  competition versus, 319
  formal institutions governing international competition with focus on, 310–11
antidumping duty, defined, 140
antitrust laws
  defined, 305
  Sherman Act, 1890, 305, 319, 320
antitrust policy
  defined, 309
  formal institutions governing domestic competition with focus on, 309–10
  managers versus antitrust policymakers, 319–20
ANZCERTA (Australia-New Zealand Closer Economic Relations Trade Agreement; CER), 226
APEC. *See* Asia-Pacific Economic Cooperation (APEC)
Argentina and Hong Kong currency boards case, 197
ASEAN. *See* Association of Southeast Asian Nations (ASEAN)
Asia Pacific
  ANZCERTA and CER and, 226
  APEC and, 227–28
  ASEAN and, 226–27
  Asia Trade Exports to Russian Far East case, 265

Asia Pacific, *continued*
Four Tigers and, 12, 74, 123
Portman Ritz-Carlton Hotel's best employer in Asia case, 437–38
regional economic integration map, 227
tips about corruption around the Pacific integrative case, 116–18
Asia-Pacific Economic Cooperation (APEC), 227–28
Association of Southeast Asian Nations (ASEAN), 226–27
attack, defined, 314
Australia
Bosch Report, 477
Incat's warship names Joint Venture defense technology firm case, 277
Australia-New Zealand Closer Economic Relations Trade Agreement (ANZCERTA/CER), 226
Austria. *See* AGRANA integrative case
automobile industry. *See also* American auto industry integrative case; China, and competition in auto industry integrative case
counterfeiting in China and, 250n2
making cars in Central Europe case, 282
awareness, counterattacks in competitive dynamics and, 315

B

balance of payments, defined, 187
balance of trade, defined, 126
balance sheet approach
defined, 446
hypothetical expatriate compensation package using, 447
versus going rate on expatriate compensation, 446
bandwagon effect, defined, 189
Bangladesh. *See* DHL Bangladesh integrative case
Barbarians at the Gate (Burrough), 484
bargaining power
defined, 168
Intel bargaining with Israel and, 169
MNE bargaining with host governments, 168–70
obsolescing bargain, 169
three Cs of MNE bargaining with host governments, 170
base of pyramid
defined, 7
mobile phones and, 7
BEE (Black Economic Empowerment), 29, 30
beefing up management capabilities in Africa case, 258
benchmarking, defined, 91
bid rate, defined, 194
Black Economic Empowerment (BEE), 29, 30
board of directors
board composition and, 469
board interlocks and, 470
CEO duality and, 469
CG and, 469–71
inside director and, 469
leadership structure and, 469–70
outside director and, 469
role of, 470–71
Boeing versus Airbus case, 303–4
born global
defined, 261
slow internationalizers versus born global start-ups, 267–68
Bosch Report, 477
BOT (build-operate-transfer), defined, 289
Brazil, Embraer small commercial and military aircraft case and, 336
Bretton Woods system, defined, 190
BRIC, defined, 13
"Bright Ideas" (video), 106
build-operate-transfer (BOT), defined, 289
business, defined, 4–5
Buy American, The Untold Story of Economic Nationalism (Frank), 237

C

CAA (Clean Air Act), 497
Cadbury Report, 477
CAFTA (United States-Dominican Republic-Central America Free Trade Agreement), defined, 225
Canada
automakers using American and Canadian parts, 237
Dey Report, 477
salmon, chicken of the sea case, 492
capabilities
counterattacks in competitive dynamics and, 316
cross-border, 99–100
defined, 89
domestic resources versus international capabilities, 99–100
ethics and, 91
examples of financial resources and, 90
examples of physical resources and, 90
examples of tangible resources and, 90
financial resources and, 89
Hainan Airlines and, 87–88
human resources and, 89–90
imitability and, 97–98
innovation resources and, 90
intangible resources and, 90
organizational resources and, 89, 90
organization of firm and, 98–99
physical resources and, 89
reputational resources and, 90
resources, and VRIO framework for analyzing, 95–99
resources and, 89–90
technological resources and, 89, 90
value-adding, 95–96
VRIO framework for analyzing resources and, 95
capacity to punish, defined, 307
capital flight, defined, 189
captive sourcing, defined, 94
car industry. *See* automobile industry
cartel, defined, 305
causal ambiguity, defined, 97
CEE (Central and Eastern European), 241, 242, 243, 244n1
center of excellence, defined, 362
Central and Eastern European (CEE), 241, 242, 243, 244n1
Central Europe, making cars in, 282
CEO duality, defined, 469
CER (Australia-New Zealand Closer Economic Relations Trade Agreement; ANZCERTA), 226
CG. *See* corporate governance (CG)
CG Forum of Japan Code, 477
China. *See also* Computime integrative case; soybean industry in China integrative case
Chinese menu for development integrative case, 110–11
Chinese refrigerator plant in Camden, SC and, 162
Code of CG for Listed Companies, 477
competing for talent in China case, 445
counterfeiting and, 40, 250n2
debate on US trade deficit with, 145
Dow Chemical Company in China case, 496
first five years in WTO, 213
Lenovo and IBM case, 353–54
Li Ning sporting goods company case, 433
making M&As fly in China case, 337
slapping quotas on, 144
US-China Business Council, 147

yuan and Wal-Mart case, 181–82
China, and competition in auto industry integrative case, 245–50
auto production volume and growth rate in China, 245
emerging domestic players and, 249
evolution of FDI in auto industry and, 245–46
evolution of relative market share among major auto manufacturers in China and, 247
future of auto industry in China and, 249–50
GM and, 248
Honda and, 248–49
market and, 245
Peugeot and, 248
timing and initial investment of major auto producers and, 246
VW and, 247
Citigroup financial services case, 81–82
civilization
defined, 62
Huntington civilizations, 62, 63
civil law
application of, 36
countries with, 37
defined, 36
classical trade theories
defined, 127
new realities versus, 143–46
Clean Air Act (CAA), 497
clean (free) float, defined, 188
cluster
defined, 62
GLOBE clusters, 62, 63
Ronen and Shenkar clusters, 62, 63
CMEA (Council for Mutual Economic Assistance), 123
Code of CG for Listed Companies, 477
Code of Corporate Conduct, 477
codes of conduct, defined, 68, 499
codes of ethics, defined, 499
cognitive pillar
defined, 31
informal institutions and, 57
collaborative capability, defined, 335
collectivism, defined, 66
in-group members and, 76
opportunism versus individualism and collectivism debate, 75–77
out-group members and, 76
collusion, defined, 305
collusive price setting, defined, 310
co-marketing, defined, 289
command economy, 39–40
defined, 40
commoditization, defined, 91
common law
countries with, 37
defined, 36
interpretation of, 36
common market, defined, 217
Communist totalitarianism, 35
comparative advantage, 129–31, 137
defined, 129
comparative advantage theory
defined, 129
individual use of, 131
compensation
across-the-board pay cut versus reduction in force and, 454–55
defined, 444
for expats, 445–46
going rate versus balance sheet approach on expatriate, 446
for HCNs, 446–48
hypothetical expatriate compensation package using balance sheet approach, 447
competing in Chinese auto industry integrative case, 245–50
competition policy, defined, 309
competitive advantage, implications for actions of management and, 103
competitive analysis, 304–5
defined, 304
competitive dynamics
antitrust laws and, 305
attack and counterattack and, 315–16
attacks and, 314
Boeing versus Airbus case, 303–4
capacity to punish and, 307
cartel and, 305
collusion and, 305
competition policy and, 309
competition versus antidumping and, 319
concentration ratio and, 307
contender strategy and, 318
cooperation and collusion and, 305–8
cooperation and signaling and, 316–17
counterattacks and, 314
cross-market retaliation and, 308
defender strategy and, 317
defined, 304
dodger strategy and, 318
explicit collusion and, 305
extender strategy and, 318
feint and, 315
formal institutions governing domestic competition with focus on antitrust policy and, 309–10
framework for competitor analysis between pair of rivals and, 313
gambit and, 315
game theory and, 305
global vitamin cartel and, 306
imitability of resources and, 312
industry characteristics and possibility of collusion vis-à-vis competition and, 307
institutions, recourses and, 308
institutions governing domestic and international competition, 309–11
international price comparisons and, 309
local firms versus multinational enterprises and, 317–18, 393–99
management savvy and, 320–21
managers versus antitrust policymakers and, 319–20
market commonality and, 308
military terms and, 305
multimarket competition and, 308
mutual forbearance and, 308
organization and, 312–13
price leader and, 307
prisoners' dilemma and, 305
prisoners' dilemma for airlines and, 307
rarity of resources and, 312
resource similarity and, 313
resources influencing, 311–14
tacit collusion and, 305
thrust and, 314
tips on competitive intelligence and counterintelligence and, 321
types of attack and, 314–15
value of resources and, 311–12
complementary assets, defined, 98
Computime integrative case, 515–23
business mix and, 517
competition in electronics OEM industry and, 519
customer focus and, 517
family businesses and, 515–16
HRM and, 518
management philosophy and, 518
operational areas and, 516–17
organizational structure and, 518–19
Pearl River Delta in Southern China and, 516
phases of restructuring business and, 519–22
reorganization plan and, 522
restructuring business and, 519
social, employee, and environmental policies, 518
strategic challenges and, 523
vendors and, 517–18
concentrated ownership, defined, 465

concentration ratio, defined, 307
Confederation of Indian Industry Code of CG, 477
contagion effect, defined, 167
contender strategy, defined, 318
context, defined, 61
contractual (nonequity-based) alliances defined, 331
  equity-based versus, 340
copyright, defined, 38
corporate governance (CG)
  board of directors and, 469–71
  Computime integrative case, 515–23
  cross-listing and, 479
  David Webb as shareholder activist in Hong Kong case, 479
  defined, 464
  executive compensation at SAP case, 471
  formal institutional frameworks and, 475–76
  global convergence versus divergence and, 478–80
  global perspective on governance mechanisms and, 473–74
  governance mechanisms and, 471–73
  implications for actions of management and, 480
  informal institutions frameworks and, 476–77
  institutions and, 475–77
  internal/external governance mechanisms with global perspective and, 474
  listing in New York case, 464–65
  management savvy and, 480–81
  managerial human capital and, 478
  managers and, 466–68
  opportunistic agents versus managerial stewards and, 478
  owners and, 465–66
  private equity challenge case, 484–85
  resources, institutions and, 475
  resources and, 477–78
  selected CG codes around the world since the 1990s, 477
  stewardship theory and, 478
  tripod of, 464
  two primary families of systems of, 474
corporate social responsibility (CSR)
  accommodative strategy and, 498–99
  active versus inactive CSR engagement overseas and, 504
  codes of conduct and, 499
  defensive strategy and, 498
  defined, 489–90
  domestic versus overseas social responsibility and, 502–3
  Dow Chemical Company in China case, 496
  economic performance link to, 502
  global sustainability and, 491–92
  imitability and, 501
  implications for actions of management and, 505
  institutions, resources and, 497
  institutions and, 496–97
  management savvy and, 505
  for MNEs recommended by international organizations and, 493
  nature of firm in society and, 494–95
  offsetting carbon emission case, 508–9
  organization and, 501–2
  primary and secondary stakeholder groups and, 494
  proactive strategy and, 499–500
  race to bottom versus race to top and, 503–4
  reactive strategy and, 497–98
  resources and, 497, 500–502
  salmon, chicken of the sea case, 492
  social issue participation and, 500
  stakeholders and, 490–95
  Starbucks and CSR case, 489–90
  US chemical industry responds to environmental pressures and, 497
  value and, 500–501
Corporate Social Responsibility Annual Report (Starbucks), 490
corruption
  defined, 70
  ethics and, 70–71
  FCPA, 70
  tips about corruption around the Pacific integrative case, 116–18
  transparency international rankings of corruption perceptions, 71
cotton farmers in West Africa and Mississippi case, 234
Council for Mutual Economic Assistance (CMEA), 123
counterattack, defined, 314
counterfeiting
  China and, 40, 250n2
  worldwide, 39, 123
country and regional manager, defined, 364
country-of-origin, defined, 416
crawling bands, defined, 188
"Creating Financial Acumen with Your Company" (video), 202
cross-border capabilities, 99–100
cross-listing, defined, 479
cross-market retaliation, defined, 308
cross-shareholding, 330–31
  defined, 330
CSR. *See* corporate social responsibility (CSR)
cultural distance, defined, 283
cultural intelligence defined, 77
  five profiles of, 77
  implications for action using six rules of thumb when venturing overseas and, 78
  management savvy and, 77–78
culture
  context approach to, 61–62
  convergence versus divergence debate over cultural change, 74–75
  cultural clusters, 62–63
  defined, 57–58
  dimension approach to, 64–66
  femininity and, 66
  global business and, 66–68
  high-context versus low-context, 61
  Hofstede's dimensions of culture, 64–65, 67
  individualism and, 64–65
  language, 58–59
  long-term orientation and, 64–65
  low-context cultures, 61
  masculinity and, 64–65
  North Vietnam versus South Vietnam and, 57
  power distance and, 64–65
  religion, 59–61
  uncertainty avoidance and, 64–65
currency board, defined, 196
currency hedging, defined, 194
currency risk, defined, 195
currency swap, defined, 194
customs union, defined, 217

D

Daewoo and GM from alliance to acquisition case, 329–30
Dallas versus Delhi employment case, 459
Danish cartoons of Muhammad case, 55–56
David Webb as shareholder activist in Hong Kong case, 479
deadweight costs, defined, 138
defender strategy, defined, 317
defensive strategy, defined, 498
Delphi, and going bankrupt and then going overseas case, 176–77
democracy, defined, 34
demonstration effect, defined, 167
DenTek's UK decision integrative case, 386–89

mass market sales and, 389
time line of DenTek product development, 387
development
defined, 442
repatriates and repatriation and, 443–44
Dey Report, 477
DHL Bangladesh integrative case, 403–8
DHLB matrix structure and, 407
history of DHLB, 403–4
HQ and HRIS at DHL, 404–5
HR department at DHLB, 404
HRIS at DHLB, 404
HRIS decision and, 408
HRIS search at DHLB, 405
Karachi meeting and, 405–6
regional HQ at DHLB, 407–8
DHL chases the sun case, 94
diamond theory, 135–36, 137
defined, 135
Porter diamond and, 135
dictatorship, 34–35
defined, 34
diffused ownership, defined, 465
direct export, defined, 262
direct ownership, benefits of, 159
dirty (managed) float, defined, 188
dissemination risks, defined, 159
distribution channel, defined, 418
dodger strategy, defined, 318
Doha Round
cotton farmers in West Africa and Mississippi case, 234
defined, 213
WTO and, 213–15
domestic competition
collusive price setting and, 310
formal institutions governing domestic competition with focus on antitrust policy and, 309–10
predatory pricing and, 310
procompetition policy and, 309
proconsumer policy and, 309
proincumbent policy and, 309
proproducer policy and, 309
Dow Chemical Company in China case, 496
downstream vertical FDI, defined, 156
DP World integrative case, 111–15
drapery business case, 253, 254
Dubai, DP World integrative case and, 111–15
dumping
competition versus antidumping, 319
defined, 311
formal institutions governing international competition with focus on antidumping, 310–11

E

The East Asian Miracle (World Bank), 74
Eastern values versus Western values debate, 73–74, 75
economic development
Chinese menu for development integrative case, 110–11
drivers of, 41–43
Western values versus Eastern values debate and, 73–74, 75
economic system, 39–41
defined, 39
economic union, defined, 217
economy. *See also* world economy
command, 40
market, 39
mixed, 40
Economist Intelligence Unit, 25, 26n6, 44, 299n9
"Effective Corporate Governance" (video), 483
efficiency seeking
defined, 282
making cars in Central Europe case, 282
Embraer small commercial and military aircraft case, 336
emerging economies
BRIC, 13
contributions of, 5
defined, 5
Four Tigers, 12
emerging markets
BRIC, 13
contributions of, 5
defined, 5
Four Tigers, 12
Employee Free Choice Act, 449
enterprise resources planning (ERP) software, 96
entrepreneurial firms. *See also* firms
born global and, 261
costs of starting up new, 256
direct export and, 262
entrepreneurship and, 254–55
export and import transaction and, 263
export intermediary and, 265
financing and, 259–61
franchising and, 264
growing, 258–61
growth and, 258
Illycaffé, perfection from bean to cup case, 259
implications for actions of management and, 269
indirect exports and, 265
informal investment as a percentage of GDP and, 260
innovation and, 258–59
internationalization strategies for markets and, 262
internationalizing, 261–66
international strategies for entering foreign markets and, 262–65
international strategies for staying in domestic markets and, 265–66
L/C and, 263
licensing and franchising and, 263
management savvy and, 269
sporadic exporting and, 262
stage models and, 264
transaction costs and entrepreneurial opportunities, 261–62
venture capital investment as a percentage of GDP and, 260
entrepreneurs
defined, 254
implications for actions of management and, 269
management savvy and, 269
entrepreneurship
antifailure bias versus entrepreneur-friendly bankruptcy laws and, 268–69
defined, 254
entrepreneurial firms and, 254–55
institutions, resources and, 255
institutions and, 255–58
Kiva revolutionizes microfinance case, 272–73
microfinance cases and, 261, 272–73
resources and, 255, 256–58
slow internationalizers versus born global start-ups and, 267–68
traits versus institutions and, 266–67
entry modes. *See* modes of entry
Environmental Protection Agency (EPA), 497, 498
equity-based alliance
defined, 330, 331
equity-based versus nonequity-based alliances, 340
equity mode
advantages and disadvantages of modes of entry and, 287
defined, 286
ERP (enterprise resources planning) software, 96
ethical dilemmas
A-B goes from minority shareholder to aggressive bidder case, 348
IMF's actions and criticisms case, 193
microfinancing and macro success case, 261
quotas on China and, 144
subsidiary initiative at Honeywell Canada and, 376

ethical dilemmas, *continued*
tips about corruption around the Pacific integrative case, 116–18
ethical imperialism, defined, 69
ethical relativism, defined, 69
ethics
cartoons of Muhammad and, 56
Citigroup financial services case, 81–82
corruption and, 70–71
CSR codes of, 499
defined, 68
Exxon Valdez oil spill and, 69
global vitamin cartel and, 306
impact of, 68–69
L'Oreal acquires the Body Shop case, 91
middle-of-the-road approaches to managing ethics overseas, 69
norms and, 72–73
overseas management of, 69–70
strategic responses to ethical challenges, 72
ethnocentric approach, defined, 439
ethnocentrism, defined, 56
euro
benefits and costs of adopting, 221
defined, 219
European Union (EU)
benefits and costs of adopting euro and, 221
challenges, 222–23
defined, 208
euro and, 219
euro zone and, 219
map, 219
Schengen and, 219
waves of expansion of, 220
euro zone, defined, 219
executive compensation at SAP case, 471
exit-based governance mechanisms, defined, 471
expatriate (expat) manager, defined, 7
expatriates (expats)
compensation for, 445–46
defined, 438
development for returning, 443–44
differences in cost of living for expats in selected cities, 447
going rate versus balance sheet approach on expatriate compensation, 446
hypothetical expatriate compensation package using balance sheet approach, 447
training for, 442–43
expatriation, defined, 440
inpatriation versus, 454
explicit collusion, defined, 305
explicit knowledge, defined, 371
exporting, defined, 124
export intermediary, defined, 265
expropriation, defined, 170, 467
extender strategy, defined, 318
external (exit-based) governance mechanisms, 472–73
LBO and, 472–73
market for corporate control and, 472
market for private equity and, 472–73
private equity and, 472
Exxon Valdez oil spill, 69

F

factor endowment, defined, 131
factor endowment theory, defined, 131
family ownership
family ownership and control case, 469
owners and, 465–66
FCPA (Foreign Corruption Practices Act), defined, 70
FDI. *See* foreign direct investment (FDI)
feint, defined, 315
femininity, defined, 66
"Fijación Oral volumen 1" (album), 512, 513
financial resources
capabilities and, 89
examples of capabilities and, 90
firm behaviors
firms and, 33
institutions and, 33
firms. *See also* entrepreneurial firms
firm behaviors and, 33
German firms invest abroad directly case, 153–54
implications for actions of management and, 103
institutions and, 33
opportunism versus individualism and collectivism debate and, 75–77
first-mover advantages, 284–85
defined, 132, 284
fixed exchange rate policy, defined, 189
fixed versus floating exchange rates, 196–97
floating (flexible) exchange rate policy, defined, 188
floating versus fixed exchange rates, 196–97
foreign-born bosses case, 369
Foreign Corruption Practices Act (FCPA), defined, 70
foreign direct investment (FDI)
American auto industry integrative case, 236–38
annual FDI inflow, 157
benefits and costs to home countries of, 168, 176–77
benefits and costs to host countries of, 166–68
changes in national regulations of, 166–68, 176–77
combating market failure through FDI with one company (MNE) in two countries, 165
competing in Chinese auto industry integrative case, 245–50
defined, 4, 94
Delphi, and going bankrupt and then going overseas case, 176–77
DHL chases the sun case, 94
downstream vertical, 156
effects on home and host countries, 167
engaging in FDI to become MNE, 158–59
estimated average hourly wage, 154
evolution of FDI in auto industry, 245–46
flow, 156, 157
free market view on, 166
German firms invest abroad directly case, 153–54
horizontal, 155–56
inflow, 156, 157
international market transaction between two companies in two countries and, 164
inward FDI stock, 157
IPRs leading to, 39
licensing versus, 159–60
management savvy and, 172–73
MNE versus non-MNE, 156–57
OLI framework for engaging in FDI to become MNE, 158
outflow, 156
outsourcing versus, 170–71
overcoming market failure through, 163–64
political views of, 165–66
radical view on, 165
realities of, 165–68
Sabre Travel and FDI versus outsourcing case, 171
soybean industry in China integrative case, 238–41
stock, 156
stock and flow, 156
upstream, 156
upstream vertical, 156
vertical, 155–56
vocabulary of, 154–57
foreign direct investment (FDI) flow
annual inflow, 157
defined, 156
inflow, 156
outflow, 156
stock and, 156
foreign direct investment (FDI) inflow
annual, 157
defined, 156

foreign direct investment (FDI) outflow, defined, 156
foreign direct investment (FDI) stock
defined, 156
flow and, 156
inward, 157
foreign exchange market, defined, 193
foreign exchange movements
strategic responses to, 192–96
strategies for financial companies and, 193–95
strategies for nonfinancial companies and, 195–96
foreign exchange rates
Big Mac index, 185–86
currency hedging versus not hedging and, 198–200
defined, 183
examples of key currency exchange rates, 183
exchange rate policies and, 184, 188–89
factors determining, 183–89
fixed exchange rate policy and, 189
fixed versus floating exchange rates, 196–97
floating exchange rate policy and, 188
floating versus fixed exchange rates, 196–97
foreign-exchange reserves case, 199
interest rates and money supply, 184, 186
investor psychology and, 184, 189
management savvy and, 200
Markel Corporation fights currency fluctuations case, 203–4
productivity and balance of payments, 184, 186–88
relative price differences and PPP, 184–86
role of US dollar outside the United States, 184
strong dollar versus weak dollar, 197–98
supply and demand, 183–84
target exchange rates and, 188
US balance of payments, 2006, 187
yuan and Wal-Mart case, 181–82
foreign-exchange reserves case, 199
foreign market entries
advantages and disadvantages of modes of entry for, 287
Amazon in Japan case, 297–98
comprehensive model for choice of modes of entry for, 288
cultural and institutional distances and locations for, 283–84
cultural distance and, 283
cyberspace versus conventional entries and, 293
equity and nonequity modes of, 285–90
equity mode and, 286
first-mover and late-mover advantages, 284–85
geographic diversification of the largest MNEs by sales, 292
global versus regional geographic diversification and, 291–92
implications for actions of management and, 294
institutional distance and, 283
institutions, resources and, 279
liability versus asset of foreignness and, 291
locations for, 279–84
location-specific advantages and strategic goals and, 279–83
management savvy and, 293–94
modes of entry and, 286
modes of entry and first step on equity versus nonequity modes for, 286
modes of entry and second step on making actual selections for, 286–90
nonequity mode and, 286
overcoming liability of foreignness and, 278–79
scale of entry and, 286
scale of entry and commitment and experience for, 286
timing considerations for, 284–85
Yahoo! in France case, 293
foreign portfolio investment, defined, 155
formal external institutions, multinational strategies and structures and, 367–68
formal institutions
alliances and acquisitions and, 332–33
CG and, 475–76
cyberspace versus conventional entries and, 293
defined, 31
formal rules and, 10, 30, 33
governing domestic competition with focus on antitrust policy and, 309–10
governing international competition with focus on antidumping, 310–11
regulatory pillar and, 57
forward discount, defined, 194
forward premium, defined, 194
forward transaction, defined, 194
Four Tigers, 12, 74, 123
France
Shiseido smells at innovations in France case, 372
Yahoo! in France case, 293
franchising
defined, 264
licensing and franchising, 263
free float, defined, 188
free market view on FDI, defined, 166
free trade
defined, 127
economic arguments against, 140–41
political arguments against, 142
free trade area (FTA), defined, 217
Free Trade Area of the Americas (FTAA), defined, 225

G

gambit, defined, 315
game theory, defined, 305
GDP (gross domestic product), defined, 5, 6
General Agreement on Tariffs and Trade (GATT)
defined, 209
1948-1994, 211
General Agreement on Trade in Services (GATS), defined, 212
General Motors (GM) and Daewoo, from alliance to acquisition case, 329–30
geocentric approach, defined, 440
geographic area structure
defined, 364
at Mittal Steel, 364
Germany
executive compensation at SAP case, 471
German firms invest abroad directly case, 153–54
German Panel on CG Code, 477
Siemens' ShareNet knowledge management system case, 381–82
global account structure, defined, 377
global business
defined, 5
global business and emerging economies case, 24–25
importance of, 7–9
institution-based view of, 33–34
success and failure of, 9
unified framework of, 8–9
global economic integration, 209–11
benefits of, 210
contraction of world trade during the Great Depression and, 209
defined, 208

global economic integration, *continued*
economic benefits of, 210–11
implications for actions of management and, 230
management savvy and, 230–31
political benefits for, 209–10
regional economic integration as building versus stumbling blocks for, 228–29
global economic pyramid, 6
globalization
American general public vs. business students' views of, 20
antiglobalization protests, 16–17
bias towards, 19–20
defined, 11
pendulum view of, 12–13
of publishing industry case, 3–4
terrorism, protectionism and Homeland Security case, 19
terrorist attacks and, 17, 19
views of, 12–13
"The Globalization of Markets" (Levitt), 360, 413
global knowledge management at Accenture integrative case, 400–402
balancing global integration and local responsiveness and, 402
inadequate support for challenges at local offices and, 401–2
insufficient allowances for local control and, 402
KX and, 400–402
lack of appreciation for regional knowledge and, 400–401
global mandate, defined, 362
global matrix. *See also* DHL Bangladesh integrative case defined, 365
hypothetical global matrix structure, 365
multinational strategies and structures and, 365–66
global product division
defined, 364
at EADS, 365
multinational strategies and structures, 364–65
global standardization strategy, defined, 362
global sustainability, defined, 492
global virtual teams
defined, 374
knowledge management and, 374–75
GLOBE clusters, 62, 63
GM and Daewoo, from alliance to acquisition case, 329–30
GNI. *See* gross national income (GNI)
GNP (gross national product), defined, 6
going rate approach
defined, 445
versus balance sheet approach on expatriate compensation and, 446
gold standard, defined, 190
governance mechanisms
CG and, 471–73
external, 471, 472–73
global perspective on, 473–74
internal, 471–72
internal and external governance mechanisms with global perspective, 474
internal plus external mechanisms equals governance package, 473
shareholder capitalism and, 473
governance package, internal plus external mechanisms equals, 473
governing corporations. *See* corporate governance
green-field operation, defined, 290
gross domestic product (GDP) defined, 5, 6
gross national income (GNI) defined, 6
richest and poorest countries by, 42
gross national product (GNP), defined, 6

H

HCNs. *See* host country nationals (HCNs)
Heckscher-Ohlin theory, defined, 131
herd mentality, defined, 46
high-context culture, defined, 62
Hindustan Lever Limited Corporate Profile, 529n1
Hofstede's dimensions of culture, 64–65, 67
home country national, defined, 439
home replication strategy, defined, 361
Hong Kong. *See also* Ocean Park confronts Hong Kong Disneyland integrative case
David Webb as shareholder activist in Hong Kong case, 479
Hong Kong and Argentina currency boards case, 197
horizontal FDI, 155–56
defined, 155
host country nationals (HCNs)
compensation for, 446–48
defined, 438
training and development, 438
HR. *See* human resources (HR)
HRIS. *See* human resources information system (HRIS)
HRM. *See* human resource management (HRM)
hubris, defined, 344
human resource management (HRM)
across-the-board pay cut versus reduction in force and, 454–55
best fit versus best practice and, 453–54
compensation and, 444–48
Dallas versus Delhi employment case, 459
defined, 438
differences in cost of living for expats in selected cities and, 447
Employee Free Choice Act and, 449
expatriate failure and selection, 441–42
expatriates and, 440
expatriation versus inpatriation and, 454
factors in expatriate selection, 442
going rate approach and, 445
going rate versus balance sheet approach on expatriate compensation and, 446
implications for actions of management and, 456
institutions and, 450–52
labor relations and, 448–50
management savvy and, 455–56
Manpower case, 451
Ocean Park HRM policy, 397–98
performance appraisal and, 444, 445, 448
Portman Ritz-Carlton Hotel's best employer in Asia case, 437–38
resources and, 453
roles of expatriates and, 441
some blunders in international, 452
staffing and, 438–42
training for expatriates and, 442–43
Unemployment Act case, 449
human resources (HR)
capabilities and, 89–90
at DHLB, 404
examples of capabilities and, 90
human resources information system (HRIS)
at DHLB, 403, 404
DHL regional HQ and, 404–5
Huntington civilizations, 62, 63
Hyundai's uphill battle case, 97

I

IB. *See* international business (IB)
"If You're in a Fight, Make Sure You Win" (video), 324
Illycaffé's perfection from bean to cup case, 259
IMF. *See* International Monetary Fund (IMF)

imitability
acquisitions and, 336
alliances and, 335
capabilities and, 97–98
CSR and, 501
Hyundai's uphill battle case, 97
imitability of resources, competitive dynamics and, 312
imitation effect, defined, 167
importing, defined, 124
import quota, defined, 140
import tariff, defined, 138
Incat's warship Joint Venture defense technology firm case, 277, 278
An Inconvenient Truth, 508
India. *See also* Shakti and Unilever collaborates with women entrepreneurs in rural India integrative case
Confederation of Indian Industry Code of CG, 477
Dallas versus Delhi employment case, 459
India's forthcoming retail and supply chain revolution case, 424
indirect export, defined, 265
individualism
defined, 66
Hofstede's dimensions of culture and, 64–65
in-group members and, 76
opportunism versus individualism and collectivism debate, 75–77
out-group members and, 76
infant industry argument, defined, 141
informal external institutions, multinational strategies and structures and, 367–68
informal institutions
alliances and acquisitions and, 333
CG and, 476–77
cognitive pillar and, 57
cyberspace versus conventional entries and, 293
defined, 31, 56–57
informal rules and, 10, 30, 33
normative pillar and, 57
information asymmetries, defined, 467
in-group, defined, 76
innovation resources
capabilities and, 90
examples of capabilities and, 90
innovation seeking, defined, 283
inpatriation
defined, 454
expatriation versus, 454
inshoring
defined, 94
offshoring versus, 100–102
inside director, defined, 469
institutional distance, defined, 283
institutional framework, defined, 31
institutional transition
defined, 32
Russia puzzle and institutional transition case, 50–52
speed and effectiveness of, 43–44
institution-based view
defined, 30
external environment, 10
formal rules and, 10, 33
of global business, 33–34
informal rules and, 10, 33
management savvy and, 46–47
rational choices and, 33
institutions
AGRANA integrative case, 241–44
alliances, acquisitions, resources and, 332
alliances and acquisitions and, 332–33
CG, resources and, 475–77
CSR, resources and, 497
dimensions of, 31
DP World integrative case, 111–15
firm behaviors and, 33
formal, 10, 30, 31, 33, 57
formal rules and, 30
how institutions and resources affect multinational structures, learning and innovation, 367
HRM and, 450–52
informal, 10, 30, 31, 33, 56–57
informal rules and, 10, 30, 33
institutional framework and, 31
institutional transitions and, 32, 43–44
key role of, 32
marketing, supply chain management and, 423–25
multinational strategies and structures and, 367–69
PMC dogs of war and pussycats of peace integrative case, 118–20
rational choices and, 33
resources and, 332, 367, 450, 475, 497
Shakti and Unilever collaborate with women entrepreneurs in rural India integrative case, 524–29, 529n10
some blunders in international HRM, 452
intangible resources
defined, 89
examples of resources and capabilities, 90
integration-responsiveness framework, defined, 360
multinational strategies and structures and, 360, 361
intellectual property, defined, 38
intellectual property rights (IPRs), 38–39
Paris Convention for the Protection of Industrial Property and, 38
interlocking directorate, defined, 470
internal (voice-based) governance mechanisms, 471–72
internalization, defined, 158
internalization advantages, 163–65
market failure and, 163
international, defined, 4–5
international air travel case, 207–9
international business (IB)
defined, 4
global business and, 4–7
"International Business" (video), 23
international competition, dumping and, 311
international division
defined, 363
multinational strategies and structures and, 363
structure at Cardinal Health, 364
international entrepreneurship, defined, 254
International Monetary Fund (IMF), 191–92
actions and criticisms case, 193
defined, 182
typical IMF conditions on loan recipient countries, 192
international monetary system
Bretton Woods system, 190
evolution of, 190–96
gold standard and, 190
post-Bretton Woods system, 190–91
international premium, defined, 7–8
international trade
bilateral trading relationship of Canada and US, 150
chewing gum sales restrictions in Singapore and, 141
classical theories versus new realities and, 143–46
debate on US trade deficit with China, 145
evaluating theories of, 136–38
growth in world trade outpaces growth in GDP, 126
leading trading nations, 124
management savvy and, 146–47
North Korea versus South Korea and, 123–24
realities of, 138–46

international trade, *continued*
reasons for, 124–27
quotas on China ethical dilemma and, 144
theories of, 127
trade deficit versus trade surplus and, 142–43
intrafirm trade, defined, 165
IPRs. *See* intellectual property rights (IPRs)
Ireland, agglomeration of financial services firms in, 281
Islamic traditions and Danish cartoons case, 55–56
Italy, Illycaffé's perfection from bean to cup case and, 259

J
Japan
Amazon in Japan case, 297–98
CG Forum of Japan Code, 477
preferential regional trade agreements case, 216
tariff on rice imports in, 139
joint venture (JV)
A-B goes from minority shareholder to aggressive bidder case, 348
defined, 289
Incat's warship names Joint Venture defense technology firm case, 277, 278
majority JVs as control mechanisms versus minority JVs as real options debate, 347–48
modes of entry and, 289–90
Joint Venture (HSV-X1), 277
Jyllands-Posten (Jutland Post), 55, 56

K
Kalashnikov and swords into vodka integrative case, 514–15
King Kong, 146
King Report, 477
Kiva revolutionizes microfinance case, 272–73
knowledge management
defined, 370
global knowledge management at Accenture integrative case, 400–402
global virtual teams and, 374–75
MNE and, 371–72
multinational strategies and structures and, 370–71
problems and solutions in, 374–75
knowledge spillover, defined, 162
Korea. *See also* LG-Nortel JV integrative case
Hyundai's uphill battle case, 97
Korean Stock Exchange Code of Best Practice, 477
North Korea versus South Korea and international trade, 123–24
Kyoto Protocol, 1997, 508

L
labor relations
defined, 448
HRM and, 448–50
managing abroad, 449–50
managing at home, 448–49
laissez faire, 40, 127
defined, 39
language, 58–59
lingua franca, 58
world output by language, 59
world population by language, 58
late-mover advantages, 284–85
defined, 284
"Laundry Service" (album), 512–513
learning by doing, defined, 339
learning race, defined, 334
legal system, defined, 36
Lenovo and IBM case, 353–54
letter of credit (L/C), defined, 263
leveraged buyout (LBO), defined, 472
The Lexus and the Olive Tree (Friedman), 36
LG-Nortel JV integrative case, 390–93
description of JV, 391–92
future of JV and, 393
initial issues in JV and, 392
LG Electronics' background and, 390
Nortel-LGE leadership team and, 392
Nortel's background and, 390
Nortel's experience in new markets and, 391
Peter Mackinnon bio and, 391
telecom in South Korea industry overview and, 391
wireless in South Korea as accelerating industry and, 391
liability of foreignness, defined, 11
licensing
defined, 158, 263
FDI versus, 159–60
licensing and franchising, 263, 289
defined, 289
lingua franca, defined, 58
Li Ning sporting goods company case, 433
listing in New York case, 464–65
local content requirement, defined, 140
localization (multidomestic) strategy, defined, 362
local responsiveness, defined, 360
location
defined, 158
value chain and, 95
location-specific advantages, 161–63, 279–83
acquiring and neutralizing, 162–63
agglomeration and, 280
agglomeration of financial services firms in Ireland and, 281
Chinese refrigerator plant in Camden, SC and, 162
defined, 279
efficiency seeking and, 282
geographic, 161
innovation seeking and, 282–83
making cars in Central Europe case, 282
market seeking and, 280
matching strategic goals with locations and, 281
natural resource seeking and, 280
strategic goals and, 279–83
long-term orientation
defined, 66
Hofstede's dimensions of culture and, 64–65
L'Oreal acquires the Body Shop case, 91
Lord of the Rings, 146
low-context cultures, defined, 61

M
make-or-buy decisions
defined, 419
in making luxury cars case, 420
making M&As fly in China case, 337
managed float, defined, 188
management control rights, defined, 155
managerial human capital, defined, 478
managers
agency relationship and, 466
agency theory and, 466
agent and, 466
antitrust policymakers versus, 319–20
beefing up management capabilities in Africa case, 258
country and regional, 364
expatriate, 7
opportunistic agents versus managerial stewards and, 478
principal-agent conflicts and, 466–67
principal and, 466
principal-principal conflicts and, 467–68
TMT and, 466
managing risks in South Africa case, 29–30
Manpower case, 451
manufacturing, services versus, 426–27

Markel Corporation fights currency fluctuations case, 203–4
market commonality, defined, 308
market economy, defined, 39
market failure
combating market failure through FDI with one company (MNE) in two countries, 165
defined, 158
internalization advantages and, 163
overcoming market failure through FDI, 163–64
market imperfection, defined, 158
marketing
blunders in international, 417
country-of-origin and, 416
defined, 412
do's and don'ts to avoid blunders in international, 429
four Ps of marketing mix, 412
implications for actions of management and, 429
institutions, supply chain management and, 423–25
Kalashnikov and swords into vodka integrative case, 514–15
management savvy and, 428–30
manufacturing versus services and, 426–27
market versus relationship orientation and, 427–28
price and, 415–16
product and, 413–15
promotion and, 416–17
resources, supply chain management and, 425–26
segmentation of consumers as related to global brands and, 415
Shakira and dilemma of going global integrative case, 512–13
South African firms' foreign market entries case, 280
top-20 global brands and, 414
total cost of ownership and, 416
Zara rewriting rules on supply chain management case, 411–12
marketing mix, defined, 412
market orientation, defined, 427
market seeking, defined, 280
market segmentation
of consumers as related to global brands, 415
defined, 414
market transition debate, defined, 43
M&As. *See* mergers and acquisitions (M&As)
masculinity
defined, 66
Hofstede's dimensions of culture and, 64–65
McDonald's theory and political risk case, 36
medium-sized enterprises. *See* small and medium-sized enterprises (SMEs)
mercantilism theory, 127, 137
defined, 127
merchandise, defined, 124
Mercosur, defined, 224
mergers
defined, 331
variety of cross-border mergers and acquisitions, 331
mergers and acquisitions (M&As)
alliances and, 347
defined, 331
stakeholder concerns during M&As, 346
"Messiness" (video), 233
Mexican Code of CG, 477
MFA (Multifiber Agreement), 140
microfinance
defined, 261
Kiva revolutionizes microfinance case, 272–73
microfinancing and macro success case, 261
micro-macro link, defined, 375
mixed economy, defined, 40
MNC (multinational corporation). *See* multinational enterprise (MNE)
MNE. *See* multinational enterprise (MNE)
mobile (cell) phones, base of pyramid and, 7
modern trade theories, defined, 127
modes of entry
advantages and disadvantages of, 287
BOT, 289
co-marketing, 289
comprehensive model for choice of, 288
defined, 286
equity mode and, 287
first step on equity versus nonequity modes foreign market entries, 286
green-field operation, 290
JV, 289–90
licensing and franchising, 289
R&D contract, 289
second step on making actual selections foreign market entries, 286–90
turnkey project, 289
WOS, 290
monetary union, defined, 217
"Monitor Your Business Environment and Anticipate Change" (video), 50
moral hazard, defined, 193
motivation, counterattacks in competitive dynamics and, 315
multidomestic strategy, defined, 362
Multifiber Agreement (MFA), 140
multilateral trading system, defined, 210
multimarket competition, defined, 308
multinational corporation (MNC). *See* multinational enterprise (MNE)
multinational enterprise (MNE)
combating market failure through FDI with one company (MNE) in two countries, 165
cyberspace versus conventional entries and, 293
defined, 4, 154
engaging in FDI to become, 158–59
host governments bargaining with, 168–70
knowledge management and, 371–72, 374–75
multinational strategies and structures and, 362
non-MNE versus, 156–57
Ocean Park confronts Hong Kong Disneyland integrative case, 393–99
OLI framework for engaging in FDI to become, 158
staffing and, 440
three Cs of MNE bargaining with host governments, 168–70
multinational strategies and structures
absorptive capacity and, 375
center of excellence and, 362
corporate controls versus subsidiary initiatives and, 375–76
country and regional manager and, 364
customer-focused dimensions versus integration, responsiveness, learning and, 376–77
DenTek's UK decision integrative case, 386–89
explicit knowledge and, 371
foreign-born bosses case, 369
formal external institutions and, 367–68
formal internal institutions and, 368–69
geographic area structure and, 364
geographic area structure at Mittal Steel, 364
global account structure and, 377
globalizing R&D and, 372–74
global matrix and, 365–66
global product division and, 364
global product division at EADS and, 365
global standardization strategy and, 362

multinational strategies and structures, *continued*
global virtual teams and, 374–75
home replication strategy and, 361–62
how institutions and resources affect learning, innovation and, 367
hypothetical global matrix structure and, 365
implications for actions of management and, 377
informal external institutions and, 367–68
informal internal institutions and, 368–69
institution-based considerations and, 367–69
integration-responsiveness framework and, 360, 361
international division and, 363–64
international division structure at Cardinal Health and, 364
knowledge management and, 371–72, 374–75
localization strategy and, 362
local responsiveness and, 360
management savvy and, 377–78
micro-macro link and, 375
Motorola's global R&D network map and, 373
organizational structures and, 363–66
pressures for cost reductions and local responsiveness, 360–61
reciprocal relationship between, 366–67
resource-based considerations and, 370
Shiseido smells at innovations in France case, 372
Siemens' ShareNet knowledge management system case, 381–82
social capital and, 375
solutions-based structure and, 377
staffing approaches and, 440
strategic choices and, 361–63
strategic choices for MNEs, 362
subsidiary initiative at Honeywell Canada case, 376
tacit knowledge and, 371
transnational strategy and, 363
ups and downs at Ford case, 359, 360
worldwide mandate and, 362
Muslim traditions and Danish cartoons case, 55–56
mutual forbearance, defined, 308

N

NAFTA. *See* North American Free Trade Agreement (NAFTA)
national competitive advantage of industries theory, 135–36, 137
defined, 135
Porter diamond and, 135
natural resource seeking, defined, 280
"The Need to Measure and Explain CSR" (video), 508
new trade theory. *See* strategic trade theory
NGOs (non-government organizations), defined, 20
nondiscrimination, defined, 210
nonequity-based alliances
defined, 331
equity-based versus, 340
nonequity mode
advantages and disadvantages of modes of entry and, 287
defined, 286
non-government organizations (NGOs), defined, 20
nontariff barriers (NTBs), 139–40
defined, 138
normative pillar
defined, 31
informal institutions and, 57
norms
Danish cartoons of Muhammad case, 55–56
defined, 72
DP World integrative case, 111–15
ethical challenges and, 72–73
North America. *See also* Canada; United States
American general public vs. business students' views of globalization, 20
FTAA and, 225
Mexican Code of CG, 477
North American Free Trade Agreement (NAFTA)
bilateral trading relationship of Canada and U.S., 150
defined, 223
managing labor relations and, 448
multinational strategies and structures and, 376
regional economic integration and, 217, 223–24, 225, 228
NTBs. *See* nontariff barriers (NTBs)

O

OBMs (original brand manufacturers), defined, 102
obsolescing bargain, defined, 169
Ocean Park Annual Report, 399n2
Ocean Park confronts Hong Kong Disneyland integrative case, 393–99
brand repositioning at Ocean Park, 395
competition between parks, 396–97
employee resistance to change at Ocean Park, 395–96
future strategic challenges at Ocean Park, 398–99
history of Hong Kong Disneyland, 396
history of Ocean Park, 394
HRM policy, 397–98
initial reaction of Ocean Park to Hong Kong Disneyland, 397
Mr. Whiskers during SARS outbreak and, 394
potential obstacles at Ocean Park, 398
pricing strategy at Ocean Park, 398
revamping product line of Ocean Park, 395
ocean shipping maxing out case, 422
ODM. *See* original design manufacturers (ODM)
OECD (Organization for Economic Cooperation and Development), 123
OECD and Development Guidelines for Multinational Enterprises, 493
OECD Principles of Corporate Governance, 477
OEM (original equipment manufacturer), 101
offer rate, defined, 194
offsetting carbon emission case, 508–9
offshoring
benefit of $1 US spending on offshoring to India, 100
defined, 94
not offshoring versus, 100–102
OLI advantages, defined, 158
oligopoly
competing in Chinese auto industry integrative case, 245–50
defined, 163
opportunism
defined, 32
opportunism versus individualism and collectivism debate, 75–77
opportunity cost, defined, 148
"Oral Fixation volume 2" (album), 512
organization
acquisitions and, 336
alliances and, 335
capabilities and, 98–99
CSR and, 501–2
organizational fit, 336
Polygram and Universal Music Group's star search case, 106–7
strategic fit and, 336

organizational fit, defined, 336
organizational resources
capabilities and, 89
examples of capabilities and, 90
Organization for Economic Cooperation and Development (OECD), 123
original brand manufacturer (OBM), defined, 102
original design manufacturer (ODM)
defined, 101
from original equipment manufacturer to original design manufacturer, 101
original equipment manufacturer (OEM), 101
from original equipment manufacturer to, 101
out-group
collectivism and, 76
defined, 76
individualism and, 76
outside director, defined, 469
outsourcing
analysis of in-house versus, 91–95
defined, 92
FDI versus, 170–71
Sabre Travel and FDI versus outsourcing case, 171
value chain with some, 92
owners
CG and, 465–66
concentrated versus diffused ownership, 465
family ownership, 465–66
separation of ownership and control, 465
state ownership, 466
ownership
benefits of direct ownership, 159
defined, 158

P

parent (home) country national (PCN), defined, 439
Paris Convention for the Protection of Industrial Property, 38, 39
passive exporting, defined, 262
patent, defined, 38
path dependency, defined, 44
PBS/Frontline, 182
PCN. *See* parent (home) country national (PCN)
peg, defined, 189
performance appraisal
defined, 445
HRM and, 444, 445, 448
physical resources
capabilities and, 89
examples of capabilities and, 90
piracy, defined, 39
place, defined, 418
PMC (private military companies)
entrepreneurship and, 257
PMC dogs of war or pussycats of peace integrative case, 118–20
POLCON (political constraint index), 44
political constraint index (POLCON), 44
political risk
defined, 35
McDonald's theory and political risk case, 36
measures of, 44–46
perception versus objectivity and, 45
political system, defined, 34
political union, defined, 217
polycentric approach, defined, 439
Polygram and Universal Music Group's star search case, 106–7
Portman Ritz-Carlton Hotel's best employer in Asia case, 437–38
post-Bretton Woods system, 190–91
defined, 191
power distance
defined, 66
Hofstede's dimensions of culture and, 64–65
PPP (purchasing power parity), defined, 5, 6, 184
pragmatic nationalism, defined, 166
predatory pricing, defined, 310
preferential regional trade agreements
Japanese preferential regional trade agreements case, 216
shrimp-turtle case of WTO and, 142
price
defined, 415, 429
marketing and, 415–16
price elasticity, defined, 415, 429
price leader, defined, 307
primary stakeholder groups, defined, 494
principal, defined, 466
principal-agent conflicts
agency costs, 467
agency relationship and, 466
agency theory and, 466
agent and, 466
defined, 466
information asymmetries and, 467
principal and, 466
principal-principal conflicts and, 468
principal-principal conflicts versus, 468
TMT and, 466
principal-principal conflicts
defined, 467
expropriation and, 467
managers and, 467–68
principal-agent conflicts and, 468
principal-agent conflicts versus, 468
related transaction and, 468
tunneling and, 467–68
prisoners' dilemma
for airlines, 307
defined, 305
private equity
defined, 472
private equity challenge case, 484–85
private military companies. *See* PMC (private military companies)
proactive strategy
CSR and, 499–500
defined, 499
procompetition policy, domestic competition and, 309
proconsumer policy, domestic competition and, 309
product
defined, 413
marketing and, 413–15
product life cycle theory, 132, 133, 137
defined, 132
proincumbent policy, domestic competition and, 309
promotion
country-of-origin and, 416
defined, 416
marketing and, 416–17
property, defined, 38
property rights, 37–38
defined, 37
proproducer policy, domestic competition and, 309
protectionism, defined, 127
psychological contract, defined, 443
publishing industry globalization case, 3–4
purchasing power parity (PPP), defined, 5, 6, 184

R

radical view on FDI, defined, 165
radio frequency identification (RFID) tags, 96
rarity
acquisitions and, 336
alliances and, 335
relational capability and, 335
R&D. *See* research and development (R&D)
reactive strategy, defined, 497
real option, defined, 334
reexpatriation
defined, 443
development for returning expatriates, 443–44
regional and country manager, defined, 364
regional economic integration
in Africa, 228, 229
in Americas, 223–25
as building versus stumbling blocks for global integration, 228–29

regional economic integration, *continued*
common market, 217
customs union, 217
defined, 208
economic union, 217
FTA, 217
implications for actions of management and, 230
international air travel case, 207–9
management savvy and, 230–31
monetary union, 217
regional economic integration in Americas
Andean Community, 224
CAFTA and, 225
FTAA, 225
map of South America, 225
Mercosur and, 224
NAFTA and, 217, 223–24, 225, 228
North America, 223–24
political union, 217
pros and cons for, 215–17
South America, 224–25
types of, 217–18
regional economic integration in Asia Pacific, 226–28
ANZCERTA and CER and, 226
APEC and, 227–28
ASEAN and, 226–27
regional economic integration in Europe, 218–23
benefits and costs of adopting euro and, 221
current description of, 218–22
EU challenges and, 222–23
EU map, 219
euro and, 219
euro zone and, 219
EU waves of expansion and, 220
origin and evolution of, 218
Schengen and, 219
regional integration. *See* regional economic integration
regulatory pillar
defined, 31
formal institutions and, 57
related transaction, defined, 468
relational (collaborative) capability, defined, 335
relationship orientation, defined, 428
religion, 59–61
world religious heritages, 60
repatriation
defined, 443
development and, 443–44
problems associated with, 443
reputational resources
capabilities and, 90
examples of capabilities and, 90
research and development (R&D)
contract defined, 289
globalizing, 372–74
Motorola's global R&D network map, 373
resources
acquisitions and, 335–36
AGRANA integrative case, 241–44
alliances, acquisitions, institutions and, 332
alliances and, 333–35
capabilities and, 89–90
CG, institutions and, 475
CG and, 477–78
CSR, institutions and, 497
CSR and, 500–502
defined, 89
domestic resources versus international capabilities, 99–100
DP World integrative case, 111–15
ERP software, 96
financial, 89, 90
HRM and, 453
human, 89–90
innovation, 90
institutions and, 332, 423, 475, 497
intangible, 89, 90, 97
managerial human capital and, 478
marketing, supply chain management, institutions and, 423
multinational strategies and structures and, 370
organizational, 89, 90
physical, 89, 90
PMC dogs of war and pussycats of peace integrative case, 118–20
rarity of, 96–97
reputational, 90
Shakti and Unilever collaborate with women entrepreneurs in rural India integrative case, 524–29, 529n10
supply chain management, marketing and, 423, 425–26
tangible, 89, 90
technological, 89, 90
value-adding, 95–96
VRIO framework for analyzing capabilities and, 95–99
resources-based view
defined, 88
of individual students, 103–4
internal resources, 10–11
management savvy and, 102–4
resource similarity
defined, 313
framework for competitor analysis between pair of rivals and, 313
US TV broadcasting industry and, 313, 314
resources mobility, defined, 138
right-wing totalitarianism, 35
Ronen and Shenkar clusters, 62, 63
Russia
Asia Trade Exports to Russian Far East case, 265
Kalashnikov and swords into vodka integrative case, 514–15
Russian puzzle and institutional transition case, 50–52

S

Sabre Travel and FDI versus outsourcing case, 171
salmon, chicken of the sea case, 492
Sarbanes-Oxley (SarbOx) Act, 463–64, 476, 477, 478, 485
scale of entry, defined, 286
Schengen, defined, 219
secondary stakeholder groups, defined, 494
"Seek Out Ways to Share Best Practice" (video), 380
semiglobalization, defined, 13
separation of ownership and control, defined, 465
services, defined, 124
Sew What? A Global Brand drapery business case, 253, 254
Shakira and dilemma of going global integrative case, 512–13
Shakti and Unilever collaborate with women entrepreneurs in rural India integrative case
development of new Shakti initiative and, 524–29, 529n10
distribution of rural income by household and, 525
HLL's millennium plan and, 525
rural India's challenges and opportunities and, 525–26
selling to wealthy people and, 524
slowdown in growth and, 524–25
solution to growth crisis at HLL and, 529
Unilever in India and, 524
shareholder capitalism
A-B goes from minority shareholder to aggres-sive bidder case, 348
David Webb as shareholder activist in Hong Kong case, 479
defined, 473
Sherman Act, 1890, 305, 319, 320
shipping industry
Incat's warship names Joint Venture defense technology firm case, 277, 278
ocean shipping maxing out case, 422
Shiseido smells at innovations in France case, 372

shrimp-turtle case of WTO, 142, 212, 214
Siemens' ShareNet knowledge management system case, 381–82
"The Six Components of Ethical Decision Making" (video), 81
small and medium-sized enterprises (SMEs)
defined, 254
international entrepreneurship and, 254–55
SMEs. *See* small and medium-sized enterprises (SMEs)
Snow White and the Seven Dwarfs, 397
social capital, defined, 375
social complexity
defined, 98
organization and, 98–99
social issue participation, defined, 500
social responsibility. *See* corporate social responsibility (CSR)
solutions-based structure, defined, 377
South Africa. *See also* Africa
foreign market entries case, 280
King Report, 477
managing risks in South Africa case, 29–30
South America. *See also* specific countries
Andean Community and, 224
CAFTA and, 225
FTAA and, 225
map of regional economic integration in, 225
Mercosur and, 224
soybean industry in China integrative case, 238–41
exports and imports and, 238–39
future of soybean industry in China, 240–41
international competition and, 240
production, consumption, and imports, 239
soybean value chain and, 240
subsidies and imports and, 239–40
subsidy ratio variances and, 240
Spain, Zara rewriting rules on supply chain management case and, 411–12
Spiderman, 136
sporadic (passive) exporting, defined, 262
sporting goods Li Ning company case, 433
spot transaction, defined, 194
spread, defined, 194
staffing
across-the-board pay cut versus reduction in force and, 454–55
defined, 438
ethnocentric, polycentric, and geocentric approaches to, 439–40
ethnocentric approach and, 439
expatriates and, 438
geocentric approach and, 440
HCNs and, 438
HRM and, 438–42
MNEs and, 440
parent, third and host country nationals and, 439
PCN and, 439
polycentric approach and, 439
TCN and, 439
stage models, defined, 264
stakeholders
defined, 490
nature of firm in society and, 494–95
perspective of, 491–92
primary and secondary stakeholder groups, 494
triple bottom line and, 494
Starbucks and CSR case, 489–90
Star Wars, 146
stewardship theory, defined, 478
strategic alliances
advantages and disadvantages of, 333
defined, 329
LG-Nortel JV integrative case, 390–93
variety of, 330
strategic fit, defined, 336
strategic hedging, defined, 195
strategic investment, defined, 329
strategic trade policy, defined, 135
strategic trade theory, 132, 134–35, 137
defined, 132
entering the very large, superjumbo aircraft market, 134
strategies and structures, multinational. *See* multinational strategies and structures
structures and strategies, multinational. *See* multinational strategies and structures
students
implications for actions of management and, 103
resources-based view of individuals and, 103–4
subsidiary initiative
defined, 376
at Honeywell Canada case, 376
subsidies
cotton farmers in West Africa and Mississippi case, 234
defined, 139
sunk cost, defined, 170
"Supplier Relationships" (video), 432
supply chain, defined, 412
supply chain management
adaptability and, 419–20
agility and, 419
alignment and, 420–23
defined, 412
distribution channel and, 418
implications for actions of management and, 429
India's forthcoming retail and supply chain revolution case, 424
institutions, marketing and, 423–25
Li Ning sporting goods company case, 433
make-or-buy decisions and, 419
make-or-buy decisions in making luxury cars case, 420
management savvy and, 428–30
manufacturing versus services and, 426–27
market versus relationship orientation and, 427–28
ocean shipping maxing out case, 422
place and, 418
resources, marketing and, 425–26
source for components for BMW's mini-assembly plant in England and, 422
Zara rewriting rules on marketing case, 411–12
Swift (HSV-2), 277
SWOT analysis
defined, 88
Hainan Airlines and, 87–88

T

tacit collusion, defined, 305
tacit knowledge, defined, 371
tangible resources
defined, 89
examples of capabilities and, 90
tariff barriers, 138–41
defined, 138
tariff on rice imports in Japan, 139
technological resources
capabilities and, 89
examples of capabilities and, 90
technology spillover, defined, 167
television broadcasting industry, resource similarity in US TV, 313, 314
terrorism, protectionism and Homeland Security case, 19
theocratic law
countries with, 37
defined, 37
theocratic totalitarianism, 35
third country national, defined, 439

third-party logistics (3PL), defined, 420
thrust, defined, 314
"Timing Your Entry into New Markets" (video), 296
tips about corruption around the Pacific integrative case, 116–18
TMT (top management team), defined, 466
TNC (transnational corporation). *See* multinational enterprise (MNE)
top management team (TMT), defined, 466
total cost of ownership, defined, 416
totalitarianism, 34–35
  defined, 34
trade agreements. *See also* specific trade agreements
  preferential regional trade agreements case, 216
  shrimp-turtle case of WTO, 142, 212, 214
trade deficit, defined, 124
trade embargo, defined, 142
trademark, defined, 39
Trade-Related Aspects of Intellectual Property Rights (TRIPS), 38, 40
  defined, 212
trade surplus, defined, 124
trade theories, classical and modern, 127
training
  defined, 442
  expatriates and, 442–43
  HCNs and, 444
transaction costs, defined, 32
transnational corporation (TNC). *See* multinational enterprise (MNE)
transnational strategy, defined, 363
Triad, defined, 6
tribal totalitarianism, 35
triple bottom line, defined, 494
TRIPS. *See* Trade-Related Aspects of Intellectual Property Rights (TRIPS)
tunneling, defined, 467
turnkey project, defined, 289
turtle-shrimp case of WTO, 142

U

uncertainty avoidance
  defined, 66
  Hofstede's dimensions of culture and, 64–65
Unemployment Act case, 449
Unilever and Shakti collaboration. *See* Shakti and Unilever collaborate with women entrepreneurs in rural India integrative case
United Kingdom
  Cadbury Report, 477
  DenTek's UK decision integrative case, 386–89
  source for components for BMW's mini-assembly plant in England, 422
United States
  air capital in Wichita, Kans. case, 161
  CAA and, 497
  chemical industry responds to environmental pressures in, 497
  Chinese refrigerator plant in Camden, SC and, 162
  cotton farmers in West Africa and Mississippi case, 234
  Dallas versus Delhi employment case, 459
  DP World integrative case, 111–15
  Employee Free Choice Act, 449
  EPA and, 497, 498
  global knowledge management at Accenture integrative case, 400–402
  listing in New York case, 464–65
  Markel Corporation fights currency fluctuations case, 203–4
  salmon, chicken of the sea case, 492
  SarbOx Act, 463–64, 476, 477, 478, 485
  strong dollar versus weak dollar and foreign exchange rates, 197–98
  terrorism, protectionism and Homeland Security case, 19
  Unemployment Act case, 449
  US-China Business Council, 147
  US Federal Reserve, 197
United States-Dominican Republic-Centtral America Free Trade Agreement (CAFTA), defined, 225
ups and downs at Ford case, 359, 360
upstream vertical FDI, defined, 156

V

value
  acquisition premium and, 335
  acquisitions and, 335–36
  alliances and, 333–35
  CSR and, 500–501
value chain
  analysis of in-house versus outsourcing and, 91–95
  defined, 91
  with firm boundaries, 92
  location advantages and, 95
  with some outsourcing, 92
  soybean value chain, 240
  two-stage decision model in analysis of, 93
VERs (voluntary export restraints), defined, 140
vertical FDI, 155–56
  defined, 155
  downstream, 156
voice-based mechanisms, defined, 471
voluntary export restraints (VERs), defined, 140
VRIO framework
  for analyzing capabilities and resources, 95–99
  defined, 95
  implications for actions of management and, 103
  resources and capabilities evaluation and, 96

W

Wal-Mart and yuan case, 181–82
Western values versus Eastern values debate, 73–74, 75
wholly owned subsidiaries (WOS), defined, 290
world economy. *See also* economy
  changes in Fortune global 500, 1990-2006, 16–17
  Fortune Global 500, 1996, 18
  Fortune Global 500, 2006, 18
  history of, 14–19
  top 100 economies (GNP) and companies (sales), 14–15
  top-ten MNEs (based on revenues) in select industries, 19
The World Is Flat (Friedman), 23, 27n37, 36, 104, 109n53, 421
World Trade Organization (WTO)
  China's first five years in, 213
  cotton farmers in West Africa and Mississippi case, 234
  defined, 209
  Doha Round and, 213–15
  importance of, 230
  main areas of, 212
  1995-present, 211–12
  shrimp-turtle case, 142
  trade dispute settlement and, 212–13
worldwide (global) mandate, defined, 362

Y

Yahoo! in France case, 293
Yearbook of China's Automobile Industry, 245
"Your Business Is the Training and Development of Your People" (video), 458
yuan and Wal-Mart case, 181–82

Z

Zara rewriting rules on supply chain management case, 411–12

CREDITS

This page constitutes an extension of the copyright page. We have made every effort to trace the ownership of all copyrighted material and to secure permission from copyright holders. In the event of any question arising as to the use of any material, we will be pleased to make the necessary corrections in future printings. Thanks are due to the following authors, publishers, and agents for permission to use the material indicated.

Chapter 1. "The Chinese Menu (For Development)" by Douglass C. North. Reprinted from the Wall Street Journal (April 7, 2005) by permission of the author. With respect to Ivey cases, Ivey Management Services prohibits any form of reproduction, storage or transmittal without its written permission. This material is not covered under authorization from any reproduction rights organization. To order copies or request permission to reproduce materials, contact Ivey Publishing, Ivey Management Services, c/o Richard Ivey School of Business, The University of Western Ontario, London, Ontario, Canada, N6A 3K7; phone (519) 661-3208, fax (519) 661-3882, e-mail cases@ivey .uwo.ca. One time permission to reproduce granted by Ivey Management Services on Dec. 7, 2007.

Chapter 2. USA TODAY. March 22, 2007. Reprinted with permission.

Chapter 3. ACADEMY OF MANAGEMENT EXECUTIVE by Paik and Choi. Copyright 2005 by Academy of Management (NY). Reproduced with permission of Academy of Management (NY) in the format Textbook via Copyright Clearance Center.

Chapter 4. ECONOMIST by Economist. Copyright 2005 by Economist Newspaper Group. Reproduced with permission of the Economist Newspaper Group in the format Textbook via Copyright Clearance Center.

Chapter 5. Reprinted from the December 8, 2003, issue of Business Week by special permission, copyright © 2003 by The McGraw-Hill Companies, Inc.

Chapter 6. Reprinted from the April 24, 2006, issue of Business Week by special permission, copyright © 2006 by The McGraw-Hill Companies, Inc.

Chapter 7. Economist by Economist Staff. Copyright 2006 by Economist Newspaper Group. Reproduced with permission of Economist Newspaper Group in the format Textbook via Copyright Clearance Center.

Chapter 8. Reprinted from the May 8, 2006, issue of Business Week by special permission, copyright © 2006 by The McGraw-Hill Companies, Inc.

Chapter 9. "Click and Change the World: Microfinance for the Masses" by Mary K. Pratt, from Computerworld (January 29, 2007), pp. 31–32. Reprinted by permission of the YGS Group on behalf of Computerworld Magazine. Copyright 2006 U.S. News & World Report, L.P. Reprinted with permission.

Chapter 15. From "Setting People Up for Success" by Arthur Yeung, Human Resource Management 452 (2006), pp. 267–75. Reprinted by permission of John Wiley & Sons, Inc.

Chapter 16. Economist by Economist Staff. Copyright 2007 by Economist Newspaper Group. Reproduced with permission of Economist Newspaper Group in the format Textbook via Copyright Clearance Center.